Excel 2002 VBA Programmer's Reference

Rob Bovey
Stephen Bullen
John Green
Robert Rosenberg

Excel 2002 VBA Programmer's Reference

Published by
Wiley Publishing, Inc.
10475 Crosspoint Boulevard
Indianapolis, IN 46256
www.wiley.com

Published simultaneously in Canada

Library of Congress Card Number: 2003107072

ISBN: 0-7645-4371-7

Manufactured in the United States of America

10 9 8 7 6 5 4

1B/RQ/QW/QT/IN

For general information on our other products and services or to obtain technical support, please contact our Customer Care Department within the U.S. at (800) 762-2974, outside the U.S. at (317) 572-3993 or fax (317) 572-4002.

Wiley also publishes its books in a variety of electronic formats. Some content that appears in print may not be available in electronic books.

Trademark Acknowledgements

Wrox has endeavored to provide trademark information about all the companies and products mentioned in this book by the appropriate use of capitals. However, Wrox cannot guarantee the accuracy of this information.

Credits

Authors
Rob Bovey
Stephen Bullen
John Green
Robert Rosenberg

Category Manager
Sonia Mullineux

Technical Editors
Timothy Briggs
Dan Maharry
Nick Manning
Matthew Moodie

Author Agent
Trish Weir

Project Administrator
Vicky Idiens

Production Coordinator
Emma Eato

Figures
Natalie O' Donnell

Technical Reviewers
Robert Affleck
Alan Barasch
David C. Hager
Thomas Ivarsson
Terrence Joubert
Duncan MacKenzie
Bill Manville
Tom Ogilvy
Ryan Payet
Donna Payne
Jan Karel Pieterse
Stan Scott

Cover
Dawn Chellingworth

Index
Catherine Alexander
Andrew Criddle

Proof Reader
Chris Smith
Agnes Wigger

About the Authors

Rob Bovey

Rob Bovey is a software developer specializing in Microsoft Office, Visual Basic, and SQL Server applications. He is founder and president of the custom application development firm Application Professionals. Rob developed several Addins shipped by Microsoft for Excel. He also co-authored the Microsoft Excel 97 Developers Kit. Rob earned his Bachelor of Science degree from The Rochester Institute of Technology and his MBA from the University of North Carolina at Chapel Hill. He is a Microsoft Certified Systems Engineer (MCSE) and a Microsoft Certified Solution Developer (MCSD). Microsoft has awarded him the title of Most Valuable Professional each year since 1995.

I would like to thank my wife Michelle for putting up with my insatiable computer habit and my dog Harley for keeping my feet warm while I work.

Stephen Bullen

Stephen Bullen lives and works in Carlow, Ireland and is the father of twins Jane and Katie. After graduating from Oxford University in 1992 with an MA in Engineering, Economics and Management, Stephen joined Price Waterhouse Management Consultants where he spent five years developing Excel applications for a wide range of multinational corporations.

In 1997, Stephen started his own company, Business Modelling Solutions Ltd., specializing in Excel and Access development and consulting. The BMS web site, http://www.BMSLtd.ie, contains a large number of examples of his work, including tools and utilities to extend Excel's functionality and many examples of Excel development techniques.

Stephen enjoys helping other Excel users and devotes a lot of his spare time to answering questions in the CompuServe Excel forum and Microsoft's Internet Newsgroups. In recognition of his contributions and knowledge, Microsoft has awarded him the status of Most Valuable Professional every year since 1996.

Stephen can be contacted by e-mail at Stephen@BMSLtd.co.uk, though any Excel support questions should be asked in the newsgroups.

I would like to start by thanking all those who purchased a copy of the Excel 2000 VBA Programmer's Reference and sent e-mails of congratulations and suggestions for this update. It is your support that convinced us to comprehensively update the book for Excel 2002. I'd like to thank John Green for agreeing to co-author the update, Rob Bovey for contributing the ADO chapter, and Robert Rosenberg for taking over the Reference sections. As always, the people at Wrox Press and the book's technical reviewers worked wonders, and it is their contribution that has made this the excellent book that I hope you'll agree it is.

On a personal note, I'd like to dedicate my chapters to the eye specialists, doctors, and nurses at the Temple Street Children's Hospital in Dublin for dealing with Jane's tumour so well, and to everyone in the Ford ProPrima team for their friendship and support over the past year.

John Green

John Green lives and works in Sydney, Australia, as an independent computer consultant, specializing in Excel and Access. With 30 years of computing experience, a Chemical Engineering degree and an MBA, he draws from a diverse background. He wrote his first programs in FORTRAN, took a part in the evolution of specialized planning languages on mainframes and, in the early 80s, became interested in spreadsheet systems including Excel and Lotus 1-2-3.

John established his company, Execuplan Consulting, in 1980, specializing in developing computer-based planning applications and in training. He has led training courses for software applications and operating systems both in Australia and overseas.

John has had regular columns in a number of Australian magazines and has contributed chapters to a number of books including *Excel Expert Solutions* and *Using Visual Basic for Applications 5*, published by Que.

Since 1995 he has been accorded the status of Most Valuable Professional by Microsoft for his contributions to the CompuServe Excel forum and MS Internet newsgroups. Contact him at jgreen@enternet.com.au.

Robert Rosenberg

Robert Rosenberg runs his own consulting business which specializes in Microsoft Office advanced training and custom solutions for numerous entertainment, financial, and legal organizations. As a Microsoft Valuable Professional in Excel, he also continually offers advanced online support on Excel on behalf of Microsoft to users of their Internet newsgroups.

He has also been involved in several other published materials on Excel. He's been the technical editor for all of QUE publishing's intermediate Excel books for the last four years and has been involved in the creation of several training manuals for Excel, PowerPoint, and Word.

He enjoys computers (of course), golf, bowling, and still plays hockey. Robert can be contacted at rrosenberg@r-cor.com. Visit his website at http://www.r-cor.com.

I'd like to thank John Green, Stephen Bullen, and Rob Bovey for allowing me on the same project as three of the most brilliant minds in Excel today. It was an honor to take up the challenge. Special thanks goes to Rob Bovey, my mentor, who has always been there for me, answered all of my annoying questions, taught me countless techniques, and provided me with this opportunity.

To my best friend and brother Elliot, who has stuck by me through thick and thin.

And finally, for my Mom and Dad, their love never stops.

Table of Contents

1

Introduction to Excel

Excel made its debut on the Macintosh in 1985 and has never lost its position as the most popular spreadsheet application in the Mac environment. In 1987, Excel was ported to the PC, running under Windows. It took many years for Excel to overtake Lotus 1-2-3, which was one of the most successful software systems in the history of computing at that time.

There were a number of spreadsheet applications that enjoyed success prior to the release of the IBM PC in 1981. Among these were VisiCalc and Multiplan. VisiCalc started it all, but fell by the wayside early on. Multiplan was Microsoft's predecessor to Excel, using the R1C1 cell addressing which is still available as an option in Excel. But it was 1-2-3 that shot to stardom very soon after its release in 1982 and came to dominate the PC spreadsheet market.

Early Spreadsheet Macros

1-2-3 was the first spreadsheet application to offer spreadsheet, charting, and database capabilities in one package. However, the main reason for its run-away success was its macro capability. Legend has it that the 1-2-3 developers set up macros as a debugging and testing mechanism for the product. It is said that they only realized the potential of macros at the last minute, and included them into the final release pretty much as an afterthought.

Whatever their origins, macros gave non-programmers a simple way to become programmers and automate their spreadsheets. They grabbed the opportunity and ran. At last they had a measure of independence from the computer department.

The original 1-2-3 macros performed a task by executing the same keystrokes that a user would use to carry out the same task. It was, therefore, very simple to create a macro as there was virtually nothing new to learn to progress from normal spreadsheet manipulation to programmed manipulation. All you had to do was remember what keys to press and write them down. The only concessions to traditional programming were eight extra commands, the `/x` commands. The `/x` commands provided some primitive decision making and branching capabilities, a way to get input from a user, and a way to construct menus.

One major problem with 1-2-3 macros was their vulnerability. The multi-sheet workbook had not yet been invented and macros had to be written directly into the cells of the spreadsheet they supported, along with input data and calculations. Macros were at the mercy of the user. For example, they could be inadvertently disrupted when a user inserted or deleted rows or columns. Macros were also at the mercy of the programmer. A badly designed macro could destroy itself quite easily while trying to edit spreadsheet data.

Despite the problems, users reveled in their newfound programming ability and millions of lines of code were written in this cryptic language, using arcane techniques to get around its many limitations. The world came to rely on code that was often badly designed, nearly always poorly documented, and at all times highly vulnerable, often supporting enterprise-critical control systems.

The XLM Macro Language

The original Excel macro language required you to write your macros in a macro sheet that was saved in a file with an `.xlm` extension. In this way, macros were kept separate from the worksheet, which was saved in a file with an `.xls` extension. These macros are now often referred to as XLM macros, or Excel 4 macros, to distinguish them from the VBA macro language introduced in Excel Version 5.

The XLM macro language consisted of function calls, arranged in columns in the macro sheet. There were many hundreds of functions necessary to provide all the features of Excel and allow programmatic control. The XLM language was far more sophisticated and powerful than the 1-2-3 macro language, even allowing for the enhancements made in 1-2-3 Releases 2 and 3. However, the code produced was not much more intelligible.

The sophistication of Excel's macro language was a two edged sword. It appealed to those with high programming aptitude, who could tap the language's power, but was a barrier to most users. There was no simple relationship between the way you would manually operate Excel and the way you programmed it. There was a very steep learning curve involved in mastering the XLM language.

Another barrier to Excel's acceptance on the PC was that it required Windows. The early versions of Windows were restricted by limited access to memory, and Windows required much more horsepower to operate than DOS. The Graphical User Interface was appealing, but the tradeoffs in hardware cost and operating speed were perceived as problems.

Lotus made the mistake of assuming that Windows was a flash in the pan, soon to be replaced by OS/2, and did not bother to plan a Windows version of 1-2-3. Lotus put its energy into 1-2-3/G, a very nice GUI version of 1-2-3 that only operated under OS/2. This one horse bet was to prove the undoing of 1-2-3.

By the time it became clear that Windows was here to stay, Lotus was in real trouble as it watched users flocking to Excel. The first attempt at a Windows version of 1-2-3, released in 1991, was really 1-2-3 Release 3 for DOS in a thin GUI shell. Succeeding releases have closed the gap between 1-2-3 and Excel, but have been too late to stop the almost universal adoption of Microsoft Office by the market.

Excel 5

Microsoft took a brave decision to unify the programming code behind its Office applications by introducing **VBA (Visual Basic for Applications)** as the common macro language in Office. Excel 5, released in 1993, was the first application to include VBA. It has been gradually introduced into the other Office applications in subsequent versions of Office. Excel, Word, Access, PowerPoint, and Outlook all use VBA as their macro language in Office XP.

Since the release of Excel 5, Excel has supported both the XLM and the VBA macro languages, and the support for XLM should continue into the foreseeable future, but will decrease in significance as users switch to VBA.

VBA is an object-oriented programming language that is identical to the Visual Basic programming language in the way it is structured and in the way it handles objects. If you learn to use VBA in Excel, you know how to use it in the other Office applications.

The Office applications differ in the objects they expose to VBA. To program an application, you need to be familiar with its **object model**. The object model is a hierarchy of all the objects that you find in the application. For example, part of the Excel Object Model tells us that there is an `Application` object that contains a `Workbook` object that contains a `Worksheet` object that contains a `Range` object.

> *VBA is somewhat easier to learn than the XLM macro language, is more powerful, is generally more efficient, and allows us to write well-structured code. We can also write badly structured code, but by following a few principles, we should be able to produce code that is readily understood by others and is reasonably easy to maintain.*

In Excel 5, VBA code was written in modules, which were sheets in a workbook. Worksheets, chart sheets, and dialog sheets were other types of sheets that could be contained in an Excel 5 workbook.

> **A module is really just a word-processing document with some special characteristics that help you write and test code.**

Excel 97

In Excel 97, Microsoft introduced some dramatic changes in the VBA interface and some changes in the Excel Object Model. From Excel 97 onwards, modules are not visible in the Excel application window and modules are no longer objects contained by the `Workbook` object. Modules are contained in the VBA project associated with the workbook and can only be viewed and edited in the Visual Basic Editor (VBE) window.

In addition to the standard modules, class modules were introduced, which allow you to create your own objects and access application events. Commandbars were introduced to replace menus and toolbars, and UserForms replaced dialog sheets. Like modules, UserForms can only be edited in the VBE window. As usual, the replaced objects are still supported in Excel, but are considered to be hidden objects and are not documented in the Help screens.

In previous versions of Excel, objects such as buttons embedded in worksheets could only respond to a single event, usually the `Click` event. Excel 97 greatly increased the number of events that VBA code can respond to and formalised the way in which this is done by providing event procedures for the workbook, worksheet and chart sheet objects. For example, workbooks now have 20 events they can respond to, such as `BeforeSave`, `BeforePrint`, and `BeforeClose`. Excel 97 also introduced ActiveX controls that can be embedded in worksheets and UserForms. ActiveX controls can respond to a wide range of events such as `GotFocus`, `MouseMove`, and `DblClick`.

The VBE provides users with much more help than was previously available. For example, as we write code, popups appear with lists of appropriate methods and properties for objects, and arguments and parameter values for functions and methods. The **Object Browser** is much better than previous versions, allowing us to search for entries, for example, and providing comprehensive information on intrinsic constants.

Microsoft has provided an Extensibility library that makes it possible to write VBA code that manipulates the VBE environment and VBA projects. This makes it possible to write code that can directly access code modules and UserForms. It is possible to set up applications that indent module code or export code from modules to text files, for example.

Excel 97 has been ported to the Macintosh in the form of Excel 98. Unfortunately, many of the VBE help features that make life easy for programmers have not been included. The VBE Extensibility features have not made it to the Mac either.

Excel 2000

Excel 2000 did not introduce dramatic changes from a VBA programming perspective. There were a large number of improvements in the Office 2000 and Excel 2000 user interfaces and improvements in some Excel features such as PivotTables. A new PivotChart feature was added. Web users benefited the most from Excel 2000, especially through the ability to save workbooks as web pages. There were also improvements for users with a need to share information, through new online collaboration features.

One long awaited improvement for VBA users was the introduction of modeless UserForms. Previously, Excel only supported modal dialog boxes, which take the focus when they are on screen so that no other activity can take place until they are closed. Modeless dialog boxes allow the user to continue with other work while the dialog box floats above the worksheet. Modeless dialog boxes can be used to show a "splash" screen when an application written in Excel is loaded and to display a progress indicator while a lengthy macro runs.

Excel 2002

Excel 2002 has also introduced only incremental changes. Once more, the major improvements have been in the user interface rather than in programming features. Microsoft continues to concentrate on improving web-related features to make it easier to access and distribute data using the Internet. New features that could be useful for VBA programmers include a new `Protection` object, SmartTags, RTD (Real Time Data), and improved support for XML.

The new `Protection` object lets us selectively control the features that are accessible to users when we protect a worksheet. We can decide whether users can sort, alter cell formatting, or insert and delete rows and columns, for example. There is also a new `AllowEditRange` object that we can use to specify which users can edit specific ranges and whether they must use a password to do so. We can apply different combinations of permissions to different ranges.

SmartTags allow Excel to recognize data typed into cells as having special significance. For example, Excel 2002 can recognize stock market abbreviations, such as MSFT for Microsoft Corporation. When Excel sees an item like this, it displays a SmartTag symbol that has a popup menu. We can use the menu to obtain related information, such as the latest stock price or a summary report on the company. Microsoft provides a kit that allows developers to create new SmartTag software, so we could see a whole new class of tools appearing that use SmartTags to make data available throughout an organization or across the Internet.

RTD allows developers to create sources of information that users can draw from. Once you establish a link to a worksheet, changes in the source data are automatically passed on. An obvious use for this is to obtain stock prices that change in real time during the course of trading. Other possible applications include the ability to log data from scientific instruments or industrial process controllers. As with SmartTags, we will probably see a host of applications developed to make it easy for Excel users to gain access to dynamic information.

Improved XML support means it is getting easier to create applications that exchange data through the Internet and intranets. As we all become more dependent on these burgeoning technologies, this will become of increasing importance.

Excel 2002 VBA Programmer's Reference

This book is aimed squarely at Excel users who want to harness the power of the VBA language in their Excel applications. At all times, the VBA language is presented in the context of Excel, not just as a general application programming language.

The pages that follow have been divided into three sections:

- Primer
- Working with Specific Objects
- Object Model References

The Primer has been written for those who are new to VBA programming and the Excel Object Model. It introduces the VBA language and the features of the language that are common to all VBA applications. It explains the relationship between collections, objects, properties, methods, and events and shows how to relate these concepts to Excel through its object model. It also shows how to use the Visual Basic Editor and its multitude of tools, including how to obtain help.

The middle section of the book takes the key objects in Excel and shows, through many practical examples, how to go about working with those objects. The techniques presented have been developed through the exchange of ideas of many talented Excel VBA programmers over many years and show the best way to gain access to workbooks, worksheets, charts, ranges, etc. The emphasis is on efficiency, that is how to write code that is readable and easy to maintain and that runs at maximum speed. In addition Rob Bovey has written a chapter on Excel and ADO that details techniques for accessing data, independent of its format.

The final four chapters of this section, written by Stephen Bullen, address the following advanced issues: linking Excel to the Internet, writing code for international compatibility, programming the Visual Basic Editor, and how to use the functions in the Win32 API (Windows 32 bit Application Programming Interface).

The final section of the book is a comprehensive reference to the Excel 2002 Object Model, as well as the Visual Basic Editor and Office Object Models. All the objects in the models are presented together with all their properties, methods, and events. I trust that this book will become a well-thumbed resource that you can dig into, as needed, to reveal that elusive bit of code that you must have right now.

Version Issues

This book was first written for Excel 2000 and has now been extended to Excel 2002 as a component of Office XP. As the changes in the Excel Object Model, compared to Excel 97, have been relatively minor most of this book is applicable to all three versions. Where we discuss a feature that is not supported in previous versions, we make that clear.

What You Need to Use this Book

Nearly everything discussed in this book has examples with it. All the code is written out and there are plenty of screenshots where they are appropriate. The version of Windows you use is not important. It is important to have a full installation of Excel and, if you want to try the more advanced chapters involving communication between Excel and other Office applications, you will need a full installation of Office. Make sure your installation includes access to the Visual Basic Editor and the VBA Help files. It is possible to exclude these items during the installation process.

Note that Chapters 17 and 18 also require you to have VB6 installed as they cover the topics of COM Addins and SmartTags.

Conventions Used

We've used a number of different styles of text and layout in the book, to help differentiate between different kinds of information. Here are some of the styles and an explanation of what they mean:

> **These boxes hold important, not-to-be forgotten, mission-critical details that are directly relevant to the surrounding text.**

Background information, asides, and references appear in text like this.

- **Important Words** are in a bold font
- Words that appear on the screen, such as menu options, are in a similar font to the one used on screen, for example, the Tools menu
- All object names, function names, and other code snippets are in this style: `SELECT`

Code that is new or important is presented like this:

```
SELECT CustomerID, ContactName, Phone
FROM Customers
```

whereas code that we've seen before or has little to do with the matter being discussed, looks like this:

```
SELECT ProductName FROM Products
```

In Case of a Crisis...

There are number of places you can turn to if you encounter a problem. The best source of information on all aspects of Excel is from your peers. You can find them in a number of newsgroups across the Internet. Try pointing your newsreader to the following site where you will find us all actively participating:

- msnews.microsoft.com

Subscribe to `microsoft.public.excel.programming` or any of the groups that appeal. You can submit questions and generally receive answers within a hour or so.

Stephen Bullen and Rob Bovey maintain very useful web sites, where you will find a great deal of information and free downloadable files, at the following addresses:

- http://www.bmsltd.co.uk
- http://www.appspro.com

Another useful site is maintained by John Walkenbach at:

- http://www.j-walk.com

Wrox can be contacted directly at:

- http://www.wrox.com – for downloadable source code and support
- http://p2p.wrox.com/list.asp?list=vba_excel – for open Excel VBA discussion

Other useful Microsoft information sources can be found at:

- http://www.microsoft.com/office/ – for up-to-the-minute news and support
- http://msdn.microsoft.com/office/ – for developer news and good articles about how to work with Microsoft products
- http://www.microsoft.com/technet – for Microsoft Knowledge Base articles, security information, and a bevy of other more admin-related items

Feedback

We've tried, as far as possible, to write this book as though we were sitting down next to each other. We've made a concerted effort to keep it from getting "too heavy" while still maintaining a fairly quick pace. We'd like to think that we've been successful at it, but encourage you to e-mail us and let us know what you think one way or the other. Constructive criticism is always appreciated, and can only help future versions of this book. You can contact us either by e-mail (`support@wrox.com`) or via the Wrox web site.

Questions?

Seems like there are always some, eh? From the last edition of this book, we received hundreds of questions. We have tried to respond to every one of them as best as possible. What we ask is that you give it your best shot to understand the problem based on the explanations in the book.

If the book fails you, then you can either e-mail Wrox (`support@wrox.com`) or us personally (`jgreen@enternet.com.au`, `RobBovey@AppsPro.com`, `Stephen@BMSLtd.ie`). You can also ask questions on the vba_excel list at http://p2p.wrox.com. Wrox has a dedicated team of support staff and we personally **try** (no guarantees!) to answer all the mail that comes to us. For the last book, we responded to about 98% of the questions asked – but life sometimes becomes demanding enough that we can't get to them all. Just realize that the response may take a few days (as we get an awful lot of mail).

2

Primer in Excel VBA

This chapter is intended for those who are not familiar with Excel and the Excel macro recorder, or who are inexperienced with programming using the Visual Basic language. If you are already comfortable with navigating around the features provided by Excel, have used the macro recorder, and have a working knowledge of Visual Basic and the Visual Basic Editor, you might want to skip straight to Chapter 3.

If this is not the case, this chapter has been designed to provide you with the information you need to be able to move on comfortably to the more advanced features presented in the following chapters. We will be covering the following topics:

- The Excel macro recorder
- User-defined functions
- The Excel Object Model
- VBA programming concepts

Excel VBA is a programming application that allows you to use Visual Basic code to run the many features of the Excel package, thereby allowing you to customize your Excel applications. Units of VBA code are often referred to as **macros**. We will be covering more formal terminology in this chapter, but we will continue to use the term macro as a general way to refer to any VBA code.

In your day-to-day use of Excel, if you carry out the same sequence of commands repetitively, you can save a lot of time and effort by automating those steps using macros. If you are setting up an application for other users, who don't know much about Excel, you can use macros to create buttons and dialog boxes to guide them through your application as well as automate the processes involved.

If you are able to perform an operation manually, you can use the **macro recorder** to capture that operation. This is a very quick and easy process and requires no prior knowledge of the VBA language. Many Excel users record and run macros and feel no need to learn about VBA.

However, the recorded results might not be very flexible, in that the macro can only be used to carry out one particular task on one particular range of cells. In addition, the recorded macro is likely to run much more slowly than code written by someone with knowledge of VBA. To set up interactive macros that can adapt to change and also run quickly, and to take advantage of more advanced features of Excel such as customized dialog boxes, you need to learn about VBA.

Don't get the impression that we are dismissing the macro recorder. The macro recorder is one of the most valuable tools available to VBA programmers. It is the fastest way to generate working VBA code. But you must be prepared to apply your own knowledge of VBA to edit the recorded macro to obtain flexible and efficient code. A recurring theme in this book is to record an Excel Macro and then show how to adapt the recorded code.

In this chapter you will learn how to use the macro recorder and you will see all the ways Excel provides to run your macros. You will see how to use the **Visual Basic Editor** to examine and change your macros, thus going beyond the recorder and tapping into the power of the VBA language and the **Excel Object Model**.

You can also use VBA to create your own worksheet functions. Excel comes with hundreds of built-in functions, such as `SUM` and `IF`, which you can use in cell formulas. However, if you have a complex calculation that you use frequently and that is not included in the set of standard Excel functions – such as a tax calculation or a specialized scientific formula – you can write your own **user-defined function**.

Using the Macro Recorder

Excel's macro recorder operates very much like the recorder that stores the greeting on your telephone answering machine. To record a greeting, you first prepare yourself by rehearsing the greeting, to ensure that it says what you want. Then you switch on the recorder and deliver the greeting. When you have finished, you switch off the recorder. You now have a recording that automatically plays when you leave a call unanswered.

Recording an Excel macro is very similar. You first rehearse the steps involved and decide at what points you want to start and stop the recording process. You prepare your spreadsheet, switch on the Excel recorder, carry out your Excel operations, and switch off the recorder. You now have an automated procedure that you and others can reproduce at the press of a button.

Recording Macros

Say you want a macro that types six month names as three letter abbreviations, "Jan" to "Jun", across the top of your worksheet, starting in cell B1. I know this is rather a silly macro as you could do this easily with an AutoFill operation, but this example will serve to show us some important general concepts:

- First think about how you are going to carry out this operation. In this case, it is easy – you will just type the data across the worksheet. Remember, a more complex macro might need more rehearsals before you are ready to record it.
- Next, think about when you want to start recording. In this case, you should include the selection of cell B1 in the recording, as you want to always have "Jan" in B1. If you don't select B1 at the start, you will record typing "Jan" into the active cell, which could be anywhere when you play back the macro.
- Next, think about when you want to stop recording. You might first want to include some formatting such as making the cells bold and italic, so you should include that in the recording. Where do you want the active cell to be after the macro runs? Do you want it to be in the same cell as "Jun", or would you rather have the active cell in column A or column B, ready for your next input? Let's assume that you want the active cell to be A2, at the completion of the macro, so we will select A2 before turning off the recorder.
- Now you can set up your screen, ready to record.

In this case, start with an empty worksheet with cell A1 selected. If you like to work with toolbars, use View | Toolbars to select and display the Visual Basic toolbar as shown below in the top right of the screen. Press the Record Macro button, with the dark blue dot, to start the recorder. If you prefer, start the recorder with Tools | Macro | Record New Macro... from the Worksheet menu bar.

In the Macro name: box, replace the default entry, such as Macro1, with the name you want for your macro. The name should start with a letter and contain only letters, numbers and the underscore character with a maximum length of 255 characters. The macro name must not contain special characters such as ! or ?, or blank spaces. **It is also best to use a short but descriptive name that you will recognize later.** You can use the underscore character to separate words, but it is easy to just use capitalization to distinguish words.

Call the macro `MonthNames1`, because we will create another version later:

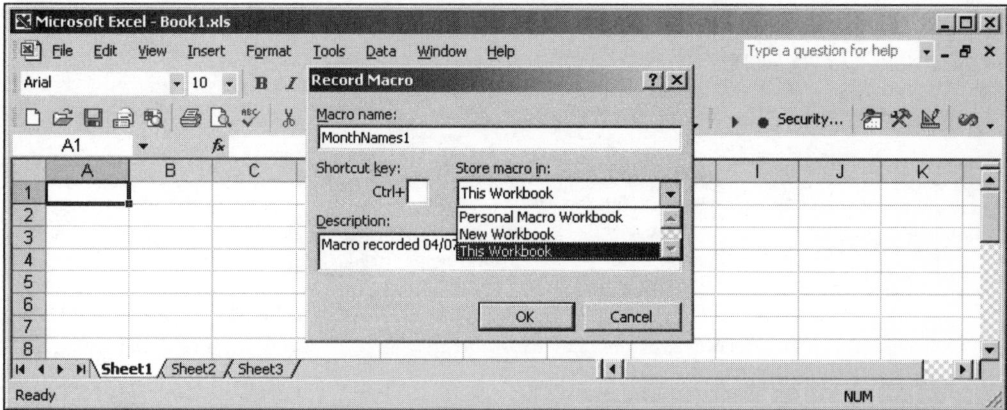

In the Shortcut key: box, you can type in a single letter. This key can be pressed later, while holding down the Ctrl key, to run the macro. We will use a lower case m. Alternatively, you can use an upper case M. In this case, when you later want to run the macro, you need to hold down the *Ctrl* key and the *Shift* key while you press *M*. It is not mandatory to provide a shortcut key. You can run a macro in a number of other ways, as we will see.

In the Description: box, you can accept the default comments provided by the recorder, or type in your own comments. These lines will appear at the top of your macro code. They have no significance to VBA but provide you and others with information about the macro. You can edit these comments later, so there is no need to change them now. All Excel macros are stored in workbooks.

You are given a choice regarding where the recorded macro will be stored. The Store macro in: combo box lists three possibilities. If you choose New Workbook, the recorder will open a new empty workbook for the macro. Personal Macro Workbook refers to a special hidden workbook that we discuss below. We will choose This Workbook to store the macro in the currently active workbook.

When you have filled in the Record Macro dialog box, click the OK button. You will see the word Recording on the left side of the Status Bar at the bottom of the screen and the Stop Recording toolbar should appear on the screen. Note that the Stop Recording toolbar will not appear if it has been previously closed during a recording session. If it is missing, refer to the instructions below under the heading **Absolute and Relative Recording** to see how to re-instate it. However, you don't really need it for the moment because we can stop the recording from the Visual Basic toolbar or the Tools menu.

*If you have the **Stop Recording** toolbar visible, make sure that the second button, the **Relative Reference** button, is not selected. It shouldn't have a border, that is it should not be as it appears in this screenshot. By default the macro recorder uses absolute cell references when it records.*

You should now click on cell B1 and type in Jan and fill in the rest of the cells as shown below. Then select B1:G1 and click the Bold and Italic buttons on the Formatting toolbar. Click the A2 cell and then stop the recorder:

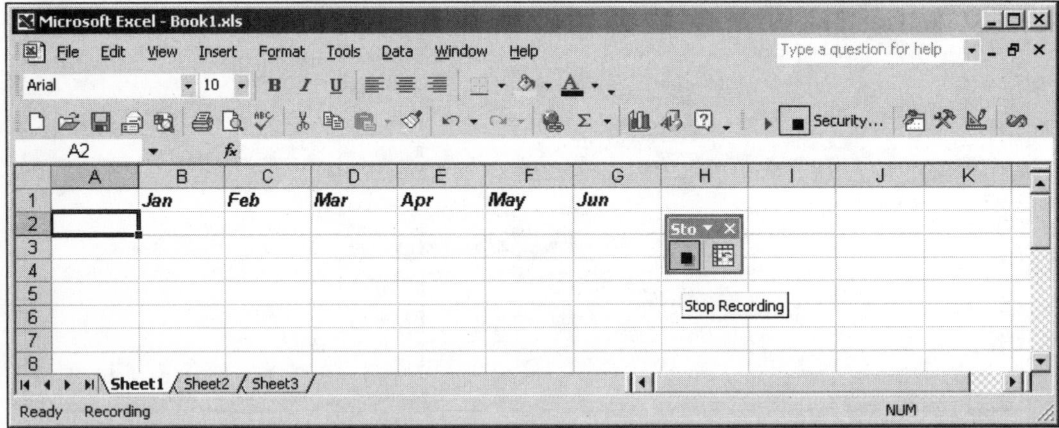

You can stop the recorder by pressing the Stop Recording button on the Stop Recording toolbar, by pressing the square Stop Recording button on the Visual Basic toolbar – the round Start Recording button changes to the Stop Recording button while you are recording – or you can use Tools | Macro | Stop Recording from the menu bar. Save the workbook as `Recorder.xls`.

It is important to remember to stop the recorder. If you leave the recorder on, and try to run the recorded macro, you can go into a loop where the macro runs itself over and over again. If this does happen to you, or any other error occurs while testing your macros, hold down the *Ctrl* key and press the Break key to interrupt the macro. You can then end the macro or go into debug mode to trace errors. You can also interrupt a macro with the *Esc* key, but it is not as effective as *Ctrl+Break* for a macro that is pausing for input.

The Personal Macro Workbook

If you choose to store your recorded macro in the Personal Macro Workbook, the macro is added to a special file called `Personal.xls`, which is a hidden file that is saved in your Excel Startup directory when you close Excel. This means that `Personal.xls` is automatically loaded when you launch Excel and, therefore, its macros are always available for any other workbook to use.

If `Personal.xls` does not already exist, the recorder will create it for you. You can use **Window | Unhide** to see this workbook in the Excel window, but it is seldom necessary or desirable to do this as you can examine and modify the `Personal.xls` macros in the Visual Basic Editor window.

An exception, where you might want to make `Personal.xls` visible, is if you need to store data in its worksheets. You can hide it again, after adding the data, with **Window | Hide**. If you are creating a general purpose utility macro, which you want to be able to use with any workbook, store it in `Personal.xls`. If the macro relates to just the application in the current workbook, store the macro with the application.

Running Macros

To run the macro, either insert a new worksheet in the `Recorder.xls` workbook, or open a new empty workbook, leaving `Recorder.xls` open in memory. You can only run macros that are in open workbooks, but they can be run from within any other open workbook.

You can run the macro by holding down the *Ctrl* key and pressing *m*, the shortcut that we assigned at the start of the recording process. You can also run the macro by clicking **Tools | Macro | Macros...** on the **Worksheet** menu bar and double-clicking the macro name, or by selecting the macro name and clicking **Run**:

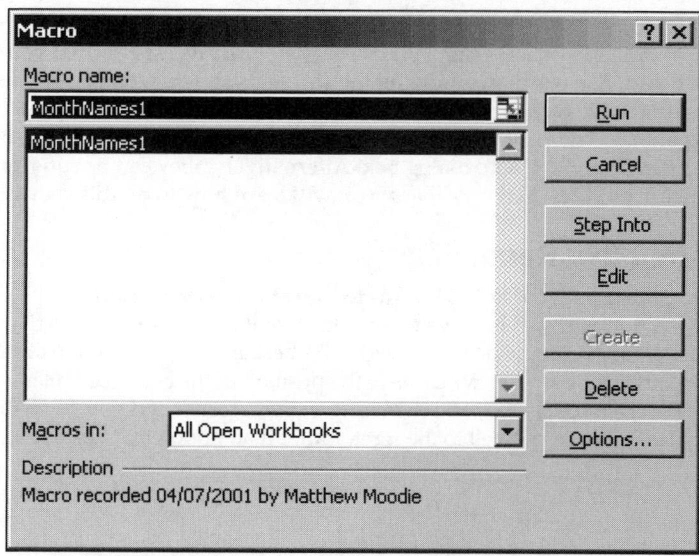

The same dialog box can be opened by pressing the **Run Macro** button on the **Visual Basic** toolbar:

Shortcut Keys

You can change the shortcut key assigned to a macro by first bringing up the **Macro** dialog box, by using **Tools | Macro | Macros**, or the **Run Macro** button on the **Visual Basic** toolbar. Select the macro name and press **Options**. This opens the following dialog box:

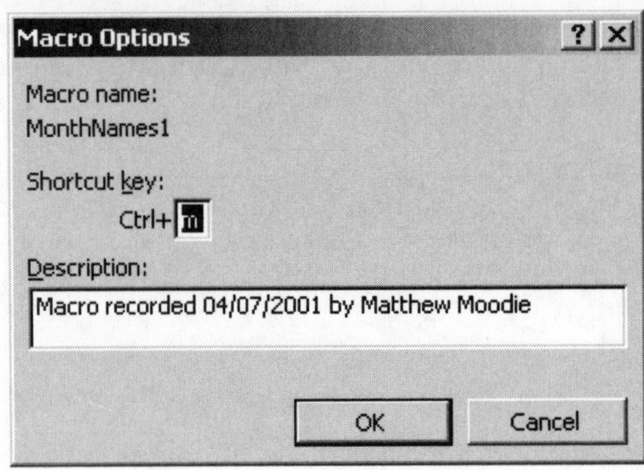

It is possible to assign the same shortcut key to more than one macro in the same workbook using this dialog box (although the dialog box that appears when you start the macro recorder will not let you assign a shortcut that is already in use).

It is also quite likely that two different workbooks could contain macros with the same shortcut key assigned. If this happens, which macro runs when you use the shortcut? The answer is, it is always the macro that comes first alphabetically that runs.

Shortcuts are appropriate for macros that you use very frequently, especially if you prefer to keep your hands on the keyboard. It is worth memorizing the shortcuts so you won't forget them if you use them regularly. Shortcuts are **not** appropriate for macros that are run infrequently or are intended to make life easier for less experienced users of your application. It is better to assign meaningful names to those macros and run them from the Macro dialog box. Alternatively, they can be run from buttons that you add to the worksheet, or place on the toolbars. You will learn how to do this shortly.

Absolute and Relative Recording

When you run `MonthNames1`, the macro returns to the same cells you selected while typing in the month names. It doesn't matter which cell is active when you start, if the macro contains the command to select cell B1, then that is what it selects. The macro selects B1 because you recorded in **absolute** record mode. The alternative, **relative** record mode, remembers the position of the active cell relative to its previous position. If you have cell A10 selected, and then turn on the recorder and you go on to select B10, the recorder notes that you moved one cell to the right, rather than noting that you selected cell B10.

We will record a second macro called `MonthNames2`. There will be three differences in this macro compared with the previous one:

- We will use the Relative Reference button on the Stop Recording toolbar as our first action after turning on the recorder.
- We will not select the "Jan" cell before typing. We want our recorded macro to type "Jan" into the active cell when we run the macro.
- We will finish by selecting the cell under "Jan", rather than A2, just before turning off the recorder.

Start with an empty worksheet and select the B1 cell. Turn on the macro recorder and specify the macro name as `MonthNames2`. Enter the shortcut as uppercase M – the recorder won't let you use lowercase m again. Click the OK button and select the Relative Reference button on the Stop Recording toolbar.

> **If the Stop Recording toolbar does not automatically appear when you start recording, click on View | Toolbars from the worksheet's menu and select Stop Recording. The Stop Recording toolbar will now appear. However, you will need to immediately click the Stop Recording button on the Stop Recording toolbar and start the recording process again. Otherwise, the recorded macro will display the Stop Recording toolbar every time it is run. The Stop Recording toolbar will now synchronize with the recorder, as long as you never close it while recording.**

If you needed to re-synchronize the Stop Recording toolbar using the instructions above, upper case M will already be assigned. If you have difficulties assigning the uppercase M shortcut to `MonthNames2` on the second recording, use another key such as uppercase N, and change it back to M after finishing the recording. Use Tools | Macro | Macros... and, in the Macro dialog box, select the macro name and press the Options button, as explained in the *Shortcut Keys* section above.

Type "Jan" and the other month names, as you did when recording `MonthNames1`. Select cells B1:G1 and press the Bold and Italic buttons on the Formatting toolbar.

> **Make sure you select B1:G1 from left to right, so that B1 is the active cell. There is a small kink in the recording process that can cause errors in the recorded macro if you select cells from right to left or from bottom to top. Always select from the top left hand corner when recording relatively. This has been a problem with all versions of Excel VBA.**

Finally, select cell B2, the cell under Jan, and turn off the recorder.

Before running `MonthNames2`, select a starting cell, such as A10. You will find that the macro now types the month names across row 10, starting in column A and finishes by selecting the cell under the starting cell.

Before you record a macro that selects cells, you need to think about whether to use absolute or relative reference recording. If you are selecting input cells for data entry, or for a print area, you will probably want to record with absolute references. If you want to be able to run your macro in different areas of your worksheet, you will probably want to record with relative references.

If you are trying to reproduce the effect of the *Ctrl+Arrow* keys to select the last cell in a column or row of data, you should record with relative references. You can even switch between relative and absolute reference recording in the middle of a macro, if you want. You might want to select the top of a column with an absolute reference, switch to relative references and use *Ctrl+Down Arrow* to get to the bottom of the column and an extra *Down Arrow* to go to the first empty cell.

> *Excel 2000 was the first version of Excel to let you successfully record selecting a block of rcells of variable height and width using the* Ctrl *key. If you start at the top left hand corner of a block of data, you can hold down the* Shift+Ctrl *keys and press* Down Arrow *and then* Right Arrow *to select the whole block (as long as there are no gaps in the data). If you record these operations with relative referencing, you can use the macro to select a block of different dimensions. Previous versions of Excel recorded an absolute selection of the original block size, regardless of recording mode.*

The Visual Basic Editor

It is now time to see what has been going on behind the scenes. If you want to understand macros, be able to modify your macros, and tap into the full power of VBA, you need to know how to use the **Visual Basic Editor (VBE)**. The VBE runs in its own window, separate from the Excel window. You can activate it in many ways.

First, you can activate it by pressing the Visual Basic Editor button on the Visual Basic toolbar. You can also activate it by holding down the *Alt* key and pressing the *F11* key. *Alt+F11* acts as a toggle, taking you between the Excel Window and the VBE window. If you want to edit a specific macro, you can use Tools | Macro | Macros… to open the Macro dialog box, select the macro, and press the Edit button. The VBE window will look something like the following:

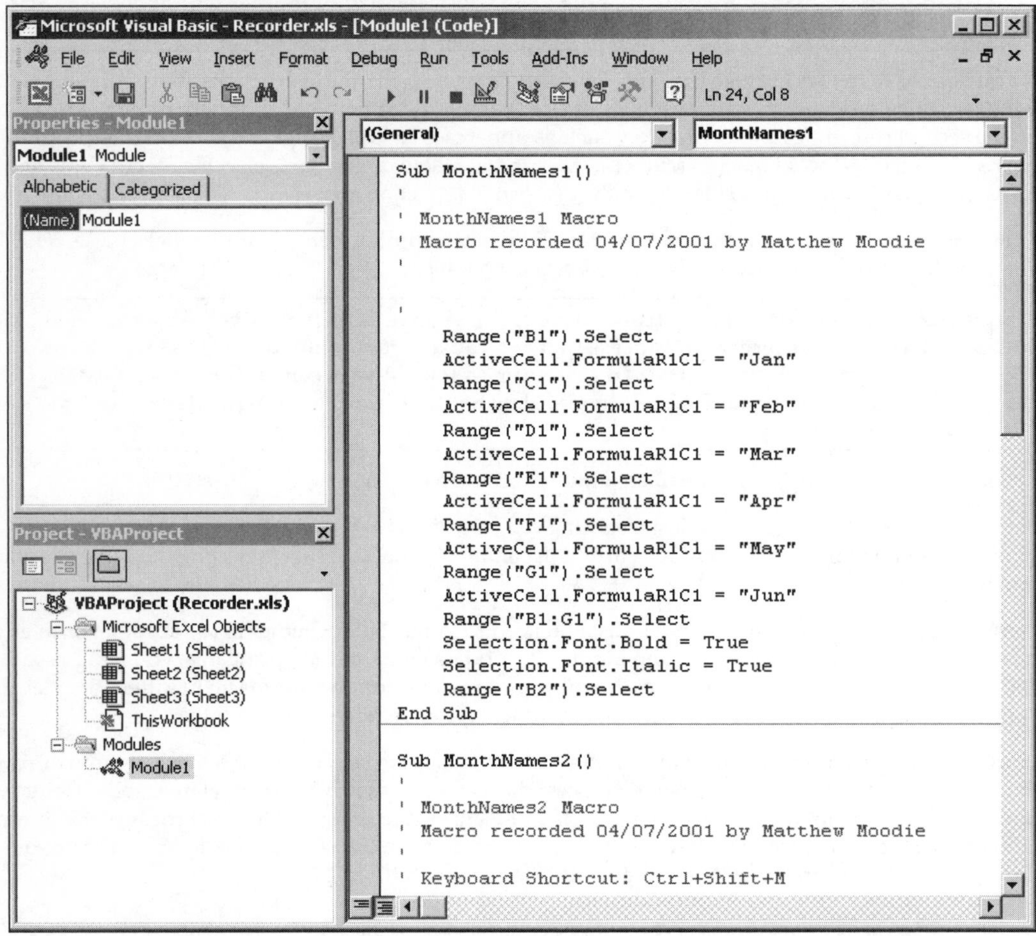

It is quite possible that you will see nothing but the menu bar when you switch to the VBE window. If you can't see the toolbar, use View | Toolbars *and click on the* Standard *toolbar. Use* View | Project Explorer *and* View | Properties Window *to show the windows on the left. If you can't see the code module on the right, double-click the icon for* Module1 *in the Project Explorer window.*

Code Modules

All macros reside in **code modules** like the one on the right of the VBE window above. There are two types of code modules – **standard modules** and **class modules**. The one you see on the right is a standard module. You can use class modules to create your own objects. You won't need to know much about class modules until you are working at a very advanced level. See Chapter 15 for more details on how to use class modules.

Some class modules have already been set up for you. They are associated with each worksheet in your workbook and there is one for the entire workbook. You can see them in the Project Explorer window, in the folder called "Microsoft Excel Objects". You will find out more about them later in this chapter.

You can add as many code modules to your workbook, as you like. The macro recorder has inserted the one above, named Module1. Each module can contain many macros. For a small application, you would probably keep all your macros in one module. For larger projects, you can organize your code better by filing unrelated macros in separate modules.

Procedures

In VBA, macros are referred to as **procedures**. There are two types of procedures – **sub procedures** and **function** procedures. You will find out about function procedures in the next section. The macro recorder can only produce sub procedures. You can see the `MonthNames1` sub procedure set up by the recorder in the above screenshot.

Sub procedures start with the keyword `Sub` followed by the name of the procedure and opening and closing parentheses. The end of a sub procedure is marked by the keywords `End Sub`. Although it is not mandatory, the code within the sub procedure is normally indented, to make it stand out from the start and end of the procedure, so that the whole procedure is easier to read. Further indentation is normally used to distinguish sections of code such as `If` tests and looping structures.

Any lines starting with a single quote are comment lines, which are ignored by VBA. They are added to provide documentation, which is a very important component of good programming practice. You can also add comments to the right of lines of code. For example:

```
Range("B1").Select   'Select the B1 cell
```

At this stage, the code may not make perfect sense, but you should be able to make out roughly what is going on. If you look at the code in `MonthNames1`, you will see that cells are being selected and then the month names are assigned to the active cell formula. You can edit some parts of the code, so if you had spelled a month name incorrectly, you could fix it; or you could identify and remove the line that sets the font to bold; or you can select and delete an entire macro.

Notice the differences between `MonthNames1` and `MonthNames2`. `MonthNames1` selects specific cells such as B1 and C1. `MonthNames2` uses `Offset` to select a cell that is zero rows down and one column to the right from the active cell. Already, you are starting to get a feel for the VBA language.

The Project Explorer

The Project Explorer is an essential navigation tool. In VBA, each workbook contains a project. The Project Explorer displays all the open projects and the component parts of those projects, as you can see here:

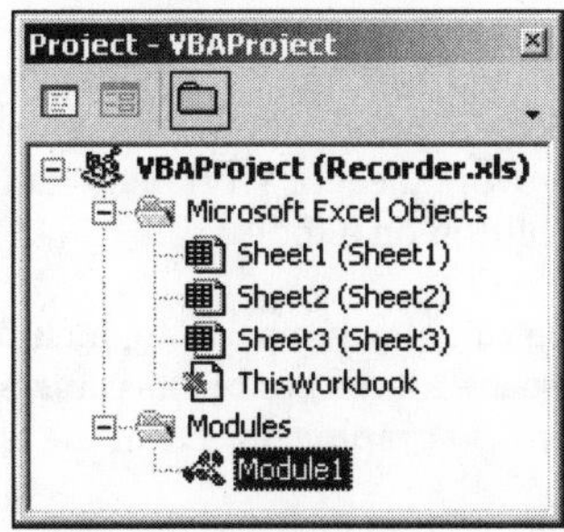

You can use the Project Explorer to locate and activate the code modules in your project. You can double click a module icon to open and activate that module. You can also insert and remove code modules in the Project Explorer. Right-click anywhere in the Project Explorer window and click Insert to add a new standard module, class module, or UserForm.

To remove Module1, right-click it and choose Remove Module1.... Note that you can't do this with the modules associated with workbook or worksheet objects. You can also export the code in a module to a separate text file, or import code from a text file.

The Properties Window

The Properties window shows you the properties that can be changed at design time for the currently active object in the Project Explorer window. For example, if you click on Sheet1 in the Project Explorer, the following properties are displayed in the Properties window. The ScrollArea property has been set to A1:D10, to restrict users to that area of the worksheet:

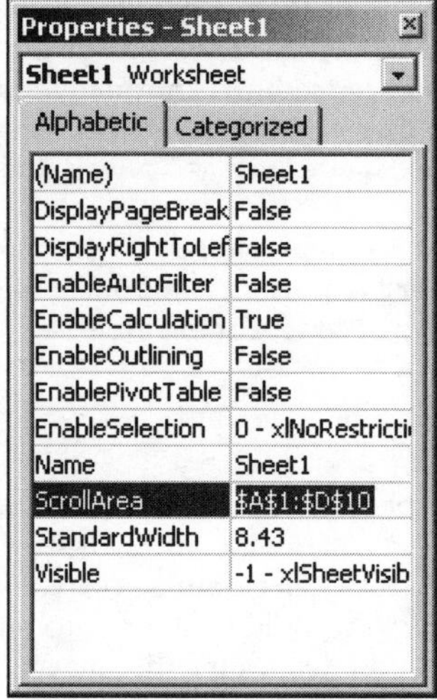

You can get to the help screen associated with any property very easily. Just select the property, such as the ScrollArea property, which is selected above, and press *F1*.

Other Ways to Run Macros

You have seen how to run macros with shortcuts and how to run them from the Tools menu. Neither method is particularly friendly. You need to be very familiar with your macros to be comfortable with these techniques. You can make your macros much more accessible by attaching them to buttons.

If the macro is worksheet specific, and will only be used in a particular part of the worksheet, then it is suitable to use a button that has been embedded in the worksheet at the appropriate location. If you want to be able to use a macro in any worksheet or workbook and in any location in a worksheet, it is appropriate to attach the macro to a button on a toolbar.

There are many other objects that you can attach macros to, including combo boxes, listboxes, scrollbars, checkboxes and option buttons. These are all referred to as **controls**. See Chapter 11 for more information on controls. You can also attach macros to graphic objects in the worksheet, such as shapes created with the Drawing toolbar.

Worksheet Buttons

Excel 2002 has two different sets of controls that can be embedded in worksheets. One set is on the Forms toolbar and the other is on the Control Toolbox toolbar. The Forms toolbar has been inherited from Excel 5 and 95. The Forms controls are also used with Excel 5 and 95 dialog sheets to create dialog boxes. Excel 97 introduced the newer ActiveX controls that are selected from the Control Toolbox toolbar. You can also use these on UserForms, in the VBE, to create dialog boxes.

For compatibility with the older versions of Excel, both sets of controls and techniques for creating dialog boxes are supported in Excel 97 and above. If you have no need to maintain backward compatibility with Excel 5 and 95, you can use just the ActiveX controls, except when you want to embed controls in a chart. At the moment, charts only support the Forms controls.

Forms Toolbar

Another reason for using the Forms controls is that they are simpler to use than the ActiveX controls, as they do not have all the features of ActiveX controls. For example, Forms controls can only respond to a single, predefined event, which is usually the mouse-click event. ActiveX controls can respond to many events, such as a mouse click, a double-click or pressing a key on the keyboard. If you have no need of such features, you might prefer the simplicity of Forms controls. To create a Forms button in a worksheet, click the fourth button from the left in the Forms toolbar shown below:

You can now draw the button in your worksheet by clicking where you want a corner of the button to appear and dragging to where you want the diagonally opposite corner to appear. The following dialog box will show, and you can select the macro to attach to the button:

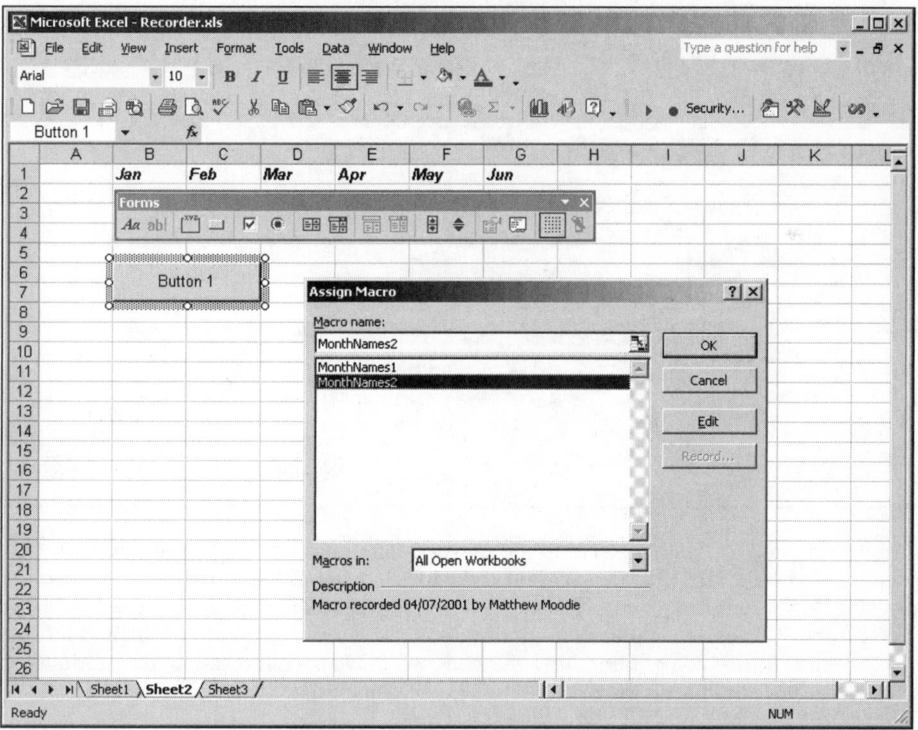

Click OK to complete the assignment. You can then edit the text on the button to give a more meaningful indication of its function. After you click on a worksheet cell, you can click the button to run the attached macro. If you need to edit the button, you can right-click on it. This selects the control and you get a shortcut menu. If you don't want the shortcut menu, hold down *Ctrl* and left-click the button to select it. (Don't drag the mouse while you hold down *Ctrl*, or you will create a copy of the button.)

If you want to align the button with the worksheet gridlines, hold down *Alt* as you draw it with the mouse. If you have already drawn the button, select it and hold down *Alt* as you drag any of the white boxes that appear on the corners and edges of the button. The edge or corner you drag will snap to the nearest gridline.

Control Toolbox Toolbar

To create an ActiveX command button control, click the sixth button on the Control Toolbox toolbar shown below:

When you draw your button in the worksheet, you enter into design mode. When you are in design mode, you can select a control with a left-click and edit it. You must turn off design mode if you want the new control to respond to events. This can be achieved by unchecking the design mode icon on the Control Toolbox toolbar or the Visual Basic toolbar:

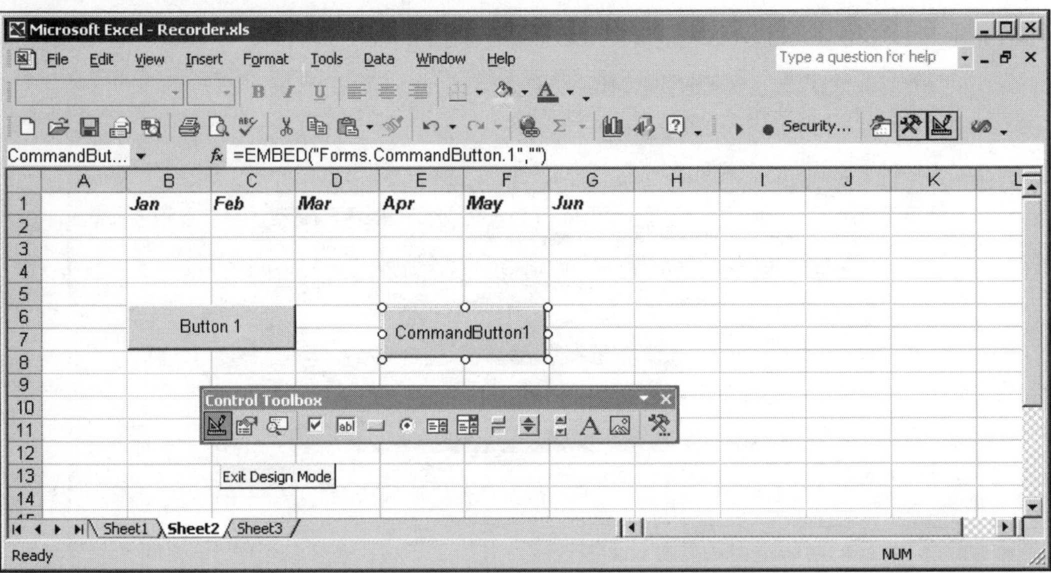

You are not prompted to assign a macro to the ActiveX command button, but you do need to write a click-event procedure for the button. An **event procedure** is a sub procedure that is executed when, for example, you click on a button. To do this, make sure you are still in design mode and double-click the command button. This will open the VBE window and display the code module behind the worksheet. The `Sub` and `End Sub` statement lines for your code will have been inserted in the module and you can add in the code necessary to run the `MonthName2` macro, as shown:

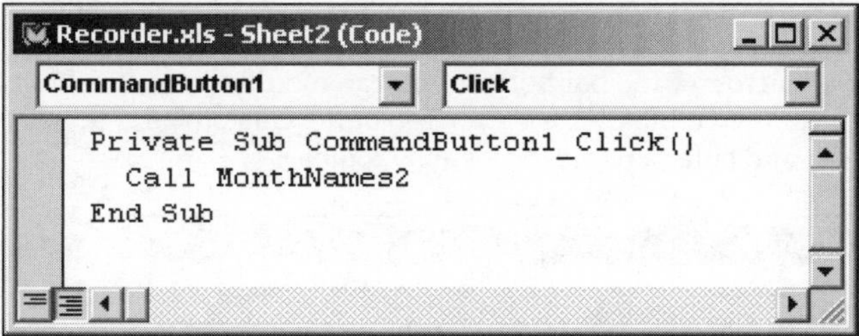

To run this code, switch back to the worksheet, turn off design mode, and click the command button.

If you want to make changes to the command button, you need to return to design mode by pressing the **Design Mode** button. You can then select the command button and change its size and position on the worksheet. You can also display its properties by right-clicking on it and choosing **Properties** to display the following window:

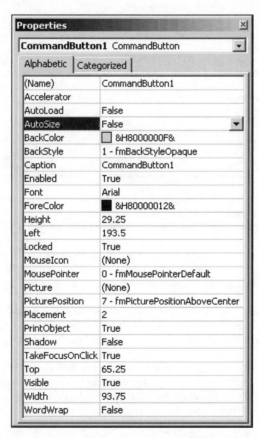

Properties

CommandButton1 CommandButton

Alphabetic | Categorized

(Name)	CommandButton1
Accelerator	
AutoLoad	False
AutoSize	False
BackColor	&H8000000F&
BackStyle	1 - fmBackStyleOpaque
Caption	CommandButton1
Enabled	True
Font	Arial
ForeColor	&H80000012&
Height	29.25
Left	193.5
Locked	True
MouseIcon	(None)
MousePointer	0 - fmMousePointerDefault
Picture	(None)
PicturePosition	7 - fmPicturePositionAboveCenter
Placement	2
PrintObject	True
Shadow	False
TakeFocusOnClick	True
Top	65.25
Visible	True
Width	93.75
WordWrap	False

To change the text on the command button, change the **Caption** property. You can also set the font for the caption and the foreground and background colors. If you want the button to work satisfactorily in Excel 97, it is a good idea to change the **TakeFocusOnClick** property from its default value of `True` to `False`. If the button takes the focus when you click on it, Excel 97 does not allow you to assign values to some properties such as the **NumberFormat** property of the `Range` object.

Toolbars

If you want to attach a macro to a toolbar button, you can modify one of the built in toolbars or create your own. To create your own toolbar, use **View | Toolbars | Customize...** to bring up the **Customize** dialog box, click **New...** and enter a name for the new toolbar:

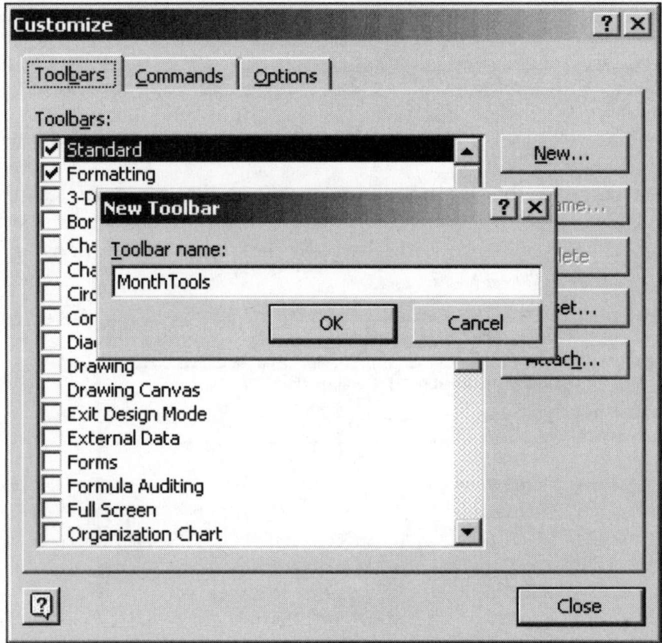

Staying in the **Customize** dialog box, click on the **Commands** tab and select the **Macros** category. Drag the **Custom Button** with the smiley face icon to the new toolbar, or an existing toolbar. Next, either click the **Modify Selection** button, or right-click the new toolbar button to get a shortcut menu.

Click on **Assign Macro...** and select the name of the macro, **MonthNames2** in this case, to be assigned to the button. You can also change the button image by clicking on **Change Button Image** and choosing from a library of 42 preset images, or you can open the icon editor with **Edit Button Image**.

Note that the **Customize** dialog box must stay open while you make these changes. It is a good idea to enter some descriptive text into the **Name** box, which will appear as the ScreenTip for the button. You can now close the **Customize** dialog box.

To run the macro, select a starting cell for your month names and click the new toolbar button. If you want to distribute the new toolbar to others, along with the workbook, you can attach the toolbar to the workbook. It will then pop up automatically on the new user's PC as soon as they open the workbook, as long as they do not already have a toolbar with the same name.

There is a potential problem when you attach a toolbar to a workbook. As Excel will not replace an existing toolbar, you can have a toolbar that is attached to an older version of the workbook than the one you are trying to use. A solution to this problem is provided in the next section on event procedures.

To attach a toolbar to the active workbook, use View | Toolbars | Customize… to bring up the Customize dialog box, click the Toolbars tab, if necessary and click Attach… to open the Attach Toolbars dialog box as follows:

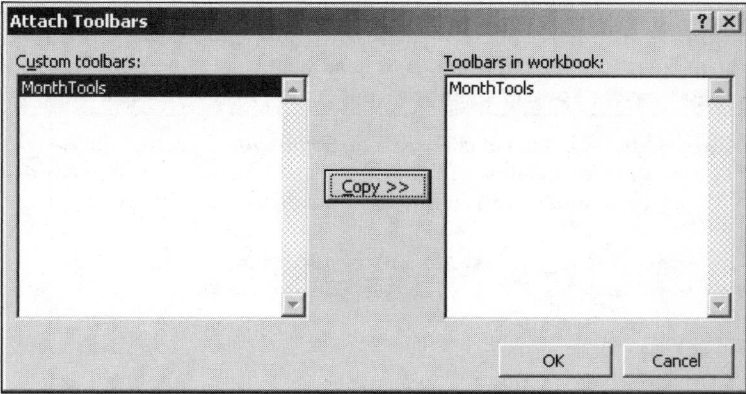

Select the toolbar name in the left list box and press the middle button, which has the caption Copy>>.

If an older copy of the toolbar is already attached to the workbook, select it in the right hand list box and press Delete to remove it. Then select the toolbar name in the left list box and press the middle button again, which will now have the caption Copy >>. Click OK to complete the attachment and then close the Customize dialog box.

Event Procedures

Event procedures are special macro procedures that respond to the events that occur in Excel. Events include user actions, such as clicking the mouse on a button, and system actions, such as the recalculation of a worksheet. Versions of Excel since Excel 97 expose a wide range of events for which we can write code.

The click-event procedure for the ActiveX command button that ran the `MonthNames2` macro, which we have already seen, is a good example. We entered the code for this event procedure in the code module behind the worksheet where the command button was embedded. All event procedures are contained in the class modules behind the workbook, worksheets, charts, and UserForms.

We can see the events that are available by activating a module, such as the ThisWorkbook module, choosing an object, such as Workbook, from the left drop-down list at the top of the module and then activating the right drop down, as shown:

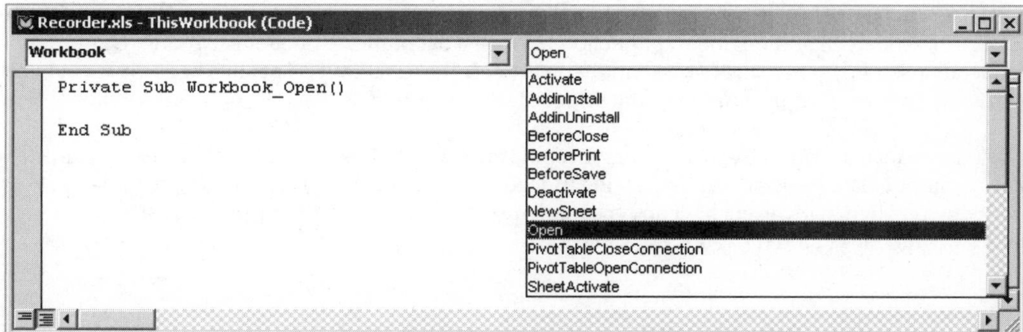

The `Workbook_Open()` event can be used to initialize the workbook when it is opened. The code could be as simple as activating a particular worksheet and selecting a range for data input. The code could be more sophisticated and construct a new menu bar for the workbook.

> **For compatibility with Excel 5 and 95, you can still create a sub procedure called `Auto_Open()`, in a standard module, that runs when the workbook is opened. If you also have a `Workbook_Open()` event procedure, the event procedure runs first.**

As you can see, there are many events to choose from. Some events, such as the `BeforeSave` and `BeforeClose` events, allow cancelation of the event. The following event procedure stops the workbook from being closed until cell A1 in Sheet1 contains the value `True`:

```
Private Sub Workbook_BeforeClose(Cancel As Boolean)
  If ThisWorkbook.Sheets("Sheet1").Range("A1").Value <> True _
                                                  Then Cancel = True
End Sub
```

This code even prevents the closure of the Excel window.

Removing an Attached Toolbar

As mentioned previously in this chapter, if you have attached a custom toolbar to a workbook, there can be a problem if you send a new version of the toolbar attached to a workbook, or the user saves the workbook under a different name. The old toolbar is not replaced when you open the new workbook, and the macros that the old toolbar runs are still in the old workbook.

One approach that makes it much less likely that problems will occur, is to delete the custom toolbar when the workbook is closed:

```
Private Sub Workbook_BeforeClose(Cancel As Boolean)
   On Error Resume Next
   Application.CommandBars("MonthsTools").Delete
End Sub
```

The `On Error` statement covers the situation where the user might delete the toolbar manually before closing the workbook. Omitting the `On Error` statement would cause a run time error when the event procedure attempts to delete the missing toolbar. `On Error Resume Next` is an instruction to ignore any run-time error and continue with the next line of code.

User Defined Functions

Excel has hundreds of built-in worksheet functions that we can use in cell formulas. You can select an empty worksheet cell and use Insert | Function… to see a list of those functions. Among the most frequently used functions are `SUM`, `IF`, and `VLOOKUP`. If the function you need is not already in Excel, you can write your own user defined function (or UDF) using VBA.

UDFs can reduce the complexity of a worksheet. It is possible to reduce a calculation that requires many cells of intermediate results down to a single function call in one cell. UDFs can also increase productivity when many users have to repeatedly use the same calculation procedures. You can set up a library of functions tailored to your organization.

Creating a UDF

Unlike manual operations, UDFs cannot be recorded. We have to write them from scratch using a standard module in the VBE. If necessary, you can insert a standard module by right-clicking in the Project Explorer window and choosing **Insert | Module**. A simple example of a UDF is shown here:

```
Function CtoF(Centigrade)
   CtoF = Centigrade * 9 / 5 + 32
End Function
```

Here, we have created a function called `CtoF()` that converts degrees Centigrade to degrees Fahrenheit. In the worksheet we could have column A containing degrees Centigrade, and column B using the `CtoF()` function to calculate the corresponding temperature in degrees Fahrenheit. You can see the formula in cell B2 by looking at the Formula bar:

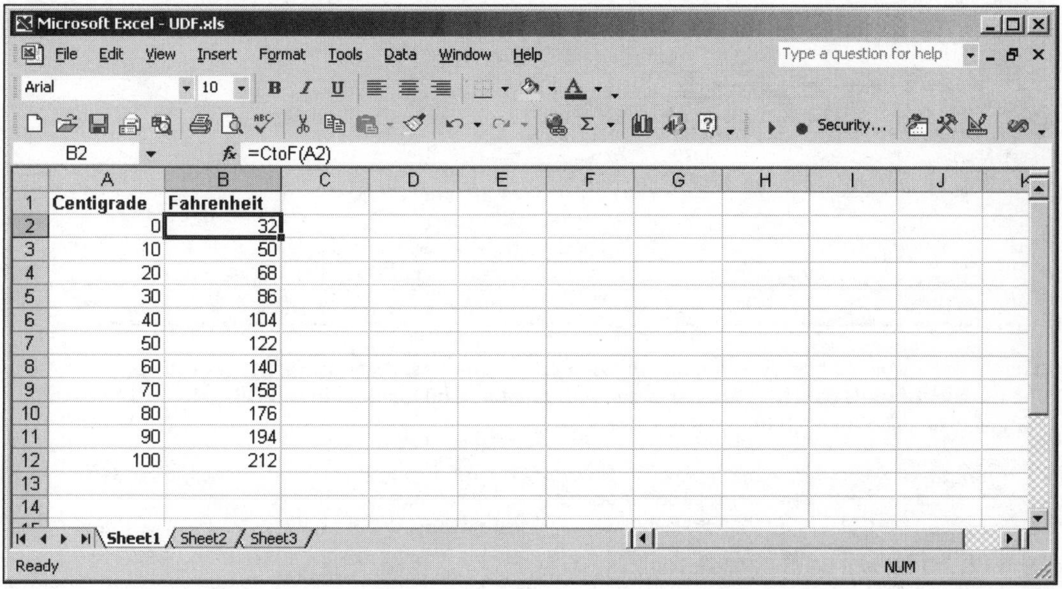

Microsoft Excel - UDF.xls

B2 =CtoF(A2)

	A	B
1	Centigrade	Fahrenheit
2	0	32
3	10	50
4	20	68
5	30	86
6	40	104
7	50	122
8	60	140
9	70	158
10	80	176
11	90	194
12	100	212

The formula has been copied into cells **B3:B13**.

The key difference between a sub procedure and a function procedure is that a function procedure returns a value. `CtoF()` calculates a numeric value, which is returned to the worksheet cell where `CtoF()` is used. A function procedure indicates the value to be returned by setting its own name equal to the return value.

Function procedures normally have one or more input parameters. `CtoF()` has one input parameter called `Centigrade`, which is used to calculate the return value. When you enter the formula, `=CtoF(A2)`, the value in cell **A2** is passed to `CtoF()` through `Centigrade`. In the case where the value of `Centigrade` is zero, `CtoF()` sets its own name equal to the calculated result, which is 32. The result is passed back to cell **B2**, as shown above. The same process occurs in each cell that contains a reference to `CtoF()`.

A different example that shows how you can reduce the complexity of spreadsheet formulas for users is shown below. The lookup table in cells **A1:D5** gives the price of each product, the discount sales volume (above which a discount will be applied), and the percent discount for units above the discount volume. Using normal spreadsheet formulas, users would have to set up three lookup formulas together with some logical tests to calculate the invoice amount:

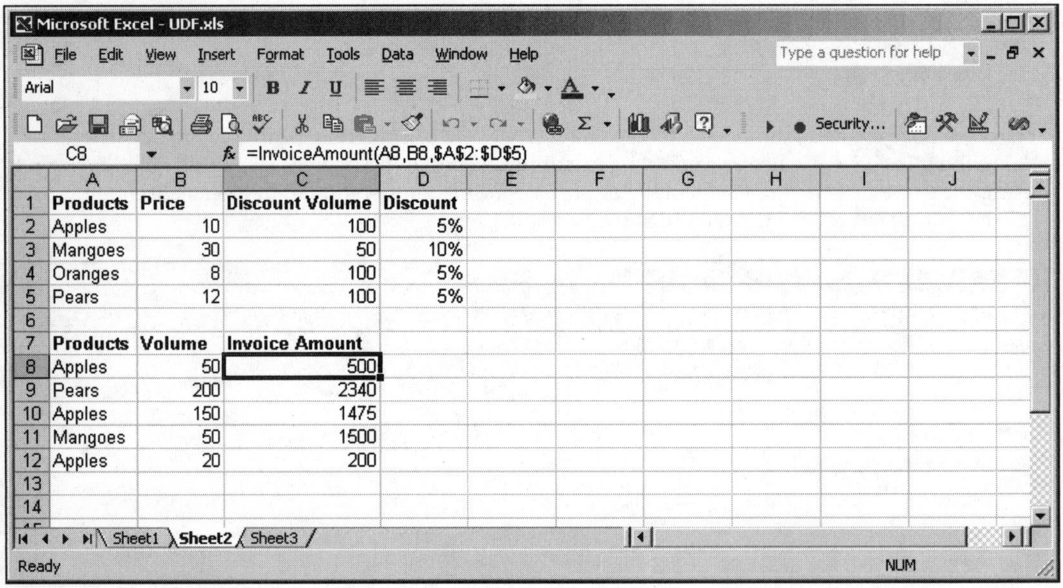

Microsoft Excel - UDF.xls

C8 =InvoiceAmount(A8,B8,$A$2:$D$5)

	A	B	C	D
1	Products	Price	Discount Volume	Discount
2	Apples	10	100	5%
3	Mangoes	30	50	10%
4	Oranges	8	100	5%
5	Pears	12	100	5%
6				
7	Products	Volume	Invoice Amount	
8	Apples	50	500	
9	Pears	200	2340	
10	Apples	150	1475	
11	Mangoes	50	1500	
12	Apples	20	200	

The `InvoiceAmount()` function has three input parameters: `Prod` is the name of the product; `Vol` is the number of units sold and `Table` is the lookup table. The formula in cell **C8**, above, defines the ranges to be used for each input parameter:

```
Function InvoiceAmount(Prod, Vol, Table)
   Price = WorksheetFunction.VLookup(Prod, Table, 2)
   DiscountVol = WorksheetFunction.VLookup(Prod, Table, 3)
   If Vol > DiscountVol Then
      DiscountPct = WorksheetFunction.VLookup(Prod, Table, 4)
      InvoiceAmount = Price * DiscountVol + Price * _
                      (1 - DiscountPct) * (Vol - DiscountVol)
   Else
      InvoiceAmount = Price * Vol
   End If
End Function
```

The range for the table is absolute so that the copies of the formula below cell **C8** refer to the same range. The first calculation in the function uses the `VLookup` function to find the product in the lookup table and return the corresponding value from the second column of the lookup table, which it assigns to the variable `Price`.

If you want to use an Excel worksheet function in a VBA procedure, you need to tell VBA where to find it by preceding the function name with `WorksheetFunction` *and a period. For compatibility with Excel 5 and 95, you can use* `Application` *instead of* `WorksheetFunction`*. Not all worksheet functions are available this way. In these cases, VBA has equivalent functions, or mathematical operators, to carry out the same calculations.*

In the next line of the function, the discount volume is found in the lookup table and assigned to the variable DiscountVol. The If test on the next line compares the sales volume in Vol with DiscountVol. If Vol is greater than DiscountVol, the calculations following, down to the Else statement, are carried out. Otherwise, the calculation after the Else is carried out.

If Vol is greater than DiscountVol, the percent discount rate is found in the lookup table and assigned to the variable DiscountPct. The invoice amount is then calculated by applying the full price to the units up to DiscountVol plus the discounted price for units above DiscountVol. Note the use of the underscore character, preceded by a blank space, to indicate the continuation of the code on the next line.

The result is assigned to the name of the function, InvoiceAmount, so that the value will be returned to the worksheet cell. If Vol is not greater than DiscountVol, the invoice amount is calculated by applying the price to the units sold and the result is assigned to the name of the function.

Direct Reference to Ranges

When you define a UDF, it is possible to directly refer to worksheet ranges rather than through the input parameters of the UDF. This is illustrated in the following version of the InvoiceAmount() function:

```
Function InvoiceAmount2(Prod, Vol)
   Set Table = ThisWorkbook.Worksheets("Sheet2").Range("A2:D5")
   Price = WorksheetFunction.VLookup(Prod, Table, 2)
   DiscountVol = WorksheetFunction.VLookup(Prod, Table, 3)
   If Vol > DiscountVol Then
      DiscountPct = WorksheetFunction.VLookup(Prod, Table, 4)
      InvoiceAmount2 = Price * DiscountVol + Price * _
                       (1 - DiscountPct) * (Vol - DiscountVol)
   Else
      InvoiceAmount2 = Price * Vol
   End If
End Function
```

Note that Table is no longer an input parameter. Instead, the Set statement defines Table with a direct reference to the worksheet range. While this method still works, the return value of the function will not be recalculated if you change a value in the lookup table. Excel does not realize that it needs to recalculate the function when a lookup table value changes, as it does not see that the table is used by the function.

Excel only recalculates a UDF when it sees its input parameters change. If you want to remove the lookup table from the function parameters, and still have the UDF recalculate automatically, you can declare the function to be volatile on the first line of the function as shown:

```
Function InvoiceAmount2(Prod, Vol)
   Application.Volatile
   Set Table = ThisWorkbook.Worksheets("Sheet2").Range("A2:D5")
   ...
```

However, you should be aware that this feature comes at a price. If a UDF is declared volatile, the UDF is recalculated every time any value changes in the worksheet. This can add a significant recalculation burden to the worksheet if the UDF is used in many cells.

What UDFs Cannot Do

A common mistake made by users is to attempt to create a worksheet function that changes the structure of the worksheet by, for example, copying a range of cells. **Such attempts will fail**. No error messages are produced because Excel simply ignores the offending code lines, so the reason for the failure is not obvious.

> **UDFs, used in worksheet cells, are not permitted to change the structure of the worksheet. This means that a UDF cannot return a value to any other cell than the one it is used in and it cannot change a physical characteristic of a cell, such as the font color or background pattern. In addition, UDFs cannot carry out actions such as copying or moving spreadsheet cells. They cannot even carry out some actions that imply a change of cursor location, such as an Edit | Find. A UDF can call another function procedure, or even a sub procedure, but that procedure will be under the same restrictions as the UDF. It will still not be permitted to change the structure of the worksheet.**

A distinction is made (in Excel VBA) between UDFs that are used in worksheet cells, and function procedures that are not connected with worksheet cells. As long as the original calling procedure was not a UDF in a worksheet cell, a function procedure can carry out any Excel action, just like a sub procedure.

It should also be noted that UDFs are not as efficient as the built-in Excel worksheet functions. If UDFs are used extensively in a workbook, recalculation time will be greater compared with a similar workbook using the same number of built-in functions.

The Excel Object Model

The Visual Basic for Applications programming language is common across all the Microsoft Office applications. In addition to Excel, you can use VBA in Word, Access, PowerPoint, and Outlook. Once you learn it, you can apply it to any of these. However, to work with an application, you need to learn about the **objects** it contains. In Word, you deal with documents, paragraphs, and words. In Access, you deal with databases, recordsets, and fields. In Excel you deal with workbooks, worksheets, and ranges.

Unlike many programming languages, you don't have to create your own objects in Office VBA. Each application has a clearly defined set of objects that are arranged according to the relationships between them. This structure is referred to as the application's **object model**. This section is an introduction to the Excel Object Model, which is fully documented in Appendix A.

Objects

First, let's cover a few basics about Object-Oriented Programming (OOP). This not a complete formal treatise on the subject, but it covers what you need to know to work with the objects in Excel.

OOP's basic premise is that we can describe everything known to us as objects. You and I are objects, the world is an object and the universe is an object. In Excel, a workbook is an object, a worksheet is an object, and a range is an object. These objects are only a small sample of around two hundred object types available to us in Excel. Let us look at some examples of how we can refer to `Range` objects in VBA code. One simple way to refer to cells B2:C4 is as follows:

```
Range("B2:C4")
```

If you give the name `Data` to a range of cells, you can use that name in a similar way:

```
Range("Data")
```

There are also ways to refer to the currently active cell and selection using shortcuts:

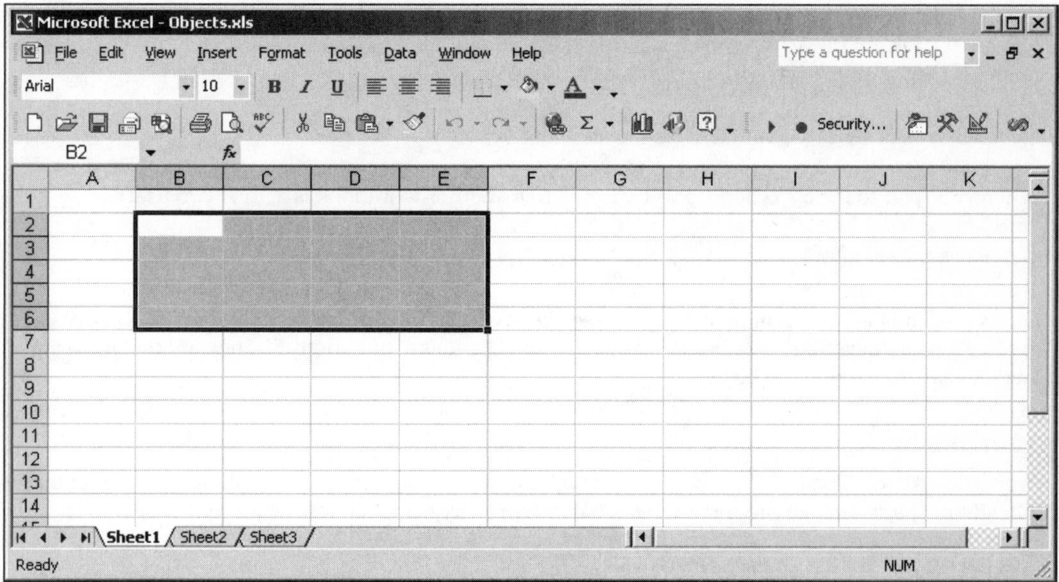

In the screenshot above, `ActiveCell` refers to the B2 cell, and `Selection` refers to the range B2:E6. For more information on `ActiveCell` and `Selection`, see Chapter 3.

Collections

Many objects belong to **collections**. A city block is a collection of high-rise buildings. A high-rise building has a collection of floor objects. A floor is a collection of room objects. Collections are objects themselves – objects that contain other objects that are closely related. Collections and objects are often related in a hierarchical or tree structure.

Excel is an object itself, called the `Application` object. In the Excel `Application` object, there is a `Workbooks` collection that contains all the currently open `Workbook` objects. Each `Workbook` object has a `Worksheets` collection that contains the `Worksheet` objects in that workbook.

> **Note that you need to make a clear distinction between the plural `Worksheets` object, which is a collection, and the singular `Worksheet` object. They are quite different objects.**

If you want to refer to a member of a collection, you can refer to it by its position in the collection, as an index number starting with 1, or by its name, as quoted text. If you have opened just one workbook called `Data.xls`, you can refer to it by either of the following:

```
Workbooks(1)
Workbooks("Data.xls")
```

If you have three worksheets in the active workbook that have the names North, East, and South, in that order, you can refer to the second worksheet by either of the following:

```
Worksheets(2)
Worksheets("East")
```

If you want to refer to a worksheet called DataInput in a workbook called Sales.xls, and Sales.xls is not the active workbook, you must qualify the worksheet reference with the workbook reference, separating them with a period, as follows:

```
Workbooks("Sales.xls").Worksheets("DataInput")
```

When you refer to the B2 cell in DataInput, while another workbook is active, you use:

```
Workbooks("Sales.xls").Worksheets("DataInput").Range("B2")
```

Let us now look at objects more closely and see how we can manipulate them in our VBA code. There are two key characteristics of objects that you need to be aware of to do this. They are the **properties** and **methods** associated with an object.

Properties

Properties are the physical characteristics of objects, and can be measured or quantified. You and I have a height property, an age property, a bank balance property, and a name property. Some of our properties can be changed fairly easily, such as our bank balance. Other properties are more difficult or impossible to change, such as our name and age.

A worksheet Range object has a RowHeight property and a ColumnWidth property. A Workbook object has a Name property, which contains its file name. Some properties can be changed easily, such as the Range object's ColumnWidth property, by assigning the property a new value. Other properties, such as the Workbook object's Name property, are read-only. You can't change the Name property by simply assigning a new value to it.

You refer to the property of an object by referring to the object, then the property, separated by a period. For example, to change the width of the column containing the active cell to 20 points, you would assign the value to the ColumnWidth property of the ActiveCell using:

```
ActiveCell.ColumnWidth = 20
```

To enter the name Florence into cell C10, you assign the name to the Value property of the Range object:

```
Range("C10").Value = "Florence"
```

If the Range object is not in the active worksheet in the active workbook, you need to be more specific:

```
Workbooks("Sales.xls").Worksheets("DataInput").Range("C10").Value = 10
```

VBA can do what is impossible for us to do manually. It can enter data into worksheets that are not visible on the screen. It can copy and move data without having to make the sheets involved active. Therefore, it is very seldom necessary to activate a specific workbook, worksheet, or range to manipulate data using VBA. The more you can avoid activating objects, the faster your code will run. Unfortunately, the macro recorder can only record what we do and uses activation extensively.

In the examples above, we have seen how we can assign values to the properties of objects. We can also assign the property values of objects to variables or to other objects' properties. We can directly assign the column width of one cell to another cell on the active sheet using:

```
Range("C1").ColumnWidth = Range("A1").ColumnWidth
```

We can assign the value in C1 in the active sheet to D10 in the sheet named `Sales`, in the active workbook, using:

```
Worksheets("Sales").Range("D10").Value = Range("C1").Value
```

We can assign the value of a property to a variable so that it can be used in later code. This example stores the current value of cell M100, sets M100 to a new value, prints the auto recalculated results and sets M100 back to its original value:

```
OpeningStock = Range("M100").Value
Range("M100").Value = 100
ActiveSheet.PrintOut
Range("M100").Value = OpeningStock
```

Some properties are read-only, which means that you can't assign a value to them directly. Sometimes there is an indirect way. One example is the `Text` property of a `Range` object. You can assign a value to a cell using its `Value` property and you can give the cell a number format using its `NumberFormat` property. The `Text` property of the cell gives you the formatted appearance of the cell. The following example displays `$12,345.60` in a Message box:

```
Range("B10").Value = 12345.6
Range("B10").NumberFormat = "$#,##0.00"
MsgBox Range("B10").Text
```

This is the only means by which we can set the value of the `Text` property .

Methods

While properties are the quantifiable characteristics of objects, methods are the actions that can be performed by objects or on objects. If you have a linguistic bent, you might like to think of objects as nouns, properties as adjectives, and methods as verbs. Methods often change the properties of objects. I have a walking method that takes me from A to B, changing my location property. I have a spending method that reduces my bank balance property and a working method that increases my bank balance property. My dieting method reduces my weight property, temporarily.

A simple example of an Excel method is the `Select` method of the `Range` object. To refer to a method, as with properties, we put the object first, add a period, and then the method. The following selects cell G4:

```
Range("G4").Select
```

Another example of an Excel method is the `Copy` method of the `Range` object. The following copies the contents of range A1:B3 to the clipboard:

```
Range("A1:B3").Copy
```

Methods often have parameters that we can use to modify the way the method works. For example, we can use the `Paste` method of the `Worksheet` object to paste the contents of the clipboard into a worksheet, but if we do not specify where the data is to be pasted, it is inserted with its top left hand corner in the active cell. This can be overriden with the `Destination` parameter (parameters are discussed later in this section):

```
ActiveSheet.Paste Destination:=Range("G4")
```

Note that the value of a parameter is specified using :=, not just =.

Often, Excel methods provide shortcuts. The previous examples of `Copy` and `Paste` can be carried out entirely by the `Copy` method:

```
Range("A1:B3").Copy Destination:=Range("G4")
```

This is far more efficient than the code produced by the macro recorder:

```
Range("A1:B3").Select
Selection.Copy
Range("G4").Select
ActiveSheet.Paste
```

Events

Another important concept in VBA is that objects can respond to events. A mouse click on a command button, a double-click on a cell, a recalculation of a worksheet, and the opening and closing of a workbook are examples of events.

All of the ActiveX controls from the Control Toolbox toolbar can respond to events. These controls can be embedded in worksheets and in UserForms to enhance the functionality of those objects. Worksheets and workbooks can also respond to a wide range of events. If we want an object to respond to an event, we enter VBA code into the appropriate event procedure for that object. The event procedure resides in the code module behind the `Workbook`, `Worksheet`, or `UserForm` object concerned.

For example, we might want to detect that a user has selected a new cell and highlight the cell's complete row and column. We can do this by entering code in the `Worksheet_SelectionChange()` event procedure:

- First activate the VBE window and double-click the worksheet in the Project Explorer
- From the drop-down lists at the top of the worksheet code module, choose `Worksheet` and `SelectionChange`, and enter the following code:

```
Private Sub Worksheet_SelectionChange(ByVal Target As Range)
  Rows.Interior.ColorIndex = xlColorIndexNone
  Target.EntireColumn.Interior.ColorIndex = 36
  Target.EntireRow.Interior.ColorIndex = 36
End Sub
```

This event procedure runs every time the user selects a new cell, or block of cells. The parameter, `Target`, refers to the selected range as a `Range` object. The first statement sets the `ColorIndex` property of all the worksheets cells to no color, to remove any existing background color. The second and third statements set the entire columns and entire rows that intersect with the selected cells to a background color of pale yellow. This color can be different, depending on the color palette set up in your workbook.

The use of properties in this example is more complex than we have seen before. Let's analyze the component parts. If we assume that `Target` is a `Range` object referring to cell B10, then the following code uses the `EntireColumn` property of the B10 `Range` object to refer to the entire B column, which is the range B1:B65536, or B:B for short:

```
Target.EntireColumn.Interior.ColorIndex = 36
```

Similarly the next line of code changes the color of row 10, which is the range A10:IV10, or 10:10 for short:

```
Target.EntireRow.Interior.ColorIndex = 36
```

The `Interior` property of a `Range` object refers to an `Interior` object, which is the background of a range. Finally, we set the `ColorIndex` property of the `Interior` object equal to the index number for the required color.

This code might appear to many to be far from intuitive. So how do we go about figuring out how to carry out a task involving an Excel object?

Getting Help

The easiest way to discover the required code to perform an operation is to use the macro recorder. The recorded code is likely to be inefficient, but it will indicate the objects required and the properties and methods involved. If you turn on the recorder to find out how to color the background of a cell, you will get something like the following:

```
With Selection.Interior
    .ColorIndex = 36
    .Pattern = xlSolid
End With
```

This `With...End With` construction is discussed in more detail later in this chapter. It is equivalent to:

```
Selection.Interior.ColorIndex = 36
Selection.Interior.Pattern = xlSolid
```

The second line is unnecessary, as a solid pattern is the default. The macro recorder is not sophisticated enough to know what the user does or doesn't want so it includes everything. The first line gives us some of the clues we need to complete our code. We only need to figure out how to change the `Range` object, `Selection`, into a complete row or complete column. If this can be done, it will be accomplished by using a property or method of the `Range` object.

The Object Browser

The Object Browser is a valuable tool for discovering the properties, methods, and events applicable to Excel objects. To display the Object Browser, you need to be in the VBE window. You can use **View | Object Browser**, press F2, or click the **Object Browser** button on the **Standard** toolbar to see the following window:

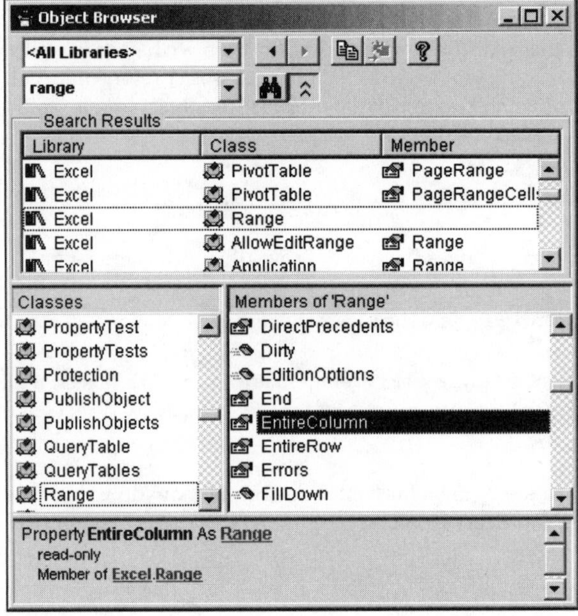

The objects are listed in the window with the title **Classes**. You can click in this window and type an r to get quickly to the `Range` object.

Alternatively, you can click in the search box, second from the top with the binoculars to its right, and type in `range`. When you press Enter or click the binoculars, you will see a list of items containing this text. When you click on **Range**, under the **Class** heading in the **Search Results** window, **Range** will be highlighted in the **Classes** window below. This technique is handy when you are searching for information on a specific property, method, or event.

We now have a list of all the properties, methods and events (if applicable) for this object, sorted alphabetically. If you right-click this list, you can choose **Group Members**, to separate the properties, methods, and events, which makes it easier to read. If you scan through this list, you will see the `EntireColumn` and `EntireRow` properties, which look likely candidates for our requirements. To confirm this, select `EntireColumn` and click the ? icon at the top of the Object Browser window to go to the following window:

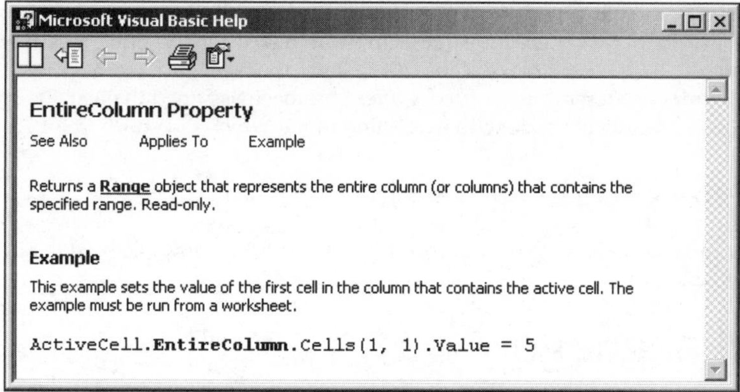

See Also can often lead to further information on related objects and methods. Now, all we have to do is connect the properties we have found and apply them to the right object.

Experimenting in the Immediate Window

If you want to experiment with code, you can use the VBE's Immediate window. Use View | Immediate Window, press *Ctrl+G*, or press the Immediate Window button on the Debug toolbar to make the Immediate window visible. You can tile the Excel window and the VBE window so that you can type commands into the Immediate window and see the effects in the Excel window as shown:

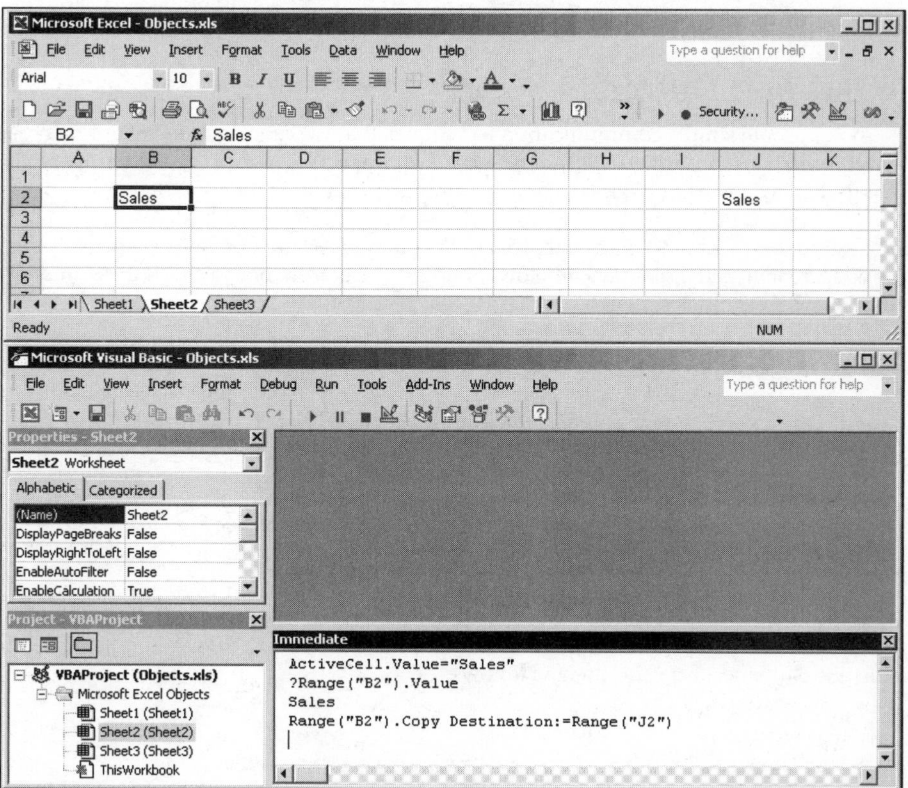

When a command is typed in, and *Enter* is pressed, the command is immediately executed. To execute the same command again, click anywhere in the line with the command and press *Enter* again.

Here, the `Value` property of the `ActiveCell` object has been assigned the text `"Sales"`. If you want to display a value, you precede the code with a question mark, which is a shortcut for `Print`:

```
?Range("B2").Value
```

This code has printed "Sales" on the next line of the **Immediate** window. The last command has copied the value in **B2** to **J2**.

The VBA Language

In this section you will see the elements of the VBA language that are common to all versions of Visual Basic and the Microsoft Office applications. We will use examples that employ the Excel Object Model, but our aim is to examine the common structures of the language. Many of these structures and concepts are common to other programming languages, although the syntax and keywords can vary. We will look at:

- Storing information in variables and arrays
- Decision making in code
- Using loops
- Basic error handling

Basic Input and Output

First, let's look at some simple communication techniques that we can use to make our macros more flexible and useful. If we want to display a message, we can use the `MsgBox` function. This can be useful if we want to display a warning message or ask a simple question.

In our first example, we want to make sure that the printer is switched on before a print operation. The following code generates the dialog box below, giving the user a chance to check the printer. The macro pauses until the **OK** button is pressed:

```
MsgBox "Please make sure that the printer is switched on"
```

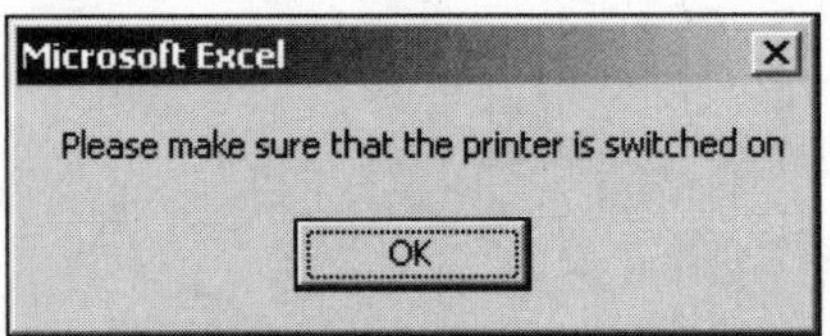

If you want to experiment, you can use the Immediate window to execute single lines of code. Alternatively, you can insert your code into a standard module in the VBE window. In this case, you need to include `Sub` and `End  Sub` lines as follows:

```
Sub Test1()
  MsgBox "Please make sure that the printer is switched on"
End Sub
```

An easy way to execute a sub procedure is to click somewhere in the code to create an insertion point, then press *F5*.

`MsgBox` has many options that control the type of buttons and icons that appear in the dialog box. If you want to get help on this, or any VBA word, just click somewhere in the word and press the *F1* key. The Help screen for the word will immediately appear. Among other details, you will see the input parameters accepted by the function:

```
MsgBox(prompt[, buttons] [, title] [, helpfile, context])
```

Parameters in square brackets are optional, so only the `prompt` message is required. If you want to have a `title` at the top of the dialog box, you can specify the third parameter. There are two ways to specify parameter values, by **position** and by **name**.

Parameters Specified by Position

If we specify a parameter by position, we need to make sure that the parameters are entered in the correct order. We also need to include extra commas for missing parameters. The following code provides a title for the dialog box, specifying the title by position:

```
MsgBox "Is the printer on?", , "Caution!"
```

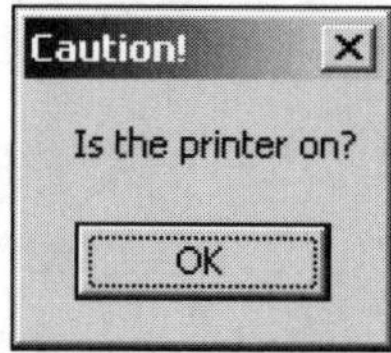

Parameters Specified by Name

There are some advantages to specifying parameters by name:

- We can enter them in any order and do not need to include extra commas with nothing between them to allow for undefined parameters
- We do need to use := rather than just = between the parameter name and the value, as we have already pointed out

The following code generates the same dialog box as the last one:

```
MsgBox Title:="Caution!", Prompt:="Is the printer on?"
```

Another advantage of specifying parameters by name is that the code is better documented. Anyone reading the code is more likely to understand it.

If you want more information on `buttons`, you will find a table of options in the help screen as follows:

Constant	Value	Description
vbOKOnly	0	Display OK button only
vbOKCancel	1	Display OK and Cancel buttons
vbAbortRetryIgnore	2	Display Abort, Retry, and Ignore buttons
vbYesNoCancel	3	Display Yes, No, and Cancel buttons
vbYesNo	4	Display Yes and No buttons
vbRetryCancel	5	Display Retry and Cancel buttons
vbCritical	16	Display Critical Message icon
vbQuestion	32	Display Warning Query icon
vbExclamation	48	Display Warning Message icon
vbInformation	64	Display Information Message icon
vbDefaultButton1	0	First button is default
vbDefaultButton2	256	Second button is default
vbDefaultButton3	512	Third button is default
vbDefaultButton4	768	Fourth button is default
vbApplicationModal	0	Application modal; the user must respond to the message box before continuing work in the current application
vbSystemModal	4096	System modal; all applications are suspended until the user responds to the message box
vbMsgBoxHelpButton	16384	Adds Help button to the message box
vbMsgBoxSet Foreground	65536	Specifies the message box window as the foreground window
vbMsgBoxRight	524288	Text is right aligned
vbMsgBoxRtlReading	1048576	Specifies text should appear as right-to-left reading on Hebrew and Arabic systems

Values zero to five control the buttons that appear. A value of 4 gives Yes and No buttons:

```
MsgBox Prompt:="Delete this record?", Buttons:=4
```

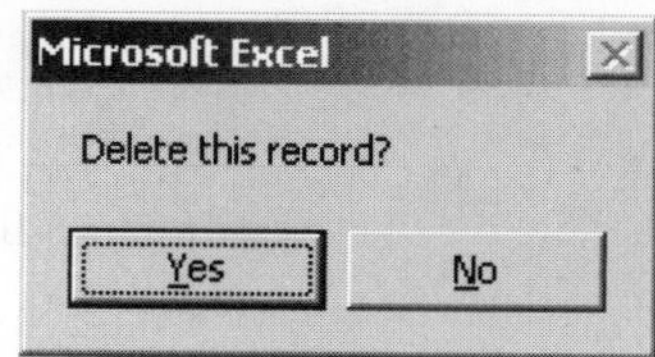

Values 16 to 64 control the icons that appear. 32 gives a question mark icon. If we wanted both value 4 and value 32, we add them:

```
MsgBox Prompt:="Delete this record?", Buttons:=36
```

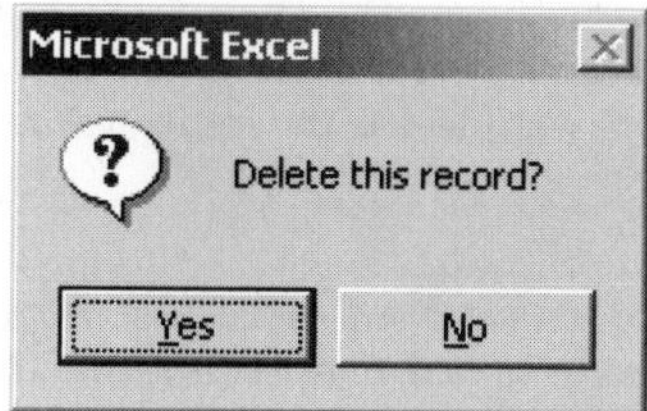

Constants

Specifying a `Buttons` value of 36 ensures that our code is indecipherable to all but the most battle hardened programmer. This is why VBA provides the **constants** shown to the left of the button values in the help screen. Rather than specifying `Buttons` by numeric value, we can use the constants, which provide a better indication of the choice behind the value. The following code generates the same dialog box as the previous example:

```
MsgBox Prompt:="Delete this record?", Buttons:=vbYesNo + vbQuestion
```

> **The VBE helps you as you type by providing a pop-up list of the appropriate constants after you type `Buttons:=`. Point to the first constant and press + and you will be prompted for the second constant. Choose the second and press the Spacebar or Tab to finish the line. If there is another parameter to be specified, enter a "," rather than Space or Tab.**

Constants are a special type of variable that do not change, if that makes sense. They are used to hold key data and, as we have seen, provide a way to write more understandable code. VBA has many built-in constants that are referred to as **intrinsic constants**. We can also define our own constants, as we will see later in this chapter:

Return Values

There is something missing from our last examples of `MsgBox`. We are asking a question, but failing to capture the user's response to the question. That is because we have been treating `MsgBox` as a statement, rather than a function. This is perfectly legal, but we need to know some rules if we are to avoid syntax errors. We can capture the return value of the `MsgBox` function by assigning it to a variable.

However, if we try the following, we will get a syntax error:

```
Answer = MsgBox Prompt:="Delete this record?", Buttons:=vbYesNo + vbQuestion
```

The error message, "Expected: End of Statement", is not really very helpful. You can press the Help button on the error message, to get a more detailed description of the error, but even then you might not understand the explanation.

Parentheses

The problem with the above line of code is that there are no parentheses around the function arguments. It should read as follows:

```
Answer = MsgBox(Prompt:="Delete this record?", Buttons:=vbYesNo + vbQuestion)
```

The general rule is that if we want to capture the return value of a function, we need to put any arguments in parentheses. If we don't want to use the return value, we should not use parentheses, as with our original examples of using `MsgBox`.

> *The parentheses rule also applies to methods used with objects. Many methods have return values that you can ignore or capture. See the section on object variables later in this chapter for an example.*

Now that we have captured the return value of `MsgBox`, how do we interpret it? Once again, the help screen provides the required information in the form of the following table of return values:

Constant	Value	Description
`vbOK`	1	OK
`vbCancel`	2	Cancel
`vbAbort`	3	Abort
`vbRetry`	4	Retry
`vbIgnore`	5	Ignore
`vbYes`	6	Yes
`vbNo`	7	No

If the Yes button is pressed, `MsgBox` returns a value of six. We can use the constant `vbYes`, instead of the numeric value, in an `If` test:

```
Answer = MsgBox(Prompt:="Delete selected Row?", Buttons:=vbYesNo + vbQuestion)
If Answer = vbYes Then ActiveCell.EntireRow.Delete
...
```

InputBox

Another useful VBA function is `InputBox`, which allows us to get input data from a user in the form of text. The following code generates the dialog box shown:

```
UserName = InputBox(Prompt:="Please enter your name")
```

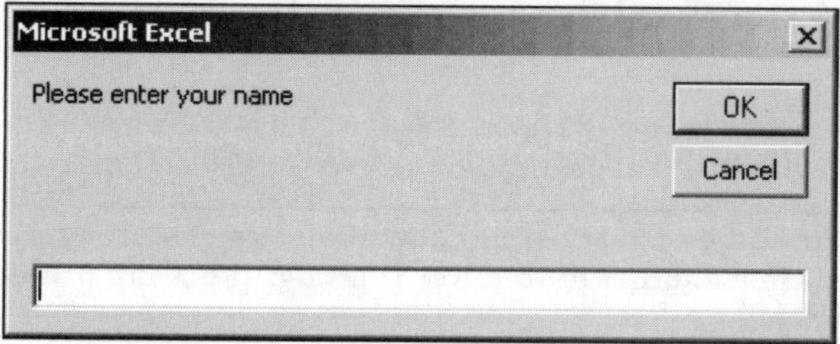

InputBox returns a text (string) result. Even if a numeric value is entered, the result is returned as text. If you press Cancel or OK without typing anything into the text box, InputBox returns a zero length string. It is a good idea to test the result before proceeding so that this situation can be handled. In the following example, the sub procedure does nothing if Cancel is pressed. The Exit Sub statement stops the procedure at that point. Otherwise, it places the entered data into cell B2:

```
Sub GetData()
   Sales = InputBox(Prompt:="Enter Target Sales")
   If Sales = "" Then Exit Sub
   Range("B2").Value = Sales
End Sub
```

In the code above, the If test compares Sales with a zero length string. There is nothing between the two double quote characters. Don't be tempted to put a blank space between the quotes.

There is a more powerful version of InputBox that is a method of the Application object. It has the ability to restrict the type of data that you can enter. It is covered in Chapter 3.

Calling Functions and Sub Procedures

When you develop an application, you should not attempt to place all your code in one large procedure. You should write small procedures that carry out specific tasks, and test each procedure independently. You can then write a master procedure that runs your task procedures. This approach makes the testing and debugging of the application much simpler and also makes it easier to modify the application later.

The following code illustrates this modular approach, although, in a practical application your procedures would have many more lines of code:

```
Sub Master()
   SalesData = GetInput("Enter Sales Data")
   If SalesData = False Then Exit Sub
   PostInput SalesData, "B3"
End Sub

Function GetInput(Message)
   Data = InputBox(Message)
   If Data = "" Then GetInput = False Else GetInput = Data
End Function

Sub PostInput(InputData, Target)
   Range(Target).Value = InputData
End Sub
```

Master uses the GetInput function and the PostInput sub procedure. GetInput has one input parameter, which passes the prompt message for the InputBox function, and tests for a zero length string in the response. A value of False is returned if this is found. Otherwise, GetInput returns the response.

Master tests the return value from GetInput and exits if it is False. Otherwise, Master calls PostInput, passing two values that define the data to be posted and the cell the data is to be posted to.

Note that sub procedures can accept input parameters, just like function procedures, if they are called from another procedure. You can't run a sub procedure with input parameters directly.

Also note that, when calling PostInput and passing two parameters to it, Master does not place parentheses around the parameters. As sub procedures do not generate a return value, you should not put parentheses around the arguments when one is called, except when using the Call statement that is discussed below.

When calling your own functions and subs, you can specify parameters by name, just as you can with built-in procedures. The following version of Master uses this technique:

```
Sub Master()
   SalesData = GetInput(Message:="Enter Sales Data")
   If SalesData = False Then Exit Sub
   PostInput Target:="B3", InputData:=SalesData
End Sub
```

The Call Statement

When running a sub procedure from another procedure, we can use the Call statement. There is no particular benefit in doing this, it is just an alternative to the method used above. Master can be modified as follows:

```
Sub Master()
  SalesData = GetInput("Enter Sales Data")
  If SalesData = False Then Exit Sub
  Call PostInput(SalesData, "B3")
End Sub
```

Note that, if we use Call, we must put parentheses around the parameters we pass to the called procedure, regardless of the fact that there is no return value from the procedure. We can also use Call with a function, but only if the return value is not used.

Parentheses and Argument Lists

As we have seen, the use of parentheses around arguments when calling procedures is a bit of a mine field, so let's summarize, at the risk of opening a can of worms and getting lost in mixed metaphors. Bear in mind that the same rules apply to argument lists of methods.

Without the Call Statement

Only place parentheses around the arguments when you are calling a function procedure and are also making use of the return value from the function procedure:

```
    SalesData = GetInput("Enter Sales Data")
```

Don't place parentheses around the arguments when you are calling a function procedure and are not making use of the return value from the function procedure:

```
GetInput "Enter Sales Data"
```

Don't place parentheses around the arguments when you are calling a sub procedure:

```
PostInput SalesData, "B3"
```

An Important Subtlety

The following is correct syntax and leads to untold confusion:

```
MsgBox ("Insert Disk")
```

It is not what it appears and it is not a negation of the parentheses rules. VBA has inserted a space between `MsgBox` and the left parenthesis, which it does not insert in the following:

```
Response = MsgBox("Insert Disk")
```

The extra space indicates that the parentheses are around the argument, not around the argument list. If we pass two input parameters, the following is not valid syntax:

```
MsgBox ("Insert Disk", vbExclamation)
```

The following is valid syntax :

```
MsgBox ("Insert Disk"), (vbExclamation)
```

It is fine to place parentheses around individual arguments, but not around the argument list. However, you might not get the result you expect.

Apologies if you are bored, but this is important stuff. It is more important when we get to refer to objects in parameter lists. Placing an object reference in parentheses causes VBA to convert the object reference to the object's default property. For example, `(Range("B1"))` is converted to the value in the B1 cell and is not a reference to a `Range` object. The following is valid syntax to copy A1 to B1:

```
Range("A1").Copy Range("B1")
```

The following is valid syntax but causes a run-time error:

```
Range("A1").Copy (Range("B1"))
```

With the Call Statement

If you use the `Call` statement, you must place parentheses around the arguments you pass to the called procedure:

```
Call PostInput(SalesData, "B3")
```

As `Call` is of limited use, not being able to process a return value, and muddies the water with its own rules, it is preferable not to use it.

Variable Declaration

We have seen many examples of the use of variables for storing information. Now we will discuss the rules for creating variable names, look at different types of variables and talk about the best way to define variables.

> **Variable names can be constructed from letters and numbers, and the underscore character. The name must start with a letter and can be up to 255 characters in length. It is a good idea to avoid using any special characters in variable names. To be on the safe side, you should only use the letters of the alphabet (upper and lower case) plus the numbers 0-9 plus the underscore (_). Also, variable names can't be the same as VBA Key words, such as `Sub` and `End`, or VBA function names.**

So far we have been creating variables simply by using them. This is referred to as **implicit variable declaration**. Most computer languages require us to employ **explicit variable declaration**. This means that we must define the names of all the variables we are going to use, before we use them in our code. VBA allows both types of declaration. If we want to declare a variable explicitly, we do so using a `Dim` statement or one of its variations, which we will see shortly. The following `Dim` statement declares a variable called `SalesData`:

```
Sub GetData()
   Dim SalesData
   SalesData = InputBox(Prompt:="Enter Target Sales")
   ...
```

Most users find implicit declaration easier than explicit declaration, but there are advantages in being explicit, the main one being capitalization.

> **You might have noticed that, if you enter VBA words, such as inputbox, in lower case, they are automatically converted to VBA's standard capitalization when you move to the next line. This is a valuable form of feedback that tells you the word has been recognized as valid VBA code. It is a good idea to always type VBA words in lower case and look for the change.**

If we do not explicitly declare a variable name, we can get odd effects regarding its capitalization. Say you write the following code:

```
Sub GetData()
   SalesData = InputBox(Prompt:="Enter Target Sales")
   If salesdata = "" Then Exit Sub
   ...
```

You will find that, as you press *Enter* at the end of the line 3, the original occurrence of `SalesData` loses its capitalization and the procedure reads as follows:

```
Sub GetData()
   salesdata = InputBox(Prompt:="Enter Target Sales")
   If salesdata = "" Then Exit Sub
   ...
```

In fact, any time you edit the procedure and alter the capitalization of `salesdata`, the new version will be applied throughout the procedure. If you declare `SalesData` in a `Dim` statement, the capitalization you use on that line will prevail throughout the procedure. You can now type the variable name in lower case in the body of the code and obtain confirmation that it has been correctly spelled as you move to a new line.

Option Explicit

There is a way to force explicit declaration in VBA. We place the statement `Option Explicit` in the Declarations section of our module, which is at the very top of our module, before any procedures, as follows:

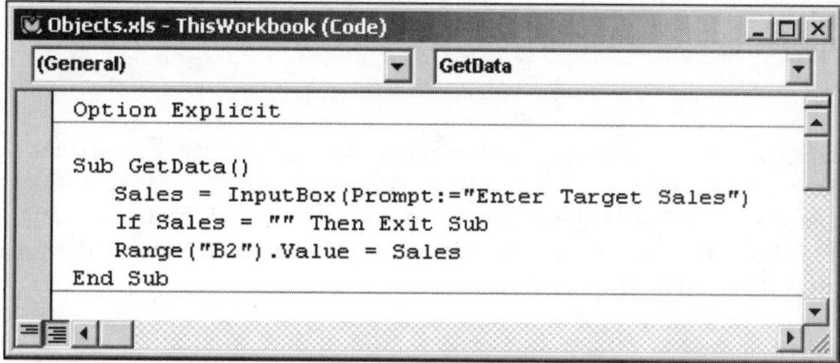

Objects.xls - ThisWorkbook (Code)
(General)
GetData
Option Explicit
Sub GetData()
Sales = InputBox(Prompt:="Enter Target Sales")
If Sales = "" Then Exit Sub
Range("B2").Value = Sales
End Sub

`Option Explicit` only applies to the module it appears in. Each module requiring explicit declaration of variables must repeat the statement in its declaration section.

When you try to compile your module or run a procedure, using explicit variable declaration, VBA will check for variables that have not been declared, highlight them, and show an error message. This has an enormous benefit. It picks up spelling mistakes, which are among the most common errors in programming. Consider the following version of `GetData`, where there is no `Option Explicit` at the top of the module and, therefore, implicit declaration is used:

```
Sub GetData()
   SalesData = InputBox(Prompt:="Enter Target Sales")
   If SaleData = "" Then Exit Sub
   Range("B2").Value = SalesData
End Sub
```

This code will never enter any data into cell B2. VBA happily accepts the misspelled `SaleData` in the `If` test as a new variable that is empty, and thus considered to be a zero length string for the purposes of the test. Consequently, the `Exit Sub` is always executed and the final line is never executed. This type of error, especially when embedded in a longer section of code, can be very difficult to see.

If you include `Option Explicit` in your declarations section, and `Dim SalesData` at the beginning of `GetData`, you will get an error message, "Variable not defined", immediately after you attempt to run `GetData`. The undefined variable will be highlighted so that you can see exactly where the error is.

You can have `Option Explicit` automatically added to any new modules you create. In the VBE, use Tools | Options... and click the Editor tab. Check the box against Require Variable Declaration. This is a highly recommended option. Note that settting this option will not affect any existing modules, where you will need to insert `Option Explicit` manually.

Scope and Lifetime of Variables

There are two important concepts associated with variables:

- The **scope** of a variable defines which procedures can use that variable
- The **lifetime** of a variable defines how long that variable retains the values assigned to it

The following procedure illustrates the lifetime of a variable:

```
Sub LifeTime()
  Dim Sales
  Sales = Sales + 1
  MsgBox Sales
End Sub
```

Every time `LifeTime` is run, it displays a value of one. This is because the variable `Sales` is only retained in memory until the end of the procedure. The memory `Sales` uses is released when the `End Sub` is reached. Next time `LifeTime` is run, `Sales` is recreated and treated as having a zero value. The lifetime of `Sales` is the time taken to run the procedure. We can increase the lifetime of `Sales` by declaring it in a `Static` statement:

```
Sub LifeTime()
  Static Sales
  Sales = Sales + 1
  MsgBox Sales
End Sub
```

The lifetime of `Sales` is now extended to the time that the workbook is open. The more times `LifeTime` is run, the higher the value of `Sales` will become.

The following two procedures illustrate the scope of a variable:

```
Sub Scope1()
  Static Sales
  Sales = Sales + 1
  MsgBox Sales
End Sub

Sub Scope2()
  Static Sales
  Sales = Sales + 10
  MsgBox Sales
End Sub
```

The variable `Sales` in `Scope1` is not the same variable as the `Sales` in `Scope2`. Each time `Scope1` is executed, the value of its `Sales` will increase by one, independently of the value of `Sales` in `Scope2`. Similarly, the `Sales` in `Scope2` will increase by 10 with each execution of `Scope2`, independently of the value of `Sales` in `Scope1`. Any variable declared within a procedure has a scope that is confined to that procedure. A variable that is declared within a procedure is referred to as a **procedure-level** variable.

Variables can also be declared in the declarations section at the top of a module as shown in the following version of our code:

```
Option Explicit
Dim Sales

Sub Scope1()
  Sales = Sales + 1
  MsgBox Sales
End Sub

Sub Scope2()
  Sales = Sales + 10
  MsgBox Sales
End Sub
```

`Scope1` and `Scope2` are now processing the same variable, `Sales`. A variable declared in the declarations section of a module is referred to as a **module-level** variable and its scope is now the whole module. Therefore, it is visible to all the procedures in the module. Its lifetime is now the time that the workbook is open.

If a procedure in the module declares a variable with the same name as a module-level variable, the module-level variable will no longer be visible to that procedure. It will process its own procedure-level variable.

Module-level variables, declared in the declarations section of the module with a `Dim` statement, are not visible to other modules. If you want to share a variable between modules, you need to declare it as `Public` in the declarations section:

```
Public Sales
```

`Public` variables can also be made visible to other workbooks, or VBA projects. To accomplish this, a **reference** to the workbook containing the `Public` variable is created in the other workbook, using Tools, References... in the VBE.

Variable Type

Computers store different types of data in different ways. The way a number is stored is quite different from the way text, or a character string, is stored. Different categories of numbers are also stored in different ways. An integer (a whole number with no decimals) is stored differently from a number with decimals. Most computer languages require that you declare the type of data to be stored in a variable. VBA does not require this, but your code will be more efficient if you do declare variable types. It is also more likely that you will discover any problems that arise when data is converted from one type to another, if you have declared your variable types.

The following table has been taken directly from the VBA Help files. It defines the various data types available in VBA and their memory requirements. It also shows you the range of values that each type can handle:

Data type	Storage size	Range
`Byte`	1 byte	0 to 255
`Boolean`	2 bytes	`True` or `False`
`Integer`	2 bytes	-32,768 to 32,767
`Long` (long integer)	4 bytes	-2,147,483,648 to 2,147,483,647
`Single` (single-precision floating-point)	4 bytes	-3.402823E38 to -1.401298E-45 for negative values; 1.401298E-45 to 3.402823E38 for positive values
`Double` (double-precision floating-point)	8 bytes	-1.79769313486231E308 to -4.94065645841247E-324 for negative values; 4.94065645841247E-324 to 1.79769313486232E308 for positive values
`Currency` (scaled integer)	8 bytes	-922,337,203,685,477.5808 to 922,337,203,685,477.5807
`Decimal`	14 bytes	+/-79,228,162,514,264,337,593,543,950,335 with no decimal point; +/-7.9228162514264337593543950335 with 28 places to the right of the decimal; the smallest non-zero number is +/-0.0000000000000000000000000001
`Date`	8 bytes	January 1, 100 to December 31, 9999
`Object`	4 bytes	Any Object reference
`String` (variable-length)	10 bytes + string length	0 to approximately 2 billion characters
`String` (fixed-length)	Length of string	1 to approximately 65,400 characters
`Variant` (with numbers)	16 bytes	Any numeric value up to the range of a `Double`
`Variant` (with characters)	22 bytes + string length	Same range as for variable-length `String`
User-defined (using `Type`)	Number required by elements	The range of each element is the same as the range of its data type

If you do not declare a variable's type, it defaults to the `Variant` type. `Variants` take up more memory than any other type because each `Variant` has to carry information with it that tells VBA what type of data it is currently storing, as well as store the data itself.

`Variants` use more computer overhead when they are processed. VBA has to figure out what types it is dealing with and whether it needs to convert between types in order to process the number. If maximum processing speed is required for your application, you should declare your variable types, taking advantage of those types that use less memory when you can. For example, if you know your numbers will be whole numbers in the range of -32000 to +32000, you would use an `Integer` type.

Declaring Variable Type

You can declare a variable's type on a `Dim` statement, or related declaration statements such as `Public`. The following declares `Sales` to be a double precision floating-point number:

```
Dim Sales As Double
```

You can declare more than one variable on a `Dim`:

```
Dim SalesData As Double, Index As Integer, StartDate As Date
```

The following can be a trap:

```
Dim Col, Row, Sheet As Integer
```

Many users assume that this declares each variable to be `Integer`. This is not true. `Col` and `Row` are `Variants` because they have not been given a type. To declare all three as `Integer`, the line should be as follows:

```
Dim Col As Integer, Row As Integer, Sheet As Integer
```

Declaring Function and Parameter Types

If you have input parameters for sub procedures or function procedures, you can define each parameter type in the first line of the procedure as follows:

```
Function IsHoliday(WhichDay As Date)

Sub Marine(CrewSize As Integer, FuelCapacity As Double)
```

You can also declare the return value type for a function. The following example is for a function that returns a value of `True` or `False`:

```
Function IsHoliday(WhichDay As Date) As Boolean
```

Constants

We have seen that there are many intrinsic constants built into VBA, such as `vbYes` and `vbNo` discussed earlier. You can also define your own constants. Constants are handy for holding numbers or text that do not change while your code is running, but that you want to use repeatedly in calculations and messages. Constants are declared using the `Const` keyword, as follows:

```
Const Pi = 3.14159265358979
```

You can include the constant's type in the declaration:

```
Const Version As String = "Release 3.9a"
```

Constants follow the same rules regarding scope as variables. If you declare a constant within a procedure, it will be local to that procedure. If you declare it in the declarations section of a module, it will be available to all procedures in the module. If you want to make it available to all modules, you can declare it to be `Public` as follows:

```
Public Const Error666 As String = "You can't do that"
```

Variable Naming Conventions

You can call your variables and user-defined functions anything you want, except where there is a clash with VBA keywords and function names. However, many programmers adopt a system whereby the variable or object type is included, in abbreviated form, in the variable name, usually as a prefix, so instead of declaring:

```
Dim SalesData As Double
```

you can use:

```
Dim dSalesData As Double
```

Wherever `dSalesData` appears in your code, you will be reminded that the variable is of type `Double`. Alternatively, you could use this line of code:

```
Dim dblSalesData As Double
```

For the sake of simplicity this approach has not been used in this chapter, but from Chapter 3 onwards, one or two letter prefixes are added to **most** variable names. This is the convention used in this book:

- One letter prefixes for the common data types:

```
Dim iColumn As Integer
Dim lRow As Long
Dim dProduct As Double
Dim bChoice As Boolean
```

- Two letter prefixes for `Strings`, `Variants`, and most object types:

```
Dim stName As String          ' Some code in later chapters uses just s-
Dim vaValue As Variant        ' Some code in later chapters uses just v-
Dim rgSelect As Range
```

- No prefix for loop counters and general (rather than specific) object names:

```
Dim i As Integer
Dim Rng As Range
Dim Wkb As Workbook
```

Object Variables

The variables we have seen so far have held data such as numbers and text. You can also create **object variables** to refer to objects such as worksheets and ranges. The `Set` statement is used to assign an object reference to an object variable. Object variables should also be declared and assigned a type as with normal variables. If you don't know the type, you can use the generic term `Object` as the type:

```
Dim MyWorkbook As Object
Set MyWorkbook = ThisWorkbook
MsgBox MyWorkbook.Name
```

It is more efficient to use the specific object type if you can. The following code creates an object variable `Rng` referring to cell B10 in Sheet1, in the same workbook as the code. It then assigns values to the object and the cell above:

```
Sub ObjectVariable()
  Dim Rng As Range
  Set Rng = ThisWorkbook.Worksheets("Sheet1").Range("C10")
  Rng.Value = InputBox("Enter Sales for January")
  Rng.Offset(-1, 0).Value = "January Sales"
End Sub
```

If you are going to refer to the same object more than once, it is more efficient to create an object variable than to keep repeating a lengthy specification of the object. It is also makes code easier to read and write.

Object variables can also be very useful for capturing the return values of some methods, particularly when you are creating new instances of an object. For example, with either the `Workbooks` object or the `Worksheets` object, the `Add` method returns a reference to the new object. This reference can be assigned to an object variable so that you can easily refer to the new object in later code:

```
Sub NewWorkbook()
  Dim Wkb As Workbook, Wks As Worksheet

  Set Wkb = Workbooks.Add
  Set Wks = Wkb.Worksheets.Add(After:=Wkb.Sheets(Wkb.Sheets.Count))
  Wks.Name = "January"
  Wks.Range("A1").Value = "Sales Data"
  Wkb.SaveAs Filename:="JanSales.xls"
End Sub
```

This example creates a new empty workbook and assigns a reference to it to the object variable `Wkb`. A new worksheet is added to the workbook, after any existing sheets, and a reference to the new worksheet is assigned to the object variable `Wks`. The name on the tab at the bottom of the worksheet is then changed to "January", and the heading "Sales Data" is placed in cell A1. Finally, the new workbook is saved as `JanSales.xls`.

Note that the parameter after the `Worksheets.Add` is in parentheses. As we are assigning the return value of the `Add` method to the object variable, any parameters must be in parentheses. If the return value of the `Add` method was to be ignored, the statement would be without parentheses as follows:

```
Wkb.Worksheets.Add After:=Wkb.Sheets(Wkb.Sheets.Count)
```

With...End With

Object variables provide a useful way to refer to objects in short hand, and are also more efficiently processed by VBA than fully qualified object strings. Another way to reduce the amount of code you write, and also increase processing efficiency, is to use a `With...End With` structure. The last example above could be re-written as follows:

```
With Wkb
  .Worksheets.Add After:=.Sheets(.Sheets.Count)
End With
```

VBA knows that anything starting with a period is a property or a method of the object following the `With`. You can re-write the entire `NewWorkbook` procedure to eliminate the `Wkb` object variable, as follows:

```
Sub NewWorkbook()
  Dim Wks As Worksheet
  With Workbooks.Add
    Set Wks = .Worksheets.Add(After:=.Sheets(.Sheets.Count))
    Wks.Name = "January"
    Wks.Range("A1").Value = "Sales Data"
    .SaveAs Filename:="JanSales.xls"
  End With
End Sub
```

You can take this a step further and eliminate the `Wks` object variable:

```
Sub NewWorkbook()
  With Workbooks.Add
    With .Worksheets.Add(After:=.Sheets(.Sheets.Count))
      .Name = "January"
      .Range("A1").Value = "Sales Data"
    End With
    .SaveAs Filename:="JanSales.xls"
  End With
End Sub
```

If you find this confusing, you can compromise with a combination of object variables and `With...End With`:

```
Sub NewWorkbook4()
  Dim Wkb As Workbook, Wks As Worksheet

  Set Wkb = Workbooks.Add
  With Wkb
    Set Wks = .Worksheets.Add(After:=.Sheets(.Sheets.Count))
    With Wks
      .Name = "January"
      .Range("A1").Value = "Sales Data"
    End With
    .SaveAs Filename:="JanSales.xls"
  End With
End Sub
```

`With...End With` is useful when references to an object are repeated in a small section of code.

Making Decisions

VBA provides two main structures for making decisions and carrying out alternative processing, represented by the `If` and the `Select Case` statements. `If` is the more flexible, but `Select Case` is better when you are testing a single variable.

If Statements

`If` comes in three forms: the `IIf` function, the one line `If` statement, and the block `If` structure. The following `Tax` function uses the `IIf` (Immediate `If`) function:

```
Function Tax(ProfitBeforeTax As Double) As Double
  Tax = IIf(ProfitBeforeTax > 0, 0.3 * ProfitBeforeTax, 0)
End Function
```

`IIf` is similar to the Excel worksheet `IF` function. It has three input arguments: the first is a logical test, the second is an expression that is evaluated if the test is true, and the third is an expression that is evaluated if the test is false.

In this example, the `IIf` function tests that the `ProfitBeforeTax` value is greater than zero. If the test is true, `IIf` calculates 30% of `ProfitBeforeTax`. If the test is false, `IIf` calculates zero. The calculated `IIf` value is then assigned to the return value of the `Tax` function. The `Tax` function can be re-written using the single line `If` statement as follows:

```
Function Tax(ProfitBeforeTax As Double) As Double
  If ProfitBeforeTax > 0 Then Tax = 0.3 * ProfitBeforeTax Else Tax = 0
End Function
```

One difference between `IIf` and the single line `If` is that the `Else` section of the single line `If` is optional. The third parameter of the `IIf` function must be defined. In VBA, it is often useful to omit the `Else`:

```
If ProfitBeforeTax < 0 Then MsgBox "A Loss has occured", , "Warning"
```

Another difference is that, while `IIf` can only return a value to a single variable, the single line `If` can assign values to different variables:

```
If JohnsScore > MarysScore Then John = John + 1 Else Mary = Mary + 1
```

Block If

If you want to carry out more than one action when a test is true, you can use a **block If** structure, as follows:

```
If JohnsScore > MarysScore Then
  John = John + 1
  Mary = Mary - 1
End If
```

Using a block If, you must not include any code after the Then, on the same line. You can have as many lines after the test as required, and you must terminate the scope of the block If with an End If statement. A block If can also have an Else section, as follows:

```
If JohnsScore > MarysScore Then
  John = John + 1
  Mary = Mary - 1
Else
  John = John - 1
  Mary = Mary + 1
End If
```

A block If can also have as many ElseIf sections as required:

```
If JohnsScore > MarysScore Then
  John = John + 1
  Mary = Mary - 1
ElseIf JohnsScore < MarysScore Then
  John = John - 1
  Mary = Mary + 1
Else
  John = John + 1
  Mary = Mary + 1
End If
```

When you have a block If followed by one or more ElseIfs, VBA keeps testing until it finds a true section. It executes the code for that section and then proceeds directly to the statement following the End If. If no test is true, the Else section is executed.

A block If does nothing when all tests are false and the Else section is missing. Block Ifs can be nested, one inside the other. You should make use of indenting to show the scope of each block. This is vital – you can get into an awful muddle with the nesting of If blocks within other If blocks and If blocks within Else blocks etc. If code is unindented, it isn't easy, in a long series of nested If tests, to match each End If with each If:

```
If Not ThisWorkbook.Saved Then
  Answer = MsgBox("Do you want to save your changes", vbQuestion + _
                                                           vbYesNo)
  If Answer = vbYes Then
    ThisWorkbook.Save
    MsgBox ThisWorkbook.Name & " has been saved"
  End If
End If
```

This code uses the Saved property of the Workbook object containing the code to see if the workbook has been saved since changes were last made to it. If changes have not been saved, the user is asked if they want to save changes. If the answer is yes, the inner block If saves the workbook and informs the user.

Select Case

The following block If is testing the same variable value in each section:

```
Function Price(Product As String) As Variant
  If Product = "Apples" Then
    Price = 12.5
  ElseIf Product = "Oranges" Then
    Price = 15
  ElseIf Product = "Pears" Then
    Price = 18
  ElseIf Product = "Mangoes" Then
    Price = 25
  Else
    Price = CVErr(xlErrNA)
  End If
End Function
```

If `Product` is not found, the `Price` function returns an Excel error value of `#NA`. Note that `Price` is declared as a `Variant` so that it can handle the error value as well as numeric values. For a situation like this, `Select Case` is a more elegant construction. It looks like this:

```
Function Price(Product As String) As Variant
  Select Case Product
    Case "Apples"
      Price = 12.5
    Case "Oranges"
      Price = 15
    Case "Pears"
      Price = 18
    Case "Mangoes"
      Price = 25
    Case Else
      Price = CVErr(xlErrNA)
  End Select
End Function
```

If you have only one statement per case, the following format works quite well. You can place multiple statements on a single line by placing a colon between statements:

```
Function Price(Product As String) As Variant
  Select Case Product
    Case "Apples":  Price = 12.5
    Case "Oranges": Price = 15
    Case "Pears":   Price = 18
    Case "Mangoes": Price = 25
    Case Else:      Price = CVErr(xlErrNA)
  End Select
End Function
```

`Select Case` can also handle ranges of numbers or text, as well as comparisons using the keyword `Is`. The following example calculates a fare of zero for infants up to 3 years old and anyone older than 65, with two ranges between. Negative ages generate an error:

```
Function Fare(Age As Integer) As Variant
  Select Case Age
    Case 0 To 3, Is > 65
      Fare = 0
    Case 4 To 15
```

```
        Fare = 10
      Case 16 To 65
        Fare = 20
      Case Else
        Fare = CVErr(xlErrNA)
    End Select
  End Function
```

Looping

All computer languages provide a mechanism for repeating the same, or similar, operations in an efficient way. VBA has two main structures that allow us to loop through the same code over and over again. They are the `Do...Loop` and the `For...Next` loop.

The `Do...Loop` is for those situations where the loop will be terminated when a logical condition applies, such as reaching the end of your data. The `For...Next` loop is for situations where you can predict in advance how many times you want to loop, such as when you want to enter expenses for the 10 people in your department.

VBA also has an interesting variation on the `For...Next` loop that is used to process all the objects in a collection – the `For Each...Next` loop. You can use it to process all the cells in a range or all the sheets in a workbook, for example.

Do...Loop

To illustrate the use of a `Do...Loop`, we will construct a sub procedure to shade every second line of a worksheet, as shown below, to make it more readable. We want to apply the macro to different report sheets with different numbers of products, so the macro will need to test each cell in the A column until it gets to an empty cell to determine when to stop:

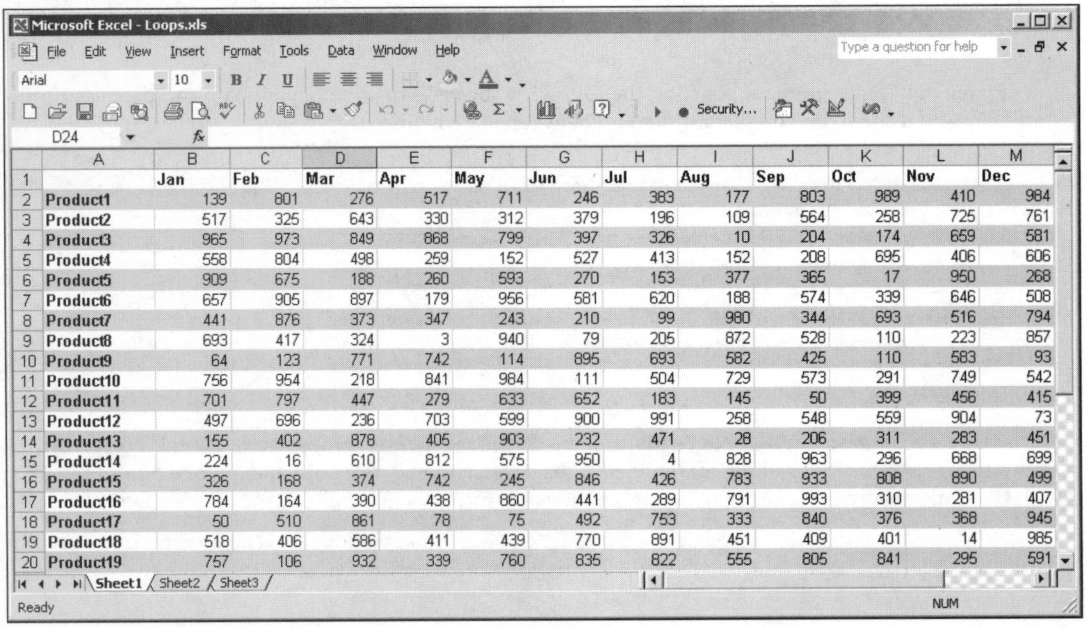

Microsoft Excel - Loops.xls

	A	B	C	D	E	F	G	H	I	J	K	L	M
1		Jan	Feb	Mar	Apr	May	Jun	Jul	Aug	Sep	Oct	Nov	Dec
2	Product1	139	801	276	517	711	246	383	177	803	989	410	984
3	Product2	517	325	643	330	312	379	196	109	564	258	725	761
4	Product3	965	973	849	868	799	397	326	10	204	174	659	581
5	Product4	558	804	498	259	152	527	413	152	208	695	406	606
6	Product5	909	675	188	260	593	270	153	377	365	17	950	268
7	Product6	657	905	897	179	956	581	620	188	574	339	646	508
8	Product7	441	876	373	347	243	210	99	980	344	693	516	794
9	Product8	693	417	324	3	940	79	205	872	528	110	223	857
10	Product9	64	123	771	742	114	895	693	582	425	110	583	93
11	Product10	756	954	218	841	984	111	504	729	573	291	749	542
12	Product11	701	797	447	279	633	652	183	145	50	399	456	415
13	Product12	497	696	236	703	599	900	991	258	548	559	904	73
14	Product13	155	402	878	405	903	232	471	28	206	311	283	451
15	Product14	224	16	610	812	575	950	4	828	963	296	668	699
16	Product15	326	168	374	742	245	846	426	783	933	808	890	499
17	Product16	784	164	390	438	860	441	289	791	993	310	281	407
18	Product17	50	510	861	78	75	492	753	333	840	376	368	945
19	Product18	518	406	586	411	439	770	891	451	409	401	14	985
20	Product19	757	106	932	339	760	835	822	555	805	841	295	591

Sheet1 / Sheet2 / Sheet3

Our first macro will select every other row and apply the formatting:

```
Sub ShadeEverySecondRow()
  Range("A2").EntireRow.Select
  Do While ActiveCell.Value <> ""
    Selection.Interior.ColorIndex = 15
    ActiveCell.Offset(2, 0).EntireRow.Select
  Loop
End Sub
```

`ShadeEverySecondRow` begins by selecting row 2 in its entirety. When you select an entire row, the left-most cell (in column A) becomes the active cell. The code between the `Do` and the `Loop` statements is then repeated `While` the value property of the active cell is not a zero length string, that is. the active cell is not empty. In the loop, the macro sets the interior color index of the selected cells to 15, which is gray. Then the macro selects the entire row, two rows under the active cell. When a row is selected that has an empty cell in column A, the `While` condition is no longer true and the loop terminates.

You can make `ShadeEverySecondRow` run faster by avoiding selecting. It is seldom necessary to select cells in VBA, but you are led into this way of doing things because that's the way you do it manually and that's what you get from the macro recorder.

The following version of `ShadeEverySecondRow` does not select cells, and it runs about six times faster. It sets up an index `i`, which indicates the row of the worksheet and is initially assigned a value of two. The `Cells` property of the worksheet allows you to refer to cells by row number and column number, so when the loop starts, `Cells(i,1)` refers to cell A2. Each time around the loop, `i` is increased by two. We can, therefore, change any reference to the active cell to a `Cells(i,1)` reference and apply the `EntireRow` property to `Cells(i,1)` to refer to the complete row:

```
Sub ShadeEverySecondRow()
  Dim i As Integer
  i = 2
  Do Until IsEmpty(Cells(i, 1))
    Cells(i, 1).EntireRow.Interior.ColorIndex = 15
    i = i + 2
  Loop
End Sub
```

To illustrate some alternatives, two more changes have been made on the `Do` statement line in the code above. Either `While` or `Until` can be used after the `Do`, so we have changed the test to an `Until` and we have used the VBA `IsEmpty` function to test for an empty cell.

The `IsEmpty` function is the best way to test that a cell is empty. If you use `If Cells(i,1) = ""`, the test will be true for a formula that calculates a zero length string.

It is also possible to exit a loop using a test within the loop and the `Exit Do` statement, as shown below, which also shows another way to refer to entire rows:

```
Sub ShadeEverySecondRow()
  i = 0
  Do
    i = i + 2
    If IsEmpty(Cells(i, 1)) Then Exit Do
    Rows(i).Interior.ColorIndex = 15
  Loop
End Sub
```

Yet another alternative is to place the `While` or `Until` on the `Loop` statement line. This ensures that the code in the loop is executed at least once. When the test is on the `Do` line, it is possible that the test will be false to start with, and the loop will be skipped.

Sometimes, it makes more sense if the test is on the last line of the loop. In the following example, it seems more sensible to test `PassWord` after getting input from the user, although the code would still work if the `Until` statement were placed on the `Do` line.

```
Sub GetPassword()
  Dim PassWord As String, i As Integer
  i = 0
  Do
    i = i + 1
    If i > 3 Then
      MsgBox "Sorry, Only three tries"
      Exit Sub
    End If
    PassWord = InputBox("Enter Password")
    Loop Until PassWord = "XXX"
  MsgBox "Welcome"
End Sub
```

`GetPassword` loops until the password `XXX` is supplied, or the number of times around the loop exceeds three.

For...Next Loop

The `For...Next` loop differs from the `Do...Loop` in two ways. It has a built-in counter that is automatically incremented each time the loop is executed and it is designed to execute until the counter exceeds a pre-defined value, rather than depending on a user-specified logical test. The following example places the full file path and name of the workbook into the center footer for each worksheet in the active workbook:

```
Sub FilePathInFooter()
  Dim i As Integer, FilePath As String

  FilePath = ActiveWorkbook.FullName
  For i = 1 To Worksheets.Count Step 1
    Worksheets(i).PageSetup.CenterFooter = FilePath
  Next i
End Sub
```

Versions of Excel prior to Excel 2002 do not have an option to automatically include the full file path in a custom header or footer, so this macro inserts the information as text. It begins by assigning the `FullName` property of the active workbook to the variable `FilePath`. The loop starts with the `For` statement and loops on the `Next` statement. `i` is used as a counter, starting at one and finishing when `i` exceeds `Worksheets.Count`, which uses the `Count` property of the `Worksheets` collection to determine how many worksheets there are in the active workbook.

The `Step` option defines the amount that `i` will be increased, each time around the loop. `Step 1` could be left out of this example, as a step of one is the default value. In the loop, `i` is used as an index to the `Worksheets` collection to specify each individual `Worksheet` object. The `PageSetup` property of the `Worksheet` object refers to the `PageSetup` object in that worksheet so that the `CenterFooter` property of the `PageSetup` object can be assigned the `FilePath` text.

The following example shows how you can step backwards. It takes a complete file path and strips out the filename, excluding the file extension. The example uses the `FullName` property of the active workbook as input, but the same code could be used with any file type. It starts at the last character in the file path and steps backwards until it finds the period between the filename and its extension and then the backslash character before the filename. It then extracts the characters between the two:

```
Sub GetFileName()
   Dim BackSlash As Integer, Point As Integer
   Dim FilePath As String, FileName As String
   Dim i As Integer

   FilePath = ActiveWorkbook.FullName
   For i = Len(FilePath) To 1 Step -1
      If Mid$(FilePath, i, 1) = "." Then
         Point = i
         Exit For
      End If
   Next i
   If Point = 0 Then Point = Len(FilePath) + 1
   For i = Point - 1 To 1 Step -1
      If Mid$(FilePath, i, 1) = "\" Then
         BackSlash = i
         Exit For
      End If
   Next i
   FileName = Mid$(FilePath, BackSlash + 1, Point - BackSlash - 1)
   MsgBox FileName
End Sub
```

The first `For...Next` loop uses the `Len` function to determine how many characters are in the `FilePath` variable and `i` is set up to step backwards, counting from the last character position, working towards the first character position. The `Mid$` function extracts the character from `FilePath` at the position defined by `i` and tests it to see if it is a period.

When a period is found, the position is recorded in `Point` and the first `For...Next` loop is exited. If the file name has no extension, no period is found and `Point` will have its default value of zero. In this case, the `If` test records an imaginary period position in `Point` that is one character beyond the end of the file name.

The same technique is used in the second `For...Next` loop as the first, starting one character before the period, to find the position of the backslash character, and storing the position in `BackSlash`. The `Mid$` function is then used to extract the characters between the backslash and the period.

For Each...Next Loop

When you want to process every member of a collection, you can use the `For Each...Next` loop. The following example is a re-work of the `FilePathInFooter` procedure:

```
Sub FilePathInFooter()
   Dim FilePath As String, Wks As Worksheet

   FilePath = ActiveWorkbook.FullName
   For Each Wks In Worksheets
      Wks.PageSetup.CenterFooter = FilePath
   Next Wks
End Sub
```

The loop steps through all the members of the collection. During each pass a reference to the next member of the collection is assigned to the object variable `Wks`.

The following example lists all the files in the root directory of the C drive. It uses the Microsoft Office `FileSearch` object to generate a `Foundfiles` object containing the names of the required files. The example uses a `For Each...Next` loop to display the names of all the files:

```
Sub FileList()
  Dim File As Variant
  With Application.FileSearch
    .LookIn = "C:\"
    .FileType = msoFileTypeAllFiles
    .Execute
    For Each File In .FoundFiles
      MsgBox File
    Next File
  End With
End Sub
```

If you test this procedure on a directory with lots of files, and get tired of clicking OK, don't forget that you can break out of the code with *Ctrl+Break*.

Arrays

Arrays are VBA variables that can hold more than one item of data. An array is declared by including parentheses after the array name. An integer is placed within the parentheses, defining the number of elements in the array:

```
Dim Data(2)
```

You assign values to the elements of the array by indicating the element number as follows:

```
Data(0) = 1
Data(1) = 10
Data(2) = 100
```

The number of elements in the array depends on the array base. The default base is zero, which means that the first data element is item zero. `Dim Data(2)` declares a three element array if the base is zero. Alternatively, you can place the following statement in the declarations section at the top of your module to declare that arrays are one based:

```
Option Base 1
```

With a base of one, `Dim Data(2)` declares a two element array. Item zero does not exist.
You can use the following procedure to test the effect of the `Option Base` statement:

```
Sub Array1()
  Dim Data(10) As Integer
  Dim Message As String, i As Integer

  For i = LBound(Data) To UBound(Data)
    Data(i) = i
  Next i
```

```
    Message = "Lower Bound = " & LBound(Data) & vbCr
    Message = Message & "Upper Bound = " & UBound(Data) & vbCr
    Message = Message & "Num Elements = " & WorksheetFunction.Count(Data) _
                                                                   & vbCr
    Message = Message & "Sum Elements = " & WorksheetFunction.Sum(Data)
    MsgBox Message
  End Sub
```

`Array1` uses the `LBound` (lower bound) and `UBound` (upper bound) functions to determine the lowest and highest index values for the array. It uses the `Count` worksheet function to determine the number of elements in the array. If you run this code with `Options Base 0`, or no `Options Base` statement, in the declarations section of the module, it will show a lowest index number of zero and 11 elements in the array. With `Options Base 1`, it shows a lowest index number of one and 10 elements in the array.

Note the use of the intrinsic constant `vbCr`, which contains a carriage return character. `vbCr` is used to break the message text to a new line.

If you want to make your array size independent of the `Option Base` statement, you can explicitly declare the lower bound as well as the upper bound as follows:

```
Dim Data(1 To 2)
```

Arrays are very useful for processing lists or tables of items. If you want to create a short list, you can use the `Array` function as follows:

```
Dim Data As Variant
Data = Array("North", "South", "East", "West")
```

You can then use the list in a `For...Next` loop. For example, you could open and process a series of workbooks called `North.xls`, `South.xls`, `East.xls`, and `West.xls`:

```
Sub Array2()
  Dim Data As Variant, Wkb As Workbook
  Dim i As Integer

  Data = Array("North", "South", "East", "West")
  For i = LBound(Data) To UBound(Data)
    Set Wkb = Workbooks.Open(FileName:=Data(i) & ".xls")
    'Process data here
    Wkb.Close SaveChanges:=True
  Next i
End Sub
```

Multi-Dimensional Arrays

So far we have only looked at arrays with a single dimension. You can actually define arrays with up to 60 dimensions, although few people would use more than two or three dimensions. The following statements declare two-dimensional arrays:

```
Dim Data(10,20)
Dim Data(1 To 10,1 to 20)
```

You can think of a two-dimensional array as a table of data. The last example defines a table with 10 rows and 20 columns.

Arrays are very useful in Excel for processing the data in worksheet ranges. It can be far more efficient to load the values in a range into an array, process the data, and write it back to the worksheet, than to access each cell individually.

The following procedure shows how you can assign the values in a range to a `Variant`. The code uses the `LBound` and `UBound` functions to find the number of dimensions in `Data`. Note that there is a second parameter in `LBound` and `UBound` to indicate which index you are referring to. If you leave this parameter out, the functions refer to the first index:

```
Sub Array3()
  Dim Data As Variant, X As Variant
  Dim Message As String, i As Integer

  Data = Range("A1:A20").Value
  i = 1
  Do
    Message = "Lower Bound = " & LBound(Data, i) & vbCr
    Message = Message & "Upper Bound = " & UBound(Data, i) & vbCr
    MsgBox Message, , "Index Number = " & i
    i = i + 1
    On Error Resume Next
    X = UBound(Data, i)
    If Err.Number <> 0 Then Exit Do
    On Error GoTo 0
  Loop
  Message = "Number of Non Blank Elements = _
            " & WorksheetFunction.CountA(Data) & vbCr
  MsgBox Message
End Sub
```

The first time round the `Do...Loop`, `Array3` determines the upper and lower bounds of the first dimension of `Data`, as `i` has a value of one. It then increases the value of `i` to look for the next dimension. It exits the loop when an error occurs, indicating that no more dimensions exist.

By substituting different ranges into `Array3`, you can determine that the array created by assigning a range of values to a `Variant` is two-dimensional, even if there is only one row or one column in the range. You can also determine that the lower bound of each index is one, regardless of the `Option Base` setting in the declarations section.

Dynamic Arrays

When writing your code, it is sometimes not possible to determine the size of the array that will be required. For example, you might want to load the names of all the `.xls` files in the current directory into an array. You won't know in advance how many files there will be. One alternative is to declare an array that is big enough to hold the largest possible amount of data – but this would be inefficient. Instead, you can define a dynamic array and set its size when the procedure runs.

You declare a dynamic array by leaving out the dimensions:

```
Dim Data()
```

You can declare the required size at run time with a `ReDim` statement, which can use variables to define the bounds of the indexes:

```
ReDim Data(iRows, iColumns)
ReDim Data(minRow to maxRow, minCol to maxCol)
```

`ReDim` will re-initialize the array and destroy any data in it, unless you use the `Preserve` keyword. `Preserve` is used in the following procedure that uses a `Do...Loop` to load the names of files into the dynamic array called `FNames`, increasing the upper bound of its index by one each time to accommodate the new name.

The `Dir` function returns the first filename found that matches the wild card specification in `FType`. Subsequent usage of `Dir`, with no parameter, repeats the same specification, getting the next file that matches, until it runs out of files and returns a zero length string:

```
Sub FileNames()
  Dim FName As String
  Dim FNames() As String
  Dim FType As String
  Dim i As Integer

  FType = "*.xls"
  FName = Dir(FType)
  Do Until FName = ""
    i = i + 1
    ReDim Preserve FNames(1 To i)
    FNames(i) = FName
    FName = Dir
  Loop
  If i = 0 Then
    MsgBox "No files found"
  Else
    For i = 1 To UBound(FNames)
      MsgBox FNames(i)
    Next i
  End If
End Sub
```

If you intend to work on the files in a directory, and save the results, it is a good idea to get all the filenames first, as in the `FileNames` procedure, and use that list to process the files. It is not a good idea to rely on the `Dir` function to give you an accurate file list while you are in the process of reading and over-writing files.

Run-Time Error Handling

When you are designing an application, you should try to anticipate any problems that could occur when the application is used in the real world. You can remove all the bugs in your code and have flawless logic that works with all permutations of conditions, but a simple operational problem could still bring your code crashing down with a less than helpful message displayed to the user.

For example, if you try to save a workbook file to the floppy disk in the A drive, and there is no disk in the A drive, your code will grind to a halt and display a message that will probably not mean anything to the average user.

If you anticipate this particular problem, you can set up your code to gracefully deal with the situation. VBA allows you to trap error conditions using the following statement:

```
On Error GoTo LineLabel
```

`LineLabel` is a marker that you insert at the end of your normal code, as shown below with the line label `errTrap`. Note that a colon follows the line label. The line label marks the start of your error recovery code and should be preceded by an `Exit` statement to prevent execution of the error recovery code when no error occurs:

```
Sub ErrorTrap1()
  Dim Answer As Long, MyFile As String
  Dim Message As String, CurrentPath As String

  On Error GoTo errTrap
  CurrentPath = CurDir$

  ChDrive "A"
  ChDrive CurrentPath
  ChDir CurrentPath
  MyFile = "A:\Data.xls"
  Application.DisplayAlerts = False
  ActiveWorkbook.SaveAs FileName:=MyFile
TidyUp:
  ChDrive CurrentPath
  ChDir CurrentPath
Exit Sub
errTrap:
  Message = "Error No: = " & Err.Number & vbCr
  Message = Message & Err.Description & vbCr & vbCr
  Message = Message & "Please place a disk in the A: drive" & vbCr
  Message = Message & "and press OK" & vbCr & vbCr
  Message = Message & "Or press Cancel to abort File Save"
  Answer = MsgBox(Message, vbQuestion + vbOKCancel, "Error")
  If Answer = vbCancel Then Resume TidyUp
  Resume
End Sub
```

Once the `On Error` statement is executed, error trapping is enabled. If an error occurs, no message is displayed and the code following the line label is executed. You can use the `Err` object to obtain information about the error. The `Number` property of the `Err` object returns the error number and the `Description` property returns the error message associated with the error. You can use `Err.Number` to determine the error when it is possible that any of a number of errors could occur. You can incorporate `Err.Description` into your own error message, if appropriate.

In Excel 5 and 95, `Err` was not an object, but a function that returned the error number. As `Number` is the default property of the `Err` object, using `Err`, by itself, is equivalent to using `Err.Number` and the code from the older versions of Excel still works in Excel 97 and later versions.

The code in `ErrorTrap1`, after executing the `On Error` statement, saves the current directory drive and path into the variable `CurrentPath`. It then executes the `ChDrive` statement to try to activate the A drive. If there is no disk in the A drive, error 68 (Device unavailable) occurs and the error recovery code executes. For illustration purposes, the error number and description are displayed and the user is given the opportunity to either place a disk in the A drive, and continue, or abort the save.

If the user wishes to stop, we branch back to `TidyUp` and restore the original drive and directory settings. Otherwise the `Resume` statement is executed. This means that execution returns to the statement that caused the error. If there is still no disk in the A drive, the error recovery code is executed again. Otherwise the code continues normally.

The only reason for the `ChDrive "A"` statement is to test the readiness of the A drive, so the code restores the stored drive and directory path. The code sets the `DisplayAlerts` property of the `Application` object to `False`, before saving the active workbook. This prevents a warning if an old file called `Data.xls` is being replaced by the new `Data.xls`. (See Chapter 3 for more on `DisplayAlerts`.)

The `Resume` statement comes in three forms:

- `Resume` – causes execution of the statement that caused the error
- `Resume Next` – returns execution to the statement following the statement that caused the error, so the problem statement is skipped
- `Resume LineLabel` – jumps back to any designated line label in the code, so that you can decide to resume where you want

The following code uses `Resume Next` to skip the `Kill` statement, if necessary. The charmingly named `Kill` statement removes a file from disk. In the following code, we have decided to remove any file with the same name as the one we are about to save, so that there will be no need to answer the warning message about over-writing the existing file.

The problem is that `Kill` will cause a fatal error if the file does not exist. If `Kill` does cause a problem, the error recovery code executes and we use `Resume Next` to skip `Kill` and continue with `SaveAs`. The `MsgBox` is there for educational purposes only. You would not normally include it:

```
Sub ErrorTrap2()
  Dim MyFile As String, Message As String
  Dim Answer As String

  On Error GoTo errTrap

  Workbooks.Add
  MyFile = "C:\Data.xls"
  Kill MyFile
  ActiveWorkbook.SaveAs FileName:=MyFile
  ActiveWorkbook.Close

  Exit Sub
errTrap:
  Message = "Error No: = " & Err.Number & vbCr
  Message = Message & Err.Description & vbCr & vbCr
  Message = Message & "File does not exist"
  Answer = MsgBox(Message, vbInformation, "Error")
  Resume Next
End Sub
```

On Error Resume Next

As an alternative to `On Error GoTo`, you can use:

```
On Error Resume Next
```

This statement causes errors to be ignored, so it should be used with caution. However, it has many uses. The following code is a re-work of `ErrorTrap2`:

```
Sub ErrorTrap3()
  Dim MyFile As String, Message As String

  Workbooks.Add
  MyFile = "C:\Data.xls"
  On Error Resume Next
  Kill MyFile
  On Error GoTo 0
  ActiveWorkbook.SaveAs FileName:=MyFile
  ActiveWorkbook.Close
End Sub
```

We use `On Error Resume Next` just before the `Kill` statement. If our `C:\Data.xls` does not exist, the error caused by `Kill` is ignored and execution continues on the next line. After all, we don't care if the file does not exist. That's the situation we are trying to achieve.

`On Error GoTo 0` is used to turn normal VBA error handling on again. Otherwise, any further errors would be ignored. It is best not to try to interpret this statement, which appears to be directing error handling to line zero. Just accept that it works.

You can use `On Error Resume Next` to write code that would otherwise be less efficient. The following sub procedure determines whether a name exists in the active workbook:

```
Sub TestForName()
  If NameExists("SalesData") Then
    MsgBox "Name Exists"
  Else
    MsgBox "Name does not exist"
  End If
End Sub

Function NameExists(myName As String) As Boolean
  Dim X As String
  On Error Resume Next
  X = Names(myName).RefersTo
  If Err.Number <> 0 Then
    NameExists = False
    Err.Clear
  Else
    NameExists = True
  End If
End Function
```

`TestForName` calls the `NameExists` function, which uses `On Error Resume Next` to prevent a fatal error when it tries to assign the name's `RefersTo` property to a variable. There is no need for `On Error GoTo 0` here, because error handling in a procedure is disabled when a procedure exits, although `Err.Number` is not cleared.

If no error occurred, the `Number` property of the `Err` object is zero. If `Err.Number` has a non-zero value, an error occurred, which can be assumed to be because the name did not exist, so `NameExists` is assigned a value of `False` and the error is cleared. The alternative to this single pass procedure is to loop through all the names in the workbook, looking for a match. If there are lots of names, this can be a slow process.

Summary

In this chapter we have seen those elements of the VBA language that enable you to write useful and efficient procedures. We have seen how to add interaction to macros with the `MsgBox` and `InputBox` functions, how to use variables to store information and how to get help about VBA keywords.

We have seen how to declare variables and define their type, and the effect on variable scope and lifetime of different declaration techniques. We have also used the block `If` and `Select Case` structures to perform tests and carry out alternative calculations, and `Do...Loop` and `For...Next` loops that allow us to efficiently repeat similar calculations. We have seen how arrays can be used, particularly with looping procedures. We have also seen how to use `On Error` statements to trap errors.

When writing VBA code for Excel, the easiest way to get started is to use the macro recorder. We can then modify that code, using the VBE, to better suit our purposes and to operate efficiently. Using the Object Browser, Help screens, and the reference section of this book, you can discover objects, methods, properties, and events that can't be found with the macro recorder. Using the coding structures provided by VBA, we can efficiently handle large amounts of data and automate tedious processes.

You now have the knowledge required to move on to the next chapter, where you will find a rich set of practical examples showing you how to work with key Excel objects. You will discover how to create your own user interface, setting up your own toolbars, menus, and dialog boxes and embedding controls in your worksheets to enable yourself and others to work more productively.

3

The Application Object

In this chapter we will examine a range of Excel functionality, looking at features that are not necessarily related to each other. In general, the Excel object model contains objects designed to address quite specific tasks. The `Application` object sits at the top of the Excel object model hierarchy and contains all the other objects in Excel. It also acts as a catch-all area for properties and methods that do not fall neatly into any other object, but are necessary for programmatic control of Excel. There are `Application` properties that control screen updating and toggle alert messages, for example. There is an `Application` method that calculates the formulas in the open workbooks.

Globals

Many of the `Application` object's methods and properties are also members of `<globals>`, which can be found at the top of the list of classes in the Object Browser as shown in the following screen:

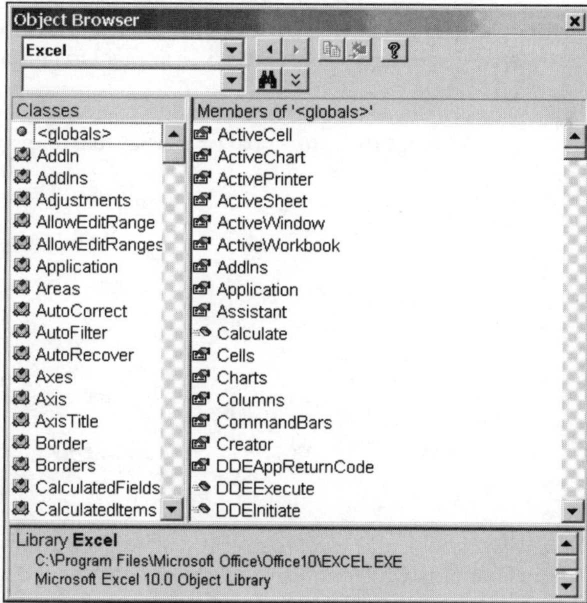

If a property or method is in `<globals>`, you can refer to that property or method without a preceding reference to an object. For example, the following two references are equivalent:

```
Application.ActiveCell
```

```
ActiveCell
```

However, you do need to be careful. It is easy to assume that frequently used `Application` object **properties**, such as `ScreenUpdating`, are globals when they are not. The following code is correct:

```
Application.ScreenUpdating = False
```

You will get unexpected results with the following:

```
ScreenUpdating = False
```

This code sets up a new variable and assigns the value `False` to it. You can easily avoid this error by having the line of code `Option Explicit` at the top of each module so that such references are flagged as undefined variables when your code is compiled.

> **Remember that you can have `Option Explicit` automatically inserted in new modules if you use Tools | Options in the VBE window and, under the Editor tab, tick the Require Variable Declaration check box.**

The Active Properties

The `Application` object provides many short cuts that allow you to refer to active objects without naming them explicitly. This makes it possible to discover what is currently active when your macro runs. It also makes it easy to write generalized code that can be applied to objects of the same type with different names.

The following `Application` object properties are global properties that allow you to refer to active objects:

- `ActiveCell`
- `ActiveChart`
- `ActivePrinter`
- `ActiveSheet`
- `ActiveWindow`
- `ActiveWorkbook`
- `Selection`

If you have just created a new workbook and want to save it with a specific filename, using the `ActiveWorkbook` property is an easy way to return a reference to the new `Workbook` object:

```
Workbooks.Add
ActiveWorkbook.SaveAs Filename:="C:\Data.xls"
```

If you want to write a macro that can apply a bold format to the currently selected cells, you can use the `Selection` property to return a reference to the `Range` object containing the selected cells:

```
Selection.Font.Bold = True
```

Be aware that `Selection` will not refer to a `Range` object if another type of object, such as a `Shape` object, is currently selected or the active sheet is not a worksheet. You might want to build a check into a macro to ensure that a worksheet is selected before attempting to enter data into it:

```
If TypeName(ActiveSheet) <> "Worksheet" Or _
   TypeName(Selection) <> "Range" Then _
      MsgBox "You can only run this macro in a range", vbCritical
   Exit Sub
End If
```

Display Alerts

It can be annoying to have to respond to system alerts while a macro runs. For example, if a macro deletes a worksheet, an alert message appears and you have to press the **OK** button to continue. However, there is also the possibility of a user clicking the **Cancel** button, which would abort the delete operation and could adversely affect subsequent code where the delete operation was assumed to have been carried out.

You can suppress most alerts by setting the `DisplayAlerts` property to `False`. When you suppress an alert dialog box, the action that is associated with the default button in that box is automatically carried out, as follows:

```
Application.DisplayAlerts = False
ActiveSheet.Delete
Application.DisplayAlerts = True
```

> **It is not necessary to reset `DisplayAlerts` to `True` at the end of your macro as VBA does this automatically. However, it is usually a good idea, after suppressing a particular message, to turn the alerts back on so that any unexpected warnings do appear on screen.**

`DisplayAlerts` is commonly used to suppress the warning that you are about to overwrite an existing file using **File | SaveAs**. When you suppress this warning, the default action is taken and the file is overwritten without interrupting the macro.

Screen Updating

It can be annoying to see the screen change and flicker while a macro is running. This happens with macros that select or activate objects and is typical of the code generated by the macro recorder.

> **It is better to avoid selecting objects in VBA. It is seldom necessary to do this and your code will run faster if you can avoid selecting or activating objects. Most of the code in this book avoids selecting where possible.**

If you want to freeze the screen while your macro runs, you use the following line of code:

```
Application.ScreenUpdating = False
```

The screen remains frozen until you assign the property a value of `True`, or when your macro finishes executing and returns control to the user interface. There is no need to restore `ScreenUpdating` to `True`, unless you want to display screen changes while your macro is still running.

There is one situation where it is a good idea to set `ScreenUpdating` to `True` while your macro is running. If you display a user form or built-in dialog box while your macro is running, you should make sure screen updating is on before showing the object. If screen updating is off, and the user drags the user form around the screen, the user form will act as an eraser on the screen behind it. You can turn screen updating off again after showing the object.

> **A beneficial side effect of turning off screen updating is that your code runs faster. It will even speed up code that avoids selecting objects, where little screen updating is required. Your code runs at maximum speed when you avoid selecting *and* turn off screen updating.**

Evaluate

The `Evaluate` method can be used to calculate Excel worksheet formulas and generate references to `Range` objects. The normal syntax for the `Evaluate` method is as follows:

```
Evaluate("Expression")
```

There is also a short cut format you can use where you omit the quotes and place square brackets around the expression, as follows:

```
[Expression]
```

`Expression` can be any valid worksheet calculation, with or without the equal sign on the left, or it can be a reference to a range of cells. The worksheet calculations can include worksheet functions that are not made available to VBA through the `WorksheetFunction` object, or they can be worksheet array formulas. You will find more information about the `WorksheetFunction` object later in this chapter.

For instance, the `ISBLANK` function, which you can use in your worksheet formulas, is not available to VBA through the `WorksheetFunction` object, because the VBA equivalent function `IsEmpty` provides the same functionality. All the same, you can use `ISBLANK`, if you need to. The following two examples are equivalent and return `True` if A1 is empty or `False` if A1 is not empty:

```
MsgBox Evaluate("=ISBLANK(A1)")
```

```
MsgBox [ISBLANK(A1)]
```

The advantage of the first technique is that you can generate the string value using code, which makes it very flexible. The second technique is shorter, but you can only change the expression by editing your code. The following procedure displays a `True` or `False` value to indicate whether the active cell is empty or not, and illustrates the flexibility of the first technique:

```
Sub IsActiveCellEmpty()
  Dim stFunctionName As String, stCellReference As String
  stFunctionName = "ISBLANK"
  stCellReference = ActiveCell.Address
  MsgBox Evaluate(stFunctionName & "(" & stCellReference & ")")
End Sub
```

Note that you cannot evaluate an expression containing variables using the second technique.

The following two lines of code show you two ways you can use `Evaluate` to generate a reference to a `Range` object, and assign a value to that object:

```
Evaluate("A1").Value = 10
```

```
[A1].Value = 10
```

The first expression is unwieldy and is rarely used, but the second is a convenient way to refer to a `Range` object, although it is not very flexible. You can further shorten the expressions by omitting the `Value` property, as this is the default property of the `Range` object:

```
[A1] = 10
```

More interesting uses of `Evaluate` include returning the contents of a workbook's `Names` collection and efficiently generating arrays of values. The following code creates a hidden name to store a password. Hidden names cannot be seen in the **Insert | Name | Define** dialog box, so they are a convenient way to store information in a workbook without cluttering the user interface:

```
Names.Add Name:="PassWord", RefersTo:="Bazonkas", Visible:=False
```

You can then use the hidden data in expressions like the following:

```
UserInput = InputBox("Enter Password")
If UserInput = [PassWord] Then
...
```

The use of names for storing data is discussed in more detail in Chapter 6.

The `Evaluate` method can also be used with arrays. The following expression generates a `Variant` array with two dimensions, 100 rows and one column, containing the values from 101 to 200. This process is carried out more efficiently than using a `For...Next` loop:

```
RowArray = [ROW(101:200)]
```

Similarly, the following code assigns the values 101 to 200 to the range **B1:B100**, and again does it more efficiently than a `For...Next` loop:

```
[B1:B100] = [ROW(101:200)]
```

InputBox

VBA has an `InputBox` **function** that provides an easy way to prompt for input data. There is also the `InputBox` **method** of the `Application` object that produces a very similar dialog box for obtaining data, but which is more powerful. It allows you to control the type of data that must be supplied by the user, and allows you to detect when the Cancel key is pressed.

If you have an unqualified reference to `InputBox` in your code, as follows, you are using the VBA `InputBox` function:

```
Answer = InputBox(prompt:="Enter range")
```

The user can only type data into the dialog box. It is not possible to point to a cell with the mouse. The return value from the `InputBox` function is always a string value and there is no check on what that string contains. If the user enters nothing, a zero length string is returned. If the user clicks the Cancel button, a zero length string is also returned. Your code cannot distinguish between no entry and the result of pressing Cancel.

The following example uses the `Application` object's `InputBox` method to prompt for a range:

```
Answer = Application.InputBox(prompt:="Enter range", Type:=8)
```

The `Type` parameter can take the following values, or any sum of the following values if you want to allow for multiple types.

Value of Type	Meaning
0	A formula
1	A number
2	Text (a string)
4	A logical value (`True` or `False`)
8	A cell reference, as a `Range` object
16	An error value, such as `#N/A`
64	An array of values

The user can point to cells with the mouse or type in data. If the input is of the wrong type, the `InputBox` method displays an error message and prompts for the data again. If the user clicks the Cancel button, the `InputBox` method returns a value of `False`.

If you assign the return value to a `Variant`, you can check to see if the value is `False`, for most return types, to detect a Cancel. If you are prompting for a range, the situation is not so simple. You need to use code like the following:

```
Sub GetRange()
  Dim Rng As Range

  On Error Resume Next
  Set Rng = Application.InputBox(prompt:="Enter range", Type:=8)
  If Rng Is Nothing Then
    MsgBox "Operation Cancelled"
  Else
    Rng.Select
  End If
End Sub
```

When you run this code, the output should look something like the following:

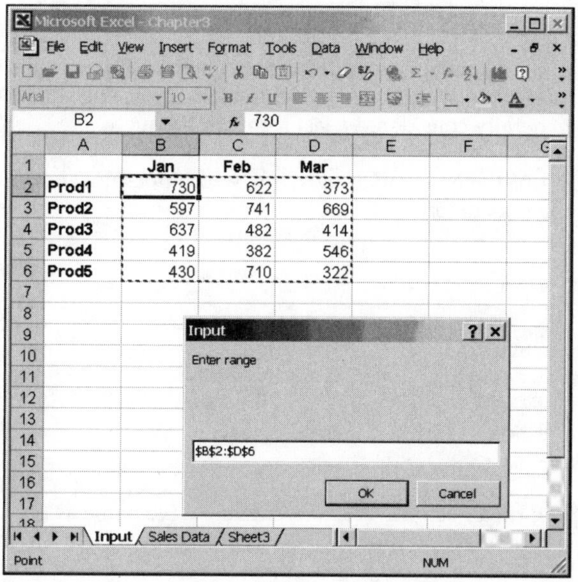

The problem is that you must use the `Set` statement to assign a range object to an object variable. If the user clicks Cancel, and a `False` value is returned, the `Set` fails and you get a run-time error. Using the `On Error Resume Next` statement, you can avoid the run-time error and then check to see if a valid range was generated. You know that the in-built type checking of the `InputBox` method ensures a valid range will be returned if the user clicks OK, so an empty range indicates that Cancel was pressed.

StatusBar

The `StatusBar` property allows you to assign a text string to be displayed at the left-hand side of the Excel status bar at the bottom of the screen. This is an easy way to keep users informed of progress during a lengthy macro operation. It is a good idea to keep users informed, particularly if you have screen updating turned off and there is no sign of activity on the screen. Even though you have turned off screen updating, you can still display messages on the status bar.

The following code shows how you can use this technique in a looping procedure:

```
Sub ShowMessage()
  Dim i As Long
  For i = 0 To 10000000
    If i Mod 1000000 = 0 Then
      Application.StatusBar = "Processing Record " & i
    End If
  Next i
  Application.StatusBar = False
End Sub
```

At the end of your processing, you must set the `StatusBar` property to `False` so that it returns to normal operation. Otherwise, your last message will stay on the screen.

SendKeys

`SendKeys` allows you to send keystrokes to the currently active window. It is used to control applications that do not support any other form of communication, such as DDE (Dynamic Data Exchange) or OLE. It is generally considered a last resort technique.

The following example opens the Notepad application, which does not support DDE or OLE, and writes a line of data to the notepad document:

```
Sub SKeys()
  Dim ReturnValue
  ReturnValue = Shell("NOTEPAD.EXE", vbNormalFocus)
  AppActivate ReturnValue
  Application.SendKeys "Copy Data.xls c:\", True
  Application.SendKeys "~", True
  Application.SendKeys "%FABATCH~", True
End Sub
```

`SKeys` uses *Alt+FA* to perform a **File | SaveAs** and enters the file name as `BATCH`. The symbol `%` is used to represent *Alt* and ~ represents *Enter*. The symbol ^ is used to represent *Ctrl* and other special keys are specified by putting their names in braces, for example, the *Del* is represented by `{Del}` as shown in the example below.

You can also send keystrokes directly to Excel. The following procedure clears the VBE's Immediate window. If you have been experimenting in the Immediate window or using `Debug.Print` to write to the Immediate window, it can get cluttered with old information. This procedure switches focus to the Immediate window and sends *Ctrl+a* to select all the text in the window. The text is then deleted by sending *Del*:

```
Sub ImmediateWindowClear()
   Application.VBE.Windows.Item("Immediate").SetFocus
   Application.SendKeys "^a"
   Application.SendKeys "{Del}"
End Sub
```

It is necessary for you to have programmatic access to your Visual Basic project for this macro to work. This can be set from the Excel (not VBE) menu Tool | Macros | Security and selecting the Trusted Sources tab.

OnTime

You can use the OnTime method to schedule a macro to run sometime in the future. You need to specify the date and time for the macro to run, and the name of the macro. If you use the Wait method of the Application object to pause a macro, all Excel activity, including manual interaction, is suspended. The advantage of OnTime is that it allows you to return to normal Excel interaction, including running other macros, while you wait for the scheduled macro to run.

Say you have an open workbook with links to Data.xls, which exists on your network server but is not currently open. At 3 p.m. you want to update the links to Data.xls. The following example schedules the RefreshData macro to run at 3 p.m., which is 15:00 hours using a 24 hour clock, on the current day. Date returns the current date and the TimeSerial function is used to add the necessary time:

```
Sub RunOnTime()
  Application.OnTime Date + TimeSerial(15, 0, 0), "RefreshData"
End Sub
```

It is worth noting that if you attempt to run this macro when it is currently after 3 p.m. you will receive an error message as you cannot schedule a task to run in the past. If necessary change the time to one in the future.

The following RefreshData macro updates the links to Data.xls that exist in ThisWorkbook using the UpdateLink method. ThisWorkbook is a convenient way to refer to the workbook containing the macro:

```
Sub RefreshData()
  ThisWorkbook.UpdateLink Name:="C:\Data.xls", Type:=xlExcelLinks
End Sub
```

If you want to keep refreshing the data on a regular basis, you can make the macro run itself as follows:

```
Dim dtScheduledTime As Date

Sub RefreshData()
  ThisWorkbook.UpdateLink Name:="C:\Data.xls", Type:= xlExcelLinks
  dtScheduledTime = Now + TimeSerial(0, 1, 0)
  Application.OnTime dtScheduledTime, "RefreshData"
End Sub

Sub StopRefresh()
  Application.OnTime dtScheduledTime, "RefreshData", , False
End Sub
```

Once you run RefreshData, it will keep scheduling itself to run every minute. In order to stop the macro, you need to know the scheduled time, so the module level variable dtScheduledTime is used to store the latest scheduled time. StopRefresh sets the fourth parameter of OnTime to False to cancel the scheduled run of RefreshData.

When you schedule a macro to run at a future time using the `OnTime` method, you must make sure that Excel keeps running in memory until the scheduled time occurs. It is not necessary to leave the workbook containing the OnTime macro open. Excel will open it, if it needs to.

The `OnTime` method is also useful when you want to introduce a delay in macro processing to allow an event to occur that is beyond your control. For example, you might want to send data to another application through a DDE link and wait for a response from that application before continuing with further processing. To do this you would create two macros. The first macro sends the data and schedules the second macro, which processes the response, to run after sufficient time has passed. The second macro could keep running itself until it detected a change in the worksheet or the environment caused by the response from the external application.

OnKey

You can use the `OnKey` method to assign a macro procedure to a single keystroke or any combination of *Ctrl*, *Shift*, and *Alt* with another key. You can also use the method to disable key combinations.

The following example shows how to assign the `DownTen` macro to the *Down Arrow* key. Once `AssignDown` has been run, the *Down Arrow* key will run the `DownTen` macro and move the cell pointer down ten rows instead of one:

```
Sub AssignDown()
  Application.OnKey "{Down}", "DownTen"
End Sub

Sub DownTen()
  ActiveCell.Offset(10, 0).Select
End Sub

Sub ClearDown()
  Application.OnKey "{Down}"
End Sub
```

`ClearDown` returns the *Down Arrow* key to its normal function.

`OnKey` can be used to disable existing keyboard short cuts. You can disable the *Ctrl+c* short cut, normally used to copy, with the following code that assigns a null procedure to the key combination:

```
Sub StopCopyShortCut()
  Application.OnKey "^c", ""
End Sub
```

Note that a lower case `c` is used. If you used an upper case `C`, it would apply to *Ctrl+Shift+c*. Once again, you can restore the normal operation of *Ctrl+c* with the following code:

```
Sub ClearCopyShortCut()
   Application.OnKey "^c"
End Sub
```

The key assignments made with the `OnKey` method apply to all open workbooks and only persist during the current Excel session.

Worksheet Functions

There are two sources of built-in functions that you can use directly in your Excel VBA code. One group of functions is part of the VBA language. The other group of functions is a subset of the Excel worksheet functions.

Excel and the Visual Basic language, in the form of VBA, were not merged until Excel 5. Each system independently developed its own functions, so there are inevitably some overlaps and conflicts between the two series of functions. For example, Excel has a `DATE` function and VBA also has a `Date` function. The Excel `DATE` function takes three input arguments (year, month, and day) to generate a specific date. The VBA `Date` function takes no input arguments and returns the current date from the system clock. In addition, VBA has a `DateSerial` function that takes the same input arguments as the Excel `DATE` function and returns the same result as the Excel `DATE` function. Finally, Excel's `TODAY` function takes no arguments and returns the same result as the VBA `Date` function.

As a general rule, if a VBA function serves the same purpose as an Excel function, the Excel function is not made directly available to VBA macros (although, you can use the `Evaluate` method to access any Excel function, as pointed out previously in this chapter). There is also a special case regarding the Excel `MOD` function. `MOD` is not directly available in VBA, but VBA has a `Mod` operator that serves the same purpose. The following line of code uses the `Evaluate` method short cut and displays the day of the week as a number, using the Excel `MOD` function and the Excel `TODAY` function:

```
MsgBox [MOD(TODAY(),7)]
```

The same result can be achieved more simply with the VBA `Date` function and the `Mod` operator as follows:

```
MsgBox Date Mod 7
```

The Excel `CONCATENATE` function is also not available in VBA. You can use the `&` operator as a substitute, just as you can in an Excel worksheet formula. If you insist on using the `CONCATENATE` function in VBA, you can write code like the following:

```
Sub ConcatenateExample1()
   Dim X As String, Y As String
   X = "Jack "
   Y = "Smith"
   MsgBox Evaluate("CONCATENATE(""" & X & """,""" & Y & """)")
End Sub
```

On the other hand, you can avoid being absurd and get the same result with the following code:

```
Sub ConcatenateExample2()
   Dim X As String, Y As String
   X = "Jack "
   Y = "Smith"
   MsgBox X & Y
End Sub
```

The VBA functions, such as `Date`, `DateSerial`, and `IsEmpty` can be used without qualification, as they are members of `<globals>`. For example, you can use the following:

```
StartDate = DateSerial(1999, 6, 1)
```

The Excel functions, such as `VLOOKUP` and `SUM`, are methods of the `WorksheetFunction` object and are used with the following syntax:

```
Total = WorksheetFunction.Sum(Range("A1:A10"))
```

For compatibility with Excel 5 and Excel 95, you can use `Application` rather than `WorksheetFunction`:

```
Total = Application.Sum(Range("A1:A10"))
```

> **`WorksheetFunction.Vlookup` does not work properly in all versions of VBA. The errors can be avoided by using `Application.Vlookup`.**

For a complete list of the worksheet functions directly available in VBA, see the `WorksheetFunction` object in the reference section.

Caller

The `Caller` property of the `Application` object returns a reference to the object that called or executed a macro procedure. It had a wide range of uses in Excel 5 and Excel 95, where it was used with menus and controls on dialog sheets. From Excel 97 onwards, command bars and ActiveX controls on user forms have replaced menus and controls on dialog sheets. The `Caller` property does not apply to these new features.

`Caller` still applies to the `Forms` toolbar controls, drawing objects that have macros attached and user-defined functions. It is particularly useful in determining the cell that called a user-defined function. The following worksheet uses the `WorksheetName` function to display the name of the worksheet in B2:

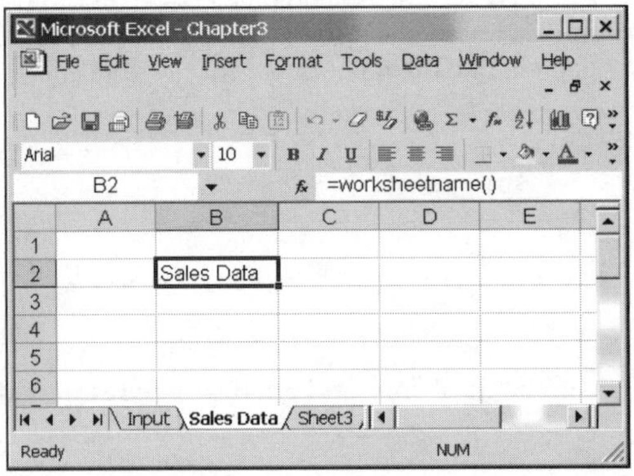

When used in a function, `Application.Caller` returns a reference to the cell that called the function, which is returned as a `Range` object. The following `WorksheetName` function uses the `Parent` property of the `Range` object to generate a reference to the `Worksheet` object containing the `Range` object. It assigns the `Name` property of the `Worksheet` object to the return value of the function. The `Volatile` method of the `Application` object forces Excel to recalculate the function every time the worksheet is recalculated, so that if you change the name of the sheet, the new name is displayed by the function:

```
Function WorksheetName()
   Application.Volatile
   WorksheetName = Application.Caller.Parent.Name
End Function
```

It would be a mistake to use the following code in the `WorksheetName` function:

```
WorksheetName = ActiveSheet.Name
```

If a recalculation takes place while a worksheet is active that is different from the one containing the formula, the wrong name will be returned to the cell.

Summary

In this chapter we have highlighted some of the more useful properties and methods of the `Application` object. As `Application` is used to hold general-purpose functionality that does not fall clearly under other objects, it is easy to miss some of these very useful capabilities.

The following properties and methods have been covered:

- `ActiveCell` – contains a reference to the active cell
- `ActiveChart` – contains a reference to the active chart
- `ActivePrinter` – contains a reference to the active printer
- `ActiveSheet` – contains a reference to the active worksheet
- `ActiveWindow` – contains a reference to the active window
- `ActiveWorkbook` – contains a reference to the active workbook
- `Caller` – contains reference to the object that called a macro
- `DisplayAlerts` – determines whether alert dialogs are displayed or not
- `Evaluate` – used to calculate Excel functions and generate `Range` objects
- `InputBox` – used to prompt a user for input
- `OnKey` – assigns a macro to a single keystroke, or a combination (with *Ctrl*, *Alt*, etc.)
- `OnTime` – used to set the time for a macro to run
- `ScreenUpdating` – determines whether screen updating is turned on or off
- `Selection` – contains a reference to the selected range
- `SendKeys` – send keystrokes to the active window
- `StatusBar` – allows messages to be displayed on the status bar
- `WorksheetFunction` – contains the Excel functions available to VBA

This is but a small sample of the total number of properties and methods of the `Application` object – there are over two hundred of them in Excel 2002. A full list is given in Appendix A.

Workbooks and Worksheets

In this chapter you will see how to create new Workbook objects and how to interact with the files that you use to store those workbooks. To do this, some basic utility functions will be presented. You will also see how to handle the Sheet objects within the workbook, and how some important features must be handled through the Window object. Finally, you will see how to synchronize your worksheets as you move from one worksheet to another.

The Workbooks Collection

The Workbooks collection consists of all the currently open Workbook objects in memory. Members can be added to the Workbooks collection in a number of ways. You can create a new empty workbook based on the default properties of the Workbook object, or you can create a new workbook based on a template file. Finally, you can open an existing workbook file.

To create a new empty workbook based on the default workbook, use the Add method of the Workbooks collection:

```
Workbooks.Add
```

The new workbook will be the active workbook, so you can refer to it in the following code as ActiveWorkbook. If you immediately save the workbook, using the SaveAs method, you can give it a filename that can be used to refer to the workbook in later code, even if it is no longer active:

```
Workbooks.Add
ActiveWorkbook.SaveAs Filename:="C:\Data\SalesData1.xls"
Workbooks.Add
ActiveWorkbook.SaveAs Filename:="C:\Data\SalesData2.xls"
Workbooks("SalesData1.xls").Activate
```

However, a better technique is to use the return value of the Add method to create an object variable that refers to the new workbook. This provides a short cut way to refer to your workbook and you can keep track of a temporary workbook, without the need to save it:

```
Sub NewWorkbooks()
    Dim Wkb1 As Workbook
    Dim Wkb2 As Workbook

    Set Wkb1 = Workbooks.Add
    Set Wkb2 = Workbooks.Add
    Wkb1.Activate
End Sub
```

The Add method allows you to specify a template for the new workbook. The template does not need to be a file saved as a template, with an .xlt extension – it can be a normal workbook file with an .xls extension. The following code creates a new, unsaved workbook called SalesDataX, where X is a sequence number that increments as you create more workbooks based on the same template, in the same way that Excel creates workbooks called Book1, Book2, etc. when you create new workbooks through the user interface:

```
Set Wkb1 = Workbooks.Add(Template:="C:\Data\SalesData.xls")
```

To add an existing workbook file to the Workbooks collection, you use the Open method. Once again, it is a good idea to use the return value of the Open method to create an object variable that you can use later in your code to refer to the workbook:

```
Set Wkb1 = Workbooks.Open(Filename:="C:\Data\SalesData1.xls")
```

Many of our examples have data, such as filenames, "hard coded". That is, we place the data inside the code instead of putting it into a variable and using the variable in the code. This is not good programming practice, in general, and isn't to be recommended. However, we will continue to show examples in this format in order to simplifying the code.

Getting a FileName from a Path

When you deal with workbooks in VBA, you often need to specify directory paths and filenames. Some tasks require that you know just the path – for example, if you set a default directory. Some tasks require you to know just the filename – for example, if you want to activate an open workbook. Other tasks require both path and filename – for example, if you want to open an existing workbook file that is not in the active directory.

Once a workbook is open, there is no problem getting its path, getting its full path and file name, or just getting the filename. For example, the following code displays "SalesData1.xls" in the message box:

```
Set Wkb = Workbooks.Open(FileName:="C:\Data\SalesData1.xls")
MsgBox Wkb.Name
```

`Wkb.Path` returns "`C:\Data`" and `Wkb.FullName` returns "`C:\Data\SalesData1.xls`".

However, if you are trying to discover whether a certain workbook is already open, and you have the full path information, you need to extract the filename from the full path to get the value of the `Name` property of the `Workbook` object. The following `GetFileName` function returns the name "`SalesData1.xls`" from the full path "`C:\Data\SalesData1.xls`":

```
Function GetFileName(stFullName As String) As String
   'GetFileName returns the file name, such as Cash.xls from
   'the end of a full path such as C:\Data\Project1\Cash.xls
   'stFullName is returned if no path separator is found
   Dim stPathSep As String          'Path Separator Character
   Dim iFNLength As Integer         'Length of stFullName
   Dim i As Integer

   stPathSep = Application.PathSeparator
   iFNLength = Len(stFullName)
   'Find last path separator character, if there is one
   For i = iFNLength To 1 Step -1
      If Mid(stFullName, i, 1) = stPathSep Then Exit For
   Next i
   GetFileName = Right(stFullName, iFNLength - i)
End Function
```

So that `GetFileName` works on the Macintosh as well as under Windows, the path separator character is obtained using the `PathSeparator` property of the `Application` object. This returns : on the Macintosh and \ under Windows. The `Len` function returns the number of characters in `stFullName` and the `For...Next` loop searches backwards from the last character in `stFullName`, looking for the path separator. If it finds one, it exits the `For...Next` loop, and the index `i` is equal to the character position of the separator. If it does not find a separator, `i` will have a value of zero when the `For...Next` loop is completed.

When a `For...Next` loop is permitted to complete normally, the index variable will not be equal to the `Stop` value. It will have been incremented past the end value.

`GetFileName` uses the `Right` function to extract the characters to the right of the separator in `stFullName`. If there is no separator, all the characters from `stFullName` are returned. Once you have the file name of a workbook, you can use the following `IsWorkbookOpen` function to see if the workbook is already a member of the `Workbooks` collection:

```
Function IsWorkbookOpen(stName As String) As Boolean
   'IsWorkbookOpen returns True if stName is a member
   'of the Workbooks collection. Otherwise, it returns False
   'stName must be provided as a file name without path
   Dim Wkb As Workbook

   On Error Resume Next
   Set Wkb = Workbooks(stName)
   If Not Wkb Is Nothing Then
      IsWorkbookOpen = True
   End If
End Function
```

In the above code IsWorkbookOpen tries to assign a reference to the workbook to an object variable, and then sees whether that attempt was successful or not. An alternative way to achieve the same result would be to search through the WorkBooks collection to see if any Workbook object had the name required.

In the code above, the On Error Resume Next ensures that no run-time error occurs when the workbook is not open. If the named document is found, IsWorkbookOpen returns a value of True. If you do not define the return value of a Boolean function, it will return False. In other words, if no open workbook of the given name is found, False is returned.

You might prefer to use the following more lengthy but more explicit code to define the return value of IsWorkbookOpen. It is also easier to understand as it avoids the double negative. Despite this, my own preference is for the shorter code as presented above, because it is shorter.

```
If Wkb Is Nothing Then
   IsWorkbookOpen = False
Else
   IsWorkbookOpen = True
End If
```

The following code uses the user-defined functions GetFileName and IsWorkbookOpen functions described above. ActivateWorkbook1 is designed to activate the workbook file in the path assigned to the variable stFullName:

```
Sub ActivateWorkbook1()
   Dim stFullName As String
   Dim stFileName As String
   Dim Wkb As Workbook

   stFullName = "C:\Data\SalesData1.xls"
   stFileName = GetFileName(stFullName)
   If IsWorkbookOpen(stFileName) Then
      Set Wkb = Workbooks(stFileName)
      Wkb.Activate
   Else
      Set Wkb = Workbooks.Open(FileName:=stFullName)
   End If
End Sub
```

ActivateWorkbook1 first uses GetFileName to extract the workbook file name, SalesData1.xls, from stFullName and assigns it to stFileName. Then it uses IsWorkbookOpen to determine whether SalesData1.xls is currently open. If the file is open, it assigns a reference to the Workbook object to the Wkb object variable and activates the workbook. If the file is not open, it opens the file and assigns the return value of the Open method to Wkb. When the workbook is opened, it will automatically become the active workbook.

Note that the above code assumes that the workbook file exists at the specified location. It will fail if this is not the case. You will find a function, called FileExists, in the *"Overwriting an Existing Workbook"* section that you can use to test for the files existence.

Files in the Same Directory

It is common practice to break up an application into a number of workbooks and keep the related workbook files in the same directory, including the workbook containing the code that controls the application. In this case, you could use the common directory name in your code when opening the related workbooks. However, if you "hard wire" the directory name into your code, you will have problems if the directory name changes, or you copy the files to another directory on the same PC or another PC. You will have to edit the directory path in your macros.

To avoid maintenance problems in this situation, you can make use of `ThisWorkbook.Path`. `ThisWorkbook` is a reference to the workbook that contains the code. No matter where the workbook is located, the `Path` property of `ThisWorkbook` gives you the required path to locate the related files, as demonstrated in the following code:

```
Sub ActivateWorkbook2()
   Dim stPath As String
   Dim stFileName As String
   Dim stFullName As String
   Dim Wkb As Workbook

   stFileName = "SalesData1.xls"
   If IsWorkbookOpen(stFileName) Then
      Set Wkb = Workbooks(stFileName)
      Wkb.Activate
   Else
      stPath = ThisWorkbook.Path
      stFullName = stPath & "\" & stFileName
      Set Wkb = Workbooks.Open(FileName:= stFullName)
   End If
End Sub
```

Overwriting an Existing Workbook

When you want to save a workbook using the `SaveAs` method and using a specific filename, there is the possibility that a file with that name will already exist on disk. If the file does already exist, the user receives an alert message and has to make a decision about overwriting the existing file. If you want, you can avoid the alert and take control programmatically.

If you want to overwrite the existing file every time, you can just suppress the alert with the following code:

```
Set Wkb1 = Workbooks.Add
Application.DisplayAlerts = False
Wkb1.SaveAs Filename:="C:\Data\SalesData1.xls"
Application.DisplayAlerts = True
```

If you want to check for the existing file and take alternative courses of action, you can use the `Dir` function. If this is a test that you need to perform often, you can create the following `FileExists` function:

```
Function FileExists(stFile As String) As Boolean
   If Dir(stFile) <> "" Then FileExists = True
End Function
```

The `Dir` function attempts to match its input argument against existing files. `Dir` can be used with wild cards under Windows for matches such as "`*.xls`". If it finds a match, it returns the first match found and can be called again without an input argument to get subsequent matches. Here, we are trying for an exact match that will either return the same value as the input argument or a zero length string if there is no match. The `FileExists` function has been declared to return a `Boolean` type value, and as explained earlier, is set to the default value of `False` if no return value is defined. The `If` test assigns a value of `True` to the return value if `Dir` does not return a zero length string.

The following code shows how you can use the `FileExists` function to test for a specific filename and take alternative courses of action:

```
Sub TestForFile()
   Dim stFileName As String
   stFileName = "C:\Data\SalesData9.xls"
   If FileExists(stFileName) Then
      MsgBox stFileName & " exists"
   Else
      MsgBox stFileName & " does not exist"
   End If
End Sub
```

What you actually do in each alternative depends very much on the situation you are dealing with. One alternative could be to prompt the user for a new filename if the name already exists. Another approach could be to compute a new file name by finding a new sequence number to be appended to the end of the text part of the filename as shown here:

```
Sub CreateNextFileName()
   Dim Wkb1 As Workbook
   Dim i As Integer
   Dim stFileName As String

   Set Wkb1 = Workbooks.Add(Template:="C:\Data\SalesData.xls")
   i = 0
   Do
      i = i + 1
      stFileName = "C:\Data\SalesData" & i & ".xls"
   Loop While FileExists(stFileName)
   Wkb1.SaveAs FileName:= stFileName
End Sub
```

Here, the code in the `Do...Loop` is repeated, increasing the value of `i` by one for each loop, as long as the file name generated exists. When `i` reaches a value for which there is no matching file name, the loop ends and the file is saved using the new name.

Saving Changes

You can close a workbook using the `Close` method of the `Workbook` object as shown:

```
ActiveWorkbook.Close
```

If changes have been made to the workbook, the user will be prompted to save the changes when an attempt is made to close the workbook. If you want to avoid this prompt, you can use several techniques, depending on whether you want to save the changes or not.

If you want to save changes automatically, you can specify this as a parameter of the `Close` method:

```
Sub CloseWorkbook()
   Dim Wkb1 As Workbook

   Set Wkb1 = Workbooks.Open(FileName:="C:\Data\SalesData1.xls")
   Range("A1").Value = Format(Date, "ddd mmm dd, yyyy")
   Range("A1").EntireColumn.AutoFit
   Wkb1.Close SaveChanges:=True
End Sub
```

If you don't want to save changes, you can set the `SaveChanges` parameter of the `Close` method to `False`.

Another situation that could arise is where you want to leave a changed workbook open to view but you don't want to save those changes or be prompted to save the changes when you close the workbook or Excel. In this situation, you can set the `Saved` property of the workbook to `True` and Excel will think that there are no changes to be saved. You should make doubly sure you would want to do this before you add this line of code:

```
ActiveWorkbook.Saved = True
```

The Sheets Collection

Within a `Workbook` object there is a `Sheets` collection whose members can be either `Worksheet` objects or `Chart` objects. For compatibility with older versions of Excel, they can also be DialogSheets, `Excel4MacroSheets` and Excel4InternationalMacroSheets. Excel 5 and Excel 95 included modules as part of the `Sheets` collection, but since Excel 97, modules have moved to the VBE.

Modules in workbooks created under Excel 5 or Excel 95 are considered by later versions of Excel to belong to a hidden `Modules` collection and can still be manipulated by the code originally set up in the older versions.

`Worksheet` objects and `Chart` objects also belong to their own collections, the `Worksheets` collection and the `Charts` collection, respectively. The `Charts` collection only includes chart sheets, that is charts that are embedded in a worksheet are **not** members of the `Charts` collection. Charts embedded in worksheets are contained in `ChartObject` objects, which are members of the `ChartObjects` collection of the worksheet. See Chapter 9 for more details.

Worksheets

You can refer to a worksheet by its name or index number in the `Sheets` collection and the `Worksheets` collection. If you know the name of the worksheet you want to work on, it is appropriate, and usually safer, to use that name to specify the required member of the `Worksheets` collection. If you want to process all the members of the `Worksheets` collection, in a `For...Next` loop for example, you would usually reference each worksheet by its index number.

The index number of a worksheet in the `Worksheets` collection can be different from the index number of the worksheet in the `Sheets` collection. In the following workbook, `Sheet1` can be referenced by any of the following:

```
ActiveWorkbook.Sheets("Sheet1")
```

```
ActiveWorkbook.Worksheets("Sheet1")
```

```
ActiveWorkbook.Sheets(2)
```

```
ActiveWorkbook.Worksheets(1)
```

Workbooks

	A	B	C	D	E	F	G
1							
2		**Jan**	**Feb**	**Mar**			
3		122	212	232			
4							
5							
6							
7							
8							
9							

Chart1 | **Sheet1** | Chart2 | Sheet2 | Sheet3

There is a trap, however, concerning the `Index` property of the `Worksheet` object. The `Index` property of the `Worksheet` object returns the value of the index in the `Sheets` collection, not the `Worksheets` collection. The following code tells you that `Worksheets(1)` is `Sheet1` with index 2, `Worksheets(2)` is `Sheet2` with index 4 and `Worksheets(3)` is `Sheet3` with index 5:

```
Sub WorksheetIndex()
   Dim i As Integer

   For i = 1 To ThisWorkbook.Worksheets.Count
      MsgBox ThisWorkbook.Worksheets(i).Name & _
             " has Index = " & _
             ThisWorkbook.Worksheets(i).Index
   Next i
End Sub
```

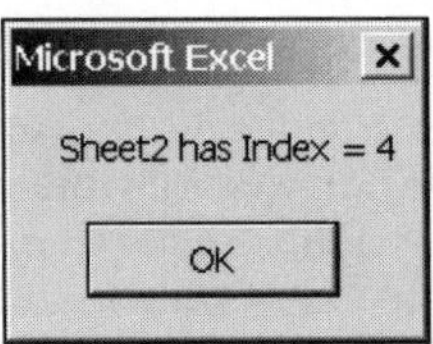

You should avoid using the `Index` property of the worksheet, if possible, as it leads to confusing code. The following example shows how you must use the worksheet `Index` as an index in the `Sheets` collection, not the `Worksheets` collection. The macro adds a new empty chart sheet to the left of every worksheet in the active workbook:

```
Sub InsertChartsBeforeWorksheets()
   Dim Wks As Worksheet

   For Each Wks In Worksheets
      Charts.Add Before:=Sheets(Wks.Index)
   Next Wks
End Sub
```

In most cases you can avoid using the worksheet `Index` property. The code above should have been written as follows:

```
Sub InsertChartsBeforeWorksheets2()
   Dim Wks As Worksheet

   For Each Wks In Worksheets
      Charts.Add Before:=Wks
   Next Wks
End Sub
```

Strangely enough, Excel will not allow you to add a new chart after the last worksheet, although it will let you move a chart after the last worksheet. If you want to insert chart sheets after each worksheet, you can use code like the following:

```
Sub InsertChartsAfterWorksheets()
   Dim Wks As Worksheet
   Dim Cht As Chart

   For Each Wks In Worksheets
      Set Cht = Charts.Add
      Cht.Move After:=Wks
   Next Wks
End Sub
```

Chart sheets are covered in more detail in Chapter 8.

Copy and Move

The `Copy` and `Move` methods of the `Worksheet` object allow you to copy or move one or more worksheets in a single operation. They both have two optional parameters that allow you to specify the destination of the operation. The destination can be either before or after a specified sheet. If you do not use one of these parameters, the worksheet will be copied or moved to a new workbook.

`Copy` and `Move` do not return any value or reference, so you have to rely on other techniques if you want to create an object variable referring to the copied or moved worksheets. This is not generally a problem as the first sheet created by a `Copy` operation, or the first sheet resulting from moving a group of sheets, will be active immediately after the operation.

Say you have a workbook like the following and want to add another worksheet for February – and then more worksheets for the following months. The numbers on rows 3 and 4 are the input data, but row 5 contains calculations to give the difference between rows 3 and 4. When you copy the worksheet, you will want to clear the input data from the copies but retain the headings and formulas:

	A	B	C	D	E
1					
2		**Apples**	**Mangoes**	**Bananas**	**Lychees**
3	**Production**	907	956	937	961
4	**Sales**	964	947	915	917
5		**-57**	**9**	**22**	**44**

The following code creates a new monthly worksheet that is inserted into the workbook after the latest month. It copies the first worksheet, removes any numeric data from it but leaves any headings or formulas in place and then renames the worksheet to the new month and year:

```
Sub NewMonth()
   'Copy the first worksheet in the active workbook
   'to create a new monthly sheet with name having format "mmm yyyy".
   'The first worksheet must have a name that is in a recognisable
   'date format.
   Dim Wks As Worksheet
   Dim dtFirstDate As Date
   Dim iFirstMonth As Integer
   Dim iFirstYear As Integer
   Dim iCount As Integer

   'Initialise counter to number of worksheets
   iCount = Worksheets.Count

   'Copy first worksheet after last worksheet and increase count
   Worksheets(1).Copy After:=Worksheets(iCount)
   iCount = iCount + 1

   'Assign last worksheet to Wks
   Set Wks = Worksheets(iCount)

   'Calculate date for first worksheet
   dtFirstDate = DateValue(Worksheets(1).Name)

   'Extract month and year components of date
   iFirstMonth = Month(dtFirstDate)
   iFirstYear = Year(dtFirstDate)

   'Compute and assign new date to name of Wks
   Wks.Name = Format(DateSerial(iFirstYear, iFirstMonth + iCount - 1, 1), _
           "mmm yyyy")

   'Clear data cells in Wks, avoiding error if there is no data
   On Error Resume Next
   Wks.Cells.SpecialCells(xlCellTypeConstants, 1).ClearContents
End Sub
```

The result of the copy is as follows:

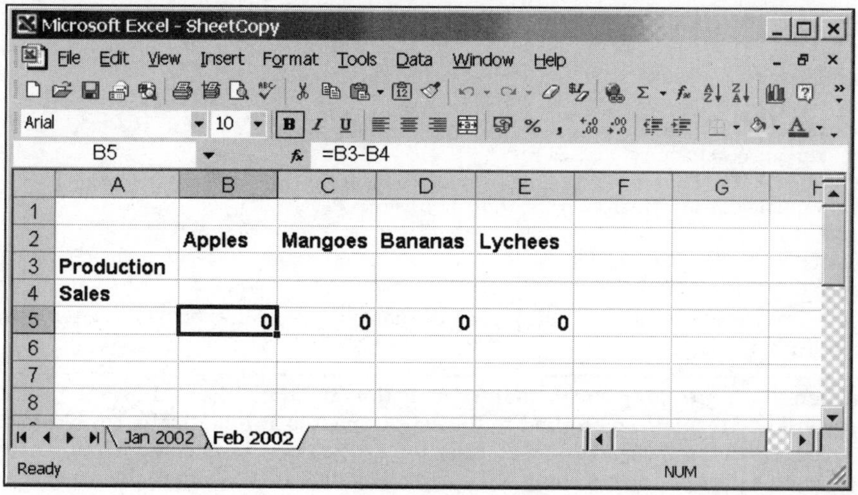

`NewMonth` first determines how many worksheets are in the workbook and then copies the current worksheet, appending it to the workbook. It updates the number of worksheets in `iCount` and creates an object variable `Wks` that refers to the copied sheet. It then uses the `DateValue` function to convert the name of the January worksheet to a date.

`NewMonth` extracts the month and year of the date into the two integer variables `iFirstMonth` and `iFirstYear` using the `Month` and `Year` functions. It then uses the `DateSerial` function to calculate a new date that follows on from the last one. This calculation is valid even when new years are created, as `DateSerial`, like the worksheet `DATE` function, treats month numbers greater than 12 as the appropriate months in the following year.

`NewMonth` uses the VBA `Format` function to convert the new date into `"mmm yyyy"` format as a string. It assigns the text to the `Name` property of the new worksheet. Finally, `NewMonth` clears the contents of any cells containing numbers using the `SpecialCells` method to find the numbers. `SpecialCells` is discussed in more detail in the following chapter on the `Range` object. The `On Error Resume Next` statement suppresses a run-time error when there is no numeric data to be cleared.

Grouping Worksheets

You can manually group the sheets in a workbook by clicking on a sheet tab then, holding down *Shift* or *Ctrl*, clicking on another sheet tab. *Shift* groups all the sheets between the two tabs. *Ctrl* adds just the new sheet to the group. You can also group sheets in VBA by using the `Select` method of the `Worksheets` collection in conjunction with the `Array` function. The following code groups the first, third, and fifth worksheets and makes the third worksheet active:

```
Worksheets(Array(1, 3, 5)).Select
Worksheets(3).Activate
```

In addition to this, you can also create a group using the `Select` method of the `Worksheet` object. The first sheet is selected in the normal way. Other worksheets are added to the group by using the `Select` method while setting its `Replace` parameter to `False`:

```
Sub Groupsheets()
   Dim stNames(1 To 3) As String
   Dim i As Integer

   stNames(1) = "Sheet1"
   stNames(2) = "Sheet2"
   stNames(3) = "Sheet3"
   Worksheets(stNames(1)).Select
   For i = 2 To 3
      Worksheets(stNames(i)).Select Replace:=False
   Next i
End Sub
```

The above technique is particularly useful when the names have been specified by user input, via a multi-select list box, for example.

> **One benefit of grouping sheets manually, is that any data inserted into the active sheet and any formatting applied to the active sheet is automatically copied to the other sheets in the group. However, only the active sheet is affected when you apply changes to a grouped sheet using VBA code. If you want to change the other members of the group, you need to set up a `For Each...Next` loop and carry out the changes on each member.**

The following code places the value `100` into the A1 cell of worksheets with index numbers `1`, `3`, and `5` and bolds the numbers:

```
Sub FormatGroup()
   Dim shSheets As Sheets
   Dim Wks As Worksheet
   Set shSheets = Worksheets(Array(1, 3, 5))
   For Each Wks In shSheets
      Wks.Range("A1").Value = 100
      Wks.Range("A1").Font.Bold = True
   Next Wks
End Sub
```

The Window Object

In VBA, if you want to detect what sheets are currently grouped, you use the `SelectedSheets` property of the `Window` object. You might think that `SelectedSheets` should be a property of the `Workbook` object, but, that is not the case. `SelectedSheets` is a property of the `Window` object because you can open many windows on the same workbook and each window can have different groups, as the following screen shows:

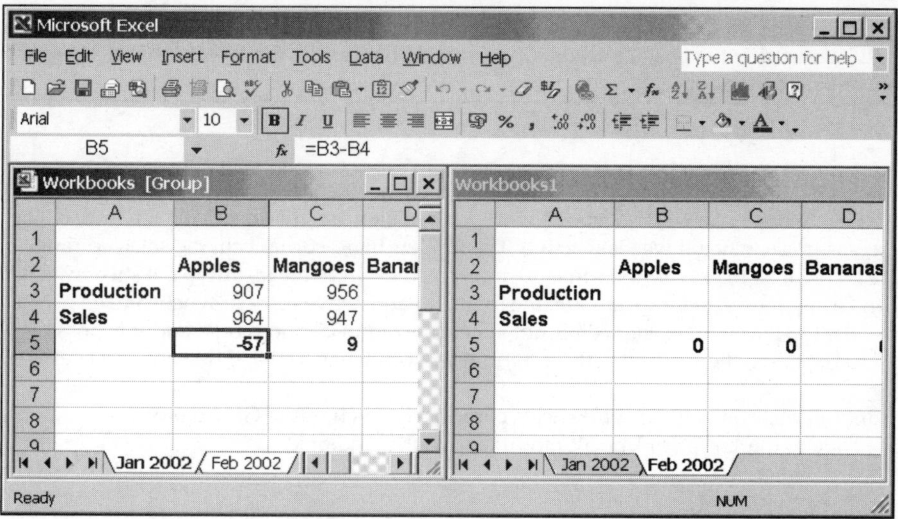

There are many other common workbook and worksheet properties that you might presume to be properties of the `Workbook` object or the `Worksheet` object, but which are actually `Window` object properties. Some examples of these are `ActiveCell`, `DisplayFormulas`, `DisplayGridlines`, `DisplayHeadings`, and `Selection`. See the `Window` object in Appendix A for a full list.

The following code determines which cells are selected on the active sheet, makes them bold and then goes on to apply bold format to the corresponding ranges on the other sheets in the group:

```
Sub FormatSelectedGroup()
   Dim Sht As Object
   Dim stAddress As String

   stAddress = Selection.Address
   For Each Sht In ActiveWindow.SelectedSheets
      If TypeName(Sht) = "Worksheet" Then
         Sht.Range(stAddress).Font.Bold = True
      End If
   Next Sht
End Sub
```

The address of the selected range on the active sheet is captured in `stAddress` as a string. It is possible to activate only the selected sheets and apply bold format to the selected cells. Group mode ensures that the selections are the same on each worksheet. However, activating sheets is a slow process. By capturing the selection address as a string, you can generate references to the same range on other sheets using the `Range` property of the other sheets. The address is stored as a string in the form "`$B$2:$E$2,$A$3:$A$4`", for example, and need not be a single contiguous block.

`FormatSelectedGroup` allows for the possibility that the user can include a chart sheet or another type of sheet in the group of sheets. It checks that the `TypeName` of the sheet is indeed "`Worksheet`" before applying the new format.

It is necessary to `Dim Sht` as the generic `Object` type, if you want to allow it to refer to different sheet types. There is a `Sheets` collection in the Excel Object Model, but there is no `Sheet` object.

Synchronizing Worksheets

When you move from one worksheet in a workbook to another, the sheet you activate will be configured as it was when it was last active. The top left-hand corner cell, the selected range of cells, and the active cell will be in exactly the same positions as they were the last time the sheet was active, unless you are in Group mode. In Group mode, the selection and active cell are synchronized across the group. However, the top left-hand corner cell is not synchronized in Group mode, and it is possible that you will not be able to see the selected cells and the active cell when you activate a worksheet.

If you want to synchronize your worksheets completely, even out of Group mode, you can add the following code to the `ThisWorkbook` module of your workbook:

```
Dim OldSheet As Object

Private Sub Workbook_SheetDeactivate(ByVal Sht As Object)
   'If the deactivated sheet is a worksheet,
   'store a reference to it in OldSheet
   If TypeName(Sht) = "Worksheet" Then Set OldSheet = Sht
End Sub

Private Sub Workbook_SheetActivate(ByVal NewSheet As Object)
   Dim lCurrentCol As Long
   Dim lCurrentRow As Long
   Dim stCurrentCell As String
   Dim stCurrentSelection As String

   On Error GoTo Fin
   If OldSheet Is Nothing Then Exit Sub
   If TypeName(NewSheet) <> "Worksheet" Then Exit Sub
   Application.ScreenUpdating = False
   Application.EnableEvents = False

   OldSheet.Activate     'Get the old worksheet configuration
   lCurrentCol = ActiveWindow.ScrollColumn
   lCurrentRow = ActiveWindow.ScrollRow
   stCurrentSelection = Selection.Address
   stCurrentCell = ActiveCell.Address

   NewSheet.Activate     'Set the new worksheet configuration
   ActiveWindow.ScrollColumn = lCurrentCol
   ActiveWindow.ScrollRow = lCurrentRow
   Range(stCurrentSelection).Select
   Range(stCurrentCell).Activate
Fin:
   Application.EnableEvents = True
End Sub
```

The `Dim OldSheet as Object` statement must be at the top of the module in the declarations area so that `OldSheet` is a module-level variable that will retain its value while the workbook is open and can be accessed by the two event procedures. The `Workbook_SheetDeactivate` event procedure is used to store a reference to any worksheet that is deactivated. The deactivate event occurs after another sheet is activated, so it is too late to store the active window properties. The procedure's `Sht` parameter refers to the deactivated sheet and its value is assigned to `OldSheet`.

The `Workbook_SheetActivate` event procedure executes after the `Deactivate` procedure. The `On Error GoTo Fin` statement ensures that, if an error occurs, there are no error messages displayed and that control jumps to the `Fin:` label where event processing is enabled, just in case event processing has been switched off.

The first `If` tests check that `OldSheet` has been defined, indicating that a worksheet has been deactivated during the current session. The second `If` test checks that the active sheet is a worksheet. If either `If` test fails, the procedure exits. These tests allow for other types of sheets, such as charts, being deactivated or activated.

Next, screen updating is turned off to minimize screen flicker. It is not possible to eliminate all flicker, because the new worksheet has already been activated and the user will get a brief glimpse of its old configuration before it is changed. Then, event processing is switched off so that no chain reactions occur. To get the data it needs, the procedure has to re-activate the deactivated worksheet, which would trigger the two event procedures again.

After reactivating the old worksheet, the `ScrollRow` (the row at the top of the screen), the `ScrollColumn` (the column at the left of the screen), the addresses of the current selection, and the active cell are stored. The new worksheet is then reactivated and its screen configuration is set to match the old worksheet. As there is no `Exit Sub` statement before the `Fin`: label, the final statement is executed to make sure event processing is enabled again.

Summary

In this chapter, we have seen many techniques for handling workbooks and worksheets in VBA code. We have seen how to:

- Create new workbooks and open existing workbooks
- Handle saving workbook files and overwriting existing files
- Move and copy worksheets and interact with Group mode

You have also seen that you access some workbook and worksheet features through the `Window` object, and have been shown that you can synchronize your worksheets using workbook events procedures. See Chapter 10 for more discussion on this topic.

In addition, a number of utility macros have been presented including routines to check that a workbook is open, to extract a file name from the full file path, and a simple macro that confirms that a file does indeed exist.

5

Using Ranges

The `Range` object is probably the object you will utilize the most in your VBA code. A `Range` object can be a single cell, a rectangular block of cells, or the union of many rectangular blocks (a non-contiguous range). A `Range` object is contained within a `Worksheet` object.

The Excel object model does not support three-dimensional `Range` objects that span multiple worksheets – every cell in a single `Range` object must be on the same worksheet. If you want to process 3D ranges, you must process a `Range` object in each worksheet separately.

In this chapter we will examine the most useful properties and methods of the `Range` object.

Activate and Select

The `Activate` and `Select` methods cause some confusion, and it is sometimes claimed that there is no difference between them. To understand the difference between them, we need to first understand the difference between the `ActiveCell` and `Selection` properties of the `Application` object. The following screen illustrates this:

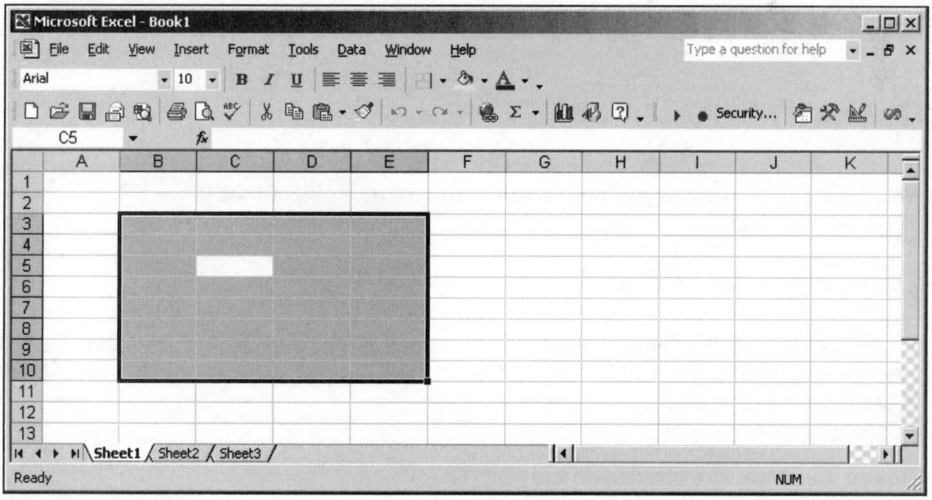

`Selection` refers to B3:E10. `ActiveCell` refers to C5, the cell where data will be inserted if the user types something. `ActiveCell` only ever refers to a single cell, while `Selection` can refer to a single cell or a range of cells. The active cell is usually the top left-hand cell in the selection, but can be any cell in the selection, as shown above. You can manually change the position of the active cell in a selection by pressing *Tab*, *Enter*, *Shift+Tab*, or *Shift+Enter*.

You can achieve the combination of selection and active cell shown above by using the following code:

```
Range("B3:E10").Select
Range("C5").Activate
```

If you try to activate a cell that is outside the selection, you will change the selection, and the selection will become the activated cell.

Confusion also arises because you are permitted to specify more than one cell when you use the `Activate` method. Excel's behavior is determined by the location of the top left cell in the range you activate. If the top-left cell is within the current selection, the selection does not change and the top left cell becomes active. The following example will create the screen above:

```
Range("B3:E10").Select
Range("C5:Z100").Activate
```

If the top-left cell of the range you activate is not in the current selection, the range that you activate replaces the current selection as shown by the following:

```
Range("B3:E10").Select
Range("A2:C5").Activate
```

In this case the `Select` is overruled by the `Activate` and A2:C5 becomes the selection.

> **To avoid errors, it is recommended that you don't use the `Activate` method to select a range of cells. If you get into the habit of using `Activate` instead of `Select`, you will get unexpected results when the top-left cell you activate is within the current selection.**

Range Property

You can use the `Range` property of the `Application` object to refer to a `Range` object on the active worksheet. The following example refers to a `Range` object that is the B2 cell on the currently active worksheet:

```
Application.Range("B2")
```

Note that you can't test code examples like the one above as they are presented. However, as long as you are referring to a range on the active worksheet, these examples can be tested by the immediate window of the VBE, as follows:

```
Application.Range("B2").Select
```

It is important to note that the above reference to a Range object will cause an error if there is no worksheet currently active. For example, it will cause an error if you have a chart sheet active.

As the Range property of the Application object is a member of <globals>, you can omit the reference to the Application object, as follows:

```
Range("B2")
```

You can refer to more complex Range objects than a single cell. The following example refers to a single block of cells on the active worksheet:

```
Range("A1:D10")
```

And this code refers to a non-contiguous range of cells:

```
Range("A1:A10,C1:C10,E1:E10")
```

The Range property also accepts two arguments that refer to diagonally opposite corners of a range. This gives you an alternative way to refer to the A1:D10 range:

```
Range("A1","D10")
```

Range also accepts names that have been applied to ranges. If you have defined a range of cells with the name SalesData, you can use the name as an argument:

```
Range("SalesData")
```

The arguments can be objects as well as strings, which provides much more flexibility. For example, you might want to refer to every cell in column A from cell A1 down to a cell that has been assigned the name LastCell:

```
Range("A1",Range("LastCell"))
```

Shortcut Range References

You can also refer to a range by enclosing an A1 style range reference or a name in square brackets, which is a shortcut form of the Evaluate method of the Application object. It is equivalent to using a single string argument with the Range property, but is shorter:

```
[B2]
[A1:D10]
[A1:A10,C1:C10,E1:E10]
[SalesData]
```

This shortcut is convenient when you want to refer to an absolute range. However, it is not as flexible as the `Range` property as it cannot handle variable input as strings or object references.

Ranges on Inactive Worksheets

If you want to work efficiently with more than one worksheet at the same time, it is important to be able to refer to ranges on worksheets without having to activate those worksheets. Switching between worksheets is slow, and code that does this is more complex than it need be. This also leads to code that is harder to read and debug.

All our examples so far apply to the active worksheet, because they have not been qualified by any specific worksheet reference. If you want to refer to a range on a worksheet that is not active, simply use the `Range` property of the required `Worksheet` object:

```
Worksheets("Sheet1").Range("C10")
```

If the workbook containing the worksheet and range is not active, you need to further qualify the reference to the `Range` object as follows:

```
Workbooks("Sales.xls").Worksheets("Sheet1").Range("C10")
```

However, you need to be careful if you want to use the `Range` property as an argument to another `Range` property. Say you want to sum **A1:A10** on **Sheet1**, while **Sheet2** is the active sheet. You might be tempted to use the following code, which results in a run-time error:

```
MsgBox WorksheetFunction.Sum(Sheets("Sheet1").Range(Range("A1"), _
                                                       Range("A10")))
```

The problem is that `Range("A1")` and `Range("A10")` refer to the active sheet, `Sheet2`. You need to use fully qualified properties:

```
MsgBox WorksheetFunction.Sum(Sheets("Sheet1").Range( _
                             Sheets("Sheet1").Range("A1"), _
                             Sheets("Sheet1").Range("A10")))
```

In this situation it is more elegant, and more efficient, to use a `With...End With` construct:

```
With Sheets("Sheet1")
   MsgBox WorksheetFunction.Sum(.Range(.Range("A1"), .Range("A10")))
End With
```

Range Property of a Range Object

The `Range` property is normally used as a property of the `Worksheet` object. You can also use the `Range` property of the `Range` object. In this case, it acts as a reference relative to the `Range` object itself. The following is a reference to the D4 cell:

```
Range("C3").Range("B2")
```

If you consider a virtual worksheet that has C3 as the top left hand cell, and B2 is one column across and one row down on the virtual worksheet, you arrive at D4 on the real worksheet

You will see this "`Range` in a `Range`" technique used in code generated by the macro recorder when relative recording is used (discussed in Chapter 2). For example, the following code was recorded when the active cell and the four cells to its right were selected while recording relatively:

```
    ActiveCell.Range("A1:E1").Select
```

As the code above is obviously very confusing, it is best to avoid this type of referencing. The `Cells` property is a much better way to reference relatively.

Cells Property

You can use the `Cells` property of the `Application`, `Worksheet`, or `Range` objects to refer to the `Range` object containing all the cells in a `Worksheet` object or `Range` object. The following two lines of code each refer to a `Range` object that contains all the cells in the active worksheet:

```
ActiveSheet.Cells
```

```
Application.Cells
```

As the `Cells` property of the `Application` object is a member of `<globals>`, you can also refer to the `Range` object containing all the cells on the active worksheet as follows:

```
Cells
```

You can use the `Cells` property of a `Range` object as follows:

```
Range("A1:D10").Cells
```

However, this code achieves nothing as it simply refers to the original `Range` object it qualifies.

You can refer to a specific cell relative to the `Range` object by using the `Item` property of the `Range` object and specifying the relative row and column positions. The row parameter is always numeric. The column parameter can be numeric or you can use the column letters entered as a string. The following are both references to the `Range` object containing the B2 cell in the active worksheet:

```
Cells.Item(2,2)
Cells.Item(2,"B")
```

As the `Item` property is the default property of the `Range` object, you can omit it as follows:

```
Cells(2,2)
Cells(2,"B")
```

The numeric parameters are particularly useful when you want to loop through a series of rows or columns using an incrementing index number. The following example loops through rows 1 to 10 and columns A to E in the active worksheet, placing values in each cell:

```
Sub FillCells()
  Dim i As Integer, j As Integer

  For i = 1 To 10
    For j = 1 To 5
      Cells(i, j).Value = i * j
    Next j
  Next i
End Sub
```

This is what you get:

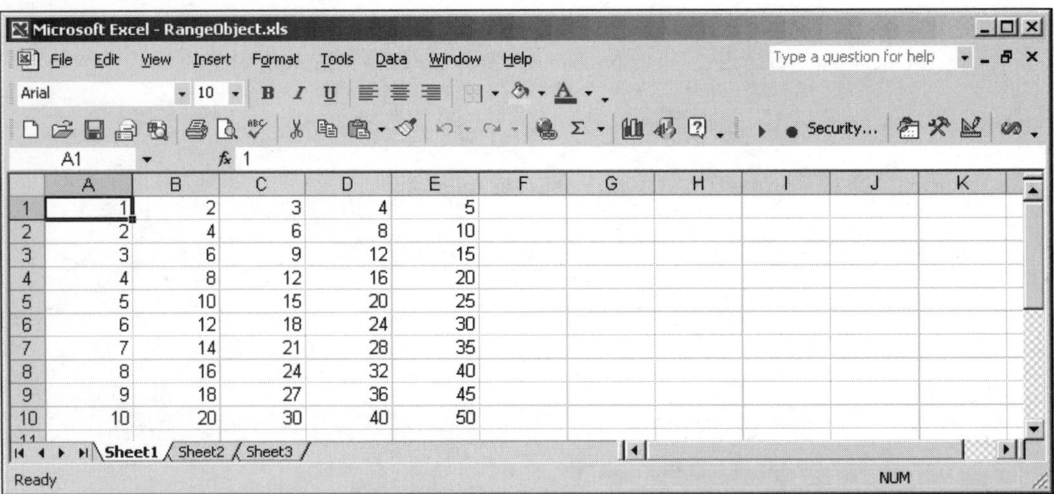

	A	B	C	D	E	F	G	H	I	J	K
1	1	2	3	4	5						
2	2	4	6	8	10						
3	3	6	9	12	15						
4	4	8	12	16	20						
5	5	10	15	20	25						
6	6	12	18	24	30						
7	7	14	21	28	35						
8	8	16	24	32	40						
9	9	18	27	36	45						
10	10	20	30	40	50						

Cells used in Range

You can use the Cells property to specify the parameters within the Range property to define a Range object. The following code refers to **A1:E10** in the active worksheet:

```
Range(Cells(1,1), Cells(10,5))
```

This type of referencing is particularly powerful because you can specify the parameters using numeric variables as shown in the previous looping example.

Ranges of Inactive Worksheets

As with the Range property, you can apply the Cells property to a worksheet that is not currently active:

```
Worksheets("Sheet1").Cells(2,3)
```

If you want to refer to a block of cells on an inactive worksheet using the Cells property, the same precautions apply as with the Range property. You must make sure you qualify the Cells property fully. If **Sheet2** is active, and you want to refer to the range **A1:E10** on **Sheet1**, the following code will fail because Cells(1,1) and Cells(10,5) are properties of the active worksheet:

```
Sheets("Sheet1").Range(Cells(1,1), Cells(10,5)).Font.Bold = True
```

A With...End With construct is an efficient way to incorporate the correct sheet reference:

```
With Sheets("Sheet1")
    .Range(.Cells(1, 1), .Cells(10, 5)).Font.Bold = True
End With
```

More on the Cells Property of the Range Object

The Cells property of a Range object provides a nice way to refer to cells relative to a starting cell, or within a block of cells. The following refers to cell **F11**:

```
Range("D10:G20").Cells(2,3)
```

If you want to examine a range with the name SalesData and color any figure under 100 red, you can use the following code:

```
Sub ColorCells()
  Dim rgSales As Range
  Dim i As Long, j As Long

  Set rgSales = Range("SalesData")
  For i = 1 To rgSales.Rows.Count
    For j = 1 To rgSales.Columns.Count
      If rgSales.Cells(i, j).Value < 100 Then
        rgSales.Cells(i, j).Font.ColorIndex = 3
      Else
        rgSales.Cells(i, j).Font.ColorIndex = 1
```

```
        End If
      Next j
    Next i
End Sub
```

This is the result:

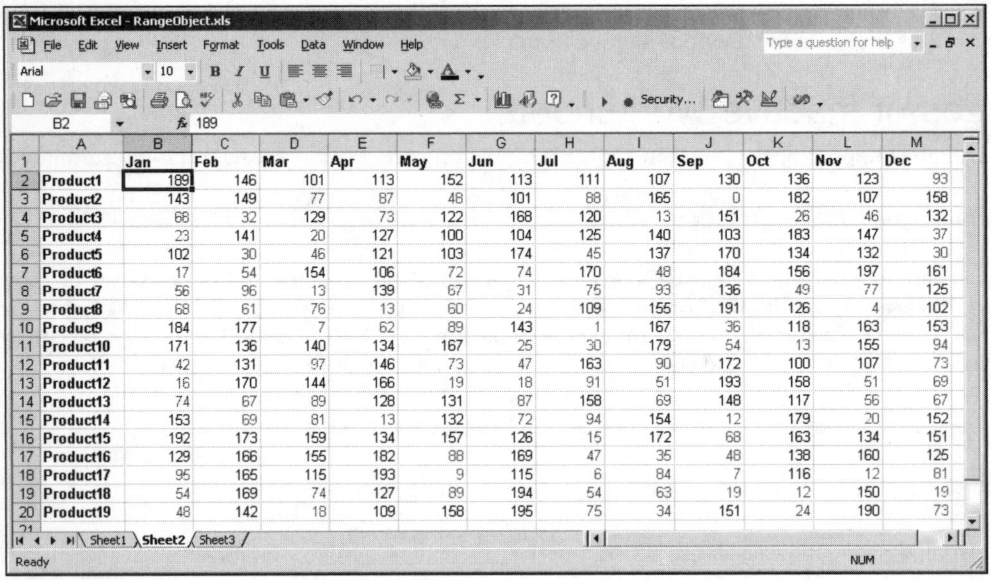

Microsoft Excel - RangeObject.xls

	Jan	Feb	Mar	Apr	May	Jun	Jul	Aug	Sep	Oct	Nov	Dec
Product1	189	146	101	113	152	113	111	107	130	136	123	93
Product2	143	149	77	87	48	101	88	165	0	182	107	158
Product3	68	32	129	73	122	168	120	13	151	26	46	132
Product4	23	141	20	127	100	104	125	140	103	183	147	37
Product5	102	30	46	121	103	174	45	137	170	134	132	30
Product6	17	54	154	106	72	74	170	48	184	156	197	161
Product7	56	96	13	139	67	31	75	93	136	49	77	125
Product8	68	61	76	13	60	24	109	155	191	126	4	102
Product9	184	177	7	62	89	143	1	167	36	118	163	153
Product10	171	136	140	134	167	25	30	179	54	13	155	94
Product11	42	131	97	146	73	47	163	90	172	100	107	73
Product12	16	170	144	166	19	18	91	51	193	158	51	69
Product13	74	67	89	128	131	87	158	69	148	117	56	67
Product14	153	69	81	13	132	72	94	154	12	179	20	152
Product15	192	173	159	134	157	126	15	172	68	163	134	151
Product16	129	166	155	182	88	169	47	35	48	138	160	125
Product17	95	165	115	193	9	115	6	84	7	116	12	81
Product18	54	169	74	127	89	194	54	63	19	12	150	19
Product19	48	142	18	109	158	195	75	34	151	24	190	73

It is not, in fact, necessary to confine the referenced cells to the contents of the `Range` object. You can reference cells outside the original range. This means that you really only need to use the top-left cell of the `Range` object as a starting point. This code refers to F11, as in the earlier example:

```
Range("D10").Cells(2,3)
```

You can also use a shortcut version of this form of reference. The following is also a reference to cell F11:

```
Range("D10")(2,3)
```

Technically, this works because it is an allowable shortcut for the `Item` property of the `Range` object, rather than the `Cells` property, as described previously:

```
Range("D10").Item(2,3)
```

It is even possible to use zero or negative subscripts, as long as you don't attempt to reference outside the worksheet boundaries. This can lead to some odd results. The following code refers to cell C9:

```
Range("D10")(0,0)
```

The following refers to B8:

```
Range("D10")(-1,-1)
```

The previous `Font.ColorIndex` example using `rgSales` can be written as follows, using this technique:

```
Sub ColorCells()
  Dim rgSales As Range
  Dim i As Long, j As Long

  Set rgSales = Range("SalesData")
  For i = 1 To rgSales.Rows.Count
    For j = 1 To rgSales.Columns.Count
      If rgSales(i, j).Value < 100 Then
        rgSales(i, j).Font.ColorIndex = 4
      Else
        rgSales(i, j).Font.ColorIndex = 1
      End If
    Next j
  Next i
End Sub
```

There is actually a small increase in speed, if you adopt this shortcut. Running the second example, the increase is about 5% on my PC when compared to the first example.

Single-Parameter Range Reference

The shortcut range reference accepts a single parameter as well as two. If you are using this technique with a range with more than one row, and the index exceeds the number of columns in the range, the reference wraps within the columns of the range, down to the appropriate row.

The following refers to cell E10:

```
Range("D10:E11")(2)
```

The following refers to cell D11:

```
Range("D10:E11")(3)
```

The index can exceed the number of cells in the `Range` object and the reference will continue to wrap within the `Range` object's columns. The following refers to cell D12:

```
Range("D10:E11")(5)
```

Qualifying a `Range` object with a single parameter is useful when you want to step through all the cells in a range without having to separately track rows and columns. The `ColorCells` example can be further rewritten as follows, using this technique:

```
Sub ColorCells()
  Dim rgSales As Range
  Dim i As Long
```

```
    Set rgSales = Range("SalesData")
      For i = 1 To rgSales.Cells.Count
        If rgSales(i).Value < 100 Then
          rgSales(i).Font.ColorIndex = 5
        Else
          rgSales(i).Font.ColorIndex = 1
        End If
    Next i
  End Sub
```

In the fourth and final variation on the `ColorCells` theme, you can step through all the cells in a range using a `For Each...Next` loop, if you do not need the index value of the `For...Next` loop for other purposes:

```
Sub ColorCells()
  Dim Rng As Range

  For Each Rng In Range("SalesData")
    If Rng.Value < 100 Then
      Rng.Font.ColorIndex = 6
    Else
      Rng.Font.ColorIndex = 1
    End If
  Next Rng
End Sub
```

Offset Property

The `Offset` property of the `Range` object returns a similar object to the `Cells` property, but is different in two ways. The first difference is that the `Offset` parameters are zero based, rather than one based, as the term 'offset' implies. These examples both refer to the A10 cell:

```
Range("A10").Cells(1,1)
```

```
Range("A10").Offset(0,0)
```

The second difference is that the `Range` object generated by `Cells` consists of one cell. The `Range` object referred to by the `Offset` property of a range has the same number of rows and columns as the original range. The following refers to B2:C3:

```
Range("A1:B2").Offset(1,1)
```

`Offset` is useful when you want to refer to ranges of equal sizes with a changing base point. For example, you might have sales figures for January to December in B1:B12 and want to generate a three-month moving average from March to December in C3:C12. The code to achieve this is:

```
Sub MoveAvg()
  Dim Rng As Range
  Dim i As Long
```

```
    Set Rng = Range("B1:B3")
    For i = 3 To 12
      Cells(i, "C").Value = WorksheetFunction.Round _
                                            (WorksheetFunction.Sum(Rng) / 3, 0)
      Set Rng = Rng.Offset(1, 0)
    Next i
  End Sub
```

The result of running the code is:

	A	B	C	D
1	Jan	100		
2	Feb	123		
3	Mar	115	113	
4	Apr	140	126	
5	May	120	125	
6	Jun	132	131	
7	Jul	124	125	
8	Aug	120	125	
9	Sep	115	120	
10	Oct	132	122	
11	Nov	143	130	
12	Dec	128	134	
13				

Resize Property

You can use the Resize property of the Range object to refer to a range with the same top left-hand corner as the original range, but with a different number of rows and columns. The following refers to D10:E10:

```
Range("D10:F20").Resize(1,2)
```

Resize is useful when you want to extend or reduce a range by a row or column. For example, if you have a data list, which has been given the name Database, and you have just added another row at the bottom, you need to redefine the name to include the extra row. The following code extends the name by the extra row:

```
With Range("Database")
  .Resize(.Rows.Count + 1).Name = "Database"
End With
```

When you omit the second parameter, the number of columns remains unchanged. Similarly, you can omit the first parameter to leave the number of rows unchanged. The following refers to A1:C10:

```
Range("A1:B10").Resize(, 3)
```

You can use the following code to search for a value in a list and, having found it, copy it and the two columns to the right to a new location. The code to do this is:

```
Sub FindIt()
  Dim Rng As Range

  Set Rng = Range("A1:A12").Find(What:="Jun", LookAt:=xlWhole, _
                                                              LookIn:=xlValues)
  If Rng Is Nothing Then
    MsgBox "Data not found"
    Exit Sub
  Else
    Rng.Resize(1, 3).Copy Destination:=Range("G1")
  End If
End Sub
```

And this is the result:

	A	B	C	D	E	F	G	H	I	J	K
1	Jan	100					Jun	132	131		
2	Feb	123									
3	Mar	115	113								
4	Apr	140	126								
5	May	120	125								
6	Jun	132	131								
7	Jul	124	125								
8	Aug	120	125								
9	Sep	115	120								
10	Oct	132	122								
11	Nov	143	130								
12	Dec	128	134								

The `Find` method does not act like the Edit | Find command. It returns a reference to the found cell as a `Range` object but it does not select the found cell. If `Find` does not locate a match, it returns a `null` object that you can test for with the `Is Nothing` expression. If you attempt to copy the `null` object, a run-time error occurs.

SpecialCells Method

When you press the *F5* key in a worksheet, the **Go To** dialog box appears. You can then press the **Special…** button to show the following dialog box:

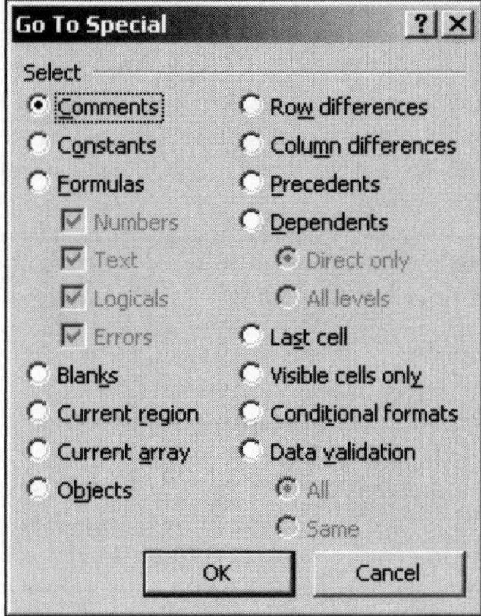

This dialog allows you to do a number of useful things, such as find the last cell in the worksheet or all the cells with numbers rather than calculations. As you might expect, all these operations can be carried out in VBA code. Some have their own methods, but most of them can be performed using the `SpecialCells` method of the `Range` object.

Last Cell

The following code determines the last row and column in the worksheet:

```
Set rgLast = Range("A1").SpecialCells(xlCellTypeLastCell)
lLastRow = rgLast.Row
lLastCol = rgLast.Column
```

The last cell is considered to be the intersection of the highest numbered row in the worksheet that contains information and the highest numbered column in the worksheet that contains information. Excel also includes cells that have contained information during the current session, even if you have deleted that information. The last cell is not reset until you save the worksheet.

Excel considers formatted cells and unlocked cells to contain information. As a result, you will often find the last cell well beyond the region containing data, especially if the workbook has been imported from another spreadsheet application, such as Lotus 1-2-3. If you want to consider only cells that contain data in the form of numbers, text, and formulas, you can use the following code:

```
Sub GetRealLastCell()
  Dim lRealLastRow As Long
  Dim lRealLastColumn As Long
  Range("A1").Select
```

```
    On Error Resume Next
    lRealLastRow = Cells.Find("*", Range("A1"), xlFormulas, , xlByRows, _
                                                              xlPrevious).Row
    lRealLastColumn = Cells.Find ("*",Range("A1"), xlFormulas, , _
                                              xlByColumns, xlPrevious).Column
    Cells(lRealLastRow, lRealLastColumn).Select
  End Sub
```

In this example, the `Find` method searches backwards from the **A1** cell (which means that Excel wraps around the worksheet and starts searching from the last cell towards the **A1** cell) to find the last row and column containing any characters. The `On Error Resume Next` statement is used to prevent a run-time error when the spreadsheet is empty.

> **Note that it is necessary to `Dim` the row number variables as `Long`, rather than `Integer`, as integers can only be as high as 32,767 and worksheets can contain 65,536 rows.**

If you want to get rid of the extra rows containing formats, you should select the entire rows, by selecting their row numbers, and then use **Edit | Delete** to remove them. You can also select the unnecessary columns by their column letters, and delete them. At this point, the last cell will not be reset. You can save the worksheet to reset the last cell, or execute `ActiveSheet.UsedRange` in your code to perform a reset. The following code will remove extraneous rows and columns and reset the last cell:

```
  Sub DeleteUnusedFormats()
    Dim lLastRow As Long, lLastColumn As Long
    Dim lRealLastRow As Long, lRealLastColumn As Long

    With Range("A1").SpecialCells(xlCellTypeLastCell)
      lLastRow = .Row
      lLastColumn = .Column
    End With
    lRealLastRow = _
        Cells.Find("*", Range("A1"), xlFormulas, , xlByRows, xlPrevious).Row
    lRealLastColumn = _
        Cells.Find("*", Range("A1"), xlFormulas, , _
                                              xlByColumns, xlPrevious).Column
    If lRealLastRow < lLastRow Then
      Range(Cells(lRealLastRow + 1, 1), Cells(lLastRow, 1)).EntireRow.Delete
    End If
    If lRealLastColumn < lLastColumn Then
      Range(Cells(1, lRealLastColumn + 1), _
                                Cells(1, lLastColumn)).EntireColumn.Delete
    End If

    ActiveSheet.UsedRange 'Resets LastCell
  End Sub
```

The `EntireRow` property of a `Range` object refers to a `Range` object that spans the entire spreadsheet, that is columns 1 to 256 (or **A** to **IV** on the rows contained in the original range. The `EntireColumn` property of a `Range` object refers to a `Range` object that spans the entire spreadsheet (rows **1** to **65536**) in the columns contained in the original object).

Deleting Numbers

Sometimes it is useful to delete all the input data in a worksheet or template so that it is more obvious where new values are required. The following code deletes all the numbers in a worksheet, leaving the formulas intact:

```
On Error Resume Next
Cells.SpecialCells(xlCellTypeConstants, xlNumbers).ClearContents
```

The code above should be preceded by the `On Error` statement if you want to prevent a run-time error when there are no numbers to be found.

Excel considers dates as numbers and they will be cleared by the above code. If you have used dates as headings and want to avoid this, you can use the following code:

```
For Each Rng In Cells.SpecialCells(xlCellTypeConstants, xlNumbers)
  If Not IsDate(Rng.Value) Then Rng.ClearContents
Next Rng
```

CurrentRegion Property

If you have tables of data that are separated from surrounding data by at least one empty row and one empty column, you can select an individual table using the `CurrentRegion` property of any cell in the table. It is equivalent to the manual *Ctrl+** keyboard short cut. In the following worksheet, you could select the `Bananas` table by clicking on the A9 cell and pressing *Ctrl+**:

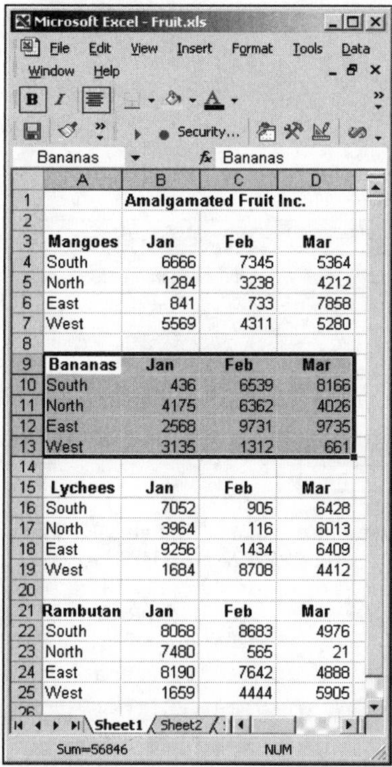

	A	B	C	D
1		Amalgamated Fruit Inc.		
2				
3	Mangoes	Jan	Feb	Mar
4	South	6666	7345	5364
5	North	1284	3238	4212
6	East	841	733	7858
7	West	5569	4311	5280
8				
9	Bananas	Jan	Feb	Mar
10	South	436	6539	8166
11	North	4175	6362	4026
12	East	2568	9731	9735
13	West	3135	1312	661
14				
15	Lychees	Jan	Feb	Mar
16	South	7052	905	6428
17	North	3964	116	6013
18	East	9256	1434	6409
19	West	1684	8708	4412
20				
21	Rambutan	Jan	Feb	Mar
22	South	8068	8683	4976
23	North	7480	565	21
24	East	8190	7642	4888
25	West	1659	4444	5905

The same result can be achieved with the following code, given that cell A9 has been named `Bananas`:

```
Range("Bananas").CurrentRegion.Select
```

This property is very useful for tables that change size over time. You can select all the months up to the current month as the table grows during the year, without having to change the code each month. Naturally, in your code, there is rarely any need to select anything. If you want to perform a consolidation of the fruit figures into a single table in a sheet called `Consolidation`, and you have named the top left corner of each table with the product name, you can use the following code:

```
Sub Consolidate()
  Dim vaProducts As Variant
  Dim rgCopy As Range 'Range to be copied
  Dim rgDestination As Range
  Dim i As Long

  Application.ScreenUpdating = False
  vaProducts = Array("Mangoes", "Bananas", "Lychees", "Rambutan")
  Set rgDestination = Worksheets("Consolidation").Range("B4")
  For i = LBound(vaProducts) To UBound(vaProducts)
    With Range(vaProducts(i)).CurrentRegion
      'Exclude headings from copy range
      Set rgCopy = .Offset(1, 1).Resize(.Rows.Count - 1, .Columns.Count - 1)
    End With
    rgCopy.Copy
    If i = LBound(vaProducts) Then
      'Paste the first product values
      rgDestination.PasteSpecial xlPasteValues, xlPasteSpecialOperationNone
    Else
      'Add the other product values
      rgDestination.PasteSpecial xlPasteValues, xlPasteSpecialOperationAdd
    End If
  Next i
  Application.CutCopyMode = False 'Clear the clipboard
End Sub
```

This gives the following output:

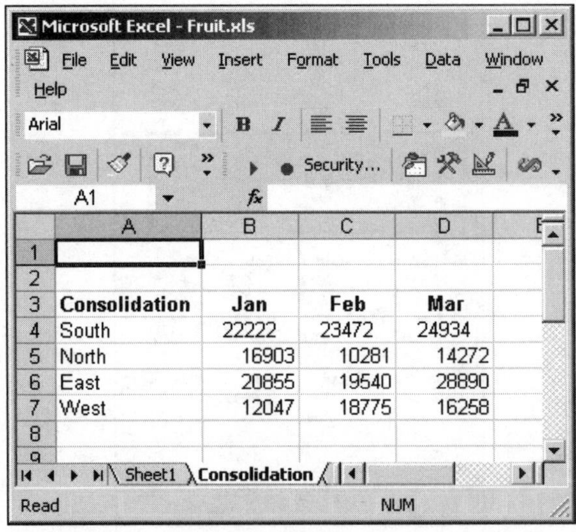

Screen updating is suppressed to cut out screen flicker and speed up the macro. The `Array` function is a convenient way to define relatively short lists of items to be processed. The `LBound` and `UBound` functions are used to avoid worrying about which `Option Base` has been set in the declarations section of the module. The code can be reused in other modules without a problem.

The first product is copied and its values are pasted over any existing values in the destination cells. The other products are copied and their values added to the destination cells. The clipboard is cleared at the end to prevent users accidentally carrying out another paste by pressing the *Enter* key.

End Property

The `End` property emulates the operation of *Ctrl+Arrow* Key. If you have selected a cell at the top of a column of data, *Ctrl+Down Arrow* takes you to the next item of data in the column that is before an empty cell. If there are no empty cells in the column, you go to the last data item in the column. If the cell after the selected cell is empty, you jump to the next cell with data, if there is one, or the bottom of the worksheet.

The following code refers to the last data cell at the bottom of column A if there are no empty cells between it and A1:

```
Range("A1").End(xlDown)
```

To go in other directions, you use the constants `xlUp`, `xlToLeft`, and `xlToRight`.

If there are gaps in the data, and you want to refer to the last cell in column A, you can start from the bottom of the worksheet and go up, as long as data does not extend as far as A65536:

```
Range("A65536").End(xlUp)
```

In the section on rows, later in this chapter, you will see a way to avoid the A65536 reference and generalize the code above for different versions of Excel.

Referring to Ranges with End

You can refer to a range of cells from the active cell to the end of the same column with:

```
Range(ActiveCell, ActiveCell.End(xlDown)).Select
```

Say you have a table of data, starting at cell B3, which is separated from surrounding data by an empty row and an empty column. You can refer to the table, as long as it has continuous headings across the top and continuous data in the last column, using this line of code:

```
Range("B3", Range("B3").End(xlToRight).End(xlDown)).Select
```

The effect, in this case, is the same as using the `CurrentRegion` property, but `End` has many more uses as you will see in the following examples.

As usual, there is no need to select anything if you want to operate on a `Range` object in VBA. The following code copies the continuous headings across the top of Sheet1 to the top of Sheet2:

```
With Worksheets("Sheet1").Range("A1")
  .Range(.Cells(1), .End(xlToRight)).Copy Destination:= _
                                       Worksheets("Sheet2").Range("A1")
End With
```

This code can be executed, no matter what sheet is active, as long as the workbook is active.

Summing a Range

Say you want to place a `SUM` function in the active cell to add the values of the cells below it, down to the next empty cell. You can do that with the following code:

```
With ActiveCell
  Set Rng = Range(.Offset(1), .Offset(1).End(xlDown))
  .Formula = "=SUM(" & Rng.Address & ")"
End With
```

The `Address` property of the `Range` object returns an absolute address by default. If you want to be able to copy the formula to other cells and sum the data below them, you can change the address to a relative one and perform the copy as follows:

```
With ActiveCell
  Set Rng = Range(.Offset(1), .Offset(1).End(xlDown))
  .Formula = "=SUM(" & Rng.Address(RowAbsolute:=False, _
                                        ColumnAbsolute:=False) & ")"
  .Copy Destination:=Range(.Cells(1), .Offset(1).End(xlToRight).Offset(-1))
End With
```

The end of the destination range is determined by dropping down a row from the `SUM`, finding the last data column to the right, and popping back up a row.

And this is what you get:

Microsoft Excel - RangeObject.xls

B2 =SUM(B3:B21)

	A	B	C	D	E	F	G	H	I	J	K	L	M
1		Jan	Feb	Mar	Apr	May	Jun	Jul	Aug	Sep	Oct	Nov	Dec
2	Total	1555	2098	1681	1942	2023	2071	1711	2180	1960	1686	1670	2071
3	Product1	123	94	71	28	160	55	103	142	49	77	35	161
4	Product2	156	149	87	103	65	129	66	62	76	39	22	113
5	Product3	32	150	189	193	195	170	174	160	79	65	2	41
6	Product4	162	80	24	112	161	100	52	30	105	83	30	42
7	Product5	41	181	129	182	135	38	52	119	54	31	75	73
8	Product6	191	149	70	131	181	179	36	191	116	124	38	115
9	Product7	13	18	21	88	175	75	69	49	42	20	196	69
10	Product8	12	127	37	139	83	65	1	188	16	41	174	106
11	Product9	159	143	16	13	25	154	148	23	179	139	116	85
12	Product10	76	3	87	151	191	44	168	197	22	101	146	115
13	Product11	93	86	192	140	159	89	56	127	130	37	29	10
14	Product12	24	80	108	99	139	47	141	120	180	198	52	110
15	Product13	23	55	99	31	80	176	81	181	46	94	6	41
16	Product14	35	197	195	45	3	122	162	115	190	1	166	193
17	Product15	10	161	44	65	34	75	148	49	169	85	157	187
18	Product16	143	139	76	157	33	78	88	172	88	58	158	199
19	Product17	107	84	79	10	102	172	16	15	98	151	67	168
20	Product18	112	147	56	104	81	117	82	88	154	178	90	82
21	Product19	43	55	101	151	21	186	68	152	167	164	111	161

Sheet1 Sheet2 Sheet4 Sheet3

Ready NUM

Columns and Rows Properties

`Columns` and `Rows` are properties of the `Application`, `Worksheet`, and `Range` objects. They return a reference to all the columns or rows in a worksheet or range. In each case, the reference returned is a `Range` object, but this `Range` object has some odd characteristics that might make you think there are such things as a "`Column` object" and a "`Row` object", which do not exist in Excel. They are useful when you want to count the number of rows or columns, or process all the rows or columns of a range.

Excel 97 increased the number of worksheet rows from the 16,384 in previous versions to 65,536. If you want to write code to detect the number of rows in the active sheet, you can use the `Count` property of `Rows`:

```
Rows.Count
```

This is useful if you need a macro that will work with all versions of Excel VBA, and detect the last row of data in a column, working from the bottom of the worksheet:

```
Cells(Rows.Count, "A").End(xlUp).Select
```

If you have a multi-column table of data in a range named `Data`, and you want to step through each row of the table making every cell in each row bold where the first cell is greater than 1000, you can use:

```
For Each rgRow In Range("Data").Rows
  If rgRow.Cells(1).Value > 1000 Then
    rgRow.Font.Bold = True
  Else
    rgRow.Font.Bold = False
  End If
Next rgRow
```

This gives us:

	A	B	C	D	E	F	G	H	I	J	K	L	M
1		**Jan**	**Feb**	**Mar**	**Apr**	**May**	**Jun**	**Jul**	**Aug**	**Sep**	**Oct**	**Nov**	**Dec**
2	**Product1**	41	165	199	186	79	190	81	115	135	49	142	57
3	**Product2**	137	180	137	58	164	163	135	16	93	53	174	39
4	**Product3**	82	126	137	44	131	152	160	83	6	29	134	14
5	**Product4**	41	149	78	17	46	94	110	112	190	175	70	65
6	**Product5**	122	181	72	97	193	30	25	122	7	199	47	169
7	**Product6**	188	124	130	97	67	70	74	34	36	83	50	123
8	**Product7**	95	168	170	63	132	194	80	159	141	155	177	151
9	**Product8**	**1210**	**53**	**194**	**3**	**164**	**128**	**192**	**139**	**139**	**3**	**173**	**134**
10	**Product9**	192	28	130	55	128	97	103	126	148	154	93	173
11	**Product10**	25	155	190	116	49	16	118	23	103	148	98	129
12	**Product11**	98	12	146	172	84	170	162	44	128	14	123	132
13	**Product12**	47	164	58	23	75	9	153	181	63	114	120	51
14	**Product13**	35	26	17	4	148	80	54	159	166	6	155	96
15	**Product14**	155	23	142	100	175	41	13	94	123	92	57	187
16	**Product15**	182	69	95	184	198	23	84	163	94	135	65	124
17	**Product16**	20	56	40	152	105	119	16	73	148	138	90	26
18	**Product17**	88	11	35	174	192	195	21	179	20	25	107	173
19	**Product18**	131	134	46	165	92	11	92	192	87	10	65	8
20	**Product19**	104	187	156	106	150	16	158	49	73	99	99	159

Curiously, you cannot replace `rgRow.Cells(1)` with `rgRow(1)`, as you can with a normal `Range` object as it causes a run-time error. It seems that there is something special about the `Range` object referred to by the `Rows` and `Columns` properties. You may find it helps to think of them as `Row` and `Column` objects, even though such objects do not officially exist.

Areas

You need to be careful when using the `Columns` or `Rows` properties of non-contiguous ranges, such as those returned from the `SpecialCells` method when locating the numeric cells or blank cells in a worksheet, for example. Recall that a non-contiguous range consists of a number of separate rectangular blocks. If the cells are not all in one block, and you use the `Rows.Count` properties, you only count the rows from the first block. The following code generates an answer of 5, because only the first range, A1:B5, is evaluated:

```
Range("A1:B5,C6:D10,E11:F15").Rows.Count
```

The blocks in a non-contiguous range are `Range` objects contained within the `Areas` collection and can be processed separately. The following displays the address of each of the three blocks in the `Range` object, one at a time:

```
For Each Rng In Range("A1:B5,C6:D10,E11:F15").Areas
  MsgBox Rng.Address
Next Rng
```

The worksheet shown below contains sales estimates that have been entered as numbers. The cost figures are calculated by formulas. The following code copies all the numeric constants in the active sheet to blocks in Sheet3, leaving an empty row between each block:

```
Sub CopyAreas()
  Dim Rng As Range, rgDestination As Range

  Set rgDestination = Worksheets("Sheet3").Range("A1")
  For Each Rng In Cells.SpecialCells(xlCellTypeConstants, _
                                                     xlNumbers).Areas
    Rng.Copy Destination:=rgDestination
    ' Set next destination under previous block copied
    Set rgDestination = rgDestination.Offset(rng.Rows.Count + 1)
  Next Rng
End Sub
```

This gives us:

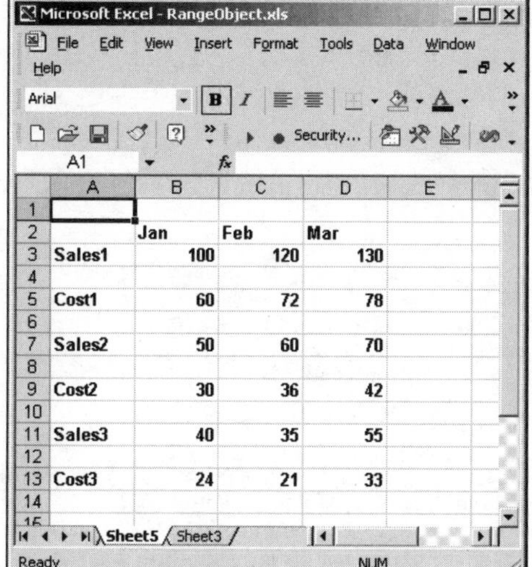

	A	B	C	D	E
1					
2		Jan	Feb	Mar	
3	Sales1	100	120	130	
4					
5	Cost1	60	72	78	
6					
7	Sales2	50	60	70	
8					
9	Cost2	30	36	42	
10					
11	Sales3	40	35	55	
12					
13	Cost3	24	21	33	
14					

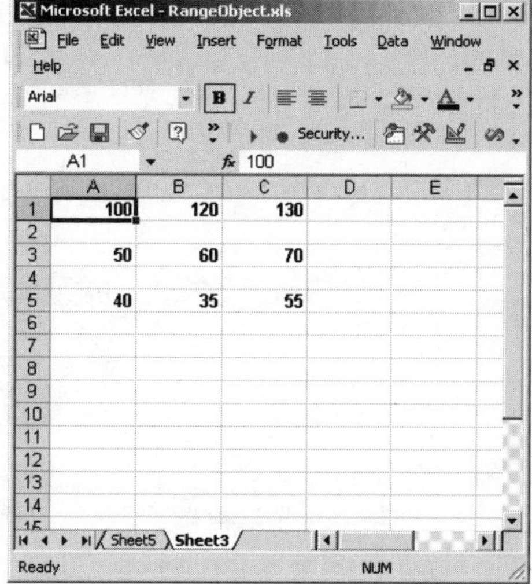

	A	B	C	D	E
1	100	120	130		
2					
3	50	60	70		
4					
5	40	35	55		

Union and Intersect Methods

`Union` and `Intersect` are methods of the `Application` object, but they can be used without preceding them with a reference to `Application` as they are members of `<globals>`. They can be very useful tools, as we shall see.

You use `Union` when you want to generate a range from two or more blocks of cells. You use `Intersect` when you want to find the cells that are common to two or more ranges, or in other words, where the ranges overlap. The following event procedure, entered in the module behind a worksheet, illustrates how you can apply the two methods to prevent a user selecting cells in two ranges B10:F20 and H10:L20. One use for this routine is to prevent a user from changing data in these two blocks:

```
Private Sub Worksheet_SelectionChange(ByVal Target As Range)
  Dim rgForbidden As Range

  Set rgForbidden = Union(Range("B10:F20"), Range("H10:L20"))
  If Intersect(Target, rgForbidden) Is Nothing Then Exit Sub
  Range("A1").Select
  MsgBox "You can't select cells in " & rgForbidden.Address, vbCritical
End Sub
```

If you are not familiar with event procedures, refer to the *Events* section in Chapter 2. For more information on event procedures see Chapter 10.

The `Worksheet_SelectionChange` event procedure is triggered every time the user selects a new range in the worksheet associated with the module containing the event procedure. The above code uses the `Union` method to define a forbidden range consisting of the two non-contiguous ranges. It then uses the `Intersect` method, in the `If` test, to see if the `Target` range, which is the new user selection, is within the forbidden range. `Intersect` returns `Nothing` if there is no overlap and the `Sub` exits. If there is an overlap, the code in the two lines following the `If` test are executed – cell A1 is selected and a warning message is issued to the user.

Empty Cells

You have seen that if you want to step through a column or row of cells until you get to an empty cell, you can use the End property to detect the end of the block. Another way is to examine each cell, one at a time, in a loop structure and stop when you find an empty cell. You can test for an empty cell with the VBA IsEmpty function.

In the spreadsheet shown below, you want to insert blank rows between each week to produce a report that is more readable:

	A	B	C	D	E	F
1	Date	Customer	Product	NumberSold	Price	Revenue
2	Mon Jan 01, 2001	Kee	Apples	659	12.5	8237.5
3	Fri Jan 05, 2001	Pradesh	Pears	195	18	3510
4	Sat Jan 06, 2001	Smith	Mangoes	928	20	18560
5	Sat Jan 06, 2001	Smith	Mangoes	608	20	12160
6	Mon Jan 08, 2001	Pradesh	Pears	191	18	3438
7	Fri Jan 12, 2001	Roberts	Apples	605	12.5	7562.5
8	Sun Jan 14, 2001	Kee	Apples	785	12.5	9812.5
9	Thu Jan 18, 2001	Kee	Oranges	167	15	2505
10	Thu Jan 18, 2001	Kee	Oranges	978	15	14670
11	Fri Jan 19, 2001	Kee	Pears	301	18	5418
12	Sat Jan 20, 2001	Smith	Apples	947	12.5	11837.5
13	Sun Jan 21, 2001	Smith	Mangoes	437	20	8740
14	Thu Jan 25, 2001	Kee	Mangoes	972	20	19440
15	Fri Jan 26, 2001	Smith	Oranges	607	15	9105
16	Sun Jan 28, 2001	Kee	Mangoes	763	20	15260
17	Thu Feb 01, 2001	Pradesh	Mangoes	50	20	1000
18	Thu Feb 01, 2001	Smith	Oranges	615	15	9225
19	Sat Feb 03, 2001	Kee	Mangoes	196	20	3920
20	Mon Feb 05, 2001	Roberts	Apples	13	12.5	162.5

The following macro compares dates, using the VBA Weekday function to get the day of the week as a number. By default, Sunday is day 1 and Saturday is day 7. If the macro finds today's day number is less than yesterday's, it assumes a new week has started and inserts a blank row:

```
Sub ShowWeeks()
  Dim iToday As Integer
  Dim iYesterday As Integer

  Range("A2").Select
  iYesterday = Weekday(ActiveCell.Value)
  Do Until IsEmpty(ActiveCell.Value)
    ActiveCell.Offset(1, 0).Select
    iToday = Weekday(ActiveCell.Value)
    If iToday < iYesterday Then
      ActiveCell.EntireRow.Insert
```

```
        ActiveCell.Offset(1, 0).Select
      End If
      iYesterday = iToday
    Loop
  End Sub
```

The result is the following:

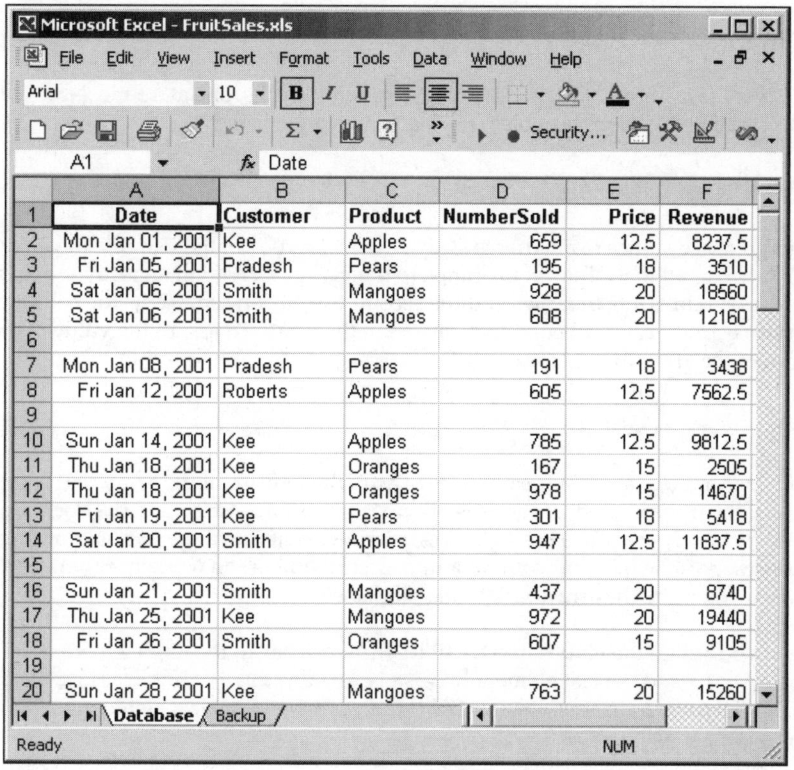

Microsoft Excel - FruitSales.xls

	A	B	C	D	E	F
1	Date	Customer	Product	NumberSold	Price	Revenue
2	Mon Jan 01, 2001	Kee	Apples	659	12.5	8237.5
3	Fri Jan 05, 2001	Pradesh	Pears	195	18	3510
4	Sat Jan 06, 2001	Smith	Mangoes	928	20	18560
5	Sat Jan 06, 2001	Smith	Mangoes	608	20	12160
6						
7	Mon Jan 08, 2001	Pradesh	Pears	191	18	3438
8	Fri Jan 12, 2001	Roberts	Apples	605	12.5	7562.5
9						
10	Sun Jan 14, 2001	Kee	Apples	785	12.5	9812.5
11	Thu Jan 18, 2001	Kee	Oranges	167	15	2505
12	Thu Jan 18, 2001	Kee	Oranges	978	15	14670
13	Fri Jan 19, 2001	Kee	Pears	301	18	5418
14	Sat Jan 20, 2001	Smith	Apples	947	12.5	11837.5
15						
16	Sun Jan 21, 2001	Smith	Mangoes	437	20	8740
17	Thu Jan 25, 2001	Kee	Mangoes	972	20	19440
18	Fri Jan 26, 2001	Smith	Oranges	607	15	9105
19						
20	Sun Jan 28, 2001	Kee	Mangoes	763	20	15260

Database / Backup

Ready NUM

Note that many users detect an empty cell by testing for a zero length string:

```
    Do Until ActiveCell.Value = ""
```

This test works in most cases, and would have worked in the example above, had we used it. However, problems can occur if you are testing cells that contain formulas that can produce zero length strings, such as the following:

```
  =IF(B2="Kee","Trainee","")
```

The zero length string test does not distinguish between an empty cell and a zero length string resulting from a formula. It is better practice to use the VBA `IsEmpty` function when testing for an empty cell.

Transferring Values between Arrays and Ranges

If you want to process all the data values in a range, it is much more efficient to assign the values to a VBA array and process the array rather than process the `Range` object itself. You can then assign the array back to the range.

You can assign the values in a range to an array very easily, as follows:

```
vaSalesData = Range("A2:F10000").Value
```

The transfer is very fast compared with stepping through the cells, one at a time. Note that this is quite different from creating an object variable referring to the range using:

```
Set rgSalesData = Range("A2:F10000")
```

When you assign range values to a variable such as `vaSalesData`, the variable must have a `Variant` data type. VBA copies all the values in the range to the variable, creating an array with two dimensions. The first dimension represents the rows and the second dimension represents the columns, so you can access the values by their row and column numbers in the array. To assign the value in the first row and second column of the array to `Customer`, use:

```
Customer = vaSalesData(1, 2)
```

When the values in a range are assigned to a `Variant`, the indexes of the array that is created are always one-based, not zero-based, regardless of the `Option Base` setting in the declarations section of the module. Also, the array always has two dimensions, even if the range has only one row or one column. This preserves the inherent column and row structure of the worksheet in the array and is an advantage when you write the array back to the worksheet.

For example, if you assign the values in **A1:A10** to `vaSalesData`, the first element is `vaSalesData(1,1)` and the last element is `vaSalesData(10,1)`. If you assign the values in **A1:E1** to `vaSalesData`, the first element is `vaSalesData(1,1)` and the last element is `vaSalesData(1,5)`.

You might want a macro that sums all the **Revenues** for **Kee** in our last example. The following macro uses the traditional method to directly test and sum the range of data:

```
Sub KeeTotal1()
  Dim dTotal As Double
  Dim i As Long

  With Range("A2:F73")
    For i = 1 To .Rows.Count
      If .Cells(i, 2) = "Kee" Then dTotal = dTotal + .Cells(i, 6)
    Next i
  End With
  MsgBox "Kee Total = " & Format(dTotal, "$#,##0")
End Sub
```

The following macro does the same job by first assigning the `Range` values to a `Variant` and processing the resulting array. The speed increase is very significant. It can be fifty times faster, which can be a great advantage if you are handling large ranges:

```
Sub KeeTotal2()
   Dim vaSalesData As Variant
   Dim dTotal As Double
   Dim i As Long

   vaSalesData = Range("A2:F73").Value
   For i = 1 To UBound(vaSalesData, 1)
      If vaSalesData(i, 2) = "Kee" Then dTotal = dTotal + vaSalesData(i, 6)
   Next i
   MsgBox "Kee Total = " & Format(dTotal, "$#,##0")
End Sub
```

You can also assign an array of values directly to a `Range`. Say you want to place a list of numbers in column G of the `FruitSales.xls` example above, containing a 10% discount on Revenue for customer Kee only. The following macro, once again, assigns the range values to a `Variant` for processing:

```
Sub KeeDiscount()
  Dim vaSalesData As Variant
  Dim vaDiscount() As Variant
  Dim i As Long

  vaSalesData = Range("A2:F73").Value
  ReDim vaDiscount(1 To UBound(vaSalesData, 1), 1 To 1)
  For i = 1 To UBound(vaSalesData, 1)
    If vaSalesData(i, 2) = "Kee" Then
      vaDiscount(i, 1) = vaSalesData(i, 6) * 0.1
    End If
  Next i
  Range("G2").Resize(UBound(vaSalesData, 1), 1).Value = vaDiscount
End Sub
```

The code sets up a dynamic array called `vaDiscount`, which it `ReDim`s to the number of rows in `vaSalesData` and one column, so that it retains a two-dimensional structure like a range, even though there is only one column. After the values have been assigned to `vaDiscount`, `vaDiscount` is directly assigned to the range in column G. Note that it is necessary to specify the correct size of the range receiving the values, not just the first cell as in a worksheet copy operation.

The outcome of this operation is:

	Date	Customer	Product	NumberSold	Price	Revenue	Kee Discount
2	Mon Jan 01, 2001	Kee	Apples	659	12.5	8237.5	823.75
3	Fri Jan 05, 2001	Pradesh	Pears	195	18	3510	
4	Sat Jan 06, 2001	Smith	Mangoes	928	20	18560	
5	Sat Jan 06, 2001	Smith	Mangoes	608	20	12160	
6							
7	Mon Jan 08, 2001	Pradesh	Pears	191	18	3438	
8	Fri Jan 12, 2001	Roberts	Apples	605	12.5	7562.5	
9							
10	Sun Jan 14, 2001	Kee	Apples	785	12.5	9812.5	981.25
11	Thu Jan 18, 2001	Kee	Oranges	167	15	2505	250.5
12	Thu Jan 18, 2001	Kee	Oranges	978	15	14670	1467
13	Fri Jan 19, 2001	Kee	Pears	301	18	5418	541.8
14	Sat Jan 20, 2001	Smith	Apples	947	12.5	11837.5	
15							
16	Sun Jan 21, 2001	Smith	Mangoes	437	20	8740	
17	Thu Jan 25, 2001	Kee	Mangoes	972	20	19440	1944
18	Fri Jan 26, 2001	Smith	Oranges	607	15	9105	
19							
20	Sun Jan 28, 2001	Kee	Mangoes	763	20	15260	1526

It is possible to use a one-dimensional array for `vaDiscount`. However, if you assign the one-dimensional array to a range, it will be assumed to contain a row of data, not a column. It is possible to get around this by using the worksheet `Transpose` function when assigning the array to the range. Say you have changed the dimensions of `vaDiscount` as follows:

```
ReDim vaDiscount(1 To Ubound(vaSalesData,1))
```

You could assign this version of `vaDiscount` to a column with:

```
Range("G2").Resize(UBound(vaSalesData, 1), 1).Value = _
                                WorkSheetFunction.Transpose(vaDiscount)
```

Deleting Rows

A commonly asked question is "What is the best way to delete rows that I do not need from a spreadsheet?" Generally, the requirement is to find the rows that have certain text in a given column and remove those rows. The best solution depends on how large the spreadsheet is and how many items are likely to be removed.

Say that you want to remove all the rows that contain the text "Mangoes" in column C. One way to do this is to loop through all the rows, and test every cell in column C. If you do this, it is better to test the last row first and work up the worksheet row by row. This is more efficient because Excel does not have to move any rows up that would later be deleted, which would not be the case if you worked from the top down. Also, if you work from the top down, you can't use a simple `For...Next` loop counter to keep track of the row you are on because, as you delete rows, the counter and the row numbers no longer correspond:

```
Sub DeleteRows1()
  Dim i As Long
  Application.ScreenUpdating = False
  For i = Cells(Rows.Count, "C").End(xlUp).Row To 1 Step -1
    If Cells(i, "C").Value = "Mangoes" Then Cells(i, "C").EntireRow.Delete
  Next i
End Sub
```

A good programming principal to follow is this: if there is an Excel spreadsheet technique you can utilize, it is likely to be more efficient than a VBA emulation of the same technique, such as the `For...Next` loop used here.

Excel VBA programmers, especially when they do not have a strong background in the user interface features of Excel, often fall into the trap of writing VBA code to perform tasks that Excel can handle already. For example, you can write a VBA procedure to work through a sorted list of items, inserting rows with subtotals. You can also use VBA to execute the `Subtotal` method of the `Range` object. The second method is much easier to code and it executes in a fraction of the time taken by the looping procedure.

It is much better to use VBA to harness the power built into Excel than to re-invent existing Excel functionality.

However, it isn't always obvious which Excel technique is the best one to employ. A fairly obvious Excel contender to locate the cells to be deleted, without having to examine every row using VBA code, is the Edit | Find command. The following code uses the `Find` method to reduce the number of cycles spent in VBA loops:

```
Sub DeleteRows2()
  Dim rgFoundCell As Range
  Application.ScreenUpdating = False
  Set rgFoundCell = Range("C:C").Find(what:="Mangoes")
  Do Until rgFoundCell Is Nothing
    rgFoundCell.EntireRow.Delete
    Set rgFoundCell = Range("C:C").FindNext
  Loop
End Sub
```

This code is faster than the first procedure when there are not many rows to be deleted. As the percentage increases, it becomes less efficient. Perhaps we need to look for a better Excel technique.

The fastest way to delete rows, that I am aware of, is provided by Excel's `AutoFilter` feature:

```
Sub DeleteRows3()
  Dim lLastRow As Long          'Last row
  Dim Rng As Range

  Application.ScreenUpdating = False
  Rows(1).Insert                'Insert dummy row for dummy field name
  Range("C1").Value = "Temp" 'Insert dummy field name
  With ActiveSheet
    .UsedRange                  'Reset Last Cell
    'Determine last row
    lLastRow = .Cells.SpecialCells(xlCellTypeLastCell).Row
    'Set Rng to the C column data rows
    Set Rng = Range("C1", Cells(lLastRow, "C"))
    'Filter the C column to show only the data to be deleted
    Rng.AutoFilter Field:=1, Criteria1:="Mangoes"
    'Delete the visible cells, including dummy field name
    Rng.SpecialCells(xlCellTypeVisible).EntireRow.Delete
    .UsedRange 'Reset the last cell
  End With
End Sub
```

This is a bit more difficult to code, but it is significantly faster than the other methods, no matter how many rows are to be deleted. To use `AutoFilter`, you need to have field names at the top of your data. A dummy row is first inserted above the data and a dummy field name supplied for column C. The `AutoFilter` is only carried out on column C, which hides all the rows except those that have the text "Mangoes".

The `SpecialCells` method is used to select only the visible cells in column C. This is extended to the entire visible rows and they are deleted, including the dummy field name row. The `AutoFilter` is automatically turned off when the dummy row is deleted.

Summary

In this chapter we have seen the most important properties and methods that can be used to manage ranges of cells in a worksheet. The emphasis has been on those techniques that are difficult or impossible to discover using the macro recorder. The properties and methods discussed were:

- `Activate` method
- `Cells` property
- `Columns` and `Rows` properties
- `CurrentRegion` property
- `End` property
- `Offset` property
- `Range` property
- `Resize` property
- `Select` method
- `SpecialCells` method
- `Union` and `Intersect` methods

We have also seen how to assign a worksheet range of values to a VBA array for efficient processing, and how to assign a VBA array of data to a worksheet range.

This chapter has also emphasized that it is very rarely necessary to select cells or activate worksheets, which the macro recorder invariably does as it can only record what we do manually. Activating cells and worksheets is a very time consuming process and should be avoided if we want our code to run at maximum speed.

The final examples showed that it is usually best to utilize Excel's existing capabilities, tapping into the Excel object model, rather than write a VBA-coded equivalent. And bear in mind, some Excel techniques are better than others. Experimentation might be necessary to get the best code when speed is important.

VBAProgrammersReferenceExcel20
mersReferenceExcel2002VB
ReferenceExcel2002VBAPro
ProgrammersReferenceExc
rammersReferenceExcel20
ReferenceExcel2002VB
ferenceExcel
nceExcel2002VBA
xcel2002VBAProgrammer
2002VBAProgrammersReferenceExce
VBAProgrammersReferen
rogrammersReferenceExcel
ammersReferencerammersR
2002VBAProgrammersReferenceExce

6

Using Names

One of the most useful features in Excel is the ability to create names. You can create a name using the Insert | Name | Define... dialog box. If the name refers to a range, you can create it by selecting the range, typing the name into the Name box at the left-hand side of the Formula Bar and pressing *Enter*. However, in Excel, names can refer to more than just ranges.

A name can contain a number, text, or a formula. Such a name has no visible location on the worksheet and can only be viewed in the Insert | Name | Define... dialog box. Therefore, you can use names to store information in a workbook without having to place the data in a worksheet cell. Names can be declared hidden so that they don't appear in the Insert | Name | Define... dialog box. This can be a useful way to keep the stored information unseen by users.

The normal use of names is to keep track of worksheet ranges. This is particularly useful for tables of data that vary in size. If you know that a certain name is used to define the range containing the data you want to work on, your VBA code can be much simpler than it might otherwise be. It is also relatively simple, given a few basic techniques, to change the definition of a name to allow for changes that you make to the tables in your code.

The Excel Object Model includes a `Names` collection and a `Name` object that can be used in VBA code. Names can be defined globally, at the workbook level, or they can be local, or worksheet-specific. If you create local names, you can repeat the same name on more than one worksheet in the workbook. To make a `Name` object worksheet-specific, you precede its `Name` property by the name of the worksheet and an exclamation mark. For example, you can type "Sheet1!Costs" into the top edit box of the Insert | Name | Define... dialog box to define a name Costs that is local to Sheet1:

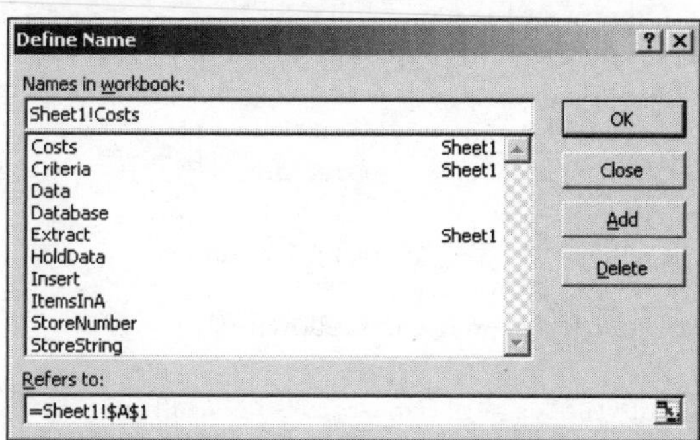

When you display the Insert | Name | Define... dialog box you see the global names in the workbook and the local names for the active worksheet. The local names are identified by the worksheet name to the right of the name. If a local name is the same as a global name, you will only see the local name.

A great source of confusion with names is that they also have names. You need to distinguish between a Name object and the Name property of that object. The following code returns a reference to a Name object in the Names collection:

```
Names("Data")
```

If you want to change the Name property of a Name object, you use code like the following:

```
Names("Data").Name = "NewData"
```

Having changed its Name property, you would now refer to this Name object as follows:

```
Names("NewData")
```

Global names and local names belong to the Names collection associated with the Workbook object. If you use a reference such as Application.Names or Names, you are referring to the Names collection for the active workbook. If you use a reference such as Workbooks("Data.xls").Names, you are referring to the Names collection for that specific workbook.

Local names, but not global names, also belong to the Names collection associated with the WorkSheet object to which they are local. If you use a reference such as Worksheets("Sheet1").Names or ActiveSheet.Names, you are referring to the local Names collection for that worksheet.

There is also another way to refer to names that refer to ranges. You can use the Name property of the Range object. More on this later.

Naming Ranges

You can create a global name that refers to a range using the Add method of the Workbook object's Names collection:

```
Names.Add Name:="Data", RefersTo:="=Sheet1!$D$10:$D$12"
```

It is important to include the equals sign in front of the definition and to make the cell references absolute, using the $ signs. Otherwise, the name will refer to an address relative to the cell address that was active when the name was defined. You can omit the worksheet reference if you want the name to refer to the active worksheet:

```
Names.Add Name:="Data", RefersTo:="=$D$10:$D$12"
```

If the name already exists, it will be replaced by the new definition.

If you want to create a local name, you can use the following:

```
Names.Add Name:="Sheet1!Sales", RefersTo:="=Sheet1!$E$10:$E$12"
```

Alternatively, you can add the name to the Names collection associated with the worksheet, which only includes the names that are local to that worksheet:

```
Worksheets("Sheet1").Names.Add Name:="Costs", RefersTo:="=Sheet1!$F$10:$F$12"
```

Using the Name Property of the Range Object

There is a much simpler way to create a name that refers to a Range. You can directly define the Name property of the Range object:

```
Range("A1:D10").Name = "SalesData"
```

If you want the name to be local, you can include a worksheet name:

```
Range("F1:F10").Name = "Sheet1!Staff"
```

It is generally easier, in code, to work with Range objects in this way, than to have to generate the string address of a range, preceded by the equals sign that is required by the RefersTo parameter of the Add method of the Names collection. For example, if you created an object variable Rng and want to apply the name Data to it, you need to get the Address property of Rng and append it to an =:

```
Names.Add Name:="Data", RefersTo:="=" & Rng.Address
```

The alternative method is:

```
Rng.Name = "Data"
```

You cannot completely forget about the Add method, however, because it is the only way to create names that refer to numbers, formulas, and strings.

Special Names

Excel uses some names internally to track certain features. When you apply a print range to a worksheet, Excel gives that range the name Print_Area as a local name. If you set print titles, Excel creates the local name Print_Titles. If you use the Data | Filter | Advanced Filter... feature to extract data from a list to a new range, Excel creates the local names Criteria and Extract.

In older versions of Excel, the name Database was used to name the range containing your data list (or database). Although it is no longer mandatory to use this name, Database is still recognized by some Excel features such as Advanced Filter.

If you create a macro that uses the Data | Form... feature to edit your data list, you will find that the macro does not work if the data list does not start within A1:B2. You can rectify this by applying the name Database to your data list.

You need to be aware that Excel uses these names and, in general, you should avoid using them unless you want the side effects they can produce. For example, you can remove the print area by deleting the name Print_Area. The following two lines of code have the same effect if you have defined a print area:

```
ActiveSheet.PageSetup.PrintArea = ""
```

```
ActiveSheet.Names("Print_Area").Delete
```

To summarize, you need to take care when using the following names:

- Criteria
- Database
- Extract
- Print_Area
- Print_Titles

Storing Values in Names

The use of names to store data items has already been mentioned in Chapter 3, specifically under the `Evaluate` method topic. Now it's time to look at it in a bit more detail.

When you use a name to store numeric or string data, you should **not** precede the value of the `RefersTo` parameter with =. If you do, it will be taken as a formula. The following code stores a number and a string into `StoreNumber` and `StoreString`, respectively:

```
Dim X As Variant
X = 3.14159
Names.Add Name:="StoreNumber", RefersTo:=X
X = "Sales"
Names.Add Name:="StoreString", RefersTo:=X
```

This provides you with a convenient way to store the data you need in your VBA code from one Excel session to another, so that it does not disappear when you close Excel. When storing strings, you can store up to 255 characters.

You can retrieve the value in a name using the `Evaluate` method equivalent as follows:

```
X = [StoreNumber]
```

You can also store formulas into names. The formula must start with =. The following places the `COUNTA` function into a name:

```
Names.Add Name:="ItemsInA", RefersTo:="=COUNTA($A:$A)"
```

This name can be used in worksheet cell formulas to return a count of the number of items in column A:

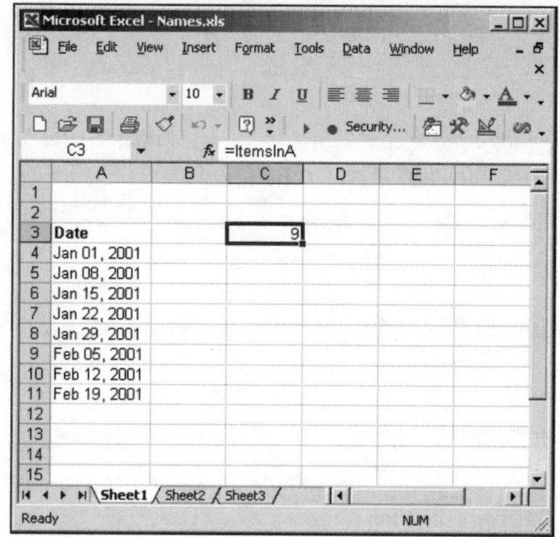

Once again, you can use the `Evaluate` method equivalent to evaluate the name in VBA:

```
MsgBox [ItemsInA]
```

Storing Arrays

You can store the values in an array variable in a name just as easily as you can store a number or a label. The following code creates an array of numbers in `MyArray` and stores the array values in `MyName`:

```
Sub ArrayToName()
   Dim MyArray(1 To 200, 1 To 3)
   Dim i as Integer
   Dim j as Integer

   For i = 1 To 200
      For j = 1 To 3
         MyArray(i, j) = i + j
      Next j
   Next i
   Names.Add Name:="MyName", RefersTo:=MyArray
End Sub
```

There is a limit to the size of an array that can be assigned to a name in Excel 97 and Excel 2000. The maximum number of columns is 256 and the total number of elements in the array cannot exceed 5461. In Excel 2002 the size is only limited by memory.

The `Evaluate` method can be used to assign the values in a name that holds an array to a `Variant` variable. The following code assigns the contents of `MyName`, created in `ArrayToName`, to `MyArray` and displays the last element in the array:

```
Sub NameToArray()
   Dim MyArray As Variant
   MyArray = [MyName]
```

```
    MsgBox MyArray(200, 3)
End Sub
```

*The array created by assigning a name containing an array to a variant is always one-based, even if you have an `Option Base 0` statement in the **Declarations** section of your module.*

Hiding Names

You can hide a name by setting its `Visible` property to `False`. You can do this when you create the name:

```
Names.Add Name:="StoreNumber", RefersTo:=x, Visible:=False
```

You can also hide the name after it has been created:

```
Names("StoreNumber").Visible = False
```

The name cannot now be seen by users in the **Insert | Name | Define...** dialog box. This is not a highly secure way to conceal information, as anyone with VBA skills can detect the name. But it is an effective way to ensure that users are not confused by the presence of strange names.

You should also be aware that if, through the Excel user interface, a user creates a `Name` object with a `Name` property corresponding to your hidden name, the hidden name is destroyed. You can prevent this by protecting the worksheet.

Despite some limitations, hidden names do provide a nice way to store information in a workbook.

Working with Named Ranges

The following spreadsheet contains a data list in **B4:D10** that has been given the name `Database`. There is also a data input area in **B2:D2** that has been given the name `Input`:

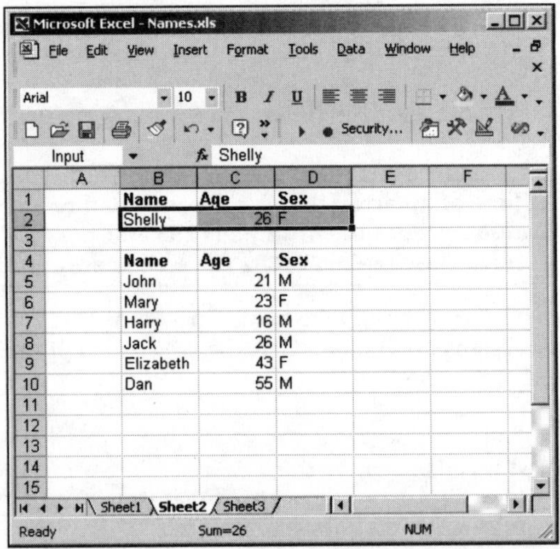

If you want to copy the Input data to the bottom of the data list and increase the range referred to by the name Database to include the new row, you can use the following code:

```
Sub AddNewData()
   Dim lRows As Long

   With Range("Database")
      lRows = .Rows.Count + 1
      Range("Input").Copy Destination:=.Cells(lRows, 1)
      .Resize(lRows).Name = "Database"
   End With
End Sub
```

The output resulting from this code will be the same as the screenshot above but with the data "Shelley 26 F" in cells B11:D11. The range Database will now refer to B4:D11.

The variable lRows is assigned the count of the number of rows in Database plus one, to allow for the new record of data. Input is then copied. The destination of the copy is the B11 cell, which is defined by the Cells property of Database, being lRows down from the top of Database, in column 1 of Database. The Resize property is applied to Database to generate a reference to a Range object with one more row than Database and the Name property of the new Range object is assigned the name Database.

The nice thing about this code is that it is quite independent of the size or location of Database in the active workbook and the location of Input in the active workbook. Database can have seven or 7,000 rows. You can add more columns to Input and Database and the code still works without change. Input and Database can even be on different worksheets and the code will still work.

Searching for a Name

If you want to test to see if a name exists in a workbook, you can use the following function. It has been designed to work both as a worksheet function and as a VBA callable function, which makes it a little more complex than if it were designed for either job alone:

```
Function IsNameInWorkbook(stName As String) As Boolean
   Dim X As String
   Dim Rng As Range

   Application.Volatile
   On Error Resume Next
   Set Rng = Application.Caller
   Err.Clear
   If Rng Is Nothing Then
      X = ActiveWorkbook.Names(stName).Name
   Else
      X = Rng.Parent.Parent.Names(stName).Name
   End If
   If Err.Number = 0 Then IsNameInWorkbook = True
End Function
```

IsNameInWorkbook has an input parameter stName, which is the required name as a string. The function has been declared volatile, so that it recalculates when it is used as a worksheet function and the referenced name is added or deleted. The function first determines if it has been called from a worksheet cell by assigning the Application.Caller property to Rng.

If it has been called from a cell, `Application.Caller` returns a `Range` object that refers to the cell containing the function. If the function has not been called from a cell, the `Set` statement causes an error, which is suppressed by the preceding `On Error Resume Next` statement. That error, should it have occurred, is cleared because the function anticipates further errors that should not be masked by the first error.

Next, the function uses an `If` test to see if `Rng` is undefined. If so, the call was made from another VBA routine. In this case, the function attempts to assign the `Name` property of the `Name` object in the active workbook to the dummy variable `X`. If the name exists, this attempt succeeds and no error is generated. Otherwise an error does occur, but is once again suppressed by the `On Error Resume Next` statement.

If the function has been called from a worksheet cell, the `Else` clause of the `If` test identifies the workbook containing `Rng` and attempts to assign the `Name` property of the required `Name` object to `X`. The parent of `Rng` is the worksheet containing `Rng` and the parent of that worksheet is the workbook containing `Rng`. Once again, an error will be generated if the name does not exist in the workbook.

Finally, `IsNameInWorkbook` checks the `Number` property of the `Err` object to see if it is zero. If it is, the return value of the function is set to `True` as the name does exist. If there is a non-zero error number, the function is left to return its default value of `False` as the name does not exist.

You could use `IsNameInWorkbook` in a spreadsheet cell as follows:

```
=IF(IsNameInWorkbook("John"),"John is ","John is not ")&"an existing name"
```

You could use the following procedure to ask the user to enter a name and determine its existence:

```
Sub TestName()
   If IsNameInWorkbook(InputBox("What Name")) Then
      MsgBox "Name exists"
   Else
      MsgBox "Name does not exist"
   End If
End Sub
```

Note that, if you are searching for a local name, you must include its sheet name, in the form `Sheet1!Name`, in the above examples.

If you invoke `IsNameInWorkbook` as a worksheet function *and* if the name "John" is present, you will get output like this:

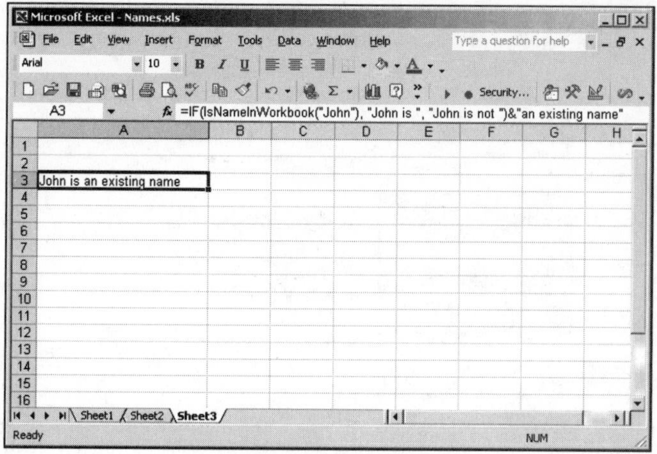

Searching for the Name of a Range

The `Name` property of the `Range` object returns the name of the range, if the range has a name and the `RefersTo` property of the `Name` object corresponds exactly to the range.

You might be tempted to display the name of a range `Rng` with the following code:

```
MsgBox Rng.Name
```

This code fails because the `Name` property of a `Range` object returns a `Name` object. The above code will display the default property value of the `Name` object, which is its `RefersTo` property. What you want is the `Name` property of the `Name` object, so you must use:

```
MsgBox Rng.Name.Name
```

This code only works if `Rng` has a name. It will return a run-time error if `Rng` does not have one. You can use the following code to display the name of the selected cells in the active sheet:

```
Sub TestNameOfRange()
   Dim nmName As Name
   On Error Resume Next
   Set nmName = Selection.Name
   If nmName Is Nothing Then
      MsgBox " Selection has no name"
   Else
      MsgBox nmName.Name
   End If
End Sub
```

If a range has more than one name, the first of the names, in alphabetical order, will be returned.

When this macro is run, the output will look something like this:

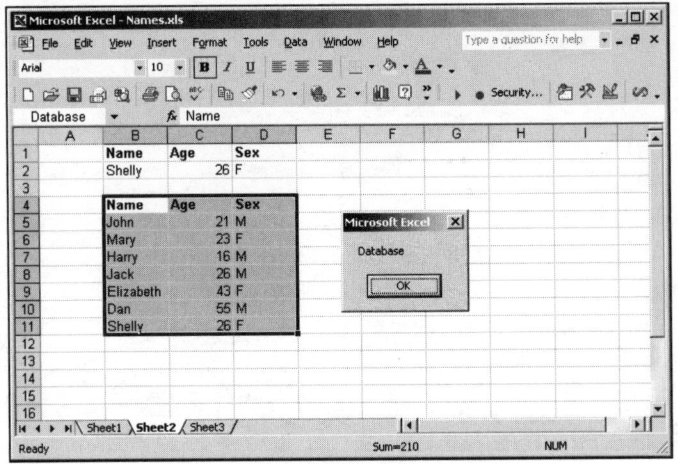

Determining which Names Overlap a Range

When you want to check the names that have been applied to ranges in a worksheet, it can be handy to get a list of all the names that are associated with the currently selected cells. You might be interested in names that completely overlap the selected cells, or names that partly overlap the selected cells. The following code lists all the names that completely overlap the selected cells of the active worksheet:

```
Sub SelectionEntirelyInNames()
   Dim stMessage As String
   Dim nmName As Name
   Dim rgNameRange As Range
   Dim Rng As Range

   On Error Resume Next
   For Each nmName In Names
      Set rgNameRange = Nothing
      Set rgNameRange = nmName.RefersToRange
      If Not rgNameRange Is Nothing Then
         If rgNameRange.Parent.Name = ActiveSheet.Name Then
            Set Rng = Intersect(Selection, rgNameRange)
            If Not Rng Is Nothing Then
               If Selection.Address = Rng.Address Then
                  stMessage = stMessage & nmName.Name & vbCr
               End If
            End If
         End If
      End If
   Next nmName
   If stMessage = "" Then
      MsgBox "The selection is not entirely in any name"
   Else
      MsgBox stMessage
   End If
End Sub
```

SelectionEntirelyInNames starts by suppressing errors with On Error Resume Next. It then goes into a For Each...Next loop that processes all the names in the workbook. It sets rgNameRange to Nothing to get rid of any range reference left in it from one iteration of the loop to the next. It then tries to use the Name property of the current Name object as the name of a Range object and assign a reference to the Range object to rgNameRange. This will fail if the name does not refer to a range, so the rest of the loop is only carried out if a valid Range object has been assigned to rgNameRange.

The next If test checks that the range that rgNameRange refers to is on the active worksheet. The parent of rgNameRange is the worksheet containing rgNameRange. The inner code is only executed if the name of the parent worksheet is the same as the name of the active sheet. Rng is then assigned to the intersection (the overlapping cells) of the selected cells and rgNameRange. If there is an overlap and Rng is not Nothing, the innermost If is executed.

This final If checks that the overlapping range in Rng is identical to the selected range. If this is the case, then the selected cells are contained entirely in rgNameRange and the Name property of the current Name object is added to any names already in stMessage. In addition, a carriage return character is appended, using the VBA intrinsic constant vbCr, so that each name is on a new line in stMessage.

When the For Each...Next loop terminates, the following If tests to see if there is anything in stMessage. If stMessage is a zero length string, MsgBox displays an appropriate message to say that no names were found. Otherwise, the list of found names in stMessage is displayed.

When this code is run in a spreadsheet with three named ranges – Data, Fred, and Mary – you get the following result on running SelectionEntirelyInNames:

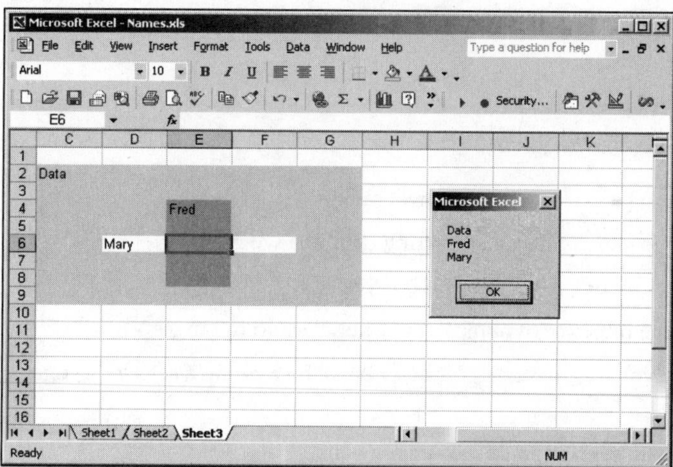

If you want to find out which names are overlapping the selected cells, regardless of whether they entirely contain the selected cells, you can remove the second innermost If test as in the following code:

```
Sub NamesOverlappingSelection()
   Dim stMessage As String
   Dim nmName As Name
   Dim rgNameRange As Range
   Dim Rng As Range
```

```
    On Error Resume Next
    For Each nmName In Names
       Set rgNameRange = Nothing
       Set rgNameRange = Range(nmName.Name)
       If Not rgNameRange Is Nothing Then
          If rgNameRange.Parent.Name = ActiveSheet.Name Then
             Set Rng = Intersect(Selection, rgNameRange)
             If Not Rng Is Nothing Then
                stMessage = stMessage & nmName.Name & vbCr
             End If
          End If
       End If
    Next nmName
    If stMessage = "" Then
       MsgBox "No Names are overlapping the selection"
    Else
       MsgBox stMessage
    End If
End Sub
```

Note that `SelectionEntirelyInNames` and `NamesOverlappingSelection` use different techniques to assign the range referred to by the name to the object variable `rgNameRange`. The following statements are equivalent:

```
Set rgNameRange = nmName.RefersToRange
```

```
Set rgNameRange = Range(nmName.Name)
```

Summary

This chapter has presented an in-depth discussion of using names in Excel VBA. We have seen how to:

- Use names to keep track of worksheet ranges
- Use names to store numeric and string data in a worksheet
- Make names hidden from the user if necessary
- Check for the presence of names in workbooks and in ranges
- Determine which names completely or partially overlap a selected range

VBAProgrammersReferenceExcel20
fe mersReferenceExcel2002VB
ReferenceExcel2002VBAPro
ProgrammersReferenceExc
ammersReferenceExcel20
ersReferenceExcel2002VB
eExcel2002VBAPro
Excel2002VBAProgram
nceExcel2002VBAProgra
xcel2002VBAProgramme VBAProgram
2002VBAProgrammersReferenceExce
VBAProgrammersReferen
rogrammersReferenceExcel
ammersReferenceammersExcel2000VBAProgra
2002VBAProgrammersRefersReferenceExce

7

PivotTables

PivotTables are an extension of the cross tabulation tables used in presenting statistics, and can be used to summarize complex data in a table format. An example of cross tabulation is a table showing the number of employees in an organisation, broken down by age and sex. PivotTables are more powerful and can show more than two variables, so they could be used to show employees broken down by age, sex, and alcohol, to quote an old statistician's joke.

The input data to a PivotTable can come from an Excel worksheet, a text file, an Access database, or a wide range of external database applications. They can handle up to 256 variables, if you can interpret the results. They can perform many types of standard calculations such as summing, counting, and averaging. They can produce subtotals and grand totals.

Data can be grouped as in Excel's outline feature and you can hide unwanted rows and columns. You can also define calculations within the body of the table. PivotTables are also very flexible if you want to change the layout of the data and add or delete variables. In Excel 2000 and 2002, you can create charts that are linked to your PivotTable results in such a way that you can manipulate the data layout from within the chart.

PivotTables are designed so that you can easily generate and manipulate them manually. If you want to create many of them, or provide a higher level of automation to users, you can tap into the Excel Object Model. In this chapter, we will examine the following objects:

- `PivotTables`
- `PivotCaches`
- `PivotFields`
- `PivotItems`
- `PivotCharts`

The PivotTable feature has evolved more than most other established Excel features. With each new version of Excel, PivotTables have been made easier to use and provided with new features. As it is important for many users to maintain compatibility in their code between Excel 97 and Excel 2002, we will discuss the differences in PivotTables between these versions.

Creating a PivotTable Report

PivotTables can accept input data from a spreadsheet, or from an external source such as an Access database. When using Excel data, the data should be structured as a data list, as explained at the beginning of Chapter 8, although it is also possible to use data from another PivotTable or from multiple consolidation ranges. The columns of the list are fields and the rows are records, apart from the top row that defines the names of the fields.

Let's take the following list as our input data:

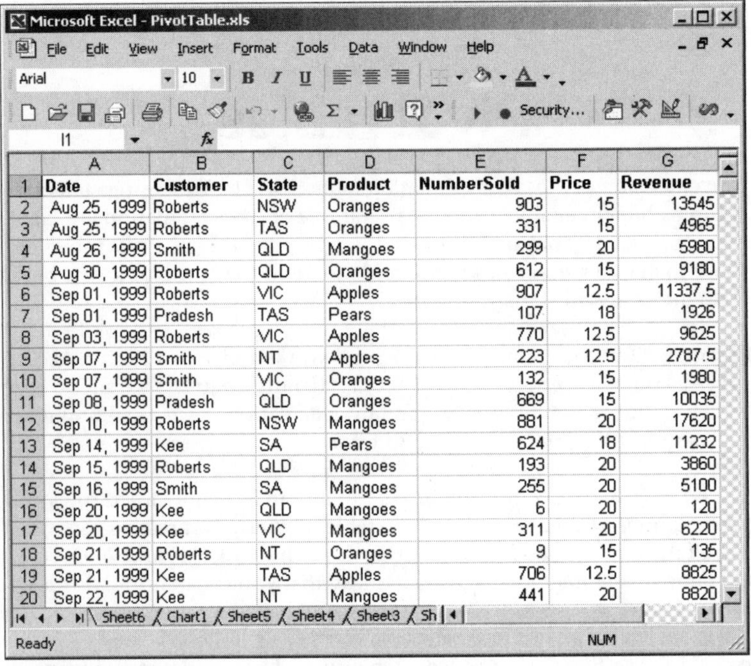

Date	Customer	State	Product	NumberSold	Price	Revenue
Aug 25, 1999	Roberts	NSW	Oranges	903	15	13545
Aug 25, 1999	Roberts	TAS	Oranges	331	15	4965
Aug 26, 1999	Smith	QLD	Mangoes	299	20	5980
Aug 30, 1999	Roberts	QLD	Oranges	612	15	9180
Sep 01, 1999	Roberts	VIC	Apples	907	12.5	11337.5
Sep 01, 1999	Pradesh	TAS	Pears	107	18	1926
Sep 03, 1999	Roberts	VIC	Apples	770	12.5	9625
Sep 07, 1999	Smith	NT	Apples	223	12.5	2787.5
Sep 07, 1999	Smith	VIC	Oranges	132	15	1980
Sep 08, 1999	Pradesh	QLD	Oranges	669	15	10035
Sep 10, 1999	Roberts	NSW	Mangoes	881	20	17620
Sep 14, 1999	Kee	SA	Pears	624	18	11232
Sep 15, 1999	Roberts	QLD	Mangoes	193	20	3860
Sep 16, 1999	Smith	SA	Mangoes	255	20	5100
Sep 20, 1999	Kee	QLD	Mangoes	6	20	120
Sep 20, 1999	Kee	VIC	Mangoes	311	20	6220
Sep 21, 1999	Roberts	NT	Oranges	9	15	135
Sep 21, 1999	Kee	TAS	Apples	706	12.5	8825
Sep 22, 1999	Kee	NT	Mangoes	441	20	8820

The list contains data from August, 1999 to December, 2001. As usual in Excel, it is a good idea to identify the data by giving it a name so that it becomes easier to reference in your code. The list has been named `Database`. This name will be picked up and used automatically by Excel when creating our PivotTable. It is not necessary to use the name `Database`, but it is recognized by Excel to have special meaning, and can assist in setting up a PivotTable.

We want to summarize **NumberSold** within the entire time period by **Customer** and **Product**. With the cell pointer in the data list, click **Data | Pivot Table and PivotChart Report...** and, in the third step of the Wizard, click **Layout** (this is not necessary in Excel 97). Drag the **Customer** button to the **Row** area, the **Product** button to the **Column** area, and the **NumberSold** button to the **Data** area, as shown opposite:

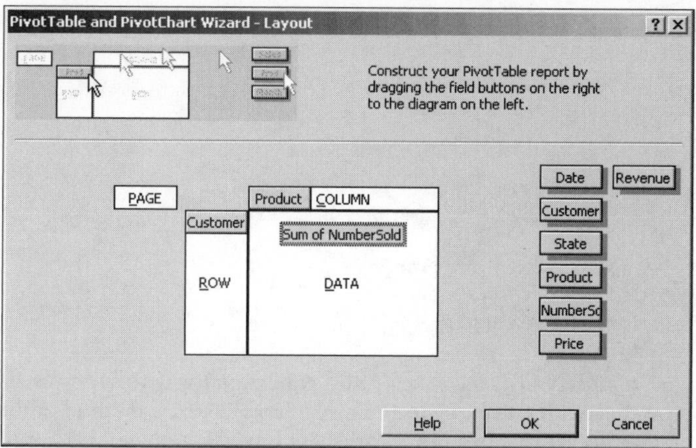

If you choose the option to place the PivotTable in a new worksheet, you will create a PivotTable report like the following:

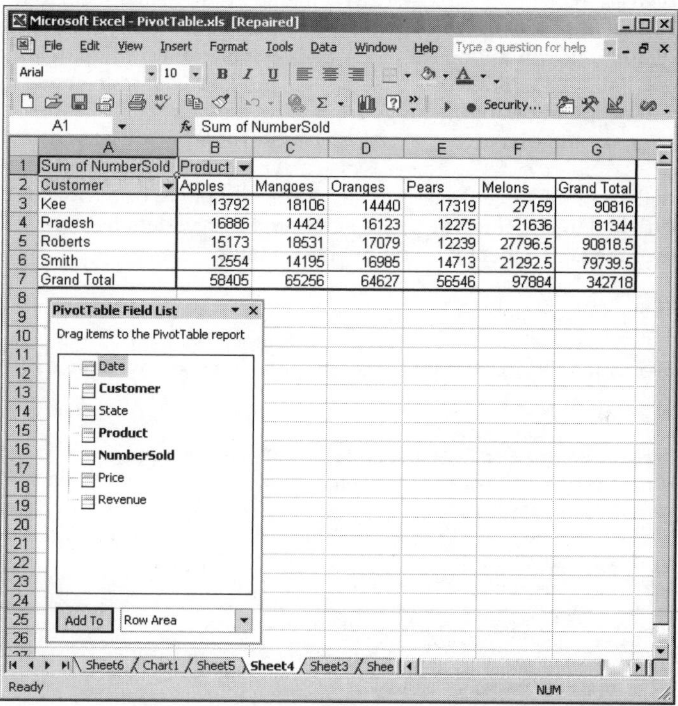

Sum of NumberSold	Product					
Customer	Apples	Mangoes	Oranges	Pears	Melons	Grand Total
Kee	13792	18106	14440	17319	27159	90816
Pradesh	16886	14424	16123	12275	21636	81344
Roberts	15173	18531	17079	12239	27796.5	90818.5
Smith	12554	14195	16985	14713	21292.5	79739.5
Grand Total	58405	65256	64627	56546	97884	342718

If you use the macro recorder to create a macro to carry out this operation in Excel 2002, it will look similar to the following code that we have reformatted to be slightly more readable:

```
ActiveWorkbook.PivotCaches.Add _
    (SourceType:=xlDatabase, SourceData:="Database"). _
    CreatePivotTable TableDestination:="", _
    TableName:="PivotTable1", _
```

```
    DefaultVersion:=xlPivotTableVersion10

ActiveSheet.PivotTableWizard _
    TableDestination:=ActiveSheet.Cells(3, 1)
ActiveSheet.Cells(3, 1).Select

ActiveSheet.PivotTables("PivotTable1").AddFields _
    RowFields:="Customer", ColumnFields:="Product"

ActiveSheet.PivotTables("PivotTable1"). _
    PivotFields("NumberSold"). _
    Orientation = xlDataField
```

The code uses the `Add` method of the `PivotCaches` collection to create a new `PivotCache`. We will discuss `PivotCaches` below. It then uses the `CreatePivotTable` method of the `PivotCache` object to create an empty PivotTable in a new worksheet starting in the A1 cell, and names the PivotTable `PivotTable1`. The code also uses a parameter that is new to Excel 2002, declaring the `DefaultVersion`. This parameter causes a compile error in previous versions.

The next line of code uses the `PivotTableWizard` method of the worksheet to move the main body of the PivotTable to A3, leaving room for page fields above the table. Page fields are discussed below. The wizard acts on the PivotTable containing the active cell, so it is important that your code does not select a cell outside the new PivotTable range before using this method. The code above has no problem because, by default, the top-left cell of the range containing the PivotTable is selected after the `CreatePivotTable` method executes.

The `AddFields` method of the table declares the `Customer` field to be a row field and the `Product` field to be a column field. Finally, `NumberSold` is declared to be a data field, which means that it appears in the body of the table where it is summed by default.

Excel 2000

Recording the same operation in Excel 2000 gives the following code, which we have reformatted:

```
ActiveWorkbook.PivotCaches.Add _
    (SourceType:=xlDatabase, SourceData:="Database"). _
    CreatePivotTable TableDestination:="", _
    TableName:="PivotTable1"

ActiveSheet.PivotTableWizard _
    TableDestination:=ActiveSheet.Cells(3, 1)

ActiveSheet.Cells(3, 1).Select

ActiveSheet.PivotTables("PivotTable1").SmallGrid = False

ActiveSheet.PivotTables("PivotTable1").AddFields _
    RowFields:="Customer", ColumnFields:="Product"

ActiveSheet.PivotTables("PivotTable1"). _
    PivotFields("NumberSold"). _
    Orientation = xlDataField
```

There are two differences in the Excel 2000 code. The Excel 2002 `DefaultVersion` parameter of the `CreatePivotTable` method does not appear and there is an extra line setting the `SmallGrid` property of the table to `False`. The `SmallGrid` property controls the appearance and functionality of the table. If the property is `True`, the table appears in the Excel 97 format, which does not allow you to drag fields from the Field List window to the table. If `SmallGrid` is `False`, a blank stencil outline is generated, as shown in the screenshot above, and you can drag fields from the Field List window to the outline.

Setting the `DefaultVersion` parameter in the Excel 2002 code has the same effect as setting the `SmallGrid` property to `False`. However, you only need to concern yourself with these features if you want to present the unfinished PivotTable to the user. If you do use these features, your code will not be compatible with Excel 97.

Excel 97

If you record the creation of the PivotTable in Excel 97, you get the following code (reformatted again):

```
ActiveSheet.PivotTableWizard _
    SourceType:=xlDatabase, _
    SourceData:="Database", _
    TableDestination:="", _
    TableName:="PivotTable1"

ActiveSheet.PivotTables("PivotTable1").AddFields _
    RowFields:="Customer", _
    ColumnFields:="Product"

ActiveSheet.PivotTables("PivotTable1"). _
    PivotFields("NumberSold"). _
    Orientation = xlDataField
```

This PivotTable is created quite differently, compared with the later versions of Excel. Although Excel 97 has `PivotCaches`, the `PivotCaches` collection does not have an `Add` method. A `PivotCache` is created indirectly when you create a PivotTable in Excel 97, but you can't create one directly. When you use the macro recorder while creating a PivotTable, Excel 97 records the `PivotTableWizard` method of the Worksheet.

If you want to have code that is compatible with Excel 97 upwards, you need to use the `PivotTableWizard` method. If you are not concerned about the name of the table, you can omit it and it will be given a default name. This can help generalize the code. The following code is adapted from the recorded code and is more flexible. It works in any version of Excel from 97 up:

```
Sub CreatePivotTable97()
  'CreatePivotTable
  With ActiveSheet.PivotTableWizard(SourceType:=xlDatabase, _
         SourceData:=ThisWorkbook.Names("Database").RefersToRange, _
         TableDestination:=ActiveCell)

    'Add Row & Column fields
    .AddFields RowFields:="Customer", ColumnFields:="Product"
    'Add Data field
    .PivotFields("NumberSold").Orientation = xlDataField
```

```
    End With
  End Sub
```

This code must be in a module in the workbook containing the range named `Database`, but can be used to create a PivotTable at any selected location in any open workbook. The code defines `SourceData` to be in `ThisWorkbook`, the workbook containing the code. It defines the `TableDestination` to be the active cell in the active workbook.

PivotCaches

A `PivotCache` is a buffer, or holding area, where data is stored and accessed as required from a data source. It acts as a communication channel between the data source and the PivotTable.

Although `PivotCaches` are automatically created in Excel 97, you can't create them explicitly, and you don't have as much control over them as you have in later versions.

In Excel 2000 and 2002, you can create a `PivotCache` using the `Add` method of the `PivotCaches` collection, as seen in our recorded code. You have extensive control over what data you draw from the source when you create a `PivotCache`. Particularly in conjunction with **ADO (ActiveX Data Objects)**, which we will demonstrate at the end of this chapter, you can achieve high levels of programmatic control over external data sources. Chapter 20 will show you the great flexibility of ADO and you can use the techniques from that chapter to construct data sources for PivotTables.

You can also use a `PivotCache` to generate multiple PivotTables from the same data source. This is more efficient than forcing each PivotTable to maintain its own data source.

When you have created a `PivotCache`, you can create any number of PivotTables from it using the `CreatePivotTable` method of the `PivotCache` object.

PivotTables Collection

Excel 2000 and 2002 give you the opportunity to use another method to create a PivotTable from a `PivotCache`, using the `Add` method of the `PivotTables` collection:

```
Sub AddTable()
  Dim PC As PivotCache
  Dim PT As PivotTable

  Set PC = ActiveWorkbook.PivotCaches.Add(SourceType:=xlDatabase, _
             SourceData:="Database")

  Set PT = ActiveSheet.PivotTables.Add(PivotCache:=PC, _
             TableDestination:="")

End Sub
```

There is no particular advantage in using this method compared with the `CreatePivotTable` method. It's just another thread in the rich tapestry of Excel.

PivotFields

The columns in the data source are referred to as fields. When the fields are used in a PivotTable, they become `PivotField` objects and belong to the `PivotFields` collection of the `PivotTable` object. The `PivotFields` collection contains all the fields in the data source and any calculated fields you have added, not just the fields that are visible in the PivotTable report. Calculated fields are discussed below.

You can add PivotFields to a report using two different techniques. You can use the `AddFields` method of the `PivotTable` object, or you can assign a value to the `Orientation` property of the `PivotField` object, as shown below:

```
Sub AddFieldsToTable()

  With ActiveSheet.PivotTables(1)

    .AddFields RowFields:="State", AddToTable:=True
    .PivotFields("Date").Orientation = xlPageField

  End With
End Sub
```

If you run this code on our example PivotTable, you will get the following result:

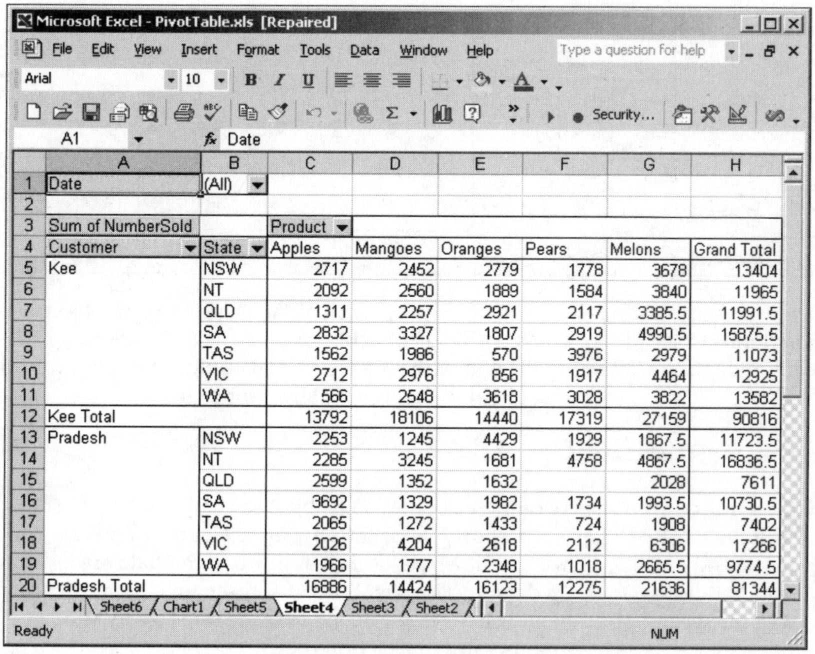

	A	B	C	D	E	F	G	H
1	Date	(All)						
2								
3	Sum of NumberSold		Product					
4	Customer	State	Apples	Mangoes	Oranges	Pears	Melons	Grand Total
5	Kee	NSW	2717	2452	2779	1778	3678	13404
6		NT	2092	2560	1889	1584	3840	11965
7		QLD	1311	2257	2921	2117	3385.5	11991.5
8		SA	2832	3327	1807	2919	4990.5	15875.5
9		TAS	1562	1986	570	3976	2979	11073
10		VIC	2712	2976	856	1917	4464	12925
11		WA	566	2548	3618	3028	3822	13582
12	Kee Total		13792	18106	14440	17319	27159	90816
13	Pradesh	NSW	2253	1245	4429	1929	1867.5	11723.5
14		NT	2285	3245	1681	4758	4867.5	16836.5
15		QLD	2599	1352	1632		2028	7611
16		SA	3692	1329	1982	1734	1993.5	10730.5
17		TAS	2065	1272	1433	724	1908	7402
18		VIC	2026	4204	2618	2112	6306	17266
19		WA	1966	1777	2348	1018	2665.5	9774.5
20	Pradesh Total		16886	14424	16123	12275	21636	81344

The `AddFields` method can add multiple row, column, and page fields. These fields replace any existing fields, unless you set the `AddToTable` parameter to `True`, as in the example above. However, `AddFields` can't be used to add or replace Data fields. The following code redefines the layout of the fields in our existing table, apart from the data field:

```
Sub RedefinePivotTable()
  Dim PT As PivotTable

  Set PT = ActiveSheet.PivotTables(1)
  PT.AddFields RowFields:=Array("Product", "Customer"), _
      ColumnFields:="State", PageFields:="Date"

End Sub
```

Note that you can use the array function to include more than one field in a field location. The result is as follows:

	A	B	C	D	E	F	G	H	I	J	K
1	Date	(All)									
2											
3				State							
4	Product	Customer	Data	NSW	NT	QLD	SA	TAS	VIC	WA	Grand Total
5	Apples	Kee	Sum of Revenue	33963	26150	16388	35400	19525	33900	7075	172400
6			Count of NumberSold	7	5	2	7	2	5	2	30
7		Pradesh	Sum of Revenue	28163	28563	32488	46150	25813	25325	24575	211075
8			Count of NumberSold	5	6	4	5	4	3	4	31
9		Roberts	Sum of Revenue	6100	34888	25825	44650	24575	37688	15938	189663
10			Count of NumberSold	3	6	4	5	6	8	3	35
11		Smith	Sum of Revenue	26963	15388	21625	21275	13550	34513	23613	156925
12			Count of NumberSold	4	3	3	4	4	4	3	25
13	Apples Sum of Revenue			95188	104988	96325	147475	83463	131425	71200	730063
14	Apples Count of NumberSold			19	20	13	21	16	20	12	121
15	Mangoes	Kee	Sum of Revenue	49040	51200	45140	66540	39720	59520	50960	362120
16			Count of NumberSold	3	6	7	6	3	6	4	35
17		Pradesh	Sum of Revenue	24900	64900	27040	26580	25440	84080	35540	288480
18			Count of NumberSold	3	6	3	3	3	8	5	31
19		Roberts	Sum of Revenue	71480	33920	20900	48000	80560	48560	67200	370620
20			Count of NumberSold	6	5	3	6	8	4	5	37
21		Smith	Sum of Revenue	37720	48940	64020	37220	5940	51360	38700	283900
22			Count of NumberSold	4	5	5	5	1	7	4	31
23	Mangoes Sum of Revenue			183140	198960	157100	178340	151660	243520	192400	1305120
24	Mangoes Count of NumberSold			16	22	18	20	15	25	18	134

You can use the `Orientation` and `Position` properties of the `PivotField` object to reorganize the table. Position defines the order of fields within a particular part of the table, counting from the one on the left. The following code, added to the end of the `RedefinePivotTable` code, would move the Customer field to the left of the Product field in the figure above, for example:

```
PT.PivotFields("Customer").Position = 1
```

You can use the `Function` property of the `PivotField` object to change the way a data field is summarised and the `NumberFormat` property to set the appearance of the numbers. The following code, added to the end of `RedefinePivotTable`, adds `Revenue` to the data area, summing it and placing it second to `NumberSold` by default. The next lines of code change the position of `NumberSold` to the second position and changes `"Sum of NumberSold"` to `"Count of NumberSold"`, which tells us how many sales transactions occurred:

```
Sub AddDataField()
  Dim PT As PivotTable

  Set PT = ActiveSheet.PivotTables(1)
```

```
    'Add and format new Data field
    With PT.PivotFields("Revenue")
      .Orientation = xlDataField
      .NumberFormat = "0"
    End With

    'Edit existing Data field
    With PT.DataFields("Sum of NumberSold")
      .Position = 2
      .Function = xlCount
      .NumberFormat = "0"
    End With

End Sub
```

Note that we need to refer to the name of the data field in the same way as it is presented in the table – Sum of NumberSold. If any further code followed, it would need to now refer to Count of NumberSold. Alternatively, you could refer to the data field by its index number or assign it a name of your own choosing.

The result of all these code changes is as follows:

Microsoft Excel - PivotTable.xls

Date	(All)							
			Product					
Customer	State	Data	Apples	Mangoes	Oranges	Pears	Melons	Grand Total
Kee	NSW	Sum of Revenue	33963	49040	41685	32004	73560	230252
		Count of NumberSold	7	3	4	2	5	21
	NT	Sum of Revenue	26150	51200	28335	28512	76800	210997
		Count of NumberSold	5	6	4	3	9	27
	QLD	Sum of Revenue	16388	45140	43815	38106	67710	211159
		Count of NumberSold	2	7	5	5	11	30
	SA	Sum of Revenue	35400	66540	27105	52542	99810	281397
		Count of NumberSold	7	6	4	5	9	31
	TAS	Sum of Revenue	19525	39720	8550	71568	59580	198943
		Count of NumberSold	2	3	2	6	5	18
	VIC	Sum of Revenue	33900	59520	12840	34506	89280	230046
		Count of NumberSold	5	6	3	3	9	26
	WA	Sum of Revenue	7075	50960	54270	54504	76440	243249
		Count of NumberSold	2	4	9	6	6	27
Kee Sum of Revenue			172400	362120	216600	311742	543180	1606042
Kee Count of NumberSold			30	35	31	30	53	179
Pradesh	NSW	Sum of Revenue	28163	24900	66435	34722	37350	191570
		Count of NumberSold	5	3	7	6	5	26
	NT	Sum of Revenue	28563	64900	25215	85644	97350	301672
		Count of NumberSold	6	6	3	9	9	33
	QLD	Sum of Revenue	32488	27040	24480		40560	124568
		Count of NumberSold	4	3	4		5	16
	SA	Sum of Revenue	46150	26580	29730	31212	39870	173542
		Count of NumberSold	5	3	4	3	5	20
	TAS	Sum of Revenue	25813	25440	21495	13032	38160	123940
		Count of NumberSold	4	3	4	3	5	19
	VIC	Sum of Revenue	25325	84080	39270	38016	126120	312811
		Count of NumberSold	3	8	4	4	12	31
	WA	Sum of Revenue	24575	35540	35220	18324	53310	166969
		Count of NumberSold	4	5	4	3	8	24
Pradesh Sum of Revenue			211075	288480	241845	220950	432720	1395070
Pradesh Count of NumberSold			31	31	30	28	47	167

CalculatedFields

You can create new fields in a PivotTable by performing calculations on existing fields. For example, you might want to calculate the weighted average price of each product. You could create a new field called `AveragePrice` and define it to be `Revenue` divided by `NumberSold`, as in the following code:

```
Sub CalculateAveragePrice()
  Dim PT As PivotTable

  'Add new Worksheet and PivotTable
  Worksheets.Add
  Set PT = ActiveWorkbook.PivotCaches(1).CreatePivotTable( _
           TableDestination:=ActiveCell, TableName:="AveragePrice")
  With PT

    'Remove AveragePrice if it exists
    On Error Resume Next
    .PivotFields("AveragePrice").Delete
    On Error GoTo 0

    'Create new AveragePrice
    .CalculatedFields.Add Name:="AveragePrice", _
       Formula:="=Revenue/NumberSold"

    'Add Row and Column fields
    .AddFields RowFields:="Customer", ColumnFields:="Product"

    'Add AveragePrice as Data field
    With .PivotFields("AveragePrice")
      .Orientation = xlDataField
      .NumberFormat = "0.00"
    End With

    'Remove grand totals
    .ColumnGrand = False
    .RowGrand = False

  End With

End Sub
```

`CalculateAveragePrice` adds a new worksheet and uses the `CreatePivotTable` method of our previously created `PivotCache` to create a new PivotTable in the new worksheet. So that you can run this code repeatedly, it deletes any existing `PivotField` objects called `AveragePrice`. The `On Error` statements ensure that the code keeps running if `AveragePrice` does not exist.

The `CalculatedFields` collection is accessed using the `CalculatedFields` method of the PivotTable. The `Add` method of the `CalculatedFields` collection is used to add the new field. Note that the new field is really added to the `PivotCache`, even though it appears to have been added to the PivotTable. It is now also available to our first PivotTable and deleting the new PivotTable would not delete `AveragePrice` from the `PivotCache`. Once the new field exists, you treat it like any other member of the `PivotFields` collection. The final lines of code remove the grand totals that appear by default.

The following table results. As the prices do not vary in our source data, it is not surprising that the weighted average prices for each product in the PivotTable do not vary either:

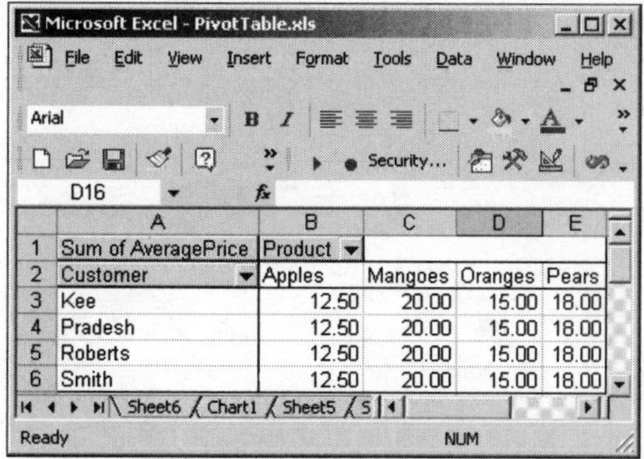

	A	B	C	D	E
1	Sum of AveragePrice	Product			
2	Customer	Apples	Mangoes	Oranges	Pears
3	Kee	12.50	20.00	15.00	18.00
4	Pradesh	12.50	20.00	15.00	18.00
5	Roberts	12.50	20.00	15.00	18.00
6	Smith	12.50	20.00	15.00	18.00

Take care when creating `CalculatedFields`. You need to appreciate that the calculations are performed AFTER the source data has been summed. In our example, `Revenue` and `NumberSold` were summed and one sum divided by the other sum. This works fine for calculating a weighted average price and is also suitable for simple addition or subtraction. Other calculations might not work as you expect

For example, say you don't have `Revenue` in the source data and you decide to calculate it by defining a `CalculatedField` equal to `Price` multiplied by `NumberSold`. This would not give the correct result. You can't get `Revenue` by multiplying the sum of `Price` by the sum of `NumberSold`, except in the special case where only one record from the source data is represented in each cell of the PivotTable.

PivotItems

Each `PivotField` object has a `PivotItems` collection associated with it. You can access the `PivotItems` using the `PivotItems` method of the `PivotField` object. It is a bit peculiar that this is a method and not a property, and is in contrast to the `HiddenItems` property and `VisibleItems` property of the `PivotField` object that return subsets of the `PivotItems` collection.

The `PivotItems` collection contains the unique values in a field. For example, the `Product` field in our source data has four unique values – "`Apples`", "`Mangoes`", "`Oranges`", and "`Pears`", which constitute the `PivotItems` collection for that field.

Grouping

We can group the items in a field in any way we like. For example, `NSW`, `QLD`, and `VIC` could be grouped as `EasternStates`. This can be very useful when we have many items in a field. We can also group dates, which have a predefined group structure including years, quarters, and months.

If we bring the `Date` field from our source data into the PivotTable as a row field, we will have nearly 400 rows in the table as there are that many unique dates:

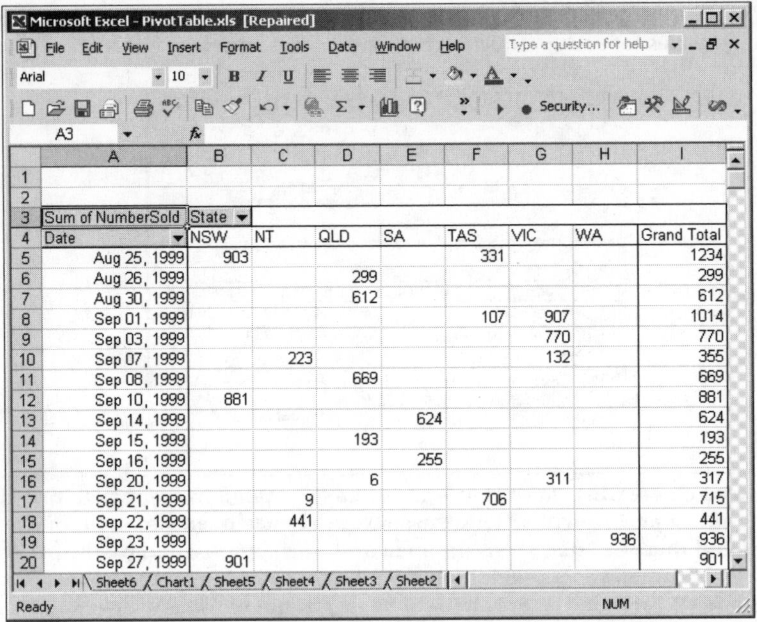

We can group the `Date` items to get a more meaningful summary. You can do this manually by selecting a cell in the PivotTable containing a date item, right-clicking the cell, and clicking Group and Show Detail | Group.... The following dialog box appears where you can select both Months and Years:

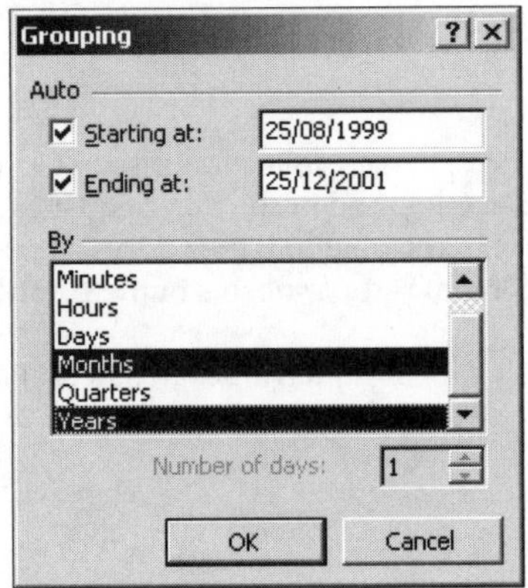

When you click OK, you will see the following:

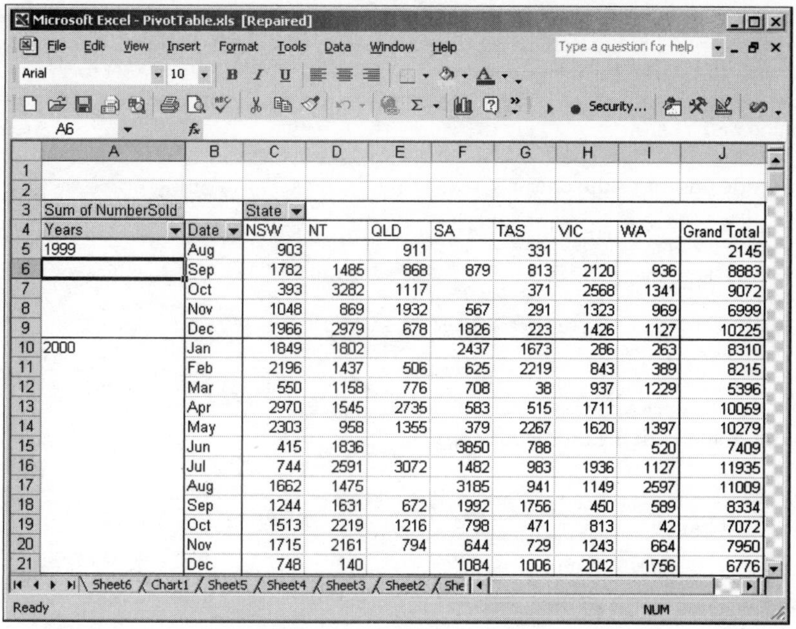

Sum of NumberSold		State							
Years	Date	NSW	NT	QLD	SA	TAS	VIC	WA	Grand Total
1999	Aug	903		911		331			2145
	Sep	1782	1485	868	879	813	2120	936	8883
	Oct	393	3282	1117		371	2568	1341	9072
	Nov	1048	869	1932	567	291	1323	969	6999
	Dec	1966	2979	678	1826	223	1426	1127	10225
2000	Jan	1849	1802		2437	1673	286	263	8310
	Feb	2196	1437	506	625	2219	843	389	8215
	Mar	550	1158	776	708	38	937	1229	5396
	Apr	2970	1545	2735	583	515	1711		10059
	May	2303	958	1355	379	2267	1620	1397	10279
	Jun	415	1836		3850	788		520	7409
	Jul	744	2591	3072	1482	983	1936	1127	11935
	Aug	1662	1475		3185	941	1149	2597	11009
	Sep	1244	1631	672	1992	1756	450	589	8334
	Oct	1513	2219	1216	798	471	813	42	7072
	Nov	1715	2161	794	644	729	1243	664	7950
	Dec	748	140		1084	1006	2042	1756	6776

The following code can be used to perform the same grouping operation:

```
Sub GroupDates()
 Dim PT As PivotTable
 Dim Rng As Range

 'Create new PivotTable in A1 of active sheet
 Set PT = ActiveSheet.PivotTableWizard(SourceType:=xlDatabase, _
     SourceData:=ThisWorkbook.Names("Database").RefersToRange, _
     TableDestination:=Range("A1"))

 With PT
   'Add data
   .AddFields RowFields:="Date", ColumnFields:="State"
   .PivotFields("NumberSold").Orientation = xlDataField

   'Find Date label
   Set Rng = .PivotFields("Date").LabelRange

   'Group all Dates by Month & Year
   Rng.Group Start:=True, End:=True, _
       Periods:=Array(False, False, False, False, True, False, True)

 End With
End Sub
```

The grouping is carried out on the `Range` object underneath the labels for the field or its items. It does not matter whether you choose the label containing the name of the field, or one of the labels containing an item name, as long as you choose only a single cell. If you choose a number of item names, you will group just those selected items.

`GroupDates` creates an object variable, `Rng`, referring to the cell containing the `Date` field label. The `Group` method is applied to this cell, using the parameters that apply to dates. The `Start` and `End` parameters define the start date and end date to be included. When they are set to `True`, all dates are included. The `Periods` parameter array corresponds to the choices in the **Grouping** dialog box, selecting **Months** and **Years**.

The following code ungroups the dates:

```
Sub UnGroupDates()
  Dim Rng As Range

  Set Rng = ActiveSheet.PivotTables(1).PivotFields("Date").LabelRange
  Rng.Ungroup
End Sub
```

You can regroup them with the following code:

```
Sub ReGroupDates()
  Dim Rng As Range

  Set Rng = ActiveSheet.PivotTables(1).PivotFields("Date").LabelRange
  Rng.Group Start:=True, End:=True, _
      Periods:=Array(False, False, False, False, True, False, True)

End Sub
```

Visible Property

You can hide items by setting their `Visible` property to `False`. Say you are working with the grouped dates from the last exercise, and you want to see only Jan 2000 and Jan 2001:

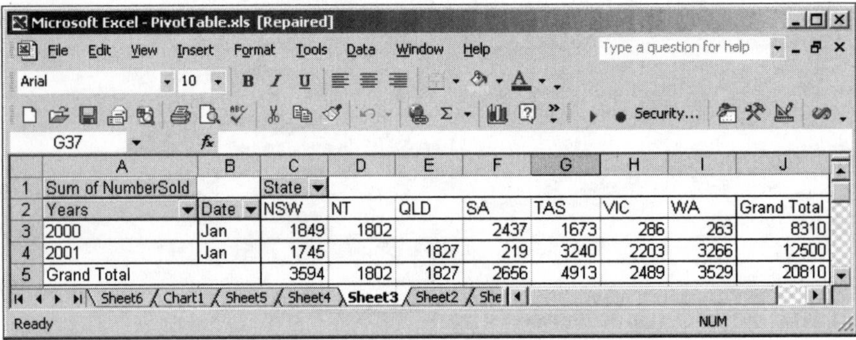

Sum of NumberSold		State							
Years	Date	NSW	NT	QLD	SA	TAS	VIC	WA	Grand Total
2000	Jan	1849	1802		2437	1673	286	263	8310
2001	Jan	1745		1827	219	3240	2203	3266	12500
Grand Total		3594	1802	1827	2656	4913	2489	3529	20810

You could use the following code:

```
Sub CompareMonths()
  Dim PT As PivotTable
  Dim PI As PivotItem
  Dim sMonth As String

  sMonth = "Jan"
  Set PT = ActiveSheet.PivotTables(1)
```

```
    For Each PI In PT.PivotFields("Years").PivotItems
      If PI.Name <> "2000" And PI.Name <> "2001" Then
        PI.Visible = False
      End If
    Next PI

    PT.PivotFields("Date").PivotItems(sMonth).Visible = True
    For Each PI In PT.PivotFields("Date").PivotItems
      If PI.Name <> sMonth Then PI.Visible = False
    Next PI
  End Sub
```

`CompareMonths` loops through all the items in the `Years` and `Date` fields setting the `Visible` property to `False` if the item is not one of the required items. The code has been designed to be reusable for comparing other months by assigning new values to `sMonth`. Note that the required month is made visible before processing the items in the `Date` field. This is necessary to ensure that the required month is visible and also so we don't try to make all the items hidden at once, which would cause a run-time error.

CalculatedItems

You can add calculated items to a field using the `Add` method of the `CalculatedItems` collection. Say you wanted to add a new product – melons. You estimate that you would sell 50% more melons than mangoes. This could be added to the table created by `CreatePivotTable97` using the following code:

```
Sub AddCalculatedItem()

  With ActiveSheet.PivotTables(1).PivotFields("Product")
    .CalculatedItems.Add Name:="Melons", Formula:="=Mangoes*1.5"
  End With

End Sub
```

This would give the following result:

Microsoft Excel - PivotTable.xls [Repaired]

File Edit View Insert Format Tools Data Window Help

A1 Sum of NumberSold

	A	B	C	D	E	F	G
1	Sum of NumberSold	Product					
2	Customer	Apples	Mangoes	Oranges	Pears	Melons	Grand Total
3	Kee	13792	18106	14440	17319	27159	90816
4	Pradesh	16886	14424	16123	12275	21636	81344
5	Roberts	15173	18531	17079	12239	27796.5	90818.5
6	Smith	12554	14195	16985	14713	21292.5	79739.5
7	Grand Total	58405	65256	64627	56546	97884	342718

Sheet6 / Chart1 / Sheet5 / Sheet4 / Sheet3 / She

Ready NUM

You can remove the `CalculatedItem` by deleting it from either the `CalculatedItems` collection or the `PivotItems` collection of the `PivotField`:

```
Sub DeleteCalculatedItem()
  With ActiveSheet.PivotTables(1).PivotFields("Product")
    .PivotItems("Melons").Delete
  End With
End Sub
```

PivotCharts

PivotCharts were introduced in Excel 2000. They follow all the rules associated with `Chart` objects, except that they are linked to a `PivotTable` object. If you change the layout of a PivotChart, Excel automatically changes the layout of the linked PivotTable. Conversely, if you change the layout of a PivotTable that is linked to a PivotChart, Excel automatically changes the layout of the chart.

The following code creates a new PivotTable, based on the same PivotCache used in the PivotTable in Sheet1 and then creates a PivotChart based on the table:

```
Sub CreatePivotChart()
  Dim PC As PivotCache
  Dim PT As PivotTable
  Dim Cht As Chart

  'Get reference to existing PivotCache
  Set PC = Worksheets("Sheet1").PivotTables(1).PivotCache

  'Add new Worksheet
  Worksheets.Add Before:=Worksheets(1)

  'Create new PivotTable based on existing Cache
  Set PT = PC.CreatePivotTable(TableDestination:=ActiveCell)

  'Add new Chart sheet based on active PivotTable
  Set Cht = Charts.Add(Before:=Worksheets(1))

  'Format PivotChart
  With Cht.PivotLayout.PivotTable

    .PivotFields("Customer").Orientation = xlRowField
    .PivotFields("State").Orientation = xlColumnField
    .PivotFields("NumberSold").Orientation = xlDataField
    '.AddDataField .PivotFields("NumberSold"), "Sum of NumberSold", xlSum

  End With

End Sub
```

The code produces the following chart:

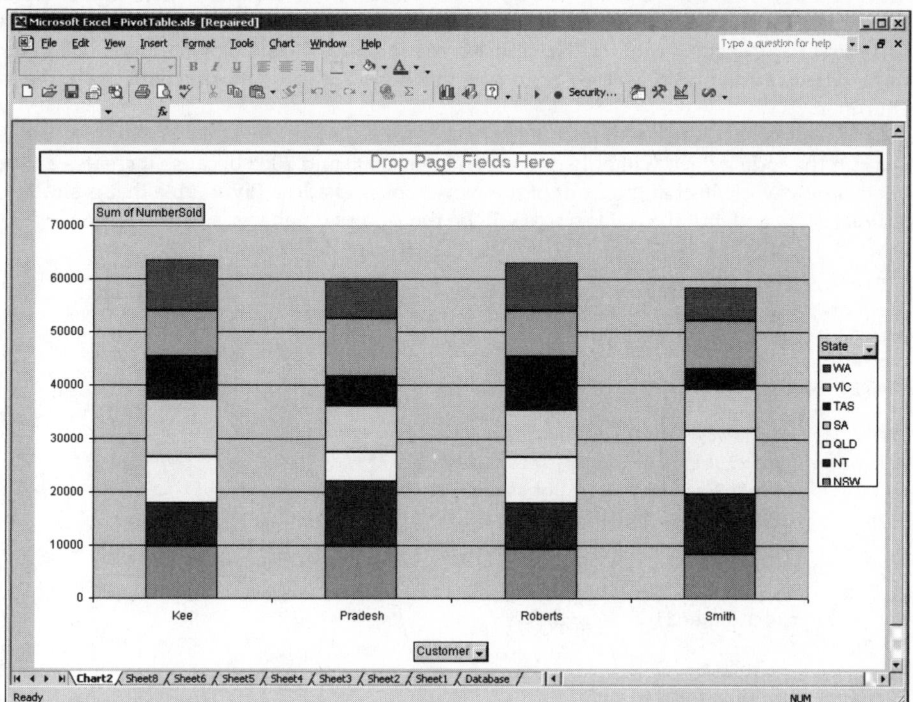

After creating the new PivotTable in a new worksheet, the code creates a new chart using the `Add` method of the `Charts` collection. It is important that the active cell is in a PivotTable when the `Add` method is executed. This causes Excel to automatically link the new chart to the PivotTable.

Once the PivotChart is created, you can link to the associated PivotTable using the `PivotLayout` object, which is now associated with the chart. It is then only a matter of setting up the fields required in the PivotTable, using the same techniques we have already used.

The last line before the `End With` has been commented out. It is an alternative way of adding the data field and can replace the line of code immediately before it. However, `AddDataField` is a new method of the `PivotTable` object that applies only to Excel 2002.

Any further programmatic manipulation of the data in the chart needs to be done through the associated PivotTable. Formatting changes to the chart can be made through the properties and methods of the `Chart` object.

External Data Sources

Excel is ultimately limited in the quantity of data it can store, and it is very poor at handling multiple related tables of data. Therefore, you might want to store your data in an external database application and draw out the data you need as required. The most powerful way to do this is to use ADO (ActiveX Data Objects). We will be covering ADO in greater depth in chapter 20.

The following example shows how to connect to an Access database called SalesDB.mdb containing similar data to that we have been using, but potentially much more comprehensive and complex. In order to run the following code, you must create a reference to ADO. To do this, go to the VBE window and click **Tools | References**. From the list, find '**Microsoft ActiveX Data Objects**' and click in the checkbox beside it. If you find multiple versions of this library, choose the one with the highest version number.

When you run the code, which will only execute in Excel 2000 and 2002 because it creates a PivotCache, it will create a new worksheet at the front of the workbook and add a PivotTable that is similar to those we have already created, but the data source will be the Access database:

```
Sub PivotTableDataViaADO()
  Dim Con As New ADODB.Connection
  Dim RS As New ADODB.Recordset
  Dim sql As String
  Dim PC As PivotCache
  Dim PT As PivotTable

  Con.Open "Provider=Microsoft.Jet.OLEDB.4.0;" & _
           "Data Source=C:\My Documents\SalesDB.mdb;"
  sql = "Select * From SalesData"

  'Open the recordset...
  Set RS = New ADODB.Recordset
  Set RS.ActiveConnection = Con
  RS.Open sql

  'Create the PivotTable cache....
  Set PC = ActiveWorkbook.PivotCaches.Add(SourceType:=xlExternal)
  Set PC.Recordset = RS

  'Create the PivotTable ....
  Worksheets.Add Before:=Sheets(1)
  Set PT = ActiveSheet.PivotTables.Add(PivotCache:=PC, _
             TableDestination:=Range("A1"))

  With PT
    .NullString = "0"
    .SmallGrid = False
    .AddFields RowFields:="State", ColumnFields:="Product"
    .PivotFields("NumberSold").Orientation = xlDataField
  End With
End Sub
```

First we create a Connection object linking us to the Access database using the Open method of the ADO Connection object. We then define an SQL (Structured Query Language) statement that says we want to select all the data in a table called SalesData in the Access database. The table is almost identical to the one we have been using in Excel, having the same fields and data. See Chapter 20 to get more information on the SQL language and the terminology that is used in ADO.

We then assign a reference to a new ADO Recordset object to the object variable RS. The ActiveConnection property of RS is assigned a reference to the Connection object. The Open method then populates the recordset with the data in the Access SalesData table, following the instruction in the SQL language statement.

We then open a new PivotCache, declaring its data source as external by setting the `SourceType` parameter to `xlExternal`, and set its `Recordset` property equal to the ADO recordset `RS`. The rest of the code uses techniques we have already seen to create the PivotTable using the PivotCache.

Chapter 20 goes into much more detail about creating recordsets and with much greater explanation of the techniques used. Armed with the knowledge in that chapter, and knowing how to connect a recordset to a PivotCache from the above example, you will be in a position to utilize an enormous range of data sources.

Summary

You use PivotTables to summarize complex data. In this chapter we have examined various techniques that you can use to create PivotTables from a data source such as an Excel data list using VBA. We have explained the restrictions that apply if your code needs to be compatible with different versions of Excel.

We have covered using the PivotTable wizard in Excel 97, and setting up PivotCaches in later versions, to create PivotTables. You can add fields to PivotTables as row, column, or data fields. You can calculate fields from other fields, and items in fields. You can group items. You might do this to summarize dates by years and months, for example. You can hide items, so that you see only the data required.

You can link a PivotChart to a PivotTable so that changes in either are synchronized. A `PivotLayout` object connects them.

Using ADO, you can link your PivotTables to external data sources.

8

Filtered Lists

In this chapter we will see how to set up VBA code to manage data in lists and code to filter information from lists. The features we will be looking at are:

- Data Form
- AutoFilter
- Advanced Filter

As always, you can use the macro recorder to generate some basic code for the above operations. However, the recorded code needs modification to make it useful and the recorder can even generate erroneous code in some cases. You will see that dates can be a problem, if not handled properly, especially in an international setting.

Structuring the Data

Before you can apply Excel's list management tools, your data must be set up in a very specific way. The data must be structured like a database table, with headings at the top of each column, which are the field names, and the data itself must consist of single rows of information, which are the equivalent of database records. The following screen shows a typical list that holds information on the sales of fruit products:

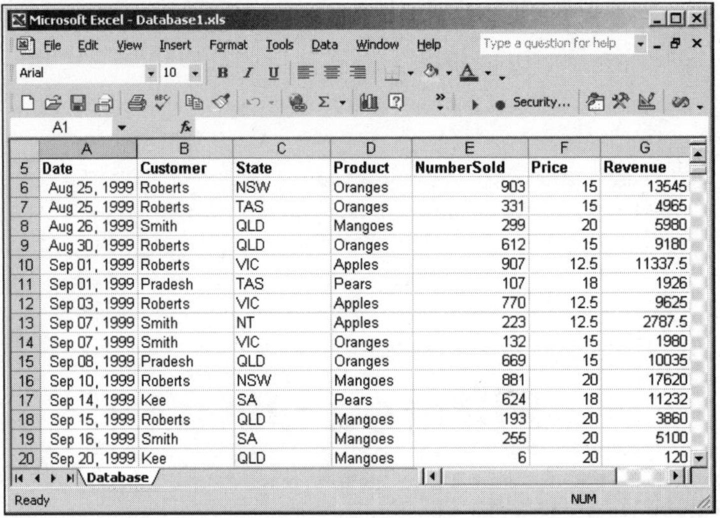

	Date	Customer	State	Product	NumberSold	Price	Revenue
6	Aug 25, 1999	Roberts	NSW	Oranges	903	15	13545
7	Aug 25, 1999	Roberts	TAS	Oranges	331	15	4965
8	Aug 26, 1999	Smith	QLD	Mangoes	299	20	5980
9	Aug 30, 1999	Roberts	QLD	Oranges	612	15	9180
10	Sep 01, 1999	Roberts	VIC	Apples	907	12.5	11337.5
11	Sep 01, 1999	Pradesh	TAS	Pears	107	18	1926
12	Sep 03, 1999	Roberts	VIC	Apples	770	12.5	9625
13	Sep 07, 1999	Smith	NT	Apples	223	12.5	2787.5
14	Sep 07, 1999	Smith	VIC	Oranges	132	15	1980
15	Sep 08, 1999	Pradesh	QLD	Oranges	669	15	10035
16	Sep 10, 1999	Roberts	NSW	Mangoes	881	20	17620
17	Sep 14, 1999	Kee	SA	Pears	624	18	11232
18	Sep 15, 1999	Roberts	QLD	Mangoes	193	20	3860
19	Sep 16, 1999	Smith	SA	Mangoes	255	20	5100
20	Sep 20, 1999	Kee	QLD	Mangoes	6	20	120

Excel should never be considered a fully equipped database application. It is limited in the amount of data it can handle and it cannot efficiently handle multiple related database tables. However, Excel can work with other database applications to provide you with the data you need and it has some powerful tools, such as Data Form, AutoFilter, Advanced Filter, SubTotal and PivotTables, for analyzing, manipulating, and presenting that data. See Chapters 8 and 15.

Data Form

Excel has a built-in form that you can use to view, find, and edit data in a list. If you select a single cell in the list, or select the entire list, and click on Data | Form... you will see a form like the following:

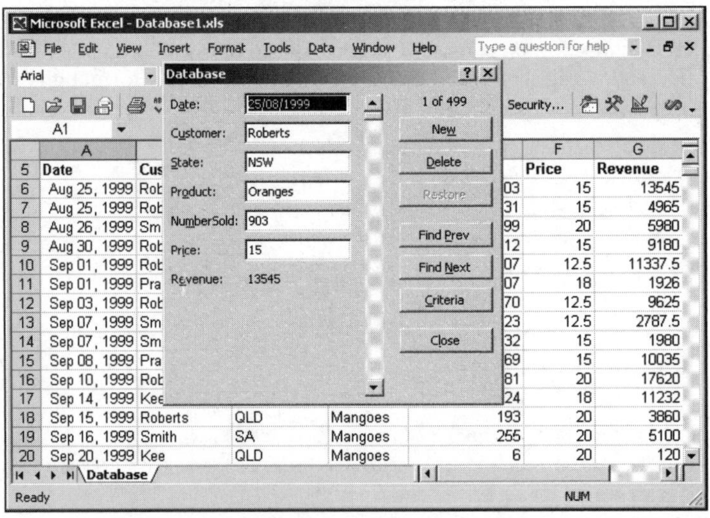

If you record this process, you will get code like the following:

```
Range("B2").Select
ActiveSheet.ShowDataForm
```

If your list starts in the range of A1:B2, and you record selecting the first cell and showing the Data Form, then the recorded macro works. If your list starts in any cell outside the range A1:B2, and you record while selecting the top left hand corner and showing the Data Form, the recorded macro will give an error message when you try to run it. You can overcome this problem by applying the name `Database` to your list.

> **If you don't work entirely with US date and number formats, the Data Form feature is quite dangerous, when displayed by VBA code using the `ShowDataForm` method. The Data Form, when invoked by VBA, displays dates and numbers only in US format. On the other hand, any dates or numbers typed in by a user are interpreted according to the regional settings in the Windows Control Panel. Therefore, if you set the date in the British format (dd/mm/yyyy), when you use the Data Form, the dates become corrupted. See Chapter 22 for more details.**

AutoFilter

The AutoFilter feature is a very easy way to select data from a list. You can activate AutoFilter by selecting a cell in your data list and clicking Data | Filter | AutoFilter. Drop-down menu buttons will appear beside each field name as shown below. If you want an exact match on a field such as `Customer`, all you need to do is click the dropdown beside the field and click on the required match, as shown below:

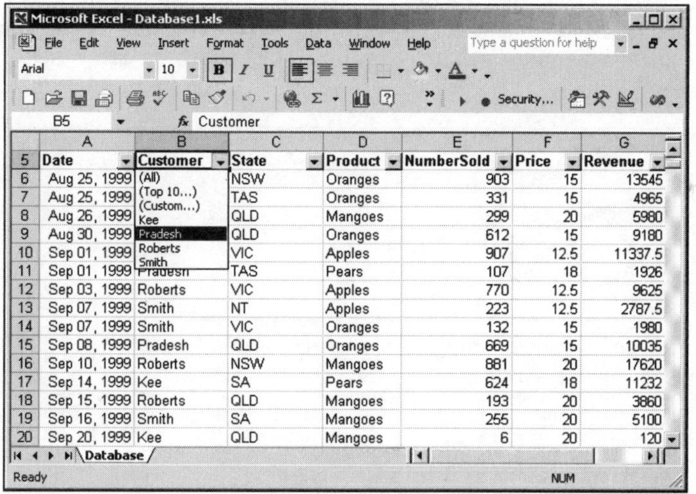

Custom AutoFilter

If you want something a bit more complex, such as a range of dates, you need to do a bit more work. The following screen shows how you can manually filter the data to show a particular month. Click on the drop-down button beside Date and choose Custom. You can then fill in the dialog box as shown:

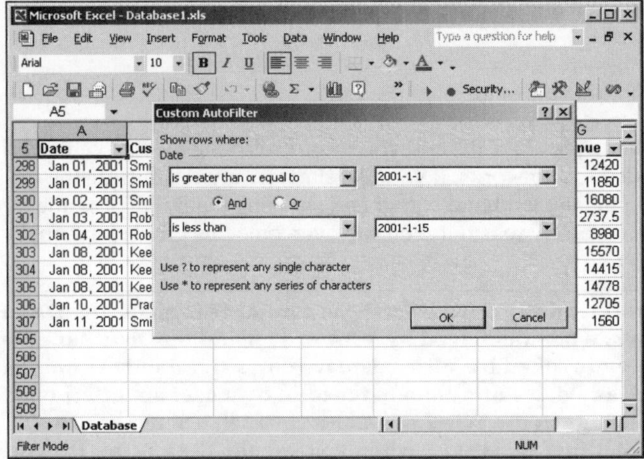

> **The format you use when you type in dates in the Custom AutoFilter dialog box depends on your regional settings. You can use a `dd/mm/yy` format if you work with UK settings, or a `mm/dd/yy` format if you work with US settings. Some formats that are more international, such `yyyy-m-d`, are also recognized.**

Adding Combo Boxes

You can make filtering even easier for a user by placing controls in the worksheet to run AutoFilter. This also gives you the opportunity to do far more with the data than filter it. You could copy the filtered data to another worksheet and generate a report, you could chart the data or you could delete it. The following screen shows two ActiveX combo box controls that allow the user to select the month and year required:

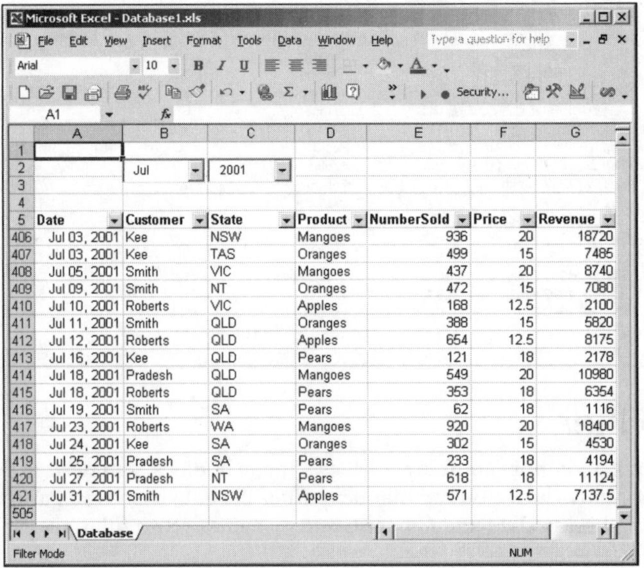

The combo boxes have the default names of ComboBox1 and ComboBox2. To place list values into the combo boxes, you can enter the list values into a worksheet column and define the ListFillRange property of the ComboBox object as something like "=Sheet2!A1:A12". Alternatively, you can use the following Workbook_Open event procedure in the ThisWorkbook module of the workbook, to populate the combo boxes when the workbook is opened:

```
Private Sub Workbook_Open()
  Dim Months
  Dim Years
  Dim i As Integer

  Months = Array("Jan", "Feb", "Mar", "Apr", "May", "Jun", "Jul", "Aug", "Sep",_
                                                           "Oct", "Nov", "Dec")
  Years = Array(1999, 2000, 2001)
  For i = LBound(Months) To UBound(Months)
    Sheet1.ComboBox1.AddItem Months(i)
  Next i
  Sheet1.ComboBox2.List = WorksheetFunction.Transpose(Years)
End Sub
```

The AddItem method of the ComboBox object adds the Months array values to the ComboBbox1 list. To show an alternative technique, the worksheet Transpose function is used to convert the Years array from a row to a column, and the values are assigned to the List property of ComboBox2.

Note that the programmatic name of Sheet1, which you can see in the **Project Explorer** window or the **Properties** window of the VBE, has been used to define the location of the combo boxes. Even though the name of the worksheet is Database, the programmatic name is still Sheet1, unless you change it at the top of the **Properties** window where it is identified by **(Name)**, rather than **Name**, as shown here:

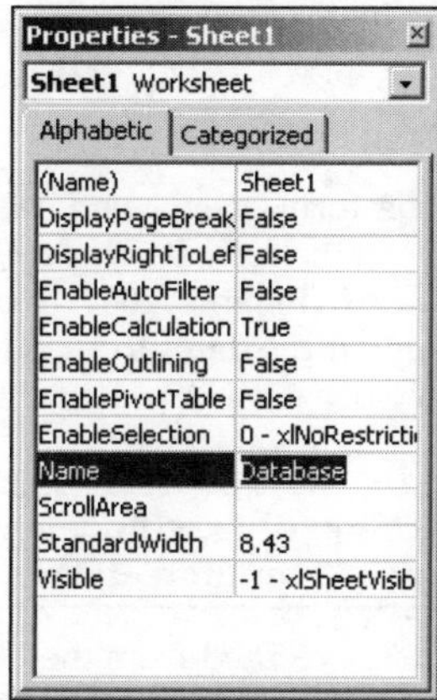

In the code module behind the worksheet, the following code is entered:

```
Private Sub ComboBox1_Click()
   Call FilterDates
End Sub

Private Sub ComboBox2_Click()
   Call FilterDates
End Sub
```

When you click on an entry in their drop-down lists, each combo box executes the `FilterDates` procedure, which is described below. `FilterDates` can be in the same module, and declared `Private` if you do not want any other modules to be able to use it, or it can be in a standard code module if you want to use it as a general utility procedure.

So, how do you construct the `FilterDates` procedure? As we have shown in previous chapters, you can use the macro recorder to get something to start with, and then refine the code to make it more flexible and efficient. If you use the macro recorder to record the process of filtering the dates, you will get code like this:

```
    Range("A6").Select
    Selection.AutoFilter
    Selection.AutoFilter Field:=1, Criteria1:=">=1/01/2001", Operator:= _
        xlAnd, Criteria2:="<28/01/2001"
```

As usual, the macro recorder selects ranges and produces redundant code. If your list has the name `Database`, you can translate this code to:

```
Sub FilterDates()
   Range("Database").AutoFilter Field:=1, _
                     Criteria1:=">=1/01/2001", _
                     Operator:=xlAnd, _
                     Criteria2:="<28/01/2001"
End Sub
```

You might also notice that the dates have been translated to the format of the regional settings – in this case that of Australia, which uses the same format as the UK. The format generated by the recorder is `d/mm/yyyy`. Also note that the dates are formatted as text, rather than dates, because the criteria must include the logical operators.

Date Format Problems

Unfortunately, the above code does not perform as expected. When you run the recorded macro, the dates are interpreted by VBA as US dates in the format `mm/dd/yyyy`. The above code selects dates greater than or equal to Jan 1, 2001 and less than Jan 2, 2001. In other words Jan 1, 2001. To make this macro perform properly, you need to convert the dates to a US format. Of course, you will not have this problem with your recorded code if you work with US date formats, in your regional settings, in the first place.

Trying to make your VBA code compatible with dates in all language versions of Excel is very difficult. See Chapter 22 for more details.

The following `FilterDates` procedure is executed from the `Click` event procedures of the combo boxes, and computes the start and end dates required for the criteria of the `AutoFilter` method. `FilterDates` has been placed in the same module as the combo box event procedures and declared as `Private` so that it does not appear in the **Tools | Macro | Macros** dialog box:

```
Private Sub FilterDates()
   Dim iStartMonth As Integer
   Dim iStartYear As Integer
   Dim dtStartDate As Date
   Dim dtEndDate As Date
   Dim stStartCriterion As String
```

```
    Dim stEndCriterion As String

    iStartMonth = Me.ComboBox1.ListIndex + 1
    iStartYear = Me.ComboBox2.Value
    dtStartDate = DateSerial(iStartYear, iStartMonth, 1)
    dtEndDate = DateSerial(iStartYear, iStartMonth + 1, 1)
    stStartCriterion = ">=" & Format(dtStartDate, "mm/dd/yyyy")
    stEndCriterion = "<" & Format(dtEndDate, "mm/dd/yyyy")
    Range("Database").AutoFilter Field:=1, Criteria1:=stStartCriterion, _
                                           Operator:=xlAnd, _
                                           Criteria2:=stEndCriterion
End Sub
```

`FilterDates` assigns the values selected in the combo boxes to `iStartMonth` and `iStartYear`. The `Me` keyword has been used to refer to the sheet containing the code, rather than the object name `Sheet1`. This makes the code portable, which means it can be used in other sheet modules without worrying about the name of the sheet.

`iStartMonth` uses the `ListIndex` property of `ComboBox1` to obtain the month as a number. As the `ListIndex` is zero based, 1 is added to give the correct month number. The `DateSerial` function translates the year and month numbers into a date and assigns the date to `dtStartDate`. The second `DateSerial` function calculates a date that is one month ahead of `dtStartDate` and assigns it to `dtEndDate`.

The `Format` function is used to turn `dtStartDate` and `dtEndDate` back into strings in the US date format of `mm/dd/yyyy`. The appropriate logical operators are placed in front and the resulting strings are assigned to `stStartCriterion` and `stEndCriterion`, respectively. `FilterDates` finally executes the `AutoFilter` method on the range `Database`, using the computed criteria.

Getting the Exact Date

There is another tricky problem with AutoFilter that occurs with dates in all language versions of Excel. The problem arises when you want to get an exact date, rather than a date within a range of dates. In this case, AutoFilter matches your date with the formatted appearance of the dates in the worksheet, not the underlying date values.

Excel holds dates as numeric values equal to the number of days since Jan 1, 1900. For example, Jan 1, 2002 is held as 37257. When you ask for dates greater than or equal to Jan 1, 2002, Excel looks for date serial numbers greater than or equal to 37257. However, when you ask for dates equal to Jan 1, 2002, Excel does not look for the numeric value of the date. Excel checks for the string value "Jan 1, 2002" as it appears formatted in the worksheet.

The following adaptation of `FilterDates` will handle an exact date match in our list, because `stExactCriterion` is assigned the date value, as a string in the format "`mmm dd, yyyy`" and the dates are formatted in the worksheet as `mmm dd, yyyy`:

```
Private Sub FilterExactDate()
   Dim iExactMonth As Integer
   Dim iExactYear As Integer
   Dim dtExactDate As Date
   Dim stExactCriterion As String

   iExactMonth = Sheet1.ComboBox1.ListIndex + 1
```

```
    iExactYear = Sheet1.ComboBox2.Value
    dtExactDate = DateSerial(iExactYear, iExactMonth, 1)
    stExactCriterion = Format(dtExactDate, "mmm dd, yyyy")
    Range("Database").AutoFilter Field:=1, Criteria1:=stExactCriterion
End Sub
```

Note that if you change the date format used in the worksheet you also need to change the date format in the code or the code will no longer work.

> *The code above will give all the entries for the first of the month, as 1 is specified as the third parameter in the `DateSerial` function. To select any day of the month, a third combo box could be added to cell **A2** and some code added to the `ComboBox1_Click event` procedure to list the correct number of days for the month specified in `ComboBox1`.*

Copying the Visible Rows

If you want to make it easy to create a new worksheet containing a copy of the filtered data, you can place an ActiveX command button at the top of the worksheet and enter the following `Click` event procedure in the worksheet module. This procedure copies the entire `Database` range, knowing that, by default, only the visible cells will be copied:

```
Private Sub CommandButton1_Click()
    Dim wsNew As Worksheet
    Dim stWksName As String
    Dim stMonth As String
    Dim stYear As String
    Dim wsDummyWks As Worksheet

    stMonth = Sheet1.ComboBox1.Value
    stYear = Sheet1.ComboBox2.Value
    On Error Resume Next
    stWksName = Format(DateValue(stYear & "-" & stMonth & "-1"), "mmm yyyy")
    Set wsDummyWks = Worksheets(stWksName)
    If Err.Number = 0 Then
        MsgBox "This data has already been copied"
        Exit Sub
    End If
    On Error GoTo 0
    Set wsNew = Worksheets.Add
    Range("Database").Copy Destination:=wsNew.Range("A1")
    wsNew.Columns("A:G").AutoFit
    wsNew.Name = stWksName
End Sub
```

The `Click` event procedure first calculates a name for the new worksheet in the format `mmm yyyy`. It then checks to see if this worksheet already exists by setting a dummy object variable to refer to a worksheet with the new name. If this does not cause an error, the worksheet already exists and the procedure issues a message and exits.

If there is no worksheet with the new name, the event procedure adds a new worksheet at the end of the existing worksheets. It copies the `Database` range to the new sheet and `AutoFits` the column widths to accommodate the copied data. The procedure then names the new worksheet.

Finding the Visible Rows

When you use AutoFilter, Excel simply hides the rows that do not match the current filters. If you want to process just the rows that are visible in your code, you need to look at each row in the list and decide if it is hidden or not. There is a trick to this. When referring to the `Hidden` property of a `Range` object, the `Range` object must be an entire row, extending from column A to column IV, or an entire column, extending from row 1 to row 65536. You can't use the `Hidden` property with a single cell or a 7 column row from the list shown below:

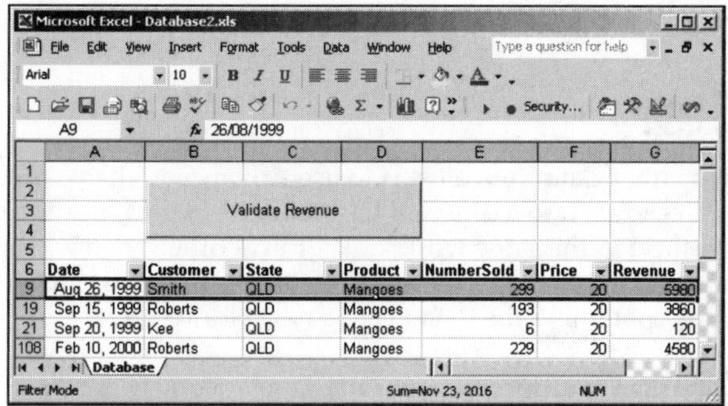

The following code checks each row that is visible on the screen and shades the background of any row that has an invalid `Revenue` calculation:

```
Private Sub CommandButton1_Click()
   Dim rgDB As Range
   Dim rgRow As Range
   Dim dNumberSold As Double
   Dim dPrice As Double
   Dim dRevenue As Double

   With Range("Database")
      Set rgDB = .Offset(1, 0).Resize(.Rows.Count - 1)
   End With
   For Each rgRow In rgDB.Rows
      If rgRow.EntireRow.Hidden = False Then
         dNumberSold = rgRow.Cells(5).Value
         dPrice = rgRow.Cells(6).Value
         dRevenue = rgRow.Cells(7).Value
         If Abs(dNumberSold * dPrice - dRevenue) > 0.000001 Then
            rgRow.Select
            MsgBox "Error in selected row"
            rgRow.Interior.ColorIndex = 15
         End If
      End If
   Next rgRow
End Sub
```

The `Click` event procedure for the command button first defines an object variable `rgDB` referring to the range named `Database`, excluding the Header Row. It then uses a `For Each...Next` loop to process all the rows in `rgDB`. The first `If` test ensures that only rows that are not hidden are processed. The `dNumberSold`, `dPrice`, and `dRevenue` values for the current row are assigned to variables and the second `If` tests that the `dRevenue` figure is within a reasonable tolerance of the product of `dNumberSold` and `dPrice`.

As worksheet computations are done with binary representations of numbers to an accuracy of about 15 significant figures, it is not always appropriate to check that two numbers are equal to the last decimal point, especially if the input figures have come from other worksheet calculations. It is better to see if they differ by an acceptably small amount. As the difference can be positive or negative, the `Abs` *function is used to convert both positive and negative differences to a positive difference before comparison.*

If the test shows an unacceptable difference, the row is selected and a message displayed. The row is also given a background color of light gray.

Advanced Filter

The most powerful way to filter data from a list is to use Advanced Filter. You can filter the list in place, like AutoFilter, or you can extract it to a different location. The extract location can be in the same worksheet, another worksheet in the same workbook, or in another open workbook. In the following example, we have extracted the data for NSW and VIC for the first quarter of 2001. The data has been copied from the workbook containing the data list to a new workbook.

When you use Advanced Filter, you specify your criteria in a worksheet range. An example of a `Criteria` range is shown in A1:C3 of the following screen. This worksheet is in a workbook called `Extract.xls`. The data list is in `Database.xls` that contains data that is the same as the data we used in the AutoFilter examples:

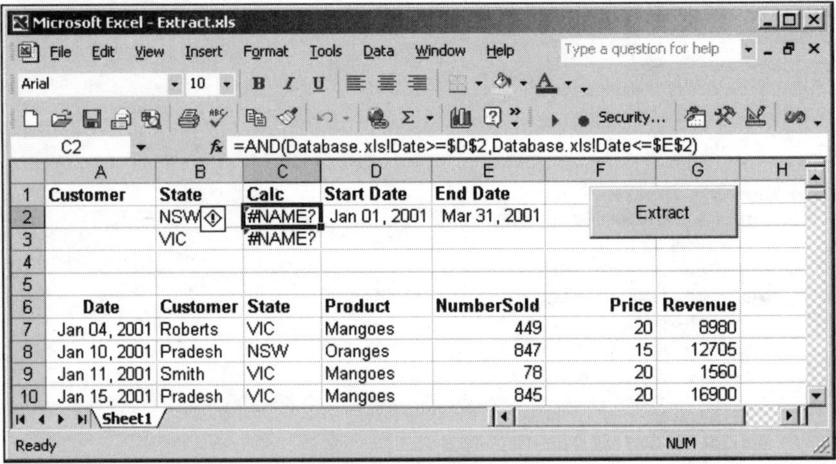

The top row of the `Criteria` range contains the field names from the list that you want to filter on. You can have as many rows under the field names as you need. Criteria on different rows are combined using the `OR` operator. Criteria across a row are combined using the `AND` operator. You can also use computed criteria in the form of logical statements that evaluate to `True` or `False`. In the case of computed criteria, the top row of the `Criteria` range must be empty or contain a label that is not a field name in the list, such as `Calc` in this case.

When you create computed criteria, you can refer to the data list field names in your formulas, as you can see in the formula bar above the worksheet. The formula bar shows the contents of C2, which is as follows:

```
=AND(Database.xls!Date>=$D$2,Database.xls!Date<=$E$2)
```

The formula in **C3** is identical to the formula in **C2**.

The criteria shown can be thought of as applying this filter:

```
(State=NSW AND Date>=Jan 1, 1999 AND Date<Mar 1, 1999) OR _
                      (State=VIC AND Date>=Jan 1, 1999 AND Date<Mar 1, 1999)
```

As the data list is in the file `Database.xls`, the references to the `Date` field are entered as external references, in the same format you would use to refer to workbook names in another workbook. As the field names are not workbook names, the formulas evaluate to a `#NAME?` error.

To facilitate the Advanced Filter, the data list in the `Database.xls` workbook has been named `Database`. In the `Extract.xls` workbook, **A1:C3** has been named `Criteria` and **A6:G6** has been named `Extract`. If you carry out the Advanced Filter manually, using **Data | Filter | Advanced Filter**, you see the following dialog box, where you can enter the names as shown:

To automate this process, the command button with the **Extract** caption runs the following `Click` event procedure:

```
Private Sub CommandButton1_Click()
   Dim rgDB As Range
   Dim rgCriteria As Range
   Dim rgExtract As Range

   Set rgDB = Workbooks("Database.xls").Worksheets("Database").Range("Database")
   Set rgCriteria = ThisWorkbook.Worksheets(1).Range("Criteria")
   Set rgExtract = ThisWorkbook.Worksheets(1).Range("Extract")
   rgDB.AdvancedFilter Action:=xlFilterCopy, CriteriaRange:=rgCriteria, _
                                                      CopyToRange:=rgExtract
End Sub
```

The event procedure defines three object variables referring to the `Database`, `Criteria`, and `Extract` ranges. It then runs the `AdvancedFilter` method of the `Database Range` object.

Summary

The Data Form feature makes it very easy to set up a data maintenance macro. However, you should apply the name `Database` to your data list if the top left hand corner of the list is not in the range A1:B2.

As you have seen, the AutoFilter and Advanced Filter features can be combined with VBA code to provide flexible ways for users to extract information from data lists. By combining these features with ActiveX controls, such as combo boxes and command buttons, you can make them readily accessible to all levels of users. You can use the macro recorder to get an indication of the required methods and adapt the recorded code to accept input from the ActiveX controls.

However, you need to take care, if you work with non-US date formats. You need to bear in mind that VBA requires you to use US date formats when you compare ranges of dates using AutoFilter. If this interests you, you should check out Chapter 22, which deals with international programming issues.

Also, when you want to detect which rows have been hidden by AutoFilter, you need to be aware that the `Hidden` property of the `Range` object can only be applied to entire worksheet rows.

Advanced Filter provides the most powerful filtering in Excel. You can set up much more complex criteria with Advanced Filter than you can with AutoFilter and you can copy filtered data to a specified range. You can also use Advanced Filter to copy filtered data from one workbook to another.

9

Generating Charts

In this chapter we will see how you can use the macro recorder to discover what objects, methods, and properties are required to manipulate charts. We will then improve and extend that code to make it more flexible and efficient. This chapter is designed to show you how to gain access to `Chart` objects in VBA code so that you can start to program the vast number of objects that Excel charts contain. You can find more information on these objects in Appendix A. We will look specifically at:

- Creating `Chart` objects on separate sheets
- Creating `Chart` objects embedded in a worksheet
- Editing data series in charts
- Defining series with arrays
- Defining chart labels linked to worksheet cells

You can create two types of charts in Excel: charts that occupy their own chart sheets and charts that are embedded in a worksheet. They can be manipulated in code in much the same way. The only difference is that, while the chart sheet is a `Chart` object in its own right, the chart embedded in a worksheet is contained by a `ChartObject` object. Each `ChartObject` on a worksheet is a member of the worksheet's `ChartObjects` collection. Chart sheets are members of the workbook's `Charts` collection.

> *Each `ChartObject` is a member of the `Shapes` collection, as well as a member of the `ChartObjects` collection. The `Shapes` collection provides you with an alternative way to refer to embedded charts. The macro recorder generates code that uses the `Shapes` collection rather than the `ChartObjects` collection.*

Chart Sheets

Before creating the chart as described, turn on the macro recorder. Create a new chart sheet called `Mangoes` using the Chart Wizard to create a chart from the following data in cells A3:D7. In Step 2 of the Chart Wizard, choose the "Series in Rows" option. In Step 4 of the Chart Wizard, choose the "As new sheet" option and enter the name of the chart sheet as "Mangoes":

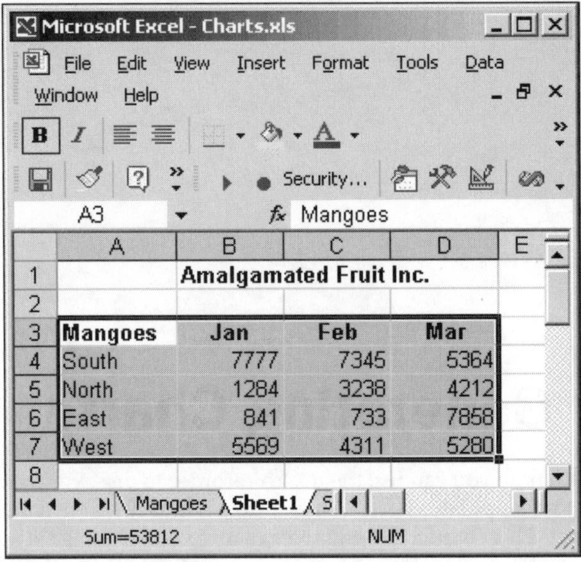

The following screen shows the chart created:

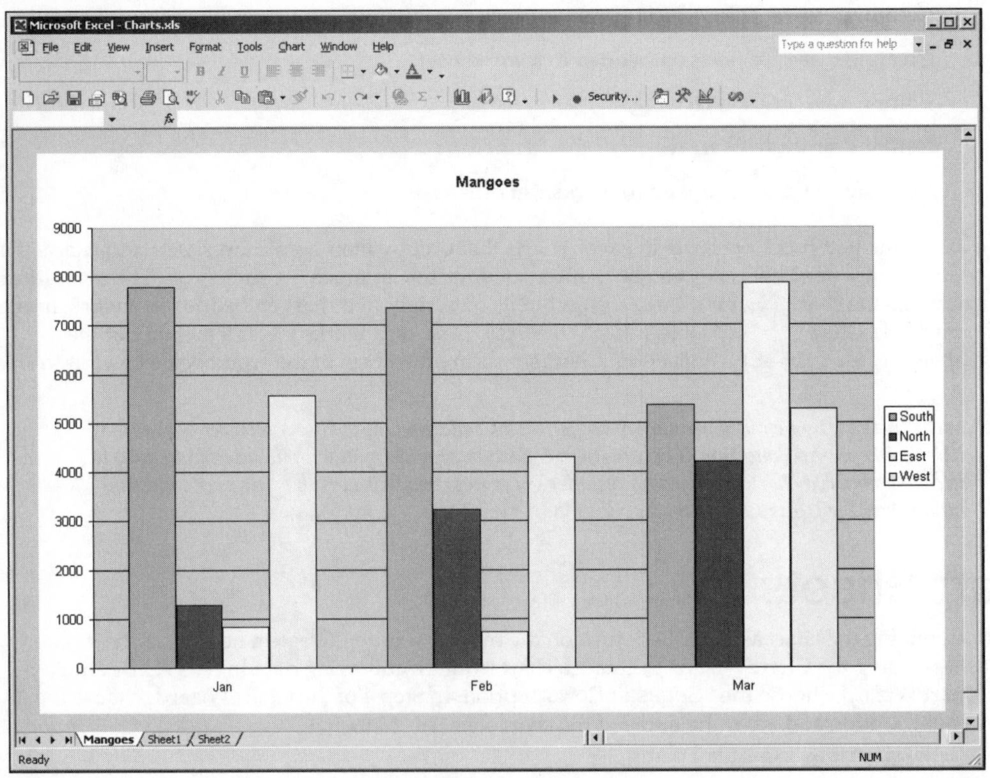

The Recorded Macro

The recorded macro should look like the following:

```
Charts.Add
ActiveChart.ChartType = xlColumnClustered
ActiveChart.SetSourceData Source:=Sheets("Sheet1").Range("A3:D7"), _
                                                            PlotBy:= xlRows
ActiveChart.Location Where:=xlLocationAsNewSheet, Name:="Mangoes"

With ActiveChart
   .HasTitle = True
   .ChartTitle.Characters.Text = "Mangoes"
   .Axes(xlCategory, xlPrimary).HasTitle = False
   .Axes(xlValue, xlPrimary).HasTitle = False
End With
```

The recorded macro uses the `Add` method of the `Charts` collection to create a new chart. It defines the active chart's `ChartType` property, and then uses the `SetSourceData` method to define the ranges plotted. The macro uses the `Location` method to define the chart as a chart sheet and assign it a name. It sets the `HasTitle` property to `True` so that it can define the `ChartTitle` property. Finally, it sets the `HasTitle` property of the axes back to `False`, a step which is not necessary.

Adding a Chart Sheet Using VBA Code

The recorded code is reasonably good as it stands. However, it is more elegant to create an object variable, so that you have a simple and efficient way of referring to the chart in subsequent code. You can also remove some of the redundant code and add a chart title that is linked to the worksheet. The following code incorporates these changes:

```
Sub AddChartSheet()
   Dim Cht As Chart

   Set Cht = Charts.Add
   With Cht
      .Name = "Mangoes"
      .ChartType = xlColumnClustered
      .SetSourceData Source:=Sheets("Sheet1").Range("A3:D7"), PlotBy:=xlRows
      .HasTitle = True
      .ChartTitle.Text = "=Sheet1!R3C1"
   End With
End Sub
```

The `Location` method has been removed, as it is not necessary. A chart sheet is produced by default. The Chart Wizard does not allow you to enter a formula to define a title in the chart, but you can separately record changing the chart title to a formula to discover that you need to set the `Text` property of the `ChartTitle` object equal to the formula. In the above code, the chart title has been defined as a formula referring to the value in cell R3C1, or A3.

When you enter a formula into a chart text element, it must be defined using the R1C1 addressing method, not the A1 addressing method.

Embedded Charts

When you create a chart embedded as a `ChartObject`, it is a good idea to name the `ChartObject` so that it can be easily referenced in later code. You can do this by manually selecting a worksheet cell, so that the chart is not selected, then holding down *Ctrl* and clicking the chart. This selects the `ChartObject`, rather than the chart, and you will see its name to the left of the Formula bar at the top of the screen.

This is how you can tell that you have selected the `ChartObject`: not only does its name appear in the name box to the left of formula bar, but you will also see white boxes (white circles in Excel 2002) at each corner of the embedded chart and the middle of each edge, as shown below. If you select the **chart**, rather than the `ChartObject`, you will see black boxes.

You can select and change the name of the `ChartObject` in the name box and press *Enter* to update it. The following embedded chart was created using the Chart Wizard. It was then dragged to its new location and had its name changed to `MangoesChart`:

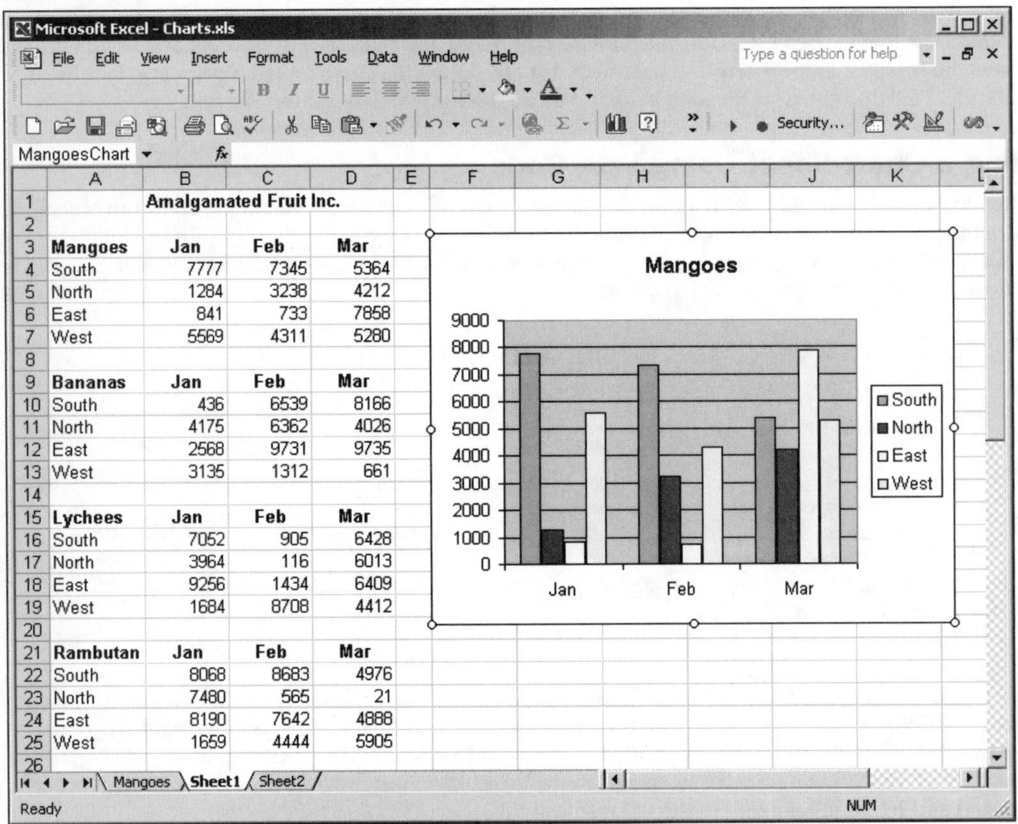

	A	B	C	D
1		Amalgamated Fruit Inc.		
2				
3	Mangoes	Jan	Feb	Mar
4	South	7777	7345	5364
5	North	1284	3238	4212
6	East	841	733	7858
7	West	5569	4311	5280
8				
9	Bananas	Jan	Feb	Mar
10	South	436	6539	8166
11	North	4175	6362	4026
12	East	2568	9731	9735
13	West	3135	1312	661
14				
15	Lychees	Jan	Feb	Mar
16	South	7052	905	6428
17	North	3964	116	6013
18	East	9256	1434	6409
19	West	1684	8708	4412
20				
21	Rambutan	Jan	Feb	Mar
22	South	8068	8683	4976
23	North	7480	565	21
24	East	8190	7642	4888
25	West	1659	4444	5905

Using the Macro Recorder

If you select cells A3:D7 and turn on the macro recorder before creating the chart above, including moving the `ChartObject` to the required location and changing its name to `MangoesChart`, you will get code like the following:

```
    Charts.Add
    ActiveChart.ChartType = xlColumnClustered
    ActiveChart.SetSourceData Source:=Sheets("Sheet1").Range("A3:D7"), _
                                                              PlotBy:= xlRows
    ActiveChart.Location Where:=xlLocationAsObject, Name:="Sheet1"
    With ActiveChart
       .HasTitle = True
       .ChartTitle.Characters.Text = "Mangoes"
       .Axes(xlCategory, xlPrimary).HasTitle = False
       .Axes(xlValue, xlPrimary).HasTitle = False
    End With
    ActiveSheet.Shapes("Chart 30").IncrementLeft 65.25
    ActiveSheet.Shapes("Chart 30").IncrementTop -54.75
    ActiveWindow.Visible = False
    Windows("Charts.xls").Activate
    Range("F17").Select
    ActiveSheet.Shapes("Chart 30").Select
    Selection.Name = "MangoesChart"
```

The recorded macro is similar to the one that created a chart sheet, down to the definition of the chart title, except that it uses the `Location` method to define the chart as an embedded chart. Up to the `End With`, the recorded code is reusable. However, the code to relocate the `ChartObject` and change its name is not reusable. The code uses the default name applied to the `ChartObject` to identify the `ChartObject`. (Note that the recorder prefers to refer to a `ChartObject` as a `Shape` object, which is an alternative that we pointed out at the beginning of this chapter.)

If you try to run this code again, or adapt it to create another chart, it will fail on the reference to `Chart 30`, or whichever shape you created when you recorded the macro. It is not as obvious how to refer to the `ChartObject` itself as how to refer to the active chart sheet.

Adding an Embedded Chart Using VBA Code

The following code uses the `Parent` property of the embedded chart to identify the `ChartObject` containing the chart:

```
Sub AddChart()
   Dim Cht As Chart

   ActiveSheet.ChartObjects.Delete
   Set Cht = Charts.Add
   Set Cht = Cht.Location(Where:=xlLocationAsObject, Name:="Sheet1")
   With Cht
      .ChartType = xlColumnClustered
      .SetSourceData Source:=Sheets("Sheet1").Range("A3:D7"), PlotBy:= _
                                                                  xlRows
      .HasTitle = True
      .ChartTitle.Text = "=Sheet1!R3C1"
      With .Parent
         .Top = Range("F3").Top
         .Left = Range("F3").Left
         .Name = "MangoesChart"
      End With
   End With
End Sub
```

`AddChart` first deletes any existing `ChartObjects`. It then sets the object variable `Cht` to refer to the added chart. By default, the new chart is on a chart sheet, so the `Location` method is used to define the chart as an embedded chart.

> **When you use the `Location` method of the `Chart` object, the `Chart` object is re-created and any reference to the original `Chart` object is destroyed. Therefore, it is necessary to assign the return value of the `Location` method to the `Cht` object variable so that it refers to the new `Chart` object.**

`AddChart` defines the chart type, source data, and chart title. Again, the chart title has been assigned a formula referring to cell A3. Using the `Parent` property of the `Chart` object to refer to the `ChartObject` object, `AddChart` sets the `Top` and `Left` properties of the `ChartObject` to be the same as the `Top` and `Left` properties of cell F3. `AddChart` finally assigns the new name to the `ChartObject` so that it can easily be referenced in the future.

Editing Data Series

The `SetSourceData` method of the `Chart` object is the quickest way to define a completely new set of data for a chart. You can also manipulate individual series using the `Series` object, which is a member of the chart's `SeriesCollection` object. The following example is designed to show you how to access individual series.

We will take the `MangoesChart` and delete all the series from it, and then replace them with four new series, one at a time. The new chart will contain product information for a region nominated by the user. To make it easier to locate each set of product data, names have been assigned to each product range in the worksheet. For example, A3:D7 has been given the name `Mangoes`, corresponding to the label in A3. The final chart will be similar to the following:

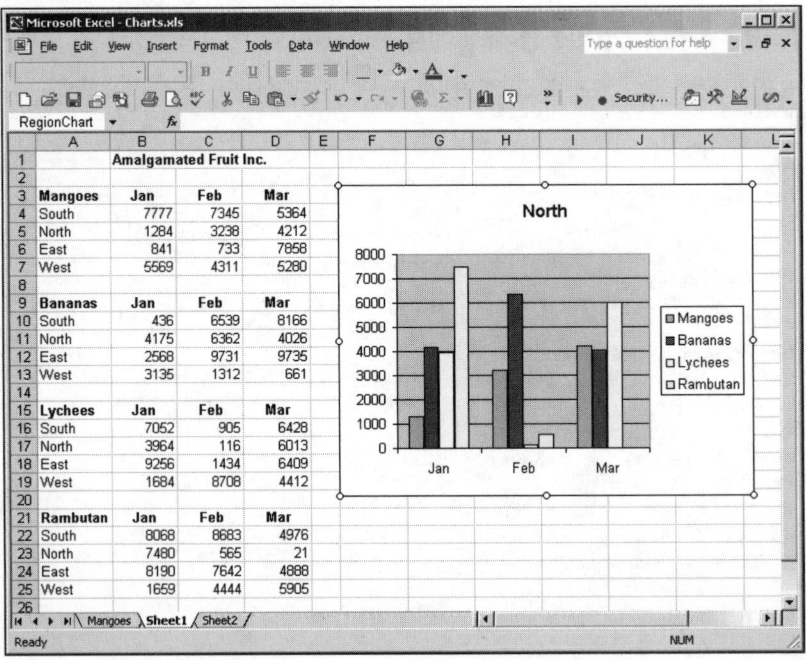

	A	B	C	D
1		Amalgamated Fruit Inc.		
2				
3	Mangoes	Jan	Feb	Mar
4	South	7777	7345	5364
5	North	1284	3238	4212
6	East	841	733	7858
7	West	5569	4311	5280
8				
9	Bananas	Jan	Feb	Mar
10	South	436	6539	8166
11	North	4175	6362	4026
12	East	2568	9731	9735
13	West	3135	1312	661
14				
15	Lychees	Jan	Feb	Mar
16	South	7052	905	6428
17	North	3964	116	6013
18	East	9256	1434	6409
19	West	1684	8708	4412
20				
21	Rambutan	Jan	Feb	Mar
22	South	8068	8683	4976
23	North	7480	565	21
24	East	8190	7642	4888
25	West	1659	4444	5905

The following code converts `MangoesChart` to include the new data (note that the original chart must still be on the spreadsheet for this to work). As `MangoesToRegion` is a fairly long procedure, we will examine it in sections:

```
Sub MangoesToRegion()
  Dim ctObject As ChartObject
  Dim Cht As Chart
  Dim scSeries As SeriesCollection
  Dim i As Integer
  Dim j As Integer
  Dim rgY As Range
  Dim rgX As Range
  Dim vaProducts As Variant
  Dim vaRegions As Variant
  Dim iRegion As Integer
  Dim Answer As Variant

  vaProducts = Array("Mangoes", "Bananas", "Lychees", "Rambutan")
  vaRegions = Array("South", "North", "East", "West")

  'Determine that MangoesChart exists
  On Error Resume Next
  Set ctObject = Worksheets("Sheet1").ChartObjects("MangoesChart")
  If ctObject Is Nothing Then
    MsgBox "MangoesChart was not found - procedure aborted", vbCritical
    Exit Sub
  End If
  On Error GoTo 0
```

`MangoesToRegion` first assigns the product names to `vaProducts` and the region names to `vaRegions`. It then tries to set the `ctObject` object variable by assigning the variable a reference to the `ChartObject` named `MangoesChart`. If this fails, the procedure is aborted. As it is not the main point of the exercise, this section of code has been kept very simple:

```
  'Get Region number
  Do 'While Answer < 1 Or Answer > 4
    Answer = InputBox("Enter Region number (1 to 4)")
    If Answer = "" Then Exit Sub
    If Answer >= 1 And Answer <= 4 Then
      Exit Do
    Else
      MsgBox "Region must be be 1, 2, 3 or 4", vbCritical
    End If
  Loop
  iRegion = CInt(Answer)
```

The user is then asked to enter the region number. The `Do...Loop` will continue until the user presses **Cancel**, presses **OK** without entering anything, or enters a number between 1 and 4. If a number between 1 and 4 is entered, the value is converted to an integer value, using the `CInt` function, and assigned to `iRegion`:

```
  'Set up new chart
  Set Cht = ctObject.Chart
  Set scSeries = Cht.SeriesCollection
```

```
'Delete all existing chart series
For i = scSeries.Count To 1 Step -1
  scSeries(i).Delete
Next i
```

Next, `Cht` is assigned a reference to the chart in the `ChartObject`. Then `scSeries` is assigned a reference to the `SeriesCollection` in the chart. The following `For...Next` loop deletes all the members of the collection. This is done backwards because deleting the lower number series first automatically decreases the item numbers of the higher series. In this case there will be no series 3 when you try to delete it, which will cause a run-time error. Alternatively, we could have deleted series 1 each time around the loop and the direction of the loop would not have mattered:

```
'Add Products for Region
For i = LBound(vaProducts) To UBound(vaProducts)
  Set rgY = Range(vaProducts(i)).Offset(iRegion, 1).Resize(1, 3)
  Set rgX = Range(vaProducts(i)).Offset(0, 1).Resize(1, 3)
  With scSeries.NewSeries
    .Name = vaProducts(i)
    .Values = rgY
    .XValues = "=" & rgX.Address _
        (RowAbsolute:=True, _
        ColumnAbsolute:=True, _
        ReferenceStyle:=xlR1C1, _
        External:=True)
  End With
Next i
```

The `For...Next` loop adds a new series to the chart for each product. The loop uses the `UBound` and `LBound` functions to avoid having to know the `Option Base` setting for the module. The range object `rgY` is assigned a reference to the chosen region data within the current product data.

`Range(vaProducts(i))` refers to the product table with the worksheet name corresponding to `vaProducts(i)`. `iRegion` is used as the row offset into the product data to refer to the correct region data. The column offset is one so that the name of the region is excluded from the data. `Resize` ensures that the data range has one row and three columns. The range object `rgX` is assigned a reference to the month names at the top of the product data table.

Following the `With` statement, `MangoesToRegion` uses the `NewSeries` method to add a new empty series to the chart. The `NewSeries` method returns a reference to the new series, which supplies the `With...End With` reference that is used by the lines between `With` and `End With`. The `Name` property of the series, which appears in the legend, is assigned the current product name.

The `Values` property of the new series is assigned a reference to `rgY`. The `XValues` property could have been assigned a direct reference to `rgX` in the same way. However, both properties can also be defined by a formula reference, as long as it is an external reference in the R1C1 style. This code has been written to show how this can be done, as it is necessary to do this with some other properties, such as the `ChartTitle` property when you want it to refer to a worksheet cell. The string value generated and assigned to the `Mangoes` series `XValues` property is:

```
=Sheet1!R3C2:R3C4
```

The final section of code is as follows:

```
    Cht.ChartTitle.Text = vaRegions(iRegion - 1 + LBound(vaRegions))
    ctObject.Name = "RegionChart"
End Sub
```

The `ChartTitle.Text` property is assigned the appropriate string value in the `vaRegions` array, using the value of `iRegion` as an index to the array. To avoid having to know the `Option Base` setting for the module, `Array(0,1)(1)` has been used to adjust the index value in `iRegion`, which ranges from 1 to 4. If the `Option Base` setting is zero, this expression returns a value of one, which adjusts the value of `iRegion` such that it ranges from 0 to 3. If the `Option Base` setting is one, the expression returns zero, which does not change the `iRegion` value so that it still has the range of 1 to 4. Another way to handle the `Option Base` is to use the following code:

```
    Cht.ChartTitle.Text = vaRegions(iRegion - 1 + LBound(vaRegions))
```

The code finally changes the name of the `ChartObject` to `RegionChart`.

Defining Chart Series with Arrays

A chart series can be defined by assigning a VBA array to its `Values` property. This can come in handy if you want to generate a chart that is not linked to the original data. The chart can be distributed in a separate workbook that is independent of the source data.

The following screenshot shows a chart of the `Mangoes` data. You can see the definition of the first data series in the Formula bar above the worksheet. The month names and the values on the vertical axis are defined by Excel arrays. The region names have been assigned as text to the series names:

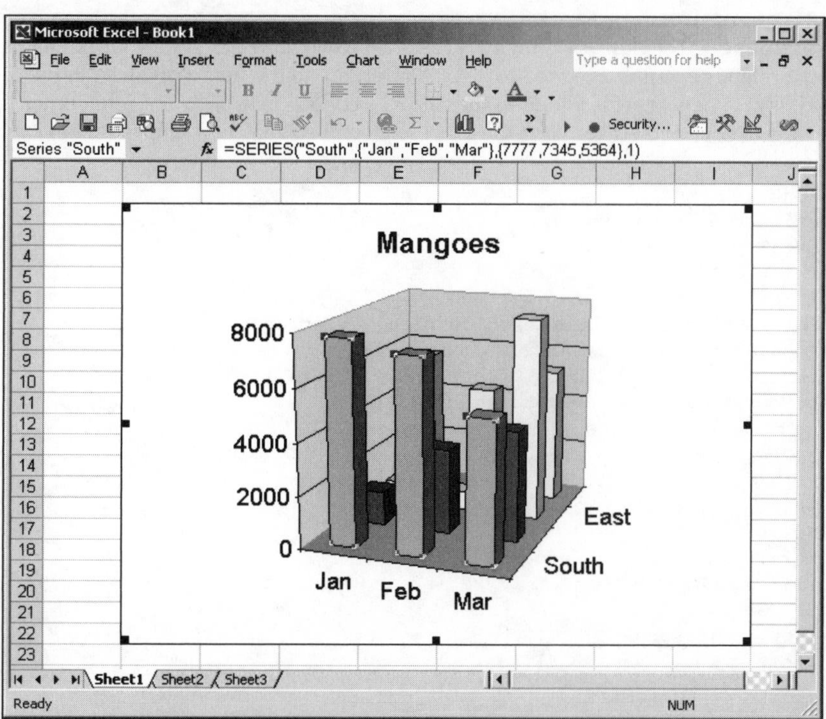

The size of an array used in the `SERIES` function is limited to around 250 characters. This limits the number of data points that can be plotted this way.

The 3D chart can be created using the following code:

```
Sub MakeArrayChart()
  Dim wsSource As Worksheet
  Dim rgSource As Range
  Dim Wkb As Workbook
  Dim Wks As Worksheet
  Dim Cht As Chart
  Dim seNewSeries As Series
  Dim i As Integer
  Dim vaSalesArray As Variant
  Dim vaMonthArray As Variant

  vaMonthArray = Array("Jan", "Feb", "Mar")
  'Define the data source
  Set wsSource = ThisWorkbook.Worksheets("Sheet1")
  Set rgSource = wsSource.Range("Mangoes")
  'Create a new workbook
  Set Wkb = Workbooks.Add
  Set Wks = Wkb.Worksheets(1)
  'Add a new chart object and embed it in the worksheet
  Set Cht = Wkb.Charts.Add
  Set Cht = Cht.Location(Where:=xlLocationAsObject, Name:="Sheet1")
```

`MakeArrayChart` assigns the month names to `vaMonthArray`. This data could have come from the worksheet, if required, like the sales data. A reference to the worksheet that is the source of the data is assigned to `wsSource`. The `Mangoes` range is assigned to `rgSource`. A new workbook is created for the chart and a reference to it is assigned to `Wkb`. A reference to the first worksheet in the new workbook is assigned to `Wks`. A new chart is added to the `Charts` collection in `Wkb` and a reference to it assigned to `Cht`. The `Location` method converts the chart to an embedded chart and redefines `Cht`:

```
  With Cht
    'Define the chart type
    .ChartType = xl3DColumn
    For i = 1 To 4
      'Create a new series
      Set seNewSeries = .SeriesCollection.NewSeries
      'Assign the data as arrays
      vaSalesArray = rgSource.Offset(i, 1).Resize(1, 3).Value
      seNewSeries.Values = vaSalesArray
      seNewSeries.XValues = vaMonthArray
      seNewSeries.Name = rgSource.Cells(i + 1, 1).Value
    Next i
    .HasLegend = False
    .HasTitle = True
    .ChartTitle.Text = "Mangoes"
    'Position the ChartObject in B2:I22 and name it
    With .Parent
      .Top = Wks.Range("B2").Top
      .Left = Wks.Range("B2").Left
      .Width = Wks.Range("B2:I22").Width
      .Height = Wks.Range("B2:I22").Height
```

```
      .Name = "ArrayChart"
    End With
  End With
End Sub
```

In the With...End With structure, the ChartType property of Cht is changed to a 3D column type. The For...Next loop creates the four new series. Each time around the loop, a new series is created with the NewSeries method. The region data from the appropriate row is directly assigned to the variant vaSalesArray, and vaSalesArray is immediately assigned to Values property of the new series.

vaMonthArray is assigned to the XValues property of the new series. The text in column A of the Mangoes range is assigned to the Name property of the new series.

The code then removes the chart legend, which is added by default, and sets the chart title. The final code operates on the ChartObject, which is the chart's parent, to place the chart exactly over B2:I22, and name the chart ArrayChart.

The result is a chart in a new workbook that is quite independent of the original workbook and its data. If the chart had been copied and pasted into the new workbook, it would still be linked to the original data.

Converting a Chart to use Arrays

You can easily convert an existing chart to use arrays instead of cell references and make it independent of the original data is was based on. The following code shows how:

```
Sub ConvertSeriesValuesToArrays()
  Dim Ser As Series
  Dim Cht As Chart

  On Error GoTo Failure

  Set Cht = ActiveSheet.ChartObjects(1).Chart
  For Each Ser In Cht.SeriesCollection
    Ser.Values = Ser.Values
    Ser.XValues = Ser.XValues
    Ser.Name = Ser.Name
  Next Ser

  Exit Sub
Failure:
  MsgBox "Sorry, the data exceeds the array limits"
End Sub
```

For each series in the chart, the Values, XValues, and Name properties are set equal to themselves. Although these properties can be assigned range references, they always return an array of values when they are interrogated. This behavior can be exploited to convert the cell references to arrays.

Bear in mind that the number of data points that can be contained in an array reference is limited to 250 characters, or thereabouts. The code will fail if the limits are exceeded, so we have set up an error trap to cover this possibility.

Determining the Ranges used in a Chart

The behavior that is beneficial when converting a chart to use arrays is a problem when you need to programmatically determine the ranges that a chart is based on. If the `Values` and `Xvalues` properties returned the strings that you use to define them, the task would be easy.

The only property that contains information on the ranges is the `Formula` property that returns the formula containing the `SERIES` function as a string. The formula would be like the following:

```
=SERIES("Mangoes", Sheet1!$B$3:$D$3, Sheet1!$B$5:$D$5,1)
```

The `XValues` are defined by the second parameter and the `Values` by the third parameter. You need to locate the commas and extract the text between them as shown in the following code, designed to work with a chart embedded in the active sheet:

```
Sub GetRangesFromChart()
  Dim Ser As Series
  Dim stSeriesFunction As String
  Dim iFirstComma As Integer, iSecondComma As Integer, _
                                                  iThirdComma As Integer
  Dim stValueRange As String, stXValueRange As String
  Dim rgValueRange As Range, rgXValueRange As Range

  On Error GoTo Oops

  'Get the SERIES function from the first series in the chart
  Set Ser = ActiveSheet.ChartObjects(1).Chart.SeriesCollection(1)
  stSeriesFunction = Ser.Formula
  'Locate the commas
  iFirstComma = InStr(1, stSeriesFunction, ",")
  iSecondComma = InStr(iFirstComma + 1, stSeriesFunction, ",")
  iThirdComma = InStr(iSecondComma + 1, stSeriesFunction, ",")
  'Extract the range references as strings
  stXValueRange = Mid(stSeriesFunction, iFirstComma + 1, _
                               iSecondComma - iFirstComma - 1)
  stValueRange = Mid(stSeriesFunction, iSecondComma + 1, _
                               iThirdComma - iSecondComma - 1)
  'Convert the strings to range objects
  Set rgXValueRange = Range(stXValueRange)
  Set rgValueRange = Range(stValueRange)
  'Colour the ranges
  rgXValueRange.Interior.ColorIndex = 3
  rgValueRange.Interior.ColorIndex = 4
  Exit Sub
Oops:
  MsgBox "Sorry, an error has ocurred" & vbCr & _
    "This chart might not contain range references"
End Sub
```

`stSeriesFunction` is assigned the formula of the series, which contains the `SERIES` function as a string. The positions of the first, second, and third commas are found using the `InStr` function. The `Mid` function is used to extract the range references as strings and they are converted to `Range` objects using the `Range` property.

The conversion of the strings to `Range` objects works even when the range references are not on the same sheet or in the same workbook as the embedded chart, as long as the source data is in an open workbook.

You could then proceed to manipulate the `Range` objects. You can change cell values in the ranges, for example, or extend or contract the ranges, once you have programmatic control over them. We have just colored the ranges for illustration purposes.

Chart Labels

In Excel, it is easy to add data labels to a chart, as long as the labels are based on the data series values or X-axis values. These options are available using Chart | Chart Options.

You can also enter your own text as labels, or you can enter formulas into each label to refer to cells, but this involves a lot of manual work. You would need to add standard labels to the series and then individually select each one and either replace it with your own text, or click in the Formula bar and enter a formula. Alternatively, you can write a macro to do it for you.

The following screenshot shows a chart of sales figures for each month, with the name of the top salesperson for each month. The labels have been defined by formulas linked to row 4 of the worksheet, as you can see for Jenny in April. The formula in the Formula bar points to cell E4:

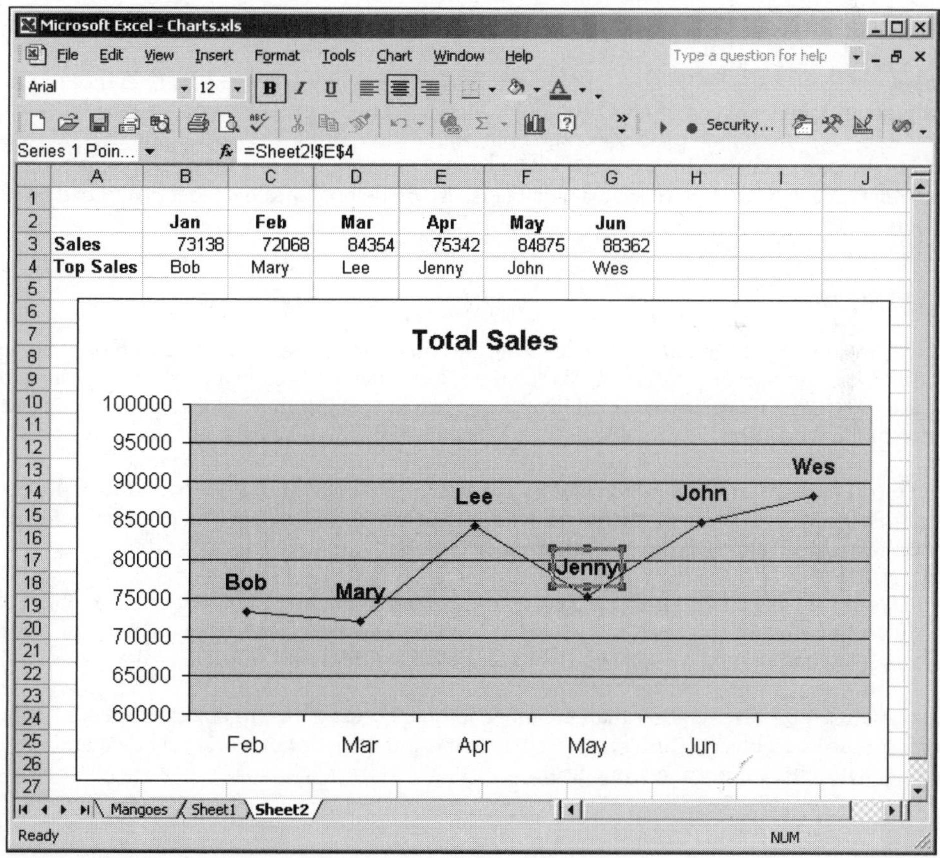

Say you have set up a line chart like the one above, but without the data labels. You can add the data labels and their formulas using the following code:

```
Sub AddDataLabels()
   Dim seSales As Series
   Dim Pts As Points
   Dim Pt As Point
   Dim Rng As Range
   Dim i As Integer

   Set Rng = Range("B4:G4")
   Set seSales = ActiveSheet.ChartObjects(1).Chart.SeriesCollection(1)
   seSales.HasDataLabels = True
   Set Pts = seSales.Points
   For Each Pt In Pts
      i = i + 1
      Pt.DataLabel.Text = "=" & Rng.Cells(i).Address _
                (RowAbsolute:=True, _
                 ColumnAbsolute:=True, _
                 ReferenceStyle:=xlR1C1, _
                 External:=True)
      Pt.DataLabel.Font.Bold = True
      Pt.DataLabel.Position = xlLabelPositionAbove
   Next Pt
End Sub
```

The object variable `Rng` is assigned a reference to B4:G4. `seSales` is assigned a reference to the first, and only, series in the embedded chart and the `HasDataLabels` property of the series is set to `True`. The `For Each...Next` loop processes each point in the data series. For each point, the code assigns a formula to the `Text` property of the point's data label. The formula refers to the worksheet cell as an external reference in R1C1 format. The data label is also made bold and the label positioned above the data point.

Summary

It is easy to create a programmatic reference to a chart on a chart sheet. The `Chart` object is a member of the `Charts` collection of the workbook. To reference a chart embedded in a worksheet, you need to be aware that the `Chart` object is contained in a `ChartObject` object that belongs to the `ChartObjects` collection of the worksheet.

You can move or resize an embedded chart by changing the `Top`, `Left`, `Width`, and `Height` properties of the `ChartObject`. If you already have a reference to the `Chart` object, you can get a reference to the `ChartObject` object through the `Parent` property of the `Chart` object.

Individual series in a chart are `Series` objects, and belong to the `SeriesCollection` object of the chart. The `Delete` method of the `Series` object is used to delete a series from a chart. You use the `NewSeries` method of the `SeriesCollection` object to add a new series to a chart.

You can assign a VBA array, rather than the more commonly used `Range` object, to the `Values` property of a `Series` object. This creates a chart that is independent of worksheet data and can be distributed without a supporting worksheet.

The `Values` and `XValues` properties return data values, not the range references used in a chart. You can determine the ranges referenced by a chart by examining the `SERIES` function in the `Formula` property of each series.

The data points in a chart are `Point` objects and belong to the `Points` collection of the `Series` object. Excel does not provide an easy way to link cell values to labels on series data points through the user interface. However, links can be easily established to data point labels using VBA code.

VBAProgrammersReferenceExcel20
mersReferenceExcel2002VB
ReferenceExcel2002VBAPro
ProgrammersReferenceExc
rammersReferenceExcel20
Excel2002VB
el2002VBAPro
cel2002VBAProgram
xcel2002VBAProgram
2002VBAProgrammersReferenceExcel
VBAProgrammersReference
rogrammersReferenceExcel
ammersReference
2002VBAProgrammersReferenceExce

10

Event Procedures

Excel makes it very easy for you to write code that runs when a range of worksheet, chart sheet, and workbook events occur. In previous chapters, we have already seen how to highlight the active row and column of a worksheet by placing code in the `Worksheet_SelectionChange` event procedure (see Chapter 2). This runs every time the user selects a new range of cells. We have also seen how to synchronize the worksheets in a workbook using the `Worksheet_Deactivate` and `Worksheet_Activate` events (see Chapter 4).

It is easy to create workbook, chart sheet, and worksheet events, because Excel automatically provides you with code modules for these objects. However, note that the chart events that are supplied automatically in a chart module apply only to chart sheets, not to embedded charts. If you want to write event procedures for embedded charts, you can do so, but it takes a bit more knowledge and effort.

There are also many other high-level events that can be accessed, for the `Application` object, for example. These events will be covered later on in Chapters 15 and 23 (*Class Modules* and *Programming the VBE*). Events associated with controls and forms will also be treated in their own chapters. In this chapter we will look, in more detail, at worksheet, chart, and workbook events and related issues.

> **Event procedures are always associated with a particular object and are contained in the class module that is associated with that object, such as the `ThisWorkbook` module or the code module behind a worksheet or a User Form. Don't try to place an event procedure in a standard module.**

Worksheet Events

The following worksheet event procedures are available in the code module behind each worksheet. `Worksheet_PivotTableUpdate` (highlighted below) is the only new addition for Excel 2002:

- `Private Sub Worksheet_Activate()`
- `Private Sub Worksheet_BeforeDoubleClick(ByVal Target As Range, Cancel As Boolean)`
- `Private Sub Worksheet_BeforeRightClick(ByVal Target As Range, Cancel As Boolean)`

- `Private Sub Worksheet_Calculate()`
- `Private Sub Worksheet_Change(ByVal Target As Range)`
- `Private Sub Worksheet_Deactivate()`
- `Private Sub Worksheet_FollowHyperlink(ByVal Target As Hyperlink)`
- **`Private Sub Worksheet_PivotTableUpdate(ByVal Target As PivotTable`**`)`
- `Private Sub Worksheet_SelectionChange(ByVal Target As Range)`

You should use the drop-down menus at the top of the code module to create the first and last lines of any procedure you want to use. For example, in a worksheet code module, you can select the `Worksheet` object from the left-hand drop-down list. This will generate the following lines of code:

```
Private Sub Worksheet_SelectionChange(ByVal Target As Range)
...
End Sub
```

The `SelectionChange` event is the default event for the `Worksheet` object. If you want a different event, select the event from the right-hand drop-down list, and delete the lines above.

As an alternative to using the dropdowns, you can type the first line of the procedure yourself, but by doing so, it's easy to make mistakes. The arguments must correspond, in number, order, and type with those shown above. You are permitted to use different parameter names, if you wish, but it is better to stick with the standard names to avoid confusion.

Most parameters must be declared with the `ByVal` keyword, which prevents your code from passing back changes to the object or item referenced by assigning a new value to the parameter. If the parameter represents an object, you can change the object's properties and execute its methods, but you cannot pass back a change in the object definition by assigning a new object definition to the parameter.

Some event procedures are executed before the associated event occurs and have a `Cancel` parameter that is passed by reference. You can assign a value of `True` to the `Cancel` parameter to cancel the associated event. For example, you could prevent a user accessing the worksheet shortcut menu by canceling the `RightClick` event in the `Worksheet_BeforeRightClick` event procedure:

```
Private Sub Worksheet_BeforeRightClick(ByVal Target As Range, _
                                        Cancel As Boolean)
   Cancel = True
End Sub
```

Enable Events

It is important to turn off event handling in some event procedures to prevent unwanted infinite recursion. For example, if a worksheet `Change` event procedure changes the worksheet, it will itself trigger the `Change` event and run itself again. The event procedure will change the worksheet again and trigger the `Change` event again, and so on.

If only one event procedure is involved, Excel 2000 and 2002 will usually detect the recursion and terminate it after some hundreds of cycles (whereas Excel 97 will stop after about 40 cycles). If more than one event procedure is involved, the process can continue indefinitely or until you press *Esc* or *Ctrl+Break* enough times to stop each process.

For example, there could be a `Calculation` event procedure active as well as a `Change` event procedure. If both procedures change a cell that is referenced in a calculation, both events are triggered into an interactive chain reaction. That is, the first event triggers the second event, which triggers the first event again, and so on. The following `Change` event procedure makes sure that it does not cause a chain reaction by turning off event handling while it changes the worksheet. It is important to turn event handling back on again before the procedure ends:

```
Private Sub Worksheet_Change(ByVal Target As Range)
   Application.EnableEvents = False
   Range("A1").Value = 100
   Application.EnableEvents = True
End Sub
```

`Application.EnableEvents = False` does not affect events outside the Excel Object Model. Events associated with ActiveX controls and user forms, for example, will continue to occur.

Worksheet Calculate

The `Worksheet_Calculate` event occurs whenever the worksheet is recalculated. It is usually triggered when you enter new data into cells that are referenced in formulas in the worksheet. You could use the `Worksheet_Calculate` event to warn you, as you enter new data assumptions into a forecast, when key results go outside their expected range of values. In the following worksheet, you want to know when the profit figure in cell N8 exceeds 600 or is lower than 500:

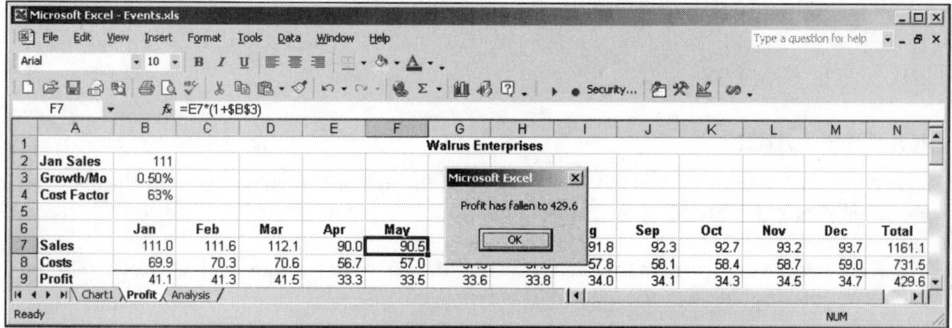

The following event procedure runs every time the worksheet recalculates, checks cell N8, which has been named `FinalProfit`, and generates messages if the figure goes outside the required band of values:

```
Private Sub Worksheet_Calculate()
   Dim dProfit As Double

   dProfit = Sheet2.Range("FinalProfit").Value
   If dProfit > 600 Then
      MsgBox "Profit has risen to " & Format(dProfit, "#,##0.0")
   ElseIf dProfit < 500 Then
      MsgBox "Profit has fallen to " & Format(dProfit, "#,##0.0")
   End If
End Sub
```

Chart Events

The following chart event procedures are available in the code module for each chart object:

- `Private Sub Chart_Activate()`
- `Private Sub Chart_BeforeDoubleClick(ByVal ElementID As Long, ByVal Arg1 As Long, ByVal Arg2 As Long, Cancel As Boolean)`
- `Private Sub Chart_BeforeRightClick(Cancel As Boolean)`
- `Private Sub Chart_Calculate()`
- `Private Sub Chart_Deactivate()`
- `Private Sub Chart_DragOver()`
- `Private Sub Chart_DragPlot()`
- `Private Sub Chart_MouseDown(ByVal Button As XlMouseButton, ByVal Shift As Long, ByVal x As Long, ByVal y As Long)`
- `Private Sub Chart_MouseMove(ByVal Button As XlMouseButton, ByVal Shift As Long, ByVal x As Long, ByVal y As Long)`
- `Private Sub Chart_MouseUp(ByVal Button As XlMouseButton, ByVal Shift As Long, ByVal x As Long, ByVal y As Long)`
- `Private Sub Chart_Resize()`
- `Private Sub Chart_Select(ByVal ElementID As XlChartItem, ByVal Arg1 As Long, ByVal Arg2 As Long)`
- `Private Sub Chart_SeriesChange(ByVal SeriesIndex As Long, ByVal PointIndex As Long)`

Before Double Click

Normally, when you double-click a chart element, you open the formatting dialog box for the element. You could provide some shortcut formatting by trapping the double-click event and writing your own code.

The following event procedure formats three chart elements when they are double-clicked. If, in the chart shown below, you double-click the legend, it is removed:

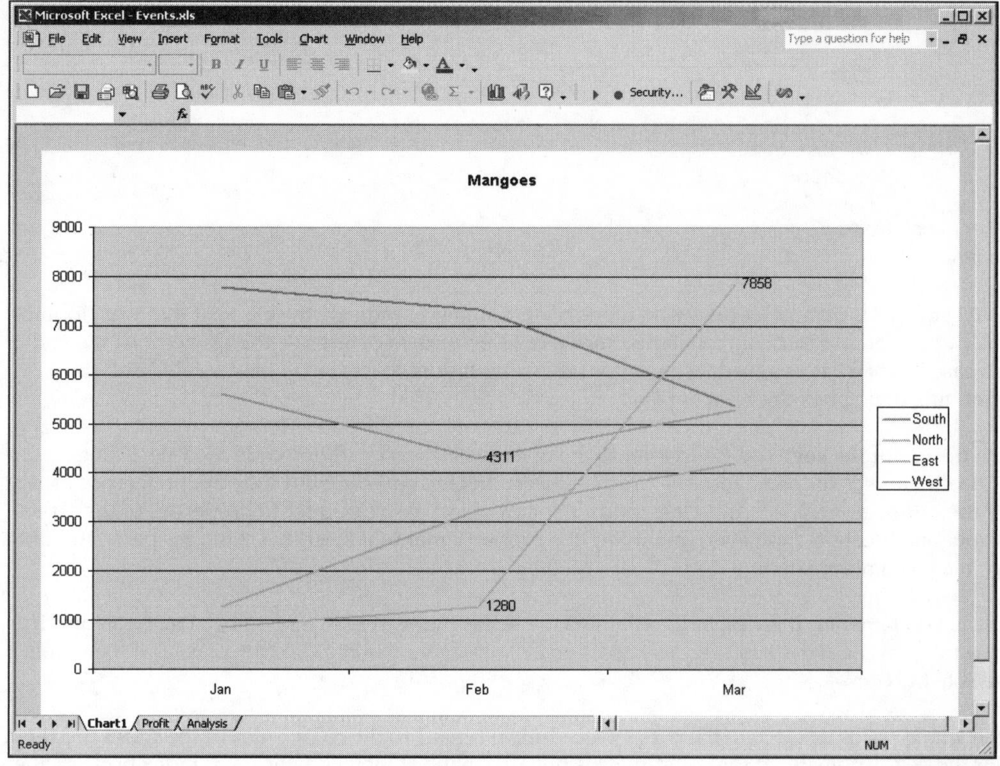

If you double-click the chart area (around the outside of the plot area), the legend is displayed. If you double-click a series line with all points selected, it changes the color of the line. If a single point in the series is selected, the data label at the point is toggled on and off:

```
Private Sub Chart_BeforeDoubleClick(ByVal ElementID As Long, _
            ByVal Arg1 As Long, ByVal Arg2 As Long, Cancel As Boolean)
   Dim Srs As Series

   Select Case ElementID
      Case xlLegend
         Me.HasLegend = False
         Cancel = True
      Case xlChartArea
         Me.HasLegend = True
         Cancel = True
      Case xlSeries
         'Arg1 is the Series index
         'Arg2 is the Point index (-1 if the entire series is selected)
         Set Srs = Me.SeriesCollection(Arg1)
         If Arg2 = -1 Then
            With Srs.Border
               If .ColorIndex = xlColorIndexAutomatic Then
                  .ColorIndex = 1
               Else
                  .ColorIndex = (.ColorIndex Mod 56) + 1
```

```
            End If
         End With
      Else
         With Srs.Points(Arg2)
            .HasDataLabel = Not .HasDataLabel
         End With
      End If
      Cancel = True
   End Select
End Sub
```

The ElementID parameter passes an identifying number to indicate the element that was double-clicked. You can use intrinsic constants, such as xlLegend, to determine the element. At the end of each case, Cancel is assigned True so that the default double-click event is canceled and the Formatting dialog box does not appear.

Note the use of the keyword Me to refer to the object associated with the code module. Using Me instead of Chart1 makes the code portable to other charts. In fact, you can omit the object reference "Me." and use "HasLegend =". In a class module for an object, you can refer to properties of the object without qualification. However, qualifying the property makes it clear that it is a property and not a variable you have created.

If the chart element is a series, Arg1 contains the series index in the SeriesCollection and if a single point in the series has been selected Arg2 contains the point index. Arg2 is -1 if the whole series is selected.

If the whole series is selected, the event procedure assigns 1 to the color index of the series border, if the color index is automatic. If the color index is not automatic, it increases the color index by 1. As there are only 56 colors available, the procedure uses the Mod operator, which divides the color index by 56 and gives the remainder, before adding 1. The only color index value that is affected by this is 56. 56 Mod 56 returns zero, which means that the next color index after 56 is 1.

If a single point is selected in the series, the procedure toggles the data label for the point. If the HasDataLabel property of the point is True, Not converts it to False. If the HasDataLabel property of the point is False, Not converts it to True.

Workbook Events

The following workbook event procedures are available. Again, those new to Excel 2002 are highlighted in bold:

- Private Sub Workbook_Activate()
- Private Sub Workbook_AddinInstall()
- Private Sub Workbook_AddinUninstall()
- Private Sub Workbook_BeforeClose(Cancel As Boolean)
- Private Sub Workbook_BeforePrint(Cancel As Boolean)
- Private Sub Workbook_BeforeSave(ByVal SaveAsUI As Boolean, Cancel As Boolean)

- `Private Sub Workbook_Deactivate()`
- `Private Sub Workbook_NewSheet(ByVal Sh As Object)`
- `Private Sub Workbook_Open()`
- **`Private Sub Workbook_PivotTableCloseConnection(ByVal Target As PivotTable)`**
- **`Private Sub Workbook_PivotTableOpenConnection(ByVal Target As PivotTable)`**
- `Private Sub Workbook_SheetActivate(ByVal Sh As Object)`
- `Private Sub Workbook_SheetBeforeDoubleClick(ByVal Sh As Object, ByVal Target As Range, Cancel As Boolean)`
- `Private Sub Workbook_SheetBeforeRightClick(ByVal Sh As Object, ByVal Target As Range, Cancel As Boolean)`
- `Private Sub Workbook_SheetCalculate(ByVal Sh As Object)`
- `Private Sub Workbook_SheetChange(ByVal Sh As Object, ByVal Target As Range)`
- `Private Sub Workbook_SheetDeactivate(ByVal Sh As Object)`
- `Private Sub Workbook_SheetFollowHyperlink(ByVal Sh As Object, ByVal Target As Hyperlink)`
- **`Private Sub Workbook_SheetPivotTableUpdate(ByVal Sh As Object, ByVal Target As PivotTable)`**
- `Private Sub Workbook_SheetSelectionChange(ByVal Sh As Object, ByVal Target As Range)`
- `Private Sub Workbook_WindowActivate(ByVal Wn As Window)`
- `Private Sub Workbook_WindowDeactivate(ByVal Wn As Window)`
- `Private Sub Workbook_WindowResize(ByVal Wn As Window)`

Some of the workbook event procedures are the same as the worksheet and chart event procedures. The difference is that when you create these procedures (such as the `Change` event procedure) in a worksheet or chart, it applies to only that sheet. When you create a workbook event procedure (such as the `SheetChange` event procedure) it applies to all the sheets in the workbook.

One of the most commonly used workbook event procedures is the `Open` event procedure. This is used to initialize the workbook when it opens. You can use it to set the calculation mode, establish screen settings, alter the menu structure, decide what toolbars should appear, or enter data into combo boxes or listboxes in the worksheets.

Similarly, the `Workbook_BeforeClose` event procedure can be used to tidy up when the workbook is closed. It can restore screen and menu settings, for example. It can also be used to prevent a workbook's closure by setting `Cancel` to `True`. The following event procedure will only allow the workbook to close if the figure in the cell named `FinalProfit` is between 500 and 600:

```
Private Sub Workbook_BeforeClose(Cancel As Boolean)
   Dim dProfit As Double
```

```
    dProfit = ThisWorkbook.Worksheets(1).Range("FinalProfit").Value
    If dProfit < 500 Or dProfit > 600 Then
       MsgBox "Profit must be in the range 500 to 600"
       Cancel = True
    End If
End Sub
```

Note that if you assign `True` to `Cancel` in the workbook `BeforeClose` event procedure, you also prevent Excel closing.

Save Changes

If you want to make sure that all changes are saved when the workbook closes, but you don't want the user to be prompted to save changes, you can save the workbook in the `BeforeClose` event procedure. You can check to see if this is really necessary using the `Saved` property of the workbook, which will be `False` if there are unsaved changes:

```
Private Sub Workbook_BeforeClose(Cancel As Boolean)
   If Not ThisWorkbook.Saved Then
      ThisWorkbook.Save
   End If
End Sub
```

If, on the other hand, you want to discard any changes to the workbook and you don't want users to be prompted to save changes in a workbook when they close it, you can set the `Saved` property of the workbook to `True` in the `BeforeClose` event procedure:

```
Private Sub Workbook_BeforeClose(Cancel As Boolean)
   ThisWorkbook.Saved = True
End Sub
```

This fools Excel into thinking that any changes have been saved.

Headers and Footers

A common need in Excel is to print information in the page header or footer that either comes from the worksheet cells, or is not available in the standard header and footer options. You might want to insert a company name that is part of the data in the worksheet and display the full path to the workbook file.

The full path and file name is available as an option in headers and footers in Excel 2002. You still need to use code like the following to insert text from worksheet cells. You can insert this information using the `BeforePrint` event procedure to ensure it is always up to date in reports. The following procedure puts the text in cell A1 of the worksheet named `Profit` in the left footer, clears the center footer and puts the full file name in the right footer. It applies the changes to every worksheet in the file:

```
Private Sub Workbook_BeforePrint(Cancel As Boolean)
   Dim Wks As Worksheet
   Dim stFullFileName As String
   Dim stCompanyName As String

   stCompanyName = Worksheets("Profit").Range("A1").Value
```

```
    stFullFileName = ThisWorkbook.FullName
    For Each Wks In ThisWorkbook.Worksheets
       With Wks.PageSetup
          .LeftFooter = stCompanyName
          .CenterFooter = ""
          .RightFooter = stFullFileName
       End With
    Next Wks
End Sub
```

The footer can be seen in a **Print Preview** as follows:

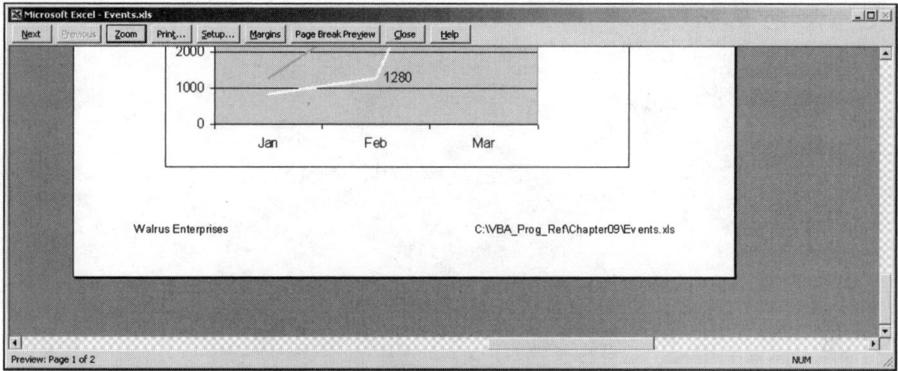

Summary

In this section you have seen some useful examples of how to utilize event procedures to respond to user actions.

You have been introduced to worksheet, chart, and workbook events. We've also delved a little deeper into the following events:

- `Worksheet_Calculate`
- `Chart_BeforeDoubleClick`
- `Workbook_BeforeClose`
- `Workbook_BeforePrint`

VBA is essentially an event-driven language, so a good knowledge of the events at your disposal can open up a whole new world of functionality you never knew existed.

To find out more, have a play with the Object Browser, and consult the object model in Appendix A.

11

Adding Controls

As we have already discussed in Chapter 2, you can add two different types of controls to Excel worksheets. You can use ActiveX controls, found on the Control Toolbox toolbar, or the controls from the Forms toolbar. The Forms toolbar is an Excel 5 and Excel 95 feature, and provided controls for the dialog sheets used in those versions, as well as controls that can be embedded in a worksheet or chart. Dialog sheets have been superseded by UserForms since the release of Excel 97, and UserForms utilize the ActiveX controls.

The Toolbars

The Forms toolbar controls and dialog sheets are still supported in Excel, however. The Forms toolbar controls even have some advantages over the ActiveX controls:

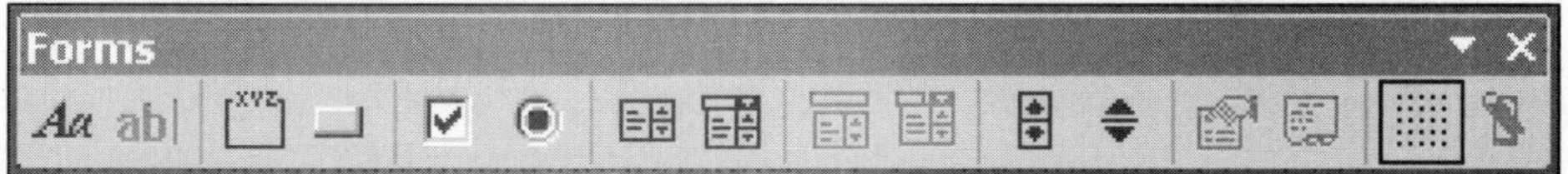

They are less complex than the ActiveX controls and, if you want to place controls on a chart sheet, you can only use the Forms toolbar controls. However, each Forms toolbar control can only respond to a single event. In most cases, that event is the `Click` event – the edit box is an exception, responding to the `Change` event.

If you want to create controls and define their event procedures in your VBA code, as opposed to creating them manually, the Forms toolbar controls are easier to work with. A big advantage over an ActiveX control is that the event procedure for a Forms toolbar control can be placed in a standard module, can have any valid VBA procedure name, and can be created when you write the code for the application, before the control is created.

You can create the control programmatically, when it is needed, and assign the procedure name to the `OnAction` property of the control. You can even assign the same procedure to more than one control. On the other hand, ActiveX event procedures must be placed in the class module behind the worksheet or user form in which they are embedded, and must have a procedure name that corresponds with the name of the control and the name of the event. For example, the click event procedure for a control named `Optionbutton1` must be as follows:

```
Sub OptionButton1_Click()
```

If you try to create an event procedure for an ActiveX control before the control exists, and you try to reference that control in your code, you will get compiler errors, so you have to create the event procedure programmatically. This is not an easy task as you will see below. In addition, see Chapter 23 for an example of adding an event procedure programmatically to a User Form control.

On the other hand, a procedure that is executed by a Forms toolbar control does not need to have a special name and can use the `Caller` property of the `Application` object to obtain a reference to the control that executes it. The control name does not need to be included in the name of the procedure or in references to the control, as you will see later in this chapter.

ActiveX Controls

The following screenshot shows four types of ActiveX controls embedded in the worksheet (`Controls.xls` is available for download from http://www.wrox.com). The scrollbar in cells C3:F3 allows you to set the value in cell B3. The spin button in cell C4 increments the growth percentage in cell B4. The checkbox in cell B5 increases the tax rate in cell B16 from 30% to 33%, if it is checked. The option buttons in column I change the cost factor in cell B15 and also change the maximum and minimum values for the scrollbar:

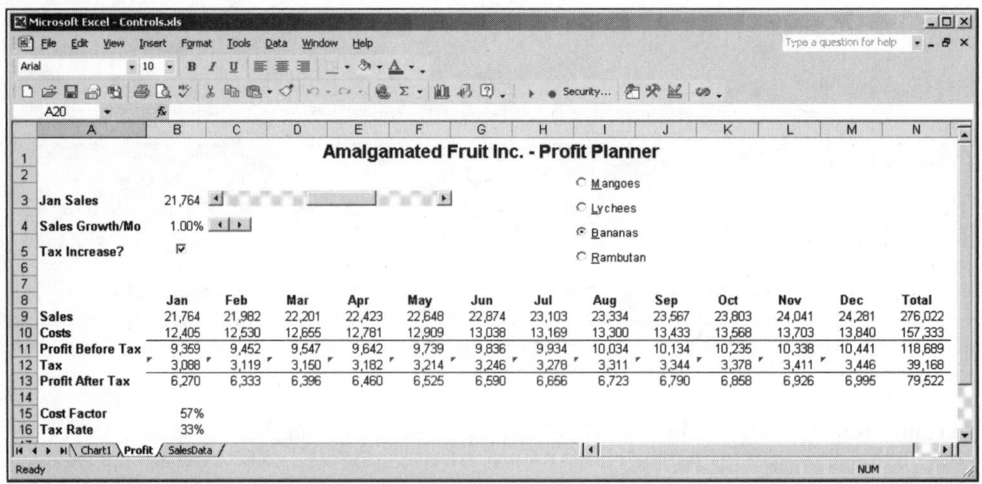

	Jan	Feb	Mar	Apr	May	Jun	Jul	Aug	Sep	Oct	Nov	Dec	Total
Sales	21,764	21,982	22,201	22,423	22,648	22,874	23,103	23,334	23,567	23,803	24,041	24,281	276,022
Costs	12,405	12,530	12,655	12,781	12,909	13,038	13,169	13,300	13,433	13,568	13,703	13,840	157,333
Profit Before Tax	9,359	9,452	9,547	9,642	9,739	9,836	9,934	10,034	10,134	10,235	10,338	10,441	118,689
Tax	3,088	3,119	3,150	3,182	3,214	3,246	3,278	3,311	3,344	3,378	3,411	3,446	39,168
Profit After Tax	6,270	6,333	6,396	6,460	6,525	6,590	6,656	6,723	6,790	6,858	6,926	6,995	79,522

An ActiveX control can be linked to a worksheet cell, using its `LinkedCell` property, so that the cell always displays the `Value` property of the control. None of the ActiveX controls shown above use a link cell, although the scrollbar could have been linked because its value is displayed in B3. Each control uses an event procedure to make its updates. This gives you far more flexibility than a simple cell link and removes the need to dedicate a worksheet cell to the task.

Scrollbar Control

The scrollbar uses the `Change` event and the `Scroll` event to assign the `Value` property of the scrollbar to cell B3. The maximum and minimum values of the scrollbar are set by the option buttons (we'll discuss that later):

```
Private Sub ScrollBar1_Change()
   Range("B3").Value = ScrollBar1.Value
End Sub

Private Sub ScrollBar1_Scroll()
   Range("B3").Value = ScrollBar1.Value
End Sub
```

The `Change` event procedure is triggered when the scrollbar value is changed by clicking the scroll arrows, by clicking above or below the scroll box (or to the left or right if it is aligned horizontally), or by dragging the scroll box. However, there is a small glitch that occurs immediately after you change the option buttons. Dragging the scroll box does not trigger the `Change` event on the first attempt. Utilizing the `Scroll` event procedure solves this problem.

The `Scroll` event causes continuous updating as you drag the scroll bar, so that you can see what figure you are producing as you drag, rather than after you have released the scroll bar. It might not be practicable to use the `Scroll` event procedure in a very large worksheet in auto-recalculation mode because of the large number of recalculations it causes.

Spin Button Control

The spin button control uses the `SpinDown` and `SpinUp` events to decrease and increase the value in cell B4:

```
Private Sub SpinButton1_SpinDown()
   With Range("B4")
     .Value = WorksheetFunction.Max(0, .Value - 0.0005)
   End With
End Sub

Private Sub SpinButton1_SpinUp()
   With Range("B4")
      .Value = WorksheetFunction.Min(0.01, .Value + 0.0005)
   End With
End Sub
```

The `Value` property of the spin button is ignored. It is not suitable to be used directly as a percentage figure because it can only be a long integer value. The events are used as triggers to run the code that operates directly on the value in B4. The growth figure is kept in the range of zero to 1 percent.

Clicking the down side of the spin button runs the `SpinDown` event procedure, which decreases the value in cell B4 by 0.05%. The worksheet `Max` function is used to ensure that the calculated figure does not become less than zero. The `SpinUp` event procedure increases the value in cell B4 by 0.05%. It uses the `Min` function to ensure that the calculated value does not exceed 1%.

CheckBox Control

The checkbox control returns a `True` value when checked, or a `False` value if it is unchecked. The `Click` event procedure that follows uses an `If` structure to set the value in cell B16:

```
Private Sub CheckBox1_Click()
   If CheckBox1.Value Then
      Range("B16").Value = 0.33
   Else
      Range("B16").Value = 0.3
   End If
End Sub
```

Option Button Controls

Each option button has code similar to the following:

```
Private Sub OptionButton1_Click()
   Call Options
End Sub
```

The processing for all the buttons is carried out in the following procedure, which is in the class module behind the `Profit` worksheet that holds the event procedures above:

```
Private Sub Options()
   Dim dCostFactor As Double
   Dim lScrollBarMax As Long
   Dim lScrollBarMin As Long

   Select Case True
      Case OptionButton1.Value
         dCostFactor = 0.63
         lScrollBarMin = 50000
         lScrollBarMax = 150000
      Case OptionButton2.Value
         dCostFactor = 0.74
         lScrollBarMin = 25000
         lScrollBarMax = 75000
      Case OptionButton3.Value
         dCostFactor = 0.57
         lScrollBarMin = 10000
         lScrollBarMax = 30000
      Case OptionButton4.Value
         dCostFactor = 0.65
         lScrollBarMin = 15000
         lScrollBarMax = 30000
   End Select
   Range("B15").Value = dCostFactor
   ScrollBar1.Min = lScrollBarMin
   ScrollBar1.Max = lScrollBarMax
   ScrollBar1.Value = lScrollBarMax
End Sub
```

The `Select Case` structure is used here in an unusual way. Normally you use a variable reference in the first line of a `Select Case` and use comparison values in the `Case` statements. Here, we have used the value `True` in the `Select Case` and referenced the option button `Value` property in the `Case` statements. This provides a nice structure for processing a set of option buttons where you know that only one can have a `True` value.

Only one option button can be selected and have a value of `True` in the worksheet above because they all belong to the same group. As you add option buttons to a worksheet, the `GroupName` property of the button is set to the name of the worksheet – `Profit`, in this case. If you want two sets of unrelated option buttons, you need to assign a different `GroupName` to the second set.

`Options` uses the `Select Case` structure to carry out any processing that is different for each option button. The code following the `End Select` carries out any processing that is common to all the option buttons. This approach also works very well when the coding is more complex and also when the code is triggered by another control, such as a command button, rather than the option button events.

Forms Toolbar Controls

The following screenshot shows a Forms toolbar control that is being used to select a product name to be entered in column D. The control appears over any cell in column D that you double-click. When you select the product, the product name is entered in the cell 'behind' the control, the price of the product is entered in column F on the same row, and the control disappears:

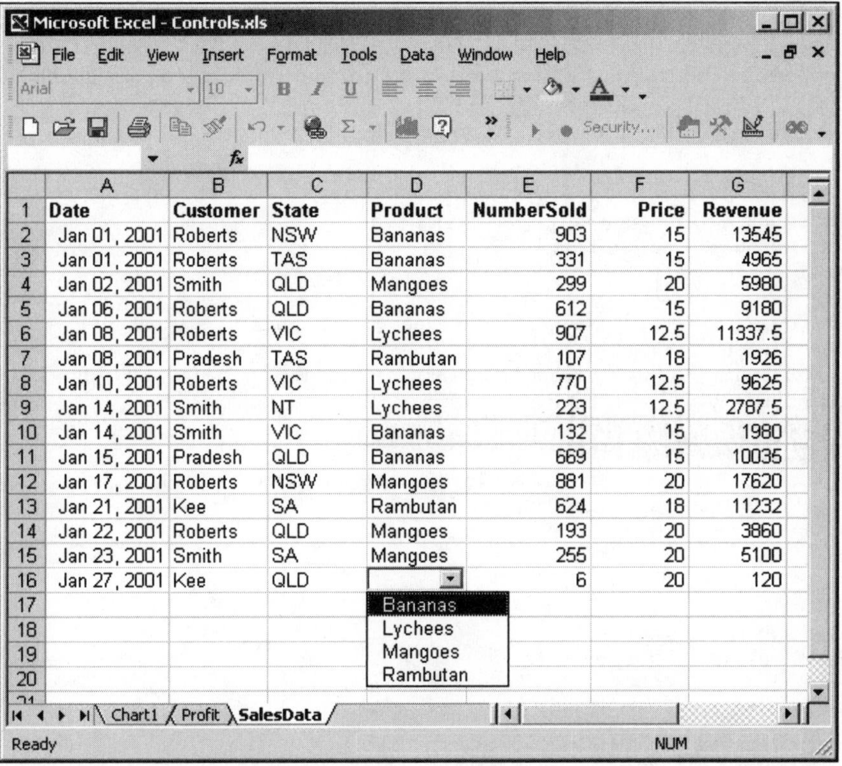

	A	B	C	D	E	F	G
1	Date	Customer	State	Product	NumberSold	Price	Revenue
2	Jan 01, 2001	Roberts	NSW	Bananas	903	15	13545
3	Jan 01, 2001	Roberts	TAS	Bananas	331	15	4965
4	Jan 02, 2001	Smith	QLD	Mangoes	299	20	5980
5	Jan 06, 2001	Roberts	QLD	Bananas	612	15	9180
6	Jan 08, 2001	Roberts	VIC	Lychees	907	12.5	11337.5
7	Jan 08, 2001	Pradesh	TAS	Rambutan	107	18	1926
8	Jan 10, 2001	Roberts	VIC	Lychees	770	12.5	9625
9	Jan 14, 2001	Smith	NT	Lychees	223	12.5	2787.5
10	Jan 14, 2001	Smith	VIC	Bananas	132	15	1980
11	Jan 15, 2001	Pradesh	QLD	Bananas	669	15	10035
12	Jan 17, 2001	Roberts	NSW	Mangoes	881	20	17620
13	Jan 21, 2001	Kee	SA	Rambutan	624	18	11232
14	Jan 22, 2001	Roberts	QLD	Mangoes	193	20	3860
15	Jan 23, 2001	Smith	SA	Mangoes	255	20	5100
16	Jan 27, 2001	Kee	QLD		6	20	120

If you hover your cursor over the Forms toolbar button that creates the control shown above, the ScreenTip that pops up describes this control as a Combo Box. However, in the Excel Object Model, it is called a `DropDown` object, and it belongs to the `DropDowns` collection.

> **The `DropDown` object is a hidden member of the Excel object model in Excel 97 and later versions. You will not find any help screens for this object and it will not normally appear in the Object Browser. You can make it visible in the Object Browser if you right-click in the Object Browser window and select Show Hidden Members from the shortcut menu. You can learn a lot about the Forms toolbar controls by using the Macro Recorder and the Object Browser, but you will need to have access to Excel 5 or Excel 95 to get full documentation on them.**

The dropdown control is created by a procedure called from the following `BeforeDoubleClick` event procedure in the `SalesData` sheet, which has the programmatic name `Sheet2`:

```
Private Sub Worksheet_BeforeDoubleClick(ByVal Target As Range, Cancel As Boolean)
   If Not Intersect(Target, Columns("D")) Is Nothing Then
      Call AddDropDown(Target)
      Cancel = True
   End If
End Sub
```

The event procedure checks that `Target` (the cell that was double-clicked) is in column D. If so, it then runs the `AddDropDown` procedure, passing `Target` as an input argument, and cancels the double-click event.

The following two procedures are in a standard module:

```
Sub AddDropDown(Target As Range)
   Dim ddBox As DropDown
   Dim vaProducts As Variant
   Dim i As Integer

   vaProducts = Array("Bananas", "Lychees", "Mangoes", "Rambutan")
   With Target
      Set ddBox = Sheet2.DropDowns.Add(.Left, .Top, .Width, .Height)
   End With
   With ddBox
      .OnAction = "EnterProdInfo"
      For i = LBound(vaProducts) To UBound(vaProducts)
         .AddItem vaProducts(i)
      Next i
   End With
End Sub

Private Sub EnterProdInfo()
   Dim vaPrices As Variant

   vaPrices = Array(15, 12.5, 20, 18)
   With Sheet2.DropDowns(Application.Caller)
      .TopLeftCell.Value = .List(.ListIndex)
      .TopLeftCell.Offset(0, 2).Value = vaPrices(.ListIndex + _
                                          LBound(vaPrices) - 1)

      .Delete
   End With
End Sub
```

The AddDropDown procedure is not declared Private, as it would not then be possible to call it from the Sheet2 code module. This would normally be a problem if you wanted to prevent users from seeing the procedure in the **Tools | Macro | Macros** dialog box. However, because it has an input argument, it will not be shown in the dialog box, anyway. Also, it does not matter whether AddDropDown is placed in the Sheet2 module or a standard module. It will operate in either location.

AddDropDown uses the Add method of the DropDowns collection to create a new dropdown. It aligns the new control exactly with Target, giving it the same Left, Top, Width, and Height properties as the cell. In the With...End With construction, the procedure defines the OnAction property of the dropdown to be the EnterProdInfo procedure. This means that EnterProdInfo will be run when an item is chosen from the dropdown. The For...Next loop uses the AddItem method of the dropdown to place the list of items in vaProducts into the dropdown list.

EnterProdInfo has been declared Private to prevent its appearance in the **Tools | Macro | Macros** dialog box. Although it is private, the dropdown can access it. EnterProdInfo could have been placed in the Sheet2 code module, but the OnAction property of the dropdown would have to be assigned "Sheet2.EnterProdInfo".

EnterProdInfo loads vaPrices with the prices corresponding to the products. It then uses Application.Caller to return the name of the dropdown control that called the OnAction procedure. It uses this name as an index into the DropDowns collection on Sheet2 to get a reference to the DropDown object itself. In the With...End With construction, EnterProdInfo uses the ListIndex property of the dropdown to get the index number of the item chosen in the dropdown list.

You cannot directly access the name of the chosen item in a DropDown object, unlike a ComboBox object that returns the name in its Value property. The Value property of a dropdown is the same as the ListIndex, which returns the numeric position of the item in the list. To get the item name from a dropdown, you use the ListIndex property as a one-based index to the List property of the dropdown. The List property returns an array of all the items in the list.

The TopLeftCell property of the DropDown object returns a reference to the Range object under the top-left corner of the DropDown object. EnterProdInfo assigns the item chosen in the list to the Value property of this Range object. It then assigns the price of the product to the Range object that is offset two columns to the right of the TopLeftCell Range object.

EnterProdInfo also uses the ListIndex property of the dropdown as an index into the Prices array. The problem with this is that the dropdown list is always one-based, while the Array function list depends on the Option Base statement in the declarations section of the module. LBound(vaPrices) – 1 is used to reduce the ListIndex value by one if Option Base 0 is in effect or by zero if Option Base 1 is in effect.

You can use the following code to ensure that the resulting array is zero-based under Option-Base-1 in Excel 97 and above:

```
vaPrices = VBA.Array(15, 12.5, 20, 18)
```

This technique does not work in Excel 5 and Excel 95 where the above expression is influenced by the Option Base statement.

Dynamic ActiveX Controls

As previously stated, it is more difficult to program the ActiveX controls than the **Forms** toolbar controls. At the same time, the ActiveX controls are more powerful, so it is a good idea to know how to program them. We will see how to construct a combo box that behaves in a similar way to the combo box in the last example. Just to be different, we will use the `BeforeRightClick` event to trigger the appearance of a combo box in the D column of the `SalesData` worksheet as follows:

```
Private Sub Worksheet_BeforeRightClick(ByVal Target As Range, _
                                                          Cancel As Boolean)
  Dim Ole As OLEObject
  Dim Ctl As MSForms.ComboBox
  Dim lLine As Long
  Dim oCodeModule As Object

  Application.ScreenUpdating = False

  'Determine if the combo box should be built
  If Intersect(ActiveCell, Columns("D")) Is Nothing Then Exit Sub
  On Error Resume Next
  Set Ole = Me.OLEObjects("Combo")
  If Not Ole Is Nothing Then
    Cancel = True
    Exit Sub
  End If
  On Error GoTo 0

  'Add the combo box to the active cell
  With ActiveCell
    Set Ole = Me.OLEObjects.Add(ClassType:="Forms.ComboBox.1", _
               Link:=False, DisplayAsIcon:=False, Left:=.Left, Top:=.Top, _
                                            Width:=.Width, Height:= .Height)
  End With
  Ole.Name = "Combo"
  Set Ctl = Ole.Object
  Ctl.Name = "Combo"
  With Ctl
    .AddItem "Bananas"
    .AddItem "Lychees"
    .AddItem "Mangoes"
    .AddItem "Rambutan"
  End With

  'Build the event procedure for the combo box click event
  Set oCodeModule = _
              ThisWorkbook.VBProject.VBComponents(Me.CodeName).CodeModule
  With oCodeModule
    lLine = .CreateEventProc("Click", "Combo")
    .ReplaceLine lLine + 1, "  ProcessComboClick"
  End With
  Cancel = True

  'Make sure the Excel window is active
  Application.Visible = False
  Application.Visible = True

End Sub
```

We first check to see that the event took place in the D column. We also check to make sure that there is no existing combo box in the worksheet, which would mean that the user has created a combo box but has not yet selected an item from it. This did not matter in our last example where the combo boxes were independent, even though they used the same `OnAction` code. Our ActiveX controls can't share the single `Click` event procedure we are going to create, so we need to ensure that we don't already have a control in the worksheet.

We are going to use the name `Combo` for our ActiveX control. The quickest way to determine if there is already a control called `Combo` is to create an object variable referring to it. If this attempt fails, then we know that the control does not exist. The error recovery code is used to ensure that the macro does not display an error message and stop running if the control does not exist. It would be friendlier to display an explanatory message before exiting the sub, but that is not the main point of this exercise. Setting `Cancel` to `True` suppresses the normal right-click menu from appearing.

If all is well, we add a new combo box in the active cell. You need to know that an ActiveX object is not added directly onto a worksheet. It is contained in an `OLEObject` object, in the same way that a chart embedded in a worksheet is contained in a `ChartObject` object as we saw in Chapter 9. The return value from the `Add` method of the `OLEObjects` collection is assigned to `Ole` to make it easy to refer to the `OLEObject` object later. The `Name` property of the `OleObject` is changed to `Combo` to make it easy to identify later.

We then create an object variable, `Ctl`, referring to the `ComboBox` object contained in the `OleObject`, which is returned by the `Object` property of the `OLEObject`. The next line of code assigns the name `Combo` to the `ComboBox` object. This is not necessary in Excel 2000 and 2002. When you assign a name to the `OLEObject`, it is also automatically assigned to the embedded object in these versions. This is not the case in Excel 97, so the name needs to be explicitly assigned.

Next we create the `Click` event procedure code for the combo box. You can't create the event procedure in advance. It will cause compile errors if the ActiveX control it refers to does not exist. The methodology for creating event procedures programmatically is explained in detail in Chapter 23, so check that chapter for full details.

`oCodeModule` is assigned a reference to the class module behind the worksheet and the `CreatEventProc` method of the code module is used to enter the first and last lines of the `Combo_Click` event procedure, with a blank line between. This method returns the line number of the first line of the procedure, which is assigned to `lLine`. The `ReplaceLine` method replaces the blank second line of the procedure with a call to a sub procedure named `ProcessComboClick`, which is listed below. The code for `ProcessComboClick` already exists in the worksheet's code module.

We set `Cancel` to `True` to ensure that the pop-up menu normally associated with a right click in a cell does not appear.

Unfortunately, when you add code to a code module as we have done, the code module is activated and the user could be left staring at a screen full of code. By setting the Excel application window's `Visible` property to `False` and then `True`, we make sure that the Excel window is active at the end of the procedure. There will still be some screen flicker, even though screen updating was suppressed at the start of the macro. It is possible to suppress this flicker by calls to the Windows API (discussed in Chapter 24).

The `Click` event procedure code that is created by the above code looks like the following:

```
Private Sub Combo_Click()
  ProcessComboClick
End Sub
```

When the user selects a value in the combo box, the `Click` event procedure executes and, in turn, executes `ProcessComboClick`. The code for `ProcessComboClick`, which is a permanent procedure in the worksheet's code module, contains the following:

```
Private Sub ProcessComboClick()
  Dim lLine As Long
  Dim oCodeModule As Object

  'Enter the chosen value
  With Me.OLEObjects("Combo")
    .TopLeftCell.Value = .Object.Value
    .Delete
  End With

  'Delete the combo box click event procedure
  Set oCodeModule = _
              ThisWorkbook.VBProject.VBComponents(Me.CodeName).CodeModule
  With oCodeModule
    lLine = .ProcStartLine("Combo_Click", 0)
    .DeleteLines lLine, 4
  End With
End Sub
```

The combo box is the object contained in the `OLEObject` named `Combo`. The above code enters the selected value from the combo box into the cell underneath the combo box and then deletes the `OLEObject` and its contents.

The code then deletes the event procedure. `oCodeModule` is assigned a reference to the worksheet's code module. The `ProcStartLine` method returns the line number of the blank line just before the `Combo_Click` event procedure. The `Delete` method removes 4 lines, including the blank line.

As you can see, dynamically coding an ActiveX control is quite complex. It is simpler to use a Forms toolbar control if you don't really need the extra power of an ActiveX control.

Controls on Charts

The following screenshot shows a chart that contains a button to remove or add the profit series from the chart, which is based on the `Profit Planner` figures of the `Profit` sheet. The control is a Forms toolbar `Button` object belonging to the `Buttons` collection (remember ActiveX controls cannot be used in charts):

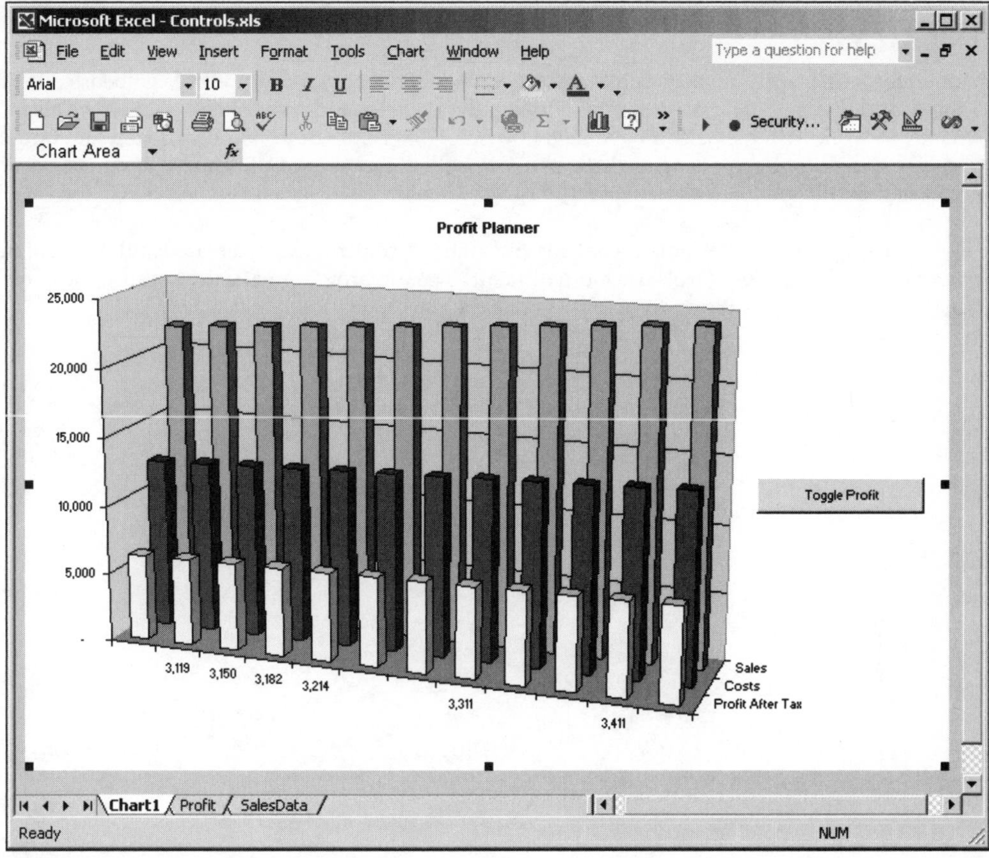

The code assigned to the `OnAction` property of the `Button` object is as follows:

```
Sub Button1_Click()
   With ActiveChart
      If .SeriesCollection.Count = 3 Then
         .SeriesCollection(1).Delete
      Else
         With .SeriesCollection.NewSeries
            .Name = Sheet1.Range("A13")
            .Values = Sheet1.Range("B13:M13")
            .XValues = Sheet1.Range("B12:M12")
            .PlotOrder = 1
         End With
      End If
   End With
End Sub
```

If the `SeriesCollection.Count` property is three, the first series is deleted. Otherwise a new series is added and the appropriate ranges assigned to it to show the profit after tax figures. The new series is added as the last series, which would plot behind the existing series, so the `PlotOrder` property of the new series is set to one to place it in front of the others.

Summary

In this chapter we have explained some of the differences between ActiveX controls embedded in worksheets and Forms toolbar controls embedded in worksheets and chart sheets, and we've also shown how to work with them. You have seen how scroll bars, spin buttons, checkboxes, and option buttons can be used to execute macros that can harness the full power of VBA and that do not need to depend on a link cell.

You also have seen how Forms toolbar controls and ActiveX controls can be created and manipulated programmatically. ActiveX controls are more difficult to create programmatically because they are contained within `OLEObjects` and you can't create their event procedures in advance.

VBAProgrammersReferenceExcel20
mmersReferenceExcel2002VB
ReferenceExcel2002VBAPro
AProgrammersReferenceExc
ammersReferenceExcel20
ReferenceExcel2002VB
enceExcel2002VBAPro
xcel2002VBAProgrammersReferenceExc
2002VBAProgrammersReferenceExce
VBAProgrammersReference
rogrammersReferenceExcel
ammersReferenceammersExcel2000VBAProgra
2002VBAProgrammersReferenceExce

12

Office Files and Folders

Most of the objects discussed in this book come from the Excel Object Model. That is not the only object model available when you are writing Excel VBA code. A number of object models, or type libraries, are automatically associated with each Excel VBA project. You can see them listed in the drop-down menu at the top of the Object Browser or by clicking Tools | References in the VB Editor window and noting the libraries with check marks. There are libraries for Excel, VBA, Office, OLE Automation and, if you attach a UserForm, there will be a Forms library. You can attach more libraries by checking items in the Tools | References dialog box. This process is discussed in later chapters such as *Programming the VBE.*

The Office Object Model is made available to all Microsoft Office applications. It contains objects that are used by all Office applications such as CommandBars, which are discussed in Chapter 14. In this chapter we will examine two objects contained in the Office Object Model that you use to search for files and to open and save files. We will also look at a number of objects associated with them:

- `FileSearch`
  - `FoundFiles`
  - `PropertyTests`
  - `FileTypes`
  - `SearchScopes`
  - `ScopeFolders`
  - `SearchFolders`
- `FileDialog`
  - `FileDialogFilters`
  - `FileDialogSelectedItems`

`FileSearch` was introduced in Office 97 and has been considerably enhanced in Office XP. It allows you to search for files with a wide range of search criteria such as file type, file size, file location, and date of last modification. `FileSearch` places the names of the files it finds in the `FoundFiles` collection.

You can use `FileSearch` instead of the VBA `Dir` function for a range of file operations. `FileSearch` is useful for maintenance of files. You can locate files of a certain age and delete them or move them to an archive directory, for example. `FileSearch` is also useful when you need to retrieve data from a number of related files. You can find all the Excel files in a certain directory that start with a client's name, before you consolidate the information in them into a summary file, for example.

FileDialog is a new object in Office XP. You use it to display the **File Open** and **File Save As** dialog boxes as well as a subdirectory browser. FileDialog is a more powerful version of the GetOpenFileName and GetSaveAsFileName methods of the Excel Application object, which have been available in all previous versions of Excel with VBA, but have not been available to other Office applications. FileDialog, being an Office object, is available to all Office XP applications.

FileSearch

The following code searches the NewClients subdirectory, including any subdirectories beneath it, looking for Excel files:

```
Sub FindClientExcelFiles()
  Dim FS As Office.FileSearch
  Dim vaFileName As Variant
  Dim stMessage As String
  Dim i As Long
  Dim iCount As Long

  Set FS = Application.FileSearch

  With FS
    'Clear old search criteria
    .NewSearch

    'Directory to search
    .LookIn = "C:\Clients\NewClients"

    'Include sub folders in search
    .SearchSubFolders = True

    'Look for Excel files
    .FileType = msoFileTypeExcelWorkbooks

    'Doesn't matter when last modified
    .LastModified = msoLastModifiedAnyTime

    'Carry out search and capture number of files found
    iCount = .Execute

    stMessage = Format(iCount, "0 ""Files Found""")

    'List the files in the FoundFiles collection
    For Each vaFileName In .FoundFiles
      stMessage = stMessage & vbCr & vaFileName
    Next vaFileName

    MsgBox stMessage

  End With
End Sub
```

We declare the object variable FS to be of the type of Office.FileSearch. The Office prefix is not required, but makes it clear that FileSearch is an object in the Office library. In the code, we use the FileSearch property of the Excel Application object to return a reference to the Office FileSearch object and assign it to FS.

We then assign values to a number of `FileSearch` properties. The `LookIn` property tells `FileSearch` which subdirectory to search. `NewSearch` is a method that clears all of the `FileSearch` properties except `LookIn`. As these properties persist while you have Excel open, it is a good idea to execute `NewSearch` each time you use `FileSearch`. The `SearchSubFolders` property controls whether we look in subdirectories below the `LookIn` subdirectory.

`FileType` determines what file extensions will be included in the search criteria. The constant `msoFileTypeExcelWorkbook` directs the search to include all the Excel file extensions .`xls`, .`xlt`, .`xlm`, .`xlc`, and .xla. See below for a table of the other constants available.

msoFileType Constants	Value
`msoFileTypeAllFiles`	1
`msoFileTypeOfficeFiles`	2
`msoFileTypeWordDocuments`	3
`msoFileTypeExcelWorkbooks`	4
`msoFileTypePowerPointPresentations`	5
`msoFileTypeBinders`	6
`msoFileTypeDatabases`	7
`msoFileTypeTemplates`	8
Excel 2002	
`msoFileTypeOutlookItems`	9
`msoFileTypeMailItem`	10
`msoFileTypeCalendarItem`	11
`msoFileTypeContactItem`	12
`msoFileTypeNoteItem`	13
`msoFileTypeJournalItem`	14
`msoFileTypeTaskItem`	15
`msoFileTypePhotoDrawFiles`	16
`msoFileTypeDataConnectionFiles`	17
`msoFileTypePublisherFiles`	18
`msoFileTypeProjectFiles`	19
`msoFileTypeDocumentImagingFiles`	20
`msoFileTypeVisioFiles`	21
`msoFileTypeDesignerFiles`	22
`msoFileTypeWebPages`	23

The `LastModified` property can use the following constants:

mso Last Modified Constants	Value
msoLastModifiedYesterday	1
msoLastModifiedToday	2
msoLastModifiedLastWeek	3
msoLastModifiedThisWeek	4
msoLastModifiedLastMonth	5
msoLastModifiedThisMonth	6
msoLastModifiedAnyTime	7

Instead of the `FileType` property, you can specify the `FileName` property, as shown below:

```
    .FileName = "*.xls"
```

> **`FileName` allows you to be more specific than the `FileType` constant. If you use both `FileType` and `FileName`, the `FileName` property overrides the `FileType` property.**

You can also search the text contained in the properties of a file or in the body of the file itself by assigning the text to the `TextOrProperty` property of `FileSearch`.

FoundFiles

The `Execute` method of `FileSearch` carries out the search and adds an object representing each file to the `FoundFiles` collection. `Execute` also returns a value that is the number of files found.

You use the `FoundFiles` collection to access the names, including the path, of the files found. The code above uses a `For Each...Next` loop to process the list, adding each name to `stMessage`, separated by a carriage return. The result could be as follows:

PropertyTests

When you use the **File | Open** dialog box in Office 97 and 2000 you can click the **Advanced** button to open the **Advanced Find** dialog box. Here you can specify one or more search criteria for locating files. In VBA, you can use the `PropertyTests` collection to set up tests that mimic the **Advanced Find** test criteria.

The **Advanced Find** dialog box has been superseded by the new **File | Search** facilities in Office XP but you can still use the `PropertyTests` collection in Office XP VBA code.

The following procedure searches for Excel files that are larger than 500,000 bytes:

```
Sub FindLargeClientExcelFiles()
  Dim FS As Office.FileSearch
  Dim vaFileName As Variant
  Dim stMessage As String
  Dim i As Long
  Dim iCount As Long

  Set FS = Application.FileSearch

  With FS
    'Clear old search criteria
    .NewSearch

    'Directory to search
    .LookIn = "C:\Clients\NewClients"

    'Include sub folders in search
    .SearchSubFolders = True

    With .PropertyTests
      'Make sure that the PropertyTests collection is empty
      For i = .Count To 1 Step -1
        .Remove i
      Next i

      'Look for Excel workbooks
      .Add Name:="Files of Type", _
           Condition:=msoConditionFileTypeExcelWorkbooks

      'Look for files over 500,000 bytes
      .Add Name:="Size", _
           Condition:=msoConditionAtLeast, _
           Value:=500000, _
           Connector:=msoConnectorAnd
    End With

    'Doesn't matter when last modified
    .LastModified = msoLastModifiedAnyTime

    'Carry out search and capture number of files found
    iCount = .Execute

    stMessage = Format(iCount, "0 ""Files Found""")

    'List the files in the FoundFiles collection
    For Each vaFileName In .FoundFiles
      stMessage = stMessage & vbCr & vaFileName
    Next vaFileName

    MsgBox stMessage

  End With

End Sub
```

The PropertyTests collection operates independently of any settings in the **Advanced Find** dialog box. It does not recognize any conditions in that dialog and it does not change the settings in that dialog. If you add tests to the PropertyTests collection, they persist until you execute NewSearch.

The Add method of the PropertyTests collection adds the new tests, which are specified by assigning a string to the Name parameter that is identical to the string that appears in the Property combo box in the **Advanced Find** dialog box. The first one added is "Files of Type", which gives us yet another way to specify that we want Excel files by providing the appropriate constant for the Condition parameter. The available constants are too numerous to tabulate here. IntelliSense ensures that they are listed automatically as you type in your code module and are self explanatory.

A trap with PropertyTests is that there is a default condition defined in the collection when you start an Excel session, and after you execute NewSearch, that specifies the "Files of Type" parameter to be msoFileTypeOfficeFiles. Therefore, it is a good idea to empty the collection before entering new tests so that you are starting from a clear base. The code in the For...Next loop removes items in the collection in reverse order. It removes the items with the highest index numbers first so that the index numbers do not change as it deletes.

The second test specifies that the "Size" of the file must be at least 500,000 bytes. The Connector parameter, msoConnectorAnd, specifies that the second test is joined to the first test with And. The alternative is msoConnectorOr. See Appendix C for a complete list of the parameters available.

If you specify msoConnectorOr instead of msoConnectorAnd in our example, and you are using Office 97 or 2000, VBA crashes with an error message when you try to execute the code. As usual, the error message is of little help in understanding the problem. The problem is that you are not allowed to combine a "File of Type" test with any other test using Or. If you try to do it manually in the Advanced Find dialog box you get a clear message telling you this. If you break this rule in your Office XP code a run-time error does not occur, but the result is based on And. So, beware.

FileTypes

In Office 97 and 2000 you can specify only a single FileType property for FileSearch. Office XP introduced a FileTypes collection that allows you to specify multiple file types. The following Office XP code finds all the Excel and Word files in the directories specified:

```
Sub FindClientExcelAndWordFiles()
  Dim FS As Office.FileSearch
  Dim vaFileName As Variant
  Dim stMessage As String
  Dim i As Long
  Dim iCount As Long

  Set FS = Application.FileSearch

  With FS
    'Clear old search criteria
    .NewSearch

    'Set first file type to search for and
    'Clear any old settings from FileTypes collection
    .FileType = msoFileTypeExcelWorkbooks
```

```
        'Add second file type to search
        .FileTypes.Add msoFileTypeWordDocuments

        'Directory to search
        .LookIn = "C:\Clients\NewClients"

        'Include sub folders in search
        .SearchSubFolders = True

        'Doesn't matter when last modified
        .LastModified = msoLastModifiedAnyTime

        'Carry out search and capture number of files found
        iCount = .Execute

        stMessage = Format(iCount, "0 ""Files Found""")

        'List the files in the FoundFiles collection
        For Each vaFileName In .FoundFiles
          stMessage = stMessage & vbCr & vaFileName
        Next vaFileName

        MsgBox stMessage

      End With

    End Sub
```

The `FileTypes` collection persists until you execute `NewSearch`, which clears the collection and places the value of `msoFileTypeOfficeFiles` in the collection. However, there is no need to empty the `FileTypes` collection before adding new entries. If you assign an entry to the `FileType` parameter any existing entries in the `FileTypes` collection are destroyed and the new entry becomes the first and only entry in the collection. You can then use the `Add` method of the collection to add more entries. You can use the same file type constants that are listed above.

SearchScopes

All of the code above assumes that you know the directory organization of the computer you are searching and can specify the subdirectories you want to search. What if you do not know the structure and need to map it for yourself? If you are designing a utility that must run on any computer, you will need to do this.

The `SearchScopes` collection, introduced in Office XP, provides a mechanism for carrying out the directory mapping process. The following code examines each member of the collection. Each member is a `SearchScope` object:

```
Sub ListSearchScopeObjects()
  Dim SS As SearchScope
  Dim stMessage As String

  'Process each member of the SearchScopes collection
  For Each SS In Application.FileSearch.SearchScopes
    stMessage = stMessage & SS.ScopeFolder.Name & vbTab
    stMessage = stMessage & " Type=" & SS.Type & vbCr
  Next SS

  MsgBox stMessage

End Sub
```

The code will produce something similar to the following message box:

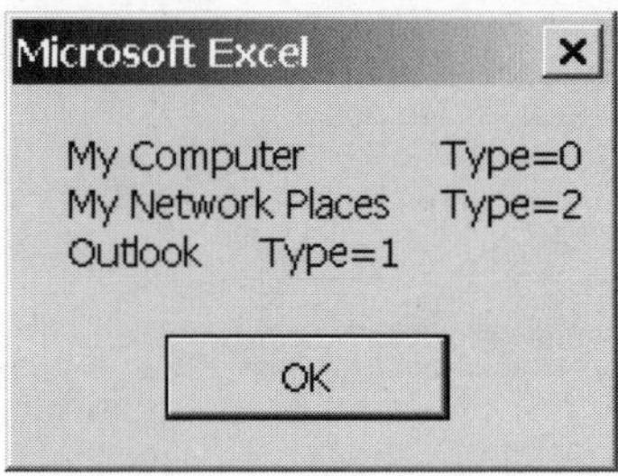

The `SearchScope` objects represent the structures you can examine. The `Type` property identifies the category of each structure. The presence of **My Computer** and **Network Places** is no surprise. It is interesting that **Outlook** is given as another structure.

Help lists the following constants that hold the possible type values:

msoSearchIn Constants	Value
`msoSearchInMyComputer`	0
`msoSearchInOutlook`	1
`msoSearchInMyNetworkPlaces`	2
`msoSearchInCustom`	3

You can't add members to or delete members from the `SearchScope` collection. The custom type is probably provided for future development.

ScopeFolder

Each `SearchScope` object has a `ScopeFolder` property that references a `ScopeFolder` object. This `ScopeFolder` object represents the top level of the structure. In the code above, the `Name` property of the `ScopeFolder` object associated with the top of each structure provides the description of that structure.

The `ScopeFolder` representing the top of the structure contains a `ScopeFolders` collection that contains more `ScopeFolder` objects. The code below displays the `Name` and `Path` properties of the `ScopeFolders` under the top-level `ScopeFolder` of each structure:

```
Sub ListScopeFolderObjects()
  Dim SS As SearchScope
  Dim SF As ScopeFolder
  Dim stMessage As String

  Application.FileSearch.RefreshScopes

  'List each member of the SearchScopes collection
  For Each SS In Application.FileSearch.SearchScopes

    'Select SearchScope object by Type
    Select Case SS.Type
```

```
        'My Computer
        Case msoSearchInMyComputer
          stMessage = SS.ScopeFolder.Name & vbCr
          For Each SF In SS.ScopeFolder.ScopeFolders
            stMessage = stMessage & SF.Name & vbTab & vbTab
            stMessage = stMessage & "Path=" & SF.Path & vbCr
          Next SF

        'My Network Places
        Case msoSearchInMyNetworkPlaces
          stMessage = stMessage & vbCr & SS.ScopeFolder.Name & vbCr
          For Each SF In SS.ScopeFolder.ScopeFolders
            stMessage = stMessage & SF.Name & vbTab
            stMessage = stMessage & "Path=" & SF.Path & vbCr
          Next SF

        'Outlook
        Case msoSearchInOutlook
          stMessage = stMessage & vbCr & SS.ScopeFolder.Name & vbCr
          For Each SF In SS.ScopeFolder.ScopeFolders
            stMessage = stMessage & SF.Name & vbTab & vbTab
            stMessage = stMessage & "Path=" & SF.Path & vbCr
          Next SF

        'Anything else
        Case Else
          stMessage = stMessage & vbCr & "Unknown SearchScope object"

      End Select

    Next SS

    MsgBox stMessage

  End Sub
```

The code produces a message box like the following:

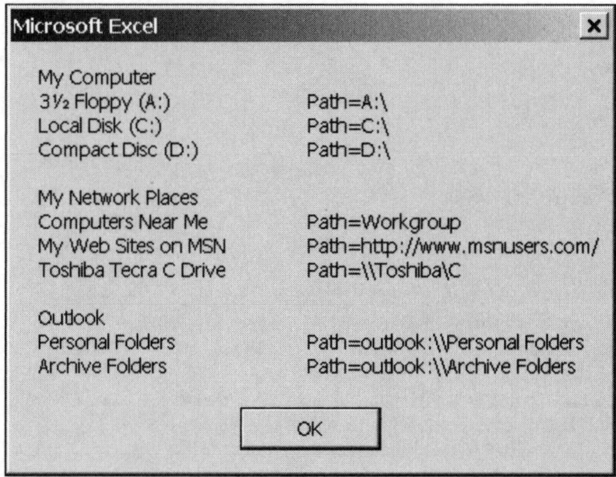

The `Select Case` statements provide a convenient way to isolate and examine each of the top-level structures. Each top level `ScopeFolders` collection contains `ScopeFolder` objects that represent the root directories of the file structures available to it. Each of these `ScopeFolder` objects contains another `ScopeFolders` collection that represents the subdirectories under it. This provides a mechanism for drilling down through the directory trees.

SearchFolders

Another new object in the Office XP object model is the SearchFolders collection. You use the LookIn property of FileSearch to define a single directory path to be searched, by assigning the directory path as a character string to the property. You use the SearchFolders collection to define additional directory paths to be searched, by adding ScopeFolder objects to the collection.

SearchFolders is not like the FileTypes collection that is re-created when you assign a value to the FileType property. SearchFolders is not affected when you assign a value to the LookIn property or when you execute NewSearch. The LookIn value is additional to the SearchFolders entries.

Because the SearchFolders collection persists during the current Excel session, it is a good idea to empty it before carrying out a new search. The following code searches through all the subdirectories in the root directory of the C drive. When it finds a directory starting with the letters "Client", it adds that directory to the SearchFolders collection:

```
Sub SetupSearchFoldersCollection()
  Dim FS As FileSearch
  Dim SS As SearchScope
  Dim SF As ScopeFolder
  Dim sfSubFolder As ScopeFolder
  Dim stMessage As String
  Dim i As Long

  Set FS = Application.FileSearch

  'Make sure that the SearchFolders collection is empty
  For i = FS.SearchFolders.Count To 1 Step -1
    FS.SearchFolders.Remove i
  Next i

  'Search the SearchScopes collection
  For Each SS In FS.SearchScopes

    'Select My Computer
    Select Case SS.Type

      Case msoSearchInMyComputer

        'Search for the C drive root directory
        For Each SF In SS.ScopeFolder.ScopeFolders

          Select Case SF.Path

            Case "C:\"

              'Search for directories starting with "Client"
              For Each sfSubFolder In SF.ScopeFolders
                If UCase(Left(sfSubFolder.Name, 6)) = "CLIENT" Then

                  'Add directory to SearchFolders collection
                  sfSubFolder.AddToSearchFolders

                End If
              Next sfSubFolder
              Exit For

          End Select
```

```
        Next SF
        Exit For

      End Select

    Next SS

    Search_SearchFolders

  End Sub
```

The code empties the `SearchFolders` collection and then drills down through the `SearchScopes` collection and `ScopeFolders` collection to locate the C drive. It then examines the `Name` property of each `ScopeFolder` in the root directory of the C drive to determine if the name begins with "`CLIENT`". It converts the name to upper case so that the comparison is not case-sensitive.

When the code finds a matching directory it uses the `AddToSearchFolders` method of the `ScopeFolder` object to add the object to the `SearchFolders` collection. The code then runs the `Search_SearchFolders` routine, which is listed below, to display the names of the Excel files in the `SearchFolders` directories.

```
  Sub Search_SearchFolders()
    Dim FS As Office.FileSearch
    Dim vaFileName As Variant
    Dim stMessage As String
    Dim iCount As Long

    Set FS = Application.FileSearch

    With FS

      'Clear old search criteria
      .NewSearch

      'Remove any old LookIn setting
      .LookIn = ""

      'Don't Include sub folders in search
      .SearchSubFolders = True

      'Look for Excel workbooks
      .FileName = "*.xls"

      'Doesn't matter when last modified
      .LastModified = msoLastModifiedAnyTime

      'Carry out search and capture number of files found
      iCount = .Execute

      stMessage = Format(iCount, "0 ""Files Found""")
      'List the files in the FoundFiles collection
      For Each vaFileName In .FoundFiles
        stMessage = stMessage & vbCr & vaFileName
      Next vaFileName

      MsgBox stMessage

    End With

  End Sub
```

Search_SearchFolders sets the LookIn property of FileSearch to a zero length string to ensure that it does not contain any directory references from previous FileSearch operations.

> **Office XP users who have used code to populate the SearchFolders collection should modify the code of the procedures presented earlier in this chapter so that the SearchFolders collection is cleared before the search is executed.**

FileDialog

Office XP introduces the FileDialog object that allows you to display the File | Open and File | Save As dialog boxes using VBA. Excel users of previous versions can use the GetOpenFileName and GetSaveAsFileName methods of the Application object to carry out similar tasks and they can continue to do so in 2002 if backwards compatibility is required. One advantage of FileDialog is that it has one extra capability that allows you to display a list of directories, rather than files and directories. FileDialog also has the advantage of being available to all Office applications.

We will set up a worksheet to display images that we will allow the user to choose through the File Open dialog box. The following screen shows how the application looks:

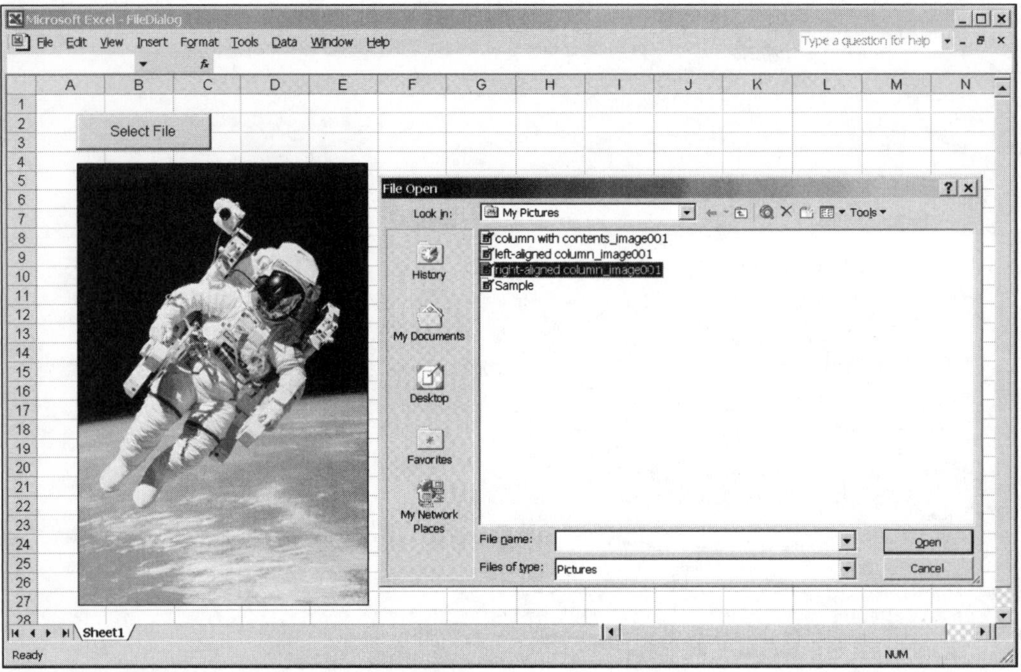

The worksheet contains an Image control created using the Control Toolbox toolbar, with the default name of "Image1". We have set the pictureSizeMode property of the control to zoom so that the picture is automatically fitted in the control. The command button above it has been named cmdGetFile.

The class module behind Sheet1 contains the following event procedure:

```
Private Sub cmdGetFile_Click()
  Dim FD As FileDialog
  Dim FFs As FileDialogFilters
  Dim stFileName As String

  On Error GoTo Problem

  'Set up File | Open dialog
  Set FD = Application.FileDialog(msoFileDialogOpen)

  With FD
    'Clear default filters and create picture filter
    Set FFs = .Filters

    With FFs
      .Clear
      .Add "Pictures", "*.jpg"
    End With

    'Allow only one file selection
    .AllowMultiSelect = False

    'Show the dialog. Exit if Cancel is pressed
    If .Show = False Then Exit Sub

   'Load selected file into Image
    Image1.Picture = LoadPicture(.SelectedItems(1))
  End With

  Exit Sub

Problem:
  MsgBox "That was not a valid picture"

End Sub
```

The `FileDialog` property of the `Application` object returns a reference to the Office `FileDialogs` object. We can use the following `msoFileDialogType` constants to specify the type of dialog:

msoFileDialog Constants	Value
msoFileDialogOpen	1
msoFileDialogSaveAs	2
msoFileDialogFilePicker	3
msoFileDialogFolderPicker	4

FileDialogFilters

We use the `Filters` property of the `FileDialog` object to return a reference to the `FileDialogFilters` collection for the `FileDialog`. The filters control the types of files that are displayed. By default there are 24 filters preset that the user can select from the drop-down menu at the bottom of the File Open dialog box. The `Clear` method of the `FileDialogFilters` collection removes the preset filters and we add our own filter that shows only `.jpg` files.

The `Show` method of the `FileDialog` object displays the dialog box. When the user clicks the **Open** button the `Show` method returns a value of "`True`". If the user clicks the **Cancel** button the `Show` method returns "`False`" and we exit from the procedure.

FileDialogSelectedItems

The `Show` method does not actually open the selected file but places the file name and path into a `FileDialogSelectedItems` collection. As we will see later, it is possible to allow multiple file selection. In the present example, the user can only select one file. The name of the file is returned from the first item in the `FileDialogSelectedItems` collection, which is referred to by the `SelectedItems` property of the `FileDialog` object.

We use the `LoadPicture` function to assign the file to the `Picture` property of the image control.

Dialog Types

There is very little difference between the four possible dialog types apart from the heading at the top of the dialog. The file picker and folder picker types show **Browse** in the title bar while the others show **File Open** and **File Save As** as appropriate. All the dialogs show directories and files except the folder picker dialog, which shows only directories.

Execute Method

As we have seen, the `Show` method displays the `FileDialog` and the items chosen are placed in the `FileDialogSelectedItems` object without any attempt to open or save any files. You can use the `Execute` method with the **File Open** and **Save As** dialogs to carry out the required `Open` or `SaveAs` operations immediately the user clicks the **Open** or **Save** button, as shown in the following code:

```
With Application.FileDialog(xlDialogOpen)
  If .Show Then .Execute
End With
```

MultiSelect

The application below has been modified to allow the user to select multiple file names by holding down *Shift* or *Control* while clicking file names. The file names are then loaded into the combo box, called *ComboBox1*, at the top of the screen, from which the files can be chosen for viewing:

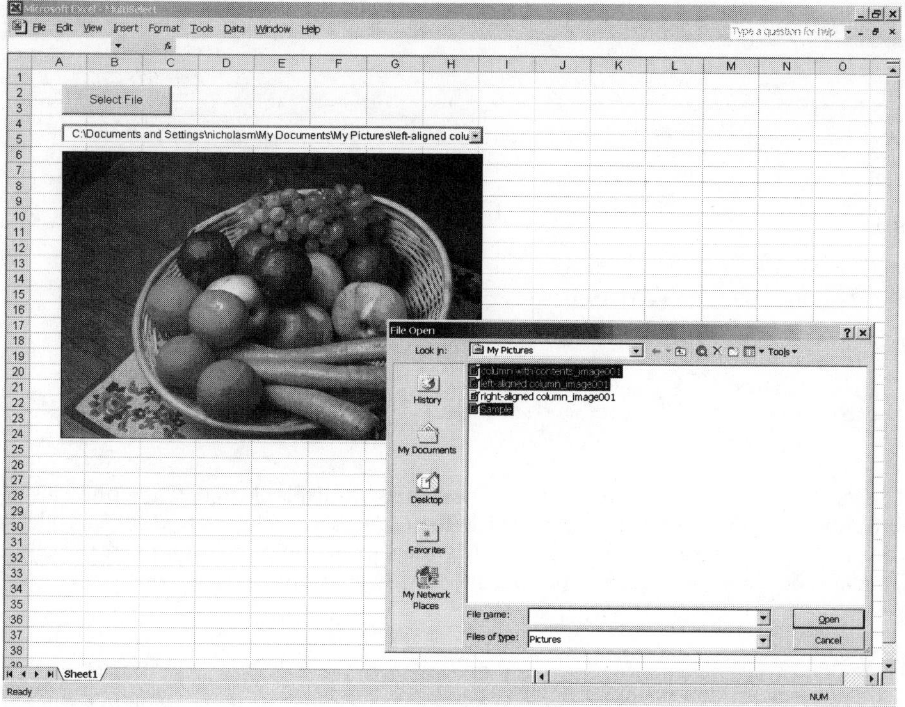

The code has been modified as follows:

```
Private Sub cmdGetFile_Click()
  Dim FD As FileDialog
  Dim FFs As FileDialogFilters
  Dim stFileName As String
  Dim vaItem

  On Error GoTo Problem

  'Set up File | Open dialog
  Set FD = Application.FileDialog(msoFileDialogOpen)

  With FD
    'Clear default filters and create picture filter
    Set FFs = .Filters

    With FFs
      .Clear
      .Add "Pictures", "*.jpg"
    End With

    'Allow multiple file selection
    .AllowMultiSelect = True

    'Show the dialog. Exit if Cancel is pressed
    If .Show = False Then Exit Sub

    'Load selected files into combo box
    ComboBox1.Clear
```

```
    For Each vaItem In .SelectedItems
      ComboBox1.AddItem vaItem
    Next vaItem

    'Display first file
    ComboBox1.ListIndex = 0

  End With

  Exit Sub

Problem:
  MsgBox "That was not a valid picture"

End Sub
```

```
Private Sub ComboBox1_Change()
  Image1.Picture = LoadPicture(ComboBox1.Text)
End Sub
```

We set the `AllowMultiSelect` property to `True`. The combo box list is cleared of any previous items and we use a `For Each...Next` loop to add the items in the `FileDialogSelectedItems` collection to the combo box list. When we set the combo box `ListIndex` property to zero, it triggers the `Change` event and the event procedure loads the first picture into the image control.

Summary

`FileSearch` and `FileDialog` provide useful facilities to VBA programmers wanting to write file handling code. Because these objects are part of the Office object model, they have the advantage of being available to all Office VBA applications.

`FileSearch` is available in Excel 97 and all later Windows versions with considerable enhancements for Office XP users. You use it to locate files with common characteristics, such as similar file names or similar locations, so that those files can be processed in subsequent code.

`FileDialog` is new to Office XP and allows you to display the **File Open** and **File Save As** dialog boxes as well as a directory browser. It provides more powerful facilities than the `GetOpenFileName` and `GetSaveAsFileName` functions that are only available in Excel.

13

UserForms

UserForms are essentially user-defined dialog boxes. You can use them to display information and to allow the user to input new data or modify the displayed data. The `MsgBox` and `InputBox` functions provide simple tools to display messages and get input data, respectively, but UserForms take you to a new dimension. With these you can implement nearly all the features that you are accustomed to seeing in normal Windows dialog boxes.

You create a UserForm in the VBE window using **Insert | UserForm**. You add controls from the **Control ToolBox** in the same way that you add controls to a worksheet. If the **Control ToolBox** is not visible, use **View | Toolbars | Control ToolBox**.

UserForms can contain labels, TextBoxes, ListBoxes, ComboBoxes, command buttons, and many other standard or ActiveX controls. You have complete control over the placement of controls and can use as many controls as you need. Naturally, each control can respond to a wide variety of events.

Displaying a UserForm

To load a UserForm called `UserForm1` into memory, without making it visible, you use the `Load` statement:

```
Load UserForm1
```

You can remove `UserForm1` from memory using the `Unload` statement:

```
UnLoad UserForm1
```

To make `UserForm1` visible, use the `Show` method of the `UserForm` object:

```
UserForm1.Show
```

If you show a UserForm that has not been loaded, it will be automatically loaded. You can use the `Hide` method to remove a UserForm from the screen without removing it from memory:

```
UserForm1.Hide
```

The following screenshot shows a simple UserForm in action. We will develop it over the course of this chapter. It has been designed to allow you to see the current values in cells B2:B6 and to make changes to those values. It is linked directly to the cells in the worksheet, which makes it very easy to set up with a minimum of VBA code:

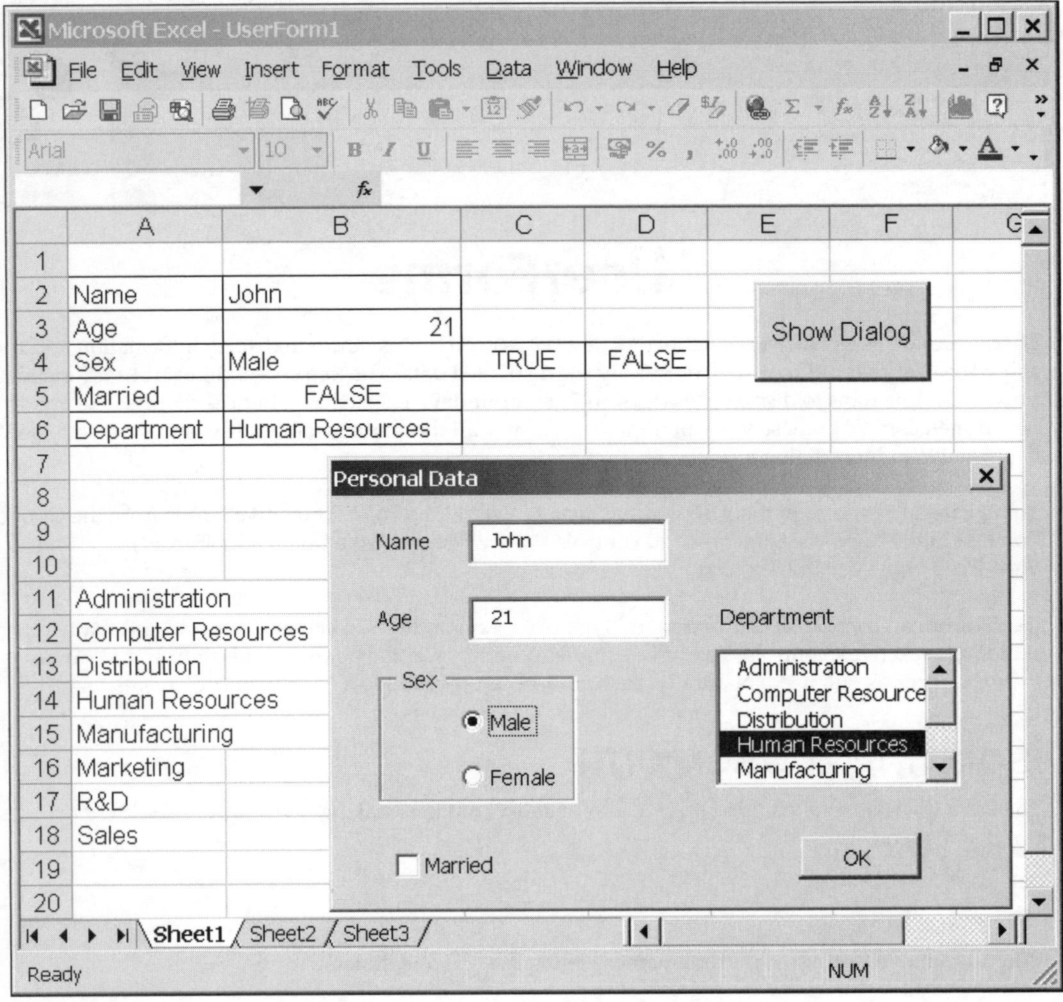

The ActiveX command button in the worksheet, with the caption Show Dialog contains the following event procedure:

```
Private Sub CommandButton1_Click()
   fmPersonal.Show
End Sub
```

The UserForm is modal by default. This means that the UserForm retains the focus until it is unloaded or hidden. The user cannot activate the worksheet or make menu choices until the UserForm is closed.

We will discuss modeless UserForms, which do allow the user to perform other tasks while they are visible, later in this chapter.

Creating a UserForm

The following screenshot shows the UserForm in the VBE window:

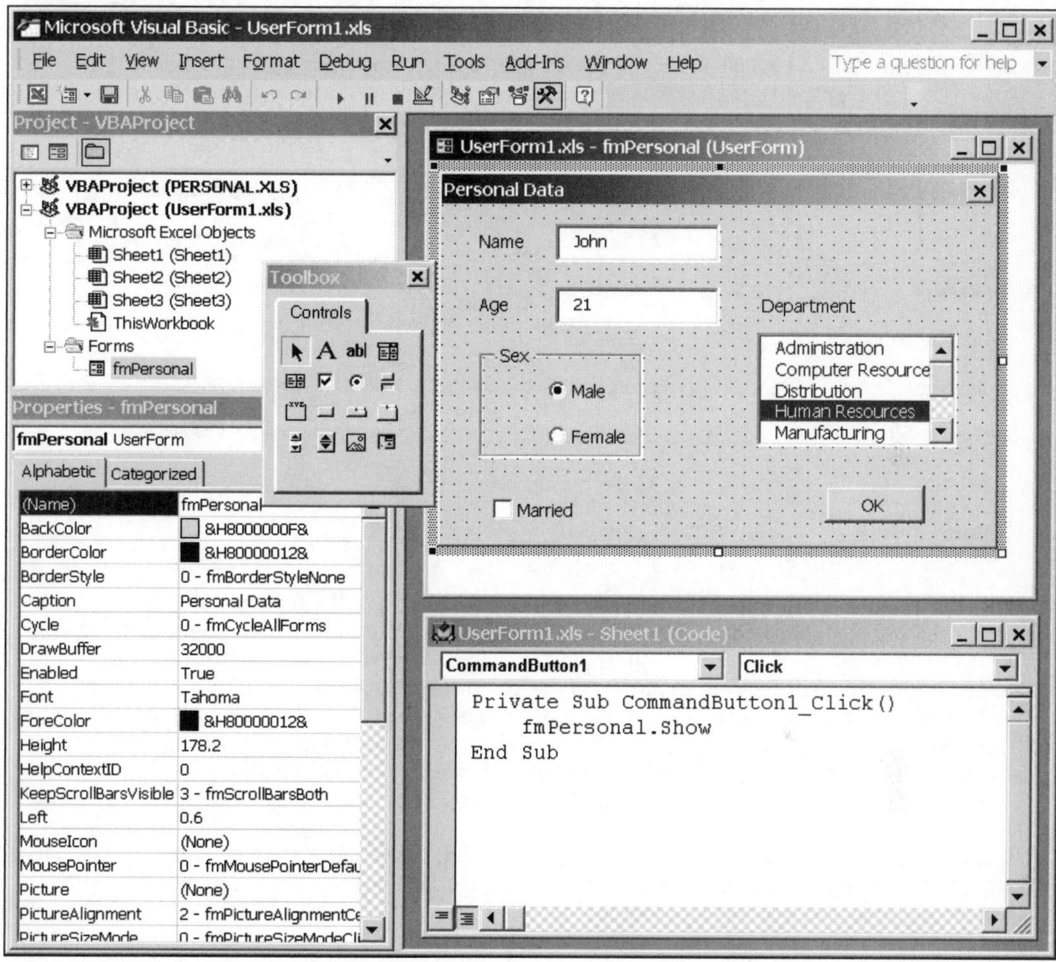

The name of the UserForm was changed from the default name `UserForm1` to `fmPersonal`. You do this in the first entry, **(Name)**, in the **Properties** window. The `Caption` property is changed to `Personal Data`. The controls were added from the **ToolBox**.

There are two TextBox controls at the top of the form for name and age data. There are two option buttons (also known as radio buttons) for **Male** and **Female**, which are inside a frame control.

When you want to have a frame around other controls, you must insert the frame first, and then insert the controls into the frame.

There is also a CheckBox for Married, a ListBox for Department and a command button for OK.

> **It is a good idea to give your UserForms and controls descriptive names that identify what type of object they are and what their purpose is. The lowercase two-character prefix identifies the object type. For example, you use `fm` for a UserForm, `sb` for a scroll bar, and `tx` for a TextBox. The capitalized words that follow identify the control's purpose. This makes it much easier to write and maintain the VBA code that manipulates these objects.**

The name of the first TextBox was changed to `txName` and the `ControlSource` property of `txName` was entered as `Sheet1!B2`. The name of the second TextBox was changed to `txAge` and the `ControlSource` property of `txAge` was entered as `Sheet1!B3`. Similar changes were made to the other main controls. The changes are summarized in the following table:

Control	Name	ControlSource
`TextBox`	`txName`	`Sheet1!B2`
`TextBox`	`txAge`	`Sheet1!B3`
`OptionButton`	`opMale`	`Sheet1!C4`
`OptionButton`	`opFemale`	`Sheet1!D4`
`CheckBox`	`ckMarried`	`Sheet1!B5`
`ListBox`	`lsDepartment`	`Sheet1!B6`
`CommandButton`	`bnOK`	

When you assign a `ControlSource` property to a worksheet cell, the cell and the control are linked in both directions. Any change to the control affects the cell and any change to the cell affects the control.

The descriptive titles on the form to the left of the TextBoxes and above the ListBox show the departments are Label controls. The `Caption` properties of the Labels were changed to `Name`, `Age`, and `Department`. The `Caption` property of the frame around the OptionButton controls was changed to `Sex` and the `Caption` properties of the option buttons were changed to `Male` and `Female`. The `Caption` property of the CheckBox was changed to `Married`.

The Male and Female option buttons can't be linked to B4. It is not appropriate to display the values of these controls directly, so the following `IF` function in cell B4 converts the `True` or `False` value in cell C4 to the required `Male` or `Female` result:

```
=IF(C4=TRUE,"Male","Female")
```

Although you only need to set cell C4 to get the required result, you need to link both option buttons to separate cells if you want the buttons to display properly when the UserForm is shown.

The `RowSource` property of `lsDepartment` was entered as `Sheet1!A11:A18`. It is good practice to create names for the linked cells and use those names in the `ControlSource`, rather than the cell references used here, but this extra step has been omitted to simplify our example.

The following `Click` event procedure was created for the button in the code module behind the UserForm:

```
Private Sub bnOK_Click()
   Unload Me
End Sub
```

`Me` is a shortcut keyword that refers to the `UserForm` object containing the code. `Me` can be used in any class module to refer to the object the class module represents. If you want to access the control values later in your VBA code, you must use the `Hide` method, which leaves the UserForm in memory. Otherwise, the `Unload` statement removes the UserForm from memory and the control values are lost. You will see examples that use `Hide` shortly.

Clicking the x in the top right corner of the UserForm will also dismiss the UserForm. This unloads the UserForm so that it is removed from memory. We will see how to prevent this later.

Directly Accessing Controls in UserForms

Linking UserForm controls to cells is not always the best way to work. You can gain more flexibility by directly accessing the data in the UserForm. The following screenshot shows a revised version of our previous example. We want to display essentially the same UserForm, but we want to store the resulting data as shown. `Sex` will be stored as a single letter code, `M` or `F`. The `Department` name will be stored as a two-character code:

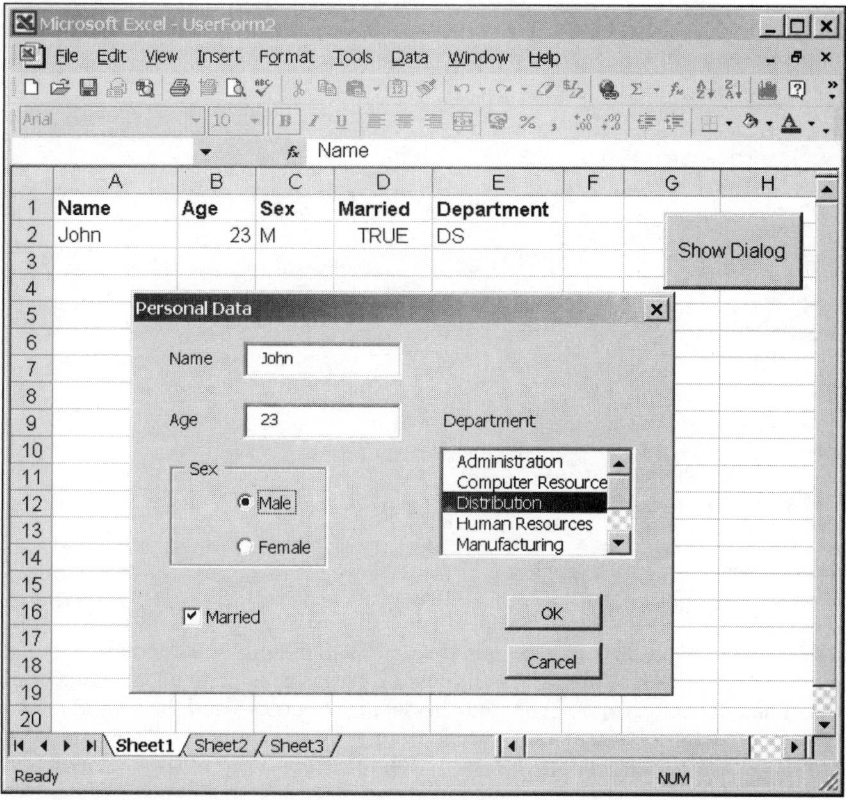

We have added a **Cancel** button to the UserForm so that any changes made to the controls while the UserForm is being shown can be discarded if the user wishes, rather than being automatically applied to the worksheet. The module behind `fmPersonal` now contains the following code:

```
Option Explicit
Public Cancelled As Boolean

Private Sub bnCancel_Click()
   Cancelled = True
   Me.Hide
End Sub

Private Sub bnOK_Click()
   Cancelled = False
   Me.Hide
End Sub
```

The `Public` variable `Cancelled` will provide a way to detect that the **Cancel** button has been pressed. If the **OK** button is pressed, `Cancelled` is assigned the value `False`. If the **Cancel** button is pressed, `Cancelled` is assigned a value of `True`. Both buttons hide `fmPersonal` so that it remains in memory. The following event procedure has also been added to the module behind `fmPersonal`:

```
Private Sub UserForm_Initialize()
   Dim vaDepartment As Variant
   Dim vaDeptCode As Variant
   Dim stDeptList() As String
   Dim i As Integer

   vaDepartment = VBA.Array("Administration", _
          "Computer Resources", _
          "Distribution", _
          "Human Resources", _
          "Manufacturing", _
          "Marketing", _
          "R&D", _
          "Sales")
   vaDeptCode = VBA.Array("AD", _
          "CR", _
          "DS", _
          "HR", _
          "MF", _
          "MK", _
          "RD", _
          "SL")
   ReDim stDeptList(0 To UBound(vaDepartment), 0 To 1)
   For i = 0 To UBound(vaDepartment)
      stDeptList(i, 0) = vaDeptCode(i)
      stDeptList(i, 1) = vaDepartment(i)
   Next i
   lsDepartment.List = stDeptList
End Sub
```

The `UserForm_Initialize` event is triggered when the UserForm is loaded into memory. It does not occur when the form has been hidden and is shown again. It is used here to load `lsDepartment` with two columns of data. The first column contains the department codes and the second contains the department names to be displayed.

vaDepartment and vaDeptCode are assigned arrays in the usual way using the Array function, except that VBA.Array has been used to ensure that the arrays are zero-based. stDeptList is a dynamic array and ReDim is used to dimension it to the same number of rows as in vaDepartment and two columns, once again zero-based.

The For...Next loop assigns the department codes and names to the two columns of stDeptList. stDeptList is then assigned directly to the List property of lsDepartment. If you prefer, you can maintain a table of departments and codes in a worksheet range and set the ListBox's RowSource property equal to the range as we saw in the first example in this chapter.

When you have a multicolumn ListBox, you need to specify which column contains the data that will appear in a link cell and be returned in the control's Value property. This column is referred to as the bound column. The BoundColumn property of lsDepartment has been set to 1. This property is one-based, so the bound column is the department code. The ColumnCount property has been set to 2, as there are two columns of data in the list.

However, we only want to see the department names in the ListBox, so we want to hide the first column. We can do that by setting the column width of the first column to 0. To do this, we only need to enter a single 0 in the ColumnWidths property, rather than, for example, 0;40. Entering a single 0 sets the first column to a width of 0 and leaves the second column to fill the ListBox width.

The following code has been placed in the module behind Sheet1:

```
Private Sub bnShowDialog_Click()
   Dim rgData As Range
   Dim vaData As Variant

   ' First block of code here
   Set rgData = Range("Database").Rows(2)
   vaData = rgData.Value
   With fmPersonal
      .txName.Value = vaData(1, 1)
      .txAge.Value = vaData(1, 2)
      Select Case vaData(1, 3)
         Case "F"
            .opFemale.Value = True
         Case "M"
            .opMale.Value = True
      End Select
      .ckMarried.Value = vaData(1, 4)
      .lsDepartment.Value = vaData(1, 5)

      ' Second block of code here
      .Show
      If Not .Cancelled Then

         ' Third block of code here
         vaData(1, 1) = .txName
         vaData(1, 2) = .txAge
         Select Case True
            Case .opFemale.Value
               vaData(1, 3) = "F"
            Case .opMale.Value
               vaData(1, 3) = "M"
         End Select
         vaData(1, 4) = .ckMarried.Value
         vaData(1, 5) = .lsDepartment.Value
```

```
            rgData.Value = vaData
         End If
      End With
      Unload fmPersonal
   End Sub
```

The code is in three blocks after the initial declaration statements. The first block loads the data from the worksheet into `fmPersonal`. The second block (only two lines) displays `fmPersonal`, then checks to see if the **Cancel** button is pressed. The third block copies the data in `fmPersonal` back to the worksheet.

At the start of the first block, `rgData` is assigned a reference to cells **A2:E2**. The range **A1:E2** has been given the name `Database`, so `Range("Database").Rows(2)` refers to the required data range. The values in `rgData` are then assigned directly to the variant `vaData`. This creates a two dimensional, one-based array of values having one row and five columns. It is much more efficient to access the worksheet data in this way rather than to access each cell individually.

Most of the remaining code is within the `With... End With` structure, which makes it possible to use shorter and more efficient references to the controls, properties, and methods associated with `fmPersonal`. The first reference to `fmPersonal` also causes `fmPersonal` to be loaded into memory, although it remains hidden at this point.

The `Value` properties of the controls on `fmPersonal` are then assigned the values in `vaData`. The option buttons are an exception because the `M` and `F` code values need to be translated to `True` values as appropriate. It is only necessary to set one of the option buttons to `True` as the other will automatically be set to `False`. You can group option buttons by assigning them the same value in their `GroupName` property, or by placing them in the same frame. The option buttons here do not have a value in their `GroupName` property. They are considered to be in the same group because they are in the same frame.

The `Show` method displays `fmPersonal`. Control then passes to `fmPersonal` until it is hidden, which occurs when the user presses the **OK** or **Cancel** button, or the **x** at the top of the UserForm. The user can also press *Esc* to activate the **Cancel** button because it has had its `Cancel` property set to `True`. The user can also press *Enter* to activate the **OK** button, as long as the **Cancel** button does not have the focus, because the OK button's `Default` property has been set to `True`.

When `fmPersonal` is hidden, the `bnShowDialog_Click` event procedure regains control, and checks to see if the **Cancel** button was pressed. It does this by examining the value of the `Public` variable `Cancelled` on `fmPersonal`.

The code modules behind UserForms (as well as those behind sheets and workbooks) are class modules. When you define a Public variable in a class module, the variable behaves as a property of the object associated with the class module. See Chapter 13 for more details.

If `Cancelled` is `False`, the procedure loads the values of the controls back into `vaData`, translating the option button settings back into an `F` or `M` value and the values in `vaData` are directly assigned back to the worksheet. The final step is to unload `fmPersonal` from memory.

Stopping the Close Button

One problem with the above code is that, if the user clicks the **x**, which is the **Close** button at the top of `fmPersonal`, the event procedure does not exit. Instead, it transfers any changes back to the worksheet. This is because the default value for `Cancelled` is `False`. Normally, clicking the **x** would also unload the form and the code would fail when it tries to access the controls on the form. However, in this case the `With...End With` structure keeps `fmPersonal` in scope, and `fmPersonal` is not unloaded until after the `End With` statement.

There are a number of simple ways in which the above problem could be corrected, but the following method gives you total control over that little **x**. You can use the `QueryClose` event of the `UserForm` object to discover what is closing the UserForm and cancel the event if necessary. Adding the following code to the `fmPersonal` module blocks the **Close** button exit:

```
Private Sub UserForm_QueryClose(Cancel As Integer, CloseMode As Integer)
   If CloseMode = vbFormControlMenu Then
      MsgBox "Please use only the OK or Cancel buttons", vbCritical
      Cancel = True
   End If
End Sub
```

The `QueryClose` event can be triggered in four ways. You can determine what caused the event by using the following intrinsic constants to test the `CloseMode` parameter:

Constant	Value	Reason for the event
`vbFormControlMenu`	0	The user clicked the **x** in the Control menu on the UserForm.
`vbFormCode`	1	The `Unload` statement was used to remove the UserForm from memory.
`vbAppWindows`	2	Windows is shutting down.
`vbAppTaskManager`	3	The application is being closed by the Windows Task Manager.

Maintaining a Data List

The code we have developed can now be extended to maintain a data list without too much extra effort. However, we will take a different approach to the last example. This time we will build all the code into `fmPersonal`, apart from the code behind the command button in the worksheet that shows the UserForm. The code behind this button now becomes the following:

```
Private Sub bnShowDialog_Click()
   fmPersonal.Show
End Sub
```

It is really much easier to maintain a data list in a proper database application, such as Microsoft Access, but it can be done in Excel without too much trouble if your requirements are fairly simple.

If we are going to manage more than one row of data, we need to be able to add new rows, delete existing rows, and navigate through the rows. `fmPersonal` needs some extra controls as shown:

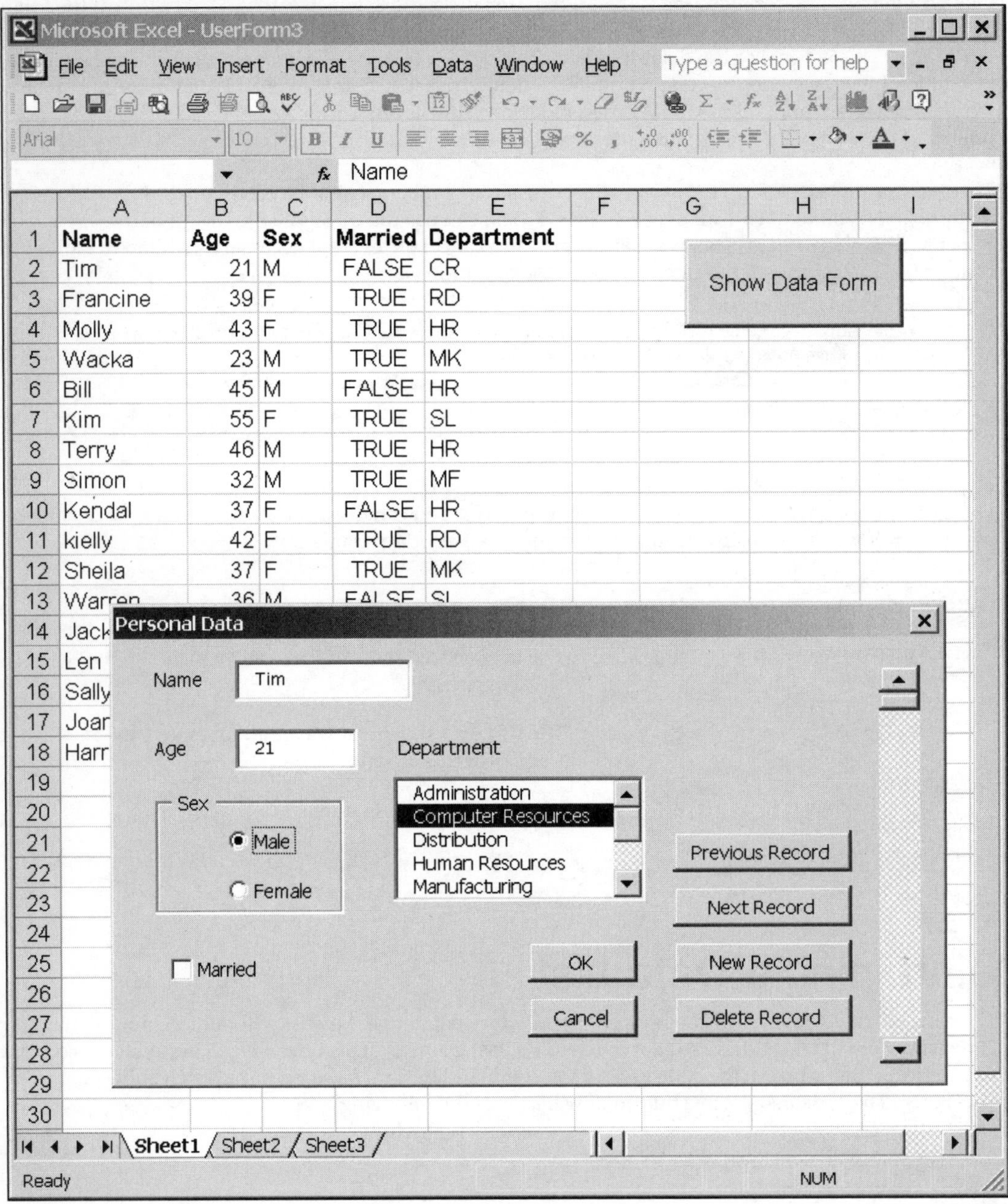

The scroll bar is a handy way to navigate through many records quickly. It also makes it easy to get to the last or first record. It can also be used to go to the next or previous record. For variety, we have included buttons to go to the next and previous records as well. The New Record button adds a record to the end of the data list and initializes some of the values in the new record. The Delete button deletes the record that is currently showing in `fmPersonal`.

The code in `fmPersonal` is discussed below. It is important to note first that the following module-level variables have been declared in the (Declarations) section at the top of the `fmPersonal` code module:

```
Dim rgData As Range
Dim vaData As Variant
```

These variables are used in exactly the same way as they were used in the previous example, except that the row referred to can vary. The object variable `rgData` is always set to the current row of data in the named range `Database`, which currently refers to A1:E18 in the worksheet shown above. `vaData` always holds the values from `rgData` as a VBA array.

The code from the command button event procedure in our previous example has been converted to two utility procedures that reside in `fmPersonal`'s code module:

```
Private Sub LoadRecord()
   'Copy values in rgData from worksheet to vaData array
   vaData = rgData.Value
   'Assign array values to fmPersonal controls
   txName.Value = vaData(1, 1)
   txAge.Value = vaData(1, 2)
   Select Case vaData(1, 3)
      Case "F"
         opFemale.Value = True
      Case "M"
         opMale.Value = True
   End Select
   ckMarried.Value = vaData(1, 4)
   lsDepartment.Value = vaData(1, 5)
End Sub

Private Sub SaveRecord()
   'Copy values from fmPersonal controls to Data array
   vaData(1, 1) = txName.Value
   vaData(1, 2) = txAge.Value
   Select Case True
      Case opFemale.Value
         vaData(1, 3) = "F"
      Case opMale.Value
         vaData(1, 3) = "M"
   End Select
   vaData(1, 4) = ckMarried.Value
   vaData(1, 5) = lsDepartment.Value
   'Assign Data array values to current record in Database
   rgData.Value = vaData
End Sub
```

As the code is in the `fmPersonal` module, there is no need to refer to `fmPersonal` when referring to a control, so all controls are directly addressed in the code.

`LoadRecord` and `SaveRecord` are the only procedures that are tailored to the data list structure and the controls. As long as the data list has the name `Database`, none of the other code in `fmPersonal` needs to change if we decide to add more fields to the data list or remove fields. It also means that we can readily apply the same code to a completely different data list. All we have to do is redesign the UserForm controls and update `LoadRecord` and `SaveRecord`.

The key navigation device in `fmPersonal` is the scroll bar, which has been named `sbNavigator`. It is used by the other buttons when a change of record is required, as well as being available to the user directly. The `Value` property of `sbNavigator` corresponds to the row number in the range named `Database`.

The minimum value of `sbNavigator` is fixed permanently at two, as the first record is the second row in `Database`, so you need to set the `Min` property of the scroll bar in the Properties window. The maximum value is altered as needed by the other event procedures in `fmPersonal` so that it always corresponds to the last row in `Database`:

```
Private Sub sbNavigator_Change()
   'When Scrollbar value changes, save current record and load
   'record number corresponding to scroll bar value
   Call SaveRecord
   Set rgData = Range("Database").Rows(sbNavigator.Value)
   Call LoadRecord
End Sub
```

When the user changes the `sbNavigator.Value` property (or when it is changed by other event procedures) the `Change` event fires and saves the current record in `fmPersonal`, redefines `rgData` to be the row in `Database` corresponding to the new value of `sbNavigator.Value`, and loads the data from that row into `fmPersonal`.

The `UserForm_Initialize` event procedure has been updated from the previous exercise to set the correct starting values for `sbNavigator`:

```
Private Sub UserForm_Initialize()
   'Sets up lsDepartment list values
   'and loads first record in Database
   Dim vaDepartment As Variant
   Dim vaDeptCode As Variant
   Dim stDeptList() As String
   Dim i As Integer

   vaDepartment = VBA.Array("Administration", _
         "Computer Resources", _
         "Distribution", _
         "Human Resources", _
         "Manufacturing", _
         "Marketing", _
         "R&D", _
         "Sales", _
         "None")
   vaDeptCode = VBA.Array("AD", _
         "CR", _
         "DS", _
         "HR", _
         "MF", _
         "MK", _
```

```
            "RD", _
            "SL", _
            "NA")
      ReDim stDeptList(0 To UBound(vaDepartment), 0 To 1)
      For i = 0 To UBound(vaDepartment)
         stDeptList(i, 0) = vaDeptCode(i)
         stDeptList(i, 1) = vaDepartment(i)
      Next i
      lsDepartment.List = stDeptList
      'Load 1st record in Database and initialize scroll bar
      With Range("Database")
         Set rgData = .Rows(2)
         Call LoadRecord
         sbNavigator.Value = 2
         sbNavigator.Max = .Rows.Count
      End With
   End Sub
```

After initializing the `lsDepartment.List` property, the code initializes `rgData` to refer to the second row of `Database`, row two being the first row of data under the field names on row one, and loads the data from that row into `fmPersonal`. It then initializes the `Value` property of `sbNavigator` to two and sets the `Max` property of `sbNavigator` to the number of rows in `Database`. If the user changes the scroll bar, they can navigate to any row from row two through to the last row in `Database`.

The buttons captioned **Next Record** and **Previous Record** have been named `bnNext` and `bnPrevious`. The `Click` event procedure for `bnNext` is as follows:

```
   Private Sub bnNext_Click()
      With Range("Database")
         If rgData.Row < .Rows(.Rows.Count).Row Then
            'Load next record only if not on last record
            sbNavigator.Value = sbNavigator.Value + 1
            'Note: Setting sbNavigator.Value runs its Change event procedure
         End If
      End With
   End Sub
```

The `If` test checks that the current row number in `Database` is less than the last row number in `Database` to ensure that we don't try to go beyond the data. If there is room to move, the value of `sbNavigator` is increased by one. This change triggers the `Change` event procedure for `sbNavigator`, which saves the current data, resets `rgData`, and loads the next row's data.

The code for `bnPrevious` is similar to `bnNext` except that there is no need for the `With...End With` as we don't need to keep repeating the reference to `Range("Database")`:

```
   Private Sub bnPrevious_Click()
      If rgData.Row > Range("Database").Rows(2).Row Then
         'Load previous record if not on first record
         sbNavigator.Value = sbNavigator.Value - 1
         'Note: Setting sbNavigator.Value runs its Change event procedure
      End If
   End Sub
```

The check ensures that we don't try to move to row numbers lower than the second row in `Database`. This, and the `bnNext` check, could have also been carried out using the `Value`, `Max`, and `Min` properties of `sbNavigator`, but the method used in `bnNext_Click` shows you how to determine the row number of the last row in a named range, which is a technique that it is very useful to know. It is important to carry out these checks as trying to set the `sbNavigator.Value` property outside the `Min` to `Max` range causes a run-time error.

The code for `bnDelete` is as follows:

```
Private Sub bnDelete_Click()
   'Deletes current record in fmPersonal

   If Range("Database").Rows.Count = 2 Then
      'Don't delete if only one record left
      MsgBox "You cannot delete every record", vbCritical
      Exit Sub
   ElseIf rgData.Row = Range("Database").Rows(2).Row Then
      'If on 1st record, move down one record and delete 1st record
      'shifting the rows below up to fill the gap
      Set rgData = rgData.Offset(1)
      rgData.Offset(-1).Delete shift:=xlUp
      Call LoadRecord
   Else
      'If on other than 1st record, move to previous record before delete
      sbNavigator.Value = sbNavigator.Value - 1
      'Note: Setting sbNavigator.Value runs its Change event procedure
      rgData.Offset(1).Delete shift:=xlUp
   End If
   sbNavigator.Max = sbNavigator.Max - 1
End Sub
```

This procedure carries out the following actions:

- It aborts if you try to delete the last remaining record in `Database`.
- If you delete the first record, `rgData` is assigned a reference to the second record. `SbNavigator.Value` is not reset, as row 2 becomes row 1, once the original row 1 is deleted. `LoadRecord` is called to load the data in `rgData` into the UserForm.
- If you delete a record that is not the first one, `sbNavigator.Value` is reduced by one. This causes the previous record to be loaded into the UserForm.
- At the end, the count of the number of rows in `Database`, held in `sbNavigator.Max`, is decreased by 1.

The code for `bnNew` is as follows:

```
Private Sub bnNew_Click()
   'Add new record at bottom of database
   Dim iRowCount As Integer

   With Range("Database")
      'Add extra row to name Database
      iRowCount = .Rows.Count + 1
      .Resize(iRowCount).Name = "Database"
      sbNavigator.Max = iRowCount
      sbNavigator.Value = iRowCount
      'Note: Setting sbNavigator.Value runs its Change event procedure
```

```
    End With
    'Set default values
    opMale.Value = True
    ckMarried = False
    lsDepartment.Value = "NA"
End Sub
```

This event procedure defines `iRowCount` to be one higher than the current number of rows in `Database`. It then generates a reference to a range with one more row than `Database` and redefines the name `Database` to refer to the larger range. It then assigns `iRowCount` to both the `Max` property of `sbNavigator` and the `Value` property of `sbNavigator`. Setting the `Value` property fires the `Change` event procedure for `sbNavigator`, which makes the new empty row the current row and loads the empty values into `fmPersonal`. Default values are then applied to some of the `fmPersonal` controls.

The only remaining code in `fmPersonal` is for the `bnOK_Click` and `bnCancel_Click` events as follows:

```
Private Sub bnOK_Click()
    'Save Current Record and unload fmPersonal
    Call SaveRecord
    Unload Me
End Sub

Private Sub bnCancel_Click()
    'Unload fmPersonal without saving current record
    Unload Me
End Sub
```

Both buttons unload `fmPersonal`. Only the **OK** button saves any changes to the current record in the UserForm.

Modeless UserForms

Excel 2000 and Excel 2002 provide the ability to show modeless UserForms. The modal UserForms that we have dealt with so far do not allow the user to change the focus away from the UserForm while it is being displayed. You cannot activate a worksheet, menu, or toolbar, for example, until the UserForm has been hidden or unloaded from memory. If you have a procedure that uses the `Show` method to display a modal UserForm, that procedure cannot execute the code that follows the `Show` method until the UserForm is hidden or unloaded.

A modeless UserForm does allow the user to activate worksheets, menus, and toolbars. It floats in the foreground until it is hidden or unloaded. The procedure that uses the `Show` method to display a modeless UserForm will immediately continue to execute the code that follows the `Show` method. `fmPersonal`, from our previous example that maintains a data list, can easily be displayed modeless. All you need to do is change the code that displays it as follows:

```
Private Sub CommandButton1_Click()
    fmPersonal.Show vbModeless
End Sub
```

When the UserForm is modeless, you can carry on with other work while it is visible. You can even copy and paste data from TextBoxes on the UserForm to worksheet cells.

Progress Indicator

One feature that has been lacking in Excel is a good progress indicator that lets you show how much work has been done, and remains to be done, while a lengthy task is carried out in the background. You can display a message on the status bar using `Application.StatusBar` as discussed in Chapter 3, but this message is not very obvious.

You can set up a good progress indicator very easily using a modeless UserForm. The following screen shows a simple progress bar indicator that moves from left to right to give a graphic indication of progress:

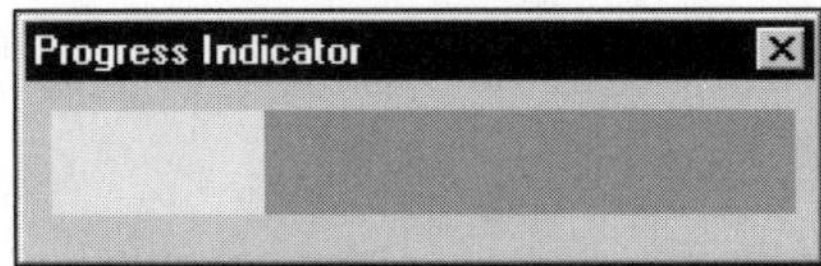

The progress indicator is a normal UserForm with two label controls, one on top of the other, which have been given contrasting background colors. The `Caption` properties of both labels are blank.

This UserForm has been given the name `fmProgress`. The longer label is named `lbFixed`, as it extends over almost all the width of the UserForm and never changes. The shorter label, which is on top of the fixed label, is named `lbIndicate`. Initially, it is given a width of 0 and its width is gradually increased until it equals the width of the fixed label. The UserForm module contains the following procedure:

```
Public Sub pcProgress(iPerCent As Integer)
   lbIndicate.Width = iPerCent / 100 * lbFixed.Width
   DoEvents
End Sub
```

When you execute `pcProgress`, you pass a number between 0 and 100 as the input argument `iPerCent`. `pcProgress` sets the width of `lbIndicate` to `iPerCent` percent of the width of `lbFixed`. The `DoEvents` statement instructs the operating system to update the UserForm.

The operating system gives priority to the running macro and holds back on updating the modeless UserForm. `DoEvents` tells the operating system to stop the macro and complete any pending events. This technique often corrects problems with screen updating or where background tasks need to be completed before a macro can continue processing.

The progress indicator can be used with a procedure like the following, which counts how many cells contain errors within a range:

```
Sub TakesAWhile()
   Dim Rng As Range
   Dim lErrorCount As Long

   For Each Rng In Range(Cells(1, 1), Cells(1000, 100))
      If IsError(Rng.Value) Then lErrorCount = lerrCount + 1
   Next Rng
   MsgBox "Error count = " & lErrorCount
End Sub
```

To incorporate the progress indicator, you can add the following code to the procedure:

```
Sub TakesAWhile()
  Dim Rng As Range
  Dim lCount As Long
  Dim lRows As Long
  Dim lErrorCount As Long

  lRows = 1000
  fmProgress.Show vbModeless
  For Each Rng In Range(Cells(1, 1), Cells(lRows, 100))
    If IsError(Rng.Value) Then lErrorCount = lErrorCount + 1
    If lCount Mod lRows = 0 Then
      fmProgress.pcProgress lCount / lRows
    End If
    lCount = lCount + 1
  Next Rng
  Unload fmProgress
  MsgBox "Error count = " & lErrorCount
End Sub
```

The changes include showing `fmProgress` as a modeless UserForm at the start. Within the `For Each...Next` loop, the variable `lCount` is used to count the loops. `lCount Mod lRows` has a value of zero when `lCount` is zero and every multiple of 1000 loops, so `fmProgress` is updated when `lCount` is zero and then at intervals of 1000 iterations. As this loop repeats 100,000 times, the `pcProgress` procedure in `fmProgress` is run 100 times with the input parameter varying from 0 to 99.

When a class module (such as the module behind a UserForm) contains a public procedure, you can execute the procedure as a method of the object represented by the class module.

The time taken by the macro will vary according to your processor. For demonstration purposes, you can alter the time taken by the procedure by changing the value of `lRows`.

Variable UserForm Name

In all our examples of UserForms, we have referred to the UserForm by its programmatic name such as `fmProgress`. There can be situations where you need to run a number of different forms with the same code, or you don't know the programmatic name of the UserForm before the code is executed. In these cases you need to be able to assign the UserForm name to a variable and use the variable as an argument. The following code allows you to do this:

```
FormName = "fmPersonal"
VBA.UserForms.Add(FormName).Show
```

Summary

In this chapter we introduced the topic of UserForms. You have seen how to:

- Directly link controls on a form to a worksheet
- Use VBA code to access UserForm controls and copy data between the form and a worksheet
- Prevent closure of a UserForm by modifying the code executed when the x button is pressed
- Set up a form to maintain a data list and the difference between modal and modeless UserForms
- Construct a progress indicator using a modeless UserForm.

14

Command Bars

The `CommandBars` collection is an object contained in the Office Object Model, documented in Appendix C. It contains all the menus, toolbars, and shortcut popup menus that are already built into Excel and the other Office applications, as well as any of those objects that you create yourself. You access commandbars through the `CommandBars` property of the `Application` object.

Commandbars were first introduced into Office in Office 97. Excel 5 and 95 supported menu bars and toolbars as separate object types. Shortcut menus, or popups, such as those which appear when you right-click a worksheet cell, were a special type of menu bar. In Excel 97 and later versions, the 'command bar' is a generic term that includes menu bars, toolbars, and shortcut menus.

Commandbars contain items that are called **controls**. When clicked, some controls execute operations, such as Copy. Until we get down to the nuts and bolts we will refer to these types of controls as **commands**. There are other controls, such as File, that produce an additional list of controls when clicked. We will refer to these controls as **menus**.

In this chapter we will show you how to create and manipulate these useful tools.

Toolbars, Menu Bars, and Popups

The screenshot overleaf shows the standard Worksheet menu bar at the top of the Excel window:

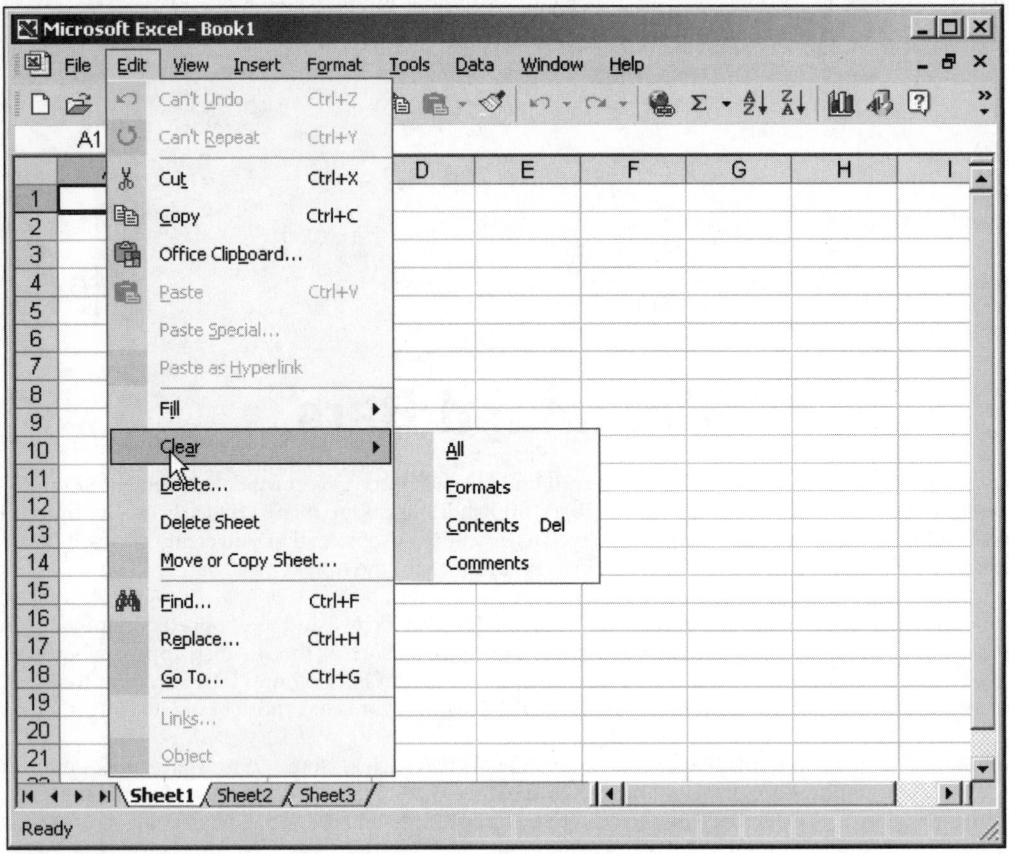

The Worksheet menu bar contains menus, such as File and Edit. When you click on a menu, you see another list containing commands and menus.

- Cut and Copy are examples of commands in the Edit menu
- Clear is an example of a menu contained within the Edit menu

The following shows the Standard toolbar:

Toolbars contain controls that can be clicked to execute Excel commands. For example, the button with the scissors icon carries out a Cut. Toolbars can also contain other types of controls such as the Zoom combobox (two from the end of the Standard toolbar in the figure above) that allows you to select, or type in, a zoom factor, displayed as a percentage. Some toolbars contain buttons that display menus, such as the PivotTable button in the PivotTable toolbar.

The following shows the shortcut menu that appears when you right-click a worksheet cell:

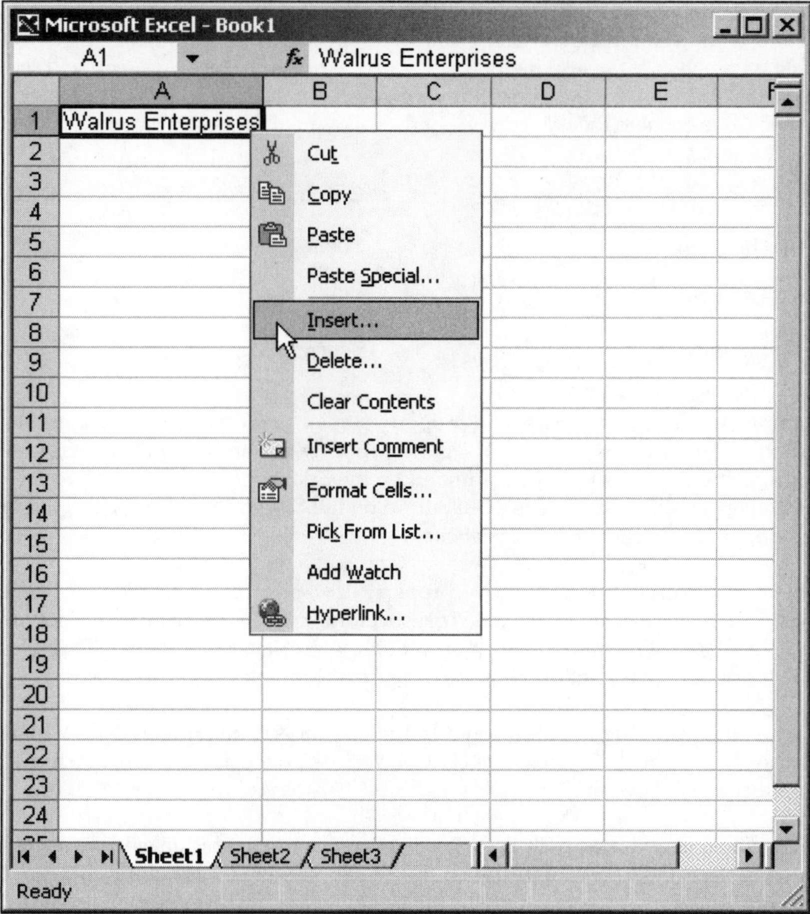

This shortcut menu contains commands, such as Paste, and menus, such as Delete..., for those operations appropriate to the selected context, in this case the a cell.

Excel 2002 has nearly 100 different built-in commandbars containing many thousands of controls. In addition, you can create your own commandbars or tailor existing commandbars to suit your needs. This can be accomplished manually using View | Toolbars | Customize..., or you can do it programmatically.

You may be able to accomplish all the customization you need manually, including attaching commandbars to workbooks, but some tasks can only be carried out using VBA code. For example, you need VBA if you want to:

- Automatically remove or hide a command bar when its related workbook is closed or deactivated
- Add a custom menu to a built-in menu bar when a workbook is opened and remove it when the workbook is closed
- Dynamically change your commandbars in response to user actions
- Use some types of controls, such as combo boxes, that can only be created and controlled using VBA

To summarize, a command bar can be any one of three types. It can be a menu, toolbar, or shortcut popup menu. When you create a command bar using VBA, you specify which of the three types it will be, using the appropriate parameters of the `Add` method of the `CommandBars` collection. You will see examples of this below. You can find out what type an existing command bar is by testing its `Type` property, which will return a numeric value equal to the value of one of the following intrinsic constants:

Constant	Command Bar Type
`msoBarTypeNormal`	Toolbar
`msoBarTypeMenuBar`	Menu Bar
`msoBarTypePopup`	Shortcut Menu

Controls on commandbars also have a `Type` property similar to the `msoXXX` constants shown above. The control that is used most frequently has a `Type` property of `msoControlButton`, which represents a command such as the Copy command on the Edit menu of the Worksheet menu bar, or a command button on a toolbar, such as the Cut button on the Standard toolbar. This type of control runs a macro or a built-in Excel action when it is clicked.

The second most common control has a `Type` property of `msoControlPopup`. This represents a menu on a menu bar, such as the Edit menu on the Worksheet menu bar, or a menu contained in another a menu, such as the Clear submenu on the Edit menu on the Worksheet menu bar. This type of control contains its own `Controls` collection, to which you can add further controls.

Controls have an `Id` property. For built-in controls, the `Id` property determines the internal action carried out by the control. When you set up a custom control, you assign the name of a macro to its `OnAction` property to make it execute that macro when it is clicked. Custom controls have an `Id` property of `1`.

Many built-in menu items and most built-in toolbar controls have a graphic image associated with them. The image is defined by the `FaceId` property. The `Id` and `FaceId` properties of built-in commands normally have the same numeric value. You can assign the built-in `FaceId` values to your own controls, if you know what numeric value to use. You can determine these values using VBA, as you will see in the next example.

Excel's Built-In Command Bars

Before launching into creating our own commandbars, it will help to understand how the built-in commandbars are structured and find out just what is already available in Excel 2002. You can use the following code to list the existing commandbars and any that you have added yourself. It lists the name of each command bar in column A and the names of the controls in the commandbar's `Controls` collection in column B as shown in the following screen. The code does not attempt to display lower level controls that belong to controls such as the File menu on the Worksheet menu bar, so the procedure has been named `ListFirstLevelControls`.

The macro also shows the control's `Id` property value, in all cases, and its image and its `FaceId` property value when such an image exists. Note that some listed controls might not be visible on your own screen. For example, the Standard toolbar's &Mail Recipient button will not be visible if you do not have a mail system.

> **Make sure you are in an empty worksheet when you run this macro and the following two examples. They contain tests to make sure they will not overwrite any data in the active sheet.**

If you are testing this code, remember that it should be placed in a standard code module, not in a class module. Don't put the code in the `ThisWorkbook` module or a class module behind a worksheet. You should also include the `IsEmptyWorksheet` function listed further down:

Microsoft Excel - ListCommandBars.xls

A1 | CommandBar

	A	B	C	D
1	**CommandBar**	**Control**	**FaceID**	**ID**
2	Worksheet Menu Bar			
3		&File		30002
4		&Edit		30003
5		&View		30004
6		&Insert		30005
7		F&ormat		30006
8		&Tools		30007
9		&Data		30011
10		A&ction		30083
11		&Window		30009
12		&Help		30010
13	Chart Menu Bar			
14		&File		30002
15		&Edit		30003
16		&View		30004
17		&Insert		30005
18		F&ormat		30006
19		&Tools		30007
20		&Chart		30022
21		A&ction		30083
22		&Window		30009
23		&Help		30010
24	Standard			
25		&New	2520	2520
26		Open	23	23
27		&Save	3	3
28		&Mail Recipient	3738	3738
29		Searc&h...	5905	5905
30		Print (\\TIMBO\Samsung 7000 Series PS)	2521	2521
31		Print Pre&view	109	109
32		&Spelling...	2	2
33		Cu&t	21	21

Sheet1 / Sheet2 / Sheet3

Ready

Here is the code to list the first level controls:

```
Sub ListFirstLevelControls()
   Dim cbCtl As CommandBarControl
   Dim cbBar As CommandBar
   Dim i As Integer
   If Not IsEmptyWorksheet(ActiveSheet) Then Exit Sub
   On Error Resume Next
   Application.ScreenUpdating = False
   Cells(1, 1).Value = "CommandBar"
   Cells(1, 2).Value = "Control"
   Cells(1, 3).Value = "FaceID"
   Cells(1, 4).Value = "ID"
   Cells(1, 1).Resize(1,4).Font.Bold = True
   i = 2
```

```
   For Each cbBar In CommandBars
      Application.StatusBar = "Processing Bar " & cbBar.Name
      Cells(i, 1).Value = cbBar.Name
      i = i + 1
      For Each cbCtl In cbBar.Controls
         Cells(i, 2).Value = cbCtl.Caption
         cbCtl.CopyFace
         If Err.Number = 0 Then
            ActiveSheet.Paste Cells(i, 3)
            Cells(i, 3).Value = cbCtl.FaceID
         End If
         Cells(i, 4).Value = cbCtl.ID
         Err.Clear
         i = i + 1
      Next cbCtl
   Next cbBar
   Range("A:B").EntireColumn.AutoFit
   Application.StatusBar = False
End Sub
```

This example, and the two following, can take a long time to complete. You can watch the progress of the code on the status bar. If you only want to see part of the output, press *Ctrl+Break* after a minute or so to interrupt the macro, click Debug and then Run | Reset.

`ListFirstLevelControls` first checks that the active sheet is an empty worksheet using the `IsEmptyWorksheet` function that is shown below. It then uses `On Error Resume Next` to avoid run-time errors when it tries to access control images that do not exist. In the outer `For Each...Next` loop, it assigns a reference to each command bar to `cbBar`, shows the `Name` property of the commandbar on the status bar so you can track what it is doing, and places the `Name` in the A column of the current row, defined by `i`.

The inner `For Each...Next` loop processes all the controls on `cbBar`, placing the `Caption` property of each control in column B. It then attempts to use the `CopyFace` method of the control to copy the control's image to the clipboard. If this does not create an error, it pastes the image to column C and places the value of the `FaceId` property in the same cell. It places the `ID` property of the control in column D. It clears any errors, increments `i` by one and processes the next control.

The `IsEmptyWorksheet` function, shown below, checks that the input parameter object `Sht` is a worksheet. If so, it checks that the count of entries in the used range is 0. If both checks succeed, it returns `True`. Otherwise, it issues a warning message and the default return value, which is `False`, is returned:

```
Function IsEmptyWorksheet(Sht As Object) As Boolean
   If TypeName(Sht) = "Worksheet" Then
      If WorksheetFunction.CountA(Sht.UsedRange) = 0 Then
         IsEmptyWorksheet = True
         Exit Function
      End If
   End If
   MsgBox "Please make sure that an empty worksheet is active"
End Function
```

Controls at All Levels

The following screenshot and code take the previous procedure to greater levels of detail. All controls are examined to see what controls are contained within them. Where possible, the contained controls are listed. Some controls, such as those containing graphics, can't be listed in greater detail. The information on sub-controls is indented across the worksheet. The code is capable of reporting to as many levels as there are, but Excel does not have controls beyond the third level:

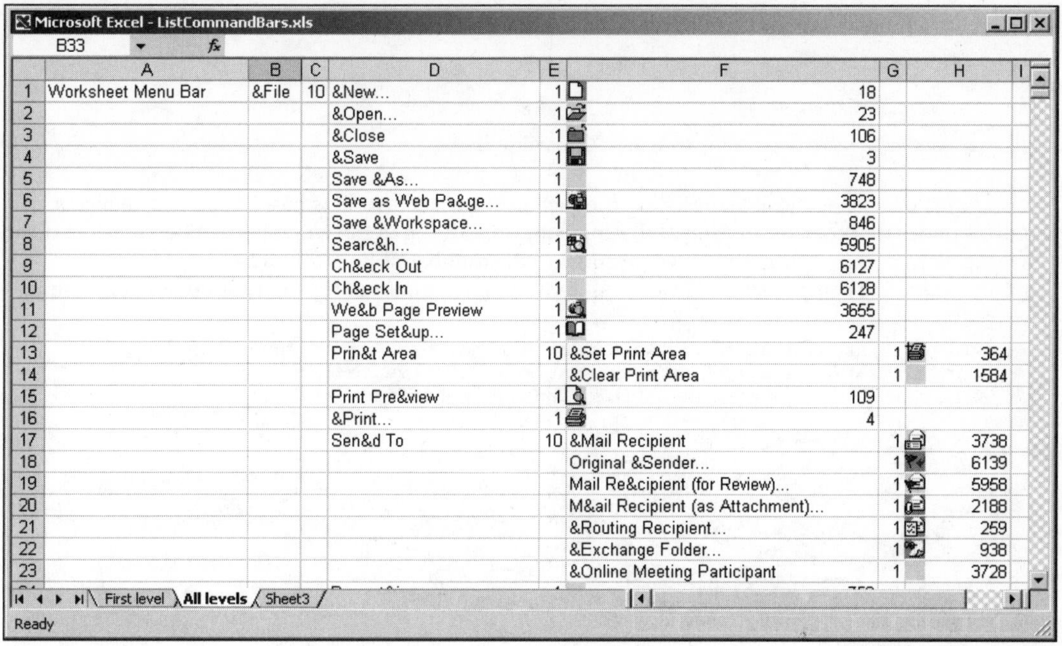

Microsoft Excel - ListCommandBars.xls

B33

	A	B	C	D	E	F	G	H	I
1	Worksheet Menu Bar	&File	10	&New...	1	18			
2				&Open...	1	23			
3				&Close	1	106			
4				&Save	1	3			
5				Save &As...	1	748			
6				Save as Web Pa&ge...	1	3823			
7				Save &Workspace...	1	846			
8				Searc&h...	1	5905			
9				Ch&eck Out	1	6127			
10				Ch&eck In	1	6128			
11				We&b Page Preview	1	3655			
12				Page Set&up...	1	247			
13				Prin&t Area	10	&Set Print Area	1	364	
14						&Clear Print Area	1	1584	
15				Print Pre&view	1	109			
16				&Print...	1	4			
17				Sen&d To	10	&Mail Recipient	1	3738	
18						Original &Sender...	1	6139	
19						Mail Re&cipient (for Review)...	1	5958	
20						M&ail Recipient (as Attachment)...	1	2188	
21						&Routing Recipient...	1	259	
22						&Exchange Folder...	1	938	
23						&Online Meeting Participant	1	3728	

First level | All levels | Sheet3

Ready

Here is the code to list controls at all levels:

```
Sub ListAllControls()
  Dim cbBar As CommandBar
  Dim Rng As Range
  Dim cbCtl As CommandBarControl

  If Not IsEmptyWorksheet(ActiveSheet) Then Exit Sub
  Application.ScreenUpdating = False
  Set Rng = Range("A1")
  For Each cbBar In Application.CommandBars
    Application.StatusBar = "Processing Bar " & cbBar.Name
    Rng.Value = cbBar.Name
    For Each cbCtl In cbBar.Controls
      Set Rng = Rng.Offset(ListControls(cbCtl, Rng))
    Next cbCtl
  Next cbBar
  Range("A:I").EntireColumn.AutoFit
  Application.StatusBar = False
End Sub
```

`ListAllControls` loops through the `CommandBars` collection, using `Rng` to keep track of the current A column cell of the worksheet it is writing to. It posts the name of the current command bar in a message on the status bar, so you can tell where it is up to, and also enters the name of the command bar at the current `Rng` location in the worksheet. It then loops through all the controls on the current `CommandBar`, executing the `ListControls` function, which is shown below.

In Chapter 23 you will need to get listings of the VBE `CommandBars`. This can be easily accomplished by changing the following line:

```
For Each cBar in Application.CommandBars
```

to:

```
For Each cBar in Application.VBE.CommandBars
```

`ListControls` is responsible for listing the details of each control it is passed and the details of any controls under that control, starting at the current `Rng` location in the worksheet. When it has performed its tasks, `ListControls` returns a value equal to the number of lines that it has used for its list. `Offset` is used to compute the new `Rng` cell location for the start of the next command bar's listing.

```
Function ListControls(cbCtl As CommandBarControl, Rng As Range) As Long
  Dim lOffset As Long 'Tracks current row relative to Rng
  Dim ctlSub As CommandBarControl 'Control contained in cbCtl

  On Error Resume Next
  lOffset = 0
  Rng.Offset(lOffset, 1).Value = cbCtl.Caption
  Rng.Offset(lOffset, 2).Value = cbCtl.Type
  'Attempt to copy control face. If error, don't paste
  cbCtl.CopyFace
  If Err.Number = 0 Then
    ActiveSheet.Paste Rng.Offset(lOffset, 3)
    Rng.Offset(lOffset, 3).Value = cbCtl.FaceId
  End If
  Err.Clear

  'Check Control Type
  Select Case cbCtl.Type
    Case 1, 2, 4, 6, 7, 13, 18
      'Do nothing for these control types
    Case Else
      'Call function recursively
      'if current control contains other controls
      For Each ctlSub In cbCtl.Controls
        lOffset = lOffset + _
            ListControls(ctlSub, Rng.Offset(lOffset, 2))
      Next ctlSub
      lOffset = lOffset - 1
  End Select
  ListControls = lOffset + 1
End Function
```

`ListControls` is a recursive function, and runs itself to process as many levels of controls as it finds. It uses `lOffset` to keep track of the rows it writes to, relative to the starting cell `Rng`. It uses very similar code to `ListFirstLevelControls`, but records the control type as well as the caption, icon, and face ID. Most of the control types are:

- 1 – `msoControlButton`
- 10 – `msoControlPopup`

However you will see other types in the list as well:

- 2 – `msoControlEdit`
- 4 – `msoControlComboBox`

- 6 – `msoControlSplitDropdown`
- 7 – `msoControlOCXDropdown`
- 13 – `msoControlSplitButtonPopup`
- 18 – `msoControlGrid`

The `Select Case` construct is used to avoid trying to list the sub-controls where this is not possible.

When `ListControls` finds a control with sub-controls it can list, it calls itself with a `Rng` starting point that is offset from its current `Rng` by `lOffset` lines down and 2 columns across. `ListControls` keeps calling itself as often as necessary to climb down into every level of sub-control and then climbs back to continue with the higher levels. Each time it is called, it returns the number of lines it has written to relative to `Rng`.

FaceIds

The following code gives you a table of the built in button faces. There are about 3,500 faces in Office 97, about 5,500 faces in Office 2000, and about 7,000 faces in Office 2002. Note that many `FaceId` values represent blank images and that the same images appear repeatedly as the numbers get higher:

Microsoft Excel - ListCommandBars.xls

A1 fx 1

	A	B	C	D	E	F	G	H	I	J
1	1	2	3	4	5	6	7	8	9	10
2	11	12	13	14	15	16	17	18	19	20
3	21	22	23	24	25	26	27	28	29	30
4	31	32	33	34	35	36	37	38	39	40
5	41	42	43	44	45	46	47	48	49	50
6	51	52	53	54	55	56	57	58	59	60
7	61	62	63	64	65	66	67	68	69	70
8	71	72	73	74	75	76	77	78	79	80
9	81	82	83	84	85	86	87	88	89	90
10	91	92	93	94	95	96	97	98	99	100
11	101	102	103	104	105	106	107	108	109	110
12	111	112	113	114	115	116	117	118	119	120
13	121	122	123	124	125	126	127	128	129	130
14	131	132	133	134	135	136	137	138	139	140
15	141	142	143	144	145	146	147	148	149	150
16	151	152	153	154	155	156	157	158	159	160
17	161	162	163	164	165	166	167	168	169	170
18	171	172	173	174	175	176	177	178	179	180
19	181	182	183	184	185	186	187	188	189	190
20	191	192	193	194	195	196	197	198	199	200
21	201	202	203	204	205	206	207	208	209	210
22	211	212	213	214	215	216	217	218	219	220
23	221	222	223	224	225	226	227	228	229	230

First level / All levels / FaceIds

Ready

Here is the code to list all the `FaceIds`:

```
Sub ListAllFaces()
  Dim i As Integer 'Tracks current FaceId
  Dim j As Integer 'Tracks current column in worksheet
  Dim k As Integer 'Tracks current row in worksheet
  Dim cbCtl As CommandBarControl
```

```
    Dim cbBar As CommandBar

    If Not IsEmptyWorksheet(ActiveSheet) Then Exit Sub
    On Error GoTo Recover
    Application.ScreenUpdating = False
    'Create temporary command bar with single control button
    'to hold control button face to be copied to worksheet
    Set cbBar = CommandBars.Add(Position:=msoBarFloating, _
                               MenuBar:=False, _
                               temporary:=True)
    Set cbCtl = cbBar.Controls.Add(Type:=msoControlButton, _
                                  temporary:=True)
    k = 1
    Do
      For j = 1 To 10
        i = i + 1
        Application.StatusBar = "FaceID = " & i
        'Set control button to current FaceId
        cbCtl.FaceId = i
        'Attempt to copy Face image to worksheet
        cbCtl.CopyFace
        ActiveSheet.Paste Cells(k, j + 1)
        Cells(k, j).Value = i
      Next j
      k = k + 1
    Loop

  Recover:
    If Err.Number = 1004 Then Resume Next
    Application.StatusBar = False
    cbBar.Delete
  End Sub
```

Note that when you run this macro your computer may well freeze for a while. The CPU has to do a lot of hard work! You can follow the macro's progress by watching the status bar

`ListAllFaces` creates a temporary toolbar, `cbBar`, using the `Add` method of the `CommandBars` collection. The toolbar is declared:

- `Temporary`, which means that it will be deleted when you exit Excel, if it has not already been deleted
- `Floating`, rather than docked at an edge of the screen or a popup
- `Not` to be a menu bar, which means that `cbBar` will be a toolbar

A temporary control is added to `cbBar` using the `Add` method of the `Controls` collection for the command bar, and assigned to `cbCtl`.

The `Do...Loop` continues looping until there are no more valid `FaceId` values. The `Do...Loop` increments `k`, which represents the row numbers in the worksheet. On every row, `j` is incremented from `1` to `10`. `j` represents the columns of the worksheet. The value of `i` is increased by one for every iteration of the code in the `For...Next` loop. `i` represents the `FaceId`. The `FaceId` property of `cbCtl` is assigned the value of `i`, and the resulting image is copied to the worksheet.

Some button images are blank and some are missing. The blank images copy without error, but the missing images cause an error number 1004. When an error occurs the code branches to the error trap at `Recover:`. If the error number is 1004, the code resumes executing at the statement after the one that caused the error, leaving an empty slot for the button image. Eventually the code gets to the last `FaceId` in Office. This causes error number –2147467259. At this point the code clears the status bar, removes the temporary command bar, and exits.

> **The information you have gathered with the last three exercises is not documented in any easily obtainable form by Microsoft. It is valuable data when you want to modify the existing command bar structures or alter command bar behavior, and as a guide to the built-in button faces at your disposal. There is an add-in application, `CBList.xla`, available with the code that accompanies this book that makes it easy to generate these lists.**

Creating New Menus

If you want to provide a user with extra functionality, without removing any of the standard commands, you can add a new menu to the existing Worksheet menu bar. The following screen shows a new menu called Custom, inserted between the Window and Help menus:

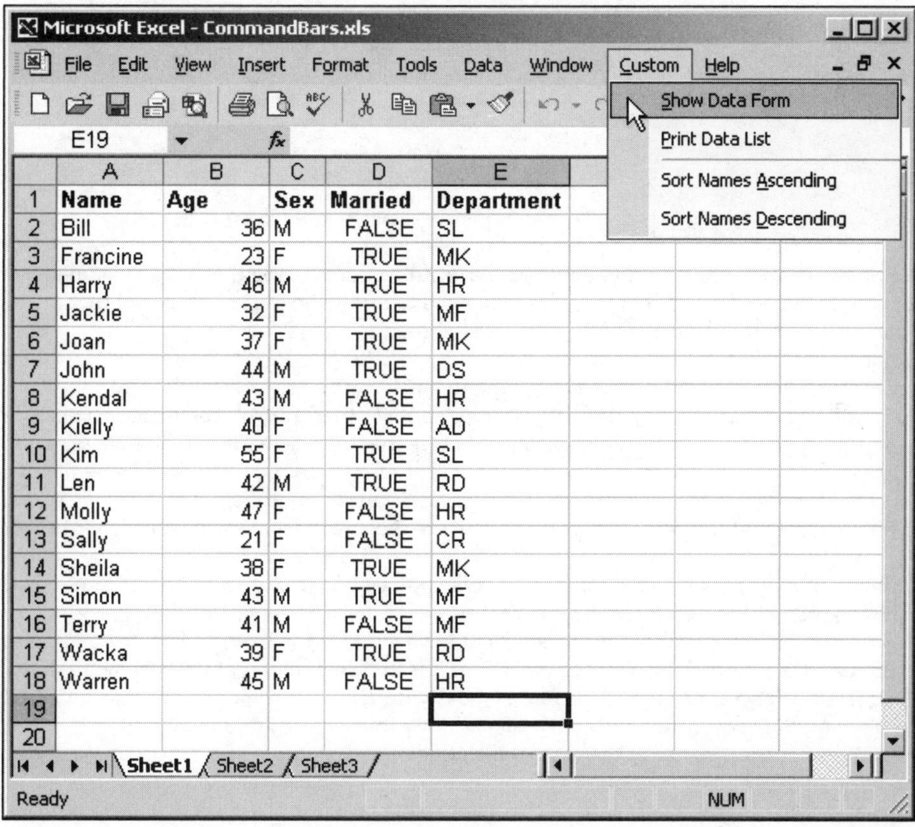

	A	B	C	D	E
1	Name	Age	Sex	Married	Department
2	Bill	36	M	FALSE	SL
3	Francine	23	F	TRUE	MK
4	Harry	46	M	TRUE	HR
5	Jackie	32	F	TRUE	MF
6	Joan	37	F	TRUE	MK
7	John	44	M	TRUE	DS
8	Kendal	43	M	FALSE	HR
9	Kielly	40	F	FALSE	AD
10	Kim	55	F	TRUE	SL
11	Len	42	M	TRUE	RD
12	Molly	47	F	FALSE	HR
13	Sally	21	F	FALSE	CR
14	Sheila	38	F	TRUE	MK
15	Simon	43	M	TRUE	MF
16	Terry	41	M	FALSE	MF
17	Wacka	39	F	TRUE	RD
18	Warren	45	M	FALSE	HR
19					
20					

The code to create this menu is as follows:

```
Public Sub AddCustomMenu()
   Dim cbWSMenuBar As CommandBar
   Dim muCustom As CommandBarControl
   Dim iHelpIndex As Integer

   Set cbWSMenuBar = Application.CommandBars("Worksheet Menu Bar")
   iHelpIndex = cbWSMenuBar.Controls("Help").Index
   Set muCustom = cbWSMenuBar.Controls.Add(Type:=msoControlPopup, _
                                            Before:=iHelpIndex)
   With muCustom
      .Caption = "&Custom"
      With .Controls.Add(Type:=msoControlButton)
         .Caption = "&Show Data Form"
         .OnAction = "ShowDataForm"
      End With
      With .Controls.Add(Type:=msoControlButton)
         .Caption = "&Print Data List"
         .OnAction = "PrintDataList"
      End With
      With .Controls.Add(Type:=msoControlButton)
         .Caption = "Sort Names &Ascending"
         .BeginGroup = True
         .OnAction = "SortList"
         .Parameter = "Asc"
      End With
      With .Controls.Add(Type:=msoControlButton)
         .Caption = "Sort Names &Descending"
         .OnAction = "SortList"
         .Parameter = "Dsc"
      End With
   End With
End Sub
```

`AddCustomMenu` creates an object variable `cbWSMenuBar` referencing the Worksheet menu bar. If you want to add a menu before an existing menu, you need to know the index number of that menu. You can determine the `Index` property of the control as shown.

`AddCustomMenu` uses the `Add` method of the menu bar's `Controls` collection to add the new menu. The `Type` property is declared `msoControlPopup` so that other controls can be attached to the menu. The `Before` parameter places the new menu just before the **Help** menu. If you do not specify the position, it will be placed at the end of the menu bar. The `Caption` property of the new menu is assigned `&Custom`. The `&` does not appear in the menu, it causes an underscore to be placed under the character it precedes and indicates that you can activate this menu from the keyboard with *Alt+C*.

The `Add` method of the new menu's `Controls` collection is then used to add four commands to the menu. They are all of type `msoControlButton` so they can each run a macro. Each is given an appropriate `Caption` property, including shortcut keys indicated with an `&`. The `OnAction` property of each command is assigned the name of the macro it is to run. The first of the sort menu items has its `BeginGroup` property set to `True`. This places the dividing line above it to mark it as the beginning of a different group. Both sort commands are assigned the same `OnAction` macro, but also have their `Parameter` properties assigned text strings which distinguish them.

The `Parameter` property is a holder for a character string. You can use it for any purpose. Here it is used to hold the strings `"Asc"`, for ascending, and `"Dsc"`, for descending. As you will see below, the `SortList` procedure will access the strings to determine the sort order required.

The OnAction Macros

The macro assigned to the `OnAction` property of the **Show Data Form** menu item is as follows:

```
Private Sub ShowDataForm()
   fmPersonal.Show
End Sub
```

It displays exactly the same data form as in the previous chapter on UserForms. The macro assigned to the **Print Data List** menu item is as follows:

```
Private Sub PrintDataList()
   Range("Database").PrintPreview
End Sub
```

`PrintDataList` shows a print preview of the list, from which the user can elect to print the list.

The macro assigned to the **Sort** menu items is as follows:

```
Private Sub SortList()
   Dim iAscDsc As Integer

   Select Case CommandBars.ActionControl.Parameter
      Case "Asc"
         iAscDsc = xlAscending
      Case "Dsc"
         iAscDsc = xlDescending
   End Select
   Range("Database").Sort Key1:=Range("A2"), Order1:=iAscDsc, Header:=xlYes
End Sub
```

`SortList` uses the `ActionControl` property of the `CommandBars` collection to get a reference to the command bar control that caused `SortList` to execute. This is similar to `Application.Caller`, used in user-defined functions to determine the `Range` object that executed the function.

Knowing the control object that called it, `SortList` can examine the control's `Parameter` property to get further information. If the `Parameter value` is `"Asc"`, `SortList` assigns an ascending sort. If the `Parameter` value is `"Dsc"`, it assigns a descending sort. Controls also have a `Tag` property that can be used, in exactly the same way as the `Parameter` property, to hold another character string. You can use the `Tag` property as an alternative to the `Parameter` property, or you can use it to hold supplementary data.

Passing Parameter Values

In the previous example we used the `Parameter` property of the control on the menu to store information to be passed to the `OnAction` macro, and pointed out that you can also use the `Tag` property. If you have more than two items of information to pass, it is more convenient to use a macro procedure that has input parameters.

Say you wanted to pass three items of data such as a product name and its cost and selling price. The macro might look like the following:

```
Sub ShowProduct(sName As String, dCost As Double, dPrice As Double)
  MsgBox "Product: " & sName & vbCr & _
      "Cost: " & Format(dCost, "$0.00") & vbCr & _
      "Price: " & Format(dPrice, "$0.00")
End Sub
```

To execute this macro from a command bar control, you need to assign something like the following code to the `OnAction` property of the control:

```
'ShowProduct "Apple", 3, 4'
```

The entire expression is enclosed in single quotes. Any string parameter values within the expression are enclosed in double quotes. In order to define this as the `OnAction` property of a control referred to by an object variable, `Ctl`, for example, you need to use the following code:

```
Ctl.OnAction = "'ShowProduct ""Apple"", 3, 4'"
```

The mix of single and double quotes is tricky to get right. The entire string is enclosed in double quotes, while any internal double quotes need to be shown twice.

Deleting a Menu

Built-in and custom controls can be deleted using the control's `Delete` method. The following macro deletes the **Custom** menu:

```
Public Sub RemoveCustomMenu()
   Dim cbWSMenuBar As CommandBar

   On Error Resume Next
   Set cbWSMenuBar = CommandBars("Worksheet Menu Bar")
   cbWSMenuBar.Controls("Custom").Delete
End Sub
```

`On Error` is used in case the menu has already been deleted.

> **You can use a built-in command bar's `Reset` method to make the entire command bar revert to its default layout and commands. This is not a good idea if users have customized their commandbars, or use workbooks or add-ins that alter the setup, as all their work will be lost.**

The following event procedures should be added to the `ThisWorkbook` module to add the **Custom** menu when the workbook is opened and delete it when the workbook is closed:

```
Private Sub Workbook_BeforeClose(Cancel As Boolean)
   Call RemoveCustomMenu
End Sub

Private Sub Workbook_Open()
   Call AddCustomMenu
End Sub
```

> **It is important to recognize that command bar changes are permanent. If you do not remove the Custom menu in this example, it will stay in the Excel Worksheet menu bar during the current session and future sessions. Trying to use this menu with another workbook active could cause unexpected results.**

Creating a Toolbar

If you are creating a simple toolbar with buttons and dropdowns, you can do it manually. However, there are more complex controls, such as those of type `msoControlEdit`, `msoControlDropdown`, and `msoControlComboBox`, which you can only fully manipulate in VBA code. The following toolbar contains three controls.

The first is of type `msoControlButton` and displays the user form for the data list:

The second control is of type `msoControlPopup` and displays two controls of type `msoControlButton`:

	Name	Age	Sex	Married	Department
2	Bill	36	M	FALSE	SL
3	Francine	23	F	TRUE	MK
4	Harry	46	M	TRUE	HR
5	Jackie	32	F	TRUE	MF
6	Joan	37	F	TRUE	MK
7	John	44	M	TRUE	DS
8	Kendal	43	M	FALSE	HR
9	Kielly	40	F	FALSE	AD
10	Kim	55	F	TRUE	SL
11	Len	42	M	TRUE	RD
12	Molly	47	F	FALSE	HR
13	Sally	21	F	FALSE	CR
14	Sheila	38	F	TRUE	MK
15	Simon	43	M	TRUE	MF
16	Terry	41	M	FALSE	MF
17	Wacka	39	F	TRUE	RD
18	Warren	45	M	FALSE	HR

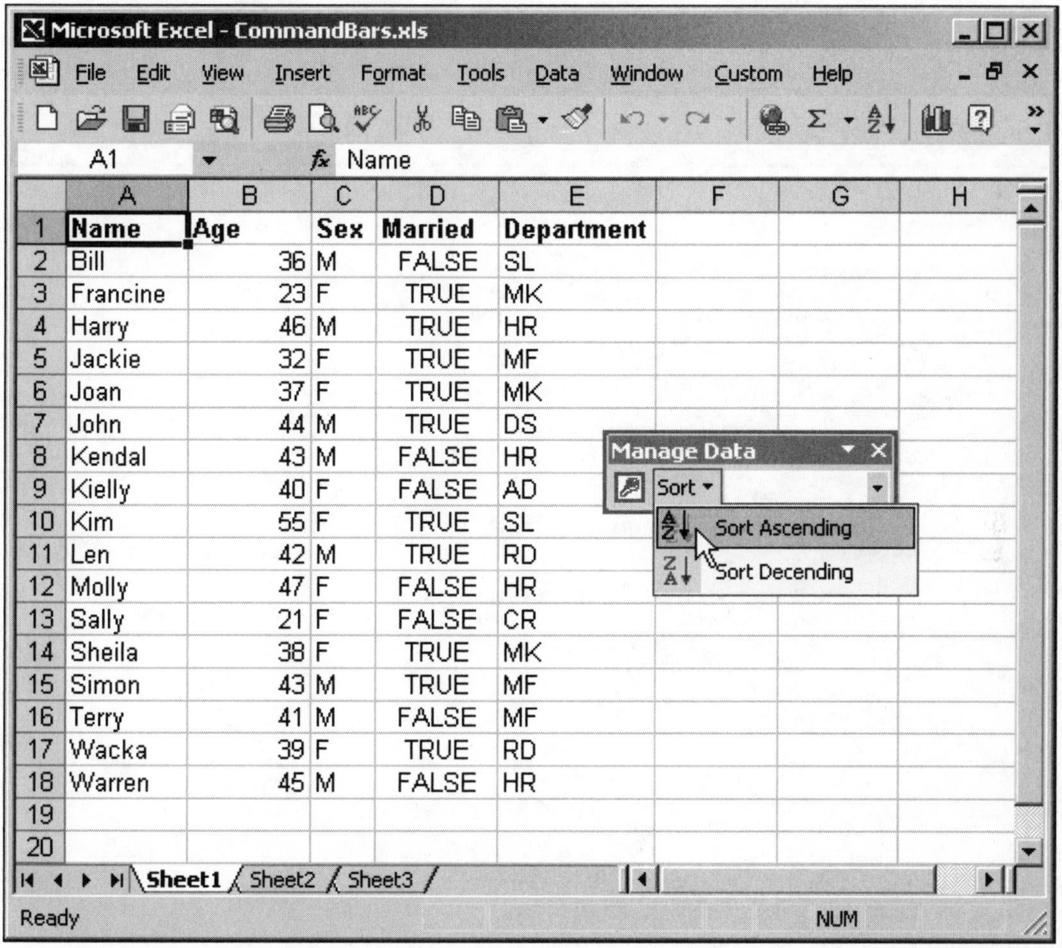

The third control is of type `msoControlDropdown` and applies an AutoFilter on Department:

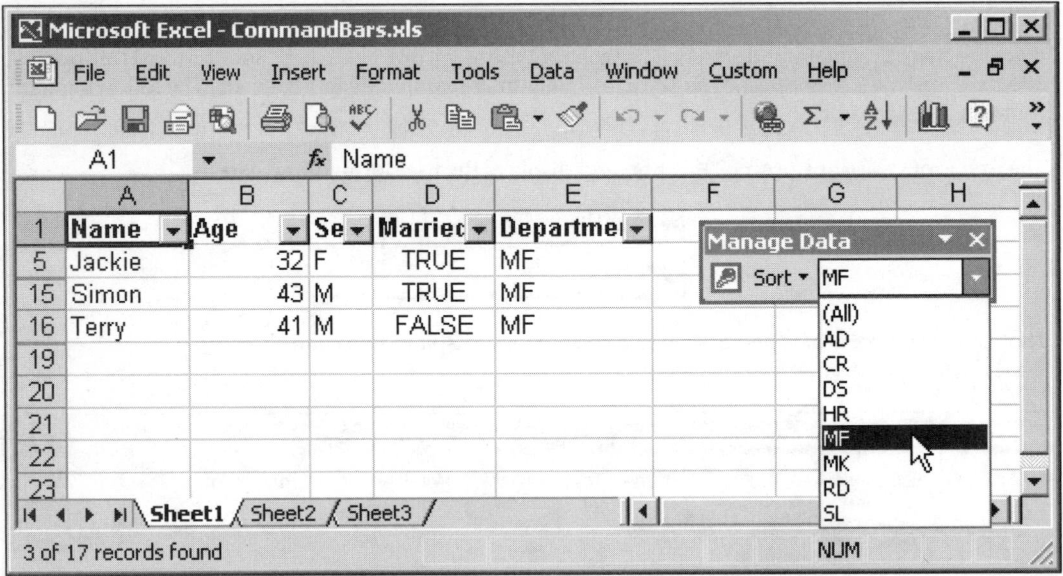

The following code creates the toolbar:

```
Public Sub CreateToolbar()
   'Get rid of any existing toolbar called Manage Data
   On Error Resume Next
   CommandBars("Manage Data").Delete
   On Error GoTo 0

  'Create new toolbar
   With CommandBars.Add(Name:="Manage Data")
      With .Controls.Add(Type:=msoControlButton)
         .OnAction = "ShowDataForm"
         .FaceID = 264
         .TooltipText = "Show Data Form"
      End With

      With .Controls.Add(Type:=msoControlPopup)
         .Caption = "Sort"
         .TooltipText = "Sort Ascending or Descending"
         With .Controls.Add(Type:=msoControlButton)
            .Caption = "Sort Ascending"
            .FaceID = 210
            .OnAction = "SortList"
            .Parameter = "Asc"
         End With
         With .Controls.Add(Type:=msoControlButton)
            .Caption = "Sort Decending"
            .FaceID = 211
            .OnAction = "SortList"
            .Parameter = "Dsc"
         End With
      End With
```

```
        With .Controls.Add(Type:=msoControlDropdown)
            .AddItem "(All)"
            .AddItem "AD"
            .AddItem "CR"
            .AddItem "DS"
            .AddItem "HR"
            .AddItem "MF"
            .AddItem "MK"
            .AddItem "RD"
            .AddItem "SL"
            .OnAction = "FilterDepartment"
            .TooltipText = "Select Department"
        End With
        .Visible = True
    End With
End Sub
```

The toolbar itself is very simple to create. `CreateToolbar` uses the `Add` method of the `CommandBars` collection and accepts all the default parameter values apart from the `Name` property. The first control button is created in much the same way as a menu item, using the `Add` method of the `Controls` collection. It is assigned an `OnAction` macro, a `FaceId`, and a ToolTip.

The second control is created as type `msoControlPopup`. It is given the `Caption` of `Sort` and a ToolTip. It is then assigned two controls of its own, of type `msoControlButton`. They are assigned the `SortList` macro and `Parameter` values, as well as `FaceIds` and captions.

Finally the control of type `msoControlDropdown` is added. Its drop-down list is populated with department codes and its `OnAction` macro is `FilterDepartment`. It is also given a ToolTip. The last action is to set the toolbar's `Visible` property to `True` to display it.

The `FilterDepartment` macro follows:

```
Sub FilterDepartment()
    Dim stDept As String

    With CommandBars.ActionControl
        stDept = .List(.ListIndex)
    End With
    If stDept = "(All)" Then
        Range("Database").Parent.AutoFilterMode = False
    Else
        Range("Database").AutoFilter Field:=5, Criteria1:=stDept
    End If
End Sub
```

A dropdown control has a `List` property that is an array of its list values and a `ListIndex` property that is the index number of the current list value. The `ActionControl` property of the `CommandBars` object, which refers to the currently active control, is a quick way to reference the control and access the `List` and `ListIndex` properties to get the department code required. The code is then used to perform the appropriate AutoFilter operation. If the (All) option is chosen, the `AutoFilterMode` property of the worksheet that is the parent of the `Database Range` object is set to `False`, removing the AutoFilter dropdowns and showing any hidden rows.

It is a good idea to run `CreateToolbar` from the `Workbook_Open` event procedure and to delete the toolbar in the `Workbook_BeforeClose` event procedure. The toolbar will remain permanently in Excel if it is not deleted and will give unexpected results if its buttons are pressed when other workbooks are active. If you do refer to `CommandBars` directly in workbook event procedures, you need to qualify the reference with `Application`:

```
Application.CommandBars("Manage Data").Delete
```

Pop-Up Menus

Excel's built-in shortcut menus are included in the command bar listing created by the macro, `ListFirstLevelControls`, which we saw earlier in this chapter. The following modified version of this macro shows only the commandbars of type `msoBarTypePopup`:

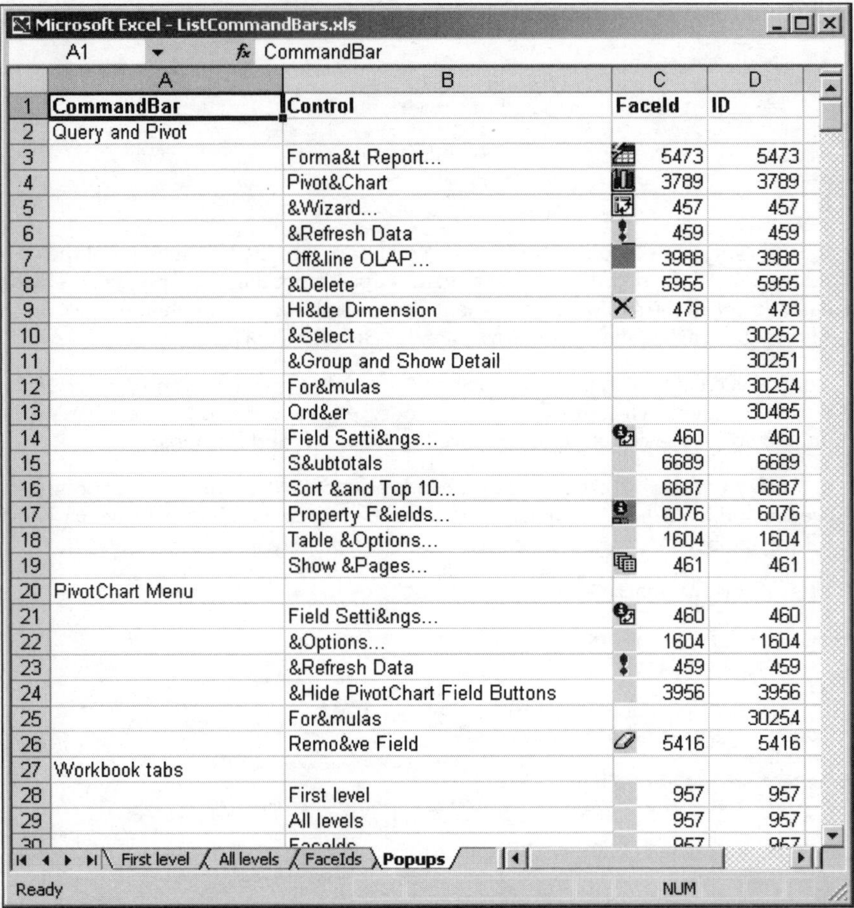

Microsoft Excel - ListCommandBars.xls

A1 | CommandBar

	A	B	C	D
1	**CommandBar**	**Control**	**FaceId**	**ID**
2	Query and Pivot			
3		Forma&t Report...	5473	5473
4		Pivot&Chart	3789	3789
5		&Wizard...	457	457
6		&Refresh Data	459	459
7		Off&line OLAP...	3988	3988
8		&Delete	5955	5955
9		Hi&de Dimension	478	478
10		&Select		30252
11		&Group and Show Detail		30251
12		For&mulas		30254
13		Ord&er		30485
14		Field Setti&ngs...	460	460
15		S&ubtotals	6689	6689
16		Sort &and Top 10...	6687	6687
17		Property F&ields...	6076	6076
18		Table &Options...	1604	1604
19		Show &Pages...	461	461
20	PivotChart Menu			
21		Field Setti&ngs...	460	460
22		&Options...	1604	1604
23		&Refresh Data	459	459
24		&Hide PivotChart Field Buttons	3956	3956
25		For&mulas		30254
26		Remo&ve Field	5416	5416
27	Workbook tabs			
28		First level	957	957
29		All levels	957	957

First level / All levels / FaceIds / Popups

Ready NUM

The code to display the popups is shown below:

```
Sub ListPopups()
    Dim cbCtl As CommandBarControl
    Dim cbBar As CommandBar
    Dim i As Integer

    If Not IsEmptyWorksheet(ActiveSheet) Then Exit Sub
    On Error Resume Next
    Application.ScreenUpdating = False
    Cells(1, 1).Value = "CommandBar"
    Cells(1, 2).Value = "Control"
    Cells(1, 3).Value = "FaceId"
    Cells(1, 4).Value = "ID"
    Cells(1, 1).Resize(1, 4).Font.Bold = True
```

```
    i = 2
    For Each cbBar In CommandBars
       Application.StatusBar = "Processing Bar " & cbBar.Name
       If cbBar.Type = msoBarTypePopup Then
          Cells(i, 1).Value = cbBar.Name
          i = i + 1
          For Each cbCtl In cbBar.Controls
             Cells(i, 2).Value = cbCtl.Caption
             cbCtl.CopyFace
             If Err.Number = 0 Then
                ActiveSheet.Paste Cells(i, 3)
                Cells(i, 3).Value = cbCtl.FaceID
             End If
             Cells(i, 4).Value = cbCtl.ID
             Err.Clear
             i = i + 1
          Next cbCtl
       End If
    Next cbBar
    Range("A:B").EntireColumn.AutoFit
    Application.StatusBar = False
 End Sub
```

The listing is identical to `ListFirstLevelControls`, apart from the introduction of a block `If` structure that processes only commandbars of type `msoBarTypePopup`. If you look at the listing produced by `ListPopups`, you will find you can identify the common shortcut menus. For example, there are commandbars named **Cell**, **Row**, and **Column** that correspond to the shortcut menus that popup when you right-click a worksheet cell, row number, or column letter.

You might be confused about the fact that the **Cell**, **Row**, and **Column** commandbars are listed twice. The first set is for a worksheet in Normal view. The second set is for a worksheet in Page Break Preview.

> **Another tricky one is the Workbook Tabs command bar. This is not the shortcut that you get when you click on an individual worksheet tab. It is the shortcut for the workbook navigation buttons to the left of the worksheet tabs. The shortcut for the tabs is the Ply command bar.**

Having identified the shortcut menus, you can tailor them to your own needs using VBA code. For example, the following screen shows a modified **Cell** command bar that includes an option to **Clear All**:

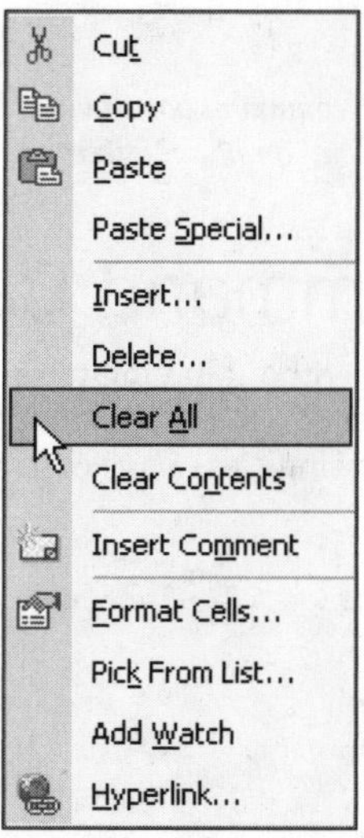

The **Clear All** control was added using the following code:

```
Public Sub AddShortCut()
   Dim cbBar As CommandBar
   Dim cbCtl As CommandBarControl
   Dim lIndex As Long

   Set cbBar = CommandBars("Cell")
   lIndex = cbBar.Controls("Clear Contents").Index
   Set cbCtl = cbBar.Controls.Add(Type:=msoControlButton, _
                                  ID:=1964, Before:=lIndex)
   cbCtl.Caption = "Clear &All"
End Sub
```

`AddShortCut` starts by assigning a reference to the `Cell` command bar to `cbBar`.

If you want to refer to the **Cell** commandbar that is shown in Page Break view in Excel 2002, you can use its `Index` property:

```
Set cbBar = CommandBars(31)
```

You need to take care here, if you want code compatible with other versions of Office. In Excel 2000, the `Index` property of the `Cell` command bar in page break view is 26 and in Excel 97 it is 24.

`AddShortCut` records the `Index` property of the `Clear Contents` control in `lIndex`, so that it can add the new control before the `Clear Contents` control. `AddShortCut` uses the `Add` method of the `Controls` collection to add the new control to `cbBar`, specifying the `ID` property of the built-in **Edit | Clear | All** menu item on the Worksheet menu bar.

*The `Add` method of the `Controls` collection allows you to specify the `Id` property of a built-in command. The listing from `ListAllControls` allows you to determine that the `Id` property, which is the same as the `FaceId` property, of the **Edit | Clear | All** menu item, is 1964.*

The built-in `Caption` property for the newly added control is **All**, so `AddShortCut` changes the `Caption` to be more descriptive.

*You can safely leave the modified **Cell** command bar in your `CommandBars` collection. It is not tied to any workbook and does not depend on having access to macros in a specific workbook.*

Showing Pop-Up Command Bars

If you want to display a shortcut menu without having to right-click on a cell, or chart, you can create code to display the shortcut in a number of ways. For example, you might like to display the shortcut **Cell** command bar from the keyboard, using *Ctrl+Shift+C*. You can do this using the following code:

```
Sub SetShortCut()
   Application.OnKey "^+c", "ShowCellShortCut"
End Sub

Private Sub ShowCellShortCut()
   CommandBars("Cell").ShowPopup x:=0, y:=0
End Sub
```

`ShowCellShortCut` uses the `ShowPopup` method to display the **Cell** shortcut menu at the top-left corner of the screen. The parameters are the x and y screen coordinates for the top left of the menu.

You can also create a popup menu from scratch. The following popup appears when you right-click inside the range named `Database`. Outside the range, the normal **Cell** popup menu appears:

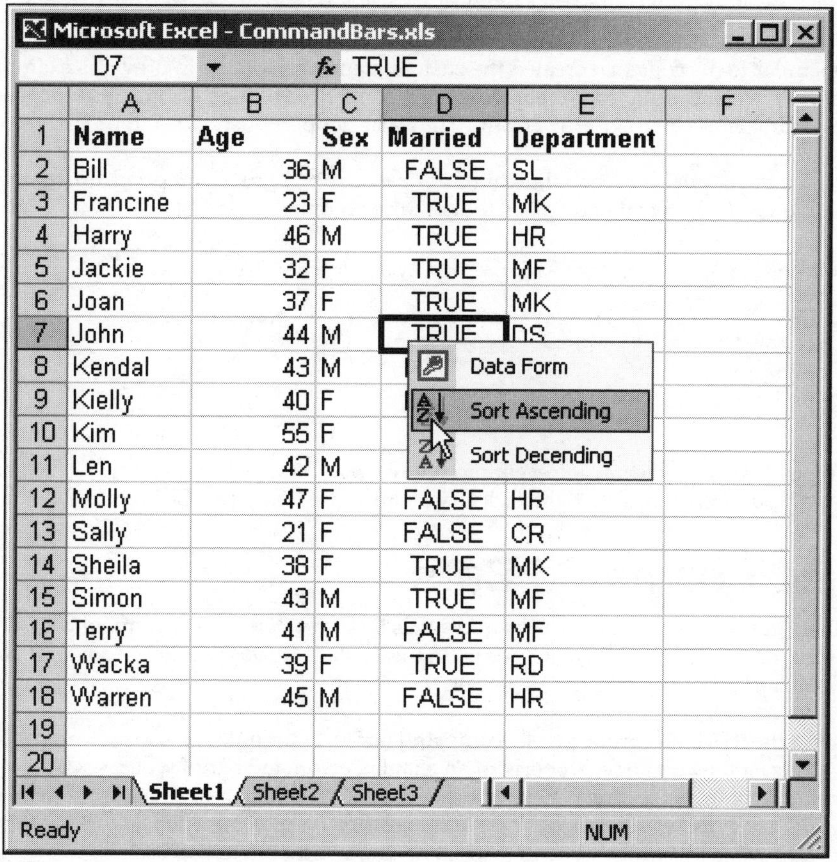

Microsoft Excel - CommandBars.xls

D7 TRUE

	A	B	C	D	E	F
1	Name	Age	Sex	Married	Department	
2	Bill	36	M	FALSE	SL	
3	Francine	23	F	TRUE	MK	
4	Harry	46	M	TRUE	HR	
5	Jackie	32	F	TRUE	MF	
6	Joan	37	F	TRUE	MK	
7	John	44	M	TRUE	DS	
8	Kendal	43	M			
9	Kielly	40	F			
10	Kim	55	F			
11	Len	42	M			
12	Molly	47	F	FALSE	HR	
13	Sally	21	F	FALSE	CR	
14	Sheila	38	F	TRUE	MK	
15	Simon	43	M	TRUE	MF	
16	Terry	41	M	FALSE	MF	
17	Wacka	39	F	TRUE	RD	
18	Warren	45	M	FALSE	HR	
19						
20						

Data Form
Sort Ascending
Sort Decending

Sheet1 Sheet2 Sheet3

Ready NUM

The following code created the popup menu:

```
Sub MakePopup()
   With CommandBars.Add(Name:="Data Popup", Position:=msoBarPopup)
      With .Controls.Add(Type:=msoControlButton)
         .OnAction = "ShowDataForm"
         .FaceID = 264
         .Caption = "Data Form"
         .TooltipText = "Show Data Form"
      End With
      With .Controls.Add(Type:=msoControlButton)
         .Caption = "Sort Ascending"
         .FaceID = 210
         .OnAction = "SortList"
         .Parameter = "Asc"
      End With
```

```
        With .Controls.Add(Type:=msoControlButton)
            .Caption = "Sort Decending"
            .FaceID = 211
            .OnAction = "SortList"
            .Parameter = "Dsc"
        End With
    End With
End Sub
```

The code is similar to the code that created the custom menu and toolbar in previous examples. The difference is that, when the popup is created by the `Add` method of the `CommandBars` collection, the `Position` parameter is set to `msoBarPopup`. The `Name` property here is set to `Data Popup`.

You can display the popup with the following `BeforeRightClick` event procedure in the code module behind the worksheet that displays the `Database` range:

```
Private Sub Worksheet_BeforeRightClick(ByVal Target As Range, _
                                       Cancel As Boolean)
   If Not Intersect(Range("Database"), Target) Is Nothing Then
      CommandBars("Data Popup").ShowPopup
      Cancel = True
   End If
End Sub
```

When you right-click the worksheet, the event procedure checks to see if `Target` is within `Database`. If so, it displays **Data Popup** and cancels the right-click event. Otherwise the normal **Cell** shortcut menu appears.

Disabling Command Bars

Commandbars have an `Enabled` property and a `Visible` property. If a command bar is enabled, and it is not of type `msoBarTypePopup`, it appears in the **Tools | Customize** dialog box. If it is checked in the **Tools | Customize** dialog box, it is visible on the screen.

You cannot set the `Visible` property of a command bar to `True` unless the `Enabled` property is also set to `True`. Setting the `Visible` property of an enabled command bar of type `msoBarTypeNormal` to `False` removes it from the screen. Setting the Worksheet menu bar's `Visible` property to `False` does not work. Excel treats it as a special case and insists on showing it when a worksheet is active. The only way to remove the Worksheet menu is to set its `Enabled` property to `False`.

The following code removes any visible toolbars and the Worksheet menu bar from the screen:

```
Sub RemoveToolbarsAndWorksheetMenuBar()
   Dim cbBar As CommandBar

   For Each cbBar In CommandBars
      If cbBar.Enabled And cbBar.Type = msoBarTypeNormal Then
         cbBar.Visible = False
      End If
   Next cbBar
   CommandBars("Worksheet Menu Bar").Enabled = False
   Application.OnKey "%-", ""
End Sub
```

This is what the screen looks like:

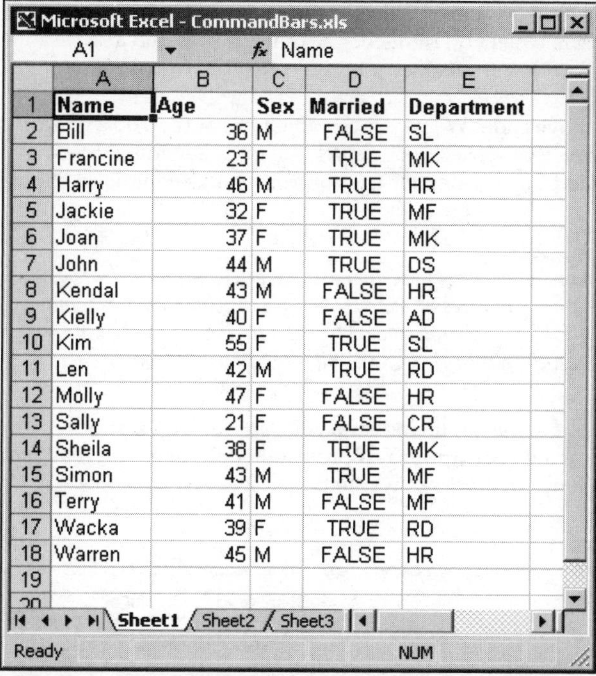
Microsoft Excel - CommandBars.xls

	A	B	C	D	E
1	Name	Age	Sex	Married	Department
2	Bill	36	M	FALSE	SL
3	Francine	23	F	TRUE	MK
4	Harry	46	M	TRUE	HR
5	Jackie	32	F	TRUE	MF
6	Joan	37	F	TRUE	MK
7	John	44	M	TRUE	DS
8	Kendal	43	M	FALSE	HR
9	Kielly	40	F	FALSE	AD
10	Kim	55	F	TRUE	SL
11	Len	42	M	TRUE	RD
12	Molly	47	F	FALSE	HR
13	Sally	21	F	FALSE	CR
14	Sheila	38	F	TRUE	MK
15	Simon	43	M	TRUE	MF
16	Terry	41	M	FALSE	MF
17	Wacka	39	F	TRUE	RD
18	Warren	45	M	FALSE	HR
19					

The final action carried out by `RemoveToolbarsAndWorksheetMenuBar` is to disable the *Alt+–* key combination that displays the workbook window's control menu. If you don't do this when you remove the Worksheet menu bar, the user can still access the control menu using *Alt+–*, and then use the cursor movement keys to make a phantom copy of the Worksheet menu bar slowly appear.

You can restore the Worksheet menu bar and the Standard and Formatting toolbars, with the following code, assuming the toolbars have not had their `Enabled` property set to `False`:

```
Sub RestoreToolbarsAndWorksheetMenuBar()
   CommandBars("Worksheet Menu Bar").Enabled = True
   Application.OnKey "%-"
   CommandBars("Standard").Visible = True
   CommandBars("Formatting").Visible = True
End Sub
```

Disabling Shortcut Access to Customize

If you want to stop users from making changes to your custom commandbars or built in commandbars, you can prevent access to the customization dialog box and toolbar with the following code. The code could be placed in the `Personal.xls` workbook so that it is automatically applied at the beginning of an Excel session:

```
Private Sub Workbook_Open()
   'Code to customize commandbars goes here...
   Application.CommandBars("Tools").Controls("Customize...").Enabled = False
   Application.CommandBars("Toolbar List").Enabled = False
End Sub
```

The first line of code disables the **Tools | Customize...** menu item. The second line of the code disables the shortcut menu that appears when you right-click a command bar and also disables the **View | Toolbars** menu item. As the code is in a workbook event procedure, the reference to `Application` is required.

Note the syntax in the above code. We have been able to treat the **Tools** control on the Worksheet menu bar as if it were a commandbar itself. If you search the table generated by `ListAllControls`, you will find a command bar called **Built-in Menus**. The controls on this command bar can be directly addressed as commandbars.

*The **Toolbar List** command bar was introduced in Excel 97 Service Release 1. You cannot use this command bar in earlier releases of Excel 97 – it is a special hidden command bar. Like the **Built-in Menus** command bar controls, `ToolBar List` has no `Index` property in the `CommandBars` collection, although it can be addressed by its `Name` property.*

If you only want to protect some commandbars, you can use the `Protect` property of the commandbars. The following code applies all protection options to the **Standard** toolbar. You can omit the constants for any options that are not wanted:

```
Sub ProtectToolbar()
   CommandBars("Standard").Protection = msoBarNoCustomize + _
                                        msoBarNoResize + _
                                        msoBarNoMove + _
                                        msoBarNoChangeVisible + _
                                        msoBarNoChangeDock + _
                                        msoBarNoVerticalDock + _
                                        msoBarNoHorizonaldock
End Sub
```

You can remove the protection with:

```
Sub UnProtectToolbar()
   CommandBars("Standard").Protection = msoBarNoProtection
End Sub
```

Table-Driven CommandBar Creation

Very few professional Excel developers write code to add their menu items and toolbars one-by-one. Most of us use a table-driven approach, whereby we fill out a table with information about the items we want to add, then have a routine which generates all the items based on this table. This makes it much easier to define and modify the design of our commandbars.

Say we want to create the **Custom** menu, which we set up earlier in this chapter, using this new method. The first thing that is needed is a table for the menu information. Insert a new worksheet, change its name to `MenuTable` and fill out the sheet as shown below. The worksheet named **Data** contains our employee database and **DataLists** will be used later to define a list of departments:

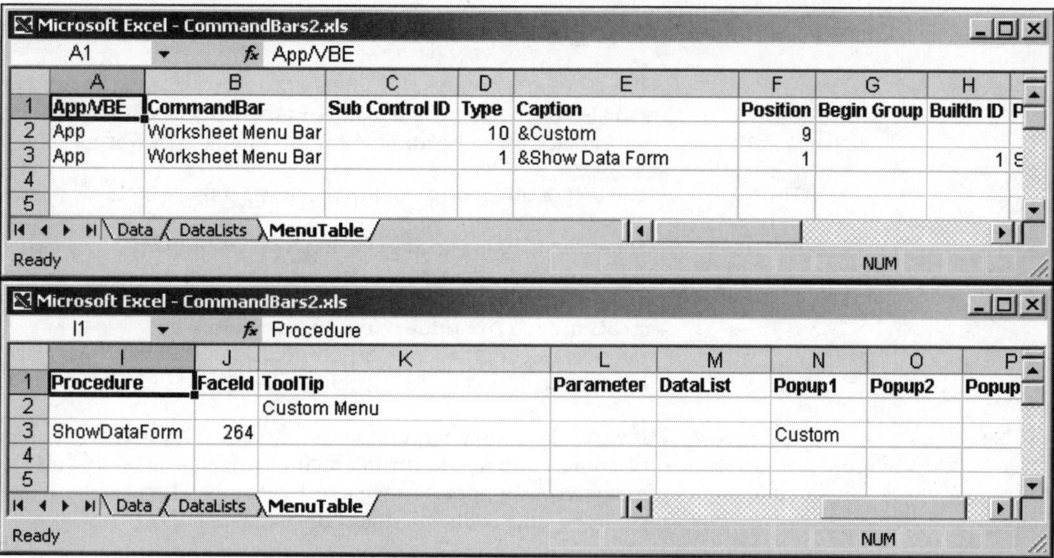

The columns of the `MenuTable` are:

Column	Title	Description
A	App / VBE	Either **App** to add items to Excel's menus or **VBE** to add them to the VBE. The code to handle VBE entries is provided in Chapter 23.
B	CommandBar	The name of the top-level command bar to add our menu to. Get these names from the listings we generated earlier in this chapter.
C	Sub Control ID	The ID number of a built-in pop-up bar to add our menu to. For example, 30002 is the ID of the **File** popup menu.
D	Type	The type of control to add: 1 for a normal button, 10 for a popup and so on. These correspond to the `msoControl...` types listed in the Object Browser.
E	Caption	The text to use for the menu item.
F	Position	The position in the command bar to add the menu item. Leave this blank to add the menu to the end of the bar.
G	Begin Group	`True` or `False` to specify whether to place a separator line before the item.
H	BuiltIn ID	If we're adding a built-in menu item, this is the ID of that menu. Use 1 for all custom menu items.
I	Procedure	The name of the procedure to run when a custom menu item is clicked.

Table continued on following page

Column	Title	Description
J	FaceId	The ID number of the built-in tool face to use for the menu. This can also be the name of a picture in the worksheet to use for the button face. 18 is the number for the standard **New** icon.
K	ToolTip	The text of the pop-up tooltip to show for the button.
L	Parameter	The string to be assigned to the `Parameter` property of the button.
M	DataList	Only used with controls that have dropdown lists, such as type `msoControlDropdown` (type 3). It contains the name of a range of cells in the worksheet called **DataLists** that contains items to be added to the dropdown list.
N+	Popup1–n	If we add our own popup menus, this is the caption of the custom popup to add further menu items to. We can include as many levels of popup as we like, by simply adding more columns – the code will detect the extra columns.

As the **MenuTable** sheet will be referred to a number of times in code, it is a good idea to give it a meaningful 'code name', such as `shMenuTable`. To do this, locate and select the sheet in the Project Explorer in the VBE, and change its name in the **Properties** window. It should now be shown as **shMenuTable (MenuTable)** in the Project Explorer. Using the code name allows you to refer directly to that sheet as an object, so the following two lines are equivalent:

```
Debug.Print ThisWorkbook.Worksheets("MenuTable").Name
```

```
Debug.Print shMenuTable.Name
```

The **DataLists** sheet needs to be renamed as `shDataLists` in the same way.

The code to create the menu from this table is shown below. The code should be copied into a new module called `modSetupBars`.

At the top of the module, a number of constants are declared, which correspond to each column of the menu table and you will use these throughout your code. If the menu table structure changes, all you need to do is renumber these constants – you don't need to search through the code:

```
'Constants for the columns in the commandbar creation table
Const miTABLE_APP_VBE           As Integer = 1
Const miTABLE_COMMANDBAR_NAME   As Integer = 2
Const miTABLE_CONTROL_ID        As Integer = 3
Const miTABLE_CONTROL_TYPE      As Integer = 4
Const miTABLE_CONTROL_CAPTION   As Integer = 5
Const miTABLE_CONTROL_POSITION  As Integer = 6
Const miTABLE_CONTROL_GROUP     As Integer = 7
Const miTABLE_CONTROL_BUILTIN   As Integer = 8
Const miTABLE_CONTROL_PROC      As Integer = 9
Const miTABLE_CONTROL_FACEID    As Integer = 10
Const miTABLE_CONTROL_TOOLTIP   As Integer = 11
Const miTABLE_CONTROL_PARAMETER As Integer = 12
```

```
Const miTABLE_CONTROL_DATALIST  As Integer = 13
Const miTABLE_POPUP_START       As Integer = 14

'Constant to determine whether commandbars are temporary or permanent
'If you set this to False, users will not loose any additional controls
'that they add to your custom commandbars
Const mbTEMPORARY               As Boolean = False

'The following Application ID is used to identify our menus, making it easy to
'remove them
Const psAppID As String = "TableDrivenCommandBars"
```

The `mbTEMPORARY` constant allows you to make the menu changes temporary or permanent. `psAppID` provides an identifying string that will be assigned to the `Tag` property of our added controls, which makes it easy to find and remove them.

The routine to actually set up the menus is called from our workbook's `Auto_Open` procedure or `Workbook_Open` event procedure:

```
' Subroutine: SetUpMenus
' Purpose:    Adds the commandbars defined in the shMenuTable worksheet'

Sub SetUpMenus()
   Dim rgRow As Range
   Dim cbAllBars As CommandBars
   Dim cbBar As CommandBar
   Dim cbBtn As CommandBarControl
   Dim iBuiltInID As Integer, iPopUpCol As Integer, vaData As Variant

   On Error Resume Next     'Just ignore errors in the table definition

   'Remove all of our menus before adding them.
   'This ensures we don't get any duplicated menus
   RemoveMenus

   'Loop through each row of our menu generation table
   For Each rgRow In shMenuTable.Cells(1).CurrentRegion.Rows
      'Ignore the header row
      If rgRow.Row > 1 Then
         'Read the row into an array of the cells' values
         vaData = rgRow.Value

         Set cbBar = Nothing
```

A single routine can be used to add menu items to both the Excel and VBE menus. The only difference is the `CommandBars` collection that is used – Excel's or the VBE's. This code does not contain all the elements necessary to add VBE menus. We will discuss the additional requirements in Chapter 23:

```
         'Get the collection of all commandbars, either in the VBE or Excel
         If vaData(1, miTABLE_APP_VBE) = "VBE" Then
            Set cbAllBars = Application.VBE.CommandBars
         Else
            Set cbAllBars = Application.CommandBars
         End If

         'Try to find the commandbar we want
         Set cbBar = cbAllBars.Item(vaData(1, miTABLE_COMMANDBAR_NAME))
```

```
'Did we find it - if not, we must be adding one!
If cbBar Is Nothing Then
   Set cbBar = cbAllBars.Add( _
       Name:=vaData(1, miTABLE_COMMANDBAR_NAME), _
                                           temporary:=mbTEMPORARY)
End If
```

If you want to look for a built-in popup menu to add your control to, you can recursively search for it in the `CommandBars` collection. For example, if you want to add a menu item to the **Edit | Clear** menu, you can enter the ID of the **Clear** menu (30021) in the **Sub Control ID** column of the table. Alternatively, you can enter one or more control name entries in the **PopUp** columns of the table. Entering **Edit** under **PopUp1** and **Clear** under **PopUp2** accomplishes the same result as placing 30021 under **Sub Control ID**. The first method is convenient when adding controls to the built-in menus. The alternative method is necessary to add items to the menus you create yourself:

```
'If set, locate the built-in popup menu bar (by ID) to add our
'control to.
'e.g. Worksheet Menu Bar > Edit
If Not IsEmpty(vaData(1, miTABLE_CONTROL_ID)) Then
   Set cbBar = cbBar.FindControl(ID:=vaData(1, _
               miTABLE_CONTROL_ID), Recursive:=True).CommandBar
End If

'Loop through the PopUp name columns to navigate down the
'menu structure
For iPopUpCol = miTABLE_POPUP_START To UBound(vaData, 2)
   'If set, navigate down the menu structure to the next popup menu
   If Not IsEmpty(vaData(1, iPopUpCol)) Then
      Set cbBar = cbBar.Controls(vaData(1, iPopUpCol)).CommandBar
   End If
Next
```

If you are adding an existing Excel control, you can specify its `Id` property value in the **BuiltIn ID** column. If you want the control to run your own procedure, you specify the name of the procedure in the **Procedure** column:

```
'Get the ID number if we're adding a built-in control
iBuiltInID = vaData(1, miTABLE_CONTROL_BUILTIN)

'If it's empty, set it to 1, indicating a custom control
If iBuiltInID = 0 Then iBuiltInID = 1

'Now add our control to the command bar
If IsEmpty(vaData(1, miTABLE_CONTROL_POSITION)) Or _
           vaData(1, miTABLE_CONTROL_POSITION) > _
                                      cbBar.Controls.Count Then
   Set cbBtn = cbBar.Controls.Add(Type:=vaData(1, _
                    miTABLE_CONTROL_TYPE), ID:=iBuiltInID, _
                                        temporary:= mbTEMPORARY)
Else
   Set cbBtn = cbBar.Controls.Add(Type:=vaData(1, _
                  miTABLE_CONTROL_TYPE), ID:=iBuiltInID, _
                  temporary:= mbTEMPORARY, _
                  before:=vaData(1, _
                  miTABLE_CONTROL_POSITION))
End If
```

```
      'Set the rest of button's properties
      With cbBtn
         .Caption = vaData(1, miTABLE_CONTROL_CAPTION)
         .BeginGroup = vaData(1, miTABLE_CONTROL_GROUP)
         .TooltipText = vaData(1, miTABLE_CONTROL_TOOLTIP)
```

You can either use one of the standard Office tool faces, by supplying the numeric `FaceId`, or provide your own picture to use. To use your own picture, just give the name of the `Picture` object in the **FaceId** column of the menu table:

```
         'The FaceId can be empty for a blank button, the number of
         'a standard button face, or the name of a picture object on
         'the sheet, which contains the picture to use.
         If Not IsEmpty(vaData(1, miTABLE_CONTROL_FACEID)) Then
            If IsNumeric(vaData(1, miTABLE_CONTROL_FACEID)) Then
               'A numeric face ID, so use it
               .FaceId = vaData(1, miTABLE_CONTROL_FACEID)
            Else
               'A textual face ID, so copy the picture to the button
               shMenuTable.Shapes(vaData(1, _
                                    miTABLE_CONTROL_FACEID)).CopyPicture
               .PasteFace
            End If
         End If
```

It is a good idea to set a property for all your menu items that identifies it as one of yours. If you use the `Tag` property to do this, you can use the `FindControl` method of the `CommandBars` object to locate all of your menu items, without having to remember exactly where you added them. This is done in the `RemoveMenus` procedure later in the module:

```
         'Set the button's tag to identify it as one we created.
         'This way, we can still find it if the user moves or renames it
         .Tag = psAppID

         'Set the control's OnAction property.
         'Surround the workbook name with quote marks, in case the
         'name includes spaces
         If Not IsEmpty(vaData(1, miTABLE_CONTROL_PROC)) Then
           .OnAction = "'" & ThisWorkbook.Name & "'!" & vaData(1, _
                                                   miTABLE_CONTROL_PROC)
         End If
```

If your procedure expects to find information in the control's `Parameter` property, you enter that information under the **Parameter** column of the table:

```
         'Assign Parameter property value, if specified
         If Not IsEmpty(vaData(1, miTABLE_CONTROL_PARAMETER)) Then
           .Parameter = vaData(1, miTABLE_CONTROL_PARAMETER)
         End If
```

For a drop-down control or combo box, you enter a list of values in the **DataLists** worksheet and assign a name to the list. You enter the name in the **DataList** column of the table:

```
            'Assign data list to ComboBox
            If Not IsEmpty(vaData(1, miTABLE_CONTROL_DATALIST)) Then
              For Each Rng In shDatalists.Range(vaData(1, _
                                                   miTABLE_CONTROL_DATALIST))
                 .AddItem Rng.Value
              Next Rng
              End If
         End With
      End If
   Next rgRow
End Sub
```

When the application workbook is closed, you need to run some code to remove your menus. Some developers just use `CommandBars.Reset`, but this removes all other customizations from the commandbars as well as their own. It is much better to locate all the menu items and commandbars that were created for your application and delete them. This takes two routines. The first removes all the menus from a specific `CommandBars` collection, by searching by its `Tag` value:

```
Private Sub RemoveMenusFromBars(cbBars As CommandBars)
   Dim cbCtl As CommandBarControl

   'Ignore errors while deleting our menu items
   On Error Resume Next

   'Using the application or VBE CommandBars ...
   With cbBars
      'Find a CommandBarControl with our tag
      Set cbCtl = .FindControl(Tag:=psAppID)

      'Loop until we don't find one
      Do Until cbCtl Is Nothing
         'Delete the one we found
         cbCtl.Delete

         'Find the next one
         Set cbCtl = .FindControl(Tag:=psAppID)
      Loop
   End With
End Sub
```

The second removal routine calls the first to remove the menu items from the Excel commandbars and the VBE commandbars and removes any custom bars that might have been created, as long as the user has not added their own controls to them:

```
Sub RemoveMenus()
   Dim cbBar As CommandBar, rgRow As Range, stBarName As String

   'Ignore errors while deleting our menu items and commandbars
   On Error Resume Next

   'Delete our menu items from the Excel and VBE commandbars
   RemoveMenusFromBars Application.CommandBars
   RemoveMenusFromBars Application.VBE.CommandBars

   'Loop through each row of our menu generation table
   For Each rgRow In shMenuTable.Cells(1).CurrentRegion.Rows
      'Ignore the header row
      If rgRow.Row > 1 Then
```

```
            stBarName = rgRow.Cells(1, miTABLE_COMMANDBAR_NAME)

            Set cbBar = Nothing
            'Find the command bar, either in the VBE or Excel
            If rgRow.Cells(1, miTABLE_APP_VBE) = "VBE" Then
               Set cbBar = Application.VBE.CommandBars(stBarName)
            Else
               Set cbBar = Application.CommandBars(stBarName)
            End If
            'If we found it, delete it if it is not a built-in bar
            If Not cbBar Is Nothing Then
               If Not cbBar.BuiltIn Then
                  'Only delete blank commandbars - in case user
                  'or other applications added menu items to the
                  'same custom bar
                  If cbBar.Controls.Count = 0 Then cbBar.Delete
               End If
            End If
         End If
      Next
   End Sub
```

You should run the `SetUpMenus` procedure from the `Auto_Open` procedure or the `Workbook_Open` event procedure and the `RemoveMenus` procedure from the `Auto_Close` procedure or the `Workbook_BeforeClose` event procedure.

You now have a complete template, which can be used as the basis for any Excel application (or just in a normal workbook where you want to modify the menu structure).

See Chapter 23 for the extra code needed to create a template that can be used with Excel and the VBE.

The first table entry shown in the figure above adds a new popup menu to the Worksheet menu bar called **Custom**. The second entry adds a menu item called **Show Data Form** to the **Custom** menu, as shown below:

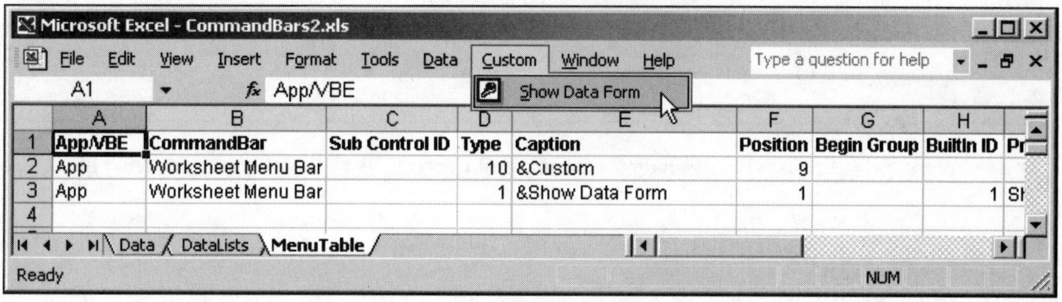

	A	B	C	D	E	F	G	H
1	App/VBE	CommandBar	Sub Control ID	Type	Caption	Position	Begin Group	BuiltIn ID
2	App	Worksheet Menu Bar		10	&Custom	9		
3	App	Worksheet Menu Bar		1	&Show Data Form	1		1
4								

You can expand the table to add more items to the custom menu and create new commandbars and controls as shown:

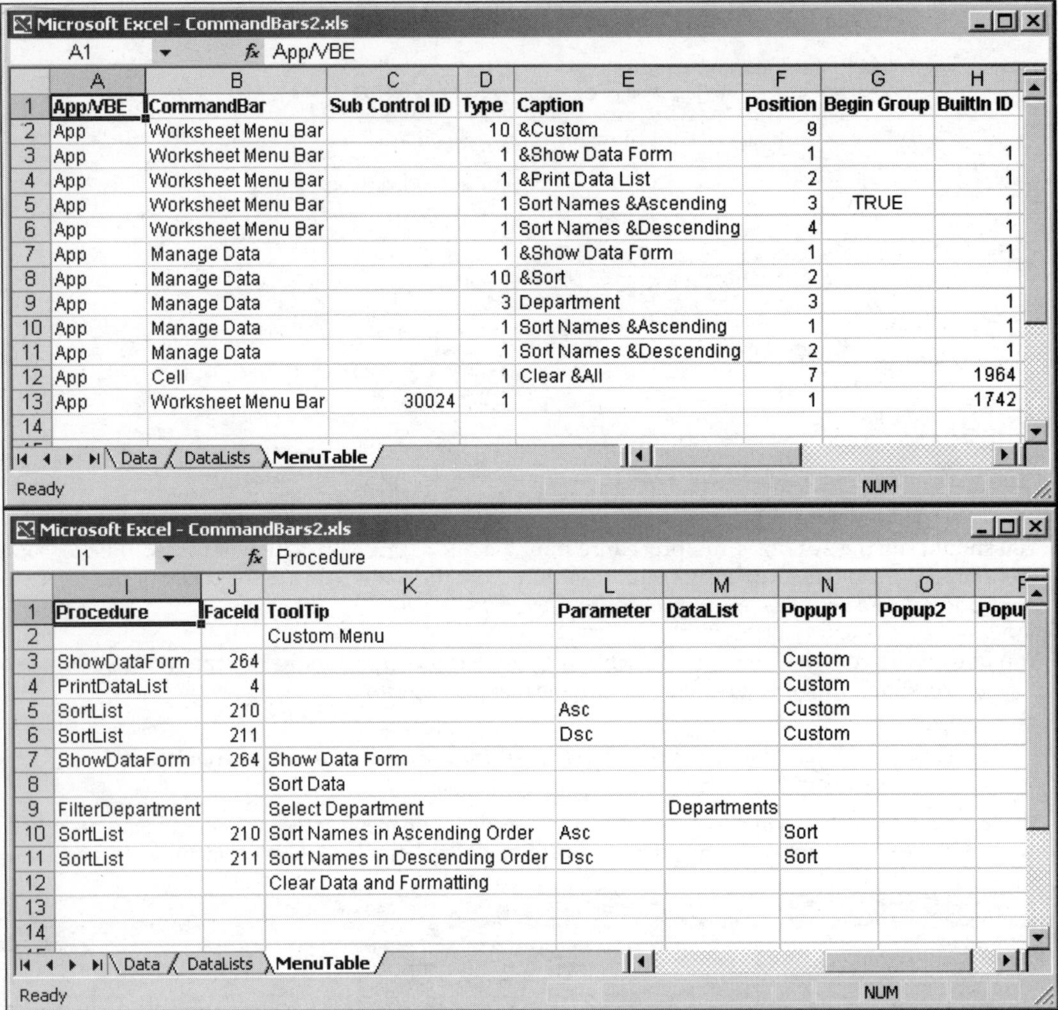

	A	B	C	D	E	F	G	H
1	App/VBE	CommandBar	Sub Control ID	Type	Caption	Position	Begin Group	BuiltIn ID
2	App	Worksheet Menu Bar		10	&Custom	9		
3	App	Worksheet Menu Bar		1	&Show Data Form	1		1
4	App	Worksheet Menu Bar		1	&Print Data List	2		1
5	App	Worksheet Menu Bar		1	Sort Names &Ascending	3	TRUE	1
6	App	Worksheet Menu Bar		1	Sort Names &Descending	4		1
7	App	Manage Data		1	&Show Data Form	1		1
8	App	Manage Data		10	&Sort	2		
9	App	Manage Data		3	Department	3		1
10	App	Manage Data		1	Sort Names &Ascending	1		1
11	App	Manage Data		1	Sort Names &Descending	2		1
12	App	Cell		1	Clear &All	7		1964
13	App	Worksheet Menu Bar	30024	1		1		1742
14								

	I	J	K	L	M	N	O	P
1	Procedure	FaceId	ToolTip	Parameter	DataList	Popup1	Popup2	Popu
2			Custom Menu					
3	ShowDataForm	264				Custom		
4	PrintDataList	4				Custom		
5	SortList	210		Asc		Custom		
6	SortList	211		Dsc		Custom		
7	ShowDataForm	264	Show Data Form					
8			Sort Data					
9	FilterDepartment		Select Department		Departments			
10	SortList	210	Sort Names in Ascending Order	Asc		Sort		
11	SortList	211	Sort Names in Descending Order	Dsc		Sort		
12			Clear Data and Formatting					
13								
14								

The following procedures will automate the running of the code as the workbook is opened and closed:

```
' Subroutine: Auto_Open
' Purpose:    Adds our menus and menuitems to the application
Sub Auto_Open()
   SetUpMenus
   CommandBars("Manage Data").Visible = True
End Sub

' Subroutine: Auto_Close
' Purpose:    Removes our menus and menu items from the application
Sub Auto_Close()
   RemoveMenus
End Sub
```

The data in rows 2 through 6 of the MenuTable table create the Custom menu shown below, which is identical to the Custom menu we created earlier in this chapter, apart from some added icons:

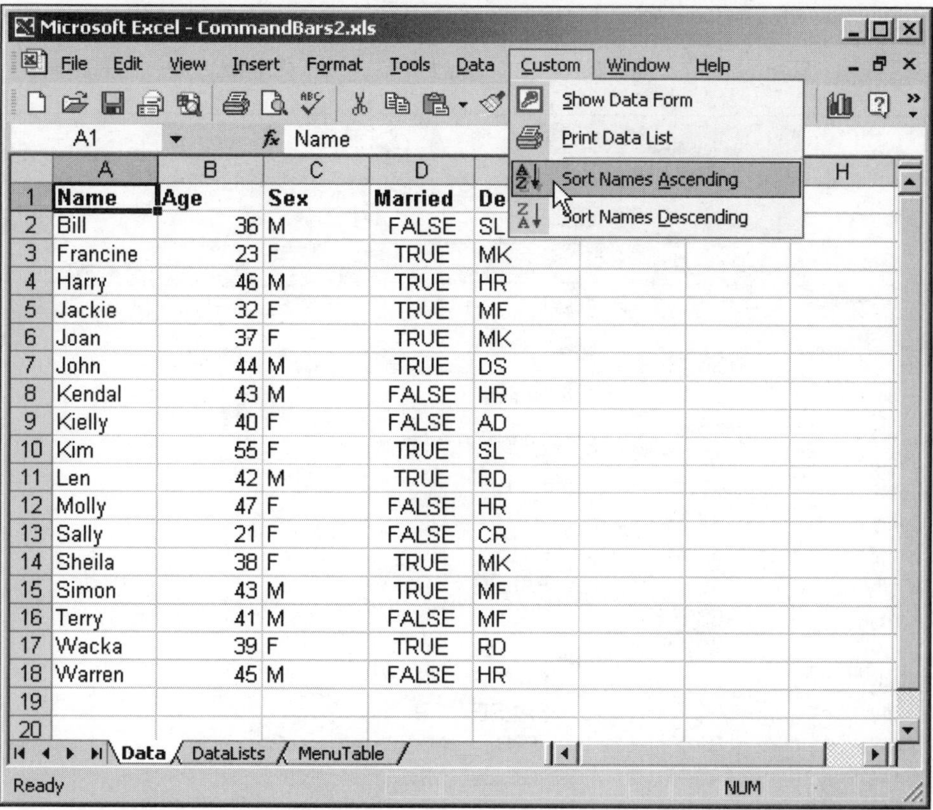

Rows 7 through 11 create a **Manage Data** toolbar identical to the one we created earlier. The data required for the drop-down list of departments is in the **DataLists** worksheet as shown below. The highlighted range has been given the name **Departments**:

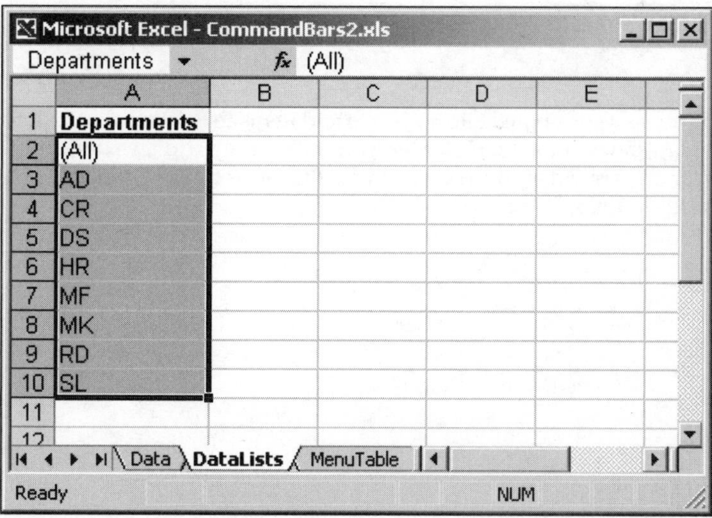

Row 12 of the table creates a Clear All entry in the popup menu that appears when you right-click a worksheet cell.

Row 13 adds the built-in Merge Across control to the Format | Row menu, as shown below:

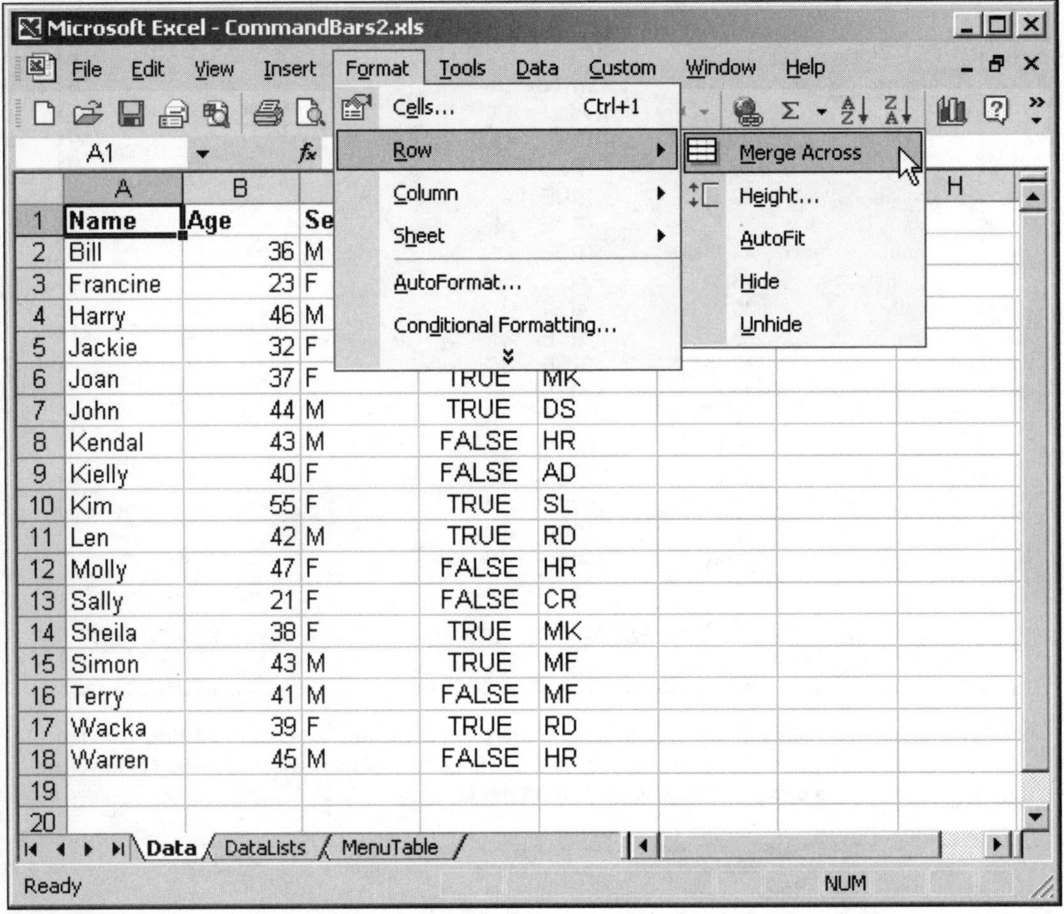

Although the code we have presented allows you to add items to existing shortcut menus, it is not able to create a new popup shortcut menu. However, you could easily add an extra column that allows you to specify this, as long as you adapt the code accordingly. The technique is flexible enough to accommodate whatever options you need.

Summary

In this chapter you have seen how the Excel commandbars are structured and learned how to create:

- Lists of the built-in control images with their `Id` and `FaceId` properties
- An entire list of the `FaceIds` that are available
- A complete list of popup menu items

You have also seen how to create your own commandbars and how to add controls to your commandbars. The differences between the three types of commandbars, that is toolbars, menu bars, and popup menus, have been described and methods of creating them programmatically have been presented. In addition, you have been shown how to enable and disable commandbars and controls, as well as how to protect commandbars so that users cannot change them.

Finally, you have seen how you can create a table to define the changes you want to make to a `CommandBar` structure while your application is open. This approach simplifies the task of customizing menus and makes it very easy to make changes.

15

Class Modules

Class modules are used in VBA to create your own customized objects. Most VBA users will never have to create their own objects because Excel already provides all of the objects they need. However, there are occasions when class modules can be very useful. You can use them to:

- Respond to application events; you can write code that is executed whenever any open workbook is saved or printed, for example
- Respond to embedded chart events
- Set up a single event procedure that can be used by a number of ActiveX controls such as text boxes in a UserForm
- Encapsulate Windows API code so that it is easy to use
- Encapsulate standard VBA procedures in a form that is easy to transport into other workbooks

In this chapter, we will create some simple (if not terribly useful) objects, to get the idea of how class modules work. Then we will apply the principles to some more useful examples. You are already familiar with Excel's built-in objects, such as the `Worksheet` object, and you know that objects often belong to collections such as the `Worksheets` collection. You also know that objects have properties and methods, such as the `Name` property and the `Copy` method of the `Worksheet` object.

Using a class module, you can create your own "blueprint" for a new object, such as an `Employee` object. You can define properties and methods for the object, such as a `Rate` property that records the employee's current rate of pay, and a `Training` method that consumes resources and increases the employee's skills. You can also create a new collection for the object, such as the `Employees` collection. The class module is a plan for the objects you want to create. From it you can create instances of your object. For example, Mary, Jack, and Anne could be instances of an `Employee` object, all belonging to the `Employees` collection.

You might not be aware of it, but you have been using some class modules already. The modules behind worksheets, charts, workbooks, and UserForms are class modules. However, they are special types of class module that behave a little differently from those you create yourself. They are designed specifically to support the object with which they are associated, and give you access to the event procedures for that object, and they cannot be deleted without deleting the associated object.

Creating Your Own Objects

Let's proceed with creating the `Employee` object we have talked about. You want to store the employee's name, hours worked per week, and rate of pay. From this information, you want to calculate the employee's weekly pay. You can create an `Employee` object with three properties to hold the required data and a method that calculates the weekly pay.

To do this, you create a class module named `clsEmployee` as shown in the top right of the following screen:

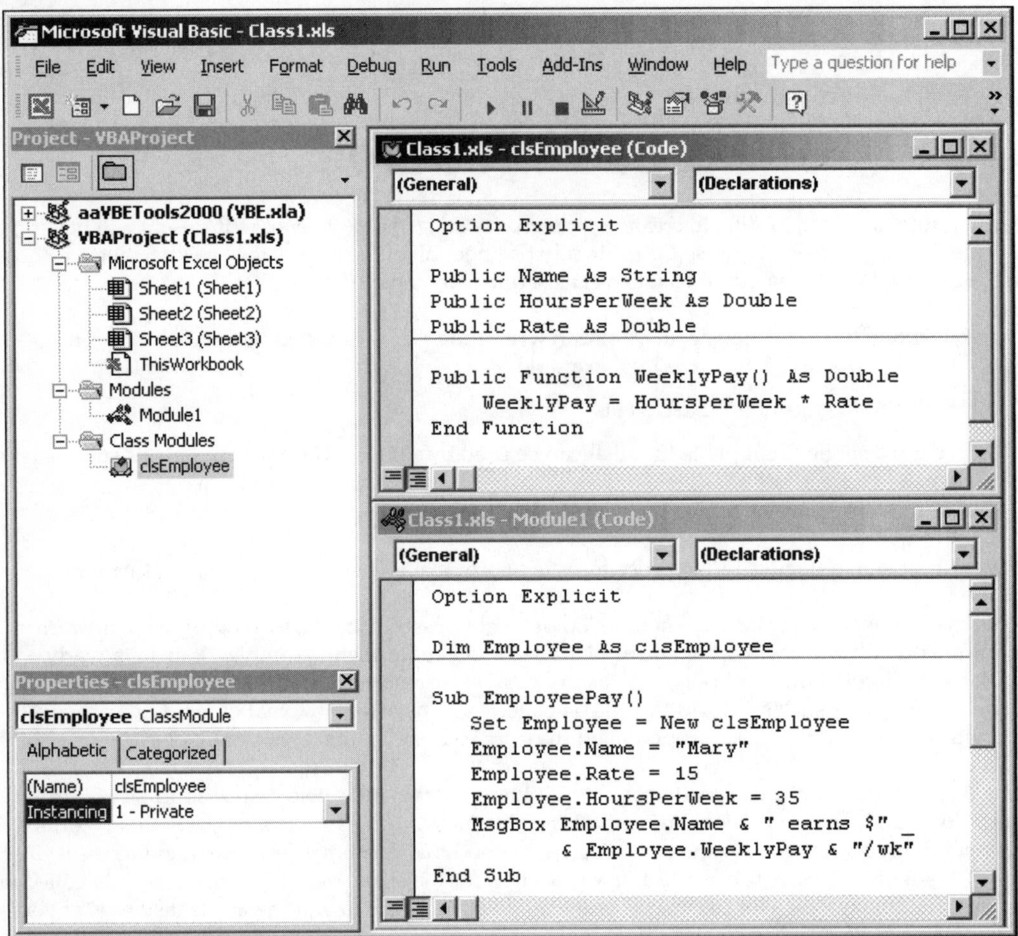

The class module declares three public variables – `Name`, `HoursPerWeek`, and `Rate` – which are the properties of the `Employee` object. There is also one public function, `WeeklyPay`. Recall, that any public function or sub procedure in the class module behaves as a method of the object. A function is a method that can generate a return value. A sub is a method that does not return a value.

The code in the standard module (at the bottom right of the screen) generates an employee object from the `clsEmployee` blueprint. The module declares `Employee` as a `clsEmployee` type. The `EmployeePay` sub procedure uses the `Set` statement to assign a new instance of `clsEmployee` to `Employee`, that is, `Set` creates the new object.

The sub then assigns values to the three properties of the object, before generating the message that appears in the message box at the bottom left of the screen. To form the message, it accesses the `Name` property of the `Employee` object and executes the `WeeklyPay` method of the `Employee` object.

An alternative way of setting up the standard code module, when you only need to create a single instance of the object variable, is as follows:

```
Dim Employee As New clsEmployee

Sub EmployeePay()
   Employee.Name = "Mary"
   Employee.Rate = 15
   Employee.HoursPerWeek = 35
   MsgBox Employee.Name & " earns $" & Employee.WeeklyPay & "/wk"
End Sub
```

Here, the keyword `New` is used on the declaration line. In this case, the `Employee` object is automatically created when it is first referenced in the code.

Property Procedures

If your properties are defined by public variables, they are read/write properties. They can be directly accessed and can be directly assigned new values, as we have seen above. If you want to perform checks or calculations on properties, you use `Property Let` and `Property Get` procedures to define the properties in your class module, instead of using public variables.

`Property Get` procedures allow the class module to control the way in which properties are accessed. `Property Let` procedures allow the class module to control the way in which properties can be assigned values. You can also use `Property Set` procedures. They are similar to `Property Let` procedures but they process objects instead of values.

For example, say you want to break up the employee hours into normal time and overtime, where the value of overtime is anything over 35 hours. You want to have an `HoursPerWeek` property, which includes both normal and overtime hours that can be read and can be assigned new values. You want the class module to split the hours into normal and overtime, and set up two properties, `NormalHours` and `OverTimeHours` that can be read, but cannot be directly assigned new values. You can set up the following code in the `clsEmployee` class module:

```
Public Name As String
Private NormalHrs As Double
Private OverTimeHrs As Double
Public Rate As Double

Public Function WeeklyPay() As Double
    WeeklyPay = NormalHrs * Rate + OverTimeHrs * Rate * 1.5
End Function

Property Let HoursPerWeek(Hours As Double)
    NormalHrs = WorksheetFunction.Min(35, Hours)
    OverTimeHrs = WorksheetFunction.Max(0, Hours - 35)
End Property

Property Get HoursPerWeek() As Double
'    HoursPerWeek = NormalHours + OverTimeHours
    HoursPerWeek = NormalHrs + OverTimeHrs
```

```
End Property

Property Get NormalHours() As Double
   NormalHours = NormalHrs
End Property

Property Get OverTimeHours() As Double
   OverTimeHours = OverTimeHrs
End Property
```

`HoursPerWeek` is no longer declared as a variable in the **(Declarations)** section. Instead, two new private variables have been added – `NormalHrs` and `OverTimeHrs`. `HoursPerWeek` is now defined by a `Property Let` procedure, which processes the input when you assign a value to the `HoursPerWeek` property. It breaks the hours into normal time and overtime. The `Property Get` procedure for `HoursPerWeek` returns the sum of normal and overtime hours when you access the property value.

`NormalHours` and `OverTimeHours` are defined only by `Property Get` procedures that return the values in the `Private` variables, `NormalHrs` and `OverTimeHrs`, respectively. This makes the properties `NormalHours` and `OverTimeHours` read-only. There is no way they can be assigned values apart from through the `HoursPerWeek` property.

The `WeeklyPay` function has been updated to calculate pay as normal hours at the standard rate and overtime hours at 1.5 times the standard rate. You can change the standard module code as follows to generate the message shown:

```
Dim Employee As New clsEmployee

Sub EmployeePay()
  Employee.Name = "Mary"
  Employee.Rate = 15
  Employee.HoursPerWeek = 45
  MsgBox Employee.Name & " earns $" _
       & Employee.WeeklyPay & "/wk" _
       & " including " & Employee.OverTimeHours _
       & " hrs overtime"
End Sub
```

Creating Collections

Now that you have an `Employee` object, you will want to have many `Employee` objects and what better way is there to organize them, but in a collection. VBA has a `Collection` object that you can use as follows, in a standard module:

```
Option Explicit
   Dim Employees As New Collection

Sub AddEmployees()
   Dim Employee As clsEmployee
```

```
    Dim lCount As Long

    For lCount = 1 To Employees.Count
       Employees.Remove 1
    Next lCount

    Set Employee = New clsEmployee
    Employee.Name = "Mary"
    Employee.Rate = 15
    Employee.HoursPerWeek = 45
    Employees.Add Employee, Employee.Name

    Set Employee = New clsEmployee
    Employee.Name = "Jack"
    Employee.Rate = 14
    Employee.HoursPerWeek = 35
    Employees.Add Employee, Employee.Name

    MsgBox "Number of Employees =  " & Employees.Count
    MsgBox "Employees(2).Name = " & Employees(2).Name
    MsgBox "Employees(""Jack"").Rate = " & Employees("Jack").Rate
    For Each Employee In Employees
       MsgBox Employee.Name & " earns $" & Employee.WeeklyPay
    Next Employee
End Sub
```

At the top of the standard module, we declare `Employees` to be a new collection. The `AddEmployees` procedure uses the `Remove` method of the collection in the `For...Next` loop to remove any existing objects. It keeps removing the first object in the collection, because as soon as you remove it, the second object automatically becomes the first object, and so on – hence the `.Remove 1` statement. This step is normally not necessary, as the collection is initialized empty. It is only here to demonstrate the `Remove` method and also allow you to run the procedure more than once without doubling-up the items in the collection.

`AddEmployees` creates the first employee, `Mary`, and uses the `Add` method of the collection to place the `Mary` object in the collection. The first parameter of the `Add` method is a reference to the object itself. The second parameter, which is optional, is an identifying key that can be used to reference the object later. In this case we have used the `Employees` collection's `Name` property. The same procedure is used with Jack.

> **If you supply a key value for each member of the collection, the keys must be unique. You will get a run-time error when you attempt to add a new member to the collection with a key value that is already in use. Using a person's name as the key is not recommended as people can have the same name. Use a unique identifier, such as a Social Security number.**

The `MsgBox` statements illustrate that you can reference the collection in the same ways as you can reference Excel's built-in collections. For instance the `Employees` collection has a `Count` property. You can reference a member of the collection by position or by key, if you have entered a key value.

Class Module Collection

You can also set up your collection in a class module. There are advantages and disadvantages in doing this. The advantages are that you get much more control over interaction with the collection, you can prevent direct access to the collection, and the code is encapsulated into a single module that makes it more transportable and easier to maintain. The disadvantages are that it takes more work to set up the collection, and that you lose some of the short-cut ways to reference members of the collection and the collection itself.

The following shows the contents of a class module `clsEmployees`:

```
Private colEmployees As New Collection

Public Function Add(Employee As clsEmployee)
    colEmployees.Add Employee, Employee.Name
End Function

Public Property Get Count() As Long
    Count = colEmployees.Count
End Property

Public Property Get Items() As Collection
    Set Items = colEmployees
End Property

Public Property Get Item(vItem As Variant) As clsEmployee
    Set Item = colEmployees(vItem)
End Property

Public Sub Remove(vItem As Variant)
    colEmployees.Remove vItem
End Sub
```

When the collection is in its own class module, you can no longer directly use the collection's four methods (`Add`, `Count`, `Item`, and `Remove`) in your standard module. You need to set up your own methods and properties in the class module, even if you have no intention of modifying the collections methods. On the other hand, you have control over what you choose to implement and what you choose to modify, as well as what you present as a method and what you present as a property.

In `clsEmployees`, `Function Add`, `Sub Remove`, `Property Get Item`, and `Property Get Count` pass on most of the functionality of the collection's methods. There is one new feature in the `Property Get Items` procedure. Whereas `Property Get Item` passes back a reference to a single member of the collection, `Property Get Items` passes back a reference to the entire collection. This is to provide the capability to use the collection in a `For Each...Next` loop.

The standard module code is now as follows:

```
Option Explicit
Dim Employees As New clsEmployees

Sub AddEmployees()
   Dim Employee As clsEmployee
   Dim lCount As Long
   Dim vaNames As Variant
   Dim vaRates As Variant
   Dim vaHours As Variant

   vaNames = Array("Mary", "Jack", "Anne", "Harry")
   vaRates = Array(15, 14, 20, 17)
   vaHours = Array(45, 35, 40, 40)

   For lCount = 1 To Employees.Count
      Employees.Remove 1
   Next lCount

   For lCount = LBound(Names) To UBound(Names)
      Set Employee = New clsEmployee
      Employee.Name = vaNames(lCount)
```

```
        Employee.Rate = vaRates(lCount)
        Employee.HoursPerWeek = vaHours(lCount)
        Employees.Add Employee
        Set Employee = Nothing
    Next lCount

    MsgBox "Number of Employees =  " & Employees.Count
    MsgBox "Employees.Item(2).Name = " & Employees.Item(2).Name
    MsgBox "Employees.Item(""Jack"").Rate = " & Employees.Item("Jack").Rate
    For Each Employee In Employees.Items
        MsgBox Employee.Name & " earns $" & Employee.WeeklyPay
    Next Employee
End Sub
```

`Employees` is declared to be an instance of `clsEmployees`. The code that follows defines three arrays as a convenient way to make it clear what data is being used. As before, the collection is cleared of objects and then a `For...Next` loop adds the four employees to the collection. As one small convenience, we no longer need to specify the key value when using the `Add` method of the `Employees` collection. The `Add` method code in `clsEmployees` does this for us.

The second, third, and fourth `MsgBox` statements show the new properties needed to reference the collection and its members. You need to use the `Item` property to reference a member and the `Items` property to reference the whole collection.

Encapsulation

Class modules allow you to encapsulate code and data in such a way that it becomes very easy to use, very easy to share, and much easier to maintain.

You hide the code that does the work from the user, who only needs to know what sort of object the class module represents, and what properties and methods are associated with the object. This is particularly useful when it is necessary to make calls to the Windows API (application programming interface) to perform tasks that are not possible in normal VBA. This topic is presented in Chapter 24 where you can see examples that encapsulate very complex code and create very useable objects.

Class modules provide a mechanism for encapsulating code that you can use in other workbooks or share with other programmers to reduce development time. You can easily copy a class module to another workbook. In the Project Explorer window it is as straightforward as dragging the class module between the projects.

You can also export the code in the class module to a file by right-clicking the module in the Project Explorer and choosing **Export File...** to create a text file that can be copied to another PC. The file can then be imported into another workbook by right-clicking its project in the Project Explorer and choosing **Import File...**.

So far, we have examined class modules from a general programming perspective. We will now see how we can use class modules to gain more control over Excel.

Trapping Application Events

You can use a class module to trap application events. Most of these events are the same as the workbook events, but they apply to all open workbooks, not just the particular workbook that contains the event procedures. For example, in a workbook there is a `BeforePrint` event that is triggered when you start to print anything in that workbook. At the application level, there is a `WorkbookBeforePrint` event that is triggered when any open workbook starts to print.

To see what application events are available, you first insert a class module into your project. The class module can have any valid module name. The one shown in the screenshot below has been named `clsAppEvents`. You then type in the following variable declaration at the top of the module:

```
Public WithEvents xlApp As Application
```

The object variable name, `xlApp`, can be any valid variable name, as long as you use it consistently in code that refers to the class module, as a property of the class. The `WithEvents` key word causes the events associated with the application object to be exposed. You can now choose `xlApp` from the left-hand side dropdown at the top of the module and then use the right-hand side dropdown to see the event list as follows:

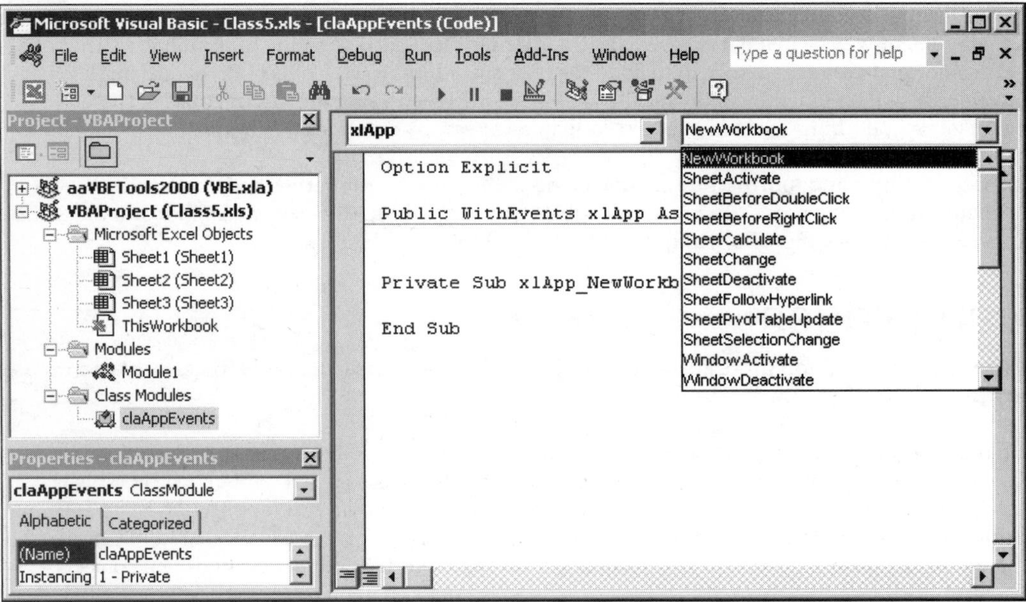

We will choose the `WorkbookBeforePrint` event and extend the event procedure that was presented in the chapter on events, using the following code in `clsAppEvents`:

```
Private Sub xlApp_WorkbookBeforePrint(ByVal Wbk As Workbook, _
                                     Cancel As Boolean)
   Dim Wks As Worksheet
   Dim stFullFileName As String
   Dim stCompanyName As String

   With Wbk
      stCompanyName = "Execuplan Consulting"
      stFullFileName = .FullName
      For Each Wks In .Worksheets
         With Wks.PageSetup
            .LeftFooter = stCompanyName
            .CenterFooter = ""
            .RightFooter = stFullFileName
         End With
      Next Wks
   End With
End Sub
```

Unlike sheet and workbook class modules, the event procedures you place in your own class modules do not automatically function. You need to create an instance of your class module and assign the `Application` object to the `xlApp` property of the new object. The following code must be set up in a standard module:

```
Public xlApplication As New clsAppEvents

Sub TrapApplicationEvents()
   Set xlApplication.xlApp = Application
End Sub
```

All you need to do now is execute the `TrapApplicationEvents` procedure. The `WorkbookBeforePrint` event procedure will then run when you use any Print or Preview commands, until you close the workbook containing the event procedure.

It is possible to terminate application event trapping during the current session. Any action that resets module-level variables and public variables will terminate application event processing, as the class module instance will be destroyed. Actions that can cause this include editing code in the VBE and executing the `End` statement in VBA code.

There have been (relatively rare) cases, in Excel 97, where bugs in Excel have caused variables to reset. It would be wise to expect that bugs could also exist in later versions.

If you want to enable application event processing for all Excel sessions, you can place your class module and standard module code in `Personal.xls` and execute `TrapApplicationEvents` in the `Workbook_Open` event procedure. You could even transfer the code in `TrapApplicationEvents` to the `Workbook_Open` event procedure. However, you must keep the `Public` declaration of `xlApplication` in a standard module.

To illustrate, you can place the following code in the (Declarations) section of a standard module:

```
Public xlApplication As New clsAppEvents
```

You can place the following event procedure in the `ThisWorkbook` module:

```
Private Sub Workbook_Open()
   Set xlApplication.xlApp = Application
End Sub
```

Embedded Chart Events

If you want to trap events for a chart embedded in a worksheet, you use a process similar to the process for trapping application events. First insert a new class module in your project, or you could use the same class module that you used for the application events. You place the following declaration at the top of the class module:

```
Public WithEvents Cht As Chart
```

We will set up the same `BeforeDoubleClick` event procedure that we used in Chapter 10. The class module should be as follows:

```
Public WithEvents Cht As Chart

Private Sub cht_BeforeDoubleClick(ByVal ElementID As Long, _
         ByVal Arg1 As Long, ByVal Arg2 As Long, Cancel As Boolean)
   Dim Srs As Series

   Select Case ElementID
      Case xlLegend
         ActiveChart.HasLegend = False
         Cancel = True
      Case xlChartArea
         ActiveChart.HasLegend = True
         Cancel = True
      Case xlSeries
         'Arg1 is the Series index
         'Arg2 is the point index (-1 if the entire series is selected)
         Set Srs = ActiveChart.SeriesCollection(Arg1)
         If Arg2 = -1 Then
            With Srs.Border
               If .ColorIndex = xlColorIndexAutomatic Then
                  .ColorIndex = 1
               Else
                  .ColorIndex = (.ColorIndex Mod 56) + 1
               End If
            End With
         Else
            With Srs.Points(Arg2)
               .HasDataLabel = Not .HasDataLabel
            End With
         End If
         Cancel = True
   End Select
End Sub
```

This code allows you to double-click the chart legend to make it disappear, or double-click in the chart area to make it re-appear. If you double-click a series line, it changes color. If you select a point in a series, by clicking on it, and then double-click it, it will toggle the data label on and off for that point.

Say your chart is contained in a `ChartObject` that is the only `ChartObject` in a worksheet called `Mangoes` and you have named your class module `clsChartEvents`. In your standard module, you enter the following:

```
Public myChart As New clsChartEvents

Sub InitializeChartEvents()
   Set myChart.Cht = ThisWorkbook.Worksheets("Mangoes").ChartObjects(1).Chart
End Sub
```

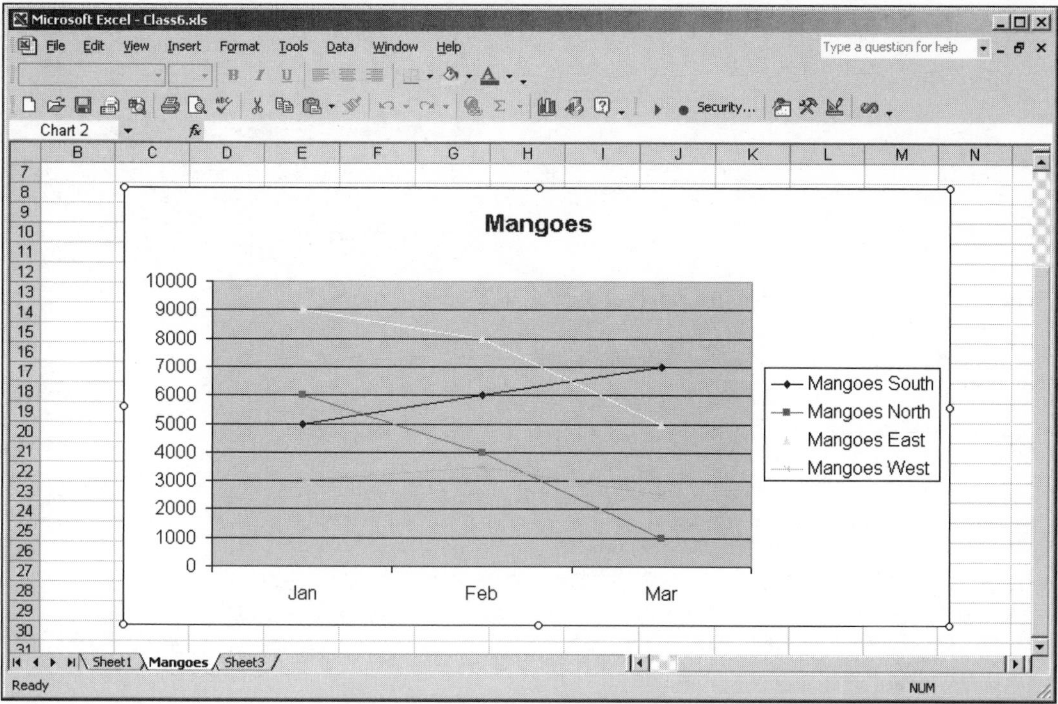

After executing `InitializeChartEvents`, you can double-click the series, points, and legend to run the `BeforeDoubleClick` event procedure.

A Collection of UserForm Controls

When you have a number of the same type of control on a form, you often write almost identical event procedures for each one. For example, say you want to be able to double-click the label to the left of each of the TextBox in the following UserForm to clear the TextBox and set the focus to the TextBox. You would normally write four, almost identical, event procedures, one for each label control:

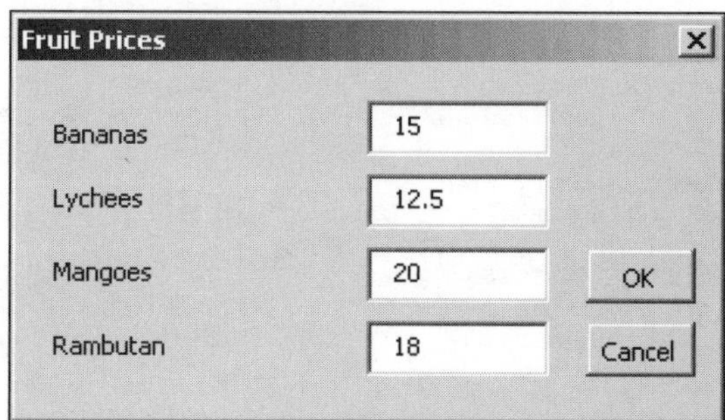

Using a class module, you can write a single generic event procedure to apply to all the label controls, or just those that need the procedure. The label controls and TextBox in the UserForm have been given corresponding names as follows:

Label	Text Box
lbBananas	txBananas
lbLychees	txLychees
lbMangoes	txMangoes
lbRambutan	txRambutan

The following code is entered in a class module `clsControlEvents`:

```
Public WithEvents Lbl As MSForms.Label
Public Frm As UserForm

Private Sub Lbl_DblClick(ByVal Cancel As MSForms.ReturnBoolean)
   Dim stProduct As String
   Dim stTextBoxName As String

   stProduct = Mid(Lbl.Name, 3)
   stTextBoxName = "tx" & stProduct
   With Frm.Controls(stTextBoxName)
      .Text = ""
      .SetFocus
   End With
End Sub
```

`Lbl` is declared with events as a UserForm label. `Frm` is declared to be the UserForm. The generic `DblClick` event procedure for `Lbl` uses the `Mid` function to get the product name starting with the third character of the label name, removing the "`lb`" identifier. It converts this to the TextBox name by appending "`tx`" in front of the product name.

The `With...End With` structure identifies the TextBox object by using the TextBox name as an index into the `Controls` collection of the UserForm. It sets the `Text` property of the TextBox to a zero length string and uses the `SetFocus` method to place the cursor in the TextBox.

The following code is entered into the class module behind the UserForm:

```
Dim colLabels As New Collection

Private Sub UserForm_Initialize()
   Dim Ctl As MSForms.Control
   Dim obEvents As clsControlEvents

   For Each Ctl In Me.Controls
      If TypeOf Ctl Is MSForms.Label Then
         Set obEvents = New clsControlEvents
         Set obEvents.Lbl = Ctl
         Set obEvents.Frm = Me
         colLabels.Add obEvents
      End If
   Next Ctl
End Sub
```

`colLabels` is declared as a new collection to hold the objects that will be created from the `clsControlEvents` class module. In the UserForm `Initialize` event procedure, the label controls are associated with instances of `clsControlEvents`.

The For Each...Next loop processes all the controls on the form. When it identifies a control that is a label, using the TypeOf key word to identify the control type, it creates a new instance of clsControlEvents and assigns it to obEvents. The Lbl property of the new object is assigned a reference to the control and the Frm property is assigned a reference to the UserForm. The new object is then added to the colLabels collection.

When the UserForm is loaded into memory, the Initialize event runs and connects the label controls to instances of the class module event procedure. Double-clicking any label clears the TextBox to the right and sets the focus to that TextBox, ready for new data to be typed in.

> **You need to be aware that some events associated with some controls are not made available in a class module using With Events. For example, the most useful events exposed by UserForm text boxes are BeforeUpdate, AfterUpdate, Enter, and Exit. None of these is available in a class module. You can only handle these events in the class module associated with the UserForm.**

Referencing Classes Across Projects

When you want to run macros in another workbook, you can use Tools | References... in the VBE window to create a reference to the other workbook's VBA project. The reference shows as a special entry in the Project Explorer as shown on the following screenshot:

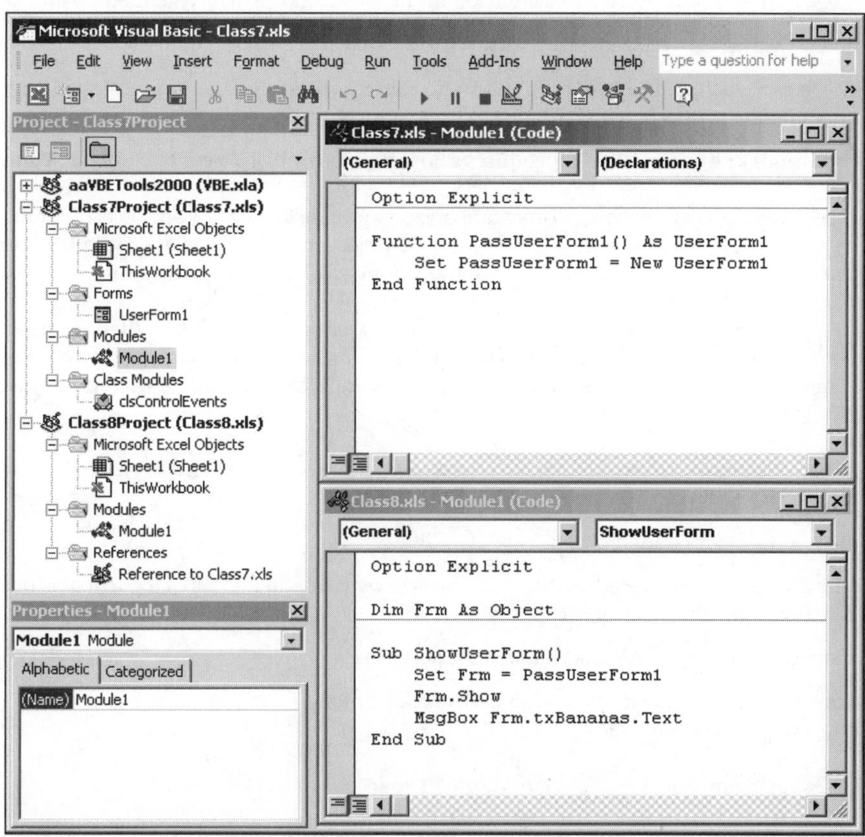

`Class8.xls` has a reference to `Class7.xls`, which contains the UserForm from our previous example. The reference allows you to run procedures in standard modules in `Class7.xls` from standard modules in `Class8.xls`. However, the reference does not allow you to create instances of class modules or UserForms in the referenced workbook.

> **When you create a reference to another workbook, you should make sure that the VBA Project in the referenced workbook has a unique name. By default, it will be named VBA Project. Click Tools | VBA Project Properties... and enter a new project name.**

There is a way to get around this. You can indirectly access a UserForm in the referenced workbook if that workbook has a function that returns a reference to the UserForm. There is an example of this type of function in the top right-hand corner of the above screen. `PassUserForm1`, in `Class7.xls`, is a function that assigns a new instance of `UserForm1` to its return value. In `Class8.xls`, `Frm` is declared as a generic `Object` type. `ShowUserform` assigns the return value of `PassUserForm1` to `Frm`. `Frm` can then be used to show the UserForm and access its control values, as long as the UserForm is hidden, not unloaded.

Summary

Class modules are used to create blueprints for new objects, such as the `Employee` object that was presented in this chapter:

- `Function` and `Sub` procedures are used in the class module to create methods for the object
- `Public` variables declare the properties for the object
- However, if you need to take programmatic control when a property is assigned a value, you can define the property using a `Property Let` procedure
- In addition, `Property Get` procedures allow you to control access to property values

To use the code in your class module, you create one or more instances of your object. For example, you can create Mary and Jack as instances of an `Employee` object. You can further customize your objects by creating your own collection, where you add all the instances of your object.

Class modules are not used to create objects to the same extent in Excel VBA as they are used in a standalone programming language such as Visual Basic. This is because Excel already contains the objects that most Excel programmers want to use. However, Excel programmers can use class modules to:

- Trap application-level events, such as the `WorkbookBeforePrint` event that allows you to control the printing of all open workbooks
- Trap events in embedded charts
- Write a single event procedure that can be used by many instances of a particular object, such as a TextBox control on a UserForm.
- Encapsulate difficult code and make it easier to use
- Encapsulate code so that you can share the code among
- different projects and users

See Chapter 24 for examples of encapsulation of API code.

VBAProgrammersReferenceExcel2D
mersReferenceExcel2002VB
ReferenceExcel2002VBAPro
ProgrammersReferenceExc
rammersReferenceExcel2D
ReferenceExcel2002VB
ceExcel2002VBAPro
Programme 2002VBAProgram
xcel2002VBAProgramme
2002VBAProgrammersReferenceExce
VBAProgrammersReference
rogrammersReferenceExce
ammersReference Excel2000VBAProgra
2002VBAProgrammersReferenceExce

16

Addins

If you want to make your workbook invisible to the user in the Excel window, you can turn it into an **Addin** file. An Addin can be loaded into memory using File | Open, but it generally makes more sense to access it via Tools | Add-Ins.... Either way, the file does not appear in the Excel Application window, but the macros it contains can be executed from the user interface. Any user-defined functions it contains can be used in worksheet calculations. The Addin's macros can be attached to menu commands and toolbar buttons, and the Addin can communicate with the user through UserForms and VBA functions such as `InputBox` and `MsgBox`.

It is widely believed that an Addin is a compiled version of a workbook. In programming, compilation involves translating the human-readable programming code into machine language. This is **not** the case with an Excel Addin. In fact, all that happens is that the workbook is hidden from the user interface. The Addin's worksheets and charts can no longer be seen by anyone. Its code modules can still be viewed, as normal, in the VBE window and remain complete with comments as well as code.

However, the Office 2000 Developer Edition and Office XP do make it possible to create a compiled version of an Addin. This is referred to as a COM (Component Object Model) Addin. COM Addins are discussed separately in Chapter 17.

For this chapter, we have taken the `CommandBars2.xls` file that we used in Chapter 14, saved it as `AddIn1.xls`, prior to converting it to `Addin1.xla`, and adapted the code to make it suitable for an Addin. We have removed the code on popup menus as it is not relevant.

> **Although it is not necessary to give an Addin file name an `.xla` extension, it is a good idea to do so. It identifies the file as an Addin and ensures that the Addin icon appears against the file in the Windows File Manager. The conversion of a workbook file to an Addin file is covered below.**

Hiding the Code

You cannot stop users from seeing a standard workbook's name, or an Addin's name, in the Project Explorer window. However, you can stop UsersFrom expanding the workbook's name, or Addin's name, to view the component modules and user forms and the code they contain.

You prevent access to your code by putting a password on the VBA project. Select the project and use Tools | <ProjectName> Properties (where <ProjectName> is the name of your particular project) or right-click the project in the Project Explorer window and click <ProjectName> Properties to see the following screen:

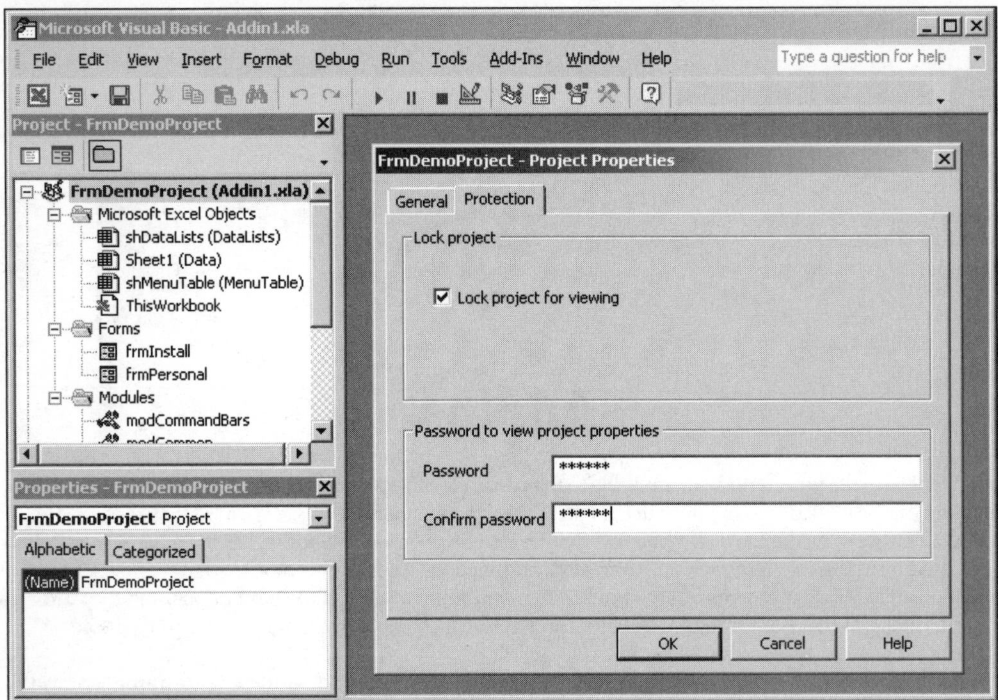

After you have entered the password and confirmed it, you will need to click OK and save the file. To see the effect, close the file and re-open it again. The top file, `VBETools.xla`, has been password protected and cannot be expanded unless you supply the password. You are prompted for the password when you try to expand the project.

It is a common misconception that Excel's passwords cannot be broken. There are programs available that can decipher file, workbook, and worksheet passwords, as well as the VBA project passwords for all versions of Excel. Since the introduction of Excel 97, the workbook file password has proven a difficult nut to crack if it contains more than just a few characters. Excel 2002 provides a number of different levels of encryption for the file password that should make it extremely difficult, if not impossible, to crack. Unfortunately, this password is useless to developers who want users to be able to open their files and actually use them.

Creating an Addin

Converting a workbook to an Addin is a trivial exercise, on the face of it. Make sure that a worksheet is active in your workbook, use the Excel window File | Save As... and scroll to the bottom of the dropdown labeled Save as type: and choose Microsoft Excel Add-In (*.xla). Excel 2000 and 2002 automatically position you in a special Addins folder, although there is no requirement that you use it. The advantage of this method is that you do not overwrite the original `.xls` file and you create a file with the `.xla` extension that distinguishes it as an Addin to the operating system.

Note that you must have a worksheet active when using File | Save As... to create an Addin. Otherwise, you will not find the `*.xla` type offered as an option.

An easier way to create an Addin is to change the `IsAddin` property of `ThisWorkbook` to `True` in the Properties window:

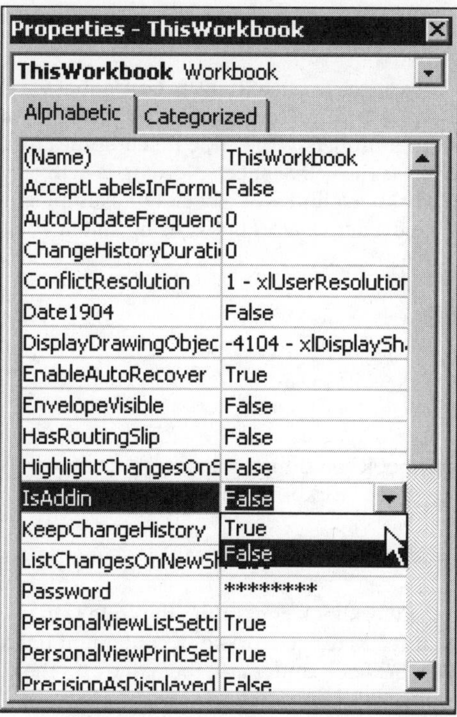

The disadvantage of this method is that you change the original `.xls` file to an Addin, but its `.xls` extension remains unchanged and, when you save the file, you are not warned that you are replacing a workbook file with an Addin file. If you want to change the file extension to `.xla`, you can exit from Excel to remove the Addin from memory, and change it manually using the Windows Explorer.

Closing Addins

If you have just converted a workbook to an Addin by changing its `IsAddin` property and saving it, or you have loaded the Addin using File | Open, there is no obvious way to close the file from the menus without closing Excel. One way to close the Addin is to go to the Immediate window and type in code that uses the `Close` method, treating the Addin as a member of the `Workbooks` collection:

```
Workbooks("Addin1.xls").Close
```

Addins do not have an `Index` property value in the `Workbooks` collection and are not included in the `Count` property of the `Workbooks` collection, but they can be addressed by name as members of the `Workbooks` collection.

Another method you can use to close an Addin is to click on the file name in the recently-used-file list at the bottom of the Excel File menu while holding down Shift. You may get a message about overwriting the copy in memory (depending on whether it has changed or not) and then you will get a message about not being able to open an Addin for editing (a hangover from previous versions). Click OK and the Addin will be removed from memory.

Code Changes

In most cases you need to make some changes to the VBA code that was written for a standard workbook to make it suitable for an Addin. This is particularly true if you reference data within your Addin workbook. Most Excel programmers write code that assumes that the workbook is the active workbook and that the worksheet is the active sheet. Nothing is active in an Addin, so your code must explicitly reference the Addin workbook and worksheet. For example, in Chapters 13 and 14, our code assumed that it was dealing with the active workbook, using statements like the following:

```
With Range("Database")
   Set rgData = .Rows(2)
   Call LoadRecord
   sbNavigator.Value = 2
   sbNavigator.Max = .Rows.Count
End With
```

This code only works if the workbook containing the name `Database` is active. In your Addin code, you need to include a reference to the workbook and worksheet. You could say:

```
With Workbooks("Addins1.xls").Sheets("Data").Range("Database")
```

A more useful way to refer to the workbook containing the code is to use the `ThisWorkbook` property of the `Application` object that refers to the workbook containing the code. This makes the code much more flexible: you can save the workbook under any file name and the code still works:

```
With ThisWorkbook.Sheets("Data").Range("Database")
```

You can also use the object name for the sheet that you see in the Project Explorer:

```
With Sheet1.Range("Database")
```

> **You can edit both the workbook's programmatic name and the sheet's programmatic name in the Properties window. If you change the sheet's programmatic name, you must also change your code. If you change the workbook's programmatic name, you can use the new name if you wish, but `ThisWorkbook` remains a valid reference, as it is a property of the `Application` object and a member of `<globals>`.**

If you want to be able to ignore the sheet name, to allow the name `Database` to exist on any sheet, you can use the following construction:

```
With ThisWorkbook.Names("Database").RefersToRange
```

Saving Changes

Another potential problem with an Addin that contains data is that changes to the data will not be saved automatically at the end of an Excel session. For example, `Addin1.xla` allows users to edit the data in the range `Database`, so it is essential to save those changes before the Addin is closed. It is one of the nice things about Addins that users are never bothered with prompts about saving changes. Therefore, you need to ensure that data is saved, by setting up a procedure in your VBA code. One way to do this is to add the following code to the `Workbook_BeforeClose` event procedure, or the `Auto_Close` procedure:

```
If Not ThisWorkbook.Saved Then ThisWorkbook.Save
```

This technique does not work in Excel 5 or Excel 95. These versions do not allow you to save changes to an Addin file.

Interface Changes

You need to bear in mind that the Addin's sheets will not be visible and you will not see the names of the Addin's macros in the Tools | Macro | Macros... dialog box. You need to create menus, toolbars, or command buttons in other workbooks to execute your macros. Luckily, we have already built a menu and toolbar interface in our `CommandBars2.xls` application, which has been converted to our `Addin1.xla` application.

It is also a good idea to make all your code as robust as possible. You should allow for abnormal events such as system crashes that could affect your code. The `CommandBars2.xls` application adds a menu and a toolbar to Excel when it is opened. Before doing this, `CommandBars2.xls` deletes any previously created versions of these commandbars, which is a very good practice. It is possible that previous versions could exist following a system crash, for example.

Finally, `CommandBars2.xls` made the data list visible on the screen, so the results of an AutoFilter were obvious. The data list is not visible when it is in an Addin so you need another way to show the results of a filter. We have adapted the Next and Previous buttons on the user form `fmPersonal` to show only the filtered data. The Addin user interface appears as follows on the screenshot:

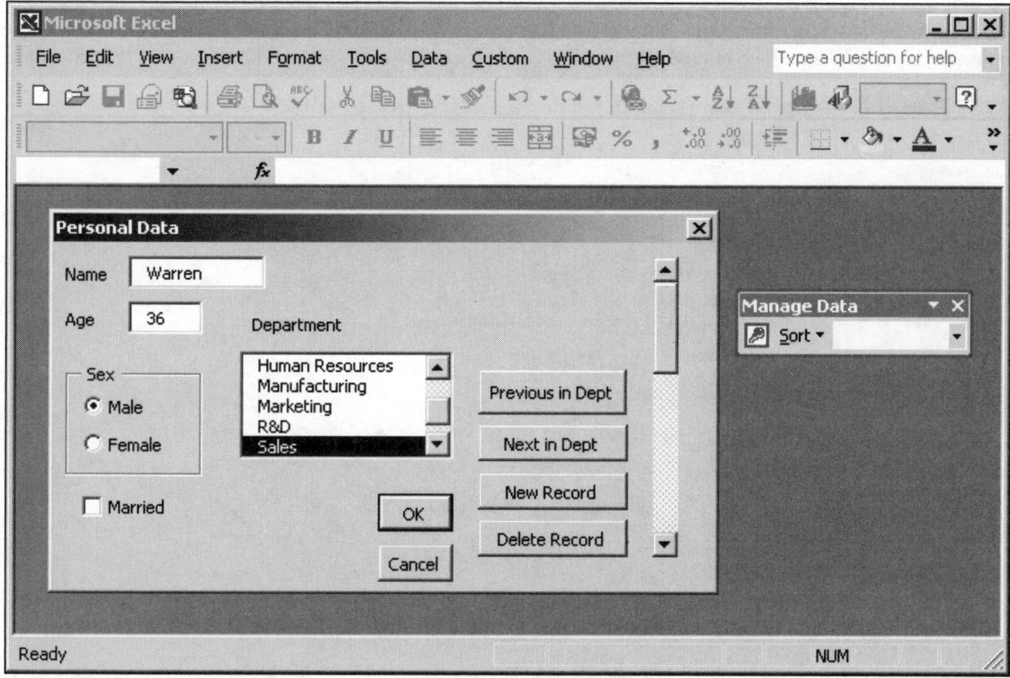

The captions on the Next and Previous buttons have been changed to Next in Dept and Previous in Dept. The code in the `Click` event procedure of the two buttons has been re-written (from that in Chapter 14) to show only the rows in the data that are not hidden by the AutoFilter:

```
Private Sub btnNext_Click()
  Dim lBottomRow As Long
  Dim lCheckRow As Long

  With ThisWorkbook.Names("Database").RefersToRange
    'Determine last row to check
    lBottomRow = .Rows(.Rows.Count).Row + 1
    'Start looking at row below current row
    lCheckRow = rngData.Row + 1
    'Look for first row down that is not hidden
    Do Until lCheckRow = lBottomRow
      If .Parent.Rows(lCheckRow).Hidden = False Then
        Exit Do
      Else
        lCheckRow = lCheckRow + 1
      End If
    Loop
    'If we found a visible row within the data, display it
    If lCheckRow <> lBottomRow Then
      sbNavigator.Value = lCheckRow + .Row - 1
    End If
  End With
End Sub
```

When we search down through the data to find a row that is not hidden, we need to take into account that there might not be one. The first visible row will then be the row after the last row of data, so we need to search that far. The first row to check is the row after the current row, which is the one we are viewing. The code in the `Do...Loop` increments the check row until we either find a visible row or reach the bottom row. If we have found the bottom row we do nothing. Otherwise, we change the scrollbar value to the found rows location in the database, which runs the scrollbar event procedure to show the data that was found:

```
Private Sub btnPrevious_Click()
  Dim lTopRow As Long
  Dim lCheckRow As Long

  With ThisWorkbook.Names("Database").RefersToRange
    'The top row to check is the database header row
    lTopRow = .Row
    'Start looking at row above current row
    lCheckRow = rngData.Row - 1
    'Look for first row up that is not hidden
    Do Until lCheckRow = lTopRow
      If .Parent.Rows(lCheckRow).Hidden = False Then
        Exit Do
      Else
        lCheckRow = lCheckRow - 1
      End If
    Loop
    'If we found a visible row within the data, display it
    If lCheckRow <> lTopRow Then
      sbNavigator.Value = lCheckRow + .Row - 1
    End If
  End With
End Sub
```

Searching up through the data to find a row that is not hidden is a similar task to searching down. We set the top row to be checked to the header record in the database because it might be the only unhidden row above the current row.

The operating procedure for these buttons may not be clear initially to users, so we will include an explanatory screen that displays when the Addin is installed, as you will see later.

Installing an Addin

An Addin can be opened from the worksheet File menu, as has been mentioned. However, you get better control over an Addin if you install it using Tools | Add-Ins, which displays the following dialog box:

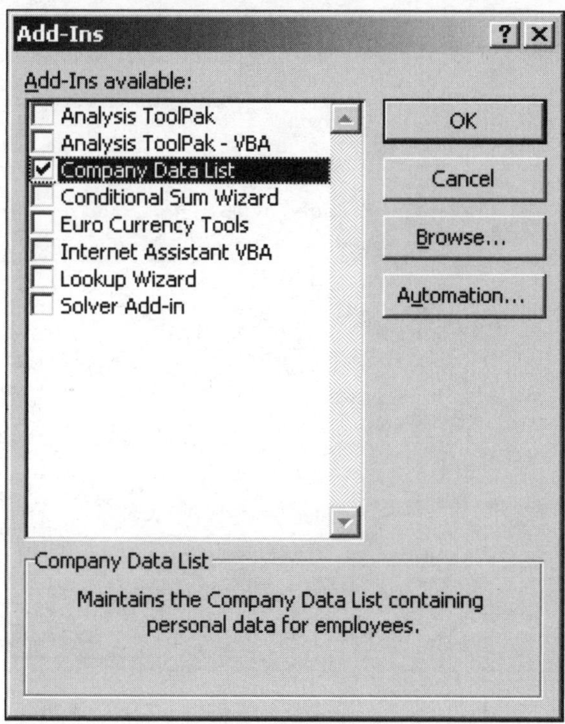

The Company Data List Addin is the `Addin1.xla file`. If it does not already appear in the list, you can click the Browse... button to locate it.

The friendly title and description are provided by filling in the workbook's Properties. If you have already converted the workbook to an Addin, you can set its `IsAddin` property to `False` to make the workbook visible in the Excel window and use File | Properties to display the following dialog box:

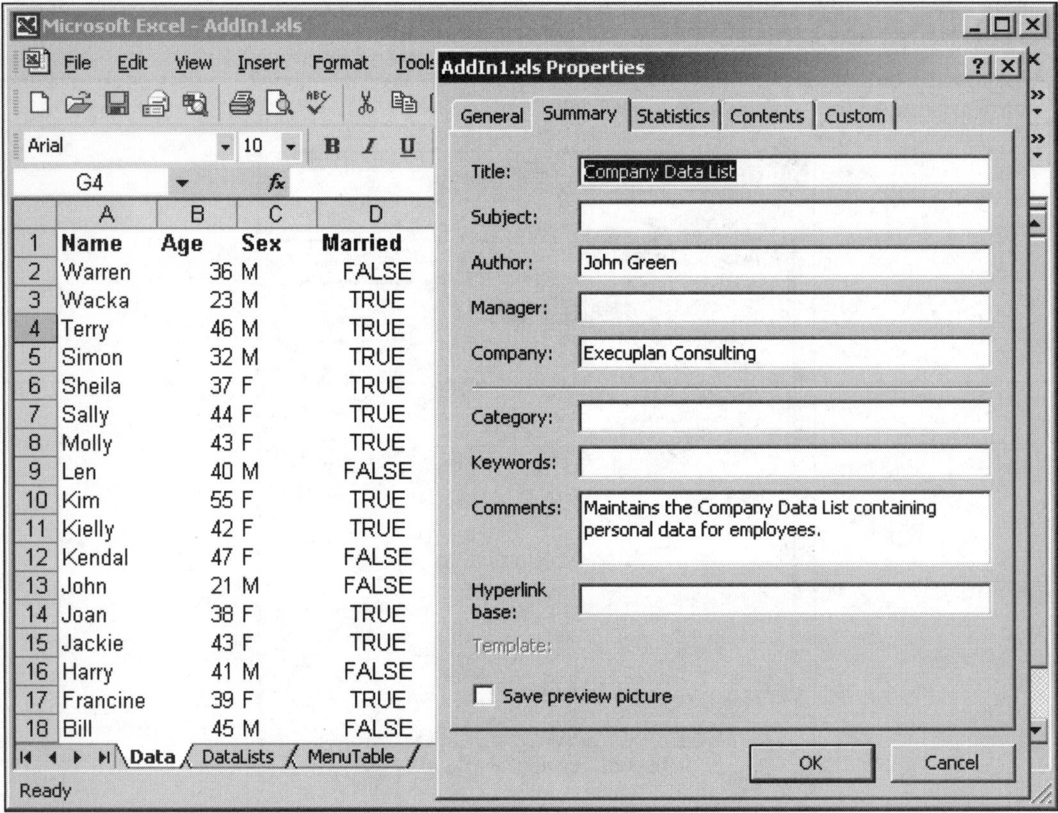

The **Title:** and **Comments:** boxes supply the information for the **Tools | Add-Ins** dialog box. When you have added the required information, you can set the `IsAddin` property back to `True` and save the file.

If you change the Addin workbook properties after adding it to the **Tools | Add-Ins** *dialog box, the friendly text will not appear. You need to remove the Addin from the list and add it back again. The removal process is covered below.*

Once the Addin is visible in the **Tools | Add-Ins** dialog box, you can install and uninstall the Addin by checking and un-checking the check box beside the Addin's description. When it is installed, it is loaded into memory and becomes visible in the VBE window and will be automatically loaded in future Excel sessions. When it is uninstalled, it is removed from memory and is no longer visible in the VBE window and will no longer be loaded in future Excel sessions.

AddinInstall Event

There are two special events that are triggered when you install and uninstall an Addin. The following code, in the `ThisWorkbook` module, shows how to display a user form when the Addin is installed:

```
Private Sub Workbook_AddinInstall()
   fmInstall.Show
End Sub
```

The user form displays the following information for the user:

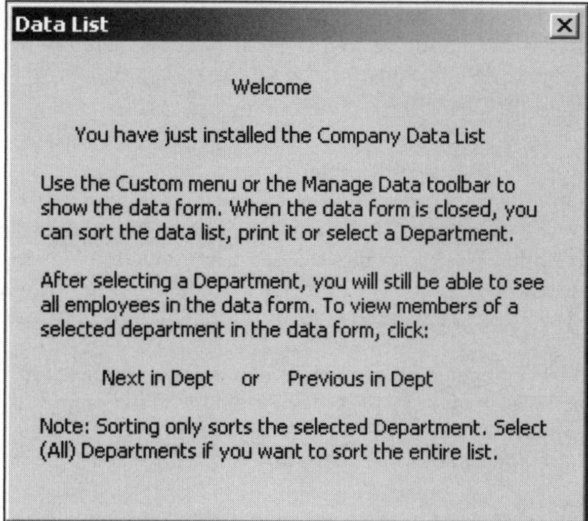

The other event is the `AddinUninstall` event.

Removing an Addin from the Addins List

There is no easy way to remove an Addin from the Tools | Add-Ins dialog box. One way you can do this is to move the Addin file from its current folder using the Windows Explorer, before opening Excel. An alternative is to change the Addin's file name before opening Excel. The following message will appear when you open Excel, and the Addin will have been deleted:

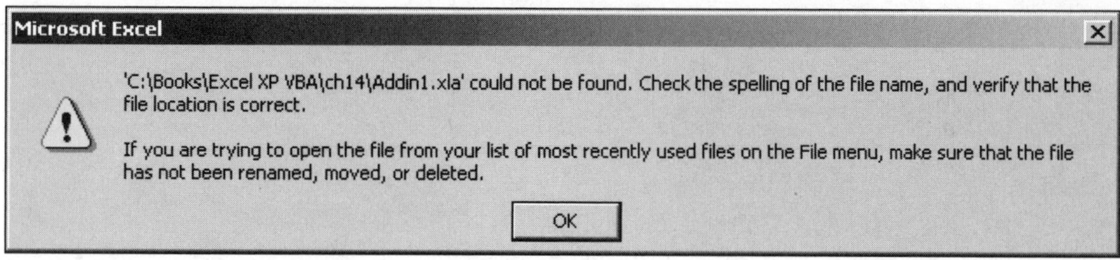

Open the Tools | Addins… dialog box and click on the check box against the Addin's entry. You will get the following message:

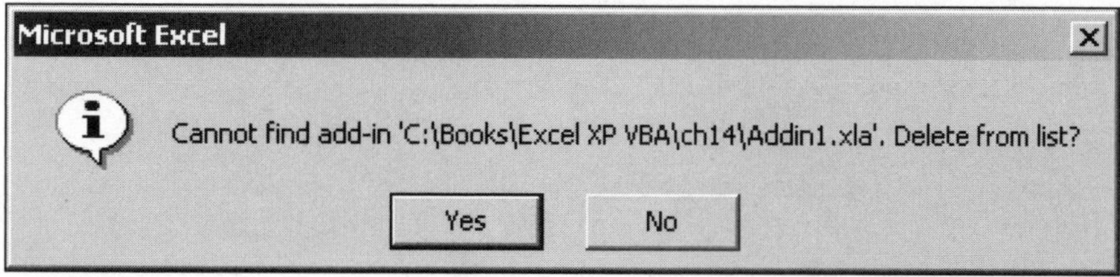

Click Yes and the Addin will be deleted from the list.

The Code for Addin1.xla

The code for `Addin1.xla` is very similar, but not identical, to that of `CommandBars1.xls` and the main differences have already been outlined in the text above. It is therefore not being presented in full in this chapter. The full set of code is included in the `Addin1.xla` file, which can be downloaded from the Wrox web site (http://www.wrox.com).

Summary

You can provide users with all the power of VBA customization, without cluttering the Excel screen with a workbook, by creating an Addin. Workbook files can be easily converted to Addin files, using File | Save As... or by changing the workbook's `IsAddin` property to `True`. It is usually necessary to make some changes to the code when converting a workbook to an Addin to be able to refer to its hidden objects.

Once a file is an Addin, it is no longer visible in the Excel window – its sheets still exist, and can be used by the Addin, but are not displayed. You can still see the Addin file in the Project Explorer in the VBE window. However, a password can be applied to lock the VBA project and prevent users viewing or editing the project's modules and UserForms, just as you can lock the VBA project of a normal workbook.

An Addin application can be accessed by users through menu commands, toolbar controls, or controls embedded in workbooks, though you cannot use popup menus. It can obtain and display information through functions such as `MsgBox` and `InputBox` and through UserForms. A workbook-based application usually needs some redesign in this area before it can be converted to an Addin application.

Although Addin files can be opened in the same way as workbooks, they work best when added to the Addins listed in the Tools | Add-Ins... dialog box. Once added, they can be installed and uninstalled using the same dialog box. If they are installed, they will open automatically in every Excel session.

17

Automation Addins and COM Addins

With the release of Office 2000, Microsoft introduced a new concept for creating custom Addins for all the Office applications. Instead of creating application-specific Addins (xlas in Excel, dots in Word, mdes in Access, etc.), we can create DLLs using Visual Basic, C++, or the Office Developer Edition that all the Office applications can use. Since these DLLs conform to Microsoft's Component Object Model, they are known as COM Addins. The second half of this chapter explains how to create and implement your own COM Addins.

The biggest failing of COM Addins is that the functions inside them can't be called from the worksheet. In Excel 2002, Microsoft extended the concept and simplified the implementation of the COM Addin mechanism, in order for their routines to be used in the same way as worksheet functions. These new Addins are known as **Automation Addins**.

Automation Addins

Automation Addins are COM DLLs (ActiveX DLLs) that have a creatable class and a public function in the creatable class. For example, when Excel can do the following with your class, you can then call FunctionName from the worksheet:

```
Dim oAutoAddin As Object

Set oAutoAddin = CreateObject("TheProgID")
TheResult = CallByName(oAutoAddin, "FunctionName", _
                       VbMethod, param1, param2, ...)
```

In other words, your function must satisfy the following conditions:

- The class must be publicly-creatable (i.e. have an Instancing property of Multi-Use or Global-Multi-Use)
- The procedure must be a Function (as opposed to a Sub or Property procedure)

A Simple Addin – Sequence

For the Excel VBA developer, the easiest way to create Automation Addins is to use Visual Basic 6. Unfortunately, it is not possible to create these Addins using the Office Developer Edition, as it does not allow classes to be set as Public-Creatable (or equivalent).

In this example, we'll create a simple Automation Addin using VB6. It will contain a single function to provide a sequence of numbers as an array (which is often used in array formulas).

Start VB6, and choose to create a new 'ActiveX DLL' project. Rename the project to `Excel2002ProgRef` and rename the class to `Simple` in the **Properties** window. Set the class's `Instancing` property to `5-MultiUse` (this should be the default setting). By setting this property, we're making the class publicly-creatable (that is Excel can create instances of this class if/when we tell it to).

Type the following code into the `Simple` class, to calculate and return a sequence of numbers:

```
'**************************************************************************
'*
'* FUNCTION NAME: Sequence
'*
'* DESCRIPTION: Returns a sequence of numbers, often used in array formulas.
'*
'* PARAMETERS:  Items    The number of elements in the sequence
'*              Start    The starting value for the sequence, default = 1
'*              Step     The step value in the sequence, default = 1
'*
'**************************************************************************
Public Function Sequence(Items As Long, Optional Start As Double = 1, _
                         Optional Step As Double = 1) As Variant

    Dim vaResult As Variant
    Dim i As Long
    Dim dValue As Double

    ' Validate entries
    If Items < 1 Then
        Sequence = CVErr(2015)          '#Value
        Exit Function
    End If

    ' Create an array for the series
    ReDim vaResult(1 To Items)

    ' Get the initial value
    dValue = Start

    ' Calculate all the values, populating the array
    For i = 1 To Items
        vaResult(i) = dValue
        dValue = dValue + Step
    Next

    ' Return the array
    Sequence = vaResult

End Function
```

By defining the function to be `Public`, Excel will be able to see it, and we'll be able to call it from the worksheet. Save the project, then use **File | Make Excel2002ProgRef.dll** to create the DLL – you've just created an Automation Addin.

Registering Automation Addins with Excel

Before we can use the `Sequence` function in a worksheet, we need to tell Excel about the DLL. Microsoft has extended the Addins paradigm to include Automation Addins, making their usage extremely similar to normal Excel `xla` Addins. The main difference is that instead of a filename, Automation Addins use the class's **ProgID**, which is the Visual Basic Project name, a period, then the class name. In our example, the ProgID of the `Simple` class is `Excel2002ProgRef.Simple`.

Through the Excel User Interface

To load an Automation Addin through Excel's dialog, we do the following:

- Click on Tools | Addins to show the Addins dialog
- Click on the Automation... button to show the Automation Addins dialog
- Find the entry for `Excel2002ProgRef.Simple` in the list, select it and OK back to the Addins dialog

You should see that our Automation Addin is now included in the list of known Addins and we can load or unload it by ticking/unticking the check box – just like any other Addin.

Using VBA

Automation Addins are loaded in the same way as normal `xla` Addins, but using the ProgID instead of the filename, as in the following code:

```
Sub InstallAutomationAddin()
    AddIns.Add Filename:="Excel2002ProgRef.Simple"
    AddIns("Excel2002ProgRef.Simple").Installed = True
End Sub
```

In the Registry

If you are creating an installation routine for your Addin, you may want to write directly to the registry in order to set the Automation Addin as installed. To do so, you need to create the following registry entry.

In the registry key:

```
HKEY_CURRENT_USER\Software\Microsoft\Office\10.0\Excel\Options
```

Create the string value:

```
Name = the first unused item in the series: Open, Open1, Open2, Open3, Open4,
Open5 etc.
Value = /A "Excel2002ProgRef.Simple"
```

If you want to add the Automation Addin to the list shown in the Addins dialog, but not have it installed, create the following registry key instead:

In the registry key:

```
HKEY_CURRENT_USER\Software\Microsoft\Office\10.0\Excel\Add-in Manager
```

Create an empty string value with the `Name = Excel2002ProgRef.Simple`.

Using Automation Addins

Like normal `xla` Addins, the functions contained in automation Addins can be used both in the worksheet and within VBA routines.

In the Worksheet

Once installed, you can just type the name of the function directly into the worksheet. To test it, start Excel 2002, install the Addin as shown above, select a horizontal range of 5 cells, type the function `=Sequence(5,10,2)`, and enter the function as an array formula by holding down *Shift* and *Ctrl*, then pressing *Enter*. You should see a sequence of numbers:

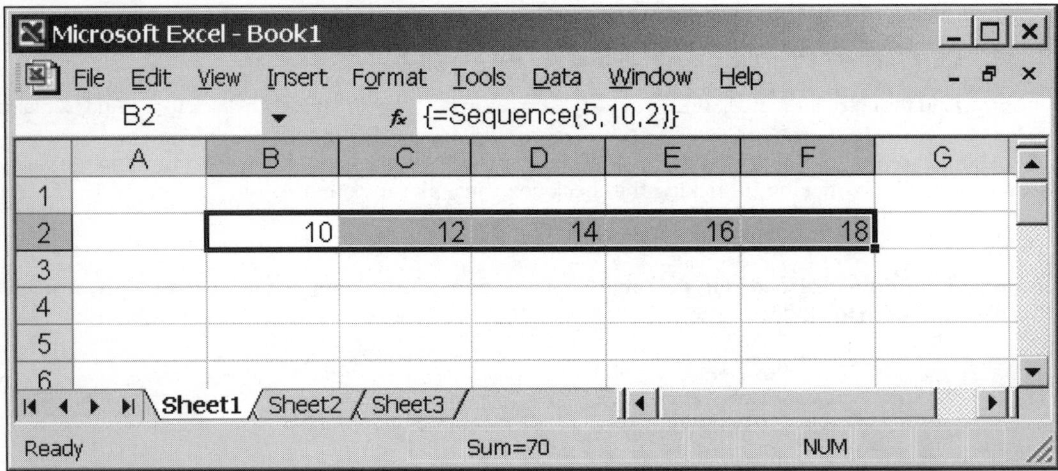

Note that if the function name in the Automation Addin conflicts with a built-in Excel function or a function defined in a normal Excel Addin, Excel will use the first one that it finds in the order of preference:

- Built-in function
- Function in *xla* Addin
- Function in Automation Addin

In order to force Excel to use the function from the Automation Addin, prefix the function name by the Addin's ProgID when typing it in, as in:

```
=Excel2002ProgRef.Simple.Sequence(5,10,2)
```

As soon as you enter the function, Excel will remove the ProgID, but will still use it to reference the function correctly. This will probably cause some confusion if you subsequently edit the function, as you must remember to re-enter the ProgID each time (or Excel will think it is the built-in function).

In VBA

There are a number of alternatives for using the function in VBA. As the DLL is a simple ActiveX DLL, we can create our own instance of it and use the function directly. This will work regardless of whether it is installed as an Addin:

```
Private Sub CommandButton1_Click()

    ' Assumes a reference has been created to the Excel2002ProgRef library,
    ' using Tools | References
    Dim oSimple As Excel2002ProgRef.Simple
    Dim vaSequence As Variant

    ' Create our own instance of the class
    Set oSimple = New Excel2002ProgRef.Simple

    ' Get the sequence
    vaSequence = oSimple.Sequence(5, 10, 2)

    ' Write the sequence to the sheet
    ActiveCell.Resize(1, 5) = vaSequence
End Sub
```

If we know that the Addin is installed, we can use the instance that Excel has created, by using `Application.Evaluate`:

```
Private Sub CommandButton1_Click()

    Dim vaSequence As Variant

    'Use Application.Evaluate - which doesn't require a reference to the DLL
    vaSequence = _
        Application.Evaluate("Excel2002ProgRef.Simple.Sequence(5,10,2)")

    'Or the shorthand:
    'vaSequence = [Excel2002ProgRef.Simple.Sequence(5,10,2)]

    'Write the sequence to the sheet
    ActiveCell.Resize(1, 5) = vaSequence
End Sub
```

When using `Application.Evaluate`, the full ProgID is only needed if there is a risk that the function name conflicts with a built-in function, or one in a loaded `xla` Addin (or workbook), so the following works equally well:

```
    vaSequence = Application.Evaluate("Sequence(5,10,2)")
```

In my opinion, it is safer and more robust to use the first method – creating and using our own instance of the class.

The IDTExtensibility2 Interface (Introduction)

The simple Addin shown above is simple for one reason – it's self-contained and doesn't need to use Excel at all. In most real-world examples, we will want to use the Excel `Application` object in a number of ways:

- Use `Application.Caller` to identify the range that the function was called from
- Use `Application.Volatile` to mark an Automation Addin function as volatile, and hence that Excel should call the function every time it recalculates the worksheet
- Use Excel's built-in functions within our Addin.

In order to use the Excel `Application` object within our Automation Addin, we need to get (or be given) a reference to it, which we can store in a private variable within our Addin class. This is achieved by implementing a specific interface within our Addin class.

An **interface** is simply a predefined and fixed set of sub procedures, functions, and properties. **Implementing an interface** means that you are including all those predefined sub procedures, functions, and properties within your class. By doing this you are providing fixed, known, and predictable entry points through which Excel can call into your class.

When Excel loads an Automation Addin, it checks to see if the Addin has implemented an interface called `IDTExtensibility2`. If that interface has been implemented, Excel calls the `OnConnection` method defined in the interface, passing a reference to itself (that is to the Excel `Application` object). In VBA terms, Excel is doing something like the following:

```
Dim oIDT2 As IDTExtensibility2
Dim oAutoAddin As Object

' Create an instance of the Automation Addin
Set oAutoAddin = CreateObject("Excel2002ProgRef.Simple")

' Does it implement the special interface?
If TypeOf oAutoAddin Is IDTExtensibility2 Then

    ' Yes it does, so get a reference to that
    ' interface within the Addin class
    Set oIDT2 = oAutoAddin

    ' And call the interface's OnConnection method,
    ' passing the Application
    oIDT2.OnConnection Me
End If
```

Within the Addin's class, we can respond to the call to `OnConnection` by storing the reference to the `Application` object in a class-level variable, and using it in our Addin's functions.

The `IDTExtensibility2` interface has five methods, each called at specific points in Excel's lifetime, though only two are used by Automation Addins (the others are used by COM Addins and are discussed later in the chapter). We have already mentioned `OnConnection`, the other method used here is `OnDisconnection`. Even though they are not used, we have to include code for every routine defined in the interface, as shown below.

The first task in implementing an interface is to create a reference to the library in which the interface is defined. In our case, the `IDTExtensibility2` interface is defined in the 'Microsoft Addin Designer' library.

Open the `Excel2002ProgRef` project in Visual Basic, select **Project | References** and put a tick mark next to the '**Microsoft Addin Designer**' item. As we're interacting with Excel, we also need a reference to the Excel object library, so find the entry for '**Microsoft Excel 10.0**' and tick that one too. Now select **Project | Excel2002ProgReg Properties** and select the **Components** tab as shown. Choose **Binary compatability** and select the file `Excel2002ProgRef.dll` that you created in the previous section. This ensures that VB updates the current DLL registry entries rather than creating new ones each time you recompile.

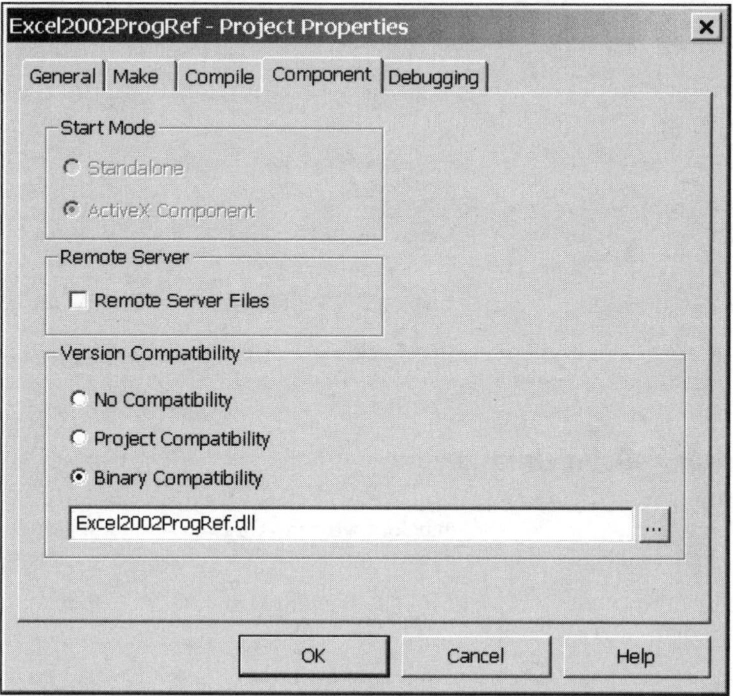

Then add a new class module to the project, call it `Complex`, set its `Instancing` property to `5-MultiUse`, and copy in the following code to implement the `IDTExtensibility2` interface and respond to Excel calling its entry points:

```
' Implement the IDTExtensibility2 interface, so Excel can call into us
Implements IDTExtensibility2

' Declare a private reference to the Excel application
Private moXL As Excel.Application

' Called by Excel when the class is loaded, passing a reference to the
' Excel object
Private Sub IDTExtensibility2_OnConnection(ByVal Application As Object, _
               ByVal ConnectMode As AddInDesignerObjects.ext_ConnectMode, _
               ByVal AddInInst As Object, custom() As Variant)

    ' Set a reference to the Excel application, for use in our functions
    Set moXL = Application

End Sub

' Called by Excel when the class is unloaded, so we destroy our reference
' to Excel
Private Sub IDTExtensibility2_OnDisconnection( _
              ByVal RemoveMode As AddInDesignerObjects.ext_DisconnectMode, _
              custom() As Variant)

    Set moXL = Nothing
End Sub
```

```
' Not used by Automation Addins, but have to be included in the class to
' implement the interface
Private Sub IDTExtensibility2_OnAddInsUpdate(custom() As Variant)
    ' Have a comment to stop VB removing the routine when doing its tidy-up
End Sub

' Not used by Automation Addins, but have to be included in the class to
' implement the interface
Private Sub IDTExtensibility2_OnBeginShutdown(custom() As Variant)
    ' Have a comment to stop VB removing the routine when doing its tidy-up
End Sub

' Not used by Automation Addins, but have to be included in the class to
' implement the interface
Private Sub IDTExtensibility2_OnStartupComplete(custom() As Variant)
    ' Have a comment to stop VB removing the routine when doing its tidy-up
End Sub
```

A Complex Addin – RandUnique

Now that we have a reference to the Excel `Application` object, we can use it in a more complex function. The `RandUnique` function shown below returns a random set of integers between two limits, without any duplicates in the set. It uses the Excel `Application` object in two ways:

- It uses `Application.Caller` to identify the range containing the function, and hence the size and shape of the array to create
- It uses `Application.Volatile` to ensure the function is recalculated each time Excel calculates the sheet.

The routine works by doing the following:

- It creates an array of all the integers between the given limits, with a random number associated with each item.
- It sorts the array by the random number, effectively putting the array into a random order.
- It reads the first n items from the jumbled-up array to fill the required range.

The function has also been written to take an optional `Items` parameter, enabling it to be called from VBA as well as from the worksheet. If the `Items` parameter is provided, the function returns a 2D array (1 , n) of unique integers. If the `Items` parameter is not provided, the function uses `Application.Caller` to identify the range to fill:

```
'***************************************************************************
'*
'* FUNCTION NAME:  RandUnique
'*
'* DESCRIPTION:    Returns an array of random integers between two limits,
'*                 without duplication
'*
'* PARAMETERS:     Min       The lower limit for the random numbers
'*                 Max       The upper limit for the random numbers
'*
'***************************************************************************
Public Function RandUnique(Min As Long, Max As Long, _
                           Optional Items As Long) As Variant

    Dim oRng As Range
    Dim vaValues() As Double, vaResult() As Double
```

```
    Dim iItems As Long, i As Long, iValue As Long
    Dim iRows As Long, iCols As Long, iRow As Long, iCol As Long

    ' Tell Excel that this function is volatile, and should be called
    ' every time the sheet is recalculated
    moXL.Volatile

    ' If we've been given the number of items required, use it...
    If Items > 0 Then
        iRows = 1
        iCols = Items
    Else
        '... Otherwise get the range of cells that this function is in
        '    (as an array formula)
        Set oRng = moXL.Caller

        iRows = oRng.Rows.Count
        iCols = oRng.Columns.Count
    End If

    ' How many cells in the range
    iItems = iRows * iCols

    ' We can't generate a unique set of numbers if there are more
    ' cells to fill than there are numbers to choose from,
    ' so return an error value in that case
    If iItems > (Max - Min + 1) Then
        RandUnique = CVErr(xlErrValue)
        Exit Function
    End If

    ' Fill an array with all the possible numbers to choose from,
    ' and a column of random numbers to sort on
    ReDim vaValues(Min To Max, 1 To 2)
    For i = Min To Max
        vaValues(i, 1) = i
        vaValues(i, 2) = Rnd()
    Next

    ' Sort by the array by the column of random numbers,
    ' jumbling up the array
    Sort2DVert vaValues, 2, "A"

    ' Dimension an array to be the same size as the range we're called from
    ReDim vaResult(1 To iRows, 1 To iCols)

    ' Start the counter at the beginning of the jumbled array
    iValue = Min

    ' Fill the result array from the jumbled array of all values
    For iRow = 1 To iRows
        For iCol = 1 To iCols
            vaResult(iRow, iCol) = vaValues(iValue, 1)
            iValue = iValue + 1
        Next
    Next

    ' Return the result
    RandUnique = vaResult

End Function
```

A QuickSort Routine

The `RandUnique` function uses a standard `QuickSort` algorithm to sort the array, reproduced below. This is one of the fastest sorting algorithms and uses a recursive divide-and-conquer approach to sorting:

- Choose one of the numbers in the array (usually the middle one)
- Group all the numbers less than it at the top of the array, and all the numbers greater than it at the bottom
- Repeat for the top half of the array, then for the bottom half.

```
'*************************************************************************
'*
'* FUNCTION NAME:  SORT ARRAY - 2D Vertically
'*
'* DESCRIPTION:    Sorts the passed array into required order, using the
'*                 given key. The array must be a 2D array of any size.
'*
'* PARAMETERS:     avArray   The 2D array of values to sort
'*                 iKey      The column to sort by
'*                 sOrder    A-Ascending, D-Descending
'*                 iLow1     The first item to sort between
'*                 iHigh1    The last item to sort between
'*
'*************************************************************************
Private Sub Sort2DVert(avArray As Variant, iKey As Integer, _
                       sOrder As String, Optional iLow1, Optional iHigh1)

    Dim iLow2 As Integer, iHigh2 As Integer, i As Integer
    Dim vItem1, vItem2 As Variant

    On Error GoTo PtrExit

    If IsMissing(iLow1) Then iLow1 = LBound(avArray)
    If IsMissing(iHigh1) Then iHigh1 = UBound(avArray)

    ' Set new extremes to old extremes
    iLow2 = iLow1
    iHigh2 = iHigh1

    ' Get value of array item in middle of new extremes
    vItem1 = avArray((iLow1 + iHigh1) \ 2, iKey)

    ' Loop for all the items in the array between the extremes
    Do While iLow2 < iHigh2

        If sOrder = "A" Then
            ' Find the first item that is greater than the mid-point item
            Do While avArray(iLow2, iKey) < vItem1 And iLow2 < iHigh1
                iLow2 = iLow2 + 1
            Loop

            ' Find the last item that is less than the mid-point item
            Do While avArray(iHigh2, iKey) > vItem1 And iHigh2 > iLow1
                iHigh2 = iHigh2 - 1
            Loop
        Else
            ' Find the first item that is less than the mid-point item
            Do While avArray(iLow2, iKey) > vItem1 And iLow2 < iHigh1
```

```
                iLow2 = iLow2 + 1
            Loop

            ' Find the last item that is greater than the mid-point item
            Do While avArray(iHigh2, iKey) < vItem1 And iHigh2 > iLow1
                iHigh2 = iHigh2 - 1
            Loop
        End If

        ' If the two items are in the wrong order, swap the rows
        If iLow2 < iHigh2 Then
            For i = LBound(avArray, 2) To UBound(avArray, 2)
                vItem2 = avArray(iLow2, i)
                avArray(iLow2, i) = avArray(iHigh2, i)
                avArray(iHigh2, i) = vItem2
            Next
        End If

        ' If the pointers are not together, advance to the next item
        If iLow2 <= iHigh2 Then
            iLow2 = iLow2 + 1
            iHigh2 = iHigh2 - 1
        End If
    Loop

    ' Recurse to sort the lower half of the extremes
    If iHigh2 > iLow1 Then Sort2DVert avArray, iKey, sOrder, iLow1, iHigh2

    ' Recurse to sort the upper half of the extremes
    If iLow2 < iHigh1 Then Sort2DVert avArray, iKey, sOrder, iLow2, iHigh1

PtrExit:

End Sub
```

You must now save and recompile your project by using File | Make Excel2002ProgRef.dll to create the updated DLL.

Note: Due to a bug in some versions of VB you may be presented with an error message stating that there is a sharing violation with the file you are trying to replace. If this occurs try closing VB (making sure you have saved your project) and then re-opening it. If this doesn't work try restarting Windows.

The complex Addin is used in the same way as the simple Sequence function shown earlier. The only difference is that we have to tell Excel to load the Excel2002ProgRef.Complex Addin, by clicking on Tools | Addins | Automation Addins and selecting it from the list. When entered as an array formula, it looks something like this:

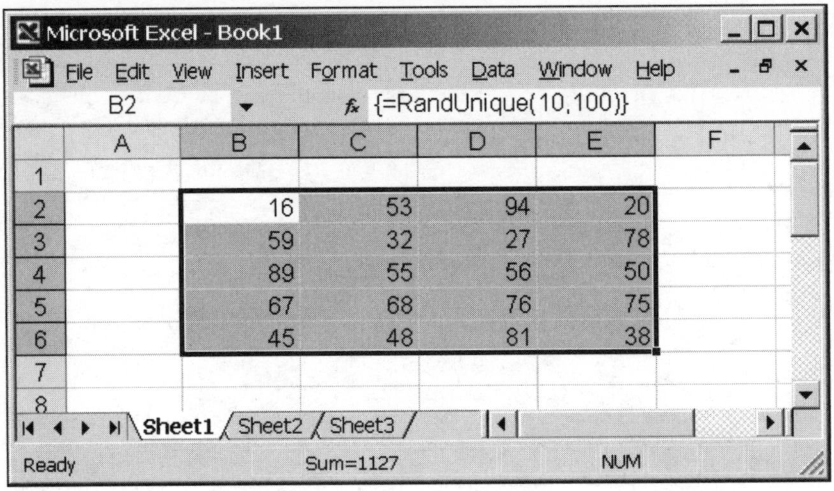

COM Addins

While Automation Addins enable us to create our own worksheet functions, COM Addins provide a way to extend the user interface of Excel and all the other Office applications. They have a number of advantages over normal `xla` Addins, including:

- They're much faster to open
- They're less obtrusive (not showing up in the VBE Project Explorer)
- They're more secure (being compiled DLLs)
- They're not specific to a single application – the same mechanism works with all the Office applications and the VBE itself (and any other application that uses VBA 6), allowing us to create a single Addin that can extend all the Office Applications

The IDTExtensibility2 Interface (Continued)

The previous section introduced the `IDTExtensibility2` interface, where we used the `OnConnection` and `OnDisconnection` methods to obtain a reference to the Excel Application. The remaining methods defined in the interface can be used by COM Addins to respond to specific events in Excel's lifetime. The methods are:

Method	Occurs	Typical usage
`OnConnection`	When the COM Addin is loaded by Excel.	Store a reference to the Excel application, add menu items to Excel's commandbars and set up event hooks.
`OnStartupComplete`	After Excel has finished loading all Addins and initial files.	Show a startup dialog (such as those in Access and PowerPoint) or to change behavior depending on whether other Addins are loaded.

Method	Occurs	Typical usage
`OnAddInsUpdate`	Whenever any other COM Addins are loaded or unloaded.	If the COM Addin depends on another Addin being loaded, this Addin can unload itself.
`OnBeginShutdown`	When Excel starts its shutdown process.	Stop the shutdown in certain circumstances or perform any pre-shutdown tidy-up routines.
`OnDisconnection`	When the COM Addin is unloaded, either by the user or by Excel shutting down.	Save settings. If unloaded by the user, delete any commandbar items that were created at connection.

Most COM Addins use only the `OnConnection` method (to add their menu items) and `OnDisconnection` method (to remove them), though code has to exist in the class module for all five methods, in order to correctly implement the interface.

Registering a COM Addin with Excel

For automation Addins, we told Excel that the Addin exists by selecting it in the Tools | Addins | Automation Addins dialog (resulting in some entries being written to the registry). We tell Excel that a COM Addin exists by writing specific keys and values to specific places in the registry. When Excel starts, it looks in those keys to see which COM Addins exist, then checks the values in those keys to see how to display them in the COM Addins list, whether to load them or not, etc. The keys for COM Addins targeted to Excel are:

- Registered for the current user:
  `HKEY_CURRENT_USER\Software\Microsoft\Office\Excel\Addins\AddinProgID`
- Registered for all users:
  `HKEY_USERS\.DEFAULT\Software\Microsoft\Office\Excel\Addins\AddinProgID`
- Registered for the machine:
  `HKEY_LOCAL_MACHINE\Software\Microsoft\Office\Excel\Addins\AddinProgID`

The values are:

Name	Type	Use
`FriendlyName`	`String`	The name shown in the COM Addins list.
`Description`	`String`	The description shown in the COM Addins dialog.
`LoadBehavior`	`Number`	Whether it is unloaded, loaded at startup, or demand-loaded.

Table continued on following page

Name	Type	Use
`SatelliteDllName`	`Number`	The name of a resource DLL that contains localized names and descriptions. If used, the name and description will be `#Num`, where `Num` is the numeric resource ID in the Satellite DLL. Most of the standard Office Addins use this technique for their localization.
`CommandLineSafe`	`String`	Whether the DLL could be called from the command line (not applicable to Office COM Addins).

Once registered correctly, the COM Addin will show up in Excel's COM Addins dialog, where it can be loaded and unloaded like any other Addin. Unfortunately, the COM Addins menu item (to show the dialog) is not on any of Excel's standard menus. You'll need to customize your commandbars to be able to access that dialog, by doing the following:

- Right-click on one of Excel's commandbars and choose **Customize**.
- Click on the **Tools** menu item to show its sub-menus.
- In the **Customize** dialog, click the **Commands** tab, select the **Tools** item in the left-hand list and scroll down the right-hand list until you find COM **Addins…**, as shown below.
- Drag the **Com Addins** item from the right-hand list and drop it on the **Tools** toolbar, below the **Addins…** menu item.
- Close the **Customize** dialog.

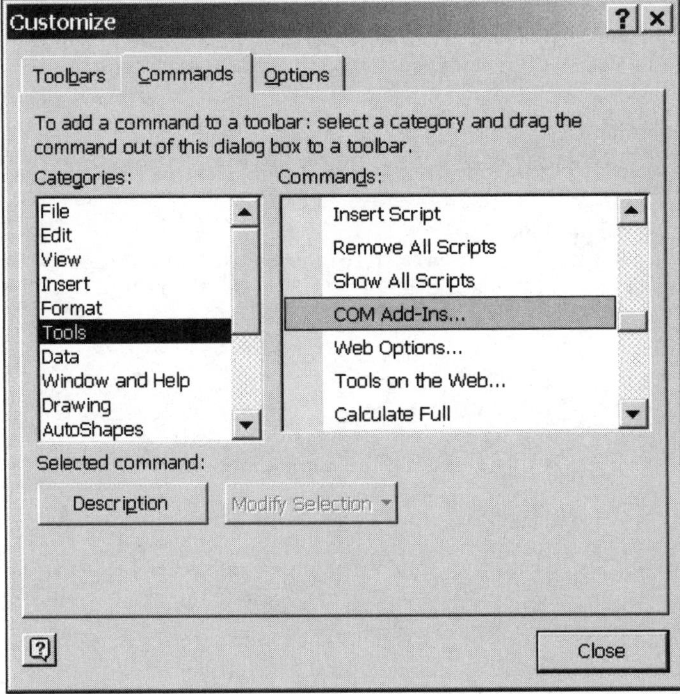

The COM Addin Designer

Microsoft has provided a COM Addin `Designer` class to assist in the creation and registration of COM Addins. It provides the following benefits:

- It implements the IDTExtensibility2 interface, exposing the methods as events that we can either hook, or ignore. We don't, therefore, have to include code for unused interface methods in our class module.
- It provides a form for us to fill in, to provide the values for the registry entries used to register the COM Addin and to select which application to target.
- When compiled, it adds code to the standard `DllRegisterServer` entry point in the DLL that writes all the registry entries for us when the DLL is registered on the system (though only for the Current User key). This greatly simplifies installation, as we can install the Addin by running the following command: `RegSvr32 c:\MyPath\MyComAddin.DLL`
- If you have Office XP Developer Edition, the Designer can be used to create COM Addins from within the VBE, instead of having to use Visual Basic. This is done by clicking **File | New Project | Addin Project** from the Office 2002 VBE.

By way of an example, we'll create a COM Addin that provides a Wizard for entering the `RandUnique` Automation Addin function that we created in the previous section. We will continue to use Visual Basic, building on the `Excel2002ProgRef` DLL from the previous section.

Open the `Excel2002ProgRef` project in Visual Basic. Add a new Addin class to the project by clicking **Project | Add Addin Class** (if that menu item doesn't exist, click on **Project | Components | Designers** and check the **Addin Class** entry). This adds a new `Designer` class and gives it the name of `AddinDesigner1`. Using the **Properties** window, change the name to `COMAddin` and set the `Public` property to `True` (ignoring any warnings). Fill in the **Designer** form as shown below:

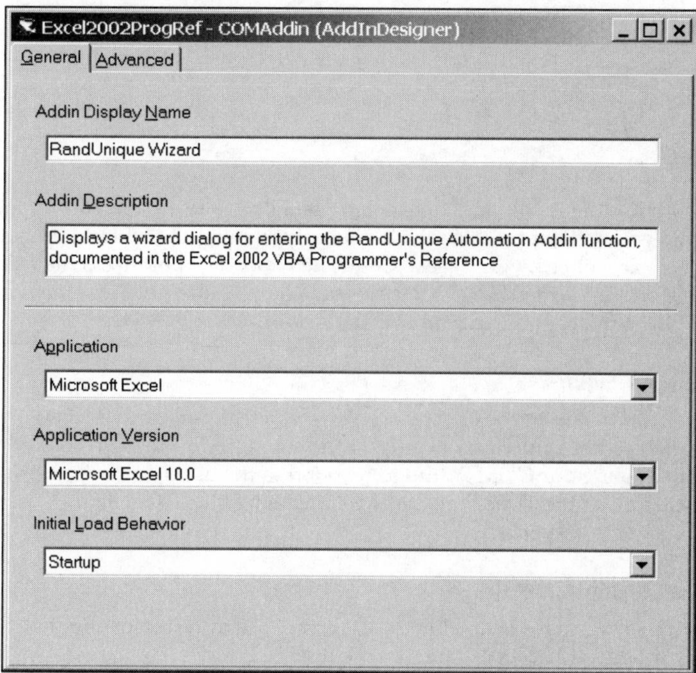

> **Note that the Designer only creates registry entries for the current user. If you wish to install the Addin for all users on the machine, you will need to add your own registry entries in the Advanced tab of the Designer form, as documented in Microsoft KnowledgeBase article Q290868, at http://support.microsoft.com/support/kb/articles/Q290/8/68.asp.**

Linking to Excel

Click on View | Code to get to the Designer's code module and copy in the following code to hook into the `IDTExtensibility2` interface and link the COM Addin to Excel, by storing a reference to the Excel `Application` object, passed to the Addin in the `OnConnection` method:

```
Dim WithEvents moXL As Excel.Application

' The IDTExtensibility2_OnConnection method is handled by the Designer,
' and exposed to us through the AddinInstance_OnConnection method
Private Sub AddinInstance_OnConnection( _
               ByVal Application As Object, _
               ByVal ConnectMode As AddInDesignerObjects.ext_ConnectMode, _
               ByVal AddInInst As Object, custom() As Variant)

    Set moXL = Application
    MsgBox "Connected"

End Sub

' The IDTExtensibility2_OnDisconnection method is handled by the Designer,
' and exposed to us through the AddinInstance_OnDisconnection method
Private Sub AddinInstance_OnDisconnection( _
              ByVal RemoveMode As AddInDesignerObjects.ext_DisconnectMode, _
              custom() As Variant)

    Set moXL = Nothing
    MsgBox "Disconnected"

End Sub
```

Save the project and make the Addin DLL by clicking on File | Make Excel2000ProgRef.dll, then open Excel 2002 (Note that you will not be able to subsequently re-build the DLL if it is being accessed by Excel at the time). As Excel opens, you'll see a 'Connected' message pop up as the Addin is connected, and a 'Disconnected' message when Excel XP is closed. You will also get these messages if you click on the Tools | COM Addins menu and load/unload the Addin.

Responding to Excel's Events

The `Designer` code module is a type of class module, which allows us to declare a variable `WithEvents`, in order to hook into their events. In the above code, we have hooked into the Excel Application events, enabling our COM Addin to respond to the users opening/closing workbooks, changing data in cells, etc. in the same way that we can in a normal Excel Addin. See Chapter 16 for more information about these events.

Adding CommandBar Controls

Once we have a reference to the Excel `Application` object, we can add our commandbars and buttons in the same way as described in Chapter 14. The only difference is how we respond to a button being clicked.

When adding a `CommandBarButton` from within Excel, we set its `OnAction` property to be the name of the procedure to run when the button is clicked.

When adding a `CommandBarButton` from outside Excel (from within a COM Addin), we have to set the `OnAction` property of the button to point to the COM Addin (so Excel knows which COM Addin is responsible for that button), then hook the button's `Click` event using a variable declared `WithEvents` inside the Addin. The sequence of events and tasks that occur when the user clicks a button is:

- User clicks the button.
- Excel checks the button's `OnAction` property, and reads the `ProgId` of the COM Addin.
- Excel checks if that Addin is loaded. If not, it loads the Addin and runs the `OnConnection` event.
- In the Addin's `OnConnection` event, a variable is declared `WithEvents` and is set to reference the commandbar button.
- Excel fires the `Click` event for the button.
- The `moBtn_Click` event in the Addin runs, performing the required action.

This sequence gives us two choices for specifying when Excel loads the Addin:

- A **demand-loaded** Addin is loaded by Excel when it is first registered and adds its menu items to Excel's menu bars, setting the `OnAction` property appropriately and leaving them in place when Excel closes. The next time Excel starts, the Addin is only loaded when/if the menu item is clicked. This is the preferred option if the Addin is only accessed through menu items. This type of Addin is specified by setting the Addin Designer's Load Behaviour dropdown to "Load on demand".
- A **startup** Addin is loaded every time Excel starts. It will typically add its menus every time Excel opens, and remove them every time Excel closes. This is the preferred option if the Addin needs to respond to Excel's `Application` events. This type of Addin it specified by setting the Addin `Designer`'s Load Behavior dropdown to "Startup".

In the following example, we'll add two menu items to show Wizard forms that will assist in the entry of our Automation Addin formulas. To use `CommandBarButtons`, we need a reference to the Office object library, so click on Project | References and check the Microsoft Office 10.0 Object Library.

Delete any code that may already exist in the Designer's code module (such as the example code added in the previous section), and replace it with the following. This defines the class-level variables we'll be using to store our reference to the Excel `Application` object, and to hook the `CommandBarButton`'s events:

```
Dim WithEvents moXL As Excel.Application
Dim WithEvents moBtn As Office.CommandBarButton

Const msAddinTag As String = "Excel2002ProgRefTag"
```

When we hook a commandbar button's events using the `WithEvents` keyword, our variable (`moBtn`) is associated with the `Tag` property of the button we set it to reference. All buttons that share the same `Tag` will cause the `Click` event to fire. In this way, we can handle the `click` events for all of our buttons using a single `WithEvents` variable, by ensuring they all have the same `Tag`. We can distinguish between buttons by giving them each a unique `Parameter` property, as we create them in the `OnConnection` method, which should be copied in to the Designer's code module.

```
' The IDTExtensibility2_OnConnection method is handled by the Designer,
' and exposed to us through the AddinInstance_OnConnection method
Private Sub AddinInstance_OnConnection( _
            ByVal Application As Object, _
            ByVal ConnectMode As AddInDesignerObjects.ext_ConnectMode, _
            ByVal AddInInst As Object, custom() As Variant)

    Dim oToolsBar As CommandBar, oBtn As CommandBarButton

    Set moXL = Application

    ' Get a reference to the Tools menus
    Set oToolsBar = moXL.CommandBars( _
                "Worksheet Menu Bar").FindControl(ID:=30007).CommandBar

    ' If our controls don't exist on the menu bar, add them

    ' Handle errors in-line (such as the button not existing)
    On Error Resume Next

    ' Check for, and add, the 'Sequence Wizard' button
    Set oBtn = oToolsBar.Controls("Sequence Wizard")
    If oBtn Is Nothing Then
        Set oBtn = oToolsBar.Controls.Add(msoControlButton, ,"SequenceWiz")
        With oBtn
            .Caption = "Sequence Wizard"
            .Style = msoButtonCaption
            .Tag = msAddinTag
            .OnAction = "!<" & AddInInst.ProgId & ">"
        End With
    End If
```

Note that the `OnAction` string has to be set to a specific text in order for Excel to recognize it as referring to a COM Addin. It must have the form `"!<ProgID>"`:

```
    ' Check for, and add, the 'RandUnique Wizard' button
    Set oBtn = Nothing
    Set oBtn = oToolsBar.Controls("RandUnique Wizard")
    If oBtn Is Nothing Then
        Set oBtn = oToolsBar.Controls.Add( _
                    msoControlButton, , "RandUniqueWiz")
        With oBtn
            .Caption = "RandUnique Wizard"
            .Style = msoButtonCaption
            .Tag = msAddinTag
            .OnAction = "!<" & AddInInst.ProgId & ">"
        End With
    End If

    ' Set the WithEvents object to hook these buttons. All buttons
    ' that share the same Tag property will fire the moBtn_Click event
    Set moBtn = oBtn

End Sub
```

The following is typical of a demand-loaded Addin, in which the menu items should only be removed if the user unloads the Addin from the COM Addins dialog. We can determine this from the `RemoveMode` property. For Addins loaded at startup, the menu items would usually be removed however the Addin is closed:

```
' The IDTExtensibility2_OnDisconnection method is handled by the Designer,
' and exposed to us through the AddinInstance_OnDisconnection method
Private Sub AddinInstance_OnDisconnection( _
            ByVal RemoveMode As AddInDesignerObjects.ext_DisconnectMode, _
            custom() As Variant)
    Dim oCtl As CommandBarControl

    ' If being unloaded by the user, remove the buttons, otherwise
    ' leave them so Excel can monitor their usage etc.
    If RemoveMode = ext_dm_UserClosed Then
        For Each oCtl In moXL.CommandBars.FindControls(Tag:=msAddinTag)
            oCtl.Delete
        Next
    End If

    Set moBtn = Nothing
    Set moXL = Nothing

End Sub
```

In the `Click` event, we check the `Parameter` property of the button that was clicked and show the appropriate form. For this example, just add two blank forms to the project, giving them the names `frmSequenceWiz` and `frmRandUniqueWiz`:

```
' The moBtn_Click event is fired when any of our commandbar buttons are
' clicked. This is because the event handler is associated with the Tag
' property of the button, not the button itself. Hence, all buttons that
' have the same Tag will fire this event.
Private Sub moBtn_Click(ByVal Ctrl As Office.CommandBarButton, _
                        CancelDefault As Boolean)

    ' Check that a cell range is selected
    If TypeOf moXL.Selection Is Range Then

        ' Run the appropriate form, depending on the control's Parameter
        Select Case Ctrl.Parameter
            Case "SequenceWiz"
                frmSequenceWiz.Show vbModal

            Case "RandUniqueWiz"
                frmRandUniqueWiz.Show vbModal
        End Select
    Else
        ' Display an error message if a range is not selected
        MsgBox "A range must be selected to run the Wizard.", vbOKOnly, _
               "Excel 2002 Prog Ref Wizards"
    End If

End Sub
```

Save the project and use File | Make Excel2002ProgRef.dll to create the DLL, which also adds the registry entries for Excel to see it. Start Excel 2002 and click on Tools | Sequence Wizard to show the Wizard form.

Using the COM Addin from VBA

It is possible (though unfortunately quite rare) for the creator of a COM Addin to provide programmatic access to the Addin from VBA. This would be done to either:

- Expose the Addin's functionality for use through code
- Provide a mechanism for controlling or customizing the Addin

It is achieved by setting the Addin instance's `Object` property to reference the COM Addin class (or a separate class within the Addin), then exposing the required functionality using `Public` properties and methods, just like any other class. In our example, we'll provide yet another way of getting to the `Sequence` and `RandUnique` functions.

Add the following lines to the bottom of the `AddinInstance_OnConnection` routine, to provide a reference to the Addin class using the Addin's `Object` property:

```
    ' Set the Addin instance's Object property to be this class, providing
    ' access to the Com Addin's object model from within VBA. Note that we
    ' don't use Set here!
   AddInInst.Object = Me
```

And add the following code to the bottom of the Designer's class module, to create and return new instances of our `Simple` and `Complex` classes:

```
' Property to return a reference to our Simple class, providing access
' from VBA:
'vaSeq = Application.ComAddins("Excel2002ProgRef.ComAddin").Object _
'        .SimpleFuncs.Sequence(...)
Public Property Get SimpleFuncs() As Simple
    Set SimpleFuncs = New Simple
End Property

' Property to return a reference to our Complex class, providing access
' from VBA:
'vaRU = Application.ComAddins("Excel2002ProgRef.ComAddin").Object _
'       .ComplexFuncs.RandUnique(...)
Public Property Get ComplexFuncs() As Complex
    Set ComplexFuncs = New Complex
End Property
```

From within Excel, we can then use the following code to access the `Sequence` function, going through the COM Addin and its `Object` property:

```
Private Sub CommandButton1_Click()

    Dim vaSequence As Variant

    ' Get the sequence using the COM Addin
    vaSequence = Application.ComAddins( _
          "Excel2002ProgRef.ComAddin").Object.SimpleFuncs.Sequence(5, 10, 2)

    ' Write the sequence to the sheet
    ActiveCell.Resize(1, 5) = vaSequence
End Sub
```

The key point about using this method is that we are accessing the same instance of the class that Excel is using for the Addin, allowing us to manipulate, query, or control that Addin from VBA. For more complex COM Addins, the same method can be used to provide access to a full object model for controlling the Addin.

Linking to Multiple Office Applications

At the start of this chapter, we mentioned that one of the fundamental advantages of COM Addins over `xla` Addins is that the same DLL can target multiple Office applications. All we need to do to achieve this is to add a new Addin `Designer` class for each application that we want to target, in exactly the same way that we added the `Designer` to target Excel previously in the chapter. Of course, we still have to handle the idiosyncrasies of each application separately.

In the following simple example, we'll make the `Sequence` function available through the COM Addins in Access and use it to populate a list box on a form.

Start by adding a new Addin class to the project. In the **Properties** window, change its name to `AccessAddin`, set its `Public` property to `True` (ignoring any warnings) and complete the Designer's form as shown below:

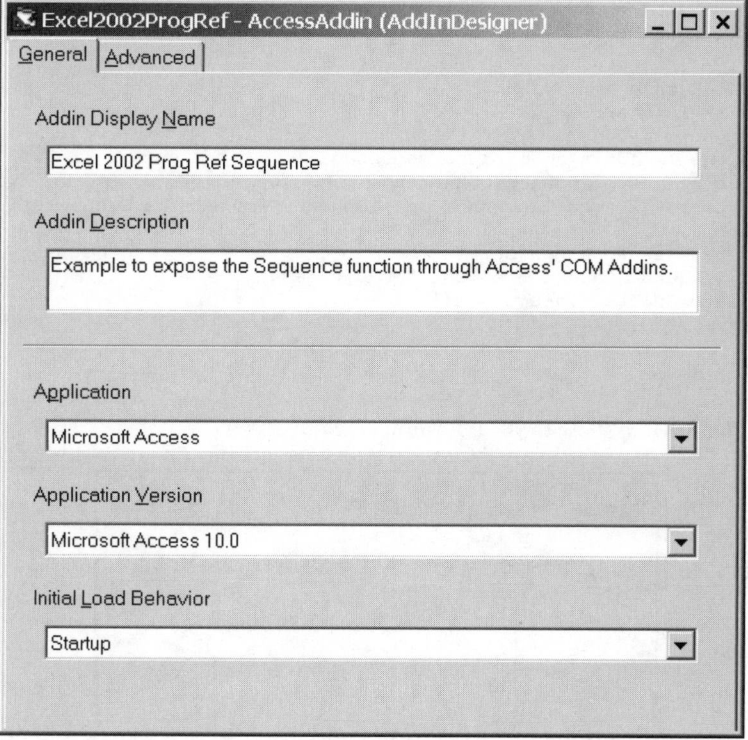

Click on **View | Code** and copy the following into the Designer's code module:

```
' Simple COM Addin to provide the Sequence function to MS Access,
' through Access' COMAddins collection

Private Sub AddinInstance_OnConnection(ByVal Application As Object, _
                ByVal ConnectMode As AddInDesignerObjects.ext_ConnectMode, _
                ByVal AddInInst As Object, custom() As Variant)

    ' Set the Addin instance's Object property to be this class,
    ' providing access to the Com Addin's object model from within VBA.
```

```
    ' Note that we don't use Set here!
    AddInInst.object = Me

End Sub

' Property to return a reference to our Simple class, providing access
' from VBA:
'vaSeq = Application.ComAddins("Excel2002ProgRef.ComAddin").Object _
'         .SimpleFuncs.Sequence(...)
Public Property Get SimpleFuncs() As Simple
    Set SimpleFuncs = New Simple
End Property
```

Save the project and use File | Make Excel2002ProgRef.dll to build the DLL. Start Access 2002 with a blank database, create a new form, add a list box and copy the following code into the form's code module:

```
Private Sub Form_Load()

    Dim vaSequence As Variant
    Dim i As Integer

    ' Use the COMAddin to get the sequence
    vaSequence = Application.COMAddIns( _
       "Excel2002ProgRef.AccessAddin").Object.SimpleFuncs.Sequence(5, 10, 2)

    ' Add the sequence to the list box
    For i = LBound(vaSequence) To UBound(vaSequence)
        List0.AddItem vaSequence(i)
    Next

End Sub
```

Save the form and run it to show the COM Addin at work:

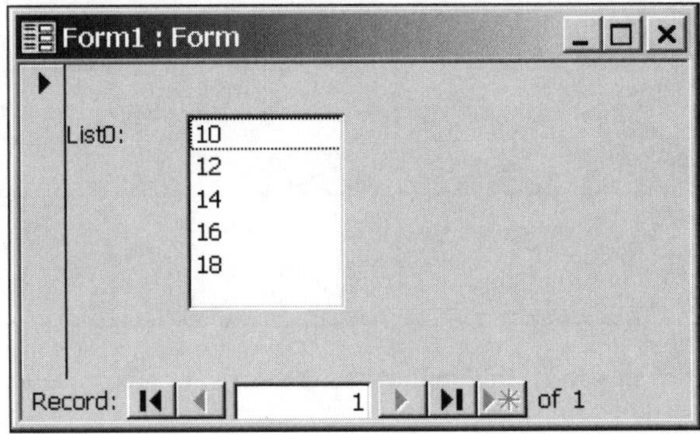

Summary

In Excel 2002, Microsoft has provided a number of ways to extend Excel using Addins written in Visual Basic, or any other language that can produce Component Object Model (COM) DLLs:

- With Automation Addins, we can add new functions for use in Excel worksheets and our VBA routines.
- With COM Addins, we can add new menu items and respond to Excel's events. We can also use these to create Addins that work across multiple Office Applications and the VBE.
- The COM Addin can provide programmatic access to the behavior of the Addin, such as enabling or disabling its actions, or using its functions.
- The performance of Automation and COM Addins is typically much faster than their VBA equivalents.

In the next chapter, we'll show a third way to extend Excel using ActiveX DLLs – SmartTags.

VBAProgrammersReferenceExcel20
mmersReferenceExcel2002VB
ReferenceExcel2002VBAPro
ProgrammersReferenceExc
rammersReferenceExcel20
mersReferenceExcel2002VB
enceExcel2002VBAPro
rogramm el2002VBAProgram
nceExcel ProgrammersReferenc
gramm 2002VBAProgrammers
Exc grammersRefe
Reference
AProgramm
renceExcel2
rogramm Prog
ammerExcel2002 ceEx
sReference BAProgramm
enceExcel2002
ferenceExcel2
nceExcel2002VBAP erenceEx
xcel2002VBAProgramm VBAProgram
2002VBAProgrammersReferenceExcel
VBAProgrammersReference
rogrammersReferenceExcel
ammersReferencerammersRe cel2002VBAProgram
2002VBAProgrammersReferenceExcel

18

SmartTags

When something is typed into a worksheet cell, Excel tries to interpret that entry, converting it to something more meaningful than a random set of characters. This is achieved using rules similar to the following:

- If the entry contains the characters 0-9, and potentially the local thousand and decimal separators, it's a number that can be used in calculations
- If the entry contains the characters 0-9 and the local date separator, it might be date that can be used in calculations (and implies a specific cell format)
- If the entry is #N/A, #Value! etc., it's an error value that should propagate through any calculations that refer to it.
- If the entry starts with an = sign, it could be a formula to be evaluated or a number
- Otherwise, it's a text string – an essentially random set of characters

In each case, Excel is recognizing the entry as a specific data type – a number, date, formula, etc. – and by doing so gives that entry a specific set of behaviors, actions, and properties (those behaviors and actions that are defined for entries of that type). For example, all entries of type 'Formula' have the following behaviors:

- They need to be checked for 'syntax' errors, such as mismatched brackets, etc.
- They need to be incorporated into Excel's calculation dependency tree
- They need to be evaluated
- The cell should show the result of the evaluation, not the text of the formula

Up until Excel 2002, the rules for recognizing entries, and the list of applicable behaviors and properties had been fixed and defined by Excel. The only ways that we were able to extend the recognition was to pre-format the cell (to force a specific data type), or by hooking `Worksheet_Change`, `Worksheet_SelectionChange`, and `Worksheet_Calculate` events for specific sheets and checking whatever was typed in, selected, or changed during the recalculation. This was rather cumbersome and it was difficult to detect and respond to every potential way of changing the contents of a cell in a worksheet.

Introduced in Office XP, SmartTags provide a mechanism for us to add our own 'data types' (such stock symbols, file names, medical terms, part numbers, etc.), to provide the recognition logic that tells Excel that an entry in a cell is a specific data type, and to provide a list of actions that can be performed on or with that data type.

When an entry is recognized as being of a specific type, the applicable actions are presented to the user as a popup menu when their mouse pointer hovers over the cell, such as the following menu from the standard stock-symbol SmartTag, where the characters MSFT are recognized as the stock symbol for Microsoft:

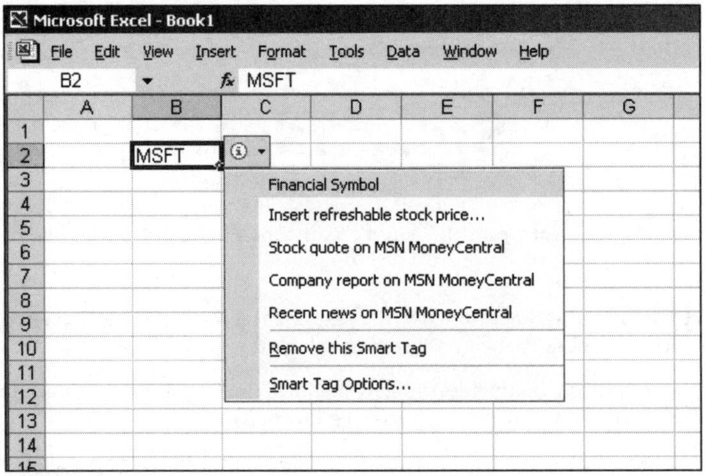

To enable SmartTags for a workbook, click on **Tools | AutoCorrect Options...**, select the **Smart Tags** tab, tick the **Label Data with Smart Tags** checkbox, and tick which of the installed SmartTag recognizers to enable.

There is an official SmartTag Software Development Kit (SDK) available from the Microsoft web site at http://msdn.microsoft.com/office/.

The FileName SmartTag

Type the following text into a worksheet cell: `C:\mydir\mypic.bmp`.

Following Excel's data entry recognition rules, it's not a number, not a date, not a formula, not an error value, and not anything else that Excel recognizes. It is as meaningful to Excel as a random jumble of characters. To us, though, it's a file, probably a picture – we've recognized that sequence of characters to be a filename and have started to think of it as a `FileName` data type, in the same way that we (and Excel) recognize 123 as an Integer, 123.456 as a Double, 10/5/2001 as a Date, etc. Once we start thinking of those characters as a filename, there are a number of actions that we may like to do with that file:

- Check that it exists
- Rename it
- Open it in its native application
- If it's a spreadsheet, open it in the same Excel instance, or a new instance of Excel

By implementing the `FileName` SmartTag that we'll be creating in this chapter, we will:

- Extend Excel's recognition routines to recognize cells containing filenames
- Provide Excel with a list of actions that can be performed on filenames (and files)
- Provide the code to perform those actions

Anatomy of a SmartTag

Most SmartTags consist of three things:

- A unique identifier for the data type (or multiple identifiers for multiple types in the same SmartTag).
- A class module that performs the recognition. Excel passes every bit of text entered in a cell to a function in this class that tags the cell with the unique identifier(s) if it passes the recognition tests.
- A class module to provide the list of actions applicable to the data type(s) and to perform the selected action when the user clicks the SmartTag action's menu item.

Note that we can extend other SmartTags by providing extra recognition routines that tag the cell with a pre-existing identifier (for example to extend the set of symbols recognized by the standard Stock Symbol SmartTag) and/or providing extra actions that apply to pre-existing identifiers (for example to retrieve stock information from providers other than MSN).

Physically, SmartTags are ActiveX DLLs, usually written in VB or C++. They will typically contain a `Recognizer` class, an `Actions` class, and a `Globals` module to hold constants and enumerations used by both the other classes. The `Recognizer` and `Actions` classes each have to implement a specific interface, to provide the hooks through which Excel can call into the class.

We'll start by creating the `FileName` SmartTag. Open VB6, create a new ActiveX DLL, and call the project `FileNameSmartTag`. The `Recognizer` and `Actions` interfaces are defined in the "Microsoft Smart Tags 1.0 Type Library", which we have to create a reference to using Project | References and selecting that item in the list.

The SmartTag Unique Identifier

When a worksheet cell is tagged, the tag is stored in the workbook in an XML-compliant format. All this means is that the identifier for the SmartTag has to be constructed in a special way – as a Uniform Resource Identifier (URI) followed by a '#' character and the specific SmartTag data type name. The URI string provides a way of identifying the source of the ID and an ID group, which together should provide a globally unique and unambiguous identifier. The full ID string for a specific data type is made up of:

```
urn:schemas-<company>-com:<group>#SmartTagName
```

In this example, we will be recognizing three types of file name:

- Files that can be opened in Excel that we'll give the ID of "`urn:schemas-wrox-com:Excel2002ProgRef#ExcelFile`"

- Files that can be opened in Word that we'll give the ID of "urn:schemas-wrox-com:Excel2002ProgRef#WordFile"
- Files that are opened by other applications, that we'll give the ID of "urn:schemas-wrox-com:Excel2002ProgRef#NonHostFile"

Add a new module called `Globals` to the Visual Basic project and add these IDs as constants:

```
'Module to hold global constants and enums used by the SmartTags

'The Uniform Resource Identifiers of the SmartTag data types
Public Const psURIExcel = "urn:schemas-wrox-com:Excel2002ProgRef#ExcelFile"
Public Const psURIWord = "urn:schemas-wrox-com:Excel2002ProgRef#WordFile"
Public Const psURINonHost = _
                         "urn:schemas-wrox-com:Excel2002ProgRef#NonHostFile"
```

Many of the SmartTag procedures that we'll be writing are called multiple times to iterate through a sequence of items – such as `Recognizer` names or SmartTag actions – passing the sequence number as a parameter. To improve readability, it is a good idea to define `Enumerations` or `Enums` in the `Globals` module to match those sequence numbers. The following `Enums` will be used later in the chapter, but should be added to the `Globals` module here:

```
'The sequence numbers for the SmartTag data types
Public Enum peTagSequence
   peTagExcel = 1
   peTagWord = 2
   peTagNonHost = 3
End Enum

'The ID numbers of the actions that we can perform
Public Enum peFileVerbs

   'Four verbs for Excel files
   peXLExists = 11
   peXLRename = 12
   peXLOpen = 13
   peXLOpenNew = 14

   'Four verbs for Word files
   peWordExists = 21
   peWordRename = 22
   peWordOpen = 23
   peWordOpenNew = 24

   'Three verbs for non-host files
   peNHExists = 31
   peNHRename = 32
   peNHOpen = 33
End Enum
```

The SmartTag Recognizer class

The interaction between Excel (or Word) and our SmartTag recognition is done through a specific interface – the `ISmartTagRecognizer` interface – that we have to implement in our class.

To create a class that implements the interface, rename the default `Class1` that was created in the VB Project to `Recognizer` and type in the following code:

```
'Module to recognize File Names
Option Explicit
Implements ISmartTagRecognizer
```

This interface has the following methods and properties, all of which need to be implemented:

Methods and Properties	Description
`ProgID`	The ID for the `Recognizer` class, defined as `<ProjectName>.<ClassName>`
`Name`	A short name for the SmartTag, shown in the SmartTag list
`Desc`	A long description for the SmartTag
`SmartTagCount`	The number of SmartTag data types that this class recognizes
`SmartTagName`	Called once for each data type, to provide the unique ID of the data type
`SmartTagDownloadURL`	If a tagged file is opened on a machine that does not have the SmartTag DLL installed, this property specifies where the `Actions` DLL can be downloaded
`Recognize`	The main routine to perform the recognition and tagging of the text

The first three items are straightforward for most SmartTags:

```
Private Property Get ISmartTagRecognizer_ProgId() As String
   ISmartTagRecognizer_ProgId = "FileNameSmartTag.Recognizer"
End Property

Private Property Get ISmartTagRecognizer_Name( _
                        ByVal LocaleID As Long) As String
   ISmartTagRecognizer_Name = "Filename SmartTag Recognizer"
End Property

Private Property Get ISmartTagRecognizer_Desc( _
                        ByVal LocaleID As Long) As String
   ISmartTagRecognizer_Desc = "SmartTag DLL to recognize filenames"
End Property
```

The SmartTagCount property just returns the number of data types recognized by this class. We're recognizing three data types – Excel files, Word files, and non-host files:

```
Private Property Get ISmartTagRecognizer_SmartTagCount() As Long
   ISmartTagRecognizer_SmartTagCount = 3
End Property
```

The SmartTagName is called multiple times, once for each data type that is being recognized, passing the sequence number of the data type (1, 2, or 3 in our case). It returns the unique ID (URI) for the data type. Many of the SmartTag interface methods use this technique of passing sequence numbers to identify the specific tag or action. To help code readability, we can use enumerated data types to match these sequence numbers; we declared the peTagSequence Enum in the Globals module above, to use in the SmartTagName property:

```
Private Property Get ISmartTagRecognizer_SmartTagName( _
                        ByVal SmartTagID As Long) As String

   'Return the required URI name for the SmartTag sequence
   Select Case SmartTagID
      Case peTagExcel
         ISmartTagRecognizer_SmartTagName = psURIExcel

      Case peTagWord
         ISmartTagRecognizer_SmartTagName = psURIWord

      Case peTagNonHost
         ISmartTagRecognizer_SmartTagName = psURINonHost
   End Select
End Property
```

The SmartTagDownloadURL can use similar code to the above routine, to provide a download location for the Action DLL. In our case, we won't provide one:

```
Private Property Get ISmartTagRecognizer_SmartTagDownloadURL( _
                        ByVal SmartTagID As Long) As String
    ISmartTagRecognizer_SmartTagDownloadURL = ""
End Property
```

The Recognizer class is where all the work is done, and is in many ways the most difficult part of the SmartTag mechanism. The best recognizers should:

- Recognize all correct cases
- Not give any 'false-positives'
- Work very quickly

If the recognition is simply a case of recognizing lists of terms (such as part numbers), it's a good idea to get the complete list into an array in one of the startup properties (for example in the ProgID property), particularly if that means reading the list from another web site, or running a database query.

However good the recognition, though, there are likely to be a number of false-positives. For example, `TRUE` is both a Boolean value in Excel and a valid stock symbol, leading to all cells that contain the Boolean `True` being tagged as stock symbols. Similarly, a recognizer for car models may recognize the numbers 106, 206, 405, etc. as valid models, even though they may be the result of calculations in Excel's cells.

For our purposes, we will define a string as being recognized as a filename if it passes one of the following tests:

- The string has the format of `<letter>:\<some text>.<some extension>`, without a space after the dot
- Alternatively, the string has the format of `\\<some text>\<some text>.<some extension>`

This could obviously lead to some files not being recognized (for example if they don't have an extension), and some false-positives. We could improve the algorithm by also checking for invalid characters within any filenames that we find, but the simple rules above are a good illustration.

We'll also define a 'HostFile' as being one with an `.xls` or `.xla` extension in Excel, or a `.doc` or `.dot` extension in Word (whichever the host is). The following code goes in the `Recognizer` class:

```
Private Sub ISmartTagRecognizer_Recognize(ByVal Text As String, _
               ByVal DataType As SmartTagLib.IF_TYPE, _
               ByVal LocaleID As Long, _
               ByVal RecognizerSite As SmartTagLib.ISmartTagRecognizerSite)

   'Variables used to locate the file name within the text
   Dim iStart As Long, iEnd As Long, iDot As Long, iSlash As Long

   'Variable to hold the file extension
   Dim sExt As String

   'Variable to hold a SmartTag's ProprtyBag
   Dim oPropBag As SmartTagLib.ISmartTagProperties

   iEnd = 1

   'A Word paragraph may contain multiple filenames, so we have to
   'loop through them all
   Do
      iDot = 0

      'Find the characters at the start of a file name
      iStart = InStr(iEnd, Text, ":\")
      If iStart > 0 Then
         iStart = iStart - 1
         iDot = InStr(iStart, Text, ".")
      Else
         iStart = InStr(iEnd, Text, "\\")
         iSlash = InStr(iStart, Text, "\")

         If iSlash > 0 Then
            iDot = InStr(iSlash, Text, ".")
         End If
```

```
      End If

      'If we found the start and the end of a file...
      If iStart > 0 And iDot > 0 Then

         '... check that there is something immediately after the dot
         If Trim$(Mid$(Text, iDot + 1, 1)) <> "" Then
            'A valid file!

            'Find the end of the file extension, which may be followed by
            'more text if we're checking a Word paragraph
            For iEnd = iDot + 1 To Len(Text)
               If InStr(1, " \/:*?""<>|", Mid$(Text, iEnd, 1)) _
                                                   <> 0 Then Exit For
            Next

            'Get the extension
            sExt = Mid$(Text, iDot + 1, iEnd - iDot)

            'Get a property bag for this SmartTag
            Set oPropBag = RecognizerSite.GetNewPropertyBag

            'Add the filename and extension to the property bag,
            'in case we use it later
            oPropBag.Write "FileName", Mid$(Text, iStart, iEnd - iStart)
            oPropBag.Write "Extension", sExt

            'Check if this is a Host or non-host file.
            'Excel's data type is IF_TYPE_CELL while Word's is
            'IF_TYPE_PARA.
            'The CommitSmartTag method is where we actually tag the text.
            If (DataType = IF_TYPE_CELL And _
                  (sExt = "xls" Or sExt = "xla")) Then

               RecognizerSite.CommitSmartTag psURIExcel, _
                                             iStart, iEnd - iStart, oPropBag

            ElseIf (DataType = IF_TYPE_PARA And _
                     (sExt = "doc" Or sExt = "dot")) Then

               RecognizerSite.CommitSmartTag psURIWord, _
                                             iStart, iEnd - iStart, oPropBag
            Else
               RecognizerSite.CommitSmartTag psURINonHost, _
                                             iStart, iEnd - iStart, oPropBag
            End If
         End If
      End If
   Loop Until iDot = 0 Or iEnd >= Len(Text)

End Sub
```

The SmartTag Actions class

Once an entry has been recognized and tagged by a SmartTag `Recognizer` class, Excel needs to find the items to show for the SmartTag popup menu – the **Actions** that are applicable to the SmartTag data type. When the user selects one of those actions, Excel needs to call the SmartTag DLL to perform the action. All of this is done through the `ISmartTagAction` interface.

To create a class that implements the interface, add a new class module to the project, make sure that its instancing is set to '`5 - Multi Use`', change its name to `Actions` and type in the following code:

```
'Module for File Names SmartTag Actions

Option Explicit
Implements ISmartTagAction
```

The `ISmartTagAction` interface has the following methods and properties, all of which need to be implemented:

Methods and Properties	Description
`ProgID`	The ID for the Recognizer class, defined as `<ProjectName>.<ClassName>`.
`Name`	A short name for the SmartTag, shown in the SmartTag list.
`Desc`	A long description for the SmartTag.
`SmartTagCount`	The number of SmartTag data types that this class recognizes.
`SmartTagName`	Called once for each data type, to provide the unique ID of the data type.
`SmartTagCaption`	Called once for each data type, to provide the caption shown on the title of the SmartTag popup menu.
`VerbCount`	Called for each data type, to provide the number of actions appropriate for that type.
`VerbID`	Called for each combination of data type and verb, to provide a unique ID number for that combination.
`VerbCaptionFromID`	Called for each verb ID, to provide the caption to show on the SmartTag popup menu.
`VerbNameFromID`	Called for each verb ID, to provide the programmatic name for the verb (so that the action can be launched using VBA – see later in this chapter for more details).
`InvokeVerb`	Called when the user clicks one of the SmartTag menus, or the action is called using VBA. This is the main routine to perform the selected action.

The first five properties are the same as the `ISmartTagRecognizer` interface:

```
Private Property Get ISmartTagAction_ProgId() As String
   ISmartTagAction_ProgId = "FileNameSmartTag.Actions"
End Property

Private Property Get ISmartTagAction_Name(ByVal LocaleID As Long) As String
   ISmartTagAction_Name = "Filename SmartTag Actions"
End Property

Private Property Get ISmartTagAction_Desc(ByVal LocaleID As Long) As String
   ISmartTagAction_Desc = "Provides actions to perform on filenames"
End Property

Private Property Get ISmartTagAction_SmartTagCount() As Long
   ISmartTagAction_SmartTagCount = 3
End Property

Private Property Get ISmartTagAction_SmartTagName( _
                        ByVal SmartTagID As Long) As String

   'Return the required URI name for the SmartTag sequence
   Select Case SmartTagID
      Case peTagExcel
         ISmartTagAction_SmartTagName = psURIExcel

      Case peTagWord
         ISmartTagAction_SmartTagName = psURIWord

      Case peTagNonHost
         ISmartTagAction_SmartTagName = psURINonHost
   End Select

End Property
```

The `SmartTagCaption` property provides the caption shown on the SmartTag popup menu:

```
Private Property Get ISmartTagAction_SmartTagCaption( _
            ByVal SmartTagID As Long, ByVal LocaleID As Long) As String

   'Return the caption for the SmartTag
   Select Case SmartTagID
      Case peTagExcel
         ISmartTagAction_SmartTagCaption = "Excel files"

      Case peTagWord
         ISmartTagAction_SmartTagCaption = "Word files"

      Case peTagNonHost
         ISmartTagAction_SmartTagCaption = "File names"
   End Select

End Property
```

The VerbCount property provides the number of actions that we define for each SmartTag. In this example, we'll provide the following actions:

- Check if the file exists
- Rename the file (in which case we'll also update the text in the document)
- Open the file in its default editor
- If we've recognized an Excel file within Excel, or a Word file within Word, we'll provide an extra action to open the file in a new instance of Excel/Word

To help readability, we defined the peFileVerbs enumeration for these actions in the Globals module, giving them IDs that correspond to their SmartTag ID and verb sequence.

In the Actions class, we use the VerbCount property to return the number of actions that we have for each data type:

```
Private Property Get ISmartTagAction_VerbCount( _
                                    ByVal SmartTagName As String) As Long

   Select Case SmartTagName
      Case psURIExcel
         ISmartTagAction_VerbCount = 4

      Case psURIWord
         ISmartTagAction_VerbCount = 4

      Case psURINonHost
         ISmartTagAction_VerbCount = 3
   End Select

End Property
```

The VerbID property is used to give a unique ID number to each of our actions. By carefully numbering the actions in our peFileVerbs enumeration, we can calculate the ID from the SmartTag and verb sequence number:

```
Private Property Get ISmartTagAction_VerbID( _
                        ByVal SmartTagName As String, _
                        ByVal VerbIndex As Long) As Long

   Select Case SmartTagName
      Case psURIExcel
         ISmartTagAction_VerbID = 10 + VerbIndex

      Case psURIWord
        ISmartTagAction_VerbID = 20 + VerbIndex

      Case psURINonHost
         ISmartTagAction_VerbID = 30 + VerbIndex
   End Select

End Property
```

Now that we've told Excel about all the verbs that we're providing, we're asked to provide a caption for each of them. This caption is the text shown in the SmartTag popup menu:

```
Private Property Get ISmartTagAction_VerbCaptionFromID( _
                    ByVal VerbID As Long, ByVal ApplicationName As String, _
                    ByVal LocaleID As Long) As String

   Select Case VerbID
      Case peXLExists, peWordExists, peNHExists
         ISmartTagAction_VerbCaptionFromID = "Check if the file exists"

      Case peXLRename, peWordRename, peNHRename
         ISmartTagAction_VerbCaptionFromID = "Rename the file"

      Case peXLOpen, peWordOpen, peNHOpen
         ISmartTagAction_VerbCaptionFromID = "Open the file"

      Case peXLOpenNew
         ISmartTagAction_VerbCaptionFromID = _
                                 "Open the file in a new instance of Excel"

      Case peWordOpenNew
         ISmartTagAction_VerbCaptionFromID = _
                                 "Open the file in a new instance of Word"

   End Select

End Property
```

Excel provides a mechanism for us to trigger the SmartTag action from VBA. The `VerbNameFromID` property is used for us to provide a programmatic name for each action. See later in this chapter for more details about using VBA to control and call SmartTags from within Excel:

```
Private Property Get ISmartTagAction_VerbNameFromID( _
                          ByVal VerbID As Long) As String

   Select Case VerbID
      Case peXLExists, peWordExists, peNHExists
         ISmartTagAction_VerbNameFromID = "CheckExists"

      Case peXLRename, peWordRename, peNHRename
         ISmartTagAction_VerbNameFromID = "Rename"

      Case peXLOpen, peWordOpen, peNHOpen
         ISmartTagAction_VerbNameFromID = "Open"

      Case peXLOpenNew, peWordOpenNew
         ISmartTagAction_VerbNameFromID = "OpenNew"

   End Select

End Property
```

The main routine of the `Actions` class is the `InvokeVerb` method, which is where we perform the selected action. Note that one of the parameters passed to the method is the `Target` object. When called from Excel, this is the `Range` object that contains the text, allowing us full access to query or modify any of Excel's objects. In our case, we'll modify the filename text when the `Rename` action is invoked.

We'll use the `ShellExecute` Windows API function to open files in their host application (see Chapter 24 for more about the Windows API). Add is declaration to the top of the `Actions` class:

```
'Use the ShellExecute API call to open a file
Private Declare Function ShellExecute Lib "shell32.dll" _
       Alias "ShellExecuteA" _
       (ByVal hwnd As Long, ByVal lpOperation As String, _
       ByVal lpFile As String, ByVal lpParameters As String, _
       ByVal lpDirectory As String, ByVal nShowCmd As Long) As Long
```

Type in the following code to perform all our actions:

```
Private Sub ISmartTagAction_InvokeVerb(ByVal VerbID As Long, _
             ByVal ApplicationName As String, ByVal Target As Object, _
             ByVal Properties As SmartTagLib.ISmartTagProperties, _
             ByVal Text As String, ByVal Xml As String)

   Dim sNewName As String
   Dim oHost As Object
   Dim a As Long

   'All our actions need a check to see if the file exists, so do that first
   If Not FileExists(Text) Then
      MsgBox "The file '" & Text & "' does not exist", _
             vbOKOnly + vbCritical, "FileName Smart Tag"
   Else
      Select Case VerbID
         Case peXLExists, peWordExists, peNHExists

         'If we got this far, the file exists, so say so
         MsgBox "The file '" & Text & "' exists", _
                vbOKOnly, "FileName Smart Tag"

         Case peXLRename, peWordRename, peNHRename

            'Get the new file name, providing the original as the default
            sNewName = InputBox("Enter the new file name below", _
                                "FileName Smart Tag", Text)

            'If the name was changed (and not cancelled)...
            If sNewName <> "" And sNewName <> Text Then
               On Error Resume Next

               '... try to rename the file to be the new name
               Name Text As sNewName

               If Err = 0 Then
                  'Successfule change of file name, so change the text
                  'in the source file
                  'Each application (Excel, Word or IE) require a
```

```
                'different syntax:

                Select Case Left$(LCase$(ApplicationName), 5)
                   Case "excel"
                      Target.Value = sNewName
                   Case "word."
                      Target.Text = sNewName
                   Case Else
                      Target.InnerText = sNewName
                End Select
             End If
          End If

       Case peXLOpen
          'Open the Excel file in Excel
          Target.Application.Workbooks.Open Text

       Case peWordOpen
          'Open the Word file in Word
          Target.Application.documents.Open Text

       Case peNHOpen
          'Use the ShellExecute API call to open the file in its
          'default editor
          On Error Resume Next
          a = ShellExecute(0, vbNullString, Text, vbNullString, _
                           vbNullString, 1)

       Case peXLOpenNew
          'Open the Excel file in a new instance of Excel
          Set oHost = CreateObject("Excel.Application")
          oHost.Workbooks.Open Text
          oHost.Visible = True

       Case peWordOpenNew
          'Open the Word file in a new instance of Word
          Set oHost = CreateObject("Word.Application")
          oHost.documents.Open Text
          oHost.Visible = True

    End Select
 End If

End Sub
```

The `InvokeVerb` routine uses a separate function to check if a file exists:

```
Private Function FileExists(sFile As String) As Boolean

   Dim sDir As String

   On Error Resume Next
   sDir = Dir(sFile)
   FileExists = (sDir <> "")

End Function
```

We're done. Save the VB Project and make the DLL file.

Registering SmartTags

Like COM Addins, we have to tell Office that our SmartTag DLL exists by adding entries to the Windows Registry. Unlike COM Addins, Microsoft has not provided us with a tool to make that a simple process. We have to resort to manually scanning the registry and creating our own keys by hand. This can be made slightly easier by using a `.reg` file to create the keys, as shown below.

When Excel starts, it scans the registry for all the keys below:

```
HKEY_CURRENT_USER\Software\Microsoft\Office\Common\Smart Tag\Recognizers
```

If it finds any, they will be either the **ProgID** or the **ClassID** of a SmartTag `Recognizer` class. It uses this ID to create an instance of the class, then uses the properties defined in the `ISmartTagRecognizer` interface to find out the remaining information about the SmartTag. Excel repeats the process for the `Actions` classes.

The first thing we need to do is to find out the ClassIDs that Visual Basic generated for our SmartTag classes. To do this, click on Start | Run and run a file called `regedit`. In the left-hand list, browse to the registry key `HKEY_CLASSES_ROOT\<ProjectName>.<ClassName>\Clsid` and note the (`Default`) value. That is the ClassID of the class. The easiest way to copy this ID is to double-click the (`Default`) label to edit the value, then use *Ctrl+C* to copy it to the clipboard.

In our `FileName` example, the `Actions` registry key is:

```
HKEY_CLASSES_ROOT\FileNameSmartTag.Actions\Clsid
```

For me, the `Actions` ClassID is:

```
{76C5099E-36E2-4BBE-BA02-6097FAF5CFA2}
```

Repeat this for the `Recognizer` class:

```
HKEY_CLASSES_ROOT\FileNameSmartTag.Recognizer\Clsid
```

Giving the `Recognizer` ClassID:

```
{76C5099E-36E2-4BBE-BA02-6097FAF5CFA2}
```

These ClassIDs are used to register the SmartTag DLL, by including them in a `.reg` file. To do this, start Notepad and copy in the following text, substituting the full ClassIDs found above instead of `ActionClassID` and `RecognizerClassID`:

```
REGEDIT4

[HKEY_CURRENT_USER\Software\Microsoft\Office\Common\Smart Tag]

[HKEY_CURRENT_USER\Software\Microsoft\Office\Common\Smart Tag\Actions]
```

```
[HKEY_CURRENT_USER\Software\Microsoft\Office\Common\Smart
Tag\Actions\ActionClassID]

[HKEY_CURRENT_USER\Software\Microsoft\Office\Common\Smart Tag\Recognizers]

[HKEY_CURRENT_USER\Software\Microsoft\Office\Common\Smart
Tag\Recognizers\RecognizerClassID]
```

Remove any blank lines from the top of the file, then save it with a `.reg` extension.

For me, the result is a file called `FileNameSmartTag.reg`, containing the following six lines:

```
REGEDIT4

[HKEY_CURRENT_USER\Software\Microsoft\Office\Common\Smart Tag]

[HKEY_CURRENT_USER\Software\Microsoft\Office\Common\Smart Tag\Actions]

[HKEY_CURRENT_USER\Software\Microsoft\Office\Common\Smart
Tag\Actions\{76C5099E-36E2-4BBE-BA02-6097FAF5CFA2}]

[HKEY_CURRENT_USER\Software\Microsoft\Office\Common\Smart Tag\Recognizers]

[HKEY_CURRENT_USER\Software\Microsoft\Office\Common\Smart
Tag\Recognizers\{76C5099E-36E2-4BBE-BA02-6097FAF5CFA2}]
```

Double-click the `.reg` file in Windows Explorer to add those entries to the registry. Excel will now see the `FileName` SmartTag.

Using the FileName SmartTag

Start Excel 2002, click on **Tools | AutoCorrect Options…**,and click on the **Smart Tags** tab. Tick the '**Label data with smart tags**' checkbox to enable SmartTags. There should be an entry in the list for the '**Filename SmartTag Recognizer**'. Tick the box and **OK** out of the dialog:

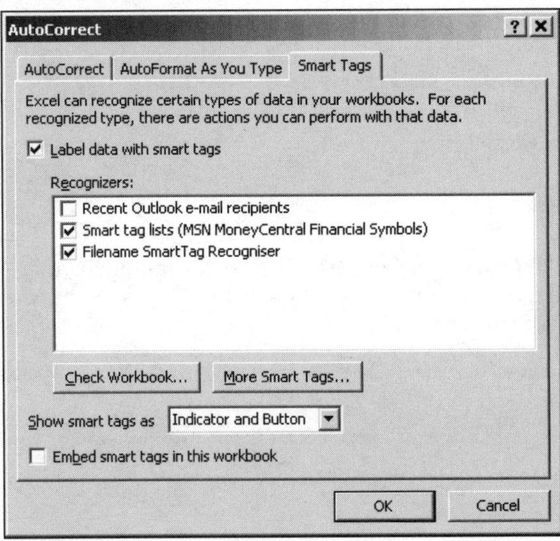

Any cells that contain text looking like a filename will then have the SmartTag indicator in the cell (a dark triangle in the bottom-right corner) and our menu of `FileName` SmartTag actions when the i button is clicked:

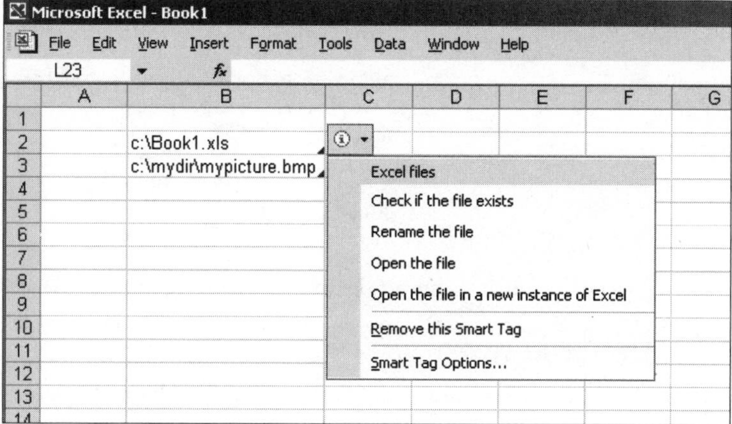

Controlling SmartTags with VBA

Historically in Excel, Microsoft has added VBA control for all new functionality and SmartTags are no exception; every action that can be performed through the user interface can also be performed through code, using the following objects and properties:

Object/Property	Description
`Workbook.SmartTagOptions`	An object to access the options on the SmartTags dialog, which are set at the workbook level.
`Application.SmartTagRecognizers`	The collection of all recognizers installed – the contents of the recognizers list in the SmartTags dialog.
`SmartTagRecognizer`	An installed recognizer (a single recognizer class), controlling whether it is enabled.
`Worksheet.SmartTags`, `Range.SmartTags`	A collection of all the SmartTags in a worksheet or range. A single range may by tagged by multiple recognizers and so have multiple SmartTags.
`SmartTag`	A single `SmartTag` object.

Table continued on following page

Object/Property	Description
`SmartTag.SmartTagActions`	The collection of actions appropriate to a specific smart tag, as defined in the SmartTag's `Actions` class.
`SmartTagAction`	A specific action of a specific SmartTag in a specific `Range`. It has an `Execute` method to invoke the action.
`Workbook.RecheckSmartTags`	A method to force Excel to re-recognize everything in the workbook.

The following examples show how to use some of the more interesting of these objects and properties.

Check if a Recognizer is Active

When working with SmartTags, the first step is often to see if a particular recognizer is installed and active:

```
Function IsRecognizerActive(sProgID As String) As Boolean

   Dim oSTR As SmartTagRecognizer

   'Loop through all the installed recognizers
   For Each oSTR In Application.SmartTagRecognizers

      'Is it the one we're looking for?
      If oSTR.ProgID = sProgID Then

         'If so, return whether it's enabled
         IsRecognizerActive = oSTR.Enabled
         Exit For
      End If
   Next

End Function
```

Remove a Tag from a Range

One of the problems with SmartTags is the issue of false-positives, where a cell is erroneously tagged. An example is the standard Stock Symbol SmartTag that recognizes TRUE as a valid stock symbol, even if that TRUE is a Boolean `True`. The following code locates all of these false-positives and removes them:

```
Sub RemoveBooleanTrue()

   Dim oSht As Worksheet
   Dim oTag As SmartTag

   'This is the URI of the StockTicker SmartTag
   Const sTicker As String = _
                "urn:schemas-microsoft-com:office:smarttags#stockticker"
```

```
    'Loop through all the worksheets in the active workbook
    For Each oSht In ActiveWorkbook.Worksheets

        'Loop through all the tags in the sheet
        For Each oTag In oSht.SmartTags

            'Is it a StockTicker tag with a Boolean value?
            If oTag.Name = sTicker And _
                          TypeName(oTag.Range.Value) = "Boolean" Then

                'Yes, so remove this SmartTag from the cell
                oTag.Delete
            End If
        Next
    Next

End Sub
```

Add a Tag to a Range

If you create a SmartTag `Recognizer` class to perform the recognition function, it has global scope. This means that the `Recognize` method will be called for every entry in all workbooks in Excel and all documents in Word. It is possible to distinguish between Word and Excel, but we can not limit the recognition to specific workbooks, sheets, or ranges.

The `SmartTags` collection has an `Add` method, by which we can tag a cell as being a specific SmartTag type. By doing so, we can completely bypass the `Recognizer` class and perform all of our recognition using VBA; we need only implement an `Actions` class to provide the popup menu and perform the action.

For example, you may find that the Stock Ticker SmartTag is too pervasive, adding lots of SmartTag indicators to cells that you'd rather not have tagged. Instead, let's assume that you have a PivotTable with a field of stock symbols and you'd like only those items SmartTagged to show the Stock Symbol actions. We first disable the Stock Symbol Recognizer in the SmartTags dialog, then use the following VBA code to recognize the stock symbols in the pivot table:

```
Sub AddTickerTagToPivotTableTitles()

    Dim oField As PivotField
    Dim oItem As PivotItem
    Dim oCell As Range

    Const sTicker As String = _
                "urn:schemas-microsoft-com:office:smarttags#stockticker"

    'Get the 'Symbol' PivotField
    Set oField = ActiveSheet.PivotTables(1).PivotFields("Symbol")

    'Loop through all the PivotItems for that field
    For Each oItem In oField.PivotItems

        'Loop through all the cells in the PivotItems label range
        For Each oCell In oItem.LabelRange
```

```
            'If the cell isn't empty ...
            If Not IsEmpty(oCell) Then

               '... tag the cell with the Stock Symbol smart tag
               oCell.SmartTags.Add sTicker
            End If
         Next
      Next

   End Sub
```

With this technique, we can combine the interface and power of the SmartTag `Actions` popup menu with the granularity and control of performing our recognition from within the Excel VBA environment. Once recognized in this way, the cells' tags can be saved within the workbook, by ticking the 'Embed Smart Tags in this Workbook' checkbox in the SmartTag Options dialog.

The Problems with SmartTags

Microsoft has done an excellent job with the new SmartTag technology, but there are a few weaknesses with the current implementation that are worth noting here.

The Recognize Method

By far the biggest problem is the relatively small amount of information that is passed to the `Recognize` method of the `ISmartTagRecognizer` interface:

```
Private Sub ISmartTagRecognizer_Recognize(ByVal Text As String, _
               ByVal DataType As SmartTagLib.IF_TYPE, _
               ByVal LocaleID As Long, _
               ByVal RecognizerSite As SmartTagLib.ISmartTagRecognizerSite)
```

Note that the text is passed to the `Recognize` method `As String`, which gives no indication of the source of that text. For example, the Boolean value `True` and the text value TRUE both come through as the string "TRUE" – the `Recognize` method can not distinguish between them.

A second weakness of the current implementation is that we are not given any informational context. We're just asked if we could recognize a single item of text. If we were able to check the cells around it, we'd be able to make a more accurate judgement. For example, if this was a 'Car Model' SmartTag, given the text "206", it would recognize that number as the Peugeot 206. If we could look at the cells around the one we're asked to recognize, we may see that the "206" is just one of a list of numbers, and is not related to models or car.

A third weakness is that we're not given any indication of 'importance', or positional context. For example, we have no way to distinguish between a list header (which we may not want to tag) and an item in the list (which we would want to tag). Similarly, we have to go back to VBA if we want to limit our tagging to specific workbooks (such as only those derived from a specific template), or only cells within PivotTable titles.

All of these problems could be solved by also passing the same `Target` parameter that is passed to the `InvokeVerb` method of the `ISmartTagAction` interface. If we were given the cell that contained the text to be recognized, we could scan the surrounding cells, check the positional context or limit the recognition to specific workbooks.

Coverage

In Office XP, the only items of text that are being passed to the SmartTag `Recognizer` class are the entire contents of worksheet cells in Excel, or full paragraphs in Word. In most Excel applications, text is presented to the user in many more forms, including:

- On charts
- On UserForms
- In comment boxes, labels, and other shapes
- On VBA `MsgBox` and `InputBox` dialogs

It would be great to see the recognition of text extended to cover those other forms of presentation.

Summary

In Office XP, Microsoft has made it possible for us to create our own recognition routines for data typed into worksheet cells or Word documents, and provide a list of actions that can be performed on cells recognized by our routines. These actions can be used to operate on the recognized cells, look up relevant information from other sources, or easily integrate our worksheet data with other applications.

SmartTag `Recognizer` and `Actions` classes are fairly easy to create for someone with an understanding of Visual Basic.

Smart Tags can be manipulated with a fine degree of precision from within the Excel VBA environment, to the extent of making a `Recognizer` class redundant in some cases.

As always with new functionality, there is room for improvement in the next release.

There are a number of web sites devoted to SmartTags, including:

- http://www.officesmarttags.com
- http://www.officezealot.com/smarttags
- http://msdn.microsoft.com/office

VBAProgrammersReferenceExcel20
ersReferenceExcel2002VB
ReferenceExcel2002VBAPro
AProgrammersReferenceExc
rammersReferenceExcel20
ReferenceExcel2002VB
ReferenceExcel2002VBAPro
rogrammer
Excel2002VBAProgram
nceExcel
ProgrammersReferenceExcel
ProgrammersReferenceExcel
nceExcel2002VBAP
xcel2002VBAPrograms
2002VBAProgrammersReferenceExcel
VBAProgrammersReferenceExc
ogrammersReferenceExcel
mmersReference
2002VBAProgrammers

19

Interacting with Other Office Applications

The Office application programs: Excel, Word, Powerpoint, Outlook, and Access all use the same VBA language. Once you understand VBA syntax in Excel, you know how to use VBA in all the other applications. Where these applications differ is in their object models.

One of the really nice things about the common VBA language is that all the Office applications are able to expose their objects to each other, and you can program interaction between all of the applications from any one of them. To work with Word objects from Excel, for example, you only need to establish a link to Word and then you have access to its objects as if you were programming with VBA in Word itself.

This chapter explains how to create the link in a number of different ways and presents some simple examples of programming the other application. In all cases, the code is written in Excel VBA, but it could easily be modified for any other Office application. The code is equally applicable to products outside Office that support the VBA language. These include other Microsoft products such as Visual Basic and SQL Server. There is also a growing list of non-Microsoft products that can be programmed in the same way.

We will also have cause to ponder on macro viruses at the end of this chapter.

> *We will not attempt to give detailed explanations of the objects, methods, and properties of the other Office applications used in the following examples. Our aim is to show how to establish communication with them, not to study their object models. You can learn about their object models in the other Wrox publications in the Office 2000 series, namely:* Word 2000 VBA Programmer's Reference *by Duncan MacKenzie (ISBN: 1-861002-55-6) and* Outlook 2000 VBA Programmer's Reference *by Dwayne Gifford (ISBN: 1-861002-53-X). In addition, Wrox Press has published a comprehensive beginner's guide to Access VBA programming, complete with compact disk:* Beginning Access 2000 VBA *by Rob Smith and Dave Sussman (ISBN: 1-861001-76-2).*

Establishing the Connection

Once you have made a connection with an Office application, its objects are exposed for automation through a type library. There are two ways to establish such a connection: **late binding** and **early binding**. In either case, you establish the connection by creating an object variable that refers to the target application, or a specific object in the target application. You can then proceed to use the properties and methods of the object referred to by the object variable.

In **late binding**, you create an object that refers to the Office application before you make a link to the Office application's type library. In earlier versions of the Office applications it was necessary to use **late binding** and you will still see it used, because it has some advantages over early binding. One advantage is that you can write code that can detect the presence or absence of the required type library on the PC running your code and link to different versions of applications based on decisions made as the code executes.

The disadvantage of late binding is that the type library for the target application is not accessed when you are writing your code. Therefore, you get no help information regarding the application, you cannot reference the intrinsic constants in the application and, when the code is compiled, the references to the target application may not be correct, as they cannot be checked. The links are only fully resolved when you try to execute the code and this takes time. It is also possible that coding errors may be detected at this point that cause your program to fail.

Early binding is supported by all the Office applications, from Office 97 onwards. Code that uses early binding executes faster than code using late binding as the target application's type library is present when you write your code. Therefore, more syntax and type checking can be performed, and more linkage details can be established, before the code executes.

It is also easier to write code for early binding because you can see the objects, methods, and properties of the target application in the Object Browser and, as you write your code, you will see automatic tips appear, such as a list of related properties and methods after you type an object reference. You can also use the intrinsic constants defined in the target application.

Late Binding

The following code creates an entry in the Outlook calendar. The code uses the late binding technique:

```
Sub MakeOutlookAppointment()
   'Example of Outlook automation using late binding
   'Creates an appointment in Outlook

   Dim olApp As Object 'Reference to Outlook
   Dim olAppointment As Object 'Reference to Outlook Appointment
   Const olAppointmentItem = 1 'Outlook intrinsic constants not available

   'Create link to Outlook
   Set olApp = CreateObject("Outlook.Application")
   Set olAppointment = olApp.CreateItem(olAppointmentItem)

   'Set details of appointment
   With olAppointment
      .Subject = "Discuss Whitefield Contract"
      .Start = DateSerial(2002, 2, 25) + TimeSerial(9, 30, 0)
```

```
        .End = DateSerial(2002, 2, 25) + TimeSerial(11, 30, 0)
        .ReminderPlaySound = True
        .Save
    End With
    'Exit Outlook
    olApp.Quit
    'Release object variable
    Set olApp = Nothing
End Sub
```

The basic technique in programming another application is to create an object variable referring to that application. The object variable in this case is `olApp`. You then use `olApp` (as you would use the `Application` object in Excel) to refer to objects in the external application's object model. In this case, the `CreateItem` method of Outlook's `Application` object is used to create a reference to a new `AppointmentItem` object.

As Outlook's intrinsic constants are not available in late binding, you need to define your own constants, such as `olAppointmentItem` here, or substitute the value of the constant as the parameter value. We go on to use the properties and methods of the `Appointment` object in the `With...End With` structure. Note the times have been defined using the `DateSerial` and `TimeSerial` functions to avoid ambiguity or problems in an international context. See Chapter 22 for more details.

By declaring `olApp` and `olAppointment` as the generic `Object` type, you force VBA to use late binding. VBA cannot resolve all the links to Outlook until it executes the `CreateObject` function.

The `CreateObject` input argument defines the application name and class of object to be created. `Outlook` is the name of the application and `Application` is the class. Many applications allow you to create objects at different levels in the object model. For example, Excel allows you to create `WorkSheet` or `Chart` objects from other applications, using `Excel.WorkSheet` or `Excel.Chart` as the input parameter of the `CreateObject` function.

It is good programming practice to close the external application when you are finished with it and set the object variable to `Nothing`. This releases the memory used by the link and the application.

If you run this macro nothing will happen in Excel at all. However, open up Outlook and in the Calendar you will find that the appointment has been added for the morning of February 25:

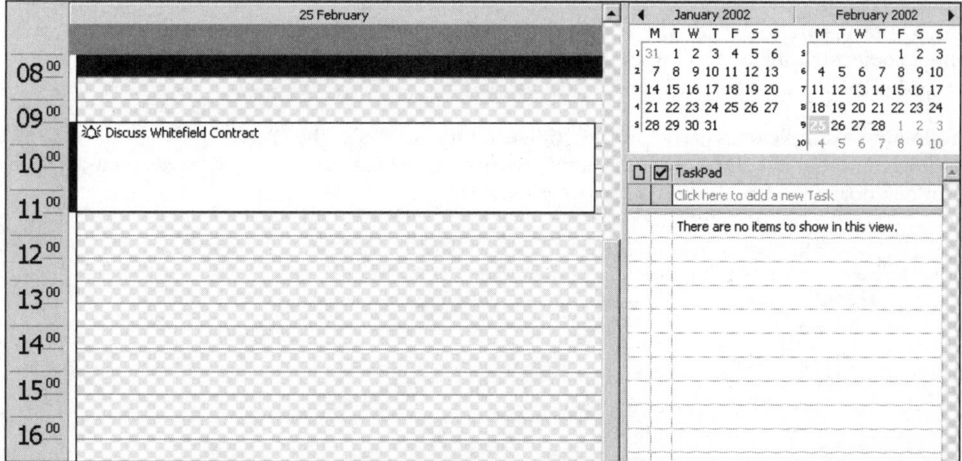

Early Binding

If you want to use early binding, you need to establish a reference to the type library of the external application in your VBA project. You do this from the VBE by selecting Tools | References, which displays the following dialog box:

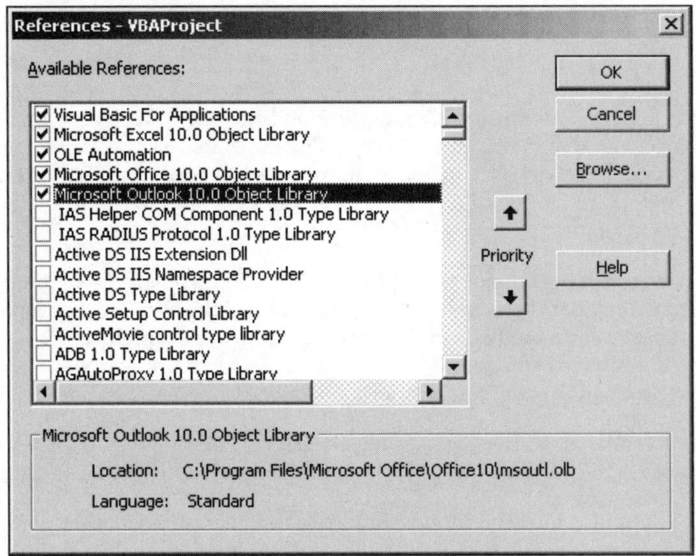

You create a reference by checking the box next to the object library. Once you have a reference to an application, you can declare your object variables as the correct type. For example, you could declare `olEntry` as an `AddressEntry` type as follows:

```
Dim olEntry As AddressEntry
```

VBA will search through the type libraries, in the order shown from the top down, to find references to object types. If the same object type is present in more than one library, it will use the first one found. You can select a library and click the Priority buttons to move it up or down the list to change the order in which libraries are searched. There is no need to depend on priority, however. You can always qualify an object by preceding it with the name of the main object in the library. For example, instead of using `AddressEntry`, use `Outlook.AddressEntry`.

The following example uses early binding. It lists all the names of the entries in the Outlook Contacts folder, placing them in column A of the active worksheet. Make sure that you have created a reference to the Outlook object library before you try to execute it:

```
Sub DisplayOutlookContactNames()
    'Example of Outlook automation using early binding
    'Lists all the Contact names from Outlook in the A column
    'of the active sheet
    Dim olApp As Outlook.Application
    Dim olNameSpace As Outlook.NameSpace
    Dim olAddresslist As AddressList
    Dim olEntry As AddressEntry
    Dim i As Long
```

```
    'Create link to Outlook Contacts folder
    Set olApp = New Outlook.Application
    Set olNameSpace = olApp.GetNamespace("MAPI")
    Set olAddresslist = olNameSpace.AddressLists("Contacts")
    For Each olEntry In olAddresslist.AddressEntries
       i = i + 1
       'Enter contacts in A column of active sheet
       Cells(i, 1).Value = olEntry.Name
    Next

    'Exit Outlook
    olApp.Quit
    'Release object variable
    Set olApp = Nothing
End Sub
```

If you are using Outlook 2002 when you run this code you will get a warning message that a program is trying to access e-mail addresses. You can allow the operation or cancel it.

Office XP has greatly increased protection against viruses. Any attempt by programs to access e-mail addresses will invoke a warning message. Every time a program tries to send an e-mail another warning is issued. If you need to avoid these warnings you should consult your system administrator.

Here, we directly declare `olApp` to be an `Outlook.Application` type. The other `Dim` statements also declare object variables of the type we need. If the same object name is used in more than one object library, you can precede the object name by the name of the application, rather than depend on the priority of the type libraries. We have done this with `Outlook.NameSpace` to illustrate the point. The `New` keyword is used when assigning a reference to `Outlook.Application` to `olApp` to create a new instance of Outlook.

The fact that we declare the variable types correctly makes VBA use early binding. You could use the `CreateObject` function to create the `olApp` object variable, instead of the `New` keyword, without affecting the early binding. However, it is more efficient to use `New`.

Opening a Document in Word

If you want to open a file created in another Office application, you can use the `GetObject` function to directly open the file. However, it is just as easy to open an instance of the application and open the file from the application. We will look at another use of `GetObject` shortly.

If you are not familiar with the Word Object Model, you can use the Word macro recorder to discover which objects, properties, and methods you need to use to perform a Word task that you can do manually.

The following code copies a range in Excel to the clipboard. It then starts a new instance of Word, opens an existing Word document, and pastes the range to the end of the document. As the code uses early binding, make sure you establish a reference to the Word object library:

```
Sub CopyTableToWordDocument()
    'Example of Word automation using early binding
    'Copies range from workbook and appends it to existing Word document
    Dim wdApp As Word.Application
```

```
    'Copy A1:B6 in Table sheet
    ThisWorkbook.Sheets("Table").Range("A1:B6").Copy

    'Establish link to Word
    Set wdApp = New Word.Application
    With wdApp
       'Open Word document
       .Documents.Open Filename:="C:\VBA_Prog_Ref\Chapter19\Chart.doc"
       With .Selection
          'Go to end of document and insert paragraph
          .EndKey Unit:=wdStory
          .TypeParagraph
          'Paste table
          .Paste

       End With
       .ActiveDocument.Save
       'Exit Word
       .Quit
    End With
    'Release object variable
    Set wdApp = Nothing
End Sub
```

The `New` keyword creates a new instance of Word, even if Word is already open. The `Open` method of the `Documents` collection is used to open the existing file. The code then selects the end of the document, enters a new empty paragraph, and pastes the range. The document is then saved and the new instance of Word is closed.

Accessing an Active Word Document

Say you are working in Excel, creating a table. You also have Word open with a document active, into which you want to paste the table you are creating. You can copy the table from Excel to the document using the following code. There is no need to establish a reference to Word if you declare `wdApp` as an `Object` type, as VBA will use late binding. On the other hand, you can establish a reference to Word, declare `wdApp` as a `Word.Application` type, and VBA will use early binding. In this example we are using early binding:

```
Sub CopyTableToOpenWordDocument()
    'Example of Word automation using late binding
    'Copies range from workbook and appends it to
    ' a currently open Word document

    Dim wdApp As Word.Application

    'Copy Range A1:B6 on sheet named Table
    ThisWorkbook.Sheets("Table").Range("A1:B6").Copy

    'Establish link to open instance of Word
    Set wdApp = GetObject(, "Word.Application")
    With wdApp.Selection
       'Go to end of document and insert paragraph
       .EndKey Unit:=wdStory
```

```
        .TypeParagraph
        'Paste table
        .Paste

     End With
     'Release object variable
     Set wdApp = Nothing
  End Sub
```

The GetObject function has two input parameters, both of which are optional. The first parameter can be used to specify a file to be opened. The second can be used to specify the application program to open. If you do not specify the first parameter, GetObject assumes you want to access a currently open instance of Word. If you specify a zero length string as the first parameter, GetObject assumes you want to open a new instance of Word.

You can use GetObject, with no first parameter, as in the code above, to access a current instance of Word that is in memory. However, if there is no current instance of Word running, GetObject with no first parameter causes a run-time error.

Creating a New Word Document

Say you want to use a current instance of Word if one exists, or if there is no current instance, you want to create one. In either case you want to open a new document and paste the table into it. The following code shows how to do this. Again, we are using early binding:

```
Sub CopyTableToAnyWordDocument()
  'Example of Word automation using early binding
  'Copies range from workbook and pastes it in
  'a new Word document, in a active instance of
  'Word, if there is one.
  'If not, opens new instance of Word

  Dim wdApp As Word.Application

  'Copy Range A1:B6 on sheet named Table
  ThisWorkbook.Sheets("Table").Range("A1:B6").Copy

  On Error Resume Next
  'Try to establish link to open instance of Word
  Set wdApp = GetObject(, "Word.Application")

  'If this fails, open Word
  If wdApp Is Nothing Then
    Set wdApp = GetObject("", "Word.Application")
  End If
  On Error GoTo 0

  With wdApp
    'Add new document
    .Documents.Add
    'Make Word visible
    .Visible = True
  End With
```

```
    With wdApp.Selection
      'Go to end of document and insert paragraph
      .EndKey Unit:=wdStory
      .TypeParagraph
      'Paste table
      .Paste

    End With
    'Release object variable
    Set wdApp = Nothing
  End Sub
```

If there is no current instance of Word, using `GetObject` with no first argument causes a run-time error and the code then uses `GetObject` with a zero length string as the first argument, which opens a new instance of Word, and then creates a new document. The code also makes the new instance of Word visible, unlike our previous examples where the work was done behind the scenes without showing the Word window. The chart is then pasted at the end of the Word document. At the end of the procedure, the object variable `wdApp` is released, but the Word window is accessible on the screen so that you can view the result.

Access and DAO

If you want to copy data from Access to Excel, you can establish a reference to the Access object library and use the Access Object Model. However, this is overkill because you don't really need most of the functionality in Access. You can also use ADO (ActiveX Data Objects), which is Microsoft's latest technology for programmatic access to relational databases, and many other forms of data storage. For examples of this, see Chapter 20.

Another simple and efficient way to get to Access data is provided by DAO (Data Access Objects). If you use Office 97, you will have DAO available but you might not have ADO, as ADO was released after Office 97 was released. You can still use ADO with Excel 97, but the powerful `CopyFromRecordset` method, which is used in the following example, is not supported in Excel 97 for ADO recordsets. Here, we will show how to use DAO.

The following screen shows an Access table named `Sales` that is in an Access database file `FruitSales.mdb`:

Sales : Table

ID	Date	Customer	State	Product	NumberSold	Price	Revenue
1	Aug 26, 1999	Roberts	NSW	Oranges	903	15	13545
2	Aug 26, 1999	Roberts	TAS	Oranges	331	15	4965
3	Aug 27, 1999	Smith	QLD	Mangoes	299	20	5980
4	Aug 31, 1999	Roberts	QLD	Oranges	612	15	9180
5	Sep 02, 1999	Roberts	VIC	Apples	907	12.5	11337.5
6	Sep 02, 1999	Pradesh	TAS	Pears	107	18	1926
7	Sep 04, 1999	Roberts	VIC	Apples	770	12.5	9625
8	Sep 08, 1999	Smith	NT	Apples	223	12.5	2787.5
9	Sep 08, 1999	Smith	VIC	Oranges	132	15	1980
10	Sep 09, 1999	Pradesh	QLD	Oranges	669	15	10035

Record: 1 of 499

The following code uses DAO to open a recordset based on the `Sales` table. It uses early binding, so a reference to the DAO object library is required:

```
Sub GetSalesDataViaDAO()
    'Example of DAO automation using early binding
    'Copies Sales table from Access database to new worksheet
    Dim daoApp As DAO.DBEngine
    Dim dbSales As DAO.Database
    Dim rsSales As DAO.Recordset
    Dim i As Integer
    Dim Wks As Worksheet
    Dim iCount As Integer

    'Establish link to DAO
    Set daoApp = New DAO.DBEngine
    'Open Access database file
    Set dbSales = daoApp.OpenDatabase _
            ("C:\VBA_Prog_Ref\Chapter19\FruitSales.mdb")
    'Open recordset based on Sales Table
    Set rsSales = dbSales.OpenRecordset("Sales")
    'Add new worksheet to active workbook
    Set Wks = Worksheets.Add
    iCount = rsSales.Fields.Count
    'Enter field names across row 1
    For i = 0 To iCount - 1
       Wks.Cells(1, i + 1).Value = rsSales.Fields(i).Name
    Next

    'Copy entire recordset data to worksheet, starting in A2
    Wks.Range("A2").CopyFromRecordset rsSales

    'Format worksheet dates in A column
    Wks.Columns("B").NumberFormat = "mmm dd, yyyy"
    'Bold row 1 and fit columns to largest entry
    With Wks.Range("A1").Resize(1, iCount)
        .Font.Bold = True
        .EntireColumn.AutoFit
    End With

    'Release object variables
    Set rsSales = Nothing
    Set dbSales = Nothing
    Set daoApp = Nothing
End Sub
```

The code opens the Access database file, creates a recordset based on the `Sales` table, and assigns a reference to the recordset to `rsSales`. A new worksheet is added to the Excel workbook, and the field names in `rsSales` are assigned to the first row of the new worksheet. The code uses the `CopyFromRecordSet` method of the `Range` object to copy the records in `rsSales` to the worksheet, starting in cell A2. `CopyFromRecordSet` is a very fast way to copy the data compared to a looping procedure that copies record by record.

Access, Excel and, Outlook

As a final example of integrating different Office applications we will extract some data from Access, chart it using Excel, and e-mail the chart using Outlook. The code has been set up as four procedures. The first procedure is a sub procedure named `EmailChart` that establishes the operating parameters and executes the other three procedures. Note that the code uses early binding and you need to create references to the DAO and Outlook object libraries:

```
Sub EmailChart()
  'Gets data from Access using SQL statement
  'Creates chart and emails chart file to recipient

  Dim stSQL As String
  Dim rgData As Excel.Range
  Dim stFileName As String
  Dim stRecipient As String

  stSQL = "SELECT Product, Sum(Revenue)"
  stSQL = stSQL & " FROM Sales"
  stSQL = stSQL & " WHERE Date>=#1/1/2000# and Date<#1/1/2001#"
  stSQL = stSQL & " GROUP BY Product;"

  stFileName = "C:\VBA_Prog_Ref\Chapter19\Chart.xls"
  stRecipient = "jgreen@enternet.com.au"

  Set rgData = rgSalesData(stSQL)
  ChartData rgData, stFileName
  SendEmail stRecipient, stFileName

End Sub
```

`stSQL` is used to hold a string that is a SQL (structured query language) command. SQL is covered in more detail in Chapter 20. In this case the SQL specifies that we want to select the unique product names and the sum of the revenues for each product from our Access database `Sales` table for all dates in the year 2000. `stFileName` defines the path and filename that will be used to hold the chart workbook. `stRecipient` holds the e-mail address of the person we are sending the chart to.

The code then executes the `rgSalesData` function that is listed below. The function accepts the SQL statement as an input parameter and returns a reference to the range containing the extracted data, which is assigned to `rgData`. The `ChartData` sub procedure is then executed, passing in the data range, as well as the path and filename for the chart workbook. Finally, the `SendEMail` sub procedure is executed, passing in the recipient's e-mail address and the location of the chart workbook to be attached to the e-mail:

```
Function rgSalesData(stSQL As String) As Excel.Range
  'Function to extract data from database using
  'SQL statement in stSQL
  'Returns a reference to the range containing
  'the data

  Dim daoApp As DAO.DBEngine
  Dim dbSales As DAO.Database
  Dim rsSales As DAO.Recordset
```

```
    'Establish link to DAO
    Set daoApp = New DAO.DBEngine

    'Open Access database file
    Set dbSales = daoApp.OpenDatabase _
        ("C:\VBA_Prog_Ref\Chapter19\FruitSales.mdb")

    'Open recordset based on Sales Table
    Set rsSales = dbSales.OpenRecordset(stSQL)

    'Clear sheet and bring in new data
    With Worksheets("Data")
      .Cells.Clear

      With .Range("A1")
        'Copy entire recordset data to worksheet, starting in A1
        .CopyFromRecordset rsSales
        'Return reference to data range
        Set rgSalesData = .CurrentRegion
      End With
    End With

    'Release object variables
    Set rsSales = Nothing
    Set dbSales = Nothing
    Set daoApp = Nothing
End Function
```

The `rgSalesData` function is similar to the `GetSalesDataViaDAO` sub procedure presented earlier. Instead of getting the entire `Sales` table from the database it uses SQL to be more selective. It clears the worksheet named `Data` and copies the selected data to a range starting in A1. It does not add the field names to the worksheet, just the product names and total revenue. It uses the `CurrentRegion` property to obtain a reference to all the extracted data and assigns the reference to the return value of the function:

```
Sub ChartData(rgData As Range, stFileName As String)
    'Procedure to create chart based on data in rgData
    'Binds data to chart as arrays
    'Saves chart to path and file in stFileName

    'Create new workbook
    With Workbooks.Add

      'Create new chart sheet
      With .Charts.Add

        'Create new data series and assign data
        With .SeriesCollection.NewSeries
          .XValues = rgData.Columns(1).Value
          .Values = rgData.Columns(2).Value
        End With

        'Format chart
        .HasLegend = False
```

```
        .HasTitle = True
        .ChartTitle.Text = "Year 2000 Revenue"

      End With

      'Save workbook and close it
      Application.DisplayAlerts = False
      .SaveAs stFileName
      Application.DisplayAlerts = True
      .Close

    End With

End Sub
```

`ChartData` has input parameters to define the range containing the data to be charted and the destination for the file it creates. It creates a new workbook and adds a chart sheet to it. It creates a new series in the chart and assigns the values from the data range as arrays to the axes of the series. `DisplayAlerts` is set to `False` to prevent a warning if it overwrites an old file of the same name.

> **Note: you could run foul of your virus checker while creating the code in `SendEmail`. Before we finish, we will look at the reasons for this.**

When is a Virus not a Virus?

The following version of `SendEmail`, created in all innocence, was identified as a virus by Norton AntiVirus. In fact, this identification of the code as the `X97.OutlookWorm.Gen` virus, set me back a few hours. When I closed Excel and saved my work, Norton AntiVirus smugly informed me that it had found the virus in my workbook and had eliminated the problem. It had deleted all the modules from the workbook. I had to turn off the AutoProtect option in Norton and start again.

Here is the code that caused the problem:

```
Sub SendEmail(stRecipient As String, stAttachment As String)
  'Send email to stRecipient
  'Attaching file in stAttachment

  Dim olApp As Outlook.Application
  Dim olNameSpace As Outlook.NameSpace
  Dim olMail As Outlook.MailItem

  Set olApp = New Outlook.Application
  'Might be necessary to Logon
  'Set olNameSpace = olApp.GetNamespace("MAPI")
  'olNameSpace.Logon Profile:="UserName", Password:="Password"
  Set olMail = olApp.CreateItem(olMailItem)
  With olMail
    .Subject = "Year 2000 Revenue Chart"
    .Recipients.Add stRecipient
    .Body = "Workbook with chart attached"

    .Attachments.Add stAttachment
```

```
        .Send
    End With
    'Release object variables
     Set olMail = Nothing
     Set olApp = Nothing
End Sub
```

After some trial and error I came up with the following code that is not identified as a virus. It escapes identification both with and without a reference to the Outlook object library. As it uses late binding, it does not require a reference to Outlook:

```
Sub SendEmail(stRecipient As String, stAttachment As String)
  'Send email to stRecipient
  'Attaching file in stAttachment

  Dim olApp As Object
  Dim olNameSpace As Object
  Dim olMail As Object

  Set olApp = CreateObject("Outlook.Application")
  'Might be necessary to Logon
  'Set olNameSpace = olApp.GetNamespace("MAPI")
  'olNameSpace.Logon "UserName", "Password"
  Set olMail = olApp.CreateItem(0)
  With olMail
    .Subject = "Year 2000 Revenue Chart"
    .Recipients.Add stRecipient
    .Body = "Workbook with chart attached"

    .Attachments.Add stAttachment
    .Send
  End With
End Sub
```

`SendEMail` has input parameters for the e-mail address of the recipient and the filename of the attachment for the e-mail. If your Outlook configuration requires you to logon you will need to uncomment the lines that get a reference to the Namespace and supply the username and password. A new mail item is created using the `CreateItem` method. Text is added for the subject line and the body of the e-mail and the recipient and attachment are specified. The `Send` method sends the e-mail.

You will need to respond to two dialog boxes when executing this code in Office XP. The first warns you that Outlook is being accessed and the second forces a five second delay and warns you that a program is sending an e-mail. The techniques you are using, while being very useful to achieve legitimate ends, are also, obviously, employed by virus writers.

While Office XP has strong protection against e-mail viruses, earlier versions of Office are more vulnerable. Patches are available from Microsoft to add protection to earlier versions of Outlook, but they might make it impossible to send e-mail programmatically. It can be very difficult to allow the legitimate use of programmatically generated e-mail and prevent viruses doing the same thing. The best answer is to have the latest virus protection software installed and keep it up to date, even if it occasionally does the dirty on you.

Summary

To automate the objects in another application, you create an object variable referring to the target application or an object in the application. You can use early binding or late binding to establish the link between VBA and the other application's objects. Early binding requires that you establish a reference to the target application's type library and you must declare any object variables that refer to the target objects using their correct type. If you declare the object variables as the generic `Object` type, VBA uses late binding.

Early binding produces code that executes faster than late binding and you can get information on the target applications objects using the Object Browser and the short cut tips that automatically appear as you type your code. Syntax and type checking is also performed as you code, so you are less likely to get errors when the code executes than with late binding where these checks cannot be done until the code is run.

You must use the `CreateObject` or `GetObject` function to create an object variable reference to the target application when using late binding. You can use the same functions when early binding, but it is more efficient to use the `New` keyword. However, if you want to test for an open instance of another application at run time, `GetObject` can be usefully employed with early binding.

The techniques presented in this chapter allow you to create powerful programs that seamlessly tap into the unique abilities of different products. The user remains in a familiar environment such as Excel while the code ranges across any product that has a type library and exposes its objects to VBA.

You need to be aware that virus writers can use the information presented here to wreak havoc on unprotected systems. Make sure that your system is adequately covered.

20

Data Access with ADO

ActiveX Data Objects, or **ADO** for short, is Microsoft's technology of choice for performing **client-server** data access between any data consumer (the client) and any data source (the server). There are other data-access technologies of which you may have heard in relation to Excel, including DAO and ODBC. However, these will not be covered in this chapter as Microsoft intends for these older technologies to be superceded by ADO, and for the most part this has occurred.

ADO is a vast topic, easily the subject of its own book. In fact Wrox has published several excellent books exclusively on ADO, including the *ADO 2.6 Programmer's Reference* (ISBN 1-861004-63-x) and *Professional ADO 2.5 Programming* (ISBN 1-861002-75-0). This chapter will necessarily present only a small subset of ADO, covering the topics and situations that I've run across most frequently in my career as an Excel programmer. For a more detailed look at ADO I strongly recommend one of the dedicated volumes mentioned above.

As a freestanding, universal data-access technology, ADO has evolved rapidly over the past several years, much more rapidly than the programs that use it. As of this writing, there are three versions of ADO in common use: 2.1, 2.5, and 2.6. This chapter will focus on ADO 2.5. This is the version of ADO that ships natively with Windows 2000 and Office 2000, or higher. If you aren't running one of these applications and don't have ADO 2.5 installed you can download it from the Microsoft Universal Data Access web site at http://www.microsoft.com/data.

An Introduction to Structured Query Language (SQL)

It's impossible to get very far into a discussion of data access without running into **SQL**, the querying language used to communicate with all databases commonly in use today. SQL is a standards-based language that has as many variations as there are databases. This chapter will use constructs compliant with the latest SQL standard, SQL-92, wherever possible. In order to properly cover data access with Microsoft SQL Server, however, the SQL Server variant of SQL called Transact SQL, or T-SQL for short, will be touched upon.

This section will provide a brief overview of basic SQL syntax. This overview is by no means complete, but will serve to introduce you to the concepts used in this chapter. For an excellent and significantly more detailed primer on SQL I would recommend *Beginning SQL Programming* (ISBN 1-861001-80-0) from Wrox Press.

There are four fundamental operations supported by SQL. These operations are:

- `SELECT`
  Used to retrieve data from a data source
- `INSERT`
  Used to add new records to a data source
- `UPDATE`
  Used to modify existing records in a data source
- `DELETE`
  Used to remove records from a data source

The terms **record** and **field** are commonly used when describing data. The data sources we'll be concerned with in this chapter can all be thought of as being stored in a two dimensional grid. A record represents a single row in that grid. A field represents a column in the grid. The intersection of a record and a field is a specific **value**. A **resultset** is the term used to describe the set of data returned by a SQL `SELECT` statement.

> **You will notice that SQL keywords such as `SELECT` and `UPDATE` are shown in upper case. This is considered good SQL programming practice. When viewing complex SQL statements, having SQL keywords in upper case makes it significantly easier to distinguish between those keywords and their operands. The subsections of a SQL statement are called clauses. In all SQL statements some clauses are required while others are optional. When describing the syntax of SQL statements, optional clauses and keywords will be surrounded with square brackets.**

We will use the `Customers` table from Microsoft's Northwind demo database, as shown below, to illustrate our SQL syntax examples. Northwind comes when you install either Access or SQL Server (it is sometimes called NWind):

Customers : Table

CustomerID	CompanyName	ContactName	Country
ALFKI	Alfreds Futterkiste	Maria Anders	Germany
ANATR	Ana Trujillo Emparedados y helados	Ana Trujillo	Mexico
ANTON	Antonio Moreno Taquería	Antonio Moreno	Mexico
AROUT	Around the Horn	Thomas Hardy	UK
BERGS	Berglunds snabbköp	Christina Berglund	Sweden
BLAUS	Blauer See Delikatessen	Hanna Moos	Germany
BLONP	Blondel père et fils	Frédérique Citeaux	France
BOLID	Bólido Comidas preparadas	Martín Sommer	Spain
BONAP	Bon app'	Laurence Lebihan	France
BOTTM	Bottom-Dollar Markets	Elizabeth Lincoln	Canada
BSBEV	B's Beverages	Victoria Ashworth	UK
CACTU	Cactus Comidas para llevar	Patricio Simpson	Argentina

The SELECT Statement

The `SELECT` statement is by far the most commonly used statement in SQL. This is the statement that allows you to retrieve data from a data source. We will use the following clauses of the `SELECT` statement in this chapter. Only the `SELECT` and `FROM` clauses are required to constitute a valid SQL statement:

```
SELECT [DISTINCT] column1, column2, …
FROM table_name
[WHERE restriction_condition]
[ORDER BY column_name [ASC|DESC]]
```

The `SELECT` clause tells the data source what fields you wish to return. The field names in the `SELECT` clause are called the `SELECT` list. The `FROM` clause tells the data source which table the records should be retrieved from. For instance, a simple example statement could look like this:

```
SELECT CompanyName, ContactName
FROM Customers
```

This statement will notify the data source that you want to retrieve all of the values for the `CompanyName` and `ContactName` fields from the `Customers` table. The `SELECT` statement provides a shorthand method for indicating that you want to retrieve all fields from the specified table. This involves placing a single asterisk as the `SELECT` list:

```
SELECT *
FROM Customers
```

This SQL statement will return all fields and all records from the `Customers` table. It's generally not considered a good practice to use `*` in the `SELECT` list as it leaves your code vulnerable to changes in field names or the order of fields in the table. It can also be very resource expensive in large tables as all columns and rows will be returned whether or not they are actually needed by the client. However, there are times when it is a useful and time saving shortcut.

Let's say that you wanted to see a list of countries where you have at least one customer located. Simply performing the following query would return one record for every customer in your table:

```
SELECT Country
FROM Customers
```

This resultset would contain many duplicate country names. The optional `DISTINCT` keyword allows you to return only unique values in your query:

```
SELECT DISTINCT Country
FROM Customer
```

If you only want to see the list of customers located in the UK, you can use the `WHERE` clause to restrict the results to only those customers:

```
SELECT CompanyName, ContactName
FROM Customers
WHERE Country = 'UK'
```

Note that the string literal UK must be surrounded in single quotes. This is also true of dates. Numeric expressions do not require any surrounding characters.

Finally, suppose that you would like to have your UK customer list sorted by `CompanyName`. This can be accomplished using the `ORDER BY` clause:

```
SELECT CompanyName, ContactName
FROM Customers
WHERE Country = 'UK'
ORDER BY CompanyName
```

The ORDER BY clause will order fields in ascending order by default. If instead you wished to sort a field in descending order, you could use the optional DESC specifier immediately after the name of the column whose sort order you wished to modify.

The INSERT Statement

The INSERT statement allows you to add new records to a table. The basic syntax of the INSERT statement is the following:

```
INSERT INTO table_name (column1, column2, …)
VALUES (value1, value2, …)
```

Use of the INSERT statement is very simple. You provide the name of the table and its columns that you'll be inserting data into and then provide a list of values to be inserted. You must provide a value in the VALUES clause for each column named in the INSERT clause and the values must appear in the same order as the column names they correspond to. Here's an example showing how to insert a new record into the Customers table:

```
INSERT INTO Customers (CustomerID, CompanyName, ContactName, Country)
VALUES ('ABCD', 'New Company', 'Owner Name', 'USA')
```

Note that as with the WHERE clause of the SELECT statement, all of the string literals in the VALUES clause are surrounded by single quotes. This is the rule throughout SQL.

If you have provided values for every field in the table in your VALUES clause, the field list in the INSERT clause can be omitted.

```
INSERT INTO Customers
VALUES ('ABCD', 'New Company', 'Owner Name', 'USA')
```

The UPDATE Statement

The UPDATE statement allows you to modify the values in one or more fields of an existing record or records in a table. The basic syntax of the UPDATE statement is the following:

```
UPDATE table_name
SET column1 = value1, column2 = value2, …
[WHERE restriction_condition]
```

Even though the WHERE clause of the UPDATE statement is optional, you must take care to specify it unless you are sure that you don't need it. Executing an UPDATE statement **without** a WHERE clause will modify the specified field(s) of every record in the specified table. For example, if we executed the following statement:

```
UPDATE Customers
SET Country = 'USA'
```

Every record in the Customers table would have its Country field modified to contain the value "USA". There are some cases where this mass update capability is useful, but it can also be very dangerous, because there is no way to undo the update if you execute it by mistake.

The more common use of the UPDATE statement is to modify the value of a specific record identified by the use of the WHERE clause. Before we look at an example of this usage, we need to discuss a very important aspect of database design called the **primary key**. The primary key is a field or group of fields in a database table whose values can be used to uniquely identify each record in that table. There is no way to identify a specific record in a table that does not have a primary key. Without that capability you cannot perform an update on a specific record.

The primary key in our sample Customers table is the CustomerID field. Each customer record in the Customers table has a unique value for CustomerID. In other words, a specific CustomerID value occurs in one, and only one, customer record in the table.

Let's say that the ContactName changed for the customer "Around the Horn", whose CustomerID is "AROUT". We could perform an UPDATE to record that change in the following manner:

```
UPDATE Customers
SET ContactName = 'New Name'
WHERE CustomerID = 'AROUT'
```

Since we used the primary key field to specify a single record in the Customers table, only this record will be updated.

The DELETE Statement

The DELETE statement allows you to remove one or more records from a table. The basic syntax of the DELETE statement is the following:

```
DELETE FROM table_name
[WHERE restriction_condition]
```

As with the UPDATE statement, notice that the WHERE clause is optional. This is probably more dangerous in the case of the DELETE statement, however, because executing a DELETE statement **without** a WHERE clause **will delete every single record in the specified table**. Once again, there is no way to undo this, so be very careful. You should always include a WHERE clause in your DELETE statements unless you have some very specific reason for wanting to remove all records from a table.

Let's assume that for some reason an entry was made into the Customers table with the CustomerID value of "BONAP" by mistake (maybe they were a supplier rather than a customer). To remove this record from the Customers table we would use the following DELETE statement:

```
DELETE FROM Customers
WHERE CustomerID = 'BONAP'
```

Once again, since we used the record's primary key in the WHERE clause, only that specific record will be affected by the DELETE statement.

An Overview of ADO

ADO is Microsoft's universal data-access technology. By universal they mean that ADO is designed to allow access to any kind of data source imaginable, from a SQL Server database, to the Windows 2000 Active Directory, to a text file saved on your local hard disk, and even to non-Microsoft products such as Oracle. All of these things and many more can be accessed by ADO. You can find a wealth of information on ADO in the ADO section of the Microsoft Universal Data Access web site: http://www.microsoft.com/data/ado/.

ADO doesn't actually access a data source directly. Instead, ADO is a data consumer that receives its data from a lower-level technology called **OLE DB**. OLE DB cannot be accessed directly using VBA, so ADO was designed to provide an interface that allows you to do so. ADO receives data from **OLE DB providers**. Most OLE DB providers are specific to a single type of data source. Each is designed to provide a common interface to whatever data its source may contain. One of the greatest strengths of ADO is that, regardless of the data source you are accessing, you use essentially the same set of commands. There's no need to learn different technologies or methods to access different data sources.

Microsoft also provides an OLE DB provider for ODBC. This general-purpose provider allows ADO to access any data source that understands ODBC, even if a specific OLE DB data provider is not available for that data source. The diagram below shows the communication path between ADO and a data source:

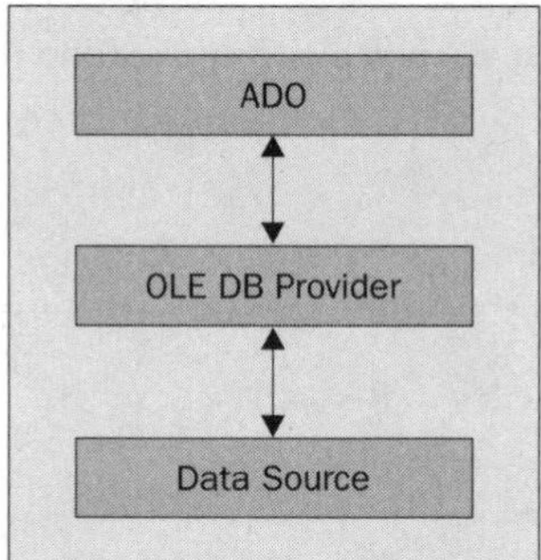

Unlike the deep, complex object models of the data access technologies that preceded it, the ADO object model is very flat and simple to understand. It achieves this simplicity without losing any of its power to access and manipulate data.

ADO consists of five top-level objects, all of which can be created independently. In this chapter we'll be covering the `Connection` object, the `Command` object, and the `Recordset` object. ADO also exposes a `Record` object (not to be confused with the `Recordset` object), as well as a `Stream` object. These objects are not commonly used in Excel applications so it's left to the interested reader to learn more about them from one of the sources mentioned at the beginning of this chapter.

In addition to the five top-level objects, ADO contains four collections. That's it. Five objects and four collections are all you need to master to gain the power of ADO at your fingertips. The diagram opposite shows the ADO object model:

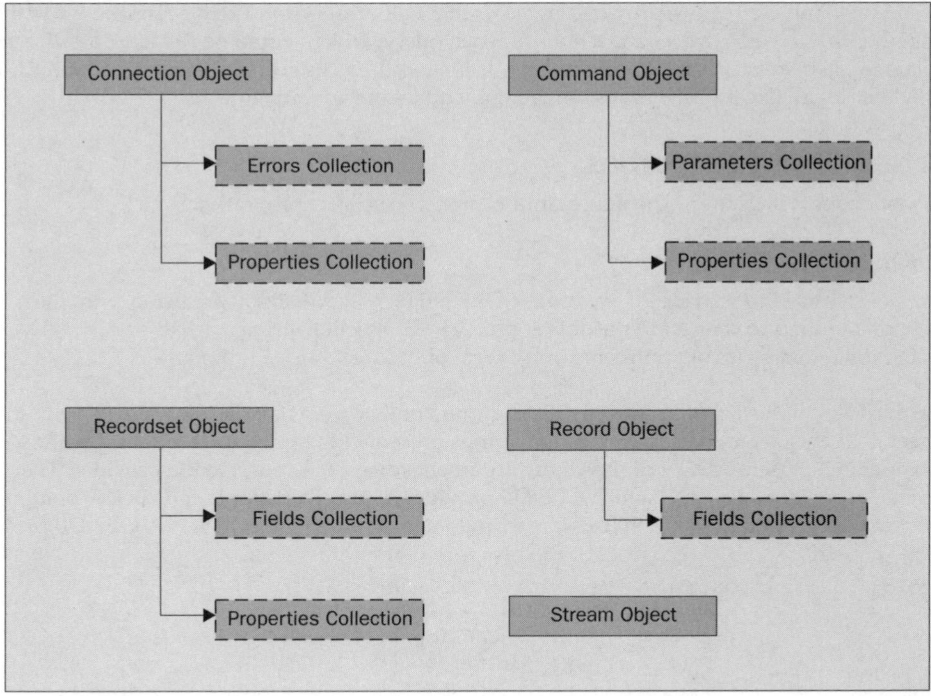

The next three sections will provide an introduction to each of the top-level ADO objects that we'll be using in this chapter. These sections will provide general information that will be applicable whenever you are using ADO. Specific examples of how to use ADO to accomplish a number of the most common data access tasks you'll encounter in Excel VBA will be covered in the sections that follow.

This is not intended to be an exhaustive reference to ADO. I will only be covering those items whose use will be demonstrated in this chapter, or which I consider particularly important to point out. ADO frequently provides you the flexibility to make the same setting in multiple ways, as both an object property and an argument to a method for instance. In these cases I will usually only cover the method I intend to demonstrate in the example sections.

The Connection Object

The `Connection` object is what provides the pipeline between your application and the data source you want to access. Like the other top-level ADO objects, the `Connection` object is extremely flexible. In some cases this may be the only object you need to use. Simple commands can easily be executed directly through a `Connection` object. In other cases you may not need to create a `Connection` object at all. The `Command` and `Recordset` objects can create a `Connection` object automatically if they need one.

Constructing and tearing down a data source connection can be a time-consuming process. If you will be executing multiple SQL statements over the course of your application you should create a publicly scoped `Connection` object variable and use it for each query. This allows you to take advantage of **connection pooling**.

Connection pooling is a feature provided by ADO that will preserve and reuse connections to the data source rather than creating new connections for each query, which would be a waste of resources. Connections can be reused for different queries as long as their connection strings are identical. This is typically the case in Excel applications so I recommend taking advantage of it.

Connection Object Properties

In this section we will examine the important `Connection` object properties.

The ConnectionString Property

This property is used to provide ADO, and the OLE DB provider that you are using, with the information required to connect to the data source. The connection string consists of a semicolon-delimited series of arguments in the form of `"name=value;"` pairs.

For the purposes of this chapter, the only ADO argument that we will be using is the `Provider` argument. All other arguments in connection strings presented in this chapter will be specific to the OLE DB provider being used. ADO will pass these arguments directly through to the provider. The `Provider` argument tells ADO which OLE DB provider to use. The sample code below demonstrates how to create a connection string to the Northwind database using the SQL Server OLE DB provider:

```
objConn.ConnectionString = "Provider=SQLOLEDB;" & _
                           "Data Source=SERVER1;" & _
                           "Initial Catalog=Northwind;" & _
                           "User Id=DemoUser;" & _
                           "Password=Password"
```

The only argument specific to ADO in this string is the `Provider` argument. All other arguments are passed directly through to the SQL Server OLE DB provider. If a different provider were being used, the arguments would be different as well. We will see this when we begin to connect to various data sources in the example sections. The `Provider` argument to the connection string is optional. If no provider is specified, ADO uses the OLE DB provider for ODBC by default.

The ConnectionTimeout Property

This property specifies how many seconds ADO will wait for a connection to complete before canceling the attempt and raising an error. The default value is 15 seconds. If you have a situation where connections normally take a long time to complete, you can increase this number so that ADO doesn't terminate the connection attempt prematurely. The following code sample changes the timeout value on the connection to 30 seconds:

```
objConn.ConnectionTimeout = 30
```

The State Property

The `State` property allows you to determine whether a connection is open, closed, connecting, or executing a command. The value will be a bit mask containing one or more of the following `ObjectStateEnum` constants:

- `AdStateClosed`
  Means the connection is closed
- `AdStateOpen`
  Means the connection is open

- `AdStateConnecting`
  Means the object is in the process of making a connection
- `AdStateExecuting`
  Means the connection is executing a command

If you attempt to close a `Connection` object that is already closed you will cause an error. You can prevent this from occurring by testing the state of the `Connection` object before closing it:

```
If CBool(objConn.State And adStateOpen) Then objConn.Close
```

Connection Object Methods

We will now look at the `Connection` object's more important methods, all of which have self-explanatory names.

The Open Method

This method opens a connection to the data source, and has the following syntax:

```
connection.Open ConnectionString, UserID, Password, Options
```

The `ConnectionString` argument serves the same purpose as the `ConnectionString` property we discussed above. ADO allows you to set this property in advance or pass it in at the time you open the connection. The `UserID` and `Password` arguments can be passed separately from the connection string if you wish.

The `Options` argument is particularly interesting. This argument allows you to make your connection **asynchronously**. That is, you can tell your `Connection` object to go off and open the connection in the background while your code continues to run. You do this by setting the `Options` argument to the `ConnectOptionEnum` value `adAsyncConnect`. The following code sample demonstrates making an asynchronous connection:

```
objConn.Open Options:=adAsyncConnect
```

This is especially useful in situations where you have lengthy connection times because it allows you to connect without freezing your application during the connection process.

The Execute Method

This method executes the command text provided to its `CommandText` argument. The `Execute` method has the following syntax for an action query (one that does not return a result set):

```
connection.Execute CommandText, [RecordsAffected], [Options]
```

And for a select query:

```
Set Recordset = connection.Execute(CommandText, _
                                   [RecordsAffected], [Options])
```

The `CommandText` argument can contain any executable string recognized by the OLE DB provider. However, it will most commonly contain a SQL statement. The optional `RecordsAffected` argument is a return value that tells you how many records the `CommandText` operation affected. It's a good idea to check this value against the number of records that you expected to be affected so that you can detect potential errors in your command text.

The `Options` argument is crucial to optimizing the execution efficiency of your command. Therefore, you should always use it even though it's nominally optional. The `Options` argument allows you to relay two different types of information to your OLE DB provider: what type of command is contained in the `CommandText` argument and how the provider should execute the contents of the `CommandText` argument.

In order to execute the `CommandText`, the OLE DB provider must know what type of command it contains. If you don't specify the type, the provider will have to determine that information for itself. This will slow down the execution of your query. You can avoid this by specifying the `CommandText` type using one of the following `CommandTypeEnum` values:

- `AdCmdText`
  The `CommandText` is a raw SQL string.
- `AdCmdTable`
  The `CommandText` is the name of a table. This sends an internally generated SQL statement to the provider that looks something like "`SELECT * FROM table_name`".
- `AdCmdStoredProc`
  The `CommandText` is the name of a stored procedure (we'll cover stored procedures in the section on SQL Server).
- `AdCmdTableDirect`
  The `CommandText` is the name of a table. However, unlike `adCmdTable`, this option does not generate a SQL statement and therefore returns the contents of the table more efficiently. Use this option if your provider supports it.

You can provide specific execution instructions to the provider by including one or more of the `ExecuteOptionEnum` constants:

- `AdAsyncExecute`
  Tells the provider to execute the command asynchronously, which returns execution to your code immediately.
- `AdExecuteNoRecords`
  Tells the provider not to construct a `Recordset` object. ADO will always construct a recordset in response to a command, even if your `CommandText` argument is not a row-returning query. In order to avoid the overhead required to create an unnecessary recordset, use this value in the `Options` argument whenever you execute a non-row-returning query.

The `CommandTypeEnum` and `ExecuteOptionEnum` values are bit masks that can be combined together in the `Options` argument using the logical `Or` operator. For example, to execute a plain text SQL command and tell ADO not to construct a `Recordset` object you would use the following syntax:

```
szSQL = "DELETE FROM Customers WHERE CustomerID = 'XXXX'"
objConn.Execute szSQL, lNumAffected, adCmdText Or adExecuteNoRecords
If lNumAffected <> 1 Then MsgBox "Error executing SQL statement."
```

The Close Method

This method closes the connection to the data source. Simply closing the connection does not destroy the `Connection` object. In order to destroy the `Connection` object and free its memory you need to set the `Connection` object variable to `Nothing`. For example, to ensure that a `Connection` object variable is closed and removed from memory you would execute the following code:

```
If CBool(objConn.State And adStateOpen) Then objConn.Close
Set objConn = Nothing
```

Connection Object Events

`Connection` object events must be trapped by creating a `WithEvents Connection` object variable in a class module. Trapping these events is necessary whenever you are using a `Connection` object asynchronously, since these events are what notify your application that the `Connection` object has completed its task.

Covering asynchronous connections is beyond the scope of this chapter. However, they are important enough to deserve mention so that you can pursue them further using one of the references mentioned at the beginning of the chapter if you like. The two most commonly used `Connection` object events are:

- `ConnectComplete`
  Triggered when an asynchronous connection has completed. You can examine the arguments passed to this event to determine if the connection was successful or not.
- `ExecuteComplete`
  Triggered when an asynchronous command has finished executing.

Connection Object Collections

The Connection Object has two collections, `Errors` and `Properties`.

Errors Collection

This collection contains a set of `Error` objects, each of which represents an OLE DB provider-specific error (ADO itself generates run-time errors). The `Errors` collection can contain not only errors, but also warnings and even messages (generated by the T-SQL `PRINT` statement, for instance). The `Errors` collection is very helpful in providing extra detail when something in your ADO code has malfunctioned. When debugging ADO problems, you can dump the contents of the `Errors` collection to the Immediate window with the following code:

```
For Each objError In objConn.Errors
    Debug.Print objError.Description
Next objError
```

The Properties Collection

This collection contains provider-specific, or **extended properties**, for the `Connection` object. Some providers add important settings that you will want to be aware of. Extended properties are beyond the scope of this chapter. You can find more information about them by consulting one of the ADO references mentioned above.

The Recordset Object

Just as the most commonly used SQL statement is the `SELECT` statement, the most commonly used ADO object is the `Recordset` object. The `Recordset` object serves as a container for the records and fields returned from a `SELECT` statement executed against a data source.

Recordset Object Properties

We will start our examination of the `Recordset` object by looking at its important properties.

The ActiveConnection Property

Prior to opening the Recordset object, you can use the ActiveConnection property to assign an existing Connection object to the Recordset or a connection string for the recordset to use to connect to the database. If you assign a connection string, the recordset will create a Connection object for itself. Once the recordset has been opened this property returns an object reference to the Connection object being used by the recordset.

The following code assigns a Connection object to the ActiveConnection property:

```
Set rsData.ActiveConnection = objConn
```

The following code assigns a connection string to the ActiveConnection property:

```
rsData.ActiveConnection = "Provider=SQLOLEDB;" & _
                          "Data Source=SERVER1;" & _
                          "Initial Catalog=Northwind;" & _
                          "User Id=DemoUser;" & _
                          "Password=Password"
```

The BOF and EOF Properties

These properties indicate whether the record pointer of the Recordset object is positioned before the first record in the recordset (BOF, or beginning of file) or after the last record in the recordset (EOF, or end of file). If the recordset is empty, both BOF and EOF will be True. The following code example demonstrates using these properties to determine if there is data in a recordset:

```
If Not rsData.EOF Then
    ' The Recordset contains data.
Else
    ' The Recordset is empty.
End If
```

Note that there is a difference between an empty recordset and a closed recordset. If you execute a query that returns no data, ADO will present you with a perfectly valid open recordset, but one that contains no data. Therefore, you should always verify that a recordset contains data using the method shown above prior to any attempt to access that data. Attempting to access data from an empty recordset will cause a run-time error.

The CursorLocation Property

This property allows you to specify whether the server-side cursor engine or the client-side cursor engine manages the records in the recordset. A cursor is the underlying object that manages the data in the recordset. Certain operations require the cursor engine to be on one side or the other. We'll explore this in more detail in the examples section.

This property must be set before the recordset is opened. If you do not specify a cursor location, the default is server side. You can set this property to one of the two CursorLocationEnum values, either adUseClient or adUseServer. The following code sample demonstrates setting the cursor location to client-side:

```
rsData.CursorLocation = adUseClient
```

The Filter Property

This property allows you to filter an open recordset so that only records that meet the specified condition are visible. The records that cannot be seen are not deleted, removed, or changed in any way, but are simply hidden from normal recordset operations. This property can be set to a string that specifies the condition you want to place on the records, or to one of the `FilterGroupEnum` constants.

You can set multiple filters, and the records exposed by the filtered recordset will be only those records that meet all of the conditions. To remove the filter from the recordset, set the `Filter` property to an empty string or the `adFilterNone` constant. The following code sample demonstrates filtering a recordset so that it displays only company names that begin with the letter B. Note that the use of wildcards is supported in a filter string:

```
rsData.Filter = "CompanyName LIKE 'B*'"
```

You can use the logical `AND`, `OR`, and `NOT` operators to set additional `Filter` property values:

```
rsData.Filter = "CompanyName LIKE 'B*' AND Country = 'UK'"
```

The State Property

This is the same as the `State` property discussed above in the section on the `Connection` object.

Recordset Object Methods

We will only be examining five of the `Recordset` object's methods, as they are the ones that you are most likely to use.

The Open Method

This method opens the `Recordset` object and retrieves the data specified by the `Source` argument. The `Open` method has the following syntax:

```
recordset.Open Source, ActiveConnection, CursorType, LockType, Options
```

The `Source` argument tells the recordset what data it should retrieve. This is most commonly a SQL string or the name of a stored procedure, but can also be the name of a table or a `Command` object.

The `ActiveConnection` argument can be a connection string or a `Connection` object that identifies the connection to be used. If you assign a connection string to the `ActiveConnection` argument, the recordset will create a `Connection` object for itself.

The `CursorType` argument specifies the type of cursor to use when opening the recordset. This is set using one of the `CursorTypeEnum` values. In this chapter we will only use the following two cursor types: `adOpenForwardOnly` and `adOpenStatic`. The first type will be used for normal queries and means that the recordset can only be navigated in one direction, from beginning to end, and is the fastest method for accessing data. Note that the data in a forward-only recordset cannot be modified. The second type will be used for disconnected recordsets and allows complete navigation. If you do not specify a cursor type, `adOpenForwardOnly` is the default.

The LockType argument specifies what type of locks the provider should place on the underlying data source when opening the recordset. This is set using one of the LockTypeEnum values. In this chapter we will only use the following two lock types, corresponding to normal and disconnected recordsets, respectively: adLockReadOnly and adLockBatchOptimistic.

The Options argument here is the same as the Options argument we covered in the Connection object's Execute method earlier in the chapter. It is used to tell the provider how to interpret and execute the contents of the Source argument.

The Close Method

This method closes the Recordset object. This does not free any memory used by the recordset. To free up the memory used by the Recordset object you must set the Recordset object variable to Nothing.

The Move Methods

When a recordset is first opened the **current record pointer** is positioned on the first record in the recordset. The Move methods are used to navigate through the records in an open recordset. They do this by repositioning the Recordset object's current record pointer. We'll be using the following move methods in this chapter:

- MoveFirst
  Positions the current record pointer on the first record of the recordset. This method will only be used with disconnected recordsets.
- MoveNext
  Positions the current record pointer to the next record in the recordset. This is the only Move method that can be used on a forward-only Recordset object.

The code sample below demonstrates common recordset navigation handling:

```
' Verify that the Recordset contains data.
If Not rsData.EOF Then
    ' Loop until we reach the end of the Recordset.
    Do While Not rsData.EOF
        ' Perform some action on the current record's data.
        Debug.Print rsData.Fields(0).Value
        ' Move to the next record.
        rsData.MoveNext
    Loop
Else
    MsgBox "Error, no records returned.", vbCritical
End If
```

Pay particular attention to the use of the MoveNext method within the Do While loop. Omitting this is a very common error and will lead to an endless loop condition in your code. The very first line of code that you should place in the Do While loop is the call to MoveNext.

The NextRecordset Method

Some providers allow you to execute commands that return multiple recordsets. The NextRecordset method is used to move through these recordsets. The NextRecordset method clears the current recordset from the Recordset object, loads the next recordset into the Recordset object, and sets the current record pointer to the first record in that recordset. If the NextRecordset method is called and there are no more recordsets to retrieve, the Recordset object is set to Nothing. The following code sample demonstrates the use of the NextRecordset method:

```
' Verify that the Recordset contains more data.
Do While Not rsData Is Nothing
    ' Loop the records in the current recordset.
    Do While Not rsData.EOF
        ' Perform some action on the current record's data.
        Debug.Print rsData.Fields(0).Value
        ' Move to the next record.
        rsData.MoveNext
    Loop
    ' Return the next recordset
    Set rsData = rsData.NextRecordset
Loop
```

Recordset Object Events

`Recordset` object events must be trapped by creating a `WithEvents Recordset` object variable in a class module. Trapping these events is necessary whenever you are using a `Recordset` object asynchronously, since these events are what notify your application that the `Recordset` object has completed its task.

Covering asynchronous recordset usage is beyond the scope of this chapter, however, the topic is important enough to deserve mention so that you can pursue it further using one of the references mentioned at the beginning of this chapter if you like. The two most commonly used `Recordset` object events are:

- `FetchComplete`
  This event is fired after all of the records have been retrieved when opening an asynchronous recordset.
- `FetchProgress`
  The provider fires this event periodically to report the number of records retrieved so far during an asynchronous open operation. It is typically used to provide a visual progress indicator to the user.

Recordset Object Collections

We will finish our look at the `Recordset` object by examining its collections.

The Fields Collection

The `Fields` collection contains the values, and information about those values, from the current record in a `Recordset` object. In Excel, the `Fields` collection is most commonly used to return the column names of each field in the recordset prior to accessing the contents of the recordset using the `CopyFromRecordset` method of the `Range` object. The following example demonstrates how to read the field names from the `Fields` collection of a `Recordset` object:

```
    With Sheet1.Range("A1")
        For Each objField In rsData.Fields
            .Offset(0, lOffset).Value = objField.Name
            lOffset = lOffset + 1
        Next objField
    End With
```

The Properties Collection

This collection contains provider-specific, or extended properties, for the `Recordset` object. Some providers add important settings that you will want to be aware of. We will cover each provider's extended properties in the section where we cover that provider. Extended properties are beyond the scope of this chapter. You can find more information about them by consulting one of the ADO references mentioned above.

The Command Object

The `Command` object is most commonly used for executing action queries. Action queries are queries that perform some action on the data source and do not return a resultset. Action queries include `INSERT`, `UPDATE`, and `DELETE` statements.

Command Object Properties

We will begin my looking at the three most important `Command` object properties.

The ActiveConnection Property

This property is identical to the `ActiveConnection` property discussed in the section on the `Recordset` object above.

The CommandText Property

This property is used to set the command that will be executed by the data provider. This property will normally be a SQL string or the name of a stored procedure. As we will see in the section on SQL Server, you must use the `CommandText` property along with the `Parameters` collection in order to take advantage of return values and output parameters in SQL Server stored procedures.

The CommandType Property

The `CommandType` property is identical to the `Options` argument to the `Connection` object's `Execute` method that we covered earlier in the chapter. It is used to tell the provider how to interpret and execute the `Command` object's `CommandText`.

Command Object Methods

We will only look at two of the `Command` object's methods, as they are the most commonly used.

The CreateParameter Method

This method is used to manually create `Parameter` objects that can then be added to the `Command` object's `Parameters` collection. The `CreateParameter` object has the following syntax:

```
Set Parameter = command.CreateParameter([Name], [Type], [Direction], _
                                        [Size], [Value])
```

`Name` is the name of the parameter object. You can use this name to reference the `Parameter` object through the `Command` object's `Parameters` collection. When working with SQL Server, the name of a `Parameter` should be the same as the name of the stored procedure argument that it corresponds to.

`Type` indicates the data type of the parameter. It is specified as one of the `DataTypeEnum` constants. There are several dozen possible data types, so I will not go into them in any detail here. We will see a few of them in the examples section. The rest can be located in the ADO help file.

`Direction` is a `ParameterDirectionEnum` value that indicates whether the parameter will be used to pass data to an input argument, receive data from an output argument, or accept a return value from a stored procedure. Direction can be one of the following values:

- `AdParamInput`
  The parameter represents an input argument
- `adParamInputOutput`
  The parameter represents an input/output argument
- `adParamOutput`
  The parameter represents an output argument
- `adParamReturnValue`
  The parameter represents a return value

`Size` is used to specify the size of `Parameter` in bytes, and is dependent on `Parameter`'s data type.

`Value` is used to provide an initial value for the `Parameter`.

The code sample below demonstrates how you can use the `CreateParameter` method in conjunction with the `Parameters` collection `Append` method to create a `Parameter` and append it to the `Parameters` collection with one line of code:

```
objCmd.Parameters.Append _
    objCmd.CreateParameter("MyParam", adInteger, adParamInput, 0)
```

The Execute Method

This method executes the command text in the `Command` object's `CommandText` property. The `Execute` method has the following syntax for an action query (one that does not return a resultset):

```
command.Execute [RecordsAffected], [Parameters], [Options]
```

And for a select query:

```
Set Recordset = command.Execute([RecordsAffected], [Parameters], [Options])
```

The `RecordsAffected` and `Options` arguments are identical to the corresponding arguments for the `Connection` object's `Execute` method described in the *Connection Object Methods* section above. If you are executing a SQL statement that requires one or more parameters to be passed, you can supply an array of values to the `Parameters` argument, one for each parameter required.

Command Object Collections

Our final section before we look at ADO in Excel will cover the `Command` object's two collections.

The Parameters Collection

This collection contains all of the `Parameter` objects associated with the `Command` object. Parameters are used to pass arguments to SQL statements and stored procedures as well as to receive output and return values from stored procedures.

The Properties Collection

This collection contains provider-specific or extended properties for the `Command` object. Some providers add important settings that you will want to be aware of. We will cover each provider's extended properties in the section where we cover that provider. Extended properties are beyond the scope of this chapter. You can find more information about them by consulting one of the ADO references mentioned above.

Using ADO in Microsoft Excel Applications

Here's where it all comes together. In this section we will combine the understanding of Excel programming that you've gained from previous chapters along with the SQL and ADO techniques discussed above. Excel applications frequently require data from outside sources. The most common of these sources are Access and SQL Server databases. However, I've created applications that required source data from mainframe text file dumps and even Excel workbooks. As we'll see, ADO makes acquiring data from these various data sources easy.

> **In the next two sections we'll be utilizing the Northwind database. This is a sample database that is provided with both Access and SQL Server. If you don't have this database available you will need to install it to run the example code.**

To run the code examples that are shown in the sections that follow, you must have a set a reference from your Excel project to the **ADO 2.5 Object Library**. To do this, select the Tools | References menu item from within the VBE. This will bring up the References dialog. Scroll down until you locate the entry labeled Microsoft ActiveX Data Objects 2.5 Library. Place a checkmark beside this entry and click OK:

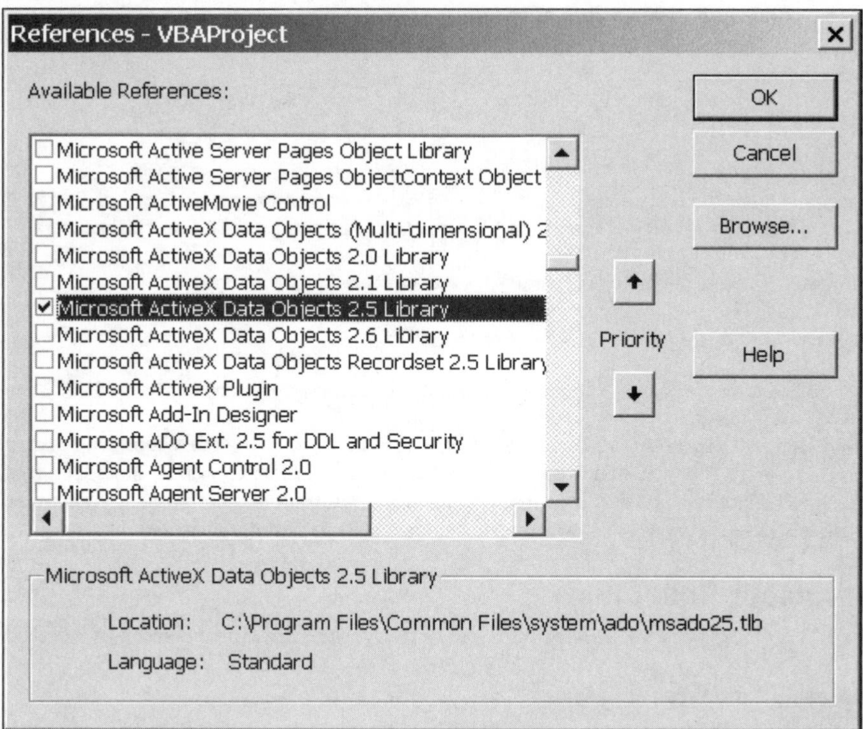

Note that it's perfectly normal to have multiple versions of the ADO object library available.

Using ADO with Microsoft Access

Since Excel applications that utilize data from Microsoft Access tend to have less complicated data access requirements than those using SQL Server, we'll use Access to introduce the basics of ADO.

Connecting to Microsoft Access

ADO connects to Microsoft Access databases through the use of the OLE DB provider for Microsoft Jet (Jet refers to the database engine used by Access). We will be using version 4.0 of this provider. To connect to a Microsoft Access database, you simply specify this provider in the ADO connection string and then include any additional provider-specific arguments required. The following is a summary of the connection string arguments you will most frequently use when connecting to an Access database:

- `Provider=Microsoft.Jet.OLEDB.4.0` (required)
- `Data Source=[full path and filename to the Access database]` (required)
- `Mode=mode` (optional)
  The three most commonly used settings for this property are:
  - `adModeShareDenyNone`
    Opens the database and allows complete shared access to other users. This is the default setting if the `Mode` argument is not specified.
  - `adModeShareDenyWrite`
    Opens the database and allows other users read access but prevents write access.
  - `adModeShareExclusive`
    Opens the database in exclusive mode, which prevents any other users from connecting to the database.
- `User ID=username` (optional)
  The username to use when connecting to the database. If the database requires a username and it is not supplied then the connection will fail.
- `Password=password` (optional)
  If a password is required to connect to the database, this argument is used to supply it. Again the connection will fail if it is required and not supplied or is incorrect.

The following example shows a connection string using all of the arguments discussed above:

```
Public Const gszCONNECTION As String = _
    "Provider=Microsoft.Jet.OLEDB.4.0;" & _
    "Data Source=C:\Files\Northwind.mdb;" & _
    "Mode=Share Exclusive;" & _
    "User ID=Admin;" & _
    "Password=password"
```

Retrieving Data from Microsoft Access Using a Plain Text Query

The following procedure demonstrates how to retrieve data from a Microsoft Access database using a plain text (sometimes referred to as ad hoc) query and place it on an Excel worksheet:

```
Public Sub PlainTextQuery()

    Dim rsData As ADODB.Recordset
    Dim szConnect As String
    Dim szSQL As String

    ' Create the connection string.
    szConnect = "Provider=Microsoft.Jet.OLEDB.4.0;" & _
                "Data Source=C:\Files\Northwind.mdb;"

    ' Create the SQL Statement.
    szSQL = "SELECT CompanyName, ContactName " & _
```

```
            "FROM Customers " & _
            "WHERE Country = 'UK' " & _
            "ORDER BY CompanyName"

    ' Create the Recordset object and run the query.
    Set rsData = New ADODB.Recordset
    rsData.Open szSQL, szConnect, adOpenForwardOnly, _
            adLockReadOnly, adCmdText

    ' Make sure we got records back
    If Not rsData.EOF Then
        ' Dump the contents of the recordset onto the worksheet.
        Sheet1.Range("A2").CopyFromRecordset rsData
        ' Close the recordset
        rsData.Close
        ' Add headers to the worksheet.
        With Sheet1.Range("A1:B1")
            .Value = Array("Company Name", "Contact Name")
            .Font.Bold = True
        End With
        ' Fit the column widths to the data.
        Sheet1.UsedRange.EntireColumn.AutoFit
    Else
        MsgBox "Error: No records returned.", vbCritical
    End If

    ' Close the recordset if it is still open.
    If CBool(rsData.State And adStateOpen) Then rsData.Close
    Set rsData = Nothing

End Sub
```

There are a number of things to note about this procedure:

- The only ADO object used was the `Recordset` object. As mentioned at the beginning of the ADO section, all of the top-level ADO objects can be created and used independently. If we were going to perform multiple queries over the course of our application we would have created a separate, publicly scoped `Connection` object in order to take advantage of ADO's connection-pooling feature.
- The syntax of the `Recordset.Open` method has been optimized for maximum performance. We've told the provider what type of command is in the `Source` argument (`adCmdText`, a plain text query) and we've opened a forward-only, read-only, server-side cursor (server-side is the default if the `Recordset.CursorLocation` property is not specified). This type of cursor is often referred to as a **firehose cursor**, because it's the fastest way to retrieve data from a database.
- We do not make any modifications to the destination worksheet until we are sure we have successfully retrieved data from the database. This avoids having to undo anything if the query fails.
- We dump the data onto the destination worksheet and close the recordset as quickly as possible. In most data-access situations you will be dealing with a multi-user environment. This is one where multiple users can access the database simultaneously. Getting in and out of the database as quickly as possible is critical to preventing contention problems, situations in which two users attempt to perform mutually incompatible actions on the same piece of data at the same time.
- Note the use of the `CopyFromRecordset` method of the Excel `Range` object. This is by far the fastest method for moving data out of a recordset and onto a worksheet. As we'll see, it doesn't fit every data-access situation, but it's the method of choice in any situation where its use is possible. Note that the `CopyFromRecordset` method does not copy the field names, only the data.

Retrieving Data from Microsoft Access Using a Stored Query

Microsoft Access allows you to create and store SQL queries in the database. You can retrieve data from these stored queries just as easily as you can use a plain text SQL statement. The procedure below demonstrates this:

```
Public Sub SavedQuery()

    Dim objField As ADODB.Field
    Dim rsData As ADODB.Recordset
    Dim lOffset As Long
    Dim szConnect As String

    ' Create the connection string.
    szConnect = "Provider=Microsoft.Jet.OLEDB.4.0;" & _
                "Data Source=C:\Files\Northwind.mdb;"

    ' Create the Recorset object and run the query.
    Set rsData = New ADODB.Recordset
    rsData.Open "[Sales By Category]", szConnect, adOpenForwardOnly, _
                adLockReadOnly, adCmdTable

    ' Make sure we got records back
    If Not rsData.EOF Then
        ' Add headers to the worksheet.
        With Sheet1.Range("A1")
            For Each objField In rsData.Fields
                .Offset(0, lOffset).Value = objField.Name
                lOffset = lOffset + 1
            Next objField
            .Resize(1, rsData.Fields.Count).Font.Bold = True
        End With
        ' Dump the contents of the recordset onto the worksheet.
        Sheet1.Range("A2").CopyFromRecordset rsData
        ' Fit the column widths to the data.
        Sheet1.UsedRange.EntireColumn.AutoFit
    Else
        MsgBox "Error: No records returned.", vbCritical
    End If

    ' Close the recordset
    rsData.Close
    Set rsData = Nothing

End Sub
```

There are two important points to note about this procedure:

- Examine the differences between the `Recordset.Open` method used in this procedure and the one used in the plain text query. In this case, rather than providing a SQL string we specified the name of the stored query that we wanted to execute. We also told the provider that the type of query being executed was a table query. The Jet OLEDB provider treats stored queries and queries of entire database tables in the same manner.
- Since we did not create the SQL statement ourselves, we did not know the names of the fields we were retrieving, or even how many fields there were. Therefore, in order to create the correct set of headers for each column in the destination worksheet we needed to loop the `Fields` collection of the `Recordset` object and determine this information dynamically. In order to accomplish this, the recordset had to be open, so we added the fields to the worksheet prior to closing the recordset in this case.

Inserting, Updating, and Deleting Records with Plain Text SQL in Microsoft Access

Executing plain text INSERT, UPDATE, and DELETE statements uses virtually identical methodology. Therefore, we'll examine these action queries by inserting a new record, updating that record, and then deleting it, all within the same procedure. This, of course, is not normally something you would do. You can take this generic procedure, however, and create a single purpose insert, update, or delete procedure by simply removing the sections that you don't need.

We're going to use the Shippers table from the Northwind database in the next procedure. The original contents of this table are shown in the screenshot below. There are two things that you'll want to keep in mind before we begin to alter this table.

First, you'll notice that the column headings in the table are slightly different from the field names that we'll use in our SQL statements. This is because Access allows you to assign a Caption property to each field in a table, which is then displayed instead of the underlying field name. However, you must use the underlying field name in SQL statements.

Second, notice that the last row in the Shipper ID column contains the value "(AutoNumber)". This isn't really a value; rather it's a prompt that alerts you to the fact that values for the Shipper ID column are automatically generated by the Jet database engine. This column is the primary key for the Shippers table and AutoNumber fields are a common method used to generate the unique value required for the primary key. As you'll see below, you don't (and can't), set or change the value of an AutoNumber field. If you need to maintain a reference to a new record that you've inserted into the table, you'll need to retrieve the value that was assigned to that record by the AutoNumber field. We'll show how this is done in the example that follows:

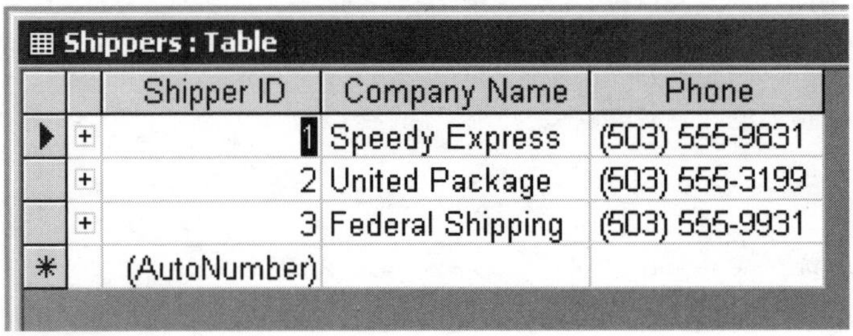

Shippers : Table

		Shipper ID	Company Name	Phone
▶	+	1	Speedy Express	(503) 555-9831
	+	2	United Package	(503) 555-3199
	+	3	Federal Shipping	(503) 555-9931
*		(AutoNumber)		

```
Public Sub InsertUpdateDelete()

    Dim objCommand As ADODB.Command
    Dim rsData As ADODB.Recordset
    Dim lRecordsAffected As Long
    Dim lKey As Long
    Dim szConnect As String

    On Error GoTo ErrorHandler

    ' Create the connection string.
    szConnect = "Provider=Microsoft.Jet.OLEDB.4.0;" & _
                "Data Source=C:\Files\Northwind.mdb;" & _
                "Mode=Share Exclusive"

    ' Create the Command object we'll use for all three queries.
    Set objCommand = New ADODB.Command
```

```
    objCommand.ActiveConnection = szConnect

    '**** INSERT a new record into the database **************
    ' Load the SQL string into the Command object.
    objCommand.CommandText = "INSERT INTO Shippers(CompanyName, Phone) " & _
                             "VALUES('Air Carriers', '(205) 555-1212');"
    ' Execute the SQL statement.
    objCommand.Execute RecordsAffected:=lRecordsAffected, _
                       Options:=adCmdText Or adExecuteNoRecords
    ' Check for errors. Only one record should have been affected.
    If lRecordsAffected <> 1 Then Err.Raise Number:=vbObjectError + 1024, _
          Description:="Error executing INSERT statement."

    ' Retrieve the primary key generated for our new record.
    objCommand.CommandText = "SELECT @@IDENTITY;"
    Set rsData = objCommand.Execute(Options:=adCmdText)
    ' Check for errors. The recordset should contain data.
    If rsData.EOF Then Err.Raise Number:=vbObjectError + 1024, _
          Description:="Error retrieving primary key value."
    ' Store the primary key value for later use.
    lKey = rsData.Fields(0).Value
    rsData.Close

    '**** UPDATE the record we just created *****************
    ' Load the SQL string into the Command object.
    objCommand.CommandText = "UPDATE Shippers " & _
                             "SET Phone='(206) 546-0086' " & _
                             "WHERE ShipperID=" & CStr(lKey) & ";"
    ' Execute the SQL statement.
    objCommand.Execute RecordsAffected:=lRecordsAffected, _
                       Options:=adCmdText Or adExecuteNoRecords
    ' Check for errors. Only one record should have been affected.
    If lRecordsAffected <> 1 Then Err.Raise Number:=vbObjectError + 1024, _
          Description:="Error executing UPDATE statement."

    '**** DELETE our record from the database ***************
    ' Load the SQL string into the Command object.
    objCommand.CommandText = "DELETE FROM Shippers " & _
                             "WHERE ShipperID = " & CStr(lKey) & ";"
    ' Execute the SQL statement.
    objCommand.Execute RecordsAffected:=lRecordsAffected, _
                       Options:=adCmdText Or adExecuteNoRecords
    ' Check for errors. Only one record should have been affected.
    If lRecordsAffected <> 1 Then Err.Raise Number:=vbObjectError + 1024, _
        Description:="Error executing DELETE statement."

ErrorExit:

    ' Destroy our ADO objects.
    Set objCommand = Nothing
    Set rsData = Nothing
    Exit Sub

ErrorHandler:
    MsgBox Err.Description, vbCritical
    Resume ErrorExit
End Sub
```

Let's quickly review what we've done in the procedure above. First we inserted a new record into the `Shippers` table. Then we retrieved the primary key that had been assigned to that new record by the database (more on this in a moment). Next we used the primary key of our new record to locate it and modify the telephone number in its `Phone` field. Finally, we used the primary key of our record to locate it and delete it from the database.

Important things to note about the procedure above include:

- We used the same ADO `Command` object throughout the procedure. All that was required to execute different commands was to load new SQL statements into the `Command.CommandText` property.
- The process of preparing and executing the command and then checking for errors upon completion was identical for all three types of action query, save for the specific SQL statement used.
- After inserting our new record in the first part of the procedure, we needed to retrieve the primary key value that had been assigned to that record in the Shipper ID AutoNumber field. We did this by querying the value of the `@@IDENTITY` system variable. This is a variable maintained by the Jet database that holds the value of the most recently assigned AutoNumber field. In most cases, you must be sure to query this value immediately after performing the insert. The `@@IDENTITY` variable is a database-wide variable, so your primary key value will be overwritten if any other user performs a similar insert before you query it. We have prevented the possibility of this occurring in the case of the procedure above by opening the database in exclusive mode (note the `Mode` argument in the connection string).

> **Note: `@@IDENTITY` will only work with Access databases that are saved in Access 2000 format or above. It does not work with Access 97.**

Using ADO with Microsoft SQL Server

In the previous section on Microsoft Access, we covered the basics of performing the various types of queried in ADO. Since ADO is designed to present a common gateway to different data sources, there isn't a lot of difference in these basic operations whether your database is in Access or in SQL Server. Therefore, after a brief introduction to the few important differences that arise when using ADO with SQL Server, in this section we'll cover more advanced topics, including stored procedures, multiple recordsets, and disconnected recordsets. We won't be going into a lot of detail on how to use SQL Server itself, as that is beyond the scope of this chapter. If you'd like to learn more about SQL Server, one of the best references available is Robert Vieira's *Professional SQL Server 2000* from Wrox press ISBN 1-861004-48-6.

Connecting to Microsoft SQL Server

To connect to a Microsoft SQL Server database, you simply specify the OLE DB provider for SQL Server in the ADO connection string, and then include any additional provider-specific arguments required. The following is a summary of the connection string arguments you will most frequently use when connecting to a SQL Server database:

- `Provider=SQLOLEDB;`
- `Data Source=server name;`
  In the case of SQL Server 7.0, this will almost always be the NetBIOS name of the computer that SQL Server is installed on. SQL Server 2000 added the ability to install multiple SQL Servers on one machine, so the server name will have the following syntax: `NetBIOS name\SQL Server name`. If SQL Server is installed on the same machine as your spreadsheet you can use the name `localhost`.

- `Initial Catalog=database name;`
  Unlike Access, one instance of SQL Server can contain many databases. This argument will be the name of the database you want to connect to.
- `User ID=username;`
  The username for SQL Server authentication.
- `Password=password;`
  The password for SQL Server authentication.
- `Network Library=netlib;`
  By default, the SQL Server OLE DB provider will attempt to use **named pipes network protocol** to connect to SQL Server. This is required for using Windows integrated security (explained below). There are many instances, however, where it is not possible to use named pipes. These include accessing SQL Server from a Windows 9x operating system and accessing SQL Server over the Internet. In these cases, the preferred protocol for connecting to SQL Server is TCP/IP. This can be specified on each machine by using the SQL Server Client Network Utility, or you can simply use the Network Library connection string argument to specify the name of the TCP/IP network library, which is `dbmssocn`.
- `Integrated Security=SSPI;`
  This connection string argument specifies that you want to use Windows integrated security rather than SQL Server authentication. The `User ID` and `Password` arguments will be ignored if this argument is present.

A Note About SQL Server Security

There are three types of security that SQL Server can be set to use: SQL Server authentication, Windows integrated security, and mixed mode. SQL Server authentication means that separate user accounts must be added to SQL Server and each user must supply a SQL Server username and password to connect.

This type of security is most commonly used when SQL Server must be accessed from outside the network. With Windows integrated security, SQL Server recognizes the same usernames and passwords that are used to log in to the Windows NT/2000 network. Mixed mode simply means you can use either one of the first two.

Below are examples of two different SQL Server connection strings. The first example shows a connection string that uses SQL Server authentication and the TCP/IP connection protocol. The second example shows a connection string that uses Windows integrated security and the named pipes connection protocol (or whatever protocol is specified by the SQL Server Client Network Utility):

```
Public Const gszCONNECTION As String = _
    "Provider=SQLOLEDB;" & _
    "Data Source=Dell500\Dell500;" & _
    "Initial Catalog=Northwind;" & _
    "User ID=User;Password=password;" & _
    "Network Library=dbmssocn"
```

```
Public Const gszCONNECTION As String = _
    "Provider=SQLOLEDB;" & _
    "Data Source=Dell500\Dell500;" & _
    "Initial Catalog=Northwind;" & _
    "Integrated Security=SSPI"
```

Microsoft SQL Server Stored Procedures

The syntax for executing plain text (or ad hoc) queries against SQL Server is identical to that which we used in the example for Access. The only difference is the contents of the connection string. When programming with SQL Server, however, it is more common to call SQL Server **stored procedures**.

Stored procedures are simply precompiled SQL statements that can be accessed by name from the database. They are much like VBA procedures in that they can accept arguments and return values. An example of a simple stored procedure that queries the `Customer` table is shown below:

```
CREATE PROC spGetCustomerNames
    @Country  nvarchar(24)
AS
    SELECT    CustomerID,
              CompanyName,
              ContactName
    FROM      Customers
    WHERE     Country = @Country
    ORDER BY  CompanyName
```

This stored procedure takes one argument, `@Country`, and returns a recordset containing the values for the fields specified in the `SELECT` list for customers whose country matches the value passed to the `@Country` argument.

ADO provides a very quick and simple way to execute stored procedures using the `Connection` object. ADO treats all stored procedures in the currently connected database as dynamic methods of the `Connection` object. You can call a stored procedure exactly like any other `Connection` object method, passing any arguments to the stored procedure as method arguments and optionally passing a `Recordset` object as the last argument if the stored procedure returns a result set.

This method is best used for "one off" procedures rather than those you will execute multiple times, since it isn't the most efficient method. However, it is significantly easier to code. The example below demonstrates executing the stored procedure shown above as a method of the `Connection` object:

```
Public Sub ExecuteStoredProcAsMethod()

    Dim objConn As ADODB.Connection
    Dim rsData As ADODB.Recordset
    Dim szConnect As String

    ' Create the connection string.
    szConnect = "Provider=SQLOLEDB;Data Source=Dell500\Dell500;" & _
                "Initial Catalog=Northwind;Integrated Security=SSPI"

    ' Create the Connection and Recordset objects.
    Set objConn = New ADODB.Connection
    Set rsData = New ADODB.Recordset

    ' Open the connection and execute the stored procedure.
    objConn.Open szConnect
    objConn.spGetCustomerNames "UK", rsData

    ' Make sure we got records back
    If Not rsData.EOF Then
        ' Dump the contents of the recordset onto the worksheet.
        Sheet1.Range("A1").CopyFromRecordset rsData
        ' Close the recordset
```

```
        rsData.Close
        ' Fit the column widths to the data.
        Sheet1.UsedRange.EntireColumn.AutoFit
    Else
        MsgBox "Error: No records returned.", vbCritical
   End If

    ' Clean up our ADO objects.
    If CBool(objConn.State And adStateOpen) Then objConn.Close
    Set objConn = Nothing
    If CBool(rsData.State And adStateOpen) Then rsData.Close
    Set rsData = Nothing

End Sub
```

In the procedure above, we executed our `spGetCustomerNames` stored procedure and passed it the value "UK" for its `@Country` argument. This populated the `rsData` recordset with all of the customers located in the UK. Note that the `Connection` object must be opened before the dynamic methods are populated and that you must instantiate the `Recordset` object prior to passing it as an argument.

The most efficient way to handle stored procedures that will be executed multiple times is to prepare a publicly scoped `Command` object to represent them. The `Connection` will be stored in the `Command` object's `ActiveConnection` property, the stored procedure name will be stored in the `Command` object's `CommandText` property, and any arguments to the stored procedure will be used to populate the `Command` object's `Parameters` collection.

Once this `Command` object has been created, it can be executed as many times as you like over the course of your application without incurring the overhead required to perform the tasks described above with each execution.

For this example, let's create a simple stored procedure that we can use to insert new records into our `Shippers` table:

```
CREATE PROC spInsertShippers
    @CompanyName  nvarchar(40),
    @Phone        nvarchar(24)
AS
    INSERT INTO Shippers(CompanyName, Phone)
    VALUES(@CompanyName, @Phone)
    RETURN @@IDENTITY
```

As you can see, the stored procedure above has two arguments, `@CompanyName` and `@Phone`, which are used to collect the values to insert into those respective fields in the `Shippers` table. However, as you may recall from our Access example, the `Shippers` table has three fields, and the stored procedure above doesn't reference the first field, Shipper ID, anywhere.

This is because, similar to the `ShipperID` field in the Access version of the Northwind database, the `ShipperID` field in the SQL Server version of Northwind is populated automatically by the database any time a new record is inserted. We also retrieve this automatically assigned value in a similar fashion; through the use of SQL Server's `@@IDENTITY` system function. In this case, however, we won't have to make a separate query to retrieve the Shipper ID value since it will be returned to us by the stored procedure.

In order to present a more realistic application scenario, the example below uses publicly scoped Connection and Command objects, procedures to create and destroy the connection, a procedure to prepare the Command object for use, and a procedure that demonstrates how to use the Command object:

```
Public Const gszCONNECTION As String = _
    "Provider=SQLOLEDB;Data Source=Dell500\Dell500;" & _
    "Initial Catalog=Northwind;Integrated Security=SSPI"

Public gobjCmd As ADODB.Command
Public gobjConn As ADODB.Connection

Private Sub CreateConnection()
    ' Create the Connection object.
    Set gobjConn = New ADODB.Connection
    gobjConn.Open gszCONNECTION
End Sub

Private Sub DestroyConnection()
    ' Check to see if connection is still open before attemping to close it.
    If CBool(gobjConn.State And adStateOpen) Then gobjConn.Close
    Set gobjConn = Nothing
End Sub

Private Sub PrepareCommandObject()

    ' Create the Command object.
    Set gobjCmd = New ADODB.Command
    Set gobjCmd.ActiveConnection = gobjConn
    gobjCmd.CommandText = "spInsertShippers"
    gobjCmd.CommandType = adCmdStoredProc

    ' Load the parameters collection. The first parameter
    ' is always the stored procedure return value.
    gobjCmd.Parameters.Append _
        gobjCmd.CreateParameter("@RETURN_VALUE", adInteger, _
                                adParamReturnValue, 0)
    gobjCmd.Parameters.Append _
        gobjCmd.CreateParameter("@CompanyName", adVarWChar, _
                                adParamInput, 40)
    gobjCmd.Parameters.Append _
        gobjCmd.CreateParameter("@Phone", adVarWChar, _
                                adParamInput, 24)

End Sub

Public Sub UseCommandObject()

    Dim lKeyValue As Long
    Dim lNumAffected As Long

    On Error GoTo ErrorHandler

    ' Create the Connection and the reusable Command object.
    CreateConnection
    PrepareCommandObject

    ' Set the values of the input parameters.
    gobjCmd.Parameters("@CompanyName").Value = "Air Carriers"
    gobjCmd.Parameters("@Phone").Value = "(206) 555-1212"

    ' Execute the Command object and check for errors.
```

```
        gobjCmd.Execute Recordsaffected:=lNumAffected, _
                        Options:=adExecuteNoRecords
        If lNumAffected <> 1 Then Err.Raise Number:=vbObjectError + 1024, _
            Description:="Error executing Command object."

        ' Retrieve the primary key value for the new record.
        lKeyValue = gobjCmd.Parameters("@RETURN_VALUE").Value
        Debug.Print "The key value of the new record is: " & CStr(lKeyValue)

    ErrorExit:

        ' Destroy the Command and Connection objects.
        Set gobjCmd = Nothing
        DestroyConnection

        Exit Sub

    ErrorHandler:
        MsgBox Err.Description, vbCritical
        Resume ErrorExit
    End Sub
```

A few things to note about the mini application above:

- In a normal application you would not create and destroy the `Connection` and `Command` objects in the `UseCommandObject` procedure. These objects are intended for reuse and therefore would typically be created when your application first started and destroyed just before it ended.
- When constructing and using the `Command` object's `Parameters` collection, keep in mind that the first parameter is always reserved for the stored procedure return value, even if the stored procedure doesn't have a return value.
- Even though we didn't make any particular use of the Shipper ID value returned from the stored procedure for the new record, in a normal application this value would be very important. The `CompanyName` and `Phone` fields are for human consumption; the primary key value is how the database identifies the record. For example, in the Northwind database the Shipper ID is a required field for entering new records into the `Orders` table. Therefore, if you planned on adding an order that was going to use the new shipper you would have to know the Shipper ID.

Multiple Recordsets

The SQL Server OLE DB provider is an example of a provider that allows you to execute a SQL statement that returns multiple recordsets. This feature comes in very handy when you need to populate multiple controls on a form with lookup-table information from the database. You can combine all of the lookup-table `SELECT` queries into a single stored procedure and then loop through the individual recordsets, assigning their contents to the corresponding controls.

For example, if you needed to create a user interface for entering information into the `Orders` table you would need information from several related tables, including `Customers` and `Shippers`:

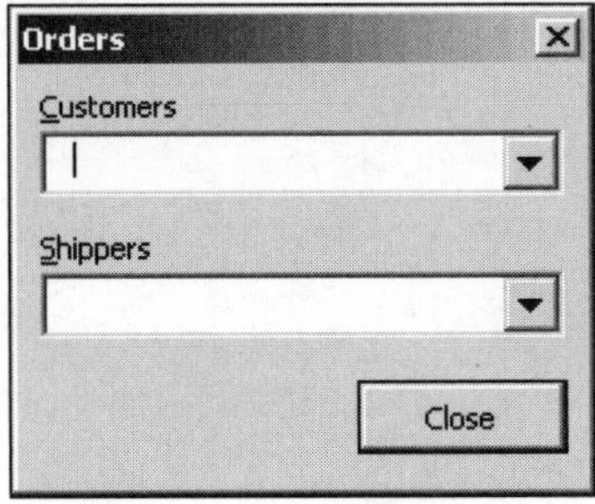

We'll create an abbreviated example of a stored procedure that returns the lookup information from these two tables and then use the result to populate dropdowns on a UserForm:

```
CREATE PROC spGetLookupValues
AS
    -- Customers lookup table info.
    SELECT    CustomerID,
              CompanyName
    FROM      Customers

    -- Shippers lookup table info.
    SELECT    ShipperID,
              CompanyName
    FROM      Shippers
```

Note that the stored procedure above contains two separate `SELECT` statements. These will populate two independent recordsets when the stored procedure is executed using ADO. The double dashes that you see at the beginning of the lines above each `SELECT` statement are T-SQL comment prefixes.

The procedure below is an example of a `UserForm_Initialize` event that populates dropdowns on the UserForm with the results of the `spGetLookupValues` stored procedure. For the purpose of this example we will assume that the public `Connection` object `gobjConn` that we used in the previous example is still open and available for use:

```
Private Sub UserForm_Initialize()

    Dim rsData As ADODB.Recordset

    ' Create and open the Recordset object.
    Set rsData = New ADODB.Recordset
    rsData.Open "spGetLookupValues", gobjConn, _
            adOpenForwardOnly, adLockReadOnly, adCmdStoredProc

    ' The first recordset contains the customer list.
    Do While Not rsData.EOF
        ' Load the dropdown with the recordset values.
        ddCustomers.AddItem rsData.Fields(1).Value
        rsData.MoveNext
    Loop
    Set rsData = rsData.NextRecordset

    ' The second recordset contains the shippers list.
    Do While Not rsData.EOF
        ' Load the dropdown with the recordset values.
        ddShippers.AddItem rsData.Fields(1).Value
        rsData.MoveNext
```

```
        Loop
        Set rsData = rsData.NextRecordset

        ' No need to clean up the Recordset object at this point,
        ' it will be closed and set to nothing after the last
        ' call to the NextRecordset method.

    End Sub
```

One thing to note about the method demonstrated above is that it requires prior knowledge of the number and order of recordsets returned by the call to the stored procedure. I have also left out any handling of the primary key values associated with the lookup table descriptions. In a real-world application you would need to maintain these keys (I prefer using a `Collection` object for this purpose) so that you could retrieve the primary key value that corresponded to the user's selection in each dropdown.

Disconnected Recordsets

In the *Returning Data from Microsoft Access Using a Plain Text Query* section above, I mentioned that getting in and out of the database as quickly as possible was an important goal. However, the `Recordset` object is a powerful tool that you would often like to hold onto and use without locking other users out of the database. The solution to this problem is ADO's disconnected recordset feature.

A disconnected recordset is a `Recordset` object whose connection to its data source has been severed, but which can still remain open. The result is a fully functional `Recordset` object that does not hold any locks in the database from which it was queried. Disconnected recordsets can remain open as long as you need them, they can be reconnected to and resynchronized with the data source, and they can even be persisted to disk for later retrieval. We will examine a few of these capabilities in the example below.

Let's say that you wanted to implement a feature that would allow users to view any group of customers they chose. Running a query against the database each time the user specified a different criterion would be an inefficient way to accomplish this. A much better alternative would be to query the complete set of customers from the database and hold them in a disconnected recordset. You could then use the `Filter` property of the `Recordset` object to quickly extract the set of customers that your user requested.

The example below shows all of the elements required to create a disconnected recordset. Again, we'll assume the availability of our public `gobjConn` `Connection` object:

```
    Public grsData As ADODB.Recordset

    Public Sub CreateDisconnectedRecordset ()

        Dim szSQL As String

        ' Create the SQL Statement.
        szSQL = "SELECT CustomerID, CompanyName, ContactName, Country " & _
                "FROM Customers"

        ' Steps to creating a disconnected recordset:
        ' 1) Create the Recordset object.
        Set grsData = New ADODB.Recordset
        ' 2) Set the cursor location to client side.
        grsData.CursorLocation = adUseClient
        ' 3) Set the cursor type to static.
        grsData.CursorType = adOpenStatic
```

```
    ' 4) Set the lock type to batch optimistic.
    grsData.LockType = adLockBatchOptimistic
    ' 5) Open the recordset.
    grsData.Open szSQL, gobjConn, , , adCmdText
    ' 6) Set the Recordset's Connection object to Nothing.
    Set grsData.ActiveConnection = Nothing

    ' grsData is now a disconnected recordset.
    Sheet1.Range("A1").CopyFromRecordset grsData

End Sub
```

Note that the `Recordset` object variable in the example above is declared with public scope. If we were to declare the `Recordset` object variable at the procedure level, VBA would automatically destroy it when the procedure ended and it would no longer be available for use.

There are six crucial steps required in order to successfully create a disconnected recordset. It's possible to combine several of them into one step during the `Recordset.Open` method, and it's more efficient to do so, but I've separated them for the sake of clarity:

- You must create a new, empty `Recordset` object to start with.
- You must set the cursor location to client-side. Since the recordset will be disconnected from the server, the cursor cannot be managed there. Note that this setting **must** be made **before** you open the recordset. It is not possible to change the cursor location once the recordset is open.
- The ADO client-side cursor engine supports only one type of cursor, the static cursor, so this is what the `CursorType` property must be set to.
- ADO has a lock type specifically designed for disconnected recordsets called Batch Optimistic. The Batch Optimistic lock type makes it possible to reconnect the disconnected recordset to the database and update the database with records that have been modified while the recordset was disconnected. This operation is beyond the scope of this chapter, so just note that the Batch Optimistic lock type is required in order to create a disconnected recordset.
- Opening the recordset is the next step. In this example I've used a plain text SQL query. This is not a requirement. You can create a disconnected recordset from almost any source that can be used to create a standard recordset. There are a few capabilities that the client side cursor engine lacks, however; multiple recordsets are one example.
- The final step is disconnecting the recordset from the data source. This is accomplished by setting the recordset's `Connection` object to `Nothing`. If you recall from the *Recordset Object Properties* section above, the `Connection` object associated with a `Recordset` object is accessed through the `Recordset.ActiveConnection` property. Setting this property to `Nothing` severs the connection between the recordset and the data source.

Now that we have a disconnected recordset to work with, what kind of things can we do with it? Just about any operation that the `Recordset` object allows is the answer. Let's say the user wanted to see a list of customers located in Germany and sorted in alphabetical order. This is how you'd accomplish that task:

```
' Set the Recordset filter to display only records
' whose Country field is Germany.
grsData.Filter = "Country = 'Germany'"
' Sort the records by CompanyName.
grsData.Sort = "CompanyName"
' Load the processed data onto Sheet1
Sheet1.Range("A1").CopyFromRecordset grsData
```

If you are working in a busy, multi-user environment, the data in your disconnected recordset may become out-of-date during the course of your application due to other users inserting, updating, and deleting records. You can solve this problem by re-querying the recordset. As demonstrated by the example below, this is a simple matter of reconnecting to the data source, executing the `Recordset.Requery` method, then disconnecting from the data source:

```
' Reconnect to the data source.
Set grsData.ActiveConnection = gobjConn
' Rerun the Recordset object's underlying query,
grsData.Requery Options:=adCmdText
' Disconnect from the data source.
Set grsData.ActiveConnection = Nothing
```

Using ADO with Non-Standard Data Sources

This section will describe how you can use ADO to access data from two common non-standard data sources (data sources that are not strictly considered databases), Excel workbooks and text files. Although the idea may seem somewhat counterintuitive, ADO is often the best choice for retrieving data from workbooks and text files because it eliminates the often lengthy process of opening them in Excel. Using ADO also allows you to take advantage of the power of SQL to do exactly what you want in the process.

Querying Microsoft Excel Workbooks

When using ADO to access Excel workbooks you use the same OLE DB provider that you used earlier in this chapter to access data from Microsoft Access. In addition to Access, this provider also supports most **ISAM data sources** (data sources that are laid out in a tabular, row, and column format). ADO will allow you to operate on workbooks that are either open or closed. However, by far the most common scenario will involve performing data access on a closed workbook.

We will be using the `Sales.xls` workbook, a picture of which is shown below, for our Excel examples. You can download this workbook, along with the rest of the examples for this book, from the Wrox web site:

Sales.xls

	A	B	C	D	E
1	**State**	**Channel**	**Type**	**Price Range**	**Quantity**
2	WA	Retail	Art	Mid	9
3	WA	Retail	Art	Low	143
4	WA	Retail	Art	High	17
5	WA	Retail	Art	Mid	23
6	WA	Retail	Art	High	26
7	WA	Retail	Art	Mid	6
8	WA	Retail	Art	Low	4
9	WA	Retail	Art	High	13
10	WA	Retail	Art	Mid	7
11	WA	Retail	Art	Low	25
12	WA	Retail	Dinosaurs	Mid	22

Sales

When using ADO to work with Excel, the workbook file takes the place of the database while worksheets within the workbook, as well as named ranges, serve as tables. Let's compare a connection string used to connect to an Access database with a connection string used to connect to an Excel workbook.

Connection string to an Access database:

```
szConnect = "Provider=Microsoft.Jet.OLEDB.4.0;" & _
            "Data Source=C:\Files\Northwind.mdb;"
```

Connection string to an Excel workbook:

```
szConnect = "Provider=Microsoft.Jet.OLEDB.4.0;" & _
            "Data Source=C:\Files\Sales.xls;" & _
            "Extended Properties=Excel 8.0;"
```

Note that the same provider is used and that the full path and filename of the Excel workbook takes the place of the full path and filename of the Access database. The only difference is that when using the OLE DB provider for Microsoft Jet to connect to data sources other than Access, you must specify the name of the data source you wish to connect to in the `Extended Properties` argument. When connecting to Excel, you set the `Extended Properties` argument to `Excel 8.0` for Excel 97 and higher.

You query data from an Excel worksheet using a plain text SQL statement exactly like you would query a database table. However, the format of the table name is different for Excel queries. You can specify the table that you wish to query from an Excel workbook in one of four different ways:

- **Worksheet Name Alone**
  When using the name of a specific worksheet as the table name in your SQL statement, the worksheet name must be suffixed with a `$` character and surrounded with square brackets. For example, `[Sheet1$]` is a valid worksheet table name. If the worksheet name contains spaces or non-alphanumeric characters you must surround it in single quotes. An example of this is: `['My Sheet$']`.

- **Worksheet-level Range Name**
  You can use a worksheet-level range name as a table name in your SQL statement. Simply prefix the range name with the worksheet name it belongs to, using the formatting conventions described above. An example of this would be: `[Sheet1$SheetLevelName]`.

- **Specific Range Address**
  You can specify the table in your SQL statement as a specific range address on the target worksheet. The syntax for this method is identical to that for a worksheet-level range name: `[Sheet1$A1:E20]`.

- **Workbook-level Range Name**
  You can also use a workbook-level range name as the table in your SQL statement. In this case there is no special formatting required. You simply use the name directly without brackets.

Although our sample workbook contains only one worksheet, this is not a requirement. The target workbook can contain as many worksheets and named ranges as you wish. You simply need to know which one to use in your query. The procedure below demonstrates all four table-specifying methods discussed above:

```
Public Sub QueryWorksheet()

    Dim rsData As ADODB.Recordset
    Dim szConnect As String
    Dim szSQL As String

    ' Create the connection string.
    szConnect = "Provider=Microsoft.Jet.OLEDB.4.0;" & _
                "Data Source=C:\Files\Sales.xls;" & _
```

```
                "Extended Properties=Excel 8.0;"

    ' Query based on the worksheet name.
    'szSQL = "SELECT * FROM [Sales$]"
    ' Query based on a sheet-level range name.
    'szSQL = "SELECT * FROM [Sales$SheetLevelName]"
    ' Query based on a specific range address.
    'szSQL = "SELECT * FROM [Sales$A1:E89]"
    ' Query based on a book-level range name.
    szSQL = "SELECT * FROM BookLevelName"

    Set rsData = New ADODB.Recordset
    rsData.Open szSQL, szConnect, adOpenForwardOnly, _
                adLockReadOnly, adCmdText

    ' Check to make sure we received data.
    If Not rsData.EOF Then
        Sheet1.Range("A1").CopyFromRecordset rsData
    Else
        MsgBox "No records returned.", vbCritical
    End If

    ' Clean up our Recordset object.
    rsData.Close
    Set rsData = Nothing

End Sub
```

By default, the OLE DB provider for Microsoft Jet assumes that the first row in the table you specify with your SQL statement contains the field names for the data. If this is the case, you can perform more complex SQL queries, making use of the `WHERE` and `ORDER BY` clauses. If the first row of your data table does not contain field names, however, you must inform the provider of this fact or you will lose the first row of data. The way to accomplish this is by providing an additional setting, `HDR=No`, to the `Extended Properties` argument of the connection string:

```
szConnect = "Provider=Microsoft.Jet.OLEDB.4.0;" & _
            "Data Source=C:\Files\Sales.xls;" & _
            "Extended Properties=""Excel 8.0;HDR=No"";"
```

Note that when you pass multiple settings to the `Extended Properties` argument the entire setting string must be surrounded with double quotes and the individual settings delimited with semi-colons. If your data table does not include column headers, you will be limited to plain `SELECT` queries.

Inserting and Updating Records in Microsoft Excel Workbooks

ADO can do more than just query data from an Excel workbook. You can also insert and update records in the workbook, just as you would with any other data source. Deleting records, however, is not supported. Updating records, although possible, is somewhat problematic when an Excel workbook is the data source, as Excel-based data tables rarely have anything that can be used as a primary key to uniquely identify a specific record. Therefore, you must specify the values of enough fields to uniquely identify the record concerned in the `WHERE` clause of your SQL statement when performing an update. If more than one record meets `WHERE` clause criteria, all such records will be updated.

Inserting is significantly less troublesome. All you do is construct a SQL statement that specifies values for each of the fields and then execute it. Note once again that your data table must have column headers in order for it to be possible to execute action queries against it. The example below demonstrates how to insert a new record into our sales worksheet data table:

```
Public Sub WorksheetInsert()

    Dim objConn As ADODB.Connection
    Dim szConnect As String
    Dim szSQL As String

    ' Create the connection string.
    szConnect = "Provider=Microsoft.Jet.OLEDB.4.0;" & _
                "Data Source=C:\Files\Sales.xls;" & _
                "Extended Properties=Excel 8.0;"

    ' Create the SQL statement.
    szSQL = "INSERT INTO [Sales$] " & _
            "VALUES('VA', 'On-Line', 'Computers', 'Mid', 30)"

    ' Create and open the Connection object.
    Set objConn = New ADODB.Connection
    objConn.Open szConnect

    ' Execute the insert statement.
    objConn.Execute szSQL, , adCmdText Or adExecuteNoRecords

    ' Close and destroy the Connection object.
    objConn.Close
    Set objConn = Nothing

End Sub
```

Querying Text Files

The last data access technique we'll discuss in this chapter is querying text files using ADO. The need to query text files doesn't come up as often as some of the other situations that we've discussed. However, when faced with an extremely large text file, the result of a mainframe database data dump, for example, ADO can be a lifesaver.

Not only will it allow you to rapidly load large amounts of data into Excel, but using the power of SQL to limit the size of the resultset can also enable you to work with data from a text file that is simply too large to be opened directly in Excel. For our discussion on text file data access we'll be using a comma-delimited text file, `Sales.csv`, whose contents are identical to the `Sales.xls` workbook we used in the Excel examples above.

The OLE DB provider for Microsoft Jet is once again used for connecting to text files with ADO. However, the connection string details are slightly different. The example below demonstrates how to construct a connection string to access a text file:

```
szConnect = "Provider=Microsoft.Jet.OLEDB.4.0;" & _
            "Data Source=C:\Files\;" & _
            "Extended Properties=Text;"
```

Note that in the case of text files, the `Data Source` argument to the provider is set to the directory that contains the text file. Do not include the name of the file in this argument. Once again, the provider is informed of the format to be queried by using the `Extended Properties` argument. In this case you simply set this argument to the value `"Text"`.

Querying a text file is virtually identical to querying an Excel workbook. The main difference is how the table name is specified in the SQL statement. When querying a text file, the filename itself is used as the table name in the query. This has the added benefit of allowing you to work with multiple text files in a single directory without having to modify your connection string.

As with Excel, you are limited to plain `SELECT` queries if the first row of your text file does not contain field names. You must also add the `HDR=No` setting to the `Extended Properties` argument if this is the case in order to avoid losing the first row of data. Our example text file has field names in the first row, and we'll assume that we need to limit the number of records we bring into Excel by adding a restriction in the form of a `WHERE` clause to our query. The procedure below demonstrates this:

```
Public Sub QueryTextFile()

    Dim rsData As ADODB.Recordset
    Dim szConnect As String
    Dim szSQL As String

    ' Create the connection string.
    szConnect = "Provider=Microsoft.Jet.OLEDB.4.0;" & _
                "Data Source=C:\Files\;" & _
                "Extended Properties=Text;"

    ' Create the SQL statement.
    szSQL = "SELECT * FROM Sales.csv WHERE Type='Art';"

    Set rsData = New ADODB.Recordset
    rsData.Open szSQL, szConnect, adOpenForwardOnly, _
                adLockReadOnly, adCmdText

    ' Check to make sure we received data.
    If Not rsData.EOF Then
        ' Dump the returned data onto Sheet1
        Sheet1.Range("A1").CopyFromRecordset rsData
    Else
        MsgBox "No records returned.", vbCritical
    End If

    ' Clean up our Recordset object.
    rsData.Close
    Set rsData = Nothing

End Sub
```

Summary

This concludes our discussion of data access with ADO. Due to space constraints we were only able to scratch the surface of possibilities in each section. If data access is, or might become, a significant part of your development effort, you are strongly recommended to obtain the additional resources mentioned throughout this chapter.

VBAProgrammersReferenceExcel20
mersReferenceExcel2002VB
ferenceExcel2002VBAPro
ProgrammersReferenceExc
ammersReferenceExcel20
ReferenceExcel2002VB
Excel2002VBAPro
el2002VBAProgram
nceExcel2002VBAP
xcel2002VBAProgram
2002VBAProgrammersReferenceExce
VBAProgrammersRefere
rogrammersReferenceExcel
ammersReference
2002VBAProgrammersReferenceExce

21

Excel and the Internet

Historically, a typical Excel-based application was almost entirely contained within Excel itself; the only external interaction would be with the user, from whom we obtained data and to whom we presented our results. If we needed to store data, we'd use separate workbooks and try to mimic a relational database as best we could.

As data access technologies developed from ODBC drivers, through DAO, to the current versions of ADO (documented in Chapter 20), it became more common-place to store data in external databases and even retrieve data from (and update data in) other systems across the network. It is now quite common to see Excel used as a front-end querying and analysis tool for large corporate databases, using QueryTables and PivotTables to retrieve the data. The data available to our Excel applications was, however, limited to that available across the company network, and to those databases that we could get permission to access.

Starting with the release of Office 97, Microsoft has slowly extended Excel's reach to include the Internet and associated technologies, either by adding native functionality directly into Excel (such as Web Queries), or by ensuring that Excel developers can easily use standard external objects (such as the Internet Transfer Control, the Web Browser control, and the MSXML parser), and including those objects within the Office installation.

In Excel 2002 we have sufficient functionality to consider rethinking our approach to developing Excel Applications. We can start to think outside of the pure Excel/ADO environment in terms of obtaining data, publishing results, monitoring our applications, and sharing data with many disparate systems, outside of the corporate network.

This chapter introduces the functionality available to us in Excel 2002 and demonstrates how to use some of it to exploit the Internet within our applications. A complete discussion of all of Excel's Internet-related functionality is beyond the scope of this book.

> **Note that throughout this chapter, the term 'Internet' is used in its broadest sense, covering both internal and external networks. The chapter assumes a basic understanding of the Internet and how it works. Throughout the examples, we will be using a web server running on a local PC. However, these techniques are equally applicable to applications running on a remote server.**

So What's all the Hype About?

In a nutshell, it's all about sharing information.

It's about publishing information to unknown consumers, using standard formats and protocols to enable them to access the information you provide in a consistent, reliable, and secure manner.

It's about making that information available globally both inside and outside the organization's networks, while maintaining control over security and access to potentially sensitive information.

It's about retrieving the information that other individuals or organizations provide, from multiple disparate sources, to use as inputs to your application.

It's about sharing information between producers and consumers, suppliers and customers, using standard formats for that exchange.

It's about looking outside of the classic Excel application and adding value to that application by sharing its results with a wider audience than simply the user sitting at the PC.

It's about using Excel as a key component of a larger business process, where that process may span multiple organizations.

Using the Internet for Storing Workbooks

The simplest way of sharing information is to store our workbooks on a web server. While Excel 97 introduced the ability to download workbooks from web sites, Excel 2000 and 2002 extended that to allow us to save workbooks as well. They do this by using the FrontPage Server Extensions, which must be running on the server. To open and save a workbook from/to a web site, we just use the URL instead of the filename:

```
Sub OpenFromWebSiteAndSaveBack()

    Dim oBk As Workbook

    'Open a workbook from a web site
    Set oBk = Workbooks.Open("http://www.MySite.com/book1.xls")

    'Save the workbook to the web site with a new name
    oBk.SaveAs "http://www.MySite.com/Book2.xls"

End Sub
```

If the server requires you to logon, you have the option of letting Excel prompt for the ID and password each time (as in the example above), or include the ID and password as part of the URL:

```
Sub OpenFromSecureWebSiteAndSaveBack()

    Dim oBk As Workbook

    'Open a workbook from a web site
    Set oBk = Workbooks.Open("http://UserID:Pwd@www.MySite.com/book1.xls")

    'Save the workbook to the web site with a new name
    oBk.SaveAs "http://UserID:Pwd@www.MySite.com/Book2.xls"

End Sub
```

The URLs can, of course, also be used in Excel's **File Open** and **Save As** dialogs.

Using the Internet as a Data Source

The 'classic' Excel application has two sources of data – databases on the network, and the user. If an item of data was not available in a database, the user was required to type it in and maintain it. To enable this, the application had to include a number of sheets and dialogs to store the information and provide a mechanism for the data entry.

A typical example of this would be maintaining exchange rate information in a financial model; it is usually the user's responsibility to obtain the latest rates and type them into the model. We can add value to the application by automating the retrieval of up-to-date exchange rate information from one of many web sites.

The following sections demonstrate different techniques for retrieving information from the web, using the USD exchange rates available from http://www.x-rates.com/tables/USD.htm as an example. The web page looks like this:

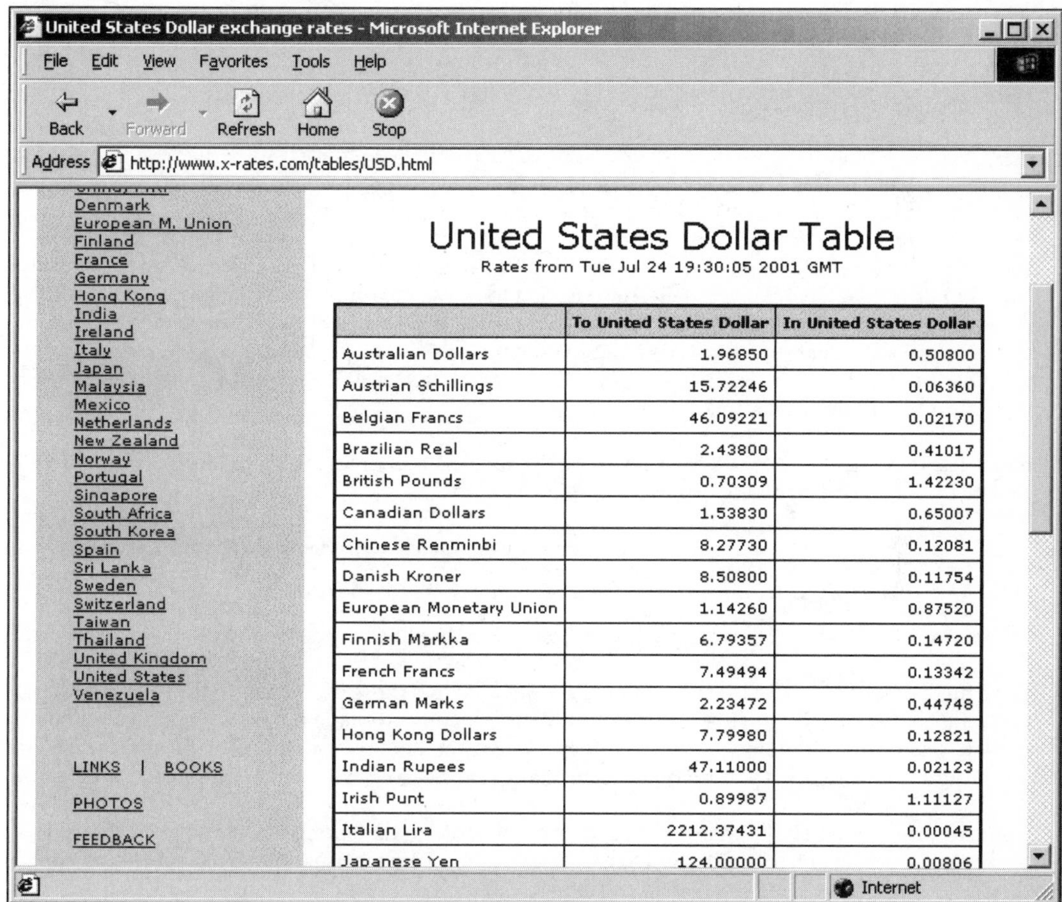

Opening Web Pages as Workbooks

The simplest solution is to open the entire web page as if it were a workbook, then scan the sheet for the required information, such the USD/GBP exchange rate:

```
Sub OpenUSDRatesPage()

    Dim oBk As Workbook
    Dim oRng As Range

    'Open the rates pages as a workbook
    Set oBk = Workbooks.Open("http://www.x-rates.com/tables/USD.HTML")

    'Find the British Pounds entry
    Set oRng = oBk.Worksheets(1).Cells.Find("British Pounds")

    'Read off the exchange rate
    MsgBox "The USD/GBP exchange rate is " & oRng.Offset(0, 1).Value

End Sub
```

The problem with using this approach is that we have to load the entire web page (including graphics, banners, etc.), which may have much more information than we want. The irrelevant data can greatly slow down the speed of data retrieval.

Using Web Queries

Web Queries were introduced in Excel 97 and have been enhanced in each subsequent version of Excel. They enable us to retrieve a single table of information from a web page, with options to automatically refresh the data each time the workbook is opened, or at frequent intervals.

One of the problems with Web Queries is that Excel uses the thousands and decimal separators specified in the Windows Regional Settings when attempting to recognize numbers in the page. If the exchange rate web page was retrieved in many European countries, the period would be treated as a thousand separator, not a decimal separator, resulting in exchange rates that are many times too large. Therefore, Web Queries could not be reliably used in versions prior to Excel 2002 in countries that used non-US decimal and thousand separators.

In Excel 2002, Microsoft added three properties to the `Application` object, to temporarily override the settings used when recognizing numbers:

- `Application.DecimalSeparator` – the character to use for the decimal separator
- `Application.ThousandsSeparator` – the same for the thousands separator
- `Application.UseSystemSeparators` – whether to use the Windows separators, or Excel's

Using these properties, we can set Excel's separators to match those on the web page, perform the query, then set them back again. If we want to use the Web Query's automatic refreshing options, we have to set these separators in the `BeforeRefresh` event, and set them back in the `AfterRefresh` event. This requires advanced VBA techniques, using class modules to trap events, as discussed in Chapter 15.

In our case, we can retrieve just the table of exchange rates, using the code shown below to create and execute a new Web Query. In practice, it's easiest to use the macro recorder to ensure the selections are correct:

```
'Retrieve USD exchange rates using a Web Query
Sub GetRatesWithWebQuery()

    Dim oBk As Workbook
    Dim oQT As QueryTable
```

```
'Store the current settings of Excel's number formatting
Dim sDecimal As String
Dim sThousand As String
Dim bUseSystem As Boolean

'Create a new workbook
Set oBk = Workbooks.Add

'Create a query table to download USD rates
With oBk.Worksheets(1)
    Set oQT = .QueryTables.Add( _
          Connection:="URL;http://www.x-rates.com/tables/USD.HTML", _
          Destination:=.Range("A1"))
End With

'Set the QueryTable's properties
With oQT
    .Name = "USD"

    'State that we're selecting a specific table
    .WebSelectionType = xlSpecifiedTables

    'Import the 5th table on the page
    .WebTables = "5"

    'Ignore the web page's formatting
    .WebFormatting = xlWebFormattingNone

    'Do not try to recognise dates
    .WebDisableDateRecognition = True

    'Don't automatically refresh the query each time the file is opened
    .RefreshOnFileOpen = False

    'Waiting for the query to complete before continuing
    .BackgroundQuery = True

    'Save the query data with the workbook
    .SaveData = True

    'Adjust column widths to autofit new data
    .AdjustColumnWidth = True
End With

With Application
    'Remember Excel's current number format settings
    sDecimal = .DecimalSeparator
    sThousand = .ThousandsSeparator
    bUseSystem = .UseSystemSeparators

    'Set Excel's separators to match those of the web site
    .DecimalSeparator = "."
    .ThousandsSeparator = ","
    .UseSystemSeparators = True

    'Ignore any errors raised by the query failing
    On Error Resume Next

    'Perform the query, waiting for it to complete
    oQT.Refresh BackgroundQuery:=False
```

```
        'Reset Excel's number format settings
        .DecimalSeparator = sDecimal
        .ThousandsSeparator = sThousand
        .UseSystemSeparators = bUseSystem
    End With

End Sub
```

The `.WebTables = 5` line in the above example tells Excel that we want the 5th table on the page. Literally, this is the 5th occurrence of a `<TABLE>` tag in the source HTML for the page.

Parsing Web Pages for Specific Information

Web Queries are an excellent way of retrieving tables of information from web pages, but are a little cumbersome if you are only interested in one or two items of information. Another way is to read the page using a hidden instance of Internet Explorer, search within the page for the required information, then return the result. The code below requires a reference to the 'Microsoft Internet Controls' object library:

```
Sub GetUSDtoGBPRateUsingIE()

    Dim oIE As SHDocVw.InternetExplorer
    Dim sPage As String
    Dim iGBP As Long, iDec As Long
    Dim iStart As Long, iEnd As Long
    Dim dRate As Double

    'Create a new (hidden) instance of IE
    Set oIE = New SHDocVw.InternetExplorer

    'Open the web page
    oIE.Navigate "http://www.x-rates.com/tables/USD.HTML"

    'Wait for the page to complete loading
    Do Until oIE.readyState = READYSTATE_COMPLETE
        DoEvents
    Loop

    'Retrieve the text of the web page into a variable
    sPage = oIE.Document.body.InnerHTML

    '**********************************************************************
    'The source HTML for the British Pounds entry looks like the following:
    '<TR>
    '   <TD BGCOLOR="#FFFFFF">
    '     <FONT FACE="Verdana, Arial" SIZE="-2">British Pounds</FONT>
    '   </TD>
    '   <TD BGCOLOR="#FFFFFF" ALIGN="right">
    '     <FONT FACE="Verdana, Arial" SIZE="-2">0.69979</FONT>
    '   </TD>
    '   <TD BGCOLOR="#FFFFFF" ALIGN="right">
    '     <FONT FACE="Verdana, Arial" SIZE="-2">1.42900</FONT>
    '   </TD>
    '</TR>
    '**********************************************************************

    'To find the exchange rate, we have to find the entry for British
    'Pounds, then work forwards to find the exchange rate
```

```
    'Find the entry for British Pounds in the HTML string.
    iGBP = InStr(1, sPage, "British Pounds")

    'Find the next decimal, which will be in the middle of the
    'exchange rate number
    iDec = InStr(iGBP, sPage, ".")

    'Find the start and end of the number
    iStart = InStrRev(sPage, ">", iDec) + 1
    iEnd = InStr(iDec, sPage, "<")

    'Evaluate the number, knowing that it's in US format
    dRate = Val(Mid$(sPage, iStart, iEnd - iStart))

    'Display the rate
    MsgBox "The USD/GBP exchange rate is " & dRate

End Sub
```

The most appropriate method to use will depend on the precise circumstances, and how much data is required. For single items, it is probably easier to use the last approach. For more than a few items, it will be easier to use a Web Query to read the page or table into a workbook, then find the required items on the sheet.

Using the Internet to Publish Results

A web server can be used as a repository of information, storing your application's results and presenting them to a wider audience than can be achieved with printed reports. By presenting results as web pages, the reader of those pages can easily use the results as sources of data for their own analysis, and easily pass those results to other interested parties.

Setting Up a Web Server

For all the examples from now on, you will require write access to a web server. As later examples use Active Server Pages (ASP), we will use Microsoft's IIS 5.0. Open IIS, and right-click the Default Web Site node. Select Properties and click on the Home Directory tab. You will be presented with various configuration options for the default web site. Make sure that the Read and Write checkboxes are selected and click OK:

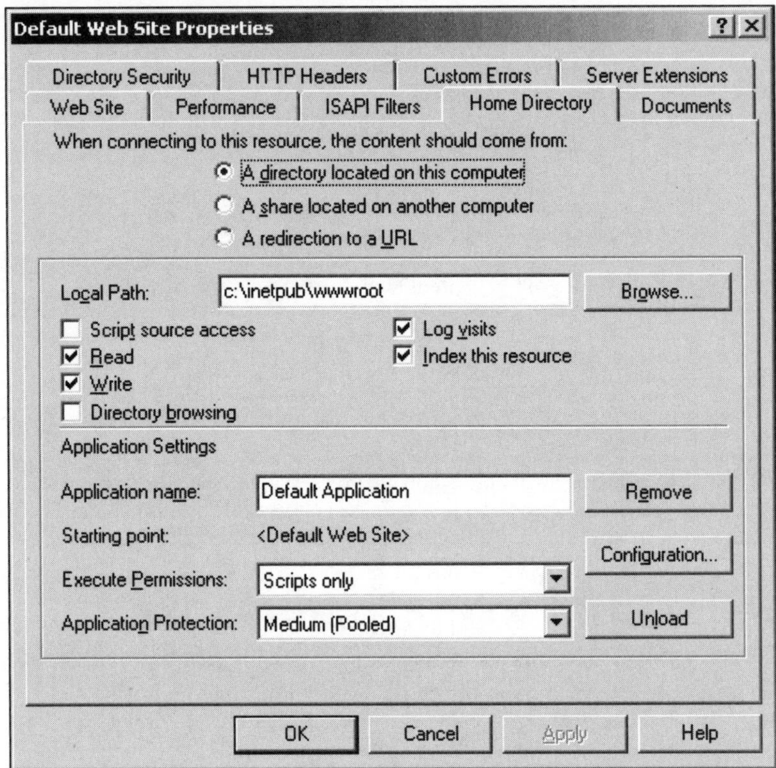

Notice the **Local Path:** box. This is where the root of your web server is located. By default it is `C:\inetpub\wwwroot\`. Any web pages placed in this directory are published at the following URL: http://localhost/PageName.html. This is where the first few examples will publish their results. The Timesheet example later in the chapter will require you to set up a Virtual Directory, but we will explain that at the time.

Saving Worksheets as Web Pages

The easiest way to present results as a web page is to create a template workbook that has all the formatting and links that you'd like to show. When your application produces its results, it is then a simple task to copy the relevant numbers to the template, then save the template direct to the web server:

```
Sub PublishResultsToWeb()

    Dim oBk As Workbook
    Dim oSht As Worksheet

    'Create a new copy of the Web Template workbook
    Set oBk = Workbooks.Add("c:\mydir\WebTemplate.xls")

    'Get the first sheet in the workbook
    Set oSht = oBk.Worksheets(1)

    'Populate the results
    oSht.Range("Profits").Value = Workbooks("Results.xls") _
            .Worksheets("Financials").Range("Profits").Value
```

```
    'Save as a web page, direct to the server
    oSht.SaveAs "http://localhost/ResultsJuly2001.htm", xlHtml

    'Close the workbook
    oBk.Close False

End Sub
```

Adding Interactivity with the Web Components

The previous example saved a static rendition of the worksheet in HTML format to the web server. In Excel 2000, Microsoft introduced the Office Web Components to create interactive web pages. When saving a worksheet in interactive form, the following conversions take place:

- The worksheet, or separate ranges on the sheet, are converted to Spreadsheet Web Components.
- Selected Charts are converted Chart Web Components
- Pivot Tables are converted to Pivot Table Web Components

These components are ActiveX controls that are embedded in the HTML page, designed to provide Excel-like levels of interaction, but from within the browser.

It is beyond the scope of this book to document the Web Components (which have all been greatly enhanced in Office XP), but the following code can be used to save a workbook as an interactive web page, where the workbook contains a range of data to be published (**A1:C30**), a pivot table, and an embedded chart:

```
Sub PublishPageInteractive()

  'The PublishObjects collection contains all the parts of the sheet that
  'will be published to web page(s)
  With ActiveWorkbook.PublishObjects

      'Delete any existing publish objects
      .Delete

      'Start with a Pivot Table web component
      .Add(xlSourcePivotTable, "http://localhost/page.htm", "Sheet1", _
             "PivotTable1", xlHtmlList).Publish True

      'Add a worksheet range to the same page
      .Add(xlSourceRange, "http://localhost/page.htm", "Sheet1", _
             "A1:C30", xlHtmlCalc).Publish False

      'Followed by a chart and its source data
      .Add(xlSourceChart, "http://localhost/page.htm", "Sheet1", _
             "Chart 1", xlHtmlChart).Publish False
  End With

End Sub
```

Note that the above example publishes all the components to the same web page. By supplying different URLs, multiple pages can be created in this way.

The resulting web pages are quite simple – being only placeholders for the various Web Components. It is likely that they would need some post-processing to create presentation-quality pages:

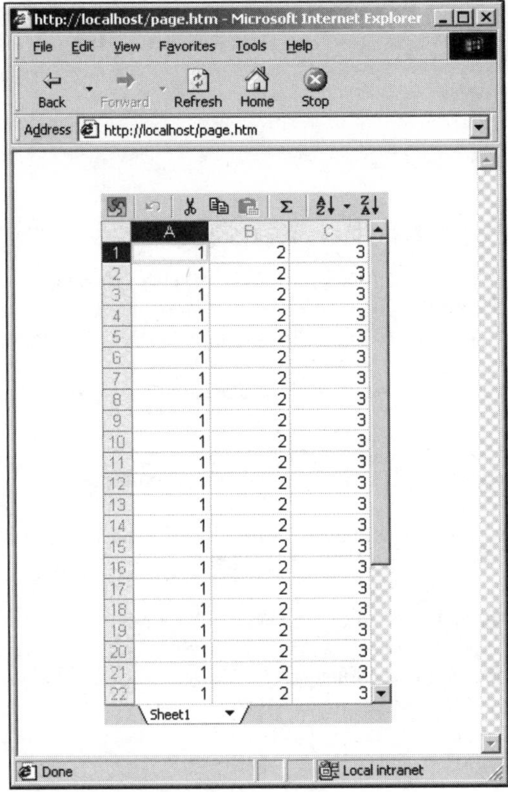

Using the Internet as a Communication Channel

Retrieving data from web pages and publishing results as web pages is in many ways a passive use of the Internet; the web server is being used primarily as a storage medium. Web servers are also able to host applications, with which we can interact in a more dynamic manner. The server application acts as a single point of contact for all the client workbooks, to perform the following functions:

- A centralized data store
- Collation of data from multiple clients
- Presentation of that data back to other clients
- Workflow management
- Calculation engines

As an example, consider a timesheet reporting system, where each member of staff has an Excel workbook to enter their time on a daily basis. At the end of each month, they connect to the Internet and send their timesheet to an application running on a web server. That application stores the submitted data in a central database. Some time later, a manager connects to the server and is sent the submitted hours for her staff. She checks the numbers and authorizes payment, sending her authorization code back to the server. The payroll department retrieves the authorized timesheet data from the same web server directly into its accounting system and processes the payments.

In this business process, Excel is used for the front-end client, providing a rich and powerful user interface, yet only fulfils a specific part of the overall process. The server application maintains the data (the completed timesheets) and presents it in whichever format is appropriate for the specific part of the process.

By using the Internet and standard data formats for this two-way communication, we can easily integrate Excel clients with completely separate systems, as in the payroll system in the example, and allow the business process to operate outside of the corporate network.

This section explains how such integration can be achieved with Excel 2002, using a simple error logging application as an example.

Communicating with a Web Server

Within a corporate network, nearly all data transfer takes place using proprietary binary formats, ranging from transferring files to performing remote database queries. Due primarily to security considerations, communication across the Internet has evolved to use textual formats, the simplest being a URL, http://www.MySite.com/MyPage.htm.

To be able to communicate with an application running on a web server we need to be able to perform some processing on the server and pass information to, and receive information from, that application.

In Excel 2002, the `Workbook` object's `FollowHyperlink` method can be used to communicate with a web server. There a few problems with using this, including:

- If an error occurs during the connection, Excel will freeze
- Any data returned from the hyperlink is automatically displayed as a new workbook
- We have very little control over the communication

A much more flexible alternative is provided by the Microsoft Internet Transfer Control, `msinet.ocx`. This ActiveX control, often referred to as the ITC, is an easy-to-use wrapper for the `wininet.dll` file, which provides low-level Internet-related services for the Windows platform.

Sending Data from the Client to the Server Application

There are two mechanisms that can be used to send information to a web server. We can either include the information as part of the URL string, or send it as a separate section of the HTTP request.

URL Encoding

Parameters can be included within the URL string by appending them to the end of the URL, with a ? between the URL and the first parameter, and an & between each parameter:
http://www.MySite.com/MyPage.asp?param1=value1¶m2=value2¶m2=value3

This has the advantage that the parameters form part of the URL and hence can be stored in the user's Favorites list or typed directly into the browser. It has the disadvantage that there is a limit to the total length of a URL (2083 characters in Internet Explorer), restricting the amount of information than can be passed in this way.

POSTing Data

Whenever a request for a web page is sent to a web server, the request contains a large amount of information in various header records. This includes things like the client application type and version, the communication protocol and version, and user IDs and passwords. It also contains a 'POST' field which can be used to send information to the server application.

As there is virtually no limit to the amount of data that can be put in a POST field, it is the preferred way of transferring information to the server, and is the method used in the example application shown later in this section.

Sending Data from the Server Application to the Client

Sending information from the application to the client is easy – the data can be presented to the client as a web page that can be read using the same techniques described earlier in this chapter.

A Web Server Application – Error Logging

There are a number of competing technologies that all provide the ability to perform processing on a web server, including PERL, CGI, JavaServer Pages (JSP), and Active Server Pages (ASP). For the VBA developer, ASP pages written with VBScript will be the most familiar.

In order to use ASP pages, the web server must be running Microsoft's Internet Information Server on Windows NT or Windows 2000, or the Personal Web Server on Windows 98 or Windows Me. See the *Setting up a Web Server* section for more details.

In the following example, we will create a web server application to provide a central error log for any run-time errors that may occur in our Excel applications (or any other application for that matter). The server application has three components:

- An Access database to store the error log
- An Active Server Page use to write to the error log
- An Active Server Page to display a page in the error log

The client, Excel, has a common error-handling routine.

An Access Database to Store the Errors

Start by creating a new database in Access 2002 called `ErrorLog.mdb`, containing a single table called `ErrorData` with the following fields:

Field Name	Data Type	Comment
`ErrorID`	`AutoNumber`	Set it to be the Primary Key
`ServerTime`	`Date/Time`	
`Application`	`Text`	50 characters
`ErrSource`	`Memo`	
`ErrNumber`	`Number`	Long Integer
`ErrDescription`	`Memo`	

In this example, we're only logging the actual error information. In practice, you're likely to store much more information, such as the user name, data file names, workbook and module name, Excel and Windows versions, and Regional settings.

Using FrontPage 2002, create a new web and import the database into the web, using File | Import.... Frontpage will automatically create an 'fpdb' folder to store it in and create a database connection for us to use, asking us for the name. Call it `ErrorLog`.

Virtual Directories

As mentioned in the *Setting up a Web Server* section, we shall be using a Virtual Directory for this example. Open IIS and right-click the Default Web Site node. Select New | Virtual Directory. This will start the Virtual Directory Creation Wizard. Click Next and fill in the alias as VBA_ProgRef:

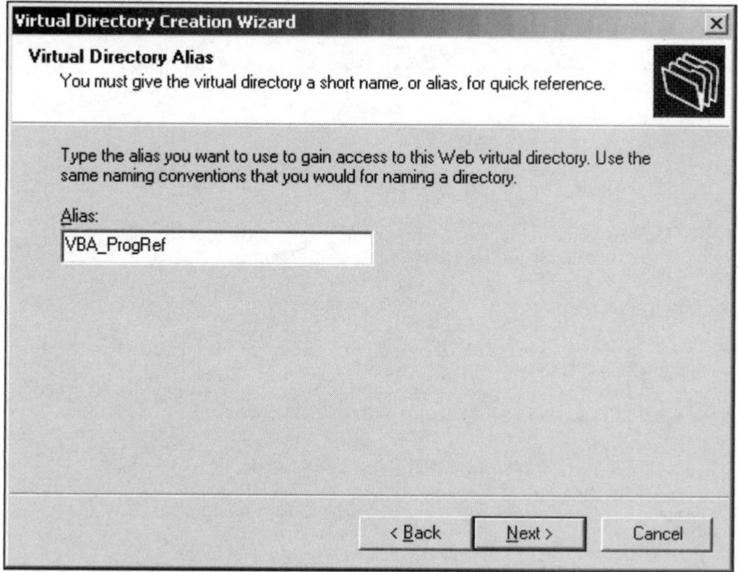

This will map the URL http://localhost/VBA_ProgRef to whatever folder on our hard drive we want. This is the next piece of information we need to give to IIS. Enter the directory where FrontPage saved the ASP pages:

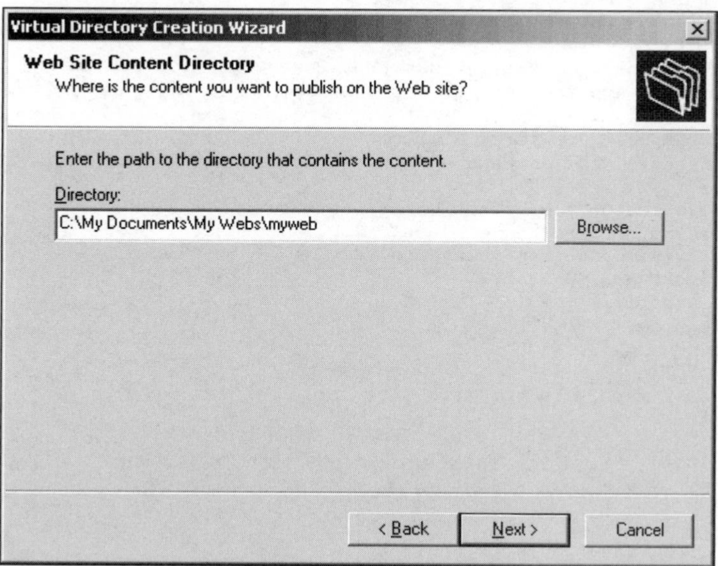

Click **Next**, and ensure that this directory gives you write access. That is the final step in the creation of our Virtual Directory. Now the URL **http://localhost/VBA_ProgRef/MyPage.asp** will map to the directory `C:\My Documents\My Webs\myweb\`.

An ASP Page to Write to the Error Log

In FrontPage 2002, create a new blank page, save it as `StoreError.asp`, click on the 'HTML' tab to edit the HTML directly and copy in the following code:

```
<%@ LANGUAGE=VBSCRIPT %>
<%
'********************************************************************************
'*
'* Page name:  StoreError.asp
'*
'* Inputs:     The information to store in the error log is supplied within a POST
'*             message (as used by Web forms).  A POST file contains information
in
'*             the form:
'*                  Name1=Value1&Name2=Value2&Name3=Value3  etc
'*
'* Outputs:    Returns the record number created to store the error information
'*
'* Purpose:    Receives error information from an application and stores it in a
database on the Server
'*
'********************************************************************************

    Dim objConn, objRS, sTable, lErrID, objField, objID

    'Ignore any errors, such as not being given a specific field in the POST info
    On Error Resume Next

    'Create a reference to the Jet Engine objects, to flush the cache
    Set objJE = Server.CreateObject("JRO.JetEngine")

    'Create a ADO connection
    Set objConn = Server.CreateObject("ADODB.Connection")

    'Use the connection string that FrontPage generated for us
    objConn.Open Application("ErrorLog_ConnectionString")

    'Flush the cache to force a write
    objJE.RefreshCache objConn

    'Create a connection to the error log table
    Set objRS = Server.CreateObject("ADODB.Recordset")
    objRS.ActiveConnection = objConn
    objRS.LockType = 3
    objRS.CursorType = 2
    objRS.Source = "ErrorData"
    objRS.Open

    'Add a new record to the error log table
    objRS.AddNew

    'Fill in all the error information
    For Each objField in objRS.Fields
```

```
        Select Case objField.Type
        Case 3    'Long Integer
            If LCase(objField.Name) <> "errorid" Then
                objField.Value = CLng(Request(objField.Name))
            End If
        Case 7, 135    'Date
            If LCase(objField.Name) = "servertime" Then
                objField.Value = Now()
            Else
                objField.Value = CDate(Request(objField.Name))
            End If
        Case 202, 203  'Char, Memo
            objField.Value = Request(objField.Name)
        End Select
    Next

    'Save the data to the database
    objRS.Update

    'Read off the error ID and return it to the client
     objRS.MoveLast
     Response.Write objRS.Fields(0).Value

     objRS.close
    Set objRS = Nothing

    'Flush the cache to force a write
    objJE.RefreshCache objConn

    objConn.Close
    Set objConn = Nothing

    Set objJE = Nothing
%>
```

The code examines the database file on the server and expects to be given a parameter in the POST string for each field in the table. The `Request` function retrieves the value of the parameter from the POST string, writing it to the database. The routine ends by using `Response.Write` to send the error ID back to the client.

An ASP Page to View the Error Log

The ASP script to view a page of the error log is fairly complex, as it generates the HTML required to view the page in the browser and provides a form to assist in navigation between errors. Create a new page called `ErrorLog.asp`, switch to the HTML view and copy in the following code:

```
<%@ LANGUAGE=VBSCRIPT %>
<%

'*******************************************************************************
'*
'* Page name:  ErrorLog.asp
'*
'* Inputs:     ErrID  - The error number to open in the browser
'*                  Op     - The navigation operation to perform
'*
'* Outputs:    Displays the error information in the browser
'*
'* Purpose:    To enable browsing of the Error Log database
'*
```

```
'*******************************************************************************

    'Any errors will just bomb through the code, returning zero
    On Error Resume Next

    'Read the parameters passed in the URL
    sOp = Request.QueryString("Op")
    iErr = Request.QueryString("ErrID")

    'Check the navigation operation
    If sOp = "" Then
        If iErr = "" Then
            sOp = "Last"
        Else
            sOp = "Go"
        End If
    End If

    If iErr = "" Then iErr = 1
    If iErr < 1 Then iErr = 1

    'Create a connection to the error log database
    Set objConn = Server.CreateObject("ADODB.Connection")
    objConn.Open Application("ErrorLog_ConnectionString")

    'Create a connection to the error log table
    Set objRS = Server.CreateObject("ADODB.Recordset")
    objRS.ActiveConnection = objConn
    objRS.CursorType = 3                        'Static cursor.

    objRS.Source = "ErrorData"
    objRS.Open

    'Work out which error to show next
    If objRS.BOF And objRS.EOF Then
        iErr = 0
    Else
      'Find the required error
        objRS.Find "ErrorID = " & iErr

        vBM = objRS.Bookmark

        'Move to the last, next or previous, depending on the required operation
        If objRS.EOF Or sOp = "Last" Then
            objRS.MoveLast

        ElseIf sOp = "Next" Then
            objRS.MoveNext

        ElseIf sOp = "Prev" Then
            objRS.MovePrevious
        End If

        If objRS.EOF Or objRS.BOF Then objRS.Bookmark = vBM

        'Remember which error number we're showing
        iErr = objRS.Fields("ErrorID")
    End If

%>
```

```
<%'Write the HTML header information for the web page %>
<HTML>

<head>
<title>Excel 2000 Prog Ref Error Browser</title>
</head>

<%'Start a Web form, so we can allow the user to go to a specific error ID number
%>
<FORM METHOD="GET" ACTION="ErrorLog.asp">

</form>

<table border="0" width="100%">
  <tr>
  <td colspan="2"><p align="center"><b>
    <font face="Arial" size="6">Excel 2002 Prog Ref</font>
    <br>
    <font face="Arial" size="4">Application Error Browser</font></b>
</td>
  </tr>
  <tr>
    <%'Populate the "Error ID" box and Go, Previous and Next links %>
    <td width="20%">Error Number: </td>
    <td width="80%"><INPUT TYPE=TEXT NAME="ErrID" VALUE="<%=iErr%>" SIZE=10>
      <INPUT TYPE=SUBMIT VALUE="Go">
      <a href="ErrorLog.asp?App=<%=sApp%>&ErrID=<%=iErr%>&Op=Prev">Previous</a> -
<a href="ErrorLog.asp?App=<%=sApp%>&ErrID=<%=iErr%>&Op=Next">Next</a> - <a
href="ErrorLog.asp?App=<%=sApp%>&Op=Last">Last</a></td>
  </tr>
<%
    'Loop through all the fields in the table, displaying the name and value to
the page
    For iField = 1 To objRS.Fields.Count - 1
%>
  <tr>
    <td width="20%"><% =objRS.Fields(iField).Name %>: </td>
    <td width="80%">
<%
    If Not objRS.EOF Then
%>
        <%=objRS.Fields(iField).Value %>
<%
    End if
%>  </td>
  </tr>
<%
    Next

    'ADO Object clean up.
    objRS.Close
    Set objRS = Nothing

    objConn.Close
    Set objConn = Nothing

%>
</FORM>
</table>

</body>
</HTML>
```

The Excel Error-Handler Routine

With the database and two ASP pages running on a server, we can now write the Excel error-handler routine to log all our run-time errors to the server database. This routine uses the Microsoft Internet Transfer Control to send the error information to the web-server application, retrieve the error number, and display it in a simple message box. In practice, you would probably want to send more information to the server, and present a more meaningful error message.

Open a new workbook in Excel 2002, add a reference to the Microsoft Internet Transfer Control (which may require browsing for the `msinet.ocx` file, usually found in the `Windows\System32` directory) and copy in the following code:

```
Option Explicit

'Common error handler
Sub ErrorHandler()

    Dim oInet As Inet
    Dim lContent As Long
    Dim sData As String
    Dim sHeader As String
    Dim sResult As String

    'Create a new instance of the Internet Transfer Control
    Set oInet = New Inet

    'Build the POST string with the error information
    sData = "Application=Excel 2002 Prog Ref" & "&" & _
            "ErrSource=" & Err.Source & "&" & _
            "ErrNumber=" & Err.Number & "&" & _
            "ErrDescription=" & Err.Description

    'Spaces must be replaced with + signs
    sData = Replace(sData, " ", "+")

    'Tell the POST that we're sending an encoded parameter list
    sHeader = "Content-Type: application/x-www-form-urlencoded"

    'Send the error information to the server
    oInet.AccessType = icDirect
    oInet.Execute "http://localhost/VBA_ProgRef/StoreError.asp", "POST", _
                  sData, sHeader

    'Wait for the server to complete its work
    Do While oInet.StillExecuting
        DoEvents
    Loop

    'Retrieve the returned text (i.e. the error ID)
    lContent = oInet.GetHeader("content-length")
    sResult = oInet.GetChunk(lContent + 100)

    'Display the error ID
    MsgBox "Error logged as number " & sResult

End Sub
```

```
'Force a division by zero error to test the error handler
Sub TestIt()

    On Error GoTo errHandler

    'Force division by zero
    Debug.Print 1 / 0

    Exit Sub

errHandler:

    'Call the common error logging routine
    ErrorHandler

End Sub
```

Run `TestIt` a few times to test the error handler. If everything was configured correctly, you will get a message showing an incrementing error number. If you open a browser and browse to http://localhost/VBA_ProgRef/ErrorLog.asp, you'll see something like the following:

The same server-side scripts can be used by many different client applications, and we're not limited to Excel as the client either. By passing the information between the server and client as a simple list of parameter/value pairs, we have made them very loosely coupled, giving us the flexibility to modify any of the components without requiring changes to any of the others. It is precisely this loose coupling between distributed applications that makes web-based applications so powerful.

XML

As systems become more and more complex, and require greater and greater amounts of information to be shared between them, it soon becomes too restrictive to pass information between them using the lists of parameter/value pairs that we used above. In order to address that restriction, yet maintain the loose coupling of the web-based architecture, a new format for data exchange was developed, called eXtensible Markup Language, or XML for short.

XML allows us to structure our data into hierarchical relationships and mark each element as being a specific data type (such as `Name`, `HoursWorked`, etc.). The XML for a simple timesheet may look something like the following (where the `TS:` prefix is used to distinguish our tags from any other):

```
<?xml version="1.0"?>
<!Excel 2002 Prog Ref Timesheet>
<TS:Timesheet xmlns:TS="urn:schemas_wrox_com:ExcelProgRef:Timesheet">
    <TS:Employee>
        <TS:FirstName>Stephen</TS:FirstName>
        <TS:LastName>Bullen</TS:LastName>
        <TS:EmployeeNumber>1234</TS:EmployeeNumber>
    </TS:Employee>
    <TS:ReportingMonth>
        <TS:Year>2001</TS:Year>
        <TS:Month>6</TS:Month>
        <TS:TotalStdHours>157.5</TS:TotalStdHours>
    </TS:ReportingMonth>
    <TS:HoursWorked>
        <TS:Day>1</TS:Day>
        <TS:StdHours>7.5</TS:StdHours>
        <TS:Overtime>2</TS:Overtime>
    </TS:HoursWorked>
    <TS:HoursWorked>
        <TS:Day>4</TS:Day>
        <TS:StdHours>7.5</TS:StdHours>
        <TS:Overtime>1</TS:Overtime>
    </TS:HoursWorked>
    <TS:HoursWorked>
        <TS:Day>5</TS:Day>
        <TS:StdHours>6</TS:StdHours>
        <TS:Overtime/>
    </TS:HoursWorked>
</TS:Timesheet>
```

To send this data to a web server application, we would use the same POST mechanism that we used above for sending our parameter/value pairs. The `<?xml version="1.0"?>` tag at the top of the data identifies it as XML. The server application could then load the XML into an XML Parser, through which the data can be extracted in a structured manner.

XML Vocabularies

In the preceding example of the XML that could be used to represent a timesheet, all the tag names (`<Timesheet>`, `<Employee>`, `<ReportingMonth>`, etc.) were completely arbitrary, invented for the example. Any application that intended to retrieve the information from the XML text would need to know what those tags were and what items of data they represented. That description of the XML data is known as an 'XML Vocabulary'. In order to exchange information, both ends of the conversation need to be using the same vocabulary.

While every organization, or individual developer, could define their own vocabulary, there are a number of standards bodies for most industry sectors that are working to define XML vocabularies for their industry's requirements. It makes sense to use these standard vocabularies whenever possible, instead of trying to reinvent the wheel. Start looking for these vocabularies at http://www.w3.org, http://www.BizTalk.org, http://www.rosettanet.org, or your industry's trade bodies.

For more information about XML, please refer to *Professional XML*, Second editon Wrox Press, ISBN 1-861005-05-9.

The XML-SS Schema

One such XML Vocabulary is the XML-SS schema that Microsoft uses to describe spreadsheet data. Both Excel 2002 and the Office 10 Spreadsheet Web Component can read and write XML using XML-SS. Until recently, the XML-SS schema documentation was available on the Microsoft web site, but was removed during one of its many reorganizations. Presumably that it is being updated for Office XP and will be made available shortly.

To obtain the XML-SS representation of an Excel `Range`, we use the new optional argument added to the `Range.Value` property:

```
Sub GetRangeXML()

    Dim sRangeXML As String

    sRangeXML = ActiveSheet.Range("A1:C40") _
                .Value(xlRangeValueXMLSpreadsheet)

    'Print to the Immediate window
    Debug.Print sRangeXML

End Sub
```

Consider the following simple timesheet:

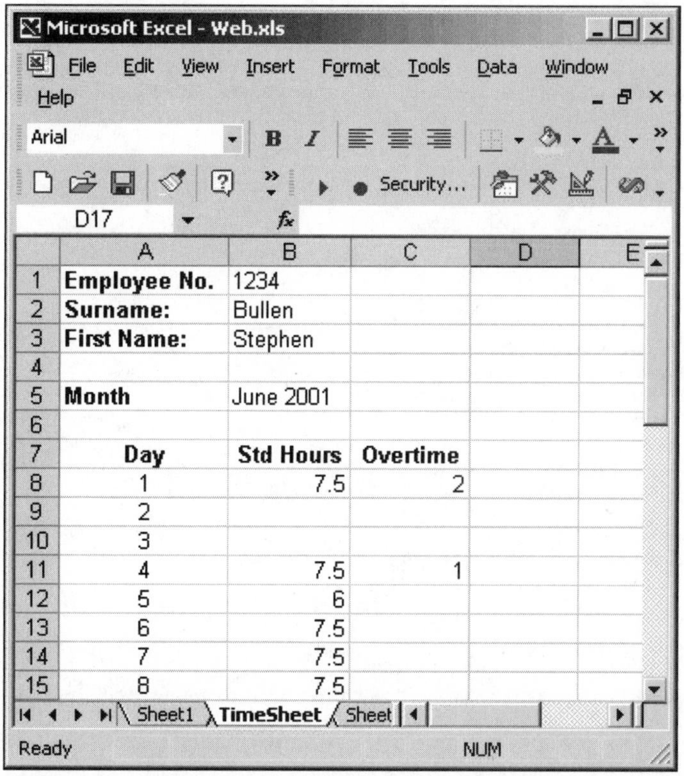

	A	B	C	D	E
1	**Employee No.**	1234			
2	**Surname:**	Bullen			
3	**First Name:**	Stephen			
4					
5	**Month**	June 2001			
6					
7	**Day**	**Std Hours**	**Overtime**		
8	1	7.5	2		
9	2				
10	3				
11	4	7.5	1		
12	5	6			
13	6	7.5			
14	7	7.5			
15	8	7.5			

This gives the following XML-SS (with some of the days removed):

```
<?xml version="1.0"?>
<Workbook xmlns="urn:schemas-microsoft-com:office:spreadsheet"
xmlns:o="urn:schemas-microsoft-com:office:office"
xmlns:x="urn:schemas-microsoft-com:office:excel"
xmlns:ss="urn:schemas-microsoft-com:office:spreadsheet"
xmlns:HTML="http://www.w3.org/TR/REC-html40">
  <Styles>
    <Style ss:ID="Default" ss:Name="Normal">
      <Alignment ss:Vertical="Bottom"/>
      <Borders/>
      <Font/>
      <Interior/>
      <NumberFormat/>
      <Protection/>
    </Style>
    <Style ss:ID="s24">
      <Alignment ss:Horizontal="Center" ss:Vertical="Bottom"/>
    </Style>
…
    <Style ss:ID="s29">
      <Alignment ss:Horizontal="Left" ss:Vertical="Bottom"/>
      <NumberFormat ss:Format="mmmm\ yyyy"/>
    </Style>
  </Styles>
  <Names>
    <NamedRange ss:Name="Days" ss:RefersTo="=TimeSheet!R8C1:R37C1"/>
    <NamedRange ss:Name="EmpNo" ss:RefersTo="=TimeSheet!R1C2"/>
    <NamedRange ss:Name="ForeName" ss:RefersTo="=TimeSheet!R3C2"/>
    <NamedRange ss:Name="Hours" ss:RefersTo="=TimeSheet!R8C2:R37C2"/>
    <NamedRange ss:Name="Month" ss:RefersTo="=TimeSheet!R5C2"/>
    <NamedRange ss:Name="Overtime" ss:RefersTo="=TimeSheet!R8C3:R37C3"/>
    <NamedRange ss:Name="StdHours" ss:RefersTo="=TimeSheet!R40C2"/>
    <NamedRange ss:Name="Surname" ss:RefersTo="=TimeSheet!R2C2"/>
  </Names>
  <Worksheet ss:Name="TimeSheet">
    <Table ss:ExpandedColumnCount="3" ss:ExpandedRowCount="40">
      <Column ss:AutoFitWidth="0" ss:Width="74.25"/>
      <Column ss:AutoFitWidth="0" ss:Width="62.25"/>
      <Column ss:AutoFitWidth="0" ss:Width="57.75"/>
      <Row>
        <Cell ss:StyleID="s27">
          <Data ss:Type="String">Employee No.</Data></Cell>
        <Cell ss:StyleID="s28">
          <Data ss:Type="Number">1234</Data>
          <NamedCell ss:Name="EmpNo"/></Cell>
      </Row>
      <Row>
        <Cell ss:StyleID="s25">
          <Data ss:Type="String">Surname:</Data></Cell>
        <Cell>
          <Data ss:Type="String">Bullen</Data>
          <NamedCell ss:Name="Surname"/></Cell>
      </Row>
…
      <Row>
        <Cell ss:StyleID="s25"><Data ss:Type="String">Month</Data></Cell>
        <Cell ss:StyleID="s29">
          <Data ss:Type="DateTime">2001-06-01T00:00:00.000</Data>
          <NamedCell ss:Name="Month"/></Cell>
      </Row>
      <Row ss:Index="7">
        <Cell ss:StyleID="s26">
```

```
          <Data ss:Type="String">Day</Data></Cell>
        <Cell ss:StyleID="s26">
          <Data ss:Type="String">Std Hours</Data></Cell>
        <Cell ss:StyleID="s26">
          <Data ss:Type="String">Overtime</Data></Cell>
      </Row>
      <Row>
        <Cell ss:StyleID="s24">
          <Data ss:Type="Number">1</Data>
          <NamedCell ss:Name="Days"/></Cell>
        <Cell>
          <Data ss:Type="Number">7.5</Data>
          <NamedCell ss:Name="Hours"/></Cell>
        <Cell>
          <Data ss:Type="Number">2</Data>
          <NamedCell ss:Name="Overtime"/></Cell>
      </Row>
      <Row>
        <Cell ss:StyleID="s24">
          <Data ss:Type="Number">2</Data>
          <NamedCell ss:Name="Days"/></Cell>
      </Row>
...
      <Row>
        <Cell ss:StyleID="s24">
          <Data ss:Type="Number">30</Data>
          <NamedCell ss:Name="Days"/></Cell>
      </Row>
      <Row ss:Index="39">
        <Cell ss:StyleID="s25"><Data ss:Type="String">Total:</Data></Cell>
        <Cell ss:StyleID="s25" ss:Formula="=SUM(R[-31]C:R[-3]C)">
          <Data ss:Type="Number">157.5</Data></Cell>
        <Cell ss:StyleID="s25" ss:Formula="=SUM(R[-31]C:R[-3]C)">
          <Data ss:Type="Number">3</Data></Cell>
      </Row>
...
    </Table>
  </Worksheet>
</Workbook>
```

The XML for a workbook contains the data, formulas, and formatting, but does not include embedded objects, charts, or VBA code.

More information about XML support in Excel 2002 is available from the Microsoft web site at http://msdn.microsoft.com/Office/.

Using XSLT to Transform XML

Examining the XML-SS data that Excel gives us, we can see that it is expressed in terms of workbooks, worksheets, tables, rows, and cells, while our timesheet XML shown earlier in this section expresses the data in terms of `Timesheets`, `Employees`, `ReportingMonths`, and `HoursWorked`. Before we can send our timesheet data to our web server, we need to transform the XML-SS schema into our `Timesheet` schema. That task is performed by XSLT, which stands for the eXtensible Stylesheet Language: Transformations.

XSLT is a declarative language, in which a stylesheet is applied to the source XML document. The stylesheet is written to select specific items of data out of the source XML in a specific order, such that the result is a new XML document that uses the target schema. In our case:

XML-SS + Custom StyleSheet = Timesheet XML

The following is the XSLT for our transformation:

```
<?xml version="1.0"?>
<xsl:stylesheet version="1.0"
    xmlns:xsl="http://www.w3.org/1999/XSL/Transform"
    xmlns:xl="urn:schemas-microsoft-com:office:spreadsheet"
    xmlns:ss="urn:schemas-microsoft-com:office:spreadsheet"
    exclude-result-prefixes="xl ss">
<xsl:template match="/xl:Workbook/xl:Worksheet/xl:Table">
<TS:Timesheet xmlns:TS="urn:schemas_wrox_com:ExcelProgRef:Timesheet">
  <TS:Employee>
    <TS:FirstName>
      <xsl:value-of
select="xl:Row/xl:Cell[xl:NamedCell[@ss:Name='ForeName']]/xl:Data"/>
    </TS:FirstName>
    <TS:LastName>
      <xsl:value-of
select="xl:Row/xl:Cell[xl:NamedCell[@ss:Name='Surname']]/xl:Data"/>
    </TS:LastName>
    <TS:EmployeeNumber>
      <xsl:value-of
select="xl:Row/xl:Cell[xl:NamedCell[@ss:Name='EmpNo']]/xl:Data"/>
    </TS:EmployeeNumber>
  </TS:Employee>
  <TS:ReportingMonth>
    <TS:Year>
      <xsl:value-of
select="substring(xl:Row/xl:Cell[xl:NamedCell[@ss:Name='Month']]/xl:Data,1,4)"/>
    </TS:Year>
    <TS:Month>
      <xsl:value-of
select="substring(xl:Row/xl:Cell[xl:NamedCell[@ss:Name='Month']]/xl:Data,6,2)"/>
    </TS:Month>
    <TS:TotalStdHours>
      <xsl:value-of
select="xl:Row/xl:Cell[xl:NamedCell[@ss:Name='StdHours']]/xl:Data"/>
    </TS:TotalStdHours>
  </TS:ReportingMonth>
  <xsl:for-each select="xl:Row/xl:Cell[xl:NamedCell[@ss:Name='Days']]">
    <xsl:if
test="string(number(../xl:Cell[xl:NamedCell[@ss:Name='Hours']]/xl:Data))!= 'NaN'">
      <TS:HoursWorked>
        <TS:Day>
          <xsl:value-of
select="../xl:Cell[xl:NamedCell[@ss:Name='Days']]/xl:Data"/>
        </TS:Day>
        <TS:StdHours>
          <xsl:value-of
select="../xl:Cell[xl:NamedCell[@ss:Name='Hours']]/xl:Data"/>
        </TS:StdHours>
        <xsl:choose>
          <xsl:when
test="string(number(../xl:Cell[xl:NamedCell[@ss:Name='Overtime']]/xl:Data))!='NaN'
">
            <TS:Overtime>
              <xsl:value-of
select="../xl:Cell[xl:NamedCell[@ss:Name='Overtime']]/xl:Data"/>
            </TS:Overtime>
```

```
            </xsl:when>
            <xsl:otherwise><TS:Overtime/></xsl:otherwise>
          </xsl:choose>
        </TS:HoursWorked>
      </xsl:if>
    </xsl:for-each>
  </TS:Timesheet>
  </xsl:template>
  </xsl:stylesheet>
```

The XSLT is almost human-readable. The key to understanding it is to realize the following:

- Only tags that start `<xsl>` and `</xsl>` are processing elements, telling the XML parser how to transform the data
- All the other tags are copied directly to the output stream
- The following expression locates the cell that has been given the range name of `ForeName` and returns its `Data` element (i.e. its value), and is equivalent to `Range("ForeName").Value` in VBA:

```
select="xl:Row/xl:Cell[xl:NamedCell[@ss:Name='ForeName']]/xl:Data"
```

- The following expression starts a `For...Each` loop through all the cells in the named range 'Days', and is equivalent to `For Each oCell In Range("Days").Cells` in VBA:

```
<xsl:for-each select="xl:Row/xl:Cell[xl:NamedCell[@ss:Name='Days']]">
```

- In the XML-SS schema, there is a tree structure of Worksheet > Rows > Cells, so the parent of a cell (`../` in XSLT) is the row, so the expression:

```
select="../xl:Cell[xl:NamedCell[@ss:Name='Hours']]/xl:Data"/>
```

  is equivalent to the VBA:

```
Application.Intersect(oCell.EntireRow, Range("Hours")).Value
```

- The transformation strips out days for which no time was entered. The expression:

```
test="string(number(…))!='NaN'"
```

  is the XSLT equivalent of `IsNumeric(...)` in VBA

We shall be referencing this code by placing it in a cell called "`XSLT`" in a worksheet called "`XSLT`", as the following screenshot shows:

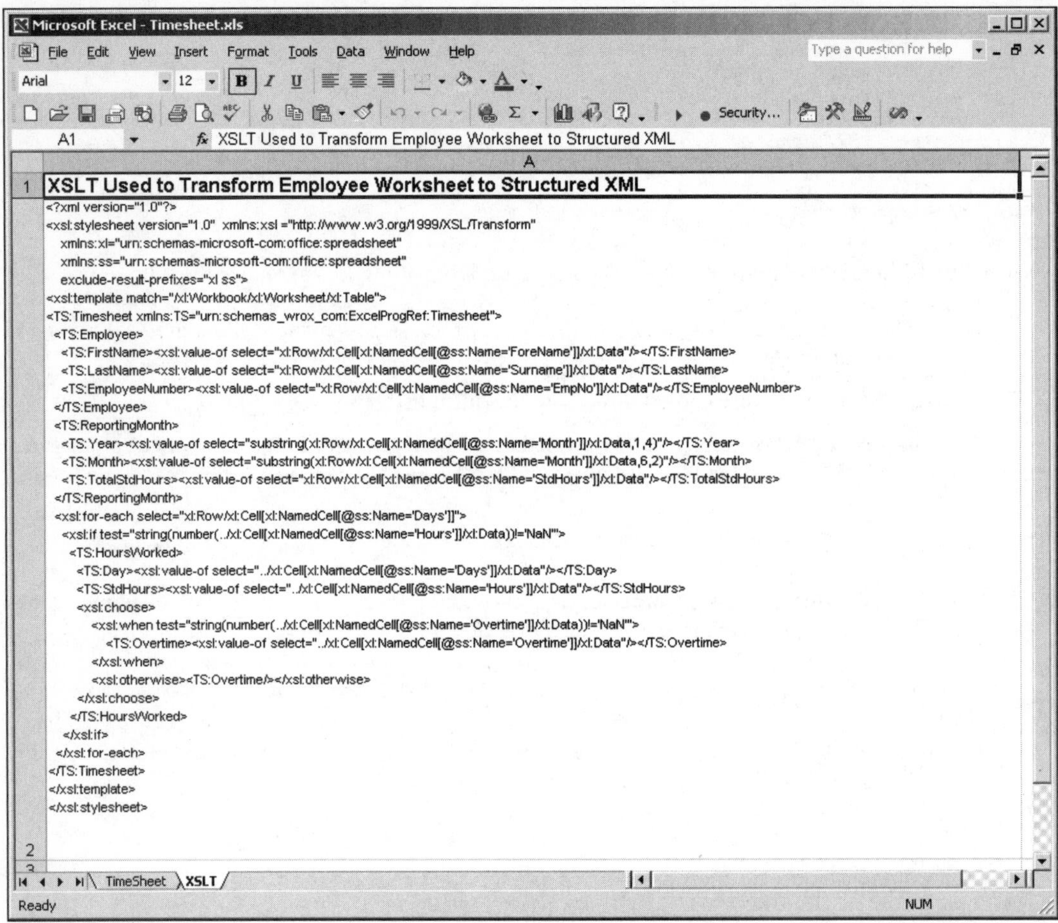

The VBA code to perform the transformation and send the Timesheet XML to a web server application is shown below. It uses the MSXML parser to perform the transformation (referenced by the 'Microsoft XML, v3.0' object library):

```
'Transfrom the spreadsheet XML-SS format to the TimeSheet XML format
Sub TransformAndPostXML()

    'Define three instances of the MSXML parser

    'One for the source XML - in XML-SS format
    Dim xmlSource As MSXML2.DOMDocument30

    'One for the XSLT transformation
    Dim xmlXSLT As MSXML2.DOMDocument30

    'One for the resultant XML - in Timesheet format
    Dim xmlTimesheet As MSXML2.DOMDocument30

    'Define an instance of the ITC for sending the XML
    Dim oInet As Inet
```

```
    Dim sTimesheetXML As String

    'Create new instances of the MSXML parsers
    Set xmlSource = New MSXML2.DOMDocument30
    Set xmlXSLT = New MSXML2.DOMDocument30
    Set xmlTimesheet = New MSXML2.DOMDocument30

    'Load the source XML from the Timesheet worksheet
    xmlSource.loadXML Worksheets("TimeSheet").Range("A1:C40") _
                      .Value(xlRangeValueXMLSpreadsheet)

    'Load the XSLT from the XSLT worksheet
    xmlXSLT.loadXML Worksheets("XSLT").Range("XSLT").Value

    'Transform the XML-SS using the XSLT, giving the Timesheet XML
    xmlSource.transformNodeToObject xmlXSLT, xmlTimesheet

    'Read the resultant Timesheet XML into a variable
    sTimesheetXML = xmlTimesheet.XML

    'Create a new instance of the Internet Transfer Control
    Set oInet = New Inet

    'Send the XML to the server
    oInet.Execute "http://localhost/MyPage.asp", "POST", sTimesheetXML

End Sub
```

A full description of XSLT is beyond the scope of this book, but much more information is available in the *XSLT Programmer's Reference*, Wrox Press, ISBN 1-861005-06-7.

Summary

In Excel 2002, Microsoft has enabled the Excel developer to use the Internet as an integral part of an application solution:

- Workbooks can be opened from and saved to web servers running the FrontPage Server Extensions
- Excel can open HTML pages as though they were workbooks
- Web Queries can be used to extract tables of data from web pages
- The Internet Explorer object library can be automated to retrieve individual items of data from a web page, without the overhead of using a workbook
- Excel workbooks can be saved as content-rich web pages
- Interactive web pages can easily be produced, providing Excel-like interaction within the web browser.
- The Microsoft Internet Transfer Control can be used to exchange data between Excel applications and web servers, either using a simple parameter list or more structured XML.
- Excel 2002 supports the XML-SS schema for describing spreadsheets, and the MSXML parser can use XSLT to transform XML-SS to other XML schemas, prior to sending the data to the web server.

Together, these tools enable us to develop new types of business solution, where Excel is one key part of a larger business process, which may span multiple organizations and geographical locations.

22

International Issues

If you think that your application may be used internationally, it has to work with any choice of Windows Regional Setting, on any language version of Windows, and with any language choice for the Excel user interface.

If you are very lucky, all your potential users will have exactly the same settings as your development machine and you don't need to worry about international issues. However, a more likely scenario is that you do not even know who all your users are going to be, let alone where in the world they will live, or the settings they will use.

Any bugs in your application that arise from the disregarding or ignoring of international issues will not occur on your development machine unless you explicitly test for them. However, they will be found immediately by your clients.

The combination of Regional Settings and Excel language is called the user's 'locale' and the aim of this chapter is to show you how to write locale-independent VBA applications. In order to do this, we include an explanation of the features in Excel that deal with locale-related issues and highlight areas within Excel where locale support is absent or limited. Workarounds are provided for most of these limitations, but some are so problematic that the only solution is to not use the feature at all.

The rules provided in this chapter should be included in your coding standards and used by you and your colleagues. It is easy to write locale-independent code from scratch; it is much more difficult to make existing code compatible with the many different locales in the world today.

Changing Windows Regional Settings and the Office XP UI Language

During this chapter, the potential errors will be demonstrated by using the following three locales:

Setting	US	UK	Norway
Decimal Separator	.	.	,
Thousand Separator	,	,	.
Date order	mm/dd/yyyy	dd/mm/yyyy	dd.mm.yyyy

Table continued on following page

Setting	US	UK	Norway
Date separator	/	/	.
Example number: 1234.56	1,234.56	1,234.56	1.234,56
Example date: Feb 10, 2001	02/10/2001	10/02/2001	10.02.2001
Windows and Excel Language	English	English	Norwegian
The text for the Boolean `True`	`True`	`True`	`Sann`

The regional settings are changed using the **Regional Settings** applet (**Regional Options** in Windows 2000) in Windows Control Panel, while the Office XP language is changed using the "Microsoft Office Language Settings" program provided with the Office XP Language Packs. Unfortunately, the only way to change the Windows language is to install a new version from scratch.

When testing your application, it is a very good idea to use some fictional regional settings, such as having # for the thousand separator, `!` for the decimal separator, and a YMD date order. It is then very easy to determine if your application is using your settings or some internal default. For completeness, you should also have a machine in your office with a different language version of Windows from the one you normally use.

Responding to Regional Settings and the Windows Language

This section explains how to write applications that work with different regional settings and Windows language versions, which should be considered the absolute minimum requirement.

Identifying the User's Regional Settings and Windows Language

Everything you need to know about your user's Windows Regional Settings and Windows language version is found in the `Application.International` property. The online help lists all of the items which can be accessed, though you are unlikely to use more than a few of them. The most notable are:

- `XlCountryCode`
  The language version of Excel (or of the currently active Office language)
- `XlCountrySetting`
  The Windows regional settings location
- `XlDateOrder`
  The choice of MDY, DMY, or YMD order to display dates

Note that there is no constant that enables us to identify which language version of Windows is installed (but we can get that information from the Windows API if required).

*Note that "Windows Regional Settings" is abbreviated to **WRS** in the rest of this chapter and is also described as 'local' settings.*

VBA Conversion Functions from an International Perspective

The online help files explain the use of VBA's conversion functions in terms of converting between different data types. This section explains their behavior when converting to and from strings in different locales.

Implicit Conversion

This is the most common form of type conversion used in VBA code and forces the VBA interpreter to convert the data using whichever format it thinks is most appropriate. A typical example of this code is:

```
Dim dtMyDate As Date
dtMyDate = DateValue("Jan 1, 2001")
MsgBox "This first day of this year is " & dtMyDate
```

When converting a number to a string in Office XP, VBA uses the WRS to supply either a date string in the user's 'ShortDate' format, the number formatted according to the WRS, or the text for `True` or `False` in the WRS language. This is fine, if you want the output as a locally formatted string. If, however, your code assumes you've got a US-formatted string, it will fail. Of course, if you develop using US formats, you won't notice the difference (though your client will).

There is a much bigger problem with using implicit conversion if you are writing code for multiple versions of Excel. In previous versions, the number formats used in the conversion were those appropriate for the Excel language being used at run time (buried within the Excel object library), which might be different from both US and local formats, and were not affected by changing the WRS.

Be very careful with the data types returned from, and used by, Excel and VBA functions. For example, `Application.GetOpenFilename` returns a `Variant` containing the Boolean value `False` if the user cancels, or a string containing the text of the selected file. If you store this result in a `String` variable, the Boolean `False` will be converted to a string in the user's WRS language, and may not equal the string `"False"` that you may be comparing it to.

To avoid these problems, use the Object Browser to check the function's return type and parameter types, then make sure to match them, or explicitly convert them to your variable's data type. Applying this recommendation gives us (at least) three solutions to using `Application.GetOpenFilename`.

Typical code running in Norway:

```
Dim stFile As String
stFile = Application.GetOpenFilename()
If stFile = "False" Then
   ...
```

If the user cancels, `GetOpenFilename` returns a variable containing the Boolean value `False`. Excel converts it to a string to put in our variable, using the Windows language. In Norway, the string will contain "`Usann`". If this is compared to the string "`False`", it doesn't match, so the program thinks it is a valid file name and subsequently crashes.

Solution 1:

```
Dim vaFile As Variant
vaFile = Application.GetOpenFileName()
If vaFile = False Then    'Compare using the same data types
   ...
```

Solution 2:

```
Dim vaFile As Variant
vaFile = Application.GetOpenFileName()
If CStr(vaFile) = "False" Then       'Explicit conversion with CStr() always
                                     'gives a US Boolean string
    ...
```

Solution 3:

```
Dim vaFile As Variant
vaFile = Application.GetOpenFileName()
If TypeName(vaFile) = "Boolean" Then      'Got a Boolean, so must have
                                          'cancelled
    ...
```

Note that in all three cases, the key point is that we are matching the data type returned by `GetOpenFilename` (a `Variant`) with our variable. If you use the `MultiSelect:=True` parameter within the `GetOpenFileName` function, the last of the above solutions should be used. This is because the `vaFile` variable will contain an array of file names, or the Boolean `False`. Attempting to compare an array with `False`, or trying to convert it to a string will result in a run-time error.

Date Literals

When coding in VBA, you can write dates using a format of `#01/01/2001#`, which is obviously Jan 1, 2001. But what is `#02/01/2001#`? Is it Jan 2 or Feb 1? Well, it is actually Feb 1, 2001. This is because when coding in Excel, we do so in American English, regardless of any other settings we may have, and hence we must use US-formatted date literals (mm/dd/yyyy format). If other formats are typed in (such as `#yyyy-mm-dd#`) Excel will convert them to `#mm/dd/yyyy#` order.

What happens if you happen to be Norwegian or British and try typing in your local date format (which you **will** do at some time, usually near a deadline)? If you type in a Norwegian-formatted date literal, `#02.01.2001#`, you get a syntax error which at least alerts you to the mistake you made. However, if you type in dates in a UK format (dd/mm/yyyy format) things get a little more interesting. VBA recognizes the date and so doesn't give an error, but 'sees' that you have the day and month the wrong way round; it swaps them for you. So, typing in dates from Jan 10, 2001 to Jan 15, 2001 results in:

You Typed	VBA Shows	Meaning
10/1/2001	10/1/2001	Oct 1, 2001
11/1/2001	11/1/2001	Nov 1, 2001
12/1/2001	12/1/2001	Dec 1, 2001
13/1/2001	1/13/2001	Jan 13, 2001
14/1/2001	1/14/2001	Jan 14, 2001
15/1/2001	1/15/2001	Jan 15, 2001

If these literals are sprinkled through your code, you will not notice the errors.

It is much safer to avoid using date literals and use the VBA functions `DateSerial(Year, Month, Day)` or `DateValue(DateString)`, where `DateString` is a non-ambiguous string such as "Jan 1, 2001". Both of these functions return the corresponding `Date` number.

The IsNumeric and IsDate Functions

These two functions test if a string can be evaluated as a number or date according to the WRS and Windows language version. You should always use these functions before trying to convert a string to another data type. We don't have an `IsBoolean` function, or functions to check if a string is a US-formatted number or date. Note that `IsNumeric` does not recognize a `%` character on the end of a number, and `IsDate` does not recognize days of the week.

The CStr Function

This is the function most used by VBA in implicit data type conversions. It converts a `Variant` to a `String`, formatted according to the WRS. When converting a `Date` type, the 'ShortDate' format is used, as defined in the WRS. Note that when converting `Booleans`, the resulting text is the English "`True`" or "`False`" and is not dependent on any Windows settings. Compare this with the implicit conversion of `Booleans`, whereby `MsgBox "I am " & True` results in the `True` being displayed in the WRS language ("`I am Sann`" in Norwegian Regional Settings).

The CDbl, CSng, CLng, CInt, CByte, CCur, and CDec Functions

All of these can convert a string representation of a number into a numeric data type (as well as converting different numeric data types into each other). The string must be formatted according to WRS. These functions do not recognize date strings or `%` characters

The CDate and DateValue Functions

These methods can convert a string to a `Date` data type (`CDate` can also convert other data types to the `Date` type). The string must be formatted according to WRS and use the Windows language for month names. It does not recognize the names for the days of the week, giving a `Type Mismatch` error. If the year is not specified in the string, it uses the current year.

The CBool

`CBool` converts a string (or a number) to a `Boolean` value. Contrary to all the other `Cxxx` conversion functions, the string must be the English "`True`" or "`False`".

The Format Function

The `Format` function converts a number or date to a string, using a number format supplied in code. The number format must use US symbols (m, d, s, etc.), but results in a string formatted according to WRS (with the correct decimal, thousand, and date separators) and the WRS language (for the weekday and month names). For example, the code below will result in "Friday 01/01/2001" in the US, but "Fredag 01.01.2001" when used with Norwegian settings:

```
MsgBox Format(DateSerial(2001, 1, 1), "dddd dd/mm/yyyy")
```

If you omit the number format string, it behaves in exactly the same way as the `CStr` function (even though online help says it behaves like `Str`), including the strange handling of `Boolean` values, where `Format(True)` always results in the English "`True`". Note that it does not change the date order returned to agree with the WRS, so your code has to determine the date order in use before creating the number format string.

The FormatCurrency, FormatDateTime, FormatNumber, and FormatPercent Functions

These functions added in Excel 2000 provide the same functionality as the `Format` function, but use parameters to define the specific resulting format instead of a custom format string. They correspond to standard options in Excel's Format | Cells | Number dialog, while the `Format` function corresponds to the Custom option. They have the same international behavior as the `Format` function above.

The Str Function

Converts a number, date or Boolean to a US-formatted string, regardless of the WRS, Windows language or Office language version. When converting a positive number, it adds a space on the left. When converting a decimal fraction, it does not add a leading zero. The following custom function is a extension of `Str` which removes the leading space and adds the zero.

The sNumToUS Function

This function converts a number, date, or Boolean variable to a US-formatted string. There is an additional parameter that can be used to return a string using Excel's `DATE` function, which would typically be used when constructing `.Formula` strings:

```
Function sNumToUS(vValue As Variant, Optional bUseDATEFunction) As String

   Dim sTmp As String

   'Don't accept strings or arrays as input
   If TypeName(vValue) = "String" Then Exit Function
   If Right(TypeName(vValue), 2) = "()" Then Exit Function

   If IsMissing(bUseDATEFunction) Then bUseDATEFunction = False

   'Do we want it returned as Excel's DATE function
   '(which we can't do with strings)?
   If bUseDATEFunction Then

      'We do, so build the Excel DATE() function string
      sTmp = "DATE(" & Year(vValue) & "," & Month(vValue) & "," & _
         Day(vValue) & ")"
   Else
      'Is it a date type?
      If TypeName(vValue) = "Date" Then
         sTmp = Format(vValue, "mm""/""dd""/""yyyy")
      Else
         'Convert number to string in US format and remove leading space
         sTmp = Trim(Str(vValue))

         'If we have fractions, we don't get a leading zero, so add one.
         If Left(sTmp, 1) = "." Then sTmp = "0" & sTmp
         If Left(sTmp, 2) = "-." Then sTmp = "-0" & Mid(sTmp, 2)
      End If
   End If

  'Return the US formatted string
   sNumToUS = sTmp
End Function
```

`vValue` is a variant containing the number to convert, which can be:

- A number to be converted to a string with US formats
- A date to be converted to a string in mm/dd/yyyy format
- A Boolean converted to the strings "True" or "False"

`bUseDATEFunction` is an optional Boolean for handling dates. When it is set to `False`, `sNumToUS` returns a date string in mm/dd/yyyy format. When it is set to `True`, `sNumToUS` returns a date as `DATE(yyyy,mm,dd)`.

The Val Function

This is the most common function that I've seen used to convert from strings to numbers. It actually only converts a **US-formatted** numerical string to a number. All the other string-to-number conversion functions try to convert the entire string to a number and raise an error if they can't. `Val`, however, works from left to right until it finds a character that it doesn't recognize as part of a number. Many characters typically found in numbers, such as `$` and commas, are enough to stop it recognizing the number. `Val` does not recognize US-formatted date strings.

`Val` also has the dubious distinction of being the only one of VBA's conversion functions to take a specific data type for its input. While all the others use `Variants`, `Val` accepts only a string. This means that anything you pass to `Val` is converted to a string (implicitly, therefore according to the WRS and Windows language), before being evaluated according to US formats.

> **The use of `Val` can have unwanted side-effects (otherwise known as bugs), which are very difficult to detect in code that is running fine on your own machine, but which would fail on another machine with different WRS.**

Here `myDate` is a `Date` variable containing Feb 10, 2001 and `myDbl` is a `Double` containing 1.234:

Expression	US	UK	Norway
`Val(myDate)`	`2`	`10`	`10.02` (or `10.2`)
`Val(myDbl)`	`1.234`	`1.234`	`1`
`Val(True)`	`0 (=False)`	`0 (=False)`	`0 (=False)`
`Val("SomeText")`	`0`	`0`	`0`
`Val("6 My St.")`	`6`	`6`	`6`

Application.Evaluate

While not normally considered to be a conversion function, `Application.Evaluate` is the only way to convert a US-formatted date string to a date number. The following two functions `IsDateUS` and `DateValueUS` are wrapper functions which use this method.

The IsDateUS Function

The built-in `IsDate` function validates a string against the Windows Regional Settings. This function provides us with a way to check if a string contains a US-formatted date:

```
Function IsDateUS(sDate As String) As Boolean

   IsDateUS = Not IsError(Application.Evaluate("DATEVALUE(""" & _
                                                           sDate & """)"))
End Function
```

sDate is a string containing a US-formatted date. `IsDateUS` returns `True` if the string contains a valid US date, and `False` if not.

The DateValueUS Function

The VBA `DateValue` function converts a string formatted according to the Windows Regional Settings to a `Date` type. This function converts a string containing a US-formatted date to a `Date` type. If the string can not be recognized as a US-formatted date, it returns an `Error` value, that can be tested for using the `IsError` function:

```
Function DateValueUS(sDate As String) As Variant

   DateValueUS = Application.Evaluate("DATEVALUE(""" & sDate & """)")

End Function
```

`sDate` is a string containing a US-formatted date. `DateValueUS` returns the date value of the given string, in a `Variant`.

Interacting with Excel

VBA and Excel are two different programs that have had very different upbringings. VBA speaks American. Excel also speaks American. However, Excel can also speak in its user's language if they have the appropriate Windows settings and Office language pack installed. On the other hand VBA knows only a little about Windows settings, and even less about Office XP language packs. So, we can either do some awkward coding to teach VBA how to speak to Excel in the user's language, or we can just let them converse in American. I very much recommend the latter.

Unfortunately, most of the newer features in Excel are not multilingual. Some only speak American, while others only speak in the user's language. We can use the American-only features if we understand their limitations; the others are best avoided. All of them are documented later in the chapter.

Sending Data to Excel

By far the best way to get numbers, dates, Booleans, and strings into Excel cells is to do so in their native format. Hence, the following code works perfectly, regardless of locale:

```
Sub SendToExcel()
   Dim dtDate As Date, dNumber As Double, bBool As Boolean, _
      stString As String

   dtDate = DateSerial(2001, 2, 13)
   dNumber = 1234.567
   bBool = True
   stString = "Hello World"

   Range("A1").Value = dtDate
   Range("A2").Value = dNumber
   Range("A3").Value = bBool
   Range("A4").Value = stString
End Sub
```

There is a boundary layer between VBA and Excel. When VBA passes a variable through the boundary, Excel does its best to interpret it according to its own rules. If the VBA and Excel data types are mutually compatible the variable passes straight through unhindered.

The problems start when Excel forces us to pass it numbers, dates, or Booleans within strings, or when we choose to do so ourselves. The answer to the latter situation is easy – don't do it. Whenever you have a string representation of some other data type, if it is possible, always explicitly convert it to the data type you want Excel to store, before passing it to Excel.

Excel requires string input in the following circumstances:

- Setting the formula for a cell, chart series, conditional format, or pivot table calculated field
- Specifying the `RefersTo` formula for a defined name
- Specifying AutoFilter criteria
- Passing a formula to `ExecuteExcel4Macro`
- Setting the number format of a cell, style, chart axis, or pivot table field
- Setting number format in the VBA `Format` function

In these cases, we have to ensure that the string that VBA sends to Excel is in US-formatted text –we must use English language formulas and US regional settings. If the string is built within the code, we must be very careful to explicitly convert all our variables to US-formatted strings.

Take this simple example:

```
Sub SetLimit(dLimit As Double)
   ActiveCell.Formula = "=IF(A1<" & dLimit & ",1,0)"
End Sub
```

We are setting a cell's formula based on a parameter supplied from another routine. Note that the formula is being constructed in the code and we are using US language and regional settings (that is the English `IF` and using a comma for the list separator). When used with different values for `dLimit` in different locales, we get the following results:

dLimit	US	UK	Norway
100	Works fine	Works fine	Works fine
100.23	Works fine	Works fine	Run-time Error 1004

It fails when run in Norway with any non-integer value for `dLimit`. This is because we are implicitly converting the variable to a string, which you'll recall uses the Windows Regional Settings number formats. The resulting string that we're passing to Excel is:

```
=IF(A1<100,23,1,0)
```

This fails because the `IF` function does not have four parameters. If we change the function to read:

```
Sub SetLimit(dLimit As Double)
   ActiveCell.Formula = "=IF(A1<" & Str(dLimit) & ",1,0)"
End Sub
```

The function will work correctly, as `Str` forces a conversion to a US-formatted string.

If we try the same routine with a `Date` instead of a `Double`, we come across another problem. The text that is passed to Excel (for example for Feb 13, 2001) is:

```
=IF(A1<02/13/2001,1,0)
```

While this is a valid formula, Excel interprets the date as a set of divisions, so the formula is equivalent to:

```
=IF(A1<0.000077,1,0)
```

This is unlikely to ever be true. To avoid this, we have to convert the `Date` data type to a `Double`, and from that to a string:

```
Sub SetDateLimit(dtLimit As Date)
   ActiveCell.Formula = "=IF(A1<" & Str(CDbl(dtLimit)) & ",1,0)"
End Sub
```

The function is then the correct (but less readable):

```
=IF(A1<36935,1,0)
```

To maintain readability, we should convert dates to Excel's `DATE` function, to give:

```
=IF(A1<DATE(2001,2,13),1,0)
```

This is also achieved by the `sNumToUS` function presented earlier on in this chapter, when the `bUseDateFunction` parameter is set to `True`:

```
Sub SetDateLimit(dLimit As Date)
   ActiveCell.Formula = "=IF(A1<" & sNumToUS(dLimit, True) & ",1,0)"
End Sub
```

If you call the revised `SetLimit` procedure with a value of 100.23 and look at the cell that the formula was put into, you'll see that Excel has converted the US string into the local language and regional settings. In Norway, for example, the cell actually shows:

```
=HVIS(A1<100,23;1;0)
```

This translation also applies to number formats. Whenever we set a number format within VBA, we can give Excel a format string which uses US characters (such as 'd' for day, 'm' for month, and 'y' for year). When applied to the cell (or style or chart axis), or used in the `Format` function, Excel translates these characters to the local versions. For example, the following code results in a number format of dd/mm/åååå when we check it using `Format`, `Cells`, and `Number` in Norwegian Windows:

```
ActiveCell.NumberFormat = "dd/mm/yyyy"
```

This ability of Excel to translate US strings into the local language and formats makes it easy for developers to create locale-independent applications. All we have to do is code in American and ensure that we explicitly convert our variables to US-formatted strings before passing them to Excel.

Reading Data from Excel

When reading a cell's value, using its `Value` property, the data type that Excel provides to VBA is determined by a combination of the cell's value and its formatting. For example, the number 3000 could reach VBA as a `Double`, a `Currency`, or a `Date` (March 18, 1908). The only international issue that concerns us here, is if the cell's value is read directly into a string variable – the conversion will then be done implicitly and you may not get what you expect (particularly if the cell contains a Boolean value).

As is the case when sending data to Excel, the translation between US and local functions and formats occurs when reading data from Excel. This means that a cell's `.Formula` or `.NumberFormat` property is given to us in English, and with US number and date formatting, regardless of the user's choice of language or regional settings.

While for most applications, it is much simpler to read and write using US formulas and formats, we will sometimes need to read exactly what the user is seeing (in their choice of language and regional settings). This is done by using the `xxxLocal` versions of many properties, which return (and interpret) strings according to the user's settings. They are typically used when displaying a formula or number format on a UserForm, and are discussed in the following section.

The Rules for Working with Excel

- Pass values to Excel in their natural format if possible (don't convert dates/numbers/Booleans to strings if you don't have to). If you have strings, convert them yourself before passing them to Excel.
- When you have to convert numbers and dates to strings for passing to Excel (such as in criteria for `AutoFilter` or `.Formula` strings), **always explicitly convert the data** to a US-formatted string, using `Trim(Str(MyNumber))`, or the `sNumToUS` function shown earlier, for all number and date types. Excel will then use it correctly and convert it to the local number/date formats.
- Avoid using `Date` literals (e.g. `#1/3/2001#`) in your code. It is better to use the VBA `DateSerial`, or the Excel `DATE` functions, which are not ambiguous.
- If possible, use the date number instead of a string representation of a date. Numbers are much less prone to ambiguity (though not immune).
- When writing formulas in code to be put into a cell (using the `.Formula` property), create the string using English functions. Excel will translate them to the local Office language for you.
- When setting number formats or using the `Format` function, use US formatting characters, for example `ActiveCell.NumberFormat = "dd mmm yyyy"`. Excel will translate these to the local number format for you.
- When reading information from a worksheet, using `.Formula`, `.NumberFormat`, etc., Excel will supply it using English formulas and US format codes, regardless of the local Excel language.

Interacting with Users

The golden rule when displaying data to your users, or getting data from them, is to always respect their choice of Windows Regional Settings and Office UI Language. They should not be forced to enter numbers dates, formulas, and/or number formats according to US settings, just because it's easier for you to develop.

Paper Sizes

One of the most annoying things for a user is discovering that their printer does not recognise the paper sizes used in your templates. If you use templates for your reports, you should always change the paper size to the user's default size. This can easily be determined by creating a new workbook and reading off the paper size from the `PageSetup` object.

Excel 2002 added the `Application.MapPaperSize` property, to automatically switch between the standard paper sizes of different countries (for example Letter in the US <–> A4 in the UK). If this is property is set to `True`, Excel 2002 should take care of paper sizes for you.

Displaying Data

Excel does a very good job of displaying worksheets according to the user's selection of regional settings and language. When displaying data in UserForms or dialog sheets, however, we have to do all the formatting ourselves.

As discussed above, Excel converts number and dates to strings according to the WRS by default. This means that we can write code like the following, and be safe in the knowledge that Excel will display it correctly:

```
tbNumber.Text = dNumber
```

There are two problems with this approach:

- Dates will get the default 'ShortDate' format, which may not include 4 digits for the year, and will not include a time component. To force a 4-digit year and include a time, use the `sFormatDate` function shown later. It may be better, though, to use a less ambiguous date format on UserForms, such as the 'mmm dd, yyyy' format used throughout this book.
- Versions of Excel prior to Excel 97 did not use the Windows Regional Settings for their default formats. If you are creating applications for use in older versions of Excel, you can't rely on the correct behavior.

The solution is simple – just use the `Format` function. This tells VBA to convert the number to a locally-formatted string and works in all versions of Excel from 5.0:

```
tbNumber.Text = Format(dNumber)
```

Interpreting Data

Your users will want to type in dates and numbers according to their choice of regional settings and your code must validate those entries accordingly and maybe display meaningful error messages back to the user. This means that you have to use the `Cxxx` conversion functions, and the `IsNumeric` and `IsDate` validation functions.

Unfortunately, these functions all have their problems (such as not recognising the `%` sign at the end of a number) which require some working around. An easy solution is to use the `bWinToNum` and `bWinToDate` functions shown at the end of this chapter to perform the validation, conversion, and error prompting for you. The validation code for a UserForm will typically be done in the OK button's `Click` event, and be something like:

```
Private Sub bnOK_Click()
   Dim dResult As Double

   'Validate the number or display an error
   If bWinToNum(tbNumber.Text, dResult, True) Then
      'It was valid, so store the number
      Sheet1.Range("A1").Value = dResult
   Else
      'An error, so set the focus back and quit the routine
      tbNumber.SetFocus
      Exit Sub
   End If

   'All OK and stored, so hide the userform
   Me.Hide
End Sub
```

The xxxLocal Properties

Up until now, we have said that you have to interact with Excel using English language functions and the default US formats. Now we present an alternative situation where your code interacts with the user in his or her own language using the appropriate regional settings. How then, can your program take something typed in by the user (such as a number format or formula) and send it straight to Excel, or display an Excel formula in a message box in the user's own language?

Microsoft has anticipated this requirement and has provided us with local versions of most of the functions we need. They have the same name as their US equivalent, with the word "`Local`" on the end (such as `FormulaLocal`, `NumberFormatLocal` etc.). When we use these functions, Excel does not perform any language or format coercion for us. The text we read and write is exactly how it appears to the user. Nearly all of the functions that return strings, or have string arguments, have local equivalents. The following table lists them all and the objects to which they apply:

Applies To	These versions of the functions use and return strings according to US number and date formats and English text	These versions of the functions use and return locally-formatted strings, and in the language used for the Office UI (or Windows version – see later)
Number/string conversion	`Str`	`CStr`
Number/string conversion	`Val`	`CDbl`, etc.
Name, Style, Command Bar	`.Name`	`.NameLocal`
Range, Chart Series	`.Formula`	`.FormulaLocal`
Range, Chart Series	`.FormulaR1C1`	`.FormulaR1C1Local`
Range, Style, Chart Data Label, Chart Axes Label	`.NumberFormat`	`.NumberFormatLocal`

Table continued on following page

Applies To	These versions of the functions use and return strings according to US number and date formats and English text	These versions of the functions use and return locally-formatted strings, and in the language used for the Office UI (or Windows version – see later)
Range	`.Address`	`.AddressLocal`
Range	`.AddressR1C1`	`.AddressR1C1Local`
Defined Name	`.RefersTo`	`.RefersToLocal`
Defined Name	`.RefersToR1C1`	`.RefersToR1C1Local`
Defined Name	`.Category`	`.CategoryLocal`

The Rules for Working with Your Users

- When converting a number or date to a text string for displaying to your users, or setting it as the `.Caption` or `.Text` properties of controls, explicitly convert numbers and dates to text according to the WRS, using `Format(myNum)`, or `CStr(MyNum)`.
- When converting dates to strings, Excel does **not** rearrange the date part order, so `Format(MyDate, "dd/mm/yyyy")` will always give a DMY date order (but will show the correct date separator). Use `Application.International(xlDateOrder)` to determine the correct date order – as used in the `sFormatDate` function shown at the end of this chapter, or use one of the standard date formats (for example ShortDate).
- If possible, use locale-independent date formats, such as `Format(MyDate, "mmm dd, yyyy")`. Excel will display month names according to the user's WRS language.
- When evaluating date or number strings which have been entered by the user, use `CDate` or `CDbl`, to convert the string to a date/number. These will use the WRS to interpret the string. Note that `CDbl` does not handle the `%` character if the user has put one at the end of the number.
- Always validate numbers and dates entered by the user before trying to convert them. See the `bWinToNum` and `bWinToDate` functions at the end of this chapter for an example.
- When displaying information about Excel objects, use the `xxxLocal` properties (where they exist) to display it in your user's language and formats.
- Use the `xxxLocal` properties when setting the properties of Excel objects with text provided by the user (which we must assume is in their native language and format).

Excel 2002's International Options

In the Tools | Options dialog, a new 'International' tab has been added in Excel 2002. This tab allows the user to specify the characters that Excel uses for the thousand and decimal separators, overriding the Windows Regional Settings. These options can be read and changed in code, using `Application.ThousandSeparator`, `Application.DecimalSeparator`, and `Application.UseSystemSeparators`.

Using these new properties we could, for example, print, save (as text), or publish a workbook using local number formats, change the separators being used, print, save (as text) or publish another version for a different target country, then change them back to their original settings. It is a great pity, though, that Microsoft didn't add the ability to override the rest of the Windows Regional Settings attributes (such as date order, date separator, whether to use (10) or -10, etc.) and it's an omission that makes this feature virtually useless in practice.

One problem with using this feature is that it does not change the number format strings used in the `=TEXT` worksheet function, so as soon as the option is changed (either in code or through the UI), all cells that use the `=TEXT` function will no longer be formatted correctly. See later in this chapter for a workaround to this problem.

The addition of this feature has a big downside for us as developers, though. The problem is that while these options affect all of Excel's `xxxLocal` properties and functions (including the `Application.International` settings), **they are ignored by VBA.**

A few examples highlight the scale of the problem:

- The VBA `Format` function – used almost every time a number is displayed to the user – ignores these options, resulting in text formatted according to the Windows Regional Settings, not those used by Excel.
- If the user types numbers into our UserForms or InputBoxes using the override separators, they will not be recognized as numbers by `IsNumeric`, `CDbl`, etc., giving us `TypeMismatch` errors.

The only way to work around this problem is to perform our own switching between WRS and Override separators before displaying numbers to the users and immediately after receiving numbers from them, using the following two functions:

```
Function WRSToOverride(ByVal sNumber As String) As String

    Dim sWRS As String, sWRSThousand As String, sWRSDecimal As String
    Dim sXLThousand As String, sXLDecimal As String

    'Only do for Excel 2002 and greater
    If Val(Application.Version) >= 10 Then

        'Only do if the user is not using System Separators
        If Not Application.UseSystemSeparators Then

            'Get the separators used by the Windows Regional Settings
            sWRS = Format(1000, "#,##0.00")
            sWRSThousand = Mid(sWRS, 2, 1)
            sWRSDecimal = Mid(sWRS, 6, 1)

            'Get the override separators used by Excel
            sXLThousand = Application.ThousandsSeparator
            sXLDecimal = Application.DecimalSeparator

            'Swap from WRS' to Excel's separators
            sNumber = Replace(sNumber, sWRSThousand, vbTab)
            sNumber = Replace(sNumber, sWRSDecimal, sXLDecimal)
            sNumber = Replace(sNumber, vbTab, sXLThousand)
        End If
    End If

    'Return the comverted string
    WRSToOverride = sNumber

End Function
```

WRSToOverride converts between WRS and Excel's number formats, and returns a string using Excel's Override formatting. sNumber is a string containing a WRS-formatted number:

```
Function OverrideToWRS(ByVal sNumber As String) As String

    Dim sWRS As String, sWRSThousand As String, sWRSDecimal As String
    Dim sXLThousand As String, sXLDecimal As String

    'Only do for Excel 2002 and greater
    If Val(Application.Version) >= 10 Then

        'Only do if the user is not using System Separators
        If Not Application.UseSystemSeparators Then

            'Get the separators used by the Windows Regional Settings
            sWRS = Format$(1000, "#,##0.00")
            sWRSThousand = Mid$(sWRS, 2, 1)
            sWRSDecimal = Mid$(sWRS, 6, 1)

            'Get the override separators used by Excel
            sXLThousand = Application.ThousandsSeparator
            sXLDecimal = Application.DecimalSeparator

            'Swap from Excel's to WRS' separators
            sNumber = Replace(sNumber, sXLThousand, vbTab)
            sNumber = Replace(sNumber, sXLDecimal, sWRSDecimal)
            sNumber = Replace(sNumber, vbTab, sWRSThousand)
        End If
    End If

    'Return the comverted string
    OverrideToWRS = sNumber

End Function
```

OverrideToWRS converts between WRS and Excel's number formats, and returns the string using WRS' formatting. sNumber is a string containing an Excel Override formatted number.

The final problem is that when we are interacting with the user, we should be doing so using the number formats that they are familiar with. By adding the ability to override the Windows Regional Settings, Excel is introducing a third set of separators for us, and our users, to contend with. We are therefore completely reliant on the user remembering that override separators have been set, and that they may not be the separators that they are used to seeing (that is according to the WRS).

I strongly recommend that your application checks if Application. UseSystemSeparators is True and displays a warning message to the user, suggesting that it be turned off, and set using Control Panel instead:

```
If Application.UseSystemSeparators Then
   MsgBox "Please set the required number formatting using Control Panel"
   Application.UseSystemSeparators = False
End If
```

Features That Don't Play by the Rules

The xxxLocal functions discussed in the previous section were all introduced during the original move from XLM functions to VBA in Excel 5.0. They cover most of the more common functions that a developer is likely to use. There were, however a number of significant omissions in the original conversion and new features have been added to Excel since then with almost complete disregard for international issues.

This section guides you through the maze of inconsistency, poor design, and omission that you'll find hidden within the following of Excel 2002's features. This table shows the methods, properties, and functions in Excel which are sensitive to the user's locale, but which do not behave according to the rules we have stated above:

Applies To	US Version	Local Version
Opening a text file	OpenText	OpenText
Saving as a text file	SaveAs	SaveAs
Application	.ShowDataForm	.ShowDataForm
Worksheet / Range		.Paste / .PasteSpecial
Pivot Table calculated fields and items	.Formula	
Conditional formats		.Formula
QueryTables (Web Queries)		.Refresh
Worksheet functions		=TEXT
Range	.Value	
Range	.FormulaArray	
Range	.AutoFilter	.AutoFilter
Range		.AdvancedFilter
Application	.Evaluate	
Application	.ConvertFormula	
Application	.ExecuteExcel4Macro	

Fortunately, workarounds are available for most of these issues. There are a few, however, that should be completely avoided.

The OpenText Function

Workbooks.OpenText is the VBA equivalent of opening a text file in Excel by using File | Open. It opens the text file, parses it to identify numbers, dates, Booleans, and strings and stores the results in worksheet cells. It is discussed in more detail elsewhere in the book. Of relevance to this chapter is the method Excel uses to parse the data file (and how it has changed over the past few versions).

In Excel 5, the text file was parsed according to your Windows Regional Settings when opened from the user interface, but according to US formats when opened in code. In Excel 97, this was changed to always use these settings from both the UI and code. Unfortunately, this meant that there was no way to open a US-formatted text file with any confidence that the resulting numbers were correct. Since Excel 5, we have been able to specify the date order to be recognised, on a column-by-column basis, which works very well for numeric dates (for example 01/02/2001).

Excel 2000 introduced the **Advanced** button on the Text Import Wizard, and the associated `DecimalSeparator` and `ThousandSeparator` parameters of the `OpenText` method. These allow us to specify the separators that Excel should use to identify numbers and are welcome additions. It is slightly disappointing to see that we can not specify the general date order in the same way:

```
Workbooks.OpenText filename:="DATA.TXT", _
    dataType:=xlDelimited, tab:=True, _
    DecimalSeparator:=",", ThousandSeparator:="."
```

While Microsoft is to be congratulated for fixing the number format problems in Excel 2000, further congratulations are due for fixing the problem of month and day names in Excel 2002, and for providing a much tidier alternative for distinguishing between US-formatted and locally-formatted text files.

Prior to Excel 2002, the `OpenText` method would only recognize month and day names according the Windows Regional Settings, and date orders had to be specified for every date field that wasn't in MDY order. In Excel 2002, the `OpenText` method has a new `Local` parameter, with which we can specify whether the text file being imported uses US English formatting throughout, or whether it uses locally-formatted dates, numbers, etc.:

- If `Local:=True`, Excel will recognize numbers, dates, and month/day names according to the Windows Regional Settings (and the Override decimal and thousand separators, if set).
- If `Local:=False`, Excel will recognize numbers, dates, and month/day name according to standard US English settings.

In either case, the extra parameters of `DecimalSeparator`, `ThousandSeparator`, and `FieldInfo` can be used to further refine the specification (overriding the `Local` parameter's defaults).

The SaveAs Function

`Workbook.SaveAs` is the VBA equivalent of saving a text file in Excel by using **File | Save As** and choosing a format of Text.

In all versions of Excel prior to Excel 2002, this resulted in a US-formatted text file, with a DMY date order, and English month and day names, etc.

In Excel 2002, the `SaveAs` method has the same `Local` parameter described in the `OpenText` method above, resulting in a US-formatted or locally-formatted text file, as appropriate. Note that if a cell has been given a locale-specific date format (that is, the number format begins with a locale-specifier, such as [$-814] for Norwegian), that formatting will be retained in the text file, regardless of whether it is saved in US or local format:

```
ActiveWorkbook.SaveAs "Data.Txt", xlText, local:=True
```

The ShowDataForm Sub Procedure

Using `ActiveSheet.ShowDataForm` is exposing yourself to one of the most dangerous of Excel's international issues. `ShowDataForm` is the VBA equivalent of the Data | Form menu item. It displays a standard dialog which allows the user to enter and change data in an Excel list/database. When run by clicking the Data | Form menu, the dates and numbers are displayed according to the WRS and changes made by the user are interpreted according to the WRS, which fully complies with the user-interaction rules above.

When used in code, `ActiveSheet.ShowDataForm` displays dates and numbers according to US formats but interprets them according to WRS. Hence, if you have a date of Feb 10, 2001, shown in the worksheet in the dd/mm/yyyy order of 10/02/2001, Excel will display it on the data form as 2/10/2001. If you change this to the 11th (2/11/2001), Excel will store Nov 2, 2001 in the sheet. Similarly, if you are using Norwegian number formats, a number of 1-decimal-234 will be displayed on the form as 1.234. Change that to read 1.235 and Excel stores 1235, one thousand times too big.

Fortunately there is an easy workaround for this if your routine only has to work with versions of Excel since Excel 97. Instead of using `ShowDataForm`, you can select the first cell in the range, then execute the Data | Form menu item itself:

```
Sub ShowForm()
   ActiveSheet.Range("A1").Select
   RunMenu 860   '860 is the CommandBarControl ID of the Data, Form menu item
End Sub
```

The following `RunMenu` routine executes a given menu item, as if it had been clicked by the user. In this case, the data form behaves correctly.

The RunMenu Sub Procedure

This routine will run a menu item by simulating clicking on it, given its `CommandBar.Control` ID (for example 860 is the ID for the Data | Form menu item):

```
Sub RunMenu(iMenuID As Long)

   Dim oCtrl As CommandBarButton

   'Ignore any errors (such as the menu ID not valid)
   On Error Resume Next

   'Create our own temporary commandbar to hold the control
   With Application.CommandBars.Add

      'Add the control and execute it
      .Controls.Add(ID:=iMenuID).Execute

      'Then delete our temporary menu bar
      .Delete
   End With

End Sub
```

`iMenuID` is the control ID of the menu item to be run.

Pasting Text

When pasting text from other applications into Excel, it is parsed according to the WRS. We have no way to tell Excel the number and date formats, and language to recognize. The only workaround is to use a `DataObject` to retrieve the text from the clipboard, parse it yourself in VBA, then write the result to the sheet. The following example assumes that the clipboard contains a single US-formatted number:

```
Sub ParsePastedNumber()

    Dim oDO As DataObject
    Dim sText As String

    'Create a new data object
    Set oDO = New DataObject

    'Read the contents of the clipboard into the DataObject
    oDO.GetFromClipboard

    'Get the text from the DataObject
    sText = oDO.GetText

    'If we know the text is in a US format,
    'use Val() to convert it to a number
    ActiveCell.Value = Val(sText)

End Sub
```

PivotTable Calculated Fields and Items, and Conditional Format Formulas

If you are used to using the `.Formula` property of a range or chart series, you'll know that it returns and accepts formula strings that use English functions and US number formats. There is an equivalent `.FormulaLocal` property which returns and accepts formula strings as they appear on the sheet (using the Office UI language and WRS number formats).

Pivot-table calculated fields and items, and conditional formats also have a `.Formula` property, but for these objects, it returns and accepts formula strings as they appear to the user, that is it behaves in the same way as the `.FormulaLocal` property of a `Range` object. This means that to set the formula for one of these objects, we need to construct it in the Office UI language, and according to the WRS.

A workaround for this is to use the cell's own `.Formula` and `.FormulaLocal` properties to convert between the formats, as shown in the `ConvertFormulaLocale` function below.

The ConvertFormulaLocale Function

This function converts a formula string between US and local formats and languages:

```
Function ConvertFormulaLocale(sFormula As String, bUSToLocal As Boolean) _
            As String

   On Error GoTo ERR_BAD_FORMULA

   'Use a cell that is likely to be empty!
   'This should be changed to suit your own situation
   With ThisWorkbook.Worksheets(1).Range("IU1")
      If bUSToLocal Then
         .Formula = sFormula
         ConvertFormulaLocale = .FormulaLocal
```

```
        Else
            .FormulaLocal = sFormula
            ConvertFormulaLocale = .Formula
        End If

      .ClearContents
    End With

    ERR_BAD_FORMULA:

End Function
```

`sFormula` is the text of the formula to convert from, while `bUSToLocal` should be set to `True` to convert US to local, and False to convert local to US.

Web Queries

While the concept behind web queries is an excellent one, they have been implemented with complete disregard to international issues. When the text of the web page is parsed by Excel, all the numbers and dates are interpreted according to your Windows Regional Settings. This means that if a European web page is opened in the US, or a US page is opened in Europe, it is likely that the numbers will be wrong. For example, if the web page contains the text 1.1, it will appear as 1st Jan on a computer running Norwegian Windows.

The `WebDisableDateRecognition` option for the `QueryTable` can be used to prevent numbers being recognized as dates. Setting Excel's override number and decimal separators can ensure that numbers are recognized correctly, if the web page is displayed in a known format

Web queries must be used with great care in a multinational application, using the following approach:

- Set `Application.UseSystemSeparators` to `False`.
- Set `Application.DecimalSeparator` and `Application.ThousandSeparator` to those used on the web page.
- Perform the query, ensuring `WebDisableDateRecognition` is set to `True`.
- Reset `Application.DecimalSeparator`, `Application.ThousandSeparator`, and `Application.UseSystemSeparators` to their original values.

=TEXT Worksheet Function

The `TEXT` worksheet function converts a number to a string, according to a specified format. The format string has to use formatting characters defined by the Windows Regional Settings (or Excel's International Options override). Hence, if you use `=TEXT(NOW(),"dd/mm/yyyy")`, you will get "01/02/yyyy" on Norwegian Windows, since Excel will only recognise 'å' as the Norwegian number-format character used for years.

Excel does not translate the number-format characters when it opens the file on a different platform. A workaround for this is to create a defined name that reads the number format from a specific cell, then use that definition within the `TEXT` function. For example, if you format cell **A1** with the date format to use throughout your sheet, you can click on **Insert | Name | Define** and define a name as:

```
Name:        DateFormat
Refers To:   =GET.CELL(7,$A$1)
```

Then use `=TEXT(Now(),DateFormat)` elsewhere in the sheet. The `GET.CELL` function is an Excel 4 macro function – which Excel lets us use within defined names, though not on the worksheet. This is equivalent to, but much more powerful than the `=CELL` worksheet function. The 7 in the example tells `GET.CELL` to return the number-format string for the cell.

Note that some people have experienced General Protection Faults when copying cells that use DateFormat to other worksheets and workbooks.

The XLM functions are documented in the XLMACR8.HLP file, available from Microsoft's web site at http://support.microsoft.com/support/kb/articles/Q143/4/66.asp

The Range.Value and Range.FormulaArray Properties

These two properties of a range only break the rules by not having local equivalents. The strings passed to (and returned by) them are in US format. Use the `ConvertFormulaLocale` function shown above to convert between US and local versions of formulas.

The Range.AutoFilter Method

The `AutoFilter` method of a `Range` object is a very curious beast. We are forced to pass it strings for its filter criteria, and hence must be aware of its string handling behavior. The criteria string consists of an operator (=, >, <, >=, etc.) followed by a value. If no operator is specified, the "=" operator is assumed.

The key issue is that when using the "=" operator, `AutoFilter` performs a textual match, while using any other operator results in a match by value. This gives us problems when trying to locate exact matches for dates and numbers. If we use "=", Excel matches on the text that is displayed in the cell, that is, the formatted number. As the text displayed in a cell will change with different regional settings and Windows language versions, it is impossible for us to create a criteria string that will locate an exact match in all locales.

There is a workaround for this problem. When using any of the other filter criteria, Excel plays by the rules and interprets the criteria string according to US formats. Hence, a search criterion of "`>=02/01/2001`" will find all dates on or after 1st Feb, 2001, in all locales. We can use this to match an exact date by using two `AutoFilter` criteria. The following code will give an exact match on 1st Feb, 2001 and will work in any locale:

```
Range("A1:D200").AutoFilter 2, ">=02/01/2001", xlAnd, "<=02/01/2001"
```

The Range.AdvancedFilter Method

The `AdvancedFilter` method does play by the rules, but in a way that may be undesirable. The criteria used for filtering are entered on the worksheet in the criteria range. In a similar way to `AutoFilter`, the criteria string includes an operator and a value. Note that when using the "=" operator, `AdvancedFilter` correctly matches by value and hence differs from `AutoFilter` in this respect.

As this is entirely within the Excel domain, the string must be formatted according to the Windows Regional Settings to work, which gives us a problem when matching on dates and numbers. An advanced filter search criterion of "`>1.234`" will find all numbers greater then 1.234 in the US, but all numbers greater than 1234 when run in Norway. A criterion of "`>02/03/2001`" will find all dates after 3rd Feb in the US, but after 2nd March in Europe.

The only workarounds are to populate the criteria strings from code, before running the `AdvancedFilter` method, or to use a calculated criteria string, using the `=TEXT` trick mentioned above. Instead of a criterion of "`>=02/03/2001`", to find all dates on or after 3rd Feb, 2001, we could use the formula:

```
=">="&TEXT(DATE(2001,2,3),DateFormat)
```

Here `DateFormat` is the defined name introduced above that returns a local date format. If the date is an integer (does not contain a time component), we could also just use the criteria string "`>=36194`", and hope that the user realizes that 36194 is actually 3rd Feb, 2001.

The Application.Evaluate, Application.ConvertFormula, and Application.ExecuteExcel4Macro Functions

These functions all play by the rules, in that we must use US-formatted strings. They do not, however, have local equivalents. To evaluate a formula that the user may have typed into a UserForm (or convert it between using relative to absolute cell ranges), we need to convert it to US format before passing it to `Application.Evaluate` or `Application.ConvertFormula`.
The `Application.ExecuteExcel4Macro` function is used to execute XLM-style functions. One of the most common uses of it is to call the XLM `PAGE.SETUP` function, which is much faster than the VBA equivalent. This takes many parameters, including strings, numbers, and Booleans. Be very careful to explicitly convert all these parameters to US-formatted strings and avoid the temptation to shorten the code by omitting the `Str` around each one.

Responding to Office XP Language Settings

One of the major advances starting with the release of Office 200 is that there is a single set of executables, with a set of plug-in language packs (whereas in prior versions, each language was a different executable, with its own set of bugs). This makes it very easy for a user of Office to have their own choice of language for the user interface, help files, etc. In fact, if a number of people share the same computer, each person can run the Office applications in a different language.

As developers of Excel applications, we must respect the user's language selection and do as much as we can to present our own user interface in their choice of language.

Where Does the Text Come From?

There are three factors that together determine the text seen by the Office user:

Regional Settings Location

The Regional Settings location is chosen on the first tab (called **Regional Settings**) of the Control Panel's **Regional Settings** applet and defines:

- The day and month names shown in Excel cells for long date formats
- The day and month names returned by the VBA `Format` function
- The month names recognized by the VBA `CDate` function and when typing dates into Excel directly

- The month names recognized by the Text Import Wizard and the VBA `OpenText` method (when the `Local` parameter is `True`)
- The number format characters used in the `=TEXT` worksheet function
- The text resulting from the implicit conversion of Boolean values to strings, such as: `"I am " & True.`

Office UI Language Settings

The Office User Interface language can be selected by using the "Microsoft Office Language Settings" applet, installed with Office XP and defines:

- The text displayed on Excel's menus and dialog boxes
- The text for the standard buttons on Excel's message boxes
- The text for Excel's built-in worksheet functions
- The text displayed in Excel's cells for Boolean values
- The text for Boolean values recognized by the Text Import Wizard, the VBA `OpenText` method, and when typing directly into Excel
- The default names for worksheets in a new workbook
- The local names for command bars

Language Version of Windows

By this, I mean the basic language version of Windows itself. This choice defines:

- The text for the standard buttons in the VBA `MsgBox` function (when using the `vbMsgBoxStyles` constants). Hence, while the text of the buttons on Excel's built-in messages respond to the Office UI language, the text of the buttons on our own messages respond to the Windows language. Note that the only way to discover the Windows language is with a Windows API call.

There are some things in Office XP which are 100% (US) English, and don't respond to any changes in Windows language, regional settings or Office UI language, namely:

- The text resulting from the explicit conversion of Boolean values to strings, that is, all of `Str(True)`, `CStr(True)`, and `Format(True)` result in "`True`". Hence, the only way to convert a Boolean variable to the same string that Excel displays for it, is to enter it into a cell, then read the cell's `.FormulaLocal` property.
- The text of Boolean strings recognized by `CBool`.

Identifying the Office UI Language Settings

The first step to creating a multilingual application is to identify the user's settings. We can identify the language chosen in Windows Regional Settings by using `Application.International(xlCountrySetting)`, which returns a number that corresponds approximately to the country codes used by the telephone system (1 is the USA, 44 is the UK, 47 is Norway, etc.).

We can also use `Application.International(xlCountryCode)` to retrieve the user interface language using the same numbering system. This method has worked well in previous versions of Excel, where there were only 30 or so languages from which to choose your copy of Office.

Beginning with Office 2000, things have changed a little. By moving all the language configuration into separate language packs, Microsoft can support many more languages with relative ease. If you use the Object Browser to look at the `msoLanguageID` constants defined in the Office object library, you'll see that there are over 180 languages and dialects listed.

We can use the following code to find out the exact Office UI language, then decide whether we can display our application in that language, a similar language, or revert to a default language (as shown in the following section):

```
lLanguageID = Application.LanguageSettings.LanguageID(msoLanguageIDUI)
```

Creating a Multilingual Application

When developing a multilingual application, you have to balance a number of factors, including:

- The time and cost spent developing the application
- The time and cost spent translating the application
- The time and cost spent testing the translated application
- The increased sales from having a translated version
- Improved ease-of-use, and hence reduced support costs
- The requirement for multi-lingual support
- Should you create language-specific versions, or use add-on language packs?

You also have to decide how much of the application to translate, and which languages to support:

- Translate nothing
- Translate only the packaging and promotional documentation
- Enable the code to work in a multilingual environment (month names etc.)
- Translate the user interface (menus, dialogs, screens, and messages)
- Translate the help files, examples, and tutorials
- Customize the application for each location (for example to use local data feeds)
- Support left-to-right languages only
- Support right-to-left languages (and hence redesign your UserForms)
- Support Double-Byte-Character-Set languages (for example Japanese)

The decision on how far to go will depend to a large extent on your users, your budget, and the availability of translators.

A Suggested Approach

It is doubtful that creating a single Excel application to support all 180+ Office languages will make economic sense, but the time spent in making your application support a few of the more common languages will often be a wise investment. This will, of course, depend on your users, and whether support for a new language is preferable to new features.

The approach that I take is to write the application to support multiple languages and provide the user with the ability to switch between the installed languages or conform to their choice of Office UI Language. I develop the application in English, then have it translated into one or two other languages depending on my target users. I will only translate it into other languages if there is sufficient demand.

How to Store String Resources

When creating multilingual applications, we cannot hard-code **any** text strings that will be displayed to the user; we must look them up in a **string resource**. The easiest form of string resource is a simple worksheet table. Give all your text items a unique identifier and store them in a worksheet, one row per identifier and one column for each supported language. You can then look up the ID and return the string in the appropriate language using a simple `VLOOKUP` function.

You will need to do the same for all your menu items, worksheet contents, and UserForm controls. The following code is a simple example, which assumes you have a worksheet called `shLanguage` that contains a lookup table that has been given a name of `rgTranslation`. It also assumes you have a public variable to identify which column to read the text from. The variable would typically be set in an Options type screen.

Note that the code shown below is not particularly fast and is shown as an example. A faster (and more complex) routine would read the entire column of IDs and selected language texts into two static VBA arrays, then work from those, only reading in a new array when the language selection was changed:

```
Public iLanguageCol As Integer

Sub Test()
   iLanguageCol = 2
   MsgBox GetText(1001)
End Sub

' lTextID - The string ID to look up
Function GetText(lTextID As Long) As String

   Dim vaTest As Variant
   Static rgLangTable As Range

   'Set an object to point to the string resource table (once)
   If rgLangTable Is Nothing Then
      Set rgLangTable = ThisWorkbook.Worksheets("shLanguage") _
         .Range("rgTranslation")
   End If

   'If the language choice is not set, assume the first language in our table
   If iLanguageCol < 2 Then iLanguageCol = 2

   'Try to locate and read off the required text
   vaTest = Application.VLookup(lTextID, rgLangTable, iLanguageCol)

   'If we got some text, return it
   If Not IsError(vaTest) Then GetText = vaTest
End Function
```

Many of your messages will be constructed at run-time. For example, you may have code to check that a number is within certain boundaries:

```
If iValue <= iMin Or iValue >= iMax Then
   MsgBox "The number must be greater than " & CStr(iMin) & _
          " and less than " & CStr(iMax) & "."
End If
```

This would mean that we have to store two text strings with different IDs in our resource sheet, which is both inefficient and much harder to translate. In the example given, we would probably not have a separate translation string for the full stop. Hence, the maximum value would always come at the end of the sentence, which may not be appropriate for many languages. A better approach is to store the combined string with placeholders for the two numbers, and substitute the numbers at run-time (using the custom `ReplaceHolders` function, shown at the end of the chapter:

```
If iValue < iMin Or iValue > iMax Then
   MsgBox ReplaceHolders( _
               "The number must be greater than %0 and less than %1.", _
                                    CStr(iMin), CStr(iMax))
End If
```

The translator (who may not understand your program) can construct a correct sentence, inserting the values at the appropriate points.

Working in a Multilingual Environment

Here are some tips on how to work in a multi-lingual environment.

Allow Extra Space

In general, most other languages use longer words than the English equivalents. When designing our UserForms and worksheets, we must allow extra room for the non-English text to fit in the controls and cells. A good rule-of-thumb is to make your controls 1.5 times the width of the English text.

Using Excel's Objects

The names that Excel gives to its objects when they are created often depend on the user's choice of Office UI Language. For example, when creating a blank workbook using `Workbooks.Add`, it will not always be called "`BookN`", and the first worksheet in it will not always be called "`Sheet1`". With the German UI, for example, they are called "`MappeN`" and "`Tabelle1`" respectively. Instead of referring to these objects by name, you should create an object reference as they are created, then use that object elsewhere in your code:

```
Dim Wkb As Workbook, Wks As Worksheet

Set Wbk = Workbooks.Add
Set Wks = Wkb.Worksheets(1)
```

Working with `CommandBarControls` can also be problematic. For example, you may want to add a custom menu item to the bottom of the **Tools** menu of the worksheet menu bar. In an English-only environment, you may write something like:

```
Sub AddHelloButton()
   Dim cbTools As CommandBarPopup
   Dim cbCtl As CommandBarButton

   Set cbTools = Application.CommandBars("Worksheet Menu Bar") _
      .Controls("Tools")

   Set cbCtl = cbTools.CommandBar.Controls.Add(msoControlButton)

   cbCtl.Caption = "Hello"
   cbCtl.OnAction = "MyRoutine"
End Sub
```

This code will fail if your user has a UI language other than English. While Excel recognises English names for command bars themselves, it does not recognise English names for the controls placed on them. In this example, the **Tools** dropdown menu is not recognised. The solution is to identify `CommandBar.Controls` by their ID and use `FindControl` to locate them. 30007 is the ID of the **Tools** popup menu:

```
Sub AddHelloButton()
   Dim cbTools As CommandBarPopup
   Dim cbCtl As CommandBarButton

   Set cbTools = Application.CommandBars("Worksheet Menu Bar") _
                 .FindControl(ID:=30007)

   Set cbCtl = cbTools.CommandBar.Controls.Add(msoControlButton)

   cbCtl.Caption = "Hello"
   cbCtl.OnAction = "MyRoutine"
End Sub
```

There is an additional problem with commandbar names in some locales and object libraries (for example the Dutch VBE commandbars), in that the commandbar name (which should always be the same US English string) has been erroneously localized. The only sure method of working with commandbars is to avoid using any names in code, using `FindControl` extensively instead. This approach is somewhat complicated, though, as the same control can occur on many commandbars and `FindControl` may not return the control that you want. Most developers use the English commandbar names.

> **Chapter 14 of this book contains a routine to show all the commandbars and the controls on them, with their names and ID numbers. Jan Karel Pieterse has compiled a workbook containing many of the commandbar translations in a file called `xlMenuFunDict`, available from http://www.BMSLtd.ie/MVP.**

Using SendKeys

In the best of cases, the use of `SendKeys` should be avoided if at all possible. It is most often used to send key combinations to Excel, in order to activate a menu item or navigate a dialog box. It works by matching the menu item or dialog control accelerator keys, in the same way that you can use *Alt+key* combinations to navigate Excel using the keyboard. When used in a non-English version of Excel, it is highly unlikely that the key combinations in the `SendKeys` string will match up with the menus and dialogs, having potentially disastrous results.

For example, SendKeys "%DB" will bring up the Subtotals dialog in English Excel, but will quit Excel when run with the German UI. Instead of using SendKeys to trigger menu items, you should use the RunMenu routine presented earlier in this chapter to execute a menu item by its CommandBarControl ID.

The Rules for Developing a Multilingual Application

- Decide early in the analysis phase the level of multilingual support that you are going to provide, then stick to it.
- Do not include any text strings within your code. Always look them up in a table.
- Never construct sentences by concatenating separate text strings, as the foreign language version is unlikely to use the same word order. Instead use place-holders in your text and replace the place-holder at run-time.
- When constructing UserForms, always make the controls bigger than you need for the English text; most other languages use longer words.
- Do not try to guess the name that Excel gives to objects that you create in code. For example, when creating a new workbook, the first sheet will not always be "Sheet1".
- Do not refer to commandbar controls by their caption. While you can refer to commandbars themselves by their English name, you must refer to the menu items by their ID (for built-in items) or tag (for custom items).
- Do not use SendKeys.

Some Helpful Functions

In addition to some of the custom functions already presented, such as RunMenu and IsDateUS, here are some more functions that are very useful when creating multinational applications. Note that the code has been written to be compatible with all versions of Excel from 5.0 to 2002 and hence avoids the use of newer VBA constructs (such as giving optional parameters specific data types).

The bWinToNum Function

This function checks if a string contains a number formatted according to the Windows Regional Settings and converts it to a Double. The function returns True or False to indicate the success of the validation, and optionally displays an error message to the user. It is best used as a wrapper function when validating numbers entered by a user, as shown in the *Interacting with Users* section above.

Note that if the user has used Excel's International Options to override the WRS decimal and thousands separator, the OverrideToWRS function must be used to ensure we send a WRS-formatted string to this function:

```
Function bWinToNum(ByVal sWinString As String, _
                   ByRef dResult As Double, _
                   Optional bShowMsg) As Boolean

   Dim dFrac As Double

   ' Take a copy of the string to play with
   sWinString = Trim(sWinString)
   dFrac = 1

   If IsMissing(bShowMsg) Then bShowMsg = True
   If sWinString = "-" Then sWinString = "0"
```

```
    If sWinString = "" Then sWinString = "0"

    ' Check for percentage, strip it out and remember to divide by 100
    If InStr(1, sWinString, "%") > 0 Then
       dFrac = dFrac / 100
       sWinString = Application.Substitute(sWinString, "%", "")
    End If
    ' Are we left with a number string in windows format?
    If IsNumeric(sWinString) Then
       ' If so, convert it to a number and return success
       dResult = CDbl(sWinString) * dFrac
       bWinToNum = True
    Else
       ' If not, display a message, return zero and failure
       If bShowMsg Then MsgBox "This entry was not recognised as a number," _
          & Chr(10) & "according to your Windows Regional Settings.", vbOKOnly
       dResult = 0
       bWinToNum = False
    End If

End Function
```

`sWinString` is the string to be converted, and `dResult` is the converted number, set to zero if the number is not valid or empty. `bShowMsg` is optional, and should be set to `True` (or missing) to show an error message, or `False` to suppress the error message.

The bWinToDate Function

This provides the same functionality as `bWinToNum`, but for dates instead of numbers:

```
Function bWinToDate(ByVal sWinString As String, _
                    ByRef dResult As Double, _
                    Optional bShowMsg) As Boolean

    If IsMissing(bShowMsg) Then bShowMsg = True

    If sWinString = "" Then
       ' An empty string gives a valid date of zero
       dResult = 0
       bWinToDate = True

    ElseIf IsDate(sWinString) Then
       ' We got a proper date, so convert it to a Double
       ' (i.e. the internal date number)
       dResult = CDbl(CDate(sWinString))
       bWinToDate = True
    Else
       ' If not, display a message, return zero and failure
       If bShowMsg Then MsgBox "This entry was not recognised as a date," & _
          Chr(10) & "according to your Windows Regional Settings.", vbOKOnly
       dResult = 0
       bWinToDate = False
    End If

End Function
```

`sWinString` is the string to be converted. `dResult` is the converted number, set to zero if the number is not valid, or empty. `bShowMsg` is optional, and should be set to `True` (or missing) to show an error message, or `False` to suppress the error message.

The sFormatDate Function

This function formats a date according to the Windows Regional Settings, using a 4-digit year and optionally including a time string in the result:

```
Function sFormatDate(dDate As Date, Optional bTimeReq) As String

   Dim sDate As String

   'Default bTimeReq to False if not supplied
   If IsMissing(bTimeReq) Then bTimeReq = False

   Select Case Application.International(xlDateOrder)
      Case 0       'month-day-year
         sDate = Format$(dDate, "mm/dd/yyyy")
      Case 1       'day-month-year
         sDate = Format$(dDate, "dd/mm/yyyy")
      Case 2       'year-month-day
         sDate = Format$(dDate, "yyyy/mm/dd")
   End Select

   If bTimeReq Then sDate = sDate & " " & Format$(dDate, "hh:mm:ss")

   sFormatDate = sDate

End Function
```

`dDate` is the Excel date number, while `bTimeReq` is an optional argument that should be set to `True` to include the time string in the result.

The ReplaceHolders Function

This function replaces the placeholders in a string with values provided to it:

```
Function ReplaceHolders(ByVal sString As String, ParamArray avReplace()) As String

   Dim i As Integer

   'Work backwards, so we don't replace %10 with our %1 text
   For i = UBound(avReplace) To LBound(avReplace) Step -1
      sString = Application.Substitute(sString, "%" & i, _
         avReplace(i - LBound(avReplace)))
   Next

   ReplaceHolders = sString

End Function
```

`sString` is the text to replace the placeholders in, and `avReplace` is a list of items to replace the placeholders.

Summary

It is possible to create an Excel application that will work on every installation of Excel in the world and support all 180-plus Office languages, but it is unlikely to be economically viable.

If you have a limited set of users and you are able to dictate their language and Windows Regional Settings, you can create your application without worrying about international issues. Even if this is the case, you should get into the habit of creating locale-independent code. The requirement for locale-independence should be included in your analysis, design, and coding standards. It is much, much easier and cheaper to write locale-independent code at the onset than to rework an existing application.

At a minimum, your application should work regardless of the user's choice of Windows Regional Settings or Windows or Office UI Language or whether they have set non-standard thousand and decimal separators using Tools | Options | International. You should be able to achieve this by following the rules listed in this chapter.

The following Excel features don't play by the rules and have to be treated very carefully:

- `OpenText`
- `SaveAs` to a text file
- `ShowDataForm`
- Pasting text from other applications
- The `.Formula` property in all its guises
- `<range>.Value`
- `<range>.FormulaArray`
- `<range>.AutoFilter`
- `<range>.AdvancedFilter`
- The `=TEXT` worksheet function
- `Application.Evaluate`
- `Application.ConvertFormula`
- `Application.ExecuteExcel4Macro`
- Web queries

There are also some features in Excel that you may have to avoid completely:

- `SendKeys`
- Using `True` and `False` in imported text files

23

Programming the VBE

Up until now, the book has focused on writing VBA procedures to automate Excel. While writing the code, you have been working in the Visual Basic Editor (VBE), otherwise known as the Visual Basic Integrated Design Environment (VBIDE).

There is an object library provided with Office XP that is shown as Microsoft Visual Basic for Applications Extensibility 5.3 in the VBE's Tools | References list. The objects in this library and their methods, properties, and events enable us to:

- Programmatically create, delete, and modify the code, UserForms, and references in our own and other workbooks
- Program the VBE itself, to create useful Addins to assist us in our development efforts and automate many of your development tasks

> **There was no change to the Visual Basic for Applications Extensibility library between Office 2000 and Office 2002, so all the examples in this chapter apply equally to both versions.**

Between Office 97 and Office 2000, the `Click` event was added to the `CommandBarButton` object, which is used to respond to the user clicking the buttons that we add to the VBE's commandbars. The Addin will not, therefore work in Office 97, although all of the code that manipulates the VBE and its objects is still applicable.

The one difference between Excel 2000 and Excel 2002 is related to security. Macro viruses work by using the methods shown in this chapter to modify the target file's code, thus infecting it. To prevent this, Microsoft has made it possible to disable access to all workbooks' `VBProjects`. By default the access is disabled, so none of the code in this chapter will work. To enable access to the `VBProjects`, tick the 'Trust Access to Visual Basic Project' check box on Excel 2002's Tools | Macros | Security | Trusted Sources dialog.

This chapter explains how to write code to automate the VBE by walking you through the development of a VBE Toolkit to speed up your application development. You will then add a few utilities to the toolkit that demonstrate how to programmatically manipulate code, UserForms, and references. For simplicity, most of the code examples in this chapter have not been provided with error handling. The completed toolkit Addin can be found on the Wrox web site at http://www.wrox.com.

Identifying VBE Objects in Code

All the objects that form the VBE, and their properties and methods, are contained in their own object library. You need to create a reference to this library before you can use the objects, by switching to the VBE, selecting the menu item **Tools | References**, checking the **Microsoft VBA Extensibility 5.3 library**, and clicking **OK**:

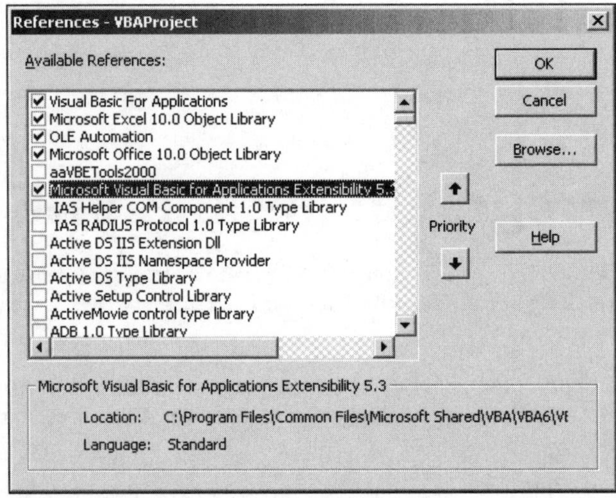

In code, this library is referred to as the VBIDE object library.

The full VBIDE Object Model is documented in Appendix B. The more important objects are summarised below.

The VBE Object

The top-level object of the Visual Basic Editor is known as the `VBE` object and is itself a property of the Excel `Application` object. Hence, to create an object variable to refer to the VBE, we need code like:

```
Dim obVBE As VBIDE.VBE
Set obVBE = Application.VBE
```

The VBProject Object

This object is the container for all the 'programming' aspects of a workbook, including UserForms, standard modules, class modules, and the code behind each worksheet and the workbook itself. Each `VBProject` corresponds to one of the top-level items in the Project Explorer. A specific `VBProject` object can be located either by iterating through the VBE's `VBProjects` collection, or through the `VBProject` property of a workbook.

To find the `VBProject` that corresponds to the workbook `Book1.xls`, the following code can be used:

```
Dim obVBP As VBIDE.VBProject
Set obVBP = Workbooks("Book1.xls").VBProject
```

When creating Addins for the VBIDE itself, we often need to know which project is currently highlighted in the Project Explorer. This is given by the `ActiveVBProject` property of the VBE:

```
Dim obVBP As VBIDE.VBProject
Set obVBP = Application.VBE.ActiveVBProject
```

Note that the `ActiveVBProject` is the project that the user is editing within the VBE. It is not related in any way to the `ActiveWorkbook` given by Excel. In fact with the Developer Editions of Office 2000 and Office XP, it is possible to create self-contained VB Projects that are not part of an Excel workbook.

The VBComponent Object

The UserForms, standard modules, class modules, and code modules behind the worksheets and workbook are all `VBComponent` objects. Each `VBComponent` object corresponds to one of the lower-level items in the Project Explorer tree. A specific `VBComponent` can be located through the `VBComponents` collection of a `VBProject`. Hence, to find the `VBComponent` that represents the `UserForm1` form in `Book1.xls`, code like this can be used:

```
Dim obVBC As VBIDE.VBComponent
Set obVBC = Workbooks("Book1.xls").VBProject.VBComponents("UserForm1")
```

The name of the `VBComponent` that contains the code behind the workbook, worksheets, and charts is given by the `CodeName` property of the related Excel object (the workbook, worksheet, or chart object). Hence, to find the `VBComponent` for the code behind the workbook (where code can be written to hook into workbook events), this code can be used:

```
Dim obVBC As VBIDE.VBComponent

With Workbooks("Book1.xls")
   Set obVBC = .VBProject.VBComponents(.CodeName)
End With
```

And for a specific worksheet:

```
Dim obVBC As VBIDE.VBComponent

With Workbooks("Book1.xls")
   Set obVBC = .VBProject.VBComponents(.Worksheets("Sheet1").CodeName)
End With
```

Note that the name of the workbook's `VBComponent` is usually "**ThisWorkbook**" in the Project Explorer. Do not be tempted to rely on this name. If your user has chosen a different language for the Office User Interface, it will be different. The name can also be easily changed by the user in the VBE. For this reason, **do not** use code like:

```
Dim obVBC As VBIDE.VBComponent

With Workbooks("Book1.xls")
   Set obVBC = .VBProject.VBComponents("ThisWorkbook")
End With
```

When developing Addins for the VBE, you often need to know the `VBComponent` that the user is editing (the one highlighted in the Project Explorer). This is given by the `SelectedVBComponent` property of the VBE:

```
Dim obVBC As VBIDE.VBComponent
Set obVBC = Application.VBE.SelectedVBComponent
```

Each VBComponent has a Properties collection, corresponding approximately to the list shown in the Properties Window of the VBE when a VBComponent is selected in the Project Explorer. One of these is the Name property, shown in the following test routine:

```
Sub ShowNames()
   With Application.VBE.SelectedVBComponent
      Debug.Print .Name & ": " & .Properties("Name")
   End With
End Sub
```

For most VBComponent objects, the text returned by .Name and .Properties("Name") is the same. However, for the VBComponent objects that contain the code behind workbooks, worksheets, and charts, .Properties("Name") gives the name of the Excel object (the workbook, worksheet or chart). You can use this to find the Excel object that corresponds to the item that the user is working on in the VBE, or the Excel workbook that corresponds to the ActiveVBProject. The code for doing this is shown later in this chapter.

The CodeModule Object

All of the VBA code for a VBComponent is contained within its CodeModule object. Through this object you can programmatically read, add, change, and delete lines of code. There is only one CodeModule for each VBComponent. In Office 2000 and Office XP, every type of VBComponent has a CodeModule, though this may not be the case in future versions. For example, you may get a tool to help design, execute and debug SQL queries that only has a graphical interface, like MS query, but does not have any code behind it.

The CodePane Object

This object gives us access to the user's view of a CodeModule. Through this object you can identify such items as the section of a CodeModule that is visible on the screen, and the text that the user has selected. You can identify which CodePane is currently being edited by using the VBE's ActiveCodePane property:

```
Dim obCP As VBIDE.CodePane
Set obCP = Application.VBE.ActiveCodePane
```

The Designer Object

Some VBComponents (such as UserForms) present both code and a graphical interface to the developer. While the code is accessed through the CodeModule and CodePane objects, the Designer object gives you access to the graphical part. In the standard versions of Office 2000 and Office XP, UserForms are the only components with a graphical interface for you to control. However, the Developer Editions include a number of other items (such as the Data Connection Designer), which have graphical interfaces; these too are exposed to us through the Designer object.

These are the main objects that we'll be using throughout the rest of this chapter, as we create our VBE Toolkit Addin.

Starting Up

There is very little difference in Excel 2002 between a normal workbook and an Addin. The code and UserForms can be modified in the same manner, and they both offer the same level of protection (locking the Project from view). The two advantages of using an Addin to hold your tools are that it is invisible within the Excel User Interface, and that it can be loaded using Excel's Tools | Add-Ins menu (though each activated Addin will slow down Excel's startup as it is loaded). This chapter uses the term 'Addin' to mean a container for tools that you're adding to Excel/VBE. In fact, during the development of the Addin, you will actually keep the file as a standard workbook, only converting it to an Addin at the end.

Most Addins have a common structure, and the one we will develop in this chapter will be no exception:

- A startup module to trap the opening and closing of the Addin
- Some code to add our menu items to the commandbars on opening and remove them when closing
- For the VBE, a class module to handle the menu items' `Click` events
- Some code to perform your menus' actions.

Start with a new workbook and delete all of the worksheets apart from the first. Press *Alt+F11* to switch to the VBE, and find your workbook in the Project Explorer. Select the `VBProject` entry for it. In the Properties Window, change the project's name to `aaVBETools2002`. The name starts with the prefix '`aa`' so that it always appears at the top of the Project Explorer, nicely out of the way of any other projects you may be developing.

Add a new module to the project, give it the name of `modCommon` and type in the following code, which runs when the workbook is opened and closed:

```
Option Explicit
Option Compare Text

'The Addin ID is used to identify our menus, making it easy to remove them
Public Const psAddinID As String = "VBEToolsXP"

'The Addin title is shown on various message boxes
Public Const psAddinTitle As String = "VBE Tools XP"

'''''''''''''''''''''''''''''''''''
' Subroutine: Auto_Open
'
' Purpose:    Adds our menus and menuitems to the VBE and sets up the objects to
trap
'             the command bar events for the new controls
'

Sub Auto_Open()
   SetUpMenus
End Sub
```

```
''''''''''''''''''''''''''''''''''
' Subroutine: Auto_Close
'
' Purpose:    Removes our menus and menu items from the VBE
'

Sub Auto_Close()
   RemoveMenus
End Sub
```

The `Auto_Open` and `Auto_Close` procedures just call some other routines (which will be created in the following section) to add and remove the menus and menu items to/from the VBE commandbars. A global constant has also been defined to uniquely identify our Addin's menus, and another to use as a standard title for the Addin's message boxes.

Adding Menu Items to the VBE

The VBE uses the same commandbar code as the rest of the Office suite, so the procedure for adding your own menus to the VBE is very little different from that documented in Chapter 14 of this book.

There is one major difference, which is how to run your routine when the menu item is clicked. When adding menu items to Excel, we set the `CommandBarButton`'s `OnAction` property to the name of the procedure to run. In the VBE, `CommandBarButtons` still have an `OnAction` property, but it is ignored.

Instead, MS has added the `Click` event to the `CommandBarButton` (and the `Change` event to the `CommandBarComboBox`). In order to use these events, we have to use a class module containing a variable of the correct type declared `WithEvents`, so add a class module to the project, give it the name of `CBarEvents`, and type in the following code:

```
'Object to trap the CommandBar events (i.e. clicking)
Public WithEvents cbBtnEvents As CommandBarButton

''''''''''''''''''''''''''''''''''
' Subroutine: cbBtnEvents_Click
'
' Purpose:    Handles clicking on the commandbar control
'

Private Sub cbBtnEvents_Click(ByVal Ctrl As Office.CommandBarButton, _
                              CancelDefault As Boolean)

   On Error Resume Next     'In case the routine is wrong/doesn't exist

   'Run the routine given by the commandbar control's OnAction property
   Application.Run Ctrl.OnAction

   'We handled it OK
   CancelDefault = True
End Sub
```

The key things to note here are:

- An object, `cbBtnEvents`, is declared to receive the `Click` event for the menu items.
- The `Click` event is raised by the `cbBtnEvents` object (the only one exposed by it).
- The `Click` event passes the `Ctrl` object (the menu item or toolbar button) that was clicked.
- The code runs the routine specified in the control's `OnAction` property. The code is simulating the behavior that occurs when adding menu items to Excel's menus.

```
'A module-level variable for our menu handler
Dim moBtnEvents As CBarEvents

Sub AddMenu()

  Dim oAddinBar As CommandBar
  Dim oBtn As CommandBarButton

  'Get the Addins menu bar
  Set oAddinBar = Application.VBE.CommandBars.FindControl(ID:=30038).CommandBar

  'Add a button to it
  Set oBtn = oAddinBar.Controls.Add(msoControlButton)

  'Set the button's properties
  With oBtn
    .Caption = "About My Addin"
    .Tag = "MyAddin"
    .OnAction = "AboutMe"
  End With

  'Create an instance of our BtnEvents class...
  Set moBtnEvents = New CBarEvents

  '... and hook it up to the button we just created
  Set moBtnEvents.cbBtnEvents = oBtn

End Sub

Sub AboutMe()
  MsgBox "About Me"
End Sub
```

In order to use this class, we have to hook it up to any `CommandBarButtons` we add, using the above code, which can be typed into a new standard module. When we hook the event handler to the `CommandBarButton` in this way, we're actually linking the event handler (the `cbBtnEvents` variable in the `CBarEvents` class) to the **button's** `.Tag` property:

```
'A module-level variable for our menu handler
Dim moBtnEvents As CBarEvents

Sub AddMenu()

  Dim oAddinBar As CommandBar
```

```
  Dim oBtn As CommandBarButton

  'Get the Addins menu bar
  Set oAddinBar = Application.VBE.CommandBars.FindControl(ID:=30038).CommandBar

  'Add a button to it
  Set oBtn = oAddinBar.Controls.Add(msoControlButton)

  'Set the button's properties
  With oBtn
    .Caption = "About My Addin"
    .Tag = "MyAddin"
    .OnAction = "AboutMe"
  End With

  'Create an instance of our BtnEvents class...
  Set moBtnEvents = New CBarEvents

  '... and hook it up to the button we just created
  Set moBtnEvents.cbBtnEvents = oBtn

  'Add a second button
  Set oBtn = oAddinBar.Controls.Add(msoControlButton)

  'Set the second button's properties.  By using the same Tag string, its click
event
  'will fire the same event handler that we set up above
  With oBtn
    .Caption = "About My Addin Too"
    .Tag = "MyAddin"
    .OnAction = "AboutMeToo"
  End With

End Sub

Sub AboutMe()
  MsgBox "About Me"
End Sub

Sub AboutMeToo()
  MsgBox "About Me Too"
End Sub
```

All buttons that have the same `Tag` will also fire the `Click` event in the single instance of our `CBarEvents` class, as shown in the above example, where we're just adding a 'Me Too' button. The clicks of both buttons are handled by the single `moBtnEvents` object. Note that the above code is not part of our VBE Toolkit Addin, so delete the module before continuing.

Table-Driven Menu Creation

Very few professional Excel developers write code to add their menu items one-by-one. Most use a table-driven approach, whereby a table is filled with information about the menu items we want to add, before a routine generates all the menu items based on this table. The same technique will be used here. Using a table-drive approach has the following advantages:

- The same menu-creation code can be reused in different projects.
- It is much easier and quicker to add lines to a table than to modify code.
- It is much easier to see the resulting menu structure by examining the table than to trace through the equivalent code.

The first thing that is needed is a table for the menu information. In Excel, rename the worksheet to `MenuTable` and fill out the sheet as shown below:

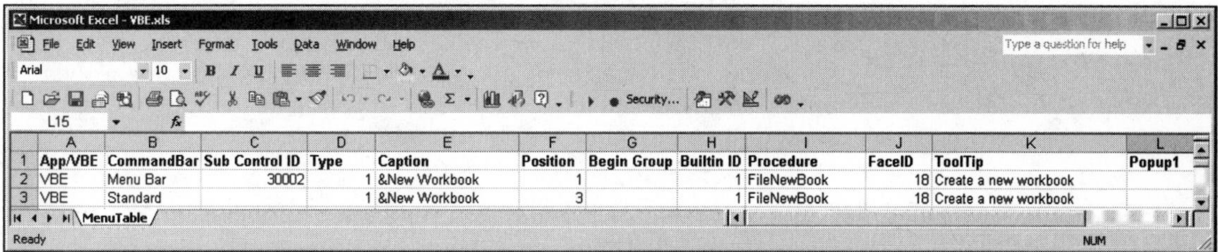

The columns of the `MenuTable` are:

Col	Title	Description
A	App / VBE	Either 'App' to add items to Excel's menus or 'VBE' to add them to the VBE.
B	CommandBar	The name of the top-level command bar to add our menu to. See below for a list of valid names and the parts of the VBE to which they apply.
C	Sub Control ID	The ID number of a built-in pop-up bar to add our menu to. For example, 30002 is the ID of the **File** popup menu.
D	Type	The type of control to add: 1 for a normal button, 10 for a popup, etc. These correspond to the `msoControl` types listed in the Object Browser.
E	Caption	The text to use for the menu item.
F	Position	The position in the command bar to add the menu item. Leave this blank to add the menu to the end of the bar.
G	Begin Group	`True` or `False` to specify whether to place a separator line before the item.
H	BuiltIn ID	If we're adding a built-in menu item, this is the ID of that menu. Use 1 for all custom menu items.

Table continued on following page

Col	Title	Description
I	Procedure	The name of the procedure to run when the menu item is clicked.
J	FaceID	The ID number of the built-in tool face to use for the menu. This can also be the name of a picture in the worksheet to use for the button face. 18 is the number for the standard New icon.
K	ToolTip	The text of the pop-up tooltip to show for the button.
L+	Popup1 – n	If we add our own popup menus, this is the caption of the custom popup to add further menu items to. See later for an example of its use. We can include as many levels of popup as we like, by simply adding more columns – the code will detect the extra columns.

The names for each of the top-level commandbars in the VBE (i.e. the names to use in column B of the menu table) are shown in the following table. Note that Excel should always recognize these names, regardless of the user's choice of language for the Office User Interface (apart from a few rare exceptions, such as the Dutch menus, in which case we'll get a run-time error). The same is not true for the menu items placed on these toolbars. The only language-independent way to locate specific built-in menu items is to use their ID number. A routine to list the ID numbers of built-in menu items is provided in Chapter 14:

Name	Description
Menu Bar	The normal VBE menu bar
Standard	The normal VBE toolbar
Edit	The VBE edit toolbar, containing useful code-editing tools
Debug	The VBE debug toolbar, containing typical debugging tools
UserForm	The VBE UserForm toolbar, containing useful form-editing tools
MSForms	The popup menu for a UserForm (shown when you right-click the UserForm background)
MSForms Control	The popup menu for a normal control on a UserForm
MSForms Control Group	The popup menu that appears when you right-click a group of controls on a UserForm
MSForms MPC	The popup menu for the Multi-Page Control
MSForms Palette	The popup menu that appears when you right-click a tool in the Control Toolbox

Name	Description
MSForms Toolbox	The popup menu that appears when you right-click one of the tabs at the top of the Control Toolbox
MSForms DragDrop	The popup menu that appears when you use the right mouse button to drag a control between tabs in the Control Toolbox, or onto a UserForm
Code Window	The popup menu for a code window
Code Window (Break)	The popup menu for a code window, when in Break (debug) mode
Watch Window	The popup menu for the Watch window
Immediate Window	The popup menu for the Immediate window
Locals Window	The popup menu for the Locals window
Project Window	The popup menu for the Project Explorer
Project Window (Break)	The popup menu for the Project Explorer, when in Break mode
Object Browser	The popup menu for the Object Browser
Property Browser	The popup menu for the Properties window
Docked Window	The popup menu that appears when you right-click the title bar of a docked window

As this sheet will be referred to a number of times in code, it is a good idea to give it a meaningful 'code name', such as `shMenuTable`. To do this, locate and select the sheet in the Project Explorer in the VBE, probably shown as **Sheet1 (MenuTable)**, and change its name in the **Properties** window. It should now be shown as **shMenuTable (MenuTable)** in the Project Explorer. Using the code name allows you to refer directly to that sheet as an object, so the following two lines are equivalent:

```
Debug.Print ThisWorkbook.Worksheets("MenuTable").Name
Debug.Print shMenuTable.Name
```

The code to create the menus from this table is shown below. The code should be copied into a new module called `modSetupBars`.

At the top of the module, a number of constants are declared, which correspond to each column of the menu table, and we will use these throughout the code. If the menu table structure changes, all you need to do is renumber these constants – you don't need to search through the code:

```
Option Explicit
Option Compare Text

'Constants for the columns in the commandbar creation table
Const miTABLE_APP_VBE          As Integer = 1
```

```
Const miTABLE_COMMANDBAR_NAME  As Integer = 2
Const miTABLE_CONTROL_ID       As Integer = 3
Const miTABLE_CONTROL_TYPE     As Integer = 4
Const miTABLE_CONTROL_CAPTION  As Integer = 5
Const miTABLE_CONTROL_POSITION As Integer = 6
Const miTABLE_CONTROL_GROUP    As Integer = 7
Const miTABLE_CONTROL_BUILTIN  As Integer = 8
Const miTABLE_CONTROL_PROC     As Integer = 9
Const miTABLE_CONTROL_FACEID   As Integer = 10
Const miTABLE_CONTROL_TOOLTIP  As Integer = 11
Const miTABLE_POPUP_START      As Integer = 12

'Define a variable to store the menu item click event handler
Dim moBarEvents As CBarEvents
```

As explained above, the `Click` event for all our commandbars can be routed through a single instance of our event handler, by ensuring they all share the same `Tag` string:

```
''''''''''''''''''''''''''''''''''''
' Subroutine: SetUpMenus
'
' Purpose:    Adds the menus to the VBE Edit menu and sets up the objects to trap
'             the command bar events for the new controls
'

Sub SetUpMenus()
  Dim rgRow As Range
  Dim cbAllBars As CommandBars
  Dim cbBar As CommandBar
  Dim cbBtn As CommandBarControl
  Dim iBuiltInID As Integer, iPopUpCol As Integer, vaData As Variant

  On Error Resume Next    'Just ignore errors in the table definition

  'Remove all of our menus to before adding them.
  'This ensures we don't get any duplicated menus
  RemoveMenus

  'Loop through each row of our menu generation table
  For Each rgRow In shMenuTable.Cells(1).CurrentRegion.Rows
    'Ignore the header row
    If rgRow.Row > 1 Then
      'Read the row into an array of the cells' values
      vaData = rgRow.Value

      Set cbBar = Nothing
```

The routine to actually set up the menus is called from our Addin's `Auto_Open` procedure:

```
      'Get the collection of all commandbars, either in the VBE or Excel
      If vaData(1, miTABLE_APP_VBE) = "VBE" Then
        Set cbAllBars = Application.VBE.CommandBars
      Else
        Set cbAllBars = Application.CommandBars
```

```
      End If

      'Try to find the commandbar we want
      Set cbBar = cbAllBars.Item(vaData(1, miTABLE_COMMANDBAR_NAME))

      'Did we find it - if not, we must be adding one!
      If cbBar Is Nothing Then
        Set cbBar = cbAllBars.Add(Name:=vaData(1, miTABLE_COMMANDBAR_NAME), _

temporary:=True)
      End If
```

A single routine can be used to add menu items to both the Excel and VBE menus. The only difference is the `CommandBars` collection that is looked in – Excel's or the VBE's:

```
      'If set, locate the built-in popup menu bar (by ID) to add our control to.
      'e.g. Menu Bar > Edit
      If Not IsEmpty(vaData(1, miTABLE_CONTROL_ID)) Then
        Set cbBar = cbBar.FindControl(ID:=vaData(1, miTABLE_CONTROL_ID), _
                                      Recursive:=True).CommandBar
      End If

      'Loop through the PopUp name columns to navigate down the menu structure
      For iPopUpCol = miTABLE_POPUP_START To UBound(vaData, 2)
        'If set, navigate down the menu structure to the next popup menu
        If Not IsEmpty(vaData(1, iPopUpCol)) Then
          Set cbBar = cbBar.Controls(vaData(1, iPopUpCol)).CommandBar
        End If
      Next

      'Get the ID number if we're adding a built-in control
      iBuiltInID = vaData(1, miTABLE_CONTROL_BUILTIN)

      'If it's empty, set it to 1, indicating a custom control
      If iBuiltInID = 0 Then iBuiltInID = 1

      'Now add our control to the command bar, passing the procedure to run
      'as the control's parameter
      If IsEmpty(vaData(1, miTABLE_CONTROL_POSITION)) Or _
         vaData(1, miTABLE_CONTROL_POSITION) > cbBar.Controls.Count
Then
        Set cbBtn = cbBar.Controls.Add(Type:=vaData(1, miTABLE_CONTROL_TYPE), _
                                       ID:=iBuiltInID, temporary:=True)
      Else
        Set cbBtn = cbBar.Controls.Add(Type:=vaData(1, miTABLE_CONTROL_TYPE), _
                                       ID:=iBuiltInID, temporary:=True, _
                                       before:=vaData(1, _
                                       miTABLE_CONTROL_POSITION))
      End If

      'Set the rest of button's properties
      With cbBtn
        .Caption = vaData(1, miTABLE_CONTROL_CAPTION)
        .BeginGroup = vaData(1, miTABLE_CONTROL_GROUP)
        .TooltipText = vaData(1, miTABLE_CONTROL_TOOLTIP)
```

If you want to add your control to a built-in popup menu, you can recursively search for it in the `CommandBars` collection. For example, if you wanted to add a menu item to the **Format | Make same size** menu, you can specify the ID of the **Make same size** menu (32790) in the `SubControlID` column of the table:

```
         'The FaceID can be empty for a blank button, the number of a standard
         'button face, or the name of a picture object on the sheet, which
         'contains the picture to use.
         If Not IsEmpty(vaData(1, miTABLE_CONTROL_FACEID)) Then
            If IsNumeric(vaData(1, miTABLE_CONTROL_FACEID)) Then
               'A numeric face ID, so use it
               .FaceId = vaData(1, miTABLE_CONTROL_FACEID)
            Else
               'A textual face ID, so copy the picture to the button
               shMenuTable.Shapes(vaData(1, miTABLE_CONTROL_FACEID)).CopyPicture
               .PasteFace

               'In Office XP, CommandBarButtons now have a Picture property, so we
               'could use:
               '.Picture = shMenuTable.Shapes(vaData(1,
miTABLE_CONTROL_FACEID)).Picture
            End If
         End If

         'Set the button's tag to identify it as one we created.
         'This way, we can still find it if the user moves or renames it.
         'Using the same ID for all buttons lets them all use the same event
handler.
         .Tag = psAddinID

         'Set the control's OnAction property.  This only really has an effect on
         'the Excel menus, but we can use it in the VBE to say which routine to
         'run in the Click event handler
         'Surround the workbook name with quote marks, in case the name includes
spaces
         .OnAction = "'" & ThisWorkbook.Name & "'!" & vaData(1,
miTABLE_CONTROL_PROC)
      End With
```

You can either use one of the standard Office tool faces, by supplying the numeric `FaceID`, or provide your own picture to use. To use your own picture, just give the name of the `Picture` object in the **FaceID** column of the menu table. The picture should be 32x32 pixels for the small icon view, or 64x64 pixels when viewing large icons:

```
      'We only need to handle events for custom controls in the VBE
      If iBuiltInID = 1 And vaData(1, miTABLE_APP_VBE) = "VBE" Then

         'Has it been set already?
         If moBarEvents Is Nothing Then

            'No, so create a new instance of our button event-handling class
            Set moBarEvents = New CBarEvents

            'Tell the class to hook into the events for all our buttons
```

```
            Set moBarEvents.cbBtnEvents = cbBtn
          End If
        End If
      End If
    Next
  End Sub
```

This is the code that sets up the menu event handler. It only needs to be done once, as it will respond to the `Click` events raised by **all** our buttons.

When the Addin is closed, you need to run some code to remove the menus from the VBE. Some developers just use `CommandBars.Reset`, but this removes all other customizations from the commandbars as well as their own. It is much better programming etiquette to locate all the menu items and commandbars that were created for your Addin and delete them. This takes two routines. The first removes all the menus from a specific `CommandBars` collection, by searching for its `Tag`:

```
Private Sub RemoveMenusFromBars(cbBars As CommandBars)
  Dim cbCtl As CommandBarControl

  'Ignore errors while deleting our menu items
  On Error Resume Next

  'Using the application or VBE CommandBars ...
  With cbBars
    'Find a CommandBarControl with our tag
    Set cbCtl = .FindControl(Tag:=psAddinID)

    'Loop until we didn't find one
    Do Until cbCtl Is Nothing
      'Delete the one we found
      cbCtl.Delete

      'Find the next one
      Set cbCtl = .FindControl(Tag:=psAddinID)
    Loop
  End With
End Sub
```

The second removal routine calls the first to remove the menu items from the Excel commandbars and the VBE commandbars, removes any custom bars that might have been created, and clears the module-level event handler:

```
Sub RemoveMenus()
  Dim cbBar As CommandBar, rgRow As Range, stBarName As String

  'Ignore errors while deleting our menu items and commandbars
  On Error Resume Next

  'Delete our menu items from the Excel and VBE commandbars
  RemoveMenusFromBars Application.CommandBars
  RemoveMenusFromBars Application.VBE.CommandBars

  'Loop through each row of our menu generation table
```

```
    For Each rgRow In shMenuTable.Cells(1).CurrentRegion.Rows
      'Ignore the header row
      If rgRow.Row > 1 Then
        stBarName = rgRow.Cells(1, miTABLE_COMMANDBAR_NAME)

        Set cbBar = Nothing
        'Find the command bar, either in the VBE or Excel
        If rgRow.Cells(1, miTABLE_APP_VBE) = "VBE" Then
          Set cbBar = Application.VBE.CommandBars(stBarName)
        Else
          Set cbBar = Application.CommandBars(stBarName)
        End If
        'If we found it, delete it if it is not a built-in bar
        If Not cbBar Is Nothing Then
          If Not cbBar.BuiltIn Then
            'Only delete blank commandbars - in case two Addins
            'added menu items to the same custom bar
            If cbBar.Controls.Count = 0 Then cbBar.Delete
          End If
        End If
      End If
    Next

    'Clear down our menu click event handler
    Set moBarEvents = Nothing
  End Sub
```

You now have a complete template, which can be used as the basis for any Excel or VBE Addin (or just in a normal workbook where you want to modify the menu structure).

Let's add this procedure, then test the Addin. Add a new module called `modMenuFile` and copy in the following code. We will be adding more file-related routines to this module later:

```
  '''''''''''''''''''''''''''''''''''
  ' Subroutine: FileNewBook
  '
  ' Purpose:    Create a new workbook
  '

  Sub FileNewBook()
     'Just ignore any errors
     On Error Resume Next

     'Create a new workbook
     Application.Workbooks.Add

     'Refresh the VBE display
     With Application.VBE.MainWindow
         .Visible = False
         .Visible = True
     End With
  End Sub
```

This just adds a new blank workbook and refreshes the VBE display. Note that the VBE Project Explorer does not always update correctly when workbooks are added and removed through code. The easiest way to refresh the VBE display is to hide and then reshow the main VBE window.

First, check that the Addin compiles, using the **Debug | Compile** menu. If any compile errors are highlighted, check your code against the listings above. To run the Addin, click on **Tools | Macros**, select the **Auto_Open** procedure and click the **Run** button. If all goes well, a new menu item will be added to the VBE **File** menu and a standard **New** icon will appear on the VBE toolbar, just to the left of the **Save** icon:

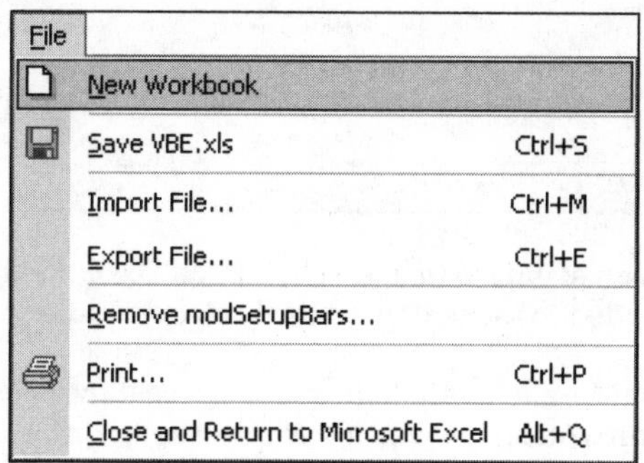

When you click the button, a new workbook will be created in Excel and you will see its `VBProject` added to the Project Explorer. Congratulations, you have programmed the VBE.

Displaying Built-In Dialogs, UserForms, and Messages

The ability to save a workbook from the VBE is built in to Office 2002, but you have also added the ability to create new workbooks. For a full complement of file operations, you need to add routines to open and close workbooks as well. Adding a "Most Recently Used" list to the VBE is left as an exercise for the reader.

By the end of this chapter, you'll have functionality within the VBE to:

- Create a new workbook
- Open an existing workbook
- Save a workbook (this is built into the VBE)
- Close a workbook
- Display a workbook's `Properties` dialog

For the `Open` routine, another menu item will be added to the **File** menu, and another standard button to the toolbar. For the `Close` routine, an item will once again be added to the **File** menu, but it will also be added to the Project Explorer popup menu, allowing you to close a `VBProject` by right-clicking on it in the Project Explorer. The following additions to the menu table will achieve this:

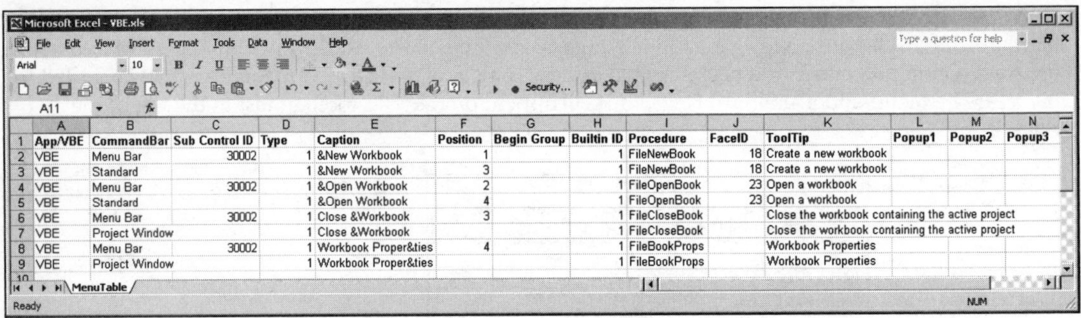

App/VBE	CommandBar	Sub Control ID	Type	Caption	Position	Begin Group	Builtin ID	Procedure	FaceID	ToolTip	Popup1	Popup2	Popup3
VBE	Menu Bar	30002	1	&New Workbook	1		1	FileNewBook	18	Create a new workbook			
VBE	Standard		1	&New Workbook	3		1	FileNewBook	18	Create a new workbook			
VBE	Menu Bar	30002	1	&Open Workbook	2		1	FileOpenBook	23	Open a workbook			
VBE	Standard		1	&Open Workbook	4		1	FileOpenBook	23	Open a workbook			
VBE	Menu Bar	30002	1	Close &Workbook	3		1	FileCloseBook		Close the workbook containing the active project			
VBE	Project Window		1	Close &Workbook			1	FileCloseBook		Close the workbook containing the active project			
VBE	Menu Bar	30002	1	Workbook Proper&ties	4		1	FileBookProps		Workbook Properties			
VBE	Project Window		1	Workbook Proper&ties			1	FileBookProps		Workbook Properties			

Note that the Close menu does not have a standard image, so the FaceID column has been left empty, and by not specifying a position, it is added to the bottom of the Project Explorer popup menu.

To accurately simulate Excel's functionality, a test should be made to see if the *Shift* key is held down when the menu button is clicked, and turn off any events if this is the case. Unfortunately, if the user holds down the *Shift* key when a workbook is opened in the VBE, the routine will stop dead (see MS KnowledgeBase article Q175223 for the gory details at http://support.microsoft.com/support/kb/articles/Q175/2/23.asp). The best that can be done is to use the *Ctrl* key for the same effect. Back in the `modCommon` module, add the following declaration at the top:

```
'Windows API call to see if the Shift, Ctrl and/or Alt keys are pressed
Private Declare Function GetAsyncKeyState Lib "user32" (ByVal vKey As Long) As
Integer
```

This tells VBA about a function available in Windows – see Chapter 24 for more information about these calls. At the bottom of the `modCommon` module, add the following function:

```
''''''''''''''''''''''''''''''''''''
' Subroutine: fnGetShiftCtrlAlt
'
' Purpose:    Uses a Windows API call to detect if the shift, ctrl and/or alt keys
are pressed
'

Function fnGetShiftCtrlAlt() As Integer
  Dim iKeys As Integer

  Const VK_SHIFT As Long = &H10
  Const VK_CONTROL As Long = &H11
  Const VK_ALT As Long = &H12

  'Check to see if the Shift, Ctrl and Alt keys are pressed
  If GetAsyncKeyState(VK_SHIFT) <> 0 Then iKeys = iKeys + 1
  If GetAsyncKeyState(VK_CONTROL) <> 0 Then iKeys = iKeys + 2
  If GetAsyncKeyState(VK_ALT) <> 0 Then iKeys = iKeys + 4

  fnGetShiftCtrlAlt = iKeys
End Function
```

For the Open routine, Excel's GetOpenFilename method will be used to retrieve the name of a file, and then open it. If the user holds down the *Ctrl* key, the application events will be turned off, so that the user can open the workbook without triggering any other code – either within the workbook being opened, or Excel's own Workbook_Open event. If the user is not holding down the *Ctrl* key, an attempt is made to run any Auto_Open routines in the workbook:

```
''''''''''''''''''''''''''''''''''''''''
' Subroutine: FileOpenBook
'
' Purpose:    Opens an existing workbook
'

Sub FileOpenBook()
  Dim vaFile As Variant, bCtrl As Boolean
  Dim Wbk As Workbook

  'Use our error handler to display a message if something goes wrong
  On Error GoTo ERR_HANDLER

  'Check if the Ctrl key is held down (1=Shift, 2=Ctrl, 4=Alt)
  bCtrl = (fnGetShiftCtrlAlt And 2) = 2

  'Hide Excel, so the Open dialog appears in the VBE
  Application.Visible = False

  'Get the filename to open (or False if cancelled)
  vaFile = Application.GetOpenFilename

  'Make Excel visible again
  Application.Visible = True

  'If the user didn't cancel, open the workbook, adding it to Excel's MRU
  If Not (vaFile = False) Then
    If bCtrl Then
      'If the user held the Ctrl key down, we should disable events and
      'not update links
      Application.EnableEvents = False

      Set Wbk = Workbooks.Open(Filename:=vaFile, updatelinks:=0, AddToMru:=True)

      'Enable events again
      Application.EnableEvents = True
    Else
      'Shift not held down, so open the book normally and run Auto_Open
      Set Wbk = Workbooks.Open(Filename:=vFile, AddToMru:=True)
      Wbk.RunAutoMacros xlAutoOpen
    End If
  End If

  'Refresh the VBE display
  With Application.VBE.MainWindow
    .Visible = False
    .Visible = True
  End With
```

```
    'No error, so Exit routine
    Exit Sub

  ERR_HANDLER:

    'Display the error message (in the VBE Window) and end the routine.
    Application.Visible = False

    MsgBox "An Error has occurred." & vbCrLf & _
              Err.Number & ": " & Err.Description, vbOKOnly, psAddinTitle

    Application.Visible = True
  End Sub
```

Whenever a dialog is used that would normally be shown in the Excel window (including the built-in dialogs, any UserForms, and even `MsgBox` and `InputBox` calls), Excel automatically switches to its own window to show the dialog. When developing applications for the VBE, however, we really want the dialog to appear within the VBE window, not Excel's. The easiest way to achieve this effect is to hide the Excel window before showing the dialog, then unhide it afterwards:

```
Function fnActiveProjectBook() As Workbook
  Dim obVBP As VBIDE.VBProject, obVBC As VBIDE.VBComponent
  Dim stName As String

  'If any errors occur (e.g. the project is locked), assume we can't find the
'workbook
  On Error GoTo ERR_CANT_FIND_WORKBOOK

  'Get the VBProject that is active in the VBE
  Set obVBP = Application.VBE.ActiveVBProject

  If obVBP.Protection = vbext_pp_locked Then
    'If the project is locked, it must have been saved, so we can read its file
'name
    stName = obVBP.Filename

    'Strip off the path
    If InStrRev(stName, "\") <> 0 Then
      stName = Mid(stName, InStrRev(stName, "\") + 1)

      'If it's the name of a workbook, we found it! (it could be the name of a VBE
'project)
      If fnIsWorkbook(stName) Then
        Set fnActiveProjectBook = Workbooks(stName)
        Exit Function
      End If
    End If
  Else
    'Loop through all the VB Components in the project.
    'The 'ThisWorkbook' component exposes the name of the workbook, but the
    'component may not be called "ThisWorkbook"!

    For Each obVBC In obVBP.VBComponents
      'Only need to check Document types (i.e. Excel objects)
```

```
      If obVBC.Type = vbext_ct_Document Then

        'Get the underlying name of the component
        stName = obVBC.Properties("Name")

        'Is it the name of an open workbook
        If fnIsWorkbook(stName) Then

          'Yes it is, but is it the correct one?
          If Workbooks(stName).VBProject Is obVBP Then

            'We found it!
            Set fnActiveProjectBook = Workbooks(stName)
            Exit Function
          End If
        End If
      End If
    Next
  End If

PTR_CANT_FIND:

  'We didn't find the workbook, so display an error message in the VBE
  Application.Visible = False
  MsgBox "Unable to identify the workbook for this project.", vbOKOnly,
psAddinTitle
  Application.Visible = True

  Set fnActiveProjectBook = Nothing
  Exit Function

ERR_CANT_FIND_WORKBOOK:

  'We had an error, so we can't find the workbook.  Continue with the clean-up
code.
  Resume PTR_CANT_FIND
End Function
```

The `Close` routine presents us with a new challenge. We are adding a **Close Workbook** menu item to the popup menu for the Project Explorer, and hence need to determine which `VBProject` was clicked. The `ActiveVBProject` property of the VBE provides this, but a way is needed to get from the `VBProject` object to the workbook containing it. The method for doing this was described in the *Identifying VBE Objects in Code* section at the start of this chapter and the code is shown below. Add it to the `modCommon` module, along with the `Auto_Open` and `Auto_Close` routines, as you will be needing it again later:

```
Function fnIsWorkbook(stBook As String) As Boolean
  Dim stName As String

  'Use inline error handling to check for a workbook
  On Error Resume Next

  Err.Clear
  stName = Workbooks(stBook).Name
  fnIsWorkbook = (Err.Number = 0)
End Function
```

Note that the Excel window is being hidden before displaying our error message, and is "unhidden" afterwards. The following routine is needed to check if the result is the name of a workbook:

```
''''''''''''''''''''''''''''''''''
' Subroutine: FileCloseBook
'
' Purpose:    Closes the workbook containing the active VB Project
'

Sub FileCloseBook()
  Dim Wbk As Workbook, bCtrl As Boolean

  'Use our error handler to display a message if something goes wrong
  On Error GoTo ERR_HANDLER

  'Try to get the workbook containing the active VB Project
  Set Wbk = fnActiveProjectBook

  'If we didn't find it, just quit
  If Wbk Is Nothing Then Exit Sub

  'Check if the Ctrl key is held down (1=Shift, 2=Ctrl, 4=Alt)
  bCtrl = (fnGetShiftCtrlAlt And 2) = 2

  If bCtrl Then
    'Ctrl key is held down, so disable events and don't run Auto_Close
    'Disable events, so we we don't run anything in the workbook being closed
    Application.EnableEvents = False

    'Close the workbook - Excel will ask to save changes etc.
    Wbk.Close

    'Enable events again
    Application.EnableEvents = True
  Else
    'Normal close so run any Auto_Close macros and close the workbook
    Wbk.RunAutoMacros xlAutoClose
    Wbk.Close
  End If

  'Exit procedure, bypass error handling routine
  Exit Sub

ERR_HANDLER:

  'Display the error message (in the VBE Window) and end the routine.
  Application.Visible = False

  MsgBox "An Error has occurred." & vbCrLf & _
           Err.Number & ": " & Err.Description, vbOKOnly, psAddinTitle

  Application.Visible = True
End Sub
```

Now that you can get the workbook that corresponds to the active VB Project, you can use it in the `Close` routine, which should be added to the `modMenuFile` module:

```
''''''''''''''''''''''''''''''''''''''
' Subroutine: FileBookProps
'
' Purpose:    Displays the workbook properties dialog for the active VB Project
'

Sub FileBookProps()
  Dim Wbk As Workbook, bAddin As Boolean, bVis As Boolean

  'Just ignore any errors
  On Error Resume Next

  'Try to get the workbook containing the active VB Project
  Set Wbk = fnActiveProjectBook

  'If we didn't find it, just quit
  If Wbk Is Nothing Then Exit Sub

  'Hide the Excel window, so the dialog seems to appear within the VBE environment
  Application.Visible = False

  'Using the workbook...
  With Wbk
    'If it is an Addin, convert it to a normal workbook temporarily
    bAddin = .IsAddin
    .IsAddin = False

    'Make sure its window is visible
    bVis = .Windows(1).Visible
    .Windows(1).Visible = True

    'Display the Workbook Properties dialog
    Application.Dialogs(xlDialogProperties).Show

    'Restore the workbook's visibility and Addin Status
    .Windows(1).Visible = bVis
    .IsAddin = bAddin
  End With

  'Make Excel visible again
  Application.Visible = True
End Sub
```

The last workbook-related tool to be defined displays the **File Properties** dialog for the active VB Project's workbook. One of the main uses for the workbook properties is to provide the information shown in the **Tools | Add-Ins** dialog. The list box shows the Addin's title from its **Properties** dialog, while the description shown when an Addin is selected, is obtained from its **Comments** box.

Excel's built-in **Properties** dialog can be used for this, but we cannot tell it which workbook to show the properties for – the active workbook is used. Therefore any Addins need to be temporarily converted to normal workbooks and "unhidden" if they are hidden. After showing the **Properties** dialog, the workbooks must be converted back to Addins.

To test the Addin so far, just run the `Auto_Open` routine using **Tools | Macros** to recreate our menu items, then check that each item works as intended.

Note that attempting to close the Addin itself using the menu might cause the computer to lock up.

Working with Code

So far in this chapter, we have been working at a fairly high level in the VBIDE and Excel Object Models (limiting ourselves to the `VBProject` and `Workbook` objects), to add typical file operations to the Visual Basic environment. You now have the ability to create new workbooks (and hence their VB Projects), open existing workbooks, change a workbook's properties, and save and close workbooks from within the VBE.

In this section, we will plunge to the lowest level of the VBE Object Model and learn how to work with the user's code. We will limit ourselves to detecting the line of code the user is editing (and even identifying the selected characters within that line), and getting information about the procedure, module, and project containing that line of code. We will leave adding and changing code until the next section, where we'll be creating a UserForm, adding some buttons to it and adding code to handle the buttons' events.

To demonstrate how to identify the code that the user is working on, right-click access will be added to provide a print routine, with individual buttons to print the current selection, current procedure, module, or project. First some additional rows will be added to our menu table:

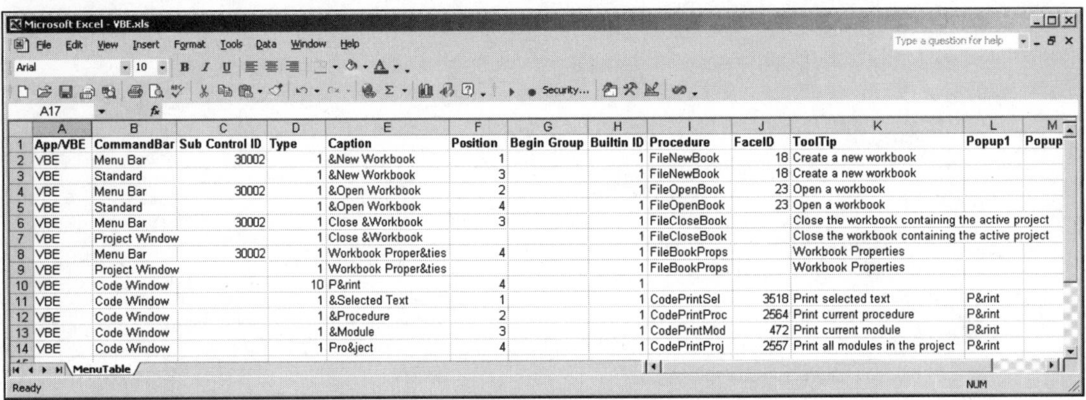

App/VBE	CommandBar	Sub Control ID	Type	Caption	Position	Begin Group	Builtin ID	Procedure	FaceID	ToolTip	Popup1	Popup
VBE	Menu Bar	30002	1	&New Workbook	1		1	FileNewBook	18	Create a new workbook		
VBE	Standard		1	&New Workbook	3		1	FileNewBook	18	Create a new workbook		
VBE	Menu Bar	30002	1	&Open Workbook	2		1	FileOpenBook	23	Open a workbook		
VBE	Standard		1	&Open Workbook	4		1	FileOpenBook	23	Open a workbook		
VBE	Menu Bar	30002	1	Close &Workbook	3		1	FileCloseBook		Close the workbook containing the active project		
VBE	Project Window		1	Close &Workbook			1	FileCloseBook		Close the workbook containing the active project		
VBE	Menu Bar	30002	1	Workbook Proper&ties	4		1	FileBookProps		Workbook Properties		
VBE	Project Window		1	Workbook Proper&ties			1	FileBookProps		Workbook Properties		
VBE	Code Window		10	P&rint	4		1					
VBE	Code Window		1	&Selected Text	1		1	CodePrintSel	3518	Print selected text	P&rint	
VBE	Code Window		1	&Procedure	2		1	CodePrintProc	2564	Print current procedure	P&rint	
VBE	Code Window		1	&Module	3		1	CodePrintMod	472	Print current module	P&rint	
VBE	Code Window		1	Pro&ject	4		1	CodePrintProj	2557	Print all modules in the project	P&rint	

The first thing to note is that we're adding our own cascading menu to the Code Window popup menu (type 10 is a custom popup menu), then adding four menu items to the cascading menu, each of which has its own face ID. The result is:

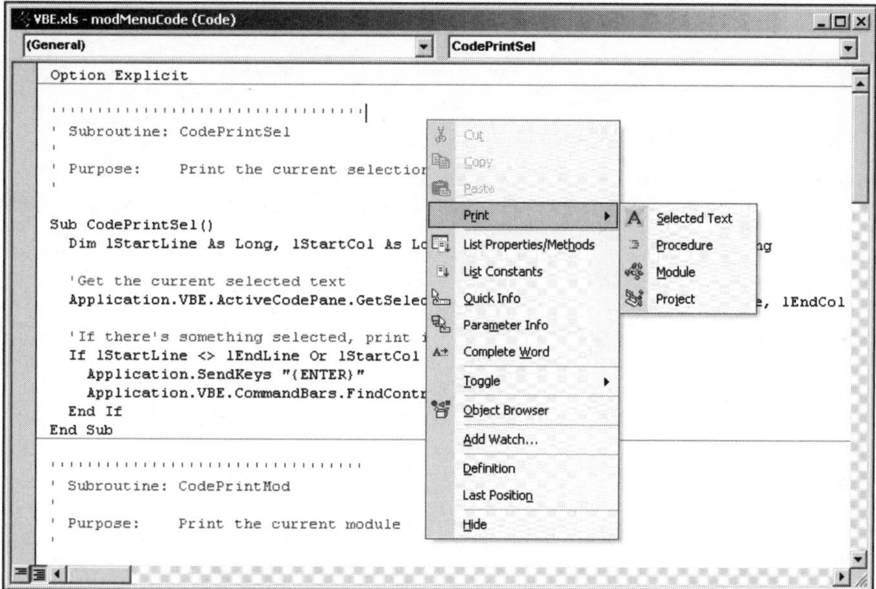

The code for the four printing routines will be placed into their own module, so add a new module to the project called `modMenuCode`.

Unfortunately, the VBIDE Object Model does not include a `Print` method for any of its objects. To provide right-click printing, there are three options:

- Show the VBE's `Print` dialog and operate it using `SendKeys`
- Copy the code to a worksheet range and print it from there
- Copy the code to a private instance of Word, reformat to show the Excel reserved words, etc. in their correct colors and then print it from Word

For the sake of simplicity, the first option will be implemented. The main problem that this presents is how to select the **Selected Text**, **Module**, or **Project** option buttons on the **Print** dialog, using `SendKeys`, especially as the **Selected Text** option is only enabled when some text is actually selected.

The answer is to identify if any text is selected, then send the appropriate number of *DownArrow* keys to the dialog to select either the **Module** or **Project** options. If we could rely on our users only ever having an English user interface language, we could send *Alt+M* or *Alt+J* keystrokes – sending *DownArrows* works with any choice of user interface language.

The code for the **Selected Text** menu item is the simplest and is presented below. All that is required is to identify if the user has actually selected anything and if so, to send some keystrokes to the **Print** dialog to print it:

```
Option Explicit

''''''''''''''''''''''''''''''''''''''
' Subroutine: CodePrintSel
'
```

```
' Purpose:    Print the current selection
'

Sub CodePrintSel()
  Dim lStartLine As Long, lStartCol As Long, lEndLine As Long, lEndCol As Long

  'Get the current selected text
  Application.VBE.ActiveCodePane.GetSelection lStartLine, lStartCol, lEndLine,
lEndCol

  'If there's something selected, print it
  If lStartLine <> lEndLine Or lStartCol <> lEndCol Then
    Application.SendKeys "{ENTER}"
    Application.VBE.CommandBars.FindControl(ID:=4).Execute
  End If
End Sub
```

The main items to note are:

- The `ActiveCodePane` property of the VBE is being used to identify which module the user is editing.
- The variables sent to the `GetSelection` method are sent `ByRef` and actually get filled by the method. After the call to `GetSelection`, they contain the start and ending line numbers and start and ending columns of the currently selected text.
- A simple *Enter* keystroke is sent to the keyboard buffer. Then the VBE Print dialog is immediately shown by running the File | Print menu item (ID = 4) directly. This technique of running menu items directly was introduced in Chapter 22, in connection with the `RunMenu` routine presented there. By default (if some text is selected) when the VBE Print dialog is shown, the Selected Text option is selected so this does not need to be changed.

It should be noted that while no method in the Excel Object Model changes the value of the variables passed to it, this technique is quite common in the VBIDE Object Model and is getting more common in Windows applications generally.

```
''''''''''''''''''''''''''''''''''
' Subroutine: CodePrintMod
'
' Purpose:    Print the current module
'

Sub CodePrintMod()
  Dim lStartLine As Long, lStartCol As Long, lEndLine As Long, lEndCol As Long

  'Get the current selection
  Application.VBE.ActiveCodePane.GetSelection lStartLine, lStartCol, lEndLine,
lEndCol

  If lStartLine <> lEndLine Or lStartCol <> lEndCol Then
    'If there's something selected, make sure the 'Module' item is selected
    Application.SendKeys "{DOWN}{ENTER}"
  Else
    'If there's nothing selected, the 'Module' item is selected by default
    Application.SendKeys "{ENTER}"
```

```
  End If

  Application.VBE.CommandBars.FindControl(ID:=4).Execute
End Sub

''''''''''''''''''''''''''''''''''
' Subroutine: CodePrintProj
'
' Purpose:    Print the current project

Sub CodePrintProj()
  Dim lStartLine As Long, lStartCol As Long, lEndLine As Long, lEndCol As Long

  'Get the current selection
  Application.VBE.ActiveCodePane.GetSelection lStartLine, lStartCol, lEndLine,
_lEndCol

  'Make sure the 'Project' item is selected
  If lStartLine <> lEndLine Or lStartCol <> lEndCol Then
    Application.SendKeys "{DOWN}{DOWN}{ENTER}"
  Else
    Application.SendKeys "{DOWN}{ENTER}"
  End If

  Application.VBE.CommandBars.FindControl(ID:=4).Execute
End Sub
```

To print the current module and project, very similar code can be used. The only difference is to check if any text is selected (that is, if the Selected Text option in the Print dialog is enabled), then send a number of down keystrokes to the dialog to select the correct option. Both of these routines can be added to the modMenuCode module:

```
''''''''''''''''''''''''''''''''''
' Subroutine: CodePrintProc
'
' Purpose:    Print the current procedure

Sub CodePrintProc()
  Dim lStartLine As Long, lStartCol As Long, lEndLine As Long, lEndCol As Long
  Dim lProcType As Long, stProcName As String, lProcStart As Long, lProcEnd As
Long

  With Application.VBE.ActiveCodePane
    'Get the current selection, so we know what to print and can restore it later
    .GetSelection lStartLine, lStartCol, lEndLine, lEndCol

    With .CodeModule
      If lStartLine <= .CountOfDeclarationLines Then
        'We're in the declarations section
        lProcStart = 1
        lProcEnd = .CountOfDeclarationLines
      Else
        'We're in a procedure, so find its start and end
        stProcName = .ProcOfLine(lStartLine, lProcType)
        lProcStart = .ProcStartLine(stProcName, lProcType)
```

```
        lProcEnd = lProcStart + .ProcCountLines(stProcName, lProcType)
      End If
    End With

    'Select the text to print
    .SetSelection lProcStart, 1, lProcEnd, 0

    'Print it
    Application.SendKeys "{ENTER}"
    Application.VBE.CommandBars.FindControl(ID:=4).Execute

    'The VBE Printing code is on another thread, so we need to let it do its stuff
    'before setting the selection back.
    DoEvents

    'And select the original text again
    .SetSelection lStartLine, lStartCol, lEndLine, lEndCol
  End With
End Sub
```

The code to print the current procedure is slightly more complex, as the Print dialog does not have a Current Procedure option. The steps we need to perform are:

- Identify and store away the user's current selection
- Identify the procedure (or declaration lines) containing the user's selection
- Expand the selection to encompass the full procedure (or all the declaration lines)
- Show the Print dialog to print this expanded selection
- Restore the user's original selections

Doing this on some PCs raises an interesting issue – the final step of restoring the user's original selection sometimes gets run before the Print dialog has been shown. This is presumably because the printing is done on a separate thread of execution and Excel 2002 is having a concurrency problem. The easy fix is to include a `DoEvents` statement immediately after showing the Print dialog, to let the print routine carry out its task. This will also yield control to the operating system, allowing it to process any pending or queued events.

The main item to note in this code is that the `ProcOfLine` method accepts the start line as input, fills the `lProcType` variable with a number to identify the procedure type (`Sub`, `Function`, `Property Let`, `Property Get`, etc.), and returns the name of the procedure. The procedure type and name are used to find the start of the procedure (using `ProcStartLine`) and the number of lines within the procedure (`ProcCountLines`), which are then selected and printed.

Working with UserForms

The code examples presented in this chapter so far have been extending the VBE, to provide additional tools for the developer. In this section, we move our attention to programmatically creating and manipulating UserForms, adding controls, and adding procedures to the UserForm's code module to handle the controls' events. While the example provided in this section continues to extend the VBE, the same code and techniques can be applied in end-user applications, including:

- Adding UserForms to workbooks created by the application
- Sizing the UserForm and moving and sizing its controls to make the best use of the available screen space
- Adding code to handle events in UserForms created by the application
- Changing the controls shown on an existing UserForm in response to user input
- Creating UserForms on-the-fly, as they are needed (for example, when the number and type of controls on the UserForm will vary significantly depending on the data to be shown)

The above techniques will be demonstrated by writing code to add a UserForm to the active project, complete with standard-sized **OK** and **Cancel** buttons, as well as code to handle the buttons' `Click` events and the UserForm's `QueryClose` event. The UserForm's size will be set to 2/3 of the width and height of the Excel window and the **OK** and **Cancel** buttons' position will be adjusted accordingly.

The example shown here is the difficult way to achieve the desired result, and is intended to be an educational, rather than a practical, example. The easy way to add a standardized UserForm is to create it manually and export it to disk as a `.frm` file, then import it using the following code (do not type this in):

```
Dim oVBC As VBComponent
Set oVBC = Application.VBE.ActiveVBProject.VBComponents.Import ("MyForm.frm")
```

When you need to include it in another project, just import it again. The only advantage to doing it through code is that the UserForm can be given a size appropriate to the user's screen resolution and size, and its controls positioned correctly.

Start by adding another row to the menu table, which should now look like:

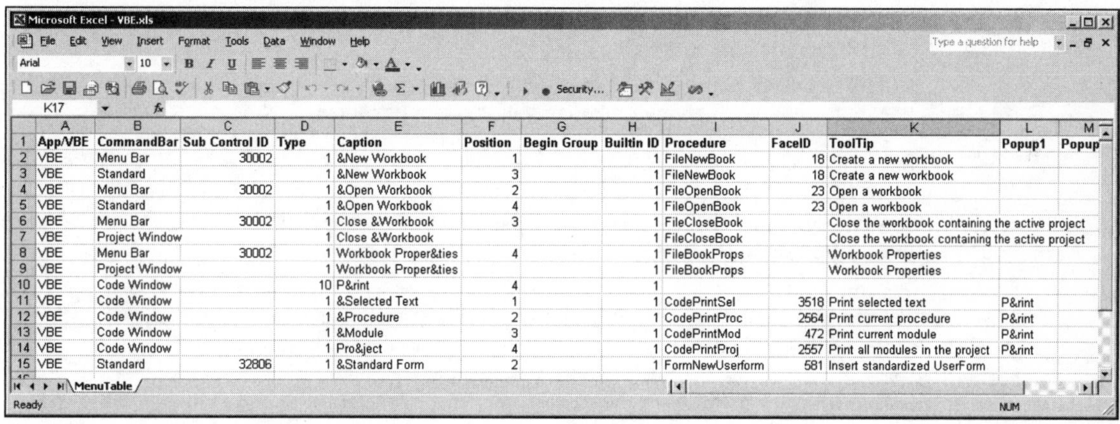

	A	B	C	D	E	F	G	H	I	J	K	L	M
1	App/VBE	CommandBar	Sub Control ID	Type	Caption	Position	Begin Group	Builtin ID	Procedure	FaceID	ToolTip	Popup1	Popup
2	VBE	Menu Bar	30002	1	&New Workbook	1		1	FileNewBook	18	Create a new workbook		
3	VBE	Standard		1	&New Workbook	3		1	FileNewBook	18	Create a new workbook		
4	VBE	Menu Bar	30002	1	&Open Workbook	2		1	FileOpenBook	23	Open a workbook		
5	VBE	Standard		1	&Open Workbook	4		1	FileOpenBook	23	Open a workbook		
6	VBE	Menu Bar	30002	1	Close &Workbook	3		1	FileCloseBook		Close the workbook containing the active project		
7	VBE	Project Window		1	Close &Workbook			1	FileCloseBook		Close the workbook containing the active project		
8	VBE	Menu Bar	30002	1	Workbook Proper&ties	4		1	FileBookProps		Workbook Properties		
9	VBE	Project Window		1	Workbook Proper&ties			1	FileBookProps		Workbook Properties		
10	VBE	Code Window		10	P&rint	4		1					
11	VBE	Code Window		1	&Selected Text	1		1	CodePrintSel	3518	Print selected text	P&rint	
12	VBE	Code Window		1	&Procedure	2		1	CodePrintProc	2564	Print current procedure	P&rint	
13	VBE	Code Window		1	&Module	3		1	CodePrintMod	472	Print current module	P&rint	
14	VBE	Code Window		1	Pro&ject	4		1	CodePrintProj	2557	Print all modules in the project	P&rint	
15	VBE	Standard	32806	1	&Standard Form	2		1	FormNewUserform	581	Insert standardized UserForm		

The result of this addition will be the **Standard Form** item:

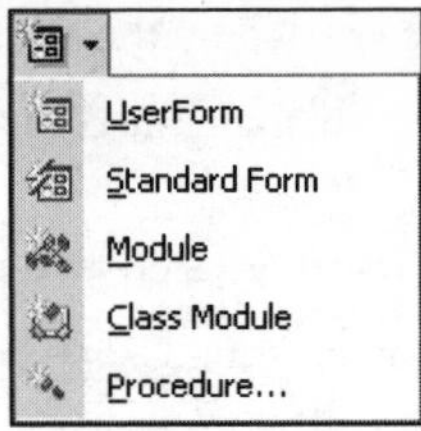

Add a new module for this routine, called `modMenuForm` and copy in the code below:

```
Option Explicit
Option Compare Text

'Window API call to freeze a window
'It does the same as Application.ScreenUpdating, but for the VBE
Private Declare Function LockWindowUpdate Lib "user32" (ByVal hwndLock As Long) _
                                                                              As
Long
```

`Application.ScreenUpdating` does not affect the VBE, and `FormNewUserform` results in quite a lot of screen activity as the form is sized and the controls are drawn. A simple Windows API call can be used to freeze the VBE window at the start of the routine and unfreeze it at the end. See the next chapter for more information about using this and other API functions:

```
''''''''''''''''''''''''''''''''''''
' Subroutine: FormNewUserform
'
' Purpose:    Creates a new userform, adding standard OK and Cancel buttons
'             and code to handle their events
'

Sub FormNewUserform()
  Dim obVBC As VBIDE.VBComponent, fmFrmDesign As UserForm, lLine As Long
  Dim cbBtn As CommandBarButton, cbPopup As CommandBarPopup

  Const dGap As Double = 6
```

Microsoft's Windows design guidelines recommend a gap of 6 points (approximately 4 pixels) between buttons, and between a button and the edge of a form:

```
  'Use our error handler to display a message if something goes wrong
  On Error GoTo ERR_HANDLER
```

This is one of the more complex routines in the Addin, so some error handling code will be added to it. Every routine in this chapter should really be given similar error-handling code:

```
  'Freeze the VBE window - same as Application.ScreenUpdating = False
  LockWindowUpdate Application.VBE.MainWindow.HWnd
```

We will use the Windows API call to freeze the VBE's window. Note that `HWnd` is a hidden property of the `MainWindow` object. To display the hidden properties for an object, open the Object Browser, right-click in its window, and click the **Show Hidden Members** item:

```
'Add a new userform to the active VB Project
Set obVBC = Application.VBE.ActiveVBProject.VBComponents.Add(vbext_ct_MSForm)

'Set the form's height and width to 2/3 that of the Excel application.
obVBC.Properties("Width") = Application.UsableWidth * 2 / 3
obVBC.Properties("Height") = Application.UsableHeight * 2 / 3
```

The `VBComponent` object (`obVBC` in the code) provides the 'canvas' (background) of the UserForm, its `Properties` collection, and its `CodeModule`. When a new UserForm is added to a project, a `VBComponent` object is passed back that contains the form. The `VBComponent's Properties` collection can be used to change the size (as shown here), colour, font, caption, etc. of the form's background:

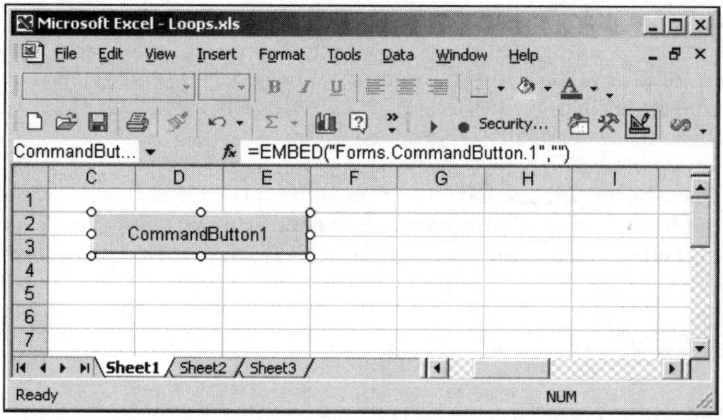


```
'Get the UserForm's Designer
Set fmFrmDesign = obVBC.Designer

'Use the designer to add the standard controls
With fmFrmDesign
  'Add an OK button, according to standard Windows size
  With .Controls.Add("Forms.CommandButton.1", "bnOK")
    .Caption = "OK"
    .Default = True
    .Height = 18
    .Width = 54
  End With

  'Add a Cancel button, according to standard Windows size
  With .Controls.Add("Forms.CommandButton.1", "bnCancel")
    .Caption = "Cancel"
    .Cancel = True
    .Height = 18
    .Width = 54
  End With
```

The `VBComponent's Designer` object provides access to the **content** of the UserForm and is responsible for the area inside the form's borders and below its title bar. In this code, two controls are added to the normal blank UserForm, to provide standard **OK** and **Close** buttons. The name to use for the control (`Forms.CommandButton.1` in this case) can be found by adding the control from Excel's **Control Toolbox** to a worksheet, then examining the resulting `=EMBED` function:

```
    'Move the OK and Cancel buttons to the bottom-right of the UserForm,
    'with a standard-width gap around and between them
    With .Controls("bnOK")
      .Top = fmFrmDesign.InsideHeight - .Height - dGap
      .Left = fmFrmDesign.InsideWidth - .Width * 2 - dGap * 2
    End With

    With .Controls("bnCancel")
      .Top = fmFrmDesign.InsideHeight - .Height - dGap
      .Left = fmFrmDesign.InsideWidth - .Width - dGap
    End With
  End With
```

This could be extended to add ListBoxes, labels, checkboxes, etc. From this point on, you could just as easily be working with an existing UserForm, changing its size and the position and size of its controls to make the best use of the available screen resolution. The code above just moves the OK and Cancel buttons to the bottom-right corner of the UserForm, without adjusting their size. The same technique can be used to move and size all of a UserForm's controls.

Now that buttons have been added to the UserForm at the correct place (i.e. bottom-right hand corner), some code can be added to the UserForm's module to handle the buttons' and UserForm's events. In this example, the code is being added from strings. Alternatively, the code could be kept in a separate text file and imported into the UserForm's module:

```
      .AddFromString "Sub bnOK_Click()"
```

We'll first add simple code for the OK and Cancel buttons' `Click` events. Code like this could be used to create the routine:

```
  ' Now add some code to the userform's code module
  With obVBC.CodeModule
    'Add the code for the OK button's Click event
    lLine = .CreateEventProc("Click", "bnOK")
    .InsertLines lLine, "'Standard OK button handler"
    .ReplaceLine lLine + 2, "    mbOK = True" & vbCrLf & "    Me.Hide"

    'Add the code for the Cancel button's Click event
    .AddFromString vbCrLf & _
             "'Standard Cancel button handler" & vbCrLf & _
             "Private Sub bnCancel_Click()" & vbCrLf & _
             "    mbOK = False" & vbCrLf & _
             "    Me.Hide" & vbCrLf & _
             "End Sub"
```

However, if `CreateEventProc` is used, all of the procedure's parameters are filled in on our behalf. There is very little difference between the two techniques. Note that the `CreateEventProc` adds the '`Private Sub...`' line, the '`End Sub`' line, and a space between them. **Do not** type this code snippet into the Addin:

```
  Private Sub bnOK_Click()

  End Sub
```

`CreateEventProc` returns the number of the line in the module where the `'Private Sub...'` was added, which is then used to insert a comment line and to replace the default blank line with the code:

```
      'Add the code for the UserForm's Close event - just call the Cancel code
      lLine = .CreateEventProc("QueryClose", "UserForm")
      .InsertLines lLine, "'Standard Close handler, treat same as Cancel"
      .ReplaceLine lLine + 2, "    bnCancel_Click"

      'And close the code window that was automatically opened by Excel
      'when we created the event procedures
      .CodePane.Window.Close
   End With

   'Unfreeze the VBE window - same as Application.ScreenUpdating = True
   LockWindowUpdate 0&

Exit Sub
```

The code for the UserForm's `QueryClose` event is the same as that of the **Cancel** button, so some code will be added just to call the `bnCancel_Click` routine:

```
ERR_HANDLER:

   'Unfreeze the VBE window - same as Application.ScreenUpdating = True
   LockWindowUpdate 0&

   'Display the error message (in the VBE Window) and end the routine.
   Application.Visible = False

   MsgBox "An Error ocurred while creating the standard userform." & vbCrLf & _
           Err.Number & ": " & Err.Description, vbOKOnly, psAddinTitle

   Application.Visible = True
End Sub
```

The standard error handler unfreezes the window, displays the error message and closes. Such error handling should be added to all the routines in the Addin.

The Addin is now complete. Switch back to Excel and save the workbook as an Addin (at the bottom of the list of available file types), with an `.xla` extension. Then use **Tools | Add-Ins** to install it.

Working with References

One of the major enhancements in recent versions of VBA is the ability to declare a reference to an external object library (using the **Tools | References** dialog), then use the objects defined in that library as if they were built into Excel. In this chapter, for example, you have been using the objects defined in the VBA Extensibility library without thinking about where they came from.

The term for this is 'early binding', so named because we are binding the external object library to our application at design-time. Using early binding gives the following benefits:

- The code is much faster, as all the links between the libraries have been checked and compiled
- The `New` operator can be used to create instances of the external objects

- All of the constants defined in the object library can be utilized, thus avoiding numerous 'magic numbers' throughout the code
- Excel displays the Auto List Members, Auto Quick Info, and Auto Data Tips information for the objects while the application is being developed

This has been explained in more detail in Chapter 24.

There is, however, one major disadvantage. If you try to run your application on a computer that does not have the external object library installed, you will get a compile-time error which cannot be trapped using standard error-handling techniques – usually showing a perfectly valid line of code as being the culprit. Excel will display the error when it runs some code in a module, which contains:

- An undeclared variable in a procedure – and you didn't use `Option Explicit`
- A declaration of a type defined in the missing object library
- A constant defined in the missing object library
- A call to a routine, object, method, or property defined in the missing object library

The VBIDE `References` collection provides a method of checking that all the application's references are functioning correctly, and that all the required external object libraries are installed and are the correct version. The code to check this should be put in your `Auto_Open` routine and the module that contains the `Auto_Open` must not contain any code that uses the external object libraries. If there is a broken reference, it is unlikely that any other code will run, so the routine simply stops after displaying which references are missing. Typical `Auto_Open` code is:

```
Sub Auto_Open()
  Dim obRef As Object, bBroken As Boolean, stDescn As String

  For Each obRef In ThisWorkbook.VBProject.References
    'Is the link broken?
    If obRef.IsBroken Then
      'Some broken links don't have descriptions, so ignore the error
      On Error Resume Next
      stDescn = "<Not known>"
      stDescn = obRef.Description
      On Error GoTo 0

      'Display a message, asking the user to install the missing item
      MsgBox "Missing reference to:" & vbCrLf & _
             "    Name: " & stDescn & vbCrLf & _
             "    Path: " & obRef.FullPath & vbCrLf & _
             "Please reinstall this file."

      bBroken = True
    End If
  Next

  'If everything present and correct, carry on with the initialising code
  If Not bBroken Then
    '...Continue to open
  End If
End Sub
```

COM Addins

The VBE is common to all the Office 2002 applications, so it would be convenient for us to be able to create Addins for the VBE in a way that is not specific to a single Office application. In this chapter, we have created the VBE Toolkit as an Excel Addin, with the result that the added functionality will only be available when using the VBE from within Excel. This was an appropriate choice, as the Addin provides some Excel-specific functionality (such as opening and closing workbooks), but is a poor choice for the other functions we've added.

COM Addins provide a different way of extending the VBE and other Office applications, in a way that is not necessarily specific to a single application. By using a COM Addin, we can create a single Addin that targets the VBE specifically, and hence works across all the Office applications.

Chapter 17 explains how to create COM Addins.

Summary

The Microsoft Visual Basic for Applications Extensibility 5.3 object library provides a rich set of objects, properties, methods, and events for controlling the VBE itself. Using these objects, developers can create their own labour-saving Addins to help in their daily development tasks.

Many end-user applications can also utilize these objects to manipulate their own code modules, UserForms and references, to provide a feature-rich, flexible, and robust set of functionality.

The example Addin developed in this chapter can be downloaded from http://www.wrox.com.

VBAProgrammersReferenceExcel20
mersReferenceExcel2002VB
eferenceExcel2002VBAPro
ProgrammersReferenceExc
ammersReferenceExcel20
ReferenceExcel2002VB
Excel2002VBAPro
Programmer
el2002VBAProgram
enceExce
ogrammersReferen
ammers
ReferenceExce
rsReferenc
rammer
ammersRefe
ceExcel2002VBAPro
ferenceExce
nceExcel2002VBAPro ferenceExc
xcel2002VBAProgram VBAProgram
2002VBAProgrammersReferenceExce
VBAProgrammersReferenceEx
rogrammersReferenceExcel
ammersReferencerammersExcel2002VBAProgra
2002VBAProgrammersReferenceExce

24

Programming with the Windows API

Visual Basic for Applications is a high-level language that provides us with a rich, powerful, yet quite simple set of functionality for controlling the Office suite of products, as well as many other applications. We are insulated, some would say protected, from the "mundane minutiae" of Windows programming that, say, a C++ programmer has to contend with.

The price we pay for this protection is an inability to investigate and control many elements of the Windows platform. We can, for example, use `Application.International` to read most of the Windows Regional Settings and read the screen dimensions from `Application.UsableWidth` and Application.`UsableHeight`, but that's about it. All the Windows-related items available to us are properties of the `Application` object and are listed in Appendix A.

The Windows platform includes a vast amount of low-level functionality that is not normally accessible from VBA, from identifying the system colors to creating a temporary file. Some of the functionality has been exposed in VBA but only to a limited extent, such as creating and using an Internet connection (for example we can open a page from the Internet using `Workbooks.Open "<URL>"`, but we can't just download it to disk). There are also a number of other object libraries typically available on a Windows computer that provide high-level, VBA-friendly access to the underlying Windows functionality. Examples of these are the Windows Scripting Runtime and the Internet Transfer Control.

There are times, though, when we need to go beyond the limits of VBA and the other object libraries and delve into the files that contain the low-level procedures provided and used by Windows. The Windows Operating System is made up of a large number of separate files, mostly dynamic link libraries (DLLs), each containing code to perform a discrete set of inter-related functions. DLLs are files that contain functions that can be called by other Windows programs or other DLLs. They can not be 'run' like a program themselves.

These files are collectively known as the Windows Application Programming Interface, or Windows API. Some of the most common files you'll use in the Windows API are:

File	Function Group(s)
USER32.EXE	User-interface functions (such as managing windows, the keyboard, clipboard, etc.)
KERNEL32.DLL	File and system-related functions (such as managing programs)
GDI32.DLL	Graphics and display functions
SHELL32.DLL	Windows shell functions (such as handling icons and launching programs)
COMDLG32.DLL	Standard Windows dialog functions.
ADVAPI32.DLL	Registry and NT Security functions
MPR.DLL and NETAPI32.DLL	Network functions
WININET.DLL	Internet functions
WINMM.DLL	Multimedia functions
WINSPOOL.DRV	Printing functions

This chapter explains how to use the functions contained in these files in your VBA applications and includes a number of useful examples. All of the Windows API functions are documented in the 'Platform SDK' section of the MSDN Library at: http://msdn.microsoft.com/library/default.asp, which can be thought of as the online help for the Windows API.

Anatomy of an API Call

Before we can use the procedures contained in the Windows DLLs, we need to tell the VBA interpreter where they can be found, the parameters they take, and what they return. We do this using the `Declare` statement, which VBA help shows as:

```
[Public | Private] Declare Sub name Lib "libname" [Alias "aliasname"]
[([arglist])]
```

```
[Public | Private] Declare Function name Lib "libname" [Alias "aliasname"]
[([arglist])] [As type]
```

The VBA Help gives a good explanation of the syntax of these statements, but does not include any examples. The following is the declaration used to find the Windows `TEMP` directory:

```
Private Declare Function GetTempPath Lib "kernel32" _
        Alias "GetTempPathA" ( _
        ByVal nBufferLength As Long, _
        ByVal lpBuffer As String) As Long
```

This tells VBA that:

- The function is going to be referred to in the code as `GetTempPath`
- The procedure can be found in `kernel32.dll`
- It goes by the name of `GetTempPathA` in the DLL (case sensitive)
- It takes two parameters, a Long and a String (more about these later)
- It returns a Long

The declarations for most of the more common API functions can be found in the file `win32api.txt`. The Developer version of Office XP and any of the more recent versions of Visual Basic include this file and a small API Viewer applet to help locate the declarations. At the time of writing, the text file can be downloaded from the 'Free Stuff' page of the Office Developer section of Microsoft's web site, http://www.microsoft.com/officedev/o-free.htm, or directly from http://www.microsoft.com/OfficeDev/Articles/Exe/Win32api.exe.

Interpreting C-Style Declarations

The MSDN library is the best source for information about the functions in the Windows API, but is primarily targeted towards C and C++ programmers and displays the function declarations using C notation. The `win32api.txt` file contains most of the declarations for the core Windows functions in VBA notation, but has not been updated to include some of the newer Windows DLLs (such as the OLE functions in `olepro32.dll` and the Internet functions in `WinInet.dll`). It is usually possible to convert the C notation to a VBA `Declare` statement, using the method shown below.

The declaration shown in MSDN for the `GetTempPath` function (at http://msdn.microsoft.com/library/psdk/winbase/filesio_78fc.htm) is:

```
DWORD GetTempPath(
   DWORD nBufferLength,  // size, in characters, of the buffer
   LPTSTR lpBuffer       // pointer to buffer for temp. path
);
```

This should be read as:

```
<Return data type> <Function name>(
    <Parameter data type> <Parameter name>,
    <Parameter data type> <Parameter name>,
);
```

Rearranging the C-style declaration to a VBA `Declare` statement gives the following (where the C-style `DWORD` and `LPSTR` are converted to VBA data types below):

```
Declare Function <Our Name> Lib "???" Alias "GetTempPath" ( _
        nBufferLength As DWORD, _
        lpBuffer As LPTSTR _
        ) As DWORD
```

On the Windows platform, there are two types of character sets. The ANSI character set has been the standard for many years and uses one byte to represent one character, which only gives 255 characters available at any time. To provide simultaneous access to a much wider range of characters (such as Far Eastern alphabets), the Unicode character set was introduced. This allocates two bytes for each character, allowing for 65,535 characters.

To provide the same functionality for both character sets, the Windows API includes two versions of all the functions that involve strings, denoted by the 'A' suffix for the ANSI version and 'W' for the Unicode (or Wide) version. VBA always uses ANSI strings, so we will always be using the 'A' version of the functions – in this case GetTempPathA. The C-style declarations also use different names for their data types, which we need to convert. While not an exhaustive list, the following table shows the most common data types:

C Data Type	VBA Declaration
BOOL	ByVal <Name> As Long
BYTE	ByVal <Name> As Byte
BYTE *	ByRef <Name> As Byte
Char	ByVal <Name> As Byte
char _huge *	ByVal <Name> As String
char FAR *	ByVal <Name> As String
char NEAR *	ByVal <Name> As String
DWORD	ByVal <Name> As Long
HANDLE	ByVal <Name> As Long
HBITMAP	ByVal <Name> As Long
HBRUSH	ByVal <Name> As Long
HCURSOR	ByVal <Name> As Long
HDC	ByVal <Name> As Long
HFONT	ByVal <Name> As Long
HICON	ByVal <Name> As Long
HINSTANCE	ByVal <Name> As Long
HLOCAL	ByVal <Name> As Long
HMENU	ByVal <Name> As Long
HMETAFILE	ByVal <Name> As Long

C Data Type	VBA Declaration
HMODULE	ByVal <Name> As Long
HPALETTE	ByVal <Name> As Long
HPEN	ByVal <Name> As Long
HRGN	ByVal <Name> As Long
HTASK	ByVal <Name> As Long
HWND	ByVal <Name> As Long
Int	ByVal <Name> As Long
int FAR *	ByRef <Name> As Long
LARGE_INTEGER	ByVal <Name> As Currency
LONG	ByVal <Name> As Long
LPARAM	ByVal <Name> As Long
LPCSTR	ByVal <Name> As String
LPCTSTR	ByVal <Name> As String
LPSTR	ByVal <Name> As String
LPTSTR	ByVal <Name> As String
LPVOID	ByRef <Name> As Any
LRESULT	ByVal <Name> As Long
UINT	ByVal <Name> As Integer
UINT FAR *	ByRef <Name> As Integer
WORD	ByVal <Name> As Integer
WPARAM	ByVal <Name> As Integer
Other	It is a probably a user-defined type, which you need to define

Some API definitions on the MSDN also include the `IN` and `OUT` identifiers. If the VBA type is shown in the table as '`ByVal <Name> As Long`', it should be changed to '`ByRef...`' for the `OUT` parameters.

> **Note that strings are *always* passed `ByVal` (by value) to API functions. This is because VBA uses its own storage mechanism for strings, which the C DLLs do not understand. By passing the string `ByVal`, VBA converts its own storage structure into one that the DLLs can use.**

Putting these into the declaration, gives:

```
Declare Function GetTempPath Lib "???" _
        Alias "GetTempPathA" ( _
        ByVal nBufferLength As Long, _
        ByVal lpBuffer As String _
        ) As Long
```

The only thing that the declaration doesn't tell you is the DLL that contains the function. Looking at the bottom of the MSDN page, the 'Requirements' section includes the line:

Library: Use kernel32.lib.

This tells you that the function is in the file `kernel32.dll`, giving the final declaration of:

```
Declare Function GetTempPath Lib "kernel32.dll" _
        Alias "GetTempPathA" ( _
        ByVal nBufferLength As Long, _
        ByVal lpBuffer As String _
        ) As Long
```

This is the same as that shown in the `win32api.txt` file, which should be your first reference point for all API function definitions.

Warning: using an incorrect function declaration is likely to crash Excel. When developing with API calls, save your work as often as possible.

Constants, Structures, Handles, and Classes

Most of the API functions include arguments that accept a limited set of predefined constants. For example, to get information about the operating system's capabilities, you can use the `GetSystemMetrics` function:

```
Declare Function GetSystemMetrics Lib "user32" ( _
        ByVal nIndex As Long) As Long
```

Note that in the `win32api.txt` file, the `GetSystemMetrics` function is shown including an `Alias` clause:

```
Declare Function GetSystemMetrics Lib "user32" Alias "GetSystemMetrics" ( _
        ByVal nIndex As Long) As Long
```

The `Alias` clause is not required when the function name is the same as the alias, and is automatically removed when the function is copied into a code module.

The value that you pass in the `nIndex` argument tells the function which metric you want to be given, and must be one of a specific set of constants that the function knows about. The applicable constants are listed in the MSDN documentation, but their values are often not shown. Fortunately, the `win32api.txt` file contains most of the constants that you are likely to need. There are over 80 constants for `GetSystemMetrics` including `SM_CXSCREEN` and `SM_CYSCREEN` to retrieve the screen's dimensions:

```
Const SM_CXSCREEN As Long = 0    'Screen width
Const SM_CYSCREEN As Long = 1    'Screen height

Private Declare Function GetSystemMetrics Lib "user32" _
               (ByVal nIndex As Long) As Long

Sub ShowScreenDimensions()
   Dim lScreenX As Long, lScreenY As Long

   'Get the screen's dimensions
   lScreenX = GetSystemMetrics(SM_CXSCREEN)
   lScreenY = GetSystemMetrics(SM_CYSCREEN)

   MsgBox "Screen resolution is " & lScreenX & "x" & lScreenY
End Sub
```

Many of the Windows API functions pass information using **structures**, which is the C term for a User-Defined Type (UDT). For example, the `GetWindowRect` function is used to return the size of a window, and is defined as:

```
Declare Function GetWindowRect Lib "user32" ( _
        ByVal hwnd As Long, _
        lpRect As RECT) As Long
```

The `lpRect` parameter is a `RECT` structure that is filled in by the `GetWindowRect` function with the window's dimensions. The `RECT` structure is defined on MSDN as:

```
typedef struct tagRECT {
   LONG left;
   LONG top;
   LONG right;
   LONG bottom;
} RECT;
```

This can be converted to a VBA UDT using the same data-type conversion shown in the previous section, giving:

```
Type RECT
    Left As Long
    Top As Long
    Right As Long
    Bottom As Long
End Type
```

The UDT definitions for most of the common structures are also included in the `win32api.txt` file.

The first parameter of the `GetWindowRect` function is shown as '`hwnd`', and represents a handle to a window. A handle is simply a pointer to an area of memory that contains information about the object being pointed to (in this case, a window). Handles are allocated dynamically by Windows and are unlikely to be the same between sessions. You cannot, therefore, hard-code the handle number in your code, but must use other API functions to give you the handle you need. For example, to obtain the dimensions of the Excel window, you need to get the Excel window's `hwnd`. The API function `FindWindow` gives it to you:

```
'API call to find a window
Public Declare Function FindWindow Lib "user32" _
        Alias "FindWindowA" (_
        ByVal lpClassName As String, _
        ByVal lpWindowName As String) As Long
```

This function looks through all the open windows until it finds one with the class name and caption that you ask for. In Excel 2002, the `hWnd` property has been added to the `Application` object, so we no longer need to use `FindWindow` for that case. All of the code examples in this chapter use `FindWindow`, to be compatible with previous versions of Excel.

There are many different types of windows in Windows applications, ranging from Excel's application window, to the windows used for dialog sheets, UserForms, ListBoxes, or buttons. Each type of window has a unique identifier, known as its **class**. Some common class names in Excel are:

Window	Class name
Excel's main window	`XLMAIN`
Excel worksheet	`EXCEL7`
Excel UserForm	`ThunderDFrame` (in Excel 2002 and 2000) `ThunderRT6DFrame` (in Excel 2002 and 2000, when running as a COM Add-in) `ThunderXFrame` (in Excel 97)
Excel dialog sheet	`bosa_sdm_xl9` (in Excel 2002 and 2000) `bosa_sdm_xl8` (in Excel 97) `bosa_sdm_xl` (in Excel 5 and 95)
Excel status bar	`EXCEL4`

The `FindWindow` function uses this class name and the window's caption to find the window.

Note that the class names for some of Excel's standard items have changed with every release of Excel. You therefore need to include version checking in your code to determine which class name to use:

```
Select Case Val(Application.Version)
  Case Is >= 9    'Use Excel 2000/2002 class names
  Case Is >= 8    'Use Excel 97 class names
  Case Else       'Use Excel 5/95 class names
End Select
```

This gives us a forward-compatibility problem. It would be nice if we could write code with a reasonable amount of confidence that it will work in the next version of Excel, but we don't know what the class names are going to be. Fortunately, the class names didn't change between Excel 2000 and Excel 2002.

Putting these items together, you can use the following code to find the location and size of the Excel main window (in pixels):

```
'UDT to hold window dimensions
Type RECT
    Left As Long
    Top As Long
    Right As Long
    Bottom As Long
End Type

'API function to locate a window
Declare Function FindWindow Lib "user32" _
        Alias "FindWindowA" ( _
        ByVal lpClassName As String, _
        ByVal lpWindowName As String) As Long

'API function to retrieve a window's dimensions
Declare Function GetWindowRect Lib "user32" ( _
        ByVal hWnd As Long, _
        lpRect As RECT) As Long

Sub ShowExcelWindowSize()
   Dim hWnd As Long, uRect As RECT

   'Get the handle on Excel's main window
   hWnd = FindWindow("XLMAIN", Application.Caption)

   'Get the window's dimensions into the RECT structure
   GetWindowRect hWnd, uRect

   'Display the result
   MsgBox "The Excel window has the following dimensions:" & _
        vbCrLf & " Left: " & uRect.Left & _
        vbCrLf & " Right: " & uRect.Right & _
        vbCrLf & " Top: " & uRect.Top & _
        vbCrLf & " Bottom: " & uRect.Bottom & _
        vbCrLf & " Width: " & (uRect.Right - uRect.Left) & _
        vbCrLf & " Height: " & (uRect.Bottom - uRect.Top)

End Sub
```

Resize the Excel window to cover a portion of the screen and run the `ShowExcelWindowSize` routine. You should be given a message box showing the window's dimensions. Now try it with Excel maximized – you may get negative values for the top and left. This is because the `GetWindowRect` function returns the size of the Excel window, measuring around the edge of its borders. When maximized, the borders are off the screen, but still part of the window.

What if Something Goes Wrong?

One of the hardest parts of working with the Windows API functions is identifying the cause of any errors. If an API call fails for any reason, it **should** return some indication of failure (usually a zero result from the function) and register the error with Windows. You should then be able to use the VBA function `Err.LastDLLError` to retrieve the error code and use the `FormatMessage` API function to retrieve the descriptive text for the error:

```
'Windows API declaration to get the API error text
Private Declare Function FormatMessage Lib "kernel32" _
        Alias "FormatMessageA" ( _
        ByVal dwFlags As Long, _
        ByVal lpSource As Long, _
        ByVal dwMessageId As Long, _
        ByVal dwLanguageId As Long, _
        ByVal lpBuffer As String, _
        ByVal nSize As Long, _
        Arguments As Long) As Long

'Constant for use in the FormatMessage API function
Private Const FORMAT_MESSAGE_FROM_SYSTEM As Long = &H1000

Sub ShowExcelWindowSize()
   'Define some variables to use in the API calls
   Dim hWnd As Long, uRect As RECT

   'Get the handle on Excel's main window
   hWnd = FindWindow("XLMAIN", Application.Caption)

   If hWnd = 0 Then
      'An error occured, so get the text of the error
      MsgBox LastDLLErrText(Err.LastDllError)
   Else
      'Etc.
   End If
End Sub

Function LastDLLErrText(ByVal lErrorCode As Long) As String
'*****************************************************
'*
'* Function Name:   LastDLLErrText
'*
'* Input:           lErrorCode - a Windows error number
'*
'* Output:          Returns the description corresponding to the error
'*
'* Purpose:         Retrieve a Windows error description
'*
'*****************************************************

   Dim sBuff As String * 255, iAPIResult As Long

   'Get the text of the error and return it
   iAPIResult = FormatMessage(FORMAT_MESSAGE_FROM_SYSTEM, 0&, lErrorCode, _
               0, sBuff, 255, 0)

   LastDLLErrText = Left(sBuff, iAPIResult)
End Function
```

The full code for this example can be found in the module `'m1_ExcelWindowSize'` in the API `Examples.xls` workbook, available on the Wrox web site at http://www.wrox.com.

Unfortunately, this technique does not always work. For example, if you change the class name to `XLMAINTEST` in the `FindWindow` function call, you may expect to get an error message of 'Unable to find window'. This is the case on Windows NT 4, but when using `FindWindow` under Windows 98, the error information is not populated and you get the standard message 'The operation completed successfully'. In most cases, you do get some error information, as will be seen in the next section.

Wrapping API Calls in Class Modules

If you need to use lots of API calls in your application, your code can get very messy, very quickly. Most developers prefer to encapsulate the API calls within class modules, which provides a number of benefits:

- The API declarations and calls are removed from your core application code.
- The class module can perform a number of initialization and clean-up tasks, improving your system's robustness.
- Many of the API functions take a large number of parameters, most of which are not used in your situation. The class module need expose only those properties that need to be changed by your calling routine.
- Class modules can be stored as text files or in the Code Librarian (if you're using Office XP Developer), providing a self-contained set of functionality that is easy to reuse in future projects.

The code below is an example of a class module for working with temporary files, allowing the calling code to:

- Create a temporary file in the Windows default `TEMP` directory
- Create a temporary file in a user-specified directory
- Retrieve the path and file name of the temporary file
- Retrieve the text of any errors that may have occurred while creating the temporary file
- Delete the temporary file after use.

Create a class module called `CTempFile` and copy in the code below (this class can also be found in the API `Examples.xls` file, on the Wrox web site at http://www.wrox.com):

```
'***************************************************************************
'*
'* MODULE NAME:     EXCEL 2002 PROG REF - TEMP FILE CLASS
'* AUTHOR:          STEPHEN BULLEN, Business Modelling Solutions Ltd.
'*
'* CONTACT:         Stephen@BMSLtd.co.uk
'* WEB SITE:        http://www.BMSLtd.co.uk
'*
'* DESCRIPTION:     Encapsulates API calls for handling temporary files
'*
'***************************************************************************
Option Explicit

'Windows API declaration to find the Windows Temporary directory
Private Declare Function GetTempPath Lib "kernel32" _
        Alias "GetTempPathA" ( _
```

```
        ByVal nBufferLength As Long, _
        ByVal lpBuffer As String) As Long

'Windows API declaration to create, and return the name of,
'a temporary filename
Private Declare Function GetTempFileName Lib "kernel32" _
        Alias "GetTempFileNameA" ( _
        ByVal lpszPath As String, _
        ByVal lpPrefixString As String, _
        ByVal wUnique As Long, _
        ByVal lpTempFileName As String) As Long

'Windows API declaration to get the text for an API error code
Private Declare Function FormatMessage Lib "kernel32" _
        Alias "FormatMessageA" ( _
        ByVal dwFlags As Long, _
        ByVal lpSource As Long, _
        ByVal dwMessageId As Long, _
        ByVal dwLanguageId As Long, _
        ByVal lpBuffer As String, _
        ByVal nSize As Long, _
        Arguments As Long) As Long

'Constant for use in the FormatMessage API function
Const FORMAT_MESSAGE_FROM_SYSTEM As Long = &H1000

'Variables to store the path, file and error message
Dim stTempPath As String
Dim stTempFile As String
Dim stErrMsg As String
Dim bTidyUp As Boolean
```

One advantage of using a class module is that you can perform some operations when the class is initialized. In this case, you will identify the default Windows `TEMP` directory. The temporary file will be created in this directory, unless the calling code tells you otherwise:

```
'Get the Windows temporary path when the class is initialised
Private Sub Class_Initialize()
   'Define some variables to use in the API calls
   Dim stBuff As String * 255, lAPIResult As Long

   'Call the Windows API function to get the TEMP path
   lAPIResult = GetTempPath(255, stBuff)

   If lAPIResult = 0 Then
      'An error occured, so get the text of the error
      stErrMsg = LastDLLErrText(Err.LastDllError)
   Else
      'Store the TEMP path
      stTempPath = Left(stBuff, lAPIResult)
   End If
End Sub
```

This is the routine to create the temporary file, returning its name (including the path). In its simplest use, the calling routine can just call this one method to create a temporary file:

```
'Create a temporary file, returning its name (including the path)
Public Function CreateFile() As String
   'Define some variables to use in the API calls
   Dim stBuff As String * 255, lAPIResult As Long

   'Try to get a temporary file name (also creates the file)
   lAPIResult = GetTempFileName(stTempPath, "", 0, stBuff)

   If lAPIResult = 0 Then
      'An error occured, so get the text of the error
      stErrMsg = LastDLLErrText(Err.LastDllError)
   Else
      'Created a temp file OK, so store the file and "OK" error message
      stTempFile = Left(stBuff, InStr(1, stBuff, Chr(0)) - 1)
      stErrMsg = "OK"
      bTidyUp = True

      CreateFile = stTempFile
   End If
End Function
```

In a class module, you can expose a number of properties that allow the calling routine to retrieve and modify the temporary file creation. For example, you may want to enable the calling program to set which directory to use for the temporary file. You could extend this to make the property read-only after the file has been created, raising an error in that case. The use of `Property` procedures in class modules is described in more detail in Chapter 15:

```
'Show the TEMP path as a property of the class
Public Property Get Path() As String
   'Return the path, without the final '\'
   Path = Left(stTempPath, Len(stTempPath) - 1)
End Property

'Allow the user to change the TEMP path
Public Property Let Path(stNewPath As String)
   stTempPath = stNewPath

   'Ensure path ends with a \
   If Right(stTempPath, 1) <> "\" Then
      stTempPath = stTempPath & "\"
   End If
End Property
```

You can also give the calling routine read-only access to the temporary file's name and full name (that is including the path):

```
'Show the temporary file name as a property
Public Property Get Name() As String
   Name = Mid(stTempFile, Len(stTempPath) + 1)
End Property

'Show the full name (directory and file) as a property
Public Property Get FullName() As String
   FullName = stTempFile
End Property
```

Give the calling program read-only access to the error messages:

```
'Show the error message as a property of the class
Public Property Get ErrorText() As String
   ErrorText = stErrMsg
End Property
```

You'll also allow the calling program to delete the temporary file after use:

```
'Delete the temporary file
Public Sub Delete()
   On Error Resume Next  'In case it has already been deleted
   Kill stTempFile
   bTidyUp = False
End Sub
```

By default, you will delete the temporary file that you created when the class is destroyed. The calling application may not want you to, so provide some properties to control this:

```
'Whether or not to delete the temp file when the
'class is deleted
Public Property Get TidyUpFiles() As Boolean
   TidyUpFiles = bTidyUp
End Property

'Allow the user to prevent the deletion of his/her own files
Public Property Let TidyUpFiles(bNew As Boolean)
   bTidyUp = bNew
End Property
```

In the class's `Terminate` code, you'll delete the temporary file, unless told not to. This code is run when the instance of the class is destroyed. If declared within a procedure, this will be when the class variable goes out of scope at the end of the procedure. If declared at a module level, it will occur when the workbook is closed:

```
Private Sub Class_Terminate()
   If bTidyUp Then Delete
End Sub
```

The same function you saw in the previous section is used to retrieve the text associated with a Windows API error code:

```
'Get the text associated with a Windows API error code
Private Function LastDLLErrText(ByVal lErrorCode As Long) As String
   Dim stBuff As String * 255, lAPIResult As Long

   'Get the text of the error and return it
   lAPIResult = FormatMessage(FORMAT_MESSAGE_FROM_SYSTEM, _
            0&, lErrorCode, 0, stBuff, 255, 0)

   LastDLLErrText = Left(stBuff, lAPIResult)
End Function
```

Once this class module is included in a project, the calling routine does not need to know anything about any of the API functions you're using:

```
Sub TestCTempFile()
   Dim obTempFile As New CTempFile

   If obTempFile.CreateFile = "" Then
      MsgBox "An error occured while creating the temporary file:" & _
           vbCrLf & obTempFile.ErrorText
  Else
      MsgBox "Temporary file " & obTempFile.FullName & " created"
  End If
End Sub
```

This results in a message like:

Temporary file C:\WINDOWS\TEMP\5024.TMP created

Note that the temporary file is created during the call to `CreateFile`. When the procedure ends, the variable `obTempFile` goes out of scope and hence is destroyed by VBA. The `Terminate` event in the class module ensures the temporary file is deleted – the calling procedure does not need to know about any clean-up routines. If `CreateFile` is called twice, only the last temporary file is deleted. A new instance of the class should be created for each temporary file required.

You can force an error by amending `TestCTempFile` to specify a non-existent directory for the temp file:

```
Sub TestCTempFile()
   Dim obTempFile As New CTempFile

   'Tell the class to use a non-existent path
   obTempFile.Path = "C:\NoSuchPath"

   If obTempFile.CreateFile = "" Then
      MsgBox "An error occured while creating the temporary file:" & _
          Chr(10) & obTempFile.ErrorText
   Else
      MsgBox "Temporary file " & obTempFile.FullName & " created"
   End If
End Sub
```

This time, you get a meaningful error message:

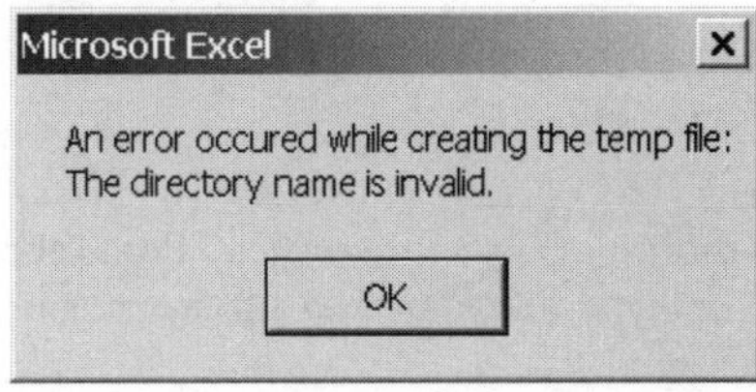

Some Example Classes

This section provides a number of common API calls to include in your projects. Note that in each case the function and constant definitions must be put in the `Declarations` section at the top of a module.

A High-Resolution Timer Class

When testing your code, it is a good idea to time the various routines, in order to identify and eliminate any bottlenecks. VBA includes two functions that can be used as timers:

- The `Now` function returns the current time and has a resolution of about 1 second
- The `Timer` function returns the number of milliseconds since midnight, with a resolution of approximately 10 milliseconds

Neither of these are accurate enough to time VBA routines, unless the routine is repeated many times.

Most modern PCs include a high-resolution timer, which updates many thousands of times per second, accessible through API calls. You can wrap these calls in a class module to provide easy access to a high-resolution timer.

Class Module CHighResTimer

```
Option Explicit

'How many times per second is the counter updated?
Private Declare Function QueryFrequency Lib "kernel32" _
        Alias "QueryPerformanceFrequency" ( _
        lpFrequency As Currency) As Long

'What is the counter's value
Private Declare Function QueryCounter Lib "kernel32" _
        Alias "QueryPerformanceCounter" ( _
        lpPerformanceCount As Currency) As Long
```

Note that the `win32api.txt` file shows these definitions using the '`LARGE_INTEGER`' data type, but they are defined as `Currency` above. The `LARGE_INTEGER` is a 64-bit data type, usually made up of two Longs. The VBA Currency data type also uses 64-bits to store the number, so you can use it in place of a `LARGE_INTEGER`. The only differences are that the `Currency` data type is scaled down by a factor of 10,000 and that VBA can perform standard maths operations with `Currency` variables:

```
'Variables to store the counter information
Dim cyFrequency As Currency
Dim cyOverhead As Currency
Dim cyStarted As Currency
Dim cyStopped As Currency
```

The API call itself takes a small amount of time to complete. For accurate timings, you should take this delay into account. You find this delay and the counter's frequency in the class's `Initialize` routine:

```
'When first initialized, determine the overhead incurred when retrieving the
'high-performance counter value
```

```
Private Sub Class_Initialize()
   Dim cyCount1 As Currency, cyCount2 As Currency

   'Get the counter frequency
   QueryFrequency cyFrequency

   'Call the hi-res counter twice, to check how long it takes
   QueryCounter cyCount1
   QueryCounter cyCount2

   'Store the call overhead
   cyOverhead = cyCount2 - cyCount1
End Sub

Public Sub StartTimer()
   'Get the time that you started
   QueryCounter cyStarted
End Sub

Public Sub StopTimer()
   'Get the time that you stopped
   QueryCounter cyStopped
End Sub

Public Property Get Elapsed() As Double
   Dim cyTimer As Currency

   'Have you stopped or not?
   If cyStopped = 0 Then
      QueryCounter cyTimer
   Else
      cyTimer = cyStopped
   End If

   'If you have a frequency, return the duration, in seconds
   If cyFrequency > 0 Then
      Elapsed = (cyTimer - cyStarted - cyOverhead) / cyFrequency
   End If
End Property
```

When you calculate the elapsed time, both the timer and the frequency contain values that are a factor of 10,000 too small. As the numbers are divided, the factors cancel out to give a result in seconds.

The High-Resolution Timer class can be used in a calling routine like:

```
Sub TestCHighResTimer()
   Dim i As Long
   Dim obTimer As New CHighResTimer

   obTimer.StartTimer

   For i = 1 To 10000
   Next i
```

```
    obTimer.StopTimer

    Debug.Print "10000 iterations took " & obTimer.Elapsed & " seconds"
End Sub
```

Freeze a UserForm

When working with UserForms, the display may be updated whenever a change is made to the form, such as adding an item to a ListBox, or enabling/disabling controls. `Application.ScreenUpdating` has no effect on UserForms; this class provides a useful equivalent.

Class Module CFreezeForm

```
Option Explicit

'Find a window
Private Declare Function FindWindow Lib "user32" _
        Alias "FindWindowA" ( _
        ByVal lpClassName As String, _
        ByVal lpWindowName As String) As Long

'Freeze the window to prevent continuous redraws
Private Declare Function LockWindowUpdate Lib "user32" ( _
        ByVal hwndLock As Long) As Long

Public Sub Freeze(oForm As UserForm)
   Dim hWnd As Long

   'Get a handle to the UserForm window,
   'using the class name appropriate for the XL version
   If Val(Application.Version) >= 9 Then
      hWnd = FindWindow("ThunderDFrame", oForm.Caption)
   Else
      hWnd = FindWindow("ThunderXFrame", oForm.Caption)
   End If

   'If you got a handle, freeze the window
   If hWnd > 0 Then LockWindowUpdate hWnd
End Sub

'Allow the calling routine to unfreeze the UserForm
Public Sub UnFreeze()
   LockWindowUpdate 0
End Sub

'If they forget to unfreeze the form, do it at the end
'of the calling routine (when you go out of scope)
Private Sub Class_Terminate()
   UnFreeze
End Sub
```

To demonstrate this in action, create a new UserForm and add a listbox and a command button. Add the following code for the command button's `Click` event:

```
Private Sub CommandButton1_Click()
   Dim i As Integer

   For i = 1 To 1000
      ListBox1.AddItem "Item " & i
      DoEvents
   Next i
End Sub
```

The `DoEvents` line forces the UserForm to redraw, to demonstrate the problem. In more complicated routines, the UserForm may redraw itself without using `DoEvents`. To prevent the redrawing, you can modify the routine to use the `CFreezeForm` class as shown below:

```
Private Sub CommandButton1_Click()
   Dim obFF As New CFreezeForm, i As Integer
   'Freeze the UserForm
   obFF.Freeze Me

   For i = 1 To 1000
      ListBox1.AddItem "Item " & i
      DoEvents
   Next i
End Sub
```

This is much easier than including several API calls in every function. The class's `Terminate` event ensures that the UserForm is unfrozen when the `obFF` object variable goes out of scope. Freezing a UserForm in this way can result in a dramatic performance improvement. For example, the non-frozen version takes approximately 3.5 seconds to fill the ListBox, while the frozen version of the routine takes approximately 1.2 seconds. This should be weighted against user interaction; they may think the computer has frozen if they see no activity for some time. Consider using `Application.StatusBar` to keep them informed of progress in that case.

A System Info Class

The classic use of a class module and API functions is to provide all the information about the Windows environment that you cannot get at using VBA. The following properties are typical components of such a `CSysInfo` class.

> **Note that the declarations for the constants and API functions used in these procedures must all be placed together at the top of the class module. For clarity, they are shown here with the corresponding routines.**

Obtaining the Screen Resolution (in Pixels)

```
Option Explicit

Private Const SM_CYSCREEN As Long = 1    'Screen height
Private Const SM_CXSCREEN As Long = 0    'Screen width

'API Call to retrieve system information
Private Declare Function GetSystemMetrics Lib "user32" ( _
        ByVal nIndex As Long) As Long
```

```
'Retrieve the screen height, in pixels
Public Property Get ScreenHeight() As Long
   ScreenHeight = GetSystemMetrics(SM_CYSCREEN)
End Property

'Retrieve the screen width, in pixels
Public Property Get ScreenWidth() As Long
   ScreenWidth = GetSystemMetrics(SM_CXSCREEN)
End Property
```

Obtaining the Color Depth (in Bits)

```
Private Declare Function GetDC Lib "user32" ( _
        ByVal hwnd As Long) As Long

Private Declare Function GetDeviceCaps Lib "Gdi32" ( _
        ByVal hDC As Long, _
        ByVal nIndex As Long) As Long

Private Declare Function ReleaseDC Lib "user32" ( _
        ByVal hwnd As Long, _
        ByVal hDC As Long) As Long

Private Const BITSPIXEL = 12

Public Property Get ColourDepth() As Integer
   Dim hDC As Long

   'A device context is the canvas on which a window is drawn
   hDC = GetDC(0)
   ColourDepth = GetDeviceCaps(hDC, BITSPIXEL)
   ReleaseDC 0, hDC
End Property
```

Obtaining the Width of a Pixel in UserForm Coordinates

```
'Same as the ColourDepth API declares, repeated here for clarity
Private Declare Function GetDC Lib "user32" ( _
        ByVal hwnd As Long) As Long

Private Declare Function GetDeviceCaps Lib "Gdi32" ( _
        ByVal hDC As Long, _
        ByVal nIndex As Long) As Long

Private Declare Function ReleaseDC Lib "user32" ( _
        ByVal hwnd As Long, _
        ByVal hDC As Long) As Long

Private Const LOGPIXELSX = 88

'The width of a pixel in Excel's UserForm coordinates
Public Property Get PointsPerPixel() As Double
    Dim hDC As Long

    hDC = GetDC(0)
```

```
    'A point is defined as 1/72 of an inch and LOGPIXELSX returns
    'the number of pixels per logical inch, so divide them to give
    'the width of a pixel in Excel's UserForm coordinates
    PointsPerPixel = 72 / GetDeviceCaps(hDC, LOGPIXELSX)

    ReleaseDC 0, hDC

End Property
```

Reading the User's Login ID

```
Private Declare Function GetUserName Lib "advapi32.dll" _
        Alias "GetUserNameA" ( _
        ByVal lpBuffer As String, _
        ByRef nSize As Long) As Long

Public Property Get UserName() As String
   Dim stBuff As String * 255, lAPIResult As Long
   Dim lBuffLen As Long

   lBuffLen = 255

   '  The second parameter, lBuffLen is both In and Out.
   '  On the way in, it tells the function how big the string buffer is
   '  On the way out, it tells us how long the user name is (including
   '  a terminating Chr(0))
   lAPIResult = GetUserName(stBuff, lBuffLen)

   'If you got something, return the text of the user name
   If lBuffLen > 0 Then UserName = Left(stBuff, lBuffLen - 1)
End Property
```

Reading the Computer's Name

```
Private Declare Function GetComputerName Lib "kernel32" _
        Alias "GetComputerNameA" ( _
        ByVal lbbuffer As String, _
        nsize As Long) As Long

Public Property Get ComputerName() As String
   Dim stBuff As String * 255, lAPIResult As Long
   Dim lBuffLen As Long

   lBuffLen = 255
   lAPIResult = GetComputerName(stBuff, lBuffLen)
   If lBuffLen > 0 Then ComputerName = Left(stBuff, lBuffLen)
End Property
```

These can be tested by using the following routine (in a standard module):

```
Sub TestCSysInfo()
   Dim obSysInfo As New CSysInfo
```

```
    Debug.Print "Screen Height = " & obSysInfo.ScreenHeight
    Debug.Print "Screen Width = " & obSysInfo.ScreenWidth
    Debug.Print "Colour Depth = " & obSysInfo.ColourDepth
    Debug.Print "One pixel = " & obSysInfo.PointsPerPixel & " points"
    Debug.Print "User name = " & obSysInfo.UserName
    Debug.Print "Computer name = " & obSysInfo.ComputerName
End Sub
```

Modifying UserForm Styles

UserForms in Excel do not provide any built-in mechanism for modifying their appearance. Our only choice is a simple pop-up dialog with a caption and an x button to close the form, though we can choose to show it modally or non-modally.

Using API calls, we can modify the UserForm's window, to do any combination of:

- Switching between modal and non-modal while the form is showing
- Making the form resizable
- Showing or hiding the form's caption and title bar
- Showing a small title bar, like those on a floating toolbar
- Showing a custom icon on the form
- Showing an icon in the task bar for the form
- Removing the x button to close the form
- Adding standard maximize and/or minimize buttons

An example workbook demonstrating all these choices can be found on the Wrox web site at http://www.wrox.com, with the key parts of the code explained below.

Windows Styles

The appearance and behavior of a window is primarily controlled by its **style** and **extended style** properties. These styles are both Long values, in which each bit of the value controls a specific aspect of the window's appearance – either on or off. We can change the window's appearance using the following process:

- Use `FindWindow` to get the UserForm's window handle
- Read its style using the `GetWindowLong` function
- Toggle one or more of the style bits
- Set the window to use this modified style using the `SetWindowLong` function
- For some changes, tell the window to redraw itself using the `ShowWindow` function

Some of the main constants for each bit of the basic window style are:

```
'Style to add a titlebar
Private Const WS_CAPTION As Long = &HC00000
```

```
'Style to add a system menu
Private Const WS_SYSMENU As Long = &H80000

'Style to add a sizable frame
Private Const WS_THICKFRAME As Long = &H40000

'Style to add a Minimize box on the title bar
Private Const WS_MINIMIZEBOX As Long = &H20000

'Style to add a Maximize box to the title bar
Private Const WS_MAXIMIZEBOX As Long = &H10000

'Cleared to show a task bar icon
Private Const WS_POPUP As Long = &H80000000

'Cleared to show a task bar icon
Private Const WS_VISIBLE As Long = &H10000000
```

While some of those for the extended window style are:

```
'Controls if the window has an icon
Private Const WS_EX_DLGMODALFRAME As Long = &H1

'Application Window: shown on taskbar
Private Const WS_EX_APPWINDOW As Long = &H40000

'Tool Window: small titlebar
Private Const WS_EX_TOOLWINDOW As Long = &H80
```

Note that this is only a subset of all the possible window style bits. See the MSDN documentation for Window Styles for the full list (http://msdn.microsoft.com/library/psdk/winui/ windows_2v90.htm) and the `win32api.txt` file for their values.

The following example uses the above process to remove a UserForm's close button and can be found in the `NoCloseButton.xls` example in the code download:

```
'Find the UserForm's Window
Private Declare Function FindWindow Lib "user32" _
        Alias "FindWindowA" ( _
        ByVal lpClassName As String, _
        ByVal lpWindowName As String) As Long

'Get the current window style
Private Declare Function GetWindowLong Lib "user32" _
        Alias "GetWindowLongA" ( _
        ByVal hWnd As Long, _
        ByVal nIndex As Long) As Long

'Set the new window style
Private Declare Function SetWindowLong Lib "user32" _
        Alias "SetWindowLongA" ( _
        ByVal hWnd As Long, _
        ByVal nIndex As Long, _
        ByVal dwNewLong As Long) As Long
```

```
Const GWL_STYLE = -16              'The standard syle
Const WS_SYSMENU = &H80000         'The system menu style bit

Private Sub UserForm_Initialize()
    Dim hWnd As Long, lStyle As Long

    '1. Find the UserForm's window handle
    If Val(Application.Version) >= 9 Then
        hWnd = FindWindow("ThunderDFrame", Me.Caption)
    Else
        hWnd = FindWindow("ThunderXFrame", Me.Caption)
    End If

    '2. Get the current window style
    lStyle = GetWindowLong(hWnd, GWL_STYLE)

    '3. Toggle the SysMenu bit, to turn off the system menu
    lStyle = (lStyle And Not WS_SYSMENU)

    '4. Set the window to use the new style
    SetWindowLong hWnd, GWL_STYLE, lStyle
End Sub
```

The CFormChanger Class

As mentioned previously in this chapter, API calls are much easier to use when they are encapsulated within a class module. The `CFormChanger` class included in the `FormFun.xls` file on the Wrox web site (at http://www.wrox.com) repeats the above code snippet for all the windows style bits mentioned in the previous section, presenting them as the following properties of the class:

- `Modal`
- `Sizeable`
- `ShowCaption`
- `SmallCaption`
- `ShowIcon`
- `IconPath` (to show a custom icon)
- `ShowCloseBtn`
- `ShowMaximizeBtn`
- `ShowMinimizeBtn`
- `ShowSysMenu`
- `ShowTaskBarIcon`

To use the class on your own forms, copy the entire class module into your project and call it from your form's `Activate` event, as in the following example. This example can be found in the `ToolbarForm.xls` workbook at http://www.wrox.com:

```
Private Sub UserForm_Activate()

    Dim oChanger As CFormChanger

    'Create a new instance of the CFormChanger class
    Set oChanger = New CFormChanger

    'Set the form changer's properties
    oChanger.SmallCaption = True
    oChanger.Sizeable = True

    'Tell the changer which form to apply the style changes to.
    'Also acts as the trigger for applying them
    Set oChanger.Form = Me

End Sub
```

Resizable Userforms

In Office XP, Microsoft made the File Open and Save As dialogs resizable. They remember their position and size between sessions, greatly improving their usability. Using the same API calls shown in the previous section and a class module to do all the hard work, you can give your users the same experience when interacting with your UserForms.

One of the curiosities of the `UserForm` object is that it has a `Resize` event, but it doesn't have a property to specify whether or not it is resizable – in theory, the `Resize` event will never fire. As shown in the previous example, you can provide your own `Sizeable` property by toggling the `WS_THICKFRAME` window style bit; when you do this, the `Userform_Resize` event comes to life, triggered every time the user changes the size of the form (though not when they move it around the screen). You can respond to this event by changing the size and/or position of all the controls on the form, such that they make the best use of the UserForm's new size.

There are two approaches that can be used to change the size and/or position of all the controls on the form, absolute and relative.

Absolute Changes

Using an absolute approach, code has to be written to set the size and position of all the controls on the form, relative to the form's new dimensions and to each other. Consider a very simple form showing just a ListBox and an OK button:

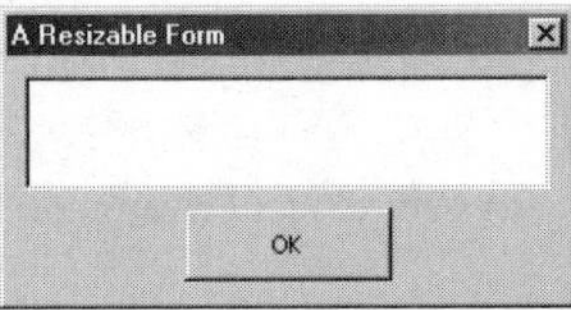

The code to resize and reposition the two controls using absolute methods is:

```
Private Sub UserForm_Resize()

    'Handle the form's resizing by specifying the new size and position
    'of all the controls
```

```
    'Use a standard gap of 6 points between controls
    Const dGap = 6

    'Ignore errors caused by controls getting too small
    On Error Resume Next

    'The OK button is in the middle ...
    btnOK.Left = (Me.InsideWidth - btnOK.Width) / 2

    '... and at the bottom of the form, with a standard gap below it
    btnOK.Top = Me.InsideHeight - dGap - btnOK.Height

    'The list's width is the form's width,
    'minus two gaps for the left and right edges
    lstItems.Width = Me.InsideWidth - dGap * 2

    'The list should fill the space between the top of the form
    'and the top of the OK button, minus a gap top and bottom
    lstItems.Height = btnOK.Top - dGap * 2

End Sub
```

It works, but has a few major problems:

- Specific code has to be written for every control that changes size and/or position, which can be a daunting task for more complex forms. See the resize code in the `FormFun.xls` for an example of this.
- The size and position of controls are often dependent on the size and position of other controls (such as the height of the ListBox being dependent on the top of the OK button in the example above).
- If you modify the appearance of the form by adding or moving controls, you have to make corresponding changes to the resize code. For example, to add a Cancel button alongside the OK button, you have to add code to handle the Cancel button's repositioning and also change the code for the OK button.
- There is no opportunity for code reuse.

Relative Changes

Using a relative approach, information is added to each control to specify by how much that control's size and position should change as the UserForm's size changes. In the same dialog, the two controls have the following relative changes:

- The OK button should move down by the full change in the form's height (to keep it at the bottom)
- The OK button should move across by half the change in the form's width (to keep it in the middle)
- The List's height and width should change by the full change in the form's height and width

These statements can be encoded into a single string to state the percentage change for each control's `Top`, `Left`, `Height`, and `Width` properties, and stored against the control. A convenient place to store it is the control's Tag property, which allows the resizing behavior of the control to be set at design time. Using the letters T, L, H, and W for the four properties, and a decimal for the percentage change if not 100%, gives the following `Tag` properties for the simple form:

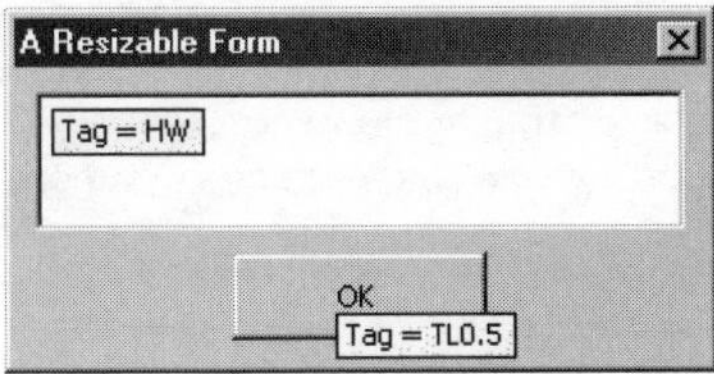

When the `UserForm_Resize` event fires, the code can calculate the change in the form's height and width and iterate through all the controls adjusting their `Top`, `Left`, `Height`, and `Width` as specified by their Tags. The `CFormResizer` class to do this is shown below.

There are a number of benefits to this approach:

- The resize behavior of each control is set at design time, while the form is being viewed, just like all the other properties of the control
- The change in size and position of each control is independent of any other control
- Controls can be added, moved, or deleted without having to modify the `Resize` code or change other controls' resize behavior.
- The resize code can treat every control in exactly the same way, hence
- Every UserForm uses exactly the same `Resize` code, which can be encapsulated in a separate class module

The CFormResizer Class

By encapsulating all the resize code in a separate class module, any UserForm can be made resizable by adding just six lines of code, to instantiate and call into the class, and setting the resize behavior for each control in its Tag property.

The `CFormResizer` class provides the following functionality:

- Sets the form to be resizable
- Sets the initial size and position of the form, if it has been shown before
- Resizes and repositions all the controls on the form, according to their Tag resizing string
- Stores the form's size and position in the registry, for use when the same form is shown again
- Allows the calling code to specify a key name for storing the form dimensions in the registry
- Prevents a form being resized in either direction if none of the controls are set to respond to changes in height and/or width
- Stops resizing when any control is moved to the left or top edge of the form, or when any control is reduced to zero height or width

The code for the `CFormResizer` class is shown below, with comments in the code to explain each section. It is available for download in the `FormResizer.xls` workbook at http://www.wrox.com:

```
Option Explicit

'Find the UserForm's window handle
Private Declare Function FindWindow Lib "user32" _
              Alias "FindWindowA" ( _
              ByVal lpClassName As String, _
              ByVal lpWindowName As String) As Long

'Get the UserForm's window style
Private Declare Function GetWindowLong Lib "user32" _
              Alias "GetWindowLongA" ( _
              ByVal hWnd As Long, _
              ByVal nIndex As Long) As Long

'Set the UserForm's window style
Private Declare Function SetWindowLong Lib "user32" _
              Alias "SetWindowLongA" ( _
              ByVal hWnd As Long, _
              ByVal nIndex As Long, _
              ByVal dwNewLong As Long) As Long


'The offset of a window's style
Private Const GWL_STYLE As Long = (-16)

'Style to add a sizable frame
Private Const WS_THICKFRAME As Long = &H40000

Dim moForm As Object
Dim mhWndForm As Long
Dim mdWidth As Double
Dim mdHeight As Double
Dim msRegKey As String

'Default for the registry key to store the dimensions
Private Sub Class_Initialize()
   msRegKey = "Excel 2002 Prog Ref"
End Sub

'Properties to identify where in the registry to store the UserForm
'position information
Public Property Let RegistryKey(sNew As String)
   msRegKey = sNew
End Property

Public Property Get RegistryKey() As String
    RegistryKey = msRegKey
End Property

'We're told which form to handle the resizing for,
'set in the UserForm_Initialize event.
'Make the form resizable and set its size and position
Public Property Set Form(oNew As Object)
```

```
    Dim sSizes As String, vaSizes As Variant
    Dim iStyle As Long

    'Remember the form for later
    Set moForm = oNew

    'Get the UserForm's window handle
    If Val(Application.Version) < 9 Then
        'XL97
        mhWndForm = FindWindow("ThunderXFrame", moForm.Caption)
    Else
        'XL2000 and 2002
        mhWndForm = FindWindow("ThunderDFrame", moForm.Caption)
    End If

    'Make the form resizable
    iStyle = GetWindowLong(mhWndForm, GWL_STYLE)
    iStyle = iStyle Or WS_THICKFRAME
    SetWindowLong mhWndForm, GWL_STYLE, iStyle

    'Read its dimensions from the registry (if there)
    'The string has the form of "<Top>;<Left>;<Height>;<Width>"
    sSizes = GetSetting(msRegKey, "Forms", moForm.Name, "")

    'Remember the current size for use in the Resize routine
    mdWidth = moForm.Width
    mdHeight = moForm.Height

    If sSizes <> "" Then
        'If we got a dimension string, split it into its parts
        vaSizes = Split(sSizes, ";")

        'Make sure we got 4 elements!
        ReDim Preserve vaSizes(0 To 3)

        'Set the form's size and position
        moForm.Top = Val(vaSizes(0))
        moForm.Left = Val(vaSizes(1))
        moForm.Height = Val(vaSizes(2))
        moForm.Width = Val(vaSizes(3))

        'Set to manual startup position
        moForm.StartUpPosition = 0
    End If

End Property

'Called from the User_Form resize event, also triggered when we change
'the size ourself.

'This is the routine that performs the resizing, by checking each control's
'Tag property, and moving/sizing it accordingly.
Public Sub FormResize()

    Dim dWidthAdj As Double, dHeightAdj As Double
```

```
    Dim bSomeWidthChange As Boolean
    Dim bSomeHeightChange As Boolean
    Dim sTag As String, sSize As String
    Dim oCtl As MSForms.Control

    Static bResizing As Boolean

    'Resizing can be triggered from within this routine,
    'so use a flag to prevent recursion
    If bResizing Then Exit Sub
    bResizing = True

    'Calculate the change in height and width
    dHeightAdj = moForm.Height - mdHeight
    dWidthAdj = moForm.Width - mdWidth

    'Check if we can perform the adjustment
    '(i.e. widths and heights can't be negative)
    For Each oCtl In moForm.Controls

        'Read the control's Tag property, which contains the resizing info
        sTag = UCase(oCtl.Tag)

        'If we're changing the Top, check that it won't move off the top
        'of the form
        If InStr(1, sTag, "T", vbBinaryCompare) Then
            If oCtl.Top + dHeightAdj * ResizeFactor(sTag, "T") <= 0 Then
                moForm.Height = mdHeight
            End If

            bSomeHeightChange = True
        End If

        'If we're changing the Left, check that it won't move off the
        'left of the form
        If InStr(1, sTag, "L", vbBinaryCompare) Then
            If oCtl.Left + dWidthAdj * ResizeFactor(sTag, "L") <= 0 Then
                moForm.Width = mdWidth
            End If

            bSomeWidthChange = True
        End If

        'If we're changing the Height, check that it won't go negative
        If InStr(1, sTag, "H", vbBinaryCompare) Then
            If oCtl.Height + dHeightAdj * ResizeFactor(sTag, "H") <= 0 Then
                moForm.Height = mdHeight
            End If

            bSomeHeightChange = True
        End If

        'If we're changing the Width, check that it won't go negative
        If InStr(1, sTag, "W", vbBinaryCompare) Then
            If oCtl.Width + dWidthAdj * ResizeFactor(sTag, "W") <= 0 Then
                moForm.Width = mdWidth
```

```
            End If

            bSomeWidthChange = True
        End If
    Next        'Control

    'If none of the controls move or size,
    'don't allow the form to resize in that direction
    If Not bSomeHeightChange Then moForm.Height = mdHeight
    If Not bSomeWidthChange Then moForm.Width = mdWidth

    'Recalculate the height and width changes,
    'in case the previous checks reset them
    dHeightAdj = moForm.Height - mdHeight
    dWidthAdj = moForm.Width - mdWidth

    'Loop through all the controls on the form,
    'adjusting their position and size
    For Each oCtl In moForm.Controls
        With oCtl
            sTag = UCase(.Tag)

            'Changing the Top
            If InStr(1, sTag, "T", vbBinaryCompare) Then
                .Top = .Top + dHeightAdj * ResizeFactor(sTag, "T")
            End If

            'Changing the Left
            If InStr(1, sTag, "L", vbBinaryCompare) Then
                .Left = .Left + dWidthAdj * ResizeFactor(sTag, "L")
            End If

            'Changing the Height
            If InStr(1, sTag, "H", vbBinaryCompare) Then
                .Height = .Height + dHeightAdj * ResizeFactor(sTag, "H")
            End If

            'Changing the Width
            If InStr(1, sTag, "W", vbBinaryCompare) Then
                .Width = .Width + dWidthAdj * ResizeFactor(sTag, "W")
            End If
        End With
    Next        'Control

    'Remember the new dimensions of the form for next time
    mdWidth = moForm.Width
    mdHeight = moForm.Height

    'Store the size and position in the registry
    With moForm
        SaveSetting msRegKey, "Forms", .Name, Str(.Top) & ";" & _
                                              Str(.Left) & ";" & _
                                              Str(.Height) & ";" & _
                                              Str(.Width)
    End With
```

```
    'Reset the recursion flag, now that we're done
    bResizing = False

End Sub

'Function to locate a property letter (T, L, H or W) in the Tag string
'and return the resizing factor for it
Private Function ResizeFactor(sTag As String, sChange As String)

    Dim i As Integer, d As Double

    'Locate the property letter in the tag string
    i = InStr(1, sTag, sChange, vbBinaryCompare)

    'If we found it...
    If i > 0 Then

        '... read the number following it
        d = Val(Mid$(sTag, i + 1))

        'If there was no number, use a factor of 100%
        If d = 0 Then d = 1
    End If

    'Return the factor
    ResizeFactor = d

End Function
```

Using the CFormResizer Class

The code to use the `CFormResizer` class in a UserForm's code module is as follows:

```
'Declare an object for our CFormResizer class to handle
'resizing for this form
Dim moResizer As CFormResizer

'The Resizer class is set up in the UserForm_Initialize event
Private Sub UserForm_Initialize()

    'Create the instance of the class
    Set moResizer = New CFormResizer

    'Tell it where to store the form dimensions
    moResizer.RegistryKey = "Excel 2002 Prog Ref"

    'Tell it which form it's handling
    Set moResizer.Form = Me

End Sub

'When the form is resized, the UserForm_Resize event is raised,
'which we just pass on to the Resizer class
Private Sub UserForm_Resize()
```

```
    moResizer.FormResize
End Sub

'The OK button unloads the form
Private Sub btnOK_Click()
    Unload Me
End Sub

'The QueryClose event in called whenever the form is closed.
'We call the FormResize method one last time, to store the form's
'final size and position in the registry
Private Sub UserForm_QueryClose(Cancel As Integer, CloseMode As Integer)
    moResizer.FormResize
End Sub
```

There are a few points to remember when using this approach in your own UserForms:

- The resizer works by changing the control's `Top`, `Left`, `Height`, and `Width` properties in response to changes in the UserForm size, according to the control's resizing information.
- The control's resizing information is set in its `Tag` property, using the letters T, L, H, and/or W followed by a number specifying the resizing factor (if not 100%).
- The resizing factors must be in US format, using a period as the decimal separator.
- If there are no controls that have T or H in their `Tag` strings, the form will not be allowed to resize vertically.
- If there are no controls that have L or W in their `Tag` strings, the form will not be allowed to resize horizontally.
- The smallest size for the form is set by the first control to be moved to the top or left edge, or to have a zero width or height.
- This can be used to set a minimum size for the form, by using a hidden label with a `Tag` of 'HW', where the size of the label equals the amount that the form can be reduced in size. If the label is set to zero height and width to start with, the UserForm can only be enlarged from its design-time size.

Other Examples

You are not forced to put all your API calls into class modules, though it is usually a good idea. This section demonstrates a few examples where the API calls would typically be used within a standard module.

Change Excel's Icon

When developing an application that takes over the entire Excel interface, you can use the following code to give Excel your own icon:

```
'Get the handle for a window
Declare Function FindWindow Lib "user32" _
        Alias "FindWindowA" ( _
        ByVal lpClassName As String, _
        ByVal lpWindowName As String) As Long
```

```
'Extract an icon from a file
Declare Function ExtractIcon Lib "shell32.dll" _
        Alias "ExtractIconA" ( _
        ByVal hInst As Long, _
        ByVal lpszExeFileName As String, _
        ByVal nIconIndex As Long) As Long

'Send a Windows message
Declare Function SendMessage Lib "user32" _
        Alias "SendMessageA" ( _
        ByVal hWnd As Long, _
        ByVal wMsg As Long, _
        ByVal wParam As Integer, _
        ByVal lparam As Long) As Long

'Windows message types
Const WM_SETICON = &H80

Sub SetExcelIcon(stIconPath As String)
   Dim A As Long, hWnd As Long, hIcon As Long

   'Get the handle of the Excel window
   hWnd = FindWindow("XLMAIN", Application.Caption)

   'Get the icon from the source file
   hIcon = ExtractIcon(0, stIconPath, 0)

   '1 means invalid icon source, 0 means no icons in source
   If hIcon > 1 Then
      'Set the big (32x32) and small (16x16) icons
      SendMessage hWnd, WM_SETICON, True, hIcon
      SendMessage hWnd, WM_SETICON, False, hIcon
   End If
End Sub

'Example routine to change the Excel application icon
Sub TestExcelIcon()
   SetExcelIcon "c:\MyDir\MyIcon.ico"
End Sub
```

Play a .wav file

Excel does not include a built-in method of playing sounds. This is a simple API call to play a `.wav` file. The `uFlags` argument can be used to play the sound asynchronously or in a continuous loop, though we use a value of zero in this example to play the sound once, synchronously:

```
'API Call to play a wav file
Declare Function sndPlaySound Lib "winmm.dll" _
        Alias "sndPlaySoundA" ( _
        ByVal lpszSoundName As String, _
        ByVal uFlags As Long) As Long

'Wrapper routine to call the API function
Sub PlayWav(stWavFileName As String)
```

```
   sndPlaySound stWavFileName, 0
End Sub

'Example routine to demonstrate calling the PlayWav procedure
Sub TestWav()
   PlayWav "c:\MyDir\MySound.wav"
End Sub
```

Summary

The functions defined in the Windows API provide a valuable and powerful extension to the VBA developer's tool set. The `win32api.txt` file provides the VBA definitions for most of the core functions. The definitions for the remaining functions can be converted from the C-style versions shown in the online MSDN library.

Class modules enable the user to encapsulate both the API definitions and their use into simple chunks of functionality that are easy to use and reuse in VBA applications. A number of example classes and routines have been provided in this chapter to get you started using the Windows API functions within your applications. These include:

- Creating a `TEMP` file
- A high-resolution timer
- Freezing a UserForm
- Getting system information
- Modifying a UserForm's appearance
- Making UserForms resizable, with a minimum of code in the form
- Changing Excel's icon
- Playing a `.wav` file

Excel 2002 Object Model

Most of the objects in the Excel Object Model have objects with associated collections. The collection object is usually the plural form of the associated object. For example, the Worksheets collection holds a collection of Worksheet objects. For simplicity, each object and associated collection will be grouped together under the same heading.

Common Properties with Collections and Associated Objects

In most cases the purpose of the collection object is only to hold a collection of the same objects. The common properties and methods of the collection objects are listed below. Only unique properties, methods or events will be mentioned in each object section.

Common Collection Properties

Name	Returns	Description
`Application`	`Application`	Read Only. Returns a reference to the owning Application of the current object. Excel in this case.
`Count`	`Long`	Read Only. Returns the number of objects in the collection.
`Creator`	`Long`	Read Only. Returns a `Long` number that describes whether the object was created in Excel or not.
`Parent`	`Object`	The `Parent` object is the owning object of the collection object. For example, Workbooks. `Parent` returns a reference to the `Application` object.

Common Collection Methods

Name	Returns	Parameters	Description
`Item`	`Single`	`Index as Variant`	Returns the object from the collection with the `Index` value specified by the `Index` parameter. The `Index` value may also specify a unique string key describing one of the objects in the collection.

Common Object Properties

Objects also have some common properties. To avoid redundancy the common properties and methods of all objects are listed below. They will be mentioned in each object description as existing but are only defined here:

Name	Returns	Description
`Application`	`Application`	Read Only. Returns a reference to the owning Application of the current object – Excel in this case.
`Creator`	`Long`	Read Only. Returns a `Long` number that describes whether the object was created in Excel or not.
`Parent`	`Object`	Read Only. The owning object of the current object. For example `Characters. Parent` may return a reference to a `Range` object, since a `Range` object is one of the possible owners of a `Characters` object.

Excel Objects and Their Properties, Methods and Events

The objects are listed in alphabetical order. Each object has a general description of the object and possible parent objects. This is followed by a table format of each of the object's properties, methods and events. The last section of each object describes some code examples of the object's use.

Addin Object and the Addins Collection

The `Addins` collection holds all of the `Addin` objects available to Excel. Each `Addin` object represents an Addin shown in Excel's **Add-Ins** dialog box under the **Tools | Add-Ins...** menu. The Addin must be installed (`AddIn.Installed = True`) to be able to use it in the current session. Examples of available `Addin` objects in Excel include the Analysis Toolpack, the MS Query Addin, and the Conditional Sum Wizard.

The `Add` method of the `Addins` collection can be used to add a new `Addin` to the collection. The `Add` method requires a `FileName` to be specified (usually with a XLL or XLA file extension). The `Count` property of the `Addins` collection returns the number of Addins that are available for use by the current Excel session.

Addin Common Properties

The `Application`, `Creator`, and `Parent` properties are defined at the beginning of this appendix.

Addin Properties

Name	Returns	Description
`CLSID`	`String`	Read Only. Returns a unique identifier for the Addin.
`FullName`	`String`	Read Only. Returns the full path and filename of the associated Addin.
`Installed`	`Boolean`	Set/Get whether the Addin can be used in the current session.
`Name`	`String`	Read Only. Returns the filename of the Addin.
`Path`	`String`	Read Only. Returns the full file path of the associated Addin
`Title`	`String`	Read Only. This hidden property returns the string shown in the Addin Manager dialog box.

Example: AddIn Object and the AddIns Collection

This example ensures that the Analysis Toolpack is installed:

```
Sub UseAnalysisToolpack()
   Dim oAddin As AddIn

   'Make sure the Analysis Toolpack is installed
   For Each oAddin In AddIns
      If oAddin.Name = "ANALYS32.XLL" Then
         oAddin.Installed = True
      End If
   Next
End Sub
```

Note that instead of looping through the `Addins` collection, you could follow the on-line help and use:

```
AddIns("Analysis Toolpak").Installed = True
```

Unfortunately, this approach may not work with a non-English User-Interface language, if the Addin's title has been localised.

Adjustments Object

The `Adjustments` object holds a collection of numbers used to move the adjustment 'handles' of the parent `Shape` object. Each `Shape` object can have up to 8 different adjustments. Each specific adjustment handle can have one or two adjustments associated with it depending on if it can be moved both horizontally and vertically (two) or in just one dimension. Adjustment values are between 0 and 1 and hence are percentage adjustments – the absolute magnitude of a 100% change is defined by the shape being adjusted.

Adjustments Common Properties

The `Application`, `Creator`, and `Parent` properties are defined at the beginning of this appendix.

Adjustments Properties

Name	Returns	Description
`Count`	`Long`	Read Only. Returns the number of adjustments values associated with the parent `Shape` object.
`Item`	`Single`	Parameters: `Index As Long`. Set/Get the adjustment value or values indicated by the `Index` parameter.

Example: Adjustments Object

This example draws a block arrow on the sheet, then modifies the dimensions of the arrow head:

```
Sub AddArrow()
    Dim oShp As Shape

    'Add an arrow head to the sheet
    Set oShp = ActiveSheet.Shapes.AddShape( _
                mSoShapeRightArrow, 10, 10, 100, 50)

    'Set the 'head' of the arrow to start 30% of the way across
    'and the 'shaft' to start 40% of the way down.
    oShp.Adjustments(1) = 0.3        'Left/right
    oShp.Adjustments(2) = 0.4        'Up/down
End Sub
```

AllowEditRange Object and the AllowEditRanges Collection

The `AllowEditRange` object represents a range of cells on a worksheet that can still be edited when protected. Each `AllowEditRange` object can have permissions set for any number of users on your network and can have a separate password.

Be aware of the `Locked` property of the `Range` object when using this feature. When you unlock cells, then protect the worksheet, you are allowing any user access to those cells, regardless of the `AllowEditRange` objects. When each `AllowEditRange` object's cells are locked, any user can still edit them unless you assign a password or add users and deny them permission without using a password.

The `AllowEditRanges` collection represents all `AllowEditRange` objects that can be edited on a protected worksheet. See the `AllowEditRange` object for more details.

AllowEditRanges Collection Properties

Name	Returns	Description
`Count`	`Long`	Read Only. Returns the number of `AllowEditRange` objects that are contained in the area.
`Item`	`AllowEdit Range`	Parameter: `Index As Variant`. Returns a single `AllowEditRange` object in the `AllowEditRanges` collection.

AllowEditRanges Collection Methods

Name	Returns	Parameters	Description
Add	AllowEdit Range	Title As String, Range As Range, [Password]	Adds an AllowEditRange object to the AllowEditRanges collection

AllowEditRange Properties

Name	Returns	Description
Range	Range	Returns a subset of the ranges that can be edited on a protected worksheet
Title	String	Returns or sets the title of the web page when the document is saved as a web page
Users	UserAccess List	Returns the list of users who are allowed access to the protected range on a worksheet

AllowEditRange Methods

Name	Returns	Parameters	Description
ChangePassword		Password As String	Sets the password for a range that can be edited on a protected worksheet
Delete			Deletes the object
Unprotect		[Password]	Removes any protection from a sheet or workbook

Example: AllowEditRange Object

The following routine loops through a list of range names in a worksheet and adds an `AllowEditRange` item for each one whose name begins with "`pc`". It also denies access to the `pcNetSales` range to all but one user, who can only edit the range with a password:

```
Sub CreateAllowRanges()

    Dim lPos As Long
    Dim nm As Name
    Dim oAllowRange As AllowEditRange
    Dim sName As String

    With wksAllowEditRange
        'Loop through the worksheet level
        ' range names
        For Each nm In .Names
            'Store the name
            sName = nm.Name

            'Locate the position of the "!"
```

```
                lPos = InStr(1, sName, "!", vbTextCompare)

                'If there was an "!"...
                If lPos > 0 Then
                    'Is there a "pc" just after the exclamation point
                    'If so, it's a range we want to create an AllowEditRange
                    ' object for
                    If Mid(sName, lPos + 1, 2) = "pc" Then
                        'Make sure the cells are locked
                        'Unlocking them will allow any user
                        ' access to them.
                        nm.RefersToRange.Locked = True

                        'Pull out the worksheet reference (including the "!")
                        ' from the range name
                        sName = Right(sName, Len(sName) - lPos)

                        'Create the AllowEditRange
                        'Remove the old one if it exists
                        On Error Resume Next
                            Set oAllowRange = Nothing
                            Set oAllowRange = .Protection.AllowEditRanges(sName)
                        On Error GoTo 0
                        If Not oAllowRange Is Nothing Then oAllowRange.Delete
                        Set oAllowRange = .Protection.AllowEditRanges.Add(sName, _
                                                                  nm.RefersToRange)
                        'If it's the sales range name...
                        If sName = "pcNetSales" Then
                            'Add a password, then
                            'Add a user and deny them from editing the range
                            ' without the password
                            oAllowRange.ChangePassword "pcnsw"
                            oAllowRange.Users.Add "RCR\AgamaOffice", False
                        End If
                    End If
                End If
            Next nm
        End With

    End Sub
```

Application Object

The `Application` object is the root object of the Excel Object Model. All the other objects in the Excel Object Model can only be accessed through the `Application` object. Many objects, however, are globally available. For example, the `ActiveSheet` property of the `Application` object is also available globally. That means that the active WorkSheet can be accessed by at least two ways: `Application.ActiveSheet` and `ActiveSheet`.

The `Application` object holds most of the application level attributes that can be set through the **Tools | Options** menu in Excel. For example, the `DefaultFilePath` is equivalent to the **Default File Location** text box in the **General** tab of the **Options** dialog box.

Many of the `Application` object's properties and methods are equivalent to things that can be set with the **Options** dialog box.

The Application object is also used when automating Excel from another application, such as Word. The CreateObject function, GetObject function or the New keyword can be used to create a new instance of an Excel Application object from another application. Please refer to Chapter 19 for examples of automation from another application.

The Application object can also expose events. However, Application events are not automatically available for use. The following three steps must be completed before Application events can be used:
Create a new class module, say called cAppObject, and declare a Public object variable in a class, say called AppExcel, to respond to events. For example:

```
Public WithEvents AppExcel As Excel.Application
```

Now the Application object events will be available in the class for the AppExcel object variable. Write the appropriate event handling code in the class. For example if you wanted a message to appear whenever a worksheet is activated then you could write the following:

```
Private Sub AppExcel_SheetActivate(ByVal Sh As Object)
    'display worksheet name
    MsgBox "The " & Sh.Name & " sheet has just been activated."
End Sub
```

Finally, in a procedure in a standard module instantiate the class created above with a current Application object:

```
Private App As New cAppObject 'class with the above code snippets
Sub AttachEvents()
    Set App.AppExcel = Application
End Sub
```

The EnableEvents property of the Application object must also be set to True for events to trigger at the appropriate time.

Application Common Properties

The Application, Creator, and Parent properties are defined at the beginning of this appendix.

Application Properties

Name	Returns	Description
ActiveCell	Range	Read Only. Returns the cell in the active sheet where the cursor is located.
ActiveChart	Chart	Read Only. Returns the currently selected chart in the active workbook. If no chart is currently selected, nothing is returned.
ActivePrinter	String	Set/Get the name of the printer currently being used.
ActiveSheet	Object	Read Only. Returns the currently active sheet in the active workbook.

Table continued on following page

Name	Returns	Description
ActiveWindow	Window	Read Only. Returns the currently selected Excel window, if any.
ActiveWorkbook	Workbook	Read Only. Returns the workbook that is currently active, if any.
AddIns	AddIns	Read Only. Returns the collection of Addins currently available for use in Excel.
AlertBefore Overwriting	Boolean	Set/Get whether a message pops up any time an attempt to overwrite non-blank cells by a drag-and-drop operation is made.
AltStartupPath	String	Set/Get the alternative startup file location folder for Excel.
AnswerWizard	Answer Wizard	Read Only. Returns an object allowing manipulation of the Answer Wizard.
AskToUpdate Links	Boolean	Set/Get whether the user is prompted to update links whenever a workbook with links is opened.
Assistant	Assistant	Read Only. Returns an object allowing manipulation of the Office Assistant.
AutoCorrect	AutoCorrect	Read Only. Returns an object allowing modification of Excel's AutoCorrect features.
AutoFormatAs You TypeReplace Hyperlinks	Boolean	Set/Get whether Excel automatically formats/creates hyperlinks as you type.
Automation Security	Mso Automation Security	Set/Get the level of macro security used when Excel opens a file programmatically. This setting is independent of the macro security setting found in Security dialog box in the Tools | Macro command, though the msoAutomationSecurityByUI constant instructs the property to use the setting found there.
AutoPercent Entry	Boolean	Set/Get whether Excel automatically adds a % sign when typing a number into a cell that has a Percentage format applied.
AutoRecover	AutoRecover	Set/Get AutoRecover options such as Path and Time interval.
Build	Long	Read Only. Returns the exact build number of Excel.
Calculate BeforeSave	Boolean	Set/Get whether workbooks are calculated before they are saved to disk. This assumes that formula calculation is not set to automatic (Calculation property).
Calculation	Xl Calculation	Set/Get when calculations are made automatically, manually, or semi-automatically.

Name	Returns	Description
Calculation InterruptKey	Xl Calculation Interrupt Key	Set/Get the key that can interrupt Excel when performing calculations.
Calculation State	Xl Calculation State	Read Only. Indicates whether Excel calculations are in progress, pending, or done.
Calculation Version	Long	Read Only. Returns the Excel version and calculation engine version used when the file was last saved.
Caller	Variant	Read Only. Parameters: `[Index]`. Returns information describing what invoked the current Visual Basic code (for example cell function, document event).
CanPlaySounds	Boolean	Read Only. Returns whether sound notes are heard in Excel. Property unused from Excel 2000 onwards.
CanRecord Sounds	Boolean	Read Only. Returns whether sound notes can be recorded in Excel. Property unused from Excel 2000 onwards.
Caption	String	Set/Get the caption that appears in the main Excel window.
CellDragAnd Drop	Boolean	Set/Get whether dragging and dropping cells is possible.
Cells	Range	Read Only. Returns all the cells in the active sheet.
Charts	Sheets	Read Only. Returns all the charts in the active workbook.
Clipboard Formats	Variant	Read Only. Parameters: `[Index]`. Returns an array of format values (`XlClipboardFormat`) that are currently in the clipboard.
Columns	Range	Read Only. Returns all the columns in the currently active sheet.
COMAddIns	COMAddIns	Read Only. Returns the collection of installed COM Addins.
CommandBars	CommandBars	Read Only. Returns the collection of command bars available to Excel.
Command Underlines	XlCommand Underlines	Set/Get how commands are underlined in Excel. Used only on Macintosh systems.
Constrain Numeric	Boolean	Set/Get whether only numbers and punctuation marks are recognized by handwriting recognition. Used only by Windows for Pen Computing.

Table continued on following page

Name	Returns	Description
Control Characters	Boolean	Set/Get whether control characters are displayed for right-to-left languages. (Language support must be installed).
CopyObjects WithCells	Boolean	Set/Get whether objects (such as embedded objects) can be cut, copied, and sorted along with cell data.
Cursor	XlMouse Pointer	Set/Get which mouse pointer is seen in Microsoft Excel.
CursorMovement	Long	Set/Get what type of cursor is used: visual or logical.
CustomList Count	Long	Read Only. Returns the number of custom and built-in lists used in Excel (for example Monday, Tuesday, Wednesday…).
CutCopyMode	XlCutCopy Mode	Set/Get whether a cut or copy operation is currently happening.
DataEntry Mode	Long	Set/Get whether locked cells can be edited (`xlOff` for editing allowed, `xlOn` for editing of unlocked cells only, `xlStrict` for editing of unlocked cells only that can not be canceled by pressing Escape).
DDEAppReturn Code	Long	Read Only. Returns the result (confirmation/error) of the last DDE message sent by Excel.
DefaultFile Path	String	Set/Get the default folder used when opening files.
DefaultSave Format	XlFile Format	Set/Get the default file format used when saving files.
DefaultSheet Direction	Long	Set/Get which direction new sheets will appear in Excel.
DefaultWeb Options	DefaultWeb Options	Read Only. Returns an object allowing manipulation of the items associated with the Web Options dialog.
Decimal Separator	String	Set/Get the character used for the decimal separator. This is a global setting and will affect all workbooks when opened. Use `Application UseSystemSeparators = True` to globally reset custom separators.
Dialogs	Dialogs	Read Only. Returns a collection of all the built-in dialog boxes.
DisplayAlerts	Boolean	Set/Get whether the user is prompted by typical Excel messages (for example 'Save Changes to Workbook?') or no prompts appear and the default answer is always chosen.
Display Clipboard Window	Boolean	Set/Get whether the Clipboard window is displayed. Used in Microsoft Office Macintosh Edition.
DisplayComment Indicator	XlComment DisplayMode	Set/Get how Excel displays cell comments and indicators.

Name	Returns	Description
DisplayExcel4 Menus	Boolean	Set/Get whether Excel display Excel 4.0 menus.
DisplayFormula Bar	Boolean	Set/Get whether the formula bar is displayed.
DisplayFull Screen	Boolean	Set/Get whether the Excel is in full screen mode.
Display Function ToolTips	Boolean	Set/Get whether tooltips for arguments appear in the cell when typing a function.
DisplayInsert Options	Boolean	Set/Get whether the Insert Options dropdown button appears next to a range after inserting cells, rows, or columns.
DisplayNote Indicator	Boolean	Set/Get whether comments inserted into cells have a little note indicator at the top right corner of the cell.
DisplayPaste Options	Boolean	Set/Get whether the Paste Options dropdown button appears next to a range after a paste operation. This is an Office XP setting and therefore affects all other Office applications that use this feature.
DisplayRecent Files	Boolean	Set/Get whether the most recently opened files are displayed under the File menu.
DisplayScroll Bars	Boolean	Set/Get whether scroll bars are displayed for all open workbooks in the current session.
DisplayStatu sBar	Boolean	Set/Get whether the status bar is displayed.
EditDirectly InCell	Boolean	Set/Get whether existing cell text can be modified directly in the cell. Note that cell text can still be overwritten directly.
EnableAnimat ions	Boolean	Set/Get whether adding and deleting cells, rows, and columns are animated.
EnableAuto Complete	Boolean	Set/Get whether the `AutoComplete` feature is enabled.
EnableCancel Key	XlEnable CancelKey	Set/Get how an Excel macro reacts when the user tries to interrupt the macro (for example Ctrl-Break). This can be used to disable any user interruption, send any interruption to the error handler, or to just stop the code (default). **Use with care.**
EnableEvents	Boolean	Set/Get whether events are triggered for any object in the Excel Object Model that supports events.

Table continued on following page

Name	Returns	Description
EnableSound	Boolean	Set/Get whether sounds are enabled for Excel.
ErrorChecking Options	Error Checking Options	Set/Get error checking properties such as BackgroundChecking, IndicatorColorIndex, and InconsistentFormula. These options mirror rules found on the Error Checking tab of the Tools | Options command.
Excel4Intl MacroSheets	Sheets	Read Only. Returns the collection of sheets containing Excel 4 International macros.
Excel4Macro Sheets	Sheets	Read Only. Returns the collection of sheets containing Excel 4 macros.
ExtendList	Boolean	Set/Get whether formatting and formulas are automatically added when adding new rows or columns to existing lists of rows or columns.
FeatureInstall	MsoFeature Install	Set/Get how Excel reacts when an Excel feature is accessed that is not installed (through the interface or programmatically).
FileConverters	Variant	Read Only. Parameters: [Index1], [Index2]. Returns an array of all the file converters available in Excel.
FileDialog	FileDialog	Parameters: [fileDialogType]. Returns an object that represents an instance of one of several types of file dialogs.
FileFind	IFind	Returns an object that can be used to search for files. Used in Microsoft Office Macintosh Edition.
FileSearch	FileSearch	Read Only. Returns an object that can be used to search for files.
FindFormat	FindFormat	Set/Get search criteria for the types of cell formats to look for when using the Find and Replace methods.
FixedDecimal	Boolean	Set/Get whether any numbers entered in the future will have the decimal points specified by FixedDecimalPlaces.
FixedDecimal Places	Long	Set/Get the decimals places used for any future numbers.
GenerateGet PivotData	Boolean	Set/Get whether Excel can get PivotTable report data.
Height	Double	Set/Get the height of Excel's main application window. The value cannot be set if the main window is maximized or minimized.
Hinstance	Long	Read Only. Returns the instance handle of the instance that is calling Excel. Used mainly by other custom applications like those written in Visual Basic.

Name	Returns	Description
Hwnd	Long	Read Only. Returns the top-level window handle of the Excel window. Used mainly by other custom applications like those written in Visual Basic.
IgnoreRemote Requests	Boolean	Set/Get whether remote requests through DDE are ignored.
Interactive	Boolean	Set/Get whether Excel accepts keyboard and mouse input.
International	Variant	Read Only. Parameters: [Index]. Returns international settings for Excel. Use the XlApplicationInternational constants as one of the values of Index.
Iteration	Boolean	Set/Get whether Excel will iterate through and calculate all the cells in a circular reference trying to resolve the circular reference. Use with MaxIterations and MaxChange.
Language Settings	Language Settings	Read Only. Returns an object describing the language settings in Excel.
Left	Double	Set/Get the left edge of Excel's main application window. The value cannot be set if the main window is maximized or minimized.
LibraryPath	String	Read Only. Returns the directory where Addins are stored.
MailSession	Variant	Read Only. Returns the hexadecimal mail session number or Null if mail session is active.
MailSystem	XlMail System	Read Only. Returns what type of mail system is being used by the computer (for example xlMapi, xlPowerTalk).
MapPaperSize	Boolean	Set/Get whether documents formatted for another country's/region's standard paper size (for example, A4) are automatically adjusted so that they're printed correctly on your country's/region's standard paper size (for example, Letter).
Math Coprocessor Available	Boolean	Read Only. Returns whether a math coprocessor is available.
MaxChange	Double	Set/Get the minimum change between iterations of a circular reference before iterations stop.
MaxIterations	Long	Set/Get the maximum number of iterations allowed for circular references before iterations stop.
MemoryFree	Long	Read Only. Returns how much free memory (in bytes) Excel can use.
MemoryTotal	Long	Read Only. Returns how much total memory (in bytes) is available to Excel (including memory in use).

Table continued on following page

Name	Returns	Description
MemoryUsed	Long	Read Only. Returns how much memory (in bytes) Excel is using.
MouseAvailable	Boolean	Read Only. Returns whether the mouse is available.
MoveAfter Return	Boolean	Set/Get whether the current cell changes when the user hits Enter.
MoveAfter Return Direction	XlDirection	Set/Get which direction the cursor will move when the user hits Enter changing the current cell.
Name	String	Read Only. Returns "Microsoft Excel".
Names	Names	Read Only. Returns the collection of defined names in an active workbook.
Network Templates Path	String	Read Only. Returns the location on the network where the Excel templates are kept, if any.
NewWorkbook	Start Working	Read Only. Returns a StartWorking object.
ODBCErrors	ODBCErrors	Read Only. Returns the collection of errors returned by the most recent query or PivotTable report that had an ODBC connection.
ODBCTimeout	Long	Set/Get how long, in seconds, an ODBC connection will be kept before timing out.
OLEDBErrors	OLEDBErrors	Read Only. Returns the collection of errors returned by the most recent query or PivotTable report that had an OLEDB connection.
OnWindow	String	Set/Get the procedure that is executed every time a window is activated by the end user.
Operating System	String	Read Only. Returns the name and version of the operating system.
Organization Name	String	Read Only. Returns the organization name as seen in the About Microsoft Excel dialog box.
Path	String	Read Only. Returns the path where Excel is installed.
PathSeparator	String	Read Only. Returns a backslash ("\") on a PC or a colon ":" on a Macintosh.
PivotTable Selection	Boolean	Set/Get whether pivot tables use structured selection. For example, when selecting a Row field title the associated data is selected with it.
Previous Selections	Variant	Read Only. Parameters: [Index]. Returns an array of the last four ranges or named areas selected by using Name dialog box or Goto feature.

Name	Returns	Description
ProductCode	String	Read Only. Returns the GUID for Excel.
PromptFor SummaryInfo	Boolean	Set/Get whether the user is prompted to enter summary information when trying to save a file.
Range	Range	Read Only. Parameters: `Cell1, [Cell2]`. Returns a `Range` object containing all the cells specified by the parameters.
Ready	Boolean	Read Only. Determines whether the Excel application is ready.
RecentFiles	RecentFiles	Read Only. Returns the collection of recently opened files.
RecordRelative	Boolean	Read Only. Returns whether recorded macros use relative cell references (`True`) or absolute cell references (`False`).
ReferenceStyle	XlReference Style	Set/Get how cells are referenced: Letter-Number (for exampleA1, A3) or RowNumber-ColumnNumber (for example. R1C1, R3C1).
Registered Functions	Variant	Read Only. Parameters: `[Index1], [Index2]`. Returns the array of functions and function details relating to external DLLs or code resources. Using Addins will add external DLLs to your workbook.
ReplaceFormat	Replace Format	Set/Get replacement criteria for the types of cell formats to replace when using the `Replace` method.
RollZoom	Boolean	Set/Get whether scrolling with a scroll mouse will zoom instead of scroll.
Rows	Range	Read Only. Returns all the rows in the active sheet.
RTD	RTD	Read Only. Returns a reference to a real-time date (RTD) object connected to a RTD Server.
ScreenUpdating	Boolean	Set/Get whether Excel updates its display while a procedure is running. This property can be used to speed up procedure code by turning off screen updates (setting the property to `False`) during processing. Use with the `ScreenRefresh` method to manually refresh the screen.
Selection	Object	Read Only. Returns whatever object is currently selected (for example sheet, chart).
Sheets	Sheets	Read Only. Returns the collection of sheets in the active workbook.
SheetsInNew Workbook	Long	Set/Get how many blank sheets are put in a newly created workbook.
ShowChartTip Names	Boolean	Set/Get whether charts show the tip names over data points.

Table continued on following page

Name	Returns	Description
ShowChartTip Values	Boolean	Set/Get whether charts show the tip values over data points.
ShowStartup Dialog	Boolean	Set/Get whether the New Workbook task pane appears when loading the Excel application.
ShowToolTips	Boolean	Set/Get whether tool tips are shown in Excel.
ShowWindowsIn Taskbar	Boolean	Set/Get whether each workbook is visible on the taskbar (True) or only one Excel item is visible in the taskbar (False).
SmartTag Recognizers	SmartTag Recognize rs	Read Only. Returns a collection of smart tag recognition engines (recognizers) currently being used in the application.
Speech	Speech	Read Only. Allows access to the properties and methods used to programmatically control the Office speech tools.
Spelling Options	Spelling Options	Read Only. Allows access to the spelling options of the application.
StandardFont	String	Set/Get what font is used as the standard Excel font.
StandardFontSi ze	Double	Set/Get what font size is used as the standard Excel font size (in points).
StartupPath	String	Read Only. Returns the folder used as the Excel startup folder.
StatusBar	Variant	Set/Get the status bar text. Returns False if Excel has control of the status bar. Set to False to give control of the status bar to Excel.
TemplatesPath	String	Read Only. Returns the path to the Excel templates.
ThisCell	Range	Set/Get the cell in which a user-defined function is being called.
ThisWorkbook	Workbook	Read Only. Returns the workbook that contains the currently running VBA code.
Thousands Separator	String	Set/Get the character used for the thousands separator. This is a global setting and will affect all workbooks when opened. Use Application UseSystemSeparators = True to globally reset custom separators.
Top	Double	Set/Get the top of Excel's main application window. The value cannot be set if the main window is maximized or minimized.
Transition MenuKey	String	Set/Get what key is used to bring up Excel's menu. The forward slash key ("/") is the default.

Name	Returns	Description
TransitionMenuKeyAction	Long	Set/Get what happens when the Transition Menu Key is pressed. Either Excel menus appear (xlExcelMenu) or the Lotus help dialog box (xlLotusHelp) appears.
TransitionNavigKeys	Boolean	Set/Get whether the Transition Navigation Keys are active. These provide different key combinations for moving and selecting within a worksheet.
UsableHeight	Double	Read-Only. Returns the vertical space available in Excel's main window, in points, that is available to a sheet's Window. The value will be 1 if there is no space available.
UsableWidth	Double	Read-Only. Returns the horizontal space available in Excel's main window, in points, that is available to a sheet's Window. This property's value will be invalid if no space is available. Check the value of the UsableHeight property to check to see if there is any space available (>1).
UsedObjects	UsedObjects	Read Only. Represents objects allocated in a workbook.
UserControl	Boolean	Read-Only. True if the current Excel session was started by a user, and False if the Excel session was started programmatically.
UserLibraryPath	String	Read Only. Returns the location of Excel's COM-Addins.
UserName	String	Set/Get the user name in Excel. Note that this is the name shown in the **General** tab of the **Options** dialog box and **not** the current user's network ID or the name shown in the Excel splash screen.
UseSystemSeparators	Boolean	Set/Get whether the system operators in Excel are enabled. When set to False, you can use Application.DecimalSeparator and Application.ThousandsSeparator to override the system separators, which are located in the Regional Settings/Options applet in the Windows Control Panel.
Value	String	Read Only. Returns "Microsoft Excel".
VBE	VBE	Read Only. Returns an object allowing manipulation of the Visual Basic Editor.
Version	String	Read Only. Returns the version of Excel.
Visible	Boolean	Set/Get whether Excel is visible to the user.
Watches	Watches	Read Only. Returns a Watches object that represents all of the ranges that are tracked when a worksheet is calculated.

Table continued on following page

Name	Returns	Description
Width	Double	Set/Get the width of Excel's main application window. The value cannot be set if the main window is maximized or minimized.
Windows	Windows	Read Only. Returns all the Windows open in the current Excel session.
WindowsForPens	Boolean	Read Only. Returns whether Excel is running in a Windows for Pen Computing environment.
WindowState	XlWindow State	Set/Get whether the window is maximized, minimized, or in a normal state.
Workbooks	Workbooks	Read Only. Returns all the open workbooks (not including Addins) in the current Excel session.
Worksheet Function	Worksheet Function	Read Only. Returns an object holding all the Excel's worksheet functions that can be used in VBA.
Worksheets	Sheets	Read Only. Returns all the worksheets in the active workbook.

Application Methods

Name	Returns	Parameters	Description
Activate MicrosoftApp		Index As XlMS Application	Activates an application specified by XlMSApplication. Opens the application if it is not open. Acts in a similar manner as the GetObject function in VBA.
AddChartAuto Format		Chart, Name As String, [Description]	Adds the formatting and legends of the Chart specified by the parameter to the custom chart types.
AddCustomList		ListArray, [ByRow]	Adds the array of strings specified by ListArray to Excel's custom lists. The ListArray may also be a cell range.
Calculate			Calculates all the formulas in all open workbooks that have changed since the last calculation. Only applicable if using manual calculation.
CalculateFull			Calculates all the formulas in all open workbooks. Forces recalculation of every formula in every workbook, regardless of whether or not it has changed since the last calculation.

Name	Returns	Parameters	Description
CalculateFull Rebuild			Completely calculates all open workbooks, including all formulas with dependencies.
CalculateFull Rebuild			Forces a full calculation of the data and rebuilds the dependencies for all open workbooks. Note that dependencies are the formulas that depend on other cells.
CentimetersTo Points	Double	Centimeters As Double	Converts the `Centimeters` parameter to points where 1 cm = 28.35 points.
CheckAbort		[KeepAbort]	Stops any recalculations in an Excel application.
CheckSpelling	Boolean	Word As String, [Custom Dictionary], [Ignore Uppercase]	Checks the spelling of the `Word` parameter and returns `True` if the spelling is correct or `False` if there are errors.
Convert Formula	Variant	Formula, FromReference Style As XlReference Style, [ToReference Style], [ToAbsolute], [RelativeTo]	Converts the `Formula` parameter between R1C1 references and A1 references and returns the converted formula. Also can change the `Formula` parameter between relative references and absolute references using the `ToReferenceStyle` parameter and the `XlReferenceStyle` constants.
DDEExecute		Channel As Long, String As String	Sends a `Command` to an application using DDE through the given `Channel` number. The properties starting with DDE are associated with the older technology, Dynamic Data Exchange, which was used to share data between applications.
DDEInitiate	Long	App As String, Topic As String	Returns a channel number to use for DDE given an application name and the DDE topic.
DDEPoke		Channel As Long, Item, Data	Sends `Data` to an item in an application using DDE through the given `Channel` number.
DDERequest	Variant	Channel As Long, Item As String	Returns information given a specific DDE channel and a requested item.

Table continued on following page

Name	Returns	Parameters	Description
DDETerminate		Channel As Long	Closes the specified DDE channel.
DeleteChart AutoFormat		Name As String	Deletes the custom chart type specified by the Name parameter.
DeleteCustom List		ListNum As Long	Deletes the custom list specified by the list number. The first four lists are built-in to Excel and cannot be removed.
DoubleClick			Triggered by a double-click to the active cell in the active sheet.
Evaluate	Variant	Name	Evaluates the Name string expression as if it were entered into a worksheet cell.
ExecuteExcel4 Macro	Variant	String As String	Executes the Excel 4 macro specified by the String parameter and returns the results.
FindFile	Boolean		Shows the Open dialog box allowing the user to choose a file to open. True is returned if the file opens successfully.
GetCustomList Contents	Variant	ListNum As Long	Returns the custom list specified by the ListNum parameter as an array of strings.
GetCustom ListNum	Long	ListArray	Returns the list number for the custom list that matches the given array of strings. A zero is returned if nothing matches.
GetOpen Filename	Variant	[FileFilter], [FilterIndex], [Title], [ButtonText], [MultiSelect]	The Open dialog box is displayed with the optional file filters, titles, and button texts specified by the parameters. The filename and path are returned from this method call. Optionally can return an array of filenames if the MultiSelect parameter is True. Does not actually open the file.
GetPhonetic	String	[Text]	Returns the phonetic text of the Japanese characters in the Text parameter. If no Text parameter is specified then an alternate phonetic text of the previous Text parameter is returned.

Name	Returns	Parameters	Description
`GetSaveAs Filename`	`Variant`	`[Initial Filename], [FileFilter], [FilterIndex], [Title], [ButtonText]`	The Save As dialog box is displayed with the optional default file name, file filters, titles, and button texts specified by the parameters. The filename and path are returned from this method call. Does not actually save the file.
`Goto`		`[Reference], [Scroll]`	Selects the object specified by the `Reference` parameter and activates the sheet containing that object. The `Reference` parameter can be a cell, range, or the name of a VBA procedure. The `Scroll` parameter, if set to `True`, will scroll the selected object to the top left corner of the Excel window.
`Help`		`[HelpFile], [HelpContext ID]`	Displays the help topic specified by the `HelpContextID` parameter in the help file `HelpFile`.
`InchesTo Points`	`Double`	`Inches As Double`	Converts the `Inches` parameter to points and returns the new value. (1 inch = 72 points).
`InputBox`	`Variant`	`Prompt As String, [Title], [Default], [Left], [Top], [HelpFile], [HelpContext ID], [Type]`	Displays a simple input box very similar to a standard VBA one. However, the `[Type]` parameter can be used to set the return type to a formula (0), number (1), text (2), Boolean (4), cell reference (8), an error value (16), or an array of values (64).
`Intersect`	`Range`	`Arg1 As Range, Arg2 As Range, [Arg3], ... [Arg30]`	Returns the intersection or overlap of the ranges specified by the parameters as a `Range` object.

Table continued on following page

Name	Returns	Parameters	Description
MacroOptions		[Macro], [Description], [HasMenu], [MenuText], [HasShortcut Key], [ShortcutKey], [Category], [StatusBar], [HelpContext ID], [HelpFile]	Allows modification of macro attributes such as the name, description, shortcut key, category and associated help file. Equivalent to the Macro Options dialog box.
MailLogoff			Logs off the current MAPI mail session (for example Exchange, Outlook)
MailLogon		[Name], [Password], [DownloadNew Mail]	Logs on to the default MAPI mail client (for example Exchange, Outlook). Credentials such as name and password can be specified.
NextLetter	Workbook		Used in Macintosh systems with PowerTalk mail extensions to open the oldest unread workbook from the In Tray. Generates an error in Windows.
OnKey		Key As String, [Procedure]	Executes the procedure specified by the Procedure parameter whenever the keystroke or key combination described in the `Key` parameter is pressed.
OnRepeat		Text As String, Procedure As String	Specifies the text to appear by the Edit | Repeat menu item and the procedure to run when the user chooses Edit | Repeat.
OnTime		EarliestTime, Procedure As String, [LatestTime], [Schedule]	Chooses a procedure to run at the time specified by the `EarliestTime` parameter. Uses the `LatestTime` parameter to specify a time range.
OnUndo		Text As String, Procedure As String	Specifies the text to appear by the Edit | Undo menu item and the procedure to run when the user chooses Edit | Undo.
Quit			Shuts down Microsoft Excel.

Name	Returns	Parameters	Description
RecordMacro		[BasicCode], [XlmCode]	If the user is currently recording a macro, running this statement will put the code specified in the `BasicCode` parameter into the currently recording macro.
RegisterXLL	Boolean	Filename As String	Loads the code resource specified by the `Filename` parameter and registers all the functions and procedures in that code resource.
Repeat			Repeats the last user action made. Must be the first line of a procedure.
Run	Variant	[Macro], [Arg1], [Arg2], ... [Arg30]	Runs the macro or procedure specified by the Macro parameter. Can also run Excel 4.0 macros with this method.
SaveWorkspace		[Filename]	Saves the current workspace to the `Filename` parameter.
SendKeys		Keys, [Wait]	Sends the keystrokes in the `Keys` parameter to Microsoft Excel user interface.
SetDefault Chart		[FormatName], [Gallery]	Set the default chart type added when programmatically adding a chart. The `FormatName` parameter can be a built-in chart type or a custom chart type name.
Undo			Undoes the last action done with the user interface.
Union	Range	Arg1 As Range, Arg2 As Range, [Arg3], ... [Arg30]	Returns the union of the ranges specified by the parameters.
Volatile		[Volatile]	Sets the function that currently contains this statement to be either volatile (`Volatile` parameter to `True`) or not. A volatile function will be recalculated whenever the sheet containing it is calculated, even if its input values have not changed.
Wait	Boolean	Time	Pauses the macro and Excel until the time in the `Time` parameter is reached.

Application Events

Name	Parameters	Description
NewWorkbook	Wb As Workbook	Triggered when a new workbook is created. The new workbook is passed into the event.
SheetActivate	Sh As Object	Triggered when a sheet is activated (brought up to front of the other sheets). The activated sheet is passed into the event.
SheetBefore DoubleClick	Sh As Object, Target As Range, Cancel As Boolean	Triggered when a sheet is about to be double-clicked. The sheet and the potential double-click spot are passed into the event. The double-click action can be canceled by setting the `Cancel` parameter to `True`.
SheetBefore RightClick	Sh As Object, Target As Range, Cancel As Boolean	Triggered when a sheet is about to be right-clicked. The sheet and the potential right-click spot are passed into the event. The right-click action can be canceled by setting the `Cancel` parameter to `True`.
Sheet Calculate	Sh As Object	Triggered when a sheet is recalculated passing in the recalculated sheet.
SheetChange	Sh As Object, Target As Range	Triggered when a range on a sheet is changed, for example by clearing the range, entering data, deleting rows or columns, pasting data etc. **Not** triggered when inserting rows/columns.
Sheet Deactivate	Sh As Object	Triggered when a sheet loses focus. Passes in the sheet.
SheetFollow Hyperlink	Sh As Object, Target As Hyperlink	Triggered when the user clicks on a hyperlink on a sheet. Passes in the sheet and the clicked hyperlink.
SheetPivot TableUpdate	ByVal Sh As Object, Target As PivotTable	Triggered by an update of the `PivotTable` report. Passes in the sheet and the `PivotTable` report.
Sheet Selection Change	Sh As Object, Target As Range	Triggered when the user selects a new cell in a worksheet. Passes in the new range and the sheet where the change occurred.
Window Activate	Wb As Workbook, Wn As Window	Triggered when a workbook window is activated (brought up to the front of other workbook windows). The workbook and the window are passed in.
Window Deactivate	Wb As Workbook, Wn As Window	Triggered when a workbook window loses focus. The related workbook and the window are passed in.

Name	Parameters	Description
WindowResize	Wb As Workbook, Wn As Window	Triggered when a workbook window is resized. The resized workbook and window are passed into the event. Not triggered when Excel is resized.
Workbook Activate	Wb As Workbook	Triggered when a workbook is activated (brought up to the front of other workbook windows). The workbook is passed in.
WorkbookAddin Install	Wb As Workbook	Triggered when an Addin is added to Excel that is also a workbook. The Addin workbook is passed into the event.
WorkbookAddin Uninstall	Wb As Workbook	Triggered when an Addin is removed to Excel that is also a workbook. The Addin workbook is passed into the event.
Workbook BeforeClose	Wb As Workbook, Cancel As Boolean	Triggered just before a workbook is closed. The workbook is passed into the event. The closure can be canceled by setting the `Cancel` parameter to `True`.
Workbook BeforePrint	Wb As Workbook, Cancel As Boolean	Triggered just before a workbook is printed. The workbook is passed into the event. The printing can be canceled by setting the `Cancel` parameter to `True`.
Workbook BeforeSave	Wb As Workbook, SaveAsUI As Boolean, Cancel As Boolean	Triggered just before a workbook is saved. The workbook is passed into the event. The saving can be canceled by setting the `Cancel` parameter to `True`. If the `SaveAsUI` is set to `True` then the **Save As** dialog box appears.
Workbook Deactivate	Wb As Workbook	Triggered when a workbook loses focus. The related workbook and the window are passed in.
WorkbookNew Sheet	Wb As Workbook, Sh As Object	Triggered when a new sheet is added to a workbook. The workbook and new sheet are passed into the event.
WorkbookOpen	Wb As Workbook	Triggered when a workbook is opened. The newly opened workbook is passed into the event.
WorkbookPivot TableClose Connection	ByVal Wb As Workbook, Target As PivotTable	Triggered when a `PivotTable` report connection is closed. The selected workbook and `PivotTable` report are passed in to this event.
WorkbookPivot TableOpen Connection	ByVal Wb As Workbook, Target As PivotTable	Triggered when a `PivotTable` report connection is opened. The selected workbook and `PivotTable` report are passed in to this event.

Example: Application Object

This example demonstrates how to use `Application.GetOpenFilename` to get the name of a file to open. The key to using this function is to assign its return value to a `Variant` data type:

```
Sub UsingGetOpenFilename()
   Dim sFilter As String
   Dim vaFile As Variant

   'Build a filter list.  If you omit the space before the first comma,
   'Excel will not display the pattern, (*.New)
   sFilter = "New Files (*.New) ,*.new," & _
             "Old Files (*.Old) ,*.old," & _
             "All Files (*.*) ,*.*"

   'Display the File Open dialog, putting the result in a Variant
   vaFile = Application.GetOpenFilename(FileFilter:=sFilter, FilterIndex:=1, _
                              Title:="Open a New or Old File",
MultiSelect:=False)

   'Did the user cancel?
   If vaFile <> False Then
      MsgBox "You want to open " & vaFile
   End If
End Sub

The Application object is used to store and retrieve custom sort orders:

Sub UsingACustomSortOrder()
   Dim vaSortList As Variant
   Dim iListNum As Integer
   Dim bAdded As Boolean

   'Sort the products in this order
   vaSortList = Array("Oranges", "Mangoes", "Apples", "Pears")

   'Get the number of this custom sort, if it exists.
   iListNum = Application.GetCustomListNum(vaSortList)

   'If it doesn't exist, we get zero, NOT an error
   If iListNum = 0 Then
      'Create a custom list for this sort order
      Application.AddCustomList vaSortList

      'And retrieve its number (the last one!)
      iListNum = Application.CustomListCount

      'Remember that we added it - delete it after use
      bAdded = True
   End If

   'Sort the range using this custom list.  Note that we have to
   'add 1 to the list number, as 'ordercustom:=1' means to use the
   'standard sort order (which is not a custom list)
   ActiveCell.CurrentRegion.Sort key1:=ActiveCell, _
                              ordercustom:=iListNum + 1, header:=xlYes

   'If we added the list, remove it.
   If bAdded Then Application.DeleteCustomList iListNum
End Sub
```

Chapter 3 in the first section of this book contains more examples of using the `Application` object.

Areas Collection

The `Areas` collection holds a collection of `Range` objects. Each `Range` object represents a block of cells (for example A1:A10) or a single cell. The `Areas` collection can hold many ranges from different parts of a workbook. The parent of the `Areas` collection is the `Range` object.

Areas Common Properties

The `Application`, `Creator`, and `Parent` properties are defined at the beginning of this appendix.

Areas Properties

Name	Returns	Description
`Count`	`Long`	Read Only. Returns the number of `Range` objects that are contained in the area.
`Item`	`Range`	Parameter: `Index As Long`. Returns a single `Range` object in the `Areas` collection. The `Index` parameter corresponds to the order of the ranges selected.

Example: Areas Collection

When using a `Range` containing a number of different areas, we cannot use code like `rgRange.Cells(20).Value` if the twentieth cell is not inside the first area in the range. This is because Excel only looks at the first area, implicitly doing `rgRange.Areas(1).Cells(20).Value`, as this example shows – with a function to provide a workaround:

```
Sub TestMultiAreaCells()
   Dim oRNg As Range

   'Define a multi-area range
   Set oRNg = Range("D2:F5,H2:I5")

   'The 12th cell should be F5.
   MsgBox "Rng.Cells(12) is " & oRNg.Cells(12).Address & _
          vbCrLf & "Rng.Areas(1).Cells(12) is " & _
                   oRNg.Areas(1).Cells(12).Address & _
          vbCrLf & "MultiAreaCells(Rng, 12) is " & _
                   MultiAreaCells(Rng, 12).Address

   'The 13th cell of the multi-area range should be H2,
   'that is the first cell in the second area.
   MsgBox "Rng.Cells(13) is " & oRNg.Cells(13).Address & _
           vbCrLf & "Rng.Areas(1).Cells(13) is " & _
                    oRNg.Areas(1).Cells(13).Address & _
           vbCrLf & "MultiAreaCells(Rng, 13) is " & _
                    MultiAreaCells(Rng, 13).Address
End Sub

Function MultiAreaCells(oRange As Range, iCellNum As Long) As Range
   Dim iTotCells As Long, oArea As Range

   'Loop through all the areas in the range,
   'starting again from the first if we run out
   Do
      For Each oArea In oRange.Areas
```

```
            'Is the cell we want in this area?
            If iTotCells + oArea.Cells.Count >= iCellNum Then

               'Yes - return it and exit the function
               Set MultiAreaCells = oArea.Cells(iCellNum - iTotCells)
               Exit Function
            Else
               'No - count up the cells we've checked and carry on
               iTotCells = iTotCells + oArea.Cells.Count
            End If
         Next
      Loop
   End Function
```

AutoCorrect Object

The `AutoCorrect` object represents all of the functionality of the Excel's `AutoCorrect` features.

AutoCorrect Common Properties

The `Application`, `Creator`, and `Parent` properties are defined at the beginning of this appendix.

AutoCorrect Properties

Name	Returns	Description
`CapitalizeNamesOfDays`	`Boolean`	Set/Get whether the first letter of days of the weeks are capitalized.
`CorrectCapsLock`	`Boolean`	Set/Get whether typing mistakes made with leaving the Caps Lock on are automatically corrected.
`CorrectSentenceCap`	`Boolean`	Set/Get whether the first letter of a sentence is capitalized if accidentally left in small case.
`DisplayAutoCorrectOptions`	`Boolean`	Displays / Hides the **AutoCorrect Options** button. The default value is `True`. This is an Office-wide setting. Changing it in Excel will also affect all the other Office applications.
`ReplaceText`	`Boolean`	Set/Get whether Excel will automatically replace certain words with words from the `AutoCorrect` list.
`TwoInitialCapitals`	`Boolean`	Set/Get whether Excel will automatically change the second letter of a word to lowercase if the first letter is uppercase.

AutoCorrect Methods

Name	Returns	Parameters	Description
Add Replacement	Variant	What As String, Replacement As String	Adds a word (the `What` parameter) that will be automatically replaced with another word (the `Replacement` parameter) to the `ReplacementList` list array.
Delete Replacement	Variant	What As String	Deletes a word from the `ReplacementList` list so that it does not get replaced with another word automatically.
Replacement List	Variant	[Index]	Returns a multidimensional array of strings. The first column of the array holds the word that will be changed and the second column holds the replaced text. The `Index` parameter can be used to return an array containing a single word and its replacement.

Example: AutoCorrect Object

This example uses the `AutoCorrect` object to find the replacement to use for a given word:

```
Sub TestAutoCorrect()
   MsgBox "'(c)' is replaced by " & UseAutoCorrect("(c)")
End Sub

Function UseAutoCorrect(ByVal sWord As String) As String
   Dim i As Integer
   Dim vaRepList As Variant
   Dim sReturn As String

   'Default to returning the word we were given
   sReturn = sWord

   'Get the replacement list into an array
   vaRepList = Application.AutoCorrect.ReplacementList

   'Go through the replacement list
   For i = LBound(vaRepList) To UBound(vaRepList)
      'Do we have a match?
      If vaRepList(i, 1) = sWord Then

         'Return the replacement text
         sReturn = vaRepList(i, 2)

         'Jump out of the loop
         Exit For
      End If
   Next

   'Return the word, or its replacement if it has one
   UseAutoCorrect = sReturn
End Function
```

AutoFilter Object

The `AutoFilter` object provides the functionality equivalent to the `AutoFilter` feature in Excel. This object can programmatically filter a range of text for specific types of rows, hiding the rows that do not meet the filter criteria. Examples of filters include top 10 rows in the column, rows matching specific values, and non-blank cells in the row. Using the **Data | Filter | AutoFilter** submenu in Excel can access this feature. The parent of the `AutoFilter` object is the `Worksheet` object (implying that a worksheet can have only one `AutoFilter`).

The `AutoFilter` object is used with the `AutoFilter` method of the `Range` object and the `AutoFilterType` property of the `Worksheet` object.

AutoFilter Common Properties

The `Application`, `Creator`, and `Parent` properties are defined at the beginning of this appendix.

AutoFilter Properties

Name	Returns	Description
`Filters`	`Filters`	Read Only. Returns the collection of filters associated with the range that was autofiltered (for example non-blank rows)
`Range`	`Range`	Read Only. Returns the group of cells that have an `AutoFilter` applied to it.

Example: AutoFilter Object

This example demonstrates how to use the `AutoFilter`, `Filters` and `Filter` objects, by displaying the complete set of auto-filters currently in use:

```
Sub ShowAutoFilterCriteria()
   Dim oAF As AutoFilter, oFlt As Filter
   Dim sField As String
   Dim sCrit1 As String, sCrit2 As String
   Dim sMsg As String, i As Integer

   'Check if the sheet is filtered at all
   If ActiveSheet.AutoFilterMode = False Then
      MsgBox "The sheet does not have an AutoFilter"
      Exit Sub
   End If

   'Get the sheet's AutoFilter object
   Set oAF = ActiveSheet.AutoFilter

   'Loop through the Filters of the AutoFilter
   For i = 1 To oAF.Filters.Count

      'Get the field name from the first row
      'of the AutoFilter range
      sField = oAF.Range.Cells(1, i).Value

      'Get the Filter object
      Set oFlt = oAF.Filters(i)
```

```
        'If it is on...
        If oFlt.On Then

            'Get the standard filter criteria
            sMsg = sMsg & vbCrLf & sField & oFlt.Criteria1

            'If it's a special filter, show it
            Select Case oFlt.Operator
                Case xlAnd
                    sMsg = sMsg & " And " & sField & oFlt.Criteria2

                Case xlOr
                    sMsg = sMsg & " Or " & sField & oFlt.Criteria2

                Case xlBottom10Items
                    sMsg = sMsg & " (bottom 10 items)"

                Case xlBottom10Percent
                    sMsg = sMsg & " (bottom 10%)"

                Case xlTop10Items
                    sMsg = sMsg & " (top 10 items)"

                Case xlTop10Percent
                    sMsg = sMsg & " (top 10%)"

            End Select
        End If
    Next

    If sMsg = "" Then
        'No filters are applied, so say so
        sMsg = "The range " & oAF.Range.Address & " is not filtered."
    Else
        'Filters are applied, so show them
        sMsg = "The range " & oAF.Range.Address & " is filtered by:" & sMsg
    End If

    'Display the message
    MsgBox sMsg
End Sub
```

AutoRecover Object

This object allows access to the `AutoRecover` settings for the Excel application. These settings can be found on the **Save** tab of the **Tools | Options** command and apply to all workbooks. Note that each workbook can choose whether or not to have `AutoRecover` applied to it – also located on the **Save** tab.

AutoRecover Common Properties

The `Application`, `Creator`, and `Parent` properties are defined at the beginning of this appendix.

AutoRecover Properties

Name	Returns	Description
Enabled	Boolean	True if the AutoRecover object is enabled.
Path	String	Set/Get the complete path to where the AutoRecover temporary files are saved.
Time	Long	Set/Get the time interval for the AutoRecover object. Permissible values are integers from 1 to 120 minutes (default 10).

Example: AutoRecover Object

The following subroutine and function sets AutoRecover properties, then ensures that the workbook the code is in uses them:

```
Sub SetAutoRecoverOptions()
    'Set the AutoRecover options for the application
    ChangeAutoRecoverSettings True, "C:\Documents and Settings\AgamaOffice\My
Documents\Backup Files\AutoRecover\Excel", 2

    'Make sure this workbook uses them
    ThisWorkbook.EnableAutoRecover = True
End Sub

Function ChangeAutoRecoverSettings(Optional ByVal vEnable As Variant, Optional
ByVal vPath As Variant, Optional ByVal vTime As Variant)
    With Application.AutoRecover
        'Only set the property if a value was passed
        If Not IsMissing(vEnable) Then
            'Enable AutoRecover
            .Enabled = vEnable
        End If

        'Only set the property if a value was passed
        If Not IsMissing(vPath) Then
            'Change the path to a central backup files area
            .Path = vPath
        End If

        'Only set the property if a value was passed
        If Not IsMissing(vTime) Then
            'Save every AutoRecover file every 2 minutes
            .Time = vTime
        End If
    End With
End Function
```

Axis Object and the Axes Collection

The Axes collection represents all the of Axes in an Excel chart. Each Axis object is equivalent to an axis in an Excel chart (for example X axis, Y axis, etc). The parent of the Axes collection is the Chart object.

Besides the typical properties and methods associated with a collection object, the Axes collection also has a Count property that returns the number of Axis objects in the collection. Also, unlike most other collections, the Item method of the Axes collection has two parameters: Type and AxisGroup. Use one of the xlAxisType constants for the Type parameter (xlValue, xlCategory, or xlSeriesAxis). The optional second parameter, AxisGroup, can take one of the xlAxisGroup constants (xlPrimary or xlSecondary).

Axis Common Properties

The Application, Creator, and Parent properties are defined at the beginning of this appendix.

Axis Properties

Name	Returns	Description
AxisBetween Categories	Boolean	Set/Get whether the value axis crosses the category axis between categories (as in Column charts) or aligned with the category label (as in Line charts).
AxisGroup	XlAxis Group	Read Only. Returns whether the current axis is of the primary group (xlPrimary) or the secondary group (xlSecondary).
AxisTitle	AxisTitle	Read Only. Returns an object manipulating the axis title properties.
BaseUnit	XlTime Unit	Set/Get what type of base units to have for a category axis. Use with BaseUnitIsAuto property. Fails on a value axis.
BaseUnitIsAuto	Boolean	Set/Get whether the Excel automatically chooses the base units for a category axis. Fails on a value axis.
Border	Border	Read Only. Returns the border's properties around the selected axis.
CategoryNames	Variant	Set/Get the category names for the axis as a string array.
CategoryType	XlCategory Type	Set/Get what type of axis to make the category axis. Fails on a value axis.
Crosses	XlAxis Crosses	Set/Get where one axis crosses with the other axis: at the minimum value, maximum value, Excel automatic, or some custom value.
CrossesAt	Double	Set/Get what value the other axis crosses the current one. Use when the Crosses property is xlAxisCrossesCustom.
DisplayUnit	XlDisplay Unit	Set/Get what sort of unit to display for the axis (for example xlThousands).

Table continued on following page

Name	Parameters	Description
DisplayUnit Custom	Double	Set/Get the value to display units if the DisplayUnit property is set to xlCustom.
DisplayUnit Label	DisplayUnit Label	Read Only. Returns an object that manipulates a unit label for an axis.
HasDisplay UnitLabel	Boolean	Set/Get whether a display unit label created using the DisplayUnit or DisplayUnitCustom property is visible on the axis.
HasMajor Gridlines	Boolean	Set/Get whether major gridlines are displayed on the axis.
HasMinor Gridlines	Boolean	Set/Get whether minor gridlines are displayed on the axis
HasTitle	Boolean	Set/Get whether the axis has a title.
Height	Double	Read Only. Returns the height of the axis.
Left	Double	Read Only. Returns the position of the axis from the left edge of the chart.
Major Gridlines	Gridlines	Read Only. Returns an object to manipulate the major gridlines formatting associated.
MajorTickMark	XlTickMark	Set/Get how the major ticks should look like (for example inside the axis, outside the axis).
MajorUnit	Double	Set/Get what the value is between major blocks of a unit.
MajorUnitIs Auto	Boolean	Set/Get whether the value of MajorUnit is set automatically.
MajorUnit Scale	XlTimeUnit	Set/Get what type to set for the major units.
MaximumScale	Double	Set/Get what the maximum value is for the axis.
MaximumScale IsAuto	Boolean	Set/Get whether the maximum value for the axis is determined automatically.
MinimumScale	Double	Set/Get what the minimum value is for the axis.
MinimumScale IsAuto	Boolean	Set/Get whether the minimum value for the axis is determined automatically.
Minor Gridlines	Gridlines	Read Only. Returns an object to manipulate major gridline formatting associated.
MinorTickMark	XlTickMark	Set/Get what the minor ticks should look like (for example inside the axis, outside the axis).
MinorUnit	Double	Set/Get what the value is between minor blocks of a unit.
MinorUnitIs Auto	Boolean	Set/Get whether the value of MinorUnit is set automatically.
MinorUnitScale	XlTimeUnit	Set/Get what scale to set for the minor units.

Name	Parameters	Description
ReversePlot Order	Boolean	Set/Get whether the unit values on the axis should be reversed.
ScaleType	XlScale Type	Set/Get the type of scale to use for the units: Linear or Logarithmic.
TickLabel Position	XlTickLabel Position	Set/Get the position that the tick marks will appear in relation to the axis (for example low, high).
TickLabels	TickLabels	Read Only. Returns an object to manipulate properties of the tick labels of an axis.
TickLabel Spacing	Long	Set/Get how often to display the tick labels.
TickMark Spacing	Long	Set/Get how often to display tick marks on an axis. Fails on a value axis.
Top	Double	Read Only. Returns the top of the axis in relation to the top edge of the chart.
Type	XlAxisType	Set/Get the type of axis (`xlCategory`, `xlSeriesAxis`, or `xlValue`).
Width	Double	Read Only. Returns the width of the axis.

Axis Methods

Name	Returns	Parameters	Description
Delete	Variant		Deletes the axis from the axes collection
Select	Variant		Selects the axis on the chart

Example: Axis Object and the Axes Collection

This example sets the labels for the X-axis (independently of the data that's plotted) and applies some formatting:

```
Sub FormatXAxis()
   Dim oCht As Chart, oAxis As Axis

   'Get the first embedded chart on the sheet
   Set oCht = ActiveSheet.ChartObjects(1).Chart

   'Get it's X axis
   Set oAxis = oCht.Axes(xlCategory)

   'Format the X axis
   With oAxis
      .CategoryNames = Array("Item 1", "Item 2", "Item 3")
      .TickLabels.Orientation = 45
      .AxisBetweenCategories = True
      .ReversePlotOrder = False
      .MinorTickMark = xlTickMarkNone
```

```
        .MajorTickMark = xlTickMarkCross
    End With
End Sub
```

AxisTitle Object

The AxisTitle object contains the formatting and words associated with a chart axis title. The parent of the AxisTitle object is the Axis object. The AxisTitle object is used in coordination with the HasTitle property of the parent Axis object. The HasTitle property must be True for a child AxisTitle object to exist.

AxisTitle Common Properties

The Application, Creator, and Parent properties are defined at the beginning of this appendix.

AxisTitle Properties

Name	Returns	Description
AutoScaleFont	Variant	Set/Get whether the font size will change automatically if the parent chart changes sizes.
Border	Border	Read Only. Returns the border's properties around the selected axis title.
Caption	String	Set/Get the axis title's text.
Characters	Characters	Read Only. Parameters: [Start], [Length]. Returns an object containing all the characters in the axis title. Allows manipulation on a character-by-character basis.
Fill	ChartFill Format	Read Only. Returns an object containing fill formatting options for the chart axis title.
Font	Font	Read Only. Returns an object containing Font options for the chart axis title.
Horizontal Alignment	Variant	Set/Get how you want the axis title horizontally aligned. Use the xlAlign constants.
Interior	Interior	Read Only. Returns an object containing options to format the area in the chart title text area (for example interior color).
Left	Double	Set/Get the distance from the left edge of the axis title text area to the chart's left edge.
Name	String	Read Only. Returns the name of the axis title object.
Orientation	Variant	Set/Get the angle of the text for the axis title. The value can be in degrees (from –90 to 90) or one of the XlOrientation constants.
ReadingOrder	Long	Set/Get how the text is read (from left to right or right to left). Only applicable in appropriate languages.

Name	Returns	Description
Shadow	Boolean	Set/Get whether the axis title has a shadow effect.
Text	String	Set/Get the axis title's text.
Top	Double	Set/Get the distance from the top edge of the axis title text area to the chart's top edge.
Vertical Alignment	Variant	Set/Get how you want the axis title horizontally aligned. Use the xlVAlign constants.

AxisTitle Methods

Name	Returns	Parameters	Description
Delete	Variant		Deletes the axis title from the axis
Select	Variant		Selects the axis title on the chart

Example: AxisTitle Object

This example ensures the X-axis has a title and sets the X-axis title's caption and formatting:

```
Sub FormatXAxisTitle()
   Dim oCht As Chart, oAT As AxisTitle

   'Get the first embedded chart on the sheet
   Set oCht = ActiveSheet.ChartObjects(1).Chart

   'Give the X axis a title
   oCht.Axes(xlCategory).HasTitle = True

   'Get the title
   Set oAT = oCht.Axes(xlCategory).AxisTitle

   'Format the title
   With oAT
      .AutoScaleFont = False
      .Caption = "X Axis Title"
      .Font.Bold = True
   End With
End Sub
```

Border Object and the Borders Collection

The Borders collection contains the properties associated with four borders around the parent object. Parent objects of the Borders collection are the Range and the Style object. A Borders collection always has four borders. Use the xlBordersIndex constants with the Item property of the Borders collection to access one of the Border objects in the collection.

Each Border object corresponds to a side or some sides of a border around a parent object. Some objects only allow access to all four sides of a border as a whole (for example left side of border can not be accessed independently). The following objects are parents of the Border object (not the Borders collection): Axis, AxisTitle, ChartArea, ChartObject, ChartTitle, DataLabel, DataTable, DisplayUnitLabel, Downbars, DropLines, ErrorBars, Floor, GridLines, HiLoLines, LeaderLines, Legend, LegendKey, OleObject, PlotArea, Point, Series, SeriesLines, TrendLine, UpBars, and Walls. The following collections are also possible parents of the Border object: DataLabels, ChartObjects, and OleObjects.

The Borders collection has a few properties besides the typical collection attributes. They are listed in the following table.

Borders Collection Properties

Name	Returns	Description
Color	Variant	Set/Get the color for all four of the borders in the collection. Use the RGB function to set the color.
ColorIndex	Variant	Set/Get the color for all four of the borders in the collection. Use the index number of a color in the current color palette to set the Color value.
Count	Long	Read Only. Returns the number of Border objects in the collection. Always returns four.
LineStyle	Variant	Set/Get the style of line to use for the borders (for example xlDash). Use the xlLineStyle constants to set the value.
Value	Variant	Set/Get the style of line to use for the borders (for example xlDash). Use the xlLineStyle constants to set the value. Same as LineStyle.
Weight	Variant	Set/Get how thick to make the borders in the collection (for example xlThin, xlThick). Use the xlBorderWeight constants.

Border Common Properties

The Application, Creator, and Parent properties are defined at the beginning of this appendix.

Border Properties

Name	Returns	Description
Color	Variant	Set/Get the color for a border. Use the RGB function to set the color.
ColorIndex	Variant	Set/Get the color for a border. Use the index number of a color in the current color palette to set the color value.
LineStyle	Variant	Set/Get the style of line to use for a border (for example xlDash). Use the xlLineStyle constants to set the value.
Weight	Variant	Set/Get how thick to make the border (for example. xlThin, xlThick). Use the xlBorderWeight constants.

Example: Border Object and the Borders Collection

Applies a 3D effect to a range:

```
Sub TestFormat3D()
   'Format the selected range as 3D sunken
   Format3D Selection
End Sub

Sub Format3D(oRange As Range, Optional bSunken As Boolean = True)
   'Using the range...
   With oRange
      'Surround it with a white border
      .BorderAround Weight:=xlMedium, Color:=RGB(255, 255, 255)

      If bSunken Then
         'Sunken, so make the left and top dark-grey
         .Borders(xlEdgeLeft).Color = RGB(96, 96, 96)
         .Borders(xlEdgeTop).Color = RGB(96, 96, 96)
      Else
         'Raised, so make the right and bottom dark-grey
         .Borders(xlEdgeRight).Color = RGB(96, 96, 96)
         .Borders(xlEdgeBottom).Color = RGB(96, 96, 96)
      End If
   End With
End Sub
```

CalculatedFields Collection

See the *PivotField Object, PivotFields Collection and the CalculatedFields Collection* section.

CalculatedItems Collection

See the *PivotItem Object, PivotItems Collection, and the CalculatedItems Collection* section.

CalculatedMember Object and the CalculatedMembers Collection

The `CalculatedMembers` collection is a collection of all the `CalculatedMember` objects on the specified `PivotTable`. Each `CalculatedMember` object represents a calculated field, or calculated item.

CalculatedMembers Common Properties

The `Application`, `Creator`, and `Parent` properties are defined at the beginning of this appendix.

CalculatedMembers Collection Properties

Name	Returns	Description
`Count`	`Long`	Returns the number of objects in the collection.
`Item`	`Calculated Member`	Parameter: `Index As Variant`. Returns a single `CalculatedMember` object in the `CalculatedMembers` collection.

CalculatedMembers Collection Methods

Name	Returns	Parameters	Description
`Add`	`Calculated Member`	`Name As String, Formula As String, [SolveOrder], [Type]`	Adds a `CalculatedField` or `CalculatedItem` to a `PivotTable`

CalculatedMember Common Properties

The `Application`, `Creator`, and `Parent` properties are defined at the beginning of this appendix.

CalculatedMember Properties

Name	Returns	Description
`Formula`	`String`	Returns the `CalculatedMember`'s formula in multidimensional expressions (MDX) syntax.
`IsValid`	`Boolean`	Indicates whether the specified `CalculatedMember` object has been successfully instantiated with the OLAP provider during the current session. Will return `True` even if the `PivotTable` is not connected to its data source.
`Name`	`String`	Set/Get the name of the object.
`SolveOrder`	`Long`	Gets the value of the `CalculatedMember`'s MDX (multidimensional expression) argument (default is zero).
`SourceName`	`String`	Gets the object's name as it appears in the original source data for the specified `PivotTable` report.
`Type`	`Xl Calculated MemberType`	Gets the `CalculatedMember` object's type.

CalculatedMember Methods

Name	Returns	Parameters	Description
`Delete`			Deletes the selected object

Example: CalculatedMembers Collection and CalculatedMember Object

The following routine returns information about each `CalculatedMember` from the data source used by the PivotTable on the `wksPivotTable` worksheet. It returns messages if either the data source is not an OLAP type or if there are no `CalculatedMembers`:

```
Sub ReturnCalculatedMembers()

    Dim lIcon As Long, lCount As Long
    Dim ptTable As PivotTable
    Dim oCalcMember As CalculatedMember
    Dim oCalcMembers As CalculatedMembers
    Dim sInfo As String

    'Set the reference to the PivotTable
    Set ptTable = wksPivotTable.PivotTables("WroxSales1")

    On Error Resume Next
        Set oCalcMembers = ptTable.CalculatedMembers
    On Error GoTo 0

    'Did we return a reference to Calculated Members?
    If Not oCalcMembers Is Nothing Then
        'If there's at least one Calculated Member...
        If oCalcMembers.Count > 0 Then
            'Initialize the Count
            ' and message variables
            lCount = 1
            lIcon = vbInformation

            'Loop through each Calculated Member
            ' And store its name and formula
            For Each oCalcMember In oCalcMembers
                With oCalcMember
                    sInfo = sInfo & lCount & ") " & .Name & ": " & .Formula
                    lCount = lCount + 1
                End With
            Next oCalcMember

        Else
            'It's a valid OLAP data source, but no
            ' Calculated Members are there
            lIcon = vbExclamation
            sInfo = "No Calculated Members found."
        End If
    Else
        'oCalcMembers returned nothing. Not an OLAP data source
        lIcon = vbCritical
        sInfo = "Could not retrieve Calculated Members. Data Source may not be
OLAP type."
    End If

    MsgBox sInfo, lIcon, "Calculated Members"

End Sub
```

CalloutFormat Object

The `CalloutFormat` object corresponds to the line callouts on shapes. The parent of the `CalloutFormat` object is the `Shape` object.

CalloutFormat Common Properties

The `Application`, `Creator`, and `Parent` properties are defined at the beginning of this appendix.

CalloutFormat Properties

Name	Returns	Description
Accent	MsoTriState	Set/Get whether a vertical accent bar is used to separate the callout box from the line.
Angle	MsoCallout AngleType	Set/Get the angle of the callout line in relation to the callout box.
AutoAttach	MsoTriState	Set/Get whether a callout line automatically changes where it is attached to the callout box depending on the where the line is pointing (left or right of the callout box).
AutoLength	MsoTriState	Read Only. Return whether the callout line changes size automatically if the multi-segment callout box is moved.
Border	MsoTriState	Set/Get whether the callout box has a border around it.
Drop	Single	Read Only. Returns the distance from the callout box to the spot where the callout line is pointing.
DropType	MsoCallout DropType	Read Only. Returns the spot on the callout box that attaches to the callout line.
Gap	Single	Set/Get the distance between the callout line end and the callout box.
Length	Single	Read Only. Returns the length of the first part of a callout line. `AutoLength` must be `False`.
Type	MsoCallout Type	Set/Get the type of line callout used.

CalloutFormat Methods

Name	Returns	Parameters	Description
Automatic Length			Sets the `AutoLength` property to `True`.
CustomDrop		Drop As Single	Uses the `Drop` parameter to set the distance from the callout box to the spot where the callout line is pointing.
CustomLength		Length As Single	Sets the length of the first part of a callout line to the `Length` parameter and sets `AutoLength` to `False`.
PresetDrop		DropType As MsoCallout DropType	Sets the spot on the callout box that attaches to the callout line using the `DropType` parameter.

Example: CalloutFormat Object

This example applies the same formatting to all the callouts in a worksheet:

```
Sub FormatAllCallouts()
   Dim oShp As Shape
   Dim oCF As CalloutFormat

   'Loop through all the shapes in the sheet
   For Each oShp In ActiveSheet.Shapes

      'Is this a callout?
      If oShp.Type = msoCallout Then

         'Yes - set its text box to autosize
         oShp.TextFrame.AutoSize = True

         'Get the CalloutFormat object
         Set oCF = oShp.Callout

         'Format the callout
         With oCF
            .Gap = 0
            .Border = msoFalse
            .Accent = msoTrue
            .Angle = msoCalloutAngle30
            .PresetDrop msoCalloutDropCenter
         End With
      End If
   Next
End Sub
```

CellFormat Object

Represents both the `FindFormat` and `ReplaceFormat` property settings of the `Application` object, which are then used by the `Find` and `Replace` methods (respectively) of the `Range` object.

Set the `FindFormat` property settings before using the `Find` method to search for cell formats within a range. Set the `ReplaceFormat` property settings if you want the `Replace` method to replace formatting in cells. Any values specified in the `What` or `Replacement` arguments of either the `Find` or `Replace` methods will involve an `And` condition. For example, if you are searching for the word "wrox" and have set the `FindFormat` property to search for Bold, only those cells containing both will be found.

When searching for formats, make sure the `SearchFormat` argument of the `Find` method is set to `True`. When replacing formats, make sure the `ReplaceFormat` argument of the `Replace` method is set to `True`.

When you want to search for formats only, make sure the `What` argument of the `Find` method contains nothing. When you only want to replace formats, make sure the `Replace` argument of the `Replace` method contains nothing.

When replacing one format with another, make sure you explicitly specify formats you no longer want. For example, if you are searching for cells containing both bold and red and want to replace both formats with just blue, you'll need to make sure you set the bold property of the `ReplaceFormat` property to `False`. If you don't, you'll end up with blue and bold text.

When you need to search or replace using different format settings (or none at all), be sure to use the `Clear` method of either the `CellFormat` object – if you've declared a variable as such, or by directly accessing the `Clear` methods of the `FindFormat` and `ReplaceFormat` properties. Setting the `SearchFormat` and `ReplaceFormat` arguments to `False` for the `Find` and `Replace` methods will **not** prevent the `FindFormat` and/or `ReplaceFormat` settings from being used.

CellFormat Common Properties

The `Application`, `Creator`, and `Parent` properties are defined at the beginning of this appendix.

CellFormat Properties

Name	Returns	Description
`AddIndent`	`Variant`	Gets whether the text in a cell is automatically indented when the text alignment is set to equal distribution either horizontally or vertically.
`Borders`	`Borders`	Set/Get the search criteria based on the cell's border format.
`Font`	`Font`	Set/Get the search criteria based on the cell's font format.
`FormulaHidden`	`Variant`	Gets whether the formula will be hidden when the worksheet is protected. Returns `Null` if the specified range contains some cells with hidden formulas and some cells without.
`HorizontalAlignment`	`Variant`	Set/Get the horizontal alignment for the specified object.
`IndentLevel`	`Variant`	Set/Get the indent level for the cell or range.
`Interior`	`Interior`	Set/Get the search criteria based on the cell's interior format.
`Locked`	`Variant`	Set/Get whether cells in the range can be modified if the sheet is protected. Returns `Null` if only some of the cells in the range are locked.
`MergeCells`	`Variant`	Returns `True` if the range or style contains merged cells.
`NumberFormat`	`Variant`	Set/Get the number format associated with the cells in the range. `Null` if all the cells don't have the same format.
`NumberFormatLocal`	`Variant`	Set/Get the number format associated with the cells in the range in the language of the end user. `Null` if all the cells don't have the same format.
`Orientation`	`Variant`	Set/Get the text orientation for the cell text. A value from -90 to 90 degrees can be specified, or use an `XlOrientation` constant.
`ShrinkToFit`	`Variant`	Set/Get whether the cell text will automatically shrink to fit the column width. Returns `Null` if the rows in the range have different `ShrinkToFit` properties.
`VerticalAlignment`	`Variant`	Set/Get how the cells in the range are vertically aligned. Use the `XLVAlign` constants.
`WrapText`	`Variant`	Set/Get whether cell text wraps in the cell. Returns `Null` if the cells in the range contain different text wrap properties.

CellFormat Methods

Name	Returns	Parameters	Description
`Clear`			Removes the criteria set in the `FindFormat` and `ReplaceFormat` properties

Example: CellFormat Object

The following routine searches through the used range in a worksheet replacing any cells containing both a Tahoma font and a light blue background with Arial light green background:

```
Sub ReplaceFormats()

    Dim oCellFindFormat As CellFormat
    Dim oCellReplaceFormat As CellFormat
    Dim rngReplace As Boolean, sMessage As String

    'Define variables for Find and Replace formats
    Set oCellFindFormat = Application.FindFormat
    Set oCellReplaceFormat = Application.ReplaceFormat

    'Set the Search criteria for the Find Formats
    With oCellFindFormat
        .Clear
        .Font.Name = "Tahoma"
        .Interior.ColorIndex = 34
    End With

    'Set the Replace criteria for the Replace Formats
    With oCellReplaceFormat
        .Clear
        .Font.Name = "Arial"
        .Interior.ColorIndex = 35
    End With

    'Perform the replace
    wksAllowEditRange.UsedRange.Replace What:="", Replacement:="", _
                                        SearchFormat:=True, _
                                        ReplaceFormat:=True

    'Reset the Find and Replace formats
    oCellFindFormat.Clear
    oCellReplaceFormat.Clear

End Sub
```

Characters Object

The `Characters` object allows access to individual characters in a string of text. Characters can have some of the visual properties modified with this object. Possible parents of the `Characters` object are the `AxisTitle`, `ChartTitle`, `DataLabel`, and the `Range` object. Each of the parent objects can use the `Characters([Start], [Length])` property to access a part of their respective texts. The `Start` parameter can specify which character to start at and the `Length` parameter can specify how many to take from the `Start` position.

Characters Common Properties

The `Application`, `Creator`, and `Parent` properties are defined at the beginning of this appendix.

Characters Properties

Name	Returns	Description
`Caption`	`String`	Set/Get the full string contained in the `Characters` object.
`Count`	`Long`	Read Only. Returns the number of characters in the object.
`Font`	`Font`	Read Only. Returns an object allowing manipulation of the character's font.
`Phonetic Characters`	`String`	Set/Get the phonetic characters contained in the `Characters` object.
`Text`	`String`	Set/Get the full string contained in the `Characters` object.

Characters Methods

Name	Returns	Parameters	Description
`Delete`	`Variant`		Deletes the characters in the collection.
`Insert`	`Variant`	`String As String`	Replaces the characters in the collection with the specified string.

Example: Characters Object

This example formats all the capital letters in the active cell in red with 16 point bold text:

```
Sub FormatCellCapitals()
   Dim sText As String
   Dim oChars As Characters
   Dim i As Integer

   'Get the text of the active cell
   sText = ActiveCell.Text

   'Loop through the text
   For i = 1 To Len(sText)
      'Is this character a capital letter?
      If Asc(Mid(sText, i, 1)) > 64 And Asc(Mid(sText, i, 1)) < 91 Then

         'Yes, so get the Characters object
         Set oChars = ActiveCell.Characters(i, 1)

         'Format the Characters object in Red, 16pt Bold.
         With oChars
            .Font.Color = RGB(255, 0, 0)
            .Font.Size = 16
```

```
            .Font.Bold = True
          End With
        End If
      Next
    End Sub
```

Chart Object and the Charts Collection

The `Charts` collection holds the collection of chart sheets in a workbook. The `Workbook` object is always the parent of the `Charts` collection. The `Charts` collection only holds the chart sheets. Individual charts can also be embedded in worksheets and dialog sheets. The `Chart` objects in the `Charts` collection can be accessed using the `Item` property. Either the name of the chart can be specified as a parameter to the `Item`'s parameter or an index number describing the position of the chart in the workbook (from left to right).

The `Chart` object allows access to all of the attributes of a specific chart in Excel. This includes chart formatting, chart types, and other charting properties. The `Chart` object also exposes events that can be used programmatically.

The `Charts` collection has a few properties and methods besides the typical collection attributes. These are listed in the following table.

Charts Collection Properties and Methods

Name	Returns	Description
`Count`	`Long`	Read Only. Returns the number of charts in the collection.
`HPageBreaks`	`HPageBreaks`	Read Only. Returns a collection holding all the horizontal page breaks associated with the `Charts` collection.
`VPageBreaks`	`VPageBreaks`	Read Only. Returns a collection holding all the vertical page breaks associated with the `Charts` collection.
`Visible`	`Variant`	Set/Get whether the charts in the collection are visible. Also can set this to `xlVeryHidden` to not allow a user to make the charts in the collection visible.
`Add`	`Chart`	Method. Parameters: `[Before], [After], [Count]`. Adds a chart to the collection. You can specify where the chart goes by choosing which sheet object will be before the new chart object (`Before` parameter) or after the new chart (`After` parameter). The `Count` parameter decides how many charts are created.
`Copy`		Method. Parameters: `[Before], [After]`. Adds a new copy of the currently active chart to the position specified at the `Before` or `After` parameters.
`Delete`		Method. Deletes all the charts in the collection.
`Move`		Method. Parameters: `[Before], [After]`. Moves the current chart to the position specified by the parameters.

Table continued on following page

Name	Returns	Description
PrintOut		Method. Parameters: [From], [To], [Copies], [Preview], [ActivePrinter], [PrintToFile], [Collate], [PrToFileName]. Prints out the charts in the collection. The printer, number of copies, collation, and whether a print preview is desired can be specified with the parameters. Also, the sheets can be printed to a file using the PrintToFile and PrToFileName parameters. The From and To parameters can be used to specify the range of printed pages.
PrintPreview		Method. Parameters: [EnableChanges]. Displays the current chart in the collection in a print preview mode. Set the EnableChanges parameter to False to disable the **Margins** and **Setup** buttons, hence not allowing the viewer to modify the chart's page setup.
Select		Method. Parameters: [Replace]. Selects the current chart in the collection.

Chart Common Properties

The Application, Creator, and Parent properties are defined at the beginning of this appendix.

Chart Properties

Name	Returns	Description
Area3DGroup	ChartGroup	Read Only. Returns a ChartGroup object containing the area chart group for a 3-D chart.
AutoScaling	Boolean	Set/Get whether Excel will stretch a 3-D chart to match its 2-D chart equivalent. RightAngleAxes must be true.
Bar3DGroup	ChartGroup	Read Only. Returns a ChartGroup object containing the bar chart group for a 3-D chart.
BarShape	XlBarShape	Set/Get the basic shape used in 3D bar or column charts (for example box, cylinder, pyramid, etc).
ChartArea	ChartArea	Read Only. Returns the part of a chart containing axes, titles, legends, and formatting properties.
ChartTitle	ChartTitle	Read Only. Returns an object manipulating the chart title's properties. Use with the HasTitle property.
ChartType	XlChart Type	Set/Get what the type of chart is. This property determines what other chart properties are valid. For example, if the ChartType is set to xl3DBarClustered then the Bar3DGroup property can be used to access the chart group properties.

Name	Returns	Description
CodeName	String	Read Only. Returns the programmatic name of the chart set at design time in the VBA editor.
Column3DGroup	ChartGroup	Read Only. Returns a ChartGroup object containing the column chart group for a 3-D chart.
Corners	Corners	Read Only. Returns an object holding all the corners of a 3D chart.
DataTable	DataTable	Read Only. Returns an object to manipulate a chart's data table.
DepthPercent	Long	Set/Get the percentage that a 3D chart depth (y-axis) is in relation to its width (x-axis).
Display BlanksAs	XlDisplay BlanksAs	Set/Get how blank cells are treated when plotting data in a chart. (for example xlNotPlotted, xlZero, or xlInterpolated).
Elevation	Long	Set/Get what angle of elevation, in degrees, the viewer sees a 3D chart. Valid degrees vary depending on the type of 3D chart.
Floor	Floor	Read Only. Returns an object with the formatting properties of the floor (base) of a 3D chart.
GapDepth	Long	Set/Get the percentage depth of a data series in relation to the marker width.
HasAxis	Variant	Parameters: [Index1], [Index2]. Set/Get whether axes exist for the chart. The parameters can be used to specify the axis type (using the xlAxisType constants with the first parameter) and the axis group (using the xlAxisGroup constants with the second parameter).
HasDataTable	Boolean	Set/Get whether a data table is associated (and therefore displayed). Use with the DataTable property.
HasLegend	Boolean	Set/Get whether the chart has a legend. Use with the Legend property.
HasPivot Fields	Boolean	Set/Get whether PivotChart controls are displayed for the PivotChart. Can only set to True if using a PivotChart report.
HasTitle	Boolean	Set/Get whether the chart has a title. Use with the ChartTitle property.
Height Percent	Long	Set/Get the percentage that a 3D chart height (z-axis) is in relation to its width (x-axis).
Hyperlinks	Hyperlinks	Read Only. Returns the collection of hyperlinks associated with the chart.
Index	Long	Read Only. Returns the spot in the parent collection where the current chart is located.

Table continued on following page

Name	Returns	Description
Legend	Legend	Read Only. Returns the formatting properties for a Legend. Use with the HasLegend property.
Line3DGroup	ChartGroup	Read Only. Returns a ChartGroup object containing the line chart group for a 3-D chart.
MailEnvelope	MsoEnvelope	Set/Get the e-mail header for a document.
Name	String	Set/Get the name of the chart.
Next	Object	Read Only. Returns the next sheet in the workbook (from left to right) as an object.
PageSetup	PageSetup	Read Only. Returns an object to manipulate the page setup properties for the chart.
Perspective	Long	Sets the perspective, in degrees, that a 3D chart will be viewed as if the RightAngleAxes property is set to False.
Pie3DGroup	ChartGroup	Read Only. Returns a ChartGroup object containing the pie chart group for a 3-D chart.
PivotLayout	Pivot Layout	Read Only. Returns an object to manipulate the location of fields for a PivotChart report.
PlotArea	PlotArea	Read Only. Returns an object to manipulate formatting, gridlines, data markers and other visual items for the area where the chart is actually plotted. Inside the chart area.
PlotBy	XlRowCol	Set/Get whether columns in the original data are used as individual data series (xlColumns) or if the rows in the original data are used as data series (xlRows).
PlotVisible Only	Boolean	Set/Get whether only visible cells are plotted or if invisible cells are plotted too (False).
Previous		Read Only. Returns the previous sheet in the workbook (from right to left) as an object.
Protect Contents	Boolean	Read Only. Returns whether the chart and everything in it is protected from changes.
ProtectData	Boolean	Set/Get whether the source data can be redirected for a chart.
Protect Drawing Objects	Boolean	Read Only. Returns whether the shapes in the chart can be modified (ProtectDrawingObjects = False).
Protect Formatting	Boolean	Set/Get whether formatting can be changed for a chart.
Protect GoalSeek	Boolean	Set/Get whether the user can modify the points on a chart with a mouse action.

Name	Returns	Description
Protection Mode	Boolean	Read Only. Returns whether protection has been applied to the user interface. Even if a chart has user interface protection on, any VBA code associated with the chart can still be accessed.
Protect Selection	Boolean	Set/Get whether parts of a chart can be selected and if shapes can be put into a chart.
RightAngle Axes	Variant	Set/Get whether axes are fixed at right angles for 3D charts even if the perspective of the chart changes.
Rotation	Variant	Set/Get what angle of rotation around the z-axis, in degrees, the viewer sees on a 3D chart. Valid degrees vary depending on the type of 3D chart.
Scripts	Scripts	Read Only. Returns the collection of VBScript code associated with a chart (typically to later use on web pages).
Shapes	Shapes	Read Only. Returns all the shapes contained by the chart.
ShowWindow	Boolean	Set/Get whether an embedded chart is shown in a separate window and not as an embedded object in the worksheet.
SizeWith Window	Boolean	Set/Get whether chart sheets automatically change sizes to match the window size.
SurfaceGroup	ChartGroup	Read Only. Returns a `ChartGroup` object containing the surface chart group for a 3-D chart.
Tab	Tab	Read Only. Returns a `Tab` object for a chart or a worksheet.
Visible	XlSheet Visibility	Set/Get whether the chart is visible or not. The `Visible` property can also be set to `xlVeryHidden` to make the chart inaccessible to the end user.
Walls	Walls	Read Only. Returns an object to manipulate the formatting of the walls on a 3D chart.
WallsAnd Gridlines2D	Boolean	Set/Get whether gridlines and walls are drawn in a 2D manner on a 3D bar charts, 3D stacked area charts, and 3D clustered column charts.

Chart Methods

Name	Returns	Parameters	Description
Activate			Activates the chart making it the `ActiveChart`.
ApplyCustom Type		ChartType As XlChartType, [TypeName]	Changes the chart type to the one specified in the `ChartType` parameter. If the `ChartType` is `xlUserDefined` then the second parameter can specify the custom chart type name.

Table continued on following page

Name	Returns	Parameters	Description
ApplyData Labels		[Type As Xl DataLabels Type],[Legend Key], [Auto Text], [Has LeaderLines], [ShowSeries Name], [Show CategoryName], [ShowValue], [Show Percentage], [ShowBubble Size], [Separator]	Sets the point labels for a chart. The Type parameter specifies whether no label, a value, a percentage of the whole, or a category label is shown. The legend key can appear by the point by setting the LegendKey parameter to True.
AreaGroups	Object	[Index]	Returns either a single area chart group (ChartGroup) or a collection of area chart groups (ChartGroups) for a 2D chart.
Axes	Object	Type, AxisGroup As XlAxisGroup	Returns the Axis object or the Axes collection for the associated chart. The type of axis and the axis group can be specified with the parameters.
BarGroups	Object	[Index]	Returns either a single bar chart group (ChartGroup) or a collection of bar chart groups (ChartGroups) for a 2D chart.
ChartGroups	Object	[Index]	Returns either a single chart group (ChartGroup) or a collection of chart groups (ChartGroups) for a chart.
ChartObjects	Object	[Index]	Returns either a single embedded chart (ChartObject) or a collection of embedded charts (ChartObjecs) in a chart.
ChartWizard		[Source], [Gallery], [Format], [PlotBy], [Category Labels], [Series Labels], [HasLegend], [Title], [Category Title], [ValueTitle], [ExtraTitle]	A single method to modify the key properties associated with a chart. Specify the properties that you want to change. The Source specifies the data source. Gallery specifies the chart type. Format can specify one of the 10 built-in chart auto-formats. The rest of the parameters set up how the source will be read, the source of category labels, the source of the series labels, whether a legend appears, and the titles of the chart and the axis. If Source is not specified this method can only be used if the sheet containing the chart is active.

Name	Returns	Parameters	Description
CheckSpelling		[Custom Dictionary], [Ignore Uppercase], [Always Suggest], [SpellLang]	Checks the spelling of the text in the chart. A custom dictionary can be specified (CustomDictionary), all **uppercase** words can be ignored (IgnoreUppercase), and Excel can be set to display a list of suggestions (AlwaysSuggest).
ColumnGroups	Object	[Index]	Returns either a single column chart group (ChartGroup) or a collection of column chart groups (ChartGroups) for a 2D chart.
Copy		[Before], [After]	Adds a new copy of the chart to the position specified at the Before or After parameters.
CopyPicture		[Appearance As XlPicture Appearance], [Format As XlCopyPictur e Format], [Size As XlPicture Appearance]	Copies the chart into the clipboard as a picture. The Appearance parameter can be used to specify whether the picture is copied as it looks on the screen or when printed. The Format parameter can specify the type of picture that will be put into the clipboard. The Size parameter is used when dealing with chart sheets to describe the size of the picture.
Create Publisher		Edition, Appearance As XlPicture Appearance, Size As XlPictureA ppearance, [Contains PICT], [Contains BIFF], [Contains RTF], [Contains VALU]	Used on the Macintosh to create an image of the chart in a standard format. Equivalent to CopyPicture on the PC.
Delete			Deletes the chart.
Deselect			Unselects the chart object.
Doughnut Groups	Object	[Index]	Returns either a single doughnut chart group (ChartGroup) or a collection of doughnut chart groups (ChartGroups) for a 2D chart.

Table continued on following page

Name	Returns	Parameters	Description
Evaluate	Variant	Name	Evaluates the Name string expression as if it were entered into a worksheet cell.
Export	Boolean	Filename As String, [FilterName], [Interactive]	Saves the chart as a picture (jpg or gif format) at the name specified by Filename.
GetChartElement		x As Long, y As Long, ElementID As Long, Arg1 As Long, Arg2 As Long	Returns what is located at the coordinates x and y of the chart. Only the first two parameters are sent. Variables must be put in the last three parameters. After the method is run the last three parameters can be checked for return values. The ElementID parameter will return one of the XlChartItem parameters. The Arg1 and Arg2 parameters may or may not hold data depending on the type of element.
LineGroups	Object	[Index]	Returns either a single line chart group (ChartGroup) or a collection of line chart groups (ChartGroups) for a 2D chart.
Location	Chart	Where As XlChart Location, [Name]	Moves the chart to the location specified by the Where and Name parameters. The Where can specify if the chart is moving to become a chart sheet or an embedded object.
Move		[Before], [After]	Moves the chart to the position specified by the parameters.
OLEObjects	Object	[Index]	Returns either a single OLE Object. (OLEObject) or a collection of OLE objects (OLEObjects) for a chart.
Paste		[Type]	Pastes the data or pictures from the clipboard into the chart. The Type parameter can be used to specify if only formats, formulas or everything is pasted.
PieGroups	Object	[Index]	Returns either a single pie chart group (ChartGroup) or a collection of pie chart groups (ChartGroups) for a 2D chart.

Name	Returns	Parameters	Description
PrintOut		[From], [To], [Copies], [Preview], [Active Printer], [PrintToFile], [Collate], [PrToFile Name]	Prints out the chart. The printer, number of copies, collation, and whether a print preview is desired can be specified with the parameters. Also, the sheets can be printed to a file by using the PrintToFile and PrToFileName parameters. The From and To parameters can be used to specify the range of printed pages.
PrintPreview		[Enable Changes]	Displays the current chart in the collection in a print preview mode. Set the EnableChanges parameter to False to disable the **Margins** and **Setup** buttons, hence not allowing the viewer to modify the page setup.
Protect		[Password], [Drawing Objects], [Contents], [Scenarios], [User Interface Only]	Protects the chart from changes. A case-sensitive Password can be specified. Also, whether shapes are protected (DrawingObjects), the entire contents are protected (Contents), and whether only the user interface is protected (UserInterfaceOnly).
RadarGroups	Object	[Index]	Returns either a single radar chart group (ChartGroup) or a collection of radar chart groups (ChartGroups) for a 2D chart.
Refresh			Refreshes the chart with the data source.
SaveAs		Filename As String, [FileFormat], [Password], [WriteRes Password], [ReadOnly Recommended], [Create Backup], [AddToMru], [Text Codepage], [TextVisual Layout], [Local]	Saves the current chart into a new workbook with the file name specified by the Filename parameter. A file format, password, write-only password, creation of backup files, and other properties of the saved file can be specified with the parameters.

Table continued on following page

Name	Returns	Parameters	Description
Select		[Replace]	Selects the chart.
Series Collection	Object	[Index]	Returns either a single series (Series) or a collection of series (SeriesCollection) for a chart.
SetBackground Picture		FileName As String	Sets the chart's background to the picture specified by the FileName parameter.
SetSourceData		Source As Range, [PlotBy]	Sets the source of the chart's data to the range specified by the Source parameter. The PlotBy parameter uses the XlRowCol constants to choose whether rows or columns of data will be plotted.
Unprotect		[Password]	Deletes the protection set up for a chart. If the chart was protected with a password, the password must be specified now.
XYGroups	Object	[Index]	Returns either a single scatter chart group (ChartGroup) or a collection of scatter chart groups (ChartGroups) for a 2D chart.

Chart Events

Name	Parameters	Description
Activate		Triggered when a chart is made to have focus.
BeforeDouble Click	ElementID As XlChartItem , Arg1 As Long, Arg2 As Long, Cancel As Boolean	Triggered just before a user double-clicks on a chart. The element that was double-clicked in the chart is passed in to event procedure as ElementID. The Arg1 and Arg2 parameters may or may not hold values depending on the ElementID. The double-click action can be canceled by setting the Cancel parameter to True.
BeforeRight Click	Cancel As Boolean	Triggered just before a user right-clicks on a chart. The right-click action can be canceled by setting the Cancel parameter to True.
Calculate		Triggered after new or changed data is plotted on the chart.
Deactivate		Triggered when the chart loses focus.

Name	Returns	Parameters	Description
DragOver			Triggered when a cell range is dragged on top of a chart. Typically used to change the mouse pointer or give a status message.
DragPlot			Triggered when a cell range is dropped onto a chart. Typically used to modify chart attributes.
MouseDown		Button As XlMouse Button, Shift As Long, x As Long, y As Long	Triggered when the mouse button is pressed down on a chart. Which mouse button is pressed is passed in with the `Button` parameter. The `Shift` parameter holds information regarding the state of the Shift, Ctrl, and Alt keys. The `x` and `y` parameters hold the x and y coordinates of the mouse pointer.
MouseMove		Button As XlMouse Button, Shift As Long, x As Long, y As Long	Triggered when the mouse is moved on a chart. Which mouse button is pressed is passed in with the `Button` parameter. The `Shift` parameter holds information regarding the state of the Shift, Ctrl, and Alt keys. The `x` and `y` parameters hold the x and y coordinates of the mouse pointer.
MouseUp		Button As XlMouse Button, Shift As Long, x As Long, y As Long	Triggered when the mouse button is released on a chart. Which mouse button is pressed is passed in with the `Button` parameter. The `Shift` parameter holds information regarding the state of the Shift, Ctrl, and Alt keys. The `x` and `y` parameters hold the x and y coordinates of the mouse pointer.
Resize			Triggered when the chart is resized.
Select		ElementID As XlChartItem, Arg1 As Long, Arg2 As Long	Triggered when one of the elements in a chart is selected. The element that was selected in the chart is passed in to event procedure as `ElementID`. The `Arg1` and `Arg2` parameters may or may not hold values depending on the `ElementID`.
SeriesChange		SeriesIndex As Long, PointIndex As Long	Triggered when the value of a point on a chart is changed. `SeriesIndex` returns the location of the series in the chart series collection. `PointIndex` returns the point location in the series.

Example: Chart Object and the Charts Collection

This example creates a 3D chart from the table containing the active cell, formats it and saves a picture of it as a `.jpg` image:

```
Sub CreateAndExportChart()
   Dim oCht As Chart

   'Create a new (blank) chart
   Set oCht = Charts.Add
```

```
    'Format the chart
    With oCht
        .ChartType = xl3DColumnStacked

        'Set the data source and plot by columns
        .SetSourceData Source:=Selection.CurrentRegion, PlotBy:=xlColumns

        'Create a new sheet for the chart
        .Location Where:=xlLocationAsNewSheet

        'Size and shape matches the window it's in
        .SizeWithWindow = True

        'Turn of stretching of chart
        .AutoScaling = False

        'Set up a title
        .HasTitle = True
        .ChartTitle.Caption = "Main Chart"

        'No titles for the axes
        .Axes(xlCategory).HasTitle = False
        .Axes(xlSeries).HasTitle = False
        .Axes(xlValue).HasTitle = False

        'Set the 3D view of the chart
        .RightAngleAxes = False
        .Elevation = 50   'degrees
        .Perspective = 30 'degrees
        .Rotation = 20    'degrees
        .HeightPercent = 100

        'No data labels should appear
        .ApplyDataLabels Type:=xlDataLabelsShowNone

        'Save a picture of the chart as a jpg image
        .Export "c:\" & .Name & ".jpg", "jpg", False
    End With
End Sub
```

ChartArea Object

The `ChartArea` object contains the formatting options associated with a chart area. For 2D charts `ChartArea` includes the axes, axes titles and chart titles. For 3D charts `ChartArea` includes the chart title and its legend. The part of the chart where data is plotted (plot area) is not part of the `ChartArea` object. Please see the `PlotArea` object for formatting related to the plot area. The parent of the `ChartArea` is always the `Chart` object.

ChartArea Common Properties

The `Application`, `Creator`, and `Parent` properties are defined at the beginning of this appendix.

ChartArea Properties

Name	Returns	Description
`AutoScaleFont`	`Variant`	Set/Get whether the font size changes in the `ChartArea` whenever the `Chart` changes sizes.

Name	Returns	Description
Border	Border	Read Only. Returns the border's attributes around the selected chart area.
Fill	ChartFill Format	Read Only. Returns an object to manipulate the fill attributes of the chart area.
Font	Font	Read Only. Returns access to `Font` properties such as `Type` and `Size`.
Height	Double	Set/Get the height of the chart area in points.
Interior	Interior	Read Only. Returns an object containing options to format the inside area of the chart area (for example interior color).
Left	Double	Set/Get the left edge of the chart area in relation to the chart in points.
Name	String	Read Only. Returns the name of the chart area.
Shadow	Boolean	Set/Get whether a shadow effect appears around the chart area.
Top	Double	Set/Get the top edge of the chart area in relation to the chart in points.
Width	Double	Set/Get the width of the chart area in points.

ChartArea Methods

Name	Returns	Parameters	Description
Clear	Variant		Clears the chart area
ClearContents	Variant		Clears the data from the chart area without affecting formatting
ClearFormats	Variant		Clears the formatting from the chart area without affecting the data
Copy	Variant		Copies the chart area into the clipboard
Select	Variant		Activates and selects the chart area

Example: ChartArea Object

Apply formatting to the chart area:

```
Sub FormatChartArea()
    Dim oCA As ChartArea

    Set oCA = Charts(1).ChartArea

    With oCA
        .Border.LineStyle = xlContinuous
        .Fill.PresetTextured msoTextureCanvas
```

```
        .Fill.Visible = msoTrue
    End With
End Sub
```

ChartColorFormat Object

The `ChartColorFormat` object describes a color of the parent `ChartFillFormat`. For example, the `ChartFillFormat` object contains a `BackColor` property that returns a `ChartColorFormat` object to set the color.

ChartColorFormat Common Properties

The `Application`, `Creator`, and `Parent` properties are defined at the beginning of this appendix.

ChartColorFormat Properties

Name	Returns	Description
`RGB`	`Long`	Read Only. Returns the red-green-blue value associated with color.
`SchemeColor`	`Long`	Set/Get the color of `ChartColorFormat` using an index value corresponding to the current color scheme.
`Type`	`Long`	Read Only. Returns whether the color is an RGB, mixed, or scheme type.

Example: ChartColorFormat Object

This example sets a chart's fill pattern to built-in colour number 6, then displays the RGB values for the color.

```
Sub SetChartColorFormat()
   Dim oCCF As ChartColorFormat

   With Charts(3).PlotArea.Fill
      'Make sure we're using a Fill pattern
      .Visible = True

      'Get the ChartColorFormat for the ForeColor
      Set oCCF = .ForeColor

      'Set it to built-in colour #6
      oCCF.SchemeColor = 6

      'Read off colour 6's RGB values
      MsgBox "ForeColor #6 RGB is:" & vbCrLf & _
      "Red = " & ((oCCF.RGB And &HFF0000) / &H10000) & vbCrLf & _
      "Green = " & ((oCCF.RGB And &HFF00) / &H100) & vbCrLf & _
      "Blue = " & ((oCCF.RGB And &HFF))
   End With
End Sub
```

ChartFillFormat Object

The ChartFillFormat object represents the fill formatting associated with its parent object. This object allows manipulation of foreground colors, background colors and patterns associated with the parent object.

ChartFillFormat Common Properties

The Application, Creator, and Parent properties are defined at the beginning of this appendix.

ChartFillFormat Properties

Name	Returns	Description
BackColor	ChartColor Format	Read Only. Returns the background color through the ChartColorFormat object.
ForeColor	ChartColor Format	Read Only. Returns the foreground color through the ChartColorFormat object.
GradientColor Type	Mso Gradient ColorType	Read Only. Returns what type of gradient fill color concept is used.
GradientDegree	Single	Read Only. Returns how dark or light the gradient fill is.
GradientStyle	Mso Gradient Style	Read Only. Returns the orientation of the gradient that is used.
Gradient Variant	Long	Read Only. Returns the variant used for the gradient from the center.
Pattern	MsoPattern Type	Read Only. Returns the pattern used for the fill, if any.
PresetGradient Type	MsoPreset Gradient Type	Read Only. Returns the type of gradient that is used.
PresetTexture	MsoPreset Texture	Read Only. Returns the non-custom texture of the fill.
TextureName	String	Read Only. Returns the custom texture name of the fill.
TextureType	MsoTexture Type	Read Only. Returns whether the texture is custom, preset, or mixed.
Type	MsoFillType	Set/Get how transparent the fill is. From 0 (opaque) to 1 (clear).
Visible	MsoTriState	Read Only. Returns if the fill is a texture, gradient, solid, background, picture or mixed.

ChartFillFormat Methods

Name	Returns	Parameters	Description
OneColor Gradient		Style As MsoGradient Style, Variant As Long, Degree As Single	Sets the style, variant and degree for a one-color gradient fill
Patterned		Pattern As MsoPattern Type	Set the pattern for a fill
Preset Gradient		Style As MsoGradient Style, Variant As Long, Preset GradientType As MsoPreset GradientType	Choose the style, variant, and preset gradient type for a gradient fill
Preset Textured		PresetTexture As MsoPreset Texture	Set the preset texture for a fill
Solid			Set the fill to a solid color
TwoColor Gradient		Style As MsoGradient Style, Variant As Long	Set the style for a two-color gradient fill
UserPicture		[PictureFile], [Picture Format], [Picture StackUnit], [Picture Placement]	Set the fill to the picture in the PictureFile format
UserTextured		TextureFile As String	Set the custom texture for a fill with the TextureFile format

Example: ChartFillFormat Object

```
Sub FormatPlotArea()
   Dim oCFF As ChartFillFormat

   'Get the ChartFillFormat for the plot area
   Set oCFF = ActiveSheet.ChartObjects(1).Chart.PlotArea.Fill

   'Format the fill area
   With oCFF
      .TwoColorGradient Style:=msoGradientDiagonalUp, Variant:=1
      .Visible = True
      .ForeColor.SchemeColor = 6
      .BackColor.SchemeColor = 7
   End With
End Sub
```

ChartGroup Object and the ChartGroups Collection

The ChartGroups collection holds all the plotting information associated with the parent chart. A chart can have more than one ChartGroup associated with it. For example, a single chart can contain both a line and a bar chart associated with it. The ChartGroups property of the Chart object can be used to access the ChartGroups collection. Also, the PieGroups and LineGroups properties of the Chart object will also return only chart groups of pie chart types and line chart types, respectively.

Besides the typical properties associated with a collection, the ChartGroups collection also has a Count property that returns the number of ChartGroup objects in the collection. The parent of the ChartGroups collection or the ChartGroup object is the Chart object.

The ChartGroup object includes all of the plotted points associated with a particular chart type. A ChartGroup can hold many series of points (each column or row of the original data). Each series can contain many points (each cell of the original data). A Chart can contain more than one ChartGroup associated with it. The Bar3DGroup, Column3DGroup, Line3DGroup, Pie3DGroup, and the SurfaceGroup properties of the Chart object can be used to access a particular chart group of the corresponding chart type. The AreaGroups, BarGroups, ColumnGroups, DoughnutGroups, LineGroups, PieGroups, RadarGroups, and XYGroups methods of the Chart object can be used to return either a ChartGroup object or a ChartGroups collection.

ChartGroup Common Properties

The Application, Creator, and Parent properties are defined at the beginning of this appendix.

ChartGroup Properties

Name	Returns	Description
AxisGroup	XlAxis Group	Set/Get whether the chart group is primary or secondary.
BubbleScale	Long	Set/Get the percentage increase in the size of bubbles from the default size. Valid values from 0 to 300 percent. Valid only for bubble chart group.
DoughnutHole Size	Long	Set/Get how large the hole in a doughnut chart group is. The value is a percentage of the size of the chart. Valid values from 10 to 90 percent. Valid only on doughnut chart groups.
DownBars	DownBars	Read Only. Returns an object to manipulate the formatting options of down bars on a line chart group. Valid only on line chart groups. Use with the HasUpDownBars property.
DropLines	DropLines	Read Only. Returns an object to manipulate the formatting options of drop lines on a line or area chart group. Valid only on line or area chart groups. Use with the HasDropLines property.
FirstSlice Angle	Long	Set/Get what angle to use for the first slice of a pie or doughnut chart groups (the first data point plotted on the chart).

Name	Returns	Description
GapWidth	Long	Set/Get how big to make the gap between the columns of different data series. Also, when dealing with Bar of Pie charts or Pie of Pie charts, the GapWidth describes the distance from the main chart to the secondary chart (when the ChartType is xlPieOfPie or xlBarOfPie for the parent chart).
Has3Dshading	Boolean	Set/Get whether 3D shading is applied to the chart group visuals.
HasDropLines	Boolean	Set/Get whether the chart group has drop lines. Use with the DownLines property.
HasHiLoLines	Boolean	Set/Get whether the chart group has high-low lines. Use with the HiLoLines property.
HasRadarAxis Labels	Boolean	Set/Get whether axis labels are put on a radar chart. Valid only for radar chart groups.
HasSeries Lines	Boolean	Set/Get whether the chart group has series lines. Use with the SeriesLines property.
HasUpDownBars	Boolean	Set/Get whether the chart group has up and down bars. Use with the DownBars and UpBars property.
HiLoLines	HiLoLines	Read Only. Returns an object to manipulate the formatting of high-low lines in a line chart. Valid only for line charts.
Index	Long	Read Only. Returns the spot in the parent collection that the current ChartGroup object is located.
Overlap	Long	Set/Get whether bars and columns in a series will overlap each other or have a gap between them. A value from –100 to 100 can be specified where –100 will put a gap between each bar / column equal to the bar / column width and 100 will stack the bars / columns on top of each other. Valid only for 2D bar and column chart groups.
RadarAxis Labels	TickLabels	Read Only. Returns an object to manipulate the formatting and labels associated with radar axis labels. Valid only for radar chart groups.
SecondPlot Size	Long	Set/Get the percentage of size of the secondary part of a Pie of Pie or Bar of Pie chart group as a percentage of the main Pie.
SeriesLines	SeriesLines	Read Only. Returns an object to manipulate the formatting associated with the series lines in a chart group. A series line connects same series of data appearing in a stacked column chart groups, stacked bar chart groups, Pie of Pie chart groups, or Bar of Pie chart groups. Use with the HasSeriesLines property.

Name	Returns	Description
ShowNegative Bubbles	Boolean	Set/Get whether bubbles with negative data values are shown. Valid only on bubble chart groups.
Size Represents	XlSize Represents	Set/Get whether the value of the data points are represented by the size or the area of bubbles on a bubble chart group. Valid only on bubble chart groups.
SplitType	XlChart SplitType	Set/Get how the two charts in Pie of Pie chart group and Bar of Pie chart group are split up. For example, the chart can be split by percentage of value (`xlSplitByPercentValue`) or be split by value (`xlSplitByValue`).
SplitValue	Variant	Set/Get the value that will be combined in the main pie chart but split up in the secondary chart in a Pie of Pie or Bar of Pie chart group.
UpBars	UpBars	Returns an object to manipulate the formatting options of up bars on a line chart group. Valid only on line chart groups. Use with the `HasUpDownBars` property.
VaryBy Categories	Boolean	Set/Get whether different colors are assigned to different categories in a single series of a chart group. The chart can only contain a single data series for this to work.

ChartGroup Methods

Name	Returns	Parameters	Description
Series Collection	Object	[Index]	Returns either a single series (`Series`) or a collection of series (`SeriesCollection`) for a chart.

Example: ChartGroup Object and the ChartGroups Collection

This sets the gap width of all column groups in the chart to 10% and set each column to have a different color:

```
Sub FormatColumns()
   Dim oCht As Chart
   Dim oCG As ChartGroup

   For Each oCG In Charts(1).ColumnGroups
      oCG.GapWidth = 10
      oCG.VaryByCategories = True
   Next
End Sub
```

ChartObject Object and the ChartObjects Collection

The ChartObjects collection holds all of the embedded Chart objects in a worksheet, chart sheet, or dialog sheet. This collection does not include the actual chart sheets themselves. Chart sheets can be accessed through the Charts collection. Each Chart in the ChartObjects collection is accessed through the ChartObject object. The ChartObject acts as a wrapper for the embedded chart itself. The Chart property of the ChartObject is used to access the actual chart. The ChartObject object also contains properties to modify the formatting of the embedded chart (for example Height, Width).

The ChartObjects collection contains many properties besides the typical collection attributes. These properties are listed below.

ChartObjects Collection Properties and Methods

Name	Returns	Description
Border	Border	Read Only. Returns the border's properties around the collection of chart objects.
Count	Long	Read Only. Returns the number of ChartObject objects in the collection.
Enabled	Boolean	Set/Get whether any macros associated with each ChartObject object in the collection can be triggered by the user.
Height	Double	Set/Get the height of the ChartObject in the collection if there is only one object in the collection.
Interior	Interior	Read Only. Returns an object containing options to format the inside area of all the Chart objects in the collection (for example interior color).
Left	Double	Set/Get the distance from the left edge of the ChartObject to the left edge of the parent sheet. This property only works if there is only one ChartObject in the collection.
Locked	Boolean	Set/Get whether the ChartObject is locked when the parent sheet is protected. This property only works if there is only one ChartObject in the collection.
Placement	Variant	Set/Get how the ChartObject object is anchored to the sheet (for example free floating, move with cells). Use the XlPlacement constants to set this property. This property only works if there is only one ChartObject in the collection.
PrintObject	Boolean	Set/Get whether the embedded chart on the sheet will be printed when the sheet is printed. This property only works if there is only one ChartObject in the collection.

Name	Returns	Description
Rounded Corners	Boolean	Set/Get whether the corners of the embedded chart are rounded (True) or right angles (False). This property only works if there is only one ChartObject in the collection.
Shadow	Boolean	Set/Get whether a shadow appears around the embedded chart. This property only works if there is only one ChartObject in the collection.
ShapeRange	ShapeRange	Read Only. Returns the ChartObjects in the collection as Shape objects.
Top	Double	Set/Get the distance from top edge of the ChartObject to the top of the parent sheet. This property only works if there is only one ChartObject object in the collection.
Visible	Boolean	Set/Get whether all the ChartObject objects in the collection are visible.
Width	Double	Set/Get the width of the ChartObject in the collection if there is only one ChartObject object in the collection.
Add	ChartObject	Method. Parameters: Left As Double, Top As Double, Width As Double, Height As Double. Adds a ChartObject to the collection of ChartObjects. The position of the new ChartObject can be specified by using the Left, Top, Width, and Height parameters.
BringToFront	Variant	Method. Brings all the ChartObject objects in the collection to the front of all the other objects.
Copy	Variant	Method. Copies all the ChartObject objects in the collection into the clipboard.
CopyPicture	Variant	Method. Parameters: Appearance As XlPictureAppearance, Format As XlCopyPictureFormat. Copies the Chart objects in the collection into the clipboard as a picture. The Appearance parameter can be used to specify whether the picture is copied as it looks on the screen or when printed. The Format parameter can specify the type of picture that will be put into the clipboard.
Cut	Variant	Method. Cuts all the ChartObject objects in the collection into the clipboard.
Delete	Variant	Method. Deletes all the ChartObject objects in the collection into the clipboard.

Table continued on following page

Name	Returns	Description
`Duplicate`		Method. Duplicates all the `ChartObject` objects in the collection into the parent sheet. (for example if you had two `ChartObject` objects in the parent sheet and used this method then you would have four `ChartObject` objects).
`Select`	`Variant`	Method. Parameters: `[Replace]`. Selects all the `ChartObject` objects in the collection.
`SendToBack`	`Variant`	Method. Brings the `ChartObject` objects in the collection to the back of other objects.

ChartObject Common Properties

The `Application`, `Creator`, and `Parent` properties are defined at the beginning of this appendix.

ChartObject Properties

Name	Returns	Description
`Border`	`Border`	Read Only. Returns the border's properties around the embedded chart.
`BottomRight Cell`	`Range`	Read Only. Returns the single cell range located under the lower-right corner of the `ChartObject`.
`Chart`	`Chart`	Read Only. Returns the actual chart associated with the `ChartObject`.
`Enabled`	`Boolean`	Set/Get whether a macro associated with the `ChartObject` is capable of being triggered.
`Height`	`Double`	Set/Get the height of embedded chart.
`Index`	`Long`	Read Only. Returns the position of the `ChartObject` among the parent collection.
`Interior`	`Interior`	Read Only. Returns an object containing options to format the inside area of the chart object (for example interior color).
`Left`	`Double`	Set/Get the distance from the left edge of the `ChartObject` to the left edge of the parent sheet.
`Locked`	`Boolean`	Set/Get whether the `ChartObject` is locked when the parent sheet is protected.
`Name`	`String`	Set/Get the name of the `ChartObject`.
`Placement`	`Variant`	Set/Get how the `ChartObject` object is anchored to the sheet (for example free floating, move with cells). Use the `XlPlacement` constants to set this property.
`PrintObject`	`Boolean`	Set/Get whether the embedded chart on the sheet will be printed when the sheet is printed.

Name	Returns	Description
ProtectChart Object	Boolean	Set/Get whether the embedded chart can change sizes, be moved, or deleted from the parent sheet.
Rounded Corners	Boolean	Set/Get whether the corners of the embedded chart are rounded (`True`) or right angles (`False`).
Shadow	Boolean	Set/Get whether a shadow appears around the embedded chart.
ShapeRange	ShapeRange	Read Only. Returns the `ChartObject` as a `Shape` object.
Top	Double	Set/Get the distance from top edge of the `ChartObject` to the top of the parent sheet.
TopLeftCell	Range	Read Only. Returns the single cell range located above the top-left corner of the `ChartObject`.
Visible	Boolean	Set/Get whether the `ChartObject` object is visible.
Width	Double	Set/Get the width of embedded chart.
ZOrder	Long	Read Only. Returns the position of the embedded chart among all the other objects on the sheet. The `ZOrder` also matches the location of the `ChartObject` in the parent collection.

ChartObject Methods

Name	Returns	Parameters	Description
Activate	Variant		Makes the embedded chart the active chart.
BringToFront	Variant		Brings the embedded chart to the front of all the other objects on the sheet. Changes the `ZOrder`.
Copy	Variant		Copies the embedded chart into the clipboard.
CopyPicture	Variant	Appearance As XlPicture Appearance, Format As XlCopyPicture Format	Copies the `Chart` object into the clipboard as a picture. The `Appearance` parameter can be used to specify whether the picture is copied as it looks on the screen or when printed. The `Format` parameter can specify the type of picture that will be put into the clipboard. The `Size` parameter is used when dealing with chart sheets to describe the size of the picture.

Name	Returns	Parameters	Description
Cut	Variant		Cuts the embedded chart into the clipboard.
Delete	Variant		Deletes the embedded chart from the sheet.
Duplicate			Duplicates the embedded chart and places the duplicate in the same parent sheet.
Select	Variant	[Replace]	Sets focus to the embedded chart.
SendToBack	Variant		Sends the embedded object to the back of the other objects on the sheet.

Example: ChartObject Object and the ChartObjects Collection

This example creates .jpg images from all the embedded charts in the active worksheet:

```
Sub ExportChartObjects()
   Dim oCO As ChartObject

   For Each oCO In ActiveSheet.ChartObjects
      'Export the chart as a jpg image, giving it the
      'name of the embedded object
      oCO.Chart.Export "c:\" & oCO.Name & ".jpg", "jpg"
   Next
End Sub
```

ChartTitle Object

The ChartTitle object contains all of the text and formatting associated with a chart's title. The parent of the ChartTitle object is the Chart object. This object is usually used along with the HasTitle property of the parent Chart object.

ChartTitle Common Properties

The Application, Creator, and Parent properties are defined at the beginning of this appendix.

ChartTitle Properties

Name	Returns	Description
AutoScaleFont	Variant	Set/Get whether the font size will change automatically if the parent chart changes sizes.
Border	Border	Read Only. Returns the border's properties around the selected chart title.
Caption	String	Set/Get the chart title's text.

Name	Returns	Description
Characters	Characters	Read Only. Parameters: [Start], [Length]. Returns an object containing all the characters in the chart title. Allows manipulation on a character-by-character basis.
Fill	ChartFill Format	Read Only. Returns an object containing fill formatting options for the chart title.
Font	Font	Read Only. Returns an object containing Font options for the chart title.
Horizontal Alignment	Variant	Set/Get how the chart title is horizontally aligned. Use the xlAlign constants.
Interior	Interior	Read Only. Returns an object containing options to format the area in the chart title text area (for example interior color).
Left	Double	Set/Get the distance from the left edge of the chart title text area to the chart's left edge.
Name	String	Read Only. Returns the name of the chart title object.
Orientation	Variant	Set/Get the angle of the text for the chart title. The value can either be in degrees (from –90 to 90) or one of the XlOrientation constants.
ReadingOrder	Long	Set/Get how the text is read (from left to right or right to left). Only applicable in appropriate languages.
Shadow	Boolean	Set/Get whether the chart title has a shadow effect.
Text	String	Set/Get the chart title's text.
Top	Double	Set/Get the distance from the top edge of the chart title text area to the chart's top edge.
Vertical Alignment	Variant	Set/Get how you want the chart title horizontally aligned. Use the xlVAlign constants.

ChartTitle Methods

Name	Returns	Parameters	Description
Delete	Variant		Deletes the chart title from the chart
Select	Variant		Selects the chart title on the chart

Example: ChartTitle Object

This example adds a chart title to a chart and formats it:

```
Sub AddAndFormatChartTitle()
   Dim oCT As ChartTitle

   'Make sure the chart has a title
   Charts(1).HasTitle = True
```

```
    'Get the ChartTitle object
    Set oCT = Charts(1).ChartTitle

    'Format the chart title
    With oCT
        .Caption = "Hello World"
        .Font.Name = "Times New Roman"
        .Font.Size = 16
        .Characters(1, 1).Font.Color = RGB(255, 0, 0)
        .Characters(7, 1).Font.Color = RGB(255, 0, 0)
        .Border.LineStyle = xlContinuous
        .Border.Weight = xlThin
        .Shadow = True
    End With
End Sub
```

ColorFormat Object

The `ColorFormat` object describes a single color used by the parent object. Possible parents of the `ColorFormat` object are the `FillFormat`, `LineFormat`, `ShadowFormat`, and `ThreeDFormat` objects.

ColorFormat Common Properties

The `Application`, `Creator`, and `Parent` properties are defined at the beginning of this appendix.

ColorFormat Properties

Name	Returns	Description
`RGB`	`Long`	Read Only. Returns the red-green-blue value associated with color.
`SchemeColor`	`Integer`	Set/Get the color of the `ColorFormat` using an index value corresponding to the current color scheme.
`TintAndShade`	`Single`	Set/Get a value that lightens or darkens the color of a specified shape. The values can be from -1 (darkest) to 1 (lightest). Zero is neutral.
`Type`	`MsoColor Type`	Read Only. Returns whether the color is an RGB, mixed, or scheme type.

Example: ColorFormat Object

Set the `ForeColor` of a shape's fill effect:

```
Sub FormatShapeColour()
    Dim oShp As Shape
    Dim oCF As ColorFormat

    Set oShp = ActiveSheet.Shapes(1)
    Set oCF = oShp.Fill.ForeColor
    oCF.SchemeColor = 53
End Sub
```

Comment Object and the Comments Collection

The `Comments` collection holds all of the cell comments in the parent `Range` object. Each `Comment` object represents a single cell comment.

Comment Common Properties

The `Application`, `Creator`, and `Parent` properties are defined at the beginning of this appendix.

Comment Properties

Name	Returns	Description
`Author`	`String`	Read Only. Returns the name of the person who created the comment.
`Shape`	`Shape`	Read Only. Returns the comment box as a `Shape` object allowing manipulation of the comment box.
`Visible`	`Boolean`	Set/Get whether the comment is visible all the time (`True`) or only when the user hovers over the cell containing the comment.

Comment Methods

Name	Returns	Parameters	Description
`Delete`			Deletes the comment from the cell.
`Next`	`Comment`		Returns the next cell comment in the parent collection.
`Previous`	`Comment`		Returns the previous cell comment in the parent collection.
`Text`	`String`	`[Text]`, `[Start]`, `[Overwrite]`	Sets the text associated with the comment. The `Text` parameter is used to set the comment text. Use the `Start` parameter to specify the starting point for `Text` in the existing comment. Set the `Overwrite` parameter to `True` to overwrite existing text.

Example: Comment Object and the Comments Collection

This example removes the user name added by Excel at the start of the comment and formats the comment to make it more readable:

```
Sub FormatComments()
   Dim oComment As Comment, i As Integer

   'Loop through all the comments in the sheet
   For Each oComment In ActiveSheet.Comments
```

```
        'Using the text of the comment...
        With oComment.Shape.TextFrame.Characters

            'Find and remove the user name inserted by Excel
            i = InStr(1, .Text, ":" & vbLf)
            If i > 0 Then
                .Text = Mid(.Text, i + 2)
            End If

            'Increase the font size
            With .Font
                .Name = "Arial"
                .Size = 10
                .Bold = False
            End With
        End With

        'Make the text frame auto-fit
        oComment.Shape.TextFrame.AutoSize = True
    Next
End Sub
```

ConnectorFormat Object

The `ConnectorFormat` object represents the connector line used between shapes. This connector line connects two shapes together. If either of shapes are moved the connector automatically re-adjusts so the shapes still look visually connected. The parent of a `ConnectorFormat` object is the `Shape` object.

ConnectorFormat Common Properties

The `Application`, `Creator`, and `Parent` properties are defined at the beginning of this appendix.

ConnectorFormat Properties

Name	Returns	Description
`Begin Connected`	`MsoTri State`	Read Only. Returns whether the beginning of the connector has a shape attached. Use with `BeginConnectedShape`.
`Begin Connected Shape`	`Shape`	Read Only. Returns the shape that is connected to the beginning of the connector. Use with `BeginConnected`.
`Begin Connection Site`	`Long`	Read Only. Returns which connection site (connection spot) on the shape that the beginning of the connector is connected to. Use with `BeginConnected`.
`EndConnected`	`MsoTri State`	Read Only. Returns whether the end of the connector has a shape attached. Use with `BeginConnectedShape`.
`EndConnected Shape`	`Shape`	Read Only. Returns the shape that is connected to the end of the connector. Use with `EndConnected`.

Name	Returns	Description
EndConnection Site	Long	Read Only. Returns which connection site (connection spot) on the shape that the end of the connector is connected to. Use with EndConnected.
Type	Mso Connector Type	Set/Get what type of connector is being used (for example msoConnectorStraight, msoConnectorCurve).

ConnectorFormat Methods

Name	Returns	Parameters	Description
BeginConnect		Connected Shape As Shape, Connection Site As Long	Sets the beginning of the connector to the shape specified by the ConnectedShape parameter at the connection site specified by the ConnectionSite parameter.
Begin Disconnect			Disconnects the shape that was at the beginning of the connection. This method does not move the connection line.
EndConnect		Connected Shape As Shape, Connection Site As Long	Sets the end of the connector to the shape specified by the ConnectedShape parameter at the connection site specified by the ConnectionSite parameter.
End Disconnect			Disconnects the shape that was at the end of the connection. This method does not move the connection line.

Example: ConnectorFormat Object

This example formats all fully-connected connectors as curved lines:

```
Sub FormatConnectors()
   Dim oShp As Shape
   Dim oCF As ConnectorFormat

   'Loop through all the Shapes in the sheet
   For Each oShp In ActiveSheet.Shapes

      'Is it a Connector?
      If oShp.Connector Then

         'Yes, so get the ConnectorFormat object
         Set oCF = oShp.ConnectorFormat

         'If the connector is connected at both ends,
         'make it a curved line.
         With oCF
```

```
            If .BeginConnected And .EndConnected Then
               .Type = msoConnectorCurve
            End If
         End With
      End If
   Next
End Sub
```

ControlFormat Object

The `ControlFormat` object contains properties and methods used to manipulate Excel controls such as textboxes and listboxes. This object's parent is always the `Shape` object.

ControlFormat Common Properties

The `Application`, `Creator`, and `Parent` properties are defined at the beginning of this appendix.

ControlFormat Properties

Name	Returns	Description
`DropDown Lines`	`Long`	Set/Get how many lines are displayed in the drop-down part of a combo box. Valid only if the control is a combo box.
`Enabled`	`Boolean`	Set/Get whether the control is enabled.
`LargeChange`	`Long`	Set/Get the value that is added or subtracted every time the user clicks inside the scroll bar area for a scroll box. Valid only if the control is a scroll box.
`LinkedCell`	`String`	Set/Get the range where the results of the control are placed.
`ListCount`	`Long`	Read Only. Returns the number of items in the list box of combo box. Valid only for list box and combo box controls.
`ListFill Range`	`String`	Set/Get the range that contains the items for a list box or combo box. Valid only for list box and combo box controls.
`ListIndex`	`Long`	Set/Get the item that is currently selected in the list box or combo box. Valid only for list box and combo box controls.
`LockedText`	`Boolean`	Set/Get whether the control text can be changed if the workbook is locked.
`Max`	`Long`	Set/Get the maximum value allowed for a scroll bar or spinner. Valid only on a control that is a scroll bar or spinner.
`Min`	`Long`	Set/Get the minimum value allowed for a scroll bar or spinner. Valid only on a control that is a scroll bar or spinner.

Name	Returns	Description
MultiSelect	Long	Set/Get how a list box reacts to user selection. The property can be set to xlNone (only one item can be selected), xlSimple (each item the user clicks one is added to the selection), or xlExtended (the user has to hold down the Ctrl key to select multiple items). Valid only on list boxes.
PrintObject	Boolean	Set/Get whether the control will be printed when the sheet is printed.
SmallChange	Long	Set/Get the value that is added or subtracted every time the user clicks on the arrow button associated with the scroll bar. Valid only if the control is a scroll box.
Value	Long	Set/Get the value of the control.

ControlFormat Methods

Name	Returns	Parameters	Description
AddItem		Text As String, [Index]	Adds the value of the Text parameter into a list box or combo box. Valid only for list box and combo box controls.
List	Variant	[Index]	Set/Get the string list array associated with a combo box or list box. Can also Set/Get individual items in the list box or combo box if the Index parameter is specified. Valid only for list box and combo box controls.
RemoveAll Items			Removes all the items from a list box or combo box. Valid only for list box and combo box controls.
RemoveItem		Index As Long, [Count]	Removes the item specified by the Index parameter from a list box or combo box. Valid only for list box and combo box controls.

Example: ControlFormat Object

This example resets all the list boxes, dropdowns, scrollbars, spinners, and check boxes on the sheet:

```
Sub ResetFormControls()
   Dim oShp As Shape
   Dim oCF As ControlFormat

   'Loop through all the shapes in the sheet
   For Each oShp In ActiveSheet.Shapes

      'Is this a Forms control?
```

```
        If oShp.Type = msoFormControl Then

           'Yes, so get the ControlFormat object
           Set oCF = oShp.ControlFormat

           'Reset the control as appropriate
           Select Case oShp.FormControlType
              Case xlListBox, xlDropDown
                 oCF.RemoveAllItems

              Case xlSpinner, xlScrollBar
                 oCF.Value = oCF.Min

              Case xlCheckBox
                 oCF.Value = xlOff

           End Select
        End If
     Next
  End Sub
```

Corners Object

The `Corners` object represents the corners of a 3D chart. The parent of the `Corners` object is the `Chart` object. The parent chart must be a 3D chart. Individual corners cannot be accessed.

Corners Common Properties

The `Application`, `Creator`, and `Parent` properties are defined at the beginning of this appendix.

Corners Properties

Name	Returns	Description
`Name`	`String`	Read Only. Returns the name of the `Corners` object – usually "`Corners`".

Corners Methods

Name	Returns	Parameters	Description
`Select`	`Variant`		Sets the corners on the chart

Example: Corners Object

No example – its only method is to select it, which is not particularly useful.

CubeField Object and the CubeFields Collection

The `CubeFields` collection holds all of the `PivotTable` report fields based on an OLAP cube. Each `CubeField` object represents a measure or hierarchy field from the OLAP cube. The parent of the `CubeFields` collection is the `PivotTable` object.

The `CubeFields` collection contains a `Count` property besides the typical collection attributes. The `Count` property returns the number of objects in the collection.

CubeFields Collection Methods

Name	Returns	Parameters	Description
AddSet	CubeField	Name As String, Caption As String	Adds a new CubeField object to the CubeFields collection

CubeField Common Properties

The Application, Creator, and Parent properties are defined at the beginning of this appendix.

CubeField Properties

Name	Returns	Description
Caption	String	Read Only. Returns the text label to use for the cube field.
CubeField Type	XlCube FieldType	Read Only. Returns whether the cube field is a hierarchy field (xlHierarchy) or a measure field (xlMeasure).
DragToColumn	Boolean	Set/Get whether the field can be dragged to a column position. False for measure fields.
DragToData	Boolean	Set/Get whether the field can be dragged to the data position.
DragToHide	Boolean	Set/Get whether the field can be dragged off the PivotTable report and therefore hidden.
DragToPage	Boolean	Set/Get whether the field can be dragged to the page position. False for measure fields.
DragToRow	Boolean	Set/Get whether the field can be dragged to a row position. False for measure fields.
Enable Multiple PageItems	Boolean	Set/Get whether multiple items in the page field area for OLAP PivotTables can be selected.
HasMember Properties	Boolean	Read Only. Returns True when there are member properties specified to be displayed for the cube field.
HiddenLevels	Long	Set/Get the top levels of the hierarchy cube field that are hidden. Set the value to 0 before setting it a value greater than 0 (displays all the levels then hide some).
LayoutForm	XlLayout FormType	Set/Get the way the specified PivotTable items appear.
Layout Subtotal Location	XlSubtotal Location Type	Set/Get the position of the PivotTable field subtotals in relation to the specified field.
Name	String	Read Only. Returns the name of the field.

Table continued on following page

Name	Returns	Description
Orientation	XlPivot Field Orientation	Set/Get where the field is located in the PivotTable report.
PivotFields	PivotFields	Read Only. Returns the PivotFields collection.
Position	Long	Set/Get the position number of the hierarchy field among all the fields in the same orientation.
ShowInField List	Boolean	Set/Get whether a CubeField object will be shown in the field list.
Treeview Control	Treeview Control	Read Only. Returns an object allowing manipulation of the cube on an OLAP PivotTable report.
Value	String	Read Only. Returns the name of the field.

CubeField Methods

Name	Returns	Parameters	Description
AddMember PropertyField		Property As String, [Property Order]	Adds a member property field to the display for the cube field. Note that the property field specified will not be viewable if the PivotTable view has no fields.
Delete			Deletes the object.

CustomProperty Object and the CustomProperties Collection

This object allows you to store information within a worksheet or SmartTag. This information can then be used as Meta Data for XML, or can be accessed by any routine that needs information specific to the worksheet or SmartTag.

More important to me as a developer is the ability of this new object to store specifics regarding a worksheet or group of worksheets so that any routine can call up the `CustomProperty`, analyze the information contained within, then make decisions on how to handle that worksheet. In the past, many developers used worksheet level range names to store information about a worksheet. Worksheet level range names only reside in that worksheet, enabling each worksheet to have the same range name, but store different values.

For example, each worksheet in a workbook containing a dozen budget worksheets and three report worksheets could contain the same range name called `IsBudget`. All of the budget sheets would store the value of `True` in the range name while the report sheets would store `False`. Routines that need to loop through the worksheets applying different formats or calculations to budget sheets can call on the value of the range name to determine if it's a budget sheet before running code on it.

This new `CustomProperty` object makes storing such information (or any information for that matter) simpler than creating worksheet level range names, or storing such information in a hidden worksheet or in the Registry.

The `CustomProperties` collection represents `CustomProperty` objects for either worksheets or

SmartTags. CustomProperties can store information within either a worksheet or SmartTag. They are similar to the DocumentProperties object in the Office XP model, except they are stored with a worksheet or SmartTag instead of the whole document.

CustomProperties Common Properties

The Application, Creator, and Parent properties are defined at the beginning of this appendix.

CustomProperties Collection Properties

Name	Returns	Description
Count	Long	Read Only. Returns the number of objects in the collection.
Item	Custom Property	Read Only. Index As Variant. Returns a single object from a collection.

CustomProperties Collection Methods

Name	Returns	Parameters	Description
Add	Custom Property	Name As String, Value As Variant	Adds custom property information

CustomProperty Common Properties

The Application, Creator, and Parent properties are defined at the beginning of this appendix.

CustomProperty Properties

Name	Returns	Description
Name	String	Set/Get the name of the object.
Value	Variant	Set/Get the style of line to use for the borders (for example xlDash). Use the xlLineStyle constants to set the value. Same as LineStyle.

CustomProperty Methods

Name	Returns	Parameters	Description
Delete			Deletes the object

Example: CustomProperty Object

This routine loops through the worksheets in a workbook and creates a CustomProperty called IsBudget. The value of IsBudget depends on whether or not the worksheet contains the phrase "Budget Analysis". It then lists the results:

```
Sub CreateCustomProperties()

    Dim bBudget As Boolean
    Dim lRow As Long
    Dim oCustomProp As CustomProperty
    Dim rng As Range, wks As Worksheet

    'Turn off the screen and clear the search formats
    With Application
        .FindFormat.Clear
        .ScreenUpdating = False
    End With

    'Clear the worksheet that will contain the
    ' Custom Property list
    wksCustomProperties.UsedRange.Offset(1, 0).ClearContents

    'Initialize the row counter
    lRow = 2    'Row 1 contains the Column Headings

    'Loop through the worksheet in this workbook
    For Each wks In ThisWorkbook.Worksheets

        'Supress errors resulting in no cells found and
        ' no Custom Property
        On Error Resume Next
            bBudget = False
            bBudget = _
                   (Len(wks.UsedRange.Find(What:="Budget Analysis").Address) > 0)

            'Unfortunately, we cannot refer to a Custom Property by
            ' its name, only its numeric index
            Set oCustomProp = wks.CustomProperties(1)
        On Error GoTo 0

        'If the Custom Property exists, delete it and
        ' add it again
        If Not oCustomProp Is Nothing Then oCustomProp.Delete

        'Note the value of bBudget is encased in double quotes.
        'If we don't, True will be stored as -1 and False 0 (their
        'numeric values).
        Set oCustomProp = wks.CustomProperties.Add(Name:="IsBudget", Value:="" _
                                                                & bBudget & "")

        'List the Custom Property settings on the worksheet
        With wksCustomProperties
            'Parent.Name returns the name of the object
            ' holding the Custom Property - the worksheet name in this case
            .Cells(lRow, 1).Value = oCustomProp.Parent.Name
            .Cells(lRow, 2).Value = oCustomProp.Name
            .Cells(lRow, 3).Value = oCustomProp.Value
        End With

        'Move down one row
        lRow = lRow + 1

    Next wks

End Sub
```

CustomView Object and the CustomViews Collection

The `CustomViews` collection holds the list of custom views associated with a workbook. Each `CustomView` object holds the attributes associated with a workbook custom view. A custom view holds settings such as window size, window position, column widths, hidden columns, and print settings of a workbook. The parent object of the `CustomViews` collection is the `Workbook` object.

The `CustomViews` collection has two other properties besides the typical collection attributes. The `Count` property returns the number of `CustomView` objects in the collection. The `Add` method adds a custom view to the `CustomViews` collection. The `Add` method accepts a name for the view with the `ViewName` parameter. Optionally the `Add` method accepts whether print settings are included (`PrintSettings`) and whether hidden rows and columns are included (`RowColSetttings`).

CustomView Common Properties

The `Application`, `Creator`, and `Parent` properties are defined at the beginning of this appendix.

CustomView Properties

Name	Returns	Description
`Name`	`String`	Read Only. Returns the name of the custom view.
`PrintSettings`	`Boolean`	Read Only. Returns whether print settings are included in the custom view.
`RowCol Settings`	`Boolean`	Read Only. Returns whether hidden rows and columns are included in the custom view.

CustomView Methods

Name	Returns	Parameters	Description
`Delete`			Deletes the custom view
`Show`			Shows the custom view and the settings associated with it

Example: CustomView Object and the CustomViews Collection

Display all the custom views in the workbook as a screen-show, pausing for 2 seconds between each one:

```
Sub ShowCustomView()
   Dim oCV As CustomView

   'Cycle through all the custom views in the sheet
   'that contain row/column information
   For Each oCV In ActiveWorkbook.CustomViews

      If oCV.RowColSettings Then
         oCV.Show
      End If

      'Pause for 2 seconds between each view
```

```
        Application.Wait Now + TimeValue("00:00:02")
    Next
End Sub
```

DataLabel Object and the DataLabels Collection

The DataLabels collection holds all the labels for individual points or trendlines in a data series. Each series has only one DataLabels collection. The parent of the DataLabels collection is the Series object. Each DataLabel object represents a single data label for a trendline or a point. The DataLabels collection is used with the HasDataLabels property of the parent Series object.

The DataLabels collection has a few properties and methods besides the typical collection attributes. They are listed in the following table.

DataLabels Collection Properties and Methods

Name	Returns	Description
AutoScaleFont	Variant	Set/Get whether the font size will change automatically if the parent chart changes sizes.
AutoText	Boolean	Set/Get whether Excel will generate the data label text automatically.
Border	Border	Read Only. Returns the border's properties around the data label collection.
Count	Long	Read Only. Returns the number of data labels in the collection.
Fill	ChartFill Format	Read Only. Returns an object containing fill formatting options for the data labels in the collection.
Font	Font	Read Only. Returns an object containing Font options for the data labels in the collection.
Horizontal Alignment	Variant	Set/Get how the data labels are horizontally aligned. Use the xlAlign constants.
Interior	Interior	Read Only. Returns an object containing options to format the inside area of the data labels in the collection (for example interior color).
Name	String	Read Only. Returns the name of the collection.
NumberFormat	String	Set/Get the numeric formatting to use if the data labels are numeric values or dates.
NumberFormat Linked	Boolean	Set/Get whether the same numerical format used for the cells containing the chart data is used by the data labels.
NumberFormat Local	Variant	Set/Get the name of the numeric format being used by the data labels in the language being used by the user.

Name	Returns	Description
Orientation	Variant	Set/Get the angle of the text for the data labels. The value can be in degrees (from –90 to 90) or one of the XlOrientation constants.
Position	XlDataLabel Position	Set/Get where the data labels are going to be located in relation to points or trendlines.
ReadingOrder	Long	Set/Get how the text is read (from left to right or right to left). Only applicable in appropriate languages.
Separator	Variant	Set/Get the separator used for the data labels on a chart.
Shadow	Boolean	Set/Get whether the data labels have a shadow effect.
ShowBubble Size	Boolean	Set/Get whether to show the bubble size for the data labels on a chart.
ShowCategory Name	Boolean	Set/Get whether to display the category name for the data labels on a chart.
ShowLegendKey	Boolean	Set/Get whether the key being used in the legend, usually a specific color, will show along with the data label.
Show Percentage	Boolean	Set/Get whether to display the percentage value for the data labels on a chart.
ShowSeries Name	Boolean	Set/Get whether to show the series name.
ShowValue	Boolean	Set/Get whether to display the specified chart's data label values.
Type	Variant	Set/Get what sort of data label to show for the collection (for example labels, percent, values).
Vertical Alignment	Variant	Set/Get how you want the data labels horizontally aligned. Use the xlVAlign constants.
Delete	Variant	Method. Deletes the data labels.
Select	Variant	Method. Selects the data labels on the chart.

DataLabel Common Properties

The Application, Creator, and Parent properties are defined at the beginning of this appendix.

DataLabel Properties

Name	Returns	Description
AutoScaleFont	Variant	Set/Get whether the font size will change automatically if the parent chart changes sizes.
AutoText	Boolean	Set/Get whether Excel will generate the data label text automatically.
Border	Border	Read Only. Returns the border's properties around the data label.
Caption	String	Set/Get the data label text.
Characters	Characters	Read Only. Parameters: [Start], [Length]. Returns an object that represents a range of characters within the text.
Fill	ChartFill Format	Read Only. Returns an object containing fill formatting options for the data label.
Font	Font	Read Only. Returns an object containing Font options for the data label.
Horizontal Alignment	Variant	Set/Get how the data labels are horizontally aligned. Use the xlAlign constants.
Interior	Interior	Read Only. Returns an object containing options to format the inside area of the data label (for example interior color).
Left	Double	Set/Get the distance from the left edge of the data label to the parent chart's left edge.
Name	String	Read Only. Returns the name of the data label.
NumberFormat	String	Set/Get the numeric formatting to use if the data label is a numeric value or a date.
NumberFormat Linked	Boolean	Set/Get whether the same numerical format used for the cells containing the chart data is used by the data label.
NumberFormat Local	Variant	Set/Get the name of the numeric format being used by the data label in the language being used by the user.
Orientation	Variant	Set/Get the angle of the text for the data label. The value can be in degrees (from –90 to 90) or one of the XlOrientation constants.
Position	XlDataLabel Position	Set/Get where the data label is going to be located in relation to points or trendlines.
ReadingOrder	Long	Set/Get how the text is read (from left to right or right to left). Only applicable in appropriate languages.

Name	Returns	Description
Separator	Variant	Set/Get the separator used for the data labels on a chart.
Shadow	Boolean	Set/Get whether the data label has a shadow effect.
ShowBubble Size	Boolean	Set/Get whether to show the bubble size for the data labels on a chart.
ShowCategory Name	Boolean	Set/Get whether to display the category name for the data labels on a chart.
ShowLegendKey	Boolean	Set/Get whether the key being used in the legend, usually a specific color, will show along with the data label.
Show Percentage	Boolean	Set/Get whether to display the percentage value for the data labels on a chart.
ShowSeries Name	Boolean	Set/Get whether to show the series name.
ShowValue	Boolean	Set/Get whether to display the specified chart's data label values.
Text	String	Set/Get the data label text.
Top	Double	Set/Get the distance from the top edge of the data label to the parent chart's top edge.
Type	Variant	Set/Get what sort of data label to show (for example labels, percent, values).
Vertical Alignment	Variant	Set/Get how you want the data label horizontally aligned. Use the `xlVAlign` constants.

DataLabel Methods

Name	Returns	Parameters	Description
Delete	Variant		Deletes the data label
Select	Variant		Selects the data label on the chart

Example: DataLabel Object and the DataLabels Collection

This example adds data labels to all the points on the chart, using the column to the left of the X values range:

```
Sub AddDataLabels()
   Dim oSer As Series
   Dim vaSplits As Variant
   Dim oXRng As Range
   Dim oLblRng As Range
   Dim oLbl As DataLabel

   'Loop through all the series in the chart
```

```
    For Each oSer In Charts(1).SeriesCollection

        'Get the series formula and split it into its
        'constituent parts (Name, X range, Y range, order)
        vaSplits = Split(oSer.Formula, ",")

        'Get the X range
        Set oXRng = Range(vaSplits(LBound(vaSplits) + 1))

        'Get the column to the left of the X range
        Set oLblRng = oXRng.Offset(0, -1)

        'Show data labels for the series
        oSer.ApplyDataLabels

        'Loop through the points
        For i = 1 To oSer.Points.Count

            'Get the DataLabel object
            Set oLbl = oSer.Points(i).DataLabel

            'Set its text and alignment
            With oLbl
                .Caption = oLblRng.Cells(i)
                .Position = xlLabelPositionAbove
            End With
        Next
    Next
End Sub
```

DataTable Object

A `DataTable` object contains the formatting options associated with a chart's data table. The parent of the `DataTable` object is the `Chart` object.

DataTable Common Properties

The `Application`, `Creator`, and `Parent` properties are defined at the beginning of this appendix.

DataTable Properties

Name	Returns	Description
`AutoScaleFont`	`Variant`	Set/Get whether the font size will change automatically if the parent chart changes sizes.
`Border`	`Border`	Read Only. Returns the border's properties around the data table.
`Font`	`Font`	Read Only. Returns an object containing `Font` options for the data table.
`HasBorder Horizontal`	`Boolean`	Set/Get whether the data table has horizontal cell borders.

Name	Returns	Description
HasBorder Outline	Boolean	Set/Get whether the data table has a border around the outside.
HasBorder Vertical	Boolean	Set/Get whether the data table has vertical cell borders.
ShowLegendKey	Boolean	Set/Get whether the legend key is shown along with the data table contents.

DataTable Methods

Name	Returns	Parameters	Description
Delete			Deletes the data table
Select			Selects the data table on the chart

Example: DataTable Object

Adds a data table to a chart and formats it to only have vertical lines between the values:

```
Sub FormatDataTable()
   Dim oDT As DataTable

   'Display the data table
   Charts(1).HasDataTable = True

   'Get the DataTable object
   Set oDT = Charts(1).DataTable

   'Format the data table to only have vertical lines
   With oDT
      .HasBorderOutline = False
      .HasBorderHorizontal = False
      .HasBorderVertical = True
   End With
End Sub
```

DefaultWebOptions Object

Allows programmatic changes to items associated with the default settings of the Web Options dialog. These options include what Excel does when opening an HTML page and when saving a sheet as an HTML page.

DefaultWebOptions Common Properties

The `Application`, `Creator`, and `Parent` properties are defined at the beginning of this appendix.

DefaultWebOptions Properties

Name	Returns	Description
AllowPNG	Boolean	Set/Get whether Portable Network Graphics Format PNG is allowed as an output format. PNG is a file format for the lossless, portable, well-compressed storage of images.
AlwaysSaveIn DefaultEncoding	Boolean	Set/Get whether web pages are always saved in the default encoding.
CheckIfOfficeIs HTMLEditor	Boolean	Set/Get whether Office is the default web editor for Office created pages.
Download Components	Boolean	Set/Get whether Office components are downloaded to the end user's machine when viewing Excel files in a web browser.
Encoding	MsoEncodin g	Set/Get the type of encoding to save a document as.
FolderSuffix	String	Read Only. Returns what the suffix name is for the support directory created when saving an Excel document as a web page. Language dependent.
Fonts	WebPage Fonts	Read Only. Returns a collection of possible web type fonts.
LoadPictures	Boolean	Set/Get whether images are loaded when opening up an Excel file.
LocationOf Components	String	Set/Get the URL or path that contains the Office web components needed to view documents in a web browser.
Organize InFolder	Boolean	Set/Get whether supporting files are organized in a folder.
PixelsPer Inch	Long	Set/Get how dense graphics and table cells should be when viewed on a web page.
RelyOnCSS	Boolean	Set/Get whether Cascading Style Sheets (CSS) is used for font formatting.
RelyOnVML	Boolean	Set/Get whether image files are not created when saving a document with drawn objects. Vector Markup Language is used to create the images on the fly. VML is an XML-based format for high-quality vector graphics on the Web.
SaveHidden Data	Boolean	Set/Get whether all hidden data is saved in the web page along with the regular data.
SaveNewWeb PagesAsWeb Archives	Boolean	Set/Get whether a new web page can be saved as a web archive.

Name	Returns	Description
`ScreenSize`	`MsoScreen Size`	Set/Get the target monitor's screen size.
`Target Browser`	`MsoTarget Browser`	Set/Get the browser version.
`UpdateLinks OnSave`	`Boolean`	Set/Get whether links are updated every time the document is saved.
`UseLongFile Names`	`Boolean`	Set/Get whether long file names are used whenever possible.

Example: DefaultWebOptions Object

This example shows how to open a web page, without loading the pictures:

```
Sub OpenHTMLWithoutPictures()
   Dim bLoadImages As Boolean
   Dim oDWO As DefaultWebOptions

   'Get the Default Web options
   Set oDWO = Application.DefaultWebOptions

   'Remember whether to load pictures
   bLoadImages = oDWO.LoadPictures

   'Tell Excel not to load pictures, for faster opening
   oDWO.LoadPictures = False

   'Open a web page, without pictures
   Workbooks.Open "http://www.wrox.com"

   'Restore the setting
   oDWO.LoadPictures = bLoadImages
End Sub
```

Diagram Object

A `Diagram` represents a preset collection of shapes surrounded by an invisible border. It's a cross between adding shapes using the Drawing toolbar and an enhanced version of the Org Chart program used in previous versions of Microsoft Office. Within each `Diagram` are `Nodes`. Each Node represents an individual shape in the `Diagram`.

There are several different types of preset `Diagrams` you can choose from: `Cycle`, `Target`, `Radial`, `Venn`, `Pyramid`, and `OrgChart`.

It's important to note that the `Diagram` object belongs to the `Shape`(s) object, which in turn belongs to the `Worksheet` object. Consequently, to add a `Diagram` object to a worksheet, you go through the `Shapes` collection using the `AddDiagram` method:

```
ActiveSheet.Shapes.AddDiagram(msoDiagramOrgChart, 2, 2, 400, 300)
```

If you set the above code to an object variable, it returns a `Shape` object. To add shapes to the `Diagram`, use the `DiagramNode` object within the `Shape` object:

```
ActiveSheet.Shapes(1).DiagramNode.Children.AddNode
```

To reference the properties and methods of the `Diagram` object itself (listed below), you access the `Diagram` object through the `Shape` object, like so:

```
ActiveSheet.Shapes(1).Diagram.Nodes(1).TextShape.Fill.BackColor.SchemeColor = 17
```

Diagram Common Properties

The `Application`, `Creator`, and `Parent` properties are defined at the beginning of this appendix.

Diagram Properties

Name	Returns	Description
`AutoFormat`	`MsoTriState`	Get / Set the automatic formatting state for a diagram
`AutoLayout`	`MsoTriState`	Get / Set the constant which determines the automatic positioning of the nodes and connectors in a diagram
`Nodes`	`Diagram Nodes`	Read Only. Returns a `DiagramNodes` object that contains a flat list of all the nodes in the specified diagram
`Reverse`	`MsoTriState`	Set/Get whether to reverse the order of the nodes
`Type`	`MsoDiagram Type`	Read Only. Returns the diagram type

Diagram Methods

Name	Returns	Parameters	Description
`Convert`		`Type As Mso DiagramType`	Converts the current diagram to a different diagram

Example: Diagram Object

The following routine creates a diagram and adds and formats several shapes (called nodes) to the diagram. The shape color and font name come from a table on a worksheet, allowing you to easily experiment with different looks.

Important Note: As of this writing, any attempt to programmatically add text to nodes in a `Diagram` results in an error:

```
Sub CreateDiagram()

    Const sRANGE_LEVELS As String = "Levels"

    Dim lCount As Long
    Dim oDiagramShape As Shape
    Dim oDiagramNode As DiagramNode
    Dim oDiagramNodeChild As DiagramNode

    'Clear the current shapes (except the Command Button)
    On Error Resume Next
        For Each oDiagramShape In wksDiagrams.Shapes
            If oDiagramShape.HasDiagram Then oDiagramShape.Delete
        Next oDiagramShape
    On Error GoTo 0
```

```
    'Turn off the screen
    Application.ScreenUpdating = False

    'Create the Diagram
    Set oDiagramShape = wksDiagrams.Shapes.AddDiagram(msoDiagramOrgChart, 2, 2,
300, 250)

    'Remove the transparent background
    oDiagramShape.Fill.Visible = msoTrue

    'Create the top level node
    Set oDiagramNode = oDiagramShape.DiagramNode.Children.AddNode

    With oDiagramNode

        'Format the top level node
        With .Shape
            .AutoShapeType = msoShapeBevel
            .TextFrame.Characters.Font.Name = _
                wksDiagrams.Range(sRANGE_LEVELS).Cells(1, 2).Text
            .Fill.ForeColor.SchemeColor = _
                wksDiagrams.Range(sRANGE_LEVELS).Cells(1, 3).Value
        End With

        'Create a child node under the top level node
        Set oDiagramNodeChild = .Children.AddNode

        'Format the child node
        With oDiagramNodeChild
            .Shape.TextFrame.Characters.Font.Name = _
                wksDiagrams.Range(sRANGE_LEVELS).Cells(2, 2).Text
            .Shape.Fill.ForeColor.SchemeColor = _
                wksDiagrams.Range(sRANGE_LEVELS).Cells(2, 3).Value
        End With

        'Place two child nodes under the top level's child
        For lCount = 1 To 2
            With oDiagramNodeChild.Children.AddNode
                .Shape.TextFrame.Characters.Font.Name = _
                    wksDiagrams.Range(sRANGE_LEVELS).Cells(3, 2).Text
                .Shape.Fill.ForeColor.SchemeColor = _
                    wksDiagrams.Range(sRANGE_LEVELS).Cells(3, 3).Value
            End With
        Next lCount

        'Create another child under the top level node
        Set oDiagramNodeChild = .Children.AddNode

        With oDiagramNodeChild
            .Shape.TextFrame.Characters.Font.Name = _
                wksDiagrams.Range(sRANGE_LEVELS).Cells(2, 2).Text
            .Shape.Fill.ForeColor.SchemeColor = _
                wksDiagrams.Range(sRANGE_LEVELS).Cells(2, 3).Value
        End With

        'Place two child nodes under this child
        '(which is under top level)
        For lCount = 1 To 2
            With oDiagramNodeChild.Children.AddNode
                .Shape.TextFrame.Characters.Font.Name = _
```

```
                        wksDiagrams.Range(sRANGE_LEVELS).Cells(3, 2).Text
                    .Shape.Fill.ForeColor.SchemeColor = _
                        wksDiagrams.Range(sRANGE_LEVELS).Cells(3, 3).Value
                End With
            Next lCount

        End With

    End Sub
```

DiagramNode Object and the DiagramNodes Collection

The DiagramNode object represents one shape inside a Diagram. Shapes underneath a specific node are called children. Use the AddNode method of the Children property of this object to add nodes to the current node.

The DiagramNodes collection consists of all of the Nodes in a Diagram object. Each Node is a shape within the Diagram.

DiagramNodes Common Properties

The Application, Creator, and Parent properties are defined at the beginning of this appendix.

DiagramNodes Collection Properties

Name	Returns	Description
Count	Long	Read Only. Returns the number of objects in the collection.

DiagramNodes Collection Methods

Name	Returns	Parameters	Description
Item	Diagram Node	Index As Variant	Returns a single object from a collection
SelectAll			Selects all the shapes in the collection

DiagramNode Common Properties

The Application, Creator, and Parent properties are defined at the beginning of this appendix.

DiagramNode Properties

Name	Returns	Description
Children	Diagram NodeChildren	Read Only. Returns the collection of child nodes of a particular node.
Diagram	IMso Diagram	Read Only. Returns a representation of a diagram.

Name	Returns	Description
`Layout`	`MsoOrg Chart LayoutType`	Set/Get the formatting style of the child nodes of an organization chart.
`Root`	`Diagram Node`	Read Only. Returns the root of the root diagram node.
`Shape`	`Shape`	Read Only. Returns the shape attached to the specified comment, diagram node, or hyperlink.
`TextShape`	`Shape`	Read Only. Returns the shape of the text box associated with a diagram node.

DiagramNode Methods

Name	Returns	Parameters	Description
`AddNode`	`Diagram Node`	`[pos As MsoRelative NodePosition], [nodeType As MsoDiagram NodeType]`	Creates a diagram node and returns a `DiagramNode` object that represents the new node
`CloneNode`	`Diagram Node`	`copyChildren As Boolean, [pTarget Node As DiagramNode], [pos As MsoRelative NodePosition]`	Clones a diagram node and returns a `DiagramNode` object representing the cloned node
`Delete`			Deletes the object
`MoveNode`		`pTargetNode As DiagramNode, pos As MsoRelative NodePosition`	Moves a diagram node and any of its child nodes, within a diagram
`NextNode`	`Diagram Node`		Selects the next diagram node in a series of nodes and returns a `DiagramNode` object representing the newly-selected node
`PrevNode`	`Diagram Node`		Returns the previous diagram node in a collection of diagram nodes
`ReplaceNode`		`pTargetNode As DiagramNode`	Replaces a target diagram node with the source diagram node

Table continued on following page

Name	Returns	Parameters	Description
SwapNode		pTargetNode As DiagramNode, [swapChildren As Boolean]	Swaps the source diagram node with a target diagram node
Transfer Children		pReceiving Node As DiagramNode	The child nodes of a source diagram node are transferred to a receiving diagram node

DiagramNodeChildren Object

The DiagramNodeChildren object represents a Child shape one level below a DiagramNode object. Each DiagramNodeChildren object is a DiagramNode object itself. If a DiagramNodeChildren object contains Children below it (in the hierchარchy), then each of those would be considered DiagramNodeChildren objects.

DiagramNodeChildren Common Properties

The Application, Creator, and Parent properties are defined at the beginning of this appendix.

DiagramNodeChildren Properties

Name	Returns	Description
Count	Long	Read Only. Returns the number of objects in the collection.
FirstChild	Diagram Node	Read Only. Returns the first child node of a parent node.
LastChild	Diagram Node	Read Only. Returns the last child node of a parent node.

DiagramNodeChildren Methods

Name	Returns	Parameters	Description
AddNode	Diagram Node	[Index], [nodeType As MsoDiagram NodeType]	Makes a new DiagramNode
SelectAll			Selects all the shapes in the collection

Dialog Object and the Dialogs Collection

The `Dialogs` collection represents the list of dialog boxes that are built-in to Excel. The `XlBuiltinDialog` constants are used to access an individual `Dialog` object in the `Dialogs` collection. A `Dialog` object represents a single built-in Excel dialog box. Each `Dialog` object will have additional custom properties depending on what type of `Dialog` object it is. Besides the typical collection attributes, the `Dialogs` collection also has a `Count` property that returns the number of `Dialog` objects in the collection.

Dialog Common Properties

The `Application`, `Creator`, and `Parent` properties are defined at the beginning of this appendix.

Dialog Methods

Name	Returns	Parameters	Description
Show	Boolean	[Arg1], [Arg2], ... [Arg30]	Displays and executes the dialog box settings. `True` is returned if the user chose OK and `False` is returned if the user chose Cancel. The arguments to pass depend on the dialog box.

Example: Dialog Object and the Dialogs Collection

```
Sub ShowPrinterSelection()
    'Show printer selection dialog
    Application.Dialogs(xlDialogPrinterSetup).Show
End Sub
```

DisplayUnitLabel Object

The `DisplayUnitLabel` object contains all of the text and formatting associated with the label used for units on axes. For example, if the values on an axis are in the millions it would be messy to display such large values on the axis. Using a unit label such as 'Millions' would allow much smaller numbers to be used. The parent of the `DisplayUnitLabel` object is the `Axis` object. This object is usually used along with the `HasDisplayUnit` property of the parent `Axis` object.

DisplayUnitLabel Common Properties

The `Application`, `Creator`, and `Parent` properties are defined at the beginning of this appendix.

DisplayUnitLabel Properties

Name	Returns	Description
AutoScaleFont	Variant	Set/Get whether the font size will change automatically if the parent chart changes sizes.
Border	Border	Read Only. Returns the border's properties around the unit label.

Table continued on following page

Name	Returns	Description
Caption	String	Set/Get the unit label's text.
Characters	Characters	Read Only. Parameters: [Start], [Length]. Returns an object containing all the characters in the unit label. Allows manipulation on a character-by-character basis.
Fill	ChartFill Format	Read Only. Returns an object containing fill formatting options for the unit label.
Font	Font	Read Only. Returns an object containing Font options for the unit label.
Horizontal Alignment	Variant	Set/Get how you want the unit label horizontally aligned. Use the xlAlign constants.
Interior	Interior	Read Only. Returns an object containing options to format the area in the unit label text area for example interior color).
Left	Double	Set/Get the distance from the left edge of the unit label text area to the chart's left edge.
Name	String	Read Only. Returns the name of the DisplayUnitLabel object.
Orientation	Variant	Set/Get the angle of the text for the unit label. The value can be in degrees (from –90 to 90) or one of the XlOrientation constants.
ReadingOrder	Long	Set/Get how the text is read (from left to right or right to left). Only applicable in appropriate languages.
Shadow	Boolean	Set/Get whether the unit label has a shadow effect.
Text	String	Set/Get the unit label's text.
Top	Double	Set/Get the distance from the top edge of the unit label text area to the chart's top edge.
Vertical Alignment	Variant	Set/Get how you want the unit label horizontally aligned. Use the xlVAlign constants.

DisplayUnitLabel Methods

Name	Returns	Parameters	Description
Delete	Variant		Deletes the unit label from the axis
Select	Variant		Selects the unit label on the chart

Example: DisplayUnitLabel Object

```
Sub AddUnitLabel()
   Dim oDUL As DisplayUnitLabel

   'Format the Y axis to have a unit label
   With Charts(1).Axes(xlValue)
      .DisplayUnit = xlThousands
      .HasDisplayUnitLabel = True

      'Get the unit label
      Set oDUL = .DisplayUnitLabel
   End With

   'Format the unit label
   With oDUL
      .Caption = "Thousands"
      .Font.Name = "Arial"
      .VerticalAlignment = xlCenter
   End With
End Sub
```

DownBars Object

The `DownBars` object contains formatting options for down bars on a chart. The parent of the `DownBars` object is the `ChartGroup` object. To see if this object exists use the `HasUpDownBars` property of the `ChartGroup` object.

DownBars Common Properties

The `Application`, `Creator`, and `Parent` properties are defined at the beginning of this appendix.

DownBars Properties

Name	Returns	Description
Border	Border	Read Only. Returns the border's properties around the down bars.
Fill	ChartFill Format	Read Only. Returns an object containing fill formatting options for the down bars.
Interior	Interior	Read Only. Returns an object containing options to format the inside area of the down bars (for example interior color).
Name	String	Read Only. Returns the name of the down bars.

DownBars Methods

Name	Returns	Parameters	Description
`Delete`	`Variant`		Deletes the down bars
`Select`	`Variant`		Selects the down bars in the chart

DropLines Object

The `DropLines` object contains formatting options for drop lines in a chart. The parent of the `DropLines` object is the `ChartGroup` object. To see if this object exists use the `HasDropLines` property of the `ChartGroup` object.

DropLines Common Properties

The `Application`, `Creator`, and `Parent` properties are defined at the beginning of this appendix.

DropLines Properties

Name	Returns	Description
`Border`	`Border`	Read Only. Returns the border's properties around the drop lines.
`Name`	`String`	Read Only. Returns the name of the drop lines.

DropLines Methods

Name	Returns	Parameters	Description
`Delete`	`Variant`		Deletes the drop lines
`Select`	`Variant`		Selects the drop lines in the chart

Example: DropLines Object

```
Sub AddAndFormatDropLines()
   Dim oDLine As DropLines

   'Show the drop lines
   Charts(1).ChartGroups(1).HasDropLines = True

   'Get the DropLines object
   Set oDLine = Charts(1).ChartGroups(1).DropLines

   'Format the drop lines
   With oDLine
      .Border.Weight = xlMedium
      .Border.LineStyle = xlDash
      .Border.ColorIndex = 3
   End With
End Sub
```

Error Object and the Errors Collection

The `Error` object contains one error in the `Errors` collection representing one error in a cell containing possible errors.

The `Errors` collection represents all the errors contained within a cell. Each cell can contain multiple errors.

These errors are analogous to the new Error Checking feature in Excel 2002. The different types of errors that Excel can check can be found on the Error Checking Tab of the Tools | Options command. In the Excel application, cells containing errors appear with a small triangle in their upper left corner. The default color of the triangle on most systems is green, but can be changed using the Error Indicator Color option on the Error Checking Tab of the Options command.

When a user selects a range containing an error, a drop down icon containing an exclamation point inside a yellow diamond appears. The user can then click the icon and choose how to handle the errors in the range. If action was taken, like ignoring the error or clicking one of the recommended choices, the green indicator disappears for all cells containing that error. Any cells still containing the green triangle indicate other error types are still present in those cells.

As of this writing, the `Errors Collection` object and `Error` object do not have the ability to handle multiple errors in a multi-cell range as described above. The Help file and object model indicate that the Parent object of the `Errors Collection` is a `Range` object. However, any attempt to reference the `Errors` in a multi-cell range results in an error. Since each cell can contain multiple errors, for all intent and purposes, the `Error Collection` object stores all the errors contained within one cell, not a range of cells. This requires that you loop through a range of cells if you need to programmatically handle errors in a multi-cell range.

Note that neither the `Error` nor `Errors` objects contains a count or Boolean property that would allow us to test whether an error even exists in a cell. For this reason, additional code would be needed to loop through each error type for every desired cell checking for the `Error` object's `Value` property, which returns `True` if that type of error occurs in the cell.

Use the `Item` property of the `Errors Collection` object to loop through the error types to determine which errors might have occurred.

Errors Common Properties

The `Application`, `Creator`, and `Parent` properties are defined at the beginning of this appendix.

Errors Collection Properties

Name	Returns	Description
`Item`	`Error`	Returns an `Error` object that is contained in the `Errors` collection

Error Common Properties

The `Application`, `Creator`, and `Parent` properties are defined at the beginning of this appendix.

Error Properties

Name	Returns	Description
`Ignore`	`Boolean`	Get / Set whether error checking is enabled for a range.
`Value`	`Boolean`	Read Only. Returns whether all the validation criteria are met.

Example: Error Object

ErrorBars Object

The `ErrorBars` object contains formatting options for error bars in a chart. The parent of the `Errors` object is the `SeriesCollection` object.

ErrorBars Common Properties

The `Application`, `Creator`, and `Parent` properties are defined at the beginning of this appendix.

ErrorBars Properties

Name	Returns	Description
`Border`	`Border`	Read Only. Returns the border's properties around the error bars.
`EndStyle`	`XlEndStyle Cap`	Set/Get the style used for the ending of the error bars.
`Name`	`String`	Read Only. Returns the name of the error bars.

ErrorBars Methods

Name	Returns	Parameters	Description
`ClearFormats`	`Variant`		Clears the formatting set on the error bar
`Delete`	`Variant`		Deletes the error bars
`Select`	`Variant`		Selects the error bars in the chart

Example: ErrorBars Object

```
Sub AddAndFormatErrorBars()
   Dim oSer As Series
   Dim oErrBars As ErrorBars

   'Add error bars to the first series (at +/- 10% of the value)
   Set oSer = Charts(1).SeriesCollection(1)
   oSer.ErrorBar xlY, xlErrorBarIncludeBoth, xlErrorBarTypePercent, 10

   'Get the ErrorBars object
   Set oErrBars = oSer.ErrorBars
```

```
    'Format the error bars
    With oErrBars
        .Border.Weight = xlThick
        .Border.LineStyle = xlContinuous
        .Border.ColorIndex = 7
        .EndStyle = xlCap
    End With
End Sub
```

ErrorCheckingOptions Collection Object

Represents all of the Error Checking possibilities found on the Error Checking Tab of the Tools | Options command. Using the `BackgroundChecking` property of this object hides all of the error indicators (small triangle in upper right corner of cells).

Use the other properties in this object to specify which type of error checking you want Excel to perform.

The `ErrorCheckingOptions` object can be referenced through the `Application` object and therefore affect all open workbooks.

ErrorCheckingOPtions Common Properties

The `Application`, `Creator`, and `Parent` properties are defined at the beginning of this appendix.

ErrorCheckingOptions Collection Properties

Name	Returns	Description
`Background Checking`	`Boolean`	Set/Get whether background error checking is set, that is whether the autocorrect button will apear in cells that contain errors
`EmptyCell References`	`Boolean`	Set/Get whether error checking is on for cells containing formulas that refer to empty cells
`EvaluateToEr ror`	`Boolean`	Set/Get whether error checking is on for cells that evaluate to an error value
`Inconsistent Formula`	`Boolean`	Set/Get whether error checking is on for cells containing an inconsistent formula in a region
`IndicatorCol or Index`	`XlColor Index`	Set/Get the color of the indicator for error checking options
`NumberAsText`	`Boolean`	Set/Get whether error checking is on for numbers written as text
`OmittedCells`	`Boolean`	Set/Get whether error checking is on for cells that contain formulas referring to a range that omits adjacent cells that could be included
`TextDate`	`Boolean`	Set/Get whether error checking is on for cells that contain a text date with a two-digit year
`UnlockedForm ulaCells`	`Boolean`	Set/Get whether error checking is on for cells that are unlocked and contain a formula

Example: ErrorCheckingOptions Object

The following routine uses a table on a worksheet to set the Error Checking Options:

```
Sub SetErrorCheckingOptions()

    Dim rngSettings As Range
    Dim vSetting As Variant

    'Locate the start of the Settings table
    Set rngSettings = wksErrors.Range("ErrorSettings")

    'Go through each ErrorChecking Property and
    ' set it according to the values placed in teh table
    With Application.ErrorCheckingOptions

        vSetting = rngSettings.Cells(1, 2).Value
        If Len(vSetting) And (vSetting = True Or vSetting = False) Then
            .BackgroundChecking = vSetting
        End If

        vSetting = rngSettings.Cells(2, 2).Value
        If Len(vSetting) And (vSetting = True Or vSetting = False) Then
            .EvaluateToError = vSetting
        End If

        vSetting = rngSettings.Cells(3, 2).Value
        If Len(vSetting) And (vSetting = True Or vSetting = False) Then
            .TextDate = vSetting
        End If

        vSetting = rngSettings.Cells(4, 2).Value
        If Len(vSetting) And (vSetting = True Or vSetting = False) Then
            .NumberAsText = vSetting
        End If

        vSetting = rngSettings.Cells(5, 2).Value
        If Len(vSetting) And (vSetting = True Or vSetting = False) Then
            .InconsistentFormula = vSetting
        End If

        vSetting = rngSettings.Cells(6, 2).Value
        If Len(vSetting) And (vSetting = True Or vSetting = False) Then
            .OmittedCells = vSetting
        End If

        vSetting = rngSettings.Cells(7, 2).Value
        If Len(vSetting) And (vSetting = True Or vSetting = False) Then
            .UnlockedFormulaCells = vSetting
        End If

        vSetting = rngSettings.Cells(8, 2).Value
        If Len(vSetting) And (vSetting = True Or vSetting = False) Then
            .EmptyCellReferences = vSetting
        End If

        vSetting = rngSettings.Cells(9, 2).Value
        If LCase(vSetting) = "xlcolorindexautomatic" Then
            .IndicatorColorIndex = xlColorIndexAutomatic
        ElseIf Len(vSetting) And (vSetting > 1 And vSetting < 100) Then
            .IndicatorColorIndex = vSetting
        End If
```

```
    End With

    'Indicators sometimes don't appear
    ' after the routine finishes unless you
    ' update the screen
    Application.ScreenUpdating = True

End Sub
```

FillFormat Object

The `FillFormat` object represents the fill effects available for shapes. For example, a `FillFormat` object defines solid, textured, and patterned fill of the parent shape. A `FillFormat` object can only be accessed through the parent `Shape` object.

FillFormat Common Properties

The `Application`, `Creator`, and `Parent` properties are defined at the beginning of this appendix.

FillFormat Properties

Name	Returns	Description
`BackColor`	`ColorFormat`	Read Only. Returns the background color through the `ColorFormat` object.
`ForeColor`	`ColorFormat`	Read Only. Returns the foreground color through the `ColorFormat` object.
`GradientColorType`	`MsoGradientColorType`	Read Only. Returns what type of gradient fill color concept is used.
`GradientDegree`	`Single`	Read Only. Returns how dark or light the gradient fill is.
`GradientStyle`	`MsoGradientStyle`	Read Only. Returns the orientation of the gradient that is used.
`GradientVariant`	`Integer`	Read Only. Returns the variant used for the gradient from the center.
`Pattern`	`MsoPatternType`	Read Only. Returns the pattern used for the fill, if any.
`PresetGradientType`	`MsoPresetGradientType`	Read Only. Returns the type of gradient that is used.
`PresetTexture`	`MsoPresetTexture`	Read Only. Returns the non-custom texture of the fill.
`TextureName`	`String`	Read Only. Returns the custom texture name of the fill.
`TextureType`	`MsoTextureType`	Read Only. Returns whether the texture is custom, preset, or mixed.
`Transparency`	`Single`	Set/Get how transparent the fill is. From `0` (opaque) to `1` (clear).

Table continued on following page

Name	Returns	Description
`Type`	`MsoFillType`	Read Only. Returns if the fill is a texture, gradient, solid, background, picture or mixed.
`Visible`	`MsoTriState`	Set/Get whether the fill options are visible in the parent shape.

FillFormat Methods

Name	Returns	Parameters	Description
`OneColor Gradient`		`Style As MsoGradient Style, Variant As Integer, Degree As Single`	Set the style, variant and degree for a one-color gradient fill
`Patterned`		`Pattern As MsoPattern Type`	Set the pattern for a fill
`Preset Gradient`		`Style As MsoGradient Style, Variant As Integer, Preset GradientType As MsoPreset GradientType`	Choose the style, variant, and preset gradient type for a gradient fill
`Preset Textured`		`Preset Texture As MsoPreset Texture`	Set the preset texture for a fill
`Solid`			Set the fill to a solid color
`TwoColor Gradient`		`Style As MsoGradient Style, Variant As Integer`	Set the style for a two-color gradient fill
`UserPicture`		`PictureFile As String`	Set the fill to the picture in the `PictureFile` format
`UserTextured`		`TextureFile As String`	Set the custom texture for a fill with the `TextureFile` format

Example: FillFormat Object

```
Sub FormatShape()
   Dim oFF As FillFormat

   'Get the Fill format of the first shape
   Set oFF = ActiveSheet.Shapes(1).Fill
```

```
    'Format the shape
    With oFF
        .TwoColorGradient msoGradientFromCorner, 1
        .ForeColor.SchemeColor = 3
        .BackColor.SchemeColor = 5
    End With
End Sub
```

Filter Object and the Filters Collection

The `Filters` collection holds all of the filters associated with the specific parent `AutoFilter`. Each `Filter` object defines a single filter for a single column in an autofiltered range. The parent of the `Filters` collection is the `AutoFilter` object.

The `Filters` collection has one other property besides the typical collection attributes. The `Count` property returns the number of `Filter` objects in the collection.

Filter Common Properties

The `Application`, `Creator`, and `Parent` properties are defined at the beginning of this appendix.

Filter Properties

Name	Returns	Description
`Criteria1`	`Variant`	Read Only. Returns the first criteria defined for the filter (for example ">=5").
`Criteria2`	`Variant`	Read Only. Returns the second criteria for the filter if defined.
`On`	`Boolean`	Read Only. Returns whether the filter is in use.
`Operator`	`XlAuto Filter Operator`	Read Only. Returns what sort of operator has been defined for the filter (for example `xlTop10Items`).

Example: Filter Object and the Filters Collection

See the `AutoFormat` object for an example of using the `Filter` object and the `Filters` collection.

Floor Object

The `Floor` object contains formatting options for the floor area of a 3D chart. The parent of the `Floor` object is the `Chart` object.

Floor Common Properties

The `Application`, `Creator`, and `Parent` properties are defined at the beginning of this appendix.

Floor Properties

Name	Returns	Description
Border	Border	Read Only. Returns the border's properties around the floor of the 3D chart.
Fill	ChartFill Format	Read Only. Returns an object containing fill formatting options for the floor of a 3D chart.
Interior	Interior	Read Only. Returns an object containing options to format the inside area of the chart floor (for example interior color).
Name	String	Read Only. Returns the name of the `Floor` object.
PictureType	Variant	Set/Get how an associated picture is displayed on the floor of the 3D chart (for example stretched, tiled). Use the `XlPictureType` constants.

Floor Methods

Name	Returns	Parameters	Description
ClearFormats	Variant		Clears the formatting made on the `Floor` object
Paste			Pastes the picture in the clipboard into the `Floor` object
Select	Variant		Selects the floor on the parent chart

Example: Floor Object

```
Sub FormatFloor()
   Dim oFlr As Floor

   'Get the chart's Floor
   Set oFlr = Charts(1).Floor

   'Format the floor in white marble
   With oFlr
      .Fill.PresetTextured msoTextureWhiteMarble
      .Fill.Visible = True
   End With
End Sub
```

Font Object

The `Font` object contains all of the formatting attributes related to fonts of the parent including font type, size and color. Possible parents of the `Font` object are the `AxisTitle`, `Characters`, `ChartArea`, `ChartTitle`, `DataLabel`, `Legend`, `LegendEntry`, `Range`, `Style`, and `TickLabels` objects. Also, the `DataLabels` collection is another possible parent of the `Font` object.

Font Common Properties

The Application, Creator, and Parent properties are defined at the beginning of this appendix.

Font Properties

Name	Returns	Description
Background	Variant	Set/Get the type of background used behind the font text (xlBackgroundAutomatic, xlBackgroundOpaque, and xlBackgroundTransparent). Use the XlBackground constants. Valid only for text on charts.
Bold	Variant	Set/Get whether the font is bold.
Color	Variant	Set/Get the color of the font. Use the RGB function to create the color value.
ColorIndex	Variant	Set/Get the color of the font. Use the XlColorIndex constants or an index value in the current color palette.
FontStyle	Variant	Set/Get what style to apply to the font (for example "Bold").
Italic	Variant	Set/Get whether the font is italic.
Name	Variant	Set/Get the name of the font.
OutlineFont	Variant	Set/Get whether the font is an outline font. Not used in Windows.
Shadow	Variant	Set/Get whether the font is a shadow font. Not used in Windows.
Size	Variant	Set/Get the font size of the font.
Strikethrough	Variant	Set/Get whether the font has a strikethrough effect.
Subscript	Variant	Set/Get whether the font characters look like a subscript.
Superscript	Variant	Set/Get whether the font characters look like a superscript.
Underline	Variant	Set/Get whether the font is underlined.

Example: Font Object

```
Sub FormatCellFont()
   Dim oFont As Font

   'Get the font of the currently selected range
   Set oFont = Selection.Font

   'Format the font
   With oFont
      .Name = "Times New Roman"
      .Size = 16          'Points
      .ColorIndex = 5     'Blue
      .Bold = True
      .Underline = xlSingle
```

```
    End With
End Sub
```

FormatCondition Object and the FormatConditions Collection

The FormatConditions collection contains the conditional formatting associated with the particular range of cells. The Parent of the FormatConditions collection is the Range object. Up to three FormatCondition objects can be contained in the FormatConditions collection. Each FormatCondition object represents some formatting that will be applied if the condition is met.

The FormatConditions collection has one property and two methods besides the typical collection attributes. The Count property returns how many FormatCondition objects are in the collection. The Add method can be used to add a formatting condition to the collection. The Type parameter must be specified (XlFormatConditionType constants) and the condition may be specified with the Operator, Formula1, and Formula2 parameters.

Name	Returns	Description
Count	Long	Read Only. Returns the number of objects in the collection.
Add	Format Condition	Method. Parameters: Type As XlFormatConditionType, [Operator], [Formula1], [Formula2].
Delete		Method.

FormatCondition Common Properties

The Application, Creator, and Parent properties are defined at the beginning of this appendix.

FormatCondition Properties

Name	Returns	Description
Borders	Borders	Read Only. Returns a collection holding all the individual border attributes for the formatting condition.
Font	Font	Read Only. Returns an object containing Font options for the formatting condition.
Formula1	String	Read Only. Returns the value that the cells must contain or an expression or formula evaluating to True/False. If the formula or expression evaluates to True then the formatting is applied.
Formula2	String	Read Only. Returns the value that the cells must contain or an expression evaluating to True/False. Valid only if the Operator property is xlBetween or xlNotBetween.
Interior	Interior	Read Only. Returns an object containing options to format the inside area for the formatting condition (for example interior color).

Name	Returns	Description
`Operator`	`Long`	Read Only. Returns the operator to apply to the `Formula1` and `Formula2` property. Use the `XlFormatConditionOperator` constants.
`Type`	`Long`	Read Only. Returns whether the `FormatCondition` is applying formatting based on cell values or a formula. Use the `XlFormatConditionType` constants.

FormatCondition Methods

Name	Returns	Parameters	Description
`Delete`			Deletes the formatting condition.
`Modify`		`Type As XlFormat Condition Type, [Operator], [Formula1], [Formula2]`	Modifies the formatting condition. Since all the properties are read only, this is the only way to modify the format condition.

Example: FormatCondition Object and the FormatConditions Collection

```
Sub AddConditionalFormat()
   Dim oFC As FormatCondition

   'Remove any existing conditions
   For Each oFC In Selection.FormatConditions
      Selection.FormatConditions(1).Delete
   Next

   'Add first condition
   Set oFC = Selection.FormatConditions.Add(Type:=xlCellValue, Operator:=xlLess, _
                                                                    Formula1:="10")
   With oFC
      .Font.ColorIndex = 2                'white
      .Font.Bold = True
      .Interior.Pattern = xlSolid
      .Interior.Color = RGB(255, 0, 0)    'red
   End With

   'Add second condition
   Set oFC = Selection.FormatConditions.Add(Type:=xlCellValue,
Operator:=xlBetween, _
                                                     Formula1:="10",
Formula2:="40")
   With oFC
      .Font.Color = RGB(0, 255, 0)
      .Font.Bold = False
      .Interior.Pattern = xlNone
   End With

   'Add third condition
   Set oFC = Selection.FormatConditions.Add(Type:=xlCellValue,
Operator:=xlGreater, _
```

```
Formula1:="40")
    With oFC
        .Font.Color = RGB(0, 0, 255)
        .Font.Bold = True
        .Interior.Pattern = xlNone
    End With
End Sub
```

FreeformBuilder Object

The `FreeformBuilder` object is used by the parent `Shape` object to create new 'free hand' shapes. The `BuildFreeform` method of the `Shape` object is used to return a `FreeformBuilder` object.

FreeformBuilder Common Properties

The `Application`, `Creator`, and `Parent` properties are defined at the beginning of this appendix.

FreeformBuilder Methods

Name	Returns	Parameters	Description
`AddNodes`		`SegmentType As MsoSegment Type, EditingType As MsoEditing Type, X1 As Single, Y1 As Single, [X2], [Y2], [X3], [Y3]`	This method adds a point in the current shape being drawn. A line is drawn from the current node being added to the last node added. `SegmentType` describes the type of line to add between the nodes. `X1, Y1, X2, Y2, X3, Y3` is used to define the position of the current node being added. The coordinates are taken from the upper left corner of the document.
`ConvertTo Shape`	`Shape`		Converts the nodes added above into a `Shape` object.

Example: FreeformBuilder Object

```
Sub MakeArch()
    Dim oFFB As FreeformBuilder

    'Create a new freeform builder
    Set oFFB = ActiveSheet.Shapes.BuildFreeform(msoEditingCorner, 100, 300)

    'Add the lines to the builder
    With oFFB
        .AddNodes msoSegmentLine, msoEditingAuto, 100, 200
        .AddNodes msoSegmentCurve, msoEditingCorner, 150, 150, 0, 0, 200, 200
        .AddNodes msoSegmentLine, msoEditingAuto, 200, 300
        .AddNodes msoSegmentLine, msoEditingAuto, 100, 300

        'Convert it to a shape
        .ConvertToShape
    End With
End Sub
```

Graphic Object

Represents a picture that can be placed in any one of the six locations of the Header and Footer in the Page Setup of a sheet. It's analogous to using both the **Insert Picture** and **Format Picture** buttons in the **Header** or **Footer** dialogs inside the **Page Setup** command.

It's important to note that none of the Property settings of this object will result in anything appearing in the Header or Footer unless you insert "`&G`" (via VBA code) in any of the six different areas of the Header or Footer.

Graphic Common Properties

The `Application`, `Creator`, and `Parent` properties are defined at the beginning of this appendix.

Graphic Properties

Name	Returns	Description
`Brightness`	`Single`	Set/Get the brightness of the specified picture. This property's value must be from 0.0 (dimmest) to 1.0 (brightest).
`ColorType`	`MsoPictureColorType`	Set/Get the color transformation applied to the specified picture or OLE object.
`Contrast`	`Single`	Set/Get the contrast of the specified picture. This property's value must be from 0.0 (least) to 1.0 (greatest).
`CropBottom`	`Single`	Set/Get the number of points that are cropped off the bottom of the specified picture or OLE object.
`CropLeft`	`Single`	Set/Get the number of points that are cropped off the left-hand side of the specified picture or OLE object.
`CropRight`	`Single`	Set/Get the number of points that are cropped off the right-hand side of the specified picture or OLE object.
`CropTop`	`Single`	Set/Get the number of points that are cropped off the top of the specified picture or OLE object.
`Filename`	`String`	Set/Get the URL or path to where the specified object was saved.
`Height`	`Single`	Set/Get the height of the object.
`LockAspectRatio`	`MsoTriState`	Set/Get whether the specified shape retains its original proportions when you resize it.
`Width`	`Single`	Set/Get the width of the object.

Example: Graphic Object

The following routine prompts the user for a graphic file. If chosen, it places the graphic in the header of the active sheet as a Watermark and sizes it to fit the page:

```
Sub AddWatermark()

    Dim oSheet As Object
    Dim sFile As String

    On Error Resume Next
        Set oSheet = ActiveSheet
    On Error GoTo 0

    'Make sure there is an active sheet
    If Not oSheet Is Nothing Then

        'Set the properties of the File Open dialog
        With Application.FileDialog(msoFileDialogFilePicker)

            'Change the default dialog title
            .Title = "Insert Graphic In Center Header"

            'Allow only one file
            .AllowMultiSelect = False

            'Clear the filters and create your own
            'Switch to the custom filter before showing the dialog
            .Filters.Add "All Pictures", "*.gif; *.jpg; *.jpeg; *.bmp; *.wmf; _
                                  *.gif; *.emf; *.dib; *.jfif; *.jpe", 1

            'Show thumbnails to display small representations
            ' of the images
            .InitialView = msoFileDialogViewThumbnail

            'Show the dialog
            '-1 means they didn't cancel
            If .Show = -1 Then
                'Store the chosen file
                sFile = .SelectedItems(1)

                'Set up the graphic in the Header
                With oSheet.PageSetup
                    With .CenterHeaderPicture
                        .Filename = sFile
                        .ColorType = msoPictureWatermark
                        .LockAspectRatio = True

                        'Make it fill the page
                        'c Assumes a letter size portrait)
                        .Width = Application.InchesToPoints(17)
                    End With

                    'Make the graphic appear
                    'Without this, nothing happens
                    .CenterHeader = "&G"
                End With

            End If

            'Remove the filter when done
            .Filters.Clear

        End With

    End If

End Sub
```

Gridlines Object

The `Gridlines` object contains formatting properties associated with the major and minor gridlines on a chart's axes. The gridlines are an extension of the tick marks seen in the background of a chart allowing the end user to more easily see what a chart object's value is. The parent of the `Gridlines` object is the `Axis` object. To make sure the object is valid and to create the `Gridlines` object use the `HasMajorGridlines` and `HasMinorGridlines` properties of the `Axis` object first.

Gridlines Common Properties

The `Application`, `Creator`, and `Parent` properties are defined at the beginning of this appendix.

Gridlines Properties

Name	Returns	Description
`Border`	`Border`	Read Only. Returns the border's properties around the gridlines.
`Name`	`String`	Read Only. Returns the name of the `Gridlines` object.

Gridlines Methods

Name	Returns	Parameters	Description
`Delete`	`Variant`		Deletes the `Gridline` object
`Select`	`Variant`		Selects the gridlines on the chart

Example: Gridlines Object

```
Sub FormatGridlines()
   Dim oGL As Gridlines

   'Make sure the Y axis has gridlines
   With Charts(1).Axes(xlValue)
      .HasMajorGridlines = True

      'Get the Gridlines object for the major gridlines
      Set oGL = .MajorGridlines
   End With

   'Format the gridlines
   With oGL
      .Border.ColorIndex = 5
      .Border.LineStyle = xlDash
      .Border.Weight = xlThin
   End With
End Sub
```

GroupShapes Collection

The `GroupShapes` collection holds all of the shapes that make up a grouped shape. The `GroupShapes` collection holds a collection of `Shape` objects. The parent of the `GroupShapes` object is the `Shape` object.

The GroupShapes collection only has two properties besides the typical collection attributes. The Count property returns the number of Shape objects in the GroupShapes collection, and the Range property returns a subset of the shapes in the Shapes collection.

HiLoLines Object

The HiLoLines object contains formatting attributes for a chart's high-low lines. The parent of the HiLoLines object is the ChartGroup object. High-low lines connect the largest and smallest points on a 2D line chart group.

HiLoLines Common Properties

The Application, Creator, and Parent properties are defined at the beginning of this appendix.

HiLoLines Properties

Name	Returns	Description
Border	Border	Read Only. Returns the border's properties around the high-low lines.
Name	String	Read Only. Returns the name of the HiLoLines object.

HiLoLines Methods

Name	Returns	Parameters	Description
Delete	Variant		Deletes the high-low lines
Select	Variant		Selects the high-low lines on the chart

Example: HiLoLines Object

```
Sub AddAndFormatHiLoLines()
    Dim oHLL As HiLoLines

    'Add high-low lines to the first group
    Charts(1).ChartGroups(1).HasHiLoLines = True

    'Get the HiLoLines object
    Set oHLL = Charts(1).ChartGroups(1).HiLoLines

    'Format the lines
    With oHLL
        .Border.Weight = xlMedium
        .Border.LineStyle = xlContinuous
        .Border.ColorIndex = 3
    End With
End Sub
```

HPageBreak Object and the HPageBreaks Collection

The HPageBreaks collection contains all of the horizontal page breaks in the printable area of the parent object. Each HPageBreak object represents a single horizontal page break for the printable area of the parent object. Possible parents of the HPageBreaks collection are the WorkSheet and the Chart objects.

The HPageBreaks collection contains one property and one method besides the typical collection attributes. The Count property returns the number of HPageBreak objects in the collection. The Add method is used to add a HPageBreak object to the collection (and horizontal page break to the sheet). The Add method has a Before parameter to specify the range above where the horizontal page break will be added.

HPageBreak Common Properties

The Application, Creator, and Parent properties are defined at the beginning of this appendix.

HPageBreak Properties

Name	Returns	Description
Extent	XlPageBreak Extent	Read Only. Returns whether the horizontal page break is full screen or only for the print area.
Location	Range	Set/Get the cell that the horizontal page break is located. The top edge of the cell is the location of the page break.
Type	XlPageBreak	Set/Get whether the page break is automatic or manually set.

HPageBreak Methods

Name	Returns	Parameters	Description
Delete			Deletes the page break.
DragOff		Direction As XlDirection, RegionIndex As Long	Drags the page break out of the printable area. The Direction parameter specifies the direction the page break is dragged. The RegionIndex parameter specifies which print region the page break is being dragged out of.

Example: HPageBreak Object and the HPageBreaks Collection

```
Sub AddHPageBreaks()
   Dim oCell As Range

   'Loop through all the cells in the first column of the sheet
   For Each oCell In ActiveSheet.UsedRange.Columns(1).Cells

      'If the font size is 16, add a page break above the cell
      If oCell.Font.Size = 16 Then
         ActiveSheet.HPageBreaks.Add oCell
      End If
   Next
End Sub
```

Hyperlink Object and the Hyperlinks Collection

The `Hyperlinks` collection represents the list of hyperlinks in a worksheet or range. Each `Hyperlink` object represents a single hyperlink in a worksheet or range. The `Hyperlinks` collection has an `Add` and `Delete` method besides the typical collection properties and methods. The `Add` method takes the text or graphic that is to be converted into a hyperlink (`Anchor`) and the URL address or filename (`Address`) and creates a `Hyperlink` object. The `Delete` method deletes the `Hyperlinks` in the collection. The `Hyperlinks` collection also has a `Count` property that returns the number of `Hyperlink` objects in the collection.

Hyperlink Common Properties

The `Application`, `Creator`, and `Parent` properties are defined at the beginning of this appendix.

Hyperlink Properties

Name	Returns	Description
`Address`	`String`	Set/Get the file name or URL address of the hyperlink.
`EmailSubject`	`String`	Set/Get the e-mail subject line if the address is an e-mail address.
`Name`	`String`	Read Only. Returns whether the `ExtraInfo` property needs to be filled.
`Range`	`Range`	Read Only. Returns the name of the hyperlink.
`ScreenTip`	`String`	Read Only. Returns the spot in the document where the hyperlink is.
`Shape`	`Shape`	Set/Get the text that appears when the mouse hovers over the hyperlink.
`SubAddress`	`String`	Read Only. Returns the shape associated with the hyperlink, if any.
`TextTo Display`	`String`	Set/Get the spot in the target location that the hyperlink points to.
`Type`	`Long`	Set/Get the target location of the HTML frame of the Address.

Hyperlink Methods

Name	Returns	Parameters	Description
`AddTo Favorites`			Adds the `Address` property to the `Favorites` folder.
`CreateNew Document`		`Filename As String, EditNow As Boolean, Overwrite As Boolean`	Creates a new document with the `FileName` name from the results of the hyperlink's address. Set the `EditNow` property to `True` to open up the document in the appropriate editor. Set `Overwrite` to `True` to overwrite any existing document with the same name.

Name	Returns	Parameters	Description
Delete			Deletes the Hyperlink object.
Follow		[NewWindow], [AddHistory], [ExtraInfo], [Method], [HeaderInfo]	Opens up the target document specified by the Address property. Setting NewWindow to True opens up a new window with the target document. Set AddHistory to True to display the item in history folder. Use the Method parameter to choose if the ExtraInfo property is sent as a Get or a Post.

Example: Hyperlink Object and the Hyperlinks Collection

This example creates a hyperlink-based 'Table of Contents' worksheet:

```
Sub CreateHyperlinkTOC()
   Dim oBk As Workbook
   Dim oShtTOC As Worksheet, oSht As Worksheet
   Dim iRow As Integer

   Set oBk = ActiveWorkbook

   'Add a new sheet to the workbook
   Set oShtTOC = oBk.Worksheets.Add

   With oShtTOC
      'Add the title to the sheet
      .Range("A1").Value = "Table of Contents"

      'Add Mail and web hyperlinks
      .Hyperlinks.Add .Range("A3"), "mailto:Me@MyISP.com", _
                  TextToDisplay:="Email your comments"
      .Hyperlinks.Add .Range("A4"), "http://www.wrox.com", _
                  TextToDisplay:="Visit Wrox Press"
   End With

   'Loop through the sheets in the workbook
   'adding location hyperlinks
   iRow = 6
   For Each oSht In oBk.Worksheets
      If oSht.Name <> oShtTOC.Name Then
         oShtTOC.Hyperlinks.Add oShtTOC.Cells(iRow, 1), "", _
                  SubAddress:="'" & oSht.Name & "'!A1", _
                  TextToDisplay:=oSht.Name
         iRow = iRow + 1
      End If
   Next
End Sub
```

Interior Object

The Interior object contains the formatting options associated with the inside area of the parent object. Possible parents of the Interior object are the AxisTitle, ChartArea, ChartObject, ChartTitle, DataLabel, DownBars, Floor, FormatCondition, Legend, LegendKey, OLEObject, PlotArea, Point, Range, Series, Style, Upbars, and Walls objects. The ChartObjects, DataLabels, and OLEObjects collections also are possible parents of the Interior object.

Interior Common Properties

The `Application`, `Creator`, and `Parent` properties are defined at the beginning of this appendix.

Interior Properties

Name	Returns	Description
`Color`	`Variant`	Set/Get the color of the interior. Use the `RGB` function to create the color value.
`ColorIndex`	`Variant`	Set/Get the color of the interior. Use the `XlColorIndex` constants or an index value in the current color palette.
`InvertIf Negative`	`Variant`	Set/Get whether the color in the interior of the parent object is inverted if the values are negative.
`Pattern`	`Variant`	Set/Get the pattern to use for the interior of the parent object. Use one of the `XlPattern` constants.
`PatternColor`	`Variant`	Set/Get the color of the interior pattern. Use the `RGB` function to create the color value.
`PatternColor Index`	`Variant`	Set/Get the color of the interior pattern. Use the `XlColorIndex` constants or an index value in the current color palette.

Example: Interior Object

```
Sub FormatRange()
   Dim oInt As Interior

   'Get the interior of the current selection
   Set oInt = Selection.Interior

   'Format the interior in solid yellow
   '(colour depends on the workbook palette)
   With oInt
      .Pattern = xlSolid
      .ColorIndex = 6
   End With
End Sub
```

IRtdServer Object

This object allows the ability to connect to a Real-Time Data Server (RTD). This type of server allows Excel to receive timed interval data updates without the need for extra coding. In prior versions of Excel, when regular updates were needed, you could use the `OnTime` method to set up regular data update intervals. RTDs send updates automatically based on an interval set within the server or by using the `HeartbeatInterval` method of the `IRTDUpdateEvent` object.

This object is similar in nature to using the RTD worksheet function, which displays data at regular intervals in a worksheet cell.

Note that to use this object you must instantiate it using the `Implements` keyword.

IRtdServer Methods

Name	Returns	Parameters	Description
ConnectData		TopicID, Strings, GetNewValues	Called when a file is opened that contains real-time data (RTD) functions or when a new formula which contains a RTD function is entered.
Disconnect Data		TopicID	Used to notify the RTD server that a topic is no longer in use.
Heartbeat	Long		Checks to see if the RTD server is still active. Negative numbers or zero are a failure, while positive numbers indicate success.
RefreshData		ByRef TopicCount As Long	This method is called to get new data, but only after being notified by the RTD server that there is new data.
ServerStart	Long	Callback Object	Called immediately after a RTD server is instantiated. Negative numbers or zero are a failure, while positive numbers indicate success.
Server Terminate			Used to terminate the connection to the server.

IRTDUpdateEvent Object

Represents Real-Time update events. This object is used to set the interval between updates for an `IrtdServer` object using the `HeartbeatInterval` property. This object is returned when you use the `ServerStart` method of the `IrtdServer` object to connect to a Real-Time Data Server.

IRTDUpdateEvent Properties

Name	Returns	Description
Heartbeat Interval	Long	Set/Get the interval between updates for RTD

IRTDUpdateEvent Methods

Name	Returns	Parameters	Description
Disconnect			Instructs the RTD server to disconnect from the specified object
UpdateNotify			Excel is informed by the RTD server that new data has been received

LeaderLines Object

The `LeaderLines` object contains the formatting attributes associated with leader lines on charts connecting data labels to the actual points. The parent of the `LeaderLines` object is the `Series` object. Use the `HasLeaderLines` property of the `Series` object to create a `LeaderLines` object and make sure one exists.

LeaderLines Common Properties

The `Application`, `Creator`, and `Parent` properties are defined at the beginning of this appendix.

LeaderLines Properties

Name	Returns	Description
`Border`	`Border`	Read Only. Returns the border's properties around the leader lines.

LeaderLines Methods

Name	Returns	Parameters	Description
`Delete`			Deletes the `LeaderLines` object
`Select`			Selects the leader lines on the chart

Example: LeaderLines Object

```
Sub AddAndFormatLeaderLines()
   Dim oLL As LeaderLines

   'Using the first series of the PIE chart
   With Charts(1).SeriesCollection(1)

      'Add labels with leader lines (if required)
      .ApplyDataLabels HasLeaderLines:=True

      'Position the labels
      .DataLabels.Position = xlLabelPositionBestFit

      'Get the LeaderLines Object.  If all labels are
      'in their default position, this will give an error
      Set oLL = .LeaderLines
   End With

   'Format the leader lines
   With oLL
      .Border.LineStyle = xlContinuous
      .Border.ColorIndex = 5
   End With
End Sub
```

Legend Object

The `Legend` object contains the formatting options and legend entries for a particular chart. The parent of the `Legend` object is the `Chart` object. Use the `HasLegend` property of the `Chart` object to create a `Legend` object and to make sure one exists.

Legend Common Properties

The Application, Creator, and Parent properties are defined at the beginning of this appendix.

Legend Properties

Name	Returns	Description
AutoScaleFont	Variant	Set/Get whether the font size will change automatically if the parent chart changes sizes.
Border	Border	Read Only. Returns the border's properties around the legend.
Fill	ChartFill Format	Read Only. Returns an object containing fill formatting options for the legend of a chart.
Font	Font	Read Only. Returns an object containing Font options for the legend text.
Height	Double	Set/Get the height of the legend box.
Interior	Interior	Read Only. Returns an object containing options to format the inside area of a legend (for example interior color).
Left	Double	Set/Get the distance from the left edge of the legend box to the left edge of the chart containing the legend.
Name	String	Read Only. Returns the name of the Legend object.
Position	XlLegend Position	Set/Get the position of the legend on the chart (for example xlLegendPositionCorner, xlLegendPositionLeft).
Shadow	Boolean	Set/Get whether the legend has a shadow effect.
Top	Double	Set/Get the distance from the top edge of the legend box to the top edge of the chart containing the legend.
Width	Double	Set/Get the width of the legend box.

Legend Methods

Name	Returns	Parameters	Description
Clear	Variant		Clears the legend.
Delete	Variant		Deletes the legend.
LegendEntries	Object	[Index]	Returns either one LegendEntry object or a LegendEntries collection depending if an Index parameter is specified. Contains all the legend text and markers.
Select	Variant		Selects the legend on the chart.

Example: Legend Object

```
Sub PlaceLegend()
    Dim oLgnd As Legend

    'Make sure the chart has a legend
    Charts(1).HasLegend = True

    'Get the Legend
    Set oLgnd = Charts(1).Legend

    'Position and format the legend
    With oLgnd
        .Position = xlLegendPositionRight
        .Border.LineStyle = xlNone
        .AutoScaleFont = False
    End With
End Sub
```

LegendEntry Object and the LegendEntries Collection

The `LegendEntries` collection contains the collection of entries in a legend. Each `LegendEntry` object represents a single entry in a legend. This consists of the legend entry text and the legend entry marker. The legend entry text is always the associated series name or trendline name. The parent of the `LegendEntries` collection is the `Legend` object.

The `LegendEntries` collection contains one property besides the typical collection attributes. The `Count` property returns the number of `LegendEntry` objects in the collection.

LegendEntry Common Properties

The `Application`, `Creator`, and `Parent` properties are defined at the beginning of this appendix.

LegendEntry Properties

Name	Returns	Description
`AutoScaleFont`	`Variant`	Set/Get whether the font size will change automatically if the parent chart changes sizes.
`Font`	`Font`	Read Only. Returns an object containing `Font` options for the legend entry text.
`Height`	`Double`	Read Only. Returns the height of the legend entry.
`Index`	`Long`	Read Only. Returns the position of the `LegendEntry` in the `LegendEntries` collection.
`Left`	`Double`	Read Only. Returns the distance from the left edge of the legend entry box to the left edge of the chart.
`LegendKey`	`LegendKey`	Read Only. Returns an object containing formatting associated with the legend entry marker.
`Top`	`Double`	Read Only. Returns the distance from the top edge of the legend entry box to the top edge of the chart.
`Width`	`Double`	Read Only. Returns the width of the legend entry.

LegendEntry Methods

Name	Returns	Parameters	Description
Delete	Variant		Deletes the LegendEntry object
Select	Variant		Selects the legend entry on the chart

Example: LegendEntry Object and the LegendEntries Collection

```
Sub FormatLegendEntries()
   Dim oLE As LegendEntry

   'Make sure the chart has a legend
   Charts(1).HasLegend = True

   'Loop through all the legend entries
   For Each oLE In Charts(1).Legend.LegendEntries

      'Format each entry with a different font style
      With oLE
         .Font.Size = 10 + .Index * 4
         .Font.Bold = (.Index Mod 2) = 0
         .Font.ColorIndex = .Index
      End With
   Next
End Sub
```

LegendKey Object

The `LegendKey` object contains properties and methods to manipulate the formatting associated with a legend key entry marker. A legend key is a visual representation, such as a color, that identifies a specific series or trendline.

LegendKey Common Properties

The `Application`, `Creator`, and `Parent` properties are defined at the beginning of this appendix.

LegendKey Properties

Name	Returns	Description
Border	Border	Read Only. Returns the border's properties around the legend key.
Fill	ChartFill Format	Read Only. Returns an object containing fill formatting options for the legend key of a series or trendline in a chart.
Height	Double	Read Only. Returns the height of the legend entry key.
Interior	Interior	Read Only. Returns an object containing options to format the inside area of the legend key (for example interior color).

Table continued on following page

Name	Returns	Description
InvertIf Negative	Boolean	Set/Get whether the color in the legend key is inverted if the values are negative.
Left	Double	Read Only. Returns the distance from the left edge of the legend key entry box to the left edge of the chart.
Marker Background Color	Long	Set/Get the color of the legend key background. Use the RGB function to create the color value.
Marker Background ColorIndex	XlColor Index	Set/Get the color of the legend key background. Use the XlColorIndex constants or an index value in the current color palette.
Marker Foreground Color	Long	Set/Get the color of the legend key foreground. Use the RGB function to create the color value.
Marker Foreground ColorIndex	XlColor Index	Set/Get the color of the legend key foreground. Use the XlColorIndex constants or an index value in the current color palette.
MarkerSize	Long	Set/Get the size of the legend key marker.
MarkerStyle	XlMarker Style	Set/Get the type of marker to use as the legend key (for example square, diamond, triangle, picture, etc.).
PictureType	Long	Set/Get how an associated picture is displayed on the legend (for example stretched, tiled). Use the XlPictureType constants.
PictureUnit	Long	Set/Get how many units a picture represents if the PictureType property is set to xlScale.
Shadow	Boolean	Set/Get whether a shadow effect appears around the legend entry key.
Smooth	Boolean	Set/Get whether the legend key has smooth curving enabled.
Top	Double	Read Only. Returns the distance from the top edge of the legend entry key box to the top edge of the chart.
Width	Double	Read Only. Returns the width of the legend entry key box.

LegendKey Methods

Name	Returns	Parameters	Description
ClearFormats	Variant		Clears the formatting made on the LegendKey object
Delete	Variant		Deletes the LegendKey object
Select	Variant		Selects the legend key on the parent chart

Example: LegendKey Object

```
Sub FormatLegendKeys()
   Dim oLE As LegendEntry
   Dim oLK As LegendKey

   'Make sure the chart has a legend
   Charts(1).HasLegend = True

   'Loop through all the legend entries
   For Each oLE In Charts(1).Legend.LegendEntries

      'Get the legend key for the entry
      Set oLK = oLE.LegendKey

      'Format each legend key with a different colour and size
      With oLK
         .MarkerForegroundColor = oLE.Index
         .MarkerSize = oLE.Index * 2 + 1
      End With
   Next
End Sub
```

LineFormat Object

The `LineFormat` object represents the formatting associated with the line of the parent `Shape` object. The `Line` property of the `Shape` object is used to access the `LineFormat` object. The `LineFormat` object is commonly used to change line properties such as arrowhead styles and directions.

LineFormat Common Properties

The `Application`, `Creator`, and `Parent` properties are defined at the beginning of this appendix.

LineFormat Properties

Name	Returns	Description
`BackColor`	`Color Format`	Read Only. Returns an object allowing manipulation of the background color of the line.
`Begin Arrowhead Length`	`Mso Arrowhead Length`	Set/Get the arrowhead length on the start of the line.
`Begin Arrowhead Style`	`Mso Arrowhead Style`	Set/Get how the arrowhead looks on the start of the line.
`Begin Arrowhead Width`	`Mso Arrowhead Width`	Set/Get the arrowhead width on the start of the line.
`DashStyle`	`MsoLine Dash Style`	Set/Get the style of the line.
`EndArrowhead Length`	`Mso Arrowhead Length`	Set/Get the arrowhead length on the end of the line.

Name	Returns	Description
EndArrowhead Style	Mso Arrowhead Style	Set/Get how the arrowhead looks on the end of the line.
EndArrowhead Width	Mso Arrowhead Width	Set/Get the arrowhead width on the end of the line.
ForeColor	Color Format	Read Only. Returns an object allowing manipulation of the background color of the line.
Pattern	MsoPattern Type	Set/Get the pattern used on the line.
Style	MsoLine Style	Set/Get the line style.
Transparency	Single	Set/Get how transparent (1) or opaque (0) the line is.
Visible	MsoTri State	Set/Get whether the line is visible.
Weight	Single	Set/Get how thick the line is.

Example: LineFormat Object

```
Sub AddAndFormatLine()
   Dim oShp As Shape
   Dim oLF As LineFormat

   'Add a line shape
   Set oShp = ActiveSheet.Shapes.AddLine(100, 100, 200, 250)

   'Get the line format object
   Set oLF = oShp.Line

   'Set the line format
   With oLF
      .BeginArrowheadStyle = msoArrowheadOval
      .EndArrowheadStyle = msoArrowheadTriangle
      .EndArrowheadLength = msoArrowheadLong
      .EndArrowheadWidth = msoArrowheadWide
      .Style = msoLineSingle
   End With
End Sub
```

LinkFormat Object

The `LinkFormat` object represents the linking attributes associated with an `OLE` object or picture. The `LinkFormat` object is associated with a `Shape` object. Only `Shape` objects that are valid `OLE` objects can access the `LinkFormat` object.

LinkFormat Common Properties

The `Application`, `Creator`, and `Parent` properties are defined at the beginning of this appendix.

LinkFormat Properties

Name	Returns	Description
`AutoUpdate`	`Boolean`	Set/Get whether the parent `Shape` object is updated whenever the source file changes or when the parent object is opened.
`Locked`	`Boolean`	Set/Get whether the parent `Shape` object does not update itself against the source file.

LinkFormat Methods

Name	Returns	Parameters	Description
`Update`			Updates the parent `Shape` object with the source file data.

Example: LinkFormat Object

```
Sub UpdateShapeLinks()
    Dim oShp As Shape
    Dim oLnkForm As LinkFormat

    'Loop through all the shapes in the sheet
    For Each oShp In ActiveSheet.Shapes

        'Is it a linked shape?
        If oShp.Type = msoLinkedOLEObject Or oShp.Type = msoLinkedPicture Then

            'Yes, so get the link format
            Set oLnkForm = oShp.LinkFormat

            'and update the link
            oLnkForm.Update
        End If
    Next
End Sub
```

Mailer Object

The `Mailer` object is used on the Macintosh to mail Excel files using the PowerTalk Mailer.

Mailer Common Properties

The `Application`, `Creator`, and `Parent` properties are defined at the beginning of this appendix.

Mailer Properties

Name	Returns	Description
`BCCRecipients`	`Variant`	Set/Get the list of blind copies.
`CCRecipients`	`Variant`	Set/Get the list of carbon copies.

Table continued on following page

Name	Returns	Description
Enclosures	Variant	Set/Get the list of enclosures.
Received	Boolean	Read Only. Returns whether the mail message was received.
SendDateTime	Date	Read Only. Returns the date and time the message was sent.
Sender	String	Read Only. Returns the name of the mail message sender.
Subject	String	Set/Get the subject line of the mail message.
ToRecipients	Variant	Set/Get the array of recipient names.
WhichAddress	Variant	Set/Get the address that the mail message originates from.

Name Object and the Names Collection

The Names collection holds the list of named ranges in a workbook. Each Name object describes a range of cells in a workbook that can be accessed by the name. Some Name objects are built-in (for example Print_Area) and others are user defined. The parent of the Names collection can be the WorkBook, Application, and Worksheet object. The Name object can also be accessed through the Range object.

The Names collection has an Add method besides the typical collection attributes. The Add method adds a Name object to the collection. The parameters of the Add method correspond to the properties of the Name object.

Name Common Properties

The Application, Creator, and Parent properties are defined at the beginning of this appendix.

Name Properties

Name	Returns	Description
Category	String	Set/Get the category of the Name in the language used to create the macro. Valid only if the Name is a custom function or command.
CategoryLocal	String	Set/Get the category of the Name in the language of the end user. Valid only if the Name is a custom function or command.
Index	Long	Read Only. Returns the spot that Name is located in the Names collection.
MacroType	XlXLMMacro Type	Set/Get if the Name refers to command, function, or just a range.

Name	Returns	Description
Name	String	Set/Get the name of the Name object in the language of the macro.
NameLocal	String	Set/Get the name of the Name object in the language of the end user.
RefersTo	Variant	Set/Get the range text that the Name refers to in the language of the macro and in A1 notation style.
RefersToLocal	Variant	Set/Get the range text that the Name refers to in the language of the user and in A1 notation style.
RefersToR1C1	Variant	Set/Get the range text that the Name refers to in the language of the macro and in R1C1 notation style.
RefersToR1C1 Local	Variant	Set/Get the range text that the Name refers to in the language of the user and in R1C1 notation style.
RefersToRange	Range	Read Only. Returns the range that the Name refers to.
ShortcutKey	String	Set/Get the shortcut key to trigger a Microsoft Excel 4.0 macro associated with a Name.
Value	String	Set/Get the range text that the Name refers to in the language of the macro and in A1 notation style.
Visible	Boolean	Set/Get whether the name of the Name object appears in the **Names Dialog** box in Excel.

Name Methods

Name	Returns	Parameters	Description
Delete			Deletes the Name object from the collection

Example: Name Object and the Names Collection

```
Sub DeleteInvalidNames()
   Dim oName As Name

   'Loop through all the names in the active workbook
   For Each oName In ActiveWorkbook.Names

      'Is it an invalid name?
      If InStr(1, oName.RefersTo, "#REF") > 0 Then

         'Yes, so log it
         Debug.Print "Deleted name " & oName.Name & " - " & oName.RefersToLocal

         'and delete it from the collection
         oName.Delete
      End If
   Next
End Sub
```

ODBCError Object and the ODBCErrors Collection

The `ODBCErrors` collection contains a list of errors that occurred by the most recent query using an ODBC connection. Each `ODBCError` object contains information describing an error that occurred on the most recent query using an ODBC connection. If the most recent query against an ODBC source did not generate any errors then the collection is empty.

The `ODBCErrors` collection has a `Count` property besides the typical collection attributes. The `Count` property returns the number of `ODBCError` objects in the collection.

ODBCError Common Properties

The `Application`, `Creator`, and `Parent` properties are defined at the beginning of this appendix.

ODBCError Properties

Name	Returns	Description
`ErrorString`	`String`	Read Only. Returns the error string generated from the ODBC connection.
`SqlState`	`String`	Read Only. Returns the SQL state error generated from the ODBC connection.

Example: ODBCError Object and the ODBCErrors Collection

```
Sub CheckODBCErrors()
   Dim oErr As ODBCError
   Dim sMsg As String

   'Continue after errors
   On Error Resume Next

   'Don't show logon prompts etc
   Application.DisplayAlerts = False

   'Update an ODBC query table
   ActiveSheet.QueryTables(1).Refresh

   'Any errors?
   If Application.ODBCErrors.Count = 0 Then

      'No, so all OK
      MsgBox "Updated OK"
   Else
      'Yes, so list them all
      sMsg = "The following error(s) occured during the update"

      For Each oErr In Application.ODBCErrors
         sMsg = sMsg & vbCrLf & oErr.ErrorString & " (" & oErr.SqlState & ")"
      Next

      MsgBox sMsg
   End If
End Sub
```

OLEDBError Object and the OLEDBErrors Collection

The `OLEDBErrors` collection contains a list of errors that occurred by the most recent query using an OLE DB provider. Each `OLEDBError` object contains information describing an error that occurred on the most recent query using an OLE DB provider. If the most recent query against an OLE DB provider did not generate any errors then the collection is empty.

The `OLEDBErrors` collection has a `Count` property besides the typical collection attributes. The `Count` property returns the number of `OLEDBError` objects in the collection.

OLEDBError Common Properties

The `Application`, `Creator`, and `Parent` properties are defined at the beginning of this appendix.

OLEDBError Properties

Name	Returns	Description
`ErrorString`	`String`	Read Only. Returns the error string generated from the OLE DB provider.
`Native`	`Long`	Read Only. Returns a provider-specific error number describing the error.
`Number`	`Long`	Read Only. Returns the error number describing the error.
`SqlState`	`String`	Read Only. Returns the SQL state error generated from the OLE DB provider.
`Stage`	`Long`	Read Only. Returns the stage of an error generated from the OLE DB provider.

Example: OLEDBError Object and the OLEDBErrors Collection

```
Sub CheckOLEDbErrors()
    Dim oErr As OLEDBError
    Dim sMsg As String

    'Continue after errors
    On Error Resume Next

    'Don't show logon prompts etc
    Application.DisplayAlerts = False

    'Update an OLE DB pivot table
    ActiveSheet.PivotTables(1).Refresh

    'Any errors?
    If Application.OLEDBErrors.Count = 0 Then

        'No, so all OK
        MsgBox "Updated OK"
    Else
        'Yes, so list them all
        sMsg = "The following error(s) occured during the update"

        For Each oErr In Application.OLEDBErrors
            sMsg = sMsg & vbCrLf & oErr.ErrorString & " (" & oErr.SqlState & ")"
```

```
        Next

        MsgBox sMsg
    End If
End Sub
```

OLEFormat Object

The OLEFormat object represents all attributes associated with an OLE object or ActiveX object for linking. Linking characteristics are taken care of by the LinkFormat object. The Shape object is the parent of the OLEFormat object. The parent Shape object must be a linked or embedded object to be able to use this object.

OLEFormat Common Properties

The Application, Creator, and Parent properties are defined at the beginning of this appendix.

OLEFormat Properties

Name	Returns	Description
Object	Object	Read Only. Returns a reference to the parent OLE object.
ProgId	String	Read Only. Returns the ProgId of the parent OLE object.

OLEFormat Methods

Name	Returns	Parameters	Description
Activate			Activates and opens the parent OLE object.
Verb		[Verb]	Performs an action on the parent OLE object that triggers a reaction in the OLE object (for example xlOpen).

Example: OLEFormat Object

```
Sub PrintEmbeddedWordDocuments1()
   Dim oShp As Shape
   Dim oOF As OLEFormat

   'Loop through all the shapes in the sheet
   For Each oShp In ActiveSheet.Shapes

      'Is it an embedded object
      If oShp.Type = msoEmbeddedOLEObject Then

         'Get the embedded object's format
         Set oOF = oShp.OLEFormat

         'Is it a Word document?
         If oOF.ProgId Like "Word.Document*" Then

            'Yes, so print the Word document.
            'The first .Object gives us the generic
```

```
                'OLEObject contained in the Shape.
                'The second .Object gives us the Word object
                'contained within the OLEObject
                oOF.Object.Object.PrintOut
            End If
        End If
    Next
End Sub
```

OLEObject Object and the OLEObjects Collection

The `OLEObjects` collection holds all the ActiveX controls, linked OLE objects and embedded OLE objects on a worksheet or chart. An OLE object represents an ActiveX control, a linked OLE object, or an embedded OLE object on a worksheet or chart.

The `OLEObjects` collection has many properties and methods besides the typical collection attributes. These are listed in the following table.

OLEObjects Collection Properties and Methods

Name	Returns	Description
`AutoLoad`	`Boolean`	Set/Get whether the `OLE` object is automatically loaded when the workbook is opened. Not valid for ActiveX controls. Usually set to `False`. This property only works if there is one `OLEObject` in the collection.
`Border`	`Border`	Read Only. Returns the border's properties around the `OLE` object. This property only works if there is one `OLEObject` in the collection.
`Count`	`Long`	Read Only. Returns the number of `OLEObject` objects in the collection.
`Enabled`	`Boolean`	Set/Get whether the `OLEObject` is enabled. This property only works if there is one `OLEObject` in the collection.
`Height`	`Double`	Set/Get the height of `OLEObject` frame. This property only works if there is one `OLEObject` in the collection.
`Interior`	`Interior`	Read Only. Returns an object containing options to format the inside area of the `OLE` object (for example interior color). This property only works if there is one `OLEObject` in the collection.
`Left`	`Double`	Set/Get the distance from the left edge of the `OLEObject` frame to the left edge of the sheet. This property only works if there is one `OLEObject` in the collection.
`Locked`	`Boolean`	Set/Get whether editing will be possible when the parent sheet is protected. This property only works if there is one `OLEObject` in the collection.

Table continued on following page

Name	Returns	Description
Placement	Variant	Set/Get how the OLEObject object is anchored to the sheet (for example free floating, move with cells). Use the XlPlacement constants to set this property. This property only works if there is one OLEObject in the collection.
PrintObject	Boolean	Set/Get whether the OLEObject on the sheet will be printed when the sheet is printed. This property only works if there is one OLEObject in the collection.
Shadow	Boolean	Set/Get whether a shadow appears around the OLE object. This property only works if there is one OLEObject in the collection.
ShapeRange	ShapeRange	Read Only. Returns the OLE object as a Shape object. This property only works if there is one OLEObject in the collection.
SourceName	String	Set/Get the link source name of the OLE object. This property only works if there is one OLEObject in the collection.
Top	Double	Set/Get the distance from top edge of the OLE object to the top of the parent sheet. This property only works if there is one OLEObject in the collection.
Visible	Boolean	Set/Get whether all the OLEObjects in the collection are visible.
Width	Double	Set/Get the width of the OLE object frame. This property only works if there is one OLEObject in the collection.
ZOrder	Long	Read Only. Returns the position of the OLE object among all the other objects on the sheet. This property only works if there is one OLEObject in the collection.
Add	OLEObject	Method. Parameters: [ClassType], [Filename], [Link], [DisplayAsIcon], [IconFileName], [IconIndex], [IconLabel], [Left], [Top], [Width], [Height]. Adds an OLE object to the collection of OLEObjects. The position of the new OLE object can be specified by using the Left, Top, Width, and Height parameters. The type of OLEObject (ClassType) or its location (FileName) can be specified as well. The other parameters have equivalent OLEObject properties.
BringToFront	Variant	Method. Brings all the OLE objects in the collection to the front of all the other objects.
Copy	Variant	Method. Copies all the OLE objects in the collection into the clipboard.

Name	Returns	Description
CopyPicture	Variant	Method. Parameters: Appearance As XlPictureAppearance, Format As XlCopyPictureFormat. Copies the OLE objects in the collection into the clipboard as a picture. The Appearance parameter can be used to specify whether the picture is copied as it looks on the screen or when printed. The Format parameter can specify the type of picture that will be put into the clipboard.
Cut	Variant	Method. Cuts all the OLE objects in the collection into the clipboard.
Delete	Variant	Method. Deletes all the OLEObject objects in the collection into the clipboard.
Duplicate		Method. Duplicates all the OLEObject objects in the collection into the parent sheet.
Select	Variant	Method. Parameters: [Replace]. Selects all the OLEObject objects in the collection.
SendToBack	Variant	Method. Brings the OLEObject objects in the collection to the back of other objects.

OLEObject Common Properties

The Application, Creator, and Parent properties are defined at the beginning of this appendix.

OLEObject Properties

Name	Returns	Description
AltHTML	String	Set/Get what HTML to use when the document is saved as a web page instead of embedding the OLE control.
AutoLoad	Boolean	Set/Get whether the OLE object is automatically loaded when the workbook is opened. Not valid for ActiveX controls. Usually set to False.
AutoUpdate	Boolean	Set/Get whether the OLE object is automatically updated when the source changes. Valid only for linked objects (OLEType=xlOLELink).
Border	Border	Read Only. Returns the border's properties around the OLE object.
BottomRight Cell	Range	Read Only. Returns the single cell range located under the lower-right corner of the OLE object.
Enabled	Boolean	Set/Get whether the OLEObject is enabled.
Height	Double	Set/Get the height of OLEObject frame.

Table continued on following page

Name	Returns	Description
Index	Long	Read Only. Returns the spot in the collection where the current OLEObject is located.
Interior	Interior	Read Only. Returns an object containing options to format the inside area of the OLE object (e.g. interior color).
Left	Double	Set/Get the distance from the left edge of the OLEObject frame to the left edge of the sheet.
LinkedCell	String	Set/Get the range that receives the value from the results of the OLE object.
ListFill Range	String	Set/Get the range that holds the values used by an ActiveX list box.
Locked	Boolean	Set/Get whether editing will be possible when the parent sheet is protected.
Name	String	Set/Get the name of the OLE object.
Object		Read Only. Returns access to some of the properties and methods of the underlying object in the OLE object.
OLEType	Variant	Read Only. Returns the type OLE object: xlOLELink or xlOLEEmbed. Use the XlOLEType constants.
Placement	Variant	Set/Get how the OLEObject object is anchored to the sheet (e.g. free floating, move with cells). Use the XlPlacement constants to set this property.
PrintObject	Boolean	Set/Get whether the OLEObject on the sheet will be printed when the sheet is printed.
ProgId	String	Read Only. Returns the programmatic identifier associated with the OLE object (e.g. "Excel.Application").
Shadow	Boolean	Set/Get whether a shadow appears around the OLE object.
ShapeRange	ShapeRange	Read Only. Returns the OLE object as a Shape object.
SourceName	String	Set/Get the link source name of the OLE object.
Top	Double	Set/Get the distance from top edge of the OLE object to the top of the parent sheet.
TopLeftCell	Range	Read Only. Returns the single cell range located above the top-left corner of the OLE object.
Visible	Boolean	Set/Get whether the OLEObject is visible
Width	Double	Set/Get the width of the OLE object frame.
ZOrder	Long	Read Only. The position of the OLE object among all the other objects on the sheet.

OLEObject Methods

Name	Returns	Parameters	Description
Activate	Variant		Sets the focus and activates the OLE object.
BringToFront	Variant		Brings the OLE object to the front of all the other objects.
Copy	Variant		Copies the OLE object into the clipboard.
CopyPicture	Variant	Appearance As XlPicture Appearance, Format As XlCopyPicture Format	Copies the OLE object into the clipboard as a picture. The Appearance parameter can be used to specify whether the picture is copied as it looks on the screen or when printed. The Format parameter can specify the type of picture that will be put into the clipboard
Cut	Variant		Cuts the OLE object into the clipboard.
Delete	Variant		Deletes the OLEObject object into the clipboard.
Duplicate			Duplicates the OLEObject object into the parent sheet.
Select	Variant	[Replace]	Selects the OLEObject object.
SendToBack	Variant		Brings the OLEObject object to the back of other objects.
Update	Variant		Updates the OLE object link if applicable.
Verb	Variant	Verb As XlOLEVerb	Performs an action on the parent OLE object that triggers a reaction in the OLE object (e.g. xlOpen).

OLEObject Events

Name	Parameters	Description
GotFocus		Triggered when the OLE object gets focus
LostFocus		Triggered when the OLE object loses focus

Example: OLEObject Object and the OLEObjects Collection

```
Sub PrintEmbeddedWordDocuments2()
   Dim oOLE As OLEObject
```

```
    'Loop through all the shapes in the sheet
    For Each oOLE In ActiveSheet.OLEObjects

        'Is it a Word document?
        If oOLE.ProgId Like "Word.Document*" Then

            'Yes, so print the Word document.
            oOLE.Object.PrintOut
        End If
    Next
End Sub
```

Outline Object

The `Outline` object represents the outline feature in Excel. The parent of the `Outline` object is the `WorkSheet` object.

Outline Common Properties

The `Application`, `Creator`, and `Parent` properties are defined at the beginning of this appendix.

Outline Properties

Name	Returns	Description
`AutomaticStyles`	`Boolean`	Set/Get whether the outline has styles automatically assigned by Excel.
`SummaryColumn`	`XlSummaryColumn`	Set/Get whether the summary columns are to the left (`xlLeft`) or the right (`xlRight`) of the detail columns.
`SummaryRow`	`XlSummaryRow`	Set/Get whether the summary rows are above (`xlAbove`) or below (`xlBelow`) the detail rows.

Outline Methods

Name	Returns	Parameters	Description
`ShowLevels`	`Variant`	`[RowLevels], [ColumnLevels]`	Show the detail of rows and columns at a higher level as specified by the `RowLevels` and `ColumnLevels` parameters, respectively. The rest of the detail for the other levels is hidden.

Example: Outline Object

```
Sub ShowOutlines()
    Dim oOutl As Outline

    'Group some rows
    ActiveSheet.Range("4:5").Group

    'Get the Outline object
    Set oOutl = ActiveSheet.Outline
```

```
    'Format the outline display
    With oOutl
        .ShowLevels 1
        .SummaryRow = xlSummaryAbove
    End With
End Sub
```

PageSetup Object

The `PageSetup` object contains the functionality of the **Page Setup** dialog box. Possible parents of the `PageSetup` object are the `Chart` and `Worksheet` object.

PageSetup Common Properties

The `Application`, `Creator`, and `Parent` properties are defined at the beginning of this appendix.

PageSetup Properties

Name	Returns	Description
`BlackAndWhite`	`Boolean`	Set/Get whether worksheet items will be printed in black and white only. Not valid when parents are `Chart` objects.
`BottomMargin`	`Double`	Set/Get the bottom margin of the page in points.
`CenterFooter`	`String`	Set/Get the text for the center part of the footer.
`CenterFooter Picture`	`Graphic`	Read Only. Returns the picture for the center section of the footer.
`CenterHeader`	`String`	Set/Get the text for the center part of the header.
`CenterHeader Picture`	`Graphic`	Read Only. Returns the picture for the center section of the footer.
`Center Horizontally`	`Boolean`	Set/Get whether the worksheet or chart will be horizontally centered on the page.
`Center Vertically`	`Boolean`	Set/Get whether the worksheet or chart will be vertically centered on the page.
`ChartSize`	`XlObject Size`	Set/Get how the chart is scaled to fit one page (`xlFullPage` or `xlFitToPage`) or the same way it appears on the screen (`xlScreenSize`). Not valid when parents are `Worksheet` objects.
`Draft`	`Boolean`	Set/Get whether graphics will be printed. `True` means graphics will not be printed.
`FirstPage Number`	`Long`	Set/Get which number will be used as the first page number. Use `xlAutomatic` to have Excel choose this (default).
`FitToPages Tall`	`Variant`	Set/Get how many pages tall the sheet will be scaled to. Setting this property to `False` will mean the `FitToPagesWide` property will be used.

Table continued on following page

Name	Returns	Description
FitToPages Wide	Variant	Set/Get how many pages wide the sheet will be scaled to. Setting this property to False will mean the FitToPagesTall property will be used.
FooterMargin	Double	Set/Get the distance from the page bottom to the footer of the page in points.
HeaderMargin	Double	Set/Get the distance from the page top to the header of the page in points.
LeftFooter	String	Set/Get the text for the left part of the footer.
LeftFooter Picture	Graphic	Read Only. Returns the picture for the left section of the footer.
LeftHeader	String	Set/Get the text for the center part of the header.
LeftHeader Picture	Graphic	Read Only. Returns the picture for the left section of the header.
LeftMargin	Double	Set/Get the left margin of the page in points.
Order	XlOrder	Set/Get the manner that Excel numbers pages for large worksheets (e.g. xlDownTheOver, xlOverThenDown). Not valid for parents that are Chart objects.
Orientation	XlPage Orientation	Set/Get the page orientation: xlLandscape or xlPortrait.
PaperSize	XlPaper Size	Set/Get the paper size (e.g. xlPaperLetter, xlPaperLegal, etc.).
PrintArea	String	Set/Get the range on a worksheet that will be printed. If this property is set to False then the entire sheet is printed. Not valid for parents that are Chart objects.
PrintComments	XlPrint Location	Set/Get how comments are printed or if they are at all (e.g. xlPrintInPlace, xlPrintNoComments).
PrintErrors	XlPrint Errors	Set/Get the type of print error displayed. This allows the suppression of error values when printing a worksheet.
Print Gridlines	Boolean	Set/Get whether cell gridlines are printed for a worksheet. Not valid for parents that are Chart objects.
PrintHeadings	Boolean	Set/Get whether row and column headings are printed.
PrintNotes	Boolean	Set/Get whether notes attached to the cells are printed at the end as endnotes. Not valid if parents are Chart objects.
PrintTitle Columns	String	Set/Get which columns to repeat on the left side of every printed page.
PrintTitleRow s	String	Set/Get which rows to repeat on the top of every page.

Name	Returns	Description
RightFooter	String	Set/Get the text for the right part of the footer.
RightFooter Picture	Graphic	Read Only. Returns the picture for the right section of the footer.
RightHeader	String	Set/Get the text for the center part of the header.
RightHeader Picture	Graphic	Read Only. Returns the picture for the right section of the header.
RightMargin	Double	Set/Get the right margin of the page in points.
TopMargin	Double	Set/Get the top margin of the page in points.
Zoom	Variant	Set/Get the percentage scaling that will occur for the worksheet. Not valid for parents that are `Chart` objects. (10 to 400 percent).

PageSetup Methods

Name	Returns	Parameters	Description
PrintQuality	Variant	[Index]	Set/Get the print quality. The `Index` parameter can be used to specify horizontal (`1`) or vertical (`2`) print quality.

Example: PageSetup Object

```
Sub SetUpPage()
   Dim oPS As PageSetup

   'Get the sheet's PageSetup object
   Set oPS = ActiveSheet.PageSetup

   'Set up the page
   With oPS
      'Set the paper size to the local default
      .PaperSize = fnLocalPaperSize
      .Orientation = xlPortrait
      'etc.
   End With
End Sub

Function fnLocalPaperSize() As XlPaperSize

   'Remember the paper size when we've read it
   Static iPaperSize As XlPaperSize

   'Is it set?
   If iPaperSize = 0 Then

      'No, so create a new workbook and read off the paper size
      With Workbooks.Add
         iPaperSize = .Worksheets(1).PageSetup.PaperSize
         .Close False
      End With
   End If
```

```
    'Return the paper size
    fnLocalPaperSize = iPaperSize
End Function
```

Pane Object and the Panes Collection

The Panes collection allows manipulation of the different panes of a window. A Pane object is equivalent to the single pane of a window. The parent object of the Panes collection is the Window object.
Besides the typical collection properties and methods the Panes collection has a Count property. The Count property returns the number of Pane objects in the collection.

Pane Common Properties

The Application, Creator, and Parent properties are defined at the beginning of this appendix.

Pane Properties

Name	Returns	Description
Index	Long	Read Only. Returns the spot in the collection where Pane object is located.
ScrollColumn	Long	Set/Get which column number is the leftmost column in the pane window.
ScrollRow	Long	Set/Get which row number is the top row in the pane window.
VisibleRange	Range	Read Only. Returns the cell range that is visible in the pane.

Pane Methods

Name	Returns	Parameters	Description
Activate	Boolean		Activates the pane.
LargeScroll	Variant	[Down], [Up], [ToRight], [ToLeft]	Causes the document to scroll in a certain direction a screen-full at a time as specified by the parameters.
ScrollInto View		Left As Long, Top As Long, Width As Long, Height As Long, [Start]	Scrolls the spot specified by the Left, Top, Width, and Height parameters to either the upper-left corner of the pane (Start = True) or the lower-right corner of the pane (Start = False). The Left, Top, Width, and Height parameters are specified in points.
SmallScroll	Variant	[Down], [Up], [ToRight], [ToLeft]	Causes the document to scroll in a certain direction a document line at a time as specified by the parameters.

Example: Pane Object and the Panes Collection

```
Sub ScrollActivePane()
    Dim oPane As Pane
    Dim oRNg As Range

    'The range to show in the pane
    Set oRNg = Range("G3:J10")

    'Get the active pane
    Set oPane = Application.ActiveWindow.ActivePane

    'Scroll the pane to show the range in the top-left corner
    oPane.ScrollColumn = oRNg.Column
    oPane.ScrollRow = oRNg.Row
End Sub
```

Parameter Object and the Parameters Collection

The `Parameters` collection holds the list of parameters associated with a query table. If no parameters exist then the collection has no `Parameter` objects inside of it. Each `Parameter` object represents a single parameter for a query table. The parent of the `Parameters` collection is the `QueryTable` object.

The `Parameters` collection has a few extra properties and methods besides the typical collection attributes. They are listed in the table below.

Parameters Collection Properties and Methods

Name	Returns	Description
`Count`	`Long`	Read Only. Returns the number of `Parameter` objects in the collection.
`Add`	`Parameter`	Method. Parameters: `Name As String, [iDataType]`. Adds a parameter to the collection creating a new query parameter for the parent query table. The type of parameter can be specified by `iDataType`. Use the `XlParamaterDataType` constants for `iDataType`.
`Delete`		Method. Deletes the parameters in the collection.

Parameter Common Properties

The `Application`, `Creator`, and `Parent` properties are defined at the beginning of this appendix.

Parameter Properties

Name	Returns	Description
`DataType`	`XlParameter DataType`	Set/Get the data type of the parameter.
`Name`	`String`	Set/Get the name of the parameter.
`PromptString`	`String`	Read Only. Returns the prompt that is displayed to the user when prompted for a parameter value.

Table continued on following page

Name	Returns	Description
RefreshOn Change	Boolean	Set/Get whether the query table results are refreshed when the parameter value changes.
SourceRange	Range	Read Only. Returns the range of text that contains the parameter value.
Type	XlParameter Type	Read Only. Returns the type of parameter (e.g. xlConstant, xlPrompt, or xlRange). XlConstant means that the Value parameter has the value of the parameter. XlPrompt means that the user is prompted for the value. XlRange means that the value defines the cell range that contains the value.
Value	Variant	Read Only. Returns the parameter value.

Parameter Methods

Name	Returns	Parameters	Description
SetParam		Type As XlParameter Type, Value	Set/Get the type of the parameter and the value of the parameter

Example: Parameter Object and the Parameters Collection

```
Sub UpdateQuery()
   Dim oParam As Parameter

   'Using the Query Table...
   With ActiveSheet.QueryTables(1)

      'Get the first parameter
      Set oParam = .Parameters(1)

      'Set its value
      oParam.SetParam xlConstant, "Company"

      'Refresh the query
      .Refresh
   End With
End Sub
```

Phonetic Object and the Phonetics Collection

The Phonetics collection holds all of the phonetic text in a range. The Phonetic object represents a single phonetic text string. The parent of the Phonetics object is the Range object.

The Phonetics collection has a few properties and methods besides the typical collection attributes. They are listed in the following table.

Phonetics Collection Properties and Methods

Name	Returns	Description
Alignment	Long	Set/Get the alignment for the phonetic text. Use the XlPhoneticAlignment constants.
CharacterType	Long	Set/Get the type of phonetic text to use. Use the XLPhoneticCharacterType constants.
Count	Long	Read Only. Returns the number of Phonetic objects in the collection.
Font	Font	Read Only. Returns an object containing Font options for the text in the Phonetics collection.
Length	Long	Read Only. Returns the number of phonetic text characters starting from the Start parameter.
Start	Long	Read Only. Returns what the position is that represents the first character of the phonetic text strings. Valid only if there is only one Phonetic object in the collection.
Text	String	Set/Get the phonetic text. Valid only if there is only one Phonetic object in the collection.
Visible	Boolean	Set/Get whether the phonetic text is visible to the end user. Valid only if there is only one Phonetic object in the collection.
Add		Method. Parameters: Start As Long, Length As Long, Text As String. Adds a Phonetic object to the collection at the cell specified by the parent Range object.
Delete		Method. Deletes all the Phonetic objects in the collection.

Phonetic Common Properties

The Application, Creator, and Parent properties are defined at the beginning of this appendix.

Phonetic Properties

Name	Returns	Description
Alignment	Long	Set/Get the alignment for the phonetic text. Use the XlPhoneticAlignment constants.
CharacterType	Long	Set/Get the type of phonetic text to use. Use the XLPhoneticCharacterType constants.
Font	Font	Read Only. Returns an object containing Font options for the phonetic text.
Text	String	Set/Get the phonetic text.
Visible	Boolean	Set/Get whether the phonetic text is visible to the end user.

PictureFormat Object

The `PictureFormat` object allows manipulation of the picture properties of the parent `Shape` object.

PictureFormat Common Properties

The `Application`, `Creator`, and `Parent` properties are defined at the beginning of this appendix.

PictureFormat Properties

Name	Returns	Description
`Brightness`	`Single`	Set/Get the brightness of the parent shape (0 to 1 where 1 is the brightest)
`ColorType`	`MsoPicture ColorType`	Set/Get the type of color setting of the parent shape
`Contrast`	`Single`	Set/Get the contrast of the parent shape (0 to 1 where 1 is the greatest contrast)
`CropBottom`	`Single`	Set/Get how much is cropped off the bottom
`CropLeft`	`Single`	Set/Get how much is cropped off the left
`CropRight`	`Single`	Set/Get how much is cropped off the right
`CropTop`	`Single`	Set/Get how much is cropped off the top
`Transparency Color`	`Long`	Set/Get the color used for transparency
`Transparent Background`	`MsoTriState`	Set/Get whether transparent colors appear transparent

PictureFormat Methods

Name	Returns	Parameters	Description
`Increment Brightness`		`Increment As Single`	Increases the brightness by the `Increment` value
`Increment Contrast`		`Increment As Single`	Increases the contrast by the `Increment` value

Example: PictureFormat Object

```
Sub SetPictureFormat()
   Dim oShp As Shape
   Dim oPF As PictureFormat

   For Each oShp In ActiveSheet.Shapes
      If oShp.Type = msoPicture Then

         'Get the PictureFormat
         Set oPF = oShp.PictureFormat

         'Format the picture
         With oPF
            .TransparentBackground = msoTrue
            .TransparencyColor = RGB(255, 0, 0)
            .ColorType = msoPictureWatermark
         End With
```

```
        End If
    Next
End Sub
```

PivotCache Object and the PivotCaches Collection

The PivotCaches collection holds the collection of memory 'caches' holding the data associated with a PivotTable report. Each PivotCache object represents a single memory cache for a PivotTable report. The parent of the PivotCaches collection is the Workbook object. Also a possible parent of the PivotCache object is the PivotTable object.

The PivotCaches has a Count property and Add method besides the typical collection attributes. The Count property returns the number of items in the collection. The Add method takes a SourceType constant (from the XlPivotTableSourceType constants) and SourceData to add a PivotCache to the collection.

PivotCache Common Properties

The Application, Creator, and Parent properties are defined at the beginning of this appendix.

PivotCache Properties

Name	Returns	Description
ADOConnection	Object	Read Only. Returns an ADO connection object if the PivotCache is connected to an OLE DB data source.
Background Query	Boolean	Set/Get if the processing of queries in a PivotTable report is done asynchronously. False for OLAP data sources.
CommandText	Variant	Set/Get the SQL command used to retrieve data.
CommandType	XlCmdType	Set/Get the type of ComandText (e.g. xlCmdSQL, xlCmdTable).
Connection	Variant	Set/Get the OLE DB connection string, the ODBC string, web data source, path to a text file, or path to a database.
EnableRefresh	Boolean	Set/Get whether the PivotTable cache data can be refreshed. Always False for OLAP data sources.
Index	Long	Read Only. Returns the spot in the collection for the specific cache.
IsConnected	Boolean	Read Only. Returns whether the PivotCache is still connected to a data source.
Local Connection	String	Set/Get the connection string to an offline cube file. Blank for non-OLAP data sources. Use with UseLocalConnection.
Maintain Connection	Boolean	Set/Get whether the connection to the data source does not close until the workbook is closed. Valid only against an OLE DB source.

Table continued on following page

Name	Returns	Description
MemoryUsed	Long	Read Only. Returns the amount of bytes used by the PivotTable cache.
MissingItems Limit	XlPivot Table Missing Items	Set/Get the maximum number of unique items that are retained per PivotTable field, even when they have no supporting data in the cache records.
OLAP	Boolean	Read Only. Returns whether the PivotCache is connected to an OLAP server.
OptimizeCache	Boolean	Set/Get whether the PivotTable cache is optimized when it is built. Always False for OLE DB data sources.
QueryType	xlQuery Type	Read Only. Returns the type of connection associated with the query table. (e.g. xlOLEDBQuery, xlDAOQuery, xlTextImport).
RecordCount	Long	Read Only. Returns the number of records in the PivotTable cache.
Recordset		Set/Get the recordset used as the data source for the PivotTable cache.
RefreshDate	Date	Read Only. Returns the date the cache was last refreshed.
RefreshName	String	Read Only. Returns the name of the person who last refreshed the cache.
RefreshOnFile Open	Boolean	Set/Get whether the PivotTable cache is refreshed when the workbook is opened.
RefreshPeriod	Long	Set/Get how long (minutes) between automatic refreshes from the data source. Set to 0 to disable.
RobustConnect	XlRobust Connect	Set/Get the method by which the PivotCache connects to its data source.
SavePassword	Boolean	Set/Get whether an ODBC connection password is saved with the query table.
Source Connection File	String	Set/Get the name of the file that was used to create the PivotTable.
SourceData	Variant	Set/Get the data source for the PivotTable report.
SourceData File	String	Read Only. Returns the name of the source data file for the PivotCache.
SourceType	XlPivot TableSource Type	Read Only. Returns a value that identifies the type of item being published.
UseLocal Connection	Boolean	Set/Get if the LocalConnection property is used to set the data source. False means the Connection property is used. Allows you to store some data sources offline.

PivotCache Methods

Name	Returns	Parameters	Description
CreatePivot Table	PivotTable	Table Destination As Variant, [TableName], [ReadData], [Default Version]	Creates a PivotTable report that is based on the current PivotCache object. The TableDestination parameter specifies where the new PivotTable report will be located. A TableName can also be specified. Set ReadData to True to fill the cache with all the records from the external database. Set ReadData to True to only retrieve some of the data. DefaultVersion is the default version of the PivotTable report.
Make Connection			Makes a connection for the specified PivotCache.
Refresh			Refreshes the data in the PivotTable cache with the latest copy of the external data. Set the BackgroundQuery parameter to True to get the data to refresh asynchronously.
ResetTimer			Resets the time for the automatic refresh set by RefreshPeriod property.
SaveAsODC		ODCFileName As String, [Description], [Keywords]	Saves the PivotCache source as an Office Data Connection (ODC) file. ODCFileName is the location where the file is to be saved. Description is the description that will be saved in the file. Keywords is a list of space-separated keywords that can be used to search for this file.

Example: PivotCache Object and the PivotCaches Collection

```
Sub RefreshPivotCache()
   Dim oPC As PivotCache

   Set oPC = ActiveWorkbook.PivotCaches(1)

   With oPC
      'Refresh in the foreground
      .BackgroundQuery = False
```

```
        'Only refresh if the data is over 1 hour old
        If .RefreshDate < Now - TimeValue("01:00:00") Then
            .Refresh
        End If
    End With
End Sub
```

PivotCell Object

Represents a cell somewhere inside a PivotTable. Use access the PivotCell object through the range object. Once obtained, you can use the various properties of the PivotCell object to retrieve data from a PivotTable. For example, you can use the PivotCellType, ColumnItems, and RowItems properties to locate a particular sales person's total sales for a specific region.

This object mirrors the functionality of the GETPIVOTDATA worksheet function and the GetPivotData method of the PivotTable object. The difference is the PivotCell object can render information about where the cell is in the report. The GETPIVOTDATA worksheet function and the GetPivotData method do just the opposite. They yield the value associated with row and column heading you provide.

PivotCell Common Properties

The Application, Creator, and Parent properties are defined at the beginning of this appendix.

PivotCell Properties

Name	Returns	Description
ColumnItems	PivotItemList	Read Only. Returns the items which represent the selected range on the column axis.
Custom Subtotal Function	Xl Consolidation Function	Read Only. Returns the custom subtotal function field setting of the PivotCell.
DataField	PivotField	Read Only. Returns the selected data field.
PivotCellType	XlPivotCell Type	Read Only. Returns the PivotTable entity that the selected cell corresponds to.
PivotField	PivotField	Read Only. Returns the PivotTable field containing the upper-left corner of the specified range.
PivotItem	PivotItem	Read Only. Returns the PivotTable item containing the upper-left corner of the specified range.
PivotTable	PivotTable	Read Only. Returns the PivotTable report containing the upper-left corner of the specified range, or the PivotTable report associated with the PivotChart report.
Range	Range	Read Only. Returns the range to which the specified PivotCell applies.
RowItems	PivotItemList	Read Only. Returns the items which represent the selected range on the row axis.

PivotField Object, PivotFields Collection and the CalculatedFields Collection

The PivotFields collection holds the collection of fields associated with the parent PivotTable report. The CalculatedFields collection holds the collection of calculated fields associated with the parent PivotTable report. Each PivotField object represents single field in a PivotTable report. The parent of the PivotFields and CalculatedFields collection is the PivotTable object.

The PivotFields and CalculatedFields collections have one extra property besides the typical collection attributes. The Count property returns the number of fields in the parent collection. The CalculatedFields collection also has an Add method that adds a new calculated field to the collection given a Name and a Formula.

PivotField Common Properties

The Application, Creator, and Parent properties are defined at the beginning of this appendix.

PivotField Properties

Name	Returns	Description
AutoShowCount	Long	Read Only. Returns the number of top or bottom items that are automatically displayed in the PivotTable field.
AutoShowField	String	Read Only. Returns the name of the data field used to figure out what top or bottom items to show automatically for a PivotTable field.
AutoShowRange	Long	Read Only. Returns either xlTop if the top items are shown automatically or xlBottom if the bottom items are shown.
AutoShowType	Long	Read Only. Returns either xlAutomatic if AutoShow is True or xlManual if AutoShow is disabled.
AutoSortField	String	Read Only. Returns the data field name that will be used to sort the PivotTable field automatically.
AutoSortOrder	Long	Read Only. Returns one of the XLSortOrder constants specifying the automatic sort order type used for the field.
BaseField	Variant	Set/Get the base field used for a calculation. Data fields only.
BaseItem	Variant	Set/Get the base item in the base field used for a calculation. Data fields only.
Calculation	XlPivotField Calculation	Set/Get the type of calculation to do on the data field.
Caption	String	Set/Get the text label to use for the field.

Table continued on following page

Name	Returns	Description
ChildField	PivotField	Read Only. Returns the child field of the current field, if any.
ChildItems	Variant	Read Only. Parameters: [Index]. Returns an object or collection containing a single PivotTable item (PivotItem) or group of PivotTable items (PivotItems) associated with the field.
CubeField	CubeField	Read Only. Returns the cube field that the current PivotTable field comes from.
CurrentPage	Variant	Set/Get the current page showing for the page field. Page fields only.
Current PageList	Variant	Set or Get an array of strings corresponding to the list of items included in a multiple-item page field of a PivotTable report.
CurrentPageNa me	String	Set/Get the displayed page of the PivotTable report.
DataRange	Range	Read Only. Returns a range containing the data or items in the field.
DataType	XlPivotField DataType	Read Only. Returns the data type of the PivotTable field.
DatabaseSort	Boolean	Set/Get whether manual repositioning of items in a PivotField is allowed. Returns True, if the field has no manually positioned items.
DragToColumn	Boolean	Set/Get whether the field can be dragged to a column position.
DragToData	Boolean	Set/Get whether the field can be dragged to the data position.
DragToHide	Boolean	Set/Get whether the field can be dragged off the PivotTable report and therefore hidden.
DragToPage	Boolean	Set/Get whether the field can be dragged to the page position.
DragToRow	Boolean	Set/Get whether the field can be dragged to a row position.
DrilledDown	Boolean	Set/Get whether the PivotTable field can be drilled down.
EnableItem Selection	Boolean	Set/Get whether the ability to use the field dropdown in the user interface is enabled.
Formula	String	Set/Get the formula associated with the field, if any.
Function	Xl Consolidation Function	Set/Get the type of function used to summarize the PivotTable field.

Name	Returns	Description
GroupLevel	Variant	Read Only. Returns how the field is placed within a group of fields.
HiddenItems	Variant	Read Only. Parameters: [Index]. Returns an object or collection containing a single hidden PivotTable item (PivotItem) or group of hidden PivotTable items (PivotItems) associated with the field.
HiddenItems List	Variant	Set/Get an array of strings that are hidden items for the PivotField.
IsCalculated	Boolean	Read Only. Returns whether the PivotTable field is calculated.
IsMember Property	Boolean	Read Only. Returns whether the PivotField contains member properties.
LabelRange	Range	Read Only. Returns the cell range containing the field's label.
LayoutBlank Line	Boolean	Set/Get whether a blank row is added just after the current row field.
LayoutForm	XlLayoutForm Type	Set/Get how the items will appear in the field.
LayoutPage Break	Boolean	Set/Get whether a page break is inserted after each field.
LayoutSubtotal Location	XlSubtotal LocationType	Set/Get the location for the field subtotals as compared to the current field.
MemoryUsed	Long	Read Only. Returns the number of bytes of computer memory being used for the field.
Name	String	Set/Get the name of the field.
NumberFormat	String	Set/Get the format used for numbers in the field.
Orientation	XlPivotField Orientation	Set/Get where the field is located in the PivotTable report.
ParentField	PivotField	Read Only. Returns the parent field of the current field, if any.
ParentItems	Variant	Read Only. Parameters: [Index]. Returns an object or collection containing a single parent PivotTable item (PivotItem) or group of parent PivotTable items (PivotItems) associated with the field.
Position	Variant	Set/Get the position number of the field among all the fields in the same orientation.

Table continued on following page

Name	Returns	Description
PropertyOrder	Long	Set/Get the display position of the member property within the cube field to which it belongs (setting will rearrange the order). Valid only for PivotField objects that are member property fields.
PropertyParent Field	PivotField	Read Only. Returns the field to which the properties in this field are linked.
ServerBased	Boolean	Set/Get whether only items that match the page field selection are retrieved from the external data source.
ShowAllItems	Boolean	Set/Get whether all items in the field are displayed.
SourceName	String	Read Only. Returns the name of the source data for the field.
Standard Formula	String	Set/Get the formulas with standard US formatting.
SubtotalName	String	Set/Get the label used for the subtotal column or row for this field.
Subtotals	Variant	Parameters: [Index]. Set/Get the subtotals displayed for the field.
TotalLevels	Variant	Read Only. Returns the total number of fields in the current field group.
Value	String	Set/Get the name of the field.
VisibleItems	Variant	Read Only. Parameters: [Index]. Returns an object or collection containing a single visible PivotTable item (PivotItem) or group of visible PivotTable items (PivotItems) associated with the field.

PivotField Methods

Name	Returns	Parameters	Description
AddPageItem		Item As String, [ClearList]	Adds an additional item to a multiple item page field. Item is the source name of a PivotItem object, corresponding to the specific OLAP member unique name. ClearList indicates whether to delete all existing items before adding the new item.
AutoShow		Type As Long, Range As Long, Count As Long, Field As String	Set the number of top or bottom items to display for a row, page, or column field. Type describes whether the items are shown as xlAutomatic or xlManual. Range is the location to start showing items. Count is the number of items to show for the field. Field is the base data field name.

Name	Returns	Parameters	Description
`AutoSort`		`Order As Long, Field As String`	Sets the field to automatically sort based on the `Order` specified (using `XlSortOrder` constants) and the base data `Field`.
`Calculated Items`	`Calculated Items`		Returns the group of calculated `PivotTable` items associated with the field.
`Delete`			Deletes the `PivotField` object.
`PivotItems`	`Variant`	`[Index]`	Returns an object or collection containing a single `PivotTable` item (`PivotItem`) or group of `PivotTable` items (`PivotItems`) associated with the field.

Example: PivotField Object, PivotFields Collection and the CalculatedFields

```
Sub AddField()
   Dim oPT As PivotTable
   Dim oPF As PivotField

   Set oPT = ActiveSheet.PivotTables(1)

      'Set the UseStandardFormula argument to true
      'This will format the field names in the formula for
      ' Standard U.S.English instead of using Local Settings
      'Note that running/debugging this workbook in versions of Excel
      ' prior to Excel 2002 will result in a "Wrong number of arguments" error.
   Set oPF = oPT.CalculatedFields.Add("Total", "=Price * Volume", True)

   oPF.Orientation = xlDataField
End Sub
```

PivotFormula Object and the PivotFormulas Collection

The `PivotFormulas` collection holds the formulas associated with the `PivotTable`. Each `PivotFormula` object represents a formula being used in a `PivotTable` report. The parent of the `PivotFormulas` collection is the `PivotTable` object.

The `PivotFormulas` collection has a `Count` property and an `Add` method besides the typical collection attributes. The `Count` property returns the number of items in the collection. The `Add` method takes a `Formula` string and adds a `PivotFormula` to the collection.

PivotFormula Common Properties

The `Application`, `Creator`, and `Parent` properties are defined at the beginning of this appendix.

PivotFormula Properties

Name	Returns	Description
`Formula`	`String`	Set/Get the formula associated with the table. Use the A1-style reference notation.
`Index`	`Long`	Read Only. Returns the order that the formulas in the parent collection will be processed.
`Standard Formula`	`String`	Set/Get the formulas with standard US formatting.
`Value`	`String`	Set/Get the formula associated with the table.

PivotFormula Methods

Name	Returns	Parameters	Description
`Delete`			Deletes the formula from the parent collection.

PivotItem Object, PivotItems Collection, and the CalculatedItems Collection

The `PivotItems` collection holds the collection of individual data entries in a field. The `CalculatedItems` collection holds the collection of individual calculated entries in a field. Each `PivotItem` object represents a single entry in a data field. The parent of the `PivotItems` and `CalculatedItems` collections is the `PivotField` object.

The `PivotItems` and `CalculatedItems` have one extra property besides the typical collection attributes. The `Count` property returns the number of objects in the collection. Also, the `Add` method of the `PivotItems` collection adds another item to the collection (only a `Name` is required). The `Add` method of the `CalculatedItems` collection adds another item to the collection but requires a `Name` and a `Formula` to be specified.

PivotItem Common Properties

The `Application`, `Creator`, and `Parent` properties are defined at the beginning of this appendix.

PivotItem Properties

Name	Returns	Description
`Caption`	`String`	Set/Get the label text associated with the item.
`ChildItems`	`Variant`	Read Only. Parameters: `[Index]`. Returns an object or collection containing a single `PivotTable` item (`PivotItem`) or group of `PivotTable` items (`PivotItems`) associated with the item.
`DataRange`	`Range`	Read Only. Returns a range containing the data or items in the item.

Name	Returns	Description
DrilledDown	Boolean	Set/Get whether the PivotTable item can be drilled down.
Formula	String	Set/Get the formula associated with item, if any.
IsCalculated	Boolean	Read Only. Returns whether the item that was calculated is a data item.
LabelRange	Range	Read Only. Returns the cell range containing the field's item.
Name	String	Set/Get the name of the item.
ParentItem	PivotItem	Read Only. Returns the parent item of the current item, if any.
ParentShowDetail	Boolean	Read Only. Returns whether the current item is being show because the one of the item's parents is set to show detail.
Position	Long	Set/Get the position number of the item among all the items in the same orientation.
RecordCount	Long	Read Only. Returns the number of records in the PivotTable cache that contain the item.
ShowDetail	Boolean	Set/Get whether the detail items are being displayed.
SourceName	Variant	Read Only. Returns the name of the source data for the item.
SourceNameStandard	String	Read Only. Returns the PivotItem's source name in standard US format settings.
StandardFormula	String	Set/Get the formulas with standard US formatting.
Value	String	Set/Get the name of the specified item.
Visible	Boolean	Set/Get whether the item is visible.

PivotItem Methods

Name	Returns	Parameters	Description
Delete			Deletes the item from the collection

Example: PivotItem Object, PivotItems Collection, and the CalculatedItems Collection

```
Sub ShowPivotItemData()
   Dim oPT As PivotTable
   Dim oPI As PivotItem

   'Get the pivot table
   Set oPT = ActiveSheet.PivotTables(1)
```

```
    'Get the pivot item
    Set oPI = oPT.PivotFields("Product").PivotItems("Oranges")

    'Show all the source data rows for that pivot item
    oPI.ShowDetail = True
End Sub
```

PivotItemList Object

Represents a list of PivotItems associated with a particular cell in a PivotTable. You access the list through the PivotCell object. PivotItemLists are accessed either through the ColumnItems or RowItems properties of the PivotCell object. How many row and column items in the PivotItemList depends on the structure of the PivotTable.

For example, cell D5 is in a PivotTable called WroxSales1. In the row area to the left of cell D5 is the row heading OR (Oregon). To the left of OR is another row label called Region1. Based on this information the following will yield 2:

```
MsgBox wksPivotTable.Range("D5").PivotCell.RowItems.Count
```

The following will yield Region1, the farthest label to the left of cell D5:

```
MsgBox wksPivotTable.Range("D5").PivotCell.RowItems(1)
```

Finally, the following will yield OR, the second farthest label to the left of cell D5:

```
MsgBox wksPivotTable.Range("D5").PivotCell.RowItems(2)
```

I have yet to find a use for both the PivotItemList and PivotCell objects. Normally I'm looking for the opposite. I want to retrieve information based on row or column items (headings) I provide, something the GetPivotData method and the GETPIVOTDATA worksheet function can obtain.

PivotItemList Common Properties

The Application, Creator, and Parent properties are defined at the beginning of this appendix.

PivotItemList Properties

Name	Returns	Description
Count	Long	Returns the number of objects in the collection

PivotItemList Methods

Name	Returns	Parameters	Description
Item	PivotItem	Index As Variant	Returns a single PivotItem from the PivotItemList

PivotLayout Object

The PivotLayout object describes how the fields of a PivotChart are placed in the parent chart. Either the Chart object or the ChartGroup object is the parent of the PivotChart object.

PivotLayout Common Properties

The Application, Creator, and Parent properties are defined at the beginning of this appendix.

PivotLayout Properties

Name	Returns	Description
ColumnFields		Read Only. Parameters: [Index]. Returns an object or collection containing the PivotTable field (PivotField) or PivotTable fields (PivotFields) associated with the columns of the PivotChart.
CubeFields	CubeFields	Read Only. Returns the collection of cube fields associated with the PivotChart.
DataFields		Read Only. Parameters: [Index]. Returns an object or collection containing the PivotTable field (PivotField) or PivotTable fields (PivotFields) associated with the data fields of the PivotChart.
HiddenFields		Read Only. Parameters: [Index]. Returns an object or collection containing the PivotTable field (PivotField) or PivotTable fields (PivotFields) associated with the hidden fields of the PivotChart.
InnerDetail	String	Set/Get the name of the field that will show the detail when the ShowDetail property is True.
PageFields		Read Only. Parameters: [Index]. Returns an object or collection containing the PivotTable field (PivotField) or PivotTable fields (PivotFields) associated with the page fields of the PivotChart.
PivotCache	PivotCache	Read Only. Returns the PivotChart's data cache.
PivotFields		Read Only. Parameters: [Index]. Returns an object or collection containing the PivotTable field (PivotField) or PivotTable fields (PivotFields) associated with the fields of the PivotChart
PivotTable	PivotTable	Read Only. Returns the PivotTable associated with the PivotChart.
RowFields		Read Only. Parameters: [Index]. Returns an object or collection containing the PivotTable field (PivotField) or PivotTable fields (PivotFields) associated with the rows of the PivotChart.
Visible Fields		Read Only. Parameters: [Index]. Returns an object or collection containing the PivotTable field (PivotField) or PivotTable fields (PivotFields) associated with the visible fields of the PivotChart.

PivotLayout Methods

Name	Returns	Parameters	Description
AddFields		[RowFields], [Column Fields], [PageFields], [AppendField]	Adds row, column, and page fields to a PivotChart report. RowFields, ColumnFields, and PageFields can hold a single string field name or an array of string field names. Set AppendField to True to add the fields to the chart. Set AppendField to False to replace the fields in the chart.

Example: PivotLayout Object

```
Sub SetPivotLayout()
   Dim oPL As PivotLayout

   'Get the pivot layout
   Set oPL = Charts(1).PivotLayout

   'Show sales of Oranges by region
   With oPL
      .AddFields RowFields:="Region", PageFields:="Product"
      .PageFields("Product").CurrentPage = "Oranges"
   End With
End Sub
```

PivotTable Object and the PivotTables Collection

The PivotTables collection contains the collection of PivotTables in the parent worksheet. Each PivotTable object in the collection allows manipulation and creation of Excel PivotTables. The parent of the PivotTables collection is the Worksheet object.

The PivotTables collection has a Count property and an Add method besides the typical collection attributes. The Count property returns the number of PivotTable objects in the collection. The Add method takes a new PivotTable cache (containing the data) and the destination single cell range determining the upper-left corner of the PivotTable report to create a new PivotTable report. The name of the new PivotTable report can also be specified in the Add method.

PivotTable Common Properties

The Application, Creator, and Parent properties are defined at the beginning of this appendix.

PivotTable Properties

Name	Returns	Description
CacheIndex	Long	Set/Get the index number pointing to the PivotTable cache of the current PivotTable.
Calculated Members	Calculated Members	Read Only. Returns all the calculated fields and calculated items for the PivotTable.

Name	Returns	Description
ColumnFields	Object	Read Only. Parameters: [Index]. Returns an object or collection containing the PivotTable field (PivotField) or PivotTable fields (PivotFields) associated with the columns of the PivotTable.
ColumnGrand	Boolean	Set/Get whether grand totals are shown for columns in the PivotTable.
ColumnRange	Range	Read Only. Returns the range of cells containing the column area in the PivotTable report.
CubeFields	CubeFields	Read Only. Returns the collection of cube fields associated with the PivotTable report.
DataBody Range	Range	Read Only. Returns the range of cells containing the data area of the PivotTable report.
DataFields	Object	Read Only. Parameters: [Index]. Returns an object or collection containing the PivotTable field (PivotField) or PivotTable fields (PivotFields) associated with the data fields of the PivotTable.
DataLabel Range	Range	Read Only. Returns the range of cells that contain the labels for the data fields in the PivotTable report.
DataPivot Field	PivotField	Read Only. Returns all the data fields in a PivotTable.
DisplayEmpty Column	Boolean	Read Only. Returns whether the non-empty MDX keyword is included in the query to the OLAP provider for the value axis.
DisplayEmpty Row	Boolean	Read Only. Returns whether the non-empty MDX keyword is included in the query to the OLAP provider for the category axis.
DisplayError String	Boolean	Set/Get whether the string in the ErrorString property is displayed in cells that contain errors.
Display Immediate Items	Boolean	Set/Get whether items in the row and column areas are visible when the data area of the PivotTable is empty.
DisplayNull String	Boolean	Set/Get whether the string in the NullString property is displayed in cells that contain null values.
EnableData ValueEditing	Boolean	Set/Get whether to show an alert when the user overwrites values in the data area of the PivotTable.
Enable Drilldown	Boolean	Set/Get whether drilldown in the PivotTable report is enabled.
EnableField Dialog	Boolean	Set/Get whether the PivotTable Field dialog box is displayed when the user double-clicks a PivotTable field.

Table continued on following page

Name	Returns	Description
EnableField List	Boolean	Set/Get whether to disable the ability to display the field well for the PivotTable. If the list was already visible, it disappears.
EnableWizard	Boolean	Set/Get whether the PivotTable Wizard is available.
ErrorString	String	Set/Get the string that is displayed in cells that contain errors. Use with the DisplayErrorString property.
GrandTotal Name	String	Set/Get the string label that will be displayed on the grand total column or row heading of a PivotTable report. Default is "Grand Total".
HasAuto Format	Boolean	Set/Get whether the PivotTable report is automatically re-formatted when the data is refreshed or the fields are moved around.
HiddenFields	Object	Read Only. Parameters: [Index]. Returns an object or collection containing the PivotTable field (PivotField) or PivotTable fields (PivotFields) associated with the hidden fields of the PivotTable.
InnerDetail	String	Set/Get the name of the field that will show the detail when the ShowDetail property is True.
MDX	String	Read Only. Returns the MDX (Multidimensional Expression) that would be sent to the provider to populate the current PivotTable view.
ManualUpdate	Boolean	Set/Get whether the PivotTable report is only recalculated manually.
MergeLabels	Boolean	Set/Get whether the outer-row item, column item, subtotal, and grand total labels of a PivotTable report have merged cells.
Name	String	Set/Get the name of the PivotTable report.
NullString	String	Set/Get the string that is displayed in cells that contain null strings. Use with the DisplayNullString property.
PageField Order	Long	Set/Get how new page fields are added to a PivotTable report's layout. Use the XLOrder constants.
PageFields	Object	Read Only. Parameters: [Index]. Returns an object or collection containing the PivotTable field (PivotField) or PivotTable fields (PivotFields) associated with the page fields of the PivotTable.
PageField Style	String	Set/Get the style used for a page field area in a PivotTable.
PageField WrapCount	Long	Set/Get how many page fields are in each column or row of the PivotTable report.

Name	Returns	Description
PageRange	Range	Read Only. Returns the range containing the page area in the PivotTable report.
PageRange Cells	Range	Read Only. Returns the range containing the page fields and item dropdown lists in the PivotTable report.
Pivot Formulas	Pivot Formulas	Read Only. Returns the collection of formulas used in the PivotTable report.
Pivot Selection	String	Set/Get the data and label selection in the PivotTable using the standard PivotTable report selection format. For example, to select the data and label for the Country equal to 'Canada' then the string would be "Country[Canada]".
Pivot Selection Standard	String	Set/Get the PivotTable selection in standard PivotTable report format using US settings.
Preserve Formatting	Boolean	Set/Get whether formatting of the PivotTable report is preserved when the report is changed, sorted, pivoted, refreshed or recalculated.
PrintTitles	Boolean	Set/Get whether the print title set on the PivotTable report is printed whenever the parent worksheet is printed.
RefreshDate	Date	Read Only. Returns the date that the PivotTable report data was refreshed last.
RefreshName	String	Read Only. Returns the name of the user who last refreshed the PivotTable report data.
RepeatItems OnEachPrinted Page	Boolean	Set/Get whether row, column, and item labels appear on the first row of each page when the PivotTable report is printed.
RowFields		Read Only. Parameters: [Index]. Returns an object or collection containing the PivotTable field (PivotField) or PivotTable fields (PivotFields) associated with the rows of the PivotTable.
RowGrand	Boolean	Set/Get whether grand totals are shown for rows in the PivotTable.
RowRange	Range	Read Only. Returns the range of cells containing the row area in the PivotTable report.
SaveData	Boolean	Set/Get whether the PivotTable report data is saved with the workbook.
Selection Mode	XlPT Selection Mode	Set/Get how the PivotTable report selection mode is set (e.g. xlLabelOnly)

Table continued on following page

Name	Returns	Description
ShowCell Background FromOLAP	Boolean	Set/Get whether the MDX that Excel asks for includes the BackColor property for each cell in the data area that corresponds to a cell in the OLAP data set.
ShowPage MultipleItem Label	Boolean	Set/Get whether "(Multiple Items)" will appear in the PivotTable cell whenever items are hidden and an aggregate of non-hidden items is shown in the PivotTable view.
SmallGrid	Boolean	Set/Get whether a two-by-two grid is used for a newly created PivotTable report (True) or a blank stencil outline (False).
SourceData	Variant	Set/Get the source of the PivotTable report data. Can be a cell reference, an array, multiple ranges, and another PivotTable report. Not valid to use with OLE DB data sources.
Subtotal HiddenPage Items	Boolean	Set/Get whether hidden page fields are included in row and column subtotals, block totals, and grand totals.
TableRange1	Range	Read Only. Returns the range containing the whole PivotTable report, not including page fields.
TableRange2	Range	Read Only. Returns the range containing the whole PivotTable report, with page fields.
TableStyle	String	Set/Get the PivotTable report body style.
Tag	String	Set/Get a string to be saved with the PivotTable report (e.g. a description of the PivotTable report).
VacatedStyle	String	Set/Get the style to use for vacated cells when a PivotTable report is refreshed.
Value	String	Set/Get the name of the PivotTable report.
Version	XlPivot Table VersionList	Read Only. Returns the version number of Excel.
View Calculated Members	Boolean	Set/Get whether calculated members for OLAP PivotTables can be viewed.
Visible Fields		Read Only. Parameters: [Index]. Returns an object or collection containing the PivotTable field (PivotField) or PivotTable fields (PivotFields) associated with the visible fields of the PivotTable.
VisualTotals	Boolean	Set/Get whether PivotTables should retotal after an item has been hidden from view.

PivotTable Methods

Name	Returns	Parameters	Description
AddDataField	PivotField	Field As Object, [Caption], [Function]	Adds a data field to a PivotTable report. Field is the unique field on the server, Caption is the label used to identify this data field, and Function is the function performed in the added data field.
AddFields	Variant	[RowFields], [Column Fields], [PageFields], [AddToTable]	Adds row, column, and page fields to a PivotTable report. The RowFields, ColumnFields, and PageFields can hold a single string field name or an array of string field names. Set AddToTable to True to add the fields to the report. Set AddToTable to False to replace the fields in the report.
Calculated Fields	Calculated Fields		Returns the collection of calculated fields in the PivotTable Report.
CreateCube File	String	File As String, [Measures], [Levels], [Members], [Properties]	Creates a cube file from a PivotTable report connected to an OLAP data source. File is the name of the cube file to be created, Measures is an array of unique names of measures that are to be part of the slice, and Levels an array of strings, where each array item is a unique level name. Members is an array of string arrays, where the elements correspond, in order, to the hierarchies represented in the Levels array. Properties should be set to False if you don't want member properties being included in the slice.
Format		Format As xlPivotFormat Type	Set the PivotTable report format to the predefined style specified in the Format parameter.
GetData	Double	Name As String	Get the value of a specific cell in the PivotTable report. The Name parameter must be in the standard PivotTable report selection format.

Table continued on following page

Name	Returns	Parameters	Description
GetPivotData	Range	[DataField], [Field1], [Item1], [Field2], [Item2], [Field3], [Item3], [Field4], [Item4], [Field5], [Item5], [Field6], [Item6], [Field7], [Item7], [Field8], [Item8], [Field9], [Item9], [Field10], [Item10], [Field11], [Item11], [Field12], [Item12], [Field13], [Item13], [Field14], [Item14]	Returns information about a data item in a PivotTable report. FieldN is the name of a column or row field in the PivotTable report, and ItemN is the name of an item in FieldN.
ListFormulas			Creates a separate worksheet with the list of all the calculated PivotTable items and fields.
PivotCache	PivotCache		Returns a data cache associated with the current PivotTable.
PivotFields	Object	[Index]	Returns an object or collection containing the PivotTable field (PivotField) or PivotTable fields (PivotFields) associated with the fields of the PivotTable.
PivotSelect		Name As String, [Mode As XlPTSelection Mode], [UseStandard Name]	Selects the part of the PivotTable specified by Name parameter in the standard PivotTable report selection format. Mode decides which part of the PivotTable to select (e.g. xlBlanks). Set UseStandardName to True for recorded macros that will play back in other locales.

Name	Returns	Parameters	Description
PivotTableWizard		[SourceType], [SourceData], [TableDestination], [TableName], [RowGrand], [ColumnGrand], [SaveData], [HasAutoFormat], [AutoPage], [Reserved], [BackgroundQuery], [OptimizeCache], [PageFieldOrder], [PageFieldWrapCount], [ReadData], [Connection]	Creates a PivotTable report. The SourceType uses the XLPivotTableSourceType constants to specify the type of SourceData being used for the PivotTable. The TableDestination holds the range in the parent worksheet that the report will be placed. TableName holds the name of the new report. Set RowGrand or ColumnGrand to True to show grand totals for rows and columns, respectively. Set HasAutoFormat to True for Excel to format the report automatically when it is refreshed or changed. Use the AutoPage parameter to set if a page field is created for consolidation automatically. Set BackgroundQuery to True for Excel to query the data source asynchronously. Set OptimizeCache to True for Excel to optimize the cache when it is built. Use the PageFieldOrder with the XLOrder constants to set how new page fields are added to the report. Use the PageFieldWrapCount to set the number of page fields in each column or row. Set ReadData to True to copy the data from the external database into a cache. Finally, use the Connection parameter to specify an ODBC connection string for the PivotTable's cache.
RefreshTable	Boolean		Refreshes the PivotTable report from the source data and returns True if successful.
ShowPages	Variant	[PageField]	Creates a new PivotTable report for each item in the page field (PageField) in a new worksheet.
Update			Updates the PivotTable report.

Example: PivotTable Object and the PivotTables Collection

```
Sub PreviewPivotTable()
   Dim oPT As PivotTable

   'Get the pivot layout
   Set oPT = ActiveSheet.PivotTables(1)

   'Add column and row titles, then printpreview the table
   With oPT
      .ColumnGrand = False
      .RowGrand = True
      .TableRange2.PrintPreview
   End With
End Sub
```

PlotArea Object

The `PlotArea` object contains the formatting options associated with the plot area of the parent chart. For 2D charts the `PlotArea` includes trendlines, data markers, gridlines, data labels, and the axis labels – but not titles. For 3D charts the `PlotArea` includes the walls, floor, axes, axis titles, tick-marks, and all of the items mentioned for the 2D charts. The area surrounding the plot area is the chart area. Please see the `ChartArea` object for formatting related to the chart area. The parent of the `PlotArea` is always the `Chart` object.

PlotArea Common Properties

The `Application`, `Creator`, and `Parent` properties are defined at the beginning of this appendix.

PlotArea Properties

Name	Returns	Description
`Border`	`Border`	Read Only. Returns the border's properties around the plot area.
`Fill`	`ChartFill Format`	Read Only. Returns an object containing fill formatting options for a chart's plot area.
`Height`	`Double`	Set/Get the height of the chart plot area.
`InsideHeight`	`Double`	Read Only. Returns the height inside the plot area that does not include the axis labels.
`InsideLeft`	`Double`	Read Only. Returns the distance from the left edge of the plot area, not including axis labels, to the chart's left edge.
`InsideTop`	`Double`	Read Only. Returns the distance from the left edge of the plot area, not including axis labels, to the chart's left edge.
`InsideWidth`	`Double`	Read Only. Returns the width inside the plot area that does not include the axis labels.
`Interior`	`Interior`	Read Only. Returns an object containing options to format the inside area of the plot area (e.g. interior color).

Name	Returns	Description
Left	Double	Set/Get the distance from the left edge of the plot area to the chart's left edge.
Name	String	Read Only. Returns the name of the plot area.
Top	Double	Set/Get the distance from the top edge of the plot area to the chart's top edge.
Width	Double	Set/Get the width of the chart plot area.

PlotArea Methods

Name	Returns	Parameters	Description
ClearFormats	Variant		Clears any formatting made to the plot area
Select	Variant		Selects the plot area on the chart

Example: PlotArea Object

This example uses the `PlotArea` object to make all the charts in the workbook have the same size and position plot area, regardless of the formatting of the axes (e.g. different fonts and number scales):

```
Sub MakeChartAreasSameSizeAsFirst()
   Dim oCht As Chart, oPA As PlotArea
   Dim dWidth As Double, dHeight As Double
   Dim dTop As Double, dLeft As Double

   'Get the dimensions of the inside of the
   'plot area of the first chart
   With Charts(1).PlotArea
      dWidth = .InsideWidth
      dHeight = .InsideHeight
      dLeft = .InsideLeft
      dTop = .InsideTop
   End With

   'Loop through the charts in the workbook
   For Each oCht In Charts

      'Get the PlotArea
      Set oPA = oCht.PlotArea

      'Size and move the plot area
      With oPA
         If .InsideWidth > dWidth Then
            'Too big, make it smaller
            .Width = .Width - (.InsideWidth - dWidth)
         Else
            'Too small, move it left and make bigger
            .Left = .Left - (dWidth - .InsideWidth)
            .Width = .Width + (dWidth - .InsideWidth)
         End If
```

```
            If .InsideHeight > dHeight Then
               'Too big, make it smaller
               .Height = .Height - (.InsideHeight - dHeight)
            Else
               'Too small, move it left and make bigger
               .Top = .Top - (dHeight - .InsideHeight)
               .Height = .Height + (dHeight - .InsideHeight)
            End If

            'Set the position of the inside of the plot area
            .Left = .Left + (dLeft - .InsideLeft)
            .Top = .Top + (dTop - .InsideTop)
         End With
      Next
   End Sub
```

Point Object and the Points Collection

The `Points` collection holds all of the data points of a particular series of a chart. In fact, a chart (`Chart` object) can have many chart groups (`ChartGroups / ChartGroup`) that can contain many series (`SeriesCollection / Series`), which, in turn, can contain many points (`Points / Point`). A `Point` object describes the particular point of a series on a chart. The parent of the `Points` collection is the `Series` object.

The `Points` collection contains a `Count` property besides the typical collection attributes. The `Count` property returns the number of `Point` objects in the collection.

Point Common Properties

The `Application`, `Creator`, and `Parent` properties are defined at the beginning of this appendix.

Point Properties

Name	Returns	Description
ApplyPictToEnd	Boolean	Set/Get whether pictures are added to the end of the point.
ApplyPictToFront	Boolean	Set/Get whether pictures are added to the front of the point.
ApplyPictToSides	Boolean	Set/Get whether pictures are added to the sides of the point.
Border	Border	Read Only. Returns the border's properties around the point.
DataLabel	DataLabel	Read Only. Returns an object allowing you to manipulate the data label attributes (e.g. formatting, text). Use with `HasDataLabel`.
Explosion	Long	Set/Get how far out a slice (point) of a pie or doughnut chart will explode out. 0 for no explosion.
Fill	ChartFillFormat	Read Only. Returns an object containing fill formatting options for a point.

Name	Returns	Description
HasDataLabel	Boolean	Set/Get whether the point has a data label. Use with DataLabel.
Interior	Interior	Read Only. Returns an object containing options to format the inside area of the point (e.g. interior color).
InvertIfNegative	Boolean	Set/Get whether the point's color will be inverted if the point value is negative.
MarkerBackgroundColor	Long	Set/Get the color of the point marker background. Use the RGB function to create the color value.
MarkerBackgroundColorIndex	XlColorIndex	Set/Get the color of the point marker background. Use the XlColorIndex constants or an index value in the current color palette.
MarkerForegroundColor	Long	Set/Get the color of the point marker foreground. Use the RGB function to create the color value.
MarkerForegroundColorIndex	XlColorIndex	Set/Get the color of the point marker foreground. Use the XlColorIndex constants or an index value in the current color palette.
MarkerSize	Long	Set/Get the size of the point key marker.
MarkerStyle	XlMarkerStyle	Set/Get the type of marker to use as the point key (e.g. square, diamond, triangle, picture, etc.)
PictureType	XlChartPictureType	Set/Get how an associated picture is displayed on the point (e.g. stretched, tiled). Use the XlPictureType constants.
PictureUnit	Long	Set/Get how many units a picture represents if the PictureType property is set to xlScale.
SecondaryPlot	Boolean	Set/Get if the point is on the secondary part of a Pie of Pie chart of a Bar of Pie chart.
Shadow	Boolean	Set/Get whether the point has a shadow effect.

Point Methods

Name	Returns	Parameters	Description
ApplyData Labels	Variant	[Type As XlDataLabels Type], [LegendKey], [AutoText], [HasLeader Lines], [ShowSeries Name], [ShowCategory Name], [ShowValue], [Show Percentage], [ShowBubble Size], [Separator]	Applies the data label properties specified by the parameters to the point. The Type parameter specifies whether no label, a value, a percentage of the whole, or a category label is shown. The legend key can appear by the point by setting the LegendKey parameter to True. Set AutoText to True if the object automatically generates appropriate text based on content. HasLeaderLines should be set to True if the series has leader lines. All the other parameters are simply the property of the data label that they describe.
ClearFormats	Variant		Clears the formatting made to a point.
Copy	Variant		Cuts the point and places it in the clipboard.
Delete	Variant		Deletes the point.
Paste	Variant		Pastes the picture in the clipboard into the current point so it becomes the marker.
Select	Variant		Selects the point on the chart.

Example: Point Object and the Points Collection

```
Sub ExplodePie()
   Dim oPt As Point

   'Get the first data point in the pie chart
   Set oPt = Charts(1).SeriesCollection(1).Points(1)

   'Add a label to the first point only and
   'set it away from the pie
   With oPt
      .ApplyDataLabels xlDataLabelsShowLabelAndPercent
      .Explosion = 20
   End With
End Sub
```

Protection Object

Represents the group of much needed sheet protection options new to Excel 2002. When you protect a sheet, you now have the option to only allow unlocked cells selected, allow cell, column, and row formatting, allow insertion and deletion of rows and columns, allow sorting, and more.

Setting Protection options is done via the `Protect` method of the `Worksheet` object. Use the `Protection` property of the `Worksheet` object to check the current protection settings:

```
MsgBox ActiveSheet.Protection.AllowFormattingCells
```

Protection Properties

Name	Returns	Description
AllowDeleting Columns	Boolean	Read Only. Returns whether the deletion of columns is allowed on a protected worksheet.
AllowDeleting Rows	Boolean	Read Only. Returns whether the deletion of rows is allowed on a protected worksheet.
AllowEdit Ranges	AllowEdit Ranges	Read Only. Returns an `AllowEditRanges` object.
Allow Filtering	Boolean	Read Only. Returns whether the user is allowed to make use of an `AutoFilter` that was created before the sheet was protected.
Allow Formatting Cells	Boolean	Read Only. Returns whether the formatting of cells is allowed on a protected worksheet.
AllowFormatting Columns	Boolean	Read Only. Returns whether the formatting of columns is allowed on a protected worksheet.
AllowFormattin gRows	Boolean	Read Only. Returns whether the formatting of rows is allowed on a protected worksheet.
AllowInserting Columns	Boolean	Read Only. Returns whether the inserting of columns is allowed on a protected worksheet.
AllowInserting Hyperlinks	Boolean	Read Only. Returns whether the inserting of hyperlinks is allowed on a protected worksheet.
AllowInserting Rows	Boolean	Read Only. Returns whether the inserting of rows is allowed on a protected worksheet.
AllowSorting	Boolean	Read Only. Returns whether the sorting option is allowed on a protected worksheet.
AllowUsingPiv otTables	Boolean	Read Only. Returns whether the manipulation of `PivotTables` is allowed on a protected worksheet.

Example: Protection Object

The following routine sets `Protection` options based on the user name found on the General tab of the Tools | Options command and that user's settings on a table on the worksheet. If the user isn't found, a message appears and the default settings are used:

```
Sub ProtectionSettings()

    Dim rngUsers As Range, rngUser As Range
    Dim sCurrentUser As String

    'Grab the current username
    sCurrentUser = Application.UserName

    'Define the list of users in the table
    With wksAllowEditRange
        Set rngUsers = .Range(.Range("Users"), .Range("Users").End(xlToRight))
    End With

    'Locate the current user on the table
    Application.FindFormat.Clear
    Set rngUser = rngUsers.Find(What:=sCurrentUser, SearchOrder:=xlByRows,
MatchCase:=False, SearchFormat:=False)

    'If current user is found on the table...
    If Not rngUser Is Nothing Then
        'Set the Protection properties based
        ' on a table
        wksAllowEditRange.Protect Password:="wrox1", _
        DrawingObjects:=True, _
        Contents:=True, _
        AllowFormattingCells:=rngUser.Offset(1, 0).Value, _
        AllowFormattingColumns:=rngUser.Offset(2, 0).Value, _
        AllowFormattingRows:=rngUser.Offset(3, 0).Value, _
        AllowSorting:=rngUser.Offset(4, 0).Value, _
        UserInterfaceOnly:=True

        'Select Unlocked cells, Locked and Unlocked cells, or neither
        ' is NOT part of the Protection object
        If rngUser.Offset(5, 0).Value = True Then
            wksAllowEditRange.EnableSelection = xlUnlockedCells
        Else
             wksAllowEditRange.EnableSelection = xlNoRestrictions
        End If

    Else
        'Current user is not on the table
        MsgBox "User not found on User Table. Default Options will be used.",
vbExclamation, "Protection Settings"
        wksAllowEditRange.Protect , True, True, False, False, False, _
                                    False, False, False, False, False, _
                                    False, False, False, False, False

        wksAllowEditRange.EnableSelection = xlNoRestrictions

    End If

End Sub
```

PublishObject Object and the PublishObjects Collection

The `PublishObjects` collection holds all of the things in a workbook that have been saved to a web page. Each `PublishObject` object contains items from a workbook that have been saved to a web page and may need some occasional refreshing of values on the web page side. The parent of the `PublishObjects` collection is the `Workbook` object.

The PublishObjects collection has a few properties and methods besides the typical collection attributes. The unique attributes are listed in the following table.

PublishObjects Properties and Methods

Name	Returns	Description
AutoRepublish	Boolean	Set/Get whether an item in the PublishObjects collection should be republished when a workbook is saved.
Count	Long	Read Only. Returns the number of PublishObject objects in the collection.
Add	Publish Object	Method. Parameters: SourceType As XlSourceType, Filename As String, [Sheet], [Source], [HtmlType], [DivID], [Title]. Adds a PublishObject to the collection.
Delete		Method. Deletes the PublishObject objects from the collection.
Publish		Method. Publishes all the items associated with the PublishObject objects to a web page.

PublishObject Common Properties

The Application, Creator, and Parent properties are defined at the beginning of this appendix.

PublishObject Properties

Name	Returns	Description
DivID	String	Read Only. Returns the id used for the <DIV> tag on a web page.
Filename	String	Set/Get the URL or path that the object will be saved to as a web page.
HtmlType	XlHtmlType	Set/Get what type of web page to save (e.g. xlHtmlStatic, xlHtmlChart). Pages saved as other than xlHtmlStatic need special ActiveX components.
Sheet	String	Read Only. Returns the Excel sheet that will be saved as a web page.
Source	String	Read Only. Returns the specific item, like range name, chart name, or report name from the base type specified by the SourceType property.
SourceType	XlSource Type	Read Only. Returns the type of source being published (e.g. xlSourceChart, xlSourcePrintArea, etc.)
Title	String	Set/Get the web page title for the published web page.

PublishObject Methods

Name	Returns	Parameters	Description
Delete			Deletes the PublishObject object.
Publish		[Create]	Publishes the source items specified by the PublishObject as a web file. Set the Create parameter to True to overwrite existing files. False will append to the existing web page with the same name, if any.

Example: PublishObject Object and the PublishObjects Collection

```
Sub UpdatePublishedCharts()
   Dim oPO As PublishObject

   For Each oPO In ActiveWorkbook.PublishObjects
      If oPO.SourceType = xlSourceChart Then
         oPO.Publish
      End If
   Next
End Sub
```

QueryTable Object and the QueryTables Collection

The QueryTables collection holds the collection of data tables created from an external data source. Each QueryTable object represents a single table in a worksheet filled with data from an external data source. The external data source can be an ODBC source, an OLE DB source, a text file, a Data Finder, a Web-based query, or a DAO / ADO recordset. The parent of the QueryTables collection is the Worksheet object.

The QueryTables collection has a few properties and methods not typical of a collection. These atypical attributes are listed below.

QueryTables Properties and Methods

Name	Returns	Description
Count	Long	Read Only. Returns the number of items in the collection.
Add	QueryTable	Method. Parameters: Connection, Destination As Range, [Sql]. Adds a QueryTable to the collection. The Connection parameter can specify the ODBC or OLE DB connection string, another QueryTable object, a DAO or ADO recordset object, a Web-based query, a Data Finder string, or a text file name. The Destination parameter specifies the upper-left corner that the query table results will be placed. The SQL parameter can specify the SQL for the connection, if applicable.

QueryTable Common Properties

The `Application`, `Creator`, and `Parent` properties are defined at the beginning of this appendix.

QueryTable Properties

Name	Returns	Description
`AdjustColumn Width`	`Boolean`	Set/Get whether the column widths automatically adjust to best fit the data every time the query table is refreshed.
`Background Query`	`Boolean`	Set/Get if the query table processing is done asynchronously.
`CommandText`	`Variant`	Set/Get the SQL command used to retrieve data.
`CommandType`	`XlCmdType`	Set/Get the type of `ComandText` (e.g. `xlCmdSQL`, `xlCmdTable`).
`Connection`	`Variant`	Set/Get the OLE DB connection string, the ODBC string, web data source, path to a text file, or path to a database.
`Destination`	`Range`	Read Only. Returns the upper-left corner cell that the query table results will be placed.
`EditWebPage`	`Variant`	Set/Get the web page URL for a web query.
`Enable Editing`	`Boolean`	Set/Get whether the query table data can be edited or only refreshed (`False`).
`Enable Refresh`	`Boolean`	Set/Get whether the query table data can be refreshed.
`FetchedRow Overflow`	`Boolean`	Read Only. Returns whether the last query table refresh retrieved more rows than available on the worksheet.
`FieldNames`	`Boolean`	Set/Get whether the field names from the data source become column headings in the query table.
`FillAdjacent Formulas`	`Boolean`	Set/Get whether formulas located to the right of the query table will update automatically when the query table data is refreshed.
`Maintain Connection`	`Boolean`	Set/Get whether the connection to the data source does not close until the workbook is closed. Valid only against an OLE DB source.
`Name`	`String`	Set/Get the name of the query table.
`Parameters`	`Parameters`	Read Only. Returns the parameters associated with the query table.
`PostText`	`String`	Set/Get the post message sent to the web server to return data from a web query.

Table continued on following page

Name	Returns	Description
PreserveColumnInfo	Boolean	Set/Get whether column location, sorting and filtering does not disappear when the data query is refreshed.
PreserveFormatting	Boolean	Set/Get whether common formatting associated with the first five rows of data are applied to new rows in the query table.
QueryType	xlQueryType	Read Only. Returns the type of connection associated with the query table. (e.g. xlOLEDBQuery, xlDAOQuery, xlTextImport).
Recordset		Read Only. Returns a recordset associated with the data source query.
Refreshing	Boolean	Read Only. Returns whether an asynchronous query is currently in progress.
RefreshOnFileOpen	Boolean	Set/Get whether the query table is refreshed when the workbook is opened.
RefreshPeriod	Long	Set/Get how long (minutes) between automatic refreshes from the data source. Set to 0 to disable.
RefreshStyle	XlCellInsertionMode	Set/Get how worksheet rows react when data rows are retrieved from the data source. Worksheet cells can be overwritten (xlOverwriteCells), cell rows can be partial inserted / deleted as necessary (xlInsertDeleteCells), or only cell rows that need to be added are added (xlInsertEntireRows).
ResultRange	Range	Read Only. Returns the cell range containing the results of the query table.
RobustConnect	XlRobustConnect	Set/Get how the PivotCache connects to its data source.
RowNumbers	Boolean	Set/Get whether a worksheet column is added to the left of the query table containing row numbers.
SaveData	Boolean	Set/Get whether query table data is saved with the workbook.
SavePassword	Boolean	Set/Get whether an ODBC connection password is saved with the query table.
SourceConnectionFile	String	Set/Get the name of the file that was used to create the PivotTable.
SourceDataFile	String	Read Only. Returns the name of the source data file for the PivotCache.
TextFileColumnDataTypes	Variant	Set/Get the array of column constants representing the data types for each column. Use the XlColumnDataType constants. Used only when QueryType is xlTextImport.

Name	Returns	Description
TextFile Comma Delimiter	Boolean	Set/Get whether a comma is the delimiter for text file imports into a query table. Used only when QueryType is xlTextImport and for a delimited text file.
TextFile Consecutive Delimiter	Boolean	Set/Get whether consecutive delimiters (e.g. ",,,") are treated as a single delimeter. Used only when QueryType is xlTextImport.
TextFile Decimal Separator	String	Set/Get the type of delimeter to use to define a decimal point. Used only when QueryType is xlTextImport.
TextFile Fixed ColumnWidths	Variant	Set/Get the array of widths that correspond to the columns. Used only when QueryType is xlTextImport and for a fixed width text file.
TextFile Other Delimiter	String	Set/Get the character that will be used to delimit columns from a text file. Used only when QueryType is xlTextImport and for a delimited text file.
TextFile ParseType	XlText ParsingType	Set/Get the type of text file that is being imported: xlDelimited or xlFixedWidth. Used only when QueryType is xlTextImport.
TextFilePlat form	XlPlatform	Set/Get which code pages to use when importing a text file (e.g. xlMSDOS, xlWindows). Used only when QueryType is xlTextImport.
TextFile PromptOn Refresh	Boolean	Set/Get whether the user is prompted for the text file to use to import into a query table every time the data is refreshed. Used only when QueryType is xlTextImport. The prompt does not appear on the initial refresh of data.
TextFile Semicolon Delimiter	Boolean	Set/Get whether the semicolon is the text file delimiter for importing text files. Used only when QueryType is xlTextImport and the file is a delimited text file.
TextFile Space Delimiter	Boolean	Set/Get whether the space character is the text file delimiter for importing text files. Used only when QueryType is xlTextImport and the file is a delimited text file.
TextFile StartRow	Long	Set/Get which row number to start importing from a text file. Used only when QueryType is xlTextImport.
TextFileTab Delimiter	Boolean	Set/Get whether the tab character is the text file delimiter for importing text files. Used only when QueryType is xlTextImport and the file is a delimited text file.

Table continued on following page

Name	Returns	Description
TextFileText Qualifier	XlText Qualifier	Set/Get which character will be used to define string data when importing data from a text file. Used only when QueryType is xlTextImport.
TextFile Thousands Separator	String	Set/Get which character is used as the thousands separator in numbers when importing from a text file (e.g. ",").
TextFile TrailingMinus Numbers	Boolean	Set/Get whether to treat numbers imported as text that begin with a "-" symbol as negative numbers.
Web Consecutive DelimitersAs One	Boolean	Set/Get whether consecutive delimiters are treated as a single delimeter when importing data from a Web page. Used only when QueryType is xlWebQuery.
WebDisable Date Recognition	Boolean	Set/Get whether data that looks like dates are parsed as text when importing web page data. Used only when QueryType is xlWebQuery.
WebDisable Redirections	Boolean	Set/Get whether web query redirections are disabled for the QueryTable object.
WebFormatting	xlWeb Formatting	Set/Get whether to keep any of the formatting when importing a web page (e.g. xlAll, xlNone). Used only when QueryType is xlWebQuery.
WebPre Formatted TextToColumns	Boolean	Set/Get whether HTML data with the <PRE> tag is parsed into columns when importing web pages. Used only when QueryType is xlWebQuery.
WebSelection Type	xlWeb Selection Type	Set/Get what data from a web page is imported. Either all tables (xlAllTables), the entire page (xlEntirePage), or specified tables (xlSpecifiedTables). Used only when QueryType is xlWebQuery.
WebSingleBlo ck TextImport	Boolean	Set/Get whether all the web page data with the <PRE> tags are imported all at once. Used only when QueryType is xlWebQuery.
WebTables	String	Set/Get a comma-delimited list of all the table names that will be imported from a web page. Used only when QueryType is xlWebQuery and WebSelectionType is xlSpecifiedTables.

QueryTable Methods

Name	Returns	Parameters	Description
CancelRefresh			Cancels an asynchronously running query table refresh.

Name	Returns	Parameters	Description
Delete			Deletes the query table.
Refresh	Boolean	[Background Query]	Refreshes the data in the query table with the latest copy of the external data. Set the BackgroundQuery parameter to True to get the data to refresh asynchronously.
ResetTimer			Resets the time for the automatic refresh set by RefreshPeriod property.
SaveAsODC		ODCFileName As String, [Description], [Keywords]	Saves the PivotCache source as an Office Data Connection file. ODCFileName is the location of the source file. Description is the description that will be saved in the file. Keywords is a list of space-separated keywords that can be used to search for this file.

Example: QueryTable Object and the QueryTables Collection

```
Sub UpdateAllWebQueries()
   Dim oQT As QueryTable

   For Each oQT In ActiveSheet.QueryTables
      If oQT.QueryType = xlWebQuery Then
         oQT.BackgroundQuery = False
         oQT.Refresh
      End If
   Next
End Sub
```

Range Object

The Range object is one of the more versatile objects in Excel. A range can be a single cell, a column, a row, a contiguous block of cells, or a non-contiguous range of cells. The main parent of a Range object is the Worksheet object. However, most of the objects in the Excel Object Model use the Range object. The Range property of the Worksheet object can be used to choose a certain range of cells using the Cell1 and Cell2 parameters.

Range Common Properties

The Application, Creator, and Parent properties are defined at the beginning of this appendix.

Range Properties

Name	Returns	Description
AddIndent	Variant	Set/Get whether text in a cell is automatically indented if the text alignment in a cell is set to equally distribute.
Address	String	Read Only. Parameters: `RowAbsolute, ColumnAbsolute, ReferenceStyle As XlReferenceStyle, [External], [RelativeTo]`. Returns the address of the current range as a string in the macro's language. The type of address (reference, absolute, A1 reference style, R1C1 reference style) is specified by the parameters.
AddressLocal	String	Read Only. Parameters: `RowAbsolute, ColumnAbsolute, ReferenceStyle As XlReferenceStyle, [External], [RelativeTo]`. Returns the address of the current range as a string in the user's language. The type of address (reference, absolute, A1 reference style, R1C1 reference style) is specified by the parameters.
AllowEdit	Boolean	Read Only. Returns `True` if the range can be edited on a protected worksheet.
Areas	Areas	Read Only. Returns an object containing the different non-contiguous ranges in the current range.
Borders	Borders	Read Only. Returns all the individual borders around the range. Each border side can be accessed individualy in the collection.
Cells	Range	Read Only. Returns the cells in the current range. The `Cells` property will return the same range as the current range.
Characters	Characters	Read Only. Parameters: `[Start], [Length]`. Returns all the characters in the current range, if applicable.
Column	Long	Read Only. Returns the column number of the first column in the range.
Columns	Range	Read Only. Returns a range of the columns in the current range.
ColumnWidth	Variant	Set/Get the column width of all the columns in the range. Returns `Null` if the columns in the range have different widths.
Comment	Comment	Read Only. Returns an object representing the range comment, if any.
Count	Long	Read Only. Returns the number of cells in the current range.
CurrentArray	Range	Read Only. Returns a `Range` object that represents the array associated with the particular cell range, if the cell is part of an array.

Name	Returns	Description
CurrentRegion	Range	Read Only. Returns the current region that contains the Range object. A region is defined as an area that is surrounded by blank cells.
Dependents	Range	Read Only. Returns the dependants of a cell on the same sheet as the range.
Direct Dependents	Range	Read Only. Returns the direct dependants of a cell on the same sheet as the range.
Direct Precedents	Range	Read Only. Returns the direct precedents of a cell on the same sheet as the range.
End	Range	Read Only. Parameters: Direction As XlDirection. Returns the cell at end of the region containing the Range object. Which end of the region is specified by the Direction parameter.
EntireColumn	Range	Read Only. Returns the full worksheet column(s) occupied by the current range.
EntireRow	Range	Read Only. Returns the full worksheet row(s) occupied by the current range.
Errors	Errors	Read Only. Returns the Errors collection associated with the Range object.
Font	Font	Read Only. Returns an object containing Font options for the text in the range.
Format Conditions	Format Conditions	Read Only. Returns an object holding conditional formatting options for the current range.
Formula	Variant	Set/Get the formula in the cells of the range.
FormulaArray	Variant	Set/Get the array formula of the cells in the range.
Formula Hidden	Variant	Set/Get whether the formula will be hidden if the workbook / worksheet is protected.
FormulaLabel	XlFormula Label	Set/Get the type of formula label to use for the specified range.
FormulaLocal	Variant	Set/Get the formula of the range in the language of the user using the A1 style references.
FormulaR1C1	Variant	Set/Get the formula of the range in the language of the macro using the R1C1 style references.
FormulaR1C1 Local	Variant	Set/Get the formula of the range in the language of the user using the R1C1 style references.
HasArray	Variant	Read Only. Returns whether a single cell range is part of an array formula.

Table continued on following page

Name	Returns	Description
HasFormula	Variant	Read Only. Returns whether all the cells in the range contain formulas (True). If only some of the cells contain formulas then Null is returned.
Height	Variant	Read Only. Returns the height of the range.
Hidden	Variant	Set/Get whether the cells in the range are hidden. Only works if the range contains whole columns or rows.
Horizontal Alignment	Variant	Set/Get how the cells in the range are horizontally aligned. Use the XLHAlign constants.
Hyperlinks	Hyperlinks	Read Only. Returns the collection of hyperlinks in the range.
ID	String	Set/Get the ID used for the range if the worksheet is saved as a web page.
IndentLevel	Variant	Set/Get the indent level for the range.
Interior	Interior	Read Only. Returns an object containing options to format the inside area of the range if applicable (e.g. interior color).
Left	Variant	Read Only. Returns the distance from the left edge of the left-most column in the range to the left edge of ColumnA.
ListHeader Rows	Long	Read Only. Returns the number of header rows in the range.
LocationIn Table	XlLocation InTable	Read Only. Returns the location of the upper-left corner of the range.
Locked	Variant	Set/Get whether cells in the range can be modified if the sheet is protected. Returns Null if only some of the cells in the range are locked.
MergeArea	range	Read Only. Returns a range containing the merged range of the current cell range.
MergeCells	Variant	Set/Get whether the current range contains merged cells.
Name	Variant	Set/Get the Name object that contains the name for the range.
Next	Range	Read Only. Returns the next range in the sheet.
NumberFormat	Variant	Set/Get the number format associated with the cells in the range. Null if all the cells don't have the same format.
NumberFormat Local	Variant	Set/Get the number format associated with the cells in the range in the language of the end user. Null if all the cells don't have the same format.

Name	Returns	Description
Offset	Range	Read Only. Parameters: [RowOffset], [ColumnOffset]. Returns the cell as a Range object that is the offset from the current cell as specified by the parameters. A positive RowOffset offsets the row downward. A negative RowOffset offsets the row upward. A positive ColumnOffset offsets the column to the right and a negative ColumnOffset offsets the column to the left.
Orientation	Variant	Set/Get the text orientation for the cell text. A value from -90 to 90 degrees can be specified, or use an XlOrientation constant.
OutlineLevel	Variant	Set/Get the outline level for the row or column range.
PageBreak	Long	Set/Get how page breaks are set in the range. Use the XLPageBreak constants.
Phonetic	Phonetic	Read Only. Returns the Phonetic object associated with the cell range.
Phonetics	Phonetics	Read Only. Returns the Phonetic objects in the range.
PivotCell	PivotCell	Read Only. Returns a PivotCell object that represents a cell in a PivotTable report.
PivotField	PivotField	Read Only. Returns the PivotTable field associated with the upper-left corner of the current range.
PivotItem	PivotItem	Read Only. Returns the PivotTable item associated with the upper-left corner of the current range.
PivotTable	PivotTable	Read Only. Returns the PivotTable report associated with the upper-left corner of the current range.
Precedents	Range	Read Only. Returns the range of precedents of the current cell range on the same sheet as the range.
Prefix Character	Variant	Read Only. Returns the character used to define the type of data in the cell range. E.g. "'" for a text label.
Previous	Range	Read Only. Returns the previous range in the sheet.
QueryTable	QueryTable	Read Only. Returns the query table associated with the upper-left corner of the current range.
Range	Range	Read Only. Parameters: Cell1, [Cell2]. Returns a Range object as defined by the Cell1 and optionally Cell2 parameters. The cell references used in the parameters are relative to the range. For example Range.Range ("A1") would return the first column in the parent range but not necessarily the first column in the worksheet.

Table continued on following page

Name	Returns	Description
ReadingOrder	Long	Set/Get whether the text is from right-to-left (xlRTL), left-to-right (xlLTR), or context-sensitive (xlContext).
Resize	Range	Read Only. Parameters: [RowSize], [ColumnSize]. Returns a new resized range as specified by the RowSize and ColumnSize parameters.
Row	Long	Read Only. Returns the row number of the first row in the range.
RowHeight	Variant	Set/Get the height of the rows in the range. Returns Null if the rows in the range have different row heights.
Rows	Range	Read Only. Returns a Range object containing the rows of the current range.
ShowDetail	Variant	Set/Get if all the outline levels in the range are expanded. Applicable only if a summary column or row is the range.
ShrinkToFit	Variant	Set/Get whether the cell text will automatically shrink to fit the column width. Returns Null if the rows in the range have different ShrinkToFit properties.
SmartTags	SmartTags	Read Only. Returns a SmartTags object representing the identifier for the specified cell.
SoundNote	SoundNote	Property is kept for backwards compatibility only.
Style	Variant	Read Only. Returns the Style object associated with the range.
Summary	Variant	Read Only. Returns whether the range is an outline summary row or column.
Text	Variant	Read Only. Returns the text associated with a range cell.
Top	Variant	Read Only. Returns the distance from the top edge of the top-most row in the range to the top edge of RowA.
UseStandard Height	Variant	Set/Get whether the row height is the standard height of the sheet. Returns Null if the rows in the range contain different heights.
UseStandard Width	Variant	Set/Get whether the column width is the standard width of the sheet. Returns Null if the columns in the range contain different widths.
Validation	Validation	Read Only. Returns the data validation for the current range.
Value	Variant	Parameters: [RangeValueDataType]. Set/Get the value of a cell or an array of cells depending on the contents of the Range object.

Name	Returns	Description
Value2	Variant	Set/Get the value of a cell or an array of cells depending on the contents of the Range object. No Currency or Date types are returned by Value2.
Vertical Alignment	Variant	Set/Get how the cells in the range are vertically aligned. Use the XLVAlign constants.
Width	Variant	Read Only. Returns the height of the range.
Worksheet	Worksheet	Read Only. Returns the worksheet that has the Range object.
WrapText	Variant	Set/Get whether cell text wraps in the cell. Returns Null if the cells in the range contain different text wrap properties.

Range Methods

Name	Returns	Parameters	Description
Activate	Variant		Selects the range cells.
AddComment	Comment	[Text]	Adds the text specified by the parameter to the cell specified in the range. Must be a single cell range.
Advanced Filter	Variant	Action As XlFilter Action, [Criteria Range], [CopyToRange], [Unique]	Copies or filters the data in the current range. The Action parameter specifies whether a copy or filter is to take place. CriteriaRange optionally specifies the range containing the criteria. CopyToRange specifies the range that the filtered data will be copied to (if Action is xlFilterCopy).
ApplyNames	Variant	Names, Ignore Relative Absolute, UseRowColumn Names, OmitColumn, OmitRow, Order As XlApplyNames Order, [AppendLast]	Applies defined names to the formulas in a range. For example, if a cell contained =$A$1*100 and $A$1 was given the name "TopLeft", you could apply the "TopLeft" name to the range, resulting in the formula changing to =TopLeft*100. Note that there is no UnApplyNames method.
ApplyOutline Styles	Variant		Applies the outline styles to the range.

Table continued on following page

Name	Returns	Parameters	Description
AutoComplete	String	String As String	Returns and tries to AutoComplete the word specified in the String parameter. Returns the complete word if found. Returns an empty string if no word or more than one word is found.
AutoFill	Variant	Destination As Range, Type As XlAutoFill Type	Uses the current range as the source to figure out how to AutoFill the range specified by the Destination parameter. The Type parameter can also be used to specify the type of fill to use (e.g. xlFillCopy, xlFillDays).
AutoFilter	Variant	Field, Criteria1, Operator As XlAutoFilter Operator, [Criteria2], [VisibleDrop Down]	Creates an auto-filter on the data in the range. See the AutoFilter object for details on the parameters.
AutoFit	Variant		Changes the column widths in the range to best fit the data in the cells. The range must contain full rows or columns.
AutoFormat	Variant	Format As XlRangeAuto Format, [Number], [Font], [Alignment], [Border], [Pattern], [Width]	Formats the range using the format specified by the Format parameter. The other parameters are Boolean indicators to specify: if numbers are formatted appropriately (Number), fonts applied (Font), alignnments applied (Alignment), border formats applied (Border), pattern formats applied (Pattern), and if row / column widths are applied from the autoformat.
AutoOutline	Variant		Creates an outline for the range.
BorderAround	Variant	LineStyle, Weight As XlBorder Weight, ColorIndex As XlColorIndex, [Color]	Creates a border around the range with the associated line style (LineStyle), thickness (Weight), and color (ColorIndex).
Calculate	Variant		Calculates all the formulas in the range.

Name	Returns	Parameters	Description
CheckSpelling	Variant	[Custom Dictionary], [Ignore Uppercase], [Always Suggest], [SpellLang]	Checks the spelling of the text in the range. A custom dictionary can be specified (CustomDictionary), all UPPERCASE words can be ignored (IgnoreUppercase), and Excel can be set to display a list of suggestions (AlwaysSuggest).
Clear	Variant		Clears the text in the cells of the range.
ClearComments			Clears all the comments in the range cells.
ClearContents	Variant		Clears the formulas and values in a range.
ClearFormats	Variant		Clears the formatting in a range.
ClearNotes	Variant		Clears comments from the cells in the range.
ClearOutline	Variant		Clears the outline used in the current range.
Column Differences	Range	Comparison	Returns the range of cells that are different to the cell specified by the Comparison parameter.
Consolidate	Variant	[Sources], [Function], [TopRow], [Left Column], [Create Links]	Consolidates the source array of range reference strings in the Sources parameter and returns the results to the current range. The Function parameter can be used to set the consolidation function. Use the XLConsolidationFunction constants.
Copy	Variant	[Destination]	Copies the current range to the range specified by the parameter or to the clipboard if no destination is specified.
CopyFrom Recordset	Long	Data As Recordset, [MaxRows], [MaxColumns]	Copies the records from the ADO or DAO recordset specified by the Data parameter into the current range. The recordset can't contain OLE objects.

Table continued on following page

Name	Returns	Parameters	Description
CopyPicture	Variant	Appearance As XlPicture Appearance, Format As XlCopyPicture Format	Copies the range into the clipboard as a picture. The Appearance parameter can be used to specify whether the picture is copied as it looks on the screen or when printed. The Format parameter can specify the type of picture that will be put into the clipboard.
CreateNames	Variant	[Top], [Left], [Bottom], [Right]	Creates a named range for the items in the current range. Set Top to True to make the first row hold the names for the ranges below. Set Bottom to True to use the bottom row as the names. Set Left or Right to True to make the left or right column contain the Names, respectively.
Create Publisher	Variant	Edition, Appearance As XlPicture Appearance, [Contains PICT], [Contains BIFF], [ContainsRTF], [Contains VALU]	Creates a publisher based on the range. Available only on the Macintosh with System 7 or later.
Cut	Variant	[Destination]	Cuts the current range to the range specified by the parameter, or to the clipboard if no destination is specified.
DataSeries	Variant	Rowcol, Type As XlDataSeries Type, Date As XlDataSeries Date, [Step], [Stop], [Trend]	Creates a data series at the current range location.
Delete	Variant	[Shift]	Deletes the cells in the current range and optionally shifts the cells in the direction specified by the Shift parameter. Use the XlDeleteShiftDirection constants for the Shift parameter.
DialogBox	Variant		Displays a dialog box defined by an Excel 4.0 macro sheet.
Dirty			Selects a range to be recalculated when the next recalculation occurs.

Name	Returns	Parameters	Description
Edition Options	Variant	Type As XlEdition Type, Option As XlEdition Options Option, Name, Reference, Appearance As XlPicture Appearance, ChartSize As XlPicture Appearance, [Format]	Used on the Macintosh. EditionOptions set how the range should act when being used as the source (publisher) or target (subscriber) of the link. Editions are basically the same as Windows' DDE links.
FillDown	Variant		Copies the contents and formatting from the top row into the rest of the rows in the range.
FillLeft	Variant		Copies the contents and formatting from the rightmost column into the rest of the columns in the range.
FillRight	Variant		Copies the contents and formatting from the leftmost column into the rest of the columns in the range.
FillUp	Variant		Copies the contents and formatting from the bottom row into the rest of the rows in the range.
Find	Range	What As Variant, [After], [LookIn], [LookAt], [SearchOrder], [Search Direction As XlSearch Direction], [MatchCase], [MatchByte], [Search Format]	Looks through the current range for the text of data type specified by the What parameter. Use a single cell range in the After parameter to choose the starting position of the search. Use the LookIn parameter to decide where the search is going to take place.
FindNext	Range	[After]	Finds the next instance of the search criteria defined with the Find method.
FindPrevious	Range	[After]	Finds the previous instance of the search criteria defined with the Find method.

Table continued on following page

Name	Returns	Parameters	Description
FunctionWizard	Variant		Displays the FunctionWizard for the upper-left cell of the current range.
GoalSeek	Boolean	Goal, ChangingCell As Range	Returns True if the value specified by the Goal parameter is returned when changing the ChangingCell cell range.
Group	Variant	[Start], [End], [By], [Periods]	Either demotes the outline in the range or groups the discontinuous ranges in the current Range object.
Insert	Variant	[Shift], [CopyOrigin]	Inserts the equivalent rows or columns in the range into the range's worksheet.
InsertIndent		InsertAmount As Long	Indents the range by the amount specified by the InsertAmount parameter.
Justify	Variant		Evenly distributes the text in the cells from the current range.
ListNames	Variant		Pastes the names of all the named ranges in the current range starting at the top-left cell in the range.
Merge		[Across]	Merges the cells in the range. Set the Across parameter to True to merge each row as a separate cell.
NavigateArrow	Variant	[TowardPrecedent], [ArrowNumber], [LinkNumber]	Moves through the tracer arrows in a workbook from the current range, returning the range of cells that make up the tracer arrow destination. Tracer arrows must be turned on. Use the ShowDependents and ShowPrecendents methods.
NoteText	String	[Text], [Start], [Length]	Set/Get the cell notes associated with the cell in the current range.
Parse	Variant	[ParseLine], [Destination]	Parses the string specified by the ParseLine parameter and returns it to the current range parsed out by column. Optionally can specify the destination range with the Destination parameter. The ParseLine string should be in the "[ColumnA] [ColumnB]" format.

Name	Returns	Parameters	Description
PasteSpecial	Variant	Paste As XlPasteType, Operation As XlPaste Special Operation, [SkipBlanks], [Transpose]	Pastes the range from the clipboard into the current range. Use the Paste parameter to choose what to paste (e.g. formulas, values). Use the Operation parameter to specifiy what to do with the paste. Set SkipBlanks to True to not have blank cells in the clipboard's range pasted. Set Transpose to True to transpose columns with rows.
PrintOut	Variant	[From], [To], [Copies], [Preview], [Active Printer], [PrintToFile], [Collate], [PrToFile Name]	Prints out the charts in the collection. The printer, number of copies, collation, and whether a print preview is desired can be specified with the parameters. Also, the sheets can be printed to a file with using the PrintToFile and PrToFileName parameters. The From and To parameters can be used to specify the range of printed pages.
PrintPreview	Variant	[Enable Changes]	Displays the current range in a print preview. Set the EnableChanges parameter to False to disable the Margins and Setup buttons, hence not allowing the viewer to modify the page setup.
Remove Subtotal	Variant		Removes subtotals from the list in the current range.
Replace	Boolean	What As Variant, Replacement As Variant, [LookAt], [SearchOrder], [MatchCase], [MatchByte], [Search Format], [Replace Format]	Finds the text specified by the What parameter in the range. Replaces the found text with the Replacement parameter. Use the SearchOrder parameters with the XLSearchOrder constants to choose whether the search occurs by rows or by columns.
Row Differences	Range	Comparison.	Returns the range of cells that are different to the cell specified by the Comparison parameter.

Table continued on following page

Name	Returns	Parameters	Description
Run	Variant	[Arg1], [Arg2], ... [Arg30]	Runs the Excel 4.0 macro specified by the current range. The potential arguments to the macro can be specified with the Argx parameters.
Select	Variant		Selects the cells in the range.
SetPhonetic			Creates a Phonetic object for each cell in the range.
Show	Variant		Scrolls the Excel window to display the current range. This only works if the range is a single cell.
ShowDependents	Variant	[Remove]	Displays the dependents for the current single cell range using tracer arrows.
ShowErrors	Variant		Displays the source of the errors for the current range using tracer arrows.
ShowPrecedents	Variant	[Remove]	Displays the precedents for the current single cell range using tracer arrows.
Sort	Variant	[Key1], [Order1 As XlSortOrder], [Key2], [Type], [Order2 As XlSortOrder], [Key3], [Order3 As XlSortOrder], [Header As XlYesNoGuess], [OrderCustom], [MatchCase], [Orientation As XlSort Orientation], [SortMethod As XlSortMethod], [DataOption1 As XlSortData Option], [DataOption2 As XlSortData Option], [DataOption3 As XlSortData Option]	Sorts the cells in the range. If the range contains only one cell then the active region is searched. Use the Key1, Key2, and Key3 parameters to set which columns will be the sort columns. Use the Order1, Order2, and Order3 parameters to set the sort order. Use the Header parameter to set whether the first row contains headers. Set the MatchCase parameter to True to sort data and to treat uppercase and lowercase characters differently. Use the Orientation parameter to choose whether rows are sorted or columns are sorted. Finally, the SortMethod parameter is used to set the sort method for other languages (e.g. xlStroke or xlPinYin). Use the SortSpecial method for sorting in East Asian languages.

Name	Returns	Parameters	Description
SortSpecial	Variant	[SortMethod As XlSortMethod], [Key1], [Order1 As XlSortOrder], [Type], [Key2], [Order2 As XlSortOrder], [Key3], [Order3 As XlSortOrder], [Header As XlYesNoGuess], [OrderCustom], [MatchCase], [Orientation As XlSort Orientation], [DataOption1 As XlSortData Option], [DataOption2 As XlSortData Option], [DataOption3 As XlSortData Option]	Sorts the data in the range using East Asian sorting methods. The parameters are the same as the Sort method.
Speak		[Speak Direction], [Speak Formulas]	Causes the cells of the range to be spoken in row order or column order.
SpecialCells	Range	Type As XlCellType, [Value]	Returns the cells in the current range that contain some special attribute as defined by the Type parameter. For example, if Type is xlCellTypeBlanks then a Range object containing all of the empty cells are returned.
SubscribeTo	Variant	Edition As String, Format As XlSubscribeTo Format	Only valid on the Macintosh. Defines the source of a link that the current range will contain.

Name	Returns	Parameters	Description
Subtotal	Variant	GroupBy As Long, Function As Xl Consolidation Function, TotalList, Replace, PageBreaks, SummaryBelow Data As XlSummaryRow	Creates a subtotal for the range. If the range is a single cell then a subtotal is created for the current region. The GroupBy parameter specifies the field to group (for subtotaling). The Function parameter describes how the fields will be grouped. The TotalList parameter uses an array of field offsets that describe the fields that will be subtotaled. Set the Replace parameter to True to replace existing subtotals. Set the PageBreaks to True for page breaks to be added after each group. Use the SummaryBelowData parameter to choose where the summary row will be added.
Table	Variant	[RowInput], [Column Input]	Creates a new data table at the current range.
TextToColumns	Variant	[Destination], [DataType As XlTextParsing Type], [Text Qualifier As XlText Qualifier], [Consecutive Delimiter], [Tab], [Semicolon], [Comma], [Space], [Other], [OtherChar], [FieldInfo], [Decimal Separator], [Thousands Separator], [Trailing MinusNumbers]	Parses text in cells into several columns. The Destination specifies the range that the parsed text will go into. The DataType parameter can be used to choose whether the text is delimited or fixed width. The TextQualifier parameter can specify which character denotes string data when parsing. Set the ConsecutiveDelimiter to True for Excel to treat consecutive delimiters as one. Set the Tab, Semicolon, Comma, or Space parameter to True to use the associated character as the delimiter. Set the Other parameter to True and specify an OtherChar to use another character as the delimiter. FieldInfo takes a two-dimensional array containing more parsing information. The DecimalSeparator and ThousandsSeparator can specify how numbers are treated when parsing.

Name	Returns	Parameters	Description
Ungroup	Variant		Either promotes the outline in the range or ungroups the range in a PivotTable report.
UnMerge			Splits up a merged cell into single cells.

Example: Range Object

See Chapter 5 for examples of working with the `Range` object.

RecentFile Object and the RecentFiles Collection

The `RecentFiles` collection holds the list of recently modified files. Equivalent to the files listed under the File menu in Excel. Each `RecentFile` object represents one of the recently modified files.

`RecentFiles` has a few attributes besides the typical collection ones. The `Maximum` property can be used to set or return the maximum number of files that Excel will 'remember' modifying. The value can range from 0 to 9. The `Count` property returns the number of `RecentFile` objects in the collection. The `Add` method is used to add a file (with the `Name` parameter) to the collection.

RecentFile Common Properties

The `Application`, `Creator`, and `Parent` properties are defined at the beginning of this appendix.

RecentFile Properties

Name	Returns	Description
Index	Long	Read Only. Returns the spot in the collection that the current object is located.
Name	String	Read Only. Returns the name of the recently modified file.
Path	String	Read Only. Returns the file path of the recently modified file.

RecentFile Methods

Name	Returns	Parameters	Description
Delete			Deletes the object from the collection
Open	Workbook		Opens up the recent file and returns the opened workbook

Example: RecentFile Object and the RecentFiles Collection

```
Sub CheckRecentFiles()
   Dim oRF As RecentFile
```

```
    'Remove any recent files that refer to the floppy drive
    For Each oRF In Application.RecentFiles
       If Left(oRF.Path, 2) = "A:" Then
          oRF.Delete
       End If
    Next
 End Sub
```

RoutingSlip Object

The RoutingSlip object represents the properties and methods of the routing slip of an Excel document. The parent object of the RoutingSlip object is the Workbook object. The HasRoutingSlip property of the Workbook object has to set to True before the RoutingSlip object can be manipulated.

RoutingSlip Common Properties

The Application, Creator, and Parent properties are defined at the beginning of this appendix.

RoutingSlip Properties

Name	Returns	Description
Delivery	XlRouting Slip Delivery	Set/Get how the delivery process will proceed.
Message	Variant	Set/Get the body text of the routing slip message.
Recipients	Variant	Parameters: [Index]. Returns the list of recipient names to send the parent workbook to.
ReturnWhen Done	Boolean	Set/Get whether the message is returned to the original sender.
Status	XlRouting SlipStatus	Read Only. Returns the current status of the routing slip.
Subject	Variant	Set/Get the subject text for the routing slip message.
TrackStatus	Boolean	Set/Get whether the message is sent to the original sender each time the message is forwarded.

RoutingSlip Methods

Name	Returns	Parameters	Description
Reset	Variant		Reset the routing slip

RTD Object

Represents a Real-Time Data object, like one referenced using the IrtdServer object. As of this writing, there was very little documentation.

RTD Properties

Name	Returns	Description
Throttle Interval	Long	Set/Get the time interval between updates

RTD Methods

Name	Returns	Parameters	Description
RefreshData	RTD		Requests an update of RTD from the RTD server
Restart Servers	RTD		Reconnects to servers for RTD

Scenario Object and the Scenarios Collection

The `Scenarios` collection contains the list of all the scenarios associated with a worksheet. Each `Scenario` object represents a single scenario in a worksheet. A scenario holds the list of saved cell values that can later be substituted into the worksheet. The parent of the `Scenarios` collection is the `Worksheet` object.

The `Scenarios` collection has a few extra properties and methods besides the typical collection attributes. These are listed in the following table.

Scenarios Properties and Methods

Name	Returns	Description
Count	Long	Read Only. Returns the number of `Scenario` objects in the collection.
Add	Scenario	Method. Parameters: `Name As String, ChangingCells, [Values], [Comment], [Locked], [Hidden]`. Adds a scenario to the collection. The `Name` parameter specifies the name of the scenario. See the `Scenario` object for a description of the parameters.
CreateSummary	Variant	Method. Parameters: `ReportType As XlSummaryReportType, [ResultCells]`. Creates a worksheet containing a summary of all the scenarios of the parent worksheet. The `ReportType` parameter can specify the report type. The `ResultCells` parameter can be a range of cells containing the formulas related to the changing cells.
Merge	Variant	Method. Parameters: `Source`. Merges the scenarios in the `Source` parameter into the current worksheet.

Scenario Common Properties

The `Application`, `Creator`, and `Parent` properties are defined at the beginning of this appendix.

Scenario Properties

Name	Returns	Description
ChangingCells	Range	Read Only. Returns the range of cells in the worksheet that will have values plugged in for the specific scenario.
Comment	String	Set/Get the scenario comment.
Hidden	Boolean	Set/Get whether the scenario is hidden.
Index	Long	Read Only. Returns the spot in the collection that the current Scenario object is located.
Locked	Boolean	Set/Get whether the scenario cannot be modified when the worksheet is protected.
Name	String	Set/Get the name of the scenario.
Values	Variant	Read Only. Parameters: `[Index]`. Returns an array of the values to plug in to the changing cells for this particular scenario.

Scenario Methods

Name	Returns	Parameters	Description
Change Scenario	Variant	Changing Cells, [Values]	Changes which set of cells in the worksheet are able to change for the scenario. Optionally can choose new values for the scenario.
Delete	Variant		Deletes the `Scenario` object from the collection.
Show	Variant		Shows the scenario results by putting the scenario values into the worksheet.

Example: Scenario Object and the Scenarios Collection

```
Sub GetBestScenario()
   Dim oScen As Scenario
   Dim oBestScen As Scenario
   Dim dBestSoFar As Double

   'Loop through the scenarios in the sheet
   For Each oScen In ActiveSheet.Scenarios

      'Show the secnario
      oScen.Show

      'Is it better?
      If Range("Result").Value > dBestSoFar Then
         dBestSoFar = Range("Result").Value

         'Yes - remember it
         Set oBestScen = oScen
```

```
        End If
    Next

    'Show the best scenario
    oBestScen.Show

    MsgBox "The best scenario is " & oBestScen.Name
End Sub
```

Series Object and the SeriesCollection Collection

The `SeriesCollection` collection holds the collection of series associated with a chart group. Each `Series` object contains a collection of points associated with a chart group in a chart. For example, a simple line chart contains a series (`Series`) of points brought in from the originating data. Since some charts can have many series plotted on the same chart, the `SeriesCollection` is used to hold that information. The parent of the `SeriesCollection` is the `ChartGroup`.

The `SeriesCollection` has a few attributes that are not typical of a collection. These are listed in the following table.

SeriesCollection Properties and Methods

Name	Returns	Description
`Add`	`Series`	Method. Parameters: `Source, Rowcol As XlRowCol, [SeriesLabels], [CategoryLabels], [Replace]`. Adds a `Series` to the collection. The `Source` parameter specifies either a range or an array of data points describing the new series (and all the points in it). The `Rowcol` parameter sets whether the row or the column of the `Source` contains a series of points. Set `SeriesLabels` or `CategoryLabels` to `True` to make the first row or column of the `Source` contain the labels for the series and category, respectively.
`Count`	`Long`	Read Only. Returns the number of `Series` objects in the collection.
`Extend`	`Variant`	Method. Parameters: `Source, [Rowcol], [CategoryLabels]`. Adds the points specified by the range or array of data points in the `Source` parameter to the `SeriesCollection`. See the `Add` method for details on the other parameters.
`Paste`	`Variant`	Method. Parameters: `Rowcol As XlRowCol, [SeriesLabels], [CategoryLabels], [Replace], [NewSeries]`. Pastes the data from the `Clipboard` into the `SeriesCollection` as a new `Series`. See the `Add` method for details on the other parameters.
`NewSeries`	`Series`	Method. Creates a new series and returns the newly created series.

Series Common Properties

The `Application`, `Creator`, and `Parent` properties are defined at the beginning of this appendix.

Series Properties

Name	Returns	Description
ApplyPictTo End	Boolean	Set/Get whether pictures are added to the end of the points in the series.
ApplyPictTo Front	Boolean	Set/Get whether pictures are added to the front of the points in the series.
ApplyPictTo Sides	Boolean	Set/Get whether pictures are added to the sides of the points in the series.
AxisGroup	XlAxis Group	Set/Get the type of axis type being used by the series (primary or secondary).
BarShape	XlBarShape	Set/Get the type of shape to use in a 3D bar or column chart (e.g. `xlBox`).
Border	Border	Read Only. Returns the collection of borders (sides) around the series. Each border's attributes can be accessed individually.
BubbleSizes	Variant	Set/Get the cell references (A1 reference style) that contain data relating to how big the bubble should be for bubble charts.
ChartType	XlChartType	Set/Get the type of chart to use for the series.
ErrorBars	ErrorBars	Read Only. Returns the error bars in a series. Use with `HasErrorBars`.
Explosion	Long	Set/Get how far out the slices (points) of a pie or doughnut chart will explode out. `0` for no explosion.
Fill	ChartFill Format	Read Only. Returns an object containing fill formatting options for the series of points on a chart.
Formula	String	Set/Get the type of formula label to use for the series.
FormulaLocal	String	Set/Get the formula of the series in the language of the user using the A1 style references.
FormulaR1C1	String	Set/Get the formula of the series in the language of the macro using the R1C1 style references.
FormulaR1C1 Local	String	Set/Get the formula of the series in the language of the user using the R1C1 style references.
Has3DEffect	Boolean	Set/Get if bubble charts have a 3D appearance.
HasDataLabels	Boolean	Set/Get if the series contains data labels.
HasErrorBars	Boolean	Set/Get if the series contains error bars. Use with the `ErrorBars` property.

Name	Returns	Description
HasLeader Lines	Boolean	Set/Get if the series contains leader lines. Use with the LeaderLines property.
Interior	Interior	Read Only. Returns an object containing options to format the inside area of the series (e.g. interior color).
InvertIf Negative	Boolean	Set/Get whether the color of the series' points should be the inverse if the value is negative.
LeaderLines	LeaderLines	Read Only. Returns the leader lines associated with the series.
Marker Background Color	Long	Set/Get the color of the series points marker background. Use the RGB function to create the color value.
Marker Background ColorIndex	XlColor Index	Set/Get the color of the series points marker background. Use the XlColorIndex constants or an index value in the current color palette.
Marker Foreground Color	Long	Set/Get the color of the series points marker foreground. Use the RGB function to create the color value.
Marker Foreground ColorIndex	XlColor Index	Set/Get the color of the series points marker foreground. Use the XlColorIndex constants or an index value in the current color palette.
MarkerSize	Long	Set/Get the size of the point key marker.
MarkerStyle	XlMarker Style	Set/Get the type of marker to use as the point key (e.g. square, diamond, triangle, picture, etc.)
Name	String	Set/Get the name of the series.
PictureType	XlChart Picture Type	Set/Get how an associated picture is displayed on the series (e.g. stretched, tiled). Use the XlPictureType constants.
PictureUnit	Long	Set/Get how many units a picture represents if the PictureType property is set to xlScale.
PlotOrder	Long	Set/Get the plotting order for this particular series in the SeriesCollection.
Shadow	Boolean	Set/Get whether the points in the series will have a shadow effect.
Smooth	Boolean	Set/Get whether scatter or line charts will have curves smoothed.
Type	Long	Set/Get the type of series.
Values	Variant	Set/Get the range containing the series values or an array of fixed values containing the series values.
XValues	Variant	Set/Get the array of x values coming from a range or an array of fixed values.

Series Methods

Name	Returns	Parameters	Description
ApplyCustom Type		ChartType As XlChartType	Changes the chart type to the one specified in the ChartType parameter.
ApplyData Labels	Variant	[Type As XlDataLabels Type], [LegendKey], [AutoText], [HasLeader Lines], [ShowSeries Name], [ShowCategory Name], [ShowValue], [Show Percentage], [ShowBubble Size], [Separator]	Applies the data label properties specified by the parameters to the series. The Type parameter specifies whether no label, a value, a percentage of the whole, or a category label is shown. The legend key can appear by the point by setting the LegendKey parameter to True. Set the HasLeaderLines to True to add leader lines to the series.
ClearFormats	Variant		Clears the formatting made on the series.
Copy	Variant		Copies the series into the clipboard.
DataLabels	Object	[Index]	Returns the collection of data labels in a series. If the Index parameter is specified then only a single data label is returned.
Delete	Variant		Deletes the series from the series collection.
ErrorBar	Variant	[Direction As XlErrorBar Direction], [Include As XlErrorBar Include], [Type As XlErrorBar Type], [Amount], [MinusValues]	Adds error bars to the series. The Direction parameter chooses whether the bar appears on the X or Y axis. The Include parameter specifies which error parts to include. The Type parameter decides the type of error bar to use. The Amount parameter is used to choose an error amount. The MinusValues parameter takes the negative error amount to use when the Type parameter is xlErrorBarTypeCustom.
Paste	Variant		Uses the picture in the Clipboard as the marker on the points in the series.

Name	Returns	Parameters	Description
Points		[Index]	Returns either the collection of points associated with the series or a single point if the Index parameter is specified.
Select	Variant		Selects the series' points on the chart.
Trendlines		[Index]	Returns either the collection of trendlines associated with the series or a single trendline if the Index parameter is specified.

Example: Series Object and the SeriesCollection Collection

See the DataLabel object for an example of using the Series object.

SeriesLines Object

The SeriesLines object accesses the series lines connecting data values from each series. This object only applies to 2D stacked bar or column chart groups. The parent of the SeriesLines object is the ChartGroup object.

SeriesLines Common Properties

The Application, Creator, and Parent properties are defined at the beginning of this appendix.

SeriesLines Properties

Name	Returns	Description
Border	Border	Read Only. Returns the border's properties around the series lines.
Name	String	Read Only. Returns the name of the SeriesLines object.

SeriesLines Methods

Name	Returns	Parameters	Description
Delete	Variant		Deletes the SeriesLines object
Select	Variant		Selects the series lines in the chart

Example: SeriesLines Object

```
Sub FormatSeriesLines()
   Dim oCG As ChartGroup
   Dim oSL As SeriesLines

   'Loop through the column groups on the chart
   For Each oCG In Charts(1).ColumnGroups
```

```
        'Make sure we have some series lines
        oCG.HasSeriesLines = True

        'Get the series lines
        Set oSL = oCG.SeriesLines

        'Format the lines
        With oSL
           .Border.Weight = xlThin
           .Border.ColorIndex = 5
        End With
     Next
  End Sub
```

ShadowFormat Object

The `ShadowFormat` object allows manipulation of the shadow formatting properties of a parent `Shape` object. Use the `Shadow` property of the `Shape` object to access the `ShadowFormat` object.

ShadowFormat Common Properties

The `Application`, `Creator`, and `Parent` properties are defined at the beginning of this appendix.

ShadowFormat Properties

Name	Returns	Description
ForeColor	ColorFormat	Read Only. Allows manipulation of the shadow fore-color.
Obscured	MsoTriState	Set/Get whether the shape obscures the shadow or not.
OffsetX	Single	Set/Get the horizontal shadow offset.
OffsetY	Single	Set/Get the vertical shadow offset.
Transparency	Single	Set/Get the transparency of the shadow (0 to 1 where 1 is clear).
Type	MsoShadow Type	Set/Get the shadow type.
Visible	MsoTriState	Set/Get whether the shadow is visible.

ShadowFormat Methods

Name	Returns	Parameters	Description
Increment OffsetX		Increment As Single	Changes the horizontal shadow offset.
Increment OffsetY		Increment As Single	Changes the vertical shadow offset.

Example: ShadowFormat Object

```
Sub AddShadow()
    Dim oSF As ShadowFormat

    Set oSF = ActiveSheet.Shapes.Range(1).Shadow

    With oSF
        .Type = msoShadow6
        .OffsetX = 5
        .OffsetY = 5
        .ForeColor.SchemeColor = 2
        .Visible = True
    End With
End Sub
```

Shape Object and the Shapes Collection

The `Shapes` collection holds the list of shapes for a sheet. The `Shape` object represents a single shape such as an `AutoShape`, a free-form shape, an OLE object (like an image), an ActiveX control or a picture. Possible parent objects of the `Shapes` collection are the `Worksheet` and Chart object.

The `Shapes` collection has a few methods and properties besides the typical collection attributes. They are listed in the following table.

Shapes Collection Properties and Methods

Name	Returns	Description
`Count`	`Long`	Read Only. Returns the number of shapes in the collection.
`Range`	`ShapeRange`	Read Only. Parameters: `Index`. Returns a `ShapeRange` object containing only some of the shapes in the `Shapes` collection.
`AddCallout`	`Shape`	Method. Parameters: `Type As MsoCalloutType, Left As Single, Top As Single, Width As Single, Height As Single`. Adds a callout line shape to the collection.
`AddConnector`	`Shape`	Method. Parameters: `Type As MsoConnectorType, BeginX As Single, BeginY As Single, EndX As Single, EndY As Single`. Adds a connector shape to the collection.
`AddCurve`	`Shape`	Method. Parameters: `SafeArrayOfPoints`. Adds a `Bezier` curve to the collection.
`AddDiagram`	`Shape`	Method. Parameters: `Type As MsoDiagramType, Left As Single, Top As Single, Width As Single, Height As Single`. Adds a new `AutoShape` to the worksheet.
`AddFormControl`	`Shape`	Method. Parameters: `Type As XlFormControl, Left As Long`, Top As Long, `Width As Long, Height As Long`. Adds an Excel control to the collection.

Table continued on following page

Name	Returns	Description
AddLabel	Shape	Method. Parameters: Orientation As MsoTextOrientation, Left As Single, Top As Single, Width As Single, Height As Single. Adds a label to the collection.
AddLine	Shape	Method. Parameters: BeginX As Single, BeginY As Single, EndX As Single, EndY As Single. Adds a line shape to the collection.
AddOLEObject	Shape	Method. Parameters: [ClassType], [Filename], [Link], [DisplayAsIcon], [IconFileName], [IconIndex], [IconLabel], [Left], [Top], [Width], [Height]. Adds an OLE control to the collection.
AddPicture	Shape	Method. Parameters: Filename As String, LinkToFile As MsoTriState, SaveWithDocument As MsoTriState, Left As Single, Top As Single, Width As Single, Height As Single. Adds a picture object to the collection.
AddPolyline	Shape	Method. Parameters: SafeArrayOfPoints. Adds an open polyline or a closed polygon to the collection.
AddShape	Shape	Method. Parameters: Type As MsoAutoShapeType, Left As Single, Top As Single, Width As Single, Height As Single. Adds a shape using the Type parameter to the collection.
AddTextbox	Shape	Method. Parameters: Orientation As MsoTextOrientation, Left As Single, Top As Single, Width As Single, Height As Single. Adds a textbox to the collection.
AddText Effect	Shape	Method. Parameters: PresetTextEffect As MsoPresetTextEffect, Text As String, FontName As String, FontSize As Single, FontBold As MsoTriState, FontItalic As MsoTriState, Left As Single, Top As Single. Adds a WordArt object to the collection.
Build Freeform	Freeform Builder	Method. Parameters: EditingType As MsoEditingType, X1 As Single, Y1 As Single. Accesses an object that allows creation of a new shape based on ShapeNode objects.
SelectAll		Method. Selects all the shapes in the collection.

Shape Common Properties

The Application, Creator, and Parent properties are defined at the beginning of this appendix.

Shape Properties

Name	Returns	Description
Adjustments	Adjustments	Read Only. An object accessing the adjustments for a shape.
Alternative Text	String	Set/Get the alternate text to appear if the image is not loaded. Used with a web page.
AutoShape Type	MsoAuto ShapeType	Set/Get the type of AutoShape used.
BlackWhite Mode	MsoBlack WhiteMode	Property used for compatibility to other drawing packages only. Does not do anything.
BottomRight Cell	Range	Read Only. Returns the single cell range that describes the cell under the lower-right corner of the shape.
Callout	Callout Format	Read Only. An object accessing the callout properties of the shape.
Child	MsoTriState	Read Only. Returns whether the specified shape is a child shape, or if all shapes in a shape range are child shapes of the same parent.
Connection SiteCount	Long	Read Only. Returns the number of potential connection points (sites) on the shape for a connector.
Connector	MsoTriState	Read Only. Returns whether the shape is a connector.
Connector Format	Connector Format	Read Only. Returns an object containing formatting options for a connector shape. Shape must be a connector shape.
Control Format	Control Format	Read Only. Returns an object containing formatting options for an Excel control. Shape must be an Excel control.
Diagram	Diagram	Read Only. Returns a Diagram object.
DiagramNode	DiagramNode	Read Only. Returns a node in the diagram.
Fill	FillFormat	Read Only. Returns an object containing fill formatting options for the Shape object.
FormControl Type	XlForm Control	Read Only. Returns the type of Excel control the current shape is (e.g. xlCheckBox). Shape must be an Excel control.
GroupItems	GroupShapes	Read Only. Returns the shapes that make up the current shape.
HasDiagram	MsoTriState	Read Only. Returns whether a shape or shape range contains a diagram.
HasDiagram Node	MsoTriState	Read Only. Returns whether a diagram node exists in a given shape or shape range.
Height	Single	Set/Get the height of the shape.

Table continued on following page

Name	Returns	Description
HorizontalFlip	MsoTriState	Read Only. Returns whether the shape has been flipped.
Hyperlink	Hyperlink	Read Only. Returns the hyperlink of the shape, if any.
ID	Long	Read Only. Returns the type for the specified object.
Left	Single	Set/Get the horizontal position of the shape.
Line	LineFormat	Read Only. An object accessing the line formatting of the shape.
LinkFormat	LinkFormat	Read Only. An object accessing the OLE linking properties.
LockAspectRatio	MsoTriState	Set/Get whether the dimensional proportions of the shape is kept when the shape is resized.
Locked	Boolean	Set/Get whether the shape can be modified if the sheet is locked (`True` = cannot modify).
Name	String	Set/Get the name of the `Shape` object.
Nodes	ShapeNodes	Read Only. An object accessing the nodes of the freeform shape.
OLEFormat	OLEFormat	Read Only. An object accessing OLE object properties if applicable.
OnAction	String	Set/Get the macro to run when the shape is clicked.
ParentGroup	Shape	Read Only. Returns the common parent shape of a child shape or a range of child shapes.
PictureFormat	PictureFormat	Read Only. An object accessing the picture format options.
Placement	XlPlacement	Set/Get how the object will react with the cells around the shape.
Rotation	Single	Set/Get the degrees rotation of the shape.
Script	Script	Read Only. Returns the VBScript associated with the shape.
Shadow	ShadowFormat	Read Only. An object accessing the shadow properties.
TextEffect	TextEffectFormat	Read Only. An object accessing the text effect properties.
TextFrame	TextFrame	Read Only. An object accessing the text frame properties.
ThreeD	ThreeDFormat	Read Only. An object accessing the 3-D effect formatting properties.
Top	Single	Set/Get the vertical position of the shape.
TopLeftCell	Range	Read Only. Returns the single cell range that describes the cell over the upper-left corner of the shape.

Name	Returns	Description
Type	MsoShape Type	Read Only. Returns the type of shape.
VerticalFlip	MsoTriState	Read Only. Returns whether the shape has been vertically flipped.
Vertices	Variant	Read Only. Returns a series of coordinate pairs describing the Freeform's vertices.
Visible	MsoTriState	Set/Get whether the shape is visible.
Width	Single	Read Only. Returns the type of shape.
ZOrder Position	Long	Read Only. Returns where the shape is in the z-order of the collection (e.g. front, back).

Shape Methods

Name	Returns	Parameters	Description
Apply			Activates the shape.
Copy			Copies the shape to the Clipboard.
CopyPicture		[Appearance As XLPicture Appearance], [Format As XlCopyPicture Format]	Copies the range into the clipboard as a picture. The `Appearance` parameter can be used to specify whether the picture is copied as it looks on the screen or when printed. The `Format` parameter can specify the type of picture that will be put into the clipboard.
Cut			Cuts the shape and places it in the clipboard.
Delete			Deletes the shape.
Duplicate	Shape		Duplicates the shape returning the new shape.
Flip		FlipCmd As MsoFlipCmd	Flips the shape using the `FlipCmd` parameter.
Increment Left		Increment As Single	Moves the shape horizontally.
Increment Rotation		Increment As Single	Rotates the shape using the `Increment` parameter as degrees.
IncrementTop		Increment As Single	Moves the shape vertically.
PickUp			Copies the format of the current shape so another shape can then apply the formats.

Table continued on following page

Name	Returns	Parameters	Description
Reroute Connections			Optimizes the route of the current connector shape connected between two shapes. Also, this method may be used to optimize all the routes of connectors connected to the current shape.
ScaleHeight		Factor As Single, RelativeTo OriginalSize As MsoTriState, [Scale]	Scales the height of the shape by the Factor parameter.
ScaleWidth		Factor As Single, RelativeTo OriginalSize As MsoTriState, [Scale]	Scales the width of the shape by the Factor parameter.
Select		[Replace]	Selects the shape in the document.
SetShapes Default Properties			Sets the formatting of the current shape as a default shape in Word.
Ungroup	ShapeRange		Breaks apart the shapes that make up the Shape object.
ZOrder		ZOrderCmd As MsoZ OrderCmd	Changes the order of the shape object in the collection.

Example: Shape Object and the Shapes Collection

The Shape object is a generic container object for other object types. Examples of using the Shapes collection and Shape object are included under the specific objects.

ShapeNode Object and the ShapeNodes Collection

The ShapeNodes collection has the list of nodes and curved segments that make up a free-form shape. The ShapeNode object specifies a single node or curved segment that makes up a free-form shape. The Nodes property of the Shape object is used to access the ShapeNodes collection.

The ShapeNodes collection has a few methods besides the typical collection attributes listed in the following table.

ShapeNodes Collection Properties and Methods

Name	Returns	Description
Count	Integer	Read Only. Returns the number of ShapeNode objects in the collection.
Delete		Method. Parameters: Index As Integer. Deletes the node specified by the Index.
Insert		Method. Parameters: Index As Integer, SegmentType As MsoSegmentType, EditingType As MsoEditingType, X1 As Single, Y1 As Single, X2 As Single, Y2 As Single, X3 As Single, Y3 As Single. Inserts a node or curved segment in the Nodes collection.
SetEditing Type		Method. Parameters: Index As Integer, EditingType As MsoEditingType. Sets the editing type for a node.
SetPosition		Method. Parameters: Index As Integer, X1 As Single, Y1 As Single. Moves the specified node.
SetSegment Type		Method. Parameters: Index As Integer, SegmentType As MsoSegmentType. Changes the segment type following the node.

ShapeNode Common Properties

The Application, Creator, and Parent properties are defined at the beginning of this appendix.

ShapeNode Properties

Name	Returns	Description
EditingType	MsoEditing Type	Read Only. Returns the editing type for the node.
Points	Variant	Read Only. Returns the positional coordinate pair.
SegmentType	MsoSegment Type	Read Only. Returns the type of segment following the node.

Example: ShapeNode Object and the ShapeNodes Collection

```
Sub ToggleArch()
    Dim oShp As Shape
    Dim oSN As ShapeNodes

    Set oShp = ActiveSheet.Shapes(1)

    'Is the Shape a freeform?
    If oShp.Type = msoFreeform Then

        'Yes, so get its nodes
        Set oSN = oShp.Nodes
```

```
        'Toggle segment 3 between a line and a curve
        If oSN.Item(3).SegmentType = msoSegmentCurve Then
           oSN.SetSegmentType 3, msoSegmentLine
        Else
           oSN.SetSegmentType 3, msoSegmentCurve
        End If
     End If
  End Sub
```

ShapeRange Collection

The ShapeRange collection holds a collection of Shape objects for a certain range or selection in a document. Possible parent items are the Range and the Selection object. The ShapeRange collection has many properties and methods besides the typical collection attributes. These items are listed below.

However, some operations will cause an error if performed on a ShapeRange collection with multiple shapes.

ShapeRange Properties

Name	Returns	Description
Adjustments	Adjustments	Read Only. An object accessing the adjustments for a shape.
Alternative Text	String	Set/Get the alternative text to appear if the image is not loaded. Used with a web page.
AutoShape Type	MsoAuto ShapeType	Set/Get the type of AutoShape used.
BlackWhite Mode	MsoBlack WhiteMode	Property used for compatibility to other drawing packages only. Does not do anything.
Callout	Callout Format	Read Only. An object accessing the callout properties of the shape.
Child	MsoTriState	Read Only. Returns whether the specified shape is a child shape, or if all shapes in a shape range are child shapes of the same parent.
Connection SiteCount	Long	Read Only. Returns the number of potential connection points (sites) on the shape for a connector.
Connector	MsoTriState	Read Only. Returns whether the shape is a connector.
ConnectorFor mat	Connector Format	Read Only. Returns an object containing formatting options for a connector shape. Shape must be a connector shape.
Count	Long	Read Only. Returns the number of shapes in the collection.
Diagram	Diagram	Read Only. Returns a Diagram object.
DiagramNode	DiagramNode	Read Only. Returns a node in the diagram.

Name	Returns	Description
Fill	FillFormat	Read Only. An object accessing the fill properties of the shape.
GroupItems	GroupShapes	Read Only. Returns the shapes that make up the current shape.
HasDiagram	MsoTriState	Read Only. Returns whether a shape or shape range contains a diagram.
HasDiagram Node	MsoTriState	Read Only. Returns whether a diagram node exists in a given shape or shape range.
Height	Single	Set/Get the height of the shape.
Horizontal Flip	MsoTriState	Read Only. Returns whether the shape has been flipped.
ID	Long	Read Only. Returns the type for the specified object.
Left	Single	Set/Get the horizontal position of the shape.
Line	LineFormat	Read Only. An object accessing the line formatting of the shape.
LockAspect Ratio	MsoTriState	Set/Get whether the dimensional proportions of the shape are kept when the shape is resized.
Name	String	Set/Get the name of the shape.
Nodes	ShapeNodes	Read Only. Returns the nodes associated with the shape.
ParentGroup	Shape	Read Only. Returns the common parent shape of a child shape or a range of child shapes.
Picture Format	Picture Format	Read Only. An object accessing the picture format options.
Rotation	Single	Set/Get the degrees rotation of the shape.
Shadow	Shadow Format	Read Only. An object accessing the shadow properties.
TextEffect	TextEffect Format	Read Only. An object accessing the text effect properties.
TextFrame	TextFrame	Read Only. An object accessing the text frame properties.
ThreeD	ThreeD Format	Read Only. An object accessing the 3-D effect formatting properties.
Top	Single	Set/Get the vertical position of the shape.
Type	MsoShape Type	Read Only. Returns the type of shape.
VerticalFlip	MsoTriState	Read Only. Returns whether the shape has been vertically flipped.
Vertices	Variant	Read Only. Returns a series of coordinate pairs describing the Freeform's vertices.

Table continued on following page

Name	Returns	Description
Visible	MsoTriState	Set/Get whether the shape is visible.
Width	Single	Set/Get the width of the shape.
ZOrderPosition	Long	Read Only. Changes the order of the object in the collection.

ShapeRange Methods

Name	Returns	Parameters	Description
Align		AlignCmd As MsoAlignCmd, RelativeTo As MsoTriState	Aligns the shapes in the collection to the alignment properties set by the parameters.
Apply			Applies the formatting that was set by the PickUp method.
Delete			Deletes the shape.
Distribute		DistributeCmd As MsoDistribute Cmd, RelativeTo As MsoTriState	Distributes the shapes in the collection evenly either horizontally or vertically.
Duplicate	ShapeRange		Duplicates the shape and returns a new ShapeRange.
Flip		FlipCmd As MsoFlipCmd	Flips the shape using the FlipCmd parameter.
Group	Shape		Groups the shapes in the collection.
IncrementLeft		Increment As Single	Moves the shape horizontally.
Increment Rotation		Increment As Single	Rotates the shape using the Increment parameter as degrees.
IncrementTop		Increment As Single	Moves the shape vertically.
PickUp			Copies the format of the current shape so another shape can then apply the formats.
Regroup	Shape		Regroups any previously grouped shapes.

Name	Returns	Parameters	Description
Reroute Connections			Optimizes the route of the current connector shape connected between two shapes. Also, this method may be used to optimize all the routes of connectors connected to the current shape.
ScaleHeight		Factor As Single, RelativeTo OriginalSize As MsoTriState, [Scale]	Scales the height of the shape by the Factor parameter.
ScaleWidth		Factor As Single, RelativeTo OriginalSize As MsoTriState, [Scale]	Scales the width of the shape by the Factor parameter.
Select		[Replace]	Selects the shape in the document.
SetShapesDef ault Properties			Sets the formatting of the current shape as a default shape in Word.
Ungroup	ShapeRange		Breaks apart the shapes that make up the Shape object.
ZOrder		ZOrderCmd As MsoZOrderCmd	Changes the order of the shape object in the collection.

Example: ShapeRange Collection

```
Sub AlignShapeRanges()
   Dim oSR As ShapeRange

   'Get the first two shapes on the sheet
   Set oSR = ActiveSheet.Shapes.Range(Array(1, 2))

   'Align the left-hand edges of the shapes
   oSR.Align msoAlignLefts, msoFalse
End Sub
```

Sheets Collection

The Sheets collection contains all of the sheets in the parent workbook. Sheets in a workbook consist of chart sheets and worksheets. Therefore, the Sheets collection holds both the Chart objects and Worksheet objects associated with the parent workbook. The parent of the Sheets collection is the Workbook object.

Sheets Common Properties

The Application, Creator, and Parent properties are defined at the beginning of this appendix.

Sheets Properties

Name	Returns	Description
Count	Long	Read Only. Returns the number of sheets in the collection (and therefore workbook).
HPageBreaks	HPageBreaks	Read Only. Returns a collection holding all the horizontal page breaks associated with the Sheets collection.
VPageBreaks	VpageBreaks	Read Only. Returns a collection holding all the vertical page breaks associated with the worksheets of the Sheets collection.
Visible	Variant	Set/Get whether the sheets in the collection are visible. Also can set this to xlVeryHidden to not allow a user to make the sheets in the collection visible.

Sheets Methods

Name	Returns	Parameters	Description
Add		[Before], [After], [Count], [Type]	Adds a sheet to the collection. You can specify where the sheet goes by choosing which sheet object will be before the new sheet object (Before parameter) or after the new sheet (After parameter). The Count parameter decides how many sheets are created. The Type parameter can be used to specify the type of sheet using the XLSheetType constants.
Copy		[Before], [After]	Adds a new copy of the currently active sheet to the position specified at the Before or After parameters.
Delete			Deletes all the sheets in the collection. Remember a workbook must contain at least one sheet.
FillAcross Sheets		Range As Range, Type As XlFillWith	Copies the values in the Range parameter to all the other sheets at the same location. The Type parameter can be used to specify whether cell contents, formulas or everything is copied.

Name	Returns	Parameters	Description
Move		[Before], [After]	Moves the current sheet to the position specified by the parameters. See the Add method.
PrintOut		[From], [To], [Copies], [Preview], [Active Printer], [PrintToFile], [Collate], [PrToFileName]	Prints out the sheets in the collection. The printer, number of copies, collation, and whether a print preview is desired can be specified with the parameters. Also, the sheets can be printed to a file using the PrintToFile and PrToFileName parameters. The From and To parameters can be used to specify the range of printed pages.
PrintPreview		[Enable Changes]	Displays the current sheet in the collection in a print preview mode. Set the EnableChanges parameter to False to disable the **Margins** and **Setup** buttons, hence not allowing the viewer to modify the page setup.
Select		[Replace]	Selects the current sheet in the collection.

SmartTag Object and the SmartTags Collection Object

The SmartTag object represents an identifier that is assigned to a cell. Excel comes with many SmartTags, such as the Stock Ticker or Date recognizer, built in. However, you may also write your own SmartTags in Visual Basic. SmartTags are covered in detail in Chapter 18, but note that a degree of familiarity with XML is required to work with SmartTags.

The SmartTags collection represents all the SmartTags assigned to cells in an application.

SmartTag Common Properties

The Application, Creator, and Parent properties are defined at the beginning of this appendix.

SmartTag Properties

Name	Returns	Description
DownloadURL	String	Read Only. Returns a URL to save along with the corresponding SmartTag.
Name	String	Read Only. Returns name of the SmartTag.
Properties	Custom Properties	Read Only. Returns the properties for the SmartTag.

Table continued on following page

Name	Returns	Description
`Range`	`Range`	Read Only. Returns the range to which the specified SmartTag applies.
`SmartTag Actions`	`SmartTag Actions`	Read Only. Returns the type of action for the selected SmartTag.
`XML`	`String`	Read Only. Returns a sample of the XML that would be passed to the action handler.

SmartTag Methods

Name	Returns	Parameters	Description
`Delete`			Deletes the object

Example: SmartTag Object

Note: this example is repeated in Chapter 18, in the *Remove a Tag from a Range* section.

One of the problems with SmartTags is the issue of false-positives, where a cell is erroneously tagged. An example is the standard Stock Symbol SmartTag that recognizes TRUE as a valid stock symbol, even if that TRUE is a Boolean `True`. The following code locates all of these false-positives and removes them:

```
Sub RemoveBooleanTrue()

   Dim oSht As Worksheet
   Dim oTag As SmartTag

   'This is the URI of the StockTicker SmartTag
   Const sTicker As String = _
                "urn:schemas-microsoft-com:office:smarttags#stockticker"

   'Loop through all the worksheets in the active workbook
   For Each oSht In ActiveWorkbook.Worksheets

      'Loop through all the tags in the sheet
      For Each oTag In oSht.SmartTags

         'Is it a StockTicker tag with a Boolean value?
         If oTag.Name = sTicker And _
                  TypeName(oTag.Range.Value) = "Boolean" Then

            'Yes, so remove this SmartTag from the cell
            oTag.Delete
         End If
      Next
   Next

End Sub
```

SmartTagAction Object and the SmartTagActions Collection Object

The `SmartTagAction` object represents an action that can be performed by a SmartTag. This may involve displaying the latest price for a stock symbol, or setting up an appointment on a certain date.

The `SmartTagActions` collection represents all of the SmartTagAction objects in the application.

SmartTagAction Common Properties

The `Application`, `Creator`, and `Parent` properties are defined at the beginning of this appendix.

SmartTagAction Properties

Name	Returns	Description
`Name`	`String`	Read Only. Returns name of the SmartTag.

SmartTagAction Methods

Name	Returns	Parameters	Description
`Execute`			Activates the SmartTag action

SmartTagOptions Collection Object

The `SmartTagOptions` collection represents all the options of a SmartTag. For instance, it holds whether SmartTags should be embedded in the worksheet, or if they should be displayed at all.

SmartTagOptions Collection Properties

Name	Returns	Description
`DisplaySmart Tags`	`XlSmartTag DisplayMode`	Set/Get the display features for SmartTags
`EmbedSmartTags`	`Boolean`	Set/Get whether to embed SmartTags on the specified workbook

SmartTagReconizer Object and the SmartTagRecognizers Collection Object

The `SmartTagReconizer` object represents the recognizer engines that label the data in the worksheet. These can be user defined, and as such any kind of information can be identified by SmartTags. See Chapter 18 for more details.

The `SmartTagRecognizers` collection represents all of the `SmartTagRecognizer` objects in the application.

SmartTagRecognizers Collection Properties

Name	Returns	Description
`Recognize`	`Boolean`	Set/Get whether data can be labeled with a SmartTag

SmartTagRecognizer Common Properties

The `Application`, `Creator`, and `Parent` properties are defined at the beginning of this appendix.

SmartTagRecognizer Properties

Name	Returns	Description
`Enabled`	`Boolean`	Set/Get whether the object is recognized.
`FullName`	`String`	Read Only. Returns the name of the object, including its path on disk, as a string.
`progId`	`String`	Read Only. Returns the programmatic identifiers for the object.

SoundNote Object

The `SoundNote` object is not used in the current version of Excel. It is kept here for compatibility purposes only. The list of its methods is shown below.

SoundNote Methods

Name	Returns	Parameters
`Delete`	`Variant`	
`Import`	`Variant`	`Filename As String`
`Play`	`Variant`	
`Record`	`Variant`	

Speech Object

Represents the Speech recognition applet that comes with Office XP. This new Speech feature allows text to be read back on demand, or when you enter data on a document. For Excel, you have the option of having each cell's contents read back as they are entered on the worksheet. Use the `SpeakCellOnEnter` property of this object to enable this feature.

`Speech` is accessible through the `Application` object.

Speech Properties

Name	Returns	Description
`Direction`	`XlSpeak Direction`	Set/Get the order in which the cells will be spoken
`SpeakCellOn Enter`	`Boolean`	Set/Get whether to turn on Excel's mode where the active cell will be spoken when the *Enter* key is pressed, or when the active cell is finished being edited

Speech Methods

Name	Returns	Parameters	Description
`Speak`		`Text As String, [SpeakAsync], [SpeakXML], [Purge]`	The `Text` is spoken by Excel. If `Purge` is `True` the current speech will be terminated and any buffered text to be purged before `Text` is spoken.

Example: Speech Object

The following routine reads off the expense totals for all items that are greater than a limit set in another cell on the sheet:

```
Sub ReadHighExpenses()

    Dim lTotal As Long
    Dim lLimit As Long
    Dim rng As Range

    'Grab the limitation amount
    lLimit = wksAllowEditRange.Range("Limit")

    'Loop through the expense totals
    For Each rng In wksAllowEditRange.Range("Expenses")
        'Store the current expense total
        lTotal = rng.Offset(0, 5).Value

        'If the current total is greater than
        ' the limit, read it off
        If lTotal > lLimit Then
            Application.Speech.Speak rng.Text
            Application.Speech.Speak lTotal
        End If
    Next rng

End Sub
```

SpellingOptions Collection Object

Represents the spelling options in Excel. These options can be found on the **Spelling** tab of the **Tools | Options** command and are accessed through the `Application` object. Hence this object is accessible through the `Application` object.

SpellingOptions Collection Properties

Name	Returns	Description
ArabicModes	XlArabic Modes	Set/Get the mode for the Arabic spelling checker
DictLang	Long	Set/Get the dictionary language used by Excel for checking spelling
GermanPost Reform	Boolean	Set/Get whether to check the spelling of words using the German post-reform rules
HebrewModes	XlHebrew Modes	Set/Get the mode for the Hebrew spelling checker
IgnoreCaps	Boolean	Set/Get whether to check for uppercase words, or lowercase words during spelling checks
IgnoreFile Names	Boolean	Set/Get whether to check for Internet and file addresses during spelling checks
IgnoreMixed Digits	Boolean	Set/Get whether to check for mixed digits during spelling checks
KoreanCombine Aux	Boolean	Set/Get whether to combine Korean auxiliary verbs and adjectives when using the spelling checker
KoreanProcess Compound	Boolean	Set/Get whether to process Korean compound nouns when using the spelling checker
KoreanUseAuto ChangeList	Boolean	Set/Get whether to use the auto-change list for Korean words when using the spelling checker
SuggestMain Only	Boolean	Set/Get whether to suggest words from only the main dictionary, for using the spelling checker
UserDict	String	Set/Get whether to create a custom dictionary to which new words can be added, when performing spelling checks

Example: SpellingOptions Collection Object

The following routine sets some spelling options and creates a new custom dictionary where added words during a spellcheck can be found:

```
Sub SetSpellingOptions()

    'This one is as simple as it gets
    With Application.SpellingOptions
        .IgnoreCaps = True
        .IgnoreFileNames = True
        .IgnoreMixedDigits = True
        .SuggestMainOnly = False

        'This property creates a custom dictionary
        ' called Wrox.dic, which can be found and directly edited
        ' in C:\WINDOWS\Application Data\Microsoft\Proof.
        'Added words during a spellcheck will now appear
        ' in this custom dictionary.
        .UserDict = "Wrox.dic"
    End With
```

Style Object and the Styles Collection

The Styles collection holds the list of user-defined and built-in formatting styles, such as Currency and Normal, in a workbook or range. Each Style object represents formatting attributes associated with the parent object. There are some Excel built-in Style objects, such as Currency. Also, new styles can be created. Possible parents of the Styles collection are the Range and Workbook objects.

Styles can be accessed by the end user using the **Style** dialog box from the **Format | Style** menu.
The Styles collection has three extra attributes besides the typical collection ones. The Count property returns the number of Style objects in the collection. The Add method uses the Name parameter to add a new style to the collection. The BasedOn parameter of the Add method can be used to specify a range that the new style will be based on. The Merge method merges the styles in the workbook specified by the Workbook parameter into the current parent workbook.

Style Common Properties

The Application, Creator, and Parent properties are defined at the beginning of this appendix.

Style Properties

Name	Returns	Description
AddIndent	Boolean	Set/Get whether text associated with the style is automatically indented if the text alignment in a cell is set to equally distribute.
Borders	Borders	Read Only. Returns the collection of borders associated with the style. Each border side can be accessed individually.
BuiltIn	Boolean	Read Only. Returns whether the style is built-in.
Font	Font	Read Only. Returns an object containing Font options for the associated style.
FormulaHidden	Boolean	Set/Get whether formulas associated with the style will be hidden if the workbook / worksheet is protected.
Horizontal Alignment	XlHAlign	Set/Get how the cells associated with the style are horizontally aligned. Use the XlHAlign constants.
IncludeAlign ment	Boolean	Set/Get whether the styles include properties associated with alignment (that is, AddIndent, HorizontalAlignment, VerticalAlignment, WrapText, and Orientation).
IncludeBorder	Boolean	Set/Get whether border attributes are included with the style (that is, Color, ColorIndex, LineStyle, and Weight).
IncludeFont	Boolean	Set/Get whether font attributes are included in the style (that is, Background, Bold, Color, ColorIndex, FontStyle, Italic, Name, OutlineFont, Shadow, Size, Strikethrough, Subscript, Superscript, and Underline).

Table continued on following page

Name	Returns	Description
IncludeNumber	Boolean	Set/Get whether the NumberFormat property is included in the style.
Include Patterns	Boolean	Set/Get whether interior pattern related properties are included in the style (that is, Color, ColorIndex, InvertIfNegative, Pattern, PatternColor, and PatternColorIndex).
Include Protection	Boolean	Set/Get whether the locking related properties are included with the style (that is, FormulaHidden and Locked).
IndentLevel	Long	Set/Get the indent level for the style.
Interior	Interior	Read Only. Returns an object containing options to format the inside area of the style (e.g. interior color).
Locked	Boolean	Set/Get whether the style properties can be changed if the workbook is locked.
MergeCells	Variant	Set/Get whether the current style contains merged cells.
Name	String	Read Only. Returns the name of the style.
NameLocal	String	Read Only. Returns the name of the style in the language of the user's computer.
NumberFormat	String	Set/Get the number format associated with the style.
NumberFormat Local	String	Set/Get the number format associated with the style in the language of the end user.
Orientation	Xl Orientation	Set/Get the text orientation for the cell text associated with the style. A value from –90 to 90 degrees can be specified or an XlOrientation constant.
ReadingOrder	Long	Set/Get whether the text associated with the style is from right-to-left (xlRTL), left-to-right (xlLTR), or context sensitive (xlContext).
ShrinkToFit	Boolean	Set/Get whether the cell text associated with the style will automatically shrink to fit the column width.
Value	String	Read Only. Returns the name of the style.
Vertical Alignment	XlVAlign	Set/Get how the cells associated with the style are vertically aligned. Use the XlVAlign constants.
WrapText	Boolean	Set/Get whether cell text wraps in cells associated with the style.

Style Methods

Name	Returns	Parameters	Description
Delete	Variant		Deletes the style from the collection

Example: Style Object and the Styles Collection

```
Sub UpdateStyles()
   Dim oStyle As Style

   Set oStyle = ActiveWorkbook.Styles("Editing")

   'Update the Editing style to be unlocked with a default background
   With oStyle
      .IncludePatterns = True
      .IncludeProtection = True
      .Locked = False
      .Interior.Pattern = xlNone
   End With
End Sub
```

Tab Object

Represents the Sheet tab at the bottom of an Excel chart sheet or worksheet. Excel 2002 now allows you to customize the sheet's tab color by using either the `Color` or `ColorIndex` properties of this object.

Note that when setting `ColorIndex` property of this object to `xlColorIndexAutomatic` (which appears on the AutoComplete list for the property), an error will occur.

Tab Common Properties

The `Application`, `Creator`, and `Parent` properties are defined at the beginning of this appendix.

Tab Properties

Name	Returns	Description
`Color`	`Variant`	Set/Get the primary color of the `Tab` object. Use the `RGB` function to create a color value.
`ColorIndex`	`XlColor Index`	Set/Get the color of the interior.

Example: Tab Object

The following routine changes the tab color for all budget worksheet in a workbook based on a setting in a custom property for each worksheet:

```
Sub ColorBudgetTabs()

    Dim bBudget As Boolean
    Dim oCustomProp As CustomProperty
    Dim oCustomProps As CustomProperties
    Dim wks As Worksheet

    'Loop through each worksheet in this workbook
    For Each wks In ThisWorkbook.Worksheets
        'Loop through all of the custom properties
        ' for the current worksheet until the
        ' "IsBudget" proeprty name is found
        For Each oCustomProp In wks.CustomProperties
            If oCustomProp.Name = "IsBudget" Then
                'Grab its value and exit the loop
```

```
                bBudget = CBool(oCustomProp.Value)
                Exit For
            End If
        Next oCustomProp

        'Use the value in the custom property to determine
        ' whether the tab should be colored.
        If bBudget Then wks.Tab.ColorIndex = 20 'Light blue

    Next wks

End Sub
```

TextEffectFormat Object

The `TextEffectFormat` object contains all the properties and methods associated with `WordArt` objects. The parent object of the `TextEffectFormat` is always the `Shape` object.

TextEffectFormat Common Properties

The `Application`, `Creator`, and `Parent` properties are defined at the beginning of this appendix.

TextEffectFormat Properties

Name	Returns	Description
`Alignment`	`MsoText Effect Alignment`	Set/Get the alignment of the `WordArt`
`FontBold`	`MsoTriState`	Set/Get whether the `WordArt` is bold
`FontItalic`	`MsoTriState`	Set/Get whether the `WordArt` is italic
`FontName`	`String`	Set/Get the font used in the `WordArt`
`FontSize`	`Single`	Set/Get the font size in the `WordArt`
`KernedPairs`	`MsoTriState`	Set/Get whether the characters are kerned in the `WordArt`
`Normalized Height`	`MsoTriState`	Set/Get whether both the uppercase and lowercase characters are the same height
`PresetShape`	`MsoPreset TextEffect Shape`	Set/Get the shape of the `WordArt`
`PresetText Effect`	`MsoPreset TextEffect`	Set/Get the effect associated with the `WordArt`
`RotatedChars`	`MsoTriState`	Set/Get whether the `WordArt` has been rotated by 90 degrees
`Text`	`String`	Set/Get the text in the `WordArt`
`Tracking`	`Single`	Set/Get the spacing ratio between characters

TextEffectFormat Methods

Name	Returns	Parameters	Description
Toggle VerticalText			Toggles the text from vertical to horizontal and back

Example: TextEffectFormat Object

```
Sub FormatTextArt()
   Dim oTEF As TextEffectFormat
   Dim oShp As Shape

   Set oShp = ActiveSheet.Shapes(1)

   If oShp.Type = msoTextEffect Then

      Set oTEF = oShp.TextEffect

      With oTEF
         .FontName = "Times New Roman"
         .FontBold = True
         .PresetTextEffect = msoTextEffect14
         .Text = "Hello World!"
      End With
   End If
End Sub
```

TextFrame Object

The `TextFrame` object contains the properties and methods that can manipulate text-frame shapes. Possible parent objects of the `TextFrame` object are the `Shape` and `ShapeRange` objects.

TextFrame Common Properties

The `Application`, `Creator`, and `Parent` properties are defined at the beginning of this appendix.

TextFrame Properties

Name	Returns	Description
AutoMargins	Boolean	Set/Get whether Excel will calculate the margins of the text frame automatically. Set this property to `False` to use the `MarginLeft`, `MarginRight`, `MarginTop`, and `MarginBottom` properties.
AutoSize	Boolean	Set/Get whether the size of the text frame changes to match the text inside.
Horizontal Alignment	XlHAlign	Set/Get how the text frame is horizontally aligned. Use the `XLHAlign` constants.
MarginBottom	Single	Set/Get the bottom spacing in a text frame.
MarginLeft	Single	Set/Get the left spacing in a text frame.

Table continued on following page

Name	Returns	Description
MarginRight	Single	Set/Get the right spacing in a text frame.
MarginTop	Single	Set/Get the top spacing in a text frame.
Orientation	MsoText Orientation	Set/Get the orientation of the text in the text frame.
ReadingOrder	Long	Set/Get whether the text in the frame is read from right-to-left (xlRTL), left-to-right (xlLTR), or context sensitive (xlContext).
Vertical Alignment	XlVAlign	Set/Get how the text frame is vertically aligned. Use the XlVAlign constants.

TextFrame Methods

Name	Returns	Parameters	Description
Characters	Characters	[Start], [Length]	Returns an object containing all the characters in the text frame. Allows manipulation on a character-by-character basis and to retrieve only a subset of text in the frame.

Example: TextFrame Object

```
Sub SetShapeAutoSized()
   Dim oTF As TextFrame
   Dim oShp As Shape

   Set oShp = ActiveSheet.Shapes(1)
   Set oTF = oShp.TextFrame

   oTF.AutoSize = True
End Sub
```

ThreeDFormat Object

The ThreeDFormat object contains all of the three-dimensional formatting properties of the parent Shape object. The ThreeD property of the Shape object is used to access the ThreeDFormat object.

ThreeDFormat Common Properties

The Application, Creator, and Parent properties are defined at the beginning of this appendix.

ThreeDFormat Properties

Name	Returns	Description
Depth	Single	Set/Get the 'depth' of a 3D shape.
ExtrusionColor	ColorFormat	Read Only. An object manipulating the color of the extrusion.
ExtrusionColor Type	MsoExtrusion ColorType	Set/Get how the color for the extrusion is set.
Perspective	MsoTriState	Set/Get whether the shape's extrusion has perspective.
Preset Extrusion Direction	MsoPreset Extrusion Direction	Read Only. Returns the direction of the extrusion.
Preset Lighting Direction	MsoPreset Lighting Direction	Set/Get the directional source of the light source.
Preset Lighting Softness	MsoPreset Lighting Softness	Set/Get the softness of the light source.
Preset Material	MsoPreset Material	Set/Get the surface material of the extrusion.
PresetThreeD Format	MsoPreset ThreeD Format	Read Only. Returns the preset extrusion format.
RotationX	Single	Set/Get how many degrees the extrusion is rotated.
RotationY	Single	Set/Get how many degrees the extrusion is rotated.
Visible	MsoTriState	Set/Get whether the 3D shape is visible.

ThreeDFormat Methods

Name	Returns	Parameters	Description
Increment RotationX		Increment As Single	Changes the `RotationX` property
Increment RotationY		Increment As Single	Changes the `RotationY` property
ResetRotation			Resets the `RotationX` and `RotationY` to 0
SetExtrusion Direction		Preset Extrusion Direction As MsoPreset Extrusion Direction	Changes the extrusion direction
SetThreeD Format		PresetThreeD Format As MsoPresetThree DFormat	Sets the preset extrusion format

Example: ThreeDFormat Object

```
Sub SetShape3D()
   Dim o3DF As ThreeDFormat
   Dim oShp As Shape

   Set oShp = ActiveSheet.Shapes(1)
   Set o3DF = oShp.ThreeD

   With o3DF
      .Depth = 10
      .SetExtrusionDirection msoExtrusionBottomRight
   End With
End Sub
```

TickLabels Object

The `TickLabels` object contains the formatting options associated with the tick-mark labels for tick marks on a chart axis. The parent of the `TickLabels` object is the `Axis` object.

TickLabels Common Properties

The `Application`, `Creator`, and `Parent` properties are defined at the beginning of this appendix.

TickLabels Properties

Name	Returns	Description
`Alignment`	`Long`	Set/Get the alignment of the tick labels. Use the `XlHAlign` constants.
`AutoScaleFont`	`Variant`	Set/Get whether the font size will change automatically if the parent chart changes sizes/
`Depth`	`Long`	Read Only. Returns how many levels of category tick labels are on the axis.
`Font`	`Font`	Read Only. Returns an object containing `Font` options for the tick label text.
`Name`	`String`	Read Only. Returns the name of the `TickLabels` object.
`NumberFormat`	`String`	Set/Get the numeric formatting to use if the tick labels are numeric values or dates.
`NumberFormat Linked`	`Boolean`	Set/Get whether the same numerical format used for the cells containing the chart data is used by the tick labels.
`NumberFormat Local`	`Variant`	Set/Get the name of the numeric format being used by the tick labels in the language being used by the user.
`Offset`	`Long`	Set/Get the percentage distance between levels of labels as compared to the axis label's font size.

Name	Returns	Description
Orientation	XlTickLabel Orientation	Set/Get the angle of the text for the tick labels. The value can be in degrees (from –90 to 90) or one of the XlTickLabelOrientation constants.
ReadingOrder	Long	Set/Get how the text is read (from left to right or right to left). Only applicable in appropriate languages.

TickLabels Methods

Name	Returns	Parameters	Description
Delete	Variant		Deletes the tick labels from the axis labels
Select	Variant		Selects the tick labels on the chart

Example: TickLabels Object

```
Sub FormatTickLabels()
   Dim oTL As TickLabels

   Set oTL = Charts(1).Axes(xlValue).TickLabels

   With oTL
      .NumberFormat = "#,##0"
      .Font.Size = 12
   End With
End Sub
```

TreeviewControl Object

The `TreeviewControl` object allows manipulation of the hierarchical member-selection of a cube field. This object is usually used by macro recordings and not when building VBA code. The parent of the `TreeviewControl` object is the `CubeField` object.

TreeviewControl Common Properties

The `Application`, `Creator`, and `Parent` properties are defined at the beginning of this appendix.

TreeviewControl Properties

Name	Returns	Description
Drilled	Variant	Set/Get a string array describing the drilled status of the members of the parent cube field
Hidden	Variant	Set/Get the hidden status of the members in a cube field

Trendline Object and the Trendlines Collection

The `Trendlines` collection holds the collection of trendlines in a chart. Each `TrendLine` object describes a trendline on a chart of a particular series. `Trendlines` are used to graphically show trends in the data and help predict future values. The parent of the `Trendlines` collection is the `Series` object.

The Trendlines collection has one property and one method besides the typical collection attributes. The Count property returns the number of TrendLine objects in the collection. The Add method adds a trendline to the current chart. The Add method has a Type, Order, Period, Forward, Backward, Intercept, DisplayEquation, DispayRSquared, and Name parameter. See the *Trendline Properties* section for more information.

Trendline Common Properties

The Application, Creator, and Parent properties are defined at the beginning of this appendix.

Trendline Properties

Name	Returns	Description
Backward	Long	Set/Get how many periods the trendline extends back.
Border	Border	Read Only. Returns the border's properties around the trendline.
DataLabel	DataLabel	Read Only. Returns an object to manipulate the trendline's data label.
Display Equation	Boolean	Set/Get whether the equation used for the trendline is displayed on the chart.
Display RSquared	Boolean	Set/Get whether the R-squared value for the trendline is displayed on the chart.
Forward	Long	Set/Get how many periods the trendline extends forward.
Index	Long	Read Only. Returns the spot in the collection that the current object is.
Intercept	Double	Set/Get at which point the trendline crosses the value (y) axis.
InterceptIs Auto	Boolean	Set/Get whether the point the trendline crosses the value axis is automatically calculated with regression.
Name	String	Set/Get the name of the Trendline object.
NameIsAuto	Boolean	Set/Get whether Excel automatically chooses the trendline name.
Order	Long	Set/Get the order of a polynomial trendline. The Type property must be xlPolynomial.
Period	Long	Set/Get what the period is for the moving-average trendline.
Type	XlTrendline Type	Set/Get the type of the trendline (e.g. xlExponential, xlLinear, etc.).

Trendline Methods

Name	Returns	Parameters	Description
ClearFormats	Variant		Clears any formatting made on the trendlines
Delete	Variant		Deletes the trendlines
Select	Variant		Selects the trendlines on the chart

Example: Trendline Object and the Trendlines Collection

```
Sub AddTrendLine()
   Dim oSer As Series
   Dim oTL As Trendline

   Set oSer = Charts(1).SeriesCollection(1)
   Set oTL = oSer.Trendlines.Add(xlLinear)

   With oTL
      .DisplayEquation = True
      .DisplayRSquared = True
   End With
End Sub
```

UpBars Object

The `UpBars` object contains formatting options for up bars on a chart. The parent of the `UpBars` object is the `ChartGroup` object. To see if this object exists use the `HasUpDownBars` property of the `ChartGroup` object.

UpBars Common Properties

The `Application`, `Creator`, and `Parent` properties are defined at the beginning of this appendix.

UpBars Properties

Name	Returns	Description
Border	Border	Read Only. Returns the border's properties around the up bars.
Fill	ChartFill Format	Read Only. Returns an object containing fill formatting options for the up bars of a chart.
Interior	Interior	Read Only. Returns an object containing options to format the inside area of the up bars (e.g. interior color).
Name	String	Read Only. Returns the name of the up bars.

UpBars Methods

Name	Returns	Parameters	Description
Delete	Variant		Deletes the up bars
Select	Variant		Selects the up bars in the chart

Example: UpBars Object

```
Sub AddAndFormatUpBars()
   Dim oUpBars As UpBars

   'Add Up/Down bars to the chart
   Charts(1).ChartGroups(1).HasUpDownBars = True

   'Get the collection of UpBars
   Set oUpBars = Charts(1).ChartGroups(1).UpBars

   'Format the up bars
   With oUpBars
      .Interior.ColorIndex = 3
      .Interior.Pattern = xlSolid
   End With
End Sub
```

UsedObjects Collection Object

Represents the total amount of objects currently being used in all open workbooks. Used objects can be worksheets, chart sheets, the workbook itself, and any ActiveX controls placed on worksheets. This object can be referenced through the `Application` object.

Note that in addition to the common collection properties defined above, `UsedObjects` has the `Item` and `Count` properties.

Example: UsedObjects Collection Object

The following routine lists all of the parent objects of the `UsedObjects` collection:

```
Sub CountUsedObjects()

    Dim lCount As Long
    Dim oUsedObjs As UsedObjects

    'Turn off the screen
    Application.ScreenUpdating = False

    'Store the used object collection
    Set oUsedObjs = Application.UsedObjects

    'Clear the old list
    wksUsedObjects.UsedRange.Offset(1, 0).Resize(, 1).ClearContents

    'Loop through and list the parents of all of the objects
    'Cannot seem to grab the name/caption/... of the object itself
    For lCount = 1 To oUsedObjs.Count
        wksUsedObjects.Range("ListStart").Cells(lCount, 1) =
oUsedObjs.Item(lCount).Parent.Name
    Next lCount

End Sub
```

UserAccess Collection Object

Represents one user within a possible group of users who have permission to access a range specified by the `AllowEditRange` object. You can refer to a user by using the `Item` property of the `UserAccessList` object. Once referenced, you use the properties of this object to change the user's settings.

UserAccess Collection Properties

Name	Returns	Description
AllowEdit	Boolean	Set/Get whether the user is allowed access to the specified range on a protected worksheet.
Name	String	Read Only. Returns the name of the UserAccess object.

UserAccess Collection Methods

Name	Returns	Parameters	Description
Delete			Deletes the object

UserAccessList Collection Object

Represents a list of users who have access to a protected range on a worksheet. This object can be accessed via the AllowEditRange object after it's been created. Use the Add method of this object to add a user to the list, which contains an argument that determines whether or not they need a password to access the range.

Note that the password is set using the ChangePassword method of the AllowEditRange object. This means that all of the users for an AllowEditRange use the same password. Note that this collection only has Count and Item properties.

UserAccessList Methods

Name	Returns	Parameters	Description
Add	UserAccess	Name As String, AllowEdit As Boolean	Adds a user access list to the collection. Name is the name of the list, and if AllowEdit is True users on the access list are allowed to edit the editable ranges on a protected worksheet.
DeleteAll			Removes all users associated with access to a protected range on a worksheet.

Example: UserAccessList Object

The following routine loops through all of the AllowEditRange objects on a specified worksheet and removes all of the users except for the range pcNetSales:

```
Sub DeleteAllUsers()

    Dim oAllowRange As AllowEditRange

    'Loop through all of the AllowEditRange objects on the
    ' specified worksheet
    For Each oAllowRange In wksAllowEditRange.Protection.AllowEditRanges
```

```
        'Remove all names from all AllowEditRanges
        ' except for the range whose AllowEditRange Title
        ' is pcNetSales
        If oAllowRange.Title <> "pcNetSales" Then
            oAllowRange.Users.DeleteAll
        End If
    Next oAllowRange

End Sub
```

Validation Object

The `Validation` object contains properties and methods to represent validation for a range in a worksheet. The `Range` object is the parent of the `Validation` object.

Validation Common Properties

The `Application`, `Creator`, and `Parent` properties are defined at the beginning of this appendix.

Validation Properties

Name	Returns	Description
`AlertStyle`	`Long`	Read Only. Returns the how the user will be alerted if the range includes invalid data. Uses the `XlDVAlertStyle` constants.
`ErrorMessage`	`String`	Set/Get the error message to show for data validation.
`ErrorTitle`	`String`	Set/Get what the title is for the error data validation dialog box.
`Formula1`	`String`	Read Only. Returns the value, cell reference, or formula used for data validation.
`Formula2`	`String`	Read Only. Returns the second part of the value, cell reference, or formula used for data validation. The `Operator` property must be `xlBetween` or `xlNotBetween`.
`IgnoreBlank`	`Boolean`	Set/Get whether a blank cell is always considered valid.
`IMEMode`	`Long`	Set/Get how the Japanese input rules are described. Use the `XlIMEMode` constants.
`InCell Dropdown`	`Boolean`	Set/Get whether a dropdown list of valid values is displayed in the parent range. Used when the `Type` property is `xlValidateList`.
`InputMessage`	`String`	Set/Get the validation input message to prompt the user for valid data.
`InputTitle`	`String`	Set/Get what the title is for the input data validation dialog box.

Name	Returns	Description
Operator	Long	Read Only. Returns the operator describing how Formula1 and Formula2 are used for validation. Uses the XlFormatConditionOperator constants.
ShowError	Boolean	Set/Get whether the error message will be displayed when invalid data is entered in the parent range.
ShowInput	Boolean	Set/Get whether the input message will be displayed when the user chooses one of the cells in the parent range.
Type	Long	Read Only. Returns the data validation type for the range. The XlDVType constants can be used (e.g. xlValidateDecimal, xlValidateTime)
Value	Boolean	Read Only. Returns whether if the validation is fulfilled for the range.

Validation Methods

Name	Returns	Parameters	Description
Add		Type As XlDVType, [AlertStyle], [Operator], [Formula1], [Formula2]	Adds data validation to the parent range. The validation type (Type parameter) must be specified. The type of validation alert (AlertStyle) can be specified with the XlDVAlertStyle constants. The Operator parameter uses the XlFormatConditionOperator to pick the type of operator to use. The Formula1 and Formula2 parameters pick the data validation formula.
Delete			Deletes the Validation method for the range.
Modify		[Type], [AlertStyle], [Operator], [Formula1], [Formula2]	Modifies the properties associated with the Validation. See the properties of the Validation object for a description of the parameters.

Example: Validation Object

```
Sub AddValidation()
    Dim oValid As Validation

    Set oValid = Selection.Validation

    With oValid
```

```
        .Delete
        .Add Type:=xlValidateWholeNumber, AlertStyle:=xlValidAlertStop, _
            Operator:=xlBetween, Formula1:="10", Formula2:="20"

        .ShowInput = False
        .ShowError = True
        .ErrorTitle = "Error"
        .ErrorMessage = "Number must be between 10 and 20"
    End With
End Sub
```

VPageBreak Object and the VPageBreaks Collection

The `VPageBreaks` collection contains all of the vertical page breaks in the printable area of the parent object. Each `VPageBreak` object represents a single vertical page break for the printable area of the parent object. Possible parents of the `VPageBreaks` collection are the `WorkSheet` and the `Chart` objects.

The `VPageBreaks` collection contains one property and one method besides the typical collection attributes. The `Count` property returns the number of `VPageBreak` objects in the collection. The `Add` method is used to add a `VPageBreak` object to the collection (and vertical page break to the sheet). The `Add` method has a `Before` parameter to specify the range to the right of where the vertical page break will be added.

VPageBreak Common Properties

The `Application`, `Creator`, and `Parent` properties are defined at the beginning of this appendix.

VPageBreak Properties

Name	Returns	Description
`Extent`	`XlPageBreak Extent`	Read Only. Returns whether the vertical page break is full screen or only for the print area.
`Location`	`Range`	Set/Get the cell wherethe vertical page break is located. The left edge of the cell is the location of the page break.
`Type`	`XlPageBreak`	Set/Get whether the page break is automatic or manually set.

VPageBreak Methods

Name	Returns	Parameters	Description
`Delete`			Deletes the page break.
`DragOff`		`Direction As XlDirection, RegionIndex As Long`	Drags the page break out of the printable area. The `Direction` parameter specifies the direction the page break is dragged. The `RegionIndex` parameter specifies which print region the page break is being dragged out of.

Example: VPageBreak Object and the VPageBreaks Collection

```
Sub AddVPageBreaks()
   Dim oCell As Range

   'Loop through all the cells in the first column of the sheet
   For Each oCell In ActiveSheet.UsedRange.Rows(1).Cells

      'If the font size is 16, add a page break to the left of the cell
      If oCell.Font.Size = 16 Then
         ActiveSheet.VPageBreaks.Add oCell
      End If
   Next
End Sub
```

Walls Object

The `Walls` object contains formatting options for all the walls of a 3D chart. The walls of a 3D chart cannot be accessed individually. The parent of the `Walls` object is the `Chart` object.

Walls Common Properties

The `Application`, `Creator`, and `Parent` properties are defined at the beginning of this appendix.

Walls Properties

Name	Returns	Description
`Border`	`Border`	Read Only. Returns the border's properties around the walls of the 3D chart.
`Fill`	`ChartFill Format`	Read Only. Returns an object containing fill formatting options for the walls of a 3D chart.
`Interior`	`Interior`	Read Only. Returns an object containing options to format the inside area of the walls (e.g. interior color).
`Name`	`String`	Read Only. Returns the name of the `Walls` object.
`PictureType`	`Variant`	Set/Get how an associated picture is displayed on the walls of the 3D chart (e.g. stretched, tiled). Use the `XlPictureType` constants.
`PictureUnit`	`Variant`	Set/Get how many units a picture represents if the `PictureType` property is set to `xlScale`.

Walls Methods

Name	Returns	Parameters	Description
`ClearFormats`	`Variant`		Clears the formatting made on the `Walls` object.
`Paste`			Deletes the `Walls` object.
`Select`	`Variant`		Selects the walls on the parent chart.

Example: Walls Object

```
Sub FormatWalls()
   Dim oWall As Walls

   Set oWall = Charts(1).Walls

   With oWall
      .Fill.PresetTextured msoTextureCork
      .Fill.Visible = True
   End With
End Sub
```

Watch Object and the Watches Collection Object

The `Watch` object represents one Watch in the Watch window (View | Toolbars | Watch Window). Each Watch can be a cell or cell range you need to keep track of as other data on the worksheet changes. A `Watch` object is an auditing tool similar to the watches you can create in the VBE. Watches do just that, they keep track of a cell or cell range, allowing you to study changes to those cells when other data on the worksheet changes.

The `Watches` collection contains all the `Watch` objects that have been set in the application.

Watches Collection Methods

Name	Returns	Parameters	Description
`Add`	`Watch`	`Source As Variant`	Adds a range which is tracked when the worksheet is recalculated
`Delete`			Deletes the object

Watch Common Properties

The `Application`, `Creator`, and `Parent` properties are defined at the beginning of this appendix.

Watch Properties

Name	Returns	Description
`Source`	`Variant`	Read Only. Returns the unique name that identifies items that have a `SourceType` property value of `xlSourceRange`, `xlSourceChart`, `xlSourcePrintArea`, `xlSourceAutoFilter`, `xlSourcePivotTable`, or `xlSourceQuery`.

Watch Methods

Name	Returns	Parameters	Description
`Delete`			Deletes the object

Example: Watch Object

The following routine prompts the user for a range, then loops through each cell in the range and adds it to the Watch Window. It then displays the Watch Window:

```
Sub AddWatches()

    Dim oWatch As Watch
    Dim rng As Range
    Dim rngWatches As Range

    'Prompt the user for a range
    'Supress the error if they cancel
    On Error Resume Next
        Set rngWatches = Application.InputBox(_
          "Please select a cell or cell range to watch", "Add Watch", , , , , , 8)
    On Error GoTo 0

    'If they selected a range
    If Not rngWatches Is Nothing Then
        'Loop through each cell and
        ' add it to the watch list
        For Each rng In rngWatches
            Application.Watches.Add rng
        Next rng
    End If

    'View the watch window based on their answer
    Application.CommandBars("Watch Window").Visible = (Not rngWatches Is Nothing)

End Sub
```

WebOptions Object

The `WebOptions` object contains attributes associated with opening or saving Wweb pages. The parent of the `WebOptions` object is the `Workbook` object. The properties set in the `WebOptions` object override the settings of the `DefaultWebOptions` object.

WebOptions Common Properties

The `Application`, `Creator`, and `Parent` properties are defined at the beginning of this appendix.

WebOptions Properties

Name	Returns	Description
`AllowPNG`	`Boolean`	Set/Get whether Portable Network Graphics Format (PNG) is allowed as an output format. PNG is a file format for the lossless, portable, well-compressed storage of images.
`Download Components`	`Boolean`	Set/Get whether Office components are downloaded to the end user's machine when viewing Excel files in a web browser.
`Encoding`	`MsoEncoding`	Set/Get the type of code page or character set to save with a document.

Table continued on following page

Name	Returns	Description
FolderSuffix	String	Read Only. Returns what the suffix name is for the support directory created when saving an Excel document as a web page. Language dependent.
LocationOf Components	String	Set/Get the URL or path that contains the Office web components needed to view documents in a web browser.
OrganizeIn Folder	Boolean	Set/Get whether supporting files are organized in a separate folder from the document.
PixelsPer Inch	Long	Set/Get how dense graphics and table cells should be when viewed on a web page.
RelyOnCSS	Boolean	Set/Get whether Cascading Style Sheets (CSS) is used for font formatting.
RelyOnVML	Boolean	Set/Get whether image files are not created when saving a document with drawn objects. Vector Markup Language is used to create the images on the fly. VML is an XML-based format for high-quality vector graphics on the Web.
ScreenSize	MsoScreen Size	Set/Get the target monitor's screen size.
Target Browser	MsoTarget Browser	Set/Get the browser version.
UseLongFile Names	Boolean	Set/Get whether links are updated every time the document is saved.

WebOptions Methods

Name	Returns	Parameters	Description
UseDefault FolderSuffix			Tells Excel to use its default naming scheme for creating supporting folders

Example: WebOptions Object

```
Sub SetWebOptions()
   Dim oWO As WebOptions

   Set oWO = ActiveWorkbook.WebOptions

   With oWO
      .ScreenSize = msoScreenSize800x600
      .RelyOnCSS = True
      .UseDefaultFolderSuffix
   End With
End Sub
```

Window Object and the Windows Collection

The Windows collection holds the list of windows used in Excel or in a workbook. Each Window object represents a single Excel window containing scrollbars and gridlines for the window. The parents of the Windows collection can be the Application object and the Workbook object.

The Windows collection has a Count property and an Arrange method besides the typical collection attributes. The Count property returns the number of Window objects in the collection. The Arrange method arranges the windows in the collection in the manner specified by the ArrangeStyle parameter. Use the XlArrangeStyle constants to set the ArrangeStyle parameter. Set the ActiveWorkbook parameter to True to arrange only the windows associated with the open workbook. Set the SyncHorizontal parameter or the SyncVertical parameter to True so the windows will scroll horizontally or vertically together, respectively.

Window Common Properties

The Application, Creator, and Parent properties are defined at the beginning of this appendix.

Window Properties

Name	Returns	Description
ActiveCell	Range	Read Only. Returns the cell in the window where the cursor is.
ActiveChart	Chart	Read Only. Returns the currently selected chart in the window. If no chart is currently selected, nothing is returned.
ActivePane	Pane	Read Only. Returns the active pane in the window.
ActiveSheet		Read Only. Returns the active sheet in the window.
Caption	Variant	Set/Get the caption that appears in the window.
Display Formulas	Boolean	Set/Get whether formulas are displayed in the window. Not valid in a Chart sheet.
Display Gridlines	Boolean	Set/Get whether worksheet gridlines are displayed.
Display Headings	Boolean	Set/Get whether row and column headings are displayed. Not valid in a Chart sheet.
Display Horizontal ScrollBar	Boolean	Set/Get whether the horizontal scrollbar is displayed in the window.
Display Outline	Boolean	Set/Get whether outline symbols are displayed.
DisplayRight ToLeft	Boolean	Set/Get whether the window contents are displayed from right to left. Valid only with languages that support right-to-left text.
Display Vertical ScrollBar	Boolean	Set/Get whether the vertical scrollbar is displayed in the window.

Table continued on following page

Name	Returns	Description
Display WorkbookTabs	Boolean	Set/Get whether workbook tabs are displayed.
DisplayZeros	Boolean	Set/Get whether zero values are displayed. Not valid with Chart sheets.
EnableResize	Boolean	Set/Get whether a user can resize the window.
FreezePanes	Boolean	Set/Get whether split panes are frozen. Not valid with Chart sheets.
GridlineColor	Long	Set/Get the color of the gridlines. Use the RGB function to create the color value.
GridlineColor Index	XlColor Index	Set/Get the color of the gridlines. Use the XlColorIndex constants or an index value in the current color palette.
Height	Double	Set/Get the height of the window.
Index	Long	Read Only. Returns the spot in the collection where the current object is located.
Left	Double	Set/Get the distance from the left edge of the client area to the window's left edge.
OnWindow	String	Set/Get the name of the procedure to run whenever a window is activated.
Panes	Panes	Read Only. Returns the panes that are contained in the window.
RangeSelecti on	Range	Read Only. Returns the selected range of cells or object in the window.
ScrollColumn	Long	Set/Get the column number of the left-most column in the window.
ScrollRow	Long	Set/Get the row number of the top-most row in the window.
SelectedSheets	Sheets	Read Only. Returns all the selected sheets in the window.
Selection	Object	Read Only. Returns the selected object in the window.
Split	Boolean	Set/Get whether the window is split into panes.
SplitColumn	Long	Set/Get at which column number the window split is going to be located.
Split Horizontal	Double	Set/Get where the horizontal split of window will be located, in points.
SplitRow	Long	Set/Get at which row number the window split is going to be located.
SplitVertical	Double	Set/Get where the vertical split of window will be located, in points.

Name	Returns	Description
TabRatio	Double	Set/Get how big a workbook's tab is as a ratio of a workbook's tab area width to the window's horizontal scrollbar width.
Top	Double	Set/Get the distance from the top edge of the client area to the window's top edge.
Type	XlWindow Type	Read Only. Returns the window type.
UsableHeight	Double	Read Only. Returns the maximum height that the window can be.
UsableWidth	Double	Read Only. Returns the maximum width that the window can be.
View	XlWindow View	Set/Get the view in the window (e.g. `xlNormalView`, `xlPageBreakPreview`).
Visible	Boolean	Set/Get whether the window is visible.
VisibleRange	Range	Read Only. Returns the range of cells that are visible in the current window.
Width	Double	Set/Get the width of the window.
WindowNumber	Long	Read Only. Returns the number associated with a window. Typically used when the same workbook is opened twice (e.g. `MyBook.xls:1` and `MyBook.xls:2`)
WindowState	XlWindow State	Set/Get the state of window: minimized, maximized, or normal.
Zoom	Variant	Set/Get the percentage window zoom.

Window Methods

Name	Returns	Parameters	Description
Activate	Variant		Sets focus to the window.
ActivateNext	Variant		Activates the next window in the z-order.
Activate Previous	Variant		Activates the previous window in the z-order.
Close	Boolean	[SaveChanges], [Filename], [Route Workbook]	Closes the window. Set `SaveChanges` to `True` to automatically save changes in the window's workbook. If `SaveChanges` is `False` then all changes are lost. The `Filename` parameter can be used to specify the filename to save to. `RouteWorkbook` is used to automatically route the workbook onto the next recipient, if applicable.

Table continued on following page

Name	Returns	Description	
LargeScroll	Variant	[Down], [Up], [ToRight], [ToLeft]	Causes the document to scroll a certain direction a screen-full at a time as specified by the parameters.
NewWindow	Window		Creates and returns a new window.
PointsTo Screen PixelsX	Long	Points As Long	Converts the horizontal document coordinate Points parameter to screen coordinate pixels.
PointsTo Screen PixelsY	Long	Points As Long	Converts the vertical document coordinate Points parameter to screen coordinate pixels.
PrintOut	Variant	[From], [To], [Copies], [Preview], [Active Printer], [PrintToFile], [Collate], [PrToFile Name]	Prints out the document in the window. The printer, number of copies, collation, and whether a print preview is desired can be specified with the parameters. Also, the sheets can be printed to a file using the `PrintToFile` and `PrToFileName` parameters. The `From` and `To` parameters can be used to specify the range of printed pages.
PrintPreview	Variant	[Enable Changes]	Displays the current workbook in the window in a print preview mode. Set the `EnableChanges` parameter to `False` to disable the **Margins** and **Setup** buttons, hence not allowing the viewer to modify the page setup.
RangeFrom Point	Object	x As Long, y As Long	Returns the shape or range located at the x and y coordinates. Returns nothing if there is no object at the x, y coordinates.
ScrollInto View		Left As Long, Top As Long, Width As Long, Height As Long, [Start]	Scrolls the spot specified by the `Left`, `Top`, `Width`, and `Height` parameters to either the upper-left corner of the window (`Start = True`) or the lower-right corner of the window (`Start = False`). The `Left`, `Top`, `Width`, and `Height` parameters are specified in points.
Scroll Workbook Tabs	Variant	[Sheets], [Position]	Scrolls through the number of sheets specified by the `Sheets` parameter or goes to the sheet specified by the position parameter (`xlFirst` or `xlLast`).

Name	Returns	Description	
SmallScroll	Variant	[Down], [Up], [ToRight], [ToLeft]	Causes the document to scroll a certain direction a document line at a time as specified by the parameters.

Example: Window Object and the Windows Collection

```
Sub MinimiseAllWindows()
   Dim oWin As Window

   For Each oWin In Windows
      oWin.WindowState = xlMinimized
   Next
End Sub
```

Workbook Object and the Workbooks Collection

The `Workbooks` collection contains the list of open workbooks. A `Workbook` object represents a single workbook. The parent of the `Workbook` is the `Application` object.

Workbooks Properties

Name	Returns	Description
Count	Long	Read Only. Returns the number of `Workbook` objects in the collection.

Workbooks Methods

Name	Returns	Parameters	Description
Add	Workbook	[Template]	Adds a new workbook to the collection. Using a template name in the `Template` parameter can specify a template. Also the `XlWBATemplate` constants can be used to open up a type of workbook.
CanCheckOut	Boolean	Filename As String	Returns whether Excel can check out a specified workbook from a server.
CheckOut		Filename As String	Returns a specified workbook from a server for editing.
Close			Closes the workbook.
Discard Conflict		Filename As String	This keyword is reserved for future use.

Table continued on following page

Name	Returns	Parameters	Description
`Offline Conflict`	`Boolean`	`Filename As String`	This keyword is reserved for future use.
`Open`	`Workbook`	`Filename As String, [UpdateLinks], [ReadOnly], [Format], [Password], [WriteRes Password], [IgnoreRead Only Recommended], [Origin], [Delimiter], [Editable], [Notify], [Converter], [AddToMru], [Local], [CorruptLoad], [OpenConflict Document]`	Opens a workbook specified by the `Filename` parameter and adds it to the collection. Use the `UpdateLinks` parameter to choose how links in the file are updated. Set `ReadOnly` to `True` to open up the workbook in read-only mode. If the file requires a password, use the `Password` or `WriteResPassword` parameters. Set `AddToMru` to `True` to add the opening workbook to the recently used files list. If the file to open is a delimited text file then there are some parameters that can be used. Use the `Format` parameter to choose the text delimiter character if opening a text file. Use the `Origin` parameter to choose the code page style of the incoming delimited text file. Use the `Delimiter` parameter to specify a delimiter if 6 (custom) was chosen for the `Format` parameter.
`OpenDatabase`	`Workbook`	`Filename As String, [CommandText], [CommandType], [Background Query], [ImportData As]`	Returns a `Workbook` representing a database specified by the `Filename` parameter. The `CommandText` and `CommandType` parameters set the text and the type of the query.

Name	Returns	Parameters	Description
OpenText		Filename As String, [Origin], [StartRow], [DataType], [Text Qualifier As XlText Qualifier], [Consecutive Delimiter], [Tab], [Semicolon], [Comma], [Space], [Other], [OtherChar], [FieldInfo], [TextVisual Layout], [Decimal Separator], [Thousands Separator], [Trailing MinusNumbers], [Local]	Opens the text file in `Filename` and parses it into a sheet on a new workbook. `Origin` is used to choose the code page style of the file (`XlPlatform` constant). `StartRow` decides the first row to parse. `DataType` decides if the file is `xlDelimited` or `xlFixedWidth`. Set `ConsecutiveDelimiter` to `True` to treat consecutive delimiters as one. Set `Tab`, `Semicolon`, `Comma`, `Space`, or `Other` to `True` to pick the delimiter character. Use the `DecimalSeparator` and `ThousandsSeparator` to pick the numeric characters to use.
OpenXML	Workbook	Filename As String, [Stylesheets]	Returns an XML file in Microsoft Excel. Use the `Stylesheets` parameter to specify which XSLT stylesheet processing instructions to apply.

Workbook Common Properties

The `Application`, `Creator`, and `Parent` properties are defined at the beginning of this appendix.

Workbook Properties

Name	Returns	Description
AcceptLabelsIn Formulas	Boolean	Set/Get whether labels can be used in worksheet formulas.
ActiveChart	Chart	Read Only. Returns the active chart in the workbook.
ActiveSheet		Read Only. Returns the active sheet (chart or workbook) in the workbook.
AutoUpdate Frequency	Long	Set/Get how often a shared workbook is updated automatically, in minutes.
AutoUpdate SaveChanges	Boolean	Set/Get whether changes made to a shared workbook are visible to other users whenever the workbook is automatically updated.

Table continued on following page

Name	Returns	Description
Builtin Document Properties	Document Properties	Read Only. Returns a collection holding all the built-in properties of the workbook. Things like title, subject, author, and number of words of the workbook can be accessed from this object.
Calculation Version	Long	Read Only. Returns the version number of Excel that was last used to recalculate the Excel spreadsheet.
ChangeHistory Duration	Long	Set/Get how far back, in days, a shared workbook's change history is visible.
Charts	Sheets	Read Only. Returns the charts in the workbook.
CodeName	String	Read Only. Returns the name of the workbook that was set at design time in the VBE.
Colors	Variant	Parameters: `[Index]`. Set/Get the color palette colors for the workbook. There are 56 possible colors in the palette.
CommandBars	CommandBars	Read Only. Returns an object to manipulate the command bars in Excel.
Conflict Resolution	XlSave Conflict Resolution	Set/Get how shared workbook conflicts are resolved when they are being updated (e.g. `xlLocalSessionChanges` means that the local user's changes are always accepted).
Container		Read Only. Returns the object that contains the workbook, if applicable.
CreateBackup	Boolean	Read Only. Returns whether a backup file is created whenever the workbook is saved.
Custom Document Properties	Document Properties	Read Only. Returns a collection holding all the user-defined properties of the workbook.
CustomViews	CustomViews	Read Only. Returns the collection of custom views in a workbook.
Date1904	Boolean	Set/Get whether the 1904 date system is used in the workbook.
Display Drawing Objects	xlDisplay Drawing Objects	Set/Get if shapes are displayed, placeholders are displayed or shapes are hidden.
EnableAuto Recover	Boolean	Set/Get whether the option to save changed files, of all formats, on a timed interval, is switched on.
Envelope Visible	Boolean	Set/Get whether the envelope toolbar and e-mail composition header are visible.
Excel4Intl MacroSheets	Sheets	Read Only. Returns the collection of Excel 4.0 international macro sheets in the workbook.

Name	Returns	Description
Excel4Macro Sheets	Sheets	Read Only. Returns the collection of Excel 4.0 macro sheets in the workbook.
FileFormat	XlFile Format	Read Only. Returns the file format of the workbook.
FullName	String	Read Only. Returns the path and file name of the workbook.
FullNameURL Encoded	String	Read Only. Returns the name of the object, including its path on disk, as a string.
HasPassword	Boolean	Read Only. Returns whether the workbook has a protection password.
HasRouting Slip	Boolean	Set/Get whether the workbook has a routing slip. Use with the `RoutingSlip` object.
Highlight Changes OnScreen	Boolean	Set/Get whether changes in a shared workbook are visibley highlighted.
HTMLProject	HTMLProject	Read Only. Returns an object to access the project explorer of the script editor.
IsAddin	Boolean	Set/Get whether the current workbook is running as an add-in.
IsInplace	Boolean	Read Only. Returns whether the workbook is being edited as an object (`True`) or in Microsoft Excel (`False`).
KeepChange History	Boolean	Set/Get whether changes are tracked in a shared workbook.
ListChangesOn NewSheet	Boolean	Set/Get whether a separate worksheet is used to display changes of a shared workbook.
Mailer	Mailer	Read Only.
MultiUser Editing	Boolean	Read Only. Returns whether a workbook is being shared.
Name	String	Read Only. Returns the file name of the workbook.
Names	Names	Read Only. Returns the collection of named ranges in the workbook.
Password	String	Set/Get the password that must be supplied to open the specified workbook.
Password Encryption Algorithm	String	Read Only. Returns the algorithm used by Excel to encrypt passwords for the specified workbook.
Password EncryptionFile Properties	Boolean	Read Only. Returns whether Excel encrypts file properties for the specified password-protected workbook.

Table continued on following page

PasswordEncryptionKeyLength	Long	Read Only. Returns the key length of the algorithm that Excel uses when encrypting passwords for the specified workbook.
PasswordEncryptionProvider	String	Read Only. Returns the name of the algorithm encryption provider that Excel uses when encrypting passwords for the specified workbook.
Path	String	Read Only. Returns the file path of the workbook.
PersonalViewListSettings	Boolean	Set/Get whether a user's view of the workbook includes filters and sort settings for lists.
PersonalViewPrintSettings	Boolean	Set/Get whether a user's view of the workbook includes print settings.
PrecisionAsDisplayed	Boolean	Set/Get whether the precision of numbers in the workbook are as displayed in the cells. Used for calculations.
ProtectStructure	Boolean	Read Only. Returns whether the sheet order cannot be changed in the workbook.
ProtectWindows	Boolean	Read Only. Returns whether the workbook windows are protected.
PublishObjects	PublishObjects	Read Only. Returns access to an object used to publish objects in the workbook as web pages.
ReadOnly	Boolean	Read Only. Returns whether the workbook is in read-only mode.
ReadOnlyRecommended	Boolean	Read Only. Returns whether the user is prompted with a message recommending that you open the workbook as read-only.
RemovePersonalInformation	Boolean	Set/Get whether personal information can be removed from the specified workbook.
RevisionNumber	Long	Read Only. Returns how many times a shared workbook has been saved while open.
Routed	Boolean	Read Only. Returns whether a workbook has been routed to the next recipient.
RoutingSlip	RoutingSlip	Read Only. Returns access to a `RoutingSlip` object that can be used to add a routing slip for the workbook. Use with the `HasRoutingSlip` property.
Saved	Boolean	Set/Get whether a workbook does not have changes that need saving.
SaveLinkValues	Boolean	Set/Get whether values linked from external sources are saved with the workbook.
Sheets	Sheets	Read Only. Returns the collection of sheets in a workbook (`Chart` or `Worksheet`).

Name	Returns	Description
ShowConflict History	Boolean	Set/Get whether the sheet containing conflicts related to shared workbooks are displayed.
ShowPivot Table FieldList	Boolean	Set/Get whether the PivotTable field list can be shown.
SmartTag Options	SmartTag Options	Read Only. Returns the options that can be performed with a SmartTag.
Styles	Styles	Read Only. Returns the collection of styles associated with the workbook.
Template Remove ExtData	Boolean	Set/Get whether all the external data references are removed after a workbook is saved as a template.
UpdateLinks	XlUpdate Links	Set/Get the workbook's setting for updating embedded OLE links.
UpdateRemote References	Boolean	Set/Get whether remote references are updated for the workbook.
UserStatus	Variant	Read Only. Returns the name of the current user.
VBASigned	Boolean	Read Only. Returns whether the VBA Project for the workbook has been digitally signed.
VBProject	VBProject	Read Only. Returns access to the VBE and associated project.
WebOptions	WebOptions	Read Only. Returns an object allowing manipulation of web related properties of the workbook.
Windows	Windows	Read Only. Returns the collection of windows that make up the workbook.
Worksheets	Sheets	Read Only. Returns the collection of worksheets that make up the workbook.
WritePassword	String	Set/Get the write password of a workbook.
WriteReserved	Boolean	Read Only. Returns whether the workbook can be modified.
Write ReservedBy	String	Read Only. Returns the name of the person with write permission to the workbook.

Workbook Methods

Name	Returns	Parameters	Description
Accept AllChanges		[When], [Who], [Where]	Accepts all the changes made by other people in a shared workbook.
Activate			Activates the workbook.

Table continued on following page

Name	Returns	Parameters	Description
AddTo Favorites			Adds the workbook shortcut to the Favorites folder.
BreakLink		Name As String, Type As XlLinkType	Converts formulas linked to other Excel sources or OLE sources to values.
CanCheckIn	Boolean		Set/Get whether Excel can check in a specified workbook to a server.
ChangeFile Access		Mode As XlFileAccess, [Write Password], [Notify]	Changes access permissions of the workbook to the one specified by the Mode parameter. If necessary, the WritePassword can be specified. Set Notify to True to have the user notified if the file cannot be accessed.
ChangeLink		Name As String, NewName As String, Type As XlLinkType	Changes the link from the workbook specified by the Name parameter to the NewName workbook. Type chooses the type of link (e.g. OLE, Excel)
CheckIn		[SaveChanges], [Comments], [MakePublic]	Performs a check-in or undo-check-out of the working copy on the server.
Close		[SaveChanges], [Filename], [Route Workbook]	Closes the workbook. Set SaveChanges to True to automatically save changes in the workbook. If SaveChanges is False then all changes are lost. The Filename parameter can be used to specify the filename to save to. RouteWorkbook is used to automatically route the workbook onto the next recipient, if applicable.
DeleteNumber Format		NumberFormat As String	Deletes the number format in the NumberFormat parameter from the workbook.
EndReview			Ends the review of a file that has been sent for review.
Exclusive Access	Boolean		Gives the current user exclusive access to a shared workbook.

Name	Returns	Parameters	Description
Follow Hyperlink		Address As String, [SubAddress], [NewWindow], [AddHistory], [ExtraInfo], [Method], [HeaderInfo]	Opens up the appropriate application with the URL specified by the Address parameter. Set NewWindow to True to open up a new window for the hyperlink. Use the ExtraInfo and Method parameters to send more information to the hyperlink (say for an ASP page). The Method parameter uses the MsoExtraInfoMethod constants.
Highlight Changes Options		[When], [Who], [Where]	Set/Get when changes are viewed in a shared workbook (When), whose workbook changes can be viewed (Who), and the range that the changes should be put in (Where). Use the XlHighlighChangesTime constants with the When parameter.
LinkInfo	Variant	Name As String, LinkInfo As XlLinkInfo, [Type], [EditionRef]	Returns the link details mentioned in the LinkInfo parameter for the link specified by the Name parameter. Use the Type parameter with the XlLinkInfoType constants to pick the type of link that will be returned.
LinkSources	Variant	[Type]	Returns the array of linked documents, editions, DDE and OLE servers in a workbook. Use the Type parameter with the XlLinkInfoType constants to pick the type of link that will be returned.
MergeWorkbook		Filename	Merges the changes from the Filename workbook into the current workbook.
NewWindow	Window		Opens up a new window with the current workbook.
OpenLinks		Name As String, [ReadOnly], [Type]	Opens the Name link and supporting documents. Set ReadOnly to True to open the documents as read-only. Use the Type parameter with the XlLinkInfoType constants to pick the type of link that will be returned.

Table continued on following page

Name	Returns	Parameters	Description
PivotCaches	PivotCaches		Returns the collection of PivotTable caches in the workbook.
Post		[DestName]	Posts the workbook into a Microsoft Exchange public folder.
PrintOut		[From], [To], [Copies], [Preview], [Active Printer], [PrintToFile], [Collate], [PrToFile Name]	Prints out the workbook. The printer, number of copies, collation, and whether a print preview is desired can be specified with the parameters. Also, the sheets can be printed to a file using the PrintToFile and PrToFileName parameters. The From and To parameters can be used to specify the range of printed pages.
PrintPreview		[Enable Changes]	Displays the current workbook in a print preview mode. Set the EnableChanges parameter to False to disable the **Margins** and **Setup** buttons, hence not allowing the viewer to modify the page setup.
Protect		[Password], [Structure], [Windows]	Protects the workbook from user changes. A protect Password can be specified. Set the Structure parameter to True to protect the relative position of the sheets. Set the Windows to True to protect the workbook windows.
Protect Sharing		[Filename], [Password], [WriteRes Password], [ReadOnly Recommended], [Create Backup], [Sharing Password]	Protects and saves the workbook for sharing. The file is saved to the Filename parameter with the optional passwords in Password, WriteResPassword, and SharingPassword parameters. Set ReadOnlyRecommended to True to display a message to the user every time the workbook is opened. Set CreateBackup to True to create a backup of the saved file.
PurgeChange HistoryNow		Days As Long, [Sharing Password]	Deletes the entries in the change log for the shared workbook. The Days parameter specifies how many days back to delete the entries. A SharingPassword may be required.

Name	Returns	Parameters	Description
RecheckSmart Tags			Does a foreground SmartTag check. Any data that was not annotated before will now be annotated.
RefreshAll			Refreshes any external data source's data into the workbook.
RejectAll Changes		[When], [Who], [Where]	Rejects all the changes in a shared workbook.
ReloadAs		Encoding As MsoEncoding	Re-opens the workbook using the web page related Encoding parameter.
RemoveUser		Index As Long	Disconnects the user (specified by the user index in the Index parameter) from a shared workbook.
ReplyAll			Replies to all recipients of the sent workbook. Valid only in the Macintosh Edition of Excel.
ReplyWith Changes		[ShowMessage]	E-mails a notification to the author of a workbook telling them that a reviewer has completed review of the workbook.
ResetColors			Resets the colors in the color palette to the default colors.
Route			Routes the workbook using the routing slip.
RunAuto Macros		Which As XlRunAuto Macro	Runs the auto macro specified by the Which parameter.
Save			Saves the workbook.

Table continued on following page

Name	Returns	Parameters	Description
SaveAs		Filename, FileFormat, Password, WriteRes Password, ReadOnly Recommended, CreateBackup, AccessMode As XlSaveAs AccessMode, [Conflict Resolution], [AddToMru], [Text Codepage], [TextVisual Layout], [Local]	Saves the workbook as FileName. The type of file to be saved can be specified with the FileFormat parameter. The file can be saved with the optional passwords in the Password and WriteResPassword parameters. Set ReadOnlyRecommended to True to display a message to the user every time the workbook is opened. Set CreateBackup to True to create a backup of the saved file. Use the AccessMode to choose how the workbook is accessed (e.g. xlShared, xlExclusive). Use the ConflictResolution parameter to decide how shared workbooks resolve change conflicts. Set the AddToMru parameter to True to add the workbook to the recently opened files list.
SaveCopyAs		[Filename]	Saves a copy of the workbook as the FileName.
SendForRevie w		[Recipients], [Subject], [ShowMessage], [Include Attachment]	Sends a workbook in an e-mail message for review to the specified recipients.
SendMail		Recipients, [Subject], [Return Receipt]	Sends the workbook through the default mail system. The recipient or recipients and subject can be specified with the parameters. Set ReturnReceipt to True to request a return receipt.
SendMailer		FileFormat, Priority As XlPriority	
SetLinkOnData		Name As String, [Procedure]	Runs the procedure in the Procedure parameter whenever the DDE or OLE link in the Name parameter is updated.

Name	Returns	Parameters	Description
SetPassword Encryption Options		[Password Encryption Provider], [Password Encryption Algorithm], [Password EncryptionKeyLength], [Password Encryption File Properties]	Sets the options for encrypting workbooks using passwords.
Unprotect		[Password]	Unprotects the workbook with the password if necessary.
Unprotect Sharing		[Sharing Password]	Unprotects the workbook from sharing and saves the workbook.
UpdateFrom File			Re-loads the current workbook from the file if the file is newer then the workbook.
UpdateLink		[Name], [Type]	Updates the link specified by the `Name` parameter. Use the `Type` parameter with the `XlLinkInfoType` constants to pick the type of link that will be returned.
WebPagePreview			Previews the workbook as a web page.

Workbook Events

Name	Parameters	Description
Activate		Triggered when the workbook is activated.
AddinInstall		Triggered when the workbook is opened as an add-in.
Addin Uninstall		Triggered when the workbook opened as an add-in is uninstalled.
BeforeClose	Cancel As Boolean	Triggered just before the workbook closes. Set the `Cancel` parameter to `True` to cancel the closing.
BeforePrint	Cancel As Boolean	Triggered just before the workbook is printed. Set the `Cancel` parameter to `True` to cancel the printing.
BeforeSave	SaveAsUI As Boolean, Cancel As Boolean	Triggered just before the workbook is saved. Set the `Cancel` parameter to `True` to cancel the saving. Set the `SaveAsUI` to `True` for the user to be prompted with the Save As dialog box.

Table continued on following page

Name	Parameters	Description
Deactivate		Triggered when the workbook loses focus.
NewSheet	Sh As Object	Triggered when a new sheet is created in the workbook. The Sh parameter passes in the new sheet.
Open		Triggered when the workbook is opened.
PivotTable Close Connection	ByVal Target As PivotTable	Triggered when a PivotTable report closes the connection to its data source. Target is the selected PivotTable.
PivotTable Open Connection	ByVal Target As PivotTable	Triggered when a PivotTable report opens the connection to its data source. Target is the selected PivotTable.
SheetActivate	Sh As Object	Triggered when a sheet is activated in the workbook. The Sh parameter passes in the activated sheet.
SheetBefore DoubleClick	Sh As Object, Target As Range, Cancel As Boolean	Triggered when a sheet is about to be double-clicked. The sheet and the potential double-click spot are passed into the event. The double-click action can be canceled by setting the Cancel parameter to True.
SheetBefore RightClick	Sh As Object, Target As Range, Cancel As Boolean	Triggered when a sheet is about to be right-clicked. The sheet and the potential right-click spot are passed into the event. The right-click action can be canceled by setting the Cancel parameter to True.
Sheet Calculate	Sh As Object	Triggered when a sheet is recalculated passing in the recalculated sheet.
SheetChange	Sh As Object, Target As Range	Triggered when the contents of a cell are changed in any worksheet in the workbook, e.g. triggered by entering new data, clearing the cell, deleting a row/column. **Not** triggered when inserting rows/columns.
Sheet Deactivate	Sh As Object	Triggered when a sheet loses focus. Passes in the sheet.
SheetFollow Hyperlink	Sh As Object, Target As Hyperlink	Triggered when the user clicks on a hyperlink on a sheet. Passes in the sheet and the clicked hyperlink.
SheetPivot TableUpdate	ByVal Sh As Object, Target As PivotTable	Triggered when the sheet of the PivotTable report has been updated.
Sheet Selection Change	Sh As Object, Target As Range	Triggered when the user selects a different cell on the sheet. Passes in the new range and the sheet where the change occurred.

Name	Parameters	Description
Window Activate	Wn As Window	Triggered when a workbook window is activated (brought up to the front of other workbook windows). The workbook and the window are passed in.
Window Deactivate	Wn As Window	Triggered when a workbook window loses focus. The related workbook and the window are passed in.
WindowResize	Wn As Window	Triggered when a workbook window is resized. The resized workbook and window are passed into the event.

Example: Workbook Object and the Workbooks Collection

Please refer to Chapter 4 for `Workbook` object examples.

Worksheet Object and the Worksheets Collection

The `Worksheets` collection holds the collection of worksheets in a workbook. The `Workbook` object is always the parent of the `Worksheets` collection. The `Worksheets` collection only holds the worksheets. The `Worksheet` objects in the `Worksheets` collection can be accessed using the `Item` property. Either the name of the worksheet can be specified as a parameter to the `Item`'s parameter or an index number describing the position of the worksheet in the workbook (from left to right).

The `Worksheet` object allows access to all of the attributes of a specific worksheet in Excel. This includes worksheet formatting and other worksheet properties. The `Worksheet` object also exposes events that can be used programmatically.

The `Worksheets` collection has a few properties and methods besides the typical collection attributes. These are listed in the following table.

Worksheets Collection Properties and Methods

Name	Returns	Description
Count	Long	Read Only. Returns the number of worksheets in the collection.
HPageBreaks	HPage Breaks	Read Only. Returns a collection holding all the horizontal page breaks associated with the `Worksheets` collection.
VpageBreaks	VPage Breaks	Read Only. Returns a collection holding all the vertical page breaks associated with the `Worksheets` collection.
Visible	Variant	Set/Get whether the worksheets in the collection are visible. Also can set this to `xlVeryHidden` to not allow a user to make the worksheets in the collection visible.
Add		Method. Parameters: `[Before]`, `[After]`, `[Count]`, `[Type]`. Adds a worksheet to the collection. You can specify where the worksheet goes by choosing which sheet object will be before the new worksheet object (`Before` parameter) or after the new worksheet (`After` parameter). The `Count` parameter decides how many worksheets are created.

Table continued on following page

Name	Returns	Description
`Copy`		Method. Parameters: `[Before]`, `[After]`. Adds a new copy of the currently active worksheet to the position specified at the `Before` or `After` parameters.
`Delete`		Method. Deletes all the worksheets in the collection.
`FillAcross Sheets`		Method. Parameters: `Range As Range`, `Type As XlFillWith`. Copies the range specified by the `Range` parameter across all the other worksheets in the collection. Use the `Type` parameter to pick what part of the range is copied (e.g. `xlFillWithContents`, `xlFillWithFormulas`).
`Move`		Method. Parameters: `[Before]`, `[After]`. Moves the current worksheet to the position specified by the parameters.
`PrintPreview`		Method. Parameters: `[EnableChanges]`. Displays the current worksheet in the collection in a print preview mode. Set the `EnableChanges` parameter to `False` to disable the **Margins** and **Setup** buttons, hence not allowing the viewer to modify the page setup.
`PrintOut`		Method. Parameters: `[From]`, `[To]`, `[Copies]`, `[Preview]`, `[ActivePrinter]`, `[PrintToFile]`, `[Collate]`, `[PrToFileName]`. Prints out the worksheets in the collection. The printer, number of copies, collation, and whether a print preview is desired can be specified with the parameters. Also, the sheets can be printed to a file using the `PrintToFile` and `PrToFileName` parameters. The `From` and `To` parameters can be used to specify the range of printed pages.
`Select`		Method. Parameters: `[Replace]`. Selects the current worksheet in the collection.

Worksheet Common Properties

The `Application`, `Creator`, and `Parent` properties are defined at the beginning of this appendix.

Worksheet Properties

Name	Returns	Description
`AutoFilter`	`AutoFilter`	Read Only. Returns an `AutoFilter` object if filtering is turned on.
`AutoFilter Mode`	`Boolean`	Set/Get whether `AutoFilter` drop-down arrows are currently displayed on the worksheet.
`Cells`	`Range`	Read Only. Returns the cells in the current worksheet.

Name	Returns	Description
CircularReference	Range	Read Only. Returns the cell range that contains the first circular reference on the worksheet.
CodeName	String	Read Only. Returns the name of the worksheet set at design time in the VBE.
Columns	Range	Read Only. Returns a range of the columns in the current worksheet.
Comments	Comments	Read Only. Returns the collection of comments in the worksheet.
ConsolidationFunction	XlConsolidationFunction	Read Only. Returns the type of consolidation being used in the worksheet (e.g. `xlSum`, xlMax, xlAverage).
ConsolidationOptions	Variant	Read Only. Returns a one-dimensional array containing three elements of booleans. The first element describes whether the labels in the top row are used; the second element describes whether the labels in the left-most column are used; and the third element describes whether links are created to the source data.
ConsolidationSources	Variant	Read Only. Returns the array of strings that describe the source sheets for the current worksheet's consolidation.
CustomProperties	CustomProperties	Read Only. Returns the identifier information associated with a worksheet.
DisplayPageBreaks	Boolean	Set/Get whether page breaks are displayed.
DisplayRightToLeft	Boolean	Set/Get whether the worksheet contents are displayed from right to left. Valid only with languages that support right-to-left text.
EnableAutoFilter	Boolean	Set/Get whether the AutoFilter arrows are enabled when a worksheet is user interface-only protected.
EnableCalculation	Boolean	Set/Get whether Excel will automatically recalculate the worksheet as necessary.
EnableOutlining	Boolean	Set/Get whether outlining symbols are enabled when a worksheet is user interface-only protected.
EnablePivotTable	Boolean	Set/Get whether `PivotTable` controls and related actions are enabled when a worksheet is user interface-only protected.
EnableSelection	XlEnableSelection	Set/Get what objects can be selected when a worksheet is protected (e.g. `xlNoSelection`, `xlNoRestrictions`).

Table continued on following page

Name	Returns	Description
FilterMode	Boolean	Read Only. Returns whether a worksheet is in a filter mode
HPageBreaks	HPageBreaks	Read Only. Returns a collection holding all the horizontal page breaks associated with the Worksheet.
Hyperlinks	Hyperlinks	Read Only. Returns the collection of hyperlinks in the worksheet.
Index	Long	Read Only. Returns the spot in the parent collection where the current worksheet is located.
MailEnvelope	MsoEnvelope	Set/Get the e-mail header for a document.
Name	String	Set/Get the name of the worksheet.
Names	Names	Read Only. Returns the collection of ranges with names in the worksheet.
Next		Read Only. Returns the next sheet in the workbook (from left to right) as an object.
Outline	Outline	Read Only. Returns an object to manipulate an outline in the worksheet.
PageSetup	PageSetup	Read Only. Returns an object to manipulate the page setup properties for the worksheet.
Previous		Read Only. Returns the previous sheet in the workbook (from right to left) as an object.
Protect Contents	Boolean	Read Only. Returns whether the worksheet and everything in it is protected from changes.
Protect Drawing Objects	Boolean	Read Only. Returns whether the shapes in the worksheet can be modified (ProtectDrawingObjects = False).
Protection	Protection	Read Only. Returns the protection options of the worksheet.
Protection Mode	Boolean	Read Only. Returns whether protection has been applied to the user interface. Even if a worksheet has user interface protection on, any VBA code associated with the worksheet can still be accessed.
Protect Scenarios	Boolean	Read Only. Returns whether the worksheet scenarios are protected.
QueryTables	QueryTables	Read Only. Returns the collection of query tables associated with the worksheet.
Range	Range	Read Only. Parameters: Cell1, [Cell2]. Returns a Range object as defined by the Cell1 and optionally Cell2 parameters.

Name	Returns	Description
`Rows`	`Range`	Read Only. Returns a `Range` object containing the rows of the current worksheet.
`Scripts`	`Scripts`	Read Only. Returns the collection of VBScript code associated with a worksheet (typically to later use on web pages).
`ScrollArea`	`String`	Sets the A1-style reference string describing the range in the worksheet that can be scrolled. Cells not in the range cannot be selected.
`Shapes`	`Shapes`	Read Only. Returns all the shapes contained by the worksheet.
`SmartTags`	`SmartTags`	Read Only. Returns the identifier for the specified cell.
`Standard Height`	`Double`	Read Only. Returns the default height of the rows in the worksheet, in points.
`Standard Width`	`Double`	Read Only. Returns the default width of the columns in the worksheet, in points.
`Tab`	`Tab`	Read Only. Returns the `Tab` object for the selected chart or worksheet.
`TransitionExp Eval`	`Boolean`	Set/Get whether evaluates expressions using Lotus 1-2-3 rules in the worksheet.
`TransitionForm Entry`	`Boolean`	Set/Get whether formula entries can be entered using Lotus 1-2-3 rules.
`Type`	`XlSheetType`	Read Only. Returns the worksheet type (e.g. `xlWorksheet, xlExcel4MacroSheet, xlExcel4IntlMacroSheet`)
`UsedRange`	`Range`	Read Only. Returns the range in the worksheet that is being used.
`Visible`	`XlSheet Visibility`	Set/Get whether the worksheet is visible. Also can set this to `xlVeryHidden` to not allow a user to make the worksheet visible.
`VPageBreaks`	`VPageBreaks`	Read Only. Returns a collection holding all the vertical page breaks associated with the worksheet.

Worksheet Methods

Name	Returns	Parameters	Description
`Activate`			Activates the worksheet.
`Calculate`			Calculates all the formulas in the worksheet.

Table continued on following page

Name	Returns	Parameters	Description
ChartObjects		[Index]	Returns either a chart object (ChartObject) or a collection of chart objects (ChartObjects) in a worksheet.
CheckSpelling		[Custom Dictionary], [Ignore Uppercase], [Always Suggest], [SpellLang]	Checks the spelling of the text in the worksheet. A custom dictionary can be specified (CustomDictionary), all uppercase words can be ignored (IgnoreUppercase), and Excel can be set to display a list of suggestions (AlwaysSuggest).
CircleInvalid			Circles the invalid entries in the worksheet.
ClearArrows			Clears out all the tracer arrows in the worksheet.
ClearCircles			Clears all the circles around invalid entries in a worksheet.
Copy		[Before], [After]	Adds a new copy of the worksheet to the position specified at the Before or After parameters.
Delete			Deletes the worksheet.
Evaluate	Variant	Name	Evaluates the Name string expression as if it were entered into a worksheet cell.
Move		[Before], [After]	Moves the worksheet to the position specified by the parameters.
OLEObjects		[Index]	Returns either a single OLE object (OLEObject) or a collection of OLE objects (OLEObjects) for a worksheet.
Paste		[Destination], [Link]	Pastes the contents of the clipboard into the worksheet. A specific destination range can be specified with the Destination parameter. Set Link to True to establish a link to the source of the pasted data. Either the Destination or the Link parameter can be used.

Name	Returns	Parameters	Description
PasteSpecial		[Format], [Link], [DisplayAs Icon], [IconFile Name], [IconIndex], [IconLabel] , [NoHTML Formatting]	Pastes the clipboard contents into the current worksheet. The format of the clipboard data can be specified with the string Format parameter. Set Link to True to establish a link to the source of the pasted data. Set DisplayAsIcon to True to display the pasted data as an icon and the IconFileName, IconIndex, and IconLabel to specify the icon and label. A destination range must be already selected in the worksheet.
PivotTables		[Index]	Returns either a single PivotTable report (PivotTable) or a collection of PivotTable reports (PivotTables) for a worksheet.
PivotTableWi zard	PivotTable	[SourceType], [SourceData], [Table Destination], [TableName], [RowGrand], [ColumnGrand], [SaveData], [HasAuto Format], [AutoPage], [Reserved], [Background Query], [Optimize Cache], [PageField Order], [PageField WrapCount], [ReadData], [Connection]	Creates a PivotTable report. The SourceType uses the XLPivotTableSourceType constants to specify the type of SourceData being used for the PivotTable. TableDestination holds the range in the parent worksheet that report will be placed. TableName holds the name of the new report. Set RowGrand or ColumnGrand to True to show grand totals for rows and columns, respectively. Set HasAutoFormat to True for Excel to format the report automatically when it is refreshed or changed. Use the AutoPage parameter to set if a page field is created automatically for consolidation. Set BackgroundQuery to True for Excel to query the data source asynchronously. Set OptimizeCache to True for Excel to optimize the cache when it is built. Use the PageFieldOrder with the xlOrder constants to set how new page fields are added to the report. Use the PageFieldWrapCount to set the number of page fields in each column or row. Set ReadData to True to copy the data from the external database into a cache. Finally, use the Connection parameter to specify an ODBC connection string for the PivotTable's cache.

Table continued on following page

Name	Returns	Parameters	Description
PrintOut		[From], [To], [Copies], [Preview], [Active Printer], [PrintToFile], [Collate], [PrToFile Name]	Prints out the worksheet. The printer, number of copies, collation, and whether a print preview is desired can be specified with the parameters. Also, the sheets can be printed to a file using the PrintToFile and PrToFileName parameters. The From and To parameters can be used to specify the range of printed pages.
PrintPreview		[Enable Changes]	Displays the worksheet in a print preview mode. Set the EnableChanges parameter to False to disable the Margins and Setup buttons, hence not allowing the viewer to modify the page setup.
Protect		[Password], [Drawing Objects], [Contents], [Scenarios], [User Interface Only], [Allow Formatting Cells], [Allow Formatting Columns], [Allow Formatting Rows], [Allow Inserting Columns], [Allow Inserting Rows], [Allow Inserting Hyperlinks], [Allow Deleting Columns], [Allow DeletingRows], [Allow Sorting], [Allow Filtering], [AllowUsing PivotTables]	Protects the worksheet from changes. A case-sensitive Password can be specified. Also, whether shapes are protected (DrawingObjects), the entire contents are protected (Contents), and whether only the user interface is protected (UserInterfaceOnly).

Name	Returns	Parameters	Description
ResetAllPage Breaks			Resets all the page breaks in the worksheet.
SaveAs		Filename As String, [FileFormat], [Password], [WriteRes Password], [ReadOnly Recommended], [Create Backup], [AddToMru], [Text Codepage], [TextVisual Layout] , [Local]	Saves the worksheet as FileName. The type of file to be saved can be specified with the FileFormat parameter. The file can be saved with the optional passwords in the Password and WriteResPassword parameters. Set ReadOnlyRecommended to True to display a message to the user every time the worksheet is opened. Set CreateBackup to True to create a backup of the saved file. Set the AddToMru parameter to True to add the worksheet to the recently-opened files list.
Scenarios		[Index]	Returns either a single scenario (Scenario) or a collection of scenarios (Scenarios) for a worksheet.
Select		[Replace]	Selects the worksheet.
SetBackground Picture		Filename As String	Sets the worksheet's background to the picture specified by the FileName parameter.
ShowAllData			Displays all of the data that is currently filtered.
ShowDataForm			Displays the data form that is part of the worksheet.
Unprotect		[Password]	Deletes the protection set up for a worksheet. If the worksheet was protected with a password, the password must be specified now.

Worksheet Events

Name	Parameters	Description
Activate		Triggered when a worksheet is made to have focus.
BeforeDouble Click	Target As Range, Cancel As Boolean	Triggered just before a user double-clicks on a worksheet. The cell closest to the point double-clicked in the worksheet is passed in to the event procedure as Target. The double-click action can be canceled by setting the Cancel parameter to True.

Table continued on following page

Name	Returns	Parameters	Description
BeforeRight Click	Cancel As Boolean	Triggered just before a user right-clicks on a worksheet. The cell closest to the point right-clicked in the worksheet is passed in to the event procedure as `Target`. The right-click action can be canceled by setting the `Cancel` parameter to `True`.	
Calculate		Triggered after the worksheet is recalculated.	
Change	Target As Range	Triggered when the worksheet cell values are changed. The changed range is passed into the event procedure as `Target`.	
Deactivate		Triggered when the worksheet loses focus.	
Follow Hyperlink	Target As Hyperlink	Triggered when a hyperlink is clicked on the worksheet. The hyperlink that was clicked is passed into the event procedure as `Target`.	
PivotTable Update	ByVal Target As Pivot Table	Triggered when a `PivotTable` report is updated on a worksheet.	
Selection Change	Target As Range	Triggered when the selection changes in a worksheet. The new selected range is passed into the event procedure as `Target`.	

Example: Worksheet Object and the Worksheets Collection

Please refer to Chapter 4 for `Worksheet` object examples.

WorksheetFunction Object

The `WorksheetFunction` object contains all of the Excel worksheet function. The `WorksheetFunction` object allows access to Excel worksheet function in Visual Basic code. The parent of the `WorksheetFunction` object is the `Application` object.

WorksheetFunction Common Properties

The `Application`, `Creator`, and `Parent` properties are defined at the beginning of this appendix.

WorksheetFunction Methods

Name	Returns	Parameters	Description
Acos	Double	Arg1 As Double	Returns the arccosine of the `Arg1` number. `Arg1` must be between –1 to 1.
Acosh	Double	Arg1 As Double	Returns the inverse hyperbolic cosine of the `Arg1` number. `Arg1` must be >= 1.
And	Boolean	Arg1, [Arg2], ... [Arg30]	Returns `True` if all the arguments (from `Arg1` up to `Arg30`) evaluate to `True`.

Name	Returns	Parameters	Description
Asc	String	Arg1 As String	Returns the half-width character equivalent of the full width characters in the Arg1 string. Not the same as the VBA Asc function which returns the ASCII code of the first character in the string.
Asin	Double	Arg1 As Double	Returns the arcsine of the Arg1 number. Arg1 must be between –1 and 1.
Asinh	Double	Arg1 As Double	Returns the inverse hyperbolic sine of the Arg1 number.
Atan2	Double	Arg1 As Double, Arg2 As Double	Returns the arctangent of the x and y coordinates specified in the Arg1 and Arg2 parameters, respectively.
Atanh	Double	Arg1 As Double	Returns the inverse hyperbolic tangent of the Arg1 number. Arg1 must be between –1 and 1.
AveDev	Double	Arg1, [Arg2], ... [Arg30]	Returns the average of the absolute deviation from the mean of the Arg1 to Arg30 number parameters.
Average	Double	Arg1, [Arg2], ... [Arg30]	Returns the average of the numbers in Arg1 to Arg30.
BahtText	String	Arg1 As Double	Returns a number in Thai text with a "Baht." suffix. Arg1 is the number to be converted.
BetaDist	Double	Arg1 As Double, Arg2 As Double, Arg3 As Double, [Arg4], [Arg5]	Returns the cumulative beta probability. Arg1 is the number to evaluate. Arg2 is the Alpha part of the distribution. Arg3 is the Beta part of the distribution. Arg4 and Arg5 can be the lower and upper bounds of the interval in Arg1.
BetaInv	Double	Arg1 As Double, Arg2 As Double, Arg3 As Double, [Arg4], [Arg5]	Returns the inverse of the cumulative beta probability density. Arg1 is the probability of the distribution. Arg2 is the Alpha part of the distribution. Arg3 is the Beta part of the distribution. Arg4 and Arg5 can be the lower and upper bounds of the evaluated number.

Table continued on following page

Name	Returns	Parameters	Description
BinomDist	Double	Arg1 As Double, Arg2 As Double, Arg3 As Double, Arg4 As Boolean	Returns the individual term binomial distribution probability. Arg1 is the number of successes in the trials. Arg2 holds the total number of trials. Arg3 is the probability of success on a single trial. Arg4 sets whether the method returns the cumulative distribution function (True) or the probability mass function (False).
Ceiling	Double	Arg1 As Double, Arg2 As Double	Returns the nearest number to Arg1 that is a multiple of Arg2, rounded positively.
ChiDist	Double	Arg1 As Double, Arg2 As Double	Returns the one-tail probability of the chi-squared distribution. Arg1 is the number to evaluate. Arg2 is the number of degrees of freedom.
ChiInv	Double	Arg1 As Double, Arg2 As Double	Returns the inverse of the one-tail probability of the chi-squared distribution. Arg1 is the probability. Arg2 is the number of degrees of freedom.
ChiTest	Double	Arg1, Arg2	Returns the chi-squared distribution test for independence. Arg1 holds the range of data that will be tested against the expected values. Arg2 holds the range of expected data.
Choose	Variant	Arg1, Arg2, [Arg3], ... [Arg30]	Returns one of the parameter values (Arg2 to Arg30) given the index value in Arg1. For example, if Arg1 is 2 then the value in Arg3 is returned.
Clean	String	Arg1 As String	Returns the string in Arg1 without any nonprintable characters.
Combin	Double	Arg1 As Double, Arg2 As Double	Returns the total possible number of combinations of a group ofArg2 items in a total number of Arg1 items.
Confidence	Double	Arg1 As Double, Arg2 As Double, Arg3 As Double	Returns a range on either side of a sample mean for a population mean. Arg1 is the Alpha value used to determine the confidence level. Arg2 is the standard deviation for the data range. Arg3 is the sample size.

Name	Returns	Parameters	Description
Correl	Double	Arg1, Arg2	Returns the correlation coefficient of the arrays in Arg1 and Arg2. The parameters can also be cell ranges.
Cosh	Double	Arg1 As Double	Returns the hyperbolic cosine of the Arg1 number.
Count	Double	Arg1, [Arg2], ... [Arg30]	Returns the number of numeric values in the arguments. Arg1 to Arg30 can be values or range references.
CountA	Double	Arg1, [Arg2], ... [Arg30]	Returns the number of non-empty values in the arguments. Arg1 to Arg30 can be values or range references.
CountBlank	Double	Arg1 As Range	Returns the number of empty values in the range in Arg1.
CountIf	Double	Arg1 As Range, Arg2	Counts the number of cells in the Arg1 range that meet the criteria in Arg2.
Covar	Double	Arg1, Arg2	Returns the covariance of the arrays or ranges in Arg1 and Arg2.
CritBinom	Double	Arg1 As Double, Arg2 As Double, Arg3 As Double	Returns the smallest value where the cumulative binomial distribution is greater than or equal to the criterion value. Arg1 is the number of Bernoulli trials. Arg2 is the probability of success for each trial. Arg3 is the criterion value.
DAverage	Double	Arg1 As Range, Arg2, Arg3	Returns the average of the column specified by Arg2 in the range of cells in Arg1. Arg3 contains the criteria used to choose rows of records to be averaged.
Days360	Double	Arg1, Arg2, [Arg3]	Returns the difference of days between the Arg1 and Arg2 dates (Arg1 – Arg2). If the Arg3 method is set to True then the European method of calculation is used. If Arg3 is set to False or omitted then the US method of calculation is used.

Table continued on following page

Name	Returns	Parameters	Description
Db	Double	Arg1 As Double, Arg2 As Double, Arg3 As Double, Arg4 As Double, [Arg5]	Returns depreciation for a specified period using the fixed-declining balance method. Arg1 is the initial cost to depreciate. Arg2 is the final salvage cost (cost at end of depreciation). Arg3 is the number of periods to depreciate. Arg4 is the specific period from Arg3 to depreciation. Arg5 can be the number of months in the first year that depreciation will start.
Dbcs	String	Arg1 As String	Returns the Double-Byte-Character-Set string of the given ASCII string. Opposite of the Asc function.
DCount	Double	Arg1 As Range, Arg2, Arg3	Returns the number of cells that match the criteria in Arg3. Arg1 specifies the range of rows and columns to count and Arg2 is used to choose the field name or number to count.
DCountA	Double	Arg1 As Range, Arg2, Arg3	Returns the number of non-blank cells that match the criteria in Arg3. Arg1 specifies the range of rows and columns to count and Arg2 is used to choose the field name or number to count.
Ddb	Double	Arg1 As Double, Arg2 As Double, Arg3 As Double, Arg4 As Double, [Arg5]	Returns depreciation for a specified period using the double-declining balance method. Arg1 is the initial cost to depreciate. Arg2 is final salvage cost (cost at end of depreciation). Arg3 is the number of periods to depreciate. Arg4 is the specific period from Arg3 to depreciation. Arg5 can be the rate at which the balance declines.
Degrees	Double	Arg1 As Double	Converts the radians in Arg1 into degrees and returns the degrees.
DevSq	Double	Arg1, [Arg2], ... [Arg30]	Returns the sum of the squares of deviations of the Arg1 to Arg30 from their mean.

Name	Returns	Parameters	Description
DGet	Variant	Arg1 As Range, Arg2, Arg3	Returns the cell value that matches the criteria in Arg3. Arg1 specifies the range of rows and columns to count and Arg2 is used to choose the field name or number to count. Criteria must match a single cell.
DMax	Double	Arg1 As Range, Arg2, Arg3	Returns the largest value that matches the criteria in Arg3. Arg1 specifies the range of rows and columns to count and Arg2 is used to choose the field name or number to count.
DMin	Double	Arg1 As Range, Arg2, Arg3	Returns the smallest value that matches the criteria in Arg3. Arg1 specifies the range of rows and columns to count and Arg2 is used to choose the field name or number to count.
Dollar	String	Arg1 As Double, [Arg2]	Returns a currency-type string of the number in Arg1 with the decimal points specified in Arg2.
DProduct	Double	Arg1 As Range, Arg2, Arg3	Returns the multiplication product of the values that match the criteria in Arg3. Arg1 specifies the range of rows and columns to count and Arg2 is used to choose the field name or number to count.
DStDev	Double	Arg1 As Range, Arg2, Arg3	Returns the estimated standard deviation of the values that match the criteria in Arg3. Arg1 specifies the range of rows and columns to count and Arg2 is used to choose the field name or number to count.
DStDevP	Double	Arg1 As Range, Arg2, Arg3	Returns the standard deviation of the values that match the criteria in Arg3 assuming the entire population is given. Arg1 specifies the range of rows and columns to count and Arg2 is used to choose the field name or number to count.
DSum	Double	Arg1 As Range, Arg2, Arg3	Returns the sum of the values that match the criteria in Arg3. Arg1 specifies the range of rows and columns to count and Arg2 is used to choose the field name or number to count.

Table continued on following page

Name	Returns	Parameters	Description
DVar	Double	Arg1 As Range, Arg2, Arg3	Returns the variance of the values that match the criteria in Arg3. Arg1 specifies the range of rows and columns to count and Arg2 is used to choose the field name or number to count.
DVarP	Double	Arg1 As Range, Arg2, Arg3	Returns the variance of the values that match the criteria in Arg3 assuming that the entire population is given. Arg1 specifies the range of rows and columns to count and Arg2 is used to choose the field name or number to count.
Even	Double	Arg1 As Double	Converts the Arg1 number into the nearest even whole number, rounded up, and returns it.
ExponDist	Double	Arg1 As Double, Arg2 As Double, Arg3 As Boolean	Returns the exponential distribution of a value. Arg1 is the value of the function. Arg2 is the Lambda parameter value. Set Arg3 to True for the method to return the cumulative distribution. Set Arg3 to False to return the probability density.
Fact	Double	Arg1 As Double	Returns the factorial of Arg1.
FDist	Double	Arg1 As Double, Arg2 As Double, Arg3 As Double	Returns the F probability distribution of a value. Arg1 is the value to evaluate the function. Arg2 is the numerator degrees of freedom and Arg3 is the denominator degrees of freedom.
Find	Double	Arg1 As String, Arg2 As String, [Arg3]	Finds the text in Arg1 from the text in Arg2 and returns the starting position of the found text. Arg3 can specify the starting position to search in Arg2.
FindB	Double	Arg1 As String, Arg2 As String, [Arg3]	Finds the text in Arg1 from the text in Arg2 and returns the starting position of the found text. Arg3 can specify the starting byte position to search in Arg2.

Name	Returns	Parameters	Description
FInv	Double	Arg1 As Double, Arg2 As Double, Arg3 As Double	Returns the inverse of the F probability distribution. Arg1 is the probability that is associated with the F cumulative distribution. Arg2 is the numerator degrees of freedom and Arg3 is the denominator degrees of freedom.
Fisher	Double	Arg1 As Double	Returns the Fisher transformation at the Arg1 value.
FisherInv	Double	Arg1 As Double	Returns the inverse of the Fisher transformation given the value of Arg1.
Fixed	String	Arg1 As Double, [Arg2], [Arg3]	Rounds the number Arg1 to the decimal points Arg2 and returns the value as a string. Set Arg3 to True to put commas in the returned text. Set Arg3 to False to not put commas in the returned text.
Floor	Double	Arg1 As Double, Arg2 As Double	Returns the nearest number to Arg1 that is a multiple of Arg2, rounded down towards 0.
Forecast	Double	Arg1 As Double, Arg2, Arg3	Returns a predicted y value for a given x value (Arg1) by using the existing value pairs. Arg2 is an array or range corresponding to the y's known values. Arg3 is an array or range corresponding to the x's known values.
Frequency	Variant	Arg1, Arg2	Returns an array of numbers describing the frequency of values in the array Arg1 that are in the intervals specified by the Arg2 array. Arg1 and Arg2 can also be references to a range.
FTest	Double	Arg1, Arg2	Returns the result of an F-test of the arrays in Arg1 and Arg2. Arg1 and Arg2 can also be references to a range.

Table continued on following page

Name	Returns	Parameters	Description
Fv	Double	Arg1 As Double, Arg2 As Double, Arg3 As Double, [Arg4], [Arg5]	Returns the future value of an investment for a time period. Arg1 is the interest rate per period. Arg2 is the total number of payment periods. Arg3 is the payment per period. Arg4 is the initial value. Arg5 determines if payments are due at the end of the period (0) or the beginning of the period (1).
GammaDist	Double	Arg1 As Double, Arg2 As Double, Arg3 As Double, Arg4 As Boolean	Returns the gamma distribution. Arg1 is the value to evaluate. Arg2 is the alpha parameter to the distribution. Arg3 is the beta parameter to the distribution. Set Arg4 to True for the method to return the cumulative distribution. Set Arg4 to False to return the probability density.
GammaInv	Double	Arg1 As Double, Arg2 As Double, Arg3 As Double	Returns the inverse of the gamma cumulative distribution. Arg1 is the gamma distribution probability. Arg2 is the alpha parameter to the distribution. Arg3 is the beta parameter to the distribution.
GammaLn	Double	Arg1 As Double	Returns the natural logarithm of the gamma function with the Arg1 number.
GeoMean	Double	Arg1, [Arg2], ... [Arg30]	Returns the geometric mean of the numbers in Arg1 to Arg30. Arg1 to Arg30 can also be a reference to a range.
Growth	Variant	Arg1, [Arg2], [Arg3], [Arg4]	Returns the predicted exponential growth of y values (Arg1) for a series of new x values (Arg3). Arg2 can be used to set the series of existing x values. Arg4 can be set to False to make the 'b' part of the equation equal to one.
HarMean	Double	Arg1, [Arg2], ... [Arg30]	Returns the harmonic mean of the numbers in Arg1 to Arg30. Arg1 to Arg30 can also be a reference to a range.

Name	Returns	Parameters	Description
HLookup	Variant	Arg1, Arg2, Arg3, [Arg4]	Looks up the value specified by Arg1in the table array (or range reference); Arg2 first row. Arg3 specifies the row number in the table array that contains the matching value. Set Arg4 to True to find approximate data or set Arg4 to False to only lookup exact values.
HypGeomDist	Double	Arg1 As Double, Arg2 As Double, Arg3 As Double, Arg4 As Double	Returns the hypergeometric distribution probability. Arg1 is the number of successes in the trials. Arg2 holds the total number of trials. Arg3 is the number of successes in the trial. Arg4 is the size of the population.
Index	Variant	Arg1, Arg2 As Double, [Arg3], [Arg4]	May return the cell or array of cells from Arg1 that has a row number of Arg2 and a column number of Arg3. May also return the cell or range of cells that have a row number of Arg2 and a column number of Arg3. If Arg1 contains many areas then Arg4 can be used to specify the area.
Intercept	Double	Arg1, Arg2	Returns the point where the x-axis and y-axis coordinates intersect. Arg1 represents the array of known y values and Arg2 represents the array of known x values.
Ipmt	Double	Arg1 As Double, Arg2 As Double, Arg3 As Double, Arg4 As Double, [Arg5], [Arg6]	Returns the interest amount paid for an investment for a time period. Arg1 is the interest rate per period. Arg2 is the period that you want to find the amount of interest for. Arg3 is the total number of payment periods. Arg4 is the initial value. Arg5 is the future value that is wanted to be attained. Arg6 determines if payments are due at the end of the period (0) or the beginning of the period (1).
Irr	Double	Arg1, [Arg2]	Returns the rate of return for an array of values in Arg1. Arg2 can be used to specify a guess of the Irr result.

Table continued on following page

Name	Returns	Parameters	Description
IsErr	Boolean	Arg1	Returns whether the cell Arg1 contains an error value (except #N/A).
IsError	Boolean	Arg1	Returns whether the cell Arg1 contains any error value.
IsLogical	Boolean	Arg1	Returns whether the cell or value Arg1 contains a logical value.
IsNA	Boolean	Arg1	Returns whether the cell Arg1 contains the #N/A value.
IsNonText	Boolean	Arg1	Returns whether the cell Arg1 does not contain text.
IsNumber	Boolean	Arg1	Returns whether the cell Arg1 contains a numeric value.
Ispmt	Double	Arg1 As Double, Arg2 As Double, Arg3 As Double, Arg4 As Double	Returns the interest amount paid for an investment at a particular period. Used for compatibility purposes. Arg1 is the interest rate per period. Arg2 is the period that you want to find the amount of interest for. Arg3 is the total number of payment periods. Arg4 is the initial value.
IsText	Boolean	Arg1	Returns whether the cell Arg1 contains a text value.
Kurt	Double	Arg1, [Arg2], ... [Arg30]	Returns the kurtosis of the values in Arg1 to Arg30. Also, Arg1 can be a reference to a cell range.
Large	Double	Arg1, Arg2 As Double	Returns the Arg2 largest value in the array or cell reference specified by Arg1 (e.g. second largest, third largest).
LinEst	Variant	Arg1, [Arg2], [Arg3], [Arg4]	Returns an array describing a straight line that best fits the data of known y values (Arg1) and known x values (Arg2). Set Arg3 to False to make the 'b' part of the calculations equal to 0. Set Arg4 to True to return additional statistics.
Ln	Double	Arg1 As Double	Returns the natural logarithm of the Arg1 number.
Log	Double	Arg1 As Double, [Arg2]	Returns the logarithm of the Arg1 number to the base specified in Arg2. Arg2 is 10 by default.

Name	Returns	Parameters	Description
`Log10`	`Double`	`Arg1 As Double`	Returns the base-10 logarithm of the `Arg1` number.
`LogEst`	`Variant`	`Arg1, [Arg2], [Arg3], [Arg4]`	Returns an array describing the curved line that best fits the data of known y values (`Arg1`) and known x values (`Arg2`). Set `Arg3` to `False` to make the 'b' part of the calculations equal to 0. Set `Arg4` to `True` to return additional statistics.
`LogInv`	`Double`	`Arg1 As Double, Arg2 As Double, Arg3 As Double`	Returns the inverse of the lognormal cumulative distribution of a value. `Arg1` is the probability that will have to be inversed. `Arg2` is the mean of ln(value). `Arg3` is the standard deviation of ln(value).
`LogNormDist`	`Double`	`Arg1 As Double, Arg2 As Double, Arg3 As Double`	Returns the cumulative lognormal distribution of `Arg1`. `Arg2` is the mean of ln(`Arg1`) and `Arg3` is the standard deviation of ln(`Arg1`).
`Lookup`	`Variant`	`Arg1, Arg2, [Arg3]`	The value `Arg1` is searched for in the single row or column in `Arg2`. A value from the matching spot in another array, `Arg3`, is returned.
`Match`	`Double`	`Arg1, Arg2, [Arg3]`	Returns the relative position of an item in an array, `Arg2`, which matches a specific value, `Arg1`. Use `Arg3` to set the type of match.
`Max`	`Double`	`Arg1, [Arg2], ... [Arg30]`	Returns the largest value in the numbers `Arg1` to `Arg30`. `Arg1` can also be a cell range.
`MDeterm`	`Double`	`Arg1`	Returns the matrix determinant of the matrix array specified by `Arg1`. `Arg1` can also be a cell range. Cell elements cannot contain text or be empty. There must be an equal amount of rows to columns.
`Median`	`Double`	`Arg1, [Arg2], ... [Arg30]`	Returns the median value in the numbers `Arg1` to `Arg30`. `Arg1` can also be a cell range.

Table continued on following page

Name	Returns	Parameters	Description
Min	Double	Arg1, [Arg2], ... [Arg30]	Returns the smallest value in the numbers Arg1 to Arg30. Arg1 can also be a cell range.
MInverse	Variant	Arg1	Returns the inverse matrix for the matrix array in Arg1. Arg1 can also be a cell range. Cell elements cannot contain text or be empty. There must be an equal amount of rows to columns.
MIrr	Double	Arg1, Arg2 As Double, Arg3 As Double	Returns the modified rate or return for a series of values in Arg1. Arg2 is the interest rate paid. Arg3 is the interest rate received as the cash flow values are re-invested.
MMult	Variant	Arg1, Arg2	Returns the matrix product of the two matrix arrays Arg1 and Arg2. The number of columns in Arg1 must be the same as the number of rows in Arg2. Arg1 and Arg2 can also be a cell range. Cell elements cannot contain text or be empty.
Mode	Double	Arg1, [Arg2], ... [Arg30]	Returns the most frequently occurring number in Arg1 to Arg30. Arg1 can also be a cell range.
NegBinomDist	Double	Arg1 As Double, Arg2 As Double, Arg3 As Double	Returns the negative binomial distribution of the arguments. Arg1 is the number of failures in the trials. Arg2 holds the threshold number of successes. Arg3 is the probability of success on a single trial.
NormDist	Double	Arg1 As Double, Arg2 As Double, Arg3 As Double, Arg4 As Boolean	Returns the normal cumulative distribution for the value to distribute (Arg1), the mean (Arg2), and the standard deviation (Arg3). Set Arg4 to True to return the cumulative distribution and False to return the probability mass.
NormInv	Double	Arg1 As Double, Arg2 As Double, Arg3 As Double	Returns the inverse of the normal cumulative distribution given a probability (Arg1), the mean (Arg2), and the standard deviation (Arg3).

Name	Returns	Parameters	Description
NormSDist	Double	Arg1 As Double	Returns the standard normal cumulative distribution for the value to distribute (Arg1).
NormSInv	Double	Arg1 As Double	Returns the inverse of the standard normal cumulative distribution for a given probability (Arg1).
NPer	Double	Arg1 As Double, Arg2 As Double, Arg3 As Double, [Arg4], [Arg5]	Returns the number of periods for an investment. Arg1 is the interest rate per period. Arg2 is the payment amount made each period. Arg3 is the initial value. Arg4 is the future value that is wanted to be attained. Arg5 determines if payments are due at the end of the period (0) or the beginning of the period (1).
Npv	Double	Arg1 As Double, Arg2, [Arg3], ... [Arg30]	Returns the net present value of an investment using a discount rate (Arg1) and many future payments and income (Arg2 to Arg30).
Odd	Double	Arg1 As Double	Converts the Arg1 number into the nearest odd whole number, rounded up, and returns it.
Or	Boolean	Arg1, [Arg2], ... [Arg30]	Returns True if any of the expressions in Arg1 to Arg30 returns True.
Pearson	Double	Arg1, Arg2	Returns the Pearson product moment correlation coefficient containing an array of values. Arg1 is the array of independent values and Arg2 is the array of dependent values. Arg1 and Arg2 can also be cell references.
Percentile	Double	Arg1, Arg2 As Double	Returns the Arg2 percentile of values in the Arg1 range of cells or array.
PercentRank	Double	Arg1, Arg2 As Double, [Arg3]	Returns how the value Arg2 ranks in the Arg1 range of cells or array. Arg3 can specify the number of significant digits for the returned percentage.

Table continued on following page

Name	Returns	Parameters	Description
Permut	Double	Arg1 As Double, Arg2 As Double	Returns the total possible number of permutations of a group of Arg2 items in a total number of Arg1 items.
Phonetic	String	Arg1 As Range	Returns the phonetic characters from the Arg1 text string.
Pi	Double		Returns pi (3.14) to 15 decimal places.
Pmt	Double	Arg1 As Double, Arg2 As Double, Arg3 As Double, [Arg4], [Arg5]	Returns the payment for a loan. Arg1 is the interest rate per period. Arg2 is the number of payments for the loan. Arg3 is the initial value. Arg4 is the future value that is wanted to be attained. Arg5 determines if payments are due at the end of the period (0) or the beginning of the period (1).
Poisson	Double	Arg1 As Double, Arg2 As Double, Arg3 As Boolean	Returns the Poisson distribution given the number of events (Arg1) and the expected numeric value (Arg2). Set Arg3 to True to return the cumulative probability and False to return the probability mass.
Power	Double	Arg1 As Double, Arg2 As Double	Returns the base number Arg1 raised to the power of Arg2.
Ppmt	Double	Arg1 As Double, Arg2 As Double, Arg3 As Double, Arg4 As Double, [Arg5], [Arg6]	Returns the payment on the principal of an investment for a given period of time. Arg1 is the interest rate per period. Arg2 specifies the period to look at. Arg3 is the total number of payments. Arg4 is the initial value. Arg5 is the future value that is wanted to be attained. Arg6 determines if payments are due at the end of the period (0) or the beginning of the period (1).
Prob	Double	Arg1, Arg2, Arg3 As Double, [Arg4]	Returns the probability that the values in the Arg1 array and associated Arg2 array are within the lower limit (Arg3) and upper limit (Arg4).

Name	Returns	Parameters	Description
Product	Double	Arg1, [Arg2], ... [Arg30]	Returns the multiplication product of all the values in Arg1 to Arg30.
Proper	String	Arg1 As String	Capitalizes the start of every word in Arg1 and makes everything else lowercase.
Pv	Double	Arg1 As Double, Arg2 As Double, Arg3 As Double, [Arg4], [Arg5]	Returns the present value of an investment. Arg1 is the interest rate per period. Arg2 is the number of payments for the loan. Arg3 is the payment amount made per period. Arg4 is the future value that is wanted to be attained. Arg5 determines if payments are due at the end of the period (0) or the beginning of the period (1).
Quartile	Double	Arg1, Arg2 As Double	Returns the quartile specified by Arg2 of the array in Arg1. Arg2 can be 0 (Minimum value), 1 (first quartile), 2 (second quartile), 3 (third quartile), or 4 (maximum value).
Radians	Double	Arg1 As Double	Converts the Arg1 number from degrees to radians and returns the new value.
Rank	Double	Arg1 As Double, Arg2 As Range, [Arg3]	Returns the rank of Arg1 in the range Arg2. Arg3 can be used to set how to rank Arg1.
Rate	Double	Arg1 As Double, Arg2 As Double, Arg3 As Double, [Arg4], [Arg5], [Arg6]	Returns the interest rate per period for a value. Arg1 is the total number of payments. Arg2 is the payment amount per period. Arg3 is the initial value. Arg4 is the future value that is wanted to be attained. Arg5 determines if payments are due at the end of the period (0) or the beginning of the period (1).
Replace	String	Arg1 As String, Arg2 As Double, Arg3 As Double, Arg4 As String	Replaces part of the text in Arg1 with the text in Arg4. The starting character of the replacement is at the number Arg2 and Arg3 specifies the number of replaced characters in Arg1.

Table continued on following page

Name	Returns	Parameters	Description
ReplaceB	String	Arg1 As String, Arg2 As Double, Arg3 As Double, Arg4 As String	Replaces part of the text in Arg1 with the text in Arg4. The starting character of the replacement is at the number Arg2 and Arg3 specifies the number of replaced bytes in Arg1.
Rept	String	Arg1 As String, Arg2 As Double	Repeats the string in Arg1 by Arg2 number of times and returns that new string.
Roman	String	Arg1 As Double, [Arg2]	Returns the number in Arg1 to a Roman numeral equivalent. Arg2 can specify the style of Roman numerals. 0 or True is the classic style. 4 or False is the simplified style. The other options are 2, 3, and 4 that set the style to varying degrees of simplification.
Round	Double	Arg1 As Double, Arg2 As Double	Returns the Arg1 number rounded to the number of digits specified in Arg2.
RoundDown	Double	Arg1 As Double, Arg2 As Double	Returns the Arg1 number rounded to the number of digits specified in Arg2. The number is rounded down towards 0.
RoundUp	Double	Arg1 As Double, Arg2 As Double	Returns the Arg1 number rounded to the number of digits specified in Arg2. The number is rounded up towards 0.
RSq	Double	Arg1, Arg2	Returns the square of the Pearson product moment correlation coefficient containing an array of values. Arg1 is the array of y values and Arg2 is the array of x values. Arg1 and Arg2 can also be cell references.

Name	Returns	Parameters	Description
RTD	Variant	progID As Variant, server As Variant, topic1 As Variant, [topic2], [topic3], [topic4], [topic5], [topic6], [topic7], [topic8], [topic9], [topic10], [topic11], [topic12], [topic13], [topic14], [topic15], [topic16], [topic17], [topic18], [topic19], [topic20], [topic21], [topic22], [topic23], [topic24], [topic25], [topic26], [topic27], [topic28]	Connects to a source to receive RTD. `progID` is the real-time server programmatic identifier, `server` is the server name, and `topic1` is the topic to look up.
Search	Double	Arg1 As String, Arg2 As String, [Arg3]	Finds the text in `Arg1` from the text in `Arg2` and returns the starting position of the found text. `Arg3` can specify the starting position to search in `Arg2`.
SearchB	Double	Arg1 As String, Arg2 As String, [Arg3]	Finds the text in `Arg1` from the text in `Arg2` and returns the starting position of the found text. `Arg3` can specify the starting byte position to search in `Arg2`.
Sinh	Double	Arg1 As Double	Returns the hyperbolic sine of the `Arg1` number.
Skew	Double	Arg1, [Arg2], ... [Arg30]	Returns how skewed the numbers in `Arg1` to `Arg30` are. The arguments can also be a range reference.

Table continued on following page

Name	Returns	Parameters	Description
Sln	Double	Arg1 As Double, Arg2 As Double, Arg3 As Double	Returns the simple straight-line depreciation of an asset costing Arg1 with a salvage value of Arg3 over Arg2 number of periods.
Slope	Double	Arg1, Arg2	Returns the slope of the linear regression line through the data points of the x values (Arg1) and y values (Arg2).
Small	Double	Arg1, Arg2 As Double	Returns the Arg2 smallest value in the array or cell reference specified by Arg1 (e.g. second smallest, third smallest).
Standardize	Double	Arg1 As Double, Arg2 As Double, Arg3 As Double	Returns the normalized value from a distribution given a value (Arg1), a mean (Arg2), and a standard deviation (Arg3).
StDev	Double	Arg1, [Arg2], ... [Arg30]	Returns the estimated standard deviation of the values in Arg1 to Arg30. The arguments can also be a range reference.
StDevP	Double	Arg1, [Arg2], ... [Arg30]	Returns the standard deviation of the values in Arg1 to Arg30 based on all the values. The arguments can also be a range reference.
StEyx	Double	Arg1, Arg2	Returns the standard error of the predicted y values for each of the x values in the regression given some know y values (Arg1) and x values (Arg2).
Substitute	String	Arg1 As String, Arg2 As String, Arg3 As String, [Arg4]	Substitutes all occurrences of the Arg2 text with the Arg3 text in the original Arg1 text string. Arg4 can be used to specify which occurrence to replace.

Name	Returns	Parameters	Description
Subtotal	Double	Arg1 As Double, Arg2 As Range, [Arg3], ... [Arg30]	Returns subtotals for the ranges or references specified in the Arg2 to Arg30 parameters. Arg1 is a number describing what type of function to use for calculating the subtotal. Valid function numbers are from 1 to 10 representing Average, Count, CountA, Max, Min, Product, StcDev, StDevP, Sum, Var, and VarP in numerical order.
Sum	Double	Arg1, [Arg2], ... [Arg30]	Returns the sum of all the numbers in Arg1 to Arg30.
SumIf	Double	Arg1 As Range, Arg2, [Arg3]	Returns the sum of the cells in the range Arg1 with the criteria matching Arg2. A different range to sum can be specified with Arg3. The columns or rows in Arg1 and Arg3 have to be the same.
SumProduct	Double	Arg1, [Arg2], ... [Arg30]	Multiplies each corresponding element in the arrays Arg1 to Arg30 and returns the sum of the products. The arrays in Arg1 to Arg30 must have the same dimension.
SumSq	Double	Arg1, [Arg2], ... [Arg30]	Returns the sum of the square roots of the number in Arg1 to Arg30.
SumX2MY2	Double	Arg1, Arg2	Subtracts the squares of the corresponding elements in the arrays Arg1 and Argc2 and returns the sum of all the new elements.
SumX2PY2	Double	Arg1, Arg2	Adds the squares of the corresponding elements in the arrays Arg1 and Arg2 and returns the sum of all the new elements.
SumXMY2	Double	Arg1, Arg2	Subtracts the corresponding elements in the arrays Arg1 and Arg2, squares the difference and returns the sum of all the new elements.

Table continued on following page

Name	Returns	Parameters	Description
Syd	Double	Arg1 As Double, Arg2 As Double, Arg3 As Double, Arg4 As Double	Returns the sum-of-years digits depreciation of an asset over a specified period. Arg1 is the initial cost. Arg2 is the salvage cost. Arg3 is the number of periods to depreciate the asset over. Arg4 is the specified period to return.
Tanh	Double	Arg1 As Double	Returns the hyperbolic tangent of the Arg1 number.
Tdist	Double	Arg1 As Double, Arg2 As Double, Arg3 As Double	Returns the probability for the student t-distribution for a value, Arg1, is a calculated value of 't'. Arg2 indicates the number of degrees of freedom. Set Arg3 to 1 to return a one-tailed distribution. Set Arg3 to 2 to return a two-tailed distribution.
Text	String	Arg1, Arg2 As String	Converts the value in Arg1 into text using the formatting in Arg2.
Tinv	Double	Arg1 As Double, Arg2 As Double	Returns the t-value of the Student's t-distribution given the probability (Arg1) and the degrees of freedom (Arg2).
Transpose	Variant	Arg1	Transposes the range specified by Arg1 from column to row or vice versa and returns the new range.
Trend	Variant	Arg1, [Arg2], [Arg3], [Arg4]	Returns the values associated with a linear trend given some y values (Arg1), some x values (Arg2), and some new x values (Arg3). Set Arg4 to False to make 'b' equal to 0 in the equation.
Trim	String	Arg1 As String	Returns the string in Arg1 without leading and trailing spaces.
TrimMean	Double	Arg1, Arg2 As Double	Returns the mean of the interior of the data array in Arg1. Use Arg2 to specify the fractional part of the data array to exclude.
Ttest	Double	Arg1, Arg2, Arg3 As Double, Arg4 As Double	Returns the probability associated with a student's t-Test given the two sets of data in Arg1 and Arg12. Set Arg3 to 1 to return a one-tailed distribution. Set Arg3 to 2 to return a two-tailed distribution. Set Arg4 to 1, 2, or 3 to set the type of t-Test to paired, two-sample equal variance, or two-sample unequal variance, respectively.

Name	Returns	Parameters	Description
USDollar	String	Arg1 As Double, Arg2 As Double	Returns a currency-type string of the number in Arg1 with the decimal points specified in Arg2.
Var	Double	Arg1, [Arg2], ... [Arg30]	Returns the estimated variance based on the numbers in Arg1 to Arg30. The arguments can also be range references.
VarP	Double	Arg1, [Arg2], ... [Arg30]	Returns the variance based on the numbers in Arg1 to Arg30 as an entire population. The arguments can also be range references.
Vdb	Double	Arg1 As Double, Arg2 As Double, Arg3 As Double, Arg4 As Double, Arg5 As Double, [Arg6], [Arg7]	Returns the double-declining balance method depreciation (unless otherwise specified) of an asset for specified periods. Arg1 is the initial cost. Arg2 is the salvage cost. Arg3 is the number of periods to depreciate the asset over. Arg4 is the starting period to calculate depreciation. Arg5 is the ending period to calculate depreciation. Arg6 is the rate at which the balance declines. Set Arg7 to True to keep the calculation using the double-declining balance method. Set Arg7 to False to have Excel switch to straight-line depreciation when necessary.
Vlookup	Variant	Arg1, Arg2, Arg3, [Arg4]	Looks up the value specified by Arg1 in the table array (or range reference) Arg2 first column Arg3 specifies the column number in the table array that contains the matching value. Set the Arg4 to True to find approximate data or set Arg4 to False to only lookup exact values.
Weekday	Double	Arg1, [Arg2]	Returns the numerical day of the week for the date in Arg1. Arg2 specifies which day is the start of the week.
Weibull	Double	Arg1 As Double, Arg2 As Double, Arg3 As Double, Arg4 As Boolean	Returns the Weibull distribution using the value (Arg1). Arg2 is the alpha parameter to the distribution. Arg3 is the beta parameter to the distribution. Set Arg4 to True to return the cumulative probability and False to return the probability mass.

Table continued on following page

Name	Returns	Parameters	Description
`Ztest`	`Double`	`Arg1, Arg2 As Double, [Arg3]`	Returns the two-tailed P-value of a z-test. `Arg1` is the array or range of data to test against `Arg2`. `Arg2` is the value to test. `Arg3` is the population standard deviation.

Example: WorksheetFunction Object

```
Sub GetBiggest()
   Dim oWSF As WorksheetFunction
   Dim vaArray As Variant

   Set oWSF = Application.WorksheetFunction

   vaArray = Array(10, 20, 13, 15, 56, 12, 8, 45)

   MsgBox "Biggest is " & oWSF.Max(vaArray)
End Sub
```

VBE Object Model

Officially known as *"Microsoft Visual Basic for Applications Extensibility 5.3"*, the VBE object library provides access to the code and forms within an application and to the various objects that compose the **Visual Basic Integrated Development Environment (VBIDE)**. By default, this object library is **not** included in the list of referenced libraries for new projects. In order to use the objects referred to in this chapter, a reference to the Microsoft Visual Basic for Applications Extensibility 5.3 library must be created using the Tools | References menu in the VBE.

Many of the objects in the VBE object model have the same names as objects in the Excel object model. To distinguish the libraries and to ensure that you have the object from the VBE library you need to include the `VBIDE` library name in any `Dim` statements you may use:

```
Dim oWinVB As VBIDE.Window        'Always gives a VBE Window
Dim oWinXL As Excel.Window        'Always gives an XL Window
Dim oWin As Window                'Gives an XL Window
```

All of the applications in Office 2002 share the same development environment – the VBE. The code and forms that belong to each Excel workbook, Word document, Access database, or PowerPoint presentation (i.e. the "host document") are grouped into Visual Basic projects (the `VBProject` object). There is one project for each host document. FrontPage and Outlook have a single Project each, which "belongs" to the application. Additionally, the Developer Edition of Office 2002 supports standalone projects, which are not linked to any of the Office applications and can be compiled into ActiveX DLLs.

Links Between the Excel and VBE Object Models

There are a number of properties of Excel objects that provide links to the VBE object model. Similarly, there are a number of properties in the VBE object model that provide a link back into Excel. Many of the code examples in this appendix and in Chapter 23 use these links:

Excel to VBE	
Excel Property	**Resulting VBE Item**
`Application.VBE`	`VBE` object
`Workbook.VBProject`	`VBProject` object

Table continued on following page

Excel to VBE	
Workbook.CodeName	The name of the workbook-level VBComponent in the workbook's VBProject, usually "ThisWorkbook" in English versions of Excel 2002.
Worksheet.CodeName Chart.CodeName	The name of the sheet-level VBComponent in the workbook's VBProject, usually "Sheet1", "Chart1" etc. in English versions of Excel 2002.

VBE to Excel	
VBE Property	**Resulting Excel Item**
VBProject.FileName	The full name of the workbook, if the VBProject is an Excel workbook project and the workbook has been saved.
VBComponent.Properties("Name")	The file name of the workbook, if the VBComponent is the workbook-level item (for example "ThisWorkbook"), or the name of the sheet for sheet-level VBComponents.
VBComponent.Properties("<Other Properties>")	The properties associated with the Excel object to which the VBComponent applies (if any).

Common Properties and Methods

Most of the objects in the VBE object library have the following common properties. To avoid redundancy, these properties will be listed for each object, but will not be explained.

Name	Returns	Description
Collection		Read Only. Returns the collection to which an object belongs. For example, a Reference object belongs to the References collection. The Collection property is used for objects that belong to collections.
Parent		Read Only. Return the object to which an object belongs. For example, a References collection belongs to a VBProject object. The Parent property is used for objects that do not belong to collections.
VBE	VBE	Read Only. Returns the Visual Basic Editor object, which is analogous to the Application object in the Excel Object Model.

Most of the objects in the VBE Object Model are contained in associated collections. The collection object is usually the plural form of the associated object. For example, the `Windows` collection holds a collection of `Window` objects. For simplicity, each object and associated collection will be grouped together under the same heading. The common properties and methods of the collection objects are the same as in the Excel Object Model, and are listed in Appendix A. Only unique properties, methods or events will be mentioned for each object.

AddIn Object and AddIns Collection

Not to be confused with Excel's `AddIn` object, VBE Addins are DLLs that conform to Microsoft's Component Object Model architecture and are more commonly known as "COM Addins". These Addins are typically created using C++, Visual Basic, or the Developer Edition of Office 2002. If you have any installed, they can be found under the VBE's **Add-Ins** menu and can be loaded and unloaded using the **Add-Ins | Add-In Manager...** menu item.

AddIn Common Properties

The `Collection` and `VBE` properties are defined at the beginning of this section.

AddIn Properties

Name	Returns	Description
`Connect`	`Boolean`	Whether the COM Addin is currently connected (i.e. active). Can be set to `True` to load and run the Addin. Similar to the `Installed` property of an Excel Addin.
`Description`	`String`	The text that appears in the "Description" box of the VBE Add-In Manager.
`Guid`	`String`	Read Only. Returns the globally unique identifier for the Addin. The `Guid` is created by Excel/VB when the Addin is compiled.
`Object`		In the AddIn's `OnConnection` method, it can expose an object to the VBE (typically the root class of its object model, if it has one). You can then use the AddIn's `Object` property to access this object and through it, the rest of the AddIn's object model. Few Addins currently expose an `Object`.
`ProgId`	`String`	Read Only. Returns the program ID for the Addin, which is comprised of the name of the Addin project and the name of the connection class (usually a connection designer). For example, if you have an Addin project called `MyAddin` and an Addin `Designer` class called `dsrMyConnection`, the `ProgId` will be `"MyAddin.dsrMyConnection"`.

AddIns Collection Methods

Name	Returns	Description
`Item`	`Addin`	Read Only. Parameters: `Item As Variant`. Returns an Addin associated with the item. The parameter can be either a number or the `ProgId` of the Addin (for example `MyAddin.dsrMyConnection`)
`Update`		Method. Updates the list of available COM Addins from the Registry. This should only need to be used if you are compiling an Addin through code (for example using `VBProject.MakeCompiledFile`).

AddIn Examples

The following example iterates through all the Addins registered for use in the VBE and prints information about those that are active.

```
Sub ListRunningAddins()
   'Define as a VBE Addin, not an Excel one
   Dim oAddin As VBIDE.Addin

   'Loop through the VBE's addins
   For Each oAddin In Application.VBE.AddIns

      'Is it active (i.e. connected)?
      If oAddin.Connect Then

         'Yes, so show it's ID and description
         Debug.Print oAddin.ProgId, oAddin.Description
     End If
   Next
End Sub
```

Note that VBE Addins do not have a property to provide their name, as shown in the list in the **Add-In Manager** dialog.

CodeModule Object

The `CodeModule` object contains all of the code for a single `VBComponent` (i.e. Module, UserForm, Class Module or Excel sheet). There is only ever one `CodeModule` for a component – its methods and properties enable you to locate, identify, modify, and add lines of code to a project's components. There can be more than one procedure of the same name in a module, if they are `Property` procedures:

```
Dim msSelection As String
Property Get TheSelection() As String
   TheSelection = msSelection
End Property

Property Let TheSelection(NewString As String)
   MsSelection = NewString
End Property
```

Hence, to uniquely identify a procedure, you need to supply both its name ("TheSelection" in this example) and the type of procedure you're looking for (vbext_pk_Get for Property Get, vbext_pk_Let for Property Let, vbext_pk_Set for Property Set, or vbext_pk_proc for Subs and Functions). The ProcOfLine function provides this information for a given line number – the name of the procedure is the return value of the function and the type of procedure is returned in the variable you supply to its ProcKind argument. It is one of the few properties in the whole of Office 2002 that returns values by modifying the arguments passed to it.

CodeModule Common Properties

The Parent and VBE properties are defined at the beginning of this section (its Parent being the VBComponent.)

CodeModule Properties

Name	Returns	Description
CodePane	CodePane	Read Only. Returns the active CodePane for the module. If there is no visible CodePane, one is created and displayed. Note that a CodeModule can have up to two code panes, but there is no CodePanes collection for them!

CountOf Declaration Lines	Long	Read Only. Returns the number of lines at the top of the module used for Dim, Type, and Option statements. If there are any such items at the top of the module, any comments following them are considered to be part of the following procedure, not the declarations. The following has two declaration lines:
		`Option Explicit`
		`Dim msSelection As String`
		
		`'My Comment`
		`Sub ProcedureStart()`
		If no such statements exist, comments appearing at the top of the module are counted as declaration lines, if they are followed by a blank line. The following has one declaration line:
		`'My Comment`
		
		`Sub ProcedureStart()`
		If the comment is immediately followed by the procedure, it is included in the procedure's lines, so the following has no declaration line:
		`'My Comment`
		`Sub ProcedureStart()`

Table continued on following page

Name	Returns	Description
CountOf Lines	Long	Read Only. Returns the total number of lines of code in the module, with line continuations counted as separate lines.
Lines	String	Read Only. Parameters: StartLine As Long, Count As Long. Returns a block of code, starting from Startline and continuing for Count lines.
Name	String	(Hidden) Read Only. Returns the name of the associated VBComponent.
ProcBody Line	Long	Read Only. Parameters: ProcName As String, ProcKind As vbext_ProcKind. Returns the line number of the start of the procedure, not including any preceding comments – that is it gives the line number of the Sub, Function, or Property statement.
ProcCount Lines	Long	Read Only. Parameters: ProcName As String, ProcKind As vbext_ProcKind. Returns the number of lines used by the procedure, including preceding comments, up to the End Sub, End Function, or End Property statement.
ProcOfLine	String	Read Only. Parameters: Line As Long [in], ProcKind As Long [out]. Returns the name of the procedure that a line is located within. The ProcKind argument is also modified to return the type of procedure (Sub/Function, Property Let, Get or Set). This is usually the first property to be called; the name and type returned from this are then used in calls to the other methods.
ProcStart Line	Long	Read Only. Parameters: ProcName As String, ProcKind As vbext_ProcKind. Returns the line number of the start of the procedure, including comments. Hence, ProcBodyLine - ProcStartLine gives you the number of preceding comment lines.

CodeModule Methods

Name	Returns	Parameters	Description
AddFromFile		FileName As String	Reads code from a text file and adds it to the end of the code module. It does not check if the names of procedures read from a file already exist in the module.
AddFrom String		String As String	Adds code from a string to the end of the code module.

Name	Returns	Parameters	Description
`CreateEventProc`	`Long`	`EventName As String, ObjectName As String`	Creates an empty event procedure in a module, filling in the event parameters for you. Cannot be used on standard modules, as they do not support events. The `ObjectName` must be a valid object for the class module, and the `EventName` must be a valid event for that object.
`DeleteLines`		`StartLine As Long, Count As Long`	Deletes lines from a code module, starting at `StartLine`, for `Count` lines.
`Find`	`Boolean`	`Target As String, StartLine As Long, StartColumn As Long, EndLine As Long, EndColumn As Long, WholeWord As Boolean, MatchCase As Boolean, PatternSearch As Boolean`	Locates a string within a code module, or section of a code module. It provides the same functionality as the VBE's Find dialog.
`InsertLines`		`Line As Long, String As String`	Adds code from a string into the middle of a code module, inserting the code before the `Line` given.
`ReplaceLine`		`Line As Long, String As String`	Adds code from a string into the middle of a code module, replacing the `Line` given.

CodeModule Examples

There are a number of `CodeModule` examples in the chapter on "*Programming the VBE*". The example below identifies the procedure for a given line and displays its type, name, and line count:

```
Sub WhichProc()
   Dim lLine As Long, iProcKind As Long, lLineCount As Long
   Dim sProc As String, sMsg As String
   Dim oActiveCM As VBIDE.CodeModule

   lLine = CLng(InputBox("Which line?"))

   'Cancelled?
   If lLine = 0 Then Exit Sub

   'Get the currently active code module
```

```
    Set oActiveCM = Application.VBE.ActiveCodePane.CodeModule

    'Get the name and type of the procedure at
    'that line - iProcKind is filled in
    sProc = oActiveCM.ProcOfLine(lLine, iProcKind)

    If sProc = "" Then
       'We didn't get a name, so you must be in the Declarations section
       sMsg = "You are in the Declarations section"
       lLineCount = oActiveCM.CountOfDeclarationLines
    Else
       sMsg = "You are in "

       'Display the type of the procedure...
       Select Case iProcKind
          Case vbext_pk_Proc
             sMsg = sMsg & "Sub or Function procedure"
          Case vbext_pk_Get
             sMsg = sMsg & "Property Get procedure"
          Case vbext_pk_Let
             sMsg = sMsg & "Property Let procedure"
          Case vbext_pk_Set
             sMsg = sMsg & "Property Set procedure"
       End Select

       '... its name ...
       sMsg = sMsg & " '" & sProc & "'"

       '... and how many lines it has.
       lLineCount = oActiveCM.ProcCountLines(sProc, iProcKind)
    End If

    'Display the message
    MsgBox sMsg & vbCrLf & "which has " & lLineCount & " lines."
End Sub
```

CodePane Object and CodePanes Collection

A `CodePane` is a view of a `CodeModule`, providing you with access to the interaction layer between the developer and the code being edited. Most VBE Addins use this layer to identify which line in which `CodePane` is currently being edited, and then modify the code at the line, using `CodeModule`'s methods and properties. Note that there can be more than one `CodePane` for a `CodeModule` (for example by splitting a code window into two panes with the horizontal splitter bar).

CodePane Common Properties

The `Collection` and `VBE` properties are defined at the beginning of this section.

CodePane Properties

Name	Returns	Description
`CodeModule`	`CodeModule`	Read Only. Returns the `CodeModule` that contains the code being viewed in the `CodePane`.
`CodePaneView`	`vbext_Code Paneview`	Read Only. Returns whether the `CodePane` is set to show one procedure at a time, or a full-module view with separator lines between procedures.

Name	Returns	Description
CountOf VisibleLines	Long	Read Only. Returns the number of lines visible in the CodePane. This and the TopLine property can be used to center a line in the CodePane window (see example below).
TopLine	Long	The CodeModule line number of the first line visible in the CodePane window.
Window	Window	Read Only. Returns the Window object containing the CodePane(s).

CodePane Methods

Name	Parameters	Description

GetSelection	StartLine As Long, StartColumn As Long, EndLine As Long, EndColumn As Long	Used to retrieve the currently selected text. All of the arguments are passed ByRef and are modified within the procedure to return the selection. All arguments are required, but it is only required to pass arguments for those items you want to retrieve. For example, to get only the start line, you can use:
		`Dim lStart As Long`
		`Application.VBE.ActiveCodePane.GetSelection - lStart, 0, 0, 0`

SetSelection	StartLine As Long, StartColumn As Long, EndLine As Long, EndColumn As Long	Used to set the position of the currently selected text. A program would typically read the selection using GetSelection, modify the code, then set the selection back again using SetSelection. See the "PrintProcedure" routine in the Chapter 23 for an example of this.
Show		Opens and displays the CodePane, making it active.

CodePanes Collection Properties

The CodePanes collection contains all of the open CodePane objects in the VBE.

Name	Returns	Description
Current	CodePane	Read Only. Returns the currently active CodePane, and is the same as Application.VBE.ActiveCodePane.

CodePane Examples

There are a number of CodePane examples in Chapter 23 of this book. The example below identifies the current selection and centers it in the CodePane window:

```
Sub CenterSelectionInWindow()
   Dim oCP As VBIDE.CodePane
   Dim lStartLine As Long, lEndLine As Long
   Dim lVisibleLines As Long, lNewTop As Long

   'Get the active CodePane
   Set oCP = Application.VBE.ActiveCodePane

   'Using the CodePane object...
   With oCP
      'Get the start and end lines of the selection
      .GetSelection lStartLine, 0, lEndLine, 0

      'How many lines fit in the window?
      lVisibleLines = .CountOfVisibleLines

      'So what should the new top line be?
      lNewTop = (lStartLine + lEndLine - lVisibleLines) \ 2

      'Set the window to display code from that line
      .TopLine = lNewTop
   End With
End Sub
```

CommandBarEvents Object

Within the VBE, the `OnAction` property of a command bar button has no effect – the routine named in this property is **not** run when the button is clicked. Instead, the VBE object model provides you with the `CommandBarEvents` object, which hooks into whichever command bar button you tell it to, either your own custom buttons or built-in items, and raises events for the button's actions. In Office 2002 it only raises the `Click` event, and hence provides exactly the same functionality as Excel's `OnAction`. The main difference is that the `Click` event has some arguments to enable you to modify its behavior. The `CommandBarEvents` object also provides an extensible interface, allowing Microsoft to provide a richer event model in future versions of the VBE (such as `BeforePopUp`, `BeforeRightClick`, and standard mouse events).

CommandBarEvents Events

Name	Parameters	Description
`Click`	`CommandBarControl As Object, handled As Boolean, CancelDefault As Boolean`	Triggered when a hooked command bar button is clicked. The `CommandBarControl` is passed to the event. A single control can be hooked by many `CommandBarEvents` objects. The events are fired in reverse order of setting up (most recently set up fires first). An event handler can set the `handled` flag to `True` to tell subsequent handlers that the event has already been processed. The `CommandBarEvents` object can also be used to hook into built-in menu items. If you want to handle the event through code, you can set the `CancelDefault` flag to `True` to stop the menu's normal action.

CommandBarEvents Examples

In a class module called `CBarEvents`, add the following code:

```
Public WithEvents oCBEvents As VBIDE.CommandBarEvents

'Hook into the Click event for the menu item
Private Sub oCBEvents_Click(ByVal CommandBarControl As Object, _
        handled As Boolean, CancelDefault As Boolean)

   Debug.Print "Clicked " & CommandBarControl.Caption
End Sub
```

In a normal module, add the following code:

```
'Declare a collection to hold all the instances of our events class
Dim ocolMenus As New Collection

Sub AddMenus()

   'Declare some CommandBar items
   Dim oBar As CommandBar
   Dim oBtn1 As CommandBarButton, oBtn2 As CommandBarButton

   'And an object to hold instances of your events class
   Dim oCBE As CBarEvents

   'Get the VBE's menu bar
   Set oBar = Application.VBE.CommandBars("Menu Bar")

   'Add a menu item to it
   Set oBtn1 = oBar.Controls.Add(Type:=msoControlButton, temporary:=True)
   oBtn1.Caption = "Menu1"
   oBtn1.Style = msoButtonCaption

   'Create a new instance of your CommandBarEvent handler
   Set oCBE = New CBarEvents

   'Link your CommandBarEvent handler to the menu item you just created
   Set oCBE.oCBEvents = Application.VBE.Events.CommandBarEvents(oBtn1)

   'And add the instance of your event handler to the collection
   ocolMenus.Add oCBE

   'Repeat for a second menu
   Set oBtn2 = oBar.Controls.Add(Type:=msoControlButton, temporary:=True)
   oBtn2.Caption = "Menu2"
   oBtn2.Style = msoButtonCaption

   Set oCBE = New CBarEvents
   Set oCBE.oCBEvents = Application.VBE.Events.CommandBarEvents(oBtn2)
   ocolMenus.Add oCBE
End Sub
```

When you run the `AddMenus` routine, two menus are added to the VBE standard menu bar, which both use your `CommandBarEvents` handling class to hook into their `Click` event. When you click each of the menu items, the Immediate window displays the menu's caption.

Events Object

The `Events` object is a high-level container for the VBE's event model. In Office 2002, it contains event objects associated with clicking a command bar button and adding/removing references. The VBE extensibility model is based on the Visual Basic extensibility model, which contains a much richer set of events.

Events Properties

Name	Returns	Description
`CommandBar Events`	`CommandBar Events`	Read Only. Parameters: `CommandBarControl`. Performs the linking required to hook a `CommandBarEvents` object to a specific command bar button.
`References Events`	`References Events`	Read Only. Parameters: `VBProject`. Performs the linking required to hook a `ReferencesEvents` object to a specific project.

Events Examples

Examples of the `Events` object are included in the `CommandBarEvents` and `ReferencesEvents` sections.

LinkedWindows Collection

The `LinkedWindows` collection contains all the docked windows in the VBE workspace. COM Addins written in VB5/6 (but not in the Developer edition of Office 2002) can add their own windows to this collection. Within the Office environment, you are limited to docking or undocking the built-in windows. Note that if you undock, then dock a built-in window, it does **not** go back to its original position.

LinkedWindows Collection Methods

Name	Returns	Description
`Add`		Method. Parameters: `Window As Window`. Docks the specified window.
`Remove`		Method. Parameters: `Window As Window`. Undocks the specified window.

Property Object and Properties Collection

All of the `VBComponents` in a project have a `Properties` collection. The properties contained in the collection correspond to the items shown in the Properties Window of the VBE. For the `VBComponents` that correspond to the Excel objects, the `Properties` collection of the `VBComponents` also includes many of the properties of the Excel object.

Property Common Properties

The `Collection`, `Parent`, and `VBE` properties are defined at the beginning of this section.

Property Properties

Name	Returns	Description
IndexedValue	Variant	Parameters: Index1, [Index2], [Index3], [Index4]. The Property's Value can be an array of up to 4 indices. The IndexedValue can be used to read a single item in the returned array.
Name	String	Read Only. Returns the name of the property, and is also used to refer to a specific property.
NumIndices	Integer	Read Only. If the Property's value is an array, this returns the number of indices (dimensions) in the array. If not an array, it returns zero.
Object	Object	The Object property is used to obtain a reference to the object returned by the Property, if any.
Value	Variant	The Property's value.

It is easy to get confused with the Name property:

Item	Refers to
Worksheet.CodeName	The code name of the VBComponent (read only).
VBComponent.Name	The code name of the VBComponent (read/write).
VBComponent .Properties("CodeName")	The code name of the VBComponent (read only).
VBComponent .Properties("_CodeName")	The code name of the VBComponent (read/write).[1]
VBComponent .Properties("Name")	The name of the worksheet (read/write).
VBComponent .Properties("Name").Name	"Name".

[1] This was the only reliable way to change a worksheet's CodeName in Excel 97.

Property Examples

This simple example identifies the workbook containing a given VBComponent:

```
Sub IdentifyWorkbook()
   Dim oBk As Workbook

   'Get the workbook containing a given VBComponent
   Set oBk =
Application.VBE.ActiveVBProject.VBComponents("Sheet1").Properties("Parent").Object

   MsgBox oBk.Name
End Sub
```

Reference Object and References Collection

A `Reference` is a link from your `VBProject` to an external file, which may be an object library (for example linking to the Word object library), a control (for example Windows Common Controls), an ActiveX DLL, or another `VBProject`. By creating a reference to the external object, you can implement early binding – meaning that the referenced objects run in the same memory area, all the links are evaluated at compile time, and Excel provides tool-tip programming help when working with the referenced objects.

When you run your application on another machine, it may not have all the objects that your application requires. The `Reference` object and `References` collection provide access to these references, allowing you to check that they are all present and working before you try to use them.

Reference Common Properties

The `Collection` and `VBE` properties are defined at the beginning of this section.

Reference Properties

Name	Returns	Description
`BuiltIn`	`Boolean`	Read Only. Returns if the reference is built-in or added by the developer. The "Visual Basic for Applications" and "Microsoft Excel 10.0 Object Library" references are built-in and cannot be removed.
`Description`	`String`	Read Only. Returns the description of the reference, which is the text shown in the Object Browser.
`FullPath`	`String`	Read Only. Returns the path to the workbook, DLL, OCX, TLB or OLB file that is the source of the reference.
`Guid`	`String`	Read Only. Returns the globally unique identifier for the reference.
`IsBroken`	`Boolean`	Read Only. Returns `True` if the reference is broken (is not available on the machine).
`Major`	`Long`	Read Only. Returns the major version number of the referenced file.
`Minor`	`Long`	Read Only. Returns the minor version number of the referenced file.
`Name`	`String`	Read Only. Returns a short name for the reference (for example "VBA" or "Excel").
`Type`	`vbext_ RefKind`	Read Only. Returns the reference type, `vbext_rk_TypeLib` for DLLs etc, or `vbext_rk_Project` for other `VBProjects`.

References Collection Methods

Name	Returns	Description
AddFromFile	Reference	Method. Parameters: `FileName As String`. Adds a reference between the `VBProject` and a specific file. This should only be used to create references between workbooks.
AddFromGuid	Reference	Method. Parameters: `Guid As String, Major As Long, Minor As Long`. Adds a reference between the `VBProject` and a specific DLL, Typelib, etc. A library's file name, location and version may change over time, but its `Guid` is guaranteed to be constant. Hence, when adding a reference to a DLL, Typelib, etc, the `Guid` should be used. If you require a specific version of the DLL, you can request the major and minor version numbers.
Remove		Method. Parameters: `Reference As Reference`. Removes a reference from the `VBProject`.

References Collection Events

The `References` collection provides two events, which you can use to detect when items are added to or removed from the collection. You could use this, for example, to create a "Top 10 References" dialog, by using the `Application`'s events to detect when a workbook is opened or created and hooking into the workbook's `VBProject`'s `References` collection events to detect when a particular `Reference` is added to a project. You could maintain a list of these and display them in a dialog box, similar to the existing **Tools | References** dialog in the VBE (but without all the clutter).

Name	Parameters	Description
ItemAdded	Reference As VBIDE.Reference	Triggered when a `Reference` is added to the `VBProject` being watched.
ItemRemoved	Reference As VBIDE.Reference	Triggered when a `Reference` is removed from the `VBProject` being watched.

Reference Examples

This example checks for broken references and alerts the user.

```
Function HasMissingRefs() As Boolean
   Dim oRef As VBIDE.Reference

   'Loop through all the references for the project
   For Each oRef In ThisWorkbook.VBProject.References

      'Is it missing?
      If oRef.IsBroken Then

         'Yes - show different messages for workbook and DLL references
```

```
            If oRef.Type = vbext_rk_Project Then
               MsgBox "Could not find the workbook " & oRef.FullPath & _
                      ", which is required by this application."
            Else
               MsgBox "This application requires the object library '" & _
                      oRef.Description & "', which has not been installed."
            End If

            'Return that there are some missing references
            HasMissingRefs = True
         End If
      Next
   End Function
```

The following example shows the core code to watch when the user adds or removes references to any project (so that you could, for example, create a "Top 10" references picker). There are four steps to take:

- When started, hook into the `References` events of the `VBProjects` in all open workbooks.
- Hook into the `Application`'s events to detect workbooks being created or opened.
- When a workbook is created or opened, hook its `VBProject`'s `References` events.
- When a `References` event is triggered, do something (here, you just print it out)

In a class module, `CRefEvents` (for the fourth step):

```
'The WithEvents object to hook the References events
Public WithEvents oRefEvt As VBIDE.References

'We'll also store the workbook you're tracking
Public oWorkbook As Workbook

'We added a reference to a workbook
Private Sub oRefEvt_ItemAdded(ByVal Reference As VBIDE.Reference)
   Debug.Print "Added Reference '" & _
               Reference.Description & _
               "' to " & oWorkbook.Name
End Sub

'We removed a reference from a workbook
Private Sub oRefEvt_ItemRemoved(ByVal Reference As VBIDE.Reference)
   Debug.Print "Removed Reference '" & _
               Reference.Description & _
               "' from " & oWorkbook.Name
End Sub
```

In a class module, `CAppEvents` (for the thrid step):

```
'WithEvents object to hook the Application's events
Public WithEvents oApp As Application

'Hook the References events for new workbooks
Private Sub oApp_NewWorkbook(ByVal Wb As Workbook)

   'A new References event handler instance
   Dim oRefEvents As New CRefEvents
```

```
    'Tell it which workbook you're hooking
    Set oRefEvents.oWorkbook = Wb

    'And give it the References object to hook into
    Set oRefEvents.oRefEvt = Wb.VBProject.References

    'Add the event handler to your collection of such handlers
    oRefHooks.Add oRefEvents
End Sub

'Hook the References events for opened workbooks
Private Sub oApp_WorkbookOpen(ByVal Wb As Workbook)
    Dim oRefEvents As New CRefEvents

    Set oRefEvents.oWorkbook = Wb
    Set oRefEvents.oRefEvt = Wb.VBProject.References
    oRefHooks.Add oRefEvents
End Sub
```

In a normal module (for the first and second steps):

```
'One instance of Application events hook
Public oAppHooks As New CAppEvents

'Lots of instances of References events hooks
Public oRefHooks As New Collection

Sub SetUpReferenceHooking()
    Dim oRefEvents As CRefEvents
    Dim oBk As Workbook

    Set oRefHooks = Nothing

    'Step 1: Loop through the existing projects,
    'hooking their references events
    For Each oBk In Workbooks
        If Not oBk Is ThisWorkbook Then
            Set oRefEvents = New CRefEvents
            Set oRefEvents.oWorkbook = oBk
            Set oRefEvents.oRefEvt = oBk.VBProject.References
            oRefHooks.Add oRefEvents
        End If
    Next

    'Step 2: Hook the Application events to watch for new projects to hook
    Set oAppHooks.oApp = Application
End Sub
```

ReferencesEvents Object

In a similar manner to the way in which the `CommandBarEvents` object provides the `Click` event for a command bar, the `ReferencesEvents` object provides two events related to a `VBProject's References` collection. The `ReferencesEvents` object appears to be redundant – all of the events it handles are also included in a `VBProject's References` object. The only difference (apart from the definition) is that the `ReferencesEvents` object works with a `VBProject` object instead of the `VBProject's References` collection. Note that a `VBProject` is compiled when a `Reference` is added or removed, resulting in the loss of any variables and instances of classes. Hence a `VBProject` cannot monitor its own `References` events.

ReferencesEvents Events

Name	Parameters	Description
ItemAdded	Reference As VBIDE.Reference	Triggered when a Reference is added to the VBProject being watched.
ItemRemoved	Reference As VBIDE.Reference	Triggered when a Reference is removed from the VBProject being watched.

ReferencesEvents Examples

The examples for the ReferencesEvents object are the same as the References Collection Events. The only difference is the way the events are handled (shown in bold in the code):

In the CRefEvents class:

```
'The WithEvents object to hook the References events
Public WithEvents oRefEvt As VBIDE.ReferencesEvents
```

In the CAppEvents class:

```
'Hook the References events for opened workbooks
Private Sub oApp_WorkbookOpen(ByVal Wb As Workbook)
   Dim oRefEvents As New CRefEvents

   Set oRefEvents.oWorkbook = Wb
   Set oRefEvents.oRefEvt = _
      Application.VBE.Events.ReferencesEvents(Wb.VBProject)
   oRefHooks.Add oRefEvents
End Sub
```

In the normal module:

```
   Set oRefEvents.oWorkbook = oBk
   Set oRefEvents.oRefEvt = _
      Application.VBE.Events.ReferencesEvents(oBk.VBProject)
```

VBComponent Object and VBComponents Collection

The VBComponents collection contains all the modules, class modules (including code behind worksheets), and UserForms in a VBProject; they are all different types of VBComponent. Every VBComponent has a CodeModule to store its code and some VBComponents (such as a UserForm) have a graphical development interface, called its Designer. Through the Designer, you can modify the graphical elements of the VBComponent, such as adding controls to a UserForm.

VBComponent Common Properties

The Collection and VBE properties are defined at the beginning of this section.

VBComponent Properties

Name	Returns	Description
CodeModule	CodeModule	Read Only. Returns the CodeModule for the component, used to store its VBA code.
Designer		Read Only. Returns the Designer object for the component, which provides access to the design-time graphical elements of the component.
DesignerID	String	Read Only. Returns an identifier for the Designer, so you know what sort of designer it is. For example, a UserForm's designer ID is Forms.Form, while that of the Addin Connection designer in Office 2002 Developer is MSAddnDr.AddInDesigner.
Designer Window	Window	Read Only. Returns a Window object, representing the Window displaying the Designer. (Shown as a method in the Object Browser, as it opens the Window if not already open).
HasOpen Designer	Boolean	Read Only. Identifies if the component's Designer is open.
Name	String	The name of the VBComponent.
Properties	Properties	Read Only. Returns the component's Properties collection, providing access to the items shown in the Property Window and to many of the associated Excel object's properties if the VBComponent represents the code behind an Excel object. See the Property Object for more information.
Saved	Boolean	Read Only. Returns whether the contents of the VBComponent has changed since the last save. It is analogous to an Excel workbook's Saved property, but applies to each component individually.
Type	vbext_ Component Type	Read Only. Returns the type of the component: vbext_ct_StdModule — Normal module vbext_ct_ClassModule — Class module vbext_ct_MSForm — UserForm vbext_ct_Document — Excel object vbext_ct_ActiveXDesigner — All other types

VBComponent Methods

Name	Parameters	Description
Activate		Displays the VBComponent's main window (code module or designer) and sets the focus to it.
Export	FileName As String	Saves the component as a file, separate from the workbook.

VBComponents Collection Methods

Name	Returns	Description
Add	VBComponent	Parameters: ComponentType. Add a new, built-in, VBComponent to the project. The ComponentType can be one of vbext_ct_StdModule, vbext_ct_ClassModule and vbext_ct_MSForm.
AddCustom	VBComponent	Parameters: ProgId. Add a new, custom, VBComponent to the project. The result is always of type vbext_ct_ActiveXDesigner. It seems that custom VB components can only be added to ActiveX DLL projects and not to Excel workbook projects.
Import	VBComponent	Parameters: FileName. Add a new VBComponent to the project from a file (usually a previously-exported VBComponent).
Remove		Parameters: VBComponent. Removes a VBComponent from a project.

VBComponent Examples

Many of the examples in this section and in Chapter 23 use the VBComponent object and its properties and methods. The example below exports a UserForm from the workbook containing the code, imports it into a new workbook and renames it. It then adds a standard module, fills in some code to show the form, then calls the routine to show the form in the new workbook:

```
Sub CopyAndShowUserForm()
   Dim oNewBk As Workbook, oVBC As VBIDE.VBComponent

   'Create a new workbook
   Set oNewBk = Workbooks.Add

   'Export a UserForm from this workbook to disk
   ThisWorkbook.VBProject.VBComponents("UserForm1").Export "c:\temp.frm"

   'Import the UserForm into the new workbook
   Set oVBC = oNewBk.VBProject.VBComponents.Import("c:\temp.frm")

   'Rename the UserForm
   oVBC.Name = "MyForm"
```

```
    'Add a standard module to the new workbook
    Set oVBC = oNewBk.VBProject.VBComponents.Add(vbext_ct_StdModule)

    'Add some code to the standard module, to show the form
    oVBC.CodeModule.AddFromString _
            "Sub ShowMyForm()" & vbCrLf & _
            "     MyForm.Show" & vbCrLf & _
            "End Sub" & vbCrLf

    'Close the code pane the Excel opened when you added code to the module
    oVBC.CodeModule.CodePane.Window.Close

    'Delete the exported file
    Kill "c:\temp.frm"

    'Run the new routine to show the imported UserForm
    Application.Run oNewBk.Name & "!ShowMyForm"
End Sub
```

VBE Object

The `VBE` object is the top-level object in the VBIDE object library and hence is analogous to the `Application` object in the Excel library. Its main jobs are to act as a container for the VBIDE's commandbars, addins, windows etc and to provide information about the objects currently being modified by the user. Unfortunately, it does not expose any of the VBIDE's options settings (code settings, edit formats, error handling etc), nor does it provide any editing events (such as selecting a different project, adding or deleting lines of code, etc).

VBE Properties

Name	Returns	Description
`ActiveCodePane`	`CodePane`	Returns or sets the `CodePane` currently being edited by the user. Typically used to identify which object is being worked on, or to force the user to work with a specific code pane.
`ActiveVBProject`	`VBProject`	Returns or sets the `VBProject` selected in the Project Explorer window. If the Project Explorer is showing a `VBComponent` selected, this property returns the `VBProject` containing the component.
`ActiveWindow`	`Window`	Read Only. Returns the active `Window`, which may be a code pane, designer or one of the VBIDE windows (i.e. Project Explorer, Immediate Window etc.)
`Addins`	`Addins`	Read Only. Returns a collection of all the COM Addins registered for use in the VBIDE. See the `AddIn` object for more information.
`CodePanes`	`CodePanes`	Read Only. Returns a collection of all the open `CodePanes` in the VBIDE. See the `CodePane` object for more information.

Table continued on following page

Name	Returns	Description
CommandBars	CommandBars	Read Only. Returns a collection of all the command bars in the VBIDE.
Events	Events	Read Only. Returns an object containing all the events in the VBIDE. See the Events object for more information.
MainWindow	Window	Read Only. Returns a Window object representing the main window of the VBIDE.
Selected VBComponent	VBComponent	Read Only. Returns the VBComponent object that is shown as selected in the Project Explorer window. Note that this usually, but not always, corresponds to the ActiveCodePane.
VBProjects	VBProjects	Read Only. Returns a collection of all the VBProjects in the VBIDE, both Excel workbooks and ActiveX DLLs.
Version	String	Read Only. Returns the version number of the Extensibility library (shows 6.0 for Office 2002).
Windows	Windows	Read Only. Returns a collection of all the open windows in the VBIDE. See the Windows object for more information.

VBE Examples

Most of the examples in this section and in Chapter 23 include the VBE's properties. The following line displays the VBE:

```
Application.VBE.MainWindow.Visible = True
```

VBProject Object and VBProjects Collection

A VBProject represents all of the code for a workbook, including code behind sheets, modules, class modules, and User Forms. In the Developer edition of Office 2002, a VBProject can also be a standalone project, compiled as an ActiveX DLL.

VBProject Common Properties

The Collection and VBE properties are defined at the beginning of this section.

VBProject Properties

Name	Returns	Description
BuildFile Name	String	For ActiveX DLLs only, get/set the name of the DLL file to compile the project into.
Description	String	For ActiveX DLLs only, the description of the DLL, as it will appear in the Tools | References list.

Name	Returns	Description
FileName	String	Read Only. For workbook projects, returns the full name of the workbook. For ActiveX DLL projects, returns the name of the source code version of the project *.vba. If the file has not been saved, a run-time error occurs if you try to read this property.
HelpContext ID	Long	Identifies the default help-file context ID for the project.
HelpFile	String	Get/Set the help file for a project. Each of the User Forms and controls within the project can be assigned a context ID to show a page from this help file.
Mode	vbext_ VBAMode	Read Only. Returns the VBProject's operation mode (Design, Run or Break). Note that VBProjects can have different execution modes (for example, an ActiveX COM Addin project can be running while you are in Design mode on a different project).
Name	String	The name of the project.
Protection	vbext_ Project Protection	Read Only. Returns whether the project is locked for viewing. Locked projects only expose their VBProject object. Any attempt to navigate below the VBProject level results in an error. Note that if a VBProject is set to **Protected**, but is unprotected by the user during a session, its Protection property shows as vbext_pp_none for the remainder of that session.
References	References	Read Only. Returns the collection of References for the VBProject. See the References object for more information
Saved	Boolean	Read Only. Returns whether the VBProject has been changed since the last save. For Excel projects, this should agree with the workbook's Saved property.
Type	vbext_ ProjectType	Read Only. Returns the type of project – host project (an Excel workbook, Word document, Access database etc.) or an ActiveX DLL project.
VBComponents	VBComponents	Read Only. Returns the collection of VBComponents in the project. See the VBComponent object for more information.

VBProject Methods

Name	Returns	Parameters	Description
MakeCompiledFile			For ActiveX DLL projects only. Compiles the project and makes the DLL file.
SaveAs		FileName As String	For ActiveX DLL projects only. Saves the project file.

VBProjects Collection Methods

Name	Returns	Description
Add	VBProject	Method. Parameters: `Type`. Adds a new project to the VBE. Can only successfully add standalone (ActiveX DLL) projects using this method.
Remove		Method. Parameters: `lpc As VBProject`. Removes a `VBProject` from the VBE. Can only be used for ActiveX DLL projects.

VBProject Examples

Most of the examples in this section use the `VBProject` object and its properties. This example lists the names of all the `VBComponents` in all the unlocked projects in the VBE:

```
Sub PrintComponents()
   Dim oVBP As VBIDE.VBProject
   Dim oVBC As VBIDE.VBComponent

   'Loop through all the projects in the VBE
   For Each oVBP In Application.VBE.VBProjects

      'If the project is not protected...
      If oVBP.Protection = vbext_pp_none Then

         '... loop through its components
         For Each oVBC In oVBP.VBComponents
            Debug.Print oVBP.Name & "." & oVBC.Name
         Next
      End If
   Next
End Sub
```

Window Object and Windows Collection

The `Window` object represents a single window in the VBE, including the VBE's main window, the built-in Project Explorer, Immediate, Debug, and Watch Windows etc., as well as all open `CodePanes` and Designer Windows.

Window Common Properties

The `Collection` and `VBE` properties are defined at the beginning of this section.

Window Properties

Name	Returns	Description
`Caption`	`String`	Read Only. Returns the caption of the `Window`, as shown in its title bar.
`Height`	`Long`	The height of the `Window`, in twips (1 twip = 1/20 points). Does not affect docked windows.
`HWnd`	`Long`	Read Only. Returns a handle to the `Window`, for use in Windows API calls.
`Left`	`Long`	The left edge of the `Window` on the screen, in twips (1 twip = 1/20 points). Does not affect docked windows.
`Linked WindowFrame`	`Window`	Read Only. Multiple windows can be linked together in the VBE (for example while docking them). This property returns another `Window` that represents the frame surrounding the docked windows. Returns `Nothing` if the window is not linked.
`Linked Windows`	`Linked Windows`	Read Only. Returns a collection of windows linked to the `Window` (for example when docked).
`Top`	`Long`	The top of the `Window` on the screen, in twips (1 twip = 1/20 points). Does not affect docked windows.
`Type`	`vbext_ WindowType`	Read Only. Returns the window type, such as `CodePane`, Immediate Window, Main Window, etc.
`Visible`	`Boolean`	Get/Set whether or not the window is visible.
`Width`	`Long`	The width of the `Window`, in twips (1 twip = 1/20 points). Does not affect docked windows.
`WindowState`	`vbext_ WindowState`	The `Window` state – minimized, maximized, or normal.

Window Methods

Name	Returns	Description
`Close`		Closes the window.
`SetFocus`		Opens and activates the window, displays it, and gives it the focus.

Windows Collection Methods

Name	Returns	Description
`CreateTool Window`	`Window`	Parameters: `AddInInst`, `ProgId`, `Caption`, `GuidPosition`, `DocObj`. This method is only used when creating COM Addins using VB5/6, to create a dockable window in the VBE.

Window Examples

This example closes all code and designer windows in the VBE:

```
Sub CloseAllCodeWindows()
   Dim oWin As VBIDE.Window

   'Loop through all the open windows in the VBE
   For Each oWin In Application.VBE.Windows

      'Close the window, depending on its type
      Select Case oWin.Type
         Case vbext_wt_Browser, vbext_wt_CodeWindow, vbext_wt_Designer

            'Close the Object Browser, code windows and designer windows
            Debug.Print "Closed '" & oWin.Caption & "' window."
            oWin.Close

         Case Else
            'Don't close any other windows
            Debug.Print "Kept '" & oWin.Caption & "' window open."
      End Select
   Next
End Sub
```

VBAProgrammersReferenceExcel20
[illegible]mmersReferenceExcel2002VB
[illegible]ReferenceExcel2002VBAPro
[illegible]AProgrammersReferenceExc
[illegible]rammersReferenceExcel20
[illegible]ReferenceExcel2002VB
[illegible]enceExcel2002VBAPro
Programmer [illegible] Excel2002VBAProgram
enceExce [illegible]
ogramme [illegible] 2002VBAProgrammers
eExce [illegible] ammersRefe
[illegible] Referen
[illegible]
rogrammer [illegible] Prog
ammersR [illegible] ceEx
rsReference [illegible] Progam
ReferenceExce [illegible]
[illegible] Progr
nceExcel2002VBA [illegible] ReferenceEx
xcel2002VBAProgram [illegible] Program
2002VBAProgrammersReferenceExcel2002VB
VBAProgrammersReferen [illegible]
[illegible] enceExcel
rogrammersReferenceEx [illegible]
[illegible] Programmer [illegible] ence
ammersReference rammers [illegible] xcel2002VBAProgra
2002VBAProgrammersReferenceExce

Office XP Object Model

Common Properties with Collections and Associated Objects

Most of the objects in the Office Object Model have objects with associated collections. The collection object is usually the plural form of the associated object. For example, the `CommandBars` collection holds a collection of `CommandBar` objects. For simplicity, each object and associated collection will be grouped together under the same heading.

In most cases the purpose of the collection object is only to hold a collection of the same objects. The common properties of the collection objects are listed below. Only unique properties, methods or events will be mentioned in each object section.

Common Collection Properties

Name	Returns	Description
`Application`	`Application`	Read Only. Returns a reference to the Application owning the current object.
`Count`	`Long`	Read Only. Returns the number of objects in the collection.
`Creator`	`Long`	Read Only. Returns a `Long` number that describes which application the object was created in. MacIntosh only.
`Parent`	`Object`	Read Only. The `Parent` object is the container object of the `collection` object. For example, `Workbooks.Parent` returns a reference to the `Application` object.

Common Object Properties

Objects also have some common properties. To avoid redundancy the common properties of all objects are listed below. They will be mentioned in each object description as existing but are only defined here.

Name	Returns	Description
`Application`	`Application`	Read Only. Returns a reference to the Application owning the current object.
`Creator`	`Long`	Read Only. Returns a `Long` number that describes which application the object was created in. MacIntosh only.
`Parent`	`Object`	Read Only. The container object of the current object. For example, in Excel `Shapes(1).Parent` may return a reference to a `Worksheet` object, since a `Worksheet` object is one of the possible containers of a `Shapes` object.

Office Objects and Their Properties and Events

The objects are listed in alphabetical order. Each object has a general description of the object and possible parent objects. This is followed by a table format of each of the object's properties and methods. The last section of each object describes some code examples of the object's use.

AnswerWizard Object

The `AnswerWizard` object is part of the `AnswerWizardFiles` collection. It's used to control which files are used when using the Answer Wizard dialog.

AnswerWizard Common Properties

The `Application`, `Creator`, and `Parent` properties are defined at the beginning of this appendix.

AnswerWizard Properties

Name	Returns	Description
`Files`	`AnswerWizardFiles`	Read Only. Returns the list of files available to the current `AnswerWizard`.

AnswerWizard Methods

Name	Returns	Parameters	Description
`ClearFileList`			Clears the list of files for the current `AnswerWizard`, including the default list of files for the Microsoft Office host application.
`ResetFileList`			Resets the list of files for the current `AnswerWizard` to the default list of files for the Microsoft Office host application.

AnswerWizardFiles Collection Object

A collection of references to Answer Wizard files. The `AnswerWizardFiles` collection contains all of the Answer Wizard files (with the file name extension .AW) available to the active Microsoft Office application.

AnswerWizardFiles Collection Common Properties

The `Application`, `Count`, `Creator`, and `Parent` properties are defined at the beginning of this appendix.

AnswerWizardFiles Properties

Name	Returns	Parameters	Description
`Item`	`String`	`Index as Long`	Read Only. Returns a file name string from an `AnswerWizardFiles` collection.

AnswerWizardFiles Collection Methods

Name	Returns	Parameters	Description
`Add`		`FileName as String`	Creates a new reference (a String value) to an Answer Wizard file and adds it to the `AnswerWizardFiles` collection.
`Delete`		`FileName as String`	Deletes the specified Answer Wizard file from the `AnswerWizardFiles` collection.

Assistant Object

The `Assistant` object controls how the Office Assistant appears and what it displays. For example, you can use the `Assistant` object to display your own custom messages as an alternative to the `MsgBox` function. Many of the `Assistant`'s properties relate to the choices found in the `Assistant`'s Options dialog.

Assistant Common Properties

The `Application`, `Creator`, and `Parent` properties are defined at the beginning of this appendix.

Assistant Properties

Name	Returns	Description
`Animation`	`Mso AnimationType`	Set/Get which animation to run for the Office Assistant.
`Assist WithAlerts`	`Boolean`	Set/Get whether the Office Assistant balloon displays application alerts when the Office Assistant is visible. When set to `False`, the alerts will appear in the Application's default dialog boxes.
`Assist WithHelp`	`Boolean`	Set/Get whether the Office Assistant appears when the user presses the F1 key to display Help. If `False`, the Microsoft Help Window displays.
`Assist WithWizards`	`Boolean`	Set/Get whether the Office Assistant appears and provides online Help when wizards appear.
`BallonError`	`MsoBalloon ErrorType`	Read Only. Returns a value that indicates the last recorded balloon error.
`FeatureTips`	`Boolean`	Set/Get whether the Office Assistant provides information about using application features more effectively.
`FileName`	`String`	Set/Get the filename and location of the current Office Assistant.
`GuessHelp`	`Boolean`	Set/Get whether the Office Assistant balloon presents a list of Help topics based on keywords the user selects before clicking the Assistant window or pressing F1. If the Assistant is disabled (see the On property overleaf), the help topics appear in the standard Help window.
`High Priority Tips`	`Boolean`	Set/Get whether the Office Assistant displays high-priority tips.
`Item`	`String`	Read Only. Returns the text associated with the object.

Name	Returns	Description
`Keyboard Shortcut Tips`	`Boolean`	Set/Get whether the Office Assistant displays Help about keyboard shortcuts.
`Left`	`Long`	Set/Get the horizontal position of the Office Assistant window (in points) from the left edge of the screen.
`MouseTips`	`Boolean`	Set/Get whether the Office Assistant provides suggestions for using the mouse effectively.
`MoveWhenIn TheWay`	`Boolean`	Set/Get whether the Office Assistant window automatically moves when it's in the way of the user's work area.
`Name`	`String`	Read Only. Returns the name of the current Office Assistant. If the Assistant is disabled either via the Assistant's Options dialog or via the `Assistant.On` property, `Name` returns `Nothing`.
`NewBalloon`	`Balloon`	Read Only. Returns a reference to a new `Balloon` object. Though you can have multiple `Balloon` objects, only one can be displayed at a time.
`On`	`Boolean`	Set/Get whether the Office Assistant is enabled.
`Reduced`	`Boolean`	Set/Get whether the Office Assistant window appears in its smaller size. This does not appear to have any effect on Office XP applications.
`SearchWhen Programming`	`Boolean`	Set/Get whether the Office Assistant displays application and programming Help while the user is working in Visual Basic.
`Sounds`	`Boolean`	Set/Get whether the Office Assistant produces the sounds that correspond to animations.
`TipOfDay`	`Boolean`	Set/Get whether the Office Assistant displays a special tip each time the Office application is opened.
`Top`	`Long`	Set/Get the distance (in points) from the top of the Office Assistant to the top edge of the screen.
`Visible`	`Boolean`	Set/Get whether the Office Assistant is visible. This property has no effect if `Assistant.On` is set to `False`.

Assistant Methods

Name	Returns	Parameters	Description
ActivateWizard		WizardID as Long, Act as MsoWizardActType, [Animation]	Resumes or suspends Office Assistant Help during a custom wizard. Use this method only with the StartWizard method.
DoAlert	Long	BstrAlertTitle as String, bstrAlertText as String, alb as MsoAlertButtonType, alc as MsoAlertIconType, ald as MsoAlertDefaultType, alq as MsoAlertCancelType, varfSysAlert as Boolean	Displays an alerts either through the Office Assistant or as a normal message box. Returns a Long that indicates which button the user pressed. When the Office Assistant is enabled, it displays the message (using a balloon). If the Assistant is disabled, the message appears and works like a regular message box. This method is very similar to the Balloon property, which only displays a message when the Office Assistant is enabled.
EndWizard		WizardID as Long, varfSuccess, Animation	Releases the variable returned by the StartWizard method. Use this method only with the StartWizard method.
Help			Displays the Office Assistant and the built-in "What would you like to do?" Assistant balloon for standard Office online Help.
Move		XLeft as Integer, yTop as Integer	Moves the Office Assistant to the specified location. Assistant must be enabled and visible for this to work, though no error occurs if either are False.
ResetTips			Resets the application tips that appear in the Office Assistant balloon.

Name	Returns	Parameters	Description
`StartWizard`	`Long`	`On as Boolean, Callback as String, PrivateX as Long, [Animation], [CustomTeaser], [Top], [Left], [Bottom], [Right]`	Starts the Office Assistant and returns a `Long` value that identifies the session. You should use this method only to run the Office Assistant in a custom wizard. The number returned by `StartWizard` method is used by the `ActivateWizard` and `EndWizard` methods.

Example: Assistant Object

The following routine uses some of the properties of the `Assistant` object to display the Assistant, ask a question, and then react to the user's response:

```
'Public user defined type used to hold current Assistant's properties
Public Type AssistInfo
    bOn As Boolean
    bVisible As Boolean
    sFileName As String
End Type

Sub Opening()

    Dim lReturnValue As Long
    Dim oBalloon As Balloon
    Dim udAssistCurr As AssistInfo

    'Store current Assistant settings
    With udAssistCurr
        .bOn = Assistant.On
        .bVisible = Assistant.Visible
        .sFileName = Assistant.Filename
    End With

    'Customize the Assistant and display a custom balloon
    With Assistant
        .On = True
        .Visible = True
        .Filename = "C:\Program Files\Microsoft Office\Office10\dot.acs"
        .Animation = msoAnimationCheckingSomething

        'Create a new balloon
        Set oBalloon = .NewBalloon

        'Customize the new balloon
        With oBalloon
            .Heading = "Wrox Press Welcomes You"
            .Text = "Do you want to load the Wrox Press custom workbook?"
            .Button = msoButtonSetYesNo
            lReturnValue = .Show
```

```
        End With

        If lReturnValue = msoBalloonButtonYes Then   'They clicked Yes
            'Open the workbook and display a custom animation
            Workbooks.Open "C:\My Documents\Wrox\Wrox Examples.xls"
            .Animation = msoAnimationGetTechy
            .Animation = msoAnimationAppear
        Else
            'Reset the Assistant properties
            If udAssistCurr.bOn Then .Animation = msoAnimationGoodbye
            If Len(udAssistCurr.sFileName) Then _
                .Filename = udAssistCurr.sFileName
            .Visible = udAssistCurr.bVisible
            .On = udAssistCurr.bOn
        End If
    End With

End Sub
```

Balloon Object

The `Balloon` object is used to reference and create messages using the Office Assistant. In most cases, it's used to create a custom balloon containing text, labels, checkboxes, and/or command buttons by setting an object variable equal to the `NewBalloon` property. See `Assistant` object for an example.

Balloon Common Properties

The `Application`, `Creator`, and `Parent` properties are defined at the beginning of this appendix.

Balloon Properties

Name	Returns	Description
`Animation`	`Mso Animation Type`	Set/Get an animation action for the Office Assistant. When this property is applied to the `Balloon` object, the Assistant is animated only while the balloon is displayed.
`Balloon Type`	`MsoBalloon Type`	Set/Get the type of balloon the Office Assistant uses. When you create a `Balloon` object, this property is initially set to `msoBalloonTypeButtons`.
`Button`	`MsoButton SetType`	Set/Get the type and number of buttons displayed at the bottom of the Office Assistant balloon. When you create a `Balloon` object, this property is initially set to `msoButtonSetOK`.

Name	Returns	Description
Callback	String	Set/Get the name of the procedure to run from a modeless balloon.If you use the Callback property with a modeless balloon, you must write the procedure to receive three arguments: the Balloon object that called the procedure; a long integer that represents the msoBalloonButtonType value of the button the user clicked; and a long integer that uniquely identifies the balloon that called the procedure, as denoted in the balloon's Private property
Heading	String	Set/Get the heading text that appears in the Office Assistant balloon.
Icon	MsoIcon Type	Set/Get the type of icon that appears in the upper-left portion of the Office Assistant balloon.
Labels	Balloon Labels	Read Only. Returns a BalloonLabels collection that represents the button labels, number labels, and bullet labels contained in the specified Office Assistant balloon.
Mode	MsoMode Type	Set/Get the modal behavior of the Office Assistant balloon. When you create a Balloon object, this property is initially set to msoModeModal, which means the balloon must be dismissed before the user can continue working with the application.
Name	String	Read Only. Returns the name of the Balloon object.
Private	Long	Set/Get an integer that identifies the Office Assistant Balloon object that initiated the callback procedure. Used to identify the modeless Balloon object when running a callback procedure, which must include this property's value as one of its arguments.
Text		Set/Get the text displayed next to a checkbox or label in the Office Assistant balloon. Applies to the BalloonLabel and BalloonCheckBox objects.

Balloon Methods

Name	Returns	Parameters	Description
`Close`	`Balloon`		Closes the active modeless balloon. You should use this method only in `callback` procedures.
`SetAvoid Rectangle`	`Assistant`	`Left as long, Top as Long, Right as Long, Bottom as Long`	Prevents the Office Assistant balloon from being displayed in a specified area of the screen.
`Show`	`MsoBalloon ButtonType`		Displays the specified `Balloon` object.

BalloonCheckBox Collection

This collection comprises all of the checkboxes that appear in a `Balloon` object. It's used to iterate through all of the `BalloonCheckBox` objects to determine which ones were checked when the `Balloon` object was closed.

BalloonCheckBox Collection Common Properties

The `Application`, `Count`, `Creator`, and `Parent` properties are defined at the beginning of this appendix.

BalloonCheckBox Collection Properties

Name	Returns	Description
`Item`	`Balloon CheckBox`	Read Only. Returns a specific item in the collection with the `Index` value specified by the `Index` parameter.
`Name`	`String`	Read Only. Returns the name of the `BalloonCheckBox` object.

BalloonCheckBox Object

Represents one of the checkboxes in a collection of checkboxes that appear in a `Balloon` object.

BalloonCheckBox Common Properties

The `Application`, `Creator`, and `Parent` properties are defined at the beginning of this appendix.

BalloonCheckBox Properties

Name	Returns	Description
Checked	Boolean	Set/Get whether the specified checkbox in the Office Assistant balloon was checked.
Item	String	Read Only. Returns a text associated with the BalloonCheck Box object.
Name	String	Read Only. Returns the name of the BalloonCheckBox object.
Text	String	Set/Get the text displayed next to a checkbox in an Office Assistant balloon.

BalloonLabels Collection

This collection comprises all of the labels that appear in a Balloon object. It's used to iterate through all of the BalloonLabels objects to determine which ones were checked when the Balloon object was closed.

BalloonLabels Collection Common Properties

The Application, Count, Creator, and Parent properties are defined at the beginning of this appendix.

BalloonLabels Collection Properties

Name	Returns	Description
Item	Balloon CheckBox	Read Only. Returns a specific item in the collection with the Index value specified by the Index parameter.
Name	String	Read Only. Returns the name of the BalloonLabels object.

BalloonLabels Object

Represents one of the checkboxes in a collection of checkboxes that appear in a Balloon object.

BalloonLabels Common Properties

The Application, Creator, and Parent properties are defined at the beginning of this appendix.

BalloonLabels Properties

Name	Returns	Description
`Checked`	`Boolean`	Set/Get whether the specified checkbox in the Office Assistant balloon was checked.
`Item`	`String`	Read Only. Returns a text associated with the `BalloonLabel` object.
`Name`	`String`	Read Only. Returns the name of the `BalloonLabels` object.
`Text`	`String`	Set/Get the text displayed next to a label in an Office Assistant balloon.

Example: BalloonCheckBox Collection Object

The following routine uses both the `BalloonCheckBox` Collection and `BalloonCheckBox` to display a list of city choices in a custom `Balloon` object, then reports the results using the `DoAlert` method of the `Assistant` object:

```
Sub CustomBalloon()

   Dim lItem As Long
   Dim lReturnValue As Long
   Dim oBalloon As Balloon
   Dim oCheckBox As BalloonCheckbox
   Dim sMessage As String
   Dim vCities As Variant

   'Create an array of cities you want displayed in the balloon
   vCities = Array("New York", "London", "Paris")

   'Display a custom balloon
   With Assistant
      .On = True
      .Visible = True

      'Create a new balloon
      Set oBalloon = .NewBalloon

      'Customize the new balloon
      With oBalloon
         'Add heading text with both blue color and underlined
         .Heading = "{cf 252}{ul 1}Wrox Press{ul 0}{cf 0}"
         'Add a picture to the balloon,
         ' then two lines below add green instructional text
         .Text = _
"{WMF ""C:\Program Files\Microsoft Office\Clipart\Office\TRAVEL.WMF""}" & _
               vbCrLf & vbCrLf & _
               "{cf 2}Please check the cities you want to visit.{cf 0}"

         'Create a series of checkboxes with each checkbox's text
```

```
            ' equal to one of the cities in the array
            For lItem = 1 To 3
               'Arrays start at 0 by default
               .CheckBoxes(lItem).Text = vCities(lItem - 1)
            Next lItem

            'Show the balloon
            .Show

            ' Loop through the BalloonCheckBox collection and
            ' determine which ones were checked
            For Each oCheckBox In .CheckBoxes
               If oCheckBox.Checked Then _
                  sMessage = sMessage & oCheckBox.Text & vbCrLf
            Next oCheckBox

         End With

         'Report the results using the .DoAlert method
         If Len(sMessage) Then
            'They chose at least one of the cities
             sMessage = "Cities chosen:" & vbCrLf & vbCrLf & sMessage
         Else
            'Report that they chose none
            sMessage = "Guess you're a hermit!"
         End If

         .DoAlert "{cf 2}Wrox{cf 0}", "{cf 1}" & sMessage & "{cf 0}", _
                  msoAlertButtonOK, msoAlertIconInfo, _
                  msoAlertDefaultFirst, msoAlertCancelDefault, False

      End With

   End Sub
```

COMAddins Collection Object

The COMAddins collection is a list of all COMAddins objects for a Microsoft Office host application, in this case Excel. COMAddins are custom solutions for use with several Office applications like Excel, Access, Word, and Outlook developed in any language (VB, C++, or J++) that supports COM (Component Object Model) components.

COMAddins Collection Common Properties

The Application, Count, Creator, and Parent properties are defined at the beginning of this appendix.

COMAddins Collection Methods

Name	Returns	Parameters	Description
`Item`	`COMAddIn`	`Index as Variant`	Returns a member of the specified `COMAddins` collection.
`Update`			Updates the contents of the `COMAddins` collection from the list of add-ins stored in the Windows registry.

COMAddinObject

Represents a single COM add-in in the Microsoft Office host application and is also a member of `COMAddins` collection. `COMAddins` are custom solutions for use with several Office applications like Excel, Access, Word, and Outlook developed in any language (VB, C++, or J++) that supports COM (Component Object Model) components.

COMAddin Common Properties

The `Application`, `Creator`, and `Parent` properties are defined at the beginning of this appendix.

COMAddinProperties

Name	Returns	Description
`Connect`	`Boolean`	Set/Get the state of the connection for the specified `COMAddIn` object.
`Description`	`String`	Set/Get a descriptive String value for the specified `COMAddIn` object.
`Guid`	`String`	Read Only. Returns the globally unique class identifier (GUID) for the specified `COMAddIn` object.
`Object`	`Object`	Set/Get the object that is the basis for the specified `COMAddIn` object. Used primarily to communicate with other `COMAddins`.
`ProgId`	`String`	Read Only. Returns the programmatic identifier (`ProgID`) for the specified `COMAddIn` object.

Example: COMAddin Object

The following routine loops through the list of `COMAddins` and displays its relevant information in a table on Sheet1 of the workbook containing the code:

```
Sub COMAddinInfo()

    Dim lRow As Long
    Dim oCom As COMAddIn

    ' Set up the headings on Sheet1 of this workbook
```

```
    With Sheet1.Range("A1:D1")
        .Value = Array("Guid", "ProgId", "Creator", "Description")
        .Font.Bold = True
        .HorizontalAlignment = xlCenter
    End With

    ' Loop through the COMAddins collection and place
    ' its information in cells below the headings
    If Application.COMAddIns.Count Then
        For Each oCom In Application.COMAddIns
            With Sheet1.Range("A2")
                .Offset(lRow, 0).Value = oCom.GUID
                .Offset(lRow, 1).Value = oCom.progID
                .Offset(lRow, 2).Value = oCom.Creator
                .Offset(lRow, 3).Value = oCom.Description
                lRow = lRow + 1
            End With
        Next oCom
    End If

    ' Autofit the table
    Sheet1.Range("A1:D1").EntireColumn.AutoFit

End Sub
```

CommandBars Collection Object

The `Commandbars` collection contains a list of all `Commandbars` (known as Toolbars to most users) in the container application. See `Commandbars` object for more information. It contains properties related to the settings found in the Options tab of the Customize command.

CommandBars Collection Common Properties

The `Application`, `Count`, `Creator`, and `Parent` properties are defined at the beginning of this appendix.

CommandBars Collection Properties

Name	Returns	Description
`Action Control`	`CommandBar Control`	Read Only. Returns the `CommandBarControl` object whose `OnAction` property is set to the running procedure. If the running procedure was not initiated by a command bar control, this property returns `Nothing`.
`Active MenuBar`	`CommandBar`	Read Only. Returns a `CommandBar` object that represents the active menu bar in the container application. This almost always returns the application's Worksheet Menu Bar.

Table continued on following page

Name	Returns	Description
AdaptiveMenus	Boolean	Set/Get whether adaptive (abbreviated) menus are enabled.
DisableAskA QuestionDrop down	Boolean	Set/Get whether the Answer Wizard dropdown menu is enabled, which appears on the right size of the container application's Worksheet Menu Bar. When set to True, the dropdown disappears from the menu bar.
Disable Customize	Boolean	Set/Get whether toolbar customization is disabled. When True, the Customize command becomes disabled on the Tools menu and disappears from the Toolbar's shortcut (right-click) menu.
DisplayFonts	Boolean	Set/Get whether the font names in the Font box are displayed in their actual fonts. Recommend setting this to False on older computer systems with fewer resources.
DisplayKeysIn Tooltips	Boolean	Set/Get whether shortcut keys are displayed in the ToolTips for each command bar control. This property has no effect on Excel's commandbars.
DisplayTool tips	Boolean	Set/Get whether ScreenTips are displayed whenever the user positions the pointer over command bar controls.
Item	CommandBar	Read Only. Returns a CommandBar object from the CommandBars collection with the Index value specified by the Index parameter. Index can also be a string representing the name of the CommandBar.
LargeButtons	Boolean	Set/Get whether the toolbar buttons displayed are larger than normal size.
MenuAnimation Style	MsoMenu Animation	Set/Get the animation type of all CommandBarPopup controls (menus) in the CommandBars Collection.

CommandBars Collection Methods

Name	Returns	Parameters	Description
Add	CommandBar	[Name], [Position], [MenuBar], [Temporary]	Creates a new command bar and adds it to the collection of command bars.
FindControl	CommandBar Control	[Type], [Id], [Tag], [Visible]	Returns a single CommandBarControl object that fits a specified criterion based on the parameters.

Name	Returns	Parameters	Description
FindControls	CommandBar Controls	[Type], [Id], [Tag], [Visible]	Returns a series of CommandBarControl objects in a collection that fits the specified criteria based on the parameters.
ReleaseFocus			Releases the user interface focus from all command bars.

CommandBars Collection Events

Name	Parameters	Description
OnUpdate		The OnUpdate event is recognized by the CommandBar object and all command bar controls. Due to the large number of OnUpdate events that can occur during normal usage, Excel developers should exercise caution when using this event.

Example: CommandBars Collection Object

The following routine sets some options for all CommandBars, then displays a count of CommandBars for the current container application as well as which menu bar is active:

```
Sub CountCommandBars()

    'Customize some settings for all CommandBars
    With CommandBars
        ' Enable the recently used menus feature
        .AdaptiveMenus = True

        ' Remove the Help box that appears on the right side of the Menu
        ' Note: This does not affect the VBE's Help box
        .DisableAskAQuestionDropdown = True

        ' Don't allow any customization of any CommandBar
        .DisableCustomize = True

        ' Don't display the look of the Fonts in the Font Dropdown button
        ' Saves resources and speeds up computer
        .DisplayFonts = False

        ' Have the menus randomly animate when clicked
        .MenuAnimationStyle = msoMenuAnimationRandom

        ' Display tooltip text when hovering over CommandBar controls
        .DisplayTooltips = True

        ' Display shortcut keys in the ToolTips (Has no effect in Excel)
        .DisplayKeysInTooltips = True

        ' Have CommandBar buttons appear large for easier readability
```

```
        .LargeButtons = True

        ' Tell the user how many CommandBars there are and which menu is active.
        MsgBox "There are " & .Count & " CommandBars in " _
               & .Parent.Name & "." & vbCrLf _
               & "The active menu is the " _
               & .ActiveMenuBar.Name & "." _
               , vbInformation, "Wrox"

    End With

End Sub
```

CommandBar Object

This object holds the properties and methods for a specific `Commandbar` in the `CommandBars` collection. The properties and methods are similar to the `Commandbars` collection but only apply to the individual `Commandbar` referenced. Use `Commandbars(Index)` to return a reference to a specific `CommandBar`, like:

```
    Dim oBar As CommandBar
    Set oBar = CommandBars("Wrox")
```

CommandBar Common Properties

The `Application`, `Creator`, and `Parent` properties are defined at the beginning of this appendix.

CommandBar Properties

Name	Returns	Description
`Adaptive Menu`	`Boolean`	Read Only. Returns a `CommandBar` object that represents the active menu bar in the container application.
`BuiltIn`	`Boolean`	Read Only. Returns `True` if the specified command bar or command bar control is a built-in command bar or control of the container application. Returns `False` if it's a custom command bar or control, or if it's a built-in control whose `OnAction` property has been set.
`Context`	`String`	Set/Get a string that determines where a command bar will be saved. The string is defined and interpreted by the application.
`Controls`	`CommandBa rControls`	Read Only. Returns a `CommandBarControl` object that represents all the controls on a command bar.
`Enabled`	`Boolean`	Set/Get whether the `CommandBar` is enabled. Setting this property to `True` causes the name of the command bar to appear in the list of available command bars.

Name	Returns	Description
Height	Long	Set/Get the height of the CommandBar.
ID	Long	Read Only. Returns the ID for a built-in command bar.
Index	Long	Read Only. Returns the index number for a CommandBar in the CommandBars collection.
Left	Long	Set/Get the distance (in pixels) of the left edge of the command bar relative to the screen.
Name	String	Set/ Get the name of the CommandBar.
NameLocal	String	Set/Get the name of a built-in command bar as it's displayed in the language version of the container application, or the name of a custom command bar.
Position	MsoBarPosi tion	Set/Get the position of the command bar.
Protection	MsoBar Protection	Set/Get the way a command bar is protected from user customization.
RowIndex	Long	Set/Get the docking order of a command bar in relation to other command bars in the same docking area. Can be an integer greater than zero, or either of the following MsoBarRow constants: msoBarRowFirst or msoBarRowLast.
Top	Long	Set/Get the distance (in points) from the top of the command bar to the top edge of the screen.
Type	MsoBar Type	Read Only. Returns the type of command bar.
Visible	Boolean	Set/Get whether the command bar is visible. The Enabled property for a command bar must be set to True before the visible property is set to True.
Width	Long	Set/Get the width (in pixels) of the specified command bar.

CommandBar Methods

Name	Returns	Parameters	Description
Delete			Deletes the specified CommandBar from the CommandBars collection.
Find Control	CommandBar Control	[Type], [Id], [Tag], [Visible], [Recursive]	Returns a CommandBar that fits the specified criteria.

Table continued on following page

Name	Returns	Parameters	Description
Reset			Resets a built-in CommandBar to its default configuration.
ShowPopup		[x], [y]	Displays the CommandBar as a shortcut menu at specified coordinates or at the current pointer coordinates.

Example: CommandBar Object

The following routine customizes a custom toolbar (CommandBar) called "Wrox":

```
Sub CustomizeWroxBar()

    Dim oBar As CommandBar
    Dim oMenu As CommandBarPopup

    ' Determine if the CommandBar exists.
    On Error Resume Next
    Set oBar = Application.CommandBars("Wrox")

    On Error GoTo Error

    ' If CommandBar exists, go ahead and customize it
    If Not oBar Is Nothing Then
        With oBar
            ' Add a separator before the 2nd control on the bar
            .Controls(2).BeginGroup = True

            ' Move it to the right
            .Position = msoBarRight

            ' Don't allow it to be customized by the user
            .Protection = msoBarNoCustomize

            ' Make it visible
            .Visible = True

            ' Obtain a reference to the first control on the Wrox bar,
            ' which is a menu holding additional controls
            Set oMenu = CommandBars("Wrox").Controls(1)
            With oMenu
                ' Change the menu text
                .Caption = "Member Info"

                ' Change the text for the popup tooltip
                .TooltipText = "Insert Member Info"

                ' Add a separator before the 3rd control on the menu
                .Controls(3).BeginGroup = True
            End With

        End With
```

```
    Else
        ' A CommandBar named "Wrox" doesn't exist.
        ' Error out and display the custom error message
        Err.Raise Number:=glERROR_CUSTOM, _
                  Description:="Wrox commandbar not found."
    End If

    Exit Sub

Error:
    ' Display the error
    MsgBox Err.Number & vbLf & Err.Description

End Sub
```

CommandBarButton Object

A `CommandBarButton` is any button or menu item on any `CommandBar`. You access a specific `CommandBarButton` by referencing the `Commandbar` it's located in and by using `Controls(Index)`. `Index` can either be the `CommandBarButton's` number position on the menu or toolbar or its `Caption`.

For example, I can refer to the first control on a `Commandbar` called "`Wrox`" using:

```
CommandBars("Wrox").Controls(1)
```

or:

```
CommandBars("Wrox").Controls("Member Info")
```

CommandBarButton Common Properties

The `Application`, `Creator`, and `Parent` properties are defined at the beginning of this appendix.

CommandBarButton Properties

Name	Returns	Description
`BeginGroup`	`Boolean`	Set/Get whether the specified `CommandBarButton` appears at the beginning of a group of controls on the command bar.
`BuiltIn`	`Boolean`	Read Only. Returns `True` if the specified command bar or command bar control is a built-in command bar or control of the container application. Returns `False` if it's a custom command bar or control, or if it's a built-in control whose `OnAction` property has been set.
`BuiltInFace`	`Boolean`	Set/Get whether the face of the `CommandBarButton` control is its original built-in face. This property can only be set to `True`, which will reset the face to the built-in face.

Table continued on following page

Name	Returns	Description
Caption	String	Set/Get the caption text of the CommandBarButton.
Description Text	String	Set/Get the description for a CommandBarButton. The description is not displayed to the user, but it can be useful for documenting the behavior of the control for other developers.
Enabled	Boolean	Set/Get whether the CommandBarButton object is enabled.
FaceId	Long	Set/Get the Id number for the face of the CommandBarButton.
Height	Long	Set/Get the height of the CommandBarButton.
HelpContextId	Long	Set/Get the Help context Id number for the Help topic attached to the CommandBarButton.
HelpFile	String	Set/Get the file name for the Help topic for the CommandBarButton.
HyperlinkType	MsoCommand BarButton Hyperlink Type	Set/Get the type of hyperlink associated with the specified CommandBarButton.
Id	Long	Read Only. Returns the ID for a built-in CommandBarButton.
Index	Long	Read Only. Returns the index number for a CommandBarButton in the CommandBars collection.
IsPriority Dropped	Boolean	Read Only. Returns whether the CommandBarButton is currently dropped from the menu or toolbar based on usage statistics and layout space. (Note that this is not the same as the control's visibility, as set by the Visible property.) A CommandBarButton with Visible set to True, will not be immediately visible on a Personalized Menu or Toolbar if IsPriorityDropped is True.
Left	Long	Read Only. Returns the horizontal position of the CommandBarButton (in pixels) relative to the left edge of the screen. Returns the distance from the left side of the docking area.
Mask	IPictureDisp	Returns an IPictureDisp object representing the mask image of a CommandBarButton object. The mask image determines what parts of the button image are transparent.

Name	Returns	Description
OLEUsage	MsoControl OLEUsage	Set/Get the OLE client and OLE server roles in which a CommandBarButton will be used when two Microsoft Office applications are merged.
OnAction	String	Set/Get the name of a Visual Basic procedure that will run when the user clicks or changes the value of a CommandBarButton.
Parameter	String	Set/Get a string that an application can use to execute a command.
Picture	IPictureDisp	Set/Get an IPictureDisp object representing the image of the CommandBarButton.
Priority	Long	Set/Get the priority of a CommandBarButton.
ShortcutText	String	Set/Get the shortcut key text displayed next to the CommandBarButton control when the button appears on a menu, submenu, or shortcut menu.
State	MsoButton State	Set/Get the appearance of the CommandBarButton.
Style	MsoButton Style	Set/Get the way a CommandBarButton is displayed.
Tag	String	Set/Get information about the CommandBarButton, for example data to be used as an argument in procedures.
TooltipText	String	Set/Get the text displayed in the CommandBarButton's ScreenTip.
Visible	Boolean	Set/Get whether the CommandBarButton is visible.
Width	Long	Set/Get the width (in pixels) of the specified CommandBarButton.

CommandBarButton Methods

Name	Returns	Parameters	Description
Copy	CommandBar Control	[Bar], [Before]	Copies a CommandBarButton to an existing command bar.
CopyFace			Copies the face of a CommandBarButton to the Clipboard.

Table continued on following page

Name	Returns	Parameters	Description
Delete		[Temporary]	Deletes the specified CommandBarButton from its collection. Set Temporary to True to delete the control for the current session only – the application will display the control again in the next session.
Execute			Runs the procedure or built-in command assigned to the specified CommandBarButton. For custom controls, use the OnAction property to specify the procedure to be run.
Move	CommandBar Conrol	[Bar], [Before]	Moves the specified CommandBarButton to an existing command bar.
PasteFace			Pastes the contents of the Clipboard onto a CommandBarButton.
Reset			Resets a built-in CommandBarButton to its default configuration, or resets a built-in CommandBarButton to its original function and face.
SetFocus			Moves the keyboard focus to the specified CommandBarButton. If the control is disabled or isn't visible, this method will fail.

CommandBarButton Events

Name	Parameters	Description
Click	ByVal Ctrl As CommandBarButton, ByVal CancelDefault As Boolean	Triggered when a user clicks a CommandBarButton. Ctrl denotes the control that initiated the event. CancelDefault is False if the default behavior associated with the CommandBarButton control occurs, unless cancelled by another process or add-in.

Example: CommandBarButton Object

The first routine below creates a CommandBarButton on the custom Wrox CommandBar, assigns it a ToolTip text and a button image, then assigns it the SelectNumericValues routine:

```
Sub AddCommandBarButton()

    Const sSELECT_NUMERIC As String = "SelectNumericValues"
```

```
    Dim ctlButton As CommandBarButton

    ' Add the CommandBarButton
    Set ctlButton = CommandBars("Wrox").Controls.Add(msoControlButton)

    With ctlButton

        ' Assign it the same button image as the
        ' Select Visible Cells button in Excel
        .FaceId = 441

        ' Add ToolTip text
        .TooltipText = "Select Numeric Values"

        ' Store a custom name in its Tag property which can be
        ' used by the FindControl method to locate the control without
        ' knowing its position
        .Tag = sSELECT_NUMERIC

        ' Assign the CommandBarButton control the routine
        .OnAction = sSELECT_NUMERIC
    End With

End Sub

Sub SelectNumericValues()

    Dim rng As Range

    ' Suppress any errors (like no worksheet/workbook active)
    On Error Resume Next

    ' Make sure the current selection is a Range
    If TypeOf Selection Is Range Then

        If Selection.Cells.Count = 1 Then
            ' If they're only selecting one cell,
            ' grab all of the numeric constants for the worksheet
            ActiveSheet.UsedRange.SpecialCells( _
                xlCellTypeConstants, xlNumbers).Select
        Else
            ' Grab the selection's numeric constants
            Selection.SpecialCells(xlCellTypeConstants, xlNumbers).Select
        End If
    End If

End Sub
```

CommandBarComboBox Object

This object represents a dropdown list, custom edit box, or ComboBox (combination of the first two) control on any CommandBar. These types of controls only appear on the Command bar when it's either floating or docked at either the top or bottom of the Application window.

CommandBarComboBox Common Properties

The `Application`, `Creator`, and `Parent` properties are defined at the beginning of this Appendix.

CommandBarComboBox Properties

Name	Returns	Description
BeginGroup	Boolean	Set/Get whether the specified CommandBarComboBox appears at the beginning of a group of controls on the command bar.
BuiltIn	Boolean	Read Only. Returns True if the specified command bar or command bar control is a built-in command bar or control of the container application. Returns False if it's a custom command bar or control, or if it's a built-in control whose OnAction property has been set.
Caption	String	Set/Get the caption text of the CommandBarComboBox.
Description Text	String	Set/Get the description for a CommandBarComboBox. The description is not displayed to the user, but it can be useful for documenting the behavior of the control for other developers.
DropDown Lines	Long	Set/Get the number of lines in a CommandBarComboBox. The ComboBox control must be a custom control. Note that an error occurs if you attempt to set this property for a ComboBox control that's an edit box or a built-in ComboBox control.
DropDown Width	Long	Set/Get the width (in pixels) of the list for the specified CommandBarComboBox. Note that an error occurs if you attempt to set this property for a built-in control.
Enabled	Boolean	Set/Get whether the CommandBarComboBox object is enabled.
Height	Long	Set/Get the height of the CommandBarComboBox.
HelpContext Id	Long	Set/Get the Help context Id number for the Help topic attached to the CommandBarComboBox.
HelpFile	String	Set/Get the file name for the Help topic for the CommandBarComboBox.
Id	Long	Read Only. Returns the ID for a built-in CommandBarComboBox.
Index	Long	Read Only. Returns a Long representing the index number for the CommandBarComboBox object in the CommandBars collection.

Name	Returns	Description
IsPriority Dropped	Boolean	Read Only. Returns whether the CommandBarComboBox is currently dropped from the menu or toolbar based on usage statistics and layout space. (Note that this is not the same as the control's visibility, as set by the Visible property.) A CommandBarComboBox with Visible set to True, will not be immediately visible on a Personalized Menu or Toolbar if IsPriorityDropped is True.
Left	Long	Read Only. Returns the horizontal position of the CommandBarComboBox (in pixels) relative to the left edge of the screen. Returns the distance from the left side of the docking area.
List	String	Set/Get a specified item in the CommandBarComboBox. Read Only for built-in CommandBarComboBox controls. Required parameter: Index as Long.
ListCount	Long	Read Only. Returns the number of list items in a CommandBarComboBox.
ListHeader Count	Long	Set/Get the number of list items in a CommandBarComboBox that appears above the separator line. Read Only for built-in ComboBox controls.
ListIndex	Long	Set/Get the index number of the selected item in the list portion of the CommandBarComboBox. If nothing is selected in the list, this property returns zero.
OLEUsage	Mso Control OLEUsage	Set/Get the OLE client and OLE server roles in which a CommandBarComboBox will be used when two Microsoft Office applications are merged.
OnAction	String	Set/Get the name of a Visual Basic procedure that will run when the user clicks or changes the value of a CommandBarComboBox.
Parameter	String	Set/Get a string that an application can use to execute a command.
Priority	Long	Set/Get the priority of a CommandBarComboBox.
Style	MsoCombo Style	Set/Get the way a CommandBarComboBox control is displayed. Can be either of the following MsoComboStyle constants: msoComboLabel or msoComboNormal.
Tag	String	Set/Get information about the CommandBarComboBox, for example, data to be used as an argument in procedures.
Text	String	Set/Get the text in the display or edit portion of the CommandBarComboBox control.

Table continued on following page

Name	Returns	Description
TooltipText	String	Set/Get the text displayed in the CommandBarComboBox's ScreenTip.
Top	Long	Read Only. Returns the distance (in pixels) from the top edge of the CommandBarComboBox to the top edge of the screen.
Type	MsoControl Type	Read Only. Returns the type of CommandBarComboBox.
Visible	Boolean	Set/Get whether the CommandBarComboBox is visible.
Width	Long	Set/Get the width (in pixels) of the specified CommandBarComboBox.

CommandBarComboBox Methods

Name	Returns	Parameters	Description
AddItem		Text as String, [Index as Variant]	Adds a list item to the specified CommandBarComboBox. The combo box control must be a custom control and must be a dropdown list box or a combo box. This method will fail if it's applied to an edit box or a built-in combo box control.
Clear			Removes all list items from a CommandBarComboBox (dropdown list box or combo box) and clears the text box (edit box or combo box). This method will fail if it's applied to a built-in command bar control.
Copy	Object	[Bar], [Before]	Copies a CommandBarComboBox to an existing command bar.
Delete		[Temporary]	Deletes the specified CommandBarComboBox from its collection. Set Temporary to True to delete the control for the current session only – the application will display the control again in the next session.
Execute			Runs the procedure or built-in command assigned to the specified CommandBarComboBox. For custom controls, use the OnAction property to specify the procedure to be run.

Name	Returns	Parameters	Description
Move	CommandBar Control	[Bar], [Before]	Moves the specified CommandBarComboBox to an existing command bar.
RemoveItem		Index As Long	Removes a specified item from a CommandBarComboBox.
Reset			Resets a built-in CommandBarComboBox to its default configuration, or resets a built-in CommandBarComboBox to its original function and face.
SetFocus			Moves the keyboard focus to the specified CommandBarComboBox. If the control is disabled or isn't visible, this method will fail.

CommandBarComboBox Events

Name	Parameters	Description
Change	ByVal Ctrl As CommandBar ComboBox	Triggered when the end user changes the selection in a CommandBarComboBox.

Example: CommandBarComboBox Object

The following routine adds a CommandBarComboBox control to a custom Commandbar named Wrox. It populates the control's list using an e-mail address list on a worksheet in the workbook containing the code. We assign a MailTo routine to the combo box, which then sends the activeworkbook to the person chosen in the combo box:

```
Sub AddComboBox()

    Const sTAG_RUN As String = "MailTo"

    Dim ctlCombo As CommandBarComboBox
    Dim lItem As Long
    Dim vaItems As Variant
    Dim szttt As String

    ' Grab the list of items from a list on a worksheet in this workbook
    vaItems = wksListData.Range("Items")

    ' Add the CommandBarComboBox
    Set ctlCombo = CommandBars("Wrox").Controls.Add(msoControlComboBox)

    With ctlCombo
        ' Add the list of items from the worksheet to
```

```
        ' the CommandBarComboBox
        For lItem = LBound(vaItems) To UBound(vaItems)
            .AddItem vaItems(lItem, 1), lItem
        Next lItem

        ' Add ToolTip text
        .TooltipText = "Send Workbook To"

        ' Store a custom name in its Tag property which can be used by the
        ' FindControl method to locate control without knowing its position
        .Tag = sTAG_RUN

        ' Assign the CommandBarComboBox control the routine
        .OnAction = sTAG_RUN
    End With

End Sub

Sub MailTo()

    Dim ctlCombo As CommandBarComboBox
    Dim lChoice As Long

    ' Suppress errors in case there is no active workbook
    On Error Resume Next

    ' Access the control
    Set ctlCombo = CommandBars.ActionControl

    ' Which one on the list did they choose?
    lChoice = ctlCombo.ListIndex

    If lChoice Then
        ' They chose someone Send the active workbook using the name chosen
        ' from the combo box
        ActiveWorkbook.SendMail _
            Recipients:=ctlCombo.List(lChoice), _
            Subject:=ActiveWorkbook.Name, ReturnReceipt:=True
    End If

End Sub
```

CommandBarControls Collection Object

This collection holds all of the controls on a `CommandBar`. This collection's name can only be seen when declaring it as a variable type. You can access all the controls for a `Commandbar` directly using:

```
CommandBars(Index).Controls
```

Where `Index` can either be an number representing its position on the list of `Commandbars` or a String representing the `Name` of the `CommandBar`.

CommandBarControls Collection Common Properties

The `Application`, `Count`, `Creator`, and `Parent` properties are defined at the beginning of this appendix.

CommandBarControls Collection Properties

Name	Returns	Parameters	Description
`Item`	`Object`	`Index as Variant`	Returns a `CommandBarControl` object from the `CommandBarControls` collection.

CommandBarControls Collection Methods

Name	Returns	Parameters	Description
`Add`	`Command Bar Control`	`[Type], [Id], [Parameter], [Before], [Temporary]`	Creates a new `CommandBarControl` object and adds it to the collection of controls on the specified command bar.

Example: CommandBarControls Collection Object

The routine below lists all of the controls on a custom `CommandBar` named `Wrox` with some of its property information on a worksheet:

```
Sub ListAllControls()

    Dim ctl As CommandBarControl
    Dim ctlAll As CommandBarControls
    Dim lRow As Long

    ' Store all of the controls for the Wrox CommandBar
    Set ctlAll = CommandBars("Wrox").Controls

    ' Initialize the Row Counter
    lRow = 2

    ' On a worksheet in this workbook...
    With wksControls
        ' Clear the old list
        .UsedRange.ClearContents

        ' Place the headings on the worksheet
        .Cells(1, 1).Value = "CAPTION"
        .Cells(1, 2).Value = "BUILTIN"
        .Cells(1, 3).Value = "ID"
        .Cells(1, 4).Value = "TAG"
        .Cells(1, 5).Value = "TOOLTIP"
        .Cells(1, 6).Value = "TYPE"

        ' Loop through all of the controls placing information about each
```

```
        ' control in columns on the worksheet
        For Each ctl In ctlAll
            .Cells(lRow, 1).Value = ctl.Caption
            .Cells(lRow, 2).Value = ctl.BuiltIn
            .Cells(lRow, 3).Value = ctl.ID
            .Cells(lRow, 4).Value = ctl.Tag
            .Cells(lRow, 5).Value = ctl.TooltipText
            .Cells(lRow, 6).Value = ctl.Type
            lRow = lRow + 1 'Increment the row counter
        Next

        ' AutoFit the columns
        .UsedRange.EntireColumn.AutoFit

    End With

End Sub
```

CommandBarControl Object

Represents a generic control on a `CommandBar`. A control usually consists of a `CommandBarButton`, `CommandBarComboBox`, or a `CommandBarPopup`. When using one of these controls, you can work with them directly using their own object reference. Doing so will yield all of the properties and methods specific to that control.

Use the `Control` object when you are unsure which type of `Commandbar` object you are working with or when using controls other than the three mentioned above. Most of the methods and properties for the `CommandBarControl` Object can also be accessed via the `CommandBarButton`, `CommandBarComboBox`, and `CommandBarPopup` controls.

CommandBarControl Common Properties

The `Application`, `Creator`, and `Parent` properties are defined at the beginning of this Appendix.

CommandBarControl Properties

Name	Returns	Description
`BeginGroup`	`Boolean`	Set/Get whether the specified `CommandBarControl` appears at the beginning of a group of controls on the command bar.
`BuiltIn`	`Boolean`	Read Only. Returns `True` if the specified command bar or command bar control is a built-in command bar or control of the container application. Returns `False` if it's a custom command bar or control, or if it's a built-in control whose `OnAction` property has been set.
`Caption`	`String`	Set/Get the caption text of the `CommandBarControl`.
`Description Text`	`String`	Set/Get the description for a `CommandBarControl`. The description is not displayed to the user, but it can be useful for documenting the behavior of the control for other developers.

Name	Returns	Description
Enabled	Boolean	Set/Get whether the CommandBarControl object is enabled.
Height	Long	Set/Get the height of the CommandBarControl.
Help ContextId	Long	Set/Get the Help context Id number for the Help topic attached to the CommandBarControl.
HelpFile	String	Set/Get the file name for the Help topic for the CommandBarControl.
Id	Long	Read Only. Returns the Id for a built-in CommandBarControl.
Index	Long	Read Only. Returns a Long representing the index number for the CommandBarControl object in the CommandBarControls collection.
IsPriority Dropped	Boolean	Read Only. Returns whether the CommandBarControl is currently dropped from the menu or toolbar based on usage statistics and layout space. (Note that this is not the same as the control's visibility, as set by the Visible property.) A CommandBarControl with Visible set to True, will not be immediately visible on a Personalized Menu or Toolbar if IsPriorityDropped is True.
Left	Long	Read Only. Returns the horizontal position of the CommandBarControl (in pixels) relative to the left edge of the screen. Returns the distance from the left side of the docking area.
OLEUsage	MsoCont rolOLEU sage	Set/Get the OLE client and OLE server roles in which a CommandBarControl will be used when two Microsoft Office applications are merged.
OnAction	String	Set/Get the name of a Visual Basic procedure that will run when the user clicks or changes the value of a CommandBarControl.
Parameter	String	Set/Get a string that an application can use to execute a command.
Priority	Long	Set/Get the priority of a CommandBarControl.
Tag	String	Set/Get information about the CommandBarControl, for example, data to be used as an argument in procedures.
Tooltip Text	String	Set/Get the text displayed in the CommandBarControl's ScreenTip.

Name	Returns	Description
Top	Long	Read Only. Returns the distance (in pixels) from the top edge of the CommandBarControl to the top edge of the screen.
Type	MsoControl Type	Read Only. Returns the type of CommandBarControl.
Visible	Boolean	Set/Get whether the CommandBarControl is visible.
Width	Long	Set/Get the width (in pixels) of the specified CommandBarControl.

CommandBarControl Methods

Name	Returns	Parameters	Description
Copy	CommandBar Control	[Bar], [Before]	Copies a CommandBarControl to an existing command bar.
Delete		[Temporary]	Deletes the specified CommandBarControl from its collection. Set Temporary to True to delete the control for the current session only – the application will display the control again in the next session.
Execute			Runs the procedure or built-in command assigned to the specified CommandBarControl. For custom controls, use the OnAction property to specify the procedure to be run.
Move	CommandBar Control	[Bar], [Before]	Moves the specified CommandBarControl to an existing command bar.
Reset			Resets a built-in CommandBarControl to its default configuration, or resets a built-in CommandBarControl to its original function and face.
SetFocus			Moves the keyboard focus to the specified CommandBarControl. If the control is disabled or isn't visible, this method will fail.

Example: CommandBarControl Object

The routine below searches for a `CommandBarControl` using its `Tag` property, then depending on the type of control found, accesses a unique property or method for that control. The `State` and `Commandbar` properties as well as the `Clear` method used below will not appear on the Properties/Methods list of a generic `CommandBarControl` object, but still work assuming the control is the correct type:

```
Sub FindCommandBarControl()

    Dim ctl As CommandBarControl

    ' Find a control on the Wrox CommandBar based on its Tag property
    ' Recursive:=True means search through the controls in any
    ' submenus(CommandBarPopup)
    Set ctl = CommandBars("Wrox").FindControl(Tag:="MailTo", _
                                              Recursive:=True)

    If Not ctl Is Nothing Then  'We found the control
        ' Access a property or method unique to that control
        Select Case ctl.Type
            Case msoControlButton
                ' Make the button appear pressed
                ctl.State = msoButtonDown
            Case msoControlComboBox
                ' Clear the items in the combo box
                ctl.Clear
            Case msoControlButtonPopup
                ' Access the 2nd control on this menu/submenu
                ' using its unique CommandBar property
                ctl.CommandBar.Controls(2).Enabled = False
            Case Else
                MsgBox ctl.Type
        End Select
    End If

End Sub
```

CommandBarPopup Object

This object represents a menu or submenu on a `CommandBar`, which can contain other `Commandbar` controls within them. For example, the **File** and **Edit** menus on the Menu Bar are both considered `CommandBarPopup` controls. The **SendTo** submenu on the **File** menu and the **Fill** submenu on the **Edit** menu are also `CommandBarPopup` controls.

Because `CommandBarPopup` controls can have other controls added to them, they are in effect a separate `CommandBar`. For example, assuming the first control on a custom `Commandbar` named `Wrox` is a `CommandBarPopup` control, the following code can be used to reference and treat the control as if it were just another `CommandBar`:

```
Dim oBar as CommandBar
Set oBar = CommandBars("Wrox").Controls(1).CommandBar
```

To reference the same control as a `CommandBarPopup`:

```
Dim ctl As CommandBarPopup
Set ctl = CommandBars("Wrox").Controls(1)
```

CommandBarPopup Common Properties

The Application, Creator, and Parent properties are defined at the beginning of this appendix.

CommandBarPopup Properties

Name	Returns	Description
BeginGroup	Boolean	Set/Get whether the specified CommandBarPopup appears at the beginning of a group of controls on the command bar.
BuilIn	Boolean	Read Only. Returns True if the specified command bar or command bar control is a built-in command bar or control of the container application. Returns False if it's a custom command bar or control, or if it's a built-in control whose OnAction property has been set.
Caption	String	Set/Get the caption text of the CommandBarPopup.
CommandBar	CommandBar	Read Only. Returns a CommandBar object that represents the menu displayed by the specified pop-up control.
Controls	CommandBar Controls	Read Only. Returns a CommandBarControls object that represents all the controls on a command bar pop-up control.
Description Text	String	Set/Get the description for a CommandBarPopup. The description is not displayed to the user, but it can be useful for documenting the behavior of the control for other developers.
Enabled	Boolean	Set/Get whether the CommandBarPopup object is enabled.
Height	Long	Set/Get the height of the CommandBarPopup.
HelpContext Id	Long	Set/Get the Help context Id number for the Help topic attached to the CommandBarPopup.
HelpFile	String	Set/Get the file name for the Help topic for the CommandBarPopup.
Id	Long	Read Only. Returns the Id for a built-in CommandBarPopup.

Name	Returns	Description
Index	Long	Read Only. Returns a Long representing the index number for the CommandBarPopup object in the CommandBars collection.
IsPriority Dropped	Boolean	Read Only. Returns whether the CommandBarPopup is currently dropped from the menu or toolbar based on usage statistics and layout space. (Note that this is not the same as the control's visibility, as set by the Visible property.) A CommandBarPopup with Visible set to True, will not be immediately visible on a Personalized Menu or Toolbar if IsPriorityDropped is True.
Left	Long	Read Only. Returns the horizontal position of the CommandBarPopup (in pixels) relative to the left edge of the screen. Returns the distance from the left side of the docking area.
OLEMenu Group	MsoOLEMen uGroup	Set/Get the menu group that the specified CommandBarPopup belongs to when the menu groups of the OLE server are merged with the menu groups of an OLE client. Read Only for built-in controls.
OLEUsage	MsoContro lOLEUsage	Set/Get the OLE client and OLE server roles in which a CommandBarPopup will be used when two Microsoft Office applications are merged.
OnAction	String	Set/Get the name of a Visual Basic procedure that will run when the user clicks or changes the value of a CommandBarPopup.
Parameter	String	Set/Get a string that an application can use to execute a command.
Priority	Long	Set/Get the priority of a CommandBarPopup.
Tag	String	Set/Get information about the CommandBarPopup, e.g. data to be used as an argument in procedures.
TooltipText	String	Set/Get the text displayed in the CommandBarPopup's ScreenTip.
Top	Long	Read Only. Returns the distance (in pixels) from the top edge of the CommandBarPopup to the top edge of the screen.

Table continued on following page

Name	Returns	Description
Type	MsoControl Type	Read Only. Returns the type of CommandBarPopup.
Visible	Boolean	Set/Get whether the CommandBarPopup is visible.
Width	Long	Set/Get the width (in pixels) of the specified CommandBarPopup.

CommandBarPopup Methods

Name	Returns	Parameters	Description
Copy	CommandBar Control	[Bar], [Before]	Copies a CommandBarPopup to an existing command bar.
Delete		[Temporary]	Deletes the specified CommandBarPopup from its collection. Set Temporary to True to delete the control for the current session only – the application will display the control again in the next session.
Execute			Runs the procedure or built-in command assigned to the specified CommandBarPopup. For custom controls, use the OnAction property to specify the procedure to be run.
Move	CommandBar Control	[Bar], [Before]	Moves the specified CommandBarPopup to an existing command bar.
Reset			Resets a built-in CommandBarPopup to its default configuration, or resets a built-in CommandBarPopup to its original function and face.
SetFocus			Moves the keyboard focus to the specified CommandBarPopup. If the control is disabled or isn't visible, this method will fail.

Example: CommandBarPopup Object

The following routine adds a custom Popup menu with three CommandBarButtons to an existing Popup menu on the custom Wrox CommandBar. The information used to add the three CommandBarButtons is drawn from a table located on a worksheet inside the workbook containing the code:

```
Sub AddCommandBarPopup()

    Dim ctlButton As CommandBarButton
    Dim ctlPopup As CommandBarPopup
    Dim ctlMenuPopup As CommandBarPopup
    Dim rngControls As Range, rngControl As Range

    ' Find the Special popup (menu) on the Wrox CommandBar
    Set ctlMenuPopup = CommandBars("Wrox").FindControl( _
                           Type:=msoControlPopup, _
                           Tag:="PopupSpecial", _
                           Recursive:=True)

    ' Continue if found
    If Not ctlMenuPopup Is Nothing Then
        ' Add a popup control to the Special popup control found,
        ' placing it in the first position
        Set ctlPopup = ctlMenuPopup.Controls.Add( _
                           Type:=msoControlPopup, _
                           Before:=ctlMenuPopup.Controls(1).Index)

        ' Set the range to the table containing the
        ' information for the controls I want added
        With wksPopup
            Set rngControls = .Range(.Range("A2"), .Range("A2").End(xlDown))
        End With

        ' Set the caption to the new popup with the letter E underlined (&E)
        ctlPopup.Caption = "&Edit"

        ' Loop through the table adding the controls to the new popup
        For Each rngControl In rngControls
            ' If it's a built-in control,
            ' use the ID parameter of the Add method
            If Len(rngControl.Offset(0, 3).Value) Then
                Set ctlButton = ctlPopup.Controls.Add( _
                                     Type:=rngControl.Offset(0, 1).Value, _
                                     ID:=rngControl.Offset(0, 3).Value)
            Else
                Set ctlButton = ctlPopup.Controls.Add( _
                                     Type:=rngControl.Offset(0, 1).Value)
            End If

            ' Set the properties for the new control
            With ctlButton
                ' Add a separator if there's something in
                ' the BeginGroup column of the table
                .BeginGroup = (Len(rngControl.Offset(0, 2).Value) > 0)

                ' Set the control's picture face if there's something
                ' in the FaceID column of the table. If it's a built-in
                ' control, there should be nothing in this column.
                If Len(rngControl.Offset(0, 4).Value) Then _
                    .FaceId = rngControl.Offset(0, 4).Value

                ' If it's a custom control, assign it a macro
```

```
                If Len(rngControl.Offset(0, 5).Value) Then _
                    .OnAction = rngControl.Offset(0, 5).Text

                ' Set a Tag value for future searches of the control
                If Len(rngControl.Offset(0, 6).Value) Then _
                    .Tag = rngControl.Offset(0, 6).Text

                ' If there's ToolTip text, use it to set the
                ' control's Caption and ToolTip
                If Len(rngControl.Offset(0, 7).Value) Then
                    .Caption = rngControl.Offset(0, 7).Text
                    .TooltipText = rngControl.Offset(0, 7).Text
                End If
            End With
        Next rngControl

    Else
        'Special Popup not found, report it
        MsgBox "Could not locate Member Info control", vbCritical, "Wrox"
    End If

End Sub
```

Below is the table used to generate the three `CommandBarButtons` in the routine above.

Sub Menu	Type	Begin Group	ID	FaceID	On Action	Tag	ToolTip Text
&Select Numeric Values	1			441	Select Numeric Values	Select Numeric Values	Select Numeric Values
Paste Special &Values	1	TRUE	370				
Paste Special &Formulas	1		5836				

DocumentProperties Collection Object

Represents all of the Document Properties listed in the host application's **Summary** and **Custom** tabs of the **Properties** command (**File** menu) for a document. The document would be the `Workbook` object in Excel and the `Document` object in Word.

The `DocumentProperties` collection consists of two distinct types: Built-in properties and Custom properties. Built-in properties are native to the host application and are found on the **Summary** tab of the **Properties** command. Custom properties are those created by the user for a particular document and are found on the **Custom** tab of the **Properties** command.

It's important to note that when accessing `DocumentProperties` for a document, you must use either the `BuiltinDocumentProperties` property for properties native to the host application, or the `CustomDocumentProperties` property for properties created by the user. Strangely enough, `BuiltinDocumentProperties` and `CustomDocumentProperties` are not found in the Office object model but are part of the host application's model. In other words, you will not find these two properties within the `DocumentProperties` or `DocumentProperty` objects of the Microsoft Office XP model.

To access the built-in author document property, you use:

```
MsgBox ActiveWorkbook.BuiltinDocumentProperties("Author").Value
```

or:

```
MsgBox ActiveWorkbook.BuiltinDocumentProperties(3).Value
```

You need to know that the `Index` value for `Author` is `3`. See the `DocumentProperties` Collection example below for more details.

To access a custom property in a document, use:

```
MsgBox ActiveWorkbook.CustomDocumentProperties("BillingNumber").Value
```

or:

```
MsgBox ActiveWorkbook.CustomDocumentProperties(1).Value
```

The assumption here is that `BillingNumber` is the first custom property.

The Custom Tab of the Properties command in Excel contains numerous suggestions for custom properties, but only those suggested custom properties that are assigned a value will be part of the `CustomDocumentProperties` list.

Several built-in properties are specific to certain host applications. For example, the `Number of Paragraphs` property is native to Microsoft Word and any attempt to reference it from another application will result in a run-time error.

DocumentProperties Collection Common Properties

The `Application`, `Count`, `Creator`, and `Parent` properties are defined at the beginning of this appendix.

DocumentProperties Collection Properties

Name	Returns	Parameters	Description
`Item`	`Document Property`	`Index as Variant`	`Index` can also be a string representing the `DocumentProperty's` name.

DocumentProperties Collection Methods

Name	Returns	Parameters	Description
Add	Document Property	Name As String, LinkToContent As Boolean, [Type], [Value], [LinkSource]	Creates a new custom document property. You can only add a new document property to the custom DocumentProperties collection.

Example: DocumentProperties Collection Object

The following routine creates a list of all document properties. It includes the property's Name, whether it's a built-in or custom property, its Type, Index and Value. The Index was obtained using a counter variable. The Index specifies its position in the list and can be used to access the property without knowing its name. For example, the code above used the number 3 to access the Author built-in property:

```
Sub ListDocumentProperties()

    Dim oProperty As DocumentProperty
    Dim lIndex As Long, lRow As Long

    ' Disable the screen
    Application.ScreenUpdating = False

    ' Start the counters
    lIndex = 1
    lRow = 2

    ' Access a worksheet within this workbook. Note that a worksheet can be
    ' accessed directly using its Property Name (in the Properties box of
    ' the VBE) so long as the code is in the same workbook as the worksheet
    With wksBuiltInProperties

        ' Clear the worksheet except for the titles in the first row
        .UsedRange.Offset(1, 0).ClearContents

        ' Supress errors when a value from a
        ' property cannot be accessed from Excel
        On Error Resume Next

        ' Loop through the Built in properties
        For Each oProperty In .Parent.BuiltinDocumentProperties
            .Cells(lRow, 1) = oProperty.Name
            .Cells(lRow, 2) = "Built in"
            .Cells(lRow, 3) = oProperty.Type
            .Cells(lRow, 4) = lIndex
            .Cells(lRow, 5) = oProperty.Value
            lIndex = lIndex + 1
            lRow = lRow + 1
        Next oProperty

        ' Reset the Index counter and loop through the custom properties
        lIndex = 1
```

```
        For Each oProperty In .Parent.CustomDocumentProperties
            .Cells(lRow, 1) = oProperty.Name
            .Cells(lRow, 2) = "Custom"
            .Cells(lRow, 3) = oProperty.Type
            .Cells(lRow, 4) = lIndex
            .Cells(lRow, 5) = oProperty.Value
            lIndex = lIndex + 1
            lRow = lRow + 1
        Next oProperty

        ' Select the 1st cell in the worksheet
        .Cells(1, 1).Select

    End With

End Sub
```

DocumentProperty Object

Represents a single property in the `DocumentProperties` collection. The property can either be a built-in or custom property. Use `BuiltinDocumentProperties` or `CustomDocumentProperties` to reference a single `DocumentProperty`.

DocumentProperty Common Properties

The `Application`, `Creator`, and `Parent` properties are defined at the beginning of this appendix.

DocumentProperty Properties

Name	Returns	Description
`LinkSource`	`String`	Set/Get the source of a linked custom document property.
`LinkTo Content`	`Boolean`	Returns whether the custom document property is linked to the content of the container document.
`Name`	`String`	Set/Get the name of the DocumentProperty.
`Type`	`MsoDoc Properties`	Set/Get the document property type. Read Only for built-in document properties; Read Write for custom document properties.
`Value`	`Variant`	Set/Get the value of a document property. If the container application doesn't define a value for one of the built-in document properties, reading the `Value` property for that document property causes an error.

DocumentProperty Methods

Name	Returns	Parameters	Description
Delete	Result		Removes a custom document property.

Example: DocumentProperty Object

The following routine adds a custom document property called `BillingNumber` and sets the `Value` property based on a user prompt:

```
Sub AddDocumentProperty()

    Dim oProperty As DocumentProperty
    Dim vAnswer As Variant
    Dim wkb As Workbook

    ' Check for an active workbook
    On Error Resume Next
        Set wkb = ActiveWorkbook
    On Error GoTo 0

    ' If a workbook is active...
    If Not wkb Is Nothing Then

        ' Prompt the user to select a cell or type a number
        ' If user selects a range, only the first cell will be used
        vAnswer = Application.InputBox("Billing Number?", _
                                       "Billing Number", , , , , , 1)

        ' If they didn't cancel...
        If vAnswer <> "False" Then

            ' Check to see if the custom property already exists
            On Error Resume Next
                Set oProperty = _
                    ActiveWorkbook.CustomDocumentProperties("BillingNumber")
            On Error GoTo 0

            ' If it doesn't exist, create it
            If oProperty Is Nothing Then
               Set oProperty = ActiveWorkbook.CustomDocumentProperties.Add _
                                    (Name:="BillingNumber", _
                                     LinkToContent:=False, _
                                     Type:=msoPropertyTypeNumber, Value:=1)
            End If

            ' Set the value based on the InputBox return value
            oProperty.Value = vAnswer

        End If

    Else
```

```
        ' No Book is active. Tell them.
        MsgBox "No Workbook active.", vbCritical, "Add Property"
    End If

End Sub
```

FileDialog Object

This object is now a more structured and more flexible alternative to both the `GetSaveAsFilename` and `GetOpenFilename` methods. It includes the ability to customize the **action** button (ex: the **Save** button in **Save As dialog**), choose from a list of different dialog types (above and beyond the **Open & Save As**), adds more flexibility when using custom file types/filters (ex: "*.bil"), and allows you to set a default view that the user will see when the dialog appears (ex: Detail or Large Icon views).

Note that some of the properties and methods for this object depend on the `MsoFileDialogType` chosen in the `FileDialogType` property. For example, the following will encounter an error when attempting to use the `Add` method of the Filters property with the `msoFileDialogSaveAs` Dialog type:

```
Application.FileDialog(msoFileDialogSaveAs).Filters.Add _
    "Billing Files", "*.bil", 1
```

FileDialog Common Properties

The `Application`, `Creator`, and `Parent` properties are defined at the beginning of this appendix.

FileDialog Properties

Name	Returns	Description
`AllowMulti Select`	`Boolean`	Set/Get whether the user is allowed to select multiple files from a file dialog box.
`ButtonName`	`String`	Set/Get the text that is displayed on the action button of a file dialog box. By default, this property is set to the standard text for the type of file dialog box.
`DialogType`	`MsoFile DialogType`	Read Only. Returns an `MsoFileDialogType` constant representing the type of file dialog box that the `FileDialog` object is set to display.
`FilterIndex`	`Long`	Set/Get the default file filter of a file dialog box. The default filter determines which types of files are displayed when the file dialog box is first opened.
`Filters`	`FileDialog Filters`	Returns a `FileDialogFilters` collection.
`InitialFile Name`	`String`	Set/Get the path and/or file name that is initially displayed in a file dialog box.

Table continued on following page

Name	Returns	Description
InitialView	MsoFile DialogView	Set/Get an MsoFileDialogView constant representing the initial presentation of files and folders in a file dialog box.
Item	String	Read Only. Returns the text associated with the FileDialog object.
SelectedItems	FileDialogSe lectedItems	Returns a FileDialogSelectedItems collection. This collection contains a list of the paths of the files that a user selected from a file dialog box displayed using the Show method of the FileDialog object.
Title	String	Set/Get the title of a file dialog box displayed using the FileDialog object.

FileDialog Methods

Name	Returns	Parameters	Description
Execute			For FileDialog objects of type msoFileDialogOpen or msoFileDialogSaveAs, carries out a user's action right after the Show method is invoked.
Show	Long		Displays a file dialog box. Returns a Long indicating whether the user pressed the action button (-1) or the cancel button (0). When the Show method is called, no more code will execute until the user dismisses the file dialog box. With Open and SaveAs dialog boxes, use the Execute method right after the Show method to carry out the user's action.

Example: FileDialog Object

The following routine prompts the user to save the active workbook using the FileDialog object. Once the user exits the Save As dialog, the routine converts the billing workbook filled with formulas and range names to values with only no range names:

```
Sub ConvertBillingStatement()

    ' Use this constant to insure that the company's keyword used for
    ' Billing remains consistent throughout this procedure
    Const sNAME_BILLING As String = "Billing"

    Dim nm As Excel.Name
```

```
Dim sPath As String
Dim wks As Excel.Worksheet
Dim wkb As Excel.Workbook

' Check whether this is a billing workbook
' by checking for the existence of a hidden name
On Error Resume Next
    Set wkb = ActiveWorkbook
On Error GoTo 0

' If a workbook is active...
If Not wkb Is Nothing Then
    On Error Resume Next
        Set nm = wkb.Names(sNAME_BILLING)

    ' If this is a billing file...
    If Not nm Is Nothing Then

        ' Store the current path
        sPath = CurDir

        ' Set the properties of the File Save As dialog
        With Application.FileDialog(msoFileDialogSaveAs)

            ' Change the default dialog title
            .Title = "Save " & sNAME_BILLING & " Number"

            ' Change the name of the Save button in the Dialog
            .ButtonName = "Save " & sNAME_BILLING

            ' Switch to the Billing folder
            .InitialFileName = "C:\" & sNAME_BILLING & "\"

            ' Display the Details view in the dialog
            .InitialView = msoFileDialogViewDetails

            ' Show the dialog -1 means they didn't cancel
            If .Show = -1 Then
                ' Convert all formulas to values
                For Each wks In wkb.Worksheets
                    wks.UsedRange.Copy
                    wks.UsedRange.PasteSpecial xlPasteValues
                Next wks

                ' Remove all range names except the one that
                ' identifies it as a Billing workbook
                For Each nm In wkb.Names
                    If nm.Name <> sNAME_BILLING Then nm.Delete
                Next nm

                ' Save the file
                .Execute

            End If

            ' Return the current path to its original state
            ChDir sPath
```

```
            End With
        Else
            ' The Billing range name is not there,
            ' so this cannot be a Billing file
            MsgBox wkb.Name & " is not a " & sNAME_BILLING & " workbook", _
                   vbInformation, "Convert " & sNAME_BILLING & " Statement"
        End If
    End If

End Sub
```

FileDialogFilters Collection Object

Represents all the filters shown in the new `FileDialog` object, including custom filters created using the `Add` method of the `Filters` property for the `FileDialog` object.

Note that filters created using the `Add` method of the `Filters` property do not appear in the standard Open and Save As dialogs.

FileDialogFilters Collection Common Properties

The `Application`, `Count`, `Creator`, and `Parent` properties are defined at the beginning of this appendix.

FileDialogFilters Collection Methods

Name	Returns	Parameters	Description
`Add`	`File Dialog Filter`	`Description As String, Extensions As String, [Position]`	Adds a new file filter to the list of filters in the Files of type dropdown list box in the File dialog box. Returns a `FileDialogFilter` object that represents the newly added file filter.
`Clear`			Removes all the file filters in the `FileDialogFilters` collection.
`Delete`		`[filter]`	Removes a specified file filter from the `FileDialogFilters` collection.
`Item`	`FileDialog Filter`	`[Index As Long]`	Returns the specified `FileDialogFilter` object from a `FileDialogFilters` collection.

Example: FileDialogFilters Collection Object

The following routine uses the `FileDialog` object to display an Open dialog. The routine uses the `Add` method of the `Filters` property to add a custom Billing file type to the Files of Type drop down in the Open dialog. Note that the custom filter is persistent, which is why this routine removes the filter once the dialog is dismissed:

```
Sub UsingFileDialogOpen()

    Const lFILTER_POSITION As Long = 1

    Dim lCount As Long
    Dim sChosen As String

    ' Set the properties of the File Open dialog
    With Application.FileDialog(msoFileDialogOpen)
        ' Change the default dialog title
        .Title = "Open Billing Files"

        ' Allow the user to select multiple files
        .AllowMultiSelect = True

        ' Set the filter description and filter position
        .Filters.Add "Billing Files", "*.bil", lFILTER_POSITION

        ' Switch to the custom filter before showing the dialog
        .FilterIndex = lFILTER_POSITION

        ' Show the dialog -1 means they didn't cancel
        If .Show = -1 Then
            ' Initialize the message string
            sChosen = "The following files were chosen:" & vbCrLf

            ' Dump filename (and path) of each file chosen in the
            ' message string
            For lCount = 1 To .SelectedItems.Count
                sChosen = sChosen & vbCrLf & .SelectedItems(lCount)
            Next lCount

            ' Display the list of each file chosen
            MsgBox sChosen, vbInformation

        End If

        ' Remove the filter when done
        .Filters.Delete lFILTER_POSITION

    End With
End Sub
```

FileDialogFilter Object

Represents a single filter in the `FileDialogFilter` collection. To reference an individual filter, use:

```
Application.FileDialog(msoFileDialogOpen).Filters(lIndex)
```

FileDialogFilter Common Properties

The `Application`, `Creator`, and `Parent` properties are defined at the beginning of this appendix.

FileDialogFilter Properties

Name	Returns	Description
`Description`	`String`	Read Only. Returns the description displayed in the file dialog box of each `Filter` object as a String value.
`Extensions`	`String`	Read Only. Returns a String value containing the extensions that determine which files are displayed in a file dialog box for each `Filter` object.

Example: FileDialogFilter Object

The following routine removes all custom billing file types from the list of filters in the `msoFileDialogSaveAs` type `FileDialog`:

```
Sub RemoveCustomBillingFilters()

    Dim lIndex As Long

    With Application.FileDialog(msoFileDialogOpen)
        ' Loop through the filter list backwards. When looping from top to
        ' bottom, deleted filters cause the filter below it (on the list)
        ' to move up one, causing the loop to skip over all filters
        ' below the deleted ones.
        For lIndex = .Filters.Count To 1 Step -1
            ' If the extension has a "bi" in it, it's our
            ' custom filter. Remove it.
            If .Filters(lIndex).Extensions Like "*.bi*" Then
                .Filters.Delete lIndex
            End If
        Next lIndex
    End With

End Sub
```

FileDialogSelectedItems Collection Object

This collection returns all of the chosen items in a `FileDialog`. It consists of more than one item when the `FileDialog`'s `AllowMultiSelect` property is set to `True`, unless the `msoFileDialogSaveAs` `FileDialog` is used (where only one item is always returned). The `FileDialogSelectedItems` collection is a collection of strings.

FileDialogSelectedItems Collection Common Properties

The `Application`, `Count`, `Creator`, and `Parent` properties are defined at the beginning of this appendix.

FileDialogSelectedItems Collection Methods

Name	Returns	Parameters	Description
`Item`	`String`	`Index as long`	Returns the path of one of the files that the user selected from a file dialog box that was displayed using the `Show` method of the `FileDialog` object.

Example: FileDialogSelectedItems Collection Object

The following routine is an altered version of the `ConvertBillingStatement` procedure above. This version uses the `SelectedItems` collection to return the path and filename from the `msoFileDialogSaveAs FileDialog`. It then checks the return value to insure that the phrase "Wrox Billing" appears and re-displays the `FileDialog` if it does not:

```
Sub ConvertBillingStatement2()

   ' Use this constant to insure that the company's keyword used for
   ' Billing remains consistent throughout this procedure
   Const sNAME_BILLING As String = "Billing"

   Dim bBillName As Boolean
   Dim nm As Excel.Name
   Dim sPath As String
   Dim wks As Excel.Worksheet
   Dim wkb As Excel.Workbook

   ' Check whether this is a billing workbook
   ' by checking for the existence of a hidden name
   On Error Resume Next
      Set wkb = ActiveWorkbook
   On Error GoTo 0

   ' If a workbook is active...
   If Not wkb Is Nothing Then
      On Error Resume Next
         Set nm = wkb.Names(sNAME_BILLING)

      ' If this is a billing file...
      If Not nm Is Nothing Then

         ' Store the current path
         sPath = CurDir

         ' Set the properties of the File Save As dialog
         With Application.FileDialog(msoFileDialogSaveAs)

            ' Change the default dialog title
            .Title = "Save " & sNAME_BILLING & " Number"

            ' Change the name of the Save button in the Dialog
            .ButtonName = "Save " & sNAME_BILLING
```

```
        ' Switch to the Billing folder
        .InitialFileName = "C:\" & sNAME_BILLING & "\"
        .AllowMultiSelect = True

        ' Display the Details view in the dialog
        .InitialView = msoFileDialogViewDetails

        ' Loop until the path or filename has the phrase
        ' Wrox Billing in it (or they cancel)
        Do
           ' Assume the path or filename does have the phrase "Wrox
           ' Billing" in it by setting the BillName check to True
           bBillName = True

           ' Show the dialog -1 means they didn't cancel
           If .Show = -1 Then

              ' Set the boolean check by searching for the
              ' phrase Wrox Billing in the path or filename
              bBillName = (InStr(1, .SelectedItems(1), _
                           "Wrox " & sNAME_BILLING, vbTextCompare) > 0)

              ' If the phrase is there...
              If bBillName Then
                 ' Convert all formulas to values
                 For Each wks In wkb.Worksheets
                    wks.UsedRange.Copy
                    wks.UsedRange.PasteSpecial xlPasteValues
                 Next wks

                 ' Remove all range names except the one that
                 ' identifies it as a Billing workbook
                 For Each nm In wkb.Names
                     If nm.Name <> sNAME_BILLING Then nm.Delete
                 Next nm

                 ' Save the file
                 .Execute

              Else
                 ' Warn them that they need the phrase "Wrox Billing"
                 ' in the path or filename
                MsgBox "The filename must contain the phrase " & _
                       "'Wrox Billing'", vbExclamation, _
                       "Convert Workbook"
              End If
           End If
        Loop Until bBillName

        ' Return the current path to its original state
        ChDir sPath
```

```
            End With
        Else
            ' Billing range name is not there, so this is not a Billing file.
            MsgBox wkb.Name & " is not a " & sNAME_BILLING & " workbook", _
                    vbInformation, "Convert " & sNAME_BILLING & " Statement"
        End If
    End If

End Sub
```

FileSearch Object

The FileSearch object programmatically mimicks the search feature in the host applications **Open dialog (Tools | Search** command). This feature allows you to search for any file type in any group of folders, based on almost any criteria. Note that search settings are persistent and should be reset using the NewSearch method each time the FileSearch object is used. Note also that the NewSearch method does not reset the LookIn property.

FileSearch Common Properties

The Application, Creator, and Parent properties are defined at the beginning of this appendix.

FileSearch Properties

Name	Returns	Description
FileName	String	Set/Get the name of the file to look for during a file search. The name of the file may include the * (asterisk) or ? (question mark) wildcards.
FileType	MsoFileType	Set/Get the type of file to look for during a file search.
FileTypes	FileTypes	Returns a FileTypes collection.
FoundFiles	FoundFiles	Read Only. Returns a FoundFiles object that contains the names of all the files found during a search.
Last Modified	MsoLastModi fied	Set/Get a constant that represents the amount of time since the specified file was last modified and saved.
LookIn	String	Set/Get the folder to be searched during the specified file search.

Table continued on following page

Name	Returns	Description
MatchAll WordForms	Boolean	Set/Get whether the file search is expanded to include all forms of the specified word contained in the body of the file, or in the file's properties.
MatchText Exactly	Boolean	Set/Get whether the specified file search will find only files whose body text or file properties contain the exact word or phrase that you've specified.
PropertyTests	Proper Tests	Read Only. Returns the PropertyTests collection that represents all the search criteria for a file search.
SearchFolders	Search Folders	Returns a SearchFolders collection.
SearchScopes	Search Scopes	Returns a SearchScopes collection.
SearchSubFolders	Boolean	Set/Get whether the search includes all the subfolders in the folder specified by the LookIn property.
TextOrProperty	String	Set/Get the word or phrase to be searched for, in either the body of a file or the file's properties, during the file search. The word or phrase can include the * (asterisk) or ? (question mark) wildcard character.

FileSearch Methods

Name	Returns	Parameters	Description
Execute	Long	[SortBy], [SortOrder], [Always Accurate]	Begins the search for the specified file(s). Returns zero if no files are found, or a positive number if one or more files are found.
NewSearch			Resets all the search criteria settings to their default settings.
RefreshScopes			Refreshes the list of currently available ScopeFolder objects.

Example: FileSearch Object

The following routine searches for any files containing the word "billing" in a billing folder that were modified in the last seven days and displays the results in a message box:

```
Sub SearchForRecentBilling()

    Dim lCount As Long
    Dim sFiles As String
```

```
    With Application.FileSearch

        ' Clear the previous search settings
        .NewSearch

        ' Search for any xls file with the word Billing
        .Filename = "*Billing*.xls"

        ' Search for Billing files this week
        .LastModified = msoLastModifiedThisWeek

        ' Look in the billing folder including subfolders
        .LookIn = "C:\Billing"
        .SearchSubFolders = True

        ' Perform the search and return the results
        If .Execute > 0 Then
            sFiles = "Files Found:" & vbCrLf
            For lCount = 1 To .FoundFiles.Count
                sFiles = sFiles & vbCrLf & .FoundFiles(lCount)
            Next lCount
            MsgBox sFiles, vbInformation, "Billing Files"
        End If

    End With

End Sub
```

FileTypes Collection Object

Represents a set of file types you want to search for when using the `FileSearch` object. The file types in this collection persist from one search to another, so when searching for new or different file types, it's important to remove all of the file types from the `FileTypes` collection by using either the `Remove` method of this `collection` object or by setting a new file type using the `FileType` property.

FileTypes Collection Common Properties

The `Application`, `Count`, and `Creator` properties are defined at the beginning of this appendix.

FileTypes Collection Properties

Name	Returns	Parameters	Description
`Item`	`MsoFile Type`	`Index as Long`	Read Only. Returns a value that indicates which file type will be searched for by the `Execute` method of the `FileSearch` object.

FileTypes Collection Methods

Name	Returns	Parameters	Description
Add		FileType As MsoFileType	Adds a new file type to a file search.
Remove		Index As Long	Removes the specified file type from the FileTypes collection.

Example: FileTypes Collection Object

The following function resets the FileSearch object by calling the NewSearch method, resetting the Lookin property to a default path of C:\ and by removing each FileType from the FileTypes collection using a backwards loop:

```
Sub NewSearch()

    ' Reset the FileSearch Object
    ResetFileSearch

    With Application.FileSearch
        ' Place code here for your new search
    End With

End Sub

Function ResetFileSearch()

    Dim lCount As Long
    Dim oFileTypes As FileTypes
    Dim oPropertyTests As PropertyTests

    With Application.FileSearch

        ' Clear the previous search settings
        .NewSearch

        ' Reset the Lookin property by setting it to a default
        ' The NewSearch method does not reset this property
        .LookIn = "C:\"

        ' Remove all FileType items from the FileTypes Collection
        Set oFileTypes = .FileTypes

        ' When removing FileTypes, PropertyTests, and SearchFolders the
        ' index of the Type below the one you remove changes (decreases by
        ' one), so you need to step backwards in the collection to prevent
        ' the Subscript Out of Range error
        For lCount = oFileTypes.Count To 1 Step -1
            oFileTypes.Remove lCount
        Next lCount

        ' Remove the Property Tests
        Set oPropertyTests = .PropertyTests
```

```
        For lCount = oPropertyTests.Count To 1 Step -1
            oPropertyTests.Remove lCount
        Next lCount

        ' Reset the SearchFolders collection
        For lCount = .SearchFolders.Count To 1 Step -1
            .SearchFolders.Remove lCount
        Next lCount

    End With

End Function
```

FoundFiles Object

The `FoundFiles` object contains the list of files returned from a file search.

FoundFiles Common Properties

The `Application`, `Creator`, and `Parent` properties are defined at the beginning of this appendix.

FileTypes Collection Properties

Name	Returns	Parameters	Description
`Item`	`String`	`Index as Long`	Read Only. Returns the file name from the list of file names represented by the `FoundFiles` object.

HTMLProject Object

Represents the HTML code used to display the Office document as an HTML document. You can use Microsoft's Script Editor to access the HTML version of the Office document.

Learning how to manipulate objects and settings using Microsoft's Script Editor and programming using HTML is beyond the scope of this book. However, a brief description is warranted before you using the Office model's HTML objects.

The Script Editor is similar the Visual Basic Editor (VBE). It contains a Project Explorer, a Properties window, a Toolbox for adding controls, and a Code window for creating HTML code, similar to the VBE. Changing settings and manipulating the document via the Script Editor changes the office document itself, similar to using the VBE to change settings and using VBA code to manipulate the document. In Excel, the data is displayed in a worksheet format, with WYSIWYG (What You See Is What You Get) formatting displayed. The Script Editor gives you access to all of the formatting, settings, data, and HTML code in one window. You don't see the formatting, but can see the HTML code that comprises the formatting.

You use the Script Editor to customize the HTML version of the Office Document similar to using the VBE to customize – a Workbook in the VBE - by adding/editing HTML code, changing object settings, adding events, etc. Editing the settings and HTML code in the Script Editor will in most cases change the Office document itself.

An HTML Project holds objects similar to that of a VBProject for a Workbook. For example, each VBProject for a Workbook contains Sheet objects for each Sheet in the Workbook. The HTML Project for the same Workbook also contains an object for each Sheet in the Workbook. The Script Editor allows you to edit the properties of the HTML objects using a Properties window, just like the Properties window in the VBE, though most of the properties between Editors don't match. For example, in the Script Editor, you can double-click one of the Sheet objects and in the Properties window change the Background setting so that it points to an image on my hard drive. When you save the project from within the Script Editor, you can see the new background appear when viewing that sheet in the Excel window. There is no such Property for the Sheet object in the VBE, but in Excel this feature can be accessed using the Format | Sheet | Background command or by using VBA code to programmatically change the background.

The HTML objects in this Office model allow access to and manipulation of the HTML objects of an Office document, similar to the VBE object model allowing access to the VBProject and its objects.

HTMLProject Common Properties

The Application, Creator, and Parent properties are defined at the beginning of this appendix.

HTMLProject Properties

Name	Returns	Description
HTMLProject Items	HTMLProject Items	Read Only. Returns the HTMLProjectItems collection that is included in the specified HTML project.
State	MsoHTMLProj ectState	Read Only. Returns the current state of an HTMLProject object.

HTMLProject Methods

Name	Returns	Parameters	Description
Open		[OpenKind As MsoHTML Project Open]	Opens the specified HTML project in the Microsoft Script Editor in one of the views specified by the optional MsoHTMLProjectOpen constants. If no constant is specified, the project item is opened in the default view.
Refresh Document		Refresh As Boolean = True	Refreshes the specified HTML project in the Microsoft Office host application. True if all changes are to be saved; False if all changes are to be ignored.

Name	Returns	Parameters	Description
`Refresh Project`		`Refresh As Boolean = True`	Using this method is equivalent to clicking the **Refresh** button on the Refresh toolbar in the Microsoft Script Editor. When refreshing the document by setting `RefreshDocument` to `True`, all changes to the HTML source made in the Office host application are saved to the HTML project in the Microsoft Script Editor. If `RefreshDocument` is set to `False`, all changes to the HTML source are ignored.

Example: HTMLProject Object

The following routine sets a reference to the `ActiveWorkbook`'s `HTMLProject` and then uses that reference to provide a count of items, the locked state of the project. It then displays the project in the Script Editor:

```
Sub HTMLProjectInfo()

    Dim oHTMLProject As HTMLProject

    ' Store a reference to the HTML project
    Set oHTMLProject = ActiveWorkbook.HTMLProject
    With oHTMLProject
        ' Display the number of items in the project and
        ' whether the document or project is locked or not
        MsgBox "Project Items: " & .HTMLProjectItems.Count & vbCrLf & _
               "Locked State: " & .State, vbInformation, _
               "HTML Project Details"

        ' Display the Project in the Script Editor
        .Open (msoHTMLProjectOpenSourceView)
    End With

End Sub
```

HTMLProjectItems Collection Object

Represents all of the objects (items) contained in an `HTMLProject`. All projects contain a `StyleSheet` object, which contains styles used by the entire project (similar to the Styles feature in Excel and Word). All projects contain an object representing the document (workbook).

For example, a workbook called "`Wrox Examples.xls`" will contain an `HTMLProjectItem` called `WroxExamples.xls` in the `HTMLProjectItems` Collection for that workbook's `HTMLProject`. This item in the project stores information about the application it runs in, the objects inside the project (ex: sheets in workbook) , as well as Document Properties (both built-in and custom) like those discussed in the `DocumentProperties` collection section of this index. In addition, each Sheet in Excel is also an object in the `HTMLProjectItems` collection.

HTMLProjectItems Collection Common Properties

The `Application`, `Count`, `Creator`, and `Parent` properties are defined at the beginning of this appendix.

HTMLProjectItems Collection Methods

Name	Returns	Parameters	Description
`Item`	`HTMLProject Item`	`Index as Variant`	Returns the `HTMLProjectItem` object that represents a particular project in the Microsoft Script Editor.

HTMLProjectItem Object

Represents one item in the `HTMLProjectItems` collection.

HTMLProjectItem Common Properties

The `Application`, `Creator`, and `Parent` properties are defined at the beginning of this appendix.

HTMLProjectItem Properties

Name	Returns	Description
`IsOpen`	`Boolean`	Read Only. Returns whether the specified HTML project item is open in the Microsoft Script Editor.
`Name`	`String`	Read Only. Returns the name of the `HTMLProjectItem` object.
`Text`	`String`	Set/Get the HTML text in the HTML editor.

HTMLProjectItem Methods

Name	Returns	Parameters	Description
`LoadFrom File`		`FileName As String`	Updates the text in the Microsoft Script Editor with text from the specified file (on disk).
`Open`		`[OpenKind As MsoHTMLProject Open]`	Opens the specified HTML project item in the Microsoft Script Editor in one of the views specified by the optional `MsoHTMLProjectOpen` constants. If no constant is specified, the project item is opened in the default view.

Name	Returns	Parameters	Description
`SaveCopyAs`		`FileName As String`	Saves the specified HTML project item using a new file name.

Example: HTMLProjectItem Object

The routine below stores the HTML code for the `Workbook` item in the `HTMLProjectItems` Collection in a text file and then displays the code in the Scrip Editor:

```
Sub OpenAndExportWorkbookItem()

    Dim oHTMLItem As HTMLProjectItem

    ' Store a reference to the Workbook object of this project
    ' Note: Use 1 when running this code in a multi-language environment
    ' 1 is always the Workbook (Document) object in the HTMLProject
    Set oHTMLItem = _
            ThisWorkbook.HTMLProject.HTMLProjectItems("WroxExamples.xls")

    With oHTMLItem
        ' Store the HTML code for the Workbook Item
        .SaveCopyAs "C:\Billing\WorkbookSettings.txt"

        ' Display it in the Scrip Editor
        .Open
    End With

End Sub
```

LanguageSettings Object

Returns information about the language settings currently being used in the host application. These are read only and can affect how data is viewed and edited in certain host applications.

LanguageSettings Common Properties

The `Application`, `Creator`, and `Parent` properties are defined at the beginning of this appendix.

HTMLProjectItem Methods

Name	Returns	Parameters	Description
LanuguageID	Long	Id As MsoAppLanguageID	Read Only. Returns the locale identifier (LCID) for the install language, the user interface language, or the Help language.
LanguagePreferredForEditing	Boolean	lid As MsoLanguageID	Read Only. Returns True if the value for the msoLanguageID constant has been identified in the Windows registry as a preferred language for editing.

Example: LanguageSettings Object

The following routine displays a message if additional language modes are not available. In Access and Excel, additional language modes can affect how the program is viewed and edited:

```
Sub ChangeLanguageID()

    Dim oLanguage As LanguageSettings

    ' Grab the reference to the Language Settings
    Set oLanguage = Application.LanguageSettings

    ' Test for any additional language support and report
    ' the result if none are available
    If oLanguage.LanguageID(msoLanguageIDExeMode) = 0 Then
        MsgBox "Support for multiple language viewing and editing is " & _
               "not currently available. Please install additional " & _
               "languages to enable. See search for LanguageID in your " & _
               "application's VBA help for more details", _
               vbInformation, "Language ID"
    End If

End Sub
```

MsoEnvelope Object

This new Office object allows you to send data from a host application using an Outlook mail item without having to reference and connect to the Outlook Object model. Using the Index property of this object allows access to a host of Outlook features not available through the SendMail feature, such as Voting Options, CC and BCC fields, Body Formatting choices (HTML, Rich text, Plain Text) and much more.

Note that the MsoEnvelope object sends the document as inline (formatted) text. It does not attach the document to an e-mail, though you can add attachments using the Attachments property of the MailItem object, which you can access via this object's Index property. For Excel, this object can only be accessed through a Worksheet or a Chart object, which means it only sends those objects (and not the entire workbook). Similar to the SendMail feature in Excel, except that this exposes a CommandBar object associated with this feature and allows for setting of Introduction text.

The properties you set are saved with the document/workbook and are therefore persistent.

MsoEnvelope Common Properties

The `Parent` property is defined at the beginning of this appendix.

MsoEnvelope Properties

Name	Returns	Description
`Command Bars`	`Command Bars`	Returns a `CommandBars` collection.
`Introduction`	`String`	Set/Get the introductory text that is included with a document that is sent using the `MsoEnvelope` object. The introductory text is included at the top of the document in the e-mail.
`Item`	`Object`	Returns a `MailItem` object that can be used to send the document as an e-mail.

MsoEnvelope Events

Name	Parameters	Description
`EnvelopeHide`		Triggered when the user interface that corresponds to the `MsoEnvelope` object is hidden.
`EnvelopeShow`		Triggered when the user interface that corresponds to the `MsoEnvelope` object is displayed.

Example: MsoEnvelope Object

The following routine creates an Outlook MailItem for a worksheet (using its `Name` property from the Properties window in the VBE) and sets the subject, introduction text and recipient, adds the entire workbook as an attachment, and sends it:

```
Sub SendSheet()
    SendMsoMail "Robert Rosenberg"
End Sub

Function SendMsoMail(ByVal strRecipient As String)

    Dim oMailEnv As MsoEnvelope
    Dim oMailItem As MailItem

    ' Grab a reference to the MsoEnvelope
    Set oMailEnv = wksIncome.MailEnvelope

    ' Set up the Envelope
    With oMailEnv

        ' Add intro text, which appears just above the data
```

```
        ' in the Outlook Mail Item
        .Introduction = "Here are the figures you asked for." & _
            "Attached is the entire workbook for your convenience."

        ' Grab a reference to the MailItem which allows us access to
        ' Oulook MailItem properties and methods
        Set oMailItem = .Item

        ' Set up the MailItem
        With oMailItem

            ' Attach this workbook
            .Attachments.Add ThisWorkbook.FullName

            ' Make sure the email format is HTML
            .BodyFormat = olFormatHTML

            ' Add the recipient name and resolve it using
            ' Outlook's Check Name feature)
            .Recipients.Add strRecipient
            .Recipients.ResolveAll

            ' Add the Subject
            .Subject = "Here is the document."

            ' Send it off. The Display method does not work
            .Send

        End With

    End With

End Function
```

NewFile Object

Represents a new document listing in the **Task** Pane of the host application. In Excel, this object allows you to add workbooks to any of the five sections in the **Task** Pane: **Open a Workbook, New, New from existing workbook, New from template,** or the bottom section (which has no name). When clicking added workbooks in **the New, New from existing workbook,** or **New from template** sections, Excel by default creates a copy of the file unless you override it using the `Action` parameter of the `Add` method.

NewFile Common Properties

The `Application` and `Creator` properties are defined at the beginning of this appendix.

NewFile Methods

Name	Returns	Parameters	Description
Add	Boolean	FileName As String, [Section], [DisplayName], [Action]	Adds a new item to the **New Item** task pane.
Remove	Boolean	FileName As String, [Section], [DisplayName], [Action]	Removes a new item to the **New Item** task pane.

Example: NewFile Object

The following routine adds a new file to the **New From Existing Workbook** section of the **Task** Pane. It will display on the **Task** Pane as New Billing Workbook, but when clicked will open a copy of the `NewFile.xls` workbook in the Billing folder on the hard drive:

```
Sub AddNewWorkbookToTaskPane()

    Dim oNewFile As NewFile

    ' Grab a reference to the NewFile object
    Set oNewFile = Application.NewWorkbook

    ' Add the file to the task pane. It places it in the New From Existing
    ' Workbook section of the Task Pane
    oNewFile.Add Filename:="C:\Billing\NewFile.xls", _
                 Section:=msoNewfromExistingFile, _
                 DisplayName:="New Billing Workbook", _
                 Action:=msoCreateNewFile

    ' The new listing on the Task Pane will not show up
    ' until you hide and display the Task pane
    Application.CommandBars("Task Pane").Visible = False
    Application.CommandBars("Task Pane").Visible = True

End Sub
```

ODSOColumns Collection Object

Represents a set of data fields (columns) in a Mail Merge Data Source.

Cannot be implemented at this time. Requires that the `OfficeDataSourceObject` be referenced via the `Application` object of the host application. No `OfficeDataSourceObject` exists in any of the `Application` objects in Microsoft Office XP.

ODSOColumn Object

Represents a single field in a MailMerge Data Source.

> **Cannot be implemented at this time. Requires that the `OfficeDataSourceObject` be referenced via the `Application` object of the host application. No `OfficeDataSourceObject` exists in any of the `Application` objects in Microsoft Office XP.**

ODSOFilters Collection Object

Represents a set of filters applied to a Mail Merge Data Source. Filters are essentially queries that restrict which records are returned when a Mail Merge is performed.

> **Cannot be implemented at this time. Requires that the `OfficeDataSourceObject` be referenced via the `Application` object of the host application. No `OfficeDataSourceObject` exists in any of the `Application` objects in Microsoft Office XP.**

ODSOFilter Object

Represents a single Filter in the ODSO (Office Data Source Object)Filters collection.

> **Cannot be implemented at this time. Requires that the `OfficeDataSourceObject` be referenced via the `Application` object of the host application. No `OfficeDataSourceObject` exists in any of the `Application` objects in Microsoft Office XP.**

OfficeDataSourceObject Object

Represents a data source when performing a Mail Merge operation. Allows you to return a set of records that meet specific criteria.

> **Cannot be implemented at this time. Requires that the `OfficeDataSourceObject` be referenced via the `Application` object of the host application. No `OfficeDataSourceObject` exists in any of the `Application` objects in Microsoft Office XP.**

PropertyTests Collection Object

This collection object represents the list of search criteria when using the `FileSearch` object. They are analogous to viewing the list of criteria on the Advanced tab of the Search dialog (accessed via the Tools | Search command inside the File | Open dialog. This object collection is used when you need to set multiple criteria during a File Search.

Use the `Add` method of this collection object to add advanced criteria to your file search.

PropertyTests Collection Common Properties

The `Application`, `Count`, and `Creator` properties are defined at the beginning of this appendix.

PropertyTests Collection Properties

Name	Returns	Parameters	Description
`Item`	`PropertyTest`	`Index as Long`	Returns a `PropertyTest` object from the `PropertyTests` collection.

PropertyTests Collection Methods

Name	Returns	Parameters	Description
`Add`		`Name As String, Condition As MsoCondition, [Value], [SecondValue], [Connector]`	Adds a `PropertyTest` object to the `PropertyTests` collection.
`Remove`		`Index As Long`	Removes a `PropertyTest` object from the `PropertyTests` collection.

Example: PropertyTests Collection Object

The following routines prompt a user for a billing number, then search for all Excel workbooks in a billing folder on the hard drive whose custom document property called `BillingNumber` is greater than or equal to their answer:

```
Sub SearchBillingNumber()

    Dim lCount As Long, lNumber As Long
    Dim oFiles As FoundFiles
    Dim sFiles As String

    ' Ask them which number they want for the lower bound of the
    ' Billing Number search
    lNumber = Application.InputBox( _
                "What billing number (starting with 1) do you" & _
                "want the search to start with?", _
                "Search for Billing Numbers", , , , , , 1)

    ' If they gave a number greater than 1...
    If lNumber > 0 Then
        ' Assume no files were found
        sFiles = "No Files found"

        ' Use the ReturnBillingNumbers function to return a list of billing
        ' files with Billing Numbers greater than lNumber
        Set oFiles = ReturnBillingNumbers(lNumber)

        ' Report the results
        If Not oFiles Is Nothing Then
```

```
            sFiles = "Files Found:" & vbCrLf
            For lCount = 1 To oFiles.Count
                sFiles = sFiles & vbCrLf & oFiles(lCount)
            Next lCount
        End If

        ' Display the search results
        MsgBox sFiles, vbInformation, "Billing Files"

    End If
End Sub

Function ReturnBillingNumbers(lNumber As Long) As FoundFiles

    With Application.FileSearch

        ' Reset the previous search including the FileTypes, Lookin values,
        ' and property tests
        ' See the FileTypes Collection example for this routine.
        ResetFileSearch

        ' Add 1st condition: Excel Workbooks only. Use the And value of
        ' Connector parameter to insure that both conditions are met
        .PropertyTests.Add _
             Name:="Files of Type", _
             Condition:=msoConditionFileTypeExcelWorkbooks, _
             Connector:=msoConnectorAnd

        ' Add 2nd Condition:
        'CustomDocumentProperty called BillingNumber is greater than lNumber
        .PropertyTests.Add _
            Name:="BillingNumber", _
            Condition:=msoConditionMoreThan, _
            Value:=lNumber

        ' Search the Billing folder
        .LookIn = "C:\Billing"

        ' Perform the search and return the results
        If .Execute > 0 Then
            Set ReturnBillingNumbers = .FoundFiles
        End If

    End With

End Function
```

PropertyTest Object

Represents a single criteria in the `PropertyTests` collection.

PropertyTest Common Properties

The `Application`, `Creator`, and `Parent` properties are defined at the beginning of this appendix.

PropertyTest Properties

Name	Returns	Description
Condition	MsoCondition	Read Only. Returns the condition of the specified search criteria.
Connector	MsoConnector	Read Only. Returns the connector between two similar property test values. The default value is msoConnectorAnd.
Name	String	Read Only. Returns the name of the PropertyTest object.
SecondValue	Variant	Read Only. Returns an optional second value property test (as in a range) for the file search.
Value	Variant	Read Only. Returns the value of a property test for a file search.

Example: PropertyTest Object

The following routine removes the `PropertyTest` that is searching for Excel workbooks:

```
Sub RemoveExcelPropertyTest()

    Dim lItem As Long
    Dim oProperty As PropertyTest

    ' Initialize the property test counter
    lItem = 1

    With Application.FileSearch
        ' Loop through the PropertTests collection
        For Each oProperty In .PropertyTests
            ' Remove the property test that's searching for Excel workbooks
            If oProperty.Condition = msoConditionFileTypeExcelWorkbooks Then
                .PropertyTests.Remove lItem
                Exit For
            Else
                lItem = lItem + 1
            End If
        Next oProperty
    End With

End Sub
```

ScopeFolders Collection Object

This collection contains a list of subfolders in a `ScopeFolder` object. It's used by the `FileSearch` object's `SearchFolders` collection to determine which folders and subfolders are used in a search. Each item in a `ScopeFolders` collection is a `ScopeFolder`, a folder that can be (but is not necessarily) used in a search. Each `ScopeFolder` that contains subfolders has in effect its own `ScopeFolders` collection, similar to folders having subfolders having more subfolders and so on.

ScopeFolders Collection Common Properties

The Application, Count, and Creator properties are defined at the beginning of this appendix.

ScopeFolders Collection Properties

Name	Returns	Parameters	Description
Item	ScopeFolder	Index as Long	Returns a ScopeFolder object that represents a subfolder of the parent object.

ScopeFolder Object

Represents a single folder in a ScopeFolders collection. Each ScopeFolder can contain a ScopeFolders collection, which represents a ScopeFolder's subfolders. Both ScopeFolder and the ScopeFolders collection can be analyzed to determine whether they will be used in a search by the FileSearch object. Any ScopeFolder you want used in a search is added to the SearchFolders collection using the ScopeFolder's AddToSearchFolders method.

ScopeFolder Common Properties

The Application and Creator properties are defined at the beginning of this appendix.

ScopeFolder Properties

Name	Returns	Description
Name	String	Read Only. Returns the name of the ScopeFolder object.
Path	String	Read Only. Returns the full path of a ScopeFolder object.
Scope Folders	Scope Folders	Returns a ScopeFolders collection. The items in this collection correspond to the subfolders of the parent ScopeFolder object.

ScopeFolder Methods

Name	Returns	Parameters	Description
AddTo SearchF olders			Adds a ScopeFolder object the SearchFolders collection.

Example: ScopeFolder Object

The following routines dump a list of Excel workbooks from all of the folders in the hard drive that contain the word billing:

```
Sub FindBillingFiles()

    Dim lCount As Long
    Dim oSearchFolders As SearchFolders
    Dim sFiles As String

    With Application.FileSearch

        ' Reset the Search. See FileTypes collection for this routine
        ResetFileSearch

        ' Search for Excel workbooks
        .FileType = msoFileTypeExcelWorkbooks

        ' Search all folders containing the word "Billing" in the hard drive
        Set oSearchFolders = BillingFolders("RCOR HD (C:)", "Billing")
        If Not oSearchFolders Is Nothing Then
            .LookIn = oSearchFolders(1)
        End If

        ' Assume no files will be found
        sFiles = "No Files found"

        ' If we found any files, list them
        If .Execute > 0 Then
            sFiles = "Files Found:" & vbCrLf
            For lCount = 1 To .FoundFiles.Count
                sFiles = sFiles & vbCrLf & .FoundFiles(lCount)
            Next lCount
        End If

    End With

    ' Report the results
    MsgBox sFiles, vbInformation, "Billing Files"

End Sub
```

This function is called by the main `FindBillingFiles` routine and creates the set of Search Folders for the `FileSearch` object.

```
Function oSetSearchFolders(sDrive As String, _
                           sKeyName As String) As SearchFolders

    Dim lCount As Long
    Dim oSearchScope As Searchscope
    Dim oScopeFolder As ScopeFolder

    With Application.FileSearch

        ' Search only the local machine (not Network neighborhood)
        For Each oSearchScope In .SearchScopes
            ' Only look in the local hard drive
            If oSearchScope.Type = msoSearchInMyComputer Then
                'Loop through each ScopeFolder in the ScopeFolders
```

```
            ' collection within the SearchScope object.
            For Each oScopeFolder In _
                      oSearchScope.ScopeFolder.ScopeFolders
                If oScopeFolder.Name = sDrive Then
                    ' This function adds any folders containing
                    ' the word Billing to the SearchFolders collection.
                    AddFolders oScopeFolder.ScopeFolders, sKeyName
                End If
            Next oScopeFolder
        End If
    Next oSearchScope

    ' If any billing folders were found pass the search folders back to
    ' the calling routine
    If .SearchFolders.Count > 0 Then
        Set oSetSearchFolders = .SearchFolders
    End If

End With

End Function
```

This routine is called by the `oSetSearchFolders` function and adds a `ScopeFolder` to the `SearchFolders` collection:

```
Sub AddFolders(ByVal oScopeFolders As ScopeFolders, ByRef sFolder As String)

    ' Declare a variable as a ScopeFolder object
    Dim oScopeFolder As ScopeFolder

    ' Loop through each ScopeFolder object in the ScopeFolders collection.
    For Each oScopeFolder In oScopeFolders
        ' Don't bother looking in the WINNT or Windows folders
        If LCase(oScopeFolder.Name) <> "winnt" And _
               LCase(oScopeFolder.Name) <> "windows" Then
            ' Test to see if the folder name of the ScopeFolder
            ' matches the value of sFolder. Use LCase to ensure
            ' that case does not affect the match.
            If InStr(1, LCase(oScopeFolder.Name), _
                     LCase(sFolder), vbTextCompare) > 0 Then

                ' Add the ScopeFolder to the SearchFolders collection.
                oScopeFolder.AddToSearchFolders

            End If

            ' Allow this process to continue handling events
            DoEvents

            ' If the current ScopeFolder has ScopeFolders (subfolders)...
            ' Supress errors resulting from certain folders not being
            ' perceived as folders
            On Error Resume Next
            If oScopeFolder.ScopeFolders.Count > 0 Then
                ' Call this routine again (recursively) to handle the
```

```
                ' subfolders
                AddFolders oScopeFolder.ScopeFolders, sFolder
            End If

            On Error GoTo 0

        End If

    Next oScopeFolder

End Sub
```

Scripts Collection Object

Represents all of the scripts in a document, like an Excel worksheet, a PowerPoint slide, or a Word document. Scripts are blocks of code written in ASP, Java, Visual Basic, or any other language able to run in an HTML environment. Scripts are run when the document they are contained within is displayed as an HTML document.

Understanding how to create HTML scripts is beyond the scope of this book.

Scripts Collection Common Properties

The `Application`, `Count`, `Creator`, and `Parent` properties are defined at the beginning of this appendix.

Scripts Collection Methods

Name	Returns	Parameters	Description
`Add`	`Script`	`[Anchor], [Location], [Language], [Id], [Extended], [ScriptText]`	Adds a `Script` object to the `Scripts` collection of `Worksheet` or `Chart` object.
`Delete`			Removes all scripts from the specified worksheet.
`Item`	`Script`	`Index As Variant`	Returns the specified member of the `Scripts` collection.

Example: Scripts Collection Object

The following routine adds a simple script to the body (cell A1) of a worksheet called Income Report. When the page is displayed in either a browser or in Excel's Web Page Preview, a simple message box is displayed warning the user that the figures are based on last year's data:

```
Sub AddScriptToReport()

   Const sSCRIPT_NAME As String = "DataWarning"

   Dim oScript As Script
```

```
    On Error Resume Next
       ThisWorkbook.Worksheets("Income Report").Scripts(sSCRIPT_NAME).Delete
    On Error GoTo 0

    ThisWorkbook.Worksheets("Income Report").Scripts.Add _
       Anchor:=ThisWorkbook.Worksheets("Income Report").Range("A1"), _
       Location:=msoScriptLocationInBody, _
       ID:=sSCRIPT_NAME, _
       ScriptText:="MsgBox ""Income Report based on last year's data"""

End Sub
```

Script Object

A `Script` object represents one block of HTML code within the `Scripts` collection. You can reference a `Script` object using the `Item` method of the `Scripts` collection object, as follows:

```
ThisWorkbook.Worksheets("Income Report").Scripts(1)
```

or:

```
ThisWorkbook.Worksheets("Income Report").Scripts.Item(1)
```

You can also reference a `Script` object by specifying its `ID`:

```
ThisWorkbook.Worksheets("Income Report").Scripts("DataWarning")
```

Script Common Properties

The `Application`, `Creator`, and `Parent` properties are defined at the beginning of this appendix.

Script Properties

Name	Returns	Description
`Extended`	`String`	Set/Get attributes added to the `<SCRIPT>` tag, with the exception of the `LANGUAGE` and `ID` attributes.
`Id`	`String`	Set/Get the `ID` of a Script object. The ID returned is the `ID` attribute of the `<SCRIPT>` tag in HTML, or an empty string if there is no `ID` attribute specified.
`Language`	`MsoScript Language`	Set/Get the scripting language of the active script.
`Location`	`MsoScriptLo cation`	Read Only. Returns the location of the script anchor in the specified HTML document.
`ScriptText`	`String`	Set/Get the text contained in a block of script.
`Shape`	`Object`	Read Only. Returns a `Shape` object.

Script Methods

Name	Returns	Parameters	Description
`Delete`			Deletes the specified Script from the `Scripts` collection.

Example: Script Object

The following routine removes all of the scripts from every sheet (chart or worksheet) in the active workbook:

```
Sub RemoveScripts()

    Dim oScript As Script
    Dim sh As Object

    ' Suppress errors (ex: no active workbook)
    On Error Resume Next

    ' Remove all of the scripts objects in this workbook
    For Each sh In ActiveWorkbook.Sheets
        For Each oScript In sh.Scripts
            oScript.Delete
        Next oScript
    Next sh

End Sub
```

SearchFolders Collection Object

Represents all of the folders used in a File Search (by the `FileSearch` object). `SearchFolders` consist of `ScopeFolder` objects (with the corresponding `ScopeFolders` collection), which are simply folders. Use the `Add` method of the `SearchFolders` object to add `ScopeFolder` objects to its collection.

SearchFolders Collection Common Properties

The `Application`, `Count`, and `Creator` properties are defined at the beginning of this appendix.

SearchFolders Collection Properties

Name	Returns	Parameters	Description
`Item`	`Scope Folder`	`Index as Long`	Returns a `ScopeFolder` object that represents a subfolder of the parent object.

SearchFolders Collection Methods

Name	Returns	Parameters	Description
`Add`		`ScopeFolder as ScopeFolder`	Adds a search folder to a file search.
`Remove`		`Index As Long`	Removes a search folder from a file search.

Example: SearchFolders Collection Object

The following routine searches for all Excel workbooks in folders containing the word "billing" on the F drive (on the network) and displays the results on a worksheet:

```
Sub ReportBillingFilesFromNetWorkDrive()

    Dim lCount As Long, lRow As Long
    Dim oSearchScope As SearchScope
    Dim oScopeFolder As ScopeFolder
    Dim oScopeSubFolder As ScopeFolder

    With Application.FileSearch

        ' Reset FileSearch object. See FileTypes collection for this routine
        ResetFileSearch

        ' Loop through the SearchScopes collection
        ' looking for the My Computer area (scope)
        For Each oSearchScope In .SearchScopes
            If oSearchScope.Type = msoSearchInMyComputer Then
                Set oScopeFolder = oSearchScope.ScopeFolder
                Exit For
            End If
        Next oSearchScope

        ' Now loop through the My computer area (scope)
        ' until we find the mapped "F Billing" drive on the network
        For Each oScopeSubFolder In oScopeFolder.ScopeFolders
            If oScopeSubFolder.Name = "Billing (F:)" Then
                Set oScopeFolder = oScopeSubFolder
                Exit For
            End If
        Next oScopeSubFolder

        ' Now loop through each top-level folder in the F drive adding any
        ' folder that contains the name Billing to the SearchFolders
        ' collection
        Set oScopeSubFolder = Nothing
        For Each oScopeSubFolder In oScopeFolder.ScopeFolders
            If InStr(1, oScopeSubFolder.Name, _
                     "billing", vbTextCompare) > 0 Then
                .SearchFolders.Add oScopeSubFolder
            End If
        Next oScopeSubFolder
```

```
        ' Look for Excel workbooks
        .FileType = msoFileTypeExcelWorkbooks

        ' Don't search subfolders. Setting this to True will override the
        ' SearchFolders collection and will search the entire contents of
        ' the F drive
        .SearchSubFolders = False

        If .Execute > 0 Then    'Files were found
            ' Dump the files found on the wksBillingFiles worksheet
            wksBillingFiles.UsedRange.Offset(1, 0).ClearContents

            ' The first row contains the column heading
            lRow = 2
            For lCount = 1 To .FoundFiles.Count
                wksBillingFiles.Cells(lRow, 1).Value = .FoundFiles(lCount)
                lRow = lRow + 1
            Next lCount
        Else
            MsgBox "No Files found", vbInformation, "Billing Files"
        End If

    End With

End Sub
```

SearchScopes Collection Object

Represents the list of top-level searchable areas when performing a File Search using the `FileSearch` object. Top level areas include My Computer, My Network Places, Outlook (folders), and Custom if available.

SearchScopes Collection Common Properties

The `Application`, `Count`, and `Creator` properties are defined at the beginning of this appendix.

SearchScopes Collection Properties

Name	Returns	Parameters	Description
`Item`	`SearchScope`	`Index as Long`	Returns a `SearchScope` object that corresponds to an area in which to perform a file search, such as local drives or Microsoft Outlook folders.

Example: SearchScopes Collection Object

The following routine lists all of the `SearchScopes` on the current computer.

```
Sub FindSearchScopes()

    Dim lRow As Long
    Dim oSearchScope As SearchScope
```

```
    With Application.FileSearch

        ' Clear the old results
        wksSearchScopes.Range("Info").ClearContents

        ' Set the starting row
        lRow = wksSearchScopes.Range("Info").Cells(1, 1).Row

        ' Loop through the SearchScopes collection
        ' looking for the My Computer area (scope)
        For Each oSearchScope In .SearchScopes
            ' Dump the info found on the wksSearchScopes worksheet
            wksSearchScopes.Cells(lRow, 1).Value = _
                oSearchScope.ScopeFolder.Name
            wksSearchScopes.Cells(lRow, 2).Value = oSearchScope.Type
            lRow = lRow + 1
        Next oSearchScope

        ' Sort the list by Scope Type
        With wksSearchScopes
            .Range("Info").Sort Key1:=.Cells(1, 2), Order1:=xlAscending
        End With

    End With

End Sub
```

SearchScope Object

An individual top-level area in the `SearchScopes` Collection object that can be searched when using the `FileSearch` object.

SearchScope Common Properties

The `Application` and `Creator` properties are defined at the beginning of this appendix.

SearchScope Properties

Name	Returns	Description
`ScopeFolder`	`ScopeFolder`	Returns a `ScopeFolder` object.
`Type`	`MsoSearchIn`	Read Only. Returns a value that corresponds to the type of `SearchScope` object. The type indicates the area in which the `Execute` method of the `FileSearch` object will search for files.

Signature Object

This object represents a digital signature attached to a document. Digital Signatures are electronic versions of handwritten signatures. They enable other users of your document to uniquely identify and validate the source of the document.

When a document containing a digital signature contains macros, users who open the document have the option of trusting the author, or source of the signature. When macro security for an Office application is set to high, only macros from trusted sources are enabled. This protects those other users from opening documents that could contain macro viruses by allowing them to choose which sources they wish to trust.

Digital Signatures also add a level protection for the author of the document by insuring that the contents of the document remained unchanged. When you digitally sign a document, an encrypted key is added to the signature. When other users change the document, a message appears informing them that they do not have the key to unlock the signature. This causes the document to lose its signature.

Note: This object is currently not accessible in Microsoft Excel, though it is available through the Document object in Microsoft Word and the Presentation object in Microsoft PowerPoint.

Signature Common Properties

The `Application`, `Creator`, and `Parent` properties are defined at the beginning of this Appendix.

Signature Properties

Name	Returns	Description
`Attach Certificate`	`Boolean`	Set/Get whether the digital certificate that corresponds to the specified `Signature` object is attached to the document.
`ExpireDate`	`Variant`	Read Only. Returns the date on which the digital signature that corresponds to the `Signature` object will expire.
`Is Certificate Expired`	`Boolean`	Read Only. Returns whether the digital certificate that corresponds to the `Signature` object has expired.
`Is Certificate Revoked`	`Boolean`	Read Only. Returns whether the digital certificate that corresponds to the `Signature` object has been revoked by the issuer of the certificate.
`Issuer`	`String`	Read Only. Returns the name of the issuer of the digital certificate that corresponds to the `Signature` object.
`IsValid`	`Boolean`	Read Only. Returns whether the digital certificate that corresponds to the `Signature` object is a valid certificate. A certificate may be invalid for several reasons ranging from its having expired to changes in the document that contains it.
`SignDate`	`Variant`	Read Only. Returns the date and time that the digital certificate corresponding to the `Signature` object was attached to the document.
`Signer`	`String`	Read Only. Returns the name of the person who attached the digital certificate that corresponds to the `Signature` object to the document.

Signature Methods

Name	Returns	Parameters	Description
`Delete`			Deletes the specified signature from the `SignatureSet` collection.

SignatureSet Collection Object

Represents all of the `Signature` objects in a document.

SignatureSet Collection Common Properties

The `Application`, `Count`, `Creator`, and `Parent` properties are defined at the beginning of this appendix.

SignatureSet Collection Properties

Name	Returns	Parameters	Description
`Item`	`Signature`	`iSig as Long`	Returns a `Signature` object that corresponds to one of the digital signatures with which the document is currently signed.

SignatureSet Collection Methods

Name	Returns	Parameters	Description
`Add`	`Signature`		Returns a `Signature` object that represents a new e-mail signature.
`Commit`			Commits all changes of the specified `SignatureSet` collection to disk. Until this method is executed, none of the changes to the collection are saved.

Example: SignatureSet Collection Object

The following routine adds a digital signature to the active PowerPoint presentation, then displays the information contained within the signature chosen. Note that the `Add` method of the `Signatures` property prompts the user with a dialog containing a list of digital signatures:

```
Sub AddSig()

    Dim lIcon As Long
    Dim ppt As Presentation
    Dim oSignature As Signature
    Dim sInfo As String

    ' Check for an active presentation
```

```
    On Error Resume Next
        Set ppt = ActivePresentation
    On Error GoTo 0

    'If there's a presentation active...
    If Not ppt Is Nothing Then

        ' Set the icon that will appear in the message box to information
        lIcon = vbInformation

        ' Add the signature to the presentation. This will prompt the user
        ' to select a signature and return all of the property settings to
        ' the oSignature object
        Set oSignature = ppt.Signatures.Add

        ' Commit the changes to disk. This will display a "Signed" message
        ' next to the presentation name
        ppt.Signatures.Commit

        ' Initialize the message string
        sInfo = "Signature Information:" & vbCrLf & vbCrLf

        ' Add the signature info to the message
        With oSignature
            sInfo = sInfo & "Issuer: " & .Issuer & vbCrLf
            sInfo = sInfo & "Signer: " & .Signer & vbCrLf
            sInfo = sInfo & "Sign Date: " & .SignDate & vbCrLf
            sInfo = sInfo & "Expire Date: " & .ExpireDate
        End With
    Else
        ' No presentation active, so set the message box icon to exclamation
        ' and the message to inform the user
        lIcon = vbExclamation
        sInfo = "No presentation is currently active"
    End If

    ' Display the message
    MsgBox sInfo, lIcon, "Add Signature"

End Sub
```

WebPageFonts Collection Object

Represents a set of `WebPageFont` objects that allow you to set both the proportional and fixed font style and size used when documents are saved as Web pages. See the `WebPageFont` object for more details.

The collection can be referenced using the `Fonts` property of the `DefaultWebOptions` property in the host's `Application` object, like so:

```
Set oWebPageFonts = Application.DefaultWebOptions.Fonts
```

Note that as of this writing, the `count` property of the `WebPageFonts` Collection object always returns zero, even though there are twelve `WebPageFont` objects (Character Sets) in the collection.

WebPageFonts Collection Common Properties

The `Application`, `Count`, and `Creator` properties are defined at the beginning of this appendix.

WebPageFonts Collection Properties

Name	Returns	Parameters	Description
`Item`	`WebPage Font`	`Index as MsoCharacter Set`	Returns a `WebPageFont` object from the `WebPageFonts` collection for a particular value of `MsoCharacterSet`.

WebPageFont Object

This object represents which fixed and proportional font and size are used when the host application's documents are saved as web pages. Microsoft Excel and Microsoft Word also use these settings when you open a web page within the application, but the settings only take effect when the web page being opened cannot display its own font settings or when no font information is contained within the HTML code.

Be aware that the `FixedWidthFont` and `ProportionalFont` properties will accept any valid String and `FixedWidthFontSize` and `ProportionalFontSize` will accept any valid Single value. For example, the following will not encounter an error, even though they aren't valid font and size settings.

```
Application.DefaultWebOptions.Fonts(msoCharacterSetEnglishWesternEuropeanOtherLati
nScript).ProportionalFont = "XXXXXXXX"

Application.DefaultWebOptions.Fonts(msoCharacterSetEnglishWesternEuropeanOtherLati
nScript).ProportionalFontSize = 1200
```

An error will occur when the application attempts to use these settings.

WebPageFont Common Properties

The `Application` and `Creator` properties are defined at the beginning of this appendix.

WebPageFont Properties

Name	Returns	Description
`FixedWidth Font`	`String`	Set/Get the fixed-width font setting in the host application.
`FixedWidth FontSize`	`Single`	Set/Get the fixed-width font size setting (in points) in the host application.
`Proportional Font`	`String`	Set/Get the proportional font setting in the host application.
`Proportional FontSize`	`Single`	Set/Get the proportional font size setting (in points) in the host application.

Example: WebPageFont Object

The following routine loops through the `WebPageFonts` collection, and for each `WebPageFont` (character set), establishes the proportional and fixed font name and size based on data entered in a `FontInfo` range located on the `wksWebPageFonts` worksheet in the workbook containing this code:

```
Sub SetWebPageFonts()

    Const sRANGE_FONT_INFO As String = "FontInfo"

    Dim lCalc As Long
    Dim lCount As Long, lRow As Long
    Dim oWebFont As WebPageFont

    ' Turn off the screen and Calculation
    With Application
        ' Store the calculation mode
        lCalc = .Calculation
        ' Turn calculation off
        .Calculation = xlCalculationManual
        ' Turn off the screen
        .ScreenUpdating = False
    End With

    ' Set the row counter based on the input range's first cell
    lRow = wksWebPageFonts.Range("InputRange").Cells(1, 1).Row

    ' Clear the old info
    wksWebPageFonts.Range("InputRange").ClearContents

    ' There are twelve Font character sets. Need to use a hard-coded upper
    ' range (12) because Application.DefaultWebOptions.Fonts.Count
    ' always returns zero
    For lCount = 1 To 12
        ' Grab a reference to a single WebPageFont (or character set)
        Set oWebFont = Application.DefaultWebOptions.Fonts(lCount)

        With oWebFont
            ' Use the settings on the wksWebPageFonts worksheet to
            ' set the WebPageFont font settings
            .ProportionalFont = _
                wksWebPageFonts.Range(sRANGE_FONT_INFO).Cells(1, 1).Value
            .ProportionalFontSize = _
                wksWebPageFonts.Range(sRANGE_FONT_INFO).Cells(1, 2).Value
            .FixedWidthFont = _
                wksWebPageFonts.Range(sRANGE_FONT_INFO).Cells(1, 3).Value
            .FixedWidthFontSize = _
                wksWebPageFonts.Range(sRANGE_FONT_INFO).Cells(1, 4).Value

            ' Display the new WebPageFont settings in a table
            ' on the wksWebPageFonts worksheet
            wksWebPageFonts.Cells(lRow, 2) = lCount
            wksWebPageFonts.Cells(lRow, 3) = .ProportionalFont
            wksWebPageFonts.Cells(lRow, 4) = .ProportionalFontSize
            wksWebPageFonts.Cells(lRow, 5) = .FixedWidthFont
            wksWebPageFonts.Cells(lRow, 6) = .FixedWidthFontSize
```

```
            ' Move one row down for the next Character set
            lRow = lRow + 1
        End With
    Next lCount

    ' Reset the calculation mode
    Application.Calculation = lCalc

End Sub
```

VBAProgrammersReferenceExcel20

mmersReferenceExcel2002VB

ReferenceExcel2002VBAPro

ProgrammersReferenceExc

grammersReferenceExcel20

rsReferenceExcel2002VB

renceExcel2002VBAPro

VBAProgram

grammers

rsRefe

ferenceExcel200

nceExcel2002VBAPro renceEx

xcel2002VBAProgram VBAProgram

2002VBAProgrammersReferenceExce

VBAProgrammersReference

rogrammersReferenceExcel

rogrammer sReferenceE

ammersReferencerammersRe nceExcel2000VBAProgra

2002VBAProgrammersRefe sReferenceExce

Index

A Guide to the Index

The index is arranged hierarchically, in alphabetical order. Most second-level entries and many third-level entries also occur as first-level entries. This is to ensure that users will find the information they require however they choose to search for it.

A

B

C

D

E

F

G

H

I

J

L

M

N

O

P

Q

R

T

V

X

Notes

Notes

Notes

Notes